HANDBOOK ON MEASUREMENT, ASSESSMENT, AND EVALUATION IN HIGHER EDUCATION

Increased demands for colleges and universities to engage in outcomes assessment for accountability purposes have accelerated the need to bridge the gap between higher education practice and the fields of measurement, assessment, and evaluation. This book provides higher education administrators, student affairs personnel, institutional researchers, and faculty with an integrated handbook of theory, method, and application to facilitate informed decision-making in higher education.

Special Features:

- **Contributing Authors** are world-renowned scholars across the fields of measurement, assessment, and evaluation, including: Robert E. Stake, Trudy W. Banta, Michael J. Kolen, Noreen M. Webb, Kurt F. Geisinger, Robert J. Mislevy, Ronald K. Hambleton, Rebecca Zwick, John W. Creswell, and Margaret D. LeCompte.
- **Depth of Coverage** includes classroom assessment and student outcomes; assessment techniques for accountability and accreditation; test theory, item response theory, validity, and reliability; qualitative, quantitative, and mixed-methods evaluation; context and ethics of assessment.
- **Questions and Exercises** follow each Section to reinforce the valuable concepts and insights presented in the preceding chapters.

This book enables educational decision-makers to engage in more sound professional judgment, providing higher education administrators with both high-level and detailed views into contemporary theories and practices, supplemented with guidance on how to apply them for the benefit of students and institutions.

Charles Secolsky is Director of Institutional Research and Planning at County College of Morris, New Jersey.

D. Brian Denison is Institutional Research Analyst at Champlain Regional College, Quebec, Canada.

HANDBOOK ON MEASUREMENT, ASSESSMENT, AND EVALUATION IN HIGHER EDUCATION

Edited by Charles Secolsky and D. Brian Denison

Routledge
Taylor & Francis Group

NEW YORK AND LONDON

First published 2012
by Routledge
711 Third Avenue, New York, NY 10017

Simultaneously published in the UK
by Routledge
2 Park Square, Milton Park, Abingdon, Oxon OX14 4RN

Routledge is an imprint of the Taylor & Francis Group, an informa business

Library of Congress Cataloging in Publication Data
Handbook on measurement, assessment, and evaluation in higher education /
[edited by] Charles Secolsky, D. Brian Denison.
p. cm.
Includes bibliographical references and index.
1. Education, Higher—Evaluation—Handbooks, manuals, etc.
2. Educational tests and measurements—Handbooks, manuals, etc.
I. Secolsky, Charles. II. Denison, D. Brian.
LB2331.62.H36 2011
378.1'66—dc23
2011028069

ISBN: 978–0–415–88075–6 (hbk)
ISBN: 978–0–415–88076–3 (pbk)
ISBN: 978–0–203–14218–9 (ebk)

Typeset in Bembo and Minion
by Swales & Willis Ltd, Exeter, Devon

Printed and bound in the United States of America on acid-free paper
by Walsworth Publishing Company, Marceline, MO

SUSTAINABLE
FORESTRY
INITIATIVE

Certified Sourcing
www.sfiprogram.org
SFI-00555
The SFI label applies to the text stock.

To Anna, Stephanie, and Barbara for motivating me; and to Bob Stake,
for his decades of friendship and sustained support—for which
I shall be eternally grateful. (CS)

To Janet G. Donald, Professor Emeritus, McGill University,
for introducing me to the fascinating world of
higher education research; and to Gohar Sahakian, for being the
balancing force in my life. (DBD)

CONTENTS

Contents

Contents

FIGURES

TABLES

FOREWORD

Edward J. Yaw, Ed.D.

PRESIDENT, COUNTY COLLEGE OF MORRIS
FORMER CHAIR, NEW JERSEY PRESIDENTS' COUNCIL

The *Handbook on Measurement, Assessment, and Evaluation in Higher Education* heralds an important milestone in the evolution of institutional research in the academy. The earliest efforts at institutional assessment and research date back to the years immediately following World War Two. Institutional research matured as a legitimate field of study and important management tool in the late sixties and early seventies. Certainly, the work of Paul L. Dressel at the University of Michigan was an important catalyst for this movement. His many publications contributed to the body of knowledge in this field, and provided a roadmap to the future. Today, nearly all colleges and universities have an active institutional research function.

These developments paralleled important innovations beyond the walls of the academy that placed increased emphasis on statistical analysis and decision making. W. Edwards Deming's ground breaking approach to total quality management, and the development of Six Sigma certifications have had an impact.

It is worth noting that this maturation of the profession comes at a time in the history of the academy when it is needed more than ever. The ever-increasing demands for public accountability and the challenges to regional accreditation require rigorous and thoughtful approaches to institutional assessment, and the assessment of student learning.

As editors of this handbook, Drs. Charles Secolsky and Brian Denison have assembled the best thinking of some of the most prominent professionals in the fields of measurement, assessment, and evaluation. Collectively, their efforts provide an outstanding resource for presidents, administrators, and faculty as they wrestle with the issues of accountability and assessment.

The handbook provides a balance of practical and theoretical approaches to the subject at hand and, where appropriate, includes exercises to foster understanding. Importantly, it recognizes the critical relationship between disciplined study and decision making. Decisions informed by rigorous study are critical to moving the enterprise forward. In the final analysis, the purpose of evaluation and assessment is continuous improvement of the academy.

PREFACE

Improving Institutional Decision Making through Educational Measurement, Assessment, and Evaluation

Charles Secolsky and D. Brian Denison

Managing an institution of higher education is a very difficult task. It necessitates attention to many administrative details arising from a mix of rational and irrational forces. Understanding of one's institution requires a wide of array of skills that presidents, vice presidents, deans, department chairpersons, faculty, and other staff must possess in order to make a college or university run smoothly and adapt to a changing external environment. When possible, higher education administrators use sound professional judgment to make decisions about their institution. At other times, they must combine this judgment with timely data to inform these decisions. While it is sometimes the case that decisions are supported by data after the decisions have been made, it would appear prudent for those who are charged with managing the operation of an institution of higher learning to have at their disposal up-to-date resources to aid in planning and deliberating decisions beforehand.

The *Handbook on Measurement, Assessment, and Evaluation in Higher Education* is intended to provide higher education administrators, student affairs personnel, faculty, the institutional researchers who generate and analyze data, and other stakeholders with an integrated handbook of theory, method, and application. This handbook brings together applied terminology, analytical perspectives, and methodological advances from the fields of measurement, assessment, and evaluation to facilitate informed decision making. It connects the latest thinking in these methodological areas with the actual practice of administration in higher education.

The authors of the chapters in this handbook include many world-renowned scholars in measurement, assessment, and evaluation. All of the authors have made a concerted effort to make their topics minimally technical and maximally accessible. By clarifying the methods and processes by which evidence gets collected and analyzed, we feel confident that this book will enable educational decision makers to engage in more sound professional judgment.

Professional judgment remains key to sound decision making in higher education. This handbook will further enhance the value and quality of that decision making by engendering a better understanding of quantitative, qualitative and mixed-methods approaches from the three fields of measurement, assessment, and evaluation. Such an enhanced understanding of these disciplines will facilitate both data driven or data informed decision making and the evaluation of others' determination of the direction of the course of a university's undertaking, especially with respect to student learning and assessment.

This handbook was designed to present complex topics in an easily understood manner. The chapters shed light on the most recent advances in measurement, assessment, and evaluation and are supported with examples from higher education at the end of six sections. Each of the chapters has been written so that it can be used as a stand-alone resource. However, the authors have also attempted to link their material to that presented in other chapters of the book.

A major challenge for developing the handbook was the integration of diverse disciplines and perspectives. Measurement is the harnessing of responses to test items or other stimuli and/or the collection and analysis of expert or examinee judgments for the purpose of making inferences and ultimately to arrive at decisions based on those inferences. It uses the developments in various sub-disciplines for reaching conclusions that enable equitable systems for such things as accepting, placing, advancing, comparing, and even rewarding students for purposes and processes of assessment and evaluation. This book attempts to bridge widening gaps between practice in higher education on the one hand and advances in measurement, assessment, and evaluation on the other. Think of common issues in higher education such as standard-setting, finding an appropriate passing score, potential bias in tests or test items, ensuring that different forms of a test yield equivalent results, diagnosing the learning or other needs of students, and developing appropriate measures of student learning or other outcomes. There are well-thought-out approaches within the field of measurement that address these kinds of issues that can and should be used for guiding assessment and evaluation efforts in higher education.

As can be seen from the chapter titles in the Table of Contents, assessment plays a major role in decision making with respect to improving learning or improving a program. In particular, formative assessment has gained in popularity over the last few years. Most educational and psychological testing can also be subsumed under the term "assessment." The assessment chapters within this handbook address issues from both the outcomes assessment perspective and the testing and measurement perspective.

Evaluation is another fundamental tool in decision making. What, then, differentiates it from assessment? Many in higher education use the terms interchangeably. We would argue, however, that the two fields are different. Assessment, at its heart, is about the collection, analysis, and interpretation of information related to a particular issue or outcome of interest. Evaluation, on the other hand, deals with determining the worth, value, or effectiveness of something—often some kind of program. From this standpoint, an evaluation may encompass an assessment initiative as the source for making judgments about program quality.

Increased demands for colleges and universities to engage in outcomes assessment for accountability purposes have accelerated opportunities for reducing the gaps between higher education practice and the fields of measurement, assessment, and evaluation. However, those working on the front lines of outcomes assessment may have had limited training in, or time to keep abreast of, key concepts and practices in these three fields. Other obstacles that may have contributed to forestalling the pace of growth of the assessment movement have been a push to stay clear of quantitative complexity on the part of various assessment constituencies for fostering greater potential acceptance from groups such as faculty, and other professional enclaves that have existed and grown over the course of time.

In higher education, in particular, assessment has grown in popularity. From the mid-1980s to the present, the outcomes assessment movement has blossomed. Take for example, the use of the rubric in assessment of portfolios. Those concerned with the inability of testing to provide more than a "snapshot" of student performance look to portfolio assessment and, in particular, electronic portfolios for greater validity and authenticity of assessment. As another example, with a more positive eye with respect to the measurement community, when tests are needed to be developed and administered, there are trends reported for test scores in higher education without the guiding principles of equating scores so that data points in the trend are comparable. This can be problematic and lead to misinterpretation of data. There is also the need to make tests and testing more fair in the various contexts in which they are used.

For users, of rubrics, there is a tendency to just want to report mean or average scores on criteria instead of the variability of ratings and inter-rater reliability. But what is a rubric and how can it be improved in a generic sense psychometrically? Rubrics have been developed for differing criteria and have different levels of rater agreement. It makes sense to use a more general psychometric framework to better understand the variability of ratings of quality that incorporates both ratings of criteria and rater agreement?

Validation runs through the three disciplines: measurement, assessment, and evaluation, but only recently has there been an attempt to unify how validation is viewed. House (1980), Kane (2006), Mislevy (2009) and others talk of a logical or evaluative argument. Others, such as Stake (2004, 2010), talk of triangulation. Both approaches call into question the validity of evidence. Both contend with the potential ambiguity that may result from varying perceptions of the legitimacy of an argument or from the filters that observers may use in carrying out an evaluation. The questions common to the approaches are: (a) who are the constituencies for the evidence, and (b) what are the consequences of potential misrepresentation or misinterpretation of such evidence? Great care is taken to keep accurate records in qualitative evaluation where it is often not possible to prespecify the variables to measure. This leads to the juxtaposition of case study methods on one hand in contrast to more technical measurement models on the other hand. These are some of the issues that convey the breadth and scope of the *Handbook on Measurement, Assessment, and Evaluation in Higher Education.*

There is a growing gap that needs to be addressed involving the scientific developments in measurement and recently developed methodologies in evaluation with respect to decision making in higher education. There is a need to address the distinctions and commonalities among measurement, assessment, and evaluation. There is a need to build a greater understanding of the differences among qualitative, quantitative and mixed-methods methodologies. There is also a great need to understand how the validation of evidence is central to logical thinking. Furthermore, there is a need to realize how politics and economics can play roles in the selection of evaluation questions and the use of evidence. And finally, decision makers need to have access to people trained in the sub-disciplines of these three fields in order to foster greater improvement in higher education.

As has been similarly stated by Robert Brennan, the editor of the fourth edition of *Educational Measurement*, complete agreement on the ideas expressed in this handbook with respect to measurement, assessment and evaluation, qualitative and quantitative, and the notions of validity and validation were virtually impossible to attain. Any inconsistencies that remain present are, in Brennan's words, "differences in opinion that . . . reflect professional disagreements that characterize any field of scientific endeavor" (2006, pp. xvi). It has been even more difficult attempting to interweave these three disciplines as applied to the field and the practice of higher education.

The handbook is divided into six sections. The first section contains topics on assessment in higher education. The contents of these chapters serve as a backdrop on which to build the foundation for the measurement, assessment, and evaluation sections that follow. The assessment topics in this first set of chapters are oriented to higher education administrators, student affairs personnel, faculty, and institutional researchers because they include the assessment of the quality of a university, classroom assessment, assessment of student learning outcomes and resistance to the use of learning outcomes by faculty, measures of institutional accountability, data sources accessible to higher education administrators, accreditation, and benchmarking. Each chapter enables these professionals to understand the assessment issues facing us in higher education.

The second section is about measurement and its technical aspects. To a certain degree, it provides in a non-technical manner, the latest thinking on theories and applications of measurement that enable decision makers to avoid pitfalls in the practice of higher educational administration.

The third section also provides a measurement focus but on how tests are constructed and analyzed in higher education. Attention is paid to what those managing the operation of an institution need to know for building into tests validity evidence, for understanding item analysis, the detection of unfairness, and the use of technology.

The fourth section provides applications of measurement and testing in various contexts. The chapters in this section detail the methods and issues involved with setting and validating a standard or passing score for different types of tests, placement testing, admissions testing, the assessment of writing skills, authentic assessment and the development of a rubric, and diagnostic assessment. They provide users of the handbook with practical guides and recent relevant information in these areas.

The fifth section of the handbook focuses on the theory of program evaluation and on evaluative methodologies. First discussed is program evaluation. The chapters on the evaluative methodologies that follow include qualitative, naturalistic, and responsive evaluation which go beyond the standards-based approaches to measurement and evaluation described in the previous sections. It also includes a chapter on case studies and validity, a major work on mixed methods evaluation, and a chapter describing the tools of survey construction.

The sixth and concluding section of the handbook focuses on important current issues in assessment and evaluation in higher education. It opens with chapters on accommodations for students with special needs and the evaluation of English-language learners. These are followed by a chapter on the evaluation of teacher quality in the K–12 system, an area of ongoing debate that may have significant consequences for teacher preparation programs in higher education. The two subsequent chapters are devoted to advising the higher education decision maker on best practices in the reporting of assessment and learning outcomes results. Revisiting reliability and validity, the next chapter raises challenging questions about how these concepts need to be reformulated in the context of higher education research and program evaluation. The final chapter in the section, and the *Handbook*, focuses on a fundamental area with which all higher education decision makers should familiarize themselves: ethical considerations in conducting assessment and evaluation activities and then using and interpreting the results.

By acquiring the knowledge contained in the sections of this handbook, the audiences for the handbook will come away with a better realization of how recent developments in measurement, assessment, and evaluation play an important role in more-informed decision making. Discussion questions and exercises for chapters appear at the end of each of the six sections.

References

Brennan, R. L. (2006). Editor's Preface. In R. L. Brennan (Ed.), *Educational measurement* (4th ed., pp. xv–xvii). Westport, CT: Praeger.

House, E. R. (1980). *Evaluating with validity*. Beverly Hills, CA: Sage.

Kane, M. (2006). Validation. In R. L. Brennan (Ed.), *Educational measurement* (4th ed., pp. 17–64). Westport, CT: Praeger.

Mislevy, R. J., Moss, P. A., & Gee, J. P. (2009). On qualitative and quantitative reasoning in validity. In K. Ercikan, & M. W. Roth (Eds.), *Generalizing from educational research: Beyond qualitative and quantitative polarization* (pp. 67–100). London, UK: Taylor & Francis.

Stake, R. E. (2004). *Standards-based and responsive evaluation*. Thousand Oaks, CA: Sage.

Stake, R. E. (2010). *Qualitative research: Studying how things work*. New York, NY: Guilford Press.

ACKNOWLEDGEMENTS

This is the first edition of the *Handbook on Measurement, Assessment, and Evaluation in Higher Education*. The contract was sealed with Routledge Press in December of 2009. However, work on the project actually began before that time as sample chapters and a proposal had to be developed. We are grateful for the hard work of Sarah Burrows, formerly of Routledge, for giving us the opportunity to undertake this endeavor. We also want to acknowledge the consistent support and patience of Heather Jarrow, our editor at Routledge, who guided us through the many stages of manuscript preparation.

An Editorial Advisory Committee, approved by Routledge, was established as part of the proposal to produce this handbook. The committee consisted of James Impara, Past President of the National Council on Measurement in Education; Nancy Petersen, Vice President of ACT; and Robert E. Stake, Professor Emeritus and Director of the Center for Instructional Research and Curriculum Evaluation (CIRCE) at the University of Illinois at Urbana-Champaign. All prominent in their fields, these individuals served to identify authors and review chapters. The input, guidance, and assistance provided by the Editorial Advisory Committee were extremely valuable to us in putting together this resource.

As co-editors, we appreciate the knowledge we have gained from our respective memberships in such organizations as the Association for Institutional Research (AIR), the American Educational Research Association (AERA), and the National Council on Measurement in Education (NCME). As lead editor, Charles Secolsky is very grateful for the associations he developed as a former employee of ETS and as a graduate of the doctoral program in Quantitative and Evaluative Research Methodologies at the University of Illinois at Urbana-Champaign. Many of the authors and reviewers involved in this handbook came from those associations.

Serving supportive roles behind the scenes were Professor Ronald K. Hambleton, University of Massachusetts at Amherst, and Professor Emeritus David A. Erlandson, Texas A & M University. Gratitude also goes to Nick Smith, Chairperson of the Instructional Design, Development and Evaluation (IDD&E) Department at Syracuse University, and to Steven Osterlind, Professor of Measurement and Statistics, University of Missouri, who reviewed the progress of the undertaking on the project's Basecamp website and provided encouragement to both of us at key points in the process.

We are grateful to Dr. Edward J. Yaw, President, and Joseph Vitale, Executive Director of College Advancement and Planning, both of County College of Morris, for their encouragement and support which helped enable this project to be completed on time. We also thank Linda Cook of

ETS and Debra Humphreys of the American Association of Colleges and Universities (AAC&U) for their recommendations of excellent authors, and Rand J. Spiro of Michigan State University for his advice at the early stages of the project's conception.

The greatest share of the credit for this *Handbook* goes to the authors, reviewers, and editors who contributed to the volume, which we believe is the first to attempt to integrate the three disciplines of measurement, assessment, and evaluation and apply them to the context of decision making in higher education. Those from County College of Morris who provided higher education review perspectives on many chapters were Dean Jane Armstrong, Denise Schmidt, and Dwight Smith III, Vice President of Academic Affairs. Kathleen Brunet Eagan of Clarus Associates served as stylistic editor for many chapters. We also acknowledge the contribution of the following individuals whose continuous and dedicated hard work as readers/reviewers provided encouragement: Kris Krishnan of Hudson County Community College, Christopher Pondish of the City University of New York, and Ellen Wentland of Northern Essex Community College. Also to be thanked are Arnold Gelfman of Brookdale Community College, Thomas Judd of the United States Military Academy, Stephen Levy of County College of Morris, and Randall Richards and Joseph Nazzaro formerly of County College of Morris. A special thanks goes to Melvin Reichler of the Sociology Department of Queens College for his long time support and encouragement as a friend and mentor.

Grateful acknowledgements are extended to all of those who served as reviewers for different chapters. Reviewers for Section 1 were Mary Ann Coughlin of Springfield College, Gabe Estill of Moraine Valley Community College, Robert Kahn of LaGuardia Community College, Bruce Keith of the United States Military Academy, Gary Nigh of the New Jersey Commission on Higher Education, Denise Schmidt of County College of Morris, Margaret Shepard of County College of Morris, and Dwight Smith III of County College of Morris.

Reviewers for Section 2 were Jane Armstrong of County College of Morris; Marc Glassman, Statistical Consultant, New York City; Nancy Petersen of ACT; and Dwight Smith III of County College of Morris.

Reviewers for Section 3 were Jane Armstrong of County College of Morris, Shelley Kurland of Montclair State University, Skip Livingston of ETS, and Michael Zieky of ETS.

Reviewers for Section 4 were Janet Eber of County College of Morris; Daniel Eignor of ETS; James Impara, Professor Emeritus of the University of Nebraska; Anthony Napoli, Professor at Suffolk County Community College; Tom Proctor of the College Board; Richard Sawyer of ACT; Kevin Sweeney of the College Board; Richard Tannenbaum of ETS; and Ellen Wentland of Northern Essex Community College.

Reviewers for Section 5 were Christopher Pondish of the City University of New York, Denise Schmidt of County College of Morris, and Robert Stake of the University of Illinois.

Reviewers for Section 6 were Thomas Judd of the United States Military Academy, David Nast of Ramapo College, and Denise Schmidt of County College of Morris.

I now want to take this opportunity to thank my co-editor Brian Denison for his tireless dedication to this project: his editorial recommendations; management of the project's Basecamp website; keeping track of the different drafts of chapters, discussion questions, section introductions, tables and figures; and assembling the manuscript and related files according to Routledge's author guidelines. For these contributions, I am most grateful.

I also would like to thank family and friends who put up with me for the last three years including Anna Bartmon, the Hasbrouck family, and Stephanie and Frank Boesch. Appreciated were the kind thoughts of Melissa, Michael, and Lindsay Rosenthal.

Charles Secolsky, June 21, 2011

SECTION 1

Assessment and Evaluation
in Higher Education

Charles Secolsky and D. Brian Denison

The eight chapters that are presented in this section reflect topics that are close to the ongoing functions of higher education administrators. They all relate to concerns that are important at different levels of higher education institutional administration and decision making. Those reading the chapters are likely to find differing perspectives presented. However, the set of chapters as a whole is intended to set the stage for more advanced applications of especially the measurement and evaluation sections that follow. From the Table of Contents, one can see that all eight chapters deal with some form of assessment, accountability, or accreditation.

There is a purpose to the order in which the chapters are presented. In Chapter 1, Stake, Contreras, and Arbesú present views on the assessment of the quality of a university, particularly its teaching. They identify barriers to successful assessment and evaluation of universities in general through the portrayal of a hypothetical university. By bringing the problems of assessment and evaluation to the forefront, this chapter sets a realistic tone that the remainder of the chapters in this section and those that follow must reckon with in order for the *Handbook* to accomplish its purpose.

Chapter 2 represents what some would consider the kernel of higher education that is closest to learning and assessment activity, namely classroom-level assessment. Drezek McConnell and Doolittle discuss embedding assessment activities within pedagogical practices that are aimed at aligning the classroom in the broadest sense with teaching and student learning.

Chapter 3 by Judd and Keith focuses on student learning outcomes at the program and institutional levels. They take the stance that learning outcomes are of the utmost importance for higher education institutions. The authors develop the most recent ideas to come forward in student learning outcomes into a cogent theoretical paper that logically integrates the issues surrounding this new and complex aspect of the field of assessment in higher education.

Chapter 4 by Banta and Pike brings out the caveats present in the notions attached to the assessment movement in higher education. They ask whether faculty will use assessment results. Why is it so difficult to derive guidance from assessment data and actually make responsive changes designed to improve instruction, curriculum, and student support services? The authors explore some reasons for this difficulty and outline strategies for addressing it, including increasing the use and technical quality of authentic measures of learning.

Chapter 5 by Palmer is on measures of accountability. This chapter is an in-depth examination of how accountability came into its present form. Starting with the use of sociological concepts that explain the etiology of accountability and, in particular, accountability in higher education, Palmer traces the development of accountability from a summative evaluation exercise to a more formative evaluation one, or from directives for corrective action to a sense that all colleges and universities seek improvement when possible.

In Chapter 6, Krishnan, Yin, Mahler, Lawson, Harris, and Ruedinger present the pros and cons of various ways to use data from national, state, and local sources in decision making, including comparisons with peers or other comparison groups. Their chapter provides a valuable resource for those needing to make the best use of such data in administrative decision making in higher education.

Chapter 7, by Fetterman, discusses empowerment evaluation, an evaluation methodology specifically intended to foster improvement and self-determination. The author uses case examples to illustrate how the use of empowerment evaluation in accreditation enables the persons at an institution to benefit from having greater ownership of the evaluation and accreditation processes.

Chapter 8, by Seybert, Weed, and Bers, covers concepts related to benchmarking in higher education. The authors present recent developments in this relatively new field of research that uses the results of traditional assessment and evaluation for purposes of peer and best-in-class comparisons across institutions. They provide case examples of how two institutions have worked with benchmarking tools.

The chapters in the five sections that follow have to do with measurement, assessment, and evaluation in different contexts. It is through the material presented in these subsequent chapters that inroads can be made in the development of new ideas by higher education decision makers to use for improving upon current practices in higher education administration, student services, and institutional research.

1

ASSESSING THE QUALITY OF A UNIVERSITY—PARTICULARLY ITS TEACHING[1]

Robert E. Stake, Gloria Contreras, and Isabel Arbesú

Universities are complex organizations, made up of semi-autonomous sectors and even more autonomous faculty members. Tradition and rules push activities toward homogeneity. Still, most administrators, staff, and students enjoy a grand leeway in which to work. Vincent Tinto (1995) noted that it would be difficult to find a single academic culture, but different cultures, different practices of evaluation and various groups of teachers and students.

Diverse Assessments Across the University

The buildings wear away, but mostly they fail the new burdens put upon them, such as for computing and collaborative instruction. The university's research seeks breakthroughs, with funding for inquiry problematically distributed (Alpert, 1985). For students, the university is partly a country club, not only the pools, but cultural exclusivity. The promises and expectations of the university vary greatly from corner to corner, and each begs for sensitivity and repair.

Assessing the quality of campus work, programs, and facilities is a responsibility shared by a vast array of stakeholders, including the trustees, the central administrators, the sector administrators, and of course, the faculty and the unions, the students and their families, the legislature and other funding bodies, the workplace, the media, and more. They all evaluate what the university does, mostly informally. Much of what the university does is complex and invisible. The great bulk of assessment is informal, structured by introspection and personal experience and framed against the long-standing reputation and culture of the university (Dressel, 1971).

The total quality[2] of any university is irregular, conditional and as complex as its many functions, classrooms, libraries, and laboratories. To rate a university as seventeenth or in the top ten or even as "very good" is a gross oversimplification, no matter the specificity of criteria or the length of acquaintance. Rankings are commonly voiced because people are comfortable with stereotypes and the reflected glow of self-adulation.

Administration

Assessment is important for managing the university and its parts. Call it assessment, call it evaluation, call it quality control, it can improve understanding when considered against thoughtful expectation and realistic standards.

Comparison of universities or departments serves curiosity but serves little the managerial or public good. The more valuable assessments are those that are formative, developmental, aimed at avoidance of dysfunction, repairing weakness, and shaping new teaching, research, and public service.

As expressed by its administrators, individual universities have their character—a mission, an organizational health, an ethic. Each has its uniqueness, integrity, and diversity. Each department, professional program, and area of aesthetics contributes to that character. Each individual in the university community, knowingly and unknowingly, contributes. The aggregated strengths and weaknesses of the whole and of the parts are difficult to know. Paying close attention to events, the flow of operational data, and the mood of the community, and more, yields good indicators. But guiding the largest and smallest of university functions depends less on formal indicators and more on experience and introspection.

There is much room for improving assessment of quality at universities nearby and around the world. There is considerable danger in representing the complexity of operations by simple indicators and criteria. Against this background, there are many topics to consider but we will limit this chapter to four, one of which will be the assessment of the special role of teaching.

Purposes

The purposes of this chapter are (a) to indicate the tension between summative and formative assessment at the university, (b) to identify barriers to comprehensive assessment at the university, (c) to overview the responsibility for assessment of university teaching as an example of accountability for the merit and the shortcoming of university functions, and (d) to analyze the role of formal and informal assessment in improving such operations as teaching.

Formative and Summative Assessment, Formal and Informal

People everywhere take notice of what they do, seeing in it the good and the bad. Evaluating is part of everyone's normal behavior. On the university campus, almost everything is evaluated, by the people in charge, by the direct beneficiaries, sometimes by the public (Stake & Cisneros, 2000). The great portion of evaluation is informal, even unintentional, whether done by administrators or others. On some occasions, and as part of some operational routines, extra effort is made to observe, measure, record, and interpret the merit and shortcoming of things. When evaluation becomes planned, routinized, recorded, and publicized, we say that the assessment is formal. Many of the functions of the university are assessed both formally and informally.

A rationale for formal evaluation should determine methods, procedures, instruments, and activities. Often there are several, sometimes competing, rationales for evaluation of any university entity or function. (Whatever is being evaluated, some call it an "evaluand.") Especially important is the anticipated use of the evaluation. People are not going to act the same with formative and summative evaluations (Contreras, 2010).

Summative Evaluation

When evaluation is done primarily to understand the quality of an existing evaluand, we call it summative evaluation. We think of it as having value, knowing that the value depends at least somewhat on its situation, and its potential uses and the users themselves, but for the time being, concentrating on how good or low bad it is. When we speak of a university's collaboration with industry, or its music program, or its library, we usually are speaking summatively of its quality at a particular time and place.

Formative Evaluation

But often we see the evaluand more as something being developed, changed, reorganized for new use—and we call for formative evaluation. The arborist trims the tree, the counselor changes protocol, the coach recruits an athlete, all of them evaluating formatively how to improve the process. In formative evaluation, not only the prospective use is considered, but also the likely situations, the new opportunities, the barriers, and possible disasters.

It would be wrong to think that summatively assessing university quality gives no attention to change and utility. And wrong to think that formative assessment gives no attention to the evaluand's merit in its immediate form. Some mix of formative and summative evaluation is common. But the different purposes call for different criteria, different explanations to informants, and different instruments.

University and department accreditation by professional associations is primarily summative assessment, but philosophically, and occasionally operationally, it is a process for improving the institution (Dressel, 1971). Some countries rely heavily on accreditation, others on inspection. Some countries rely on standardized quality control procedures set up by the central governments. Failure to attain accreditation is sometimes an indication of non-conventional operating procedures more than serious weakness. Even with thoughtful rationales, the validity of what is actually accredited is something to review. Any summary score (such as "accredited") oversimplifies the strengths and weaknesses of the evaluand.

A Hypothetical Conversation Between Administrators

A1: We are thinking of dropping accreditation by two of the three associations now accrediting us.

A2: Won't it hurt your reputation?

A1: I don't know. We agree with most of their standards, and being accredited may lower the howling, but it's too expensive.

A2: Don't you learn from their assessments?

A1: Mostly they reinforce what we already know. Sometimes we learn more from our own committees. Two of them last year really studied the problem.

A2: Committees can be worthless. And they sap staff energies.

A1: And they do little to help our reputation in the media.

A2: I suggest you find better ways to use the accreditation review process. Maybe your people show little respect for accreditation, so they treat it as political rather than evaluative.

A1. I don't know. We have to cut expenses.

Barriers to Comprehensive Assessment Across the University

In previous paragraphs, the university is said to be complex and far from homogeneous. Its parts and people have autonomy with different histories, aims, and operations. Nearly impossible, but still we do evaluate—and should do so comprehensively. Comprehensive assessment is illustrated in the following section, an example on assessment of teaching. It does not say to arrive at one summary rating, but to consider the multiple parts, their multiple features and functions, and multiple ways of knowing them. Common barriers to assessment are to be found in every institution. The order of barriers below does not indicate an order of importance.

1. *Widespread opposition to formalized assessment.* Although university people regularly evaluate their activities informally, for example, in conversations with administrators and students, often they

do not trust formal evaluation to treat them fairly. This attitude has many origins: popular distrust of authority, concern about over-simplification, lack of broad experience, doubts about the use of the information, and others.

2. *Administrators' misunderstanding of formal evaluation.* Administrators frequently associate formal evaluation with structured strategy, measurement, objective data gathering, statistical analysis, and indicators—all for control of the activities at the university. Often they have to show results quickly, so sometimes they favor techniques that capture a great amount of information in a short time.

3. *Lack of funding and training for people evaluating the functions.* Although evaluation is increasingly supported by many institutional centers at least partly dedicated to evaluation and improvement of quality, frequently staff members have only limited knowledge about the evaluation process, for example, to design studies, to fine-tune instruments, to collect data, to analyze information, or to report results. Universities do not have funds for comprehensive formal assessment of the functions.

4. *Political implications.* Evaluation is seldom recognized for its political nature, finding constraints on what will be studied, reward for favorable findings, and protective control of distribution of information (Cronbach, 1977).

5. *Expectation that the same data can be used for quite different purposes.* Data are collected from people expecting single uses, such as for research, but it ends up being used more widely. The meaning of the information is often not the same for summative and formative uses. Seeing this happen causes misinterpretation and loss of trust.

6. *The reactive effects of assessment.* Even without intention, the process of evaluation results in changing behavior. When a criterion becomes known as important for decision making, people consciously and unconsciously, sometimes unethically, act in such a way as to get better scores and improve their situations.

7. *Ethical ownership of personal data.* The confidentiality of information, especially for the people being evaluated, is a complex issue. In many ways, the institution is respectful of the privacy of personal information, but, in others, the authorities use private information to support decisions against those persons (Scriven, 1995).

8. *Self-promotion.* The increasing obligation for individuals, sectors, and the university as a whole to boast of strengths and accomplishments makes it important not to admit weakness and lack of accomplishment. Thus, assessment is denied important information needed.

Some barriers are especially apparent in the matter of evaluation of teachers (which is the topic of the next section of this chapter). The barriers above are pertinent to general assessment, including that of teaching. The barriers below, specific to teaching, are clues to obstacles to quality control throughout the rest of the university:

9. *Conceptions of teaching and evaluation of teaching.* Every instructor at the university has his or her own ways of teaching, and these ways are related to the discipline, previous professional and personal experiences, particular contexts, particular students, and some other aspects. Thus, a university may have many different conceptions about teaching and evaluation of teaching, but there is common meaning throughout, as well.

10. *Undervaluation of teaching.* Although it is said that teaching at the university is very important, it has been regularly undervalued compared to many other functions like research or public service (Canales, 2003). This situation has led to a lack of attention and resourcing of teaching, with a lack of guidelines for its evaluation.

11. *Invalid indicators.* Indicators of teaching quality may appear to have validity, such as "clarity of speaking," and may, for groups, be positively correlated with teaching effectiveness, but for individual instructors those criteria are not valid for administrative personnel decisions.

These several barriers can be overcome but they are strong and pervasive. They manifest differently in different situations. Continued study of them should be part of the institutional research of the university. Educational researchers are well positioned to study these barriers for the assessment of teaching, partly as examples of how evaluation is frustrated in all sectors of the university.

An Example: The Assessment of Teaching

Evaluation of teaching is one of the most important assessments at the university. In this section, the exclusive focus will be on assessment of teaching. Each assessment of other university functions has its special character but the points made in this section have relevance for evaluation of the other parts of the university. Assessment is a search for work needing protection from undue reorganization, reduction, and modernization. And assessment is a search for flaws needing fixing (Lehman, 1975).

Given current formal assessment procedures, a university's teaching, as a whole, or that of a department, can almost only be assessed by some aggregation of individual instructor teaching quality. Holistic self-study and committee review are possible, but direct assessment is outside reality. Good assessment of teaching quality of individuals is possible, and that is the concentration of this section.

The Complexity of Teaching

Teaching is a complex human activity fitted to common but ever-different situations. It is expected to result in student learning, but that has multiple definitions. Harry Broudy (1963) identified the modes of teaching as didactic, heuristic, and philetic. Philetic is establishing a relationship between teacher and student, resulting in motivation and perhaps love of learning what the teacher has to teach. The didactic is direct teaching, the imparting of knowledge and skill. Indirect (heuristic) teaching is the arrangement of circumstances so that students become better educated. Good teaching includes interpreting the curriculum, inspiring, scheduling, making assignments, supervising classroom interaction, testing, grading, advising, collaborating with peers, corresponding with administrators, and more (Arbesú, 2006; Arbesú, Díaz Barriga, Elizalde, Luna, Rigo, Rueda, & Torquemada, 2007; Darling-Hammond & Young, 2002; David, 2010). Doing one thing well does not assure doing all things well. Situations will vary as to how different responsibilities will be weighted.

Some teaching is open to view, but most university teaching is private within the classroom. By tradition, many instructors have come to expect privacy in the classroom and would object to having unidentified observers or electronic monitors in the room. With instructors feeling secure and protected well beyond "academic freedom," their privacy probably contributes to effective teaching. Sometimes it hides incompetent teaching. Administrators and other stakeholders of the university have a right to know the content and methods of each instructor, but monitoring which greatly diminishes the privacy of teaching would probably be an obstacle to the improvement of teaching.

Communitarian Teaching

The traditional concept of evaluating teaching is the evaluation of an autonomous instructor in an individual classroom. An additional perspective is found in practice, assessing the contribution an instructor makes to the maintenance and improvement of the instructional programs of the department. What instructors contribute to the integrity of all offerings, not just their own, is important too. A charismatic lecturer or innovative lab-organizer or personalistic mentor, that is, a star, sometimes contributes little to the upgrade of weak, misdirected, frivolous and outdated courses in the department. Both individual and team contributions need to be considered when teaching is assessed.

Collaboration across a campus faculty about matters of teaching is not new (Cruz Souza, 1999), but, in most places, it remains the exception more than the practice. Writing about a faculty as a *community of practice* became identified with John Seely Brown (1997) and others at the Institute for Research on Learning in Palo Alto (Community Intelligence Labs, 1997). Colleague Etienne Wenger said: "Even those who speak about learning organizations, life-long learning, or the information society do so mostly in terms of individual learners and information processes. The notion of communities of practice helps us break this mold" (1991, p. 7).

A Representation of the Evaluation of Teaching

Figure 1.1 is a graphic representation of both the formal and informal evaluation of teaching in higher education. It is more a representation of responsibility than a guide to assessment. It displays the responsibility for assessment of university teaching as an example of accountability for merit and shortcoming of all major university functions.

The shaded box in the middle represents responsibility for the evaluation of teaching, and to the right, responsibility for the improvement of teaching. Although potentially integrated, here they are kept separate because they are different responsibilities. At times they are merged as a comprehensive formative evaluation responsibility. For "Improvement of Teaching," we show four main areas of university support: (1) to provide counsel on improvement, (2) to foster personal self-study, (3) to provide measurement services regarding teaching effectiveness, and (4) to support mentoring by someone more experienced in teaching within the discipline. There are more, of course.

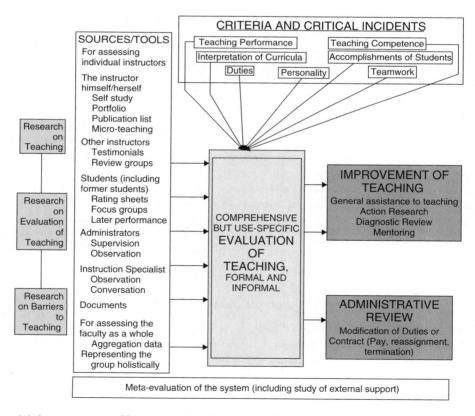

Figure 1.1 A representation of formal and informal evaluation of teaching in higher education

The box next below indicates the separate track to administrative review for the purpose of quality control—by changing instructional practice broadly as well as by modifying an individual teacher's contract. Some evaluation, summative evaluation, serves administrative review of teaching, as indicated. Much of the data are "use-specific," intentionally gathered for a specific purpose. All too often, any one measure will not serve both formative and summative purposes. In fact, data intended to improve teaching should not be automatically available to administrators because assistance to instructors can be more effective when information on weaknesses is kept private.

The range of data for evaluation is shown at the left. It comes from several sources, usually from the teacher being evaluated and his or her administrators, but also from peers in the department, from students, and from specialists in instruction. It starts with teacher reflective self-study but ranges much further (Brubacher, Case, & Reagan, 2005). Using only one or two of these sources is likely to yield a narrow view of the quality of teaching. At the top right are the criterial and critical incident data to be described in the next section. These responsibilities for evaluation need to be carried out against a background of research and professional experience, including what is pertinent to each particular university.

Some evaluation of teaching (at the bottom of the Sources/Tools box) pertains collectively to the department or sector, whether by aggregation of teaching performance of its instructors or by studying it as a unit. The three boxes at the left indicate the responsibility of drawing from research on teaching and on personnel evaluation, as well as research on barriers to teaching (mentioned earlier). The lowest box indicates the enduring necessity of backing up all evaluation with meta-evaluation—that is, evaluating the evaluation (Stufflebeam, 1981).

To repeat, this chapter is not so much a guide to evaluation practice but an identification of responsibilities shared by individuals, groups, and the university as a whole. Many of these responsibilities will be engaged in informal evaluation. Inadequate resources for formal evaluation and assistance for improvement of teaching will continue to limit engagement in these numerous obligations, but recognition of the error of using only one or two indicators will be important. The criteria and gathering of critical incidents should be comprehensive.

Criteria and Critical Incidents

Two grounds for evaluating teaching come from quantitative and qualitative perspectives: criteria and critical incidents. In a sophisticated system, both will be given attention. A criterion is a distinguishing property or characteristic of anything by which its quality can be judged or estimated, or by which a decision or classification may be made (Sadler, 2005). A criterion is often represented by a scale running from *none* to *much*. Good formal evaluation is often organized around multiple criteria drawing upon multiple data sources.

A critical incident is a distinguishing event or condition by which quality can be judged or estimated (not to be confused with the critical incident technique, Flanagan, 1954). Sometimes a single critical behavior or utterance is so important that it may overweigh other virtues and may be the primary basis for action, such as dismissal (or for an institution, loss of accreditation). In 2008, in two separate incidents, the University of Iowa removed a professor from his classrooms and duties after he had been charged, by a student, with misconduct. Isolated for a long period, each committed suicide (Franke, 2008). Each incident was a consideration for evaluating the university. Of course, other incidents will be positive, usually ordinary, such as a teacher stepping forward to defend someone. In a report, such incidents are represented by experiential detail in context rather than by measurement.

The appropriateness of criteria and critical incidents for evaluating depends on the purpose of the evaluation, the people who are evaluating, the institution, the discipline being taught, and so on (Canales, 2003; Cisneros-Cohernour, 1997). Criteria and critical incidents can be used together but will seldom converge on single pictures of teaching quality.

The most common criteria and types of critical incidents for evaluating university teaching are:

1. *Teaching performance.* To judge performance is to judge what the instructor actually did.
2. *Teaching competence.* To assess competence is to measure or estimate what the instructor is capable of doing, for example, by interview and review of portfolio, to assess the teacher's understanding of the subject matter being taught.
3. *Curriculum interpretation.* To judge teaching as to the way that teachers prioritize and interpret the topics contained in the curriculum. Here we have, for example, the capability to complete all lessons of the syllabus and to be constrained in offering objectionable interpretation of matters.
4. *Duties.* Criteria are fixed a priori by contract, assignment, or tradition on what the teacher is obligated to do. Here we have aspects like being present at classes and preparing lesson plans (Scriven, 1995).
5. *Personality.* The criteria are based on certain ideal characteristics of a teacher, like empathy, sense of humor, or relationship with the students.
6. *Teamwork.* Teamwork is a special competence, personality trait and commitment to work in a collaborative way with others, particularly other members of the faculty.
7. *Students' achievement.* One way to judge teaching is based on student grades, projects, performance, or scores on standardized tests. One might look at "value added" as seen in comparison of student test scores across years (Rosu & Stake, 2008; Rothstein, 2008). The aptitude of the students is an important consideration.

Whatever criteria or critical incidents are used, people responsible for evaluation of teaching seek widespread understanding of the means to judge teaching. This remains a problem because most teachers in higher education have extensive knowledge in their respective disciplines, but not in pedagogical methods (Troncoso & Hawes, 2006). In his or her discipline, a teacher has a special language and practice, but less so in teaching, and this can lead to problematic interpretation of quality.

Moreover, much teaching is highly contextualized, so that teachers will interpret the same criteria in different ways solely because of the classroom, media, laboratory and other contexts in which they teach.

Specialist Resources

It is common for a university to provide an office of instructional services, particularly for young and foreign speaking instructors. For example, the Pontificia Universidad Católica de Valparaiso (Chile) has a center where raising the quality of student training and the quality of teaching are the most important purposes. To these ends, the center has different units working on evaluation of teaching, quality of teaching, development of new curricula and accreditation. Some of these services, such as training teachers, are offered to teachers who volunteer, but increasingly some programs have been assigning their younger teachers to it.

Some public universities of Mexico City have centers dedicated to evaluating and improving teaching, with specialists serving teachers on campus. In some institutions, such as the Universidad Autonoma Metropolitana (UAM) at Xochimilco, no specialist staffing exists to evaluate quality of teaching or to train teachers. The professors there are assessed informally by administrators and peers designated by the director of the appropriate academic division, and formally by a student questionnaire. Results have sometimes been used to award merit pay. For formative evaluation there, on certain occasions a few professors meet to discuss their problems. Occasionally, educational researchers meet to discuss the different educational practices at the university. Of course, individual instructors are engaged in some form of self-study, a few using teaching portfolios.

A hypothetical conversation between teachers

T1. I don't like them evaluating my teaching.
T2. Too intrusive?
T1. They don't understand the experiences I want my students to have.
T2. And you do it well?
T1. I could do better.
T2. Your students don't rate you highly?
T1. Ten percent hate it. They pull me down below average.

Formative Evaluation of Teaching

Evaluation is coming to know the quality of the act of teaching, finding merit and shortcoming in each part of teaching. The learning of students may or may not be an indicator of the quality of teaching (Cisneros-Cohernour, 1997). Formative evaluation is designed to help teachers improve their daily work and course fulfillment. As things stand, professors are the most important actors in this process because they alone are in place to observe and reflect upon their own practices (sometimes with the help of specialists or peers) and to decide the changes they will make (Arbesú, 2006). At times, formative evaluation will be supported by an administration looking for change to protect its autonomy and purposes. On most occasions, summative evaluation is what administrators prefer. Sometimes it is considered by both researchers and administrators that improving education is promoted through reflection on practice and that this reflection in turn generates knowledge about teaching practice (Brubacher, Case, & Reagan, 2005; David, 2010; Rothstein, 2008).

Most researchers studying formative and comprehensive teacher evaluation are persuaded that it is useful for (a) changing methods of instruction, (b) engaging students in upgrading the quality of classroom learning, (c) promoting an aura of continuing professional education, and (d) helping the academic community (teachers, students, administrative, authorities) understand the complexities of educational practices and in particular teaching (Cronbach, 1963). Unfortunately, however clear it is for professionals to realize and support these uses, the evidence is not sufficiently strong to persuade administrators to provide the resources needed for formative evaluation of teaching. The problems will be made clear in the following section examining the function of improvement at the university when given an evaluative database.

Informally, everyone assesses teaching. Informal evaluation is constructed through perceptions and experiences of the people that participate in and observe the educational process: civil servants, teachers, students, administrators, and so forth. This type of evaluation occurs in all areas of the university and in all curricular and extracurricular activities.

Formally, assessment of teaching takes into account certain objectives and criteria a university uses to evaluate teaching quality. Educational researchers have assessed teaching for many years—but this field of knowledge is still under construction (Arbesú et al., 2007; Ashcroft & Palacio, 2010). Teaching assessment needs both formal and informal methods. Both help stakeholders refine insight into their accomplishments and problems.

Through this chapter we have highlighted the complexity of education, of teaching, and therefore, the complexity of the evaluation. Both formal and informal assessment have been found useful for understanding the activities of teaching. In the next part we present strategies for moving from assessment to improvement of university functions. Highlighted again are the complexity of the university and the people within it.

The Function of Assessment in Improving University Operations

Advocates of assessment are optimistic that gathering data about university operations will lead to improvement. It sometimes does. But at this time there is no science of university management, no theory of higher education, that has diagnostic quality. It is possible to learn much about how the university operates without understanding what could be done to improve it. From evaluation, for example, the rector may learn that the Department of Forestry is captive to commercial interests, but see no power or strategy for relief.

Figure 1.1 illustrated the responsibilities of formative evaluation of teaching, but did not show how evaluative knowledge can be converted into better teaching—and similarly for all functions of the university. Management of universities is greatly dependent on experience and intuition, however faulty those may be in some situations.

Formal assessment of most university functions, comprehensive and university-wide, lies beyond their present capacities, just, as indicated above, as complete assessment of teaching is out of reach. But it can be improved. University functions traditionally are comprehensively assessed in informal ways; some should be made more formal. Informal ways are fallible, and formal assessment also is fallible. Validating and oversight responsibilities are needed for existing and expanding assessment mechanisms.

What good evaluation reveals is not only the quality of operations but their complexity. When it becomes accepted that simple relationships do not explain much, it is easier to resist simple solutions. Each operation has educational, financial, political, ecological, aesthetic and other complexities, foreground and background, and inquiry leads toward postulation as to what might be tried and toward search for examples of where it has been tried.

Mission statements are usually not much help because they tell what has been succeeding instead of what needs fixing. They are for aspiration and energizing more than guiding. They omit most of some problems and all of others. More realistic assessment of problems, issues, and barriers is needed for better management. It is difficult to fix weaknesses in an atmosphere of self-promotion. Pressures for self-promotion have increased greatly, but good leaders will give more attention to fresh, skeptical, and sustained reflection. Quality is not sufficiently defined in any mosaic of awards and ratings. The true worth of the university is much more mundane. Both aspirations and trajectories of optimism and skepticism are indicators of institutional health.

Strategies for Formative Evaluation

Four strategic ways are available for moving from assessment to actual improvement of university operations, including student instruction but extending through all functions. All four strategies are needed, but probably not to be given equal priority. In each case there is need for attention to the heterogeneity of the university's stakeholders and the prospects of resources.

1. *The goal-based strategy.* Those responsible for campus-wide planning and operations come to agreement as to what the university should be, and prioritize shortcomings for remediation and new development as needed.
2. *The deficit strategy.* Those responsible for campus-wide planning and operations come to agreement as to where the university is falling short of expectation, missing opportunities, and in some ways hurting its community, and prioritize the shortcomings to be worked on.
3. *The sector-study strategy.* Increased support for recognition and alleviation of shortcoming is vested in departments, units, and other collectivities to come to agreement as to where their group is running smoothly, ineffective or dysfunctional.
4. *The self-study strategy.* Increased support for recognition and alleviation of shortcoming at the

level of the individual staff and faculty member is provided for self-study and coordination of improvement.

No matter how detailed the inquiry, the strategy for improvement will not come directly from indicators or ratings. Research on teaching may be suggestive; it will not be diagnostic. There is no alternative but to collect a wide array of informal and formal data for scrutiny and speculation as to where resources may best be spent. Often the individual staff member will have good guesses as to what changes in practice are feasible.

The whole and subdivisions of a university are patterned with uniqueness, with assets and contexts dissimilar. And universities differ as to the centrality of control. So it is not to be expected that evaluation and redevelopment will be the same or even visibly coordinated throughout the campus. As to the teaching function, the self-study model appears to have the greatest chance of success. Often the major function for central administrators is to demonstrate with conviction the need for assessment and to encourage sector leaders to devise their own strategies.

Evaluation of a university requires both formative and summative assessment, a recognition that the institution continues to mature and that there is a complexity of virtues and neglects that escapes easy measurement. The magnificent universities too have barriers to overcome. Assessment is not a guarantee either for protection from disarray or for quality control of growth, but comprehensive efforts to seek university quality can contribute to deliberative management. The greatest indicator of quality of a university might be the introspection of its administrators, staffs, and faculties.

Notes

1 An earlier version in Spanish of this chapter (Evaluando la calidad de la universidad, particularmente su docencia) appeared in Perfiles Educativos 2011, XXXIII (número especial), 155–168.
2 Quality means goodness, merit, and worth (Stake & Schwandt, 2006). It is not limited to the ideas of Total Quality Management (Ahire, 1997).

References

Ahire, S. L. (1997). Management science—total quality management interface: An integrative framework. *Interfaces, 27* (6), 91–105.

Alpert, D. (1985). Performance and paralysis: The organizational context of the American research university. *Journal of Higher Education, 56* (3), 241–281.

Arbesú, M. I. (2006). *La práctica de la docencia modular: El caso de la Unidad Xochimilco en la Universidad Autónoma Metropolitana.* México: UAM/Plaza y Valdés.

Arbesú, M. I., Díaz Barriga, F., Elizalde, L., Luna, E., Rigo, M. A., Rueda, M., & Torquemada, A. D. (2007). La evaluación de la docencia universitaria en México: Un estado de conocimiento del periodo 1990–2004. *Perspectiva Educacional, 48,* 27–58.

Ashcroft, K., & Palacio, D. (2010). *Researching into assessment and evaluation in colleges and universities.* London, England: Routledge.

Broudy, H. S. (1963). Historic exemplars of teaching method. In N. L. Gage (Ed.), *Handbook of research on teaching* (pp. 1–43). Chicago, IL: Rand McNally.

Brown, J. S. (1997). Common sense of purpose. In *What is a community of practice.* Community Intelligence Labs: http://www.co-i-l.com/coil/knowledge-garden/cop/definitions.shtml

Brubacher, J. W., Case, C. W., & Reagan, T. G. (2005). *Cómo ser un docente reflexivo. La construcción de una cultura de la indagación en las escuelas* (2nd ed.). Madrid, Spain: Gedisa.

Canales, A. (2003). Docencia: Tensiones estructurales en la valoración de la actividad. In M. Rueda, F. Díaz-Barriga, & M. Díaz (Eds.), *Evaluar para comprender y mejorar la docencia en la educación superior* (pp. 71–76). México: Universidad Autónoma Metropolitana-Universidad Nacional Autónoma de México-Universidad Autónoma de Baja California.

Cisneros-Cohernour, E. J. (1997). *Trade-offs: The use of student ratings results and its possible impact on instructional improvement.* University of Illinois: Unpublished report.

Community Intelligence Labs (1997). *Communities of practice.* Retrieved from http://www.co-i-l.com/coil/knowledge-garden/cop/index.shtml

Contreras, G. (2010). Diseño y operación de un sistema de evaluación del desempeño docente con fines formativos: la experiencia de la pontificia universidad Católica de Valparaíso, Chile. *Revista Iberoamericana de Evaluación Educativa, 3*(1). http://www.rinace.net/riee/numeros/vol3-num1_e/art14.pdf

Cronbach, L. J. (1963). Course improvement through evaluation. *Teachers College Record, 64,* 672–683.

Cronbach, L. J. (1977). Remarks to the new Society. *Evaluation Research Society Newsletter, 1*(1), 1–3.

Cruz Souza, F. (1999). *Psicología Comunitaria.* Buenos Aires, Argentina: Lumen/Hvanitas.

Darling-Hammond, L., & Young, P. (2002). Defining "highly qualified teachers": What does "scientifically-based research" actually tell us. *Educational Researcher, 31*(9), 13–25.

David, J. L. (2010). Using value-added measures to evaluate teachers. *Educational Leadership, 67*(8), 81–82. Retrieved from: http://www.ascd.org/publications/educational_leadership/may10/vol67/num08/Using_Value-Added_Measures_to_Evaluate_Teachers.aspx

Dressel, P. L. (1971). Accreditation and institutional self-study. *North Central Association Quarterly, 6,* 277–287.

Flanagan, J. C. (1954). The critical incident technique. *Psychological Bulletin, 51* (4), 327–358.

Franke, A. H. (2008, November 28). New lessons in dealing with sexual harassment. *Chronicle of Higher Education, 55* (14), A99.

Lehman, I. J., (1975). Evaluating teaching. In W. J. Gephart, R. B. Ingle, & G. Saretsky (Eds.), 1975. *The evaluation of teaching: National Symposium for Professors of Educational Research.* Bloomington, IN: Phi Delta Kappa.

Rosu, L. M. & Stake, R. E. (2008). The assessment of teaching and learning in USA: Reflections on school quality and the role of teacher in public schools. *Romanian Pedagogical Journal, 1*(1), 49–66.

Rothstein, J. (2008). *Student sorting and bias in value added estimation: Selection on observables and unobservables.* (CEPS Working Paper No. 170). Princeton, NJ: Center for Economic Policy Studies, Princeton University & National Bureau of Economic Research.

Sadler, R. (2005). Interpretations of criteria-based assessment and grading in higher education. *Assessment & Evaluation in Higher Education, 30*(2), 175–194.

Scriven, M. (1995). A unified theory approach to teacher evaluation. *Studies in Educational Evaluation, 21,* 111–129.

Stake, R. E. & Cisneros, E. J. (2000). Situational evaluation of teaching on campus. *New Directions for Teaching and Learning, 83,* 51–72. doi: 10.1002/tl.8305

Stake, R. E., & Schwandt, T. A. (2006). On discerning quality in evaluation. In I. F. Shaw, J. Greene, & M. Mark (Eds.), *Handbook of evaluation* (pp. 404–418). London, England: Sage.

Stufflebeam, D. L. (1981). Metaevaluation: Concepts, standards, and uses. In R. A. Berk (Ed.), *Educational evaluation methodology: The state of the art* (pp. 146–163). Baltimore, MD: Johns Hopkins University Press.

Tinto, V. (1995). El abandono en los estudios superiores: Una nueva perspectiva de las causas del abandono v su tratamiento. In *Cuadernos de planeación universitaria. 2 Época.* Mexico: UNAM-ANUIES, año 6.

Troncoso, K., & Hawes, G. (2006). A propósito de la evaluación por pares: La necesidad de semantizar la evaluación y las prácticas docentes. *Perspectiva Educacional, 48,* 59–73.

Wenger, E. (1991). Communities of practice: Where learning happens. *Benchmarks,* Fall, pp. 6–8.

2

CLASSROOM-LEVEL ASSESSMENT: ALIGNING PEDAGOGICAL PRACTICES TO ENHANCE STUDENT LEARNING

Kathryne Drezek McConnell and Peter E. Doolittle

The classroom is an intuitive unit of analysis when it comes to measuring student learning. Ask a student or recent graduate about their most meaningful learning experience in college, and you will likely hear about a specific class or favorite professor. Inquire about faculty members' most successful teaching episodes, and they may regale you with tales of a memorable lecture, seminar, or in-class activity when students' eyes lit up with comprehension, or talk about how participation in an out-of-class experience, such as a service-learning project, showcased the students' abilities to put a course's theories into action. Given this pattern, classroom-level assessment holds the promise for most directly connecting the measurement of student learning outcomes to the actual teaching and learning process.

In *The Art and Science of Classroom Assessment*—aptly subtitled *The Missing Part of Pedagogy*—Susan Brookhart (1999) delineated the multiple purposes classroom assessment may serve, from giving students feedback in order to improve their learning and shape their future academic choices, to providing faculty with data to enhance their teaching and inform larger discussions of class content and curricula. She argued that "because important decisions are based on information derived from classroom assessments, it is imperative that the information be of high-quality: accurate, dependable, meaningful, and appropriate" (p. 1). This chapter aims to further the case for classroom-level assessment by making explicit its intimate connection to teaching and learning.

A caveat before we proceed: the term *classroom-level assessment*, while descriptive, might appear to exclude out-of-classroom learning opportunities from the discussion. In this chapter, we take a more expansive view of the "classroom" as encompassing any single purposeful, organized experience offered by the institution in which students engage in order to learn. Included in this broad interpretation are the learning opportunities empirically demonstrated to promote deeper learning and greater engagement among undergraduate students, collectively known as high-impact educational practices (Kuh, 2008). Such practices include first-year seminars and experiences, common intellectual experiences, learning communities, writing-intensive courses, collaborative assignments and projects, undergraduate research, diversity or global learning, service/community-based learning, internships, and capstone courses and projects (Kuh, 2008), which need not necessarily be housed within a traditional, credit-bearing course in order to capitalize upon classroom assessment techniques (Palomba & Banta, 1999). Furthermore, considering our expansive view of the classroom, "faculty" may include co-curricular professionals in either academic or student affairs units responsible for the teaching, learning, and assessment process for non-course based experiences like these high-impact practices. Our use of the terms *classroom* and *faculty* throughout the chapter should be understood to include such non-course based learning experiences and co-curricular professionals engaged in teaching and learning.

Foundational Principles of Classroom-Level Assessment

The assessment of student learning has been studied for decades and has included both broad examinations of assessment (e.g., Palomba & Banta, 1999; Walvoord, 2004) and specific recommendations for classroom assessment (e.g., Angelo & Cross, 1993; Huba & Freed, 2000). From this scholarship, four foundational principles have been constructed to frame further discussions.

Principle #1: Classroom assessment must be defined in terms of the improvement of student learning. A definition of classroom assessment must address its three components: process, evaluation, and purpose. First, the process of classroom assessment involves the gathering of information from multiple sources and perspectives and focuses on student performance; sources of information collected from teachers, peers, and professionals may include tests and quizzes, observations and writings, reflections on research and service, projects, and activities. Second, each of these sources yield information that must be evaluated and interpreted "in order to develop a deep understanding of what students know, understand, and can do with their knowledge as a result of their educational experiences" (Huba & Freed, 2000, p. 8). And, third, the purpose of classroom assessment is the improvement of student learning through modifications in the students' and the teachers' understanding, choice of strategy, or epistemological perspective. Therefore, if truly meant to improve student learning, classroom assessment needs to be a major component of sound pedagogical practice that explicitly addresses the instructional development process.

Principle #2: Classroom assessment is the purview of those most directly responsible for the construction of instructional environments—faculty. In their seminal book on classroom assessment, Angelo and Cross (1993) argue that, in contrast to programmatic and institutional assessment efforts, classroom assessment does not necessarily require a high level of training in psychometrics or the social science research methodologies utilized by assessment professionals. Instead, faculty, as arbiters of the instructional environment of a particular course and its larger place in the curriculum (e.g., instructional design, strategies, content, and assessment) are best suited to articulate appropriate learning outcomes, design opportunities for students to demonstrate mastery of these outcomes, evaluate student performance, and make any necessary changes based on their assessment of the overall success of the class in achieving the desired outcomes (see "Seven Basic Assumptions of Classroom Assessment", Angelo & Cross, 1993, pp. 7–11). The "active, continuous, and personal involvement" of faculty, and by extension their students, in the assessment of student learning is necessary "if assessment is ever to improve substantially the quality of student learning" (Angelo, 1994, p. 1).

Principle #3: Classroom assessment is implemented through the judicious use of course assignments. Valid course assignments are those that align directly with the course's learning outcomes, pedagogical practices, course content, and student characteristics. These assignments may be formative or summative, qualitative or quantitative, and behavioral, cognitive, or affective. The nature of these assessments is limited only by the imagination of the instructor and the requirement that the assessment aligns with the course; thus, classroom assessments may include more traditional avenues (e.g., multiple-choice tests, true-false quizzes, written essays) or more alternative avenues (e.g., metacognitive reflections, service-learning projects, video essays). Each of these assignments provides information related to student learning and performance that may then be evaluated for the purpose of improving student learning.

Principle #4: Since classroom assessment is an essential element of institutional assessment, faculty members and institutional assessment administrators must collaborate. Faculty benefit from collaborating with others on campus who bring to bear empirically sound approaches to measuring student learning outcomes; moreover, those responsible for coordinating assessment at the college or university must seek out opportunities to collaborate with those on campus actively engaged in teaching and learning (Culver & Van Dyke, 2009). Faculty antipathy toward all things assessment is often taken as a truism, one reinforced by assessment efforts that emphasize accountability and accreditation over teaching and learning. Framing assessment efforts as teaching and learning efforts rather than accountability efforts helps to cultivate a culture of assessment on campuses (Suskie, 2004, p. 37). Culver and Van Dyke make the case that assessment conversations "invariably evolve into conversations about the importance of teaching" because "a stated strength of assessment is its ability to increase the transparency of teaching and learning and the educational experience" (p. 342).

Ultimately, Principles 1–4 focus on student learning through the construction of instructional environments containing embedded assignments that are used to improve both student learning and institutional effectiveness by *aligning* (a) course outcomes, content, and context; (b) students' prior knowledge and experience; (c) instructional strategies and resources; and (d) institutional improvement and accountability. It is this focus on alignment, often overlooked when considering assessment, that will serve as the backbone of this chapter. Specifically, we offer pragmatic strategies for connecting classroom assessment to the teaching and learning process through the appropriate alignment of pedagogical practices. We will address alignment issues concerning what, who, and how one teaches. Within each section, we will suggest strategies, tools, or technologies that facilitate the use of class activities and assignments—whatever the format—as measurable artifacts of learning.

The Importance of Alignment to Meaningful Classroom Assessment

In examining the essential role of alignment in creating an instructional environment focused on student learning, it is first necessary to express an assessment-based *mea culpa*. The assessment of student learning outcomes is often presented as a variation on the same cyclical theme, regardless of level (e.g., classroom, program, or institution). For the sake of clarity, we have intentionally simplified the

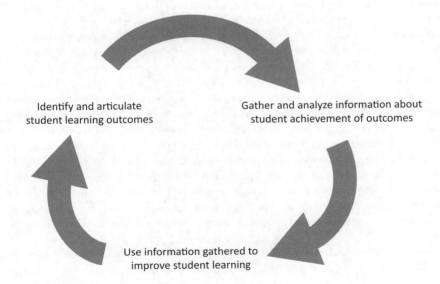

Identify and articulate
student learning outcomes

Gather and analyze information about
student achievement of outcomes

Use information gathered to
improve student learning

Figure 2.1 The assessment cycle

This figure is based on one developed by S. M. Culver & R. Van Dyke for use in workshops conducted by the Office of Academic Assessment (http://www.aap.vt.edu/index.html) at Virginia Polytechnic Institute and State University.

visualization of the standard assessment cycle at Virginia Tech (see Figure 2.1). The standard cycle includes the following constituent parts: (a) identifying and articulating student learning outcomes, (b) gathering and analyzing information about the students' achievement of these outcomes, and (c) using the information that was gathered to improve student learning.

This simple description of the assessment cycle—with its arrows linking each step in a continuously spinning circle of activity—may promote conceptual understanding; however, we have found that it often belies the complexity that exists in the spaces between writing outcomes, measuring student achievement, and making sense of the data. As professionals responsible for providing faculty development in the areas of outcomes assessment and effective pedagogy, we have been guilty of diluting its inherent complexity in order to help those with the least amount of assessment experience achieve the greatest possible level of understanding. In our estimation, less successful classroom-level initiatives suffer from a critical problem within the assessment cycle—a failure of alignment. While faculty may have learned that the measures they employ to assess student learning must correspond to the learning outcomes they have articulated, too often this is where efforts at alignment stop.

An illustrative example: Consider the well-respected academic department known for its high-quality classroom and program assessment work that decided to investigate first-year students' critical thinking skills. A group of faculty responsible for teaching multiple sections of the same first-year course decided to focus on student learning associated with critical thinking, using a course assignment—a persuasive essay—as the primary source of information related to student learning. The persuasive essay has been integrated into the course across multiple sections as a common assignment the previous semester. The faculty members spent a great deal of time developing a definition of critical thinking appropriate to their discipline and subsequently created a rubric that delineated the criteria against which students' essays would be judged that aligned with that definition. They followed appropriate procedures to establish inter-rater reliability and used multiple raters to judge essays sampled from across the previous semester's class sections. Once the scores were tallied, however, participating faculty were shocked to discover that the majority of the first-year students exhibited little to no critical thinking skills whatsoever.

Fortunately, this group's collective assessment wisdom prevented panic or angry denial from setting in; instead, they revisited their assessment process. They checked to see if their articulation of the student learning outcome (i.e., critical thinking) aligned with the measurement rubric that they had used. On the surface, their definition of critical thinking and the rubric for assessing students' critical thinking did indeed align; however, upon deeper investigation, they acknowledged several significant failures of alignment between the assignment and the rubric that provided an explanation for unexpectedly poor results. While the outcome and the criteria for assessing student achievement of the outcome aligned, they had failed to align other key elements in the teaching, learning, and assessment process. For example, they never considered whether the criteria for critical thinking that they had developed fitted the level of maturation and academic prowess of first-year college students. Additionally, there was a significant misalignment between the original directions and evaluation criteria for the persuasive essay and the subsequent rubric-based criteria for critical thinking. In other words, critical thinking as defined for the assessment process was neither communicated as a learning outcome to the students nor incorporated into the learning artifact used to judge students' skills and abilities. Faculty members were, in essence, using an assessment tool unrelated to the original assignment.

We believe that the missing links in this assessment of critical thinking were not measurement problems per se, but pedagogical problems that could have been mitigated through more sophisticated approaches to alignment. It is our contention that, for classroom assessment to generate meaningful information, all aspects of the classroom experience must align pedagogically. This alignment must take into consideration the course outcomes and content, the learners themselves, the instructional and performance contexts, and the pedagogical strategies used. In other words, assessment must be related to the *what*, *who*, and *how* of teaching and learning.

Outcomes and Content: What Are You Teaching?

Classroom assessment, as well as good pedagogical practice, "begins not with creating or implementing tests, assignments, or other assessment tools but by first deciding . . . what you want your students to learn" (Suskie, 2004, p. 73). Explicit articulation of learning outcomes is key to being successful in aligning the teaching, learning, and assessment processes. Well-crafted learning outcomes state the specific skills, abilities, knowledge, beliefs, attitudes, or dispositions that students are expected to develop as a result of completing a class. They should be ambitious, yet attainable by the students taking the course, and measurable. These outcomes answer the question, "To what end?" To what end are students writing papers, engaging in group work, or giving oral presentations before the class? Course syllabi often focus on the operational (e.g., due dates, grading policy, schedules) rather than aspirational components of a class (Doolittle & Siudzinski, 2010). Faculty sometimes confuse objectives and outcomes on a syllabus, labeling objectives like "By the end of this course, students will complete a research paper" or "By the end of the semester, students will participate in a group project" as learning outcomes. Such statements may delineate expected actions or behaviors of students, but they fail to specify the *ends* for which students are engaging in this work. Are students developing information literacy and research skills? Are the students enhancing their ability to work as part of a diverse team? Considering all the factors that learning outcomes must address, writing outcomes can be a daunting process. Fortunately, there are ample resources available to faculty to assist them in writing realistic learning outcomes. A simple Web search of peer academic departments at other institutions is a useful first stop in the search for discipline-specific learning outcomes. Disciplinary associations are another potential source for learning outcomes (Suskie, 2004). Regardless of whether they accredit programs in their field, professional associations as diverse as the American Political Science Association (APSA) and the Accreditation Board for Engineering and Technology (ABET) have begun to delineate program-level disciplinary learning outcomes that can be modified to fit individual courses. In addition to resources provided by academic associations, NASPA—Student Affairs Administrators in Higher Education—has a knowledge community dedicated to assessment, evaluation, and research that serves as a resource for those assessing co-curricular student learning (www.naspa.org/kc/saaer/default.cfm). Beyond discipline-specific or content-specific outcomes, the Association of American Colleges and Universities (AAC&U) has delineated 14 learning outcomes—from critical thinking and communication skills to ethical reasoning and integrative learning—deemed essential to undergraduate education. These Essential Learning Outcomes were articulated and further refined for assessment purposes by two of the AAC&U's most well-regarded initiatives, the Liberal Education and America's Promise (LEAP) and the Valid Assessment of Learning in Undergraduate Education (VALUE) projects (AAC&U, 2007; Rhodes, 2010). Though originally conceived to facilitate program-level assessment, the language provided in AAC&U's Web resources and many publications is an excellent starting point for developing learning outcomes for classroom-level assessment.

A final tool of note is the commercially available "critical thinking wheel" developed by Michael L. Lujan from www.MentoringMinds.com. Based on both the original Bloom's Taxonomy (1956) and the revised version (Anderson & Krathwohl, 2001), the wheel provides faculty with succinct definitions for the six levels of the taxonomy (knowledge/remember, comprehension/understand, application/apply, analysis/analyze, evaluation/evaluate, and synthesis/create), along with a bank of "power words" and questioning prompts designed to elicit student learning and engagement at each level. More convenient than a thesaurus, this tool not only helps faculty craft language for learning outcomes, but helps facilitate the alignment between outcomes, content, and sequence by reminding faculty that, if they desire learning outcomes that require higher-order thinking like synthesis or evaluation, the content they address and the sequence in which they engage the material needs to correspond to the appropriate type of learning outcomes. In other words, faculty would be hard-pressed to see student learning at the upper levels of Bloom's taxonomy if the content and sequence of the course only demanded memorization of facts and figures.

It is likely that learning outcomes will not be perfect in their first iteration; they will probably require tweaking from one semester to the next, even for the same class. Rather than focusing on linguistic perfection, however, it is more important to ensure that the outcomes reflect the expected and desired end-result of the faculty member and align with the content addressed by the class and the sequencing of content for the students. If the faculty teaching the course cannot draw a direct connection between the expected learning outcomes and the content of the class, then one or both need to be revisited.

As stated previously, course content—which includes not only the relevant knowledge, skills, and attitudes, but also the assignments required of students—must align with the learning outcomes. Thinking back to the critical thinking example: student coursework did not demonstrate critical thinking because it was not a required component of the assignment given to them. If the assignment did not explicitly include critical thinking, one expects that explicit instruction related to the development of specific critical thinking skills was lacking as well. Some may dispute the necessity of explicit instruction in the belief that, by simply engaging in certain activities, students will naturally develop desired skills and abilities. While that may be true for some students, such an approach to teaching is inherently risky and begs the question of whether individual faculty members are needed as expert guides in the learning process. Explicit instruction is not synonymous with a didactic approach to teaching either. It can be accommodated within any number of active, learner-centered pedagogical practices. Whatever the content, it must reflect the articulated learning outcomes and be part of the intellectual framework for the student assignments if it is to be meaningful for classroom assessment.

Learners and Learner Characteristics: Who Are You Teaching?

The educational psychologist David Ausubel (1968) asserted, "the most important single factor influencing learning is what the learner already knows. Ascertain this and teach . . . accordingly" (p. 18). Yet often we develop outcomes, determine content, establish expectations, and begin to teach a class without first assessing the students' prior knowledge and discovering where our students are as learners. Aligning learning outcomes, content, and strategies is unworkable if the entire alignment is not in concert with the learner. Prior knowledge includes not only content knowledge specific to the class, but also the students' beliefs, experiences, study strategies, and non-academic knowledge. All of students' prior knowledge—academic and non-academic, declarative and procedural, cognitive and metacognitive—influences how and what they learn in a course.

Faculty members have several methods available to them for getting to know their students. On the first day of class, many faculty ask students to share a bit about themselves. Are they first-year students or seniors? Are they taking the class as a major requirement or an elective? Are they traditional in age (ages 18–24) or students returning to the classroom after accumulating a range of life experiences beyond schooling? What, if anything, do students already know about the content of the class? This type of sharing may take place as a class conversation with students introducing themselves to the professor and each other, or more formally by having students fill out an index card or submit information electronically through e-mail or a short online survey. These activities not only serve to foster a learner-centered environment in a classroom (Weimer, 2002), they can also provide an opportunity for collecting data about your students' prior knowledge that may be relevant to classroom assessment. By incorporating some more detailed questions about students' academic, co-curricular, and/or professional interests, their reasons for enrolling in the course, their initial comfort level with the material, and what they hope to gain from the class, faculty gain useful insights into what their students bring to the first day of class. This information can help faculty contextualize course material to make it relevant to the specific students enrolled in the class by tapping into the interests of the students. Aligning course content to this knowledge of the students promotes the acquisition, processing, and retention of course material, including the skills of problem-solving, critical thinking, and the transferral of knowledge.

Simply structuring opportunities for students to tell you about themselves is the easiest and least costly method of data collection in terms of faculty time, effort, and resources. That said, students' prior knowledge may be directly and perhaps more accurately assessed by administering a pre-test of the material you intend to cover in the course in order to determine what students already know. Pre-tests can also be used to evaluate students' mastery of content and skills considered prerequisites for the successful completion of the class. Pre-tests, like any assignment, can take a variety of forms (e.g., multiple choice tests, open-ended reflection prompts, peer-to-peer interviews). The format of the pre-test should make sense as part of the overall course design and material to be covered. Pre-test data can help faculty both identify specific strengths and deficiencies in students' prior knowledge and respond appropriately in the design and delivery of class content. For example, the information provided by a pre-test may lead faculty to present more in-depth treatment of a topic in which students in the class demonstrated the greatest deficiencies. Topics that the students have already mastered may receive lighter treatment in the course, thereby freeing up more time for alternate content to be introduced. Data generated by pre-tests may also help faculty to adjust their expectations and reframe appropriate learning outcomes for the class. This type of adjustment in response to deficiencies need not be seen as a lowering of standards or expectations, but a sensible recalibration of what is possible within the context of a single class.

Understanding one's students as learners is not limited to measuring class content knowledge alone. Other factors may impact the students' ability to achieve the desired learning outcomes of a class. Faculty can also explore cognitive and affective characteristics early on in order to shape the direction, depth, and design of the course. One example of a potentially useful diagnostic is the *Motivated Strategies for Learning Questionnaire*, or MSLQ (McKeachie, Pintrich, & Lin, 1985; Pintrich, McKeachie, & Lin, 1987). The MSLQ was designed to assess motivation and use of learning strategies by college students (Pintrich, Smith, García, & McKeachie, 1991). Specifically designed for use at the course or class level (Duncan & McKeachie, 2005), this 81-item, self-report instrument is available at no cost in the literature and can be modified to fit the context of a specific course or subject-matter. Used as a self-diagnostic for students and in educational psychology research (Duncan & McKeachie, 2005), students rate statements from *not at all true of me* (1) to *very true of me* (7). Statements include, "If I don't understand the course material, it is because I didn't try hard enough," "I find it hard to stick to a study schedule," and "When a theory, interpretation, or conclusion is presented in the class or in the readings, I try to decide if there is good supporting evidence." Items like these form the basis of six subscales that measure the students' motivation, and nine subscales measuring students' use of learning strategies. Why should we worry about such characteristics of learners? It is the premise of the MSLQ that, in any course, the student is "an active processor of information whose beliefs and cognitions mediate important instructional input and task characteristics" (Duncan & McKeachie, 2005, p. 117). In other words, student motivation and approaches to studying effectively serve as filters for course content, helping to determine what and how students learn in any given class. Using the MSLQ, faculty can develop a profile of the students in a class and teach accordingly—playing to students' strengths, tapping into aspects of their motivation, even stretching students by explicitly offering content related to the employment of more sophisticated learning strategies.

Understanding the learners who make up a class is key to successful teaching and assessment, and provides a basis for pedagogical decisions about what and how one teaches. If instructional design is not contextualized to accommodate the actual students enrolled in the class, faculty may be setting students up to fail in the task of learning the course material. As in the case of the assessment of critical thinking described earlier, classroom assessment activities may note this failure, but the lack of alignment between characteristics of the learners and course outcomes, content, and instructional strategies may lead faculty to draw incorrect conclusions from the data. Incorrect conclusions make the improvement of student learning through assessment nearly impossible and defeat the purpose of classroom assessment.

Instructional Context and Strategies: How Are You Teaching?

As noted in the rationale for explaining the critical thinking assessment example and evident in Figure 2.1, alignment often focuses on outcomes and assessments. Focusing on alignment, however, requires that each instructional element be examined and carefully constructed. Two such elements, often overlooked, are instructional contexts and instructional strategy. Like learner characteristics, instructional contexts and strategies in the classroom serve to mediate and shape what students learn. Thus, faculty need to be as mindful of how they are teaching as they are of who and what they are teaching.

The importance of instructional contexts and instructional strategies, in relation to alignment, can be generalized within the *encoding-specificity principle* (Tulving, 1983). The encoding-specificity principle states that when, where, how, and why knowledge, skills, and attitudes are learned affects how those knowledge, skills, and attitudes will be recalled and applied. In short, this principle states that learning and performance are intricately related. The research on encoding specificity clearly indicates that, when the learning context and the performance context align, performance is enhanced (Godden & Baddeley, 1975; Ucros, 1989); moreover, when the cognitive processes employed during learning and the cognitive processes employed during performance align, performance is also enhanced (Lockhart, 2002; Tulving & Thompson, 1973). Thus, it is essential for faculty to proactively examine instructional contexts and strategies in order to align desired outcomes (learning) and learner assessments (performance).

Instructional contexts refer to the physical and affective states of the instructional environment. The physical states of instructional context include the general approach to instruction (e.g., face-to-face, online, hybrid) and the specific artifacts of instruction (e.g., location, instruments, technology). The affective states of instructional context include the physiological states (e.g., anxiety, pharmacology, stress) and emotional states (e.g., happy, sad, mood) of the learner. It has been demonstrated that misalignments in physical and emotional states between learning and performance episodes have an adverse impact on performance (see Eich, 1980; Overton, 1991, for reviews); for example, misalignments between learning and performance episodes in location (Gooden & Baddeley, 1975), instrumentation (Rosen, 2008), technology use (Doolittle & Mariano, 2008), alcohol use (Weissenborn & Duka, 2000), marijuana use (Darley, Tinklenberg, Roth, & Atkinson, 1974), nicotine use (Lowe, 1986), anxiety (Morissette, Spiegel, & Barlow, 2008), and mood (Teasdale & Russell, 1983) have all resulted in poorer performance.

Just as context has been demonstrated to be an important factor in instructional alignment, so have instructional strategies. Instructional strategies refer to the design of instructional activity and the cognitive processing that occurs during the instructional activity. It should be noted that the value of the designed instructional activity lies in its ability to motivate relevant cognitive processing, not in the mere completion of the activity; that is, a critical thinking activity is only beneficial if the learner actually thinks critically during the execution of the activity. This focus on cognitive processing plays a central role within the encoding-specificity principle in that the nature and depth of processing that occurs during learning affects the nature and degree of recall, application, and transfer of knowledge at the time of performance (Craik, 2002; Lockhart, 2002). Specifically, research into how "deeply" one processes information during a learning episode (Craik & Lockhart, 1972) and how congruent the cognitive processing is between the learning and performance episodes (Morris, Bransford, & Franks, 1977) has determined that both depth and congruence—*alignment*—are essential to learning and performance. Thus, unless instructional strategies, which motivate cognitive processing, are in alignment with both outcomes and assessments, significant learning and performance are not likely to occur.

Leveraging Technology for Classroom-Level Assessment

Alignment between what, who, and how one teaches is essential to ensuring the meaningfulness of the data collected as part of classroom-level assessment. That said, collecting information on all three dimensions of the alignment equation can be challenging. Fortunately, educational technologies exist that can support and promote a learner-centered approach to classroom-level assessment by helping faculty to collect evidence about what, who, and how they are teaching. What follows is a discussion of two very different—but equally useful—tools that hold great promise for gathering classroom assessment data.

Clickers

Student or personal response systems, colloquially known as "clickers," represent a technological innovation to the traditional in-class quiz that is particularly useful within larger classrooms (Boyle & Nichol, 2003; Mayer et al., 2009). Commercially available from a number of vendors, clickers conjure images of the gameshow *Jeopardy*, in which contestants furiously click a hand-held device in order to be the first to buzz in to answer the quiz show's questions. Rather than a tool for competition between students, however, clickers allow for mass student participation in large lecture-based courses. Clicker in hand, students respond electronically to questions posed by the instructor. Clickers have been used to monitor class attendance and more actively engage students in a given lecture; increasingly, clickers are also being recognized as a powerful tool for facilitating the assessment of student learning outcomes (Kolikant, Drane, & Calkins, 2010). Specifically, clickers offer a more convenient and adaptable in-class tool for quizzing students on more facets of a course than either pen-and-paper or Web-based questionnaires, the former requiring greater faculty time to score and the latter requiring universal computer access for enrolled students.

While the clicker allows students anonymity when they respond to questions in class, each clicker also has an assigned number that can be linked to an individual student's responses and that generate data that faculty may use later for grading and classroom assessment purposes. Faculty can directly assess student comprehension of assigned readings or concepts presented in a previous class meeting by quizzing them with three or five short multiple-choice questions at the beginning of the lecture. Students use the clickers to respond to the questions and, instantaneously, the faculty member has quantitative data to analyze and use to improve student learning. Since the instructor and students can immediately see how the majority responded to each question, the faculty member has the ability to respond to student misunderstandings in real time, while the system quietly records individual responses in a database.

From an assessment perspective, faculty can conduct clicker quizzes over the course of a semester and track student responses in order to determine what content presented more of a challenge and what content was most easily mastered. Faculty can also create questionnaires that ask students questions related to the class's instructional context and strategies, thus providing feedback on a faculty's teaching at any point during the semester and not just summatively with the traditional course evaluation form presented to students at the end of the semester. While the power of the clicker to improve student learning is still not settled (Mayer et al, 2009; Martyn, 2007), scholars note the need for faculty to take into consideration the relationship between learner characteristics, the instructional context, and the content covered as they introduce clickers as a pedagogical practice (Kolikant, Drane, and Calkins, 2010), mirroring the case made in this chapter for assuring alignment between these elements in order to promote sound classroom assessment practices.

ePortfolios

Another popular technological innovation for classroom assessment is ePortfolio. When effectively integrated into a class, it can simultaneously serve as a powerful teaching tool and a useful mechanism for assessment (Cambridge, 2010). Traditionally associated with programs in the creative arts, architecture, and teacher education (Chen & Light, 2010; Lombardi, 2008), portfolios have been used to assess student learning for decades, either showcasing a student's best work or documenting a student's learning process (Lombardi, 2008). Portfolios also provide students with an important opportunity to demonstrate both their in-class learning and the non-course based learning that they experience through the co-curriculum. As an assessment tool, the portfolio "is unique insofar as it captures evidence of student learning over time—in multiple formats and contexts—documents practice, and includes a student's own reflection on his or her learning" (Chen & Light, 2010, p. 1). Today's electronic iteration of this tool—the "e" in ePortfolio—not only taps into contemporary students' comfort with technology, but facilitates the collection and archiving of extensive samples of student work without the inconvenience of the bulky paper versions of the past.

Like the clicker, ePortfolio technology is commercially available from multiple vendors, as well as from such open source communities as Sakai. In contrast to the clicker, which is best suited to gathering quantitative data quickly through short quizzes or student questionnaires, the ePortfolio serves to organize and archive more qualitative evidence of student learning. Best practice with ePortfolios emphasizes the student reflection component, or "folio thinking" (Chen & Mazlow, 2002), with the student engaging in meaning-making and the integration of class content with his or her own knowledge and perspective. Specifically, ePortfolios can be a beneficial technology for teaching and learning in any discipline as they help promote students' ability to: (a) integrate theory and practice; (b) be explicit in their focus on the reflective purpose of an ePortfolio; (c) provide authentic, direct links between assignments and classroom practice; and (d) think critically (Parks & Kajder, 2010, p. 220). Reflections most often take written form, but need not be limited to a traditional essay; ePortfolio systems can include a student's wiki or a blog. Increasingly, faculty ask students to leverage new technologies and include digital voice or video reflections such as video logs, or Vlogs (Parks & Kajder, 2010). Regardless of ePortfolio format, opportunities to reflect upon one's learning generate cognitive benefits for students, improving their ability to engage in metacognition and synthesis (Suskie, 2004).

While there is no magic button to press that will evaluate students' work for evidence of their attainment of the desired learning outcomes, rubrics serve as a popular tool for making sense of the collection of student work assembled within an ePortfolio (Chen & Light, 2010). Rubrics are scoring tools that provide specific performance criteria and well-defined levels of achievement for each criterion (Stevens & Levi, 2005). Rubrics have long been used to grade student assignments and have multiple pedagogical benefits, including providing timely feedback, preparing students to use detailed feedback, encouraging critical thinking, facilitating communication, and helping faculty refine their teaching skills (Stevens & Levi, 2005, pp. 17–25). Using rubrics, faculty have aligned learning outcomes with specific assignments and clearly communicated the expected performance criteria to students. The same rubrics used to grade student work on an individual basis can be used to generate data for classroom-level assessment.

Developing rubrics from scratch is a difficult task. Fortunately, many rubrics are available to serve as starting points for assessing a variety of learning outcomes. Perhaps the most comprehensive rubric development project to date, the aforementioned AAC&U VALUE project has generated 15 rubrics—one for each of the 14 original essential learning outcomes, plus one to evaluate students' reading skills (http://www.aacu.org/value/index.cfm). Developed by teams of faculty and co-curricular professionals at colleges and universities around the nation, the rubrics and accompanying documentation define and operationalize essential learning outcomes, present criteria and levels of performance for learning, and provide framing language and a glossary of terms. In fact, the VALUE project made explicit the connection between using ePortfolios as a powerful mechanism for student reflection and the VALUE rubrics as useful tools for translating those reflections into assessment data (Chen & Light, 2010). Though designed initially to further program-level assessment, faculty can tweak the VALUE rubrics in order to assess learning within a single class.

Clickers and ePortfolios—while not silver bullets for assessment efforts—represent two powerful tools for faculty to use. Once faculty become adept at using these technologies, clickers and ePortfolios can help simplify the logistics of capturing evidence of student learning in class and shift faculty's focus back to the intellectual aspects of assessment and the alignment of outcomes, content, and course sequence. Though on very different scales, both clickers and ePortfolios help promote learner-centeredness by providing students with a voice and an opportunity to demonstrate learning in a meaningful way, regardless of class size. Assessment professionals can help faculty use these scalable teaching and learning technologies for data collection and provide guidance on how to make sense of the data in order to improve their students' learning. Faculty and assessment professionals can work together to determine how best to use clickers and ePortfolios and how best to ensure that the tools support, rather than drive, the teaching and learning process.

Aligning Pedagogical Practice: How Do You Pull It All Together?

Other chapters as well as entire books exist that address how to design and implement assignments and activities with the potential to serve as powerful tools for classroom-level assessment (e.g., Angelo & Cross, 1993; Banta, Lund, Black, & Oblander, 1996; Huba & Freed, 2000; Palomba & Banta, 1999; Suskie, 2004). These resources provide a much more comprehensive treatment of the range of possible classroom-level assessment techniques than is possible here, and we recommend these works as excellent references for everyone embarking upon classroom-level assessment. What follows instead is an illustrative example of "pulling it all together" to achieve the desired alignment of pedagogical practices. Embedded in this discussion are descriptions of a number of assignments we have found to elicit particularly useful data for classroom-level assessment efforts.

Imagine for a moment that you are a faculty member designing the syllabus for the first required course in your major, and you have just completed a multi-day workshop on classroom-level assessment jointly sponsored by your institution's center for teaching and learning and academic assessment office. Your head is swimming with new information, so you pull out your workshop notes to help organize your thoughts. Down the left hand side of your notes you have drafted several possible learning goals for the class under the heading *The Students Will Be Able To*, including:

- Demonstrate disciplinary content knowledge;
- Improve oral communication skills; and
- Understand research.

Down the right hand side of your notes, you have listed several types of assignments you are considering for your class instead of the traditional objective test or final essay exam:

- 25-word summaries – clear, concise statements of the main idea of a chapter, lecture, or other instructional activity (Doolittle & Sherman, 2011).

- Video logs, or "Vlogs" – a video recording of a student orally reflecting upon what she had learned related to a specific lesson/aspect of a course, usually less formal in tone (Parks & Kajder, 2010).
- Oral explanations – a clear, coherently organized 10-minute, video-recorded scholarly oral presentation constructed to: (a) explain a concept to an audience that is unfamiliar with the concept; and (b) apply the addressed concept appropriately to a problem, situation, or issue in the discipline (Doolittle, 2011b).
- Extended abstracts – a short paper (no more than three pages) reflecting the student's understanding of an empirical article addressing the article's reference information, summary of the literature/background, research question(s)/purpose of the research, research design, results, implications, and any questions or concerns the student has about the reading (Doolittle, 2011a).

Finally, at the bottom of your notes, you have written "Clickers" and "ePortfolios," technologies that interest you but have not yet integrated into any of your courses. With the mantra "align, align, align" running through your head, you begin to organize and link the what, who and how of your course.

First, Content

Students in your course are expected to develop disciplinary content knowledge; a tall order to be sure, but easily contextualized after considering the introductory nature of the course. As you are responsible for establishing a basis for students' further academic study in the major, you decide to focus on a finite number of key concepts that students must master by the end of the semester related to disciplinary content. You also want students to improve their oral communication skills, and want students to have multiple opportunities for practicing these skills without sacrificing too much in-class time. Upon further reflection, you realize that your final goal to have students "understand research" is a bit vague. You decide that you first need to introduce students to research in your discipline, which means students will need to be exposed to empirical articles in peer-reviewed journals. As such, you revise your third learning outcome to focus more specifically on having students learn how to read and evaluate empirical articles.

Considering these outcomes, you now turn to your bank of potential assignments to see what might match up with what you want the students to learn. You recognize that the objective tests from years past may not foster the development of conceptual understanding as much as they provide evidence of the existence of such understanding after it is learned. As such, you decide to have students complete 25-word summaries (Doolittle & Sherman, 2011) of the readings you assign for each key disciplinary concept you address in the class. Not only will this help ensure students take the time to read out of class, but it will also help them learn to focus on the main idea or premise behind each key disciplinary concept. Through this very short format, you hope to be able identify both students' understanding and *mis*understanding of concepts, and track the development of students' disciplinary content knowledge across the semester.

From your list of assignments, two—the Vlog (Parks & Kajder, 2010) and the oral explanation (Doolittle, 2011b)—have potential as classroom assessment techniques for oral communication. While both may help students improve their presentation skills, you are interested in more formal modes of presentation versus the more free-form reflection of the Vlog format. Additionally, you believe the requirement that students not only define but apply disciplinary concepts through illustrative examples will also promote understanding of key disciplinary concepts. Also, the requirement that oral explanations be geared toward a novice (e.g., disciplinary non-expert) audience will force students to put the disciplinary concepts into their own words, rather simply parroting the language of their professor or their texts. Finally, you decide to require your students to complete the extended abstract (Doolittle, 2011a) as it seems to be the best way to structure what is often students' first experience with empirical research in your major.

Next, Students

You begin the process of connecting the course outcomes and content to your specific students by thinking through what you already know about them, and identifying what else you need to ascertain about them as learners. Based on their high school records, you know the students in your major are academically strong, highly motivated, and performance-oriented. While there are no pre-requisites for your course and the content you address is introductory, you recognize students do come in with prior knowledge related to the discipline, but that knowledge varies greatly from student to student and year to year. You decide to use a test from a previous semester as a short objective pre-test the first day of class to get a sense of what students know so you can better shape your teaching. Despite your students' strong academic backgrounds, over the years you have noticed that many seem to struggle with moving beyond issues of knowledge and comprehension to application of disciplinary concepts. You want to begin to prepare them for upper level work in the major by giving them a bit of practice applying disciplinary concepts, even at the introductory level. Thinking back, you decide that both the 25-word summary assignment and the oral explanation assignment will help push students toward thinking more critically about disciplinary concepts. You have also heard from alumni and employers that many graduates of your program struggle while attempting to communicate complex technical information to a lay audience, a shortcoming you will begin to address through the oral explanation assignment. Lastly, over the years you have noticed that many of your students double major in a wide range of disciplines, and this has always intrigued you. You decide to ask them to respond to a few open-ended questions at the end of the pre-test regarding their motivation for choosing this major, and how it connects to other fields and disciplines, so that you can begin to incorporate relevant examples from other disciplines that may hold some intrinsic interest for your students as you help to build their conceptual understanding.

Lastly, Instruction

You turn your attention to the specific instructional context of and strategies used for your class. The class is taught in a traditional classroom that seats your 40 students comfortably. You plan to punctuate lecture-based instruction with more active learning strategies designed to get students to interact in class. Though the desks in the theater-style classroom are fixed to the floor, you intend to have students break into groups for both general discussion activities as well as peer learning groups responsible for components of the assignments delineated on the syllabus. For example, you decide to dedicate an entire class to discussing the extended abstract assignment. Knowing your students are just beginning to delve into the discipline through this course, you believe that they will benefit from some structured scaffolding for the assignment. As such, you decide to have students submit not one but two extended abstracts. The first will be on a common article assigned to all students in the class, one they will have the opportunity to dissect in class with their peers, using you as an expert resource. The second extended abstract students will complete independently on an article of their choice selected from among a list of peer-reviewed journals that you provide.

You decide students will complete three oral explanations, but allow them to choose which three disciplinary concepts from among all those covered in class to address in the assignment. This allows students to exercise some choice and autonomy within the class, while helping to alleviate some of your grading load. Furthermore, you plan to modify and use the AAC&U VALUE rubric for "oral communication" to provide feedback and score students' work for classroom assessment data. With only 40 students, you do not think the clicker will be a useful technology for the class, but you are intrigued by the possibilities for student reflection and assessment offered by the ePortfolio. You decide to have students submit their assignments through the ePortfolio, and will require them to reflect upon the development of their disciplinary content knowledge, oral communication skills, and ability to read and analyze empirical studies to help students synthesize a semester's worth of learning. You plan to reach out to your assessment and teaching and learning colleagues to secure their assistance in developing instructions for the new assignments that will frame them appropriately for the students and connect them to the course's learning outcomes so that the data generated can be used for classroom-level assessment.

Though certainly not exhaustive, the example provided demonstrates how one can meaningfully connect the course outcome, content—including assignments—students, and instructional strategies and context in the pedagogical alignment process. Outcomes, assignments, students, and instructional contexts and strategies will vary greatly; the process of alignment requires faculty to think purposefully and strategically about the best way to organize and link teaching, learning, and assessment activities at the classroom level.

Conclusion

In order to be effective and generate data that is valuable for a decision-making process, classroom assessment must exhibit alignment between the desired course outcomes, its content, the learners enrolled in the class, and the instructional contexts and strategies employed. Alignment of these pedagogical elements promotes the four foundational principles identified in this chapter. Faculty are empowered as the leaders of the process as they not only select which course assignments best represent student learning, but also as they work to align what they know about their students as learners, the instructional contexts they create, and the teaching strategies they employ. Furthermore, by grounding assessment work in the classroom as a unit of analysis, assessment professionals can create assessment opportunities that are connected to learning environments that have meaning to students and faculty. Alignment between what, who, and how we are teaching helps to ensure that classroom assessment works toward the improvement of student learning as its primary goal. By focusing on the alignment of what, who, and how we teach, faculty and their assessment professional partners will go a long way toward ensuring that the classroom is not only an intuitive unit of analysis for student learning, but—more importantly—a valid one.

References

Anderson, L. W., & Krathwohl, D. R. (Eds.). (2001). *A taxonomy for learning, teaching, and assessing: A revision of Bloom's Taxonomy of educational objectives.* New York, NY: Longman.

Angelo, T. A. (1994). Classroom assessment: Involving faculty and students where it matters most. *Assessment Update, 6* (4), p. 1–10.

Angelo, T. A., & Cross, K. P. (1993). *Classroom assessment techniques: A handbook for college teachers.* San Francisco, CA: Jossey-Bass.

Association of American Colleges and Universities. (2007). *College learning for the new global century.* Washington, DC: Author.

Ausubel, D. P. (1968). *Educational psychology: A cognitive view.* New York, NY: Holt, Rinehart & Winston.

Banta, T. W., Lund, J. P., Black, K. E., & Oblander, F. W. (1996). *Assessment in practice: Putting principles to work on college campuses.* San Francisco, CA: Jossey-Bass.

Bloom, B. (Ed.) (1956). *Taxonomy of educational objectives: The classification of educational goals (Handbook I: Cognitive Domain).* New York, NY: David McKay.

Boyle, J. T., & Nichol, D. J. (2003). Using classroom communication systems to increase interaction and discussion in large class settings. *Studies in Higher Education, 28,* 457–473.

Brookhart, S. M. (1999). *The art and science of classroom assessment: The missing part of pedagogy.* San Francisco, CA: Jossey-Bass.

Cambridge, D. (2010). *Eportfolios for lifelong learning and assessment.* San Francisco, CA: Jossey-Bass.

Chen, H., & Light, P. (2010). *Electronic portfolios and student success: Effectiveness, efficiency, and learning.* Washington, DC: Association of American Colleges and Universities.

Chen, H. L., & Mazlow, C. (2002). Electronic learning portfolios and student affairs. *Net Results.* Retrieved April 6, 2009, from www.naspa.org/netresults/PrinterFriendly.cfm?ID=825 (NASPA membership required for access.)

Craik, F. M. I. (2002). Levels of processing: Past, present . . . and future? *Memory, 10*(5/6), 305–318.

Craik, F. M. I., & Lockhart, R. S. (1972). Levels of processing: A framework for memory research. *Journal of Verbal Learning and Verbal Behavior, 11*, 671–684.

Culver, S. M., & Van Dyke, R. (2009). Developing a receptive and faculty-focused environment for assessment. In C. Schreiner (Ed.), *Handbook of research on assessment technologies, methods, and applications in higher education* (pp. 337–347). Hershey, PA: Information Science Reference.

Darley, C. F., Tinklenberg, J. R., Roth, W. T., & Atkinson, R. C. (1997). The nature of storage deficits and state-dependent retrieval under marijuana, *Psychopharmacologia, 37*, 139–149.

Doolittle, P. E. (2011a). College teaching course materials: Extended abstracts. Blacksburg, VA: Author.

Doolittle, P. E. (2011b). College teaching course materials: Oral explanations. Blacksburg, VA: Author.

Doolittle, P. E., & Mariano, G. J. (2008). Working memory capacity and mobile multimedia learning environments: Is mobile learning from portable digital media players for everyone? *Journal of Educational Multimedia and Hypermedia, 17*(4), 511–530.

Doolittle, P. E., & Sherman, T. (2011). College teaching course materials: 25 word summaries. Blacksburg, VA: Authors.

Doolittle, P. E., & Siudzinski, R. (2010). Recommended syllabus components: What do higher education faculty include on their syllabi? *Journal on Excellence in College Teaching, 21*(3), 29–60.

Duncan, T. G., & McKeachie, W. J. (2005). The making of the Motivated Strategies for Learning Questionnaire. *Educational Psychologist, 40*, 117–128.

Eich, J. E. (1980). The cue-dependent nature of state-dependent retrieval. *Memory & Cognition, 8*, 157–173.

Godden, D. R. & Baddeley, A. D. (1975). Context-dependent memory in two natural environments: On land and underwater. *British Journal of Psychology, 66*(3), 325–331.

Huba, M. E., & Freed, J. E. (2000). *Learner-centered assessment on college campuses: Shifting the focus from teaching to learning.* Boston, MA: Allyn & Bacon.

Kolikant, Y. B.-D., Drane, D., & Calkins, S. (2010). "Clickers" as Catalysts for Transformation of Teachers. *College Teaching, 58*(4), 127–135.

Kuh, G. D. (2008). *High-impact educational practices: What they are, who has access to them, and why they matter.* Washington, DC: Association of American Colleges and Universities.

Lockhart, R. S. (2002). Levels of processing, transfer-appropriate processing, and the concept of robust encoding. *Memory, 19*(5/6), 397–403.

Lombardi, J. (2008). To portfolio or not to portfolio. *College Teaching, 56*(1), 7–10.

Lowe, G. (1986). State-dependent learning effects with a combination of alcohol and nicotine. *Psychopharmacology, 89*, 105–107.

Martyn, M. (2007). Clickers in the classroom: An active learning approach. *Educause Quarterly, 2*, 71–74.

Mayer, R. E., Stull, A., DeLeeuw, K., Almeroth, K., Bimber, B., Chun, D., . . . Zhang, H. (2009). Clickers in college classrooms: Fostering learning with questioning methods in large lecture classes. *Contemporary Educational Psychology, 34*(1), 51–57.

McKeachie, W. J., Pintrich, P. R., & Lin, Y-G. (1985). Teaching learning strategies. *Educational Psychologist, 20*(3), 153–160.

Morissette, S. B., Spiegel, D. A., & Barlow, D. H. (2008). Combining exposure and pharmacotherapy in the treatment of social anxiety disorder: A preliminary study of state dependent learning. *Journal of Psychopathology and Behavioral Assessment, 30*, 211–219.

Morris, C. D., Bransford, J. D., & Franks, J. J. (1977). Levels of processing versus transfer appropriate processing. *Journal of Verbal Learning and Verbal Behavior, 16*, 519–533.

Palomba, C., & Banta, T. (1999). *Assessment essentials: Planning, implementing, and improving assessment in higher education.* San Francisco, CA: Jossey-Bass.

Parkes, K., & Kajder, S. (2010). Eliciting and assessing reflective practice: Best practices. *International Journal of Teaching and Learning in Higher Education, 22*(2), 218–228.

Pintrich, P. R., McKeachie, W. J., & Lin, Y. G. (1987). Teaching a course in learning to learn. *Teaching of Psychology, 14*, 81–86.

Pintrich, P. R., Smith, D. A. F., García, T., & McKeachie, W. J. (1991). *A manual for the use of the Motivated Strategies for Learning Questionnaire (MSLQ).* (Technical Report No. 91-B-004). Ann Arbor, MI: University of Michigan, National Center for Research to Improve Postsecondary Teaching and Learning. Retrieved from http://www.eric.ed.gov/ERICWebPortal/detail?accno=ED338122

Rhodes, T. L. (2010). *Assessing outcomes and improving achievement: Tips and tools for using rubrics*. Washington, DC: Association of American Colleges and Universities.

Rosen, K. R. (2008). The history of medical simulation. *Journal of Critical Care, 23*, 157–166.

Stevens, D. D., & Levi, A. J. (2005). *Introduction to rubrics: An assessment tool to save grading time, convey effective feedback and promote student learning*. Sterling, VA: Stylus.

Suskie, L. (2004). *Assessing student learning: A common sense guide*. Bolton, MA: Anker.

Teasdale, J. D., & Russell, M. L. (1983). Differential effects of induced mood on the recall of positive, negative and neutral words. *British Journal of Clinical Psychology, 22*, 163–171.

Tulving, E. (1983). *Elements of episodic memory*. Oxford, UK: Clarendon Press.

Tulving, E., & Thomson, D. M. (1973). Encoding specificity and retrieval processes in episodic memory. *Psychological Review, 80*, 352–373.

Ucros, C. G. (1989). Mood state-dependent memory: A meta-analysis. *Cognition and Emotion, 3*, 139–167.

Walvoord, B. E. (2004). *Assessment clear and simple: A practical guide for institutions, department, and general education*. San Francisco, CA: Jossey-Bass.

Weimer, M. G. (2002). *Learner-centered teaching: Five key changes to practice*. San Francisco, CA: Jossey-Bass.

Weissenborn, R., & Duka, T. (2000). State-dependent effects of alcohol on explicit memory: The role of semantic associations. *Psychopharmacology, 149*, 98–106.

3

STUDENT LEARNING OUTCOMES ASSESSMENT AT THE PROGRAM AND INSTITUTIONAL LEVELS

Thomas Judd and Bruce Keith

In the widely and often quoted book, *Academically Adrift: Limited Learning on College Campuses*, Richard Arum and Josipa Roksa (2010) conclude that college students "are failing to develop the higher-order cognitive skills that it is widely assumed college students should master. These findings are sobering and should be a cause for concern" (p. 121). Is this true? Are our colleges and universities failing in their mission? If so, why should an institution put scarce resources into assessing student learning outcomes when there are many other issues vying for attention? The answer to these questions lies in the very purpose of assessing student learning outcomes: using evidence for determining if students are achieving the desired outcomes, and for improving instruction based on the findings of assessment.

In this chapter, we will provide an overview of the background, purpose, context, and methodology of a system to assess the student learning outcomes of a college at the institutional and program levels. Assessment of student learning outcomes not only provides evidence regarding an institution's achievement of the mission and improves the delivery of instruction, it also informs strategic planning and facilitates change and development at the course, program and institutional levels.

We begin with a brief background of the development of assessment initiatives, followed by a discussion of mission statements and the need for alignment with student outcomes and educational activities, methodologies for effective student outcome assessment, sources of evidence that provide useful and actionable information, issues in the sustainability of an assessment system, and conclude with a case study of assessing general education student learning outcomes.

Context for Outcomes Assessment

For several decades researchers have been engaged in a wide variety of approaches to assess student learning outcomes: the education-related consequences of students' postsecondary educational experiences (U.S. Department of Education, 1997). In fact, *expansive* is the word of choice used by Pascarella and Terenzini (2005) to characterize the changes they observed in the previous decade of research on the impact of a college experience on students. Their comprehensive review documented an expansion in the sheer volume of studies, the types of institutions studied, the underlying developmental framework, the variety and influences of policy concerns and the diversity of research approaches.

With such a potentially bewildering array of purposes, contexts and methods for assessing outcomes, it is conceivable that the function and practice of assessment at an institution can become lost in complexity. It is no wonder that many assessment programs have difficulty in gaining traction, lose their focus, have little faculty buy-in, and subsequently wither on the vine for lack of effectiveness, usefulness or relevance. Indeed, several authors have taken a practical step-by-step approach in their texts to provide institutions with excellent guidance as they take their first steps into process of assessment of student learning outcomes (e.g., Leskes and Wright, 2005; Suskie, 2004; Walvoord, 2009). These authors describe a process that (a) defines the student learning outcomes, (b) articulates an alignment of the student outcomes with curriculum activities, (c) collects evidence relevant to the student outcomes, and (d) uses the results to improve student learning.

Background: Assessment Initiatives

The assessment movement gained momentum from calls for accountability in higher education at a time when there was little data available that reliably and accurately told a comprehensive story of the effects of college on students (Ewell, 1984, 2002). Ewell (2002) traces three national movements that influenced the debate over the efficacy and form of assessment, and influenced the scholarship of assessment: Value-Added, Total Quality Management (TQM), and the National Educational Goals Panel (NEGP). These movements focused debate on whether assessment should address student attainment or institutional contribution (Value-Added), on the need to address systems and processes (TQM), and on the notion of a national accountability through standard outcomes assessment at the college level (NGEP).

Partially in response to the calls for accountability, institutional accreditation has moved from an examination of fiscal solvency, faculty and administrative credentials and vitality of resources to an examination of documented institutional effectiveness and student outcomes. The evidence required for successful accreditation is focused on student outcomes and effectiveness data that is collected "within the context of the mission of the institution, the suitability and effectiveness of processes designed to accomplish institutional goals, and the institution's ability to fulfill its purposes" (Council of Regional Accrediting Commissions, 2003, p. 2).

In the broadest context, outcomes assessment is an integral component of a comprehensive planning process in which student outcomes are part of a system that encompasses the assessment of the effectiveness for the entire institution. Within a given context, each functional component of an institution has a mission and set of corresponding goals that align with those of the institution. Both student learning outcomes and institutional effectiveness data are collected to inform the institution about how successful it is in achieving its mission and to fuel a comprehensive strategic planning process (Middaugh, 2009). Therefore, the assessment of student learning outcomes is primarily about improving student learning through a systematic, intentional, and local process.

Institutional Mission and Alignment With Goals, Learning System and Student Outcomes

The mission and goals . . . are used to develop and shape its programs and practices and to evaluate its effectiveness (Middle States Commission on Higher Education [MSCHE], 2006, p. ix). The starting point for an assessment process should be a well crafted and meaningful mission statement that is embraced by all constituents of the institution. The mission provides guidance for an institution's goals and learning outcomes; the curriculum provides a framework for the process and activities that ensure the educational environment will lead to achievement of the student learning outcomes.

In one accrediting agency's definition an institution's mission "clearly defines its purpose within the context of higher education and indicates who the institution serves and what it intends to accomplish . . . [Mission statements] are developed and recognized by the institution with the participation of its members and its governing body" (MSCHE, 2006, p. ix).

The alignment of the goals with the mission statement is an indication that the institution or program has a clear sense of what it is about, and what the expectations for its program completers are. Again, in the words of an accrediting agency, "The institution's stated goals, consistent with the aspirations and expectations of higher education, clearly specify how the institution will fulfill its mission" (MSCHE, 2006, p. ix).

The mission and goals or student outcomes give us two points: the institution's or program's stated purpose at one end, and the anticipated result (goals or outcomes) of the experiences that occur during the program at the other. All that happens between these two points are what we refer to as the curriculum. In this sense, the curriculum may include experiences beyond the courses and classroom that are intentionally arranged to contribute to the outcomes. The activities that comprise the curriculum are driven by the outcomes—one should be able to discern an alignment between these activities and the outcomes to which they are contributing.

The alignment between the mission statement, the student learning outcomes, and the design of learning activities cannot be understated; the purpose of an education, as defined by the student learning outcomes, is wholly dependent on the design of the learning system (Spady & Schwahn, 2010). For example, an institution that wishes its graduates to demonstrate an increased capacity for civic responsibility should be able to show that there are activities designed to contribute to the development of that outcome, such as a service learning component, built into the context of every major.

Ancillary activities—first year experience, internships, study abroad, clubs, sports, immersion, multi/interdisciplinary, service learning, cultural events—are but a few of the activities that may contribute to general education outcomes and should be considered in the learning system design.

An important step in the assessment of student learning outcomes is the identification of places in the curriculum where activities aligned with the outcomes occur. For example, constructing a matrix of student learning outcomes and the content of course syllabi can identify locations in the curriculum where student learning outcomes are being addressed, as well as potential places for gathering direct evidence of student performance of the outcomes.

Institutional Level Student Outcomes: General Education

General Education student outcomes are the knowledge, skills and competencies all graduates of the institution can be expected to demonstrate, regardless of the major. General education outcomes can be intellectual, social, civic, political, religious, moral/ethical, physical, or occupational. They can be achieved through a series of specific courses, infused throughout the curriculum across disciplines, reinforced in the major, or through a combination of strategies.

Although individual institutions or university systems determine their own version of general education outcomes, there are several national models that can provide guidance. The Association of American Colleges and Universities (AAC&U, 2007) describes seven areas for general education: written and oral communication, critical thinking and research skills, quantitative reasoning information literacy, ethical reasoning, civic engagement, intercultural skills, application of learning, and integration of learning. AAC&U has also published a comprehensive set of rubrics for each of these outcome areas that have been developed by panels of curriculum and higher education experts. The Wabash National Study of Liberal Arts Education (2006–2009; Center of Inquiry in the Liberal Arts, n.d.), a project with 49 member institutions and 17,000 students, is examining seven liberal arts outcomes: effective reasoning and problem solving, inclination to inquire and lifelong learning, integration of learning, intercultural effectiveness, leadership, moral reasoning, and well-being.

National accrediting agencies also offer their views on appropriate general education learning outcome areas. MSCHE, for example, asks its member institution to have general education student learning outcomes in the areas of written and oral communication, scientific reasoning, quantitative reasoning, critical analysis, technological competency, values and ethics, intellectual growth, and cultural and global awareness.

The commonality of these student outcome areas at the institutional level can be viewed through several categorization systems with an eye towards comprehensiveness. Astin (1993), for example, describes a taxonomy with two dimensions: psychological/behavioral and cognitive/affective that, when combined, produce a 2×2 taxonomy of student outcomes. Ewell (1984) categorizes general education outcomes into areas of knowledge, skills, attitudes, and relationships.

While the knowledge, skills and competencies of general education are ubiquitous in higher education, there are clear indications that general education goals are moving into other more challenging affective spheres. Spady and Schwahn (2010) take a broad view of the role colleges play in preparing graduates for life by suggesting that institutions should consider eight dimensions, or spheres of living, for development of students including: personal potential and wellness, learning challenges and resources, life and resource management, close and significant relationships, group and community membership, work and productive endeavors, physical and cultural environment, and purposeful and fulfilling pursuits. W. Astin, H. Astin, and Lindholm (2010) describe the role colleges can play in developing the inner, spiritual, and affective lives of students as they develop during the college years.

Program or Majors Level Student Learning Outcomes

Program-level outcomes represent student learning outcomes for a major or discipline. They may be derived from the collective expertise of the faculty, and can be informed or directed by local needs, career requirements, and professional or accreditation standards. Program-level student learning outcomes may also provide an opportunity for reinforcement and infusion of general education outcomes.

Engineering and technology programs, for example, have to meet the standards determined by Accreditation Board for Engineering and Technologies (ABET)—the accrediting body for engineering and technology programs—which requires a set of 14 student learning outcomes in each of its accredited programs. Majors without accrediting bodies may have professional associations with recommended student learning outcomes that can guide their development for programs. With or without external sources to guide or dictate student learning outcomes, faculty in a program will need to determine the full range of student learning outcomes and standards of performance for their programs.

Institutional and program-level outcomes may look very similar, but a full set of program-level goals should have the specificity necessary to distinguish the distinctive learning outcomes of a given major. For example, there may be a quantitative reasoning student learning outcome at the institutional level, while the psychology program may have a student learning outcome for statistical analysis in a research methodology outcome. As with general education student learning outcomes, program student learning outcomes should be aligned with the program mission, the general education student learning outcomes, and the mission of the institution.

Levels of Performance/Development

While clear statements of expected student learning outcomes that are aligned with the mission are a key component of assessment, the level of performance expected is another issue that can be informed with reference to standards generated internally or externally. The standard for completing the mile run can be based on a norm for gender and age groups, referenced to personal improvement, or referenced to minimum time standard set by knowledgeable faculty. While this standard may be relatively straightforward, when the outcomes fall into some of the more complex and difficult to measure categories, the development of standards becomes increasingly challenging. When a college says that their graduates will be able to understand global issues and perspectives, or clearly communicate ideas in written and oral form, how is a standard of performance determined, and at what level? While there is some subjectivity inherent in determining a standard of performance, there are methods of clarifying aspects of the standards.

With the cognitive, affective and psychomotor domains, for example, Bloom's (1956) Taxonomy has proven to be a powerful resource for educators developing objectives that incorporate a specified level of performance in the standard. The cognitive domain, as described by Bloom has six levels of student mastery of material in this taxonomy, starting from knowledge at the simplest level, through comprehension, application, analysis, and synthesis to evaluation at the most complex. Lists of active verbs that serve as keys for performance at each of the levels abound in many sources.

Once the potential levels of performance are determined, the level that will be used as a basis for a measure of success may be specified as a standard. If a general education communication student learning outcome is assessed by an institution-wide standardized test of reading and writing skills which all students must pass prior to graduation, the standards outcomes and standards are clear, direct, easy to understand, and easy to determine if the college is achieving this goal of the mission. (See Pitoniak and Morgan, this volume, for a discussion of what constitutes passing.)

This is not the case with all outcomes. The goal to *understand global issues and perspectives* raises the question: what does it mean to *understand*, and how do we state it in such a way that it can be measured?

In Bloom's view, understanding is a part of the second level of cognitive activities he terms *comprehension*. He also provides us with verbs that describe actions that students can use to demonstrate their understanding: comprehends, converts, defends, distinguishes, estimates, explains, extends, generalizes, gives examples, infers, interprets, paraphrases, predicts, rewrites, summarizes, translates. These verbs can be used to define outcomes with a mind for creating assessment measures. Understanding global issues, for example, may then be defined as summarizing how scarce energy resources (or any other global issue) may affect international relations. An outcome embracing a higher level of cognitive skill may state that graduates *evaluate* a national policy in an international context. This could require that students compare, explain, critique, and draw conclusions about an energy policy in a global context.

The level of development that students reach through their college experiences can also be examined through one of the theories of student development and used as a basis for developing standards for assessment. Evans, Forney, Guido, Patton, & Renn (2009), Robert Kegan (1982), William Perry (1970), and Arthur Chickering and Linda Reisser (1993), for example, each describe models of developmental changes of students through the young adulthood years of college. Typically, the models show that as individuals gain experience and confidence, external controls give way to internal controls, accompanied by expanded horizons and movement from self-centered to interpersonal sensitivity, from simplicity to complexity, from dependence to independence, from impulsivity to self-control, and from instinctual to principled action. By developing student learning outcomes and standards that use a developmental modal as a basis, realistic expectations for levels of performance and the sequencing of developmental activities can be consistently defined.

Methodology: Does Assessment of Student Learning Outcomes Require Scientific Rigor?

Reliability, validity, sampling, and item construction are all components of scientific rigor, and are topics addressed elsewhere in this volume. The question for assessment is how rigorously should these concepts apply to a system of student outcomes assessment? The prime function of assessment of student outcomes is for local decision making, and does not necessarily require the full range of rigor associated with experiments designed to support cause and effect conclusions.

The notion that assessment implies a judgment also implies that the judgment is made with confidence in the supporting evidence. Judging whether an outcome has been achieved can seem quite arbitrary if the bar for success is set without reference to any level of performance that is meaningful, or with a methodology that is flawed or renders the evidence difficult or impossible to interpret. As described in a previous section, such judgments can be made from a set of standards, from peer comparisons or from documenting personal or individual growth. Standards can be derived from external sources such as professional consensus, accrediting bodies, industry needs assessments, or from agreed upon local standards. Peer comparisons, more commonly referred to as benchmarks (see Seybert, Weed, & Bers in this volume), address how well one group does in comparison to a set of their institutional, program or departmental peers. Personal growth as a point of reference depends less on how well a group does in comparison to peers or external standards, than on how much individual students have developed from their starting point at the institution.

These three contexts for judgment—standards, benchmarks and personal growth—have their appropriate place for various kinds of decision-based outcomes. For example, if an outcome requires students to demonstrate the ability to run a mile, peer comparisons and personal growth are irrelevant. The standard is completing the run, regardless of the performance of peers, or whether the student is a recruited track athlete or had never run more than a few meters prior to admission to the institution. If the outcome is to produce the best nurses in the field, benchmark comparisons of outcome measures fit the bill. On the other hand, if the outcome is to develop in students an increased capacity for civic responsibility, personal growth may be the most appropriate context for judgment. The phrase 'to develop' suggests that the institution is interested not only in where the student is at the end of the educational experience, but how much progress has been made since the student entered the institution—a central feature of a 'value-added' approach. These three types of perspectives require somewhat different sets of standards.

Frameworks for Assessment

Judgments derived from student outcome data can be made with more confidence if the methodology supports judgments of causality. Anyone steeped in research methodology can recognize designs of studies that support cause-and-effect conclusions about the agents of documented change and those that show change, but cannot attribute change to a particular agent. If outcome data show that graduates have a high level of social responsibility, can one conclude that it is due to the experiences at their college rather than characteristics of students admitted or drawn to the school? Outcome data alone may not be sufficient to support that conclusion, but if it is collected in the context of a framework of other knowledge that supports causal inferences, then it may be justified. True experimental research designs take into account all possible influences on student learning outcomes and systematically vary them to identify agents of cause. It does not seem reasonable to expect all faculty or staff from diverse disciplines involved in assessment to become facile with research designs, but it is feasible to present a conceptual framework for understanding the limits of inference that parallels the logic of experimental design.

Astin (1993) described one such framework for interpreting assessment studies that takes into account inputs, environment, and outcomes, which he calls the I-E-O model. *Inputs* are those qualities, traits, skills, attitudes, or beliefs that students bring at their entry into the program or institution being assessed. *Environment* is everything that is experienced during the course of the program, and *outcomes* are the evidence of student performance. Inputs and environment can independently and in collusion effect the outcomes. It is not difficult to see that entering students at a highly selective private college with a mean SAT score in the highest five percent is not starting at the same place as an open enrollment institution in an inner city with a low average academic performance of entering students. Inputs clearly could impact the outcome measures in the myriad ways in which entering students differ, making judgments about the comparative effectiveness of a program unclear. Even a comprehensive description of the educational experiences could not allow a claim for their contribution to the outcomes independent of the inputs.

Not only do environments differ between institutions, departments and faculty, they also can have different effects on students with differing input characteristics, resulting in outcomes that have multiple and compounded influences.

Perhaps the most useful aspect of Astin's I-E-O framework is a clarification of the kinds of inferences that can be drawn about the relationship between outcomes and differing combinations of the associated input and environmental components. The emphasis on outcome data by the accreditation and accountability movements resembles the *outcome-only* assessment model in this framework. Standardized tests and surveys given to seniors, while providing comparability to a broader population of seniors, fall into this category if they are the only source of information related to outcomes. While the outcome-only assessment model does focus on data that provides information about the success of the institution achieving its goals, it does little for identifying causal relationships between the content of programs and results. So, did those graduates with a high level of social responsibility arrive at the institution with those inclinations? Did the school contribute to the outcome, or draw students who were already on the road to social responsibility by virtue of their family and religious background and their fit with the institution's mission? Outcome-only approaches don't provide insight into these questions, but they do address the issue of whether graduates meet the standard set for that institutional student outcome.

The *environment-outcomes* approach resembles the normative approach to grading: comparisons are made between institution or programs without attention to differences at input. Comparing the written communication skills of physics majors to philosophy and music majors who all went through the same general education courses in English composition and literature may show differences between them, but ignores the fact that the students drawn to these diverse majors may have entered with different levels of skills, motivation and interests that could have influenced their written communication skill development.

The *environment-only* approach is typical of earlier accreditation standards, where the focus is on the program elements such as faculty qualifications, instructional materials, seat time, work load, textbooks, laboratory work, and facilities. While these factors may contribute to the ability of an institution to meet its mission, there is no information that tells us how well the mission is met, or if the environment had an impact.

Astin's model not only points us in the direction of the kinds of conclusion we can make from the outcome data at hand, but at the kinds of evidence an assessment process may strive to collect in the face of the kinds of conclusions the process is designed to draw. Extraordinary claims require extraordinary evidence. While the claims we make in assessment may not meet the criteria of 'extraordinary,' they certainly require appropriate evidence. In Astin's framework, an assessment that takes inputs and environment as well as student outcomes into account can provide the appropriate evidence to substantiate the claim for the effect of the program on the student outcome. Such claims for the causes of outcomes are not always required in the accreditation process, but we need to be cognizant of the limitations on interpreting the data that is produced.

Astin's model is one of several frameworks for assessment. For example, a National Center for Education Statistics (NCES, 2002) review of competency-based assessment arrays outcomes in a hierarchy, with traits and characteristics as a foundation, and with skills, abilities and knowledge developed in the learning process which are then acquired as competencies. At the peak of the hierarchy are demonstrations of the competencies, and the point for assessment of performance. This hierarchy aligns similar components of Astin's framework within a different conceptual framework.

Sources of Evidence

"I give my students grades. That is evidence of their achievement. Why do we need to collect other assessment data?" This common comment from a faculty member is understandable. Grades have a long history of providing evidence of faculty evaluation of student achievement, and do represent how individual students perform. But in the context of assessment, grades alone do not typically provide evidence that allows specific curricular decisions to be made based on the results of student learning outcome assessment. Grades represent subjective evaluation of multiple aspects of a course and an individual's predisposition toward a course and his or her external environment.

Assessment, to be useful, needs a collection of evidence that allows judgments to be made regarding the achievement of specific student outcomes. When the evidence points to a weakness in the achievement of an outcome, it should also inform the stakeholders where action can be taken to strengthen the outcome. Grades give a general sense of the faculty member's evaluation, but what can a class average of 74% on a course, final, test, paper or project tell us about how to improve outcome performance? Certainly, a well-crafted product may do just that if the component parts are structured to align with specific outcome measures and grades for the component pieces are presented as the evidence. Grades for the component parts related to the student learning outcomes can then be summarized across students and even courses to provide direct evidence of student achievement of the outcomes. Another method for examining the relevant components of a test given to students or a student project is the use of rubrics as an ancillary tool for assessment of these products, independently or in conjunction with the grading process (see Yen and Hynes in this volume).

Not all evidence collected for assessment is equally persuasive. Indeed, as Yen and Hynes note, as calls for accountability through assessment increases among the accrediting agencies, the likelihood that they will require evidence with higher levels of reliability and validity is also increased. Conveniently, Sections 2, 3, and 4 in this volume address these issues in some detail. We will continue with the distinction between indirect and direct sources of evidence and provide some examples.

Direct and Indirect Indicators

Direct evidence is "tangible, visible, self-explanatory evidence of what students have and haven't learned" (Suskie, 2004, p. 95). This evidence is based on performance of students. In contrast, indirect evidence provides an indication of learning, but lacks the clarity of direct evidence in observing actual performance. Carefully constructed surveys which align with student outcomes rely on the judgments of performance by the responders rather than actual measures of performance. Surveys requiring respondents to judge competence, skill level, or confidence in performing student learning outcomes are providing subjective judgments rather than demonstrations of performance. These are examples of indirect evidence, which provide one perspective of achievement of the student learning outcomes, but do not represent actual performance. Direct indicators are demonstrations of student performance on course products—such as tests, presentations, papers, portfolios or projects—that give direct evidence of student achievement of learning outcomes.

Embedded and Add-On Indicators

Higher education institutions routinely collect vast amounts of data, from administrative data to final exams, papers, projects, and grades on daily work. Not all of this is relevant for outcomes, but in this myriad collection there is a treasure trove that can be mined for assessment purposes. By identifying those products that relate directly to student outcomes and planning for their collection, assessment can become relatively efficient and less burdensome for faculty. By constructing the matrices of student learning outcomes and course content noted earlier, potential locations for student products can be identified. The next step is to identify the existing products that can be used for assessment. If a psychology exam in a core course asks students to apply an understanding of the development of moral decision making, faculty can compile that evidence for assessment of a student learning outcome in moral decision making. Data collected from embedded indicators aligned with the outcome statements, can grow into a body of evidence that informs outcomes assessment with little additional effort by faculty and that is clearly tied closely to the curriculum.

Embedded indicators may not always be sufficient or available for the assessment process. Although the data from embedded indicators is convenient to collect, they do not provide the opportunity for comparisons with other relevant groups. If there is a need for these comparisons, assessment may require an externally developed or nationally normed instrument such as the Defining Issues Test (Rest, Narvaez, Thoma, & Bebeau, 1999), which examines moral reasoning based on the developmental model of Kohlberg (1984), and gives national comparative data for college freshmen and seniors.

There are many nationally normed instruments available for a variety of student learning outcomes. For example, the College Learning Assessment (CLA), cited by Arum and Roksa (2010) in their assessment of the state of higher education, measures students' ability to think carefully, reason analytically, solve problems, and communicate. In determining if a given instrument is appropriate, care must be taken in examining whether the skills being evaluated align with the student outcomes of the institution or program. If an institution's student learning outcomes include the ability to think carefully, reason analytically, solve problems and communicate, and there is a desire for a comparison with other colleges, the CLA is an instrument that could be considered.

Triangulation Principles

Direct and indirect evidence that is collected for the assessment of student achievement of outcomes can vary greatly in how confident we can be that it is a valid measure of the outcome. Certainly many direct measures can be interpreted fairly confidently. Timing how fast a student can run a kilometer, measuring whether a model bridge can support a fifty pound weight, or judging the construction of a logical argument can all be deemed to be accurate measures of specific outcomes. But there are many outcomes where the use of indirect measures may be the best available or most convenient evidence. For instance, when assessing an outcome in the moral domain one could use an instrument such as the Defining Issues Test (Rest et al., 1999) to assess the level of moral reasoning ability, but this would not necessarily inform the assessment regarding moral decisions in real life circumstances. Often indirect indicators must be relied upon when direct measures are not practical. One approach is to ask graduates' supervisors in a survey their level of confidence in the graduates' decision making in situations that have a moral or ethical component. Although this is an indirect indicator and relies on subjective judgment, it does provide another data point in assessing that outcome from a source that has intimate knowledge of the performance of the graduate.

Assessing affective psychological or behavioral outcomes, in particular, poses problems in methodology and data collection that may be beyond the resources or expertise available at the institution. In these cases, indirect evidence such as survey data may be the most reasonable data accessible to the assessors. In spite of the rigorous methodology that has been developed in constructing, administering, analyzing, and interpreting survey data, there are still limitations in how much confidence we can have in concluding that responses on a survey reflect the actual abilities or outcomes. If a graduate indicates on a survey their confidence in their ability to write a coherent letter of recommendation supporting a position, how valid is that assertion? A student as a freshman and again as a senior may report a high level of confidence in their written communication skill. However, their reference point for quality written communication, applied to their own abilities, may have changed greatly over the four years. While their confidence in written communication may have remained high over that time, their skill level may have improved dramatically. Interpretations of the survey data must be tempered in some way to account for the subjective nature of the information.

This source of data, while not ideal, can still contribute to our assessment of a given outcome through the method of triangulation, in which multiple sources of evidence used together measure a construct in corroboration. If the graduate makes the assertion, the graduate's employer on a survey is comfortable with the graduate's writing, and the data from a senior thesis provides evidence of adequate writing, the three sources of evidence converge and allow the conclusion that the writing outcome indicates that the graduate has met the standard. This is the optimum situation, where all sources converge on a single conclusion. This may not always be the case, as triangulation may also result in inconsistency or contradiction among the varied data sources (Mathison, 1988). Mathison suggests that in all three cases—convergence, inconsistency and contradiction—assessment "requires embedding the empirical data . . . with a holistic understanding of the specific situation and general background knowledge" about the broader context that the researcher brings to the assessment (Mathison, p.17). By using thoughtful triangulation in assessment we can strengthen our confidence in our conclusions and recommendations, and recognize and examine the reasons for inconsistencies and contradictions.

Sampling

Assessing student learning outcomes does have costs in faculty time and survey and instrument administration. It may be cost-prohibitive and even impractical to collect data from every student, every year, for every student learning outcome, especially in large institutions; and it is not necessary. Sampling principles can be applied to get a representative group of students that gives sufficient confidence in drawing conclusions from the data. Suskie (2004) suggests that small sample sizes can make the assessment process feasible by reducing the data collection burden, but the increase in sampling error should be taken into account when interpreting the results. She includes practical suggestions for determining sample sizes and interpreting from results samples. Confidence in the accuracy of the conclusions can be bolstered by using triangulation principles and by looking for consistent results among diverse samples. Sampling techniques can be applied not only to the number of student products observed, but also to the student learning outcomes. Over successive years, data can be systematically collected from different student learning outcomes so that, in the long term, every general education and program-level student learning outcome has a body of assessment evidence.

Using and Sustaining a Process of Assessment: Faculty, Administration, and Staff Buy-In and Support

A successful student learning outcome assessment process is embedded in the culture of the institution, and is valued by the institution and supported by administration, and is useful. Key to creating a successful process is a method for reporting and responding to the evidence. While this can be done informally, and indeed, faculty collecting assessment data often revise the curriculum based on their findings, a systematic and documented reporting process can add assurance that the assessment process has validity. A report should summarize data, draw conclusions based on the evidence, and propose recommendations for curriculum and future assessments. It is crucial that leadership acknowledge and respond in a reasonable manner to the recommendations made in the report. (See Banta and Pike, this volume.)

Indeed, the ultimate purpose and success of a system that assesses student learning outcomes is determined by how it improves student learning, and this is where faculty are most likely to see assessment's usefulness.

Assessing General Education Student Learning Outcomes: A Case Study

The mission of the United States Military Academy (USMA) is "To educate, train, and inspire the Corps of Cadets so that each graduate is a commissioned leader of character committed to the values of Duty, Honor, Country and prepared for a career of professional excellence and service to the Nation as an officer in the United States Army" (USMA, 2007, p. 3). This is a clear and comprehensive mission, as all of the graduates are being prepared for the same career, yet it functions to focus the goals and activities throughout the institution. This mission guides the student learning outcomes of six developmental domains: intellectual, military, physical, social, moral/ethical, and the domain of the human spirit (USMA, 2009). The description of activities supporting the achievement of these outcomes is based on an underlying theoretical model which describes identity development as progressing from self-interest through reciprocal exchange, belonging, and on to a personal code of conduct (Kegan, 1982; Keith, 2010).

The intellectual domain is the major focus of the academic program, and is further defined by ten general education goals, described in Figure 3.1. USMA has been engaged in a robust process of assessing these general education goals of the academic program since 1989, the year in which teams of faculty leaders under the support and guidance of the academic dean defined the academic program goals and corresponding outcome statements. In 1996 a series of indirect measures in the form of surveys were developed with items that aligned with the outcome statements from the ten goals, asking freshmen and seniors their level of confidence in performing the skills defined in the outcome statements. In 1997 these questions were also posed during focus group interviews with senior military officers who were in graduate school, and in 1999 the items were incorporated into a survey for graduates and their supervisors at a point three years after graduation.

USMA Mission Statement

To educate, train, and inspire the Corps of Cadets so that each graduate is a commissioned leader of character committed to the values of Duty, Honor, Country and prepared for a career of professional excellence and service to the Nation as an officer in the United States Army.

Overarching Academic Goal

Graduates anticipate and respond effectively to the uncertainties of a changing technological, social, political, and economic world.

Academic Goals

Graduates of the Academy will:

- think and act creatively.
- recognize moral issues and apply ethical considerations in decision making.
- demonstrate the capability and desire to pursue progressive and continued intellectual development.
- listen, read, speak, and write effectively.
- draw from an appreciation of culture to understand in a global context human behavior, achievement, and ideas.
- draw on an appreciation of history to understand in a global context human behavior, achievement and ideas.

- understand patterns of human behavior, particularly how individuals, organizations, and societies pursue social, political, and economic goals.
- be scientifically literate and capable of applying scientific, mathematical, and computational modes of thought to the solution of complex problems.
- apply mathematics, science, technology, and the engineering design process to devise technological problem solutions that are effective and adaptable.
- understand and apply Information Technology concepts to acquire, manage, communicate and defend information, solve problems, and adapt to technological change.

Figure 3.1 General education goals

Since its first publication in 1997, the student learning outcomes have been codified in a document, *Educating Future Army Officers for a Changing World* (USMA, 2007). These are general education goals that are not course specific, but are infused across the set of 30 core courses and reinforced in the majors. Figure 3.1 presents a summary of the USMA Mission, the overarching academic goal, and the ten academic student learning outcome goals that support both the Mission and the overarching academic goal. Figure 3.2 gives an example of the Cultural Perspective goal statement and the student learning outcome statements. These statements were developed by faculty teams to clearly define the expected outcomes of the curriculum. An example of a character goal, also in Figure 3.2, lists the outcomes for the Moral/Ethical Goal.

In 2002 the faculty teams developed student learning outcome standards for each of the outcome statements to use for assessment. Figure 3.2 also notes the results of an analysis of a course content and student learning outcomes matrix which was prepared by the teams. Thirteen of the 30 core courses have activities directly related to one or more of the student learning outcomes of the Cultural Perspective Goal, and three courses have activities supporting the Moral/Ethical Goal. Figure 3.3 provides a more complete description of the standards of the student learning outcomes for the Cultural Perspective Goal, and the courses that were identified with activities contributing to the development of the student learning outcomes.

Examples of goals and outcomes at USMA		
	Cultural Perspective	Moral–Ethical
Goal Statement	Graduates draw from an appreciation of culture to understand in a global context, human behavior, achievements, and ideas.	Graduates who develop morally, identify moral and ethical issues, discern what is right, make proper decisions, and take appropriate action.
Outcome statements	Graduates who achieve this goal can: 1. Analyze contemporary and historical events from different cultural perspectives. 2. Apply understanding of culture wherever stationed or deployed around the world. 3. Understand diversity among people both home and abroad. 4. View the world from the perspective of someone in another culture.	Graduates will: 1. Understand, adhere to, and profess the Professional Military Ethic (e.g., Army Values) 2. Recognize moral issues and apply ethical considerations in decision-making 3. Contribute to the moral and ethical development of others
Curriculum alignment mapping	Objectives from 13 core courses identified address at least one of the four outcomes	Objectives from three core courses address at least one of the three outcomes
Direct measures	Embedded: final exams in five core courses	Embedded: Final in philosophy core course, test items and papers in psychology core courses Add-on: Defining Issues Test; ALERT, Values in Action,

Examples of goals and outcomes at USMA		
	Cultural Perspective	Moral–Ethical
Indirect measures		
Surveys	Surveys of freshmen, seniors, graduates, graduates' supervisors. Confidence in ability to: • Work with soldiers from diverse cultural backgrounds • Learn about unfamiliar cultures • View the world from the perspective of another's culture	Surveys of freshmen, seniors, graduates, graduates' supervisors. Confidence in ability to: • Lead by personal example • Assume responsibility for own actions • Examine moral implications of your actions • Recognize moral issues in decision-making
Interview/focus groups	Interviews with senior military officers in graduate school	Interviews with senior military officers in graduate school

Figure 3.2 Goals and outcomes

	WHAT GRADUATES CAN DO			
DEMONSTRATE ABILITY TO:	Analyze contemporary and historical events from different cultural perspectives.	Apply understanding of culture wherever stationed or deployed around the world.	Understand diversity among people both home and abroad.	View the world from the perspective of someone in another culture.
STANDARD	Analyze and understand the current and past events of a culture under study as well as that culture's distinctive interpretation(s) of those events. Complete this analysis by examining traditional responses to change, delineating the components of that culture, regional variations in cultural diversity/human behavior, and spatial linkages among culture systems.	Analyze and understand cultural landscapes (i.e., political, economic, military, social, cultural and religious systems), their geographic distribution(s), and be cognizant of similarities and differences as they affect decision-making processes.	Analyze and delineate cultural diversity and human behavior in domestic and international scenarios, recognize a range of similarities and differences in common cultural practices, illustrate regional dissimilarity in cultural practices and demonstrate how these differences/similarities drive choices in domestic and international relations and military/civilian law.	Analyze current and past events of the culture under study, and be able to view events, issues, and choices in international relations from multiple perspectives. Understand how individuals and cultures pursue social, political, and economic goals.
EMBEDDED INDICATORS	History 103 Final	EV203 Final	American Politics Test	History 103 Final
	Psych100 Final	Foreign Language Final	Foreign Language Final	English302 Final
	English 302 Final	American Politics Test	Law403 Test	International Relations Final
	Physical Geography Final	Physical Geography	Psych300 Test	Physical Geography Final
		English101 Test	Physical Geography	

Figure 3.3 Cultural perspective outcomes and embedded indicators

In 2003 the teams identified course products throughout the core curriculum that could be used as embedded indicators for each of the student learning outcome statements. The direct measures in Figure 3.3 show that after constructing the course and student learning matrices, faculty identified several course products that could reasonable serve as sources for collecting direct assessment evidence. Note that for the Moral/Ethical Goal, there is a combination of embedded indicators-final exams, papers, and tests- and the add-on indicators of the Defining Issues Test (DIT), and the ALERT (a locally developed version of the DIT with military scenarios).

Student learning outcome assessment began in earnest as the teams systematically collected the evidence that had been identified as embedded indicators in the course products. The last section of Figure 3.2 describes the sources of indirect indicators: surveys of students, graduates and their supervisors, and interviews, with examples of the survey items that are aligned with the student learning outcomes. The students, graduates and supervisors are asked to indicate their level of confidence in these abilities. Figure 3.4 is a rubric developed by the goal team that was applied to a direct embedded indicator: a paper prepared by a student for a core course in physical geography.

When the teams combine the evidence from the embedded indicators with the survey and interview data, they are able to see how well students and graduates are achieving the student learning outcomes for each of the goals. This combination of indirect indicators in the form of surveys and interviews, and direct evidence from student products, created a comprehensive data set for the triangulation of evidence to assess the student learning outcomes (Judd & Keith, 2009; Keith et al., 2002).

To bring the assessment cycle full circle, each goal team prepares a year-end report describing the assessment data collection activities, analyzing the results, identifying concerns, and recommending any changes deemed appropriate to the curriculum or the assessment process. The reports from the goal teams are summarized for the academic area and forwarded to the chief academic officer for review and action.

Over the course of several years, the Cultural Perspective goal team came to the consistent conclusion that while students are achieving the learning outcomes at a basic level, student achievement of the outcomes could be improved if the curriculum included the development of a framework for

GRADE EQUIVALENT➡	A	B-C	C-	D	F	--
	STRONGLY AGREE	AGREE	NEUTRAL	DISAGREE	STRONGLY DISAGREE	NOT EVALUATED
NO. STANDARD▮	5	4	3	2	1	NE
1 ANALYZE CONTEMPORARY AND HISTORICAL EVENTS						
1a Identified and analyzed discrete, culture-dependent interpretations of key historical events, which have shaped the region's modern culture.						
1c Identified significant contemporary events and explained their influence on the region's culture systems.						
1d Examined traditional responses to change by demonstrating the evolution of the culture over time.						
2 UNDERSTAND CULTURE						
2a Cadet explained the discrete components of the culture systems in the region.						
2b Cadet related the systems identified in 2a (above) to the region's relative stability.						
2d Cadet is cognizant of similarities and differences in culture systems and explained how these differences affect decision-making processes.						

GRADE EQUIVALENT➡	A	B-C	C-	D	F	--
	STRONGLY AGREE	AGREE	NEUTRAL	DISAGREE	STRONGLY DISAGREE	NOT EVALUATED
NO. STANDARD▮	5	4	3	2	1	NE
3 UNDERSTAND DIVERSITY						
3a Cadet identified cultural diversity and differences in human behavior in domestic and international scenarios.						
3b Recognized similarities and differences in cultural practices (at home and abroad) and explained how this leads to unity or fragmentation.						
3c Illustrated regional dissimilarity in cultural practices and demonstrated how this sets in motion choices in domestic and international relations.						
4 WORLD VIEW						
4a Cadet linked current and past events of the culture under study and explained how different cultures perceive those events.						
4b Cadet related multiple perspectives in international relations to the culture under study and its sensitivity to world events.						

Figure 3.4 Cultural perspective rubric for assessing embedded indicators

understanding a new cultural environment. These findings inspired discussions across the institution, and an examination of areas inside and outside the academic curriculum where the development of cultural understanding could be reinforced. In fact, numerous opportunities were identified in the academic curriculum (e.g., in language and history course coordination; psychology course treatment of cultural differences) and the military training that occurs during the summer months (Keith, 2010).

In response to the recommendations made by the assessment team, the chief academic officer asked the assessment group to define what an interculturaly competent student learning outcome should be, what is required to achieve that outcome, what elements of the current curriculum support the development of intercultural competence, and the feasibility of providing every student with an intercultural experience prior to graduation. In the true spirit of the assessment cycle, this is still a work in progress, as the institution assesses, recommends, responds, and assesses again.

Lessons Learned From the Assessment of Student Learning Outcomes

As articulated by Keith (2010), we have learned that the establishment of the student learning outcomes has defined an educated graduate from USMA, and described the learning system we have implemented to achieve those outcomes.

We have learned the value of involving all of the stakeholders in order to have universal acceptance of the system. The first iteration showed that without broad involvement across the institution in developing the model there was little sense of awareness or ownership among faculty and staff.

We have learned that the existing compartmentalization of programs has to be breached if students are expected to integrate learning across the curriculum and programs. Students tend to be risk averse, afraid of failure, and unwilling to leave their comfort zones. Therefore, we cannot wish for integration to take place; we must intentionally set the conditions and expectations for integration, and remove the institutional barriers.

We have learned that there may be limitations in how far students can be expected to develop along the model we have embraced (Lewis et al., 2005). Nevertheless, for students to continue to develop to the maximum extent while they are with us, they need to have the opportunities to assess their own performance structured into the learning system.

Our chosen learning model views development as continuing well after graduation, hence the title of our learning system begins with the words "building capacity," in the recognition that we are setting the stage for students' development well into the early years of their careers.

The process of developing and implementing a cyclical system of assessment of student learning outcomes has helped USMA determine what we intend to accomplish with our students, how we intend to accomplish it, how well we are accomplishing it, and how we can improve the preparation of our students for their careers.

References

Arum, R., & Roksa, J. (2010). *Academically adrift: Limited learning on college campuses*. Chicago, IL: University of Chicago Press.

Association of American Colleges and Universities. (2007). *College learning for the new global century*. Washington, DC: Author.

Astin, A. (1993). *Assessment for Excellence: the philosophy and practice of assessment and evaluation in higher education*. Phoenix, AZ: Oryx Press.

Astin, W., Astin, H., & Lindholm, J. (2010). *Cultivating the spirit: How college can enhance students' inner lives*. San Francisco, CA: Jossey–Bass.

Banta, T. W., & Pike, G. R. (this volume). *The bottom line: Will faculty USE assessment findings?*

Bloom, B. S. (Ed.). (1956). *Taxonomy of educational objectives: Handbook 1, Cognitive domain*. New York, NY: Longman.

Center of Inquiry in the Liberal Arts. (n.d.). Wabash National Study 2006–2009. Retrieved from: http://www. liberalarts.wabash.edu/study-overview

Chickering, A., & Reisser, L. (1993). *Education and identity*. San Francisco, CA: Jossey-Bass.

Council of Regional Accrediting Commissions. (2003). *Regional accreditation and student learning: Principles of good practice*. Retrieved from http://www.msche.org/publications/Regnlsl050208135331.pdf

Evans, N., Forney, D., Guido, F., Patton, K., & Renn, K. (2009). *Student development in college: Theory, research, and practice* (2nd ed.). San Francisco, CA: Jossey–Bass.

Ewell, P. (1984). *The self-regarding institution: Information for excellence*. Boulder, CO: National Center for Higher Education Management Systems.

Ewell, P. (2002). *An emerging scholarship: A brief history of assessment*. In T. W. Banta, & Associates (Eds.), *Building a scholarship of assessment* (pp. 3–25). San Francisco, CA: Jossey–Bass.

Judd, T., & Keith, B. (2009). Triangulation of data sources in assessing academic outcomes. In T. Banta, E. Jones, & K. Black (Eds.), *Designing effective assessment: Principles and profiles of good practice* (pp. 46–49). San Francisco, CA: Jossey-Bass.

Kegan, R. (1982). *The evolving self: Problem and process in human development*. Cambridge, MA: Harvard University Press.

Keith, B. (2010). The transformation of West Point as a liberal arts college. *Liberal Education, 96*(2), 6–13.

Keith B., LeBoeuf, J., Meese, M., Malinowski, J., Gallagher, M., Efflandt, S., Hurley, J., & Green, J. (2002). Assessing students' understanding of human behavior: A multidisciplinary outcomes-based approach for the design and assessment of an academic program goal. *Teaching Sociology, 30*(4), 430–453.

Kohlberg, L. (1984). *Essays on moral development. Volume 2: The psychology of moral development.* San Francisco, CA: Harper and Row.

Leskes, A., & Wright, B. (2005). *The art and science of assessing general education outcomes: A practical guide.* Washington, DC: Association of American Colleges and Universities.

Lewis, P., Forsythe, G., Sweeney, P., Bartone, P., Bullis, C., & Snook, S. (2005). Identity development during the college years: findings from the West Point Longitudinal Study. *Journal of College Student Development, 46*(4), 357–373.

Mathison, S. (1988). Why triangulate? *Educational Researcher, 17*(2), 12–17.

Middaugh, M. (2009). *Planning and assessment in higher education: Demonstrating educational effectiveness.* San Francisco, CA: Jossey-Bass.

Middle States Commission on Higher Education. (2006). *Characteristics of excellence in higher education.* Retrieved from http://www.msche.org/publications/CHX06060320124919.pdf.

Pascarella, E. T., & Terenzini, P. T. (2005). *How college affects students.* San Francisco, CA: Jossey-Bass.

Perry, W. (1970). *Forms of intellectual and ethical development in the college years: A scheme.* Fort Worth, TX: Harcort Brace Jovanovich.

Pitoniak, M. J., & Morgan, D. L. (this volume). *Setting and validating cut scores for tests.*

Rest, J. R., Narvaez, D., Thoma, S.J., & Bebeau, M. (1999). DIT2: Devising and testing a revised instrument of moral judgement. *Journal of Educational Psychology, 91*(4), 644–659.

Spady, W., & Schwahn, C. (2010). *Learning communities 2.0: Education in the Age of Empowerment.* Lanham, MD: Rowman & Littlefield Publishers.

Suskie, L. (2004). *Assessing student learning: A common sense guide.* Boston, MA: Anker.

U.S. Department of Education. National Center for Education Statistics. (1997). *Student outcomes information for policy making* (NCES 97–991). Washington, DC: Awnar.

U.S. Department of Education. National Center for Education Statistics. (2002). *Defining and assessing learning: Exploring competency-based initiatives* (NCES 2002–159). Washington, DC.

United States Military Academy. (2007). *Educating future army officers for a changing world.* Retrieved from: http://www.dean.usma.edu/sebpublic/EFAOCW.pdf

United States Military Academy. (2010). *Building capacity to lead: The West Point system for leader development.* Retrieved from: http://www.dean.usma.edu/documents/CLDS.2009.pdf

Walvoord, B. (2009). *Assessment clear and simple* (2nd ed.). San Francisco, CA: Jossey-Bass.

Yen, J. L., & Hynes, K. (this volume). *Authentic assessment validation: A heuristic rubrics cube.*

4

THE BOTTOM LINE: WILL FACULTY USE ASSESSMENT FINDINGS?

Trudy W. Banta and Gary R. Pike

"Closing the Loop" is a phrase heard often at annual meetings of accrediting associations and at conferences focused on outcomes assessment in higher education. The meaning of this phrase outside assessment circles may not be evident, but as calls for colleges and universities to demonstrate their accountability increase in frequency and intensity, more and more faculty will become familiar with it. Closing the loop means, simply, using assessment findings to improve the object of the assessment. For faculty this involves using what they learn about students' strengths and weaknesses from tests, projects, papers, and students' perceptions of their experiences to make warranted changes designed to improve teaching and learning in the classroom as well as curriculum and student support services. In this chapter we explore some of the reasons that closing the loop is so difficult for faculty and suggest what it will take to encourage more of this behavior.

Faculty Resistance to Assessment

Most college and university faculty members have not embraced outcomes assessment. In a 2009 survey of chief academic officers at the 2,809 regionally accredited two- and four-year undergraduate-degree-granting institutions in the U.S., two-thirds of the 1,518 respondents, and 80% of those at doctoral-research universities, said their greatest assessment-related need is "more faculty engagement" (Kuh & Ikenberry, 2009). While faculty do evaluate the work of individual students and give grades, they are reluctant—even resistant—to take a second look at student work in the aggregate to see what group strengths and weaknesses might suggest about the need for more attention to teaching a particular concept or for a different pedagogical approach.

Good reasons for faculty resistance to outcomes assessment abound (Suskie, 2004). The lives of faculty are already filled with their obligations to teach students and evaluate the students' learning for the purpose of assigning grades, to write grants and conduct research, to publish the results of their scholarship, and to render campus and community service. How can they add another time-consuming activity, especially one that might have direct, and perhaps public, implications for a very private activity—their teaching?

As some faculty dig deeper to see what outcomes assessment is all about, they find that it involves measurement and evaluation, topics most faculty have not studied and now find complex and difficult. Moreover, they begin to worry about the cost of assessment, not only in terms of the time required of themselves, their students, and involved staff, but also in connection with the purchase of commercial tests and surveys. They question how the results of assessment will be used. Will faculty or departments be punished if their students' performance is less than expected? Will some faculty be criticized or even lose their jobs? Will small departments be closed? Will the curriculum be narrowed to focus more intently on correcting weaknesses discovered in students' knowledge or skills? And finally, if individuals do spend time on outcomes assessment, will their involvement be recognized and rewarded in annual performance reviews and in promotion and tenure processes?

Faculty Criteria for Assessing Assessment Instruments

When confronted with requirements for assessment imposed by a regional or disciplinary accrediting association, or by a governor, a legislature, or members of a governing board, most faculty recognize that they must respond (Ewell, 2009). In their study, Kuh & Ikenberry (2009) found that preparing for accreditation was the most frequently cited use of assessment data by their survey respondents, followed by "revising learning goals" and "responding to accountability calls." Having recognized the need for assessment, a next step is to make decisions about the measurement instruments that will be used to provide the evidence of program and institutional quality that is sought. The first reaction to a request or a mandate to furnish a report on student learning outcomes often is to say that the evidence should be authentic; it should be a reflection of what faculty actually teach. Nevertheless, program and institutional reporting requirements usually don't lend themselves to reports from individual classrooms—and few faculty members would want to provide public reports based on evidence from a single class. So the search begins in earnest for instruments that (1) match as closely as possible what faculty are teaching and (2) yield data that are comparable across sections of the same course, courses in a curriculum, and perhaps across student class levels—freshmen and seniors, for example—in an institution (Suskie, 2009).

Selecting Tests of Generic Skills and Abilities

While it is even difficult for faculty in a given discipline to agree on the concepts students should master by the time they graduate, some progress along these lines is being made (Banta & Schneider, 1988; Walvoord, Bardes, & Denton, 1998). State-level and national exams have been developed in many professional fields such as accounting, social work, and the various health sciences. Most faculty in these disciplines find the evidence obtained via students' scores on these exams credible—certainly as indicators of the competence of individual students, and perhaps as indicators of program quality when students' scores are aggregated for a given program. Even some faculty in areas of the humanities, sciences, and social sciences, where disciplinary accreditation is rare and agreement on common learning outcomes more difficult, have come to rely on such externally developed measures as the Advanced Tests of the Graduate Record Exam, or on the shorter versions, the Major Field Tests (Educational Testing Service, 2010), as indicators of individual competence and, with reservations, of program quality.

While concerns about the appropriateness of measures of student competence in major fields cannot be minimized, they pale in comparison with those expressed in debates about how to define and assess generic, cross-cutting knowledge, skills, and abilities such as writing, quantitative reasoning, and critical thinking. The quest for acceptable measurement instruments in these areas will be our focus in the remainder of this chapter.

Some state accountability initiatives, as well as the national Voluntary System of Accountability (2010), identify generic skills such as written communication, analytic reasoning, and problem solving as essential for all college graduates to develop. So the search is on for instruments that will measure these skills and provide scores for undergraduates that can be compared across institutions. What criteria are faculty and college administrators using to decide how to address this need?

For the vast majority of faculty, who are not versed in psychometrics, the primary criterion for instrument selection will be face validity. That is, the content must look like the content the instrument says it measures and like the content faculty want students to learn in the given areas (Millett, Payne, Dwyer, Stickler, & Alexion, 2008). An early consideration in this regard is the extent to which the content of a question designed to measure a particular skill may advantage students studying in one discipline and disadvantage students studying in other fields. If, for instance, in attempting to assess their analytic reasoning skills, students are asked to answer questions related to purchasing an airplane, are students in business and engineering fields more likely to have practiced responding to such questions than those studying art or humanities? Faculty express legitimate concerns about differences among disciplines in the ways generic skills are manifested and evaluated (scientific vs. creative writing, for example) and about the real possibility that few exam questions purporting to measure generic skills can actually be content free (Perkins, 1987).

If faculty are to use data from an assessment instrument or method to improve their approaches to teaching, assessment of student work, or student support services such as advising or placement of graduates, they need to see a direct relationship between what is measured and what they need to improve (Palomba & Banta, 1999). At the least they need subscores on a test that differentiate various skills (writing vs. quantitative reasoning) and areas of knowledge (fine arts vs. science) from a global score. In addition to direct measures of what students know and can do, faculty need indirect measures of learning obtained from the students. Questionnaires, interviews, and focus groups yield students' perceptions of the effectiveness of the approaches to teaching, assessment, and support services they are experiencing. No single direct or indirect measure of student learning will provide enough evidence to convince most faculty that they have a basis for changing current practice. But considered simultaneously, multiple measures can be convincing.

As time and money are recognized as increasingly scarce resources in higher education, it will be essential to demonstrate to faculty that assessment approaches do not take too much faculty, student, and staff time and do not consume other institutional resources in ways that are not cost effective. The tests of generic skills recommended within the Voluntary System of Accountability, for instance, are quite expensive. In part to counteract arguments against using these tests that are based on their costs, the test vendors recommend using samples of 100 at each level and testing freshmen and seniors in a cross-sectional design rather than waiting four to six years for freshmen to become seniors. Such recommendations test credulity where freshman and senior classes number in the thousands and the senior class differs significantly from the freshman class due to the absence of many who have dropped out and to the presence of a large percentage of transfer students.

Using the AERA-APA-NCME Standards to Guide Test Selection

The *Standards for Educational and Psychological Testing*, developed by the American Educational Research Association (AERA), the American Psychological Association (APA), and the National Council on Measurement in Education (NCME), offer important guidance for evaluating and selecting tests of generic skills and other assessment measures. At the heart of the *Standards* is the concept of validity, which "refers to the degree to which evidence and theory support the interpretations of test scores entailed by proposed uses of tests" (American Educational Research Association, American Psychological Association, & National Council on Measurement in Education, 1999, p. 9). What is most noteworthy about this definition is that validity is presumed to inhere in the *interpretation and use* of test (or assessment) data, not in the tests themselves (see also Messick, 1989; Kane, 2006). Thus, test scores and other assessment measures may be appropriate for one interpretation or use, but not another. For example, the ACT Assessment exam and the Scholastic Aptitude Test (SAT) may provide accurate and appropriate information for making college admission decisions, but the data may be inappropriate for assessing the generic skills and abilities of college graduates.

So what types of evidence are required to establish the accuracy and appropriateness of assessment measures? Both the AERA-APA-NCME standards and measurement scholars have argued that because the focus is on the interpretation and use of assessment data, faculty and other assessment professionals must first clearly articulate the interpretations and uses that will be made of assessment data. For example, are test scores to be used to determine whether individual students have achieved specific levels of professional competence in a field (i.e., certification), or are they to be used to determine if educational programs at an institution contribute to student learning in meaningful ways (i.e., program assessment/evaluation). The validity requirements for these two uses are quite different. In the first instance, the test must provide precise information about individual students' abilities at a particular threshold or cut score. In the second instance the test must be sensitive to the effects of educational interventions on groups of students.

Once the rationale for linking student behavior on a test or assessment measure to specific inferences and actions has been clearly articulated, evidence must be collected to support this rationale (Kane, 2006). Building on the work of Samuel Messick (1989), the AERA-APA-NCME standards stress the importance of drawing on multiple sources of data about test content, the empirical structure of test scores, and the relationships between test scores and external measures to make judgments about validity. If, for example, a test is intended to provide data on students' critical thinking and writing abilities, it would be reasonable to expect the test to include questions or prompts that require the student to think critically and to write. It would also be reasonable to expect that the test would include both critical thinking and writing scores, and that these scores would be related to other measures of students' critical thinking and writing abilities.

The AERA-APA-NCME standards also include a variety of recommendations specific to using test or assessment scores for program evaluation and public policy decision making. These recommendations provide useful guidelines for faculty in interpreting and using assessment data for accountability and improvement. The standards include recommendations for providing detailed information about the sampling scheme used, information about the background characteristics of test takers if those characteristics are likely to influence assessment results, and sufficient contextual information to minimize misinterpretations of test scores. Of particular importance for outcomes assessment that focuses on learning (i.e., change) during college, Standard 15.3 states: "When change or gain scores are used, the definition of such scores should be made explicit, and their technical qualities should be reported" (American Educational Research Association, American Psychological Association, National Council on Measurement in Education, 1999, p. 167).

Using Assessment Data Where Use Is Mandated

It has been said that you can lead a horse to water, but not make it drink. In Tennessee, where both authors of this chapter were based in the 1980s and early 1990s, the Tennessee Higher Education Commission (THEC) developed a system of performance funding that based 5.45% of each public institution's state appropriation for instruction on accreditation of accreditable programs and evidence of assessing student learning in the major and in general education, reporting findings from a survey of graduates, and demonstrating in a written report that these assessment findings had been used to improve pedagogy, curriculum, and/or student services (Banta, 1986). Every year we reported our findings and on that basis the University of Tennessee, Knoxville (UTK) received a substantial proportion of the 5.45% of its budget to which that institution was entitled. But use of findings, particularly those based on scores on standardized tests of generic skills, by faculty to improve teaching and the student experience in general, was scant. Why?

In the first place, since performance funding was a state-initiated program and only a few faculty state-wide were involved in selecting the tests of generic skills to be used by all public institutions, most faculty did not feel a sense of ownership of this assessment process. We involved small groups of faculty in studying the content of the tests and the meaning of our students' scores once those became available. But we were never able to attract widespread interest among UTK faculty in the process of administering standardized tests of cross-cutting skills to freshmen and seniors and using the findings to make improvements.

During the 1987–88 academic year we conducted a study that engaged a representative group of faculty in determining how closely each of two standardized tests of generic skills recommended for use in THEC's performance funding program matched UTK's stated learning outcomes for general education. Faculty concluded that neither of the tests covered even 30% of the knowledge and skills they considered important (Banta & Pike, 1989).

From other studies based on the test scores and test-related experiences of UTK freshmen and seniors required to take the tests of generic skills, we derived the following information:

1. The tests we were giving (first the College Outcome Measures Project (COMP) exam, and later the Collegiate Assessment of Academic Proficiency (CAAP) from ACT; the Academic Profile (today's Proficiency Profile) from ETS; and the College Basic Academic Subjects Exam (C-BASE) developed at the University of Missouri-Columbia) were primarily tests of prior learning (correlations approaching .9 with entering ACT/SAT scores when aggregated at the institutional level). Therefore, differences in scores on such tests reflect individual differences in socioeconomic backgrounds and educational experiences prior to college among students taking the tests more accurately than differences in the quality of education offered at different institutions (Pike, 2006).
2. Since such tests are not content neutral, the items and the mode of response they require (e.g., writing or quantitative analysis) advantage students specializing in some disciplines and disadvantage those specializing in some others.
3. These tests cannot be given to samples of students who simply volunteer to take them if students' scores are to be interpreted as representative of all students at the institution in drawing conclusions about the presumed quality of education offered at the institution.
4. Making participation in assessment a requirement is the only way to increase confidence that the sample of students taking a given test represents the institution fairly.
5. As Sundre (2009, p. vii) observed, "Low motivation to perform well on tests is particularly manifest when the examination results hold no personal consequences for the students we ask to complete the tasks." Even when test-taking is required, lack of motivation on the part of some students to do their best work on the test may jeopardize the validity of an institution's scores unless ways are found to convince students of the importance to them of achieving their best possible score. Extrinsic incentives such as pizza, cash, or prizes do not ensure conscientious performance over time. Connecting performance to an outcome of personal import to students, such as a course grade, a diploma, or licensure in a field, appears to be most effective (see also research by Wise, 2009).

We found other measurement problems as well. In particular, the value-added measure used in the THEC's performance funding program did not appear to provide accurate and appropriate data about student learning. In Tennessee, students' ACT Assessment scores were used to calculate expected freshman scores on the College Outcome Measures Project (COMP) objective test. At graduation, students took the COMP test and the mean difference between the scores of seniors and freshmen was used as a measure of value added.

Two issues emerged from the analyses we conducted at UTK. First, the estimated gain scores used in Tennessee did not appear to be reliable measures of change. Measures of the proportion of error variance in the gain scores for individual students revealed that estimated score gain was little better than a chance measure (Pike, 1992). Although there was considerable debate about the reliability of group-mean gain scores, evidence suggested that the errors of measurement were still substantial (Pike, 1993; Steele, 1993).

The second problem with the value-added measure used in Tennessee was that gain scores were *negatively related* to entering scores. In other words, students with the lowest scores as freshmen had the largest gain scores, whereas students with the highest scores as freshmen had the smallest gains (Pike, 1992). The negative correlation between gains and initial status had serious consequences for performance funding. Colleges and universities with relatively higher ability student at entry were less likely to show significant gains in learning than institutions with less well prepared students. The negative correlations between gains and initial status also created problems for evaluating programs within an institution. For example, students majoring in STEM fields could be reasonably expected to enter the institution with better preparation in mathematics than students in the arts and humanities. When gain scores were used to evaluate mathematics-related learning, gain scores for students in STEM fields were significantly lower than gain scores for students in the arts and humanities. These findings certainly worked to undermine faculty support for trying to use the results of assessment to guide improvement at UTK and elsewhere in Tennessee.

Encouraging Faculty Use of Assessment Findings

Earlier in this chapter we outlined some of the reasons for faculty resistance to assessment. These concerns must be addressed if faculty members are to be encouraged to use assessment findings to guide improvements in teaching and learning. That is, faculty must have a reasonable degree of confidence that the assessment instruments they plan to use are reliable and valid. At the very least, the assessment tools must look like a good match for the knowledge and skills faculty are teaching. The tests, questionnaires, and interview protocols must not take much, if any, time from classroom instruction, and even if these instruments are to be given outside class, they should not take an inordinate amount of student time. Finally, faculty must perceive the costs of purchasing and administering assessment instruments to be manageable within their institution's budget.

Connecting Assessment With Valued Processes

Outcomes assessment should not spin in its own orbit, unconnected to ongoing processes that faculty understand and value (Banta & Associates, 2002). It will be perceived as a waste of time and other institutional resources, if undertaken simply to satisfy an accrediting body or state or federal government.

When faculty design a new approach to general education or to delivering instruction, most are curious as to the effectiveness of the new approach when compared with the original. Using a combination of measures of learning, questionnaires, and focus groups before and after the advent of the new approach can satisfy faculty curiosity about relative effectiveness.

At many institutions a process called program review is used to assess the effectiveness of departments and/or divisions on an annual basis or at least every few years (Bresciani, 2006). The review may be conducted by an internal team or by external reviewers who come to the campus for interviews and observations. This is usually a time-honored practice that faculty accept and may even appreciate. It requires a self study or other kind of written report. Inserting in the guidelines for preparing such reports a request for assessment data on student learning or on the effectiveness of components of the program, and for evidence that these data have guided improvements helps to ensure that personnel in departments and divisions will close the loop, that is, use assessment findings to improve academic programs and student services.

Accreditation is a special case of program review that involves preparing a self study that will be read by a team of peers appointed by an accrediting body. Following a campus visit, the team reports strengths and weaknesses that will be weighed by a central body within the association in deciding to grant or renew accreditation. Study after study, including Kuh & Ikenberry's 2009 survey, concludes that accreditation provides the most powerful stimulus for faculty to undertake outcomes assessment and apply the findings in making improvements.

Many faculty at four-year institutions are engaged in the scholarship of teaching and learning. Evidence that students are benefitting from a faculty member's approaches is an essential component of this kind of scholarship.

Most faculty are not formally prepared as **teachers** of the knowledge and skills embodied in their discipline. And if they have not received instruction on teaching, they certainly have not been trained to use assessment techniques. Thus connecting assessment with faculty development is essential if more of our colleagues are to be in a position to close the loop (Banta, Jones, & Black, 2009).

Innovation and extraordinary work in assessment can be encouraged through awards, providing summer salary, and giving small grants that involve release time, student assistance, or travel funds.

Arguably the most important connection for assessment is with promotion and tenure and other recognition and reward mechanisms. Just as students are motivated to learn and to do their best work on externally developed exams when they know their grades are influenced by their performance, so faculty are motivated to conduct assessment and use its results when they know that a promotion or the size of a raise will be determined, in part, by involvement in these activities.

Using Instruments That Have Credibility

No test or questionnaire will offer perfect reliability or validity. But this fact cannot prevent action in the field of outcomes assessment in higher education. We must start to collect evidence using instruments that faculty consider credible and work to improve them as flaws are identified. Using several sources of evidence—for instance, asking the same survey questions of students, faculty, and employers—permits triangulation and increases confidence in data-based decisions about the need for change.

As we observed at the outset, faculty prefer authentic measures of students' knowledge and skills— measures that permit students to demonstrate that they know and can do the things that faculty are trying to teach them (Walvoord, 2004). The daily assignments, the classroom tests, the papers, and the projects that faculty use to evaluate students' competence in coursework are the measures faculty generally find most credible. So the question about instrumentation for use in outcomes assessment becomes: How can we scale up the evidence collected in assignments, tests, papers, and projects from individual courses to a level that will permit faculty in a program or department, or across a campus, to view aggregated data and make decisions about needed improvements in curriculum, methods of instruction, and student support services such as advising? Currently faculty across the country are experimenting with three methods that may yield answers to this question in the years to come: student electronic portfolios, rubrics, and assessment communities (Banta, Griffin, Flateby, & Kahn, 2009).

Electronic portfolios give students a showcase for examples of their work as their competence develops over time (Hamilton & Kahn, 2009). One might argue that a portfolio enables us to **see** value added as a student moves through a sequence of learning experiences. The artifacts a student puts into a portfolio are not limited to classroom assignments, though faculty may suggest or require that certain pieces of work be included. If a student is more comfortable capturing knowledge and skills in a photograph or an oral presentation than in a piece of written work, the ePortfolio provides the opportunity to do that. In addition, metacognitive skills may be honed if students are asked to reflect on the reasons for their choice of a particular artifact to represent their attainment of specified knowledge and skills. Without question, ePortfolios can yield a far more comprehensive demonstration of what students know and can do than can standardized tests, which give only a time-bound snapshot of a small portion of what students have learned.

If one can describe a concept operationally, pulling it apart to expose its various elements, a rubric can be designed to measure gradations of each of the elements. Rubrics are essential in assessing student competence as demonstrated in ePortfolios collectively, as must be the case for outcomes assessment purposes. That is, rubrics provide the measurement tools we need to assess the work of **groups** of students as recorded in their ePortfolios. Flateby and Metzger (1999, 2001), for example, have developed a 16-trait Cognitive Level and Quality of Writing Assessment (CLAQWA) rubric that can be applied to assess cognitive level as well as a range of writing skills in coursework and in ePortfolios. Staff at the Association of American Colleges and Universities have engaged faculty across the U.S. in coming to agreement on 15 rubrics that can be applied in assessing student work in ePortfolios. Looking at common assignments and using a common rubric to evaluate them can yield outcomes assessment data useful in directing improvement decisions and demonstrating accountability at program, department, and institutional levels.

ePortfolios and rubrics have just come into widespread use within the last five years, as calls for higher education to demonstrate accountability have mounted at federal and state levels and have become more apparent to faculty in all disciplines. Assessment communities are still considered an innovation and are not yet in widespread use. Griffin (2009) is a pioneer in building online assessment communities that engage peers in applying their specialized disciplinary knowledge, years of experience, and expert judgment (Mintzberg, 2000) to create criteria for evaluating samples of student work. Since the dialogue that leads to consensus on criteria takes place online, meetings are not necessary and participants can contribute to the discussion at any time they find convenient. Moreover, faculty from other departments on a campus, or other campuses, can participate in setting criteria for assessing levels of competence in generic skills such as writing and critical thinking. Although the assessment community concept is in a very early stage, it holds promise for establishing common standards across institutions that can be applied to common assignments such as comprehensive papers or projects within or outside student electronic portfolios.

Classroom tests and other assignments are intended first and foremost to give individual students feedback about their performance and faculty a basis for assigning grades. Thus these artifacts have face validity for faculty and ensure that students are motivated to do their best work in producing them. These characteristics gives such authentic assessment methods credibility with inhabitants of the academy. But they present their own measurement challenges. If credibility is to extend beyond a given classroom, faculty groups must agree on learning outcomes, ways to measure the outcomes, and standards of achievement to employ in judging student performance. Use of rubrics demands inter-rater agreement. Secolsky and Wentland (2010) point out that different topics treated in a single student assignment constitute a source of variability that cannot be ignored in assessing the artifact. And Barrett (2009) warns us that standardized prompts mat rob us of the built-in source of student motivation that we have been associating with authentic measures! It has taken almost 80 years to build even the level of credibility that the SAT enjoys. Will it take another 80 years to bring authentic measures to the same level?

Beyond Closing the Loop

Ultimately the success of implementing outcomes assessment in higher education and using the findings to make constructive changes in curriculum, instruction, and student support services will depend on our ability to demonstrate that the changes made have actually had the desired effect on improving student learning. As Schneider and Shulman (2007, p. viii) have observed, "Assessment all by itself is an insufficient condition for powerful learning and improvement."

In 2008, Banta, Jones, and Black (2009) conducted a nation-wide search for profiles of successful assessment practice. We received 146 fully developed 1,500-word profiles, each of which contained a section on uses made of assessment findings and a second section on the long-term impact of using those findings. Examples of using findings ranged from adding ethics or appreciation of diversity components to courses, to developing new approaches to general education, to enhancing first-year seminars to provide more effective support for freshmen at risk of dropping out of college. But only 6% (9 of the 146) of the profiles we collected actually contained evidence that the long-term consequences of using the findings included improvements in student learning.

The improvements that were identified included increases in the number of faculty who were aware that outcomes assessment is important, more assessment activity, more work designed to improve assessment tools such as rubrics, additional professional development experiences designed to improve effectiveness in teaching and assessment, more use of assessment findings, redesigned assignments to address identified weaknesses of learners, accreditation granted or renewed, and funding for new faculty or staff positions to bolster areas identified as being in need of improvement (Banta, 2009).

To demonstrate accountability and to encourage more faculty to engage in assessment and use the findings to make warranted improvements, we need longer-term studies designed to assess changes in learning over time. At the University of South Florida, Flateby and colleagues have been using CLAQWA to assess student writing for a dozen years. As faculty have learned to construct assignments that develop progressively more complex levels of learning, CLAQWA ratings demonstrate that student writing has improved. Since 2003, Clayton and colleagues at North Carolina State University have documented improvements in students' reasoning and critical thinking skills in connection with outcomes such as civic learning and personal growth. Clayton employs a reflection model called DEAL (description, examination, and articulation of learning), which offers prompts to guide critical thinking and a rubric for scoring students' reflection products. At James Madison University, use of an evaluation instrument built by faculty more than a decade ago provides evidence that more students are developing requisite skills in information literacy (Banta, 2009).

We are a very long way from convincing most faculty to use assessment findings to guide needed improvements in the environment for learning on college campuses. We must begin by building faculty trust in assessment—trust that the measures they select actually evaluate the knowledge and skills they value and trust that the time spent on assessment will be recognized and appreciated. Making outcomes assessment a component of processes faculty value, such as program review and the scholarship of teaching and learning, is an important step in this process. And finally, we need support for longitudinal studies designed to demonstrate the effects on student learning of closing the loop—actually making changes on the basis of assessment findings.

References

American Educational Research Association, American Psychological Association, & National Council on Measurement in Education. (1999). *Standards for educational and psychological testing*. Washington, DC: American Educational Research Association.

Banta, T. W. (Ed.). (1986). *Performance funding in higher education: A critical analysis of Tennessee's experience*. Boulder, CO: National Center for Higher Education Management Systems. [175 pages].

Banta, T. W. (2009). Demonstrating the impact of changes based on assessment findings. *Assessment Update, 21*(2), 3–4.

Banta, T. W., & Associates. (2002). *Building a scholarship of assessment*. San Francisco, CA: Jossey-Bass.

Banta, T. W., Griffin, M., Flateby, T. L., & Kahn, S. (2009, December). *Three promising alternatives for assessing college students' knowledge and skills*. NILOA Occasional Paper No. 2. Urbana, IL: University of Illinois and Indiana University, National Institute of Learning Outcomes Assessment.

Banta, T.W., Jones, E. A., & Black, K. E. (2009). *Designing effective assessment: Principles and profiles of good practice*. San Francisco, CA: Jossey-Bass.

Banta, T. W., & Pike, G. R. (1989). Methods for comparing outcomes assessment instruments. *Research in Higher Education, 30*(5), 455–469.

Banta, T. W., & Schneider, J. A. (1988). Using faculty-developed comprehensive exams to evaluate academic programs. *Journal of Higher Education, 59*, 69–83.

Barrett, H. (2009, October 16). Limitations of portfolios [Web log post]. Retrieved from http://electronicportfolios.org/blog/2009/10/limitations-of-portfolios.html

Bresciani, M. J. (2006). *Outcomes-based academic and co-curricular program review*. Sterling, VA: Stylus.

Educational Testing Service. Retrieved March 9, 2010 from http://www.ets.org/portal/site/ets/menuitem.1488512ecfd5b8849a77b13bc3921509/?vgnextoid=f119af5e44df4010VgnVCM10000022f95190RCRD&vgnextchannel=86f346f1674f4010VgnVCM10000022f95190RCRD

Ewell, P. T. (2009). *Assessment, accountability, and improvement: Revisiting the tension*. Occasional Paper #1. Champaign, IL: National Institute for Learning Outcomes Assessment.

Flateby, T. L., & Metzger, E. (1999). Writing assessment instrument for higher order thinking skills. *Assessment Update*, *11*(2), 6–7.

Flateby, T. L., & Metzger, E. (2001). Instructional implications of the Cognitive Level and Quality of Writing Assessment. *Assessment Update*, *13*(1), 4–5.

Griffin, M. (2009). Bridging the gap between college and high school writing in an online assessment community. *Dissertation Abstracts International*, 70–10A, (UMI No. 3381255).

Hamilton, S., & Kahn, S. (2009). Demonstrating intellectual growth and development: The IUPUI ePort. In D. Cambridge, B. Cambridge, & K. B. Yancey (Eds.), *Electronic portfolios 2.0: Emergent research on implementation and impact* (pp. 91–96). Sterling, VA: Stylus Publishing.

Kane, M. T. (2006). Validation. In R. L. Brennan (Ed.), *Educational measurement* (4th ed., pp. 17–64). Westport, CT: Praeger.

Kuh, G. & Ikenberry S. (2009). *More than you think, less than we need: Learning outcomes assessment in American higher education*. Champaign, IL: National Institute for Learning Outcomes Assessment.

Messick, S. (1989). Validity. In R. L. Linn (Ed.), *Educational measurement* (3rd ed., pp. 13–104). Phoenix, AZ: Oryx Press.

Millett, C. M., Payne, D. G., Dwyer, C. A., Stickler, L. M., & Alexion, J. J. (2008). *A culture of evidence: An evidence-centered approach to accountability for student learning outcomes*. Princeton, NJ: Educational Testing Service.

Mintzberg, H. (2000). The professional bureaucracy. In M. C. Brown (Ed.), *Organization and governance in higher education* (5th ed., pp. 50–70). Boston, MA: Pearson.

Palomba, C. A., & Banta, T. W. (1999). *Assessment essentials: Planning, implementing, and improving assessment in higher education*. San Francisco, CA: Jossey-Bass.

Perkins, D. N. (1987). Thinking frames: An integrative perspective on teaching cognitive skills. In J. B. Baron & R. J. Sternberg (Eds.), *Teaching thinking skills: Theory & practice*. New York, NY: Freeman.

Pike, G. R. (1992). 'Lies, Damn Lies, and Statistics' revisited: A comparison of three methods of representing change. *Research in Higher Education*, *33*, 71–84.

Pike, G. R. (1993). The "magic" of mean gain. *Research in Higher Education*, *34*, 131–134.

Pike, G. R. (2006). Value-added models and the Collegiate Learning Assessment. *Assessment Update*, *18*(4), 5–7.

Schneider, C. G. & Shulman, L. S. (2007). Foreword. In R. J. Shavelson (Ed.), *A brief history of student learning assessment: How we got where we are and a proposal for where to go next*. Washington, DC: Association of American Colleges and Universities.

Secolsky, C., & Wentland, E. (2010). Differential effect of topic: Implications for portfolio assessment. *Assessment Update*, *22(1)*, 1–2, 15.

Steele, J. M. (1993). Truths and answers. *Research in Higher Education*, *34*, 127–130.

Sundre, D. L. (2009). Guest editor's note. *Journal of General Education*, *58*(3), vii–ix.

Suskie, L. (2004). *Assessing student learning: A common sense guide*. Bolton, MA: Anker.

Suskie, L. (2009). *Assessing student learning: A common sense guide* (2nd ed.). San Francisco, CA: Jossey-Bass.

Voluntary System of Accountability. Retrieved March 9, 2010 from http://www.voluntarysystem.org/index.cfm

Walvoord, B. E. (2004). *Assessment clear and simple*. San Francisco, CA: Jossey-Bass.

Walvoord, B. E., Bardes, B., & Denton, J. (1998). Value-added models and the collegiate learning assessment. *Assessment Update*, *10*(5), 1–2, 10–11.

Wise, S. (2009). Strategies for managing the problem of unmotivated examinees in low-stakes testing programs. *Journal of General Education*, *58*(3), 152–166.

5

THE PERENNIAL CHALLENGES OF ACCOUNTABILITY

James C. Palmer

Accountability—the process of publicly documenting institutional practices and effects—is one of three ways that higher education institutions relate to and sustain the support of the larger society. Offering evidence of institutional fidelity to societal expectations of what the academy should achieve complements and, in turn, reinforces the two other pillars of societal support: public trust in colleges and universities, and the academy's success in the marketplace (Trow, 1996). Situating accountability within this three-part framework properly focuses attention on accountability as a sociological process as well as a technical one. The key work of accountability deals with the question of how the institution presents itself to the larger community, not simply what data will be collected and how.

Nonetheless, the nature and quality of data offered to public stakeholders in the name of accountability play a large role in the academy's accountability efforts. This can be seen in the burgeoning accountability infrastructure, which incorporates regional and specialized accreditation, college rankings, licensure requirements for graduates in specific career programs, institutional and state protocols for program approval and review, follow-up studies of graduates, student outcomes assessment programs, and the development and publication of performance indicators (Bogue & Hall, 2003). Each provides a path for documenting the academy's effects, and each is the subject of an extensive literature.

But the literature also provides insights into what has been learned about the perennial challenges faced by the academy as it attempts to meaningfully document instructional impacts and communicate the results with external stakeholders. One challenge lies in the enduring difficulties of generating and communicating information that clearly teaches the public about the outcomes of the academy's core work—student learning. Despite the decades-long student outcomes movement, our capacity to generate this information lags far behind our capacity to inform society of the magnitude of the higher education enterprise (in terms of enrollments, credit hours generated, instructional expenditures, etc.). A second challenge lies in the potential misunderstanding and misuse of the data that we *do* generate. This potential is driven by a tendency to extend unwarranted meaning to outcomes data and by the tendency of organizations to confuse accountability with institutional advocacy; both muddy the waters and ultimately weaken the bonds that tie the academy to the larger society.

Information on Learning

Because colleges and universities are organizations designed to "cause learning" (Cohen, 1969, p. x), it is logical to place student learning at the heart of accountability efforts. This logic has become more compelling since the 1970s as government policymakers across the globe have tied the viability of their national economies to human capital development and attempted to balance growing national ambitions for educational attainment against government budgets constrained by recurrent recessions and competing demands for health care and other services. The sharpened concern for efficiencies in the production of human capital has increased demand for measures of that production, which are now expected to take their place alongside data on the magnitude of higher education (e.g., enrollments, revenues, and expenditures) as evidence of responsiveness to individual consumers and the larger society. In the United States, this was reflected in the report of the Secretary of Education's Commission on the Future of Higher Education (2006), which lamented the tendency to measure institutional quality on the basis of "financial inputs and resources" and called instead for clear and understandable measures of learning:

> Despite increased attention to student learning results by colleges and universities and accreditation agencies, parents and students have no solid evidence, comparable across institutions, of how much students learn in colleges or whether they learn more at one college than another. Similarly, policymakers need more comprehensive data to help them decide whether the national investment in higher education is paying off and how taxpayer dollars could be used more effectively. *(p. 14)*

Left unspoken in the Commission's report was the historical significance of its call for information on learning outcomes. The relatively scant data available on what students know and are able to do as a consequence of college attendance reflect the historical coalescence of American higher education around organizational structures rather than a shared sense of desired outcomes. The collegiate bureaucracy we are familiar with today (e.g., academic departments, faculty ranks, trustee oversight, credit hour requirements, etc.) emerged in the late 19th century as the essential signposts or symbols of academic legitimacy—the structural template that defined "college" in the eyes of the larger society (Veysey, 1965). Consequently, accountability has historically rested on form, not function. Over time, order came "to the system of higher education, not to the curriculum, but to the display of quantifiable data regarding students, faculty, physical plant, and funding" (Cohen & Kisker, p. 161). Contemporary calls for learning outcomes data thus run counter to deeply rooted norms in the modern American academy.

Also left unexamined in the Commission's report are the difficulties of moving from an applied perspective of accountability—pronouncements of what colleges should do to remain accountable—to an actionable perspective that offers insight into how and under what circumstances desired accountability efforts (in this case, the generation of learning outcomes data) might be successfully carried out.[1] Limited resources alone pose a considerable problem, because contemporary demands for data on learning have been imposed on top of continuing demands for data tied to the historical focus on structure. Indeed, society rarely substitutes one set of accountability expectations for another; instead, higher education has been "faced with different layers of expectations that gradually have been piled upon one another in keeping with . . . historical transformations" (Bleiklie, 1998, p. 310).

Political questions also need to be addressed. For example, at the state or national levels, how might a balance be struck between the generation of learning outcomes measures tied to the missions of individual institutions and cross-institutional outcomes measures that address broader public goals, such as increased science and technology skills in the general population (Wellman, 2006)? Finally, methodological challenges abound. If institutions are to calculate and report indicators of student learning as a consequence of institutional effort, how are they to negotiate "the series of inferences that need to be made to relate the student knowledge, skills, and abilities to institutional effectiveness" as opposed to the many other influences on student development (Borden & Young, 2008, p. 27)? In addition, what efforts might be undertaken to avoid an "ecological fallacy" that might emerge if measures of student learning aggregated at the institutional level inappropriately obscure "differences in effects across students or subgroups of students within the institution" (Borden & Young, 2008, p. 30)?

Despite a decades-long record of published academic scholarship on the assessment of college impacts on students (Feldman & Newcomb, 1969, 1970; Pascarella & Terenzini, 1991, 2005), institutional and policy research undertaken in the name of accountability is still in its nascent stages. The institutional and state-system efforts undertaken to systematically document those impacts in ways that will inform consumers and policymakers are tentative steps on a long road of experimentation. These efforts include the calculation and recurrent publication of indicators of student progress through the educational system, the systematic assessment of student experiences as proxies for student learning, and the development of more direct measures of student learning through testing protocols and the use of rubrics in the appraisal of student work.

Indicators of Student Progress

An indicator is a number that is calculated routinely according to a consistent definition. Indicators of the magnitude of the higher education enterprise have long been published. Examples include the Fall enrollment figures reported annually by the Integrated Postsecondary Education Data System (IPEDS) according to the specification that "students reported are those enrolled in courses creditable toward a degree or other formal award" (National Center for Education Statistics, n.d., Fall Enrollment section, para. 1). Published on a routine basis, this indicator allows us to determine if enrollment is rising or falling over time. Furthermore, the specification that the reported enrollment figure include only students in credit courses offers at least some assurance of consistency over time and across institutions—a key feature that boosts credibility and thus accountability. Other indicators of magnitude reported by IPEDS include the number of degrees awarded annually and the current fund revenues of degree-granting institutions; each is based on definitions specified by IPEDS.

The addition of indicators of student progress through the educational system, although leaving open the question of institutional impact, has offered at least some evidence of the extent to which students reach outcomes that the public associates with colleges and universities. An example can be seen in the transfer-rate data reported across states by the Center for the Study of Community Colleges in the 1980s and 1990s as a way of gauging ups and downs over time in the movement of students from community colleges to four-year colleges and universities. The transfer rate definition proposed by the Center was a response to the confused picture of transfer that emerged from disparate studies employing differing numbers in the numerator and denominator of the transfer-rate equation. In order to develop a consistent picture across states and over time, the Center rested its work on relatively simple parameters, looking at

> all students entering the community college in a given year who have no prior college experience, and who complete at least twelve credit units within four years of entry, divided into the number of that group who take one or more classes at an in-state, public university within four years [of initial entry into the community college]. *(Cohen & Brawer, 2008, p. 64)*

This definition is surely not the only one that could be employed. Others could be more "liberal" or "restrictive," looking, for example, at the transfer of community college students who earn any credits at all at the two-year institution, or, alternatively, at the transfer of only those who enrolled with the intention of preparing for transfer (Romano & Wisniewski, 2003, p. 6). One could also calculate retrospective indicators of transfer, examining, for example, the percentage of university graduates each year who had started their postsecondary careers at a community college and applied a minimum number of community college credits toward their bachelor's degrees (Romano & Wisniewski, 2003; Palmer & Pugh, 1993). Whatever the definition employed, the calculation of these types of indicators shifts our thinking from the magnitude of the higher education enterprise at any one point in time to student progress—a significant step toward the ultimate goal of providing evidence of student learning.

Recent compilations of outcomes indicators by some states have offered more comprehensive looks at student progress within and across state systems of education. Accountability efforts undertaken by the California Community Colleges are an example. In addition to statewide transfer-rate calculations and retrospective examinations of the proportion of university graduates who attended a community college along the way to the bachelor's degree, California's annual compilation of community college indicators includes those that offer institutional measures of persistence in terms of (a) fall-to-fall retention, (b) course completion as measured by the proportion of students who earn passing grades in credit vocational or basic-skills courses, (c) student basic skills improvement (i.e., successful completion of a "higher-level course in the same discipline within three years of completing the first basic-skills course" [p. 764]), and (d) overall progress and achievement as measured by the proportion of first-time students who earn a certificate or associate's degree, transfer to a four-year institution, achieve "transfer directed" status by successfully completing transfer-level courses in both mathematics and English, or achieve "transfer prepared" status by successfully completing 60 hours of coursework that is transferable to the California State University System or the University of California (California Community Colleges Chancellor's Office, 2010).

In some cases, the move to outcomes indicators may be tied to performance funding mechanisms that provide colleges and universities with fiscal incentives for increasing the number of students who are retained and eventually graduate. For example, the performance funding protocol for the Washington state community and technical colleges is based on points awarded to the colleges for the number of students who, over time, achieve significant milestones that are indicative of sustained "momentum" through the educational system (Leinbach & Jenkins, 2008; Washington State Board for Community and Technical Colleges, 2006). These points relate to pre- and post-test gains in tests of basic skills, earning a GED or high school diploma, passing "a remedial math or English course with a qualifying grade to advance toward college-level work," earning the first 15 and the first 30 college-level credits, "earning the first 5 college-level math credits," and earning a credential (a certificate or associate's degree) or completing an apprenticeship (Washington State Board for Community and Technical Colleges, n.d., p. 1). A similar performance funding system based on "success points" has been developed for the Ohio community and technical colleges. Metrics in the Ohio system are based on key indicators of student progress that include but are not limited to: completing developmental courses and moving on to college-level courses, earning the first 15 and 30 semester hours of coursework, and enrolling in a university after completing at least 15 hours of coursework at the two-year institution (Ohio Board of Regents, 2010).

Indicators of student progress through the curriculum, often used in comparisons with benchmark institutions, constitute only a small fraction of the data that are publicly available on the nation's higher education system, and at best they offer only proxy measures of student learning. In addition, their value to date has been compromised by the limited visibility they have outside of institutional research offices and education policy circles. Burke and Minassians (2004) have called this "a fatal problem of performance reporting" because "closing the accountability gap requires pushing reporting on some common indicators down to academic departments" where, after all, the college's work with students unfolds (p. 62). Still, the calculation of indicators of student progress constitutes a potentially significant change in how the academy represents itself and makes its case for continued public subsidy, highlighting institutional obligations to students. Much will depend on the extent to which efforts such as those in Washington and Ohio take hold and overcome the academy's historical resistance to funding based on student outcomes as opposed to enrollment.[2]

Assessment of Student Experience

Another set of proxy measures attempts to gauge the extent to which students exhibit behaviors that contribute to retention and degree achievement as well as the extent to which student perceptions of their colleges align with research-based understandings of what constitutes a supportive and engaging learning environment. Colleges participating in the National Survey of Student Engagement (NSSE), as well as the Community College Survey of Student Engagement (CCSSE), routinely analyze student responses to questionnaire items that reflect selected collegiate experiences. Both the NSSE and CCSSE surveys gauge student perceptions of the extent to which these experiences are academically challenging, involve active and collaborative learning, entail ongoing student-faculty interactions, and reflect an institutional commitment to student support and success. The CCSSE questionnaires also elicit student perceptions of the effort they put into their course-work, and the NSSE (which is designed for students at four-year institutions) adds questionnaire items about enriching experiences (CCSSE, 2011; NSSE, n.d.). The result is a set of survey indicators that, in addition to offering diagnostic insights that can help college educators create engaging learning environments, may also add to the information base used by colleges to communicate with external stakeholders, shifting "the conversation about college quality from topics centered on institutional resources and reputation toward dialogue about how often students are engaging in activities that relate to desired learning and personal development outcomes" (NSSE, 2011, para. 2).

There is much to be said for the NSSE and CCSSE data as indirect indicators of student learning. The psychometric properties of the questionnaires have been extensively examined, and the constructs they measure are grounded in research that has documented the correlation between student engagement in their collegiate experience and student achievement (Kuh, 2009; McClenney, 2007). In addition, by querying students about their own behaviors (among other items), the NSSE and CCSSE surveys avoid the oversimplified picture of college outcomes as the product of institutional efforts only. Indeed, the intellectual origins of these surveys can be traced back, at least partially, to the work of C. Robert Pace, a psychologist whose studies of college environments and student experiences underscored the important role played by the student's "quality of effort," which he defined as "voluntary behavior" that "reflects initiative" and that "describes the strength and scope of personal investment that students are making for their own higher education" (Pace, 1998, p. 31). The acknowledgement of the students' agency in the NSSE and CSSE surveys does not let the institution off the hook, trading one facile explanation for disappointing outcomes ("it's the college's fault") for another ("it's the student's fault"). But it does recognize learning as the product of social interaction between students and educators acting within specific organizational environments. As Kuh, Kinzie, Buckley, Bridges, and Hayek (2007) explain, "the college experience . . . includes two dimensions: student behaviors and institutional conditions" (p. 11); the latter certainly has at least a partial effect on the former.

In addition, the NSSE and CCSSE projects have endorsed the publication of survey results and carefully considered how and under what circumstances their data should be made public. Although they have taken different approaches to the publication of institution-level data (NSSE leaves this up to individual institutions; CCSSE publishes summary findings for each participating institution), both have proactively worked with the media to ensure that the survey data are appropriately represented in third-party venues. As a result, several institutions have voluntarily reported mean scores on CCSSE and NSSE benchmark constructs on a website maintained by *USA Today*, which adheres to the stipulation—established by both survey programs—that the data not be used to rank order institutions (CCSSE, 2008; *Engaging minds*, 2011; NSSE, 2011; *Searching for signs*, 2009). In the case of NSSE data, institutional averages for each of five benchmarks are "displayed [on the *USA Today* website] alongside national averages for their institutional type represented by Carnegie Classification" (NSSE, 2011, Frequently Asked Questions section, para. 3). In the case of the CCSSE, institutional averages on key benchmarks are reported alongside national averages for community colleges of a comparable size (as determined by enrollment). These data published by *USA Today* offer only a limited picture of student engagement, including only volunteer institutions and masking key variations across programs and students within colleges, as well as variations in student responses to the multiple survey items that make up the benchmarks themselves (McCormick, 2010). But it is clear that in attending to the technical tasks of creating and administering survey instruments that yield important indicators of student engagement, the NSSE and CSSE projects have not avoided the inevitable challenges of "transparency, institutional self-presentation, and the public interest" (McCormick, 2010, p. 35).

Direct Measures of Student Learning

Despite the inherent value of sound data on student engagement, calls for information on student learning have not abated. This can be seen in the Lumina Foundation's (January 2011) release of a draft *Degree Qualifications Profile* suggesting in broad terms what students should know and be able to do as they move progressively from the associate's degree, to the bachelor's degree, and the master's degree. The *Framework* takes the form of a matrix that delineates desired learning outcomes at each degree level for five overlapping areas: broad, integrative knowledge; specialized knowledge; intellectual skills; applied learning; and civic learning. Offered as a "'beta version' that will be further tested and refined by a variety of stakeholders," the Lumina *Framework* addresses a paradox inherent in the fact that "the press toward helping many more students earn degrees has not been grounded in any consistent public understanding of what these degrees ought to mean" (Lumina Foundation, p. 1). The focus on transparency and enhanced communication with the public is clear. As the Lumina Foundation notes, "Even as colleges and universities have defined their own expected student learning outcomes—typically to meet accreditation requirements—their discussions have been largely invisible to policy leaders, the public and many students" (p. 1).

This call for a common understanding of what postsecondary degrees signify in terms of student knowledge and abilities underscores the need for meaningful assessments of student learning at the program or institutional level—not just at the course level, where learning assessment has historically been centered (Pace, 1998, p. 24). One approach is the use of standardized tests to assess student learning gains over time, either longitudinally (e.g., administering the test to students in the freshman year and again to the same students in the senior year) or from a cross-sectional perspective (e.g., administering the test at the same time to a sample of freshman and a sample of seniors). Prominent examples include the three standardized tests employed by four-year colleges and universities participating in the Voluntary System of Accountability: The Collegiate Assessment of Academic Proficiency, published by ACT; the Collegiate Learning Assessment, published by the Council for Aid to Education; and the ETS Proficiency Profile, published by the Educational Testing Service. Drawing on outcomes from these assessments, a key goal of the VSA is to include data on "student learning gains in critical thinking . . . and written communication" in "college portraits" that offer consumer information for each participating institution (*Voluntary System of Accountability*, 2008, p. 2). Testing has also been employed at the national level. For example, Arum and Roksa (2011) examined the performance of a national sample of four-year college students on the Collegiate Learning Assessment, which was administered to the students in their freshman and sophomore years. The study's disappointing results, suggesting that 45% of the students experienced "no statistically significant gains in critical thinking, complex reasoning, and writing skills" (p. 45), prompted an intensive public debate about higher education's impact (or lack of impact) on student learning (see, for example, editorials by Herbert, 2011, and by Neal, 2011).

Another approach entails the direct appraisal of student work itself (e.g., papers, performances, and other artifacts that are compiled in portfolios) against criteria detailed in assessment rubrics that specify what students should know and be able to do. Although rubrics are often used by faculty members to grade student assignments in individual courses, they can also be applied to the assessment of learning that cuts across classes and programs. This is a key objective of the Valid Assessment of Learning in Undergraduate Education (VALUE) project of the Association of American Colleges and Universities (AAC&U), which has produced a set of "meta-rubrics" that synthesize assessment criteria used by faculty members nationwide to appraise student mastery of 15 "essential learning outcomes" (Rhodes, 2010, p. 17). These outcomes, which the VALUE project views as "broadly shared expectations for learning among faculty regardless of where they teach" (Rhodes, 2010, p.18), encompass "not only basic intellectual and practical abilities (such as written, oral, and graphical communication; critical thinking; problem solving; quantitative literacy; and so on) but also individual and personal responsibility outcomes . . ." (Rhodes, 2010, p. 14). The intent of the metarubrics is, among other goals, to help colleges tie institution-level outcomes assessment more closely to coursework, building a body of evidence about learning from what students do in classes as they progress from year to year. The result, potentially, is a picture of learning outcomes that offers the public a richer framework for judgment than a display of test scores or the grades on a transcript (Rhodes, 2008, 2010). As Rhodes (2008) notes:

> Communicating the results of e-portfolio learning to audiences outside the academy remains a challenge, but the criteria as presented in rubrics can be used to indicate or explain the quality of performance (for example, "95 percent of the students were able to demonstrate satisfactorily the ability to solve complex problems"), and the actual examples of student work can be packaged as both evidence and anecdote for those who need shorter documents to review or on which to base a decision, conclusion, and so on about the nature of student learning that has occurred. *(p. 61)*

But if rubrics are to be used to communicate desired outcomes and student growth as evidenced in their own work, why not replace (or at least augment) conventional transcripts with student records that describe and attest to student competencies, accounting for what they know and are able to do rather than relying on the proxies of grades and credit hours? This more encompassing approach to the documentation of learning, reminiscent of efforts in the 1960s to augment grades with written assessments at the University of California Santa Cruz (Academic Senate Committee on Educational Policy, 1970) or to document the learning of community college students with behavioral objectives (Cohen, 1969), has once again emerged in conversations about accountability. Shupe's (2011a, 2011b) work is a key example. Invoking the idea of "learning as academic currency" advanced by Johnstone, Ewell, and Paulson (2002, p. 1), Shupe argues that modern computer technology now enables colleges and universities to create student records that note evidence of the attainment of competencies set by faculty members in their courses. He points out that the compilation of these student records—alongside conventional transcripts—will help shift student attention from grades to learning, simplify student outcomes assessment by virtue of the fact that evidence for learning will pervade student record systems, and build on faculty efforts to define what students should know and be able to do (Shupe, 2011a, 2011b). The prospect of transcripts keyed to learning is the logical if ambitious apotheosis of the accountability movement in education.

The Use and Misuse of Data

The realization of our ambitious goals for public representations of institutional effects on student learning will undoubtedly require, in addition to continued attention to the technical matters involving the collection and display of data, a shift in collegiate organizational culture and the ways that culture views the purpose and use of accountability data. Ward (2008) put it bluntly: Success will only be achieved when "colleges and universities, particularly their faculties, develop a greater interest in assessment" (p. 17). An essential part of this shift will necessarily require an enhanced awareness of two deeply rooted practices in higher education that impede clear communication with external publics: the enduring tendency to associate learning outcomes assessment solely with student assessment (as opposed to assessment of the institution) and the equally enduring tendency to conflate the publication of data with institutional advocacy. The former may lead to untoward expectations of what the data tell us or forestall institution-level learning assessments altogether. The latter may displace the goal of enhancing transparency with the goal of enhancing institutional image.

Student Assessment Versus Institutional Assessment

A lingering flaw in the discourse about student outcomes is the adherence to models of assessment that are appropriate for gauging the work of individual students within specific courses but that may be inappropriate for the assessment of student outcomes at the institutional level. Pace (1998) made the important point that evaluation paradigms "appropriate for the study of large and complex institutions" with "multiple and conflicting objectives and programs" must be more open ended than the assessment paradigms used by classroom teachers to determine if students have met specific course goals (p. 24). He noted that the "central question" at the institutional level lies with overall "consequences" of attendance rather than student performance on narrow objectives, that the "style of inquiry is more aptly characterized by the word 'exploration' than by the words 'control and focus,'" that the evaluator takes on the role of a "social scientist rather than . . . a teacher . . .," and that the ultimate "purpose is to provide more complex bases for informed judgment" (p. 24). Thus, the farther one moves from the classroom focus to the institutional focus, the less one is able to make summative judgments. By itself, the finding that x% of students met a certain institutional learning objective or felt engaged with their studies says little. In the end, the strength of college-level test scores, survey results, or indicators of student progress lies in their capacity to inform discussions about what is happening at the institution and what might need to be changed.

A necessary follow-up to data collection, then, is the establishment of forums within and outside of the institution that can consider college-level outcomes measures and assess their meaning. Trow (1996), for example, has argued that accreditation—a key part of the accountability effort—should entail "searching audits of each institution's own scheme for critical self-examination, its own internal quality control procedures" (p. 8). He maintained that "the creation and operation of serious, tough internal reviews of quality can be monitored through external audits" that focus on "the procedures in place for self-study and self-criticism, and . . . the effects those internal review [sic] have on practice" (pp. 13–14). McCormick (2010) echoed this theme in his discussion of the publication of NSSE and CCSSE data, arguing that less attention should be paid to comparisons or rank ordering of colleges on the basis of "institution-level summary measures" and more attention should be paid to "what institutions actually do with assessment results . . ." (p. 36). In the end, outcomes are more appropriately viewed as a starting point for inquiry rather than as the end of inquiry. As Ewell emphasized in 1983, information on student outcomes "is ordinarily much more useful for the questions it raises than for the answers it provides" (p. 62).

Still, the pursuit of this institutional inquiry runs up against the engrained assumption that data on student learning have utility only to the extent that they inform summative judgments about individual student performance. Reflecting on their work with a group of urban community colleges that tested samples of students as a way of assessing student knowledge in liberal arts disciplines, Cohen and Brawer (1987) noted that the value of test scores that are not tied to any one student did "not square with the educator's self-appointed mission of sorting people for the benefit of employers, the senior institutions, and the professions for which they are preparing them" (pp. 124–125). As a result, the testing protocols used by the colleges never took hold as permanent features of curriculum assessment or accountability. Several years later, Bers (2007) commented on this failed case of cohort testing, pointing out that "even today . . . many faculty [members] struggle to understand that assessment can improve courses and programs" as opposed to certifying the learning of individual students (p. 175). The same may also hold for the external stakeholders (policymakers, employers, etc.) who themselves associate learning assessment with the grading and sorting they experienced as students. It remains to be seen if current testing efforts, such as those advocated by the Voluntary System of Accountability, can overcome these deeply entrenched views.[3]

Accountability Displaced by Institutional Advocacy

A second potential challenge lies in the fear that data on learning, once made public, may damage an institution's image or, at a minimum, cede control of the institution's image to others (including the media) who report the data (McCormick, 2010). Although it is difficult to gauge the extent to which this fear has actually impeded efforts to collect and report indicators of student learning, the potentially counterproductive pull of institutional advocacy is a prevailing theme in the accountability literature. Its impact can sometimes be seen in the reluctance of institutions to publicize data. For example, McCormick (2010) notes that the contrasting approaches of the CCSSE and NSSE to the publication of data—the former publishes results for all participating colleges while the latter leaves this up to the colleges themselves—might reflect the fact that "community colleges do not compete in regional or national markets for students in the same way that four-year institutions do" (p. 41); the negative consequences of publication appear to be lower for the community colleges participating in the CCSSE than they are for the four-year colleges and universities participating in the NSSE. But a more damaging consequence might entail the displacement of the goals accountability efforts are intended to advance (i.e., transparency and institutional self-improvement) with the goal of "making the grade." Examples can be seen in those instances in which colleges have increased "graduation and retention rates" by "reducing course requirements or by presenting faculty with directives that they submit detailed reports on each student who has dropped their courses" (Cohen and Brawer, 2008, p. 396).

These untoward consequences of the strong pull of advocacy can be met with equally strong ethical responses. The reluctance to make data public, though understandable in light of the possible misuse by others (McCormick, 2010), is overshadowed by the obligation of institutions that receive public funds—either directly through appropriations or indirectly through financial aid—to report the results of their institutional research efforts, especially when those efforts are tied to teaching and learning, the core work of the college. The tendency to lower standards or otherwise disregard educational obligations, to the extent that this happens, is even more untenable, representing an abandonment of professional ethics and underscoring the fact that accountability to external publics requires ethical leadership as well as technical expertise. College leaders cannot totally control how the media and policymakers will interpret data, but they can report them accurately, provide the contextual information needed to put data into a meaningful perspective, and communicate with varying audiences in ways that build what Leveille (2006, p. 36) call the "reciprocal" relationship "between the public and higher education" that is at the heart of accountability, enhancing both trust and competitiveness in the marketplace.

Attention to such ethical leadership and the reciprocity it engenders will become particularly important should outcomes data eventually drive revenues in state funding formulas or otherwise become key factors in high-stakes decisions about the future of a college and its leadership. Trow (1996, p. 56) offered a cautionary tale from Great Britain, where "severe but frequently changing request for reports and information" from government authorities led to assiduously scripted responses that were "parsimonious with the truth, especially of awkward truths that reveal problems or shortcomings in the reporting institution," and that therefore defeated the purposes of accountability. Another cautionary tales stems from the potentially corrupting influences of high-stakes testing in U.S. schools. Nichols and Berliner (2007) have argued that incidents of school educators manipulating student test responses reflect the dictum that has been referred to as "Campbell's law": "The more any quantitative social indicator is used for social decision making, the more subject it will be to corruption pressures and the more apt it will be to distort and corrupt the social processes it is intended to monitor" (Campbell, 1975, p. 35). Higher education accountability protocols in the United States have not yet ventured into this high-stakes arena, but the warnings offered by Trow and by Nichols and Berliner are instructive nonetheless. Indeed, Cohen and Brawer (2008, p. 396) also cited Campbell's warning in their discussion of how community colleges might be tempted to "game the system" when reporting outcomes data. "The accelerated drive for accountability," they concluded, "has yielded some strange fruit" (p. 396).

Moving Forward

Carefully undertaken as a genuine form of inquiry that supports institutional improvement efforts, the collection and publication of information on student learning can only be to the good. After all, if colleges and universities aren't accountable for learning, what else might they reasonably be held accountable for? Indirect or direct measures of what students know and are able to do as they progress through the curriculum can focus the attention of educators and external publics alike on higher education's core work, mitigating against the goal displacement that otherwise pushes other agendas (e.g., institutional image-building or advocacy) to the fore. The numerous efforts afoot to report indicators of student achievement over time, measures of student engagement with their work, and more direct appraisals of student learning in the form of test scores or assessments against criteria in meaningful rubrics offer promising insights into how data for accountability might be generated.

Future work in this arena will benefit from four scholarly perspectives that have received relatively little attention in the accountability literature. One is the historical perspective that can be gained through the study of previous attempts over the decades to assess student outcomes generally (as opposed to student learning in individual classes). For example, Pace (1979) detailed outcomes assessment efforts in higher education from the 1920s through the 1970s, drawing conclusions about what those experiences might teach us about effective approaches to testing student cohorts. Yet the contemporary accountability literature rarely draws on these insights, which, at the very least, might lead to meaningful discussions about why institution-level assessment of student learning—despite its long history—has yet to take hold in the academy. The historical perspective guards against the tendency to view contemporary developments as new developments, and it adds a useful dose of humility to a literature that, in the absence of an historical perspective, might overstate the promise and durability of new testing and assessment protocols.

A second perspective lies in sociological inquiry underscoring the imperfect relationship between espoused goals and the factors that boost prestige. As Lynn, Podolny, and Tao (2009) have pointed out, the desired "quality" of an actor (i.e., "any attribute, performance, or service considered desirable by the group") may be at odds with the ways prestige or status are socially constructed (p. 756); a scientist's prestige may be based on the prestige of his or her mentor rather than "scholarly merit," or job applicants may be judged "on non-merit-based criteria, such as race, gender, ties to employees, and parental status" (p. 757). The analogous imbalance between desired collegiate goals (i.e., learning or other forms of student development) and institutional prestige has long been acknowledged. Examples include Cohen (1969), who argued that the espoused goal of learning had been displaced at community colleges by prestige factors (such as the proportion of faculty members holding a doctorate), and Astin (1999), who argued that the goal of student development had been overshadowed at colleges and universities by the drive to increase resources and "move up as far as possible in the institutional pecking order" (p. 10). Further research examining the origins and enduring nature of this disconnect between quality and prestige in higher education will advance our understanding of how and under what circumstances the drive to base accountability on documented learning might eventually be realized.

A third perspective can be seen in the extensive scholarship on the use and impact of information. The aforementioned Campbell's law is an example, offering an insightful, if pessimistic, view of how the use of information in high-stakes decision making may influence the behavior of educators within colleges and universities.[4] Likewise, extant scholarship on how policymakers seek and use information to make decisions may help educators communicate their work more effectively with these important external stakeholders. Examples include the key works of Weiss and Bucuvalas (1980a, 1980b), who examined how policymakers employ social science research in decision making, and the more recent essay by Ness (2010), who examined the role of information and research in higher education policymaking specifically. The study of these and similar works can lead to realistic expectations of the messy and often indirect role of research on decisions that affect education policy. As Weiss (1982) has noted, research can be useful to policymakers, but in light of the tendency for "policy decisions to accrete through multiple disjointed steps," researchers should not expect that their work will have "direct and immediate policy effects" (p. 633). Much will depend on the capacity of educators to reach out meaningfully to policymakers, understanding their perspectives and the role information plays in their lives.

Finally, the need to reach out beyond institutional boundaries suggests the importance of research on the nature of social interaction between the education community and external stakeholders. The nascent scholarship on accountability as a function of these interactions can be seen in the work of Harbour, Davies, and Gonzales-Walker (2010), whose qualitative study of a single community college led them to the conclusion that the college's administrators "conceptualized institutional accountability as dialogic, involving ongoing communication with state authorities, employers, students, high schools, and universities about the formal and informal expectations assigned to the college" (p. 348). Another example stems from the research undertaken by Card and Tolman (2010), who interviewed policymakers in three states, noting that in addition to transparency and readily understandable data, they often valued collegial working relations and saw accountability as a process that emphasizes a partnership between the state and higher education rather than an adversarial relationship. Deil-Amen and Rosenbaum (2004) provide a third example in their examination of the different ways a sample of for-profit institutions and community colleges interacted with and responded to employers in local labor markets. The former genuinely involved employers in vocational program development and responded to their needs for qualified employees through placement services that carefully matched graduates with jobs for which they were demonstrably prepared. The latter rested their legitimacy in the job-training market on such standard academic signposts as accreditation and faculty credentials— elements of what Deil-Amen and Rosenbaum referred to as the "traditional college charter" (p. 247); employer involvement on advisory panels was perfunctory, and the colleges took a hands-off approach to the "students' transition to the labor market" (p. 258). Study of these and similar works on the social interactions that link colleges with their various stakeholders may help us understand how and under what circumstances data gathered in the name of accountability can become part of meaningful exchanges that help external constituencies understand higher education and vice versa.

Remaining accountable to the public is, of course, not simply a matter of reporting data; it encompasses "a covenant between the public and higher education" that requires ongoing attention driven by a sense of stewardship on the part of both the academy and policymakers (Leveille, 2006, p. 36). This covenant clearly extends also to students, employers, and other "consumers" in the postsecondary market. Ongoing efforts to further the transparent assessment of student learning will yield meaningful results to the extent that it is driven by the sense of give and take that this covenant implies. It will also benefit from the attempts of those studying and writing about accountability to draw on the historical and social scholarship that illuminates the nature of this reciprocity and the responsibilities it delegates to educators and the publics they serve.

Notes

1 Here I am drawing on Argyris (1993) who makes a fundamental distinction between "applicable" and "actionable" knowledge (pp. 5–6).
2 See Dougherty, Natow, Hare, & Vega (2010) for an analysis of the checkered history of performance funding.
3 Arum and Roksa (2011) noted an analogous argument made by some of their critics who questioned "the validity of general, broad-based assessments that do not focus on the specific knowledge taught in particular courses and majors" (p. 35). Clearly, the distinction between summative assessments of individuals, programs, or majors and formative assessments of institutions—or the higher education enterprise generally—has been difficult for many to grasp.
4 Campbell (1975) himself referred to his "law" as "pessimistic" (p. 35).

References

Academic Senate Committee on Educational Policy. (1970). *The grading system at UCSC—A critique.* Santa Cruz, CA: University of California, Santa Cruz. (ERIC Document Reproduction Service No. ED037174)

Argyris, C. (1993). *Knowledge for action: A guide to overcoming barriers to organizational change.* San Francisco, CA: Jossey-Bass.

Arum, R., & Roksa, J. (2011). *Academically adrift: Limited learning on college campuses.* Chicago, IL: University of Chicago Press.

Astin, A. W. (1999). Rethinking academic "excellence." *Liberal Education, 85*(2), 8–18.

Bers, T. H. (2007). Advancing research on the community college. *Community College Review, 34,* 170–183.

Bleiklie, I. (1998). Justifying the evaluative state: New public management ideals in higher education. *European Journal of Education, 33,* 299–316.

Bogue, E. G., & Hall, K. B. (2003). *Quality and accountability in higher education: Improving policy, enhancing performance.* Westport, CT: Praeger.

Borden, V. M. H., & Young, J. W. (2008). Measurement validity and accountability for student learning. In V. M. H. Borden, & G. R. Pike (Eds.), *Assessing and accounting for student learning: Beyond the Spellings Commission* (New Directions for Institutional Research, Assessment Supplement 2007, pp. 19–37). San Francisco, CA: Jossey-Bass.

Burke, J. C., & Minassians, H. P. (2004). Implications of state performance indicators for community college assessment. In A. M. Serban, & J. Friedlander (Eds.), *Developing and implementing assessment of student learning outcomes* (New Directions for Community Colleges, No. 126, pp. 53–64). San Francisco, CA: Jossey-Bass.

California Community Colleges Chancellor's Office. (2010). *Focus on results. Accountability reporting for the California community colleges.* Sacramento, CA: Author. Retrieved from http://www.cccco.edu/Portals/4/TRIS/research/ARCC/ARCC%202010,%20March%202010.pdf

Campbell, D. T. (1975). Assessing the impact of planned social change. In G. M. Lyons (Ed.), *Social research and public policies: The Dartmouth/OECD Conference* (pp. 3–45). Hanover, NH: Dartmouth College.

Card, K. A., & Tolman, J. K. (2010, May). *"Partners or adversaries": A comparative case study of higher-education systems and state-level accountability.* Paper presented at the annual convention of the American Educational Research Association, Denver, CO. (ERIC Document Reproduction Service No. ED509751)

Cohen, A. M. (1969). *Dateline '79: Heretical concepts for the community college.* Beverly Hills, CA: Glencoe Press.

Cohen, A. M., & Brawer, F. B. (1987). *The collegiate function of community colleges.* San Francisco, CA: Jossey-Bass.

Cohen, A. M., & Brawer, F. B. (2008). *The American community college* (5th ed.). San Francisco, CA: Jossey-Bass.

Cohen, A. M., with Kisker, C. B. (2010). *The shaping of American higher education* (2nd ed.). San Francisco, CA: Jossey-Bass.

Community College Survey of Student Engagement. (2008). *Memorandum of understanding for CCSSE-USA Today Initiative*. Retrieved from the Community College Survey of Student Engagement website, http://www.ccsse.org/USA_Today/Memorandum%20of%20Understanding%20For%20CCSSE-USA%20Today%20Initiative-3pages.pdf

Community College Survey of Student Engagement. (2011). *Survey results*. Retrieved from the Community College Survey of Student Engagement web site, http://www.ccsse.org/survey/survey.cfm

Deil-Amen, R., & Rosenbaum, J. E. (2004). Charter building and labor market contact in two-year colleges. *Sociology of Education, 77*, 245–265.

Dougherty, K. J., Natow, R. S., Hare, R. J., & Vega, B. E. (2010, December). *The political origins of higher education performance funding in six states* (CCR Brief No. 47). New York, NY: Community College Research Center, Teacher's College, Columbia University.

Engaging minds at community colleges (2011). Retrieved from the *USA Today* web site, http://www.usatoday.com/news/education/2008-11-16-CCSSE_N.htm

Ewell, P. T. (1983). *Information on student outcomes: How to get it and how to use it.* Boulder, CO: National Center for Higher Education Management systems. (ERIC Document Reproduction Service No. ED246827)

Feldman, K. A., & Newcomb, T. M. (1969). *The impact of college on students: Vol. 1. An analysis of four decades of research.* San Francisco, CA: Jossey-Bass.

Feldman, K. A., & Newcomb, T. M. (1970). *The impact of college on students: Vol. 2. Summary tables.* San Francisco, CA: Jossey-Bass.

Harbour, C. P., Davies, T. G., and Gonzales-Walker, R. (2010). The community college accountability network: Understanding institutional accountability at Aspen Grove Community College. *Community College Review, 37*, 348–370.

Herbert, B. (2011, March 4). College the easy way. *The New York Times.* Retrieved from http://www.nytimes.com/2011/03/05/opinion/05herbert.html

Johnstone, S. M., Ewell, P., & Paulson, K. (2002). *Student learning as academic currency.* Washington, DC: American Council on Education.

Kuh, G. D. (2009). The National Survey of Student Engagement: Conceptual and empirical foundations. In R. M. Gonyea, & G. D. Kuh (Eds.), *Using NSSE in institutional research* (New Directions for Institutional Research, No. 141, pp. 5–20). San Francisco, CA: Jossey-Bass.

Kuh, G. D., Kinzie, J., Buckley, J. A., Bridges, B. K., & Hayek, J. C. (2007). *Piecing together the student success puzzle: Research, propositions, and recommendations* (ASHE Higher Education Report, Vol. 32, No. 5). San Francisco, CA: Jossey-Bass.

Leinbach, T. D., & Jenkins, D. (2008, January). *Using longitudinal data to increase community college student success: A guide to measuring milestone and momentum point attainment* (CCRC Research Tools, No. 2, pp. 1–24). New York, NY: Community College Research Center, Teachers College, Columbia University. Retrieved from http://www.achievingthedream.org/publications/research/CCRC_Research_Tools_2.pdf

Leveille, D. E. (2006). *Accountability in higher education: A public agenda for trust and cultural change.* Berkeley, CA: Center for Studies in Higher Education, University of California, Berkeley. (ERIC Document Reproduction Service No. ED503070)

Lumina Foundation. (2011). *The degree qualifications profile.* Retrieved from the Lumina Foundation website, http://www.luminafoundation.org/publications/The_Degree_Qualifications_Profile.pdf

Lynn, F. B., Podolny, J. M., & Tao, L. (2009). A sociological (de)construction of the relationship between status and quality. *American Journal of Sociology, 115*, 755–804.

McClenney, K. M. (2007). Research update: The Community College Survey of Student Engagement. *Community College Review, 35*, 137–146.

McCormick, A. C. (2010). Here's looking at you: Transparency, institutional self-representation, and the public interest. *Change, 42* (6), 35–43.

National Center for Education Statistics. (n.d.). *Integrated postsecondary education data system glossary.* Retrieved from the National Center for Education Statistics website, http://nces.ed.gov/ipeds/glossary/?charindex=F

National Survey of Student Engagement. (n.d.). *Benchmarks of effective educational practice.* Retrieved from the National Survey of Student Engagement website, http://nsse.iub.edu/pdf/nsse_benchmarks.pdf

National Survey of Student Engagement. (2011). *NSSE and USA TODAY Initiative: Furthering dialogue on college quality.* (2011). Retrieved from the National Survey of Student Engagement website, http://nsse.iub.edu/html/USAT_initiative.cfm

Neal, A. D. (2011, January 19). Guest post: "Academically Adrift" indeed. *The Washington Post.* Retrieved from http://voices.washingtonpost.com/college-inc/2011/01/guest_post_academically_adrift.html

Ness, E. C. (2010). The role of information in the policy process: Implications for the examination of research utilization in higher education policy. In J. C. Smart (Ed.), *Higher education: Handbook of theory and research* (Vol. 25, pp. 1–50). New York, NY: Springer.

Nichols, S. L., & Berliner, D. C. (2007). *Collateral damage: How high-stakes testing corrupts America's Schools*. Cambridge, MA: Harvard University Press.

Ohio Board of Regents. (2010, July 29). *Student success initiative*. Retrieved from the Ohio Board of Regents website, http://regents.ohio.gov/hei/success_points.html

Pace, C. R. (1979). *Measuring outcomes of college: Fifty years of findings and recommendations for the future*. San Francisco, CA: Jossey-Bass.

Pace, C. R. (1998). Recollections and reflections. In J. C. Smart (Ed.), *Higher education: Handbook of theory and research* (Vol. 13, pp. 1–34). New York, NY: Agathon.

Palmer, J. C., & Pugh, M. (1993). The community college contribution to the education of baccalaureate graduates: A case study in Virginia. In J. S. Eaton (Ed.), *Probing the community college transfer function* (pp. 45–70). Washington, DC: American Council on Education.

Pascarella, E. T., & Terenzini, P. T. (1991). *How college affects students: Findings and insights from twenty years of research*. San Francisco, CA: Jossey-Bass.

Pascarella, E. T., & Terenzini, P. T. (2005). *How college affects students: Vol. 2. A third decade of research*. San Francisco, CA: Jossey-Bass.

Rhodes, T. L. (2008). VALUE: Valid assessment of learning in undergraduate education. In V. M. H. Borden, & G. R Pike (Eds.), *Assessing and accounting for student learning: Beyond the Spellings Commission* (New Directions for Institutional Research, Assessment Supplement 2007, pp. 59–70). San Francisco, CA: Jossey-Bass.

Rhodes, T. L. (2010). Since we seem to agree, why are the outcomes so difficult to achieve? In C. M. Wehlburg, & M. D. Svinicki (Eds.), *Integrated general education* (New Directions for Teaching and Learning, No. 121, pp. 13–21). San Francisco, CA: Jossey-Bass.

Romano, R. M., & Wisniewski, M. (2003, April). *Tracking community college transfers using National Student Clearinghouse data* (CHERI Working Paper #36). Ithaca, NY: Cornell Higher Education Research Institute, Cornell University. Retrieved from http://digitalcommons.ilr.cornell.edu/cheri/16/

Searching for signs of engagement. (2009). Retrieved from the *USA Today* web site, http://www.usatoday.com/news/education/nsse.htm

Secretary of Education's Commission on the Future of Higher Education (2006). *A test of leadership. Charting the future of U.S. higher education*. Washington, DC: U.S. Department of Education. Retrieved from http://www2.ed.gov/about/bdscomm/list/hiedfuture/reports/final-report.pdf

Shupe, D. (2011a, January). *Student outcomes as academic currency* [PowerPoint slides]. Presented at the 97th Annual Meeting of the Association of American Colleges and Universities, San Francisco, CA.

Shupe, D. (2011b). *The end of assessment: Outcomes as academic currency* [audio-video webcast]. Retrieved from the eLumen website, http://www.elumen.info/why-elumen/outcomes-as-currency.php

Trow, M. (1996, June). *Trust, markets and accountability in higher education: A comparative perspective* (CSHE.1.96). Berkeley, CA: Center for Studies in Higher Education, University of California, Berkeley. Retrieved from http://cshe.berkeley.edu/publications/docs/ROP.Trow.Trust.1.96.pdf

Veysey, L. R. (1965). *The emergence of the American university*. Chicago, IL: University of Chicago Press.

Voluntary System of Accountability. (2008). *Overview of college portrait*. Retrieved from The Voluntary System of Accountability Website, http://www.voluntarysystem.org/docs/cp/CollegePortraitOverview.pdf

Ward, D. (2008). *Higher education and the global knowledge economy: Affordability and accountability redefined* [David Dodds Henry Lecture]. Springfield, IL: University of Illinois at Springfield.

Washington State Board for Community and Technical Colleges. (n.d.). *Student achievement initiative momentum point calculation*. Retrieved from the Washington State Board for Community and Technical Colleges website, http://www.sbctc.ctc.edu/college/education/momentum_point_calculation_mar07.pdf

Washington State Board for Community and Technical Colleges. (2006). *Student achievement initiative*. Retrieved from the Washington State Board for Community and Technical Colleges website, http://www.sbctc.ctc.edu/college/e_studentachievement.aspx

Weis, C. H. (1982). Policy research in the context of diffuse decision making. *The Journal of Higher Education, 53*, 619–639.

Weis, C. H., & Bucuvalas, M. J. (1980a). *Social science research and decision-making*. New York, NY: Columbia University Press.

Weis, C. H., & Bucuvalas, M. J. (1980b). Truth tests and utility tests: Decision-makers' frames of reference for social science research. *American Sociological Review, 45*, 302–313.

Wellman, J. V. (2006). Accountability for the public trust. In N. B. Shulock (Ed.), *Practitioners on making accountability work for the public* (New Directions for Higher Education, No. 135, pp. 111–118). San Francisco, CA: Jossey-Bass.

6

USING NATIONAL, STATE, AND LOCAL DATA FOR ADMINISTRATIVE DECISION MAKING

Sathasivam 'Kris' Krishnan, Chengbo Yin, William Mahler,
Albertha H. Lawson, Michael Harris, and Karen Ruedinger

From its inception, higher education has operated according to tradition, intuition, and a complex set of rules and regulations. Data-informed decision making gives higher education leaders an increased ability to know what works and how to improve the areas of challenge for the benefit of their constituents. "We may intend that our decisions result in the best for our organization (to be effective), but we may not have enough information, we may not understand the information we have, or we may be influenced by ideological or even moral ideas that push us into decisions that are not the best for us or our organizations" (Hall, 2002, p. 152).

The availability of information does not necessarily lead to the obvious solution of a problem or even decreased levels of uncertainty. "In fact, the more important the strategic decisions, the higher the levels of uncertainty" (Hall, 2002, p. 153). However, having good information that is based on appropriately gathered data is preferable to making decisions based on intuition, persuasive arguments, or past practice. "[T]he amount and kind of information determine the certainty in the decision-making process. The implication is that the more certain that knowledge, the easier and better the decision making. Unfortunately, information does not flow automatically into or through an organization. Whatever is happening inside or outside an organization is subject to the perceptions and interpretations of the decision makers" (Hall, 2002, p. 155).

While this chapter strongly advocates the use of appropriate data and tries to indicate sources and uses of data, decisions can and should never be based solely on data. The whole process of deciding what data to gather, how to produce or obtain the data, and how to analyze and present the data are based on judgments that may have been made differently by other people. Decision makers inevitably must interpret the data on the basis of their own understandings and experiences. "Although information is a critical component of decision making, equally important are beliefs about cause and effect. In some areas of knowledge, certainty about cause and effect is quite well developed, whereas in others, the knowledge is probabilistic at best" (Hall, 2002, p. 156).

Even when the numbers have been verified and accepted as useful, they never tell the whole story. "Information consists of data that are useful in one or more contexts, that inform someone about something that reduce uncertainty in some way" (Brinkman & Krakower, 1983, p. 8). Decision makers need useful information that leads to greater understanding in particular circumstances, rather than simply more and more data. "The increased reliance on data for administrative purposes in colleges and universities has been motivated by both internal and external factors. Within institutions, recognition of the value of data about institutional performance has grown steadily" (Brinkman & Krakower, 1983, p. 9). However, the "external demand for data has more than kept pace, to the point where today the typical college or university administration feels overburdened with reporting tasks" (Brinkman & Krakower, 1983, p. 9).

Technology has also had an impact on the use of data for decision making. Only a few years ago, data were submitted on paper surveys distributed and returned via the postal service. The data then had to be entered into a computer or combined and analyzed by hand before static reports could then be sent through the postal service to interested decision makers. While such processes are still being used in limited circumstances, the internet now makes the gathering and sharing of data much easier. In addition, the data can be parsed, analyzed, and presented in the most useful ways with very minimal effort by anyone with the interest and skills to do so. "Another reason for the steadily expanding use of data in higher education is the significant advances made in the standardization of data collected by and from institutions. Standard definitions of data elements and widely accepted accounting procedures are necessities if comparisons are to be substantive and reliable" (Brinkman & Krakower, 1983, p. 10). Once again, technology has made such standardization more feasible.

The various calls for greater accountability, access, productivity, and contributions to society and its members by higher education (Middaugh, 2010) all require the increased use of appropriate, reliable data. "The most important (reasons for using data) are increased systemization and coordination of higher education, more emphasis on performance measures and accountability, greater interest in long-range and strategic planning, and the increasing awareness of a need for greater management control" (Brinkman & Krakower, 1983, p. 10). The whole purpose of higher education is learning and improvement. If individual institutions, higher education systems, and the entire enterprise are also going to learn and improve, they need to have and use the data that are the basis of appropriate information.

Without a doubt, the use of data in making administrative decisions has increased and should continue to do so. "There are good reasons, then, for using comparative data in higher education administration and management, even if it is not required. The rational allocation of resources and responsibilities, the establishment of a viable framework for accountability and management control, and the implementation of several aspects of strategic planning depend in part on comparative data" (Brinkman & Krakower, 1983, p. 15). The authors of this chapter strongly support this statement and are providing this chapter in the hope that it will help to increase the appropriate uses of national, state, and local data for improving the decisions made in higher education so that we can make the best use of our resources for the betterment of individuals and society.

This chapter has two major sections. The first part is a categorized list of various sources of data that have been found to be useful for administrative decision making. While most of these sources are reliable and updated at least annually, the provided list will undoubtedly be outdated by the time of publication. Fortunately, the Association for Institutional Research (AIR) now provides an online list of useful websites by selecting "IR Resources" in the left column of its home page (www.airweb. org). In addition, *Measuring Quality in Higher Education: An Inventory of Instruments, Tools and Resources* (applications.airweb.org/surveys/Default.aspx) "provides an inventory of resources designed to assist higher education faculty and staff in the challenging task of assessing academic and support programs as well as institutional effectiveness, more broadly. The items in this inventory are divided into four categories: instruments (examinations, surveys, questionnaires, etc.); software tools and platforms; benchmarking systems and data resources; projects, initiatives and services. They can be searched using keywords or through a set of filters that include the unit of analysis, the targeted level of assessment, and the subject of measurement."

The second section describes the types of decisions that can be improved by using data and the ways in which data can be used for administrative decisions. Although every decision is in some respects unique, models can be used to guide the process. The section then concludes with recommendations concerning the appropriate uses of data for administrative decisions in higher education.

Sources of Data Useful for Administrative Decision Making

National Data

Integrated Post-secondary Education Data System (IPEDS)

Because almost all institutions of higher education submit data annually and extensive efforts are used to verify the accuracy of the data, IPEDS is the most comprehensive and reliable source of comparative data available in the United States and its territories. IPEDS is "a system of interrelated surveys conducted annually by the U.S. Department's National Center for Education Statistics (NCES). IPEDS gathers information from every college, university, and technical and vocational institution that participates in the federal student financial aid programs. The Higher Education Act of 1965, as amended, requires that institutions that participate in federal student aid programs report data on enrollments, program completions, graduation rates, faculty and staff, finances, institutional prices, and student financial aid" (http://nces.ed.gov/ipeds/about/). Even though it does not gather all of the data needed for administrative decisions, it is the best place to start looking for useful information. "More than 6,700 institutions complete IPEDS surveys each year" (http://nces.ed.gov/ipeds/about/).

IPEDS data are available through several tools that range from College Navigator (nces.ed.gov/collegenavigator), a user-friendly website designed for prospective students to get basic information about individual institutions, to the Data Center (nces.ed.gov/ipeds/datacenter), where researchers can download multiple variables for almost any subset of institutions they choose, and the State Data Center (nces.ed.gov/ipeds/sdc/) that makes aggregated data at the state and national level easier to access. The chief executive officer of each participating institution receives an annual *Data Feedback Report* that contains key indicators of the institution's performance in relation to a group of comparison institutions. Online tutorials and live workshops on how to use these tools are offered by the Association for Institutional Research (www.airweb.org/IPEDS) with funding from NCES.

Data-sharing consortia

The *Higher Education Directory* lists more than 300 associations and consortia in higher education. Many of these organizations allow or require members to share data, typically on an annual basis. The data exchanges that are run by state governments are described later in this chapter in the section on *State Data*, while this section describes voluntary exchanges that may be based on region, religion, selectivity, special focus, private institutions in a state, or other characteristics. In many cases, participation is restricted to member institutions that meet certain criteria or have been invited to join the consortium. The examples shown in Table 6.1 are national in scope with varying degrees of restrictiveness for membership.

In addition, the institutional accrediting agencies gather data from their members and make at least some of that data available to the public. The U.S. Department of Education (www2.ed.gov/admins/finaid/accred/accreditation_pg6.html) recognizes 18 such accrediting agencies and provides descriptions and links to their websites.

Annual survey organizations

The growing number of annual surveys makes it impossible to list all of them in this chapter, but the *Measuring Quality in Higher Education: An Inventory of Instruments, Tools and Resources* (applications.

Table 6.1 Examples of National Data-Sharing Consortia

Consortium	URL	Description from Website
Association of American Universities Data Exchange	aaude.org	"[I]mprove[s] the quality and usability of information about higher education . . . [through] the exchange of data/information to support decision-making."
Association of Independent Technical Universities	www.theaitu.org	"[L]eading private American technological universities and colleges [that share] ideas and best practices to advance and inspire creativity, innovation and entrepreneurship within the membership."
Consortium on Financing Higher Education	web.mit.edu/cofhe	"[T]hirty-one highly selective, private liberal arts colleges and universities . . . [whose] data collection, research, and policy analysis focus on matters pertaining to access, affordability, accountability, and assessment."
Consortium for Student Retention Data Exchange	csrde.ou.edu	"[T]wo-year and four-year institutions dedicated to achieving the highest levels of student success through collaboratively sharing data, knowledge, and innovation."
Council of Independent Colleges	www.cic.edu	"[I]ndependent colleges and universities working together to support college and university leadership, advance institutional excellence, and enhance private higher education's contributions to society."
Higher Education Data Sharing Consortium	www.e-heds.org	"[P]rivate colleges and universities that assist in . . . assembling, analyzing, and sharing mutually agreed–upon and regularly updated historical information about member [and other] institutions."
National Community College Benchmark Project	www.nccbp.org	"[P]rovides community colleges with opportunities to report outcome and effectiveness data in critical performance areas, receive reports of benchmarks, and compare results with those of other colleges."
National Student Clearinghouse	www.studentclearinghouse.org	"[P]rovides . . . factual information on enrollment and graduation patterns nationwide, enabling (participants) to evaluate . . . educational policies and programs . . . and perform other educational research studies."

airweb.org/surveys/Default.aspx) is an excellent source of more detailed and current information. While some surveys do not charge the respondents, many charge for their services and then provide institution-specific data, along with appropriate comparisons, to participants. Institutional data are usually supplied by a relevant office (e.g., institutional research, human resources, financial aid), and surveys of individuals are typically coordinated by a particular office at each participating institution. With apologies for any omissions, Table 6.2 presents a list of organizations that conduct annual surveys of higher education institutions, their students, or their employees (see their websites for further information).

Table 6.2 Organizations Conducting Annual Surveys

Organization	URL
ACT's Evaluation Survey Services	www.act.org/ess
American Association of University Professors (AAUP)	www.aaup.org
American Society for Engineering Education (ASEE)	www.asee.org
Association of Physical Plant Administrators	www.appa.org
College Admissions Collaborative Highlighting Engineering & Technology (CACHET)	www.wpi.edu/News/Conf/CACHET
College and University Professional Association for Human Resources (CUPA-HR)	www.cupahr.org
College Board's Enrollment Planning Services (EPS)	www.collegeboard.com/eps
Community College Survey of Student Engagement (CCSSE)	www.ccsse.org
Council of Graduate Schools (CGS)	www.cgsnet.org
Educational Benchmarking, Inc. (EBI)	www.webebi.com
Engineering Workforce Commission (EWC)	www.ewc-online.org
Higher Education Research Institute (HERI) at UCLA	www.heri.ucla.edu
Institute of International Education (IIE)	www.iie.org
National Association for College Admission Counseling (NACAC)	www.nacacnet.org
National Center for Higher Education Management Systems (NCHEMS)	www.nchems.org
National Science Foundation (NSF)	www.nsf.gov/statistics
National Study of Instructional Costs and Productivity (Delaware Study)	www.udel.edu/IR/cost
National Survey of Student Engagement (NSSE)	www.nsse.iub.edu
Noel-Levitz, Inc.	www.noellevitz.com

Standards for decentralized databases

Three voluntary efforts provide standards so that the data from participating institutions are as comparable as possible. The Common Data Set (CDS) was developed to provide data for the publishers of college guides while minimizing the reporting burden for institutions. Although the data definitions are cooperatively reviewed and widely accepted, no single website makes the data available to participants, researchers, decision makers, or the public. The other two efforts are intended to provide "user-friendly" information for the general public. The Voluntary System of Accountability (VSA) provides a website with links to the data on each participating institution's website, while the University & College Accountability Network (U-CAN) has a website with a searchable database of its participants.

The CDS initiative is "a collaborative effort among data providers in the higher education community and publishers as represented by the College Board, Peterson's, and U.S. News & World Report. The combined goal of this collaboration is to improve the quality and accuracy of information provided to all involved in a student's transition into higher education . . . The CDS is a set of standards and definitions of data items rather than a survey instrument or set of data represented in a database" (www.commondataset.org/). Many institutions post their CDS data on their websites, where they can be accessed by anyone.

The VSA is "an initiative by public 4-year universities to supply basic, comparable information on the undergraduate student experience to important constituencies through a common web report—the College Portrait. The VSA . . . is sponsored by two higher education associations—the Association of Public and Land-grant Universities (APLU) and the Association of State Colleges and Universities (AASCU)" (http://www.voluntarysystem.org/index.cfm).

U-CAN is sponsored by the National Association of Independent Colleges and Universities and "is designed to give, in a common format, prospective students and their families concise, web-based consumer-friendly information on the nation's nonprofit, private colleges and universities" (www. ucan-network.org).

Table 6.3 Institution-Focused Measures of Student Learning

Measure	Description from Website
Collegiate Assessment of Academic Proficiency (CAAP)	"[I]s the standardized, nationally normed assessment program from ACT that enables postsecondary institutions to assess, evaluate, and enhance student learning outcomes and general education program outcomes." (www.act.org/caap)
Collegiate Learning Assessment (CLA)	"[P]resents realistic problems that require students to analyze complex materials and determine the relevance . . . and credibility. Students' written responses . . . are evaluated to assess their abilities to think critically, reason analytically, solve problems and communicate clearly and cogently." (www.collegiatelearningassessment.org)
Major Field Tests (MFT)	"[A]re comprehensive undergraduate . . . outcomes assessments designed to measure the critical knowledge and understanding . . . in a major field of study . . . [They] evaluate students' ability to analyze and solve problems, understand relationships and interpret material from their major field of study." (www.ets.org/mft)
Proficiency Profile	"[A]ssesses four core skill areas — critical thinking, reading, writing and mathematics — in a single, convenient test . . . [with] an optional essay for greater insight into students' writing skills." (www.ets.org/ proficiencyprofile)

Standardized measures of student learning

One source of relevant data for assessing student learning is tests that enable institutions to compare the performance of their students with national or other comparison groups. Certification tests for various professions and admissions tests for advanced studies are useful to the individual students, as well as the institutions, and are typically taken at the expense of the individuals. Table 6.3 presents a list of tests that are designed to provide data for the institutions and are typically paid for by the institution.

The Major Field Tests are based on the GRE Subject Tests and are used to measure learning in the designated specialty fields of study, while the other instruments listed in Table 6.3 are designed to measure the learning that typically occurs in general education programs. All such instruments should be combined with other measures of learning and interpreted in the context of the particular institution when making administrative decisions.

Environmental scanning

Decision making cannot be done effectively in a vacuum. It is all too easy for institutions to take on an insular view of the world. However, the reality is that all entities exist within a broader context of forces that impact decisions made within the institution. Social, political, educational, technological, and economic considerations are common elements of this "meta level system" context.

Traditional strategic planning processes call for a "situation analysis." Regardless of the nomenclature, the process typically involves taking a broad look at the range of factors external to an institution that can impact any decision being made. Two models that provide a structure for thinking about scanning are:

- **STEEP** = **S**ocial, **T**echnological, **E**conomics, **E**nvironmental, and **P**olitical (Morrison, 1992). Education and demographics can also be added to those five areas.
- **PINCHASTEM** = **P**olitical, **I**nformation/communication, **N**atural/macro-environmental, **C**onflict, **H**ealth/biological/micro-environmental, **A**rtistic/cultural/recreational, **S**ocial, **T**echnical/mechanical/electronic, **E**conomic, **M**oral/ethical/religious (www.audiencedialogue.net/gloss-fut.html).

Each institution must determine the variables that are particularly significant, useful, and available for their industry. Choosing the environmental factors to scan is the first step.

Once the outline of the scan is defined, environmental scanning becomes a structured process for identifying and recording from multiple respectable sources, relevant findings that suggest a trend or pattern worthy of factoring into the internal decision-making process. Think of the trend identification step as an exercise in "sense-making" which involves filtering, recognizing patterns, and making findings actionable (Gorbis, 2009).

Another decision to make is whether the institution will utilize existing sources of synthesized information or will build environmental scans based on review of direct sources of information with patterns and trends being identified by the institution. There is, of course, a continuum here, and some combination of both might produce the most efficient and relevant results. Table 6.4 provides some sources for synthesized scan content.

Web 2.0 tools are very useful in the process of modern environmental scanning. If the decision is to build your own patterns and trend analysis, it will be particularly beneficial to develop a Personal Learning Environment (PLE) which, in concert with regular RSS feeds, can do some of the heavy lifting of scanning automatically. Discovery, collaboration, and trial and error will produce a robust environmental scanning PLE over time. Some solid sources (besides those identified in Table 6.4) include:

- **Bureau of Labor Statistics** (www.bls.gov)—"The Bureau of Labor Statistics of the U.S. Department of Labor is the principal Federal agency responsible for measuring labor market activity, working conditions, and price changes in the economy. Its mission is to collect, analyze, and disseminate essential economic information to support public and private decision-making."
- **Census Bureau** (www.census.gov)—"Our Mission—To serve as the leading source of quality data about the nation's people and economy."
  - ○ **American Community Survey** (www.census.gov/ac s/www)—"The American Community Survey (ACS) is an ongoing survey that provides data every year—giving communities the current information they need to plan investments and services. Information

Table 6.4 Sources of Synthesized Scan Content

Source	URL	Description from Website
Society for College and University Planning Trends in Higher Education	www.scup.org/page/knowledge/ttw	"Members look to SCUP to find ways to successfully integrate the institution's mission into their academic plan, and then seek to integrate all other kinds of planning on campus in support of the academic plan."
Knowledge Works Foundation	www.futureofed.org/2020forecast	"Our understanding of the future of education, coupled with an underlying belief in the potential of every learner, compels us to make sure the promise of the future reaches every student."
Institute for the Future	www.iftf.org	"The Institute for the Future (IFTF) is an independent nonprofit research group. We work with organizations of all kinds to help them make better, more informed decisions about the future. We provide the foresight to create insights that lead to action."

from the survey generates data that help determine how more than $400 billion in federal and state funds are distributed each year."

- **Economic Census** (www.census.gov/econ/census02)—"The Economic Census profiles American business every 5 years, from the national to the local level."
- **State and County Quick Facts** (quickfacts.census.gov/qfd/states/00000.html)—"QuickFacts tables are summary profiles showing frequently requested data items from various Census Bureau programs. Profiles are available for the nation, states, counties, and large cities."
- **USA Counties** (censtats.census.gov/usa/usa.shtml)—"USA Counties features over 6,800 data items for the United States, States and counties from a variety of sources."

- **Occupational Supply Demand System** (www.occsupplydemand.org)—"The Occupational Supply Demand System provides information and resources that will assist with the analysis and discussion of supply and demand issues relevant to today's labor market." This site provides useful data such as the following:

  - **Programs of Study and Training**—Classification of Instructional Programs (CIP) codes and titles, programs of study and occupations by CIP.
  - **Occupations**—Standard Occupational Classification (SOC) codes and titles along with wage trends, fastest growing occupations and occupations with the most openings nationally and by state; percent wage change, percent employment growth and annual openings by SOC title and code.
  - **Career Clusters and Related Pathways**—SOC's are clustered into 16 occupational clusters which provide for a drill down to Programs of Study and Training information as well as supply and demand indicators.
  - **High Demand, High Wage, High Skill**—List of occupations by SOC code and title for select states.

- **Economic Modeling Specialists** (www.economicmodeling.com)—"Tools & data to understand employment and the local labor market. Research & reports to analyze education and the economy." (NOTE: This resource requires a paid membership.)

Be sure to refer to the government's summary of appropriate data use when using census and labor data (www.census.gov/acs/www/guidance_for_data_users/guidance_main).

The next important step is applying the results of environmental scanning to institutional decision making. The multiple approaches depend on such considerations as the level of uncertainty, the types of decisions to be made, and the culture of the institution. One approach is to utilize scanning data to inform the articulation and substantiation of key assumptions for the institution. These assumptions can be useful in sorting through uncertain outcomes by making explicit what the institution believes will come to pass.

Another approach is the development of scenarios which describe possible futures as defined by multiple factors. Scenarios allow institutions to pull together numerous variables and their possible values in a way that encourages discussion around decision options and level of uncertainty. The process can also uncover unspoken assumptions. A classic reference on this topic is the book *The Art of the Long View* by Peter Schwartz (1996).

Regardless of how scanning is incorporated into an institution's decision-making process, a connection between the two remains an important assurance that the actions of an institution are made consciously within a broader environmental context.

State Data

State higher education agencies are charged with planning and policy development for a system of public colleges and universities within a state. In that capacity, data collection is an essential function that allows informed judgments to be made by policymakers at the agency and throughout the higher education community in the state. Data management can have a major impact on the quality and quantity of information available and, therefore, may ultimately impact policy formulation. Continual assessment of data needs, exploration of new methods of collection and reporting, and examination of linkages with other data collection systems are necessary to assure decision makers of the most appropriate data to use in crafting recommendations regarding higher education. The overall objective is part of a data-based strategy by state higher education policymakers is to help ensure the state continues to meet the skills needed by employers and society in the future.

Within the state agencies, offices responsible for research and policy analysis perform most data gathering, editing, and compilation. The main sources of data are two well-established systems, IPEDS and in-house data systems; however, ad hoc surveys are regularly conducted, as needed, on specific issues. In January 2011, IPEDS released a new online application called the *IPEDS State Data Center* (nces.ed.gov/ipeds/sdc/) to meet the needs of researchers, policymakers, and others who need postsecondary data organized at the state level. Using the retrieval tools in this application one can create state groupings in predefined and customized formats.

While IPEDS and in-house data systems are at the core of a state's data capabilities, other systems provide additional insights into the state of higher education. The data systems maintained by state and regional guarantee agencies on student financial aid programs are often available for use by research and policy staff. They provide important information on a range of programs, as well as some insight into student financial status. The State Employment Training Commissions (SETC) and Labor and Workforce agencies have sought to expand cooperation among various state agencies involved in educating and assisting the state workforce. Understanding where students come from, those who choose other training paths, and the practical benefits education may create will require state policymakers to look beyond traditional higher education data sources.

Institutional data

Colleges and universities are inundated with demands for information needed to support administrative, academic, planning, regulatory, legislative, research and operational needs. Institutional stakeholders at all levels require real-time and snap-shot views of information as well as customized analysis to support their decisions. The primary source for such data is the institutional SIS (Student Information System), which can also be an ERP (Enterprise Resource Planning System). Institutions rely on the SIS to sustain functions such as enrollment management services, financial management, financial aid, human resources, administrative application management, and institutional advancement. Institutions supplement the SIS by conducting periodic surveys of students, alumni, employers, and other stakeholders.

With effective data-based decision-making capabilities, administrators and staff can identify trends and areas that need improvement, participate in data simulation, and use other decision-making processes. In order to stay competitive, institutional data sources should support timely operational decision making, optimize human resources and facility utilization, and combine with strategic and tactical planning, such as planning future degree and course offerings, to ensure alignment with community and industry needs. The major purveyors of higher educational data management systems are Sungard, Oracle, Datatel, Jenzabar, and SAP.

Assessment of student learning and institutional effectiveness are important components of an emerging accountability movement for postsecondary institutions. The publication of the Spellings

Commission report (U.S. Department of Education, 2006) suggested that changes are needed in the current practice of individual institutions of higher education designing, implementing, and evaluating their own assessment programs, monitored by their regional accrediting agencies.

The colleges are strengthening their efforts to institutionalize an assessment environment that encourages open reflection, supports innovation and experimentation in assessment methods, and promotes a culture of evidence in decision making. At many institutions, all departments or units across the campus are expected to develop and implement effective assessment plans and to report assessment results on an annual basis.

Student unit record systems

Current institutional, state, and federal reform initiatives rely heavily on the ability of states and institutions to access and use information from statewide Student Unit Record (SUR) data systems to improve student achievement. Policymakers believe that institutions and states are best positioned to achieve this by developing and implementing various policies impacting student learning outcomes using SUR databases. SUR data is useful in examining patterns of progression and completion of student cohorts.

A SUR data system is designed to strengthen the capacity of the state higher education agencies to discharge their research, planning, and coordinating responsibilities, and to assist institutions in a variety of ways, e.g., by tracking their transfers, reducing their need to fill out forms, and so forth. It is a comprehensive collection, storage, and retrieval system for computer-readable data on each student enrolled and on each graduate.

The enrollment component of SUR is typically a fall, spring and summer semester "snapshot"; the degrees conferred component captures data for an entire academic or fiscal year. Each student record includes a unique identifier that follows the student through all educational institutions, as well as various student-specific demographic, academic, and education process data. The unique identifier is typically used at all levels of education (P-20, or pre-kindergarten to doctoral degree) and could track the individual into the workforce.

SUR system data are used by the state to perform various analyses. For example, serially constructed data sets are produced for system-wide longitudinal studies of retention, attrition, and other issues where temporal relationships are important. The SUR system also produces aggregate statistics on each institution, to fulfill certain federal and state reporting requirements. In addition to supporting system-wide outcomes research and reducing institutional reporting burdens, SUR offers participating institutions opportunities to conduct their own customized research.

The National Center for Higher Education Management Systems (NCHEMS) reported in its 2006 SUR survey report (Ewell & Boeke, 2006) that 40 of the 50 states have operational SUR databases covering public institutions in their respective states. Most, if not all, of the remaining states have partial systems and are in the process of expanding them to include all levels of education.

The July 2010 report on state Student Unit Record (SUR) by State Higher Education Executive Officers (SHEEO) (Garcia & L'Orange, 2010) provides detail description of 59 SUR systems in 45 states. The report concludes that these data systems were primarily created to generate statistics and reports, facilitate research, and assist in development for policies the postsecondary system(s) in the state. Only 11 of the states have formal data-linking agreements with the K-12 systems in their respective states. Currently only 19 state SURs collect data from independent institutions.

SHEEO has also released a follow-up report (Ott & Desjardins, 2010) describing the accessibility, safeguards and privacy protection of the SURs. This report maintains that accessibility to the SUR are closely protected, limiting the data generation and reporting capabilities to employees of the agencies. However, many of the SURs provided data extracts to outside individuals. Due to commitments tied to the American Recovery and Reinvestment Act of 2009, some states are now developing or expanding SUR systems.

Local Data Sources

The most important source of local data is the office or person responsible for institutional research. If the institution is too small to have even a part-time person formally designated with such responsibilities, someone should at least be the lead person for keeping up with data requirements and coordinating relevant activities. It is highly recommended that such a person be designated as the institution's IPEDS keyholder and use the resources of the Association for Institutional Research (www.airweb.org) to learn more about IPEDS reporting. Not only will doing do so help the institution to fulfill its federally mandated responsibilities for reporting data, but the administrators and faculty will be able to make better decisions, as discussed in the next major section of this chapter.

Institutional researchers may have direct access to the institution's SIS or operational records system or may receive "snapshots" or "frozen files" of appropriate records from other offices. If they have direct access, it is strongly recommended that appropriate "snapshots" be downloaded into separate files that are controlled by the institutional researcher because the data in the operational system can change as normal activities occur. If the "snapshots" are taken at appropriate times, such as the official census date for student enrollments or November 1st for human resources data, *and* verified by appropriate people at that time, they will be more reliable and trusted by decision makers.

The variables to be included in such files will depend upon the external data reports and administrative decisions needed by that institution. Depending on the size and control (public vs. private) of the institution, such files may be kept in a data warehouse that is accessible to the public, all employees, or only selected individuals. When new questions become important, new variables may be added so that a comprehensive set of variables is available for further analyses that support future decisions.

Institutional researchers need to work with a variety of offices in order to understand the variables that are being downloaded. Typically cooperation with the offices of registrar, admissions, financial aid, human resources, intercollegiate athletics, international studies, and business/finances will be required. Other offices, such as institutional advancement/development provost, deans, and academic departments, may also be included. If the verification process identifies problems or gaps, the relevant office and the institutional researcher will need to decide if the data in the operational system or only in the downloaded files should be corrected. Sometimes the needs of the operational system are incompatible with the needs for data analysis and reporting. For example, the head of a music department may be the designated instructor for private lessons taught by adjunct instructors in order to facilitate the submission of grades, but the data on teaching loads may need to identify those instructors by name.

Accuracy, consistency, and comprehensiveness are the most important characteristics of such databases. Unfortunately these characteristics may be in opposition to each other. An administrative restructuring would require inconsistency with previous years in order to be accurate. New issues may require new variables so that the database remains comprehensive even as doing so works against the goal of consistency. If such additions suggest that some existing variables are no longer needed, continuing to download those variables for a couple of years before discarding them is recommended.

To reap the benefit of institutional databases described above, it is necessary to collect and analyze data on individual students and employees, while safeguarding the privacy of individual records. In processing data requests, institutional researchers need to be cognizant of the Family Educational Rights to Privacy Act (FERPA, 1974), as well as privacy and right to know policies.

Types of Administrative Decisions and the Use of Data

Main Areas for Administrative Decisions

As Middaugh (2010, p. 20) pointed out, "whether measuring learning or measuring the effectiveness and efficiency of human and fiscal resources deployment in support of teaching and learning, multiple measures are required, as well as multiple strategies for interpreting and communicating the results of those measurements." While recognizing the possibility of over-simplification, the decisions made at institutions of higher education can be divided into four main areas, as follows:

- the opening and closing of programs;
- the allocation of resources, including funds, personnel positions, and facilities;
- the pursuit of revenue sources, such as the setting of prices and the expenditure of resources in order to increase enrollments, gifts, grants, contracts, royalties, and revenue enhancements (i.e., profits); and
- strategic directions for the institution.

The role of data in the decisions of these areas is described below.

Opening and closing of programs

The opening of a new program, whether an academic program, student service, research direction, or any other activity associated with higher education, should be based on a variety of factors. First, there should be a demonstrated need for the program that is based on an environmental scan (as discussed earlier in this chapter in the section on environmental scanning) and a comparison with similar programs offered by other institutions. There should be well-established predictions from external sources that the program's potential outcomes will provide something that is needed by a significant segment of society. However, it is also important that existing or imminent programs at other institutions do not have sufficient or even excess capacity to meet that need. Obviously, environmental scans and comparison data are critical in deciding whether to start a new program. Secondly, the institution should have or be capable of obtaining the resources needed to establish and operate the program for the foreseeable future. While financial resources are important, personnel and physical facilities, such as building space and specialized equipment, must also be considered.

The closing of a program is typically more difficult and not done very well in higher education. Verified, generally accepted measures that support such a decision are extremely helpful, but values and adverse impacts on the affected individuals, particularly tenured faculty members, and the reputation of the institution are also important. Enrollments, costs, service for other areas of the institution, and productivity data should be compared both within the institution and with similar programs at other institutions if possible. Being part of a state system or consortium can be very helpful in obtaining such data. However, factors that are not quantifiable or even based on empirical data, such as external pressures and the inherent value of the discipline to the institution, must also be considered.

Allocation of resources

When dealing with the allocation of resources, the primary data of interest are likely to be from the institution itself. Generally accepted measures that have been used for a reasonable period of time provide the best starting point, but individual units should be allowed to add their own, verifiable data in order to present their uniqueness and special needs to the decision makers. If the institution is part of a state system with open financial records or a consortium with a high level of trust and cooperation, comparisons with the allocations at similar institutions are possible, but even in such situations, local conditions and procedures make complete, detailed comparisons difficult. Personal contact with the people who have similar responsibilities at the other institutions is a good idea so that such local factors are known and taken into account.

Pursuit of revenue sources

Setting prices, particularly student tuition and fees, can be very difficult because the decision is broadly applied, quite public, and traditionally unchangeable for a considerable length of time, and it has implications for the financial health of the institution, the ability of individual students to continue their education, and the reputation of the institution. Many businesses would reject the idea that they should publicly announce the price of their most popular model and leave it unchanged without any added incentives, price reductions, or special offers if market conditions change during an entire year. One consideration in recent years, particularly for private institutions but also for a growing number of public universities, is "sticker price" versus net price. In other words, the publicized tuition and fees are being modified more and more by grants and scholarships that generally come from either returns on the institution's endowment or the general budget. This issue has become so prominent that the Higher Education Opportunity Act of 2008 (nces.ed.gov/ipeds/resource/net_price_calculator.asp) requires that all institutions participating in the Title IV federal student aid program post a "net price calculator" on their website no later than October 29, 2011 so that prospective students and their families can get at least an estimate of the actual expenses for the individual or family. The regulations require and provide a basic template, but institutions are encouraged to add features that provide more accurate estimates on the basis of their unique cost structures and scholarship programs. While the decision makers must consider the financial implications for their institutional budgets, comparison data also need to be considered. If the tuition increase is so great that some new or existing students do not enroll, the net tuition revenue could actually decrease. On the other hand, some people believe that tuition that is too low conveys an image of poor quality that could also lower enrollment. Once again, data from the institution itself, its competitors for students, and the needs and opinions of prospective students will improve this important decision.

Almost all institutions are attempting to establish additional revenue streams to supplement the revenue from tuition and student fees. Not that long ago, most institutions were able to keep tuition and fees quite low because they were getting substantial funding from state governments, church bodies, and other organizations that wanted to support higher education. Many full-time students in those days could "work their way through college," obtain government grants, or rely on family support for the relatively minor expense, thereby graduating without any debt. Such scenarios are quite rare these days. Therefore, institutions at all levels and in all sectors are trying to establish additional revenue streams, such as money-making auxiliary enterprises, research grants, foundation grants, and individual gifts and bequests. However, investments of time and money are usually needed before such revenue streams generate appreciable income that can be used for the general budget or educational programs. Environmental scans, comparison data from similar institutions, and estimated institutional costs should be obtained before the decision is made to initiate the seeking of supplemental funds. The same factors should also be considered when contemplating new efforts to increase student enrollment. While students are the reason for higher education, their recruitment and retention do require expenditures of finances, personnel, facilities, and institutional reputation.

Strategic directions for the institution

Finally, decisions regarding strategic directions for the institution require perhaps the widest scope of data consideration. Strategic direction is typically the purview of the president working in concert with the oversight board for the institution such as a Board of Trustees. The input of multiple stakeholders must be considered. Their relative importance will vary by institution. For example, at community colleges, the input of the community which supports the institution may be weighed quite heavily; whereas, at a private institution that stakeholder may hold little influence. While different approaches to setting strategy are employed, almost all begin with a process of understanding the situation. A SWOT (Strengths, Weaknesses, Opportunities, Threats) analysis is conducted and underlying principles are articulated. Strengths and weaknesses draw from a review of internal, institutional data. Examples include the ability to effectively partner with other institutions to successfully operate programs or financial reserves of the institution. Opportunities and threats draw from data external to the institution and assess the impact on the institution. Examples include new programs or program enhancements in competitive institutions, growing or declining industries in the region the college serves, and governmental policy changes. Seybert, Weed, and Bers (this volume) discuss another important way in which data can be used in strategic planning and administrative decision making.

Decision-Making Models

Administrative decisions are often complex and difficult, and they must be made in the context of the institution's culture and political (i.e., external forces) situation. Therefore, no single or ideal process will work in all situations. Selecting the most appropriate process can be just as important and difficult as making the actual decision and may not be possible because of evolving circumstances. The various models described below suggest alternative strategies so that the decision maker can proceed with a clearer understanding of how to proceed, knowing that the process may need revision or even complete replacement before the actual decision is made. Considering the advantages and disadvantages of the various alternatives as a conscious step should lead to better decisions.

Classical model

The classical model assumes that decisions should be completely rational. Its process is a series of sequential steps involving identifying problems, establishing goals and objectives, evaluating alternatives, selecting alternatives that optimize goals and objectives, and implementing decisions (Huczynski & Buchanan, 2001; Rollinson, 2002). The classical model is ideal for seeking the best solution to an identified problem; however, most scholars consider it unrealistic. One limitation of this model is that decision makers virtually never have access to all the relevant information (Herbert, 1981; Hoy & Miskel, 2001), and they cannot be certain of the accuracy of the information they have (Robbins, 2003). This model assumes information-processing capacities, rationality, and knowledge that decision makers simply do not possess in many circumstances, and therefore it is not very useful for most decision makers (Hoy & Miskel, 2001).

Administrative model

Simon (1947) prescribed a satisfying approach which is more practical than the classical model. According to Simon, decisions that solve one problem may lead to creation of others; the rationality of the decision making is heavily reliant upon the skills, capacities and values of the decision makers. Therefore, instead of searching for the best solution as the classical model does, decision makers aspire to address bottom-line issues such as minimum objectives, musts and wants, and good-enoughs, a set of criteria for satisfactory decisions. To the extent that a fully executed decision—made, implemented and appraised—also marks the beginning of another decision making cycle, there is no such thing as a best or ultimate solution. It is a satisfactory decision for the time being and a solution for the moment.

Incremental model

Lindblom (1959) suggested that a satisfactory decision is difficult to make in reality because of the complex, uncertain and conflicting nature of many decisions. Instead of following rational steps, the incremental model emphasizes the comparison of immediately available alternatives and "muddling through" an often unfriendly political setting. Objectives and goals change as the program progresses, and decisions are constantly made and remade. Through small decisions that everyone agreed upon, the complexity of decision making is dramatically reduced and made manageable.

Mixed-scanning model

The incremental model is criticized for its aimlessness and lack of aggressiveness when it comes to higher levels of decision making, such as establishing the mission and goals for the organization. Etzioni (1967, 1986) and Goldberg (1975) presented a mixed model which addresses higher-order, fundamental decisions, such as mission and goals, and incremental lower-order decisions that serve the higher-order ones. It embodies the advantages of both the administrative and incremental models, keeping decision makers away from examining all the information or little or no information at all. In this model, satisfactory decisions still can be made with partial information in complex and uncertain situations.

"Garbage can" model

Other models try to contribute to the understanding of the dynamic and complicated processes of decision making. For instance, the "garbage can" model disconnects problems, solutions, and decision makers from each other so that decisions do not follow an orderly process from problem to solution or from question to answer (Cohen, March & Olsen, 1972). Organizations tend to produce solutions that are discarded because they do not solve an immediate problem. However, problems may eventually arise where a search of the garbage might yield fitting solutions. In the context of the operation of universities, it is criticized because it is a description rather than a prescription for decision making, and it just deals with part of the whole process of decision making (Bendor, Moe, & Shotts, 2001).

Shared governance model

In recent years, the shared decision-making model is frequently discussed and applied in higher education. In this model, decision makers involve subordinates in formulating some policies when subordinates are stakeholders and possess appropriate expertise (Hoy & Miskel, 2001). In other cases, leaders just make direct, unilateral decisions when the issue is within the zone of indifference to subordinates. This model warns of the risks of involving too many people, leading to the "groupthink syndrome" (Janis & Mann, 1977). Janis (1985) prescribed that when some conditions are present, the decision makers should either foster groupthink or avoid groupthink. In the former situation, when urgency to reach a decision is not a primary concern for the decision maker, groupthink can be an effective process. Besides, groupthink may lead to greater cohesiveness if the leader is equipped with skills to resolve conflicts among group members. However, in the latter case, a leader who lacks direct contact with subordinates often finds himself misled and therefore is forced into a groupthink process, coupled with various factors such as homogeneous nature of the group, external pressures, moral dilemmas and excessive difficulties. Either actively or passively, decision makers should expect more dangers (e.g., closed mindedness, pressure of unanimity) than benefits (e.g., effectiveness, greater cohesiveness) from such a process.

This model characterizes itself more as a guideline for actions, rather than an abstract theory, with applicability constrained by a number of factors that decision makers cannot control. In higher education settings, when it comes to aligning the assessment of learning to the overall evaluation of the institutional effectiveness, this model stands out because faculty and administrators are not in a leader-subordinate relationship. Both are stakeholders in the success of students and overall effectiveness of the institution and are trained professionals who are capable of involvement in shared decision making.

Formula funding model

States experienced the most significant adoption of formula funding between 1963 and 1973 (Carter, 2002). According to Carter, during this decade, the number of states using formula funding rose from 6 to 25. This significant growth in formula funding occurred during a time when higher education was experiencing overwhelming public support and escalating enrollment growth. Along with overwhelming public support for higher education came an increased demand for accountability. Formula funding served as one response by allowing a more systematic way for distributing public funds to higher education institutions.

By 2006, the number of states who used some form of formula funding at some point in the budgeting or resource allocation process had increased to 36 (McKeown-Moak, 2006). State formula funding has been in use in the United States for over 50 years. Its evolution has seen both an increase in usage and a decrease in usage over time. As states protected base budgets as much as possible, they attempted to eliminate formula funding during the first half of the first decade of the 21st century. Because of increasing enrollment trends and decreasing state resources, tuition and fees increased, resulting in less reliance on enrollment-driven formula funding models. In the latter half of the decade states began to return to formula funding as the funding trend began to reverse itself from tuition and fees toward more state resources.

Similar to higher education, the only constants in state formula funding models have been change and controversy. Formula funding was designed as a means to distribute funding in a rational, equitable way. According to McKeown-Moak (2006), formula funding has evolved into often complex methodologies for determining institutional funding needs and allocating public funds. Formulas are products of a political process. Therefore, formulas are not immune to compromise. It is this comprise that makes data used in formula funding models the key that validates the model.

One of the greatest roles for data is found in the use of formula funding, even though the determination of the measures to be included and the parameters of the formula still require human judgments. A primary characteristic of higher education formula funding is the need for valid and reliable data. Formula funding should be based on data that are appropriate for measuring differences in funding requirements. Any data used in formula funding should be verifiable by a third party.

Since formula funding is performance based, the formula should include sufficient data to effectively communicate to key participants in the state budget process how changes in institutional characteristics, institutional performance, and modifications to budget polices will affect funding levels. A well-designed formula funding model has the ability to impact data-driven decisions in a very positive way. Because the model recognizes that different institutional characteristics, such as program offering, degree levels, institutional size, and student readiness, require different level of funding, it has the ability to drive equitable decisions.

Formula funding is not immune to economic conditions. Therefore, economic data is a key element when it comes to formula funding. Funding formula should have the capacity to incorporate economic data to account for a variety of economic situations. A unique characteristic of a well-designed model is its ability to adjust when state appropriations for higher education are increasing, stable, or decreasing. A primary key to this flexibility is data. Data with integrity leads to a funding formula model with integrity. Uses of formula funding include the following:

- Formula funding was originally developed to help state higher education agencies distribute the state's higher education budget allocation to each institution equitably.
- Formula funding can be used to measure and reward each higher education institution's productivity.
- State higher education agencies or governing boards can use formula funding to recommend resources for each institution to the legislature.
- Formula funding can be used to evaluate higher education budget requests.

In summary, states and higher education institutions have used formula funding to allocate resources in strong economic times. During recessions, states tend to back away from the use of formula funding because of a lack of resources to sustain higher education policies and guidelines. At the core of understanding when and how formula funding is used are data. Even in formula funding, data serve as the key to historical facts and a view of future possibilities.

Closing Thoughts

Administrative decisions in higher education are often complex and difficult, especially as their importance and implications rise. Businesses must consider customer expectations, regulatory demands, resource availability, tax implications, and other factors, and governments have "checks-and balances" systems, along with political pressures. Likewise, higher education administrators must consider the often competing expectations of students, employers of the graduates, granting agencies, accrediting bodies, government regulations and funding priorities, and a tenured faculty that is responsible for the curriculum and acts as a "checks-and balances" system. The actual decision makers may not be evident to even the top administrators, and the decision is almost always subject to further change. Appropriate, verified, reliable data should improve the decision process, but they are never the whole story. As others (G. McLaughlin & J. McLaughlin, 2007) have suggested, decisions should not be "data-driven" in the sense that the numbers determine the outcome. Instead, decisions should be "data-informed" in the sense that appropriate people use their understanding of the best available data, plus their understanding of the context and institutional values, to inspirationally communicate a plan of action for all concerned individuals.

In order to use data properly, decision makers must first decide on the variables to be considered. Such decisions, which will vary according to the overall context, cannot be made in isolation by either institutional researchers, who presumably know the most about which variables are available and how they are measured, or administrators, who must interpret the data, consider the broader context, and decide on the importance of each variable. It should be an interactive process that is open, transparent, and reasonably stable so that trends and anomalies can be identified. Administrators can become frustrated by institutional researchers who always want more and better data, and institutional researchers can become frustrated when they have no advance guidance about the variables that will be the most useful or are asked for data that cannot be feasibly obtained within the necessary time frame.

For many of the most important decisions, it will take a relatively long period of time before measurable results can be expected. For example, a new academic program can take a year or more to develop, several years to have any graduates, and several more years to determine if the graduates obtain appropriate employment and make positive contributions. Decision cycles, especially budgets, are much shorter, and so intermediate measures must be used. The appropriate balance between accuracy, completeness, and urgency will always exist.

The *IPEDS Data Feedback Reports* are a starting point in identifying the most useful, long-term measures for monitoring the status and progress of all institutions, but they are certainly not accepted or even known universally. The relatively new IPEDS State Data Center (nces.ed.gov/ipeds/sdc/) provides another set of variables that should be useful for decisions beyond the individual institution. The variables used by the publications that rank institutions in their college guides must also be considered because of the influence they have had. A national discussion, based on those measures, by decision makers both inside and outside higher education is needed so that realistic, meaningful measures and "dashboards" are widely accepted.

A related issue is deciding on the appropriate comparison institutions or programs (see Seybert, Weed, & Bers, this volume). The numbers become meaningful only when they are compared with either predetermined standards, past performance, or a comparison group. If the wrong benchmarks are selected, the decision will be adversely affected and may be totally wrong. Comparison groups can be based on institutional history (e.g., a long-standing consortium), political or governmental control (e.g., the community colleges in a state), aspirations for growth in size or prestige (e.g., research universities in a region), competition for resources (e.g., students, research funds, state appropriations), or peer status, which may be subjectively or empirically determined (G. McLaughlin & J. McLaughlin, 2007). In most cases, the appropriate comparison group will vary according to the decision being made. Obviously, the earlier an agreement on the comparison group can be made, the easier the decision process will be; however, decision makers may decide to change the group membership once they examine the data.

Data reflect the past, but decisions are supposed to affect the future. Even with the best measures, the right comparison groups, and the most appropriate decision model, a decision finally has to be made. Decision paralysis caused by focusing too much on collecting more data is really a default decision to maintain the status quo. Administrators who have been researchers have to realize that they cannot expect to reach definitive conclusions before proceeding. Leadership requires making decisions that involve calculated (i.e., data-informed) risk and then convincing people to work toward accomplishing the plan. Some people who excel at the methodical, detail-oriented approach of science and scholarship are not well suited to make decisions that will inspire and lead people to desired improvements. In a recent conversation, one administrator described an ideal commute as setting the cruise-control and never having to use the brake or gas pedal, but another stated that a successful commute means passing at least 10 cars per mile. Which one should be making decisions in higher education? Or even better, how can they work together for the improvement of all?

References

American Recovery and Reinvestment Act of 2009, Pub. L. No. 111–5, 123 Stat. 115–521 (2009).

Bendor, J., Moe, T. M., & Shotts, K. W. (2001). Recycling the garbage can: An assessment of the research program. *American Political Science Review, 95,* 169–190.

Brinkman, P. and Krakower, J. (1983). *Comparative data for administrators in higher education.* Boulder, CO: National Center for Higher Education Management Systems.

Carter, M. J. (2002). A study of the discontinuance of formula funding of institutions of higher education in the Commonwealth of Virginia. (Doctoral Dissertation). Retrieved from http://scholar.lib.vt.edu/theses/available/etd-05142002-114755/unrestricted/carterfinal.pdf

Cohen, M. D., March, J. G., & Olsen, J. P. (1972). A garbage can model of organizational choice. *Administrative Science Quarterly, 17,* 1–25.

Etzioni, A. (1967). Mixed scanning: A third approach to decision making. *Public Administration Review, 27*, 387–392.

Etzioni, A. (1986). Mixed scanning revisited. *Public Administration Review, 46*, 8–15.

Ewell, P., & Boeke, M. (2006). *Tracking student progression: The state of the states* (Draft). Denver, CO: National Center for Higher Education Management Systems.

Family Educational Rights and Privacy Act of 1974, 20 U.S.C. § 1232g (1974).

Garcia, T. I., & L'Orange, H. P. (2010). *Strong foundations: The state of postsecondary data systems.* Denver, CO: State Higher Education Executive Officers.

Goldberg, M. A. (1975). On the inefficiency of being efficient. *Environment and Planning, 7*, 921–939.

Gorbis, M. (2009). *Superstructing ourselves: Finding opportunity in turmoil.* Retrieved from http://www.iftf. org/superstructing-ourselves

Hall, R. H. (2002). *Organizations: Structures, processes, and outcomes.* Upper Saddle River, NJ: Prentice Hall.

Herbert. T. T. (1981). *Dimensions of organizational behavior* (2nd ed.). New York, NY: Macmillan.

Higher Education Opportunity Act of 2008, Pub. L. No. 110–315, 122 Stat. 3078–3508 (2008).

Hoy, W., & Miskel, C. (2001), *Educational administration: Theory, research, and practice* (6th ed.). New York, NY: McGraw-Hill.

Huczynski, A., & Buchanan, D. (2001). *Organizational behavior: An introductory text* (4th ed.). Hemel Hempstead, United Kingdom: Prentice Hall Europe.

Janis, I. L. (1985). Sources of error in strategic decision making. In J. M. Pennings (Ed.), *Organizational strategy and change* (pp. 157–97). San Francisco, CA: Jossey-Bass.

Janis, I. L., and Mann, L. (1977). *Decision making: A psychological analysis of conflict, choice, and commitment.* New York, NY: Free Press.

Lindblom, C. E. (1959). The science of "muddling through". *Public Administration Review, 19*(2), 79–88.

McKeown-Moak, M. (2006). *Survey results 2006 survey of funding formula use.* Paper presented at the State Higher Education Executive Officers Professional Development Conference 2006. MGT of America, Inc. Retrieved from http://www.mgtamer.com/docs/PaperforPDC.pdf

McLaughlin, G., & McLaughlin, J. (2007). *The information mosiac: Strategic decision making for universities and colleges.* Washington, DC: Association of Governing Boards Press.

Middaugh, M. (2010). *Planning and assessment in higher education: Demonstrating institutional effectiveness.* San Francisco, CA: Jossey-Bass.

Morrison, J. L. (1992). Environmental scanning. In M. A. Whitely, J. D. Porter, & R. H. Fenske (Eds.). *A primer for new institutional researchers* (pp. 86–99). Tallahassee, FL: The Association for Institutional Research.

Ott, M., & Desjardins, S. (2010). *Protection and accessibility of state student unit record data systems at the postsecondary level.* Denver, CO: State Higher Education Executive Officers.

Robbins, S. P. (2003). *Management* (7th ed.). Upper Saddle River, NJ: Prentice-Hall.

Rollinson, D. (2002). *Organizational behavior and analysis: An integrated approach* (2nd ed.). Harlow, England: Pearson Education.

Schwartz, P. (1996). *The art of the long view: Planning for the future in an uncertain world.* New York, NY: Doubleday.

Seybert, J., Weed, E., & Bers, T. (this volume). *Benchmarking in higher education.*

Simon, H. A. (1947). *Administrative behavior.* New York, NY: Macmillan.

U.S. Department of Education. (2006). *A test of leadership: Charting the future of U.S. higher education* (A Report of the Commission Appointed by Secretary of Education Margaret Spellings). Washington, DC: Author. Retrieved from http://www2.ed.gov/about/bdscomm/list/hiedfuture/reports/final-report.pdf

EMPOWERMENT EVALUATION AND ACCREDITATION CASE EXAMPLES

California Institute of Integral Studies and Stanford University

David Fetterman

Empowerment evaluation is the use of evaluation concepts, techniques, and findings to foster improvement and self-determination (Fetterman, 1994, 2005a). It is an approach that:

> aims to increase the probability of achieving program success by (1) providing program stakeholders with tools for assessing the planning, implementation, and self-evaluation of their program, and (2) mainstreaming evaluation as part of the planning and management of the program/organization. *(Wandersman, Snell-Johns, Lentz, Fetterman, Keener, Livet, Imm, & Flaspohler, 2005, p. 28)*

Empowerment evaluation is a form of self-evaluation designed to help people accomplish their objectives through cycles of reflection and action. This approach values both processes and outcomes. It is used to enable people to establish their own goals, baselines, and benchmarks. It is well suited to accreditation self-studies, as it is designed to engage people and foster participation and collaboration in the process of conducting an evaluation. It is based on the assumption that the more closely stakeholders are engaged in interpreting and reflecting on evaluation findings in a collaborative and collegial setting, the more likely they are to take ownership of the results. Two accreditation self-study examples from opposite ends of the academic spectrum, the California Institute of Integral Studies and Stanford University's School of Medicine, will be presented to highlight the capacity of this approach to help people create their own learning organizations (Argyris, 1999; Senge, 1990).

Background

Empowerment evaluation has become a world-wide phenomenon. Empowerment evaluations are conducted in Australia, Brazil, Canada, Israel, Finland, Japan, Mexico, Nepal, New Zealand, South Africa, Spain, United Kingdom, and throughout the United States. Projects range from a large-scale $15 million Hewlett-Packard Digital Village (Fetterman, 2005b) to a series of small–scale local township health programs in South Africa. Settings range from universities and hospitals to Native American reservations. The popularity of the approach is due in part to its simplicity, transparency, and face validity.

Empowerment evaluation is guided by specific theories, principles, concepts, and steps. This approach has been particularly appropriate and effective in the creation, development, and facilitation of learning communities (Rogoff, Matusov, & White, 1998). Learning communities are instrumental in accreditation efforts, since accrediting agencies are looking for community participation, involvement, and action.

This discussion begins with an introduction to empowerment evaluation, including the theories, principles, concepts, and steps that guide it. Building on this introduction, examples of empowerment evaluation in two accreditation efforts are presented: California Institute of Integral Studies and Stanford University. The contrasting settings provide an insight into the adaptability of the approach and the common themes associated with evaluation and accreditation.

Theories

The most important theory driving empowerment evaluation is *process use. Process use* states that the more that people conduct their own evaluations the more they will buy into the findings and recommendations, because they are their findings and recommendations. This is important because one of the most significant problems in evaluation is knowledge utilization. Too often evaluation findings sit on the shelf and gather dust. Empowerment evaluation, guided by the theory of *process use*, increases the probability of evaluation data being used to inform decision making and thus improve use.

Empowerment evaluation is also guided by two additional theories: theory of action and theory of use. The theory of action is the espoused or stated program purpose or organization mission. The theory of use is the actual observed behavior. Often these two theories do not match and may even contradict each other (see Figure 7.1). Empowerment evaluation is a tool to provide continual feedback to faculty and staff members, as well as students to help them align these theories. Ideally, theories of action and use are consistent and help to ensure that people are "walking their talk."

Principles

Empowerment evaluation is also guided by principles that are designed to ensure quality (Fetterman & Wandersman, 2005). They also ensure an additional measure of consistency. The aim is to adhere to the spirit of empowerment evaluation, rather than the letter of the law. The 10 principles are:

1. *Improvement*—empowerment evaluation is not a neutral experiment; it is designed to use evaluation to help people accomplish their objectives;
2. *Community ownership*—communities have the right to make decisions about actions that affect their lives; a sense of ownership (of the evaluation) is key to knowledge utilization;

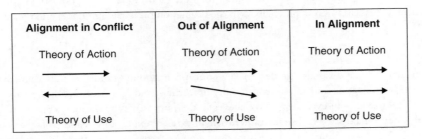

Figure 7.1 Alignment of theories of action and use

3. *Inclusion*—broad representation of participants should be recruited and asked to participate; diversity is additive not subtractive;
4. *Democratic participation*—empowerment evaluation has faith in the capacity of human beings for intelligent judgment and action if proper conditions are furnished; decisions should invite participation and be transparent;
5. *Social justice*—recognition of the fact that there are basic social inequities in society and that there is a need to strive to ameliorate these conditions by helping people use evaluation to help improve programs that impact their social conditions; there also needs to be a commitment to a fair, equitable allocation of resources, opportunities, and obligations;
6. *Community knowledge*—empowerment evaluation respects and values community knowledge —the tacit "know-how" knowledge of stakeholders;
7. *Evidence-based strategies*—empowerment evaluation respects and uses the knowledge base of scholars; communities are encouraged to adapt evidence-based knowledge, rather than adopt it; use of the literature helps to avoid reinventing the wheel;
8. *Capacity building*—enhance stakeholders' ability to conduct evaluation and to improve program planning and implementation;
9. *Organizational learning*—use data to inform decision making, implement practices based on the data, and evaluate new practices; inquire into the systemic consequences of actions rather than settle for short-term solutions that do not address the underlying problem; and
10. *Accountability*—did the program accomplish its objectives; stakeholders work together, holding each other accountable and building on each other's strengths to achieve results; empowerment evaluations exist within the context of the existing policies and standards that the program is already being held accountable to for the project/program.

The principles guide every step in the process of conducting an empowerment evaluation. For example, the principle of improvement emphasizes that this is not a neutral scientific experiment. The purpose behind empowerment evaluation is to use evaluation to help programs improve. It is not a test to see if the program works or not. The assumption is that there has been an initial screening by the funder that the program merits the "seed money" or initial investment and that evaluation can be used in the same manner as a financial counselor or advisor, to enhance the probability that the investment is paying off and serving the intended audience or population. The principle of community knowledge highlights the importance of respecting and relying on community knowledge to understand the local situation or context. Capacity building is fundamental, because if program participants are not learning how to conduct some part of their own evaluation then they are probably not building self-determination skills and experience. Finally, accountability is a critical principal because the bottom line is: did the program produce the desired results or not? The process is important but not an end in itself. The approach is designed to help programs accomplish their objectives. These principles serve as an important lens in which to view and conduct an empowerment evaluation, guiding the evaluator, participant, staff member, community member, and funder throughout the entire effort. Empowerment evaluation principles help keep the evaluation on track, authentic, and meaningful.

Concepts

Empowerment evaluation is also guided by key concepts including: critical friends, culture of evidence, cycles of reflection and action, community of learners, and reflective practitioner (see Figure 7.2). A critical friend is an evaluator who believes in the purpose of the program, but is critical and analytical. They are a trusted colleague, rather than an external expert or outsider. They can help set the tone for dialogue, helping to establish a positive and constructive learning climate. They pose questions diplomatically to ensure rigor and honesty because they want the program to be more

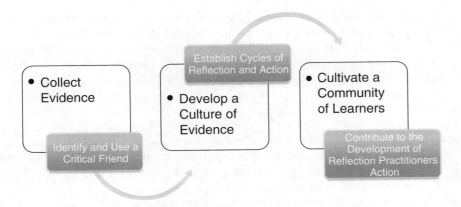

Figure 7.2 Critical concepts in empowerment evaluation

effective and accomplish its objectives. Empowerment evaluations are conducted by program participants and staff members. An empowerment evaluator is a critical friend helping to facilitate the process, rather than an external expert controlling it.

A culture of evidence is created by asking people why they believe what they believe. They are asked for evidence or documentation at every stage so that it becomes normal and expected to have data to support one's opinions and views. Cycles of reflection and action consist of the process of using evaluation data to think about program practices and then using the data to inform decision making, for example implementing new strategies, eliminating ineffective ones, and so on. The concept emphasizes the cyclical nature of the process, rather than a unilinear approach. Data are continually fed into the decision-making system with the understanding that the program is dynamic, not static, and will require continual feedback as the program changes and evolves (and periodically stabilizes). Once program changes are made, those too are monitored and evaluated. Empowerment evaluation is successful when it is institutionalized and becomes a normal part of the planning and management of the program, rather than a separate and parasitic entity operating in a "parallel universe." Once institutionalized the cycle of reflection and action is complete because it creates a continual routinized organizational feedback loop.

Empowerment evaluations facilitate an existing community of learners and cultivate new ones. This is critical to an accreditation effort because accrediting agencies are looking for wide-spread faculty, student, and staff member involvement in curricular development, review, and refinement. Empowerment evaluation is driven by the group by design. The group learns from each other, serving as their own peer review group, critical friend, resource, and norming mechanism. A community of learners is reinforcing, not dissimilar from successful weight reduction programs, which rely on peer group pressure. The groups have values held in common and hold each other accountable concerning progress toward stated goals. A community of learners also helps focus the group and keep it on track. Finally, empowerment evaluations produce and then rely on reflective practitioners. Program participants and staff members learn to use data to inform their decisions and actions concerning their own daily activities. This produces a self-aware and self-actualized individual who has the capacity to apply this worldview to all aspects of their life.

Steps

There are many ways in which to conduct an empowerment evaluation. Wanderman uses a 10-step model (Fisher, Chinman, Imm, Wandersman, & Hong, 2006). Fetterman (2001) typically uses a

3-step model. The three-step approach was adopted in both of the case examples presented in this discussion. The faculty, staff members, and students were asked to come up with their: (1) mission, (2) take stock of where they were, and (3) plan for the future. The mission consisted of value statements about their dream or ultimate goals. Taking stock had two parts: (1) prioritizing the list of activities they were engaged in; and (2) rating how well they were doing in each area. After engaging in a dialogue about the ratings and providing evidence for the ratings, the group developed their own plans for the future. That consisted of: (1) goals (associated with the activities evaluated), (2) strategies to accomplish the goals, and (3) credible evidence to document that the strategies were implemented and were successful. A second "taking stock" session was conducted six months later to compare the initial baseline taking stock ratings with a second taking stock exercise. The implemented strategies were monitored to determine if they were effective or if they needed to be replaced, allowing for mid-course corrections as needed. The second taking stock exercise was conducted after enough time had elapsed for group members to implement the new intervention (or plans for the future) and receive feedback on the implementation effort.

Two concrete and purposely different types of schools have been selected to demonstrate the value of empowerment evaluation in accreditation. The first is a progressive, rigorous, and spiritually oriented school and the second is an innovative medical school in a tier-one academic research university.

Case Example: California Institute of Integral Studies

The California Institute of Integral Studies (CIIS) is an independent accredited graduate school located in San Francisco. CIIS combines mainstream academic standards with a spiritual orientation. It has three schools: the School of Professional Psychology, the School of Consciousness and Transformation, and the School of Undergraduate Studies. It adopted an empowerment evaluation approach to prepare for an accreditation site visit. All units, including academic and administrative departments, conducted self-evaluations of their programs. Workshops were conducted to train chairs, deans, and the president on how to facilitate the process in their own areas. They developed their own mission (or sub-mission statements), prioritized the list of activities they were engaged in so that they could then select 10 to rate or evaluate. Then each member of the group evaluated each activity, rating the activities on a 1 (low) to 10 (high) scale. Individual ratings were combined to produce a group rating for each activity and one for the entire group's effort for their program. They engaged in a discussion about the ratings and assessments and then established a plan for the future (or intervention) based on their assessments. The plans for the future included specific goals, strategies, and evidence and the group monitored their strategies to determine if they were effective and helping them accomplish their objectives.

As shown in Figure 7.3, they rated themselves highly on a 10-point scale in the following categories: teaching (7.4), curriculum development (7.4), and experimental pedagogy (8). This appeared reasonable because it was a school devoted to teaching, innovation, and experimentation. Conversely, they rated themselves low in the following areas: scholarship (5.5), research (5.8), and diversity (5.4). The documentation was straightforward in both cases (e.g., student evaluations of courses, external site visit reports, record of research and publications, and numbers of students, faculty, and staff of color).

Collecting the data (with a more focused purpose in mind) helped to contribute to a culture of evidence. Discussing the data provided members with an opportunity to establish norms concerning the meaning of terms and ratings. These ratings and discussions represented one of the first baselines established in the Institute, allowing for additional data point comparisons over time.

They used this self-evaluation data to help create a strategic plan or plan for the future, which included building on strengths, such as teaching, and making a concerted effort to improve their

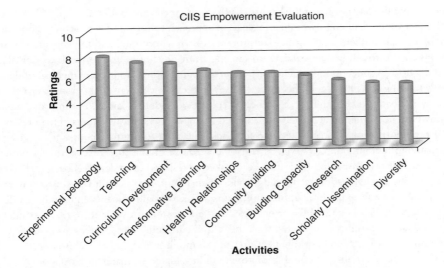

Figure 7.3 CIIS example of "taking stock" ratings

efforts in the areas of research and scholarship. They established specific goals and timelines. The dialogue was synergistic. They decided to pursue the scholarship of teaching, specifically combining their experimental pedagogy with their collaborative research. This is in alignment with the Carnegie Foundation for the Advancement of Teaching recommendation. This fusion of teaching and research prepared the groundwork for publications about their practice, including professional association presentations, articles, and books in a new area of inquiry, for example synergistic inquiry (Tang & Joiner, 2006). The process of evaluation, self-reflection, and action or cycles of reflection and action also produced significant curricular changes ranging from expanding the online component of the school to discontinuing one of its Ph.D. programs.

Concerning the Ph.D. program, the viability of the program had been a significant concern for many years. Students stated they were not getting sufficient faculty member attention. Faculty members were dedicated to the students and the program, however, they complained of burn-out. The empowerment evaluation process gave them a tool to analyze the faculty-to-student ratios and dissertation loads in a nonthreatening and unemotional manner. The answer to the conundrum was simple: there weren't enough faculty members to serve the number of graduate students in the program. It was a disservice to faculty and students to continue the program in its format and size at that time. An executive decision by the faculty and student body was made to close the program. This was a significant measure of internal accountability displayed by the institution.

The Provost institutionalized this process by requiring self-evaluations and unit plans on an annual basis to facilitate program improvement and contribute to institutional accountability. The seeds of this empowerment evaluation effort were sown in this school and adopted again many years later in the school's development, providing guidance on the future growth of its Somatic Program.

Case Example: Stanford University School of Medicine

The School of Medicine at Stanford University is one of the most highly rated medical schools in the United States, combining biomedical research with clinical education and information technology. It provides pre-clinical academic training, clerkship rotations in hospital settings, and an opportunity to explore scholarly concentrations (a mini-scholastic program designed to help students inquire about a specific medical area of research in more depth during medical school training). The School of Medicine also adopted an empowerment evaluation approach to prepare for its accreditation site visit. It involved stakeholders in an egalitarian process of review, critique, and improvement. The approach was used throughout the curriculum ranging from preclinical course work to clerkship rotations and scholarly concentrations. The purpose of the curriculum is to prepare medical students for residency training and practice. Concerning coursework, empowerment evaluation was particularly effective in creating a community of learners, a culture of evidence, and course improvement.

An empowerment evaluation approach was adopted changing five critical features of the previous process: (a) the information was collected and fed back to faculty (using mid-course focus groups and accompanying memorandum, as well as end-of-the-course online student evaluations with a minimum of an 80% response rate); (b) faculty were asked to respond to student feedback (collected and summarized by the evaluation team) and provide their own insights about the course separate from the students' views; (c) the evaluation team, course directors, and students entered into a dialogue about the findings facilitated by a critical friend (the Director of Evaluation); (d) the student assessments and faculty insights were shared with the school curriculum committees, to help build a larger community of learners and positive peer pressure to monitor and improve performance; and (e) the new strategies were implemented, monitored, and evaluated to maintain an ongoing cycle of reflection and action. This process had a dramatic impact on the quality of instruction, curricular coordination, and student ratings. In addition, the empowerment evaluation process provided faculty and students with an opportunity to collaborate between courses, improving the logical sequencing of courses and removing unintended redundancies. Empowerment evaluation helped faculty and students identify and address broader cross-cutting curricular issues.

For example, the Cells to Tissues course, a required course in the curriculum, had very low ratings which were steadily declining year after year (see Figure 7.4). The reason for the decline was that, to the extent that evaluative data were collected, the communication about the findings and recommendations was unilinear or one-way. The information was collected but rarely compiled. When it was compiled it was simply sent to the faculty and focused exclusively on student assessments of their courses. Course directors and students applied the empowerment evaluation approach to this course and engaged as a community of learners. They reviewed evaluation findings and produced viable

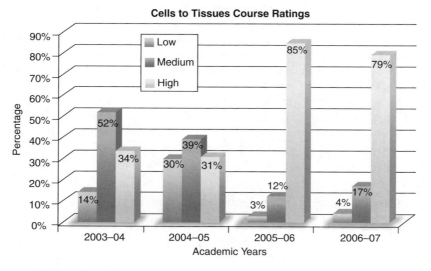

Figure 7.4 Cells to Tissues course ratings

options to respond to problems and build upon their successes. The same course ratings changed 180 degrees in one year, based on the feedback, exchange, dialogue, and action.

The same approach was used in the clerkships with similar success. For example, the obstetrics/gynecology clerkship received low student ratings and requested empowerment evaluation assistance (see Figure 7.5). The critical friend or coach facilitated the process and the faculty and students identified specific weaknesses in the curriculum and instruction. They also revised their curriculum, clarifying goals and expectations. They also improved their orientation and tutorial training modules. Student ratings of "very good/excellent" increased by 26%. (See Fetterman, 2009, for details about empowerment evaluation applied to clerkships.)

Empowerment evaluation was also used to reinvigorate the Scholarly Concentrations program. In the middle of the "taking stock" discussion and dialogue, a debate arose focusing on governance and authority. One half of the group thought they needed to take charge and begin to make policy, establish standards, and enforce existing policies. The other half did not think they had the authority to make any changes or enforce any pre-existing program requirements. This led to a stalemate in which little could be done with the scholarly concentration program. The dialogue component of the process positioned an intellectual spotlight on this "conceptual elephant in the middle of the room." It led to a review of the bylaws of the school, clearly designating the directors with the authority to create and modify program policy. The scholarly concentration directors realized they were all in charge of the program and could move forward with specific policy recommendations. The rating scales were used as a launching point in order to engage the group in an extended dialogue, as well as the baseline in which to measure future changes. The empowerment evaluation approach created an environment conducive to empowerment (no one can empower anyone but themselves). The scholarly concentration directors came to the conclusion that they were in charge of the program (a fundamental governance finding), which enabled them to make critical programmatic decisions. Previous to this epiphany, the directors were unable to make decisions concerning critical facets of the program. The insight was liberating and empowering. It also enabled the program to grow and approximate its goals.

Finally, a comparison of student ratings across the medical school curriculum before and after conducting an empowerment evaluation (see Figure 7.6) revealed a statistically significant improvement ($p = .04$; Student's 1-sample t-test). The results of this study are discussed in detail in Fetterman, Deitz, and Gesundheit (2010).

External metrics were also used to measure the effectiveness of empowerment evaluation on the curriculum, including United States Medical Licensing Examinations (focusing on clinical knowl-

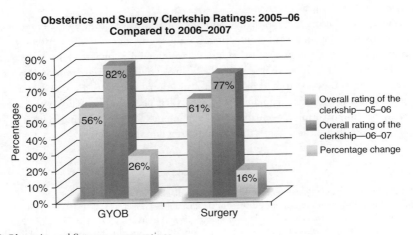

Figure 7.5 Obstetrics and Surgery course ratings

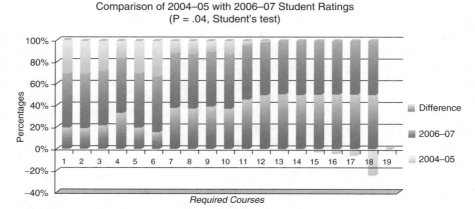

Figure 7.6 School of Medicine course ratings across the required curriculum

edge and clinical skills) as well as student/alumni performance in their first postgraduate year of residency training (Residency Director's Assessment of Clinical Performance). The aggregate measures indicate that student education was maintained at a high level or enhanced by the new curriculum and corresponding empowerment evaluation process used to refine it.

Conclusion

Empowerment evaluation was successful in helping both schools become re-accredited. In the process of applying this approach, the faculty, staff members, students, and administration became engaged in cycles of reflection and action about their own institutions. Faculty engagement made it more meaningful and fostered a sense of ownership concerning the data and the approach. There was more buy-in because the findings and recommendations were their own. They conducted the self-evaluation within the context of what the accrediting agency was holding them accountable for (the self-assessment was not conducted in a vacuum). On the surface, the approach helped people group together to tackle common curricular and administrative problems. On a deeper level, empowerment evaluation helped them coalesce as a collective agent of curricular and administrative change. The result was empowering.

External teams were also invited to review both schools. However, they were invited as additional critical friends (within the context of conducting an empowerment evaluation), providing a strategic consultation, rather than a compliance or traditional accountability review. This demonstrated how internal and external evaluations are not mutually exclusive; rather they are reinforcing and enhance each other, as long as they are rooted in internal institutional concerns. Empowerment evaluation provides educational institutions with an approach that balances accountability with a commitment to improvement. Empowerment evaluation is in alignment with the evolving culture of education and educational assessment throughout the United States and the world.

References

Argyris, C. (1999). *On organizational learning*. Malden, MA: Blackwell Business.
Fetterman, D. M. (1994). Empowerment evaluation. *Evaluation Practice, 15*(1), 1–15.
Fetterman, D. M. (2001). *Foundations of empowerment evaluation*. Thousand Oaks, CA: Sage.
Fetterman, D. M. (2005a). A window into the heart and soul of empowerment evaluation: looking through the

lens of empowerment evaluation principles. In D. M. Fetterman, & A. Wandersman (Eds.), *Empowerment evaluation principles in practice* (pp. 1–26). New York, NY: Guilford Press.

Fetterman, D. M. (2005b). Empowerment evaluation: From the digital divide to academic distress. In D. M. Fetterman, & A. Wandersman (Eds.), *Empowerment evaluation principles in practice* (pp. 92–122). New York, NY: Guilford Press.

Fetterman, D. M. (2009). Empowerment evaluation at the Stanford University School of Medicine: Using a critical friend to improve the clerkship experience. *Ensaio: Avaliação e Políticas Públicas em Educação, 17*(63), 197–204.

Fetterman, D. M., Deitz, J., & Gesundheit, N. (2010). Empowerment evaluation: A collaborative approach to evaluating and transforming a medical school curriculum. *Academic Medicine, 85*(5).

Fetterman, D.M. and Wandersman, A. (Eds.). (2005). *Empowerment evaluation principles in practice*. New York, NY: Guilford Press.

Fisher, D., Chinman, M., Imm, P., Wandersman, A., & Hong, K. (2006). *Getting to outcomes with developmental assets: Ten steps to measuring youth programs and communities*. Minneapolis, MN: Search Institute.

Rogoff, B., Matusov, E., & White, C. (1998). *Models of teaching and learning: Participation in a community of learners*. London, UK: Blackwell.

Senge, P. (1990). *The fifth discipline: The art and practice of organizational learning*. New York, NY: Doubleday.

Tang, Y. & Joiner, C. (Eds.). (2006). *Synergic inquiry: A collaborative action methodology*. Thousand Oaks, CA: Sage.

Wandersman, A., Snell-Johns, J., Lentz, B., Fetterman, D. M., Keener, D., Livet, M., Imm, P., & Flaspohler, P. (2005). The principles of empowerment evaluation. In D. M. Fetterman, & A. Wandersman (Eds.). *Empowerment evaluation principles in practice* (pp. 27–41). New York, NY: Guilford Press.

8

BENCHMARKING IN HIGHER EDUCATION

Jeffrey A. Seybert, Ellen J. Weed, and Trudy H. Bers

Higher education institutions have, in the last 10–20 years, come under increasing pressure from their various constituents to assess student learning outcomes and institutional effectiveness to facilitate continuous improvement of institutional programs, policies, and practices. A major component of these improvement initiatives is the ability to compare one's institution with similar peers. In fact, several regional accrediting organizations have introduced accreditation processes that either require or strongly suggest the use of comparative data from peer institutions. For example, the North Central Association of Colleges and Schools Higher Learning Commission offers institutions under its aegis the option of participating in an alternative quality improvement accreditation initiative known as the Academic Quality Improvement Program (AQIP). A major component of AQIP requires the institution to create a "Systems Portfolio." In each section (or category) of that Systems Portfolio, the institution must respond to the following question: "How do your results for performance of your processes for . . . compare with the performance results of other higher education organizations?" In other words, the AQIP process mandates that participating colleges and universities collect and report comparable data from peer institutions regarding each of the nine sections of the Systems Portfolio. This process of collecting data from like institutions for the purposes of comparison is generally referred to as "benchmarking" and is the focus of this chapter. The chapter is divided into three major sections: this introduction which defines benchmarking more formally and elaborates on its role in higher education, examples of benchmarking tools and processes available to colleges and universities, and a concluding section dealing with some of the challenges facing higher education institutions as they attempt to use benchmarks for comparison and improvement.

Benchmarking Defined

General definitions of benchmarking vary depending on the *definer's* perspective. According to Jackson and Lund (2000) benchmarking involves comparing organizational or industry practices, performance, and processes to improve the principal organization or business. Similarly, Bender and Schuh (2002) define benchmarking as a process of comparison for purposes of assessment and innovation. In their terms, assessment involves comparison of one's own organizational activities with those of similar other organizations to provide a context in which to measure outcomes and activities while innovation involves comparisons with peers to obtain new ideas to facilitate major change. Running through each of these conceptions of benchmarking is the theme of comparison with characteristics of similar peer organizations for purposes of institutional improvement.

Types of Benchmarking

For the purposes of this discussion, there are two major typologies of benchmarking: general benchmarking and benchmarking in higher education. According to Yarrow and Prabhu (1999), there are three types of general benchmarking: performance or metric, diagnostic, and process. Performance benchmarking is the simplest of the three and involves straightforward comparison of institutional characteristics and performance data. Diagnostic benchmarking characterizes an institution's performance status in relation to peers. It is used to identify areas for improvement. Performance benchmarking can be utilized as the initial step in diagnostic benchmarking. Process benchmarking is the most complicated, expensive, and time consuming of the three types. It involves identification of "best practices" in one or more "aspirational" peers for the purpose of developing specific improvement strategies. Usually this means sending a team of college employees to the identified peer institutions to conduct in-depth interviews or focus groups to identify the educational practices that underlie the peers' performance data. These practices may then be adopted or modified for use as improvement initiatives in the original institution.

Similarly, Upcraft and Schuh (1996) have identified three types of higher education benchmarking; internal, generic, and competitive. Internal benchmarking involves making comparisons between units within the institution. Depending on circumstances, this can sometimes be an effective aid to planning and budgeting and sometimes, when it pits units against each other, it can be disruptive.

Generic benchmarking is used to make comparisons between institutions that share similar organizational practices and procedures. Most of the initiatives identified in the "Benchmarking Tools and Processes" that follow are generally used in generic benchmarking situations.

The third type of higher education benchmarking, known as competitive benchmarking, is used to make comparisons between institutions that are direct competitors. Competitive benchmarking is usually difficult to accomplish, since competing institutions quite often attempt to hide or otherwise mask organizational data that might give them a competitive advantage, or, conversely, put them at a competitive disadvantage.

A Note about "Benchmarking" vs. "Benchmarks"

As is clear from the above discussion, benchmarking focuses on processes rather than products. Benchmarking involves activities such as tracing the way in which an institution moves students through inquiry to application to admission to orientation to registration, for example. Benchmarking—emphasis on the '*ing*'—can also be understood as the array of activities required to compile comparable data about a subject and discussing the findings. In essence, benchmarking involves identifying a variable or set of variables of interest, and then establishing a referent institution or group of institutions, and making comparisons of those variables within that referent group.

Benchmarks, on the other hand, are metrics or standards such as numbers or percentages. The emphasis here is on the product—the number—and how one institution's number compares with its own target, with peer institutions, or with the starting point from which improvement is desired. For example, a developmental math department might look at the percent of students who place into and then successfully complete the first developmental math course, compared to the same datum for peer institutions and for itself over time. Essentially, then, benchmarks are the "variables" identified above—the actual measurements used in the benchmarking process.

Benchmarking Tools: A Sample of What is Available

An increasing number of national tools have become available for colleges and universities, providing benchmarking capability for a range of variables. This section begins with descriptions of several of these tools, some in greater detail than others. Where available, URL links are provided should readers want additional information. It must be noted that this is not meant to be an exhaustive listing of all benchmarking tools available to colleges and universities in the U.S. Rather, it should be viewed as a representative sample of what institutions may find as they search for appropriate benchmarking tools.

Several of these tools measure varying aspects of student perceptions. Characteristics of three of the most widely used surveys of student perceptions—the ACT Student Opinion Survey, the Community College Survey of Student Engagement (CCSSE), and the Noel-Levitz Student Satisfaction Survey—are summarized below. All three of these tools provide options to the institution and include large national databases that enable benchmarking with confidence.

ACT Student Opinion Surveys

The ACT Student Opinion Surveys include multiple surveys designed specifically for two-year colleges. There are surveys for target populations including adult learners, entering students, alumni, and non-returning students. ACT also offers surveys that assess opinions about specific college services such as academic advising or financial aid. The college can, in most cases, add its own questions to the standardized questions and can also invite comments and suggestions from students. Most ACT surveys can be administered in paper/pencil or Web-based format. The ACT surveys take 20–25 minutes to complete and the administering college has several options about the reports it receives, including normative data reports to use for benchmarking. These reports compare the data from the individual college with data from other colleges that have used the survey. Sample surveys and additional information are available at http://act.org/ess/survey_college_two.html.

Community College Survey of Student Engagement

The Community College Survey of Student Engagement (CCSSE) measures the extent to which students in community colleges are engaged in the life of the campus. CCSSE has identified five benchmarks, each including a cluster of individual items, which are major indicators of the colleges' success in engaging its students. The benchmarks are:

- Active and Collaborative Learning;
- Student Effort;
- Academic Challenge;
- Student-Faculty Interaction; and
- Support for Learners.

The CCSSE requires about 30 minutes to complete and can be administered in paper/pencil or Web-based format. The administering college receives a report that allows comparison of college data with the national database and also with other peer groups of CCSSE participants. Data are provided separately for full-time and part-time students, and for students who have completed more or less than 24 SCH (student credit hours). Each year the CCSSE includes questions about a special focus area—technology in 2009 and deep learning in 2010. Interactive peer analysis is available to all member colleges at http://www.ccsse.org. The CCSSE website provides sample surveys and a wealth of resources and research about the importance of student engagement for student success and retention. CCSSE also offers a faculty survey and the Survey of Entering Students Engagement (SENSE). SENSE assesses students' engagement in the college campus during the first three weeks of their first semester.

Noel-Levitz

Noel-Levitz offers a variety of surveys with multiple scales for assessing the perceptions of enrolled college and university students. Specific target population surveys include the adult learner and online learners. The comprehensive Student Satisfaction Survey has 12 scales on topics such as the effectiveness of acdemic advising, instruction, admissions, financial aid, and registration. There is also a companion to the Student Satisfaction Survey for faculty and staff. The Noel-Levitz surveys require 15–20 minutes to complete and can be administered in a paper/pencil or Web-based format. Noel-Levitz publishes an annual *National Student Satisfaction and Priorities Report* to use for benchmarking purposes. Conferences and consulting opportunities on a variety of college recruiting and success issues are available through Noel-Levitz. The website at http://www.noellevitz.com includes information about available services and sample surveys.

Integrated Postsecondary Education Data System

In addition to these three survey measures of student satisfaction, benchmarking tools are now available for the Integrated Postsecondary Education Data System (IPEDS). IPEDS is the largest single database in higher education since it includes all postsecondary education providers of Title IV funds in the United States. The IPEDS surveys include institutional-level benchmarking opportunities on enrollment, program completion, faculty and staff, and financial indicators at the institutional level. An individual institution can establish one or more peer groups, either by name or institutional characteristic, and make interactive comparisons at the IPEDS website on a number of institutional measures, including student financial aid, finances, admissions, and enrollments. Trend data comparisons are also available. The Executive Peer Tool makes it easy to benchmark on the most commonly requested indicators and in-depth comparisons are also possible at http://www.nces.ed.gov/ipeds/datacenter.

Individual Development and Educational Assessment Center

One tool offered through the Individual Development and Educational Assessment (IDEA) Center at http://www.theideacenter.org is an instrument for the student evaluation of instruction. The instrument provides faculty members with feedback at the course level about the progress their students believe they have made on course objectives considered important by the faculty member. The course-level analysis that the instructor receives for each course includes comparative data for the individual course, the college as a whole, the IDEA database of 44,500 courses, and IDEA database courses in the faculty member's discipline. IDEA has also initiated an *IDEA Benchmarking for Learning Report* that analyzes responses of individual students. This report allows colleges to benchmark their student ratings against the entire IDEA database, those with the same Carnegie classification code, and those of a peer group of 6–10 similar colleges from the IDEA database.

Voluntary System of Accountability

The Voluntary System of Accountability (VSA), developed by the Association of Public and Land-Grant Universities (APLU) and the Association of State Colleges and Universities (AASCU), concentrates on consumer information related to undergraduate education in three broad areas: consumer information, student experiences and perceptions, and student learning outcomes (see http://www.voluntarysystem.org). A similar project designed for community colleges, the Voluntary Framework for Accountability (VFA), funded by the Lumina and Gates foundations, is under development as of this writing.

National Study of Instructional Costs and Productivity

The National Study of Instructional Costs and Productivity (also known as the Delaware Study) focuses on four-year college and university faculty workloads and instructional costs by department and faculty type (e.g., tenure/tenure track, teaching assistant, other) and permits participating institutions to compare their workloads and costs (see http://www.udel.edu/IR/cost/).

American Productivity and Quality Center—Open Standards Benchmarking Collaborative

The American Productivity and Quality Center provides its Open Standards Benchmarking Collaborative[SM] (OSBC) research process. The OSBC database contains over 1,200 performance metrics across multiple business functions and includes data from more than 7,000 global submissions, allowing participating institutions to compare their operations and outcomes to peers worldwide (www.apqc.org).

Council of Independent Colleges—Key Indicators Tool

The Council of Independent Colleges (CIC) Key Indicators Tool (KIT) provides a customized benchmarking report for each CIC member institution with 20 indicators of institutional performance in four key areas: (1) student enrollment and progression, (2) faculty, (3) tuition revenue and financial aid, and (4) financial resources and expenditures. Institutional performance is benchmarked by regional and national comparisons over a five-year trend (www.cic.org).

The Institute for College Access and Success—College Insight Project

The College Insight project of the Institute for College Access and Success provides user-friendly profiles with detailed information for almost 5,000 U.S. colleges and universities, and aggregates data to provide indicators of college affordability, diversity, and student success on campus to policymakers and the public. It also can create totals and averages for states, types of schools, and other groupings (www.ticas.org).

Benchmarking tools, such as those summarized above, are essential for both internal and external accountability in colleges and universities. They are useful for planning and decision making at the campus level and for accreditation documentation and reporting to external organizations.

Working With Benchmarking Tools: An Institutional Example

An ongoing source of frustration for virtually all institutional researchers is the lack of institutional use of the data and information we generate. It is therefore instructive (and gratifying) when we find instances of in-depth use of such data/information resources. What follows is a prime example of just this kind of in-depth incorporation of benchmark data in major academic operations. And, while quite detailed, it provides an excellent case study of the degree to which such data and information can have an institutional impact. Specifically, the remainder of this section will focus on ways in which two benchmarking tools have been used extensively in one institution (Nashville State Community College, NSCC) for planning, budgeting, management decision making, and to support accreditation processes.

Kansas Study of Community College Instructional Costs and Productivity

The Kansas Study of Community College Instructional Costs and Productivity was designed and implemented as a community college analog to the Delaware study. Kansas Study data are uniquely useful for staffing plans and decisions about faculty positions, for academic program planning and assessment, and for documentation of compliance for accreditation purposes. The unique advantage of the Kansas Study is its discipline-level unit of analysis. The Kansas Study provides four basic variables at the discipline level:

- Percentage of student credit hours (SCH) taught by full-time faculty members and by adjunct faculty;
- Faculty productivity for full-time and adjunct faculty, defined as SCH/FTE faculty;
- Student/Faculty ratio, a proxy for class size defined as FTE students/FTE faculty; and
- Direct cost of instruction, defined cost/SCH for each discipline.

Planning for optimal faculty staffing

The annual Kansas Study data enable a college to easily compare itself with the aggregate of all Kansas Study institutions. For example, are the student/faculty ratios of most college programs in line with the national averages? What about the costs/SCH and full-time teaching percentages? What percent of a college's programs are above/below the national student/faculty ratio? Is this basically consistent over time? An individual college can also compare itself with selected peer groups, in real time, by going to the project website: http://www.kansasstudy.org. If a particular college has math costs that look out of line compared to the total Kansas Study average math costs, these costs can be compared to only urban schools, or only schools within a similar enrollment range, or selected specific colleges. This ability to easily make comparisons with peer groups can add credibility and precision to the data.

These discipline-level data also allow a college to easily benchmark itself with all Kansas Study participants for each discipline. This allows a college to easily identify "outlier" disciplines on one or more variables and to develop plans aimed at correcting staffing or cost issues in that discipline. NSCC, for example, targets for special attention any discipline which falls below 90% or above 110% of the Kansas Study average for three consecutive years on any of the basic Kansas Study variables. Using this range and time frame, the college can then concentrate on the outlier disciplines. If, for example, business faculty productivity is below the 90% average for three or more consecutive years, it may be time to consider an increase in the maximum class size or to offer fewer sections. If 56% of biology sections are taught by full-time faculty, compared to a national average of 69%, biology should have priority for reallocation of an available faculty position. If 84% of business courses are taught by full-time faculty, compared to a national average of 66%, this suggests a possible source for reallocating a position.

The percentage SCH taught by full-time faculty, student/faculty ratio, and cost of instruction in a discipline are typically interrelated. As the percent of SCH taught by adjunct faculty increases, and as the student/faculty ratio increases, cost of instruction declines. Any exceptions to this pattern probably merit attention. For example, what is the explanation for a computer drafting program with full-time faculty percentages and student/faculty ratios that are within 10% of the Kansas Study average, but costs that are 60% above that average? Explanations might include the particular mix of courses being offered and the salaries of those faculty.

The most valuable application of Kansas Study data for academic administrators at the college and department levels is its value in making, explaining, and supporting decisions about faculty staffing. Without comparative data at the discipline level, decisions about the assignment of full-time faculty may not reflect some realities in that discipline area. The availability of qualified, willing, afford-able adjunct faculty members varies greatly across disciplines, meaning that it may be "normal" to employ 14% adjunct faculty in automotive technology and 52% in philosophy. Without some external benchmarks, however, academic leaders lack such information. Using the 90%–110% range as "normal" over a period of time, it is possible to identify which discipline areas are comparatively overstaffed or understaffed in terms of full-time faculty, and to develop a staffing plan for making adjustments over time. Similarly, the Kansas Study student/faculty ratio data can suggest the pos-sibility of making adjustments to class size, either by offering fewer/more sections of a course or by changing the maximum class size

Planning and assessing programs

Kansas Study data are useful for planning new career programs. Especially in the current economic situation, colleges must set priorities and establish new programs with great care. Kansas Study data can, in combination with local employment data, guide these decisions with information about the expected cost and faculty requirements for a new program. NSCC, for example, used the six years of national Kansas Study data to compare anticipated costs and staffing needs when considering the possibility of implementing two new programs.

Academic program evaluation/review processes typically include a self-study that includes infor-mation about staffing and cost. Including Kansas Study data in these program reviews enhances the value of the process by making it possible for program administrators and faculty to not only look at trends within their own program, but also compare themselves with other community colleges and to set benchmarks for future change where appropriate. The ability to identify peer groups composed of similar colleges within the Kansas Study database allows even greater precision in benchmarking. For example, a review of the general education program at NSCC resulted in the requirement that full-time faculty members in math and English teach more sections of develop-mental courses than was previously the case. Moving to parity so that equal percentages of devel-opmental and college-level SCH are taught by full-time faculty members was considered ideal, but impractical because of the greater availability of qualified adjuncts at the developmental levels. For that reason, the benchmark percentages for full-time faculty members are higher for college-level than for developmental courses.

Documentation for accreditation compliance

Kansas Study data proved useful for documenting compliance with several SACS standards during NSCC's 2008 reaffirmation process.

- SACS Principle 2.8 requires the college to document that the "number of full-time faculty members is adequate to support the mission of the institution" and SACS requires this infor-mation at the discipline level in order to demonstrate compliance. Kansas Study data on the percentage of SCH taught by full-time faculty at the discipline level is ideal documentation for this standard.
- SACS Principle 2.11 requires the college to demonstrate that it "has a sound financial base." NSCC could document its direct instructional expenditures by discipline area in a readable and straightforward table that allowed comparison with Kansas Study database benchmarks. Where a discipline area was out of line with the Kansas Study averages, a brief explanation was included.
- SACS Principle 3.4.9 requires documentation of appropriate academic support services. The largest support service program at NSCC is the Developmental Studies program. The Kansas

Study data enabled us to clearly and easily document that the college compares well with other community colleges in terms of full-time faculty teaching in developmental studies, average class size, and cost of delivering developmental education.

The availability of Kansas Study data saved the college significant time and effort in putting together this documentation. The data offered the important added benefit of comparative data so the college could benchmark itself against other similar institutions.

National Community College Benchmark Project

The National Community College Benchmark Project (NCCBP) collects and reports institutional-level data on approximately 130 benchmarks covering all important aspects of community college programming, practices, and outcomes. Campus-level benchmarking applications for the NCCBP differ from the Kansas Study applications in both depth and breadth. The college is the unit of analysis for NCCBP, limiting the ability to drill down to the discipline level in most cases. The NCCBP does, however, provide benchmarks down to the course level for key core and developmental courses. The NCCBP also spans a broad array of indicators commonly used by community colleges for both internal and external accountability purposes. NSCC uses NCCBP data to set benchmarks for the college strategic plan, to document student success, and to comply with SACS accreditation.

Planning for strategically important areas

NSCC is currently developing its strategic plan for 2011–2015. The plan will identify and benchmark indicators that are strategically important to the college at the campus level and/or required by external agencies, particularly the Tennessee Board of Regents and the Tennessee Higher Education Commission.

NCCBP data are critical in both areas. An overall review of NCCBP data can quickly identify indicators on which a college differs significantly from the NCCBP database. Such indicators can be identified by examining the college's percentile rank on a given set of benchmarks compared to the database and/or by comparing the college value to the median for the entire NCCBP database. This initial review identifies any "outliers." Some outliers may be explainable and some may not be important to the college. Others, however, may be strategically important. Examination of relevant NCCBP data leads to several conclusions for the college in terms of completion/transfer:

- NSCC's completion/transfer rate for full-time students should be a strategic target for study and attention.
- Tennessee community colleges as a group lag well behind the NCCBP rates. This may suggest the wisdom of system-wide initiatives. NCCBP urban colleges far lag behind non-urban colleges, suggesting that the college should use an urban peer group for setting benchmarks on this indicator.
- NSCC is much more successful with part-time students (63% of the student body), since they complete or transfer at the NCCBP median and above the urban college and Tennessee medians.
- The 2011–2015 strategic plan should establish improvement benchmarks for NSCC student completion and transfer, using urban peers. The current political climate emphasizing completion will require such benchmarks.

Measuring student success

NCCBP data offer multiple measures of student success at both the course and college levels. These indicators are used for campus purposes, for external reporting, and for accreditation documentation. NCCBP collects information on the percentage of all enrollees who complete a course, all enrollees who succeed (earn a grade of A, B, or C) in a course, and all completers who succeed in a course for:

- The aggregate of all college-level credit courses;
- The aggregate of all distance learning courses;
- Remedial/developmental math, reading, and writing courses;
- College-level math and writing courses for remedial/developmental completers; and
- English Composition I, English Composition II, College Algebra, and Speech courses for all students.

These figures are already available on many campuses. The advantage of the NCCBP data is that a college can compare and benchmark its students' success. For each of these indicators, the benchmark report includes not only the NCCBP database median, but also the figures at the 10th, 25th, 75th, and 90th percentile for the entire NCCBP database. This percentile information makes benchmarking easy.

NCCBP student success indicators also provide data at the college level. These college-wide indicators are invaluable for compiling and explaining data to various external stakeholders, including state agencies, governing boards, and college advisory committees. These indicators include:

- Next-term and fall-to-fall persistence rates;
- Three-year completion and transfer rates;
- GPA for first year at the transfer institution;
- Number of credit hours earned at the transfer institution;
- Year two persistence at the transfer institution;
- Related employment of career program completers;
- Continuing education of career program completers; and
- Employer satisfaction with career program completers.

Documentation for accreditation compliance

NSCC found multiple uses for NCCBP local and comparative information during its 2008 reaffirmation documentation. For example:

- SACS Principle 3.4.9 requires appropriate academic support services. Several years of student pass rates at or above the NCCBP median in developmental courses, and in college-level courses for developmental completers, made a strong case for the success of this academic support program.
- SACS Principle 3.3.1 requires the college to identify expected student outcomes and to assess the extent to which degree graduates achieve those outcomes. The transfer rates and transfer first-year GPA provide this documentation for transfer degree students. For career degree and certificate completers, the percent of graduates who found related employment or pursued additional education provided good evidence. In both cases, the college could provide the success rates of NSCC graduates, document how these rates compared with community college peers, and set benchmarks based on a national standard.

Challenges of Benchmarks

The perspective taken in this section is that of benchmarks as bases of comparison with other institutions rather than as institutional measures taken at one point in time that can then be compared with measures of the same variable at subsequent points in time. The former can be referred to as inter-institutional benchmarks, and the latter as intra-institutional benchmarks. Intra-institutional benchmarks are easier to compile. They demand that an institution collect and operationally define its data consistently over time—sometimes not as easy as it seems—but do not require cooperation across institutions in developing common definitions and data gathering processes. In this section the focus will be on the challenges of selecting, defining, collecting, comparing across systems and states, and using benchmarks for comparisons among institutions.

The Challenge of Selecting Benchmarks

The first challenge in developing an inter-institutional benchmark project is to come to agreement on indicators or variables. Depending on the nature of the project, existing reporting requirements already mandated within a system or state, and institutional ideas about what variables are important, coming to agreement on measures that appropriately reflect the subject of interest may be taxing. The more similar the mission and goals of an institution the more likely it is that a common set of indicators can be developed, but even here, the task is not easy. A simple example illustrates this point: graduation rates.

One of the few measures of student success reported by all Title IV institutions, the graduation rate is calculated as the percentage of first-time full-time students who complete a program within 150 percent of the time a full-time student enrolled in sequential semesters and successfully completing all courses in his original major would take. More simply put, think of a student pursuing a 120-semester credit bachelor's degree; we would expect a successful full-time student to complete the program in four years (15 credits per semester for eight semesters). For community College associate degrees, the 150 percent rule equates to three years for a 60 semester credit hour program.

Push back to the graduation rate as a meaningful measure of institutional effectiveness (graduating students) or student success (completing a degree) is rampant, especially at community colleges and four-year institutions that enroll academically underprepared, low income, commuter students. The reasons are many: students need remedial work that doesn't count toward the degree and use up time taking these courses; many degrees extend beyond 120 or 60 credits and therefore require more time than the traditional four or eight semesters; students who begin full-time don't necessarily continue as full-time students every term; full-time students change majors and as a result lose credits toward the degree and must take additional courses in their new major; and students transfer and thereby deny their first institutions the ability to 'claim' them as graduates.

The Challenge of Operationalizing Definitions

When institutions come to agreement on the measures to use as benchmarks, a second level of challenge presents itself, that of operationalizing the definitions; that is, articulating the precise way in which a value is calculated so that all institutions use the same algorithm and measure the same thing. In higher education, simple as a variable may seem, layers of complexity typically exist. Let's take a simple example: average class size. At first blush it seems easy to define and calculate. Divide the number of enrollments by the number of course sections. But, institutions use a variety of approaches in creating course schedules and course sections. How does one determine the class size of a lecture-discussion course when there are 500 students in large lectures and 20 students divided into 25 small group discussion sections? Is the class size 500 or 20? And consider a college that merges students in three courses of painting into the same studio at the same time, taught by the same instructor. If there are 8 students in each course, is the average class size 24 or is it 8? Even when conceptual agreement is reached, the mechanics of calculating class size can be daunting, particularly if manual manipulation of data is required to merge what appear on a student system as separate classes.

The Challenge of Collecting Data

Every college and university has multiple points of data entry, with individuals more or less cognizant of the importance of accuracy and policies that foster or inhibit data currency. With more self service options available to students, opportunities for typos or other errors abound, especially if they don't block students from moving forward with the transactions they seek to enact. Sometimes data entry is performed by the lowest paid, least trained institution employees—student workers—who fail to grasp the consequences of inaccurate data entry. Even regular employees frequently misunderstand or have no concept of the ways in which the data they enter into the system are used, and why accuracy is important.

Some institutions, especially those that pride themselves on ready access for students, are reluctant to place what they perceive as impediments or barriers in the way of students enrolling. Thus, for example, community colleges may not require students to update their programs of study each semester, carrying students in the program they identified when they first came to the college.

Inaccurate or out-of-date data are problematic for the institution itself, but particularly troublesome when they are used for benchmarks and comparisons. Imagine a situation where institutions believe they are comparing themselves on a measure, only to find the data are laden with errors, calcified in a history that is no longer representative of the college, and operationalized differently.

The Challenge of Comparing Across Systems and States

Even when institutions document and monitor how data are collected and verified, and when they have clear operational definitions to which they adhere, labor contracts and system requirements promote differences across institutions that weaken comparisons. For example, Minnesota and Massachusetts have statewide community college faculty contracts that limit an institution's ability to set salaries, benefits, and working conditions. Thus benchmarking faculty salaries or workloads at the institutional level may not be useful since a college has little flexibility.

Sometimes the existence of statewide or system wide policies or practices actually facilitates using benchmarks to compare. In the arena of developmental education, one of the challenges in comparing the success and progress of students from developmental through gateway courses in math and composition is that institutions use different placement tests, cut-off scores, and policies regarding advisory or mandatory placement and registration. In one institution, a student may need a score of 60 on the Compass algebra test to place out of developmental math, be barred from taking college level math until she reaches that Compass score, and be required to take developmental math within her first 12 credits. In another institution a student might need a score of only 45 to place out of developmental math, be advised to take developmental rather than college level math, and be able to avoid registering in either developmental or college level math until she chooses to do so. Students' math competencies (as measured in their Compass scores) and math course taking patterns may differ greatly between the two institutions, with the cut-off, placement and registration policies shaping students' progress and success as much if not more than the quality of teaching, the curriculum or academic support.

The Challenge of Using Benchmarks for Comparison

Using benchmarks for comparison purposes has several dimensions of challenge: technical, political and cultural. The technical dimension has been partly addressed above, in discussions of data definition and collection. Other aspects of the technical dimension include the capacity of an institution, especially a small one, to compile, store, and manipulate data. It is easy to take for granted that institutions have this capacity, but this is clearly not the case everywhere. In some states—North Carolina and Minnesota are examples—community colleges share a student data system. The ability of individual institutions, especially if they lack a skilled institutional researcher or information technology staff, to access and use data for purposes other than transactions and meeting state or federal reporting requirements, is marginal. One of the early findings of Achieving the Dream, a multi-state program to improve the success of community college students, was that more than a few participating colleges had little capacity to conduct even simple institutional research studies or to compile data to permit comparing across institutions. Many relied on their state systems to collect and produce indicators of student performance and institutional effectiveness.

The political dimension focuses more on the publication of benchmarks and the worry about consequences should benchmark values for a college decline. The furor over the *U.S. News and World Report* college rankings has diminished somewhat since they were first introduced, but even now some institutions worry greatly if they slip in the rankings. Though rare, occasional incidents of college leaders putting pressure on institutional researchers to submit data that will put the institution in a positive light have been reported. In the last few years calls for more accountability have prompted creation of institutional reports that, while not designed for benchmarking, can be used for comparative purposes. Examples include the Voluntary System of Accountability noted above, the National Association of Independent Colleges and Universities' U-CAN (http://www.ucan-network.org/), and the emerging Voluntary Framework of Accountability being developed by the American Association of Community Colleges and others. Critics argue the sites offer little more information than each institution already makes available on its websites, and do not lend themselves for easy comparison across institutions. Proponents counter by asserting the sites are consumer-friendly and offer data and information in the same format for all participating institutions, thus making it easier for users to navigate the sites and draw comparisons.

Finally, the cultural dimension relates to the receptivity of an institution to using benchmarks to gauge performance, accepting surprises when benchmark data collide with commonly held perceptions, overcoming defensiveness ("my college is unique and therefore comparisons with others are not relevant"), identifying peers that may be more effective and investigating why that may be the case, and learning from others. Some institutions have long histories of using benchmarks as aids in planning, evaluating, decision making, and policy analyses. For example, members of the Higher Education Data Sharing (HEDS) Consortium, which is composed of private colleges and universities, share data and operate with strict adherence to rules of confidentially and trust (http://www.e-heds.org/). They use HEDS data for comparing faculty salaries, admissions statistics and retention information, for example. As private institutions, members have a great deal of latitude in setting institutional policies and practices. Community colleges, on the other hand, are much newer participants in the benchmark arena, especially as they compare themselves to institutions outside their states or systems. Driven by external pressures for accountability and internal motivations to improve quality, community colleges are more interested in benchmarks than in the past, though most operate within system and contractual constraints and local perspectives that limit flexibility, at least as compared to private and many public baccalaureate-granting institutions (Bers, 2006).

Conclusions

In this era of accountability, shrinking resources, rising college costs for students, presidential advocacy for increasing the number of college graduates, and large numbers of underprepared students, the use of benchmarks can be a powerful tool for guiding institutional policies, procedure, and practices. For their utility to be optimized, it is essential that college leaders understand their benefits, their costs, and the potential for misuse and misinterpretation.

References

Bender, B. E., & Schuh, J. H. (Eds.). (2002). *Using benchmarking to inform practice in higher education* (New Directions for Higher Education, No. 118). San Francisco, CA: Jossey-Bass.

Bers, T. H. (2006). Limitations of community college benchmarking and benchmarks. In J. A. Seybert (Ed.). *Benchmarking for assessment, improvement, and accountability* (New Directions for Community Colleges, No. 134). San Francisco, CA: Jossey-Bass.

Jackson, N., & Lund, H. (Eds.). (2000). *Benchmarking for higher education.* London, UK: Open University Press.

Upcraft, M. L., & Schuh, J. H. (1996). *Assessment in student affairs: A guide for practitioners.* San Francisco, CA: Jossey-Bass.

Yarrow, D. & Prabhu, V. (1999). Collaboration to compete: Benchmarking through regional partnership. *Total Quality Management, 10*(4/5), 793–802.

QUESTIONS AND EXERCISES FOR SECTION 1

Note: Suggested answers are provided for selected questions. These questions are indicated by an asterisk (*).

(1) What problems are there if the same assessment data are being used for both formative and summative purposes?

(2) Under what circumstances is a little good evaluative information less good than none at all?

(3) Is quality of teaching a matter of similar complexity to quality of other matters across the university?

(4) What are the four principles of classroom-level assessment developed in the chapter, and how can they be understood to promote the alignment of: (a) course outcomes, content, and context; (b) students' prior knowledge and experience; (c) instructional strategies and resources; and (d) institutional improvement and accountability?

(5) What are the risks inherent to conducting classroom-level assessment without first addressing issues of alignment? What strategies can be employed to address issues of alignment before using course-level work for assessment purposes?

(6) Can you locate clearly delineated student learning outcomes for your institution? Are they in alignment with its mission?

(7) Can you locate student learning outcomes for your program? Do they support the institutional level student learning outcomes?

(8) Is it clear to you how the student learning outcomes for your course support the student learning outcomes of the program and of the institution?

(9) Is there assessment data available that provides evidence of how well students achieve the institutional and program level student learning outcomes?

(10) How does your institution's achievement of student learning outcomes compare to other similar institutions? Are there benchmarks available for comparisons?

(11) Banta and Pike discuss two different types of assessment, electronic portfolios, and standardized tests. What are the strengths and weaknesses of each approach, and under what circumstances is each approach appropriate?

(12) Banta and Pike also present a framework for assessing/evaluating assessment instruments. Describe your own framework for evaluating assessment instruments, and describe the process you would use to determine whether the Collegiate Learning Assessment (see http://www.collegiatelearningassessment.org/) is appropriate for your university.

(13) Comparison data for other institutions are available from many sources, including IPEDS, surveys by various organizations, consortia, and state record systems. Which sources are the most widely used, and which sources are the most useful for administrative decisions?

(14) Administrative decision making is usually a complex process, especially when the decisions are important. How are data from the institution itself, other institutions, and state or national sources used in these processes?

(15) What are the advantages of using an empowerment evaluation approach?*

(16) Why is it important to engage stakeholders in an evaluation?*

(17) How can peer comparison benchmark data contribute to accreditation efforts, and in what cases are benchmark data required for accreditation?

(18) Thinking of your own institution, in what areas are benchmark data needed but currently unavailable?

Suggested Answers to Selected Questions

Answer/Response for (15)

Empowerment evaluation engages a significant percentage of the community; builds evaluation capacity in the organization; contributes to organizational learning; and enhances sustainability.

Answer/Response for (16)

Engaging stakeholders in an evaluation is important in order to enhance knowledge utilization; based on the theory of process use, the more that people are engaged in conducting their own evaluation the more likely they are to use the findings and recommendations because they are their findings and recommendations.

SECTION 2

Theories and Technical Aspects of Educational Measurement

Charles Secolsky and D. Brian Denison

Higher education administrators can use principles of measurement in their work as they make decisions and direct the efforts of assessment specialists, institutional researchers, data analysts, and faculty who carry out important projects that lead to making colleges and universities function more effectively for their students. If these decision makers have access to the basic principles of measurement, they would be in a better position to identify the most relevant questions given the nature of the problems challenging them and the latest scientific thinking that has been made available by the measurement community. The eight chapters contained in the measurement theory section represent useful entities that are intended to serve administrators, current and prospective, with an array of tools by which they can tackle some of the most vexing problems related to student learning and assessment.

The study of measurement theory would also allow higher education administrators, faculty, student affairs professionals, and institutional researchers to use a broad array of concepts that will facilitate a better understanding of student academic and personal development, the foundation upon which student learning assessment processes are derived, and the methodological know-how that would enable more valid decisions regarding the improvement of teaching and learning activities. The first chapter in the section (Chapter 9), written by Schaughency, Smith, van der Meer, and Berg, provides a sensitive thesis on the importance and properties of classical test theory (CTT). The chapter is written bearing in mind the needs of those without a substantial mathematical or psychometric background, and is presented with few mathematical symbols. It provides an introduction to the other chapters in the section.

Chapter 10, written by Webb, Shavelson, and Steedle, discusses generalizability theory in higher education contexts. Generalizability (G) theory differs considerably from CTT in that the focus is on a different type of understanding of the notion of error, and has less restrictive assumptions. G theory recognizes that multiple sources of error (e.g., raters, items, occasions) may operate simultaneously in a measurement. The procedures of G theory make it possible to estimate the magnitude of the multiple sources of error and to use this information to improve the measurement. This chapter uses an example from the Collegiate Learning Assessment (CLA) to illustrate the concepts and procedures.

Chapter 11, by Osterlind and Wang, covers what is known as item response theory (IRT). It is introduced and compared to classical test theory (CTT) that is described in Chapter 9 and presented here in greater detail using a highly comprehendible approach. IRT is an approach to measurement that has a cognitive basis and appraises latent or underlying abilities and proficiencies, such as reading comprehension. A basic distinction is that with CTT both an examinee's ability and characteristics of items can vary from sample to sample, whereas with IRT they do not. While certain assumptions are needed to make such a claim, this important theory has gained prominence in the measurement field.

Chapter 12, by Kolen and Hendrickson, addresses issues of scaling, norming, and equating. These may be among the most important applications of measurement theory for higher education use. Too often it is has been our experience as higher education administrators that we do not consider the seriousness of the fact that once one or more items on a test (assessment instrument or otherwise) have been changed so that the scores are no longer comparable. This can be a real problem for administrators needing to demonstrate changes in student success to their boards of trustees. Equating methods allow the reporting of scores to be nearly comparable and much recent work in this area has led to the reduction of error in making such inferences.

Chapter 13, by Thompson and Vacha-Haase, provides greater detail on the concept of reliability, its history, and present day formulation with relevant examples. The problem of reliability is one of consistency from administration of a test to administration of the same or parallel form of the same test on a second occasion. This chapter informs the administrator of what reliability really means and how to estimate reliability from one administration of the test and the resulting obtained scores.

The following chapter (14), by Geisinger, Shaw, and McCormick, on validation of tests in higher education is at the core of the interpretations made from test scores and their uses. While the previous chapters in this section may be more technical in nature, validation of tests is primarily logical and philosophical. It answers questions as to what meaning can be derived from item and test scores. It is especially important for higher education administrators to understand the validation of tests since it is more of an all-encompassing concept that can be destroyed if the test or test scores violate assumptions of the previously discussed measurement theories.

Chapter 15, by Osterlind and Wang, on statistical modeling presents an easily accessible overview of the key concepts, statistical techniques, and methodological advances being used by higher education researchers to model phenomena of interest. This chapter will provide both consumers and practitioners of higher education research with a better understanding of when and how to use the various statistical modeling techniques presented.

Finally, Chapter 16, by McCoach, Rambo, and Welsh, presents issues in the analysis of change based on statistical modeling principles. It is common for administrators to be faced with demonstrating change or gain on some variable such as a test score and then attempt to test for the significance of that change. However, what if some students gain and others lose, resulting in a cancelling out of the effect the administrator is trying to demonstrate? Or what if the errors of measurement for the scores are large, making it difficult to determine which scores are high and which scores are truly low? This chapter takes the reader to more appropriate statistical techniques for accomplishing this purpose. A better awareness and understanding of the issues in the analysis of change is becoming increasingly important for the higher education decision maker, especially as demographics come to play a larger role in such areas as enrollment management.

In the next two sections—which are on test construction and development, and testing and assessment for decision-making—greater attention will be paid to the application of many of the principles and concepts presented in the measurement theory section, thereby providing a foundation for the ideas that follow. In order to take full advantage of these upcoming chapters, readers may benefit appreciably by spending additional time on this very important section of the handbook and the exercises that follow it.

9

CLASSICAL TEST THEORY AND HIGHER EDUCATION: FIVE QUESTIONS

Elizabeth Schaughency,[1] Jeffrey K. Smith,
Jacques van der Meer, and David Berg

It is not too difficult to measure the height of a child. But how we do measure the height of her proficiency in reading? Or how well she has mastered the first half of European History 252, or determine if her academic skills would predict that she would be successful at our university?

Classical Test Theory (CTT) refers to a body of psychometric theory about how to understand how well we have measured some mental characteristic or trait of an individual. How do we know that we have obtained a measure of unobservable qualities of a person such as knowledge, skills, or other psychological correlates of academic success on which we can rely? What would such a question even mean, exactly? These phenomena cannot be measured directly.

To be a bit more technical, CTT typically refers to issues of reliability and measurement error. As such, CTT may be considered to be a psychometric consideration, concerned with the development and refinement of educational and psychological measurement. For sake of completeness, we discuss issues of validity in this chapter as well. This is not meant to be a technical treatise on these issues, as excellent examples of those exist elsewhere in this volume; rather we want to focus on the fundamental ideas of CTT and contrast them to modern theories and approaches to measurement development, such as item response theory (IRT) and evaluating technical adequacy of approaches designed to assess learning over time or in response to instructional intervention.

CTT (which wasn't referred to as CTT until it was essentially superseded by IRT) had its statistical roots in the turn of the last century with the development of the correlation coefficient, and with most of the formulae that are used today being derived mid-20th century (Cronbach, 1951; Guttman, 1945; Hoyt, 1941; Kuder & Richardson, 1937). Perhaps the most comprehensive explication of the theories that underlie classical test theory can be found in Lord and Novick (1968). Interestingly, they also presented the fundamentals of IRT theory, which has largely replaced CTT in big test development projects, such as development of new, published norm-referenced tests. This raises the question of "Why look at CTT at all if we have a new and more sophisticated approach?" The answer to this question is that CTT works quite well for many tests developed for more limited, or local, use, and still provides useful descriptions of the consistency of measurement of assessment instruments used today.

In this chapter, we seek to do several things. First, we want to look at what kinds of testing/assessment goes on in higher education today, and how the ideas of CTT potentially contribute to those activities. Second, we want to examine how classical test theory works from a conceptual basis—what are the essential ideas behind CTT. Third, we will consider how CTT differs from IRT, especially as it applies to higher education. And finally, we will discuss how CTT impacts on measurement issues in higher education today, and the need to be mindful of the purpose of assessment when considering how best to evaluate whether assessments provide good information for educational decision making.

What Do We Test in Higher Education?

Testing serves a wide range of functions in higher education. The influence of testing in higher education begins well before students unpack their bags in their first dorm room as the first function of testing in higher education may include selection of students into universities (see Zwick, this volume). For example, in the US, this is done through what are probably the two most famous tests in American education: the SATs, and the ACTs. The SATs have been in existence in one form or another since 1926, and a precursor to it since 1901 (Donlon, 1984).

College entrance examinations serve several potential functions in the higher education admissions process. First, they give students an idea of what kinds of postsecondary institutions are likely to admit them. Students can compare their performance to the typical profile of the student body at a college or university. Next, the examinations give the institutions an independent indication of the achievement/ability level of a given student.

A second area of assessment that is common in higher education is skills testing for incoming students (see Morgan, this volume). Most American two-year colleges and many four-year colleges and universities assess the fundamental skills of students to see who would benefit from instruction in basic skill areas. Related to this type of testing is testing that occurs to place students in the proper levels of regular course sequences, for example, in which level of French should a student be enrolled?

A third area of testing is perhaps the one most familiar to higher education faculty members, and that is the testing that goes on as a natural part of instruction. We test students in courses in order to determine mastery of course content, usually so that grades can be assigned in courses (see Drezek McConnell & Doolittle, this volume). This testing may also involve assessments that are used to help students and faculty determine how well students are progressing through the course material, and what the best instructional steps to take next are. Testing of academic achievement used for grading is an example of summative assessment, and testing to determine how to tailor instruction to meet students' needs is an example of formative evaluation. Most testing that goes on at the college level is summative in nature, but faculty would probably be well advised to consider formative assessment in their courses to enhance learning and instruction.

Oftentimes, we use alternatives to testing in college and university courses, opting instead for students to write papers, make presentations, and so forth. If these are used as part of a grading program, then many of the ideas presented here will apply in theory (if not in actual application) to those types of assessments.

What Are the Characteristics of Good Measurement?

Tests are administered to serve a purpose. As can be seen in the section above, tests that are used in higher education can serve different purposes. We might want to use a test in order to pick the best students for our university, or to determine which ones need extra help to be successful, or to determine what grade a student should receive in a course. Since the purposes for tests can be different, to a degree, the evidence we consider in evaluating a test may differ as well (see chapters by Geisinger, Shaw, & McCormick; Pitoniak & Morgan, this volume). But the general ideas of what to consider when selecting a test don't change. What we want in a test is something that helps us to make good educational decisions. That decision might be to admit or reject an applicant from our university, to determine that a person should take a remedial mathematics course or not, or whether a person has earned an A or a B in our course. These are all decisions that are augmented by having test information.

In each of these cases, we want information that contributes to a good decision. We might even say "the correct decision," or "the best decision." So what should we consider in order to conclude that assessment findings have fulfilled that goal? Historically, we say that we should consider evidence supporting reliability and validity for given purpose (AERA, APA, & NCME, 1999).

Validity refers to the degree that the decisions that we make based on test information are valid ones, or ones that are sound and justifiable. Reliability is a somewhat narrower concept; the idea here is that a test should provide information that is dependable. For example, assessment results should be consistent over time if the skills and knowledge being measured have not changed for the individual. Since there are other chapters on both validity and reliability in this volume, and since CTT is primarily focused on reliability, reliability takes the lead in this discussion, but we will look at issues of validity as well, in particular as they impact on the ideas of reliability—and vice versa.

The Basic Concepts of CTT: What Do True Score, the Standard Error of Measurement, Reliability, and Validity Really Mean?

Suppose we are interested in assessing vocabulary knowledge. Vocabulary is a convenient example for a number of purposes. To begin, on the face of it, we have a notion of a definable universe of possible test items. And we can realistically think of taking a random sample of items from that universe. As noted above, CTT is largely concerned with evaluating how good the data that we obtain from test results are. A basic assumption of CTT is that test scores are the sum of two theoretical components, the true score and error (Christ & Hintze, 2007). Therefore, in order to understand the basic concepts that underlie CTT, it is probably best to start with the notion of the true score.

What Is a True Score?

Although the concept of a true score has several definitions with fine philosophical differences (Lord & Novick, 1968), we will overlook the nuances in favor of a simpler, yet accurate definition. The true score is the average score a person would get if he/she took the same test over and over again, with no opportunity for learning or skill development and all memory of having done so being erased in between administrations. Continuing with our example, suppose we wanted to know what percentage of all the words in the English language a person knew. We could randomly draw a sample of 100 words from the dictionary and ask a person to give definitions of them. We could mark them as right or wrong, and then calculate a percentage of words defined correctly. We could then sample another 100 words and repeat the process, and then do this again and again. The average percent correct after an infinite number of repetitions would be the person's true score. Or we might simply give the person all the words in the dictionary at one time. We would get the same estimate either way.

What Is Standard Error of Measurement?

Having defined a true score, we can get an idea of what a standard error of measurement is. We can think of the fact that some samples of items from the dictionary will be easier than others, and we can think that some samples might "fit" better with testees than others. Thus, there will be some variability in performance depending on the words that are sampled in the test. Additionally, our testee may be feeling better on one day than the next, or have something troubling on his mind that interferes with his performance on a given day. Therefore, there might be variability due to the testee as well as due to the set of items. In sum, CTT thinks of a test score as having two components, a true score which represents the true ability of the person, and an error score that represents the vicissitudes of the particular test and of the individual on the day of the test. Formally, we say that an observed score (X) on a test is equal to the true score (T) of the individual and an error score (E) that is peculiar to the particular administration of that test to that person on that day, or $X = T + E$.

Harkening back to our poor soul who took an infinite number of vocabulary tests, we could not only calculate a mean for that person, but indices of variability in performance around that mean as well. For example, we could calculate the standard deviation of the distribution of scores generated by giving this person an infinite number of vocabulary tests. Knowing the standard deviation would give us a very good (probabilistic) idea of how far from the true "performance" of the person any given test result might be. This provides the conceptual definition of the standard error of measurement. And it makes good sense. If we see a person get a 61% correct on the vocabulary test, and we calculate the standard error to be 4%, then, by assuming (reasonably) a normal distribution of scores (the central limit theorem comes into play here), we could say that the person's true score would be likely (68% of the time) to be between 57% and 65% (plus and minus one standard error), and be very likely (96% of the time) to be between 53% and 69%. If this level of accuracy does not seem sufficient, then we need a test with a smaller standard error of measurement (perhaps by increasing our sampling of items).

So that takes care of true score and standard error of measurement. How about reliability and validity? We've taken an initial shot at definitions above, but let us revisit and elaborate a bit on those and discuss how they relate to the concepts just discussed.

What is Reliability?

Accuracy and reliability of measurement are related, but not synonymous (Christ & Hintze, 2007). However, in general, the less evidence we have to support reliability (consistency, dependability) of measurement, the less confident that we can be that test results provide a trustworthy estimate of the student's true performance. There are a variety of ways to assess reliability, as described by Thompson and Vacha-Haase (this volume). We outline some of these below, presenting the ideas as they developed. As will be seen, a common thread across these approaches is to examine the degree to which two samples of performance correspond, or correlate. As will also be seen, however, because these reliability indices are based on types of different information, they convey different information—something to be kept in mind when selecting measures for educational decision making.

Consistency in performance across time

To begin, imagine that our vocabulary test was given to a sample of individuals, and then the following week was given again. A correlation is calculated between the two administrations, and that correlation is the estimate of the reliability coefficient. It gives us an index of how consistent scores will be from one administration to the next. It is what is called *test-retest reliability*. From a test selection perspective, the most relevant test-retest reliability periods are those that parallel the decision-making period (Macmann & Barnett, 1999). For example, if we are to use our measure of vocabulary knowledge as an indication of the student's vocabulary at entry into postsecondary education and our vocabulary measure was typically administered during the senior year of high school, ideally we would want evidence of test-retest reliability that spans that period.

But what if people become curious about the items on the test that they were not sure about? What if they found a number of the definitions? And to further complicate matters, what if some of the testees do this and others do not, how would this affect our interpretation of assessment results? The problem here is that we have what is called measurement reactivity, that is, the process of being assessed affected the test-takers' assessments in some way. It is not as severe as the Heisenberg

Principle of Uncertainty in quantum physics that acknowledges a trade-off in the precision with which we can measure some pairs of properties (the more precisely we measure position, for example, the less precisely we measure momentum), but it does hold potential for disturbing our estimate of the reliability in that those participants who took the test at Time 2 may differ from when they took the test at Time 1 due to their experience with test at Time 1.

To solve this problem, the notion of a parallel form of a test was invented. A parallel form of a test has the same number of items with roughly the same mean, standard deviation, and so forth. It is as close as possible to the original test, with all new items. This is not hard to conceptualize with vocabulary items, but is a bit tougher with introductory psychology. Now, instead of giving the same test twice, the second test is what we hope to be a parallel form of the test. We again correlate the results of the two administrations, and the correlation becomes our estimate of the reliability. It is called *parallel forms reliability*. It solves some of the problems of measurement reactivity, but not all of them. Thinking of the biology test, some testees may still decide to investigate certain areas that intrigued them on the test, and thus are not really the same people that they were (with regard to introductory biology) when they first took the test. As may be obvious, parallel forms reliability becomes an important consideration when assessments are to be conducted on more than one occasion, as in program evaluations that seek to evaluate the effectiveness of instructional strategies through the administration of pre- and post-testing to participants.

Both test-retest and parallel forms reliability, however, typically assess the stability of the measure over a short period of time, a period where we would expect there to be no change in the abilities being measured. There are additional practical problems with both test-retest and parallel forms reliability. Few people really want to come back a week later and take a test again if they don't have to.

Consistency across content

The question arises as to whether one could have testees take the test and the parallel form of the test in the same sitting, thus obviating the need for a second session? Well, if we could imagine a test twice as long as the test in which we were interested, then we could divide the results in half, correlate the two halves, and we would have our estimate of parallel forms reliability without the problem of measurement reactivity or the inconvenience of two sessions. We could, perhaps, make one form of the test be all the odd numbered items, and the other half be all the even numbered items. We then add up the odd items and then the even items, and correlate the two totals.

The only problem here is that this requires people to sit for a rather long test. To solve this problem, measurement specialists give a test of the length in which they are interested. They then correlate a test half the length in which they are interested with the other half of the test. This is called a *split-half estimate* of reliability. But there is a problem here. This is an estimate of a test half the length of the real test, and it only makes sense that a longer test would, ceteris paribus, be a more reliable test. So an adjustment formula is applied that takes the correlations from half the test and then adjusts that correlation to what it would be for full-length tests. This is done with what is called the Spearman-Brown Prophecy Formula. For an excellent and detailed explanation of this formula and all of reliability theory, see Feldt and Brennan (1989).

A test could be split in half in any of a large number of ways, not just odd items and even items. A formula was developed that essentially takes all the possible ways of splitting a test in half and estimating the reliability, and then averages all those possibilities. It is called Kuder-Richardson Formula 20 (yes, actually the twentieth formula they came up with). This formula, known as KR20, is widely used still in testing. It is based on the notion that all the items will be scored in a right/wrong fashion. Cronbach (1951) came up with a formula that generalizes KR20 to the case where the items can be scored on scales instead of just right/wrong. We call this coefficient alpha, or sometimes, Cronbach's alpha.

The split-half reliability estimate, KR20, and coefficient alpha do not look at the stability of measures over time as they all use data from a single administration of a test. Instead they provide indices of the extent to which items comprising a test seem to be tapping into a similar domain and are referred to as *internal consistency* measures of reliability. There are a variety of technical issues in the development of these concepts and the estimating algorithms of the concepts and coefficients that are not our concern here as they are described well elsewhere in this volume.

Consistency across observers

There is a final class or category of reliability coefficients that are typically associated with the classical model. These began by considering the issue that some tests do not have simple right/wrong answers such as multiple choice items, but require scoring that is based on the judgment of scorers or raters. We know that not everyone agrees on everything all the time, so there will be some variability in scores due to differences in raters. Inter-rater reliability addresses the issue of variability of raters.

Work in the area of inter-rater reliability led to the development of generalizability theory (Brennan & Kane, 1979; see also Webb, Shavelson, & Steedle, this volume). Generalizability theory provides the statistical basis for looking at variability in test performance from any possible definable source (persons, items, raters, occasions, etc.). In sum, although the various reliability indices all speak to the issue of dependability in measurement, they consider different potential sources of information in doing so. In practice, we should consider types of reliability evidence that are most relevant to our educational decisions. For example, if we are making decisions based on how someone graded a test, we are interested in evidence of inter-rater reliability. If we are interested in making decisions about a student's likely performance over time, then we are interested in evidence of test-retest reliability.

What Is Validity?

We selected assessment of vocabulary as a convenient illustrative example. With vocabulary, we seem to have a clearly defined skill set that we are measuring. Vocabulary knowledge seems a straightforward notion. If we are trying to measure knowledge of introductory biology, or readiness to take English 101, or who are the best students for our university, the notions of what it is that we are trying to assess become a bit murkier. Different teachers might not agree even on what introductory biology should consist of, much less how to generate items to measure it.

The theoretical description of the concept that we want to measure is referred to as a "construct." We use the term *construct* to acknowledge that the phenomenon that we are measuring is inferred and that we are not measuring it directly but only indirectly through our assessment (see G. T. Smith, 2005, for discussion). What is the construct to be measured in introductory biology or in who are the best students for our university? The issues related to answering those questions, and in determining whether we have done a good job of answering them fall under what is known as *construct validity* (Linn, 1994).

In general, validity evidence speaks to the degree to which our score is measuring what we want it to measure. Is it giving us the information that we are looking for? Will it lead us to make good decisions in our situation and for our purpose? Often, we hear or read about the concurrent validity, or predictive validity, or face validity of a test. But really this should be considered to be shorthand terminology for saying that we have evidence of the validity that is classified as concurrent in nature (i.e., providing information regarding the extent to which results correspond to other indicators of the construct at the same time), or predictive (providing information regarding the extent to which results predict performance at a future time), and so forth. All validity evidence essentially speaks to the same question: are we getting information that will lead to good decisions? Validity evidence accumulates as studies are conducted that speak to the issue of validity with given samples or for given purposes (AERA, APA, & NCME, 1999).

We should also consider the notions of incremental, treatment or instructional, and consequential validity evidence. *Incremental* validity evidence refers to the extent which the assessment results contribute new information and add to our decision making (Hunsley & Meyer, 2003). For example, is there value added in asking students to take a pre-enrolment placement exam or would we make the same advising decision based on available high school records?

Treatment or *instructional validity* again refers to contributions to educational decision making but asks a different question: Rather than asking whether the test predicts student performance, the question is whether assessment results inform professional decision making (L. S. Fuchs, 2004). Learning from assessment results that a student may be academically under-prepared for university study is different than learning what that student's instructional needs are and how best to support them. Instructional validity, sometimes referred to as instructional utility, refers to this latter issue. Finally, perhaps ultimately, *consequential validity* should be considered. Consequential validity considers the question of the consequences of using a particular measure as opposed to using an alternative approach, or none at all (AERA, APA, & NCME, 1999). Although we will not consider validity issues in detail here, we will return to these ideas as we explore the type of testing done in higher education.

Concluding Comments on Basic Concepts

One final important point to emphasize is that the information that is obtained on the quality of a test is only appropriately used for people who are assessed with the same form of that particular test and who are similar to those for whom the reliability estimates were obtained (and validity for that matter). That is to say, the estimates are *sample-specific*. This is more important than it might initially seem. A test that has reliability and validity evidence for predicting whether applicants who are English language learners are likely to be successful in their beginning university studies may not predict equally well for students whose first language is English. Similarly, a test that predicts grades in some university coursework may or may not predict performance in other coursework or other desired professional competencies. For example, a listening comprehension test may not predict performance in some coursework (say humanities) to the same extent that it does in others (say, science, or vice versa), or in professional contexts such as listening skills in interpersonal situations, due to the way listening comprehension was assessed. This could be due, in part, to greater overlap in the way our construct—listening comprehension—was sampled in the test and course content in some domains, than in others. Because evidence on the technical adequacy of measurement are test and sample specific, guidelines for educational assessment call for obtaining technical adequacy evidence to support each new intended use and interpretation of assessment results (AERA, APA, & NCME, 1999).

Finally, our focus here has been on reliability. As noted previously, reliability and validity are not synonymous: Good evidence to support consistency in measurement—i.e., reliability—does not guarantee validity. For example, in education, it is not uncommon to hear reference to students' preferred modality of instruction (she's a visual learner; he's a kinesthetic learner, and so on). Although assessments may identify a preferred learning style the majority of the time, the instructional validity of this assessment information—i.e., whether assessment results inform instruction in ways that are associated with beneficial educational outcomes—is a separate issue (see Kavale & Forness, 1999). As education professionals, we are often—and should be—drawn to issues of validity, particularly, instructional and consequential validity. However, we should also appreciate the implications of reliability for professional decision making: Although good evidence of reliability does not equate to good evidence of validity, reliability likely places limits on the quality of our decision making

(Macmann & Barnett, 1999). If assessment results are not consistent, the data that they provide may not be trustworthy and decisions based on that information may be misinformed.

How Does Classical Test Theory Differ From Modern Test Theory?

Modern test theory, and specifically item response theory (IRT), was developed independently along two different lines by different groups of scholars. Please refer to the chapters in this volume on IRT theory to see the issues involved here as well as the technical aspects of IRT. Here we are going to consider the essential, conceptual differences in these two approaches. For some of the testing that is done in higher education, CTT works quite adequately; for others, IRT is typically a preferable approach.

To appreciate the differences between the two approaches, we have to start by thinking about what they are trying to accomplish. Classical Test Theory looks at tests that are developed to measure traits in individuals, and tries to assess the dependability of results from those tests and help in improving these measures. It has a focus on the test and consistency of test results with a group of individuals.

Item Response Theory looks less at tests per se than it does at obtaining measures of individual performance and assessing the quality of that measurement. IRT starts with the notion that people's levels of performance are locatable along a continuum from low to high on a given construct, and that test items are locatable along that same continuum. If a person has the same proficiency as an item, that person has a 50% chance of getting that item right. In order to estimate the skill level of a person, we give that person some items, see how many they get right, and then see where they would have to be on the proficiency continuum in order for them to have had the best chance of getting the score that they obtained. This process also allows for the estimate of a standard error of measurement that is particular to this situation and this person's score. Please note that what is described here is pretty much the simplest version of IRT modeling. There are many wonderful elaborations on this model, but this model is probably used more often than not in real situations.

It requires a fair amount of work and a lot of testees to develop IRT scales in a given area. Once a set of items (item bank) exists that have been IRT "scaled," it is possible to administer basically any set of these items that seem appropriate to an individual and get an estimate of the person's skill level and an associated standard error. This has the distinct advantage of being able to tailor tests to the skill development of the individuals, and to the need for accuracy—if you need a smaller standard error in a given situation, you simply administer more items.

IRT, which is explained excellently elsewhere in this volume, has many wonderful qualities, and, when it is possible to execute, is almost always preferable to CTT. However, and this is a big "however" for higher education, it is not always possible, or even desirable, to do the work necessary to take an IRT approach to a given testing situation. A final exam in a course that does not enroll hundreds of students is such an example, as might a placement examination for courses in German where we simply want a rough idea of whether the student should take German 101 or German 102.

How Does Classical Test Theory Relate to Testing in Higher Education Today?

For this final section, let's begin by returning to the examples discussed in the opening of this chapter.

Testing Before Admission

Let's look at college entrance examinations, tests used for selection and placement into courses, and tests used to assess achievement in courses. To begin, college entrance examinations have all gone toward IRT, at any rate in the United States. These are measures that require high levels of precision and consistency across different administrations of the measures, and IRT simply provides a much more robust statistical model for doing this than CTT.

Testing for Course Planning

The second type of testing in higher education that we considered was selection into courses, perhaps developmental or perhaps part of a regular sequence, once people have been accepted into a college or university. There are some commercially available measures for making such determinations, and they might use CTT or IRT. Other measures are often developed within the institution, and they are typically developed using CTT. This process usually involves a fair amount of time defining just what is meant by constructs to be measured. Do we want to include writing skills as part of a measure to determine placement into a remedial literacy course, or just reading skills? Do we want to use reading materials from course texts, or write new materials? How will we assess the students' skills once we have the reading materials? Will we let testees refer back to the reading material, or should we have them read it once and then respond based on their memory of the material. Once these issues have been decided, a rough draft of the test is generated that usually has more items than are ultimately needed, and it is "pilot tested" on a sample of individuals who are similar to those for whom the test is intended. The pilot results are examined to determine whether the scale seems to be internally consistent and tapping into one set of skills or more than one domain, item difficulty estimates and item to total score correlations. The items are culled and refined, and an iterative process, typically involving validity evidence in addition to reliability evidence, until a final form is produced. There are many good texts available on how to produce a good test; one we would recommend is Downing and Haladyna (2006) (see also chapters in Section 3, this volume).

Testing as Part of Course Assessment

Course examinations can involve a rather special use of CTT. In developing an examination for a course, we usually cannot give it a "pilot test" before actually using it. We can, however, use the data from a given examination to refine that exam for the next year's use, and to learn about the quality of our efforts in general. A number of statistical packages such as SPSS (see, for example, Norušis, 2008) or SAS (see, for example, Cody & Smith, 2005) are available to allow you to look at the overall reliability of a test, and how well each of the items related to the total score.

As mentioned above, there are issues with the notion of reliability and how high one wants it to be in any given situation. When looking at internal consistency reliability, what one is basically measuring is how strongly all of the items on a test intercorrelate with one another. If we think we are measuring a single trait or construct that is unidimensional in nature, then we might think that the higher the internal consistency reliability, the better. But if we are measuring achievement in History 101, then we might be agglomerating knowledge and skills that are somewhat differentiated one from another. We might be interested in some facts, the ability to critique an argument about an historical situation, and the ability to write a good short essay about a topic. There is no reason to believe that these should all necessarily be highly correlated with one another. Also, there might be items that are important in the course that almost all (or even all) of the students know and get correct. These items will not contribute at all to a higher reliability estimate, but it might be the case that we want to know that the students know them, and more importantly, we want to give students credit for knowing them (if they aren't on the test, we can't give credit for our students having learned them).

Thus, in this situation, which is probably the more common situation, we are not really looking for the highest possible coefficient alpha! In fact, that might indicate to us that we have too narrowly defined our examination. There is some work to indicate that we might want to conceptualize reliability in a somewhat different fashion here, one that looks more broadly at reliability as being a measure of the sufficiency of information that we have (Shepard, 2006; J. K. Smith, 2003).

Additional Considerations When Assessing Development and Learning in Higher Education

As noted previously, the historical roots of CTT evolved in the context of trying to measure unobservable, yet typically stable, traits, like extroversion or shyness (Christ & Hintze, 2007). When our assessments occur at one point in time, as in each of the above examples, such approaches to evaluating technical adequacy work fairly well. In education, however, we are often interested in learning and change over time. By way of example, suppose students were assessed at the beginning of the semester on a measure that sampled from material that they were expected to learn across the semester. We might make two predictions about our students' performance at this point: First, we might expect that as a group they might not do very well because they hadn't yet been taught the material on which they were being assessed. Second, we still might expect variability in performance between students, due to such factors as background knowledge and the like. If we were to reassess our students on this material across the term, we could make a third prediction, and that is, that we expect our students' performance to improve across the semester. Moreover, we could plot each student's performance over time and from this extrapolate their trajectory toward end of semester performance. Thus, it may be that some students didn't know course material at the beginning of the semester but they are now making good progress toward mastering material across the semester. Other students, however, may have done poorly on our assessment at the beginning of the semester and their rate of progress is slower. They are learning but their rate of progression is such that it is unlikely that they will successfully master course material if they don't pick up their pace of progress. As professionals, we may want to influence a student's learning trajectory, perhaps via an educational program or intervention, and evaluate not only whether the student's level of performance has changed but also whether we have enhanced their learning trajectory via participation in our programs or instructional interventions. In sum, we may want to know what to do to help our students and whether our efforts are effective.

These assessment purposes raise additional methodological considerations (see, for example, McCoach, Rambo, & Welsh, this volume). Oftentimes, questions of effectiveness are equated with summative evaluation: Do program evaluations document effectiveness of the approach or practice? Considerations in designing effective program evaluations are beyond the scope of this chapter, and the interested reader is referred to Grayson (this volume).

Questions of what to do are, of course, questions of instructional utility. Assessment results and summative evaluation research on effective practice provide starting points but the uniqueness of learners and learning contexts limit the extent to which we can predict how a learner will respond to a given intervention or whether modifications would better serve student needs (Campbell & Overman, 1988). Two assessment approaches have been proposed to address this limitation: dynamic assessment (Caffrey, D. Fuchs, & L. S. Fuchs, 2008) and systematic formative evaluation (L. S. Fuchs & D. Fuchs, 1986).

In *dynamic assessment*, rather than presenting tasks to the student in one standardized condition, instruction or supports may be modified to observe student performance in different analogue learning conditions. Although dynamic assessment has been criticized as a fuzzy concept, scripted protocols may be developed and subsequently evaluated (D. Fuchs et al., 2007). Potential uses of dynamic assessment in higher education could include determining appropriate testing accommodations for students with disabilities (see Banerjee & Thurlow, this volume) and evaluation of strategies and supports that students might employ in the instructional context. When determining appropriate testing accommodations, the student might be presented with brief alternate forms of tests that incorporate the accommodations being considered, such as using a reader/writer or assistive technology to determine what is most appropriate (Braden & Joyce, 2008). In the instructional context, we might ask the student to perform an academic task, such as listening to a lecture excerpt or reading a text passage, under varying conditions and assess the student's performance for those conditions. Did the student demonstrate better listening comprehension when she sat back and listened to the lecture material? Or when she took narrative notes? Or when she took notes alongside a print-out of the lecturer's presentation slides? Did the student demonstrate better comprehension of textbook material when he followed along on an e-copy of the text as it was read aloud to him using text-to-voice software, or when he listened to an audio-recording of the text, or when he was taught pre-viewing and questioning strategies to use in approaching written texts?

Systematic formative evaluation, on the other hand, involves implementing the instructional modification in situ and assessing response following implementation of instructional intervention. Repeated assessments provide the opportunity to observe not only whether the student's level of performance has increased following intervention but also whether his learning trajectory has been enhanced (Christ & Hintze, 2007). Reflecting on progress monitoring results then informs decisions about whether instructional interventions are being effective in meeting student needs or whether modifications may be indicated to better meet learning needs (see Ervin & Schaughency, 2008; Schaughency, Alsop, & Dawson, 2010, for discussion).

Traditional approaches to measurement development that evaluate measurement by consideration of scores obtained at one point in time are still important when considering measurement tools for progress monitoring, but should be considered to be a starting point (L. S. Fuchs, 2004). In addition, we want to know whether our measures are sensitive to detecting and depicting growth and change (Hintze, 2009), whether our indices of growth and change are reliable (Christ & Hintze, 2007), and, if our results are to be used formatively, whether there is evidence to support instructional utility (L. S. Fuchs, 2004).

For reasons of efficiency, for such purposes, we may be interested in brief, repeatable indicators of relevant assessment targets. This measurement perspective is influenced by both behavior analytic and *curriculum-based measurement* approaches to assessment (Christ & Hintze, 2007; Deno, 2003). Most measurement development on this perspective has occurred in primary education settings. Work at the secondary level is underway (Twyman & Tindal, 2007), with scope for extension to higher education settings (Schaughency, Stanish, & Dickman, 2001; G. Tindal, personal communication, July 20, 2010).

Curriculum-based measurement falls under the general umbrella of curriculum-based assessment, defined as any set of measurement activities that record a student's performance in the local curriculum as a basis for gathering information to inform instructional decisions (Hintze, 2009). In higher education, this approach might be envisioned as assessing skills within the context of content area task demands (Behrman, 2000). Behrman and Street (2005), for example, describe using passages from a course text book to assess content-specific reading comprehension at the beginning of the semester to predict course grades.

In systematic formative evaluation, assessment probes would be administered in the context of ongoing instructional supports and accommodations to inform decisions about utility of those strategies and remaining learning needs. An example of systematic formative evaluation in higher education is provided by Schaughency et al. (2001), and illustrates the premises that (a) diagnostic assessment and evidence-based treatment outcome research may provide useful starting points for practice, but (b) progress monitoring may be warranted to refine accommodation or intervention plans.

Schaughency and colleagues worked with university students determined to be eligible for student disability services as students with Attention Deficit Hyperactivity Disorder (ADHD) and prescribed medication to assist with management of symptoms in the university context. They recognized that although medication may be considered to be an evidence-based treatment for ADHD, response to medication and appropriate medication dosage cannot be determined a priori, necessitating evaluation of response to medication to inform decisions about appropriate medication, dosage (American Academy of Pediatrics Subcommittee on Attention-Deficit/Hyperactivity Disorder and Committee on Quality Improvement, 2001), and remaining academic accommodation needs. Following the rationale that evaluation should encompass functional educational targets rather than focus solely on symptomology of the disorder (Pelham, Fabiano, & Massetti, 2005), measures included coding lecture notes for main points based on Spires (1993) and brief post-lecture quizzes adapted from Evans, Pelham, and Grudburg (1994–1995) (Schaughency & VanderVeen, 2000). Importantly, a first step in measurement development for this project entailed determining whether these brief indicators, collected across the semester, predicted end of semester course performance, with results suggesting that they did (Schaughency et al., 1997).

There are a number of potential benefits of systematic formative evaluation in higher education outlined by Schaughency et al. (2001). These include, but are not limited to, evaluation of the specific instructional support strategy. Engaging in the systematic formative evaluation process helps student and service providers better understand the relationship between the learner's characteristics, task demands of the university setting, and educational accommodations. Documentation of this process provides evidence of fulfillment of responsibilities by student and service providers, in the spirit of legislation relevant to providing services to students with disabilities (Bourke, Strehorn, & Silver, 2000; Foote, 2000; Shaw, McGuire, & Madaus, 1997).

Moreover, documentation may assist in accessing additional resources for students. For example, recognizing the association between higher education and employability (Graham & Stacey, 2002), state vocational rehabilitation agencies may support individuals on their caseloads who are pursuing higher education as was the case for one of the participants in the model demonstration project described by Schaughency and colleagues (2001). Upon receiving documentation that the participant experienced a specific learning disability and benefited from use of assistive technology, the state vocational rehabilitation agency supplied a laptop and specialized software to assist with the student's university coursework. In addition, the agency contacted the principal investigator to ask if she would provide these evaluation services for other clients on their caseload, commenting on the perceived helpfulness of the information provided to their decision making about allocation of resources. Post-hoc support for the agency's investment in resources for the participating student is provided by informal follow up with this student who had previous false starts at undergraduate education and a transcript peppered with grades ranging from As, hinting at his competencies, to less successful performance. Not only did he successfully complete his undergraduate degree following participation, but at last contact was enrolled in PhD study in the area of assistive technology in special education.

There is also the possibility of positive reactive effects to systematic formative evaluation. For the student, the process of participation and ongoing objective feedback can facilitate development of self-regulated learning and self-determination, important developmental tasks in higher education for all students including those with disabilities (Wehmeyer & Schwartz, 1997). Moreover, engaging in systematic formative evaluation may help faculty become aware of issues and strategies, which are then incorporated into teaching practices, thereby yielding positive reactive effects that emanate beyond the target student to potentially benefitting all students. For example, developing classroom-based assessment probes necessitated that faculty identify the main points to be covered in lectures. In so doing, one faculty member commented that it would be probably good to explicitly articulate this information to students in class, and subsequently began to do so.

To conclude, systematic formative evaluation and dynamic assessment are assessment practices designed to enhance instructional utility by examining response to intervention, and ultimately enhance outcomes for students (consequential validity). Assessing the moving target of learning and development over time or in response to intervention, however, raises additional measurement considerations. Given the importance of decisions based on these assessment results, evidence is needed to support the dependability of the assessment results used to inform these decisions.

Summary

Classical test theory has been a stalwart in higher education over the decades. Its influence has waned dramatically and appropriately in many areas of higher education, but is still useful for specific applications in higher education, and very much so for measures that are associated with specific courses. Understanding CTT also provides a solid introduction to understanding the technical issues related to testing in general. We hope this chapter has facilitated such an understanding.

Note

1 This chapter represents a collaboration of members of the Literacy Research Unit at the University of Otago. The Literacy Research Unit, housed in the Educational Assessment Research Unit of the College of Education, was formed as a partnership between faculty in the College of Education, Higher Education Development Centre, and Department of Psychology to foster a research community dedicated to learning about the literacy needs of students in higher education and to inform evidence-based practice for addressing those needs in tertiary settings. This chapter was supported in part by a grant from the University of Otago to the Literacy Research Unit. Material in the chapter referring to systematic formative evaluation in the university setting was supported by a grant from the U.S. Department of Education, Office of Special Education Programs (CFDA Award H078C6005). Opinions expressed herein are those of the authors and do not necessarily represent the opinion of the U.S. Department of Education. We would also like to acknowledge the students, faculty, and other higher education service providers with whom we have worked over the years for shaping our thinking about the importance of good data for educational decision making in higher education.

References

American Academy of Pediatrics Subcommittee on Attention-Deficit/Hyperactivity Disorder and Committee on Quality Improvement. (2001). Clinical practice guideline: Treatment of the school-aged child with attention-deficit/hyperactivity disorder. *Pediatrics, 108*, 1033–1044.

American Educational Research Association, American Psychological Association, & National Council on Measurement in Education. (1999). *Standards for educational and psychological testing*. Washington, DC: American Educational Research Association.

Banerjee, M., & Thurlow, M. L. (this volume). *Using data to find common ground between secondary and postsecondary accommodations for students with disabilities*.

Behrman, E. H. (2000). Developmental placement decisions: Content-specific reading assessment. *Journal of Developmental Education, 23*, 12–17.

Behrman, E. H., & Street, C. (2005). The validity of using a content-specific reading comprehension test for college placement. *Journal of College Reading and Learning, 25*, 5–22.

Bourke, A. B., Strehorn, K. C., & Silver, P. (2000). Faculty members' provision of instructional services to students with LD. *Journal of Learning Disabilities, 33*, 26–32.

Braden, J. P., & Joyce, L. B. (2008). Best practices in making assessment accommodations. In A. Thomas & J. Grimes (Eds.), *Best practices in school psychology V* (Vol. 2, pp. 589–604). Bethesda, MD: National Association of School Psychologists.

Brennan, R. L., & Kane, M. T. (1979). Generalizability theory: A review. In R. E. Traub (Ed.), *Methodological developments* (New Directions for Testing and Measurement, No. 4, pp. 33–51). San Francisco, CA: Jossey-Bass.

Caffrey, E., Fuchs, D., & Fuchs, L. S. (2008). The predictive validity of dynamic assessment: A review. *The Journal of Special Education, 41*, 254–270.

Campbell, D., & Overman, E. S. (Eds.). (1988). *Methodology and epistemology for social science: Selected papers by Donald T. Campbell*. Chicago. IL: University of Chicago Press.

Christ, T. J., & Hintze, J. M. (2007). Psychometric considerations when evaluating response to intervention. In

S. R. Jimerson, M. K. Burns, & A. M. VanDerHeyden (Eds.), *Handbook of response to intervention: The science and practice of assessment and intervention* (pp. 93–105). New York, NY: Springer.

Cody, R., & Smith, J. K. (2005). *Applied statistics and the SAS programming language* (5th ed.). Englewood Cliffs, NJ: Prentice-Hall.

Cronbach, L. J. (1951). Coefficient alpha and the internal structure of tests. *Psychometrika, 16,* 297–334.

Deno, S. L. (2003). Developments in curriculum-based measurement. *The Journal of Special Education, 37,* 184–192.

Donlon, T. F. (Ed.). (1984). *The College Board technical handbook for the Scholastic Aptitude Test and Achievement Tests.* New York, NY: College Entrance Examination Board.

Downing, S. M., & Haladyna, T. M. (2006). *Handbook of test development.* Mahwah, NJ: Erlbaum.

Drezek McConnell, K., & Doolittle, P. E. (this volume). *Classroom-level assessment: Aligning pedagogical practices to enhance student learning.*

Ervin, R. A., & Schaughency, E. (2008). Best practices in accessing the systems change literature. In A. Thomas & J. Grimes (Eds.), *Best practices in school psychology V* (Vol. 3, pp. 853–874). Bethesda, MD: National Association of School Psychologists.

Evans, S. W., Pelham, W., & Grudburg, M. V. (1994–1995). The efficacy of notetaking to improve behavior and comprehension of adolescents with attention deficit hyperactivity disorder. *Exceptionality, 5,* 1–17.

Feldt, L. S., & Brennan, R. L. (1989). Reliability. In R. L. Linn (Ed.), *Educational measurement* (3rd ed., pp. 105–146). New York, NY: American Council on Education.

Foote, W. E. (2000). A model for psychological consultation in cases involving the American with Disabilities Act. *Professional Psychology: Research and Practice, 31,* 190–196.

Fuchs, D., Fuchs, L. S., Compton, D. L., Bouton, B., Caffrey, E., & Hill, L. (2007). Dynamic assessment as responsiveness-to-intervention: A scripted protocol to identify young at-risk readers. *Teaching Exceptional Children, 39,* 58–63.

Fuchs, L. S. (2004). The past, present, and future of curriculum-based measurement research. *School Psychology Review, 33,* 188–192.

Fuchs, L. S., & Fuchs, D. (1986). Effects of systematic formative evaluation: A meta-analysis. *Exceptional Children, 53,* 199–208.

Geisinger, K., Shaw, L. H., & McCormick, C. (this volume). *The validation of tests in higher education.*

Graham, P. A., & Stacey, N. G. (2002). *The knowledge economy and postsecondary education: Report of a workshop.* Washington, DC: National Academy Press.

Grayson, T. E. (this volume). *Program evaluation in higher education.*

Guttman, L. A. (1945). A basis for analyzing test-retest reliability. *Psychometrika, 10,* 195–200.

Hintze, J. (2009). Curriculum-based assessment. In T. B. Gutkin, & C. R. Reynolds (Eds.), *The handbook of school psychology* (4th ed., pp. 397–409). Hoboken, NJ: Wiley.

Hoyt, C. (1941). Test reliability obtained by analysis of variance. *Psychometrika, 6,* 153–160.

Hunsley, J., & Meyer, G. J. (2003). The incremental validity of psychological testing and assessment: Conceptual, methodological, and statistical issues. *Psychological Assessment, 15,* 446–455.

Kavale, K. A., & Forness, S. R. (1999). Effectiveness of special education. In C. R. Reynolds, & T. B. Gutkin (Eds.), *The handbook of school psychology* (3rd ed., pp. 984–1024). New York, NY: Wiley.

Kuder, G. F., & Richardson, M. W. (1937). The theory of the estimation of test reliability. *Psychometrika, 2,* 151–160.

Linn, R. L. (1994). Performance assessment: Policy promises and technical measurement standards. *Educational Researcher, 23,* 4–14.

Lord, F. M., & Novick, M. R. (1968). *Statistical theories of mental test scores.* Reading, MA: Addison-Wesley.

Macmann, G. M., & Barnett, D. W. (1999). Diagnostic decision making in school psychology: Understanding and coping with uncertainty. In C. R. Reynolds & T. B. Gutkin (Eds.), *The handbook of school psychology* (3rd ed., pp. 519–548). New York, NY: Wiley.

McCoach, D. B., Rambo, K., & Welsh, M. (this volume). *Issues in the analysis of change.*

Morgan, D. L. (this volume). *College placement testing of entering students.*

Norušis, M. J. (2008). *SPSS 16.0 guide to data analysis.* Upper Saddle River, NJ: Prentice Hall.

Pelham, W. E., Jr., Fabiano, G. A., & Massetti, G. M. (2005). Evidence-based assessment of attention deficit disorder in children and adolescents. *Journal of Clinical Child and Adolescent Psychology, 34,* 449–476.

Pitoniak, M. J., & Morgan, D. L. (this volume). *Setting and validating cut scores for tests.*

Schaughency, E., Alsop, B., & Dawson, A. (2010). The school psychologist's role in assisting school staff in establishing systems to manage, understand, and use data. In G. G. Peacock, R. A. Ervin, E. J. Daly, III, & K. W. Merrell (Eds.), *Practical handbook of school psychology: Effective practices for the 21st century* (pp. 548–565). New York, NY: Guilford Press.

Schaughency, E., Stanish, H., & Dickman, H. (2001). **A**dvancement through **C**ooperative **C**ollege **E**ducation for **S**tudent **S**uccess (ACCESS): Evaluating accommodation utility and empowering the student with disabilities. Allendale, MI: Grand Valley State University. Available upon request from schaughe@psy.otago. ac.nz

Schaughency, E., Stanish, H., Dickman, K., Krum, K., Pedraza, J., & Rodriguez, S. (1997, June). *Developing ecologically valid measures to assess postsecondary students' performance in the classroom.* Paper presented at the National Transition Alliance for Youth with Disabilities 12th Annual Project Directors Meeting, Washington, DC.

Schaughency, E., & VanderVeen, K. (2000, July). *Selecting accommodations, designing environments, and empowering students through data-based decision-making (DBDM).* Paper presented at the annual meeting of the Association for Higher Education and Disability, Kansas City, MO.

Shaw, S. F., McGuire, J. M., & Madaus, J. W. (1997). Standards of professional practice. *Journal of Postsecondary Education and Disability, 12,* 26–35.

Shepard, L. A. (2006). Classroom assessment. In R. L. Brennan (Ed.), *Educational measurement* (4th ed., pp. 623–646). Westport, CT: American Council on Education/Praeger.

Smith, G. T. (2005). On construct validity: Issues of method and measurement. *Psychological Assessment, 17,* 396–408.

Smith, J. K. (2003). Reconceptualizing reliability in classroom assessment. *Educational Measurement: Issues and Practice, 22*(4), 82–88.

Spires, H. (1993). Learning from a lecture: Effects of comprehension monitoring. *Reading Research and Instruction, 32,* 19–30.

Thompson, B., & Vache-Haase, T. (this volume). *Reliability.*

Twyman, T., & Tindal, G. (2007). Extending curriculum-based measurement to middle/secondary schools. *Journal of Applied School Psychology, 24,* 49–67.

Webb, N. M., Shavelson, R. J., & Steedle, J. T. (this volume). *Generalizability theory in assessment contexts.*

Wehmeyer, M., & Schwartz, M. (1997). Self-determination and positive adult outcomes: A follow-up study of youth with mental retardation or learning disabilities. *Exceptional Children, 63,* 245–255.

Zwick, R. (this volume). *Admissions testing in higher education.*

10

GENERALIZABILITY THEORY IN ASSESSMENT CONTEXTS

Noreen M. Webb, Richard J. Shavelson, and Jeffrey T. Steedle

A central issue in higher education today is the assessment of what students learn during college. Increasingly, institutions are being asked to provide evidence of student learning, especially in broad skills such as critical thinking, communication, and problem solving (Ewell, 2009; Shavelson, 2009). Institutions are turning to assessments such as the Collegiate Learning Assessment and the Measure of Academic Proficiency and Progress (now known as the ETS Proficiency Profile) to gather data that can be used to measure their effectiveness and help improve teaching and learning at the program and institution levels (Shavelson, 2008). To inform such decisions, the data collected must be reliable. This chapter describes a statistical theory for evaluating the reliability of behavioral measurements such as scores on learning assessments.

Generalizability (G) theory is a statistical theory for evaluating the dependability ("reliability") of behavioral measurements (Cronbach, Gleser, Nanda, & Rajaratnam, 1972; see also Brennan, 2001; Shavelson & Webb, 1991). G theory permits the researcher to address such questions as: Is the sampling of tasks or judges the major source of measurement error? Can I improve the reliability of the measurement better by increasing the number of tasks or the number of judges, or is some combination of the two more effective? Are the test scores adequately reliable to make decisions about the average level of student proficiency at a particular institution?

G theory grew out of the recognition that the undifferentiated error in classical test theory (Haertel, 2006) provided too gross a characterization of the potential and/or actual sources of measurement error. In classical test theory measurement error is undifferentiated random variation; the theory does not distinguish among various possible sources. G theory pinpoints the sources of systematic and unsystematic error variation, disentangles them, and estimates each one. Moreover, in contrast to the classical parallel-test assumptions of equal observed-score means, variances and covariances, G theory assumes only randomly parallel tests sampled from the same universe. Finally, while classical test theory focuses on relative (rank-order) decisions (e.g., student admission to selective colleges), G theory distinguishes between relative ("norm-referenced") and absolute ("criterion-" or "domain-referenced") decisions for which a behavioral measurement is used.

In G theory, a behavioral measurement (e.g., a test score) is conceived of as a sample from a *universe of admissible observations*. This universe consists of all possible observations that a decision maker considers to be acceptable substitutes (e.g., scores sampled on occasions 2 and 3) for the observation at hand (scores on occasion 1). A measurement situation has characteristic features such as test form, task or item, rater, and/or test occasion. Each characteristic feature is called a *facet* of a measurement.

A universe of admissible observations, then, is defined by all possible combinations of the levels of the facets (e.g., tasks, raters, occasions).

As an example, we use a generalizability study of scores on the Collegiate Learning Assessment (CLA), which was developed to measure undergraduates' learning, in particular their ability to think critically, reason analytically, solve problems, and communicate clearly (Shavelson, 2008). One component of the CLA is a set of complex, real-world performance tasks, each of which presents students with a problem and related information and asks them either to solve the problem or recommend a course of action based on the evidence provided. For example, one of the CLA performance tasks ("Crime Reduction", Shavelson, 2008) describes a city mayor who is confronted with a rising number of crimes in the city and their association with drug use, just as he is standing for re-election. While he advocates increasing the number of police, his opponent calls instead for drug education to address the cause of crime. Students are given information regarding crime rates, drug usage, relationship between the number of police and robberies, research studies and newspaper articles and are asked to interpret the evidence to advise the mayor about whether his opponent is right about the usefulness of drug education and her interpretation of the positive relationship between the number of police and the number of crimes. Each performance task response is given a total score based on the sum of a judge's analytic and holistic ratings.

The focus here is the use of the CLA for gauging *institutions'* effectiveness at developing students' abilities. In the examples considered here, the focus is the institution rather than the individual student. Although the CLA provides students their scores so that they can gauge their own performance, the primary purpose is to make decisions about institutional-level effectiveness. Hence, in contrast to usual treatments of generalizability theory that begin with a focus on individuals (e.g., students) where the primary issue is the dependability of the scores for making decisions about, say, the level of a person's performance, we begin with a focus on institutions. Each institution's score is the mean for the group of students taking the CLA at that institution.

Consider a generalizability study of institutions' scores on six CLA performance tasks that are evaluated by two judges. For purposes of this initial example, we have simplified some things that later on will be "complexified," so assume that both judges scored all six performance tasks for all institutions in the sample (see Table 10.1 below; scores are expressed on an SAT metric, typically with mean of about 1,000 and standard deviation of about 200). Because all institutions have scores for the same six tasks and the same two judges, these three sources of variance (institutions, tasks, judges) are said to be completely crossed. At each institution, a group of students completed six tasks and their responses were evaluated by two judges. For simplicity, we assume that the same group of students at an institution responded to all six tasks. Each score in Table 10.1, then, is the mean over the students who completed that task as evaluated by one of the judges. For this example, we consider tasks and judges to be randomly selected from a large domain of such performance tasks and judges, respectively.

Table 10.1 Crossed School × Task × Judge G study of CLA Scores

School	Judge 1						Judge 2					
	Task 1	Task 2	Task 3	Task 4	Task 5	Task 6	Task 1	Task 2	Task 3	Task 4	Task 5	Task 6
1	1001	1055	930	1006	920	1004	1014	1036	967	942	956	1057
2	931	1069	828	904	988	976	935	917	980	989	1090	894
3	958	982	1032	852	1000	887	944	980	988	889	962	1086
. . .												
p	1001	1055	930	1006	920	1004	1014	1036	967	942	956	1057
. . .												
n	975	1021	1099	1034	1000	1049	996	1069	1020	1071	1006	838

In this G study, institutions (schools) are the *object of measurement* and both tasks and judges are *facets* of the measurement. The universe of admissible observations includes all possible tasks and judges that a decision maker would be equally willing to interpret as bearing on students' mean level of performance at an institution.

To pinpoint different sources of measurement error, G theory extends earlier analysis of variance approaches to reliability. It estimates the variation in scores due to the object of measurement (here, schools), each facet (here, tasks and judges), and their combinations (interactions). More specifically, G theory estimates the components of observed-score variance contributed by the object of measurement, the facets, and their combinations. In this way, the theory isolates different sources of score variation in measurements. In practice, the analysis of variance is used to estimate variance components. In contrast to experimental studies, the analysis of variance is not used to formally test hypotheses.

Now let's turn back to the CLA example. Each school's observed score is decomposed into a component for school, task, judge, and combinations (interactions) of school, task, and judge. The school component of the score reflects systematic variation in schools in students' mean performance, giving rise to variability among schools (reflected by the school variance component). The other score components reflect sources of error. Consider the component for tasks. An easy task would tend to raise all schools' scores on that task, and a difficult task would tend to lower all schools' scores on that task, giving rise to mean differences from one task to another (a non-zero task [t] variance component). While tasks did not seem to vary in difficulty in the G study presented here, as will be seen below, a non-zero effect is hypothetically possible. Or consider the component for the interaction between schools and tasks. Whether the group of students at a school finds a particular task easy or difficult may depend on the match between the students' academic focus and the academic focus of the task's scenario. For example, schools with a predominance of science and engineering majors may do well on the performance tasks based on science and engineering scenarios (and less well on the humanities-based scenarios) whereas schools with a predominance of humanities majors may do well on the performance tasks based on humanities scenarios (and less well on the science and engineering-based scenarios), giving rise to a non-zero school × task interaction ($s \times t$ variance component). The theory describes the dependability ("reliability") of generalizations made from a school's observed score (the mean of students' scores at that school) on the particular tasks administered and the particular judges evaluating the responses to the score that a school would obtain in the broad universe of possible tasks and judges—the school's "universe score" (true score in classical test theory). Hence the name, "Generalizability Theory."

G theory recognizes that an assessment might be adapted for particular decisions and so distinguishes a generalizability (G) study from a decision (D) study. In a G study, the universe of admissible observations is defined as broadly as possible (tasks, occasions, judges, etc.) to provide variance component estimates to a wide variety of decision makers. A D study typically selects only some facets for a particular purpose, thereby narrowing the score interpretation to a universe of generalization. A different generalizability (reliability) coefficient can then be calculated for each particular use of the assessment. In the performance assessment example, we might decide to use only one judge per task and perhaps four tasks for decision-making purposes, so the generalizability coefficient could be calculated to reflect this proposed use.

In the remainder of this chapter, we take up, in more detail, G studies, D studies, and the design of G and D studies. We also briefly sketch the multivariate version of G theory and end with a section on additional topics.

Generalizability Studies

A G study is designed specifically to isolate and estimate as many facets of measurement error from the universe of admissible observations as is reasonably and economically feasible. The study includes the most important facets that a variety of decision makers might wish to generalize over (e.g., tasks, judges, occasions). Typically, a G study uses "crossed" designs where, for example, all schools are measured on all levels of all facets. In our example, all schools in a sample (sample size, n) are measured on the same six tasks and evaluated by the same two judges (Table 10.1). A crossed design provides maximal information about the variation contributed by the object of measurement (universe-score or desirable variation analogous to true-score variance), the facets, and their combinations, to the total amount of variation in the observed scores.

Components of the Observed Score

An observed measurement can be decomposed into a component or effect for the universe score and one or more error components with data collected in a G study. Consider our two-facet crossed $s \times t \times j$ (school × task × judge) design where tasks and judges are considered to have been randomly selected from an indefinitely large universe of admissible tasks and judges (random-effects model). The object of measurement, here schools, is not a source of error and, therefore, is not a facet. In the $s \times t \times j$ design with generalization over all admissible tasks and judges, the components of an observed score (X_{stj}) for a particular school (s) on a particular task (t) for a particular judge (j) are:

$X_{stj} =$ (10.1)

μ	grand mean
$+\mu_s - \mu$	school effect
$+\mu_t - \mu$	task effect
$+\mu_j - \mu$	judge effect
$+\mu_{st} - \mu_s - \mu_t + \mu$	school × task effect
$+\mu_{sj} - \mu_s - \mu_j + \mu$	school × judge effect
$+\mu_{tj} - \mu_t - \mu_j + \mu$	task × judge effect
$+X_{stj} - \mu_{st} - \mu_{sj} - \mu_{tj} + \mu_s + \mu_t + \mu_j - \mu$	residual

where $\mu = E_s E_t E_j X_{stj}$ and $\mu_s = E_t E_j X_{stj}$ with E meaning expectation and other terms in (10.1) are defined analogously. In Equation 10.1 the residual is whatever is left over in the observed score after accounting for the grand mean and the effects associated with the school, task, and judge and their interactions.

Except for the grand mean, μ, each observed-score component varies from one level to another—for example, tasks on a test may vary in difficulty. Assuming a random-effects model, the distribution of each component or "effect," except for the grand mean, has a mean of zero and a variance σ^2 (called the variance component). The variance component for the school effect is $\sigma_s^2 = E_s(\mu_s - \mu)^2$, and is called the *universe-score* variance component. The variance components for the other effects are defined similarly. The residual variance component, $\sigma_{stj,e}^2$, reflects the person × task × occasion interaction confounded with residual error since there is one observation per cell (see scores in Table 10.1). The collection of observed scores, X_{stj}, has a variance, $\sigma_{X_{stj}}^2 = E_s E_t E_j (X_{stj} - \mu)^2$, which equals the sum of the variance components:

$$\sigma_{X_{stj}}^2 = \sigma_s^2 + \sigma_t^2 + \sigma_j^2 + \sigma_{st}^2 + \sigma_{sj}^2 + \sigma_{tj}^2 + \sigma_{stj,e}^2.$$ (10.2)

Each variance component can be estimated from a traditional analysis of variance (or other methods such as maximum likelihood, e.g., Searle, 1987). The relative magnitudes of the estimated variance components (denoted as $\hat{\sigma}^2$), except for $\hat{\sigma}_s^2$, provide information about potential sources of error influencing a behavioral measurement. Statistical tests are not used in G theory; instead, standard errors for variance component estimates provide information about sampling variability of estimated variance components (e.g., Brennan, 2001).

In our example (Table 10.2), the estimated school (universe-score) variance, $\hat{\sigma}_s^2$ (817.466), is fairly large compared to the other components (20.9 percent of total variation). This shows that, averaging over tasks and judges, schools in the sample differed systematically in performance. Because schools constitute the object of measurement, not error, this variability represents systematic school-to-school differences in performance. The other large estimated variance components concern the task facet more than the judge facet. The impact of judges on variability of scores is small. First, the small $\hat{\sigma}_j^2$ (1.6% of total variation) shows that judges' assessments were very similar, averaging over schools and tasks. Second, the small $\hat{\sigma}_{sj}^2$ (1.6% of the total variation) shows that the relative standings of schools across judges were quite stable. The impact of tasks on variability of scores is much larger. Although the zero $\hat{\sigma}_t^2$ shows that tasks were of equal difficulty (an artifact of scaling procedures that adjust for task difficulty in our example), averaging over schools and judges, the large $\hat{\sigma}_{st}^2$ tells a more complicated story. The large $\hat{\sigma}_{st}^2$ (17.1% of total variation) reflects different relative standings of schools across tasks, averaging over judges. For example, in Table 10.1, School 3 shows considerably higher performance on Task 3 (a mean score of 1,010, averaging over judges) than on Task 4 (a mean score of 871, averaging over judges), and it correspondingly ranks fairly high among schools on Task 3 but very low on Task 4. School 1, in contrast, shows somewhat higher performance on Task 4 than on Task 3, averaging over judges (974 vs. 949), and correspondingly a higher rank among schools on Task 4 than on Task 3. The zero $\hat{\sigma}_{tj}^2$ indicates that the rank ordering of task difficulty was the same across judges. Finally, the large $\hat{\sigma}_{stj,e}^2$ (58.8%) reflects the varying relative standing of schools across task-judge combinations and/or other sources of error not systematically incorporated into the G study.

Decision Studies

Generalizability theory distinguishes a D study from a G study. The D study uses information from a G study to design a measurement procedure that minimizes error for a particular purpose. In planning a D study, the decision maker defines the universe that he or she proposes to generalize to, called the universe of generalization, which may contain some or all of the facets and their levels in the universe of admissible observations—tasks, judges, or both in our example. In the D study, decisions usually will be based on the mean over multiple observations (e.g., multiple tasks) rather than on a single observation. The mean score over a sample of n_t' tasks and n_j' judges, for example, is denoted as X_{sTJ} in contrast to a score on a single item and occasion, X_{stj}. A two-facet, crossed D-study design where decisions are to be made on the basis of X_{sTJ} is, then, denoted as $s \times T \times J$.

Table 10.2 Estimated Variance Components in the Example s × t × j Design

Source	Variance Component	Estimate	% Total Variability
School (s)	σ_s^2	817.766	20.9
Task (t)	σ_t^2	0[a]	0
Judge (j)	σ_j^2	62.564	1.6
s × t	σ_{st}^2	671.423	17.1
s × j	σ_{sj}^2	62.178	1.6
t × j	σ_{tj}^2	0[a]	0
s × t × j, e	$\sigma_{stj,e}^2$	2305.770	58.8

a Negative estimated variance component set equal to zero.

Types of Decisions and Measurement Error

G theory recognizes that the decision maker might want to make two types of decisions based on a behavioral measurement: relative ("norm-referenced") and absolute ("criterion-" or "domain-referenced"). A relative decision focuses on the rank order of schools; an absolute decision focuses on the level of school performance, regardless of rank. In this section, we describe measurement error and reliability coefficients for a random-effects design, in which the tasks and judges are considered to be randomly sampled from the universe of all admissible tasks and judges, and the decision maker intends to generalize beyond the randomly sampled tasks and judges to all tasks and judges in the universe.

Measurement error for relative decisions

For relative decisions, the error in a random-effects s × T × J design is defined as:

$$\delta_{sTJ} = (X_{sTJ} - \mu_{TJ}) - (\mu_s - \mu) \tag{10.3}$$

where $\mu_s = E_T E_J X_{sTJ}$ and $\mu_{TJ} = E_s X_{sTJ}$. The variance of the errors for relative decisions is:

$$\sigma^2_\delta = E_s E_T E_J \delta^2_{sTJ} = \sigma^2_{sT} + \sigma^2_{sJ} + \sigma^2_{sTJ,e}$$
$$= \frac{\sigma^2_{st}}{n'_t} + \frac{\sigma^2_{sj}}{n'_j} + \frac{\sigma^2_{stj,e}}{n'_t n'_j} \tag{10.4}$$

Notice that the "main effects" of tasks and judges do not enter into error for relative decisions because, for example, all schools are measured on the same tasks so any difference in tasks influences all schools and does not change rank order. In our D study, suppose we decided to use the same number of tasks and judges as in the G study, that is, $n'_t = 6$ and $n'_j = 2$. Substituting, we have:

$$\hat{\sigma}^2_\delta = \frac{671.423}{6} + \frac{62.178}{2} + \frac{2305.770}{6 \bullet 2} = 335.140.$$

Suppose, instead, we decide to increase the number of tasks to 8 and the number of judges to 3: $n'_t = 8$ and $n'_j = 3$. Substituting those values into (10.4) yields $\hat{\sigma}^2_\delta = 200.728$. Simply put, in order to reduce $\hat{\sigma}^2_\delta$, n'_t and n'_j may be increased in a manner analogous to the Spearman-Brown prophecy formula in classical test theory and the standard error of the mean in sampling theory.

Measurement error for absolute decisions

An absolute decision focuses on the level of a school's performance independent of other schools' performance (cf. criterion-referenced or domain-referenced interpretations). For example, in California a minimum passing score on the written drivers' examination is 80% correct, regardless of how others perform on the test. For absolute decisions, the error in a random-effects $s \times T \times J$ design is defined as:

$$\Delta_{sTJ} = X_{sTJ} - \mu_s \tag{10.5}$$

and the variance of the errors is:

$$\sigma^2_\Delta = E_s E_T E_J \Delta^2_{sTJ} = \sigma^2_T + \sigma^2_J + \sigma^2_{sT} + \sigma^2_{sJ} + \sigma^2_{TJ} + \sigma^2_{sTJ,e}$$
$$= \frac{\sigma^2_t}{n'_t} + \frac{\sigma^2_j}{n'_j} + \frac{\sigma^2_{st}}{n'_t} + \frac{\sigma^2_{sj}}{n'_j} + \frac{\sigma^2_{tj}}{n'_t n'_j} + \frac{\sigma^2_{stj,e}}{n'_t n'_j} \tag{10.6}$$

Note that, with absolute decisions, the main effect of tasks and judges—how difficult a task is or how lenient a judge is—*does* affect the level of performance measured even though neither changes the rank order of schools. Consequently, they are included in the definition of measurement error. Also note that $\sigma_\Delta^2 \geq \sigma_\delta^2$ (the error for absolute decisions is greater than or equal to the effect for relative decisions). Substituting values from Table 10.2, as was done above for relative decisions, provides a numerical index for estimated measurement error for absolute decisions. For six tasks and two judges ($n_t' = 6$ and n_j'), we have:

$$\hat{\sigma}_\Delta^2 = \frac{0}{6} + \frac{62.564}{2} + \frac{671.423}{6} + \frac{62.178}{2} + \frac{0}{6 \bullet 2} + \frac{2305.770}{6 \bullet 2} = 366.422.$$

If we decide instead to increase the number of tasks to 8 and the number of judges to 3: $n_t' = 8$ and $n_j' = 3$, $\hat{\sigma}_\Delta^2 = 221.582$.

"Reliability" Coefficients

Although G theory stresses the interpretation of variance components and measurement error, it provides summary coefficients that are analogous to the reliability coefficient in classical test theory (true-score variance divided by observed-score variance, i.e., an intraclass correlation). The theory distinguishes between a Generalizability Coefficient for relative decisions and an Index of Dependability for absolute decisions.

Generalizability Coefficient

The Generalizability (G) Coefficient is analogous to the reliability coefficient in classical test theory. It is the ratio of the universe-score variance to the expected observed-score variance, i.e., an intraclass correlation. For relative decisions and an s × T × J random-effects design, the generalizability coefficient is:

$$E\rho_{X_{sTJ},\mu_s}^2 = E\rho^2 = \frac{E_s(\mu_s - \mu)^2}{E_s E_T E_J (X_{sTJ} - \mu_{TJ})^2} = \frac{\sigma_s^2}{\sigma_s^2 + \sigma_\delta^2}. \tag{10.7}$$

From Table 10.2, we can calculate an estimate of the G coefficient for six tasks and two judges:

$$E\hat{\rho}^2 = \frac{817.466}{817.466 + 335.140} = 0.709.$$

In words, the estimated proportion of observed score variance due to universe-score variance is 0.709. Increasing the number of tasks and judges to eight and three, respectively, yields $E\hat{\rho}^2 = 0.803$.

Dependability Index

For absolute decisions with an s × T × J random-effects design, the index of dependability (Brennan, 2001; see also Kane & Brennan, 1977) is:

$$\Phi = \frac{\sigma_s^2}{\sigma_s^2 + \sigma_\Delta^2}. \tag{10.8}$$

Substituting estimates from Table 10.2, we can calculate the dependability index for an assessment with six tasks and two judges evaluating each task:

$$\hat{\Phi} = \frac{817.466}{817.466 + 366.422} = 0.690.$$

Increasing the number of tasks and judges to eight and three, respectively, gives $\hat{\Phi} = 0.787$. Notice that, in our example, the dependability index is only slightly lower than the G coefficient (0.690 vs. 0.709 for six tasks and two judges; 0.787 vs. 0.803 for eight tasks and three judges) because the estimated variance components corresponding to the main effects for task and judge, and the interaction between task and judge are quite small (Table 10.2).

For criterion-referenced decisions involving a fixed cutting score, λ, and assuming that λ is a constant that is specified a priori, the error of measurement is:

$$\Delta_{sTJ} = (X_{sTJ} - \lambda) - (\mu_s - \lambda) = X_{sTJ} - \mu_s \tag{10.9}$$

and the index of dependability is:

$$\Phi_\lambda = \frac{E_s(\mu_p - \lambda)^2}{E_s E_T E_J (X_{sTJ} - \lambda)^2} = \frac{\sigma_s^2 + (\mu - \lambda)^2}{\sigma_s^2 + (\mu - \lambda)^2 + \sigma_\Delta^2}. \tag{10.10}$$

An unbiased estimator of $(\mu - \lambda)^2$ is $(\bar{X} - \lambda)^2 - \hat{\sigma}_{\bar{X}}^2$ where $\bar{X}$ is the observed grand mean over sampled objects of measurement and sampled conditions of measurement in a D study design and $\hat{\sigma}_{\bar{X}}^2$ is the error variance involved in using the observed grand mean $\bar{X}$ as an estimate of the grand mean over the population of schools and the universe of tasks and judges (μ). For the $s \times T \times J$ random-effects design, $\hat{\sigma}_{\bar{X}}^2$ is:

$$\hat{\sigma}_{\bar{X}}^2 = \frac{\hat{\sigma}_s^2}{n_s'} + \frac{\hat{\sigma}_t^2}{n_t'} + \frac{\hat{\sigma}_j^2}{n_j'} + \frac{\hat{\sigma}_{st}^2}{n_s' n_t'} + \frac{\hat{\sigma}_{sj}^2}{n_s' n_j'} + \frac{\hat{\sigma}_{tj}^2}{n_t' n_j'} + \frac{\hat{\sigma}_{stj,e}^2}{n_s' n_t' n_j'}. \tag{10.11}$$

The estimate of $\hat{\Phi}_\lambda$ is smallest when the cut score λ is equal to the observed grand mean $\bar{X}$. In the dataset presented in Table 10.1, $\bar{X} = 982.909$. For $\lambda = 1,000$, using $n_s' = 100$, $n_t' = 6$, $n_j' = 2$, and values in Table 10.2 gives $\hat{\Phi}_\lambda = 0.744$. For the same cut score, $\lambda = 1,000$, but increasing the number of tasks and judges to eight and three gives $\hat{\Phi}_\lambda = 0.830$.

Study Design in Generalizability and Decision Studies

Crossed and Nested Designs

Whenever possible, a G study should use a crossed design to provide maximal information about the components of variation in observed scores. In our example, each school has responses for all tasks and is evaluated by both judges (see Table 10.1). Consequently, seven different variance components can be estimated—one each for the main effects of school ($\hat{\sigma}_s^2$), task ($\hat{\sigma}_t^2$), and judge ($\hat{\sigma}_j^2$); two-way interactions between school and task ($\hat{\sigma}_{st}^2$), school and judge ($\hat{\sigma}_{sj}^2$), and task and judge ($\hat{\sigma}_{tj}^2$); and a residual due to the school × task × judge interaction and random error ($\hat{\sigma}_{stj,e}^2$).

In some cases, a G study will necessarily involve a nested (or partially nested) design. For example, a test may have multiple subtests (e.g., representing different content categories) with multiple items in each subtest. Because items in one subtest are different from the items in another subtest, items are nested within subtests. In this case, a fully crossed G study is not possible.

Although G studies should use crossed designs whenever possible to avoid confounding of effects, D studies may use nested designs for convenience or for increasing sample size, which typically reduces estimated error variance and, hence, increases estimated generalizability. In our example of judges rating performance tasks, it is not realistic in large-scale studies to have the same judges score all tasks, especially with a large number of institutions. Judges would be overwhelmed. Instead, in the D study we might use a different set of randomly sampled judges for each task (say, two judges per task). In this case, judges are nested within task; two judges are paired with task 1, two different judges are paired with task 2, and so on. If six tasks are to be used, then 12 judges and not just 2 judges will be sampled for the D study (see Table 10.3). The more judges, the greater the reliability (generalizability), typically.

For example, compare the error variance in a crossed $s \times T \times J$ design with the error variance in a partially nested $s \times (J:T)$ design where facet j is nested in facet t, and n' denotes the number of conditions of a facet under a decision maker's control. In a crossed $s \times T \times J$ design, the relative ($\hat{\sigma}^2_\delta$) and absolute ($\hat{\sigma}^2_\Delta$) error variances are:

$$\sigma^2_\delta = \sigma^2_{sT} + \sigma^2_{sJ} + \sigma^2_{sTJ} = \frac{\sigma^2_{st}}{n'_t} + \frac{\sigma^2_{sj}}{n'_j} + \frac{\sigma^2_{stj,e}}{n'_t n'_j} \tag{10.12a}$$

and

$$\sigma^2_\Delta = \sigma^2_T + \sigma^2_J + \sigma^2_{sT} + \sigma^2_{sJ} + \sigma^2_{TJ} + \sigma^2_{sTJ}$$

$$= \frac{\sigma^2_t}{n'_t} + \frac{\sigma^2_j}{n'_j} + \frac{\sigma^2_{st}}{n'_t} + \frac{\sigma^2_{sj}}{n'_j} + \frac{\sigma^2_{tj}}{n'_t n'_j} + \frac{\sigma^2_{stj,e}}{n'_t n'_j} \tag{10.12b}$$

In a nested $s \times (J:T)$ design, they are, respectively,

$$\sigma^2_\delta = \sigma^2_{sT} + \sigma^2_{sJ:T} = \frac{\sigma^2_{st}}{n'_t} + \frac{\sigma^2_{sj,sjt,e}}{n'_j n'_t}, \text{ and} \tag{10.13a}$$

$$\sigma^2_\Delta = \sigma^2_T + \sigma^2_{sT} + \sigma^2_{J:T} + \sigma^2_{sJ:T} = \frac{\sigma^2_t}{n'_t} + \frac{\sigma^2_{st}}{n'_t} + \frac{\sigma^2_{j,jt}}{n'_j n'_t} + \frac{\sigma^2_{sj,sjt,e}}{n'_j n'_t} \tag{10.13b}$$

In Equations 10.13a and 10.13b, σ^2_t and σ^2_{st} are directly available from a G study with design $s \times t \times j$, $\sigma^2_{j,jt}$ is the sum of σ^2_j and σ^2_{tj}, and $\sigma^2_{sj,sjt,e}$ is the sum of σ^2_{sj} and $\sigma^2_{stj,e}$. To estimate $\hat{\sigma}^2_\delta$ in a $s \times (J:T)$ design, for example, simply substitute estimated values for the variance components into Equation 10.13a; similarly for Equation 10.13b to estimate $\hat{\sigma}^2_\Delta$. Due to the difference in the designs, $\hat{\sigma}^2_\delta$ is smaller in Equation 10.13a than in Equation 10.12a and $\hat{\sigma}^2_\Delta$ is smaller in Equation 10.13b than in Equation 10.12b.

Using the estimated variance components in Table 10.2, we find that having different judges score different tasks $(j:t)$ yields slightly higher estimated generalizability than does the fully crossed design. For a fully crossed design with 6 tasks and 2 judges, $\hat{\rho}^2 = 0.709$ and $\hat{\Phi} = 0.690$. For the partially nested design $(s \times (J:T))$ with 6 tasks and 2 judges, $\hat{\rho}^2 = 0.726$ and $\hat{\Phi} = 0.722$. The fact that values of $\hat{\rho}^2$ and $\hat{\Phi}$ are larger for the partially nested design than for the fully crossed design is solely attribut-

Table 10.3 Crossed School × (Judge : Task) G study of CLA Scores

School	Task 1		Task 2		Task 3		Task 4		Task 5		Task 6	
	Judge 1	*Judge 2*	*Judge 3*	*Judge 4*	*Judge 5*	*Judge 6*	*Judge 7*	*Judge 8*	*Judge 9*	*Judge 10*	*Judge 11*	*Judge 12*
1	1001	1014	1055	967	930	967	1006	942	920	956	1004	1057
2	931	935	1069	980	828	980	904	989	988	1090	976	894
3	958	944	982	988	1032	988	852	889	1000	962	887	1086
. . .												
p	1001	1014	1055	967	930	967	1006	942	920	956	1004	1057
. . .												
n	975	996	1021	1020	1099	1020	1034	1071	1000	1006	1049	838

able to the difference between Equations 10.12a and 10.13a and the difference between Equations 10.12b and 10.13b.

Random and Fixed Facets

G theory is essentially a random effects theory. Typically a random facet is created by randomly sampling levels of a facet (e.g., tasks for a performance assessment). When the levels of a facet have not been sampled randomly from the universe of admissible observations but the intended universe of generalization is infinitely large, the concept of exchangeability may be invoked to consider the facet as random (Shavelson & Webb, 1981).

A fixed facet (cf. fixed factor in analysis of variance) arises when (a) the decision maker purposely selects certain conditions and is not interested in generalizing beyond them, (b) the decision maker finds it unreasonable to generalize beyond the levels observed, or (c) when the entire universe of levels is small and all levels are included in the measurement design. G theory typically treats fixed facets by averaging over the conditions of the fixed facet and examining the generalizability of the average over the random facets (Cronbach, et al., 1972). When it does not make conceptual sense to average over the conditions of a fixed facet, a separate G study may be conducted within each condition of the fixed facet (Shavelson & Webb, 1991) or a full multivariate analysis may be performed with the levels of the fixed facet comprising a vector of dependent variables (Brennan, 2001; see below).

G theory recognizes that the universe of admissible observations in a G study (e.g., multiple occasions) may be broader than the universe of generalization of interest in a D study (e.g., a decision maker only interested in one occasion). The decision maker may reduce the levels of a facet (creating a fixed facet), select (and thereby control) one level of a facet, or ignore a facet. A facet is fixed in a D study when $n' = N'$, where n' is the number of levels for a facet in the D study and N' is the total number of levels for a facet in the universe of generalization.

As an example, we consider the analytic writing tasks on the Collegiate Learning Assessment. Some tasks ask students to build and defend an argument about, for example, the importance of a college education preparing students for a career instead of exposing students to a range of subject matters (Shavelson, 2008). Other tasks ask students to critique an argument. The two types or categories of tasks—build and develop an argument vs. critique an argument—were purposely selected to represent analytic writing skills and so category of task constitutes a fixed facet. We present here a generalizability study of institutions' scores on eight tasks: four in the first category (make an argument) and four in the second category (critique an argument; see Table 10.4). Tasks, which are considered to be a random selection from a large domain of tasks, constitute a random facet which is nested within the fixed category facet. The G study design, then, is tasks (random) nested within category (fixed) which are both crossed with schools, or *school × (task : category)* or $s \times (t{:}c)$. In this design, generalization is over tasks, but not task categories.

Table 10.4 Crossed School × (Task : Category) G study of CLA Scores

School	Category 1 (Make-an-Argument)				Category 2 (Critique-an-Argument)			
	Task 1	Task 2	Task 3	Task 4	Task 5	Task 6	Task 7	Task 8
1	1092	976	974	1026	896	1050	1093	996
2	1270	1122	1176	1134	1107	1199	1119	1162
3	1046	995	962	988	1010	939	944	934
. . .								
p	1010	1052	1042	1099	975	1018	1085	1167
. . .								
n	1011	940	985	1007	940	866	979	985

To show the effects of fixing a facet, we contrast the fully random $s \times (t{:}c)$ design (in which category (c) is treated as random) with the $s \times (t{:}c)$ design with category c treated as fixed. For the $s \times (t{:}c)$ design with all sources of variability considered *random*, the relative and absolute error variances, respectively, are:

$$\sigma_\delta^2 = \sigma_{sC}^2 + \sigma_{sT:C}^2 = \frac{\sigma_{sc}^2}{n_c'} + \frac{\sigma_{st,stc,e}^2}{n_t'n_c'} \quad , \text{and} \tag{10.14a}$$

$$\sigma_\Delta^2 = \sigma_C^2 + \sigma_{sC}^2 + \sigma_{T:C}^2 + \sigma_{sT:C}^2 = \frac{\sigma_c^2}{n_c'} + \frac{\sigma_{sc}^2}{n_c'} + \frac{\sigma_{t,tc}^2}{n_t'n_c'} + \frac{\sigma_{st,stc,e}^2}{n_t'n_c'}. \tag{10.14b}$$

And the generalizability coefficient and index of dependability, respectively, are:

$$E\rho^2 = \frac{\sigma_s^2}{\sigma_s^2 + \frac{\sigma_{sc}^2}{n_c'} + \frac{\sigma_{st,stc,e}^2}{n_t'n_c'}}, \text{ and} \tag{10.15a}$$

$$\Phi = \frac{\sigma_s^2}{\sigma_s^2 + \frac{\sigma_c^2}{n_c'} + \frac{\sigma_{sc}^2}{n_c'} + \frac{\sigma_{t,tc}^2}{n_t'n_c'} + \frac{\sigma_{st,stc,e}^2}{n_t'n_c'}}. \tag{10.15b}$$

In contrast to the treatment of random facets, statistically G theory treats a fixed facet by averaging over the conditions of the facet. In our example, the score for an institution on analytic writing will be the average over the two types of tasks. From a random-effects G study with design $s \times (t{:}c)$ in which the universe of admissible observations is defined by facets t and c of infinite size, fixing facet c in the D study and averaging over the n_c conditions of facet c (here, two) in the G study ($n_c = n_c'$) yields the following universe-score variance:

$$\sigma_\tau^2 = \sigma_s^2 + \sigma_{sC}^2 = \sigma_s^2 + \frac{\sigma_{sc}^2}{n_c'}, \tag{10.16}$$

where σ_τ^2 denotes universe-score variance in generic terms. When facet c is fixed, the universe score is based on a school's average score over the levels of facet c, so the generic universe-score variance in Equation 10.16 is the variance over schools' *mean* scores over the two task categories. Hence, Equation 10.16 includes σ_{sC}^2 as well as σ_s^2. $\hat{\sigma}_\tau^2$ is an unbiased estimate of universe-score variance for the mixed model only when the same levels of facet c are used in the G and D studies (Brennan, 2001). The relative and absolute error variances, respectively, are:

$$\sigma_\delta^2 = \sigma_{sT:C}^2 = \frac{\sigma_{st,stc,e}^2}{n_t'n_c'}, \text{ and} \tag{10.17a}$$

$$\sigma_\Delta^2 = \sigma_{T:C}^2 + \sigma_{sT:C}^2 = \frac{\sigma_{t,tc}^2}{n_t'n_c'} + \frac{\sigma_{st,stc,e}^2}{n_t'n_c'}. \tag{10.17b}$$

And the generalizability coefficient and index of dependability, respectively, are:

$$E\rho^2 = \frac{\sigma_s^2 + \frac{\sigma_{sc}^2}{n_c'}}{\sigma_s^2 + \frac{\sigma_{sc}^2}{n_c'} + \frac{\sigma_{st,stc,e}^2}{n_t'n_c'}}, \text{ and} \tag{10.18a}$$

$$\Phi = \frac{\sigma_s^2 + \dfrac{\sigma_{sc}^2}{n_c'}}{\sigma_s^2 + \dfrac{\sigma_{sc}^2}{n_c'} + \dfrac{\sigma_{t,tc}^2}{n_t'n_c'} + \dfrac{\sigma_{st,stc,e}^2}{n_t'n_c'}}. \tag{10.18b}$$

The estimated variance components for the random *s x (t:c)* design (Table 10.5) can be substituted into Equations 10.14 and 10.15 to estimate the generalizability for the fully random design and Equations 10.17 and 10.18 for the design with task category treated as fixed. The estimated generalizability is larger for the design with category treated as fixed than for the fully random design. Using the data in Table 10.5, administering two tasks in each of two categories, for example, yields E $\hat{\rho}^2$ = 0.915 and $\hat{\Phi}$ = 0.914 for the design with category fixed and E $\hat{\rho}^2$ = 0.908 and $\hat{\Phi}$ = 0.907 for the fully random design. The difference in estimated generalizability between the two designs would be greater had the estimates of σ_c^2 and σ_{sc}^2 been larger.

Multivariate Generalizability

For behavioral measurements involving multiple scores describing individuals' or institutions' performance, multivariate generalizability can be used to (a) estimate the reliability of difference scores, observable correlations, or universe-score and error correlations for various D study designs and sample sizes (Brennan, 2001); (b) estimate the reliability of a profile of scores using multiple regression of universe scores on the observed scores in the profile (Brennan, 2001; Cronbach, et al., 1972); or (c) produce a composite of scores with maximum generalizability (Shavelson & Webb, 1981). For all of these purposes, multivariate G theory decomposes both variances and covariances into components. In a two-facet, crossed *s × t × j* design with performance divided into two dependent variables—make an argument and critique an argument, say, the observed scores for the two variables for school *s* observed under conditions *t* and *j* can be denoted as $_1X_{stj}$ and $_2X_{stj}$, respectively.

The variances of observed scores, $\sigma^2_{_1X_{stj}}$ and $\sigma^2_{_2X_{stj}}$, are decomposed as in Equation 10.2. The covariance of observed scores, $\sigma_{_1X_{stj},_2X_{stj}}$, is decomposed in analogous fashion:

$$\sigma_{_1Xstj,_2Xstj} = \sigma_{_1s,_2s} + \sigma_{_1t,_2t} + \sigma_{_1j,_2j} + \sigma_{_1st,_2st} + \sigma_{_1sj,_2sj} \tag{10.19}$$
$$+ \sigma_{_1tj,_2tj} + \sigma_{_1stj,e,_2stj,e} .$$

In Equation 10.19, the term $\sigma_{_1s,_2s}$ is the covariance between universe scores for make an argument and critique an argument. The remaining terms in Equation 10.19 are error covariance components. The term $\sigma_{_1j,_2j}$, for example, is the covariance between make an argument and critique an argument scores due to the levels of observation for the judge facet (e.g., a particularly lenient judge awards relatively high scores for both make an argument and critique an argument tasks).

An important aspect of the development of multivariate G theory is the distinction between linked and unlinked conditions. The expected values of error covariance components are zero when conditions for observing different variables are unlinked, that is, selected independently (e.g., the

Table 10.5 Estimated Variance Components in the Example s x (t:c) Random Design

Source	Variance Component	Estimate	% Total Variability
School (*s*)	σ_s^2	7243.08	71.7
Category (*c*)	σ_c^2	10.10	0.1
Task: Category (*t:c*)	$\sigma_{t,tc}^2$	34.20	0.3
s ×c	σ_{sc}^2	105.85	1.1
st:c,e	$\sigma_{st,stc,e}^2$	2710.39	26.8

tasks used to obtain scores on one variable in a profile, make an argument, are selected independently of the tasks used to obtain scores on another variable, critique an argument). The expected values of error covariance components are nonzero when levels are linked or jointly sampled (e.g., the same judges provide scores for make an argument and critique an argument tasks).

Joe and Woodward (1976) presented a G coefficient for a multivariate composite that maximizes the ratio of universe score variation to universe score plus error variation by using statistically derived weights for each dependent variable (academic and social self-concept in our example). Alternatives to maximizing the reliability of a composite are to determine variable weights on the basis of expert judgment (Short, Shavelson, & Webb, 1986; Webb & Shavelson, 1981) or a confirmatory factor analysis (Marcoulides, 1994).

Additional Topics

Here we treat a few additional topics that have practical consequences in using G theory (for details and advanced topics, see Brennan, 2001). First, given the emphasis on estimated variance components in G theory, we consider the sampling variability of estimated variance components and how to estimate variance components, especially in unbalanced designs. Second, sometimes facets are "hidden" in a G study and are not accounted for in interpreting variance components. We briefly consider an example below. Third, measurement error is not constant as often assumed but depends on the magnitude of a school's universe score and so we treat this topic briefly. Fourth, the examples we have considered thus far have focused on generalizability of school means (over students), not generalizability of individual students' scores. We show how to explicitly recognize the generalizability of group means. Finally, we briefly mention approaches for optimizing generalizability under resource constraints, as well as computer programs that are available for carrying out generalizability analyses.

Variance Component Estimates

Here we treat three concerns (among many) in estimating variance components. The first concern deals with the variability ("bounce") in variance component estimates, the second with negative variance-component estimates (variances, σ^2, cannot be negative), and the third with unbalanced designs.

Variability in variance-component estimates

The first concern is that estimates of variance components may be unstable with usual sample sizes (Cronbach, et al., 1972). In particular, when estimating variance components we use mean squares from the analysis of variance. The more mean squares that are involved in estimating variance components, the larger the variability is likely to be in these estimates from one study to the next. For example, in our school × task × judge analysis (Table 10.2), σ_s^2 is estimated using MS_s. MS_s contains not only information about σ_s^2 but it also contains information about σ_{st}^2, σ_{sj}^2, and $\sigma_{stj,e}^2$, each of which is estimated from its corresponding mean square. For the estimated variance component for schools ($\hat{\sigma}_s^2 = 817.466$), the estimated standard error is quite large (342.303). To reduce the estimated standard errors would require a larger sample than the 23 schools, 6 tasks, and 2 judges used in the example G study presented here. Although exact confidence intervals for variance components are generally unavailable (due to the inability to derive exact distributions for variance component estimates), approximate confidence intervals are available if one assumes normality or uses a resampling technique such as the bootstap (illustrated in Brennan, 2001; for details, see Wiley, 2000).

Negative estimated variance components

Negative estimates of variance components can arise because of sampling error or model misspecification (Shavelson & Webb, 1981). We can identify four possible solutions when negative estimates are small in relative magnitude: (a) substitute zero for the negative estimate and carry through the zero in other expected mean square equations from the analysis of variance, which produces biased estimates (Cronbach, et al., 1972); (b) set negative estimates to zero but use the negative estimates in expected mean square equations for other components (Brennan, 2001); (c) use a Bayesian approach that sets a lower bound of zero on the estimated variance component (Shavelson & Webb, 1981); and (d) use maximum likelihood methods, which preclude negative estimates (Searle, 1987).

Variance component estimation with unbalanced designs

An unbalanced design arises when the number of levels of a nested facet varies for each level of another facet or the object of measurement, producing unequal numbers of levels. For example, if different judges evaluate different tasks (judges are nested within tasks) and if different *numbers* of judges are assigned to each task, the unequal numbers of judges create unbalancing. Although analysis of variance methods for estimating variance components are straightforward when applied to balanced data, have the advantage of requiring few distributional assumptions, and produce unbiased estimators, problems arise with unbalanced data. They include many different decompositions of the total sums of squares without an obvious basis for choosing among them (which leads to a variety of ways in which mean squares can be adjusted for other effects in the model), biased estimation in mixed models (not a problem in G theory because G theory averages over fixed facets in a mixed model and estimates only variances of random effects, or mixed models can be handled via multivariate G theory), and algebraically and computationally complex rules for deriving expected values of mean squares. A possible solution is to exhaustively subdivide a dataset into all possible balanced subsets and then combine the variance component estimates from the different subsets (Chiu & Wolfe, 2002).

Hidden Facets

In some cases, two facets are linked such that as the levels of one facet vary, correspondingly the levels of another facet do too. This might not be readily obvious; hence the name, "hidden facet." The most notorious and easily understood hidden facet is the *occasion* facet. For example, as a person performs a series of tasks, his performance occurs over time. Typically variability in performance from task to task would be interpreted as task-sampling variability. However, while task is varying, the hidden facet, occasion, is too. It just might be that what appears to be task-sampling variability is actually occasion-sampling variability and this alternative interpretation might change prescriptions for improving the dependability of the measurement (Cronbach, Linn, Brennan, & Haertel, 1997).

In the CLA performance task example, a possible hidden facet is the field of study of the students performing the tasks at a particular school. If the field of study of the students taking the test varies from school to school (for example, at one school, students emphasizing engineering take the test; at another school, English majors take the test; at a third school, Psychology majors take the test), then what appears to be school-to-school variability may actually be variability due to examinee field of study. To avoid this confounding, it would be important to either explicitly incorporate examinee field of study as a source of variability in the design, or ensure that examinee field(s) of study is similar from school to school.

Nonconstant Error Variance for Different True Scores

The description of error variance given here, especially in Equations 10.4 and 10.6, implicitly assumes that variance of measurement error is constant for all schools, regardless of true score (universe score, here). The assumption of constant error variance for different true scores has been criticized for decades, including by Lord (1955) who derived a formula for conditional error variance that varies as a function of true score. His approach produced estimated error variances that are smaller for very high and very low true scores than true scores that are closer to the mean, producing a concave-down quadratic form. If we consider students as the object of measurement, a student with a very high true score is likely to score highly across multiple tasks (small error variance), while students with true scores close to the mean are likely to produce scores that fluctuate more from task to task (larger error variance). Stated another way, for students with very high or very low true scores, there is little opportunity for errors to influence observed scores. This issue is less likely to figure prominently when school is considered the object of measurement because true scores for school means are not likely to be very high (i.e., near the maximum possible score) or very low. Brennan (2001) discusses conditional error variances in generalizability theory and shows estimation procedures for conditional relative and absolute error variance for relative and absolute decisions, for univariate and multivariate studies, and for balanced and unbalanced designs.

Generalizability of Group Means

In our examples of the performance tasks and the analytic writing tasks on the Collegiate Learning Assessment, the school, not an individual student, is the object of study. Each score entering the analysis (see Table 10.1) is the mean over a group of students responding to the particular task. Not explicitly taken into account, for simplicity, was the fact that the sampling of students gives rise to errors of measurement. Explicitly incorporating students (persons) as a source of variation will lead to more accurate estimates of generalizability and make it possible to estimate how many students should be sampled for dependable measures of performance at the school level.

In a fully random design with persons (p) nested within schools (s) and crossed with tasks (t), denoted as $(p{:}s) \times t$, the generalizability coefficient with schools as the object of measurement and when generalizing over persons and tasks is:

$$E\rho_s^2 = \frac{\sigma_s^2}{\sigma_s^2 + \dfrac{\sigma_{p:s}^2}{n_p'} + \dfrac{\sigma_{st}^2}{n_t'} + \dfrac{\sigma_{(p:s)t,e}^2}{n_p' n_t'}}. \tag{10.20}$$

In Equation 10.20, variation among persons within schools ($\sigma_{p:s}^2$) contributes to error variation but not universe-score variation.

Alternative designs may be considered. For example, if it is not feasible for students at a school to respond to all performance tasks, different subgroups of students at a school could be assigned different tasks. In this case, schools (s) are crossed with tasks (t), but persons (p) are nested within school-task combinations, and the design is denoted as $p{:}(s \times t)$.

Optimizing the Decision (D) Study Design

When designing a decision study that will yield a reasonable level of estimated generalizability, the decision maker may consider both the design of the D study and the number of observations to be used for each facet in the design. The resources available for the D study may not accommodate the number of observations needed for a desired level of estimated generalizability, however. In this case, the decision maker may want to know the number of observations per facet that will minimize error (and maximize generalizability) for a fixed number of observations per school (Woodward & Joe, 1973) or for a given set of cost constraints. Marcoulides and Goldstein (1991, 1992); Marcoulides, 1993, 1995; see also Sanders, 1992; Sanders, Theunissen, & Baas, 1991) describe methods for minimizing error variance in decision studies under cost constraints, both total costs and per-facet costs, for univariate and multivariate designs.

Computer Programs

A number of popular computer packages and programs provide estimates of variance components in generalizability studies. These include SAS (SAS Institute, 2002), SPSS (SPSS, 2009), and S–Plus (MathSoft, 1997). (Table 10.6 gives example SPSS syntax to estimate variance components for the data in Table 10.1.) In addition, two programs have been developed specifically for generalizability theory: GENOVA (GENeralized analysis Of Variance; Brennan, 2001; Crick & Brennan, 1983) and EduG (Cardinet, Johnson, & Pini, 2010). GENOVA handles complete balanced designs (with up to five facets), urGENOVA handles designs that are unbalanced due to nesting and some designs with missing data, and mGENOVA performs multivariate generalizability and decision analyses for a selected set of designs that are balanced or unbalanced due to nesting. EduG incorporates added flexibility in univariate designs by allowing the user to consider different sources of variation as the object of measurement (the principle of *symmetry* of a behavioral measurement, Cardinet, Tourneur, & Allal, 1976).

The programs listed above use a variety of methods for estimating variance components, including the ANOVA procedure using expected mean square equations (EMS, Cornfield & Tukey, 1956), Henderson's Method 1 and Method 3 (Henderson, 1953), MINQUE (minimum norm quadratic unbiased estimation) with equal weighting of all variance components (MINQUE(0)) or equal weights for all variance components except the residual (MINQUE(1)), maximum likelihood, and restricted maximum likelihood. GENOVA also provides estimates using Cronbach et al.'s (1972) recommendation to substitute zero for negative estimated variance components wherever they appear in the EMS equations. As noted by Brennan (2001), processing times and memory requirements vary widely, depending on the complexity of the design, the numbers of observations (which can easily exceed 10,000), the estimation method used, and the computational algorithm employed.

Table 10.6 SPSS Setup for G Study of Data in Table 10.1

```
TITLE 'Variance Components for s x t x j Random-Effects Design'.
data list /1 score school task judge (4.0,x,f2.0,2(x,f1.0)).
begin data.
1001 1 1 1
1055 1 2 1
 930 1 3 1
.
.
.
1071 23 4 2
1006 23 5 2
 838 23 6 2
end data.
VARCOMP score by school task judge
/RANDOM = school task judge
/DESIGN = school task judge school*task school*judge task*judge.
```

References

Brennan, R. L. (2001). *Generalizability theory*. New York, NY: Springer-Verlag.

Cardinet, J., Johnson, S., & Pini, G. (2010). *Applying generalizability theory using EduG*. New York, NY: Routledge.

Cardinet, J., Tourneur, Y., & Allal, L. (1976). The symmetry of generalizability theory: applications to educational measurement. *Journal of Educational Measurement, 13*, 119–135.

Chiu, C. W. T., & Wolfe, E. W. (2002). A method for analyzing sparse data matrices in the generalizability theory framework. *Applied Psychological Measurement, 26*, 321–338.

Cornfield, J., & Tukey, J. W. (1956). Average values of mean squares in factorials. *Annals of Mathematical Statistics, 27*, 907–949.

Crick, J. E., & Brennan, R. L. (1983). GENOVA: A generalized analysis of variance system [Computer software and manual]. Iowa City, IA: University of Iowa. (Available from http://www.education.uiowa.edu/casma/)

Cronbach, L. J., Gleser, G. C., Nanda, H., & Rajaratnam, N. (1972). *The dependability of behavioral measurements: Theory of generalizability for scores and profiles*. New York, NY: Wiley.

Cronbach, L. J., Linn, R. L., Brennan, R. L., & Haertel, E. H. (1997). Generalizability analysis for performance assessments of student achievement or school effectiveness. *Educational and Psychological Measurement, 57*, 373–399.

Ewell, P. T. (2009). *Assessment, accountability, and improvement: Revisiting the tension*. (NILOA Occasional Paper No. 1). Urbana, IL: University of Illinois and Indiana University, National Institute for Learning Outcomes Assessment. Retrieved from http://www.learningoutcomeassessment.org/OccasionalPapers.htm

Haertel, E. H. (2006). Reliability. In R. L. Brennan (Ed.), *Educational measurement* (4th ed., pp. 65–110). Westport, CT: American Council on Education/Praeger.

Henderson, C. R. (1953). Estimation of variance and covariance components. *Biometrics, 9*, 227–252.

Joe, G. W., & Woodward, J. A. (1976). Some developments in multivariate generalizability. *Psychometrika, 41*, 205–217.

Kane, M. T., & Brennan, R. L. (1977). The generalizability of class means. *Review of Educational Research, 47*, 267–292.

Lord, F. M. (1955). Estimating test reliability. *Educational and Psychological Measurement, 16*, 325–336.

Marcoulides, G. A. (1993). Maximizing power in generalizability studies under budget constraints. *Journal of Educational Statistics, 18*, 197–206.

Marcoulides, G. A. (1994). Selecting weighting schemes in multivariate generalizability studies. *Educational and Psychological Measurement, 54*, 3–7.

Marcoulides, G. A. (1995). Designing measurement studies under budget constraints: Controlling error of measurement and power. *Educational and Psychological Measurement, 55*, 423–428.

Marcoulides, G. A., & Goldstein, Z. (1991). Selecting the number of observations in multivariate measurement studies under budget constraints. *Educational and Psychological Measurement, 51*, 573–584.

Marcoulides, G. A., & Goldstein, Z. (1992). The optimization of multivariate generalizability studies with budget constraints. *Educational and Psychological Measurement, 52*, 301–309.

MathSoft, Inc. (1997). S-Plus 4.5 standard edition [Computer software]. Cambridge, MA: Author.

Sanders, P. F. (1992). Alternative solutions for optimizing problems in generalizability theory. *Psychometrika, 57*, 351–356.

Sanders, P. F., Theunissen, T. J. J. M., & Baas, S. M. (1991). Maximizing the coefficient of generalizability under the constraint of limited resources. *Psychometrika, 56*, 87–96.

SAS Institute, Inc. (2002). The SAS system for Windows release 9.2 [Computer software]. Cary, NC: Author.

Searle, S. R. (1987). *Linear models for unbalanced data*. New York, NY: Wiley.

Shavelson, R. J. (2008). The Collegiate Learning Assessment. *Forum for the Future of Higher Education/Ford Policy Forum 2008* (pp. 18–24). Cambridge, MA.

Shavelson, R. J. (2009). *Measuring college learning responsibly: Accountability in a new era*. Stanford, CA: Stanford University Press.

Shavelson, R. J., & Webb, N. M. (1981). Generalizability theory: 1973–1980. *British Journal of Mathematical and Statistical Psychology, 34*, 133–166.

Shavelson, R. J., & Webb, N. M. (1991). *Generalizability theory: A primer*. Newbury Park, CA: Sage.

Short, L. M., Shavelson, R. J., & Webb, N. M. (1986, April). *Issues in multivariate generalizability: Weighting schemes and dimensionality*. Paper presented at the Annual Meeting of the American Educational Research Association, San Francisco, CA.

SPSS, Inc. (2009). SPSS for Windows release 17 [Computer software]. Chicago, IL: Author.

Webb, N. M., & Shavelson, R. J. (1981). Multivariate generalizability of General Education Development ratings. *Journal of Educational Measurement, 18*, 13–22.

Wiley, E. (2000). *Bootstrap strategies for variance component estimation: Theoretical and empirical results*. Unpublished doctoral dissertation, Stanford University, Stanford, CA.

Woodward, J. A., & Joe, G. W. (1973). Maximizing the coefficient of generalizability in multi-facet decision studies. *Psychometrika, 38*, 173–181.

11

ITEM RESPONSE THEORY IN MEASUREMENT, ASSESSMENT, AND EVALUATION FOR HIGHER EDUCATION

Steven J. Osterlind and Ze Wang

The scoring scale for a mental measure (e.g., educational and psychological tests) dictates the type and extent of interpretations that are possible. When a particular test is grounded in classical test theory (CTT), for example, the scale should reflect the notion of an extant true score; reliability will give important clues to the authenticity of that true score. Commonly, for CTT-based tests composed of dichotomously scored items or exercises, an examinee's score is simply the raw score, a summation of correct endorsements. Of course, the raw score need not be the only reported score. Numerous interpretations of the score are derived though transformations of the scale—to some kind of standardized score, for instance. Many such transformations are described in *Test Service Bulletin #48*, a famous early publication of the Psychological Corporation (1955).

But when a test is based on principles of cognitive psychology—the case for most modern educational and psychological tests (see Mislevy, 1996)—the measurement is more complex and a simple raw score scale may not be adequate for its interpretative task. Here, the scale must allow for reliable interpretations of latent, and exactly unknown, traits or proficiencies. The latencies may represent achievements, proficiencies, opinions, beliefs, attitudes, and so forth. These underlying cognitive aspects of an examinee are envisioned (theoretically, at least) on a continuum with range $\pm\infty$. No practical scale captures the entire range of the latency, but it does reflect some useful portion of the range, commonly three standard deviations about ($\pm$) a norm.

An Introduction to Item Response Theory

Far and away the most popular strategy for scale development in cognitive measures with sufficient audience is to use item response theory (IRT). IRT is both a theory of measurement and a concomitant set of powerful statistics useful for its implementation (Osterlind, 2010). The theory of IRT rests on cognitive psychology and posits that *both* characteristics about a mental measure's stimuli (i.e., items or exercises) *and* the ability or proficiency of examinees can be represented on a common scale that itself accurately reflects a particular latency. Hence, an IRT-based scale displays two elemental features for mental measurement: item characteristics and examinee ability/proficiency. The task for IRT's powerful statistics is to scale them simultaneously but independently, so that an item's characteristics are not directly dependent upon the particular persons who responded to them at a given testing occasion and vice versa for gauging each individual's ability. That is, the examinee's ability estimates are not tied to a particular set of items used on a testing occasion. In IRT terminology, the idea is phrased as "items are person-independent and persons are item-independent." This particular notion for independence contrasts IRT with CTT, where interpretations for items and persons are interrelated. (Later on, we elaborate upon this notion of independence.)

Imaginably, designing an IRT-based scale is demanding, encompassing many more considerations than are involved in making a scale based on CTT. IRT scales must reflect veracity to cognitive theory as well as the fit of data to a particular statistical model. Further, its complex underlying methodology must be expressed in a way that is plainly interpretable to test takers and test users who are generally not versed in sophisticated statistics—their interest, of course, is in the score's meaning as an end unto itself and not how it was calculated. For our purposes, however, we will focus on IRT's statistical underpinnings.

For implementation, the IRT statistics mathematically evaluate a correct/incorrect endorsement of an item by an examinee of a particular ability, yielding information about defined characteristics of that item. (We describe this process below.) The evaluation is repeated for many examinees, each with a different, albeit unknown, ability but who aggregate to form a normal distribution of abilities. Typically, a large number of examinees are needed for this item-evaluation process. Importantly, the item's characteristics are evaluated in relation to the underlying scale of all abilities and not just relative to the abilities of the particular tested group. The specified item characteristics to be determined are typically its difficulty, its discriminating power, and the odds of a low ability examinee guessing correctly. The aspect of determining an item's characteristics reflects the independence phenomenon mentioned above. The process is repeated for each item on the test. In this way the characteristics for the items are determined.

A converse process is simultaneously conducted for examinees in order to calibrate their abilities to the IRT scale. Here, the probability of an examinee correctly endorsing an item with particular characteristics is calculated and then repeated for many items with varying degrees of each specified characteristic. Thus, the items presented to the examinee exhibit a range of values for each item characteristic and the examinee's ability is determined in relation to his responses within the range of item characteristics. The process continues iteratively until a stopping criterion is reached.

Typically, IRT employs a criterion of .5 probability as the stopping criterion; that is, the examinee has a 50/50 chance of responding correctly to items at that level. For items above that level the examinee has a less than 50/50 chance of correctly endorsing and a greater than 50/50 chance for items lesser than that level. This value, which of course is different for each examinee, is believed to be the best estimate of a particular examinee's ability or proficiency.

IRT experts (Embretson & Reise, 2000) describe this process as a "search." Examinees are "searching" for a value to accurately reflect their ability by presenting them with a number of items, while simultaneously a converse "search" is going on for an item's characteristics by looking at the responses to it given by a distribution of examinees. The search process for examinees is termed as "ability estimates" and for items as "item calibration." Imaginably, there are a massive number of such searches going on during the process. Fortunately, working from a Bayesian perspective, the mathematics of maximum likelihood estimation can handle the search process very efficiently, and estimates of ability and item calibrations are quickly computed.

The formulas used to solve IRT searches are more than mere algorithms to run on a computer; they manifest crucial IRT assumptions. At this point, we discuss three major IRT assumptions (although there are others). Our explanation of each IRT assumption is brief but the interested reader may find a full elaboration offered by many authors (e.g., Baker, 2001; especially de Ayala, 2009; Embretson & Reise, 2000; Hambleton, Swaminathan, & Rogers, 1991; Wainer et al., 2000).

Also, at the outset of a discussion about IRT assumptions, it is worth noting counterpart CTT assumptions. While CTT also relies on assumptions, they are not often brought to the fore; in IRT, however, assumptions are front and center. In fact, for both understanding and using IRT in practical testing situations, it is imperative to understand and employ the essential assumptions.

A primary IRT assumption is for the unidimensionality of items and tests. Osterlind (2010) describes this assumption as it, "implies that within IRT estimation, a given test item or exercise is directly targeted at a single cognitive process, and in theory it fills that latent space completely" (p. 278). This means that a single ability is measured by a set of items: the latent dimension. Of course, in a practical sense, the assumption cannot be met strictly because many irrelevant factors—like anxiety, personality, testing conditions, and so forth—interact to produce a complex set of interactions influencing performance. Regardless, the assumption presumes a single latency is dominant in the mix of influencing factors. The dominance of the single (viz., unidimensional) facet is sufficient to explain an examinee's ability or proficiency. [We note, too, that complex IRT arrangement may include multidimensional assessment, but these are not part of the basic model. For discussion of complex IRT models, see van der Linden and Hambleton (1997).]

A second IRT assumption is of local independence. This assumption is scarcely unique to IRT work; it is often employed in research, particularly when discussing reliability of instruments. It means that a response to one of the test's items or exercises is wholly and uniquely a consequence of that stimulus. In other words, the assumption presumes that when an examinee responds to a given item he did not use clues from any other item or anything else. A number of implications important to IRT mathematics derive from this assumption. As we mentioned above, IRT is a probability function: the probability of an examinee endorsing a given response to an item with particular characteristics. Of course, since tests contain more than a single item, the probability multiplies for each additional test item. That is to say, the response to items is the probability of a correct endorsement of the first item times a commensurate probability for the second item, and so forth. Hence, an examinee's response to a set of items is a *joint probability*. This is an important feature to understand about IRT and we explain this further later on, after additional preliminaries.

To present this idea mathematically, let U_i represent an examinee's response to an item, say, item i. We know already that the probability of a correct endorsement by the examinee is a direct function of his ability, expressed as $P(U_i\theta)$. And, since in any test $i = (1,2,. . .,n)$, the joint probability is $P(U_1,U_2,...U_n|\theta) = P(U_1|\theta)P(U_2|\theta)...P(U_n|\theta)$. This can be stated more compactly as follows:

$$= \prod_{i=1}^{n} P(U_i|\theta)$$

.

This expression represents local independence, presuming the there is a full accounting of the latent space.

Earlier, we mentioned that items are described by their characteristics; now, we address this facet of tests more fully. In IRT, the fact that items can be so described is an important assumption because it gives a basis for the IRT scaling. Each characteristic must be specified and its parameters estimated, putting into action the "search" process described above. Typically, one, two, or three item characteristics are employed in IRT scaling, although there can be more. The three usual IRT characteristics are labeled a, b, and c for discrimination, difficulty, and pseudo-chance (also called guessing), respectively.

Fortunately, the a, b, and c item characteristics can be displayed rather simply in an item characteristic curve (ICC). Since the values for each characteristic are different for each item, there are as many ICCs for a test as there are items. Figure 11.1 presents a typical ICC for one item.

Understanding how the ICC conveys information about an item's characteristics is straightforward. First, note the two axes. The horizontal one (X axis) represents the latent trait continuum. Typically, the trait is labeled theta (θ). We know that this θ continuum ranges $(-\infty,+\infty)$ but, of course, not all the range is displayed. The scores are standardized with 1, 0 representing mean and standard deviation (in logit units), and showing just three standard deviations (SDs) is common since this amount includes most of the population. The vertical (Y) axis is used to display the probability of

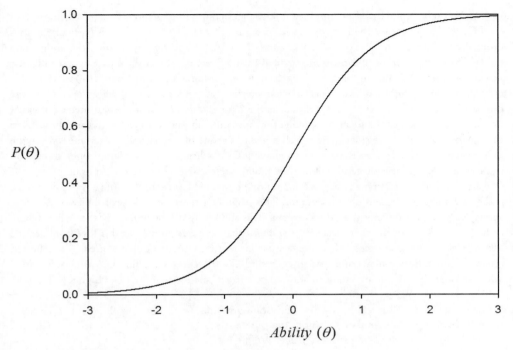

Figure 11.1 ICC for a single item

a theta, or $P(\theta)$. Obviously, probabilities go from no probability (0) to perfect (1), so this scale ranges (0, 1). Figure 11.1 displays the item's trace line (technically, an *ogive*) on these two dimensions. The ICC gives a smooth curve for the probability of a correct endorsement of the item at all trait levels within the displayed range.

Note particularly that the ICC is not perfectly linear, although it is monotonic. This means that the probability of a correct response to the item, while strongly correlated with rising trait levels, is not uniform throughout the entire range although it is always rising. For instance, in the figure note that examinees in the −2 to −3 trait range have a nearly equal probability of a correct endorsement: very low likelihood. And, in parallel fashion for highly able examinees, all of them above about 2 SDs have a virtually equal likelihood of getting the item correct. This makes logical sense, too, since test items are not equally discriminating for all examinees; commonly items discriminate very little among examinees that are of very low or of very high ability. Most discrimination is evidenced for examinees in the middle range, say ±1.5 SD in this figure, comparable to the 7th and 93rd percentile ranks.

Imaginably, some items have steeper slopes than do other items. Highly discriminating items have steep slopes, whereas low discriminating ones have more shallow slopes. An ICC displaying a flat, horizontal line (zero slope) would have no discriminating power along the entire theta range. A slope that jumped straight up vertically at some point would have perfect discrimination at that point, a deterministic scaling feature labeled Guttman scaling, so-named after its inventor (Gulliksen, 1950; Guttman, 1941, 1950). Virtually all good items in today's tests, however, are closer in feature to the one displayed in Figure 11.1. This discrimination is the *a* parameter (discrimination) in IRT scaling.

There is a point where the likelihood of a correct response is about .5, the accepted IRT criterion for identifying items as best suited to examinees. This point—called the *inflection point* because it is where the curvature of the item trace line changes concavity—is about at zero, the mean trait level for all examinees for the item displayed in Figure 11.1. In other words, this particular item is optimally suited to examinees of about average ability in the latent trait. Also, this is the point along the IRT scale where most information is gained. In IRT scaling, this is the b parameter, difficulty. Some common IRT models estimate only this difficulty parameter. Sometimes, in IRT this difficulty parameter is referred to as a "location parameter" because it locates the theta value at which the probability function is .5, $P_i(\theta = .5)$. Of course, this b point will differ from item to item. For easier items, it is to the left of the theta zero, while for more difficult one it is located to the right of zero theta. Most test makers consider an item well suited to a group of normal ability examinees when the inflection point is zero on the theta scale. Generally, ICCs will appear to shift left or right, in relation to this point. More difficult items will be shifted left, while easier items are shifted right.

A final common IRT item characteristic, but one estimated less often than the a or b parameters, is the pseudo-chance (guessing) c parameter. This parameter represents the probability of very low ability examinees endorsing the item correctly. It is shown by the beginning of the ogive, where ability is very low on the theta scale. It is thought that some examinees at this low level get the item correct by mere guessing. However, we realize that examinee guessing is itself a complicated phenomenon and they may employ many guessing-like strategies, including knowing only partial information, believing incorrect information to be correct, and much more (see Hughes & Trimble, 1965).

For comparison of several ICCs, items are sometimes displayed together. Figure 11.2 presents three ICCs in the same graphic. To note the differences, examine each characteristic, including, discrimination, difficulty, and pseudo-chance. We discuss each characteristic in turn.

First, looking at the a parameter, see that each item has a unique slope, representing its discriminating power along the theta range. More steep slopes display items with higher discrimination,

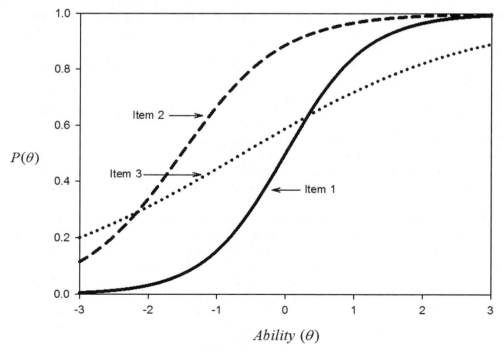

Figure 11.2 ICCs for three items

while more shallow slopes show less discrimination along the theta range. In comparing the slopes, one sees that Item 1 is steepest, Item 2 is less steep, and Item 3 has the shallowest slope. This means that Item 1 discriminates more distinctly among examinees of varying abilities; in this case, the slope is steepest in the range (−1, +1), indicating that persons with abilities in this range are more distinctly measured on the trait. Item 2 is less steep and Item 3 is relatively flat, meaning that the item has low discrimination among examinees regardless of anyone's ability.

The difficulty of the item—*b* parameter—is shown by the left-to-right shift of the ogive itself. We described above that optimal difficulty (.5) for a group normally distributed in the appraised underlying trait is when an item's inflection point is exactly at 0. Note in Figure 11.2 that while the three items inflect similarly there is still some differentiation, showing differences in difficulty. In this example, however, the items are not much different in their difficulty parameter.

Vast differences in the pseudo-chance estimation (the *c* parameter) are apparent among these items. For Item 1, the curve begins at about .05 probability; for Item 2, it is slightly above .25 probability; and, for Item 3, it is nearly at .5 probability. Obviously, for low-ability examinees, among these three items there is a huge difference in the probability of correct endorsement by mere guessing.

Various IRT approaches are identified by the number of items parameters the test makers specify for estimation. Now, we discuss commonly used IRT models, each displaying one or more item characteristic.

Key Points

Commonly Used IRT Models

One-parameter logistic model (1PL) or Rasch model

Perhaps the most common IRT model, and one of the simplest, is the one-parameter model, also called the Rasch model after its chief early proponent and developer (Rasch, 1980, original work published 1960). The only item parameter in the Rasch model is item difficulty, the *b* parameter. Using a logit link function, the probability of endorsing an item *i* by person *s* is expressed as:

$$P(X_{is} = 1 \mid \theta_s, \beta_i) = \frac{\exp(\theta_s - \beta_i)}{1 + \exp(\theta_s - \beta_i)} \tag{11.1}$$

where θ_s is person *s*'s ability/proficiency level and β_i is the difficulty level of item *i*. From Equation 11.1, an individual is more likely to endorse an easy item than to endorse a more difficult item, and a person with more ability/proficiency is more likely to endorse an item than a person with less ability/proficiency. When an item's difficulty level is the same as a person's ability/proficiency, that person has a 50 percent probability of endorsing that item. In the Rasch model, the ICCs of all items vary only in their location along the ability/proficiency continuum. Hence, we see that person-item total scores are sufficient statistics for estimating ability/proficiency.

Two-parameter logistic model (2PL)

The next most common model adds attention to item discrimination, the *a* parameter. In the 2PL model, an item discrimination parameter is added to the item characteristic function. The probability that person *s* correctly responds to item *i* is modeled as shown in Figure 11.2. This model extends Equation 11.1 (1PL model) as:

$$P(X_{is} = 1 \mid \theta_s, \beta_i, \alpha_i) = \frac{\exp[\alpha_i(\theta_s - \beta_i)]}{1 + \exp[\alpha_i(\theta_s - \beta_i)]} \tag{11.2}$$

Here, the item discrimination parameter, α_i, represents item differences in discrimination for the item along the ability scale. In the 2PL model, items are not equally related to ability/proficiency. An item with high discrimination exaggerates the discrepancy between the ability/proficiency parameter and the item difficulty parameter. Due to different discriminations, ICCs of different items may cross when put along the ability/proficiency continuum.

Three-parameter logistic model (3PL)

A third model, less commonly used but still important, considers the likelihood of low-ability examinees guessing a correct response. This pseudo-chance parameter—the c parameter—is represented by the lower-asymptote of the ICC. Equation 11.3 displays the formula for consideration of these three parameters. Note that this extends the 2PL model.

$$P(X_{is} = 1 \mid \theta_s, \beta_i, \alpha_i, \gamma_i) = \gamma_i + (1 - \gamma_i) \frac{\exp[\alpha_i(\theta_s - \beta_i)]}{1 + \exp[\alpha_i(\theta_s - \beta_i)]} \qquad (11.3)$$

In the 3PL model, a person with an infinitely low ability/proficiency level still has a non-zero chance of correctly answering an item. The guessing parameter of any item should be non-negative to reflect the fundamental concept in any measurement that a higher ability/proficiency level is related to a higher probability of correct answer. A negative estimate of the guessing parameter γ_i for an item indicates misfitting data to the model.

Researchers should be cautious when choosing to use the 3PL model because estimation problems such as non-convergence are more likely to occur. Carelessly using the 3PL model could result in instability of the estimation of item difficulty and discrimination parameters.

IRT models with polytomous items/exercises

While the three models above are the most often used models for dichotomous items, one-, two-, or three-parameter IRT models can also be expressed using a probit link function to estimate item characteristics and examinee ability in polytomous items or exercises, such as Likert scale, essays graded on a scale, and other like assessments. Here, the probability of endorsing an item is expressed as the cumulative normal ogive. Sometimes a scaling factor is added to the logistic models so that the logistic ogive function is close to the normal ogive function. It has been shown that a scaling factor of 1.7 minimizes the differences between the two functions.

In some situations, what these polytomous items represent are the degree to which people agree, magnitude of attitudes, or, simply, different types of preferences. For example, students' responses to essays are scored on a 1–6 scale; people are asked about their attitude toward abortion on a 5–, 7– or 9-point scale from strongly agree to strongly disagree; people are asked about their preferences of candidates. Polytomous IRT models are necessary for those types of responses. Some polytomous models are described in Embretson and Reise (2000). It is worth mentioning that recently polytomous response models have been developed for multiple-choice items to include information from the distractors, in addition to the correct response (Revuelta, 2004, 2005).

Estimation of Person Ability/Proficiency

Three estimation methods exist for the unknown person ability/proficiency parameter: maximum likelihood estimation (MLE), maximum a posteriori (MAP), and expected a posteriori (EAP) (see Bock & Mislevy, 1982).

In the MLE method, the ability/proficiency level which makes the person's response pattern most likely to occur is the estimate. A related concept is the likelihood function, which is the probability of observing a response pattern given the ability/proficiency level. Mathematically, it is the product of the probabilities of observing each item response in a response pattern of all items, given the ability/proficiency level. Let u_i be the observed response to the dichotomous item i, the likelihood function of a response pattern $(u_1, u_2, \ldots, u_n)$, given the ability/proficiency θ, is given in Equation 11.4:

$$L(u_1, u_2, \ldots, u_n \mid \theta) = \prod_{i=1}^{n} P_i^{u_i} (1 - P_i)^{1 - u_i} \tag{11.4}$$

where P_i is the probability of endorsing item i at the ability/proficiency level θ under the one-, two-, or three-parameter model. The MLE of θ involves searching for a value of θ which maximized the likelihood. Computationally, it is usually done by maximizing the log of the likelihood.

Both the MAP and EAP methods are Bayesian estimation methods. In the MAP method, a prior distribution is specified for ability/proficiency. Usually, persons are assumed to be sampled from a normal distribution with a mean of zero and a variance of one. The mode of the posterior distribution is the estimated ability/proficiency. The MAP estimation is usually called "Bayes modal estimation." In the EAP method, the prior distribution is discrete. That is, a finite number of ability/proficiency levels—called quadrature nodes—are extant. In these cases, the mean of the posterior distribution is the estimate of that person's ability/proficiency.

Item Calibration

As mentioned above, the procedure of estimating item parameters is the "item calibration." The most frequently used item calibration methods are joint maximum likelihood (JML), marginal maximum likelihood (MML), and conditional maximum likelihood (CML).

With JML, person parameters and item parameters are estimated jointly. The likelihood function is conditional on both sets of parameters. Through an iterative procedure, estimates for parameters are improved at each step until satisfactory results are achieved.

With MML, the ability/proficiency parameters are integrated out and only item parameters are estimated. The MML is more computationally intense due to the integration. Usually a large number of examinees are required in order to obtain a good approximate distribution of ability/proficiency.

Both JML and MML can be used in one-, two-, or three-parameter models, or together with Bayesian estimation methods when prior distributions of the items are available. CML, on the other hand, is only applicable to the Rasch model. With the Rasch model, the total scores are sufficient statistics and no integration over ability/proficiency distribution is necessary. The likelihood function is used to obtain item parameter estimates.

Item and Test Information

Information about an item can be represented by an ICC where the probability of a correct response is plotted against the continuum of ability/proficiency. Item information function (IIF) is the mathematical way to compute how much information each ICC contains. It is a function of the variability of the estimates around the parameter value. Specifically, the information is higher when the difficulty level is closer to the ability/proficiency level, the discrimination level is higher, or the low-asymptote is closer to zero. The test information function (TIF) is the sum of all IIFs in the test. The standard error of estimate, a closely related measure, is the square root of the reciprocal of TIF. Conceptually, it is similar to the standard error of measurement in CTT, except that the standard error of estimate varies with the ability/proficiency level.

Model Fit

In any application of IRT models, it is important to assess to what extent the IRT model assumptions are valid for the given data and how well the testing data fit the IRT model selected for use in that particular situation. Model fit can be assessed at the model, item, or person level.

Traditionally, goodness–of–fit statistics such as the Pearson chi-square or the likelihood ratio statistic have been used to test the overall model-data fit. Those statistics are based on chi-square distribution and, if not significant, indicate good model fit. In addition to test model fit, those statistics can also be used to compare nested models. For example, the 1PL model is nested within the 2PL model, and a chi-square difference test can be conducted based on the likelihood ratio statistics. A nonsignificant chi-square difference indicates that the simpler (1PL) model fits the data equally well as the more complex (2PL) model and the simpler model should be chosen. On the other hand, a significant chi-square difference test indicates that the simpler model does not include enough parameters that are necessary to adequately model the data and therefore the more complex model should be selected. A bootstrapping method to assess overall model fit by using several statistics together was proposed by von Davier (1997).

At the item level, the likelihood ratio test assesses the discrepancy between the expected response pattern and the actual response pattern of the examinees on a particular item in relation to their performance on the test as a whole. By comparing the estimated item response curve (IRC) based on the model and an "empirical" IRC derived from actual data, the discrepancy between them can be represented either statistically or graphically. Several statistics for the comparison between estimated IRC and empirical IRC have been developed (Bock, 1972). In the Rasch model, item fit is measured in two ways. The first is referred to as *infit*, which indicates how well an item works for a person close to it in ability/proficiency level. The second is *outfit*, which indicates how well an item works for persons far from it in ability/proficiency level.

Person fit indices are based on the consistency of a person's item response pattern with the IRT model. By analyzing response patterns, person fit statistics can identify people with aberrant responses. Aberrant response patterns may be due to fatigue, low test-taking motivation, cheating, unfamiliarity with the topic or test format, and so forth. Many person fit statistics have been proposed (see Karabatsos, 2003; Meijer & Sijtsma, 2001) although there is no agreement about which one is most effective in detecting aberrant responses.

IRT Software/Resources

There are many software programs that can estimate the IRT parameters. Some general statistical packages provide IRT procedures. For example, SAS has macros to conduct IRT with dichotomous data. However, IRT models can be most easily conducted with special programs to obtain different information. Perhaps the most popularly used software program is actually a suite of four programs, each useful for different kinds of IRT estimation. They are BILOG-MG (Zimowski, Muraki, Mislevy, & Bock, 2003), MULTILOG (Thissen, Chen, & Bock, 2003), PARSCALE (Muraki & Bock, 2003), and a companion program based on classical methodology called TESTFACT (Wood et al., 2003). (NOTE: the publisher of these programs has announced a mid-2012 release of a wholly updated version of each program.) Aside from these, a total of 54 IRT programs are listed by the Psychometric Software Exchange (http://www.psychsoft.soe.vt.edu/).

Some online resources provide a good introduction to IRT. For example, the Institute of Objective Measurement Inc. has a comprehensive site for the Rasch Model (http://www.rasch.org). Baker's (2001) ebook, together with his software, is available at http://edres.org/irt.

Conclusions

Despite its history, IRT is still an active research area. New models are being developed yearly and new applications have been frequently observed in different fields. IRT is the foundation of many state standardized tests and large-scale data sets. For example, several international databases (e.g., NAEP, TIMSS) have used IRT techniques to obtain estimates of students' achievement.

At this point, we would like you to rethink the differences between CTT and IRT. The theoretical differences clearly indicate that IRT has many good properties that CTT does not. However, the empirical differences are not necessarily big. Fan (1998) compared IRT and CTT using empirical data and found that person statistics (ability/proficiency) from CTT were highly comparable with those from IRT models. In addition, item difficulty indexes from CTT are also very comparable with those from IRT models and especially from the Rasch model. More research to empirically compare the two scoring frameworks is likely to help us gain more understanding of IRT.

References

Baker, F. B. (2001). *The basics of item response theory*. Retrieved from http://edres.org/irt/baker

Bock, R. D. (1972). Estimating item parameters and latent ability when responses are scored in two or more nominal categories. *Psychometrika, 37*, 29–51.

Bock, R. D., & Mislevy, R. J. (1982). Adaptive EAP estimation of ability in a microcomputer environment. *Applied Psychological Measurement, 6*(4), 431–444.

de Ayala, R. J. (2009). *The theory and practice of item response theory*. New York, NY: Guilford Press.

Embretson, S. E., & Reise, S. P. (2000). *Item response theory for psychologists*. Mahwah, NJ: Lawrence Erlbaum Associates.

Fan, X. (1998). Item response theory and classical test theory: an empirical comparison of their item/person statistics. *Educational and Psychological Measurement, 58*(3), 357–381.

Gulliksen, H. (1950). *Theory of mental tests*. New York, NY: Wiley.

Guttman, L. (1941). The quantification of class attributes: A theory and method of scale construction. In P. Horst (Ed.), *The prediction of personal adjustment*. New York, NY: Social Science Research Council.

Guttman, L. (1950). The basis for scalogram analysis. In S. A. Stouffer, L. Guttman, E. A. Suchrnan, P. F. Lazarsfeld, S. A. Star, & J. A. Gardner (Eds.), *Measurement and prediction* (pp. 60–90). Princeton, NJ: Princeton University Press.

Hambleton, R. K., Swaminathan, H., & Rogers, H. J. (1991). *Fundamentals of item response theory*. Newberry Park, CA: Sage.

Hughes, H. H., & Trimble, W. E. (1965). The use of complex alternatives in multiple-choice items. *Educational and Psychological Measurement* (21), 117–126.

Karabatsos, G. (2003). Comparing the aberrant response detection performance of thirty-six person-fit statistics. *Applied Measurement in Education, 16*(4), 277–298.

Meijer, R. R., & Sijtsma, K. (2001). Methodology review: Evaluating person fit. *Applied Psychological Measurement, 25*(2), 107–135.

Mislevy, R. J. (1996). Test theory reconceived. *Journal of Educational Measurement, 33*(4), 379–416.

Muraki, E., & Bock, D. (2003). PARSCALE: IRT based test scoring and item analysis for graded response items and rating scales (Version 4.1) [Computer software]. Lincolnwood, IL: Scientific Software International.

Osterlind, S. J. (2010). *Modern measurement: Theory, principles, and applications of mental appraisal* (2nd ed.). Boston, MA: Pearson Education.

Rasch, G. (1980). *Probabilistic models for some intelligence and attainment tests*. Chicago, IL: University of Chicago Press. (Original work published 1960)

Revuelta, J. (2004). Analysis of distractor difficulty in multiple-choice items. *Psychometrika, 69*, 217–234.

Revuelta, J. (2005). An item response model for nominal data based on the rising selection ratios criterion. *Psychometrika, 70*, 305–324.

The Psychological Corporation. (1955). *Methods of expressing test scores*. (Test Service Bulletin No. 48). New York, NY: Author.

Thissen, D., Chen, W., & Bock, D. (2003). MULTILOG: multiple category item analysis and test scoring using item response theory (Version 7.0) [Computer software]. Lincolnwood, IL: Scientific Software International.

van der Linden, W. J., & Hambleton, R. K. (Eds.). (1997). *Handbook of modern item response theory*. New York, NY: Springer.

von Davier, M. (1997). Bootstrapping goodness-of-fit statistics for sparse categorical data: Results of a Monte Carlo study. *Methods of Psychological Research Online, 2*(2), 29–48. Retrieved from http://www.dgps.de/fach-gruppen/methoden/mpr-online/issue3/art5/article.html

Wainer, H., Dorans, N. J., Flaughter, R., Green, B. F., Steinberg, L., & Thissen, D. (2000). *Computerized adaptive testing: A primer* (2nd ed.). Hillsdale, NJ: Lawrence Erlbaum Associates.

Wood, R., Wilson, D., Gibbons, R., Schilling, S., Muraki, E., & Bock, D. (2003). TESTFACT: Test scoring, item statistics, and item factor analysis (Version 4.0) [Computer software]. Lincolnwood, IL: Scientific Software International.

Zimowski, M., Muraki, E., Mislevy, R., & Bock, D. (2003). BILOG-MG: Multiple group IRT analysis and test maintenance for binary items (Version 3.0) [Computer software]. Lincolnwood, IL: Scientific Software International.

12

SCALING, NORMING, AND EQUATING

Michael J. Kolen and Amy B. Hendrickson

Methods for scaling, norming, and equating are considered in this chapter. The chapter begins with an overview of key points. Then the concepts of scaling, norming, and equating as they pertain to assessment in higher education are described. Issues associated with scaling, norming, and equating in admissions testing, placement testing, and assessments used for outcomes and accountability are then discussed. Detailed examples of how scaling, norming, and equating procedures are used in the ACT® (ACT, 2010a) and SAT® (College Board, 2010c) admissions testing programs and the Advanced Placement Program® (AP®, College Board, 2010b) are provided.

Key Points

A variety of scores and scales are used with educational tests. Scoring typically begins with scores on the individual items that are on the test, which are referred to as *item scores*. Item scores can be incorrect or correct or they can involve multiple score points such as when human scorers score an essay on a 5-point rubric. The *raw score* for an examinee on a test is a function of the *item scores* for that examinee. Raw scores can be as simple as a sum of the item scores or be so complicated that they depend on the entire pattern of item responses as is sometimes the case with item response theory (IRT)-based scoring (Osterlind & Wang, this volume; Yen & Fitzpatrick, 2006). Raw scores are typically transformed to *scale scores* using a process referred to as *scaling* so as to facilitate score interpretation. Incorporating information from a *norming* study into the score scale is one way to improve score interpretability.

Alternate test forms often are used with educational tests for reasons of test security and so that examinees can test more than once. Because it is impossible for test developers to build alternate test forms that are of equal difficulty, test form *equating methods* are used to provide statistical adjustments to reported scores so that scale scores from the alternate forms can be used interchangeably. Following the equating process, scores from the alternate forms are reported as scale scores. Reporting scale scores on the alternate test forms makes it more likely that the same reported score on two alternate forms is indicative of the same level of achievement.

Ideally, procedures for scoring, scaling, norming, and equating work together to facilitate the usefulness of reported scores. Without such procedures it would be difficult to properly use test scores in making important decisions in higher education. Scoring, scaling, norming, and equating procedures allow administrators to demonstrate trends in student achievement over years when assessing the outcomes of student learning and to ensure that admissions and placement criteria have the same meaning over time.

Theoretical Considerations

Theoretical considerations for scoring, scaling, norming, and equating are described in this section of the chapter. For more detailed treatments and numerical examples, refer to Angoff (1971), Flanagan (1951), Holland and Dorans (2006), Kolen (2006), Kolen and Brennan (2004), and Petersen, Kolen, and Hoover (1989). AERA/APA/NCME (1999) provides standards that should be used for scaling, norming, and equating in practice.

Scoring

Kolen (2006) distinguished unit scores from item scores. A *unit score* is the score on the smallest unit on which a score is found, which is referred to as a *scoreable* unit. An *item score* is a score over all scoreable units for an item.

For multiple-choice test questions that are scored incorrect-correct, unit scores and item scores often are the same. Such scores are either incorrect (0) or correct (1). Unit and item scores are often distinguishable when judges score the item responses. As an example, consider an essay item that is scored 1 (low) through 5 (high) by each of two judges, with the item score being the sum of scores over the two judges. In this situation, there is a unit score for judge 1 (range 1 to 5), a unit score for judge 2 (range 1 to 5), and an item score over the two judges (range 2 to 10).

Or, consider a situation in which a block of five questions is associated with a reading passage. If a test developer is using IRT and is concerned that there might be conditional dependencies among responses to questions associated with a reading passage, the developer might treat the questions associated with the passage as a single item with scores on this item being the number of questions associated with the passage that the examinee answers correctly. In this case, each question would have a unit score of 0 or 1 and the item score would range from 0 to 5. According to Kolen (2006), "the characteristic that most readily distinguishes unit scores from item scores is . . . whereas there may be operational dependencies among unit scores, item scores are considered operationally independent" (p. 157).

Raw scores are functions of the item scores. The *summed score* is a raw score that is often used. The summed score is calculated by summing the item scores. For tests that are scored correct-incorrect, the summed score is the number of items the examinee correctly answers. Sometimes test developers decide to differentially weight the item scores using positive weights that produce *weighted summed scores*. Weighted summed scores are often used with *mixed-format tests*, which are tests that contain different item types. For these tests, test developers might consider one point on a particular item type to be worth more or less than one point on another item type. The test developer might address this differential worth through weighting of the item scores. With IRT, proficiency estimates are often complex functions of the item scores. These proficiency estimates can be viewed as raw scores.

Scaling

Raw scores have limitations as primary score scales for tests. Raw scores are dependent on the particular items on a test, and so they cannot be meaningfully compared when examinees take different test forms. In addition, raw scores do not carry normative meaning and are difficult to relate to meaningful generalizations to a content domain. For these reasons, raw scores are transformed to scale scores. Linear or nonlinear transformations of raw scores are used to produce scale scores that can be meaningfully interpreted. Normative, score precision, and content information can be incorporated. Transformations that can be used to incorporate each of these types of meaning are considered next.

Incorporating normative information

Incorporating normative information begins with the administration of the test to a *norm group*. Statistical characteristics of the scale score distribution are set relative to this norm group. The scale scores are meaningful to the extent that the norm group is central to score interpretation.

For example, a twelfth grade reading test might be administered to a national norm group that is intended to be representative of twelfth graders in the nation. The mean and standard deviation of scale scores on the test might be set to particular values for this norm group. By knowing the mean and standard deviation of scale scores, test users would be able to quickly ascertain, for example, whether a particular student's score was above the mean. This information would be relevant to the extent that scores for the norm group are central to score interpretation. Kolen (2006, pp. 163–164) provided equations for linearly transforming raw scores to scale scores with a particular mean and standard deviation.

Non-linear transformations are also used to develop score scales. Normalized scores involve one such transformation. To normalize scores, percentile ranks of raw scores are found and then transformed using an inverse normal transformation. These normalized scores are then linearly transformed to have a desired mean and standard deviation. Normalized scale scores can be used by test users to quickly ascertain the percentile rank of a particular student's score, using facts about the normal distribution. For example, with normalized scores, a score that is one standard deviation above the mean has a percentile rank of approximately 84. Kolen (2006, pp. 164–165) provided a detailed description of the process of score normalization.

Incorporating score precision information

According to Flanagan (1951), scale score units should "be of an order of magnitude most appropriate to express their accuracy of measurement" (p. 246). He indicated that the use of too few score points fails to "preserve all of the information contained in raw scores" (p. 247). However, the use of too many scale score points might lead test users to attach significance to scale score differences that are predominantly due to measurement error. Kolen and Brennan (2004, pp. 346–347) provided rules of thumb for how to choose the number of score points to use.

Noting that conditional measurement error variability is typically unequal along the score scale, Kolen (1988) suggested using a transformation to equalize error variability. Kolen, Hanson, and Brennan (1992) found that this transformation adequately stabilized error variance for tests with dichotomously scored items. An application of this procedure for the ACT Assessment is described later in this chapter.

Incorporating content information

Ebel (1962) stated, "to be meaningful any test scores must be related to test content as well as to the scores of other examinees" (p. 18). Recently, there has been a focus on providing content meaningful scale scores.

One such procedure, *item mapping*, is reviewed in Zwick, Senturk, Wang, and Loomis (2001). In item mapping, test items are associated with various scale score points. For dichotomously scored items, the probability of correct response on each item is regressed on a scale score. The *response probability* (RP) level is defined as the probability (expressed as a percentage) of correct response on a test item given the scale score that is associated with mastery, proficiency, or some other category as defined by the test developer. The same RP level is used for all dichotomously scored items on the test. Using a regression of item score on scale score, an item is said to map to the scale score associated with an RP of correctly answering the item. RP values typically range from .5 to .8. Additional criteria are often used when choosing items to report on an item map, such as item discrimination and test developer judgment. Modifications of the procedures are used with polytomously scored items. The outcome of an item mapping procedure is a map that illustrates which items correspond to each of an ordered set of scale scores.

Another way to incorporate content information is to use *scale anchoring*. The first step in scale anchoring is to develop an item map. Then a set of scale score points is chosen, such as a selected set of percentiles. Subject matter experts review the items that map near each of the selected points and develop general statements that represent the skills of the examinees scoring at each point. See Allen, Carlson, and Zelenak (1999) for an example of scale anchoring with the National Assessment of Educational Progress, and ACT (2007) for an example of scale anchoring as used with ACT's College Readiness Standards.

Standard setting procedures, as recently reviewed by Hambleton and Pitoniak (2006), begin with a statement about what competent examinees know and are able to do. Structured judgmental processes are used to find the scale score point that differentiates candidates who are minimally competent from those who are less than minimally competent. In achievement testing situations, various achievement levels are often stated, such as basic, proficient, and advanced. Judgmental standard setting techniques are used to find the scale score points that differentiate between adjacent levels.

Norming

Norms relate test scores to performance of a group of examinees. *National norms* are based on drawing nationally representative samples of individuals at the age or educational level for which a test is designed. National norms typically are developed using a sampling plan that helps ensure that the sample accurately represents the population. *National norms by age or grade* are often provided for educational achievement and aptitude tests. National norming studies estimate test score characteristics, such as means, standard deviations, and percentile ranks, for a national population of examinees.

User norms are based on examinees who happen to take a test during a given time period. These user norms cannot be viewed as nationally representative because they depend on who happens to take a particular test. User norms can facilitate score interpretation. For example, college entrance testing programs in the U.S. provide norms for all students who are administered the test during a particular time period. These user groups for college entrance tests tend to be fairly stable over short periods of time and provide a reference for interpreting examinee scores. User norms can also be provided for particular colleges, allowing examinees to compare their performance to the performance of students enrolled in these colleges.

Equating

Educational and psychological tests often are developed with *alternate forms* that contain different sets of test questions. The alternate forms are administered on different occasions. *Test content specifications* detail the number of questions on a test from each of a number of content areas; *test statistical specifications* detail the statistical properties (e.g., difficulty) of the test questions (Knupp & Harris, this volume). Alternate forms of tests are built to the same content and statistical specifications so that they are very similar in content and statistical properties. Although alternate forms are built to be similar, they typically differ somewhat in difficulty. Test form equating methods are statistical methods used to adjust test scores for the differences in test difficulty among the forms. As emphasized by Kolen and Brennan (2004), "*equating adjusts for differences in difficulty, not for differences in content*" (p. 3). The goal of equating is to enable scores on the alternate test forms to be used interchangeably.

The implementation of test equating requires a process for collecting data, referred to as an *equating design*. A variety of equating designs exist, and some of the more popular ones are considered here. Statistical equating methods are also a component of the equating process.

Designs for data collection

Equating requires that data be collected and analyzed. Various data collection designs are used to conduct equating, and some of the most common designs are discussed in this section. In discussing each of these designs, assume that Form X is a new form. Also assume that Form Y is an old form, for which a transformation of raw to scale scores already has been developed. The equating process is intended to relate raw scores on Form X to raw scores on Form Y and to scale scores.

RANDOM GROUPS

In the *random groups design*, alternate test forms are randomly assigned to examinees. One way to implement the random groups design is to package the test booklets so that the forms alternate. When the forms are distributed to examinees, the first examinee receives a Form X test booklet, the second examinee a Form Y booklet, and so on. This assignment process, sometimes referred to as spiraling, leads to comparable, *randomly equivalent groups*, being administered Form X and Form Y. Assuming that the random groups are fairly large, differences between raw score means on Form X and Form Y can be attributed to differences in difficulty of the two forms.

SINGLE GROUP

In the *single group design*, the same examinees are administered two alternate forms. The forms are separately timed, and the order of the test forms is usually counterbalanced. One random half of the examinees is administered Form X followed by Form Y. The other random half is administered Form Y followed by Form X. Counterbalancing is used to control for context effects, such as practice or fatigue. Counterbalancing requires the assumption that the effect of taking Form X prior to Form Y has the same effect as taking Form Y prior to Form X. If this assumption does not hold, then *differential order effects* are said to be present, and the data on the form taken second are discarded, resulting in a considerable loss of data.

COMMON-ITEM NONEQUIVALENT GROUPS

In the *common-item nonequivalent groups design*, Form X and Form Y are administered to different (nonequivalent) groups of examinees. The two forms have items in common. Two variants of this design exist. When using an *internal set of common items*, the common items contribute to the examinee's score on the form. With an internal set, typically the common items are interspersed with the other items on the test. When using an *external set of common items*, the common items do not contribute to the examinee's score on the form taken. With an external set, the common items typically appear in a separately timed section.

When using the common-item nonequivalent groups design, the common items are used to indicate how different the group of examinees administered Form X is from the group of examinees administered Form Y. Strong statistical assumptions are used to translate the differences between the two groups of examinees on the common items to differences between the two groups on the complete forms.

Because scores on the common items are used to indicate differences between the examinee groups, it is important that the common items fully represent the content of the test forms.

Otherwise, a misleading picture of group differences is provided. In addition, it is important that the common items behave in the same manner when they are administered with Form X as with Form Y. So, the common items should be administered in similar positions in the test booklets in the two forms, and the text of the common items should be identical.

IRT CALIBRATED ITEM POOLS

The use of IRT calibrated item pools allows more flexibility in equating alternate forms of a test than the common–item nonequivalent groups design. When an IRT calibrated item pool exists, scores on a new form can be equated using items that are in common with the pool rather than being in common with a previous form or forms. As with the common–item nonequivalent groups design, the items in common with the pool should proportionally represent the content and statistical specifications of the total test.

COMPARISONS AMONG EQUATING DESIGNS

The benefits and limitations of the designs can be compared in terms of ease of test development, ease of administration, security of test administration, strength of statistical assumptions, and sample size requirements. Of the designs considered, the common–item nonequivalent groups and IRT calibrated item pool designs require the most complex test development processes. Common item sections must be developed that mirror the content of the total test, so that the score on the common item sections can be used to give an accurate reflection of examinee group proficiency. Test development is less complex for the random groups and single group designs because there is no need to construct common item sections.

However, the common–item nonequivalent groups and IRT calibrated item pool designs are the easiest of the three designs to implement. Only one test form needs to be administered on each test date. For the random groups design, multiple forms must be administered on a test date. For the single group design, each examinee must take two forms, which typically cannot be done in a regular test administration.

The common–item nonequivalent groups and IRT calibrated item pool designs tend to lead to greater test security than the other designs, because only one form needs to be administered on a given test date. With the random groups and single group designs, multiple forms are administered on a particular test date to conduct equating. However, security issues still can be of concern with the common–item nonequivalent groups and IRT calibrated item pool designs because the common items must be repeatedly administered.

The common–item nonequivalent groups design and IRT calibrated item pool designs require the strongest statistical assumptions. The random groups design requires only weak assumptions, mainly that the random assignment process was successful. The single-group design requires stronger assumptions than the random-groups design, in that it assumes no differential order effects.

As is evident from the preceding discussion, each of the designs has strengths and weaknesses. Choice of design depends on weighing the strengths and weaknesses with regard to the testing program under consideration. Each of these designs has been used to conduct equating in a variety of testing programs.

Statistical methods

Equating requires that a relationship between alternate forms be estimated. Equating methods result in a transformation of scores on the alternate forms so that the scores possess specified properties associated with each of the methods.

Traditional observed score equating methods define score correspondence on alternate forms by setting certain characteristics of score distributions equal for a specified population of examinees. In traditional *equipercentile equating*, a transformation is found such that, after equating, scores on alternate forms have the same distribution in a specified population of examinees.

Because many parameters need to be estimated in equipercentile equating (percentile ranks at each Form X and Form Y score), equipercentile equating is subject to much sampling error. For this reason, smoothing methods often are used to reduce sampling error.

Other traditional methods sometimes are used that can be viewed as special cases of the equipercentile method. In *linear equating*, a transformation is found that results in scores on Form X having the same mean and standard deviation as scores on Form Y. Unless the shapes of the score distributions for Form X and Form Y are identical, linear and equipercentile methods produce different results. However, even when the shapes of the distributions differ, equipercentile and linear methods produce similar results near the mean. When interest is in scores near the mean, linear equating often is sufficient. However, when interest is in scores all along the score scale and sample size is large, then equipercentile equating is often preferable to linear equating.

Kolen and Brennan (2004) described a few different equating methods for the common-item nonequivalent groups design. The methods differ in terms of their statistical assumptions. No method exists to directly test all of the assumptions that are made using data that are collected for equating. Methods also exist for equipercentile equating under this design that make somewhat different regression assumptions.

IRT equating methods require making strong statistical assumptions (Kolen & Brennan, 2004). One assumption that is typically made is that the proficiency estimated by the test is unidimensional. Another assumption is that the item characteristic curve, which relates probability of correctly answering an item to examinee proficiency, follows a specified form. To implement IRT methods, parameters are estimated for each item on the test. These parameters are placed on the same IRT proficiency scale using IRT linking methods. IRT true or IRT observed score equating relationships are often developed to relate raw scores on one form to raw scores on another form.

Equating error

Minimizing equating error is a major goal when developing tests that are to be equated, designing equating studies, and conducting equating. *Random equating error* is present whenever samples from populations of examinees are used to estimate equating relationships. Random error depends on the design used for data collection, the score point of interest, the method used to estimate score equivalents, and the sample size. Standard errors of equating are used to index random error. Standard error equations have been developed to estimate standard errors for most designs and methods, and resampling methods like the bootstrap can also be used. In general, standard errors diminish as sample size increases. Standard errors of equating can be used to estimate required sample sizes for equating, for comparing the precision of various designs and methods, and for documenting the amount of random error in an equating.

Systematic equating error results from violations of assumptions of the particular equating method used. For example, in the common-item nonequivalent groups design, systematic error will result if the statistical assumptions that are made are not satisfied. Systematic error typically cannot be quantified in operational equating situations.

Equating error of both types needs to be controlled because it can propagate over equatings and result in scores on later test forms not being comparable to scores on earlier forms. Choosing a large enough sample size given the design is the best way to control random error. To control systematic error, the test must be constructed and the equating implemented so as to minimize systematic error. For example, the assumptions for any of the methods for the common–item nonequivalent groups designs tend to hold better when the groups being administered the old and the new form do not differ too much from each other. The assumptions also tend to hold better when the forms to be equated are very similar to one another and when the content and statistical characteristics of the common items closely represent the content and statistical characteristics of the total test forms. One other way to help control error is to use what is often referred to as *double-linking*. In double-linking, a new form is equated to two previously equated forms. The results for the two equatings often are averaged to produce a more stable equating than if only one previously equated form had been used. Double-linking also provides for a built-in check on the adequacy of the equating.

Equating issues specific to computer-based tests

Many of the equating issues for computer-based tests are similar to those for paper-and-pencil tests. However, some testing programs have both computer and paper-and-pencil modes of their tests. In these cases, it is important to assess the extent to which different testing modes produce comparable scores.

Computer-adaptive tests are used in some testing programs (Dolan & Burling, this volume). Computer-adaptive tests typically use IRT calibrated item pools. For security purposes, alternate pools of items are sometimes used and the pools are typically refreshed over time as new items are added to the pools. In computer-adaptive testing, it is important to establish the comparability of scores from the adaptive tests from different item pools (Wang & Kolen, 2001).

The scaling and equating process

Score scales are often established using an initial form of a test. Raw scores on a subsequent alternate form are equated to raw scores on this initial form. The raw-to-scale score transformation for the initial form is then applied to the equated scores on the subsequent form. Later, raw scores on new forms are equated to previously equated forms and then transformed to scale scores. The scaling and equating process leads to scores from all forms being reported on a common scale. The intent of this process is to be able to say, for example, "a scale score of 26 indicates the same level of proficiency whether it is earned on Form X, Form Y, or Form Z."

Practical Applications

In this section, the processes of scaling, norming, and equating are described as related to large-scale admissions, placement and credit, and outcomes and accountability assessments.

Admissions Testing

Admissions tests are used to assess students' preparedness and competence for secondary and post-secondary-level work and aptitude and to supplement their grade records and other information. These tests include the SAT, ACT, Test of English as a Foreign Language (TOEFL), Graduate Record Exam (GRE), Graduate Management Admissions Test (GMAT), Law School Admissions Test (LSAT) and Medical College Admissions Test (MCAT). They provide a standardized independent measure of a defined set of tasks with results reported on a common scale for all students, unlike high school or college grades. Thus, these assessments can provide unique objective information about the student as well as confirmation or refutation of the other assessment sources. For more information on admissions tests, see Zwick (2006, this volume). The SAT and ACT assessment will be the focus of further discussion of admissions tests in this chapter.

The processes of scaling, norming, and equating are vital to large-scale standardized admissions tests, such as the SAT and ACT assessment. The large-scale high-stakes nature of these exams makes interpretability of the scores and security of the test administration procedures key elements of these testing programs. Fortunately, the large volumes also help in establishing appropriate scaling, norming, and equating processes.

Transformations of raw scores to scale scores on admissions tests are conducted to incorporate normative and in some cases, score precision, information. To incorporate normative information, the ACT and SAT assessments are administered to national norm groups chosen to be representative of college-bound high school students. The distribution of scores for the norm group is then transformed to have particular properties, such as the 200-to-800 SAT score scale that has a mean of 500 and standard deviation of 110. The resulting raw-to-scale score transformation is used to calculate reported scores for operational examinees.

Because of the high-stakes nature of these admissions tests, different forms of the assessment are administered at each testing date. To ensure the comparability of reported scores from these administrations, equating is necessary. Equating data are collected through either the common-item nonequivalent groups (SAT) or randomly equivalent groups designs (ACT), as these are the most feasible and appropriate given the large volumes and administration constraints. Generally, any equating methodology may be considered for these assessments, and the method chosen for determining the reported scores depends on how well the equated scores align with previous score distributions and reduce random equating error. For more details on the scaling and equating processes for the ACT and SAT assessments, see *Admissions Testing* in the *Examples* section later in this chapter.

Placement Testing

Large-scale placement tests used in higher education include The College Board's Advanced Placement Program (AP®, College Board, 2010b) and ACCUPLACER® (College Board, 2010c) exams and ACT's Computer-Adaptive Placement Assessment and Support System (COMPASS®, ACT, 2010c). These tests are used to assess the knowledge and skills of college-bound high school or incoming college students in order to help find the appropriate course level for students upon entering higher education institutions.

AP, ACCUPLACER, and COMPASS, although all placement tests, have different purposes and different audiences. AP is an end-of-course exam intended for high school students who have completed specific college-level coursework (e.g., biology, statistics, or psychology) while in high school. A student's score from an AP exam may allow him or her to place out of introductory-level college courses by demonstrating that he or she has already adequately completed this work. ACCUPLACER and COMPASS, on the other hand, are aimed at diagnosing students' strengths and weaknesses in more general reading, writing, and math skills to help colleges and universities make appropriate course placement decisions, including whether or not remedial work is needed. These exams can also be used to monitor student course progress and to suggest whether remediation is still needed or if a change in course assignment is recommended. For more information on placement tests in general, and the ACCUPLACER exam in particular, see Morgan (this volume). For more information on AP exams, see *Advanced Placement Program Examinations* in the *Examples* section later in this chapter.

Scaling and norming

Placement tests are used to make important decisions about which college courses students must take, relative to other students and/or to the work expected of them, thus scaling to incorporate normative and content information is very important. Since ACCUPLACER and COMPASS are administered to students already enrolled at the institution, scales that incorporate local criteria or normative information are most appropriate. AP, on the other hand, is administered to high school students but used to make decisions by institutions of higher education. Thus, scaling to incorporate normative information about representative entering college students is key in order for institutions to be able to make decisions about all entering students who have completed the AP exam.

During ACCUPLACER and COMPASS testing, which involves a computerized adaptive test based on IRT estimation, only a few questions (maximum of 20) are presented and branching occurs based on examinee performance (ACT, 2010d; College Board, 2007). After completing the test, an estimate of IRT proficiency is provided for each examinee based on the IRT three-parameter logistic model. The metric for this scale is arbitrary, and so it is typically taken to have a mean of zero and standard deviation of one. To make the scores more useful, score scales were created. For ACCUPLACER, a 20-to-120 scale was created. This scale represents a transformation from the IRT proficiency scale to a scale that describes the probability that an examinee will correctly answer 120 items, which was chosen to reflect the 120 items that were in the original item pools. For COMPASS, a 0-to-100 scale was created to represent the percentage of the entire item pool that examinees would be expected to answer correctly if they were to take all of the items. The ACCUPLACER and COMPASS score scales provide an absolute (i.e., a criterion-referenced) measure of the student's skills, independent of the distribution of skills among all test takers.

Two other measures of student performance are provided to ACCUPLACER users: the Range and the Percentile Rank. The Range uses an estimate of test score error to put a lower and upper bound around the scale score. The Percentile Rank indicates student performance in relation to a population of test takers in a specific year. The Percentile Rank score can be used to compare a student's score to a national user group of students who took the test, thus providing users with normative information.

For COMPASS, ACT suggests that institutions use local norms to compare to a student's score. Alternatively, ACT provides score distributions for two-year and four-year schools which may be used to compare to an institution's score distribution.

For AP, scale scores for new exams are established via special studies (called comparability studies) in which shortened AP exams are administered to samples of college students. The college students' results are compared to those of high school AP students and are used to establish the 1–5 AP scale, which indicates how qualified students are for college-level credit or placement based on their test performance: 5 = Extremely well qualified; 4 = Well qualified; 3 = Qualified; 2 = Possibly qualified; and 1 = No recommendation.

The score levels used for placement decisions (i.e., a student must achieve a scale score of 100 on ACCUPLACER or a 3 on the AP exam in order to place out of the introductory course) are left up to individual institutions to decide because of the unique characteristics and needs of, as well as the differences in course offerings and sequencing at, each institution. However, to help institutions establish these cut scores, testing companies may provide qualitative information, such as the College Board's "proficiency statements" that describe the knowledge and skills associated with specific ACCUPLACER scale scores or the previously mentioned qualification statements associated with AP grades.

Equating

Because of the high-stakes nature of these placement exams, different forms of the ACCUPLACER, COMPASS, and AP exams are administered at different times and these forms are equated. ACCU-PLACER and COMPASS forms are developed from IRT calibrated item pools and are equated through IRT equating to the item pool (See *IRT Calibrated Item Pools* earlier in this chapter). The equating design for AP exams is the common-item nonequivalent groups design using an anchor set of only multiple-choice (MC) items, combined with a judgmental process for considering adjustments based on constructed-response (CR) item scores. See *Advanced Placement Program Examinations* in the *Examples* section later in this chapter for more detail about the AP processes.

Assessments of Outcomes and for Accountability

Assessment is increasingly critical to the success and continuation of educational programs. Many programs engage in student assessment as part of accreditation and accountability requirements, academic program review, and/or simply out of an interest in improving their program. These assessments help to measure the impact of higher education programs and services to individual student learning, development, and student progression, and to monitor and enhance educational quality at the program or institutional level.

These assessments are used to measure students' achievement levels on a group and individual basis and can be used to compare students' achievement levels with national user norms. The assessment results then show the extent to which programs achieve their educational and developmental learning goals and objectives and can help to evaluate the strengths and weaknesses of general education programs.

These types of assessments are primarily concerned with program evaluation; therefore, the analyses focus on groups of students. However, depending on the psychometric characteristics of these exams with respect to individual-level scores (e.g., reliability of scores over forms or administrations), these assessments may or may not be appropriate vehicles for providing individual students with feedback about their mastery of particular skills or for making high-stakes classification decisions about individual students.

The General Education assessments administered by James Madison University's (JMU) Center for Assessment and Research Studies (CARS; JMU, 2010) and ACT's Collegiate Assessment of Academic Proficiency (CAAP®; ACT, 2010b) are two examples of large-scale assessments used for outcomes and accountability purposes.

JMU's General Education assessments (such as the Natural World exam [NW-9], designed to measure learning in scientific and quantitative reasoning) are primarily used to gather group-level information for evaluating JMU's general education program. Several individual student competency requirements exist as part of JMU's general education program, however, and learning objectives are routinely assessed for students in each major. These tests are generally multiple-choice tests that are developed by the appropriate university faculty and the CARS team to assess college students' skills in the relevant area. The total number of correct responses on a test is used to indicate a student's level of reasoning in that particular subject and provides criterion-referenced information. Some exams have subscores (e.g., quantitative reasoning), which give information about areas subsumed within the total test.

Whereas the total score provides criterion-referenced information, normative information is also provided in the form of percentile ranks for samples of first- and second-year JMU students. The JMU assessments are typically administered to relatively small samples (1,000–2,500) of first- and second-year students for norm studies, but these provide at least some comparison for other institutions using the instruments. JMU also provides recommended cut scores for each exam, determined by standard setting studies involving exam-specific JMU faculty, although it is recommended that institutions determine their own cut scores. One form of each JMU assessment is administered at a time and this form changes over time due to content changes or psychometric improvements. These alternate forms are not equated and thus cut score studies need to be redone whenever the form changes occur.

The CAAP is a standardized, nationally-normed assessment program from ACT with tests of writing, reading, math, science, and critical thinking for outcomes and accountability purposes. CAAP scores are reported on a scale of 40–80, with a mean of 60 and standard deviation of approximately 5. Subscores are provided for three CAAP tests to help provide insight into areas of possible weakness. These have a score range of 5–25, with a mean of 15 and standard deviation of 2.5.

Several scores and tables are reported on the CAAP institutional score reports in order to provide more content and normative meaning to these scores. These reports help institutions to make inferences about particular groups of students and about individual students. Institutions may compare groups of students at their institution to user or local norm groups (e.g., sophomores at 2- or 4-year institutions) over time, and to other groups at their institution. They may also use CAAP scores for making placement decisions for individual students after setting appropriate local cut scores. CAAP has several forms of each test that are equated through the randomly equivalent groups design. Equipercentile equating with smoothing methods are used to make adjustments to the distributions to reduce random error (See Kolen, 1984).

Examples

Admissions Testing—Contrasting Scales and Equating for the ACT Assessment and the SAT

The ACT assessment consists of four tests: English, Mathematics, Reading, Science, and an optional Writing test. These tests are MC only, scored 0 or 1, except for the writing test essay, which is scored 1–6 by two raters, resulting in a score of 2–12.

The SAT consists of three sections: Critical Reading, Mathematics, and Writing. The three sections are further broken down into three subsections for each, resulting in nine subsections, including one essay within the writing section. Most SAT forms also include a tenth unscored subsection (critical reading, mathematics, or multiple-choice writing) that is used for pretesting and equating. The subsections are MC only and formula scored, except for the writing section essay, which is scored 1–6 by two raters, resulting in a score of 2–12 (off-topic essays receive a score of 0).

Scaling

ACT MC-ONLY EXAMS

The scaling of the ACT was based on the 1988 Academic Skills Study of more than 100,000 nationally representative college-bound senior high school students. First, weighted raw scores were obtained for the sample of students, with weights chosen such that the characteristics of the sample would match those of the target population. Next, the weighted raw score distributions were smoothed. Finally, the smoothed raw score distributions were linearly transformed to an initial scale with a mean of 18 and a standard error of measurement (SEM) of 2 along the entire score scale. The process used was based on Kolen (1988) and described in detail by Kolen and Hanson (1989). These initial scale scores were rounded to integers ranging from 1 to 36 for the tests and 1 to 18 for subscores. Some adjustment of the rounded scale scores was performed to attempt to meet the specified mean and standard error of measurement and to avoid gaps in the score scale (scale scores that were not used) or to avoid having too many raw scores converting to a single scale score. This process resulted in the final raw-to-scale score conversions (ACT, 2007).

ACT WRITING

Before the launch of the ACT Writing test in February 2005, a special scaling study was conducted in which the writing test was operationally administered to over 3,800 students. A combined English/Writing score scale was created by standardizing the English scale scores (1–36) and the Writing scores (2–12) for these students, weighting them 2/3 and 1/3, respectively, and using a linear transformation to map these combined scores onto a scale that ranged from 1 through 36. These transformed scores were then rounded to integers to form the reported score scale. This approach resulted in a single conversion table that is used for all ACT English form/Writing form combinations.

SAT MC-ONLY SECTIONS

The most recent scaling of the SAT was based on exam scores from the "1990 Reference Group," which included over one million college-bound high school juniors and seniors (Dorans, 2002). These exam scores were obtained from students taking over 35 different forms of the SAT between October 1988 and June 1990. Raw-to-scale score conversions (based on the form that the examinee completed) were applied to rounded formula-scored SAT scores for these students to create unrounded scale scores (201, 202, 203, . . . 501, 502, etc.) that were then rounded at the third digit to either 0 or 5 (200, 205, 210, 215, etc). This distribution was then normalized, producing a scale with a mean of 0 and standard deviation of 1. The frequency distributions of these rounded scores were smoothed with Holland and Thayer's (1987) log-linear procedure. This discrete smoothed score distribution was made continuous by using the continuization step from Holland and Thayer's (1989) kernel method of score equating. Finally, this normalized score scale distribution was linearly transformed to a 200–800 scale with a mean of 500 and a standard deviation of 110.

SAT WRITING

Every SAT test contains a 25-minute essay. The essay subscore is reported on a 2–12 scale, resulting from summing independent scores of 1 to 6 by two readers. The essay score is scaled to the MC writing score and a linear combination of the two scores (essay weighted 30% and MC weighted 70%) is the resulting writing raw score, which is then converted to the 200–800 scale.

Norming

ACT provides norms that represent the national population of twelfth-grade students and the national subpopulation of college-bound seniors. These norms were obtained from the 1995 nationally representative weighted samples. ACT also provides rolling 3-year user norms that are based on the most recent scores of graduating seniors who took the test as 10th, 11th, or 12th graders. These norms are based on data from the last three academic years, are updated each year (oldest year of data dropped and most recent year of data added), and are included on score reports. In addition, ACT provides yearly national and state profile reports that provide percentiles and information about that year's graduating seniors who took the ACT.

SAT provides user norms in the form of percentile ranks based on the most recent scores earned by students in the previous year's high school graduating class who took the SAT. In addition, SAT

173

provides yearly national and state percentiles and information about that year's graduating seniors who took the SAT through June of that year.[1]

Both the ACT and SAT score scales were constructed to readily provide useful information to users. Normative information is also provided to help users make inferences about individual scores. ACT reports a 36-point score scale that incorporates score precision in terms of equal SEMs across the score scale and also reports national and user norms. SAT uses a 60-point normalized scale and reports only user norms.

Equating

ACT

In order to equate new forms of the ACT test, samples of examinees at one of the yearly testing dates are administered spiraled forms (over 2,000 examinees for each form), including a form that has been equated to previous forms. Thus, new forms are equated to previous forms through the use of the randomly equivalent groups data collection design. Each of the four tests of the assessment is separately equated to previous forms using the equipercentile equating method with smoothing. The composite score is then computed as a rounded average of the four test scores.

SAT

Most SAT forms contain ten subsections, one of which is a variable section (different across forms) that is used for pretesting future operational items, embedding anchor tests used for equating, or for research purposes. The different versions of the test forms (with different variable sections) are packaged in a repeating sequence and thus are administered in a spiraled fashion. The variable section is used to equate the MC subsections of new forms of the SAT through the common–item nonequivalent groups design. These forms include an anchor set of items that has been administered with a previous form and that is used to statistically adjust the scores to account for any student ability and form difficulty differences. The MC-only anchor set is a miniature version of all of SAT MC subsections but the score does not contribute to the overall test score (i.e., it is an external anchor set). Results from classical and IRT equating methods are considered for reported SAT scores. Choice of method for determining the reported scores depends on how well the equated scores align with previous score distributions and reduce random equating error. The writing essay score is then scaled to the MC writing score and a linear combination of the two scores (essay weighted 30% and MC weighted 70%) is the resulting writing raw score, which is then converted to the 200–800 scale.

SUMMARY

Both ACT and SAT assessments have multiple forms and use equating to adjust for difficulty differences among these forms. The ACT assessment uses the randomly-equivalent-groups data collection design and equipercentile equating with smoothing for the statistical adjustments. The SAT assessment uses the common–item nonequivalent groups design for data collection and considers equated scores from several of the classical and IRT equating methods.

Advanced Placement Program Examinations

The AP Program is a unique high-stakes testing program in that it is comprised of 33 summative assessments, coupled with 33 AP courses delivered by a network of over 120,000 teachers in almost

16,000 schools who use a broad array of curricula and textbooks to prepare their students for college-level work. Except for Studio Art, which is a portfolio assessment, AP exams contain both multiple-choice (MC) and constructed-response (CR) sections. Scoring, scaling, and equating of the AP exam scores takes into account both of these item types.

Number-correct scoring is used for the multiple-choice items. The constructed-response questions are scored by a single rater using rubrics with 4 to 16 points depending on the item and exam. For most of the exams, a number-correct score is calculated over all of the MC items. On some language examinations (e.g., Spanish Language), number-correct scores are calculated separately for the listening and reading comprehension items.

Scaling

A scale is established for new and modified exams at first administration and approximately once every five years for all AP exams by administering a shortened operational AP exam (i.e., some questions are left out of each section) that becomes the base form, to a sample of college students, in what is called a college comparability study. The college students' exams are scored by their professor and by AP scorers. Instructors are asked to assign a letter grade to each of their students based on their performance on the entire examination. Instructors develop their own criteria for grading and are allowed to weight different examination sections using their own judgment.

After the composite score data are available for the operationally tested high school AP examinees, composite scores on the shortened comparability study forms are linked to composite scores on the operational form. The linked scores are used to find the average score on the operational composite scale for college students who earned an A on the AP short-form as scored by their instructor. This average composite score for the college students earning an examination grade of A is used for the initial 4/5 cut score. The average composite score for college students who received an exam examination grade of B from their instructors is used for the initial 3/4 cut score, and so on for the initial 2/3 and 1/2 cut scores. Thus, the cut scores on the AP composite score scale are set such that the lowest composite score for an AP grade of 5 is roughly equal to the average composite score on the same examination for college students earning a grade of A; the lowest composite score of an AP grade of 4 is roughly equal to the average composite score for college students with a grade of B; and so forth.

Equating

The common item nonequivalent groups equating design is used for equating MC number-correct scores on the main operational AP form to MC number-correct scores on an old AP form using a MC-only anchor set. In some cases, two MC common item sets are developed that link to two different old forms. The MC-only anchor sets are built to have proportional content coverage and the same statistical specifications as the MC section of the entire form.

Equating methods that are used include linear and equipercentile methods. Choice of method for reporting results depends on a variety of criteria including the number of students, number of items on the new and old forms, and standardized mean differences on the common items.

The process described thus far equates MC number-correct scores (and thus MC cut scores) for the new form to MC number-correct scores on the base form, but the new form MC number-correct scores must still be linked to the new form composite scores. This is achieved by scaling the MC number-correct scores for the new form to the composite score for the new form using single-group equipercentile methods. Scaling functions are not produced for the entire range of scores. Only the four cut scores that determine AP grades are scaled. That is, the four MC number-correct cut scores are linked to the new form composite scores.

Standard setting/verification

Next, changes to the composite cut scores are considered to take into account any potential changes in students' performances on or difficulty of the constructed response (CR) questions from the current to previous years. A variety of evidence is considered in order to maintain AP grading standards over time, including results of the equating and the college comparability studies when available, the distribution of scores on different parts of the examinations, AP grade distributions from the past three years, and students' constructed-response answers. This continuity of AP standards helps to ensure that, for example, an AP grade of 3 on this year's examination represents, as nearly as possible, the same level of achievement as a grade of 3 on last year's examination.

Operational scores

Once the final AP cut scores have been set, scores are determined for students taking the operational exam. These students' raw composite scores are computed as a weighted linear composite of the scores from both MC and CR items. The linear composite is created from a weighted sum of the MC number-correct scores and the weighted sum of the CR scores. The weights used for calculating this composite are based on the proportion of the maximum desired number of composite score points for the MC and CR sections. The contribution of the CR section scores varies across the 33 examinations ranging from 33 to 60 percent in terms of the number of points on the composite raw score and is determined by Examination Development Committees.

The range of the weighted raw composite score differs across examinations, but ranges from 0 to as high as 150. This composite score is converted to the reported AP grade scale ranging from 1 to 5 by comparing the composite to the cut scores and assigning a grade of 1, 2, 3, 4, or 5 to the student. These grades are all that is reported for examinee overall performance (i.e., composite scores are not reported).

Through these scaling, norming, and equating processes, student-level AP scores (or grades) relay meaningful information about the student's readiness for college-level work. Whereas the AP 1–5 scale and its associated qualification definitions (5 = Extremely well qualified; 4 = Well qualified; 3 = Qualified; 2 = Possibly qualified; and 1 = No recommendation) give colleges and universities an indication of which score may be used for placement and credit decisions (i.e., scores of 3, 4, or 5), ultimately, the institutions must set their own credit and placement policies.

Note

1 The college-bound seniors cohort traditionally has included students who tested through March of their senior year. However, the College Board has observed a trend in which more students are taking the SAT for the first time in May or June of their senior year and is expanding the cohort to include this group of college-bound students.

References

ACT. (2007). *ACT technical manual.* Retrieved from http://www.act.org/aap/pdf/ACT_Technical_Manual.pdf

ACT. (2010a). The ACT®. http://act.org/aap/

ACT. (2010b). CAAP®. http://www.act.org/caap/

ACT. (2010c). [JEC3]COMPASS®. http://www.act.org/compass/

ACT. (2010d). *COMPASS® ESL internet version reference manual.* Iowa City, IA: Author.

Allen, N. L., Carlson, J. E., & Zelenak, C. A. (1999). *The NAEP 1996 technical report.* (NCES 1999–452). Washington, DC: National Center for Education Statistics.

American Educational Research Association, American Psychological Association, & National Council on Measurement in Education. (1999). *Standards for educational and psychological testing.* Washington, DC: American Educational Research Association.

Angoff, W. H. (1971). Scales, norms, and equivalent scores. In R. L. Thorndike (Ed.), *Educational measurement* (2nd ed., pp. 508–600). Washington, DC: American Council on Education.

College Board. (2007). *ACCUPLACER® OnLine: Technical manual.* New York, NY: Author.

College Board. (2010a). ACCUPLACER®. http://professionals.collegeboard.com/higher-ed/placement/ accuplacer

College Board. (2010b). AP®. http://www.collegeboard.com/student/testing/ap/about.html

College Board. (2010c). SAT®. http://sat.collegeboard.com/home

Dolan, R., & Burling, K. (this volume). *Computer-based testing in higher education.*

Dorans, N. J. (2002). *The recentering of SAT® scales and its effects on score distributions and score interpretations.* (College Board Research Report No. 2002–11, ETS RR–02–04). New York, NY: The College Board.

Ebel, R. L. (1962). Content standard test scores. *Educational & Psychological Measurement, 22*(1), 15–25.

Flanagan, J. C. (1951). Units, scores, and norms. In E. F. Lindquist (Ed.), *Educational measurement* (pp. 695–763). Washington, DC: American Council on Education.

Hambleton, R. K., & Pitoniak, M. J. (2006). Setting performance standards. In R. L. Brennan (Ed.), *Educational measurement* (4th ed., pp. 433–470). Westport, CT: American Council on Education/Praeger.

Holland, P. W., & Dorans, N. J. (2006). Linking and equating. In R. L. Brennan (Ed.), *Educational measurement* (4th ed., pp. 187–220). Westport, CT: American Council on Education/Praeger.

Holland, P. W., & Thayer, D. T. (1987). *Notes on the use of log-linear models for fitting discrete probability distributions.* (Technical Report 87–79). Princeton, NJ: Educational Testing Service.

Holland, P. W., & Thayer, D. T. (1989). *The kernel method of equating score distributions.* (Technical Report 89–84). Princeton, NJ: Educational Testing Service.

James Madison University. (2010). The Centre for Assessment and Research Studies. http://www.jmu.edu/assessment/

Knupp, T., & Harris, D. (this volume). *Building content and statistical test specifications.*

Kolen, M. J. (1984). Effectiveness of analytic smoothing in equipercentile equating. *Journal of Educational Statistics, 9*, 25–44.

Kolen, M. J. (1988). Defining score scales in relation to measurement error. *Journal of Educational Measurement, 25*(2), 97–110.

Kolen, M. J. (2006). Scaling and norming. In R. L. Brennan (Ed.), *Educational measurement* (4th ed., pp. 155–186). Westport, CT: American Council on Education/Praeger.

Kolen, M. J., & Brennan, R. L. (2004). *Test equating, scaling, and linking: Methods and practices* (2nd ed.). New York, NY: Springer-Verlag.

Kolen, M. J., & Hanson, B. A. (1989). Scaling the ACT Assessment. In R. L. Brennan (Ed.), *Methodology used in scaling the ACT Assessment and P-ACT+* (pp. 35–55). Iowa City, IA: ACT, Inc.

Kolen, M. J., Hanson, B. A., & Brennan, R. L. (1992). Conditional standard errors of measurement for scale scores. *Journal of Educational Measurement, 29*(4), 285–307.

Morgan, D. L. (this volume). *College placement testing of entering students.*

Osterlind, S. J., & Wang, Z. (this volume). *Item response theory in measurement, assessment, and evaluation for higher education.*

Petersen, N. S., Kolen, M. J., & Hoover, H. D. (1989). Scaling, norming, and equating. In R. L. Linn (Ed.), *Educational measurement* (3rd ed., pp. 221–262). New York, NY: American Council on Education.

Wang, T., & Kolen, M. J. (2001). Evaluating comparability in computerized adaptive testing: Issues, criteria, and an example. *Journal of Educational Measurement, 38*(1), 19–49.

Yen, W., & Fitzpatrick, A. R. (2006). Item response theory. In R. L. Brennan (Ed.), *Educational measurement* (4th ed., pp. 111–153). Westport, CT: American Council on Education/Praeger.

Zwick, R. (2006). Higher education admissions testing. In R. L. Brennan (Ed.), *Educational measurement* (4th ed., pp. 647–679). Westport, CT: American Council on Education/Praeger.

Zwick, R. (this volume). *Admissions testing in higher education.*

Zwick, R., Senturk, D., Wang, J., & Loomis, S. C. (2001). An investigation of alternative methods for item mapping in the National Assessment of Educational Progress. *Educational Measurement: Issues and Practice, 20*(2), 15–25.

13

RELIABILITY

Bruce Thompson and Tammi Vacha-Haase

Score reliability characterizes the degree to which scores evaluate "something" as opposed to "nothing" (e.g., are completely random). Thompson (2003b) explained the concept of score reliability using the metaphor of a bathroom scale, noting that:

> [M]any of us begin our day by stepping on a scale to measure our weight. Some days when you step on your bathroom scale you may not be happy with the resulting score. On some of these occasions, you may decide to step off the scale and immediately step back on to obtain another estimate. If the second score is half a pound lighter, you may irrationally feel somewhat happier, or if the second score is slightly higher than the first, you may feel somewhat less happy. But if your second weight measurement yields a score 25 pounds lighter than the initial measurement, rather than feeling happy, you may instead feel puzzled or perplexed. If you then measure your weight a third time and the resulting score is 40 pounds heavier, you probably will question the integrity of *all* the scores produced by your scale. It has begun to appear that your scale is exclusively producing randomly fluctuating scores. In essence, your scale measures "nothing." *(p. 4)*

Sometimes we desire protocols that yield scores that are completely random (i.e., measure nothing, and are perfectly unreliable). For example, when we enter a casino our reasonable premise is that the dice and the roulette wheels yield scores that are perfectly unreliable.

However, when we are conducting social science research, and attempting to measure constructs that we believe are relatively stable, such as intelligence, academic achievement, or self-concept, we expect the scores from our measures to measure "something" rather than "nothing," and thus expect scores to not fluctuate wildly. For example, if we measure the IQ of Steve on Monday, and again on the following Tuesday, we expect Steve's two scores to be very similar, because we do not expect Steve's IQ to fluctuate much over the course of a single routine day.

Of course, scores are never perfectly reliable, due to the inescapable influences of unavoidable measurement errors. Typically, scores from physical measurements (e.g., height, weight) tend to be more reliable than scores reflecting abstract constructs that cannot be directly observed (e.g., intelligence, academic achievement, or self-concept). But even the most sophisticated physical measures are imperfect. For example, atomic clocks gauge time by counting the vibrations (actually the microwaves caused by atomic vibrations) of certain atoms (e.g., hydrogen-1, caesium-133, rubidium-87), but even the best atomic clocks gain or lose some time (i.e., less than a second) over long time periods (e.g., a billion years)! Thus, the question is never whether scores from our measures are perfectly reliable, but rather the degree of reliability possessed by a given set of scores.

Score Reliability Coefficients as Variability Ratios

The English psychologist Charles Spearman (1904) first articulated a coherent measurement theory, sometimes called "true score theory," but now often called "classical theory," merely because this theory is older than the "modern" measurement theories. Spearman (1910) also popularized use of the term "reliability." Spearman's idea was that we needed to quantify the proportion (or the percentage) of the variability (e.g., the variance, or the sum-of-squares) in our data that is not random.

Thus, a reliability coefficient is always the ratio of [Sum-of-Squares$_{RELIABLE}$ / $(n - 1)$] / [Sum-of-Squares$_{OBSERVED}$ / $(n - 1)$] or, because for a given sample the $(n - 1)$ terms cancel, of Sum-of-Squares$_{RELIABLE}$ / Sum-of-Squares$_{OBSERVED}$. Of course, the fact that a reliability coefficient is always a ratio of two squared-metric statistics which cannot be negative implies that a reliability coefficient also theoretically cannot be negative.

For example, if we have data from four participants on a 1-to-5 scale: $X_{TOM} = 1$, $X_{DICK} = 1$, $X_{HARRY} = 5$, and $X_{SAM} = 5$, the Sum-of-Squares$_{OBSERVED}$, given $M = 3.0$, is $(1 - 3.0)^2 + (1 - 3.0)^2 + (5 - 3.0)^2 + (5 - 3.0)^2 = 2.0^2 + 2.0^2 + 2.0^2 + 2.0^2 = 4.0 + 4.0 + 4.0 + 4.0 = 16.0$. The $\sigma_{OBSERVED}^2 = 16.0 / (4 - 1) = 16.0 / 3 = 5.33$. Thus, because the most that four scores potentially ranging from 1-to-5 can be "spread out" (i.e., dispersed) is when two scores equal 1 and two scores equal 5, the Sum-of-Squares$_{OBSERVED}$ = 16.0 and the $\sigma_{OBSERVED}^2 = 5.33$ are the mathematical upper bounds on these variability statistics under the conditions that (a) $n = 4$ and (b) the scores are on a 1-to-5 scale (see Thompson, 2006a).

Obviously, obtaining variability statistics (i.e., the Sum-of-Squares$_{OBSERVED}$ and the $\sigma_{OBSERVED}^2$) for a given set of scores is quite straightforward. The real challenge is in estimating either Sum-of-Squares$_{RELIABLE}$ or $\sigma_{RELIABLE}^2$. It is in estimating the latter values that various "classical" and "modern" psychometric theories can be differentiated from each other.

Classical Theory Score Reliability Estimates

Spearman's idea was that to estimate the Sum-of-Squares$_{RELIABLE}$ or $\sigma_{RELIABLE}^2$ we needed to estimate an unknowable "true score." The true score can be conceptualized as "the mean of an infinitely large sample of repeated measurements of an individual" presuming no practice or changing motivation effects (Guilford & Fruchter, 1978, p. 408). Traditionally, three categories of classical theory reliability estimates have been considered.

Test-Retest or Stability Reliability Coefficients

One way to estimate the true scores of a given set of participants is to administer a given measure once, and then successively readminister the same measure to the same people. Of course, these readministrations might not feasibly be done immediately. The readministrations each might allow the participants to rest, conceivably even for a day or even several days.

In practice, most researchers conduct fewer than infinitely many such readministrations. Indeed, most applied researchers estimating stability reliability coefficients administer the given measure to the given set of people only twice!

Although we seek to compute a reliability coefficient always as the ratio of [Sum-of-Squares$_{RELIABLE}$ / $(n - 1)$] / [Sum-of-Squares$_{OBSERVED}$ / $(n - 1)$], it can be shown that this is mathematically equivalent to estimating the r^2 of the true scores, T, for a given group of participants with their observed scores, X. As Lord and Novick (1968) noted, the reliability coefficient "is defined as the squared correlation ρ_{XT} between observed score[s] and true score[s]" (p. 61).

In practice, when we collect two sets of scores on a given measure from a given group of people, we obtain the test-retest/stability reliability coefficient by computing the Pearson r (*not* the Pearson r^2) between the two sets of scores. Any software that computes the Pearson r can be used to obtain this stability reliability estimate (e.g., the CORRELATIONS routine within SPSS).

Of course, this discussion suggests a seeming contradiction. If a reliability coefficient is a squared correlation coefficient, how can we estimate this coefficient by computing a nonsquared Pearson r correlation coefficient? The answer to that question is very complex, and for our purposes here we merely note that "The square of the correlation between observed scores and true scores is equal to the [unsquared] correlation between parallel measurements" (Lord & Novick, 1968, pp. 58–59) and refer the interested reader to that treatment for more detail. In any case, the reliability coefficient, r_{XX}, is in a squared metric even though the symbol for the statistic does not contain a superscript 2.

Equivalence Reliability Coefficients

In some instances test developers carefully create measures that they desire to be equivalent. The availability of equivalent test forms can be useful, for example, in experiments in which both pre-tests and posttests are administered. Using equivalent forms for pre- and post-testing minimizes the contamination of performance on the posttest as a function of pretest sensitization before instruction. So two American history 10-item tests might both be developed using a table of specifications requiring 3 items that measure memory of facts about the colonies 1609–1776, 5 items that measure ability to interpret knowledge about America in the years 1777–1826, and 4 recall items about the years 1827–1945.

Both forms X and Y of the 10-item American history test might be administered to 50 students. Typically, orders of administration are counterbalanced (i.e., 25 students are randomly assigned to complete form X and then form Y, and 25 students are randomly assigned to complete form Y and then form X). The equivalence reliability coefficient is computed as the Pearson r between the X and the Y scores of the 50 students. Again, the resulting reliability coefficient is in a squared metric, notwithstanding the computational method using r (versus r^2) and the use of the symbol r_{XX} (versus r_{XX}^2).

Internal Consistency Reliability Coefficients

Logically, scores from a measure should be more likely to measure "something" rather than "nothing" when the items composing a given measure yield scores that are highly correlated with each other, such that a total score computed by totaling or averaging item scores would represent the aggregation of numbers that "go together." The internal consistency reliability coefficients are computed by taking into account these item score correlations. Two approaches can be used for these purposes.

Split-half reliability coefficients

One approach to estimating the squared-metric reliability coefficient r_{XX} for multiple item measures is to randomly split the items into two subsets, compute total scores on the items in both subsets, and then compute the Pearson r between the two sets of subset total scores. However, if the original measure had 20 items, what we have actually estimated through this process is the squared-metric reliability coefficient r_{XX} for a measure that was 10 items rather than 20 items long.

We convert the initial split–half reliability coefficient estimate by applying the Spearman-Brown correction formula:

$$r_{xx}' = (k \times r_{xx}) / (1 + (k-1) \times r_{xx}),$$

where r_{xx} is the initial reliability coefficient estimate, k is the proportion by which the measure is lengthened or shortened, and r_{xx}' is the corrected estimate. For example, if the split–half Pearson r for our 20-item measure was $r_{xx} = 0.70$, the final reliability coefficient would be estimated with $k = 2$ (because we want to convert the reliability coefficient for 10 items into the reliability coefficient for the full 20 items, and $10 \times 2 = 20$) to be

$(2 \times 0.7) / (1 + (2-1) \times 0.7)$
$(2 \times 0.7) / (1 + (1) \times 0.7)$
$1.4 / (1 + (1) \times 0.7)$
$1.4 / (1 + 0.7)$
$1.4 / (1.7) = 0.82$

For split–half applications, where k always equals 2, because $k - 1 = 1$, we can for this application simplify the Spearman-Brown formula to equal

$$r_{xx}' = (k \times r_{xx}) / (1 + r_{xx}).$$

But the Spearman-Brown formula is also useful with other coefficients, and when $k \neq 2$. For example, if our reliability coefficient for the full 20-item test is $r_{xx} = 0.82$, as in our example, we might want to estimate what the estimated score reliability would be if we made the test $k = 3$ times longer (i.e., 60 items versus the initial 20 items), assuming the new 40 items were roughly the same in quality as the initial 20 items. The estimated reliability of the scores on the longer measure would be

$(3 \times 0.82) / (1 + (3-1) \times 0.82)$
$(3 \times 0.82) / (1 + (2) \times 0.82)$
$2.46 / (1 + (2) \times 0.82)$
$2.46 / (1 + 1.64)$
$2.46 / (2.64) = 0.93$

Conversely, if the score reliability of a measure consisting of 80 items was estimated to be 0.93, we might be willing to shorten the test in the hopes that the score reliability would still remain reasonably good while requiring less testing time. If we shorten the 80-item test to 40 items, $k = 0.5$, and we obtain

$r_{xx}' = (k \times r_{xx}) / (1 + (k-1) \times r_{xx})$
$(0.5 \times 0.93) / (1 + (0.5-1) \times 0.93)$
$(0.5 \times 0.93) / (1 + (-0.5) \times 0.93)$
$0.46 / (1 + (-0.5) \times 0.93)$
$0.46 / (1 + -0.465)$
$0.46 / 0.535 = 0.87$

The Spearman-Brown formula can also be rearranged to solve for k, given as input an actual score reliability coefficient of any type, r_{xx}, and a desired score reliability, r_{xx}'. For example, if for a 25-item measure $r_{xx} = 0.7$, and $r_{xx}' = 0.9$, we have

$k = (r_{xx}' \times (1 - r_{xx})) / (r_{xx} \times (1 - r_{xx}'))$
$(0.9 \times (1 - 0.7)) / (0.7 \times (1 - 0.9))$
$(0.9 \times 0.3) / (0.7 \times (1 - 0.9))$
$(0.9 \times 0.3) / (0.7 \times 0.1)$
$0.27 / (0.7 \times 0.1)$
$0.27 / 0.07 = 3.86$

Thus, to obtain our objective of $r_{xx}' = 0.9$ we must make our 25-item test approximately 3.86 times longer, assuming our new items are roughly equal in quality to our initial 25 items, such that the test is 25 x 3.86 items long, or roughly 96 items long.

Coefficient α

A problem with split–half reliability estimates is that for a measure consisting of relatively few items there are a large number of potential item splits, each of which may yield different and potentially contradictory reliability estimates. For example, for a measure consisting of $v = 6$ items, the number of splits equals

$0.5(v!) / [(0.5(v))!]^2$
$0.5(6 \times 5 \times 4 \times 3 \times 2 \times 1) / [(0.5(6))!]^2$
$0.5(6 \times 5 \times 4 \times 3 \times 2 \times 1) / [3!]^2$
$0.5(6 \times 5 \times 4 \times 3 \times 2 \times 1) / [3 \times 2 \times 1]^2$
$0.5(6 \times 5 \times 4 \times 3 \times 2 \times 1) / 6^2$
$0.5(6 \times 5 \times 4 \times 3 \times 2 \times 1) / 36$
$0.5(720) / 36$
$360 / 36 = 10$

A measure consisting of only 12 items has a number of splits equal to

$0.5(v!) / [(0.5(v))!]^2$
$0.5(12 \times 11 \times 10 \times 9 \times 8 \times 7 \times 6 \times 5 \times 4 \times 3 \times 2 \times 1) / [(0.5(12))!]^2$
$0.5(12 \times 11 \times 10 \times 9 \times 8 \times 7 \times 6 \times 5 \times 4 \times 3 \times 2 \times 1) / [6!]^2$
$0.5(12 \times 11 \times 10 \times 9 \times 8 \times 7 \times 6 \times 5 \times 4 \times 3 \times 2 \times 1) / [6 \times 5 \times 4 \times 3 \times 2 \times 1]^2$
$0.5(12 \times 11 \times 10 \times 9 \times 8 \times 7 \times 6 \times 5 \times 4 \times 3 \times 2 \times 1) / 720^2$
$0.5(12 \times 11 \times 10 \times 9 \times 8 \times 7 \times 6 \times 5 \times 4 \times 3 \times 2 \times 1) / 518,400$
$0.5(479,001,600) / 518,400$
$239,500,800 / 518,400 = 462$

Obviously, measures consisting of more commonly encountered numbers of items (e.g., 20, 50 or 100) create a huge number of potential splits. Ideally, what we would like to estimate is the average reliability coefficient across all possible sample splits, and we would especially like to derive this estimate without having to perform all the sample splits and the related computations.

Kuder and Richardson proposed their formula number 20 for this purpose in their 1937 article:

$$\text{KR-20} = [v / (v - 1)] / [1 - ((\Sigma(p_j)(q_j)) / \sigma_x^2)],$$

where v is the number of items on the measure, p_j is the proportion of persons obtaining the first of the two possible scores on the jth dichotomously-scored item (e.g., 1 for right if the test is scored right-wrong, or 1 for agree if the item is agree-disagree), q_j is the proportion of persons obtaining the second of the two possible scores on the *j*th dichotomously-scored item (e.g., 0 for wrong if the test is scored right-wrong, or 0 for disagree if the item is agree-disagree), and σ_x^2 is the variance of the total scores on the measure. Mathematically, the variance of the scores on a given *j*th item can be computed using the formula $\sigma_j^2 = $ Sum-of-Squares $/ (n-1)$, but also can be computed using the formula $\sigma_j^2 = (p_j)(q_j)$. This (correctly) implies, for example, that the maximum variance for a dichotomously-scored item is $0.5(0.5) = 0.25$, and that the maximum item variance occurs on dichotomously-scored items when exactly half the participants score a 0, and the remaining half of the participants score a 1.

The KR-20 formula can be used with measures with *any* type (e.g., knowledge, attitude) of dichotomously-scored items, but with measures *only* using dichotomously-scored items. Of course, social scientists frequently use items that are not dichotomously-scored, such as Likert scales or cognitive measures that allow for partial credit. For this reason Cronbach (1951) proposed a more general estimate, Cronbach's α:

$$\alpha = [v / (v-1)] \times [1 - (\Sigma\sigma_j^2 / \sigma_x^2)],$$

which can be used for any combination of items scored in any way.

Table 13.1 presents the item and the total scores of eight participants on a five-item measure of attitudes about the role of mother with item responses potentially ranging from 1 to 5, and thus total scores potentially ranging from 5 to 25. On all five items half of the eight women responded 1, and half of the eight women responded 5. Thus, for each item the item Sum-of-Squares equals

Person	Item Score	−	Item Mean	=	Deviation	Deviation²
Camie	5	−	3.0	=	2.0	4.0
Deborah	5	−	3.0	=	2.0	4.0
Geri	5	−	3.0	=	2.0	4.0
Jan	5	−	3.0	=	2.0	4.0
Kathy	1	−	3.0	=	2.0	4.0
Murray	1	−	3.0	=	2.0	4.0
Peggy	1	−	3.0	=	2.0	4.0
Shawn	1	−	3.0	=	2.0	4.0
Sum						32.0

and for each item the $\sigma_j^2 = 32.0 / (8-1) = 32.0 / 7 = 4.57$. The sum of the five item-score variances equals $4.57 + 4.57 + 4.57 + 4.57 + 4.57 = 22.85$.

Table 13.1 Scores of Eight Participants on a Five-Item Measure of Attitudes About the Role of Mother: Example #1

Participant	Item					Total
	1	*2*	*3*	*4*	*5*	*Total*
Camie	5	5	5	5	5	25
Deborah	5	5	5	5	5	25
Geri	5	5	5	5	5	25
Jan	5	5	5	5	5	25
Kathy	1	1	1	1	1	5
Murray	1	1	1	1	1	5
Peggy	1	1	1	1	1	5
Shawn	1	1	1	1	1	5

And for these data for which half the total scores are 5, and half the total scores are 25, the total score variance is at its mathematical maximum for this context (i.e., $n = 8$, and potential scores range from 5 to 25), and $\sigma_X^2 = 114.28$. So we have

$\alpha = [v / (v - 1)] \times [1 - (\Sigma\sigma_j^2 / \sigma_X^2)]$,
$[5 / (5 - 1)] \times [1 - (22.85 / 114.28)]$
$[5 / 4] \times [1 - (22.85 / 114.28)]$
$1.25 \times [1 - 0.20]$
$1.25 \times 0.80 = 1.00$

The total score variance is hugely influential with respect to score reliability (see Reinhardt, 1996). Classical score reliability focuses on the stability of the rank orderings of the participants. Put simply, when people's scores on measurement #1 and measurement #2 are each both more widely dispersed, the score reliability tends to be greatest, *because then small random fluctuations on each measurement, or both, are less likely to alter the rank orderings of participants on these two sets of widely dispersed scores.* Thus, score reliability tends to be greatest when total score variance is large.

The "take home" message is that if you want highly reliable scores, measure scores in ways that lead to greater score dispersion. For example, measuring a more diverse group of participants will usually lead to greater total variance. And adding items to measures at least allows the total scores to become more dispersed.

To further illustrate these dynamics, consider the Table 13.2 example #2 data with item responses potentially ranging from 1 to 5, and thus total scores potentially ranging from 5 to 25. However, for these data the total scores are considerably more homogeneous (i.e., $\sigma_X^2 = 1.00$ versus 114.28). For these data, we have

$\alpha = [v / (v - 1)] \times [1 - (\Sigma\sigma_j^2 / \sigma_X^2)]$,
$[5 / (5 - 1)] \times [1 - (0.94 / 1.00)]$
$[5 / 4] \times [1 - (0.94 / 1.00)]$
$1.25 \times [1 - 0.94]$
$1.25 \times 0.06 = 0.078$ (unrounded)

The Table 13.3 data illustrate that Cronbach's α can mathematically be negative, even though α is in a squared metric. For these data, we have

$\alpha = [v / (v - 1)] \times [1 - (\Sigma\sigma_j^2 / \sigma_X^2)]$,

Table 13.2 Scores of Eight Participants on a Five-Item Measure of Attitudes About the Role of Father: Example #2

Participant	Item 1	2	3	4	5	Total
Steve	4	5	3	1	1	14
Cathy	5	4	3	1	1	14
Patty	5	5	2	1	1	14
Ralph	5	5	2	1	1	14
Judy	5	5	4	1	1	16
Randy	5	5	4	1	1	16
Sheri	5	5	3	2	1	16
Jay	5	5	3	1	2	16

Table 13.3 Scores of Eight Participants on a Five-Item Measure of Attitudes About the Role of Grandfather: Example #3

			Item			
Participant	1	2	3	4	5	Total
Fred	4	5	3	1	1	14
Colleen	5	4	3	1	1	14
Martha	5	5	1	1	2	14
Duane	5	5	1	2	1	14
Brinley	5	5	3	1	1	15
Parsu	5	5	3	1	1	15
Len	5	4	3	2	1	15
Valerie	4	5	3	1	2	15

$[5 / (5 - 1)] \times [1 - (1.50 / 0.25)]$
$[5 / 4] \times [1 - (1.50 / 0.25)]$
$1.25 \times [1 - 6.00]$
$1.25 \times -5.00 = -6.25$

Such a result indicates not that your computer software is in error, but rather that either your data have horrible psychometric properties, or have been incorrectly entered.

Role of Interitem Correlations

The previously presented formula for Cronbach's α does not make clear the pivotal role that the correlations of the item scores have on internal consistency reliability. Obviously, when scores across all the pairwise combinations of items are high, the items are more "internally consistent" with each other, and thus should yield more reliable total scores.

We will illustrate the computation of Cronbach's α using interitem covariances, which are related to interitem Pearson r values, given that $r_{XY} = COV_{XY} / [(SD_X) (SD_Y)]$, and $COV_{XY} = r_{XY} (SD_X) (SD_Y)$. Table 13.4 presents a fourth hypothetical set of scores of eight participants with item responses potentially ranging from 1 to 5.

Table 13.5 presents the item score variances, covariances, and Pearson r values for these data. The sum of the item score variances can be computed by adding the diagonal entries in the Table 13.5 matrix. For our data, $\Sigma\sigma_j^2 = 4.57 + 3.71 + 3.71 + 3.71 + 3.71 = 19.43$ (unrounded).

Table 13.4 Scores of Eight Participants on a Five-Item Measure of Attitudes About the Role of Grandmother: Example #4

			Item			
Participant	1	2	3	4	5	Total
Carol	5	4	5	5	5	24
Catherine	5	5	4	5	5	24
Mary	5	5	5	4	5	24
Anne	5	5	5	5	4	24
Donna	1	1	1	1	2	6
Allegra	1	1	1	2	1	6
Eileen	1	1	2	1	1	6
Nancy	1	2	1	1	1	6

Table 13.5 Item Score Variances, Covariances, and r² Values for the Table 13.4 Data

Item	\multicolumn{5}{c}{Item}				
	1	2	3	4	5
1	4.5714	0.971	0.971	0.971	0.971
2	4.0000	3.7143	0.923	0.923	0.923
3	4.0000	3.4286	3.7143	0.923	0.923
4	4.0000	3.4286	3.4286	3.7143	0.923
5	4.0000	3.4286	3.4286	3.4286	3.7143

Note. Item covariances are presented on the diagonal to 4 decimal places, item covariances are presented in the bottom left triangle to 4 decimal places, and item Pearson r values are presented in the top right triangle to 3 decimal places.

Now we will compute the variance of the total scores, σ_X^2, without even computing the total scores themselves, using only the item score variances and covariances! The crucial insight is that *the total score variance is in part a function of the item score covariances and thus the item score correlations.*

The variance of any composite score, including a total score computed by summing scores on individual items, can be computed using the formula

$$\sigma_X^2 = \Sigma\sigma_j^2 + [\Sigma COV_{jk} \text{ (for } j < k) \times 2]$$

For the Table 13.4 data, we have already determined that $\Sigma\sigma_j^2 = 4.57 + 3.71 + 3.71 + 3.71 + 3.71 = 19.43$ (unrounded). We also have

j	k	r_{jk}	×	SD_j	×	SD_k	=	COV_{jk}
1	2	0.9707		2.1381		1.9272		3.9999
1	3	0.9707		2.1381		1.9272		3.9999
1	4	0.9707		2.1381		1.9272		3.9999
1	5	0.9707		2.1381		1.9272		3.9999
2	3	0.9231		1.9272		1.9272		3.4287
2	4	0.9231		1.9272		1.9272		3.4287
2	5	0.9231		1.9272		1.9272		3.4287
3	4	0.9231		1.9272		1.9272		3.4287
3	5	0.9231		1.9272		1.9272		3.4287
4	5	0.9231		1.9272		1.9272		3.4287
Sum								36.5716
2×Sum								73.1432

Thus,

$$\sigma_X^2 = \Sigma\sigma_j^2 + [\Sigma COV_{jk} \text{ (for } j < k) \times 2]$$
$$19.43 + [36.57 \times 2]$$
$$19.43 + 73.14 = 92.57$$

So, for the Table 13.4 example,

$$\alpha = [v / (v-1)] \times [1 - (\Sigma\sigma_j^2 / \sigma_X^2)],$$
$$[5 / (5-1)] \times [1 - (19.43 / 92.57)]$$
$$[5 / 4] \times [1 - (19.43 / 92.57)]$$
$$1.25 \times [1 - 0.21]$$
$$1.25 \times 0.79 = 0.988$$

The Table 13.4 total scores are slightly less reliable than the Table 13.1 total scores, in part because the Table 13.4 scores are somewhat less dispersed (i.e., $\sigma_X{}^2 = 92.57$ versus 114.28).

Modern Measurement Theory Reliability Coefficients

Since 1970, various psychometricians have proposed new measurement models that are both more sophisticated and more complicated. For example, theorists have articulated measurement models for measures that are "strictly parallel," "tau-equivalent," "essentially tau-equivalent," "congeneric," or "multi-factor congeneric" (Feldt & Brennan, 1989, pp. 110–111; Lord & Novick, 1968, pp. 47–50). The fit of these various measurement models can be evaluated using structural equation modeling (SEM), as explained by Jöreskog and Sörbom (1989, pp. 76–96).

Perhaps the most important modern measurement theory from a score reliability perspective is Generalizability or "G" theory, as proposed by Cronbach, Gleser, Nanda and Rajaratnam (1972). The full details of "G" theory are beyond the scope of the present treatment, but are summarized in the chapter by Webb, Shavelson, and Steedle (this volume), in the accessible chapter by Thompson (2003a), or in more detail in Shavelson and Webb's (1991) book.

"G" theory uses analysis of variance (ANOVA) to partition the various sources of systematic and measurement error underlying a given set of scores (see Thompson, 2003a). For example, suppose a researcher collected data using a measure containing eight rating criteria applied by five judges to two programs skated by 10 Olympic skaters. As in classical measurement theory, in "G" theory we compute the variance in the total scores, $\sigma_X{}^2$, and we partition that variance into its two complements, reliable variance (i.e., $\sigma_{RELIABLE}{}^2$) and measurement error variance (i.e., $\sigma_{UNRELIABLE}{}^2$). And, as always, we compute a squared-metric ratio of $\sigma_{RELIABLE}{}^2 / \sigma_X{}^2$, or $[\sigma_X{}^2 - \sigma_{UNRELIABLE}{}^2] / \sigma_X{}^2$ to estimate r_{XX}.

However, when more than one source of measurement error variance is present, as in our skating example, we can further partition the measurement error into its various different subcomponents, and also into their interactions. As Jaeger (1991) explained:

> Cronbach and his associates . . . effectively demonstrated that it was no longer necessary to restrict decompensation of variation in individual's observed test scores to two components—variation attributed to true differences among individuals, and variation attributed to a conglomeration of systematic and random sources. . . . Indeed, this latter component of variation could be dissected further to gain an understanding of the systematic sources of variation that contributed to what we heretofore considered an undifferentiable mass, simply "error." *(p. ix)*

"G" theory has three important and separate advantages over classical measurement theory.

First, "G" theory estimates can simultaneously consider all the measurement error variances sources in a given protocol, while classical measurement theory reliability estimates (e.g., Cronbach's α) can each consider only a single source of measurement error variance. Yet, in many protocols multiple measurement error sources are present (e.g., measurement errors due to the rating criteria, the program skated, and the raters or judges).

Unfortunately, the sources of measurement error variance are independent and cumulative. For example, if we estimate Cronbach's α to be 90%, and stability reliability to also be 90%, these regrettably do not involve the measurement errors accounting for the same 10% of the total score variance. Instead, the more reasonable reliability estimate taking into account only these two main effect sources of measurement error variances would be 80%, not 90%!

Second, sources of measurement error variance in reality interact to create yet more error variance in the form of measurement error interaction effects. For example, some raters may more consistently apply some of the rating criteria, while other raters more consistently apply the remaining rating criteria. Or some raters might rate the first program more systematically, while other judges rate the second program more reliably. Only a modern measurement theory, such as "G" theory, can estimate and simultaneously take into account both measurement error main effects (e.g., the main effect due to rating criteria, the main effect due to raters) and measurement error interaction effects (e.g., the criteria-by-raters two-way measurement error interaction effect).

Third, "G" theory can be used to estimate different reliability coefficients for using scores to make "relative" versus "absolute" decisions. These reliability coefficients can be different (and almost always are) even for the same data when taking into account how the scores will be used. "G" theory computes a reliability coefficient called the generalizability coefficient for situations where scores are used to make "relative decisions" (e.g., the top three skaters will get trophies no matter what their scores are). "G" theory instead computes a reliability coefficient called a phi coefficient for situations where scores are used to make "absolute" decisions (e.g., any examinee with 70% or more correct answers on a licensure exam will be licensed no matter how many examinees meet this criterion).

These three advantages of "G" theory are hugely important, which is why Jaeger (1991) so strongly recommended generalizability analysis. Jaeger noted, "Thousands of social science researchers will no longer be forced to rely on outmoded reliability estimation procedures when investigating the consistency of their measurements" (p. x).

However, Hogan, Benjamin, and Brezinski's (2000) empirical study of scholarly practices found that, "Despite their prominence in the psychometric literature of the past 20 years, we encountered no reference to generalizability coefficients . . . or to the test information functions that arise from item response theory" (p. 528). As a practical matter, applied researchers tend to prefer coefficients such as Cronbach's α, because these coefficients can be estimated by administering only one test one time to one group of participants.

Tests Are Not Reliable

It is unfortunately all too common to see journal article authors describing the "reliability of the test" or stating that "the test is reliable." This "sloppy speaking" (Thompson, 1992, p. 436) at face value asserts an obvious untruth, because reliability is a property that applies to scores, and not immutably across all conceivable uses everywhere of a given measure (Thompson, 1994). The same measure, administered 100 times, may yield 100 different reliability coefficients (Thompson & Vacha-Haase, 2000).

As Wilkinson and the APA Task Force on Statistical Inference (1999) emphasized, "It is important to remember that a test is not reliable or unreliable . . . Thus, authors should provide reliability coefficients of the scores for the data being analyzed even when the focus of their research is not psychometric" (p. 596).

Various prominent measurement textbooks appropriately highlight the view that tests are *not* reliable. For example, Pedhazur and Schmelkin (1991) noted, "Statements about the reliability of a measure are . . . [inherently] inappropriate and potentially misleading" (p. 82). Similarly, Gronlund and Linn (1990) emphasized that: "Reliability refers to the *results* obtained with an evaluation instrument and not to the instrument itself . . . Thus, it is more appropriate to speak of the reliability of the 'test scores' or the 'measurement' than of the 'test' or the 'instrument'" (p. 78, emphasis in the original).

Rowley (1976) noted, "It needs to be established that an instrument itself is neither reliable nor unreliable . . . A single instrument can produce *scores* which are reliable, and other *scores* which are unreliable" (p. 53, emphasis added). In short, it must be clearly understood that "a test is not 'reliable' or 'unreliable.' Rather, reliability is a property of the scores on a test for a *particular* group of examinees" (Crocker & Algina, 1986, p. 144, emphasis added).

As Urbina (2004) emphasized, "the fact is that the quality of reliability is one that, if present, belongs not to test but to test *scores*" (p. 119). She perceptively noted that the distinction between scores versus tests being reliable is subtle, but noted:

> . . . the distinction is fundamental to an understanding of the implications of the concept of reliability with regard to the use of tests and the interpretation of test scores. If a test is described as reliable, the implication is that its reliability has been established permanently, in all respects for all uses, and with all users. *(p. 120)*

Urbina utilized a piano analogy to illustrate the fallacy of describing tests as reliable, noting that saying "the test is reliable" is similar to stating a piano will always sound the same, regardless of the type of music played, the person who is playing it, the type of the piano, or the surrounding acoustical environment.

The understanding that tests are *not* reliable led Vacha-Haase (1998) to create a new measurement meta-analytic method called "reliability generalization" (RG). RG characterizes (a) the typical score reliability yielded by a given measure across samples, (b) the degree of dispersion of the reliability coefficients for a given measure across samples, and (c) the measurement protocol features that predict variations in score reliability coefficients for a given measure.

These views have two equally important implications for scholars:

1. Do not use language referring to "the reliability of the test" or asserting that "the test is reliable" (see Thompson, 1994); and
2. Compute and report score reliability for your own data.

Sadly, a meta-analysis of Reliability Generalization (RG) meta-analyses showed that reliability is almost never discussed in published research (Vacha-Haase, Henson, & Caruso, 2002)!

Poor score reliability attenuates both $p_{CALCULATED}$ values and effect sizes (see Thompson, 2006a, 2006b). But it is the reliability of your scores, and not of the scores used to compute the reliability coefficients reported in test manuals, that dictate the integrity of your substantive analyses. It is especially egregious to attempt to "induct" the reliability coefficients reported in a test manual when your samples differ from the test manual samples in either (a) sample composition or (b) score dispersion (see Vacha-Haase, Kogan, & Thompson, 2000; Vacha-Haase & Thompson, 2011).

Reliability and Item Analysis Computations

The Table 13.6 data will be used to discuss the practical aspects of computing reliability and item analyses. The data involve scores of 10 participants on eight items that were dichotomously scored 0 or 1 (e.g., right-wrong on a cognitive test, or disagree-agree on an attitude measure).

For these data, the sum of the item score variances, $\Sigma\sigma_j^2$, equals 1.99 (0.25 + 0.25 + 0.25 + 0.25 + 0.25 + 0.25 + 0.25 + 0.24), and $\sigma_x^2 = 7.69$. Cronbach's α can be computed as

$$\alpha = [v / (v - 1)] \times [1 - (\Sigma\sigma_j^2 / \sigma_x^2)],$$
$$[8 / (8 - 1)] \times [1 - (1.99 / 7.69)]$$
$$[8 / 7] \times [1 - (1.99 / 7.69)]$$
$$1.14 \times [1 - (1.99 / 7.69)]$$
$$1.14 \times [1 - 0.25]$$
$$1.14 \times 0.74 = 0.847$$

Table 13.6 Scores of 10 Participants on an Eight-Item Measure Consisting of Dichotomously-Scored Items: Example #5

Participant/ Statistic	1	2	3	4	5	6	7	8	Total $v = 8$	Total $v = 7$
				Item						
Deborah	1	1	1	1	1	1	1	1	8	7
Geri	1	1	1	1	1	1	1	0	7	7
Kathy	1	1	1	1	1	1	1	0	7	7
Peggy	1	0	1	1	1	1	1	0	6	6
Shawn	0	1	1	1	1	1	1	0	6	6
Fred	1	0	0	0	0	0	0	1	2	1
Duane	0	1	0	0	0	0	0	1	2	1
Brinley	0	0	0	0	0	0	0	1	1	0
Len	0	0	0	0	0	0	0	1	1	0
Parsu	0	0	0	0	0	0	0	1	1	0
p	0.5	0.5	0.5	0.5	0.5	0.5	0.5	0.6		
q	0.5	0.5	0.5	0.5	0.5	0.5	0.5	0.4		
σ^2	0.25	0.25	0.25	0.25	0.25	0.25	0.25	0.24	7.69	9.85

However, commonly available statistical software readily provides Cronbach's α and additional statistics. In SPSS typing the following syntax yields the results discussed here. Alternatively, the syntax can also be produced through pointing and clicking.

```
reliability variables=V1 to V8/
scale(TOTAL)=V1 to V8/
statistics=all/summary=total .
```

The computer software also yields several additional very useful results that can be used either to evaluate the psychometric properties of scores, or during instrument development to determine which items are performing well and which items, if any, are not, so that bad items may be dropped from a measure.

α-if-Deleted Statistics

One very useful item analysis result is the α-if-item-deleted statistic. Items vary in quality, and deleting items from a measure can actually improve the reliability coefficients. In this respect items are like former girl or boyfriends: the best item is that one that hurts the most when you drop the item (i.e., the total score reliability gets the most "worse"), some items don't make much difference when you drop them (i.e., the total score unreliability is relatively unchanged either with or without the item), and the worst item is the one that makes you feel most joyous when you drop the item (i.e., the total score reliability gets the most "better"). For our data, item #8 is clearly a bad item.

For these data, as reported in Table 13.6, if we drop item #8, the sum of the item score variances, $\Sigma\sigma_j^2$, equals 1.75 (0.25 + 0.25 + 0.25 + 0.25 + 0.25 + 0.25 +0.25), and $\sigma_x^2 = 9.85$. Cronbach's α for total scores for only the first seven items can be computed as

$$\alpha = [v / (v - 1)] \times [1 - (\Sigma\sigma_j^2 / \sigma_x^2)],$$
$$[7 / (7 - 1)] \times [1 - (1.75 / 9.85)]$$
$$[7 / 6] \times [1 - (1.75 / 9.85)]$$

$$1.16 \times [1 - (1.75 \: / \: 9.85)]$$
$$1.16 \times [1 - 0.17]$$
$$1.16 \times 0.82 = 0.959$$

Clearly, because Cronbach's α when item #8 is included in the total scores is 0.847, and rises to 0.959 when item #8 is deleted, item #8 is a poor item.

The SPSS software computes α-if-deleted statistics for each item in turn in a given dataset. Thus, this useful result can be painlessly obtained even for a measure with numerous items!

"Corrected" Discrimination Coefficients

Logically, if strong reliability implies large correlations among item scores, strong reliability also implies large correlations between the scores on a given item and the total scores. For example, on a cognitive test, we expect people who get an item correct to be more likely than their counterparts to have higher total scores (i.e., we expect items to discriminate between participants who have more of a trait and those who have less of the trait). "Discrimination" coefficients are correlation coefficients that quantify how well items do in this respect. An item with a near-zero discrimination coefficient should be a candidate for item deletion during test development, and an item with a negative discrimination coefficient should certainly be deleted.

For example, the discrimination coefficient for the item #8 scores in Table 13.6 would be the Pearson r between the 10 participants' scores on the item, [1, 0, 0, 0, 0, 1, 1, 1, 1, 1], with the 10 participants' respective total scores on all eight items, [8, 7, 7, 6, 6, 2, 2, 1, 1, 1]. The discrimination coefficient for item #8 for these data is $r = -0.707$.

However, a little reflection quickly leads to a recognition that there is a problem with discrimination coefficients computed in this manner. The problem is that the scores on the item that are part of the computation, [1, 0, 0, 0, 0, 1, 1, 1, 1, 1], *are also part of the second variable involved in the correlation (i.e., the total scores)* [8, 7, 7, 6, 6, 2, 2, 1, 1, 1]. This tends to lead to spuriously inflated discrimination coefficients.

The cure for this bias is to compute "corrected" item discrimination coefficients by correlating the 10 item scores, [1, 0, 0, 0, 0, 1, 1, 1, 1, 1], not with total scores involving all the items, but instead with total scores computed by *omitting the item scores for the item being evaluated* (i.e., for total scores involving seven rather than eight items). The total scores computed only with the first seven items for these data are [7, 7, 7, 6, 6, 1, 1, 0, 0, 0]. The "corrected" item discrimination coefficient for item #8 is –0.780.

Again, SPSS painlessly computes the correlations between item scores and total scores omitting each item in turn (i.e., "corrected" discrimination coefficients). The extremely unfavorable "corrected" discrimination coefficient (i.e., –0.780) again suggests that item #8 ought to be deleted from the item pool.

Summary

Poor score reliability compromises substantive research analyses by attenuating both $p_{CALCULATED}$ values and effect sizes. Because scores, *not* tests, are reliable, it is incumbent upon the researcher using classical statistical methods to investigate the reliability of the scores in hand before conducting substantive analyses. The reliabilities of the scores in hand, and *not* the reliabilities of the scores reported in test manuals, are what potentially compromise substantive analyses (e.g., ANOVA, regression, descriptive discriminant analysis, canonical correlation analysis).

Serious scholars ought to follow two equally important admonitions for responsible practice:

1. Do not use language referring to "the reliability of the test" or asserting that "the test is reliable" (see Thompson, 1994); and
2. Compute and report score reliability for your own data.

Modern computer software makes the relevant reliability analyses relatively painless. These analyses can be augmented with item analysis statistics such as α-if-deleted and "corrected" discrimination coefficients.

References

Crocker, L., & Algina, J. (1986). *Introduction to classical and modern test theory*. New York, NY: Holt, Rinehart and Winston.

Cronbach, L. J. (1951). Coefficient alpha and the internal structure of tests. *Psychometrika, 16*, 297–334.

Cronbach, L. J., Gleser, G. C., Nanda, H., & Rajaratnam, N. (1972). *The dependability of behavioral measurements: Theory of generalizability for scores and profiles*. New York, NY: Wiley.

Feldt, L. S., & Brennan, R. L. (1989). Reliability. In R. L. Linn (Ed.), *Educational measurement* (3rd ed., pp. 105–146). New York, NY: American Council on Education.

Gronlund, N. E., & Linn, R. L. (1990). *Measurement and evaluation in teaching* (6th ed.). New York, NY: Macmillan.

Guilford, J. P., & Fruchter, B. (1978). *Fundamental statistics in psychology and education* (6th ed.). New York, NY: McGraw-Hill.

Hogan, T. P., Benjamin, A., & Brezinski, K. L. (2000). Reliability methods: A note on the frequency of use of various types. *Educational and Psychological Measurement, 60*, 523–531.

Jaeger, R. M. (1991). Forward. In R. J. Shavelson, & N. M. Webb (Eds.), *Generalizability theory: A primer* (pp. ix–x). Newbury Park, CA: Sage.

Jöreskog, K. G., & Sörbom, D. (1989). *LISREL 7: A guide to the program and applications* (2nd ed.). Chicago, IL: SPSS.

Kuder, G. F., & Richardson, M. W. (1937). The theory of the estimation of test reliability. *Psychometrika, 2*, 151–160.

Lord, F. M., & Novick, M. R. (1968). *Statistical theories of mental test scores*. Reading, MA: Addison-Wesley.

Pedhazur, E. J., & Schmelkin, L. P. (1991). *Measurement, design, and analysis: An integrated approach*. Hillsdale, NJ: Erlbaum.

Reinhardt, B. (1996). Factors affecting coefficient alpha: A mini Monte Carlo study. In B. Thompson (Ed.), *Advances in social science methodology* (Vol. 4, pp. 3–20). Greenwich, CT: JAI Press.

Rowley, G. L. (1976). The reliability of observational measures. *American Educational Research Journal, 13*, 51–59.

Shavelson, R. J., & Webb, N. M. (1991). *Generalizability theory: A primer*. Newbury Park, CA: Sage.

Spearman, C. E. (1904). The proof and measurement of association between two things. *American Journal of Psychology, 15*, 72–101.

Spearman, C. E. (1910). Correlation calculated from faulty data. *British Journal of Psychology, 3*, 271–295.

Thompson, B. (1992). Two and one-half decades of leadership in measurement and evaluation. *Journal of Counseling and Development, 70*, 434–438.

Thompson, B. (1994). Guidelines for authors. *Educational and Psychological Measurement, 54*, 837–847.

Thompson, B. (2003a). A brief introduction to Generalizability theory. In B. Thompson (Ed.), *Score reliability: Contemporary thinking on reliability issues* (pp. 43–58). Newbury Park, CA: Sage.

Thompson, B. (2003b). Understanding reliability and coefficient alpha, really. In B. Thompson (Ed.), *Score reliability: Contemporary thinking on reliability issues* (pp. 3–23). Newbury Park, CA: Sage.

Thompson, B. (2006a). *Foundations of behavioral statistics: An insight-based approach*. New York, NY: Guilford Press.

Thompson, B. (2006b). Research synthesis: Effect sizes. In J. Green, G. Camilli, & P. B. Elmore (Eds.), *Handbook of complementary methods in education research* (pp. 583–603). Washington, DC: American Educational Research Association.

Thompson, B., & Vacha-Haase, T. (2000). Psychometrics *is* datametrics: The test is not reliable. *Educational and Psychological Measurement, 60*, 174–195.

Urbina, S. (2004). *Essentials of psychological testing*. Hoboken, NJ: Wiley.

Vacha-Haase, T. (1998). Reliability generalization: Exploring variance in measurement error affecting score reliability across studies. *Educational and Psychological Measurement, 58*, 6–20.

Vacha-Haase, T., Henson, R. K., & Caruso, J. C. (2002). Reliability Generalization: Moving toward improved understanding and use of score reliability. *Educational and Psychological Measurement, 62*, 562–569.

Vacha-Haase, T., Kogan, L. R., & Thompson, B. (2000). Sample compositions and variabilities in published studies versus those in test manuals: Validity of score reliability inductions. *Educational and Psychological Measurement, 60*, 509–522.

Vacha-Haase, T. & Thompson, B. (2011). Score reliability: A retrospective look back at twelve years of Reliability Generalization (RG) studies. *Measurement and Evaluation in Counseling and Development, 44*, 159–168.

Webb, N. M., Shavelson, R. J., & Steedle, J. T. (this volume). *Generalizability theory in assessment contexts.*

Wilkinson, L., & APA Task Force on Statistical Inference. (1999). Statistical methods in psychology journals: Guidelines and explanations. *American Psychologist, 54*, 594–604.

14

THE VALIDATION OF TESTS IN HIGHER EDUCATION

Kurt F. Geisinger, Leslie H. Shaw, and Carina McCormick

Tests and other assessments are used in many ways and for different purposes in higher education. Of course, most faculty members use tests and other assessments to assign grades and guide student learning in classes. Such tests are generally not the subject of the review or consideration by testing professionals. However, tests are also used to accept students for admission to many colleges and universities, as well as to graduate programs, professional schools, and special collegiate programs; as part of the overall consideration in awarding financial aid; to evaluate the success of students to learn and achieve the outcomes that their faculty have identified and structured their students to learn; to exempt students from specific classes; to determine if students need remedial work or can advance to the courses that they want or need to take to graduate; and for many other purposes.

The professional testing community that develops standardized tests, and the best professional practices that this community supports, insists that test developers and those who use tests and test scores at the university evaluate the effectiveness of specific uses of tests. For example, if a university uses a particular test to evaluate whether students have learned the material and concepts taught as part of the general education program (or core curriculum at some institutions), they also wish to know whether the measure or measures that they are using actually cover the material taught and hopefully learned in that curriculum. Likewise, students are likely to complain if an individual faculty member administers a final examination that disproportionately covers material from one portion of the class to the exclusion of others. Such a test might not be seen as valid (or fair) by students because it does not represent the material in the course appropriately.

To determine whether our generalizations about the scores that students achieve on any kind of test are accurate portrayals of what they are intended to measure, such as one's potential to succeed at a given college, research is generally needed to justify proper test use. This kind of research is known as *validation* research—research that attempts to determine if our interpretations of test scores are accurate. Validation documents whether our uses of assessments are appropriate and fair (see Carlton, this volume). Because there are many uses of tests in higher education, we also need to use a variety of different methods to evaluate the validity and usefulness of the measures we use. This chapter seeks to enumerate and briefly explain these validation approaches with special references to common types of testing used in higher education.

This chapter begins with a brief introduction to validity as testing professionals have defined and described it. At one time, the testing community believed that there were a number of different ways to establish whether a test was valid for a given purpose and situation. Today, we hold a more unified view of validity but still believe that there are multiple ways to collect information to justify uses of tests. In general, there are three major paths for collecting evidence for validating the use of tests. These three approaches are content-related validation, criterion-related validation, and construct-related validation. As is described below, at one point these different approaches were seen as different types of validity; today we believe that they are different sources of evidence to support certain test uses. Below, each of these three approaches is briefly described and then methods for validating three specific uses of tests in higher education are provided: admissions tests, placement and exemption tests, and outcomes assessments. There have also been interesting debates in the testing literature over the extent to which unintended consequences of testing relate to the validity of a test for a specific purpose. This point too is briefly annotated.

Sources of Evidence

Content Evidence

Content-related sources of evidence deal with how well a test's content represents a defined domain, such as an academic discipline (as in Graduate Record Examination subject tests) or the material covered in a specific course. For instance, content-related evidence for a test of Spanish language proficiency would be the degree to which an exam includes appropriate and relevant Spanish language questions. Content domain evidence includes but is not limited to items, tasks, test questions, and scoring guidelines (AERA, APA, & NCME, 1999). Test developers work with content experts to outline and detail the exam components needed to evaluate the intended domain. In so doing, a carefully developed test plan (also called a test blueprint) guides the construction of the test. In fact, many consider content-related validation a superb method of constructing tests. In order to create a Spanish language test, for example, test developers consult with content experts to judge the aspects of the language that need to be covered on the test. Experts then evaluate and judge the relative importance and representativeness of test items as a measure of a specific domain.

The appropriateness of the content domain provides evidence that allows test users to make decisions and meaningful interpretations of test scores across groups of examinees. As such, it is appropriate to use scores to make decisions, such as student placement in the most appropriate college Spanish course, if there is evidence of a relationship between the content domain and specific Spanish course content. We take actions to attempt to ensure that the test covers the most representative material in the domain and that it also represents the domain inclusively. However, a limitation of the content approach is the reliance on judgments from individuals such as faculty members and the tendency for confirmatory bias (Kane, 2006). For instance, a confirmatory bias might be where someone representing a test publisher and asked to evaluate the relevance of an item might be inclined to concur with the item writer as to the relevance of an item within a domain. In this case, there is a strong tendency for the publisher to lean towards agreeing with colleagues' perceptions of item relevance.

The content approach plays a central role in achievement testing by providing evidence of how well a test measures the important knowledge and skills needed to be successful in a specific academic domain. For example, knowledge of Spanish vocabulary is an important component for success in a college-level Spanish course, thus it is appropriate to have a number of items related to vocabulary knowledge on a placement test. Content experts evaluate the correspondence between the test content and the skills needed to be successful in the language class by examining such things as the number and type of vocabulary questions on a Spanish placement exam. The correspondence between the test blueprint and the test content is an indication of the degree of validity for the use of the measure to evaluate a specific domain. For example, a common complaint about many language tests is that they overemphasize the weighting of reading and writing skills as opposed to listening and speaking.

Content-related evidence provides information as to the degree to which the test content matches the necessary exam components outlined in the test blueprint, but this information alone is limited. The content-related approach alone is generally not an appropriate approach for predicting future performance or making inferences about test scores, because the number of relevant tasks does not provide information as to how well those tasks are at measuring academic success. For example, a content evaluation of a mathematics exam can provide evidence as to the number and type of different aspects of mathematics questions on the exam, but this does not provide information as to the ability of the test scores to predict college-level mathematics skills. Additional information beyond content-related evidence needs to be collected in order to make inferences about the meaning of test scores and the potential of scores to predict performance.

Criterion-Related Evidence

In many cases where test scores are used to predict future performance, a key issue is the identification of a relevant criterion, an index that summarizes one's success, such as grade-point average (GPA). Criterion-related evidence is used to evaluate validity by determining the degree to which test scores and criterion performance are related. Two designs of criterion-related sources of evidence, predictive and concurrent, are generally used to evaluate the degree of relationship between criteria and test scores, most typically with a correlation coefficient. The difference between predictive and concurrent designs depends on the timing between the collection of the test information and criteria. If the test information is used to evaluate future proficiency, then it is considered predictive whereas concurrent measures are used to estimate relationships between two or more measures of current performance.

A common example of predictive evidence is the use of test scores on a college admissions exam to predict success in college. The relationship between test scores and future grades is a source of evidence for the appropriateness of using test scores to make certain decisions (e.g., admissions, financial aid). The ability to estimate current or future performance is valuable in terms of utility, because a test that can accurately predict performance has the potential to aid in admissions or course placement. One of the critical issues in regard to criterion-related sources of evidence is the selection of a suitable criterion measure. GPA serves as a more than acceptable measure of academic performance, yet not all criteria can be measured as objectively or conveniently and GPA makes far less sense for doctoral students than undergraduates, for example. Criterion measures are limited in the sense that they can only measure part of any variable. No criterion measure can account for all components of success, thus a suitable measure of initial or preliminary success has to be chosen to represent the desired competence one wants ultimately to predict.

Criteria are sometimes classified as immediate, intermediate, or ultimate dependent upon how long one must wait to acquire the criterion. The longer one waits, typically the better the criterion, but there are obvious concerns over the length of time required and therefore immediate or intermediate criteria, such as freshman GPA are frequently used. Often, researchers substitute a criterion that is measured sooner or more easily for the larger measure of success, such as measuring graduate student success with first-year GPA rather than a perhaps more meaningful criterion that cannot be measured until several years have passed or for which it would be more difficult to collect data, such as number of publications within five years after graduation with a Ph.D.

There are certain statistical concerns with using predictive correlation studies as validity evidence. For example, when students have already been selected for admission using a test, the students who performed poorly on the test—the same students expected to perform poorly in classes—are excluded from the predictive validity study because they were not accepted to the college and thus have no GPA to include in the calculation. This phenomenon is called range restriction or curtailment, and its effect is that it reduces the relationship that one would find in the entire group of selected and rejected applicants, sometimes substantially. Additional information on range restriction is described below in the section on validating admissions measures.

A related issue is the reduction in the correlation between a predictor and a criterion due to low reliability of one variable or both. When either measure or both measures demonstrate low reliability, the magnitude of the correlation is consequently limited (this phenomenon is known as attenuation). Corrections for attenuation due to low reliability are available but may lead to misleading results. It is the belief of the authors that it is rarely appropriate to utilize a correction for low reliability of the predictor in a validity study because high reliability is typically a prerequisite for validity. Correction for low reliability of the criterion may be more justified. An appropriate use of correction for low reliability is to estimate what the gain in prediction would be if the predictor was made more reliable, such as by adding more items.

The criterion-related model is a pragmatic approach for evaluating the degree to which test scores and a criterion are related; the stronger the relationship between test scores and performance the better. Yet, there are some situations in which adequate criteria are unavailable or proposed attributes are not easily defined. These situations require an approach that blends external variables and theory in order to measure an observed combination of skills, traits, or attributes. Although some tests do not readily lend themselves to all approaches, it is important to use multiple sources of evidence whenever possible.

Construct Evidence

Construct validity is a judgment of the extent that "empirical evidence and theoretical rationales support the adequacy and appropriateness of inferences and actions based on test scores or other modes of assessment" (Messick, 1989, p. 13). A construct is "some postulated attribute of people, assumed to be reflected in test performance" (Cronbach & Meehl, 1955, p. 283). Constructs are not directly observed; instead they are based on theoretical relationships between observed characteristics derived from psychological theory and previous research. A construct is an inferred characteristic that is given meaning through the combination of measurable skills, traits, or attributes because it cannot be observed directly. Examples of constructs include, but are not limited to, academic success, self-esteem, intelligence, or motivation.

Compared to other approaches, construct evidence may be used from the early stages of a test and throughout the lifetime of a test to investigate continually the appropriateness of the test as a measure of the intended construct. Test constructors use theory to hypothesize the pattern of relationships between the observed test scores they believe best account for the attributes, traits, or skills they are trying to measure. Construct validation is a never-ending accumulation of evidence relating test scores and the theory underlying the construct. An important component in this continual process is the exploration of the degree to which a measure represents the intended construct. Convergent evidence (i.e., when the variables are positively correlated to a moderate or high degree) among observed variables potentially reflects the construct a researcher is trying to measure, whereas a lack of convergent evidence (i.e. when the variables that are expected to be related are negatively correlated, uncorrelated, or correlated only weakly) reveals a need for further review and consideration of the test, the construct in question, or the entire theory. When measures are intended to assess different constructs (such as math and reading sections on an achievement battery), lower correlations are expected between non-related assessments than between assessments intended to measure the same construct (e.g. two different measures of reading comprehension). The presence of lower correlations with non-related assessments is considered discriminant evidence, which in turn provides support for the intended relationships between variables.

A potential source of invalidity is construct underrepresentation, which occurs when a test fails to include important construct components. An example of construct underrepresentation on a

French placement exam would be the absence of a component measuring listening skills taught and mastered in earlier courses, thus the test would underrepresent the relevant aspects that comprise the construct of French language proficiency. Another potential source of invalidity is the presence of construct-irrelevant components, which is found when a test includes variables that are irrelevant to the domain. Irrelevant information on a French placement exam would be the inclusion of English or other foreign language vocabulary items that are not necessary for success in a college-level French course. If those using a test are also creating a test, the breadth and depth of the content should be laid out in the initial test blueprint as a safeguard against such problems.

Construct validation is not a confirmatory process. Both convergent and discriminant evidence provide information as to the underlying processes, skills or attributes influencing test scores. The sources of evidence uncovered in the construct validation process provide an understanding of what influences test scores and why they might relate to each other. Such evidence might suggest the presence of influences other than the intended construct, such as test motivation for an achievement test. Results of studies that call into question the test's successful representation of the construct should also be reported.

Unified Approach to Validity

Over the last fifty years, the concept of validity has evolved from a purely pragmatic model in which validity was conceptualized primarily as the correlation between test scores, and the behavior it was supposed to measure or predict, to a more integrated model (Angoff, 1988). Initially the three components of validity (criterion-related, content-related, and construct) tended to be perceived as distinct types of validity that needed to be addressed separately. Yet, construct validity has emerged as an overarching concept that it is often seen as encompassing all other approaches to validity because almost all information contributes to the relevant understanding of the construct that a test is trying to measure. Instead of separating different sources of validity evidence into different categories as "types" of validity, most validity studies can be considered to fall under the umbrella of "construct evidence" because the purpose of such studies is to examine how successfully the test measures the intended construct while minimizing the influence of unintended constructs.

The *Standards for Educational and Psychological Testing* (AERA, APA, & NCME, 1985, 1999) is a document developed by several professional associations most involved in testing to describe best practices in testing, including validation. They have undergone several revisions from the first standards document in 1954. In the mid-1980s, these *Standards* formally accepted a unified approach to validity, built on the premise that several sources of evidence were relevant in a comprehensive evaluation of validity. By tackling the issue of test validation with a variety of approaches already described, test makers and test users better answer the question of how appropriate decisions based on test scores are for their intended uses.

The current edition of the *Standards* advocates for an explicit validation plan, detailing the interpretations, rationale, and relevance of the proposed uses of the test scores. This specific plan forms the basis of the argument-based approach, in which the goal is to evaluate the claims made in regards to the proposed uses and interpretations drawn from scores. According to Kane (2006, p. 23), "the argument-based approach to validity reflects the general principles inherent in construct validity without an emphasis on formal theories." By explicitly lining up the arguments for the test one is validating, this approach provides direction as well as a gauge by which to judge the relevant sources of evidence used during the validation process.

In addition to the general argument-based approach, researchers have also suggested a design-based argument, which takes into account conceptions of individual test-takers' actions in the assessment situation, aspects of the test-taking situation, and additional information regarding the individual's history (Mislevy, 2007). Evidence Centered Design (ECD) has a focus beyond test scores, in that it includes the interaction between the test-taker and the assessment situation. Tests are designed and built with the intended uses in mind from the start of the construction process. This type of test-taker-situation interaction model offers guidance for task and test design as well as construct representation validity evidence which can be used throughout the test development process (Mislevy, 2007).

Potential Consequences of Testing

The idea that both intended and unintended consequences of test use should be included as part of the fuller evaluation of a test is one of the more significant additions to validation theory in the past 30 years, compared to early beliefs about validity. This addition is typically attributed to Messick (1980, 1989), though of course fairness itself has long been a concern taken seriously in testing. Because a full chapter in this handbook is devoted to bias and fairness, we defer the complete discussion of the complex and thorny issues of test fairness to the authors of that chapter. Here, we emphasize the connection between the issues of bias and fairness and the goal of test validation: to ensure that the use of the test reflects the intended construct and minimizes unintended constructs. If a test is not entirely fair, it means that the validity of interpretations of test scores differs for groups based upon gender, ethnic, or racial group status, for example. The current *Standards* clearly address the issue of consequences: "evidence about consequences may be directly relevant to validity when it can be traced to a source of invalidity" (APA, AERA, NCME, 1999, p. 16). An effort should be made to understand the reasons that use of the test resulted in unintended consequences.

Validation of Test Uses in Higher Education

Validation of Admission Tests

The use of standardized tests for selecting students for undergraduate, graduate school, or professional school admissions is widespread among colleges of all types and size. The use of tests in selection situations is often controversial (e.g., Lemann, 1999) because of the importance of these decisions and because, in some cases, ethnic and racial groups differ in their average test performance. Therefore, while all tests should be validated, test validation for admissions tests is especially critical because few tests have such a life-changing impact as those that affect whether a student will be admitted to a given institution of higher education.

The two most commonly used undergraduate admissions tests are the ACT and the SAT; the GRE is in widespread use for graduate schools; and professional schools such as business, law and medical schools utilize the GMAT, LSAT and MCAT, respectively. We expect most readers of this *Handbook* are generally familiar with the admissions tests used in their organizations. In this section, we focus on procedures for gathering validation evidence for admissions tests and refer the reader to Zwick (this volume) for more detailed information about other aspects of these fine tests. Because the processes of validation are similar for undergraduate, graduate school, and professional school admissions tests, we for the most part limit our discussion to undergraduate admissions, allowing the reader to generalize the process to other admissions decisions as appropriate.

For admissions tests, the most commonly used validation approach is criterion-related evidence. In particular, the correlation coefficient is typically calculated between scores on the tests, either alone or in conjunction with other predictors, and first-year GPA. When the test score is the only predictor, a strong correlation between the score and GPA provides evidence for the use of the test scores in admissions decisions. For undergraduate admissions tests, validity studies consistently find moderately high and positive correlations between first year college GPA and both high school GPA and these admissions test scores when correlated individually.

Similarly, when the admissions test score is combined with other predictors, such as high school GPA in undergraduate admissions, one would look for an increase in the multiple correlation due to the addition of the test score or a significant regression weight for the test score. When high school GPA and admissions tests scores are included in the equation together to predict collegiate perform-ance using the statistical techniques of multiple regression or multiple correlation, there is usually a small to moderate significant increase in the multiple correlation or R^2. (R^2 is a measure of the pro-portion of variance in the outcome accounted for by predictors.) When multiple regression is used, an increase in R^2 shows the increased utility of admissions tests over and above high school GPA alone for making effective admissions decisions. In a situation such as this, one attempts to determine whether a test has incremental validity.

Even though high school grades tend to predict college grades, high school grades are rendered less useful as a single predictor due to inconsistency in grading practices and grade inflation. Because admissions tests are standardized and are scored using the same process for all test-takers, they serve as a common metric for comparing students in a way that high school grades cannot. Additionally, because they measure related but different traits than high school grades, admissions tests provide a useful complement. We emphasize that the procedures for validation within each institution depend on how the scores will be used in admissions decisions, recognizing that different institutions have different needs that are reflected in their admissions policies.

Studies consistently show that adding admissions tests scores to the prediction equation does increase the magnitude of the prediction, despite the fact that high school GPA and admissions test scores are at least moderately correlated with each other. For example, a large and recent study conducted by the College Board regarding validity of the SAT (Kobrin, Patterson, Shaw, Mat-tern, & Barbuti, 2008) calculated the correlations between predictors and first-year GPA, averaged them across schools, and adjusted them for range restriction. The average adjusted correlation rose from .54 using high school GPA alone to .62 using the three scores from the SAT (i.e., mathematics, critical reading, and writing). Interestingly, the increase of including writing in addition to the other two sections only raised the adjusted correlation from .61 to .62, despite the fact that, of the three sections, writing had the highest correlation with first-year GPA (adjusted $r = .51$), further illustrat-ing the distinction between incremental validity and validity of a single predictor.

When colleges have only a limited number of positions in a freshman class, graduate program, or professional program, it is good practice to combine the GPA of earlier educational experiences with admissions tests scores in the validation study, especially when applicants will likely be selected with a combination of these predictors. In order to understand the effectiveness of even a small increase in prediction power, we turn to a classic psychometrics calculation from personnel selec-tion illustrated in the Taylor-Russell Tables (Taylor & Russell, 1939). From this perspective, how useful a selection measure is depends on three variables: the correlation between the predictor and success in the criterion, the rate of selection, and the base rate of success in the population. We have already discussed the first variable, though our calculations are based on the continuous variables and not dichotomized into "successful" and "not successful." The rate of selection is the percent of applicants admitted, and the base rate of success is the percent of applicants that would be successful if no admissions criteria were used to filter applicants.

As shown, when the selection rate is low (i.e., a school is highly selective), even a moderate cor-relation between the predictor and the criteria drastically improves upon the base rate. Further, each incremental increase in the correlation continues to improve the utility of using the measure. From the approach of a combined high-school GPA and admissions test score predictor set, the useful-ness of the incremental increase in the correlation of the combined predictor set over GPA alone is clearly important when the selection rate is low, as it is for prestigious schools or graduate programs.

However, the benefit of using these measures decreases as the selection rate increases; if almost all applicants are accepted, the composition of the student body has not changed substantially from the use of the test.

Other schools accept students who meet their minimum admission requirements rather than selecting only a certain limited number of applicants. In addition to high school course requirements, students at these types of institutions are typically selected if they have a GPA in certain percent of their graduating class and/or an ACT/SAT score above a certain value. A second common approach is to combine these measures in a compensatory manner in which strengths in one area can make up for weaknesses in the other, but all scores are included in the final decision (Haladyna & Hess, 1999). Such approaches include use of a regression equation or a table with high school GPA percentile along the columns and test scores along the rows, with a diagonal line representing the cut-off point for admissions decisions. Thus, a student with a low SAT score could be admitted if his or her GPA was high or another student whose GPA was low could be admitted on the basis of a high SAT score. For instance, at one state university, students are admitted if they meet any of three conditions: (a) their GPA is in the top half of their class, (b) their composite ACT score is at least 20 or (c) their SAT (mathematics and critical reading combined) score is at least 950. Under this approach, students need to show success on only one measure in order to qualify. A more stringent approach than the two methods previously described is sometimes called the multiple cutoff or hurdle approach (Levy, 2009), in which a student must have both a GPA above a certain value or percentile as well as a test score above a certain value.

When high school GPA and admissions test scores are considered separately in admissions decisions, the validation study should mirror the process used in practice. That is, instead of focusing only on the combined predictive value of the test score with high school GPA, the *individual* correlations between test scores and first year GPA should be examined. Much of the literature on admissions tests emphasizes the incremental increase in prediction by adding admissions tests to high school GPA as a predictor, but if the school in question does not select among applicants using a parallel process, that is not the most relevant result from the validity study. If tests and high school GPA are used separately as gatekeepers, they need to each demonstrate moderate to high correlations with success in postsecondary education.

As previously mentioned, validation studies for admissions measures are challenged by the fact that, by nature of the selection measure, the distribution of scores in the selected sample has been constricted and is thus smaller than that in the population. That is, if a school has a minimum required admissions test score or when very selective schools admit only the top portion of their applicants, the dataset used for the validation study will not include first-year GPA for students who scored in the lower ranges because they were not admitted. Moreover, at some schools, students with very high scores are likely to choose more selective schools, further decreasing the total range of scores for students within a school. This combination leads to a restriction in the total range of scores included at a given institution. In Figure 14.1, the difference between what the correlation would be if all students were included is contrasted with a more realistic scenario in which students with low test scores are not admitted, some students with high test scores go elsewhere, and some students with very low academic performance do not complete the first year. In these situations, corrections for curtailment—such as in the College Board study described—are appropriate but must be done cautiously. Classic measurement texts (e.g., Thorndike, 1982) explain the procedure more fully. Additionally, the researcher must have information about the full population, which is not always available. If corrections to correlations, such as for range restriction, are used, both the uncorrected and corrected correlations should be reported.

So far, we have focused on criterion-related approaches to validation for admissions tests. The use of admissions tests is also supported by content evidence. The ACT and SAT each assess skills and reasoning abilities that students should have acquired by the completion of secondary school. The ACT's four sections parallel the academic subjects of reading, English, math, and science. Since the

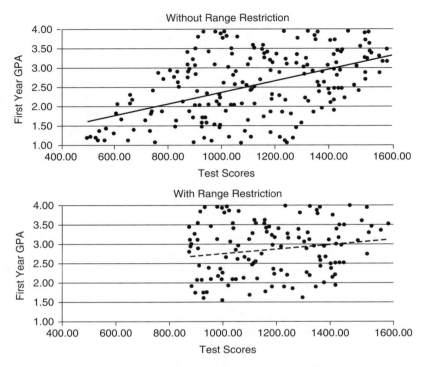

Figure 14.1 Illustration of the relationship between admissions test scores and first-year GPA, with and without range restriction

SAT's first administrations, the test has been transformed to become more like an achievement test rather than an intelligence test. Further, the SAT was revised beginning with the 2005 administration so that it was more closely aligned with high school curricula and emphasized those abilities considered important for university coursework, including removing antonyms in favor of more reading passages and assessment of more advanced mathematics skills (Lawrence, Rigol, Van Essen, & Jackson, 2003).

Recall that validity now includes consideration of consequences of testing. It is generally agreed that strong writing skills are necessary for success in postsecondary education in most majors. As such, the inclusion of writing tests on the SAT and ACT (where it is optional) provide further evidence of construct match with the knowledge and skills acquired in high school and needed in college. A further benefit of including a writing assessment in admissions measures is that high school curricula cannot ignore the teaching of writing if schools desire their students to attain high scores on the tests. In turn, there is hope that students will reach college better prepared for the writing tasks required of them in college with less remedial instruction—a positive consequence—than if writing continued to be omitted from the assessments. These considerations go beyond simple correlations between tests and criteria.

The technique of meta-analysis has been applied to correlational results of the type found in most criterion-related validation studies. Meta-analysis is a widely used research technique that combines the results of numerous studies, typically weighting results by the number of subjects involved in the individual studies. When applied to the results of validation studies, it is typically called validity generalization (e.g., Murphy, 2003). Results of several validity generalization studies (e.g., Kuncel, Hezlett & Ones, 2001) have shown that tests such as the SAT, ACT, and GRE are generally quite valid across a wide variety of institutional settings.

Validation in Placement and Exemption Testing

Unlike selection testing for undergraduate and graduate/professional study, placement testing (see Morgan, this volume) normally presumes that a student is or will be enrolled at or admitted to an institution and has some knowledge that permits him or her to pass over a given class and take the next course in a curricular sequence. These courses are often sequenced in a manner where the material in each course is required to be able to succeed in the next; such sequences are common in mathematics, English, foreign languages, and, sometimes, the sciences. At the collegiate level, the Advanced Placement (AP) and College-Level Examination Program (CLEP) examinations of the College Board are perhaps best known, and some colleges and universities have built their own institutional placement measures. In some cases, the student who earns an adequate score on such a test receives credit for the course work accompanying a passed placement test, and in other cases the student is permitted simply to avoid taking the earlier class and takes the subsequent one. These models are perhaps best described in Willingham (1974). We describe two primary kinds of placement decisions here and the means to validate the data used to help make these decisions. The first relates to the most common example of placement testing, where students are positioned in an appropriate course within a sequence. The second concerns a related situation, where the student receives an exemption from requirements that the student has already mastered. Each of these is described below in turn, and each has its own validation implications.[1]

The most important issue is placing a student in the most appropriate course in a sequence given his or her knowledge and skills level. First, we need to assess the criterion-related validation (in this case, predictive validation) of the test for all courses into which a student might be placed. The second is that we wish to know if the student actually knows the content of any courses from which he or she might be exempted. This latter type of decision making draws upon content-related evidence for validation support.

Placing students can be based upon specific course-related knowledge or a more generalized trait, as described below. In the case of the former instance, a student who studies the textbook and all the material in a course, whether alone or as part of an organized instructional experience such as Advanced Placement, might be able to pass a test similar to a final examination and be exempted from that class, and, depending upon academic regulations, receive credit for that course. In the case of a generalized trait, based on one's ability in a given discipline, for example, one might be able to skip a first course in a sequence. Alternatively, a student might be placed in a remedial course based on low performance on a test of a more generalized ability. In the case of placement based upon a general trait or ability, however, a measure such as the SAT, the ACT or ACCUPLACER might be used to help place a student into the appropriate class.

Imagine students differing in their aptitude to learn mathematics. Perhaps students high on a mathematics ability test might be exempted from taking college algebra prior to taking calculus, but students who have lower math aptitude are required to take this college algebra class. In both cases, the validation study might be similar. A validity study to demonstrate the appropriateness of such an academic strategy would probably show two regression lines, one representing those who have taken college algebra prior to calculus and the other those who do not take it. The predictor variables in each instance (whether a more general test of mathematics aptitude or a more specific test of college algebra mathematics knowledge) would be the mathematics aptitude test and the criterion, performance in the calculus class. Figures 14.2 and 14.3 provide a view of this analysis. There would be two general expectations. The first would be that mathematics aptitude and performance in the course would be correlated positively in both examples. The second would be that the two lines may cross, with students low in mathematics ability performing lower in the situation where they did not have the college algebra course and those higher in mathematics aptitude surpassing those required to take the preliminary course. It is, of course, also possible that the students higher

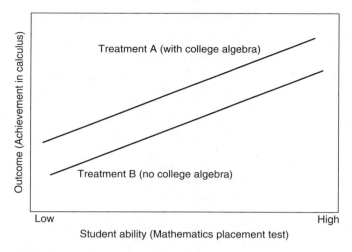

Figure 14.2 Example of no interaction between ability and treatment

Source: Willingham, Warren W. *College Placement & Exemption*. Copyright © 1974. The College Board. Reproduced with permission. www.collegeboard.com.

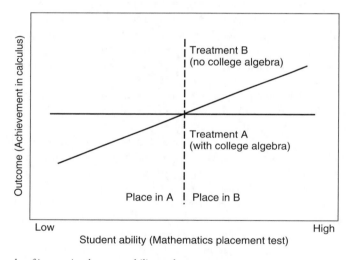

Figure 14.3 Example of interaction between ability and treatment

Source: Willingham, Warren W. *College Placement & Exemption*. Copyright © 1974. The College Board. Reproduced with permission. www.collegeboard.com.

in mathematics ability would score higher if they did take the college algebra course. However, if they scored about the same, they would have saved some time and permitted themselves to benefit from a different course.

A similar situation could be envisioned where a remediation course is possible prior to taking a course of more consequence. For example, some students might benefit from a remedial English course prior to taking freshman composition. Some institutions use the SAT, the ACT, ACCUPLACER, or another similar test to help decide whether a student is ready to take the freshman English composition course, for example. Thus, placement tests can be validated through the use of criterion–related validation with grades in freshman English as the criterion, although this model is somewhat more complex than that found in college admissions testing because there are two regression lines, one for placing students in the higher level course first and one for placing them in the remedial or lower course first. Although the primary purpose of the validation study is simply to demonstrate that using the test increases the number of students who succeed in the sequence and who master the upper-level course in the sequence, a second purpose of the validation study is to determine at what score level a student should earn on the placement test to take the upper-level course.

Course exemptions are usually based on a measure that assesses whether a student's knowledge level is functionally equivalent to that of students who have been successful in the class. This approach requires a content-oriented evidence approach. One must carefully delineate what students learn in a class (not what they are supposed to learn, but what they actually learn). A test is developed that parallels this learning maximally. Development of such a test requires that the learning domain is mapped carefully, each component area of the domain is weighted in terms of how important it is (often how much instructional time is devoted to it), and the test is built to measure this domain through a representative sampling of questions from this domain. A test that permits a student to exempt a course should ultimately be functionally equivalent to a comprehensive final examination in a given course, assuming that the final is representative of the full extent of learning expected of a student. This model is what the Advanced Placement and CLEP tests provide.

At some institutions, it may be advantageous to utilize an item bank that houses many test items, which can then be used to construct multiple test forms. A major benefit of such an item bank is that item statistics, such as difficulty and discrimination, may already be known and can be taken into account when constructing an operational test form or the set of items to be administered to an individual student (as in the case of a computer-adaptive test for which the computer system selects subsequent items based upon the test-taker's previous responses). In effect, typically pretesting has already been completed for all items, and test construction can proceed accordingly. It is likely that reviewers have also examined the items' content and potential for bias or insensitivity. Professionals or trained item writers may also have written items in item banks, which is another desirable quality.

When used properly, item banks can facilitate the process of test construction leading to quality tests, corresponding with the discussion of validity already provided in this chapter. However, there is no guarantee that tests resulting from item banks will produce reliable scores or have strong evidence of validity. The program used to ensure that test forms created from item banks appropriately sample from the range and depth of the content outline in the test blueprint is crucial. To the extent test forms produced from a single item bank substantially differ from each other (in terms of content coverage, difficulty of items selected, interactions among test items, and the like), validation must either proceed for the different forms or be done on the basis of the entire item bank. If this latter approach is used, the representation of validity for the entire item bank may not represent the operational form provided to individual students. For example, if two colleges draw from the same national item bank using their own beliefs about what course content was important to assess, their two tests could be quite different from each other, and each would be subject to individual scrutiny. The same thing could happen to two different instructors of the same course at the same institution if they select different items from the item bank. If test forms created from item banks are very similar to each other and are constructed using the same process and specifications, the validation process can typically be shared among the alternate forms. We emphasize that while drawing from an item bank may increase the quality of tests used by an institution, the fact that the items were drawn from the bank does not obviate the need for other steps in the validation process.

Validation in Outcomes Assessment

As accreditation agencies increasingly evaluate collegiate programs on the basis of outcomes assessment, colleges and universities must develop, acquire, and utilize measures to assess student learning, to compare that learning to what has been expected, and assess the results both in formative and summative manners (see Palmer, this volume). To build or acquire and utilize such measures requires that faculty and appropriate administrators have faith in these measures. Without such faith, relevant parties will not review their results with confidence, consider the results of the assessment carefully, and make the needed or suggested changes to improve the curriculum or its delivery. To enhance this faith, several processes are needed, and meaningful involvement of all relevant parties is required.

The validation paradigm that is required is content-related, and it is only modified in one major way: it is critical that multiple individuals and parties participate in the validation. If an institution builds its own outcome measure, for example, it is critical that all parties involved or their representatives take part in the mapping of the content domain, the development of test questions or assessment devices, scoring of these measures, and interpretation of results and a determination of the manner in which the curriculum or its delivery should be altered in the attempt to improve results the following year. Therefore, the content-related approach to validation is changed because the relevant parties (e.g., faculty members) are involved in the mapping of the domain and weighting of its components, in addition to the determination of whether specific test questions actually are assessing the intended components of the domain. This latter determination is more typically the basis of content validation; in the case of outcomes assessment it is also critical that relevant parties participate in the domain specification.

It is important to note that this type of situation is different than other types of assessment situations because it is considered low-stakes, due in large measure to the lack of consequences for the test-taker. Test scores obtained under low-stakes conditions may be suspect due to the condition in which assessments were administered. As noted by V. L. Wise, S. L. Wise, and Bhola (2006), the validity of scores from assessments administered under low-stakes conditions is susceptible to construct-irrelevant variance due to disparity in test-taker motivation. Scores obtained from this type of situation may underrepresent students' knowledge and as such impact the validity of the decisions made on the scores. Wise et al. suggest strategies such as motivation filtering, having tests/items that are less mentally complex, including incentives, and changing the stakes of the assessment as potential methods by which to manage low test-taker motivation. Many schools also embed such assessments in courses required by students majoring in an individual field. In such cases, a paper or final examination may doubly count in the course and as the outcomes assessment; in such an instance, the level of student motivation is obviously increased.

Final Thoughts

The concept and operationalization of validity have changed throughout its history. Near the beginning of formal psychometrics, perhaps early in the middle of the 20th century, criterion-related validation was the primary approach to establishing test validity, although content-related validation was considered appropriate for many tests of educational achievement. The field has moved to a position where construct-related validation appears to have become the superordinate general approach to validation, subsuming both criterion-related and content-related techniques in the opinion of many theorists. However, regardless of the approach employed, the key concern is that we must validate test results; that is, we must study how effectively test scores meet the intents of the test user, or in some cases, the test developer.

Most of the professionally developed tests employed in higher education have undergone extensive evaluation efforts, including reviews of some of their unintended consequences. To do less is to fail to conform to acceptable professional practices, as mandated by the *Standards* that professional associations have written over more than the past 50 years. It is critical for the professionalism of the testing community and for the benefit of the higher education community that we continue to validate the uses to which we put tests. These efforts must happen regularly, not just once, and with differing populations and special populations, like underserved groups and those with disabilities. If validation research continues, tests can continue to be used appropriately, validly, and fairly.

Note

1 Willingham also discusses some other placement decisions which the terms, assignment, that are not discussed in this chapter, such as placement into alternate pedagogies and alternate pacing.

References

American Educational Research Association, American Psychological Association, & National Council on Measurement in Education. (1985). *Standards for educational and psychological tests*. Washington, DC: American Educational Research Association.

American Educational Research Association, American Psychological Association, & National Council on Measurement in Education. (1999). *Standards for educational and psychological tests*. Washington, DC: American Educational Research Association.

Angoff, W. (1988). Validity: An evolving concept. In H. Wainer, & H. Braun (Eds.), *Test validity* (pp. 19–32). Mahway, NJ: Erlbaum.

Carlton, S. (this volume). *Using content specialists for detecting item and test unfairness*.

Cronbach, L., & Meehl, P. (1955). Construct validity in psychological tests. *Psychological Bulletin, 52*, 281–302.

Haladyna, T., & Hess, R. (1999). An evaluation of conjunctive and compensatory standard-setting strategies for test decisions. *Educational Assessment, 6*(2), 129–153.

Kane, M. (2006). Validity. In R. L. Brennan (Ed.), *Educational measurement* (4th ed., pp. 17–64). Westport, CT: American Council on Education/Praeger.

Kobrin, J. L., Patterson, B. F., Shaw, E. J., Mattern, K. D., & Barbuti, S. M. (2008). *Validity of the SAT for predicting first-year college grade point average*. (College Board Report No. 2008–5). New York, NY: The College Board.

Kuncel, N. R., Hezlett, S. A., & Ones, D. S. (2001). A comprehensive meta-analysis of the predictive validity of the Graduate Record Examinations: Implications for graduate student selection and performance. *Psychological Bulletin, 127*, 162–181.

Lawrence, I.M., Rigol, G.W., Van Essen, T., & Jackson, C.A. (2003). *A historical perspective on the content of the SAT*. (College Board Research Report No. 2003–3). New York, NY: The College Board.

Lemann, N. (1999). *The big test: The secret history of the American meritocracy*. New York, NY: Farrar, Straus and Giroux.

Levy, P. (2009). *Industrial/Organizational Psychology* (3rd ed.). New York, NY: Worth.

Messick. S. (1980). Test validity and the ethics of assessment. *American Psychologist, 35*, 1012–1027.

Messick, S. (1989). Validity. In R. Linn (Ed.), *Educational measurement* (3rd ed., pp. 13 – 103). The American Council on Education/Macmillan series on higher education. New York, NY: Macmillan.

Mislevy, R. J. (2007). Validity by design. *Educational Researcher, 36*(8), pp. 463–469.

Morgan, D. L. (this volume). *College placement testing of entering students*.

Murphy, K. R. (Ed.). (2003). *Validity generalization: A critical review*. Mahway, NJ: Erlbaum.

Palmer, J. C. (this volume). *The perennial challenges of accountability*.

Taylor, H. C., & Russell, J. T. (1939). The relationship of validity coefficients to the practical effectiveness of tests in selection: Discussion and tables. *Journal of Applied Psychology, 23*(5), 565–578.

Thorndike, R. L. (1982). *Applied psychometrics*. Boston, MA: Houghton Mifflin.

Willingham, W. W. (1974). *College placement and exemption*. New York. NY: College Entrance Examination Board.

Wise, V. L., Wise, S. L., & Bhola, D. S. (2006). The generalizability of motivation filtering in improving test score validity. *Educational Assessment, 11*, pp. 65–83.

Zwick, R. (this volume). *Admissions testing in higher education*.

15

STATISTICAL MODELING IN MEASUREMENT, ASSESSMENT, AND EVALUATION FOR HIGHER EDUCATION

Steven J. Osterlind and Ze Wang

Understanding higher education endeavors, regardless of whether from a status or change perspective, is fraught with complexity and intricacy in interpretation, and generally marked by ambiguity at its conclusion. Three concepts in our search for understanding in relevant education questions dominate. They are: (a) measurement, (b) assessment, and (c) evaluation. In brief, measurement is the most practical of these terms, marked by its attempt to quantify some cognitive latency or proficiency. Assessment, another concept directed by a methodology, seeks to garner information relevant to a specified goal or objective. Most educational and psychological tests can be considered subsumed under this term (see Kizlik, 2010). Evaluation, in contrast, is a more complex notion usually guided by some methodology that seeks to address aspects of the value of an educational enterprise.

Not long ago, a researcher, program evaluator or other professional involved in measuring, assessing, and evaluating would reference their work by pointing to the "models" of House (1980), Madaus, Scriven, and Stufflebeam (1983), and almost certainly to Bloom, Hastings, and Madaus (1974). (Many other figures prominent in measurement, evaluation, and assessment could be named, too.) The basic thrust of influence for these leaders was to encourage systematic approaches to applied research in higher education, which in such contexts is nearly always quantitative. Typically, there was heavy reliance upon descriptive statistics as well as inferential, classical statistics with null hypothesis significance testing (NHST). Sir Ronald Fisher's ANOVA (analysis of variance) tests, and Student's t-tests along with confidence intervals, were the near-universal reporting genre.

Today, however, work in measurement, assessment, and evaluation is more commonly girded by other "models;" specifically, mathematical and statistical models. Here, "model" is ". . . a set of assumptions together with implications drawn from them by mathematical reasoning" (Neimark & Estes, 1967, p. v). And, described by Pearl as, ". . . an idealized representation of reality" (Pearl, 2000, p. 202). A key characterization of these kinds of models is their attention to random variables and associated probability distributions. Generally, the variables are classed as dependent variables (DVs) being described ("explained") by independent variables (IVs). When represented by an equation, these are canonical sets, one on either side. A particular situation may call for but a single IV or DV, or it may be appropriate to use many IVs and DVs. The variables employed as DVs and IVs can correspond to a continuous phenomenon with range $(-\infty, \infty)$ like latent traits (e.g., achievement, opinion, preference) or they can just as suitably be about dichotomous or polytomous attributes (e.g., sex or gender, race/ethnic-heritage, categories of income). Relationships among DVs can also be incorporated in the model. For example, a mediator variable is another DV because it is affected by an IV(s) and also affects another DV(s).

Statistical modeling is considered a quiet methodological revolution (Rodgers, 2010) as more researchers begin to emphasize examining and comparing hypothesized substantive models based on data. This change in focus for measurement, assessment, and evaluation is not to suggest that the methodological models of earlier leaders are the same type of models as are statistical models. Clearly, we are talking about two different kinds of models; and, just as clearly, statistical models do not replace methodological ones. The point to garner is that measurement, assessment, and evaluation in higher education have moved their focus from methodological models to statistical modeling of the GLM type, mostly either general linear models or generalized linear models.[1]

The simple linear regression model is one of the most important of all statistical models. As is long-familiar to professionals in the field, it assumes a relationship between one IV and a DV. The stochastic part of simple linear regression models is of special interest, and each stochastic part is syntactically given a unique term. This term (generally the last one in an equation) represents the unpredicted or unexplained variability in a phenomenon. (In some mathematical contexts, this is called a disturbance.) The importance of the stochastic part of a statistical model is its quantification of what is *not* hypothesized/certain about the relationship between the IVs and the DVs as well as certain of its distributional characteristics. In many educational contexts, this unexplained variance highlights that our predictions/explanations are imperfect representations of reality. We learn much by realizing what is not known.

The notion of quantifying and studying the unexplained variance in a phenomenon figures prominently in the evolution of measurement, evaluation, and assessment to statistical models. Before the emphasis on statistical modeling, professionals usually only talked about the study design and assumed that a particular statistical technique was appropriate for that design. For example, in program evaluation in third-level education contexts, repeated measures design is used widely to assess the effectiveness of a particular program, and researchers often assumed that a paired t-test is typically suited for this design. But, such thinking is not necessarily the case; nor does it fit with best practices today in higher education assessment. Now, statistical modeling considerations are paramount.

In the remainder of this chapter, we describe several mathematical and statistical models that can be appropriately employed in measurement, evaluation, and assessment in higher education. To understand them, however, it is useful to explain briefly their foundation. Even before we explain modern mathematical (and mainly likelihood) models, however, it is useful to appreciate that the new models represent a direction for modern work in measurement, evaluation, and assessment in higher education and not a wholesale abandonment of traditional approaches. In fact, they are often used side-by-side.

Background into Modern Statistical Modeling

Working from the mathematical bases for statistical models, it is useful to note underpinning principles. Here, we observe that statistical models derive from either classical or Bayesian statistics. A brief explanation of the differences in approach follows but, due to space, many relevant details are omitted. Interested readers can explore the concepts further in a list of references proffered by Spiegelhalter and Rice (2009). We begin by explaining models based on Bayesian approaches to data analysis.

Many modern statistical models employed in measurement, evaluation, and assessment in higher education derive from Bayes' theorem, a mathematical explanation of conditional probabilities. More completely, this theorem has both a philosophical underpinning and a mathematical expression. The theory posits a logical positivism about ontology in science (details can be found in

Hawthorne, 2009). Our interest focuses on its application in practical testing problems: the theory's syntactic expression.

Here, Bayes' theorem computes a best solution to a hypothesis. This solution derives from iteratively testing the hypothesis with samples of data, seeking ever more precision until a criterion of satisfaction for the solution is reached. The logic of this approach is to explore by mathematical means the probability that a particular hypothesis is true in light of present evidence. Sometimes this is expressed as *P (Hypothesis | Data)*. Technically, Bayesian mathematics estimate conditional distributions of parameters given observed data, At the most basic level, Bayes' theorem is expressed for two random quantities *A* and *B*:

$$P(A|B_j) = \frac{P(B_j|A)P(B_j)}{P(A)}.$$ (15.1)

When used with data, the probabilities assume likelihoods. Initially, the likelihood is termed a *prior*. This prior probability is tested against observed data, yielding a refined likelihood, the next prior. The process is iteratively continued until solution, the final likelihood (called a *posterior*) is reached. The focus of the approach is always on whether the primary hypotheses can be evidenced by observed data (i.e., "What is the likelihood for a particular hypothesis given the observed data?"). Various maximum likelihood algorithms are available for computations. Sometimes in the algorithms of maximum likelihood estimation, values of a variable are transformed to a log scale, making the mathematics easier and the ratio of *true to not-true* more meaningful.

This theory is most commonly viewed in contrast to statistical approaches based on classical assumptions, which take an exactly opposite approach to hypothesis development and data analysis. In classical approaches to statistics (sometimes called *frequentist statistics*), the question-development process can be represented logically by *P (Data | Hypothesis)*. This is the probability of observing the data or more extreme data when the null hypothesis is true (the null hypothesis is usually the hypothesis of no effect, no difference, etc.). When this probability is low, researchers conclude that the null hypothesis is unlikely to be true ("reject the null hypothesis"). In classical statistics, a hypothesis is not developed until data are first considered. Here, the researcher or evaluator initially has data from a population (or, more practically, a sample representing the population) in mind. From this sample data, the researcher begins to ponder questions about the degree of influence of particular variables on some facet of the population. For example, in a higher education context, a researcher may have a sample of college freshmen, from whom he notices inconsistent smoking habits: some routinely smoke many cigarettes each day, some others smoke only erratically and still others do not smoke at all. The researcher may investigate whether different smoking patterns are significant in the student's academic achievement; and, the researcher may test his hypothesis in the observed data by any number of difference-in-variance tests (e.g., ANOVA). The point to note, however, is that classical statistics begin with data and seek to then test a hypothesis, while Bayesian approaches run the opposite by starting with a hypothesis and exploring its veracity by calculating conditional probabilities.

In Bayesian statistics, researchers calculate the probability of the hypothesized model being plausible given the observed data. Since the probability is of models, not of data, we can also compare competing models.

Another related concept is likelihood, which can be thought of something between classical and Bayesian statistics. In fact, classical likelihood-based inferences closely resemble Bayesian inferences. The likelihood is the probability of observing data with a given model. The maximum likelihood estimation is an estimation method used to find the estimates of model parameters that maximize the probability of observing the data under a given model.

This difference between classical and Bayesian approaches to data analysis is highlighted in the evolution of statistical models used for measurement, evaluation, and assessment in higher education. We see this change especially in application of modern statistical models to test data as widely used in higher education for admissions and selection (e.g., ACT, MCAT, GRE) and occasionally used for assessing achievement (e.g., CBASE). Today, scores from such tests are often employed by professors and researchers in empirical research. Further, most of these tests have scaling schemes based on the item response theory (IRT) as a measure of students' latent proficiency. Recently, statistical advances and more availability of software have made it possible to incorporate statistical modeling in measurement, assessment, and evaluation.

Modeling Strategies

Manifold modeling strategies exist and here we mention only a few, those more prominently employed in today's work in measurement, evaluation, and assessment.

Correlation/Regression

Perhaps the most common undergirding of modern approaches is the correlation. Simply, but significantly, a correlation is an index of the relationship between two variables (bivariate relationship). Four types of correlations are most common in social science studies: (a) the Pearson r, which is used for correlation between two interval variables; (b) Spearman's ρ, which is used for ordinal variables; (c) phi (ϕ), which is appropriate when both variables are dichotomous; and (d) point-biserial correlation (r_{pb}), which is used when one variable is dichotomous and the other variable is interval. There are still many other ways to view a bivariate relationship. Rodgers and Nicewander (1988) identified thirteen ways to look at the correlation coefficient.

As a special case and foundation of the broader general linear models (GLMs), regression is a statistical technique that is used to investigate relationships between a single outcome variable and one or more than one predictor. Most of the statistics from simple regression (with only one predictor) can be obtained from bivariate statistics. Multiple regression models (with two or more than two predictors) can be used to assess the unique contribution or the contribution of a predictor after controlling for the other predictor(s).

Regression is used for two purposes: prediction and explanation. In higher education institutions, the admission decisions are based on various categories of information about the applicants, because the admission committees believe that applicants' standing on the criteria will predict future outcomes. Most of the time, researchers also want to know why the prediction works. Theory development is an essential part of science. Regression, together with other techniques (see later discussion about SEM, mediation and moderation), can be useful to test theories.

Multilevel Modeling

In higher education, oftentimes researchers are studying subjects within their specific contexts. The multilevel feature of those studies is highly relevant for designing and implementing the assessments and for analyses of data.

When multilevel data are collected and analyzed, it is typically either at an aggregated or disaggregated level. This fact brings forward a caution for researchers: they should be aware that *ecological fallacy* (Robinson, 1950) may happen. This fallacy draws attention to the fact that a relationship found on an aggregate level cannot be generalized to the individual level.

Another modern strategy for statistical modeling is to place study variables in a contextual reference. For example, students' achievements may be studied within the context of a particular classroom, which in turn may be analyzed within the context of differing school environments. This approach to organizing variables is referred to as *nesting*. Such multilevel modeling (Raudenbush & Bryk, 2002) has gained increased popularity in studying students' performance, teacher effects, and family-related constructs (Mylonas, Pavlopoulos, & Georgas, 2008). The outcome is usually at the lowest level (such as students). Predictors at this level can be added to help explain the variability of the outcome within a higher-level unit (e.g. institution). The differences or variability between higher-level units, usually in terms of level-1 intercepts and slopes, are further explained using predictors at the higher level.

Multilevel modeling can also handle longitudinal data and does not require that all subjects are measured at the same time or with the same time intervals (Singer & Willett, 2002). Not only the initial value of a measure can be modeled as a function of subjects' characteristics, but also the change rate (linear, quadratic, etc.) can be specified as a function of other variables and be tested. The outcome can be continuous, ordinal, categorical, or count data.

Sometimes, there is not a real hierarchy of the data. Instead, individuals may have multiple memberships or change classifications (e.g., students change schools). Modeling those data is more complicated than dealing with completely nested data but possible (see Browne, Goldstein, & Rasbash, 2001; Raudenbush & Bryk, 2002).

With recent development in measurement models, hierarchical models are incorporated with measurement theory, especially item response theory. Hierarchical IRT has been used to model item difficulty, discrimination, and to detect differential item functioning (DIF).

Structural Equation Modeling

Structural equation modeling (SEM) is yet another important multivariate technique that grows out of factor analysis and path models. Factor analysis can be traced back to the early 1900s when exploratory factor analysis was introduced by Charles Spearman (1904). Path analysis was first developed by a geneticist, Sewall Wright (1918), and later introduced to other fields. The integration of factor analysis and path analysis, which later was referred to as the JKW model, was credited to Jöreskog (1973), Keesling (1972), & Wiley (1973). Here, models can help explain or even develop theories for cognitive functioning, such as when one studies learning or motivation. SEM can help explain the "why"s and can include mediating and moderating variables. Many general linear models are realized in SEM. However, SEM is probably used most often to test the feasibility of hypothesized conceptual models. SEM is most useful when an a priori theory (e.g., psychological theory) is hypothesized and researchers would like to test if the theory is supported by data collected from a representative sample of the target population. A major advantage of SEM is that many model fit indices have been developed.

Many more advanced techniques have later been included under the general term of SEM. For example, growth models, mixture models, and multilevel models are carried out in the framework of SEM (Kaplan, 2009). Different types of data such as ordinal, nominal and count data can be analyzed together. In addition, different estimation methods are developed to accommodate various types of SEM analyses.

The popular specialized software programs for conducting SEM analyses include Amos (Arbuckle, 2006), EQS (Bentler, 2003), LISREL (Jöreskog & Sörbom, 2003) and Mplus (L. K. Muthén & B.O. Muthén, 1998–2009). General statistical software such as SAS and R also has SEM functions available.

Non-Parametric Methods

Most statistical models assume that the dependent variable(s) follow certain statistical distributions (most commonly, a normal distribution). Statistical inferences, that is, inferences about population parameters from the sample are based on the statistical distribution of the DV(s). Non-parametric models, on the other hand, do not assume normality of the dependent variable and are alternatives when the distribution assumption is not met. There are non–parametric versions of t–test and ANOVA to compare group means (e.g., Wilcoxon Rank–Sum test, Mann–Whitney test; see Higgins, 2004). Another example is that Betebenner (2009) has used the non–parametric method of quantile regression to calculate student growth percentiles.

Residual Analysis

Sometimes researchers are interested in how the actual performance of a subject compares to his/her predicted performance based on the statistical models. Residuals indicate lack of fit of the model to the data. However, if used properly, residual analysis can provide information about whether a unit (individual, school, etc.) has exceeded expectation.

Additional Considerations

Of course, modeling strategies can be implemented only in a context, such as with particular variables or with prescribed demographics for a sample or population. A number of technical issues are relevant to consider at this point, some of which are discussed here.

Effect Size

A related topic in statistical modeling is effect size (Kline, 2009). Effect size is a measure of the magnitude of impact of the causal (independent) variable on the outcome (dependent variable). It also sometimes refers to the covariation between variables. The most widely cited publications about effect sizes in social sciences are by Cohen (1988, 1992).

Effect size is introduced in statistics textbooks for general linear models. With development of new statistical models, definitions and calculations of effect size for more complex situations have been introduced (e.g., Hedges, 2007).

Statistical Power

Statistical power is the probability of correctly detecting an effect in the population. Depending on the purposes, there are three types of power analysis: (a) a priori power analysis, which is usually conducted before data collection and helps decide the sample size necessary to detect a population effect with a prescribed significance level and power; (b) post hoc power analysis, which is used after a study has been conducted to assess whether a published statistical test in fact had a fair chance to detect an effect; and (c) compromise power analysis, which can be used before or after data collection. The researcher specifies the ratio of Type I and Type II errors in compromise power analysis (Faul, Edgar, Albert-Georg, & Axel, 2007).

Moderation and Mediation

A variable is a moderator variable when it affects the relationship between the independent variable and the dependent variable. For example, when a particular teaching strategy works for one ethnicity group of students but not another, ethnicity moderates the effect of this teaching strategy on student outcome.

A mediating variable is an intervening variable between the independent variable and the dependent variable and helps explain why there is a relationship between them. Statistical methods to test mediation include regression (Baron & Kenny, 1986) and SEM.

The difference between moderation and mediation is important and sometimes can be subtle.

Interesting discussion on the distinction between moderating and mediation variables is offered by many authors (e.g., Fairchild & MacKinnon, 2009; Hayes, 2009; James & Brett, 1984). Mediation effects are considered as addressing the mechanisms by which a relationship between the causal variable and the effect variable exists. On the other hand, moderation effects provide information on conditions when a relationship between variables exists (MacKinnon, 2008).

Model Fit

The purpose of conducting statistical modeling is to test if a model fits the data. If the model is supported by the data, we have more confidence about the model. The closeness of a concept/statistical model to the observed data can be measured by some model fit indexes. Studies on model fit indexes can be best exemplified in the development of SEM. Recently, model fit statistics have been discussed in the literature of multilevel modeling (e.g., deviance statistic; see Wu, West, & Taylor, 2009) and IRT (e.g., person fit statistics). Bayesian statistics have an additional way to test model fit through Bayes factor (Gelman, Carlin, Stern, & Rubin, 2004).

Conclusions and Implications for the Future

The evolution of approaches to understanding higher education endeavors has been profound and carries with it a number of implications. First, we point out that statistical analysis should serve the research questions, not vice versa. This is foundational to good research practice in measurement, evaluation, and assessment.

Second, however, we note that evolution of research in higher education form early approaches to modern, sophisticated modeling that allows more detailed and precise analyses. Through them, we have at hand better methods to understand psychological and educational phenomena in higher education.

Note

1 As generally conceived, the difference between general linear models and generalized linear models is that the former has continuous DVs while DVs in the later can be ordinal, categorical, or count data; and, a link function is used in generalized linear models to model the stochastic component.

References

Arbuckle, J. L. (2006). Amos (Version 7.0) [Computer software]. Chicago, IL: SPSS.

Baron, R. M., & Kenny, D. A. (1986). The moderator-mediator variable distinction in social psychological research: Conceptual, strategic, and statistical considerations. *Journal of Personality and Social Psychology, 51*, 1173–1182.

Bentler, P. M. (2003). EQS 6.1 for Windows [Computer software]. Encino, CA: Multivariate Software.

Betebenner, D. (2009). Norm- and criterion-referenced student growth. *Educational Measurement: Issues and Practice, 28*(4), 42–51.

Bloom, B. S., Hastings, T. J., & Madaus, G. (1974). *Handbook on formative and summative evaluation of student learning*. New York, NY: McGraw-Hill.

Browne, W. J., Goldstein, H., & Rasbash, J. (2001). Multiple membership multiple classification (MMMC) models. *Statistical Modelling, 1*(2), 103–124.

Cohen, J. (Ed.). (1988). *Statistical power analysis for the behavioral sciences* (2nd ed.). Hillsdale, NJ: Erlbaum.

Cohen, J. (1992). A power primer. *Psychological Bulletin, 112*, 155–159.

Fairchild, A. J., & MacKinnon, D. P. (2009). A general model for testing mediation and moderation effects. *Prevention Science, 10*, 87–99.

Faul, F., Edgar, E., Albert-Georg, L., & Axel, B. (2007). G*Power 3: A flexible statistical power analysis program for the social, behavioral, and biomedical sciences. *Behavior Research Methods, 39*(2), 175–191.

Gelman, A., Carlin, J. B., Stern, H. S., & Rubin, D. B. (2004). *Bayesian data analysis* (2nd ed.). Boca Raton, FL: Chapman & Hall/CRC.

Hawthorne, J. (2009). Inductive logic. In E. N. Zalta (Ed.), *The Stanford Encyclopedia of Philosophy* (Fall 2009 ed.). Retrieved from http://plato.stanford.edu/archives/fall2009/entries/logic-inductive/

Hayes, A. F. (2009). Beyond Baron and Kenny: Statistical mediation analysis in the new millennium. *Communication Monographs, 76*(4), 408–420.

Hedges, L. V. (2007). Effect size in cluster-randomized designs. *Journal of Educational and Behavioral Statistics, 32*, 341–370.

Higgins, J. J. (2004). *An introduction to modern nonparametric statistics.* Pacific Grove, CA: Brooks/Cole.

House, E. H. (1980). *Evaluating with validity.* Beverly Hills, CA: Sage.

James, L. R., & Brett, J. M. (1984). Mediators, moderators, and tests for mediation. *Journal of Applied Psychology, 69*(2), 307–321.

Jöreskog, K. G. (1973). A general method for estimating a linear structural equation system. In A. S. Goldberger, & O. D. Duncan (Eds.), *Structural equation models in the social sciences* (pp. 85–112). New York, NY: Academic Press.

Jöreskog, K. G., & Sörbom, D. (2003). LISREL 8.54 for Windows [Computer software]. Lincolnwood, IL: Scientific Software International.

Kaplan, D. (2009). *Structural equation modeling: Foundation and extensions* (2nd ed.). Thousand Oaks, CA: Sage.

Keesling, J. W. (1972). *Maximum likelihood approaches to causal analysis.* Unpublished doctoral dissertation, University of Chicago.

Kizlik, B. (2010). Measurement, assessment, and evaluation in education. Retrieved February 25, 2010, from http://www.adprima.com/measurement.htm

Kline, R. B. (2009). *Becoming a behavioral science researcher.* New York, NY: Guilford Press.

MacKinnon, D. P. (2008). *Introduction to statistical mediation analysis.* Oxford, UK: Routledge/Taylor & Francis.

Madaus, G. G., Scriven, M., & Stufflebeam, D. L. (Eds.). (1983). *Evaluation models: Viewpoints on educational and human services evaluation.* Boston, MA: Kluwer-Hijhoff.

Muthén, L. K., & Muthén, B. O. (1998–2009). *Mplus user's guide* (5th ed.). Los Angeles, CA: Muthén & Muthén.

Mylonas, K., Pavlopoulos, V., & Georgas, J. (2008). Multilevel structure analysis for family-related constructs. In F. J. R. van de Vijver, D. A. van Hemert, & Y. H. Poortinga (Eds.), *Multilevel analysis of individuals and cultures* (pp. 345–377). New York, NY: Lawrence Erlbaum Associates.

Neimark, E. D., & Estes, W. K. (1967). *Stimulus sampling theory.* San Francisco, CA: Holden-Day.

Pearl, J. (2000). *Causality: Models, reasoning, and inference.* Cambridge, UK: Cambridge University Press.

Raudenbush, S. W., & Bryk, A. S. (2002). *Hierarchical Linear Models: Applications and data analysis methods* (2nd ed.). Newbury Park, CA: Sage.

Robinson, W. S. (1950). Ecological correlations and the behavior of individuals. *American Sociological Review, 15*(3), 351–357.

Rodgers, J. L. (2010). The epistemology of mathematical and statistical modeling: A quiet methodological revolution. *American Psychologist, 65*(1), 1–12.

Rodgers, J. L., & Nicewander, W. A. (1988). Thirteen ways to look at the correlation coefficient. *The American Statistician, 42*(1), 59–66.

Singer, J. B., & Willett, J. B. (2002). *Applied longitudinal data analysis: Modeling change and event occurrence.* New York, NY: Oxford University Press.

Spearman, C. (1904). The proof and measurement of association between two things. *American Journal of Psychology, 15*, 72–101.

Spiegelhalter, D., & Rice, K. (2009). Bayesian statistics. *Scholarpedia, 4*(8), 5230. doi: 10.4249/ scholarpedia. 5230

Wiley, D. E. (1973). The identification problem for structural equation models with unmeasured variables. In A. S. Goldberger, & O. D. Duncan (Eds.), *Structural equation models in the social sciences* (pp. 69–83). New York, NY: Academic Press.

Wright, S. G. (1918). On the nature of size factors. *Genetics, 3*, 367–374.

Wu, W., West, S. G., & Taylor, A. B. (2009). Evaluating model fit for growth curve models: Integration of fit indices from SEM and MLM frameworks. *Psychological Methods, 14*(3), 183–201.

16

ISSUES IN THE ANALYSIS
OF CHANGE

D. Betsy McCoach, Karen E. Rambo, and Megan Welsh

Many of the most interesting research questions in education and the social sciences involve the measurement of change. Often educational researchers want to understand how people develop or change over time. As Willett (1988) rightly points out, "the very notion of learning implies growth and change" (p. 346). Thus, anytime we ask questions about the way in which learning occurs or about people's growth or decline in some area, we are implicitly asking questions that involve the measurement of change. Such questions might include: How do students' skills grow over time? Is this growth steady or does the rate of growth change over time? What is the shape of this growth trajectory? Do people (or units) tend to change in the same way over time? Or is there a great deal of variability between people in terms of their rate of change over time? Finally, we often want to understand what factors help to predict the rate at which change occurs, or which variables help us to understand inter-individual differences in the rate of change. In higher education, there are many research questions that involve change over time. Do student grade point averages increase over time? Do the grade point averages of males and females increase at the same rate? To what degree has the diversity on college campuses increased over the last two decades? Why are some universities more successful than others in increasing the diversity on their campuses? With enrollment declines, institutions also ask about the demographics of their student populations for planning purposes. Such questions are best answered using analysis methods that explicitly model change over time.

Over the past decade, modern models that allow for nuanced analyses of change, using an individual growth perspective, have become more commonplace. It is our goal in this chapter to briefly introduce readers to three of the most common of these models and to highlight common issues in the analysis of change. This brief chapter serves as an amuse-bouche, rather than a full treatment of the topic. Readers who are interested in pursuing such models in more depth are encouraged to consult Bollen & Curran (2006), T. E. Duncan, S. C. Duncan, & Stryker (2006), Raudenbush & Bryk, (2002), or Singer & Willett (2003).

Why Do We Need Growth Curve Modeling?

Before we embark on our journey into individual growth curve modeling, it is important to understand the inadequacies inherent in using two-wave studies to measure change. The simplest type of change is a difference score, which attempts to model the difference between post-test and pre-test achievement as a function of the presence of a treatment or some other educational variable.

Although simple to calculate, there are inherent difficulties in using difference scores to examine student growth (Cronbach & Furby, 1970).

First, measurement error in pre-test or post-test scores reduces the precision of the estimate of the treatment effect (Rogosa, Brandt, & Zimowski, 1982; Raudenbush, 2001). When measurement error is intertwined with the pre-test or post-test scores (or both), then "true" change and measurement error become confounded, and the observed change between two scores may either overestimate or underestimate the degree of "true" change. For example, a student's pre-test score could be too high and his or her post-test score could be too low because of measurement error, leading to an erroneous conclusion that the treatment had little or no effect when, in reality, measurement error is masking the true effect. Multiple data points are needed to extricate the confounded nature of the measurement error and true change (Singer & Willett, 2003). In addition, with only two time points, all change must be linear (and perfectly so). Thus, there is no way to examine the shape of the change trajectory across time.

Rogosa et al. (1982) recommend that "when used wisely, multiwave data will yield far better determinations of individual change than two-wave data" (p. 745). The conceptualization of growth as how individuals change across time and interest in modeling the variables that predict change between, as well as change within, people allows for a much fuller picture of change; however, such models require the use of longitudinal data (Singer & Willett, 2003). In addition, in non-randomized designs, it is nearly impossible to extricate potential confounding factors from the actual effect of the treatment in pre-test/post-test designs. For example, natural maturation is likely to be confounded with treatment effects making it impossible to determine whether improved scores were due to growth that would have occurred in the absence of treatment (Raudenbush, 2001). Therefore, analyses of growth or change require data collected across at least three time points.

Multivariate Repeated Measures

Another common way to examine change is to use multivariate repeated measures (MRM) designs, of which the most common analysis is repeated measures analysis of variance. Although MRM allows for several waves of data collection, there are several restrictions that MRM places on the measurement of change. One problematic restriction of MRM for measuring student growth is the requirement of a fixed time-series design. The distance between time points must be consistent across all persons, and the data collection must occur at the same time for all persons (Raudenbush & Bryk, 2002). If any student is missing data at any time point during the data collection schedule, that student is listwise deleted and all information provided by that student is lost (Raudenbush & Bryk, 2002). When working with students in higher education, this is likely to be a major issue. If a student's data is not collected on the same schedule as the other students, then the researcher must either (a) ignore that fact or (b) all of the observations for that student. For example, imagine that a researcher collects data from participants every semester. However, a student takes a semester off, making the spacing between the first and second time points 12 months, instead of the three months between semesters observed for other students. The researcher might ignore the fact that a year elapsed between waves 1 and 2 of data collection for that student, distorting that individual's trajectory. Alternatively, she can throw that student out of the sample. This has two adverse consequences. First, it decreases statistical power and lowers the precision of the estimates of growth. Second, it introduces a selection bias issue into the data analysis. People with an interrupted school experience are likely to be systematically different from people with continuous enrollment. Therefore, by eliminating these people from the analysis, we are likely to introduce bias into our estimates of growth. Luckily, there is a class of models that has the flexibility to retain student data even when some time points are missing and that allows for the collection of time unstructured data.

Further, MRM does not account for the nested nature of educational data. This is problematic because the MRM assumption that observations are independent is violated with nested observations. When we violate the assumptions on which analyses are based, the accuracy of results is jeopardized. Students who take the same course or who are taught by the same instructor may be similar to each other in terms of their achievement, and more similar than students taught by different instructors. Such similarities might also occur in other groups such as dormitory residents, members of campus organizations, or students pursuing the same degree. Also, when conducting research across multiple institutions, we would expect students from a given school to be more similar to each other than students attending different universities. These correlations among students are almost impossible to capture within an MRM framework (Raudenbush & Bryk, 2002). Ignoring the clustering of students within contexts results in underestimation of the standard errors, thereby increasing the effective Type I error rate.

What Do We Need to Measure Change?

To study change, we need data collected from the same individuals across multiple time points. Cross-sectional data, which compare the scores of different people, do not meet this requirement. For example, we cannot infer anything about the growth in student motivation by comparing the motivation level of a group of college juniors and that of college freshmen at the same school. If the juniors currently exhibit higher motivation levels, it does not necessarily imply that the freshmen will become more motivated as they mature. As alluded to earlier, using growth modeling techniques also requires collecting at least three waves of data. However, growth curve models with only three time points only allow for the estimation of linear growth trajectories. The estimation of curvilinear growth trajectories (as shown in Figure 16.1) requires data collected across four or more time points. With larger numbers of time points, it is possible to fit increasingly complex growth functions, which can be very informative if we want to understand how people change over time. When designing longitudinal studies, it is important to consider both the number and the spacing of

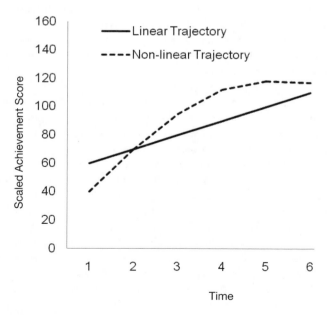

Figure 16.1 Graphical depiction of linear and non-linear growth trajectories

data collection points to accurately capture change across time. When data points are too infrequent, or when there are too few data points, it may not be possible to accurately model the functional form of the change.

In addition to collecting data on the same individuals over at least three waves, growth curve modeling requires two more conditions. First, there must be an accurate measure of time. If scores are collected across three time points, we need to know how much time elapsed between time point one and time point two and how much time elapsed between time point two and time point three. In essence, time is on the x-axis in a growth curve model (see Figure 16.1), and the score is plotted on the y-axis. We need to know the distance between testing occasions so that we can plot scores from the assessment, or the "y" score, on the correct location of the x-axis to correctly model the functional form of the growth. In education, several measures of time are equally reasonable: the student age in months for each administration of the assessment, or the number of weeks/months/ years between testing occasions.

The second requirement is that the assessment score must be psychometrically sound (e.g., scores are valid and reliable) and must be comparable over time (Singer & Willett, 2003). To be comparable over time, tests must measure the same skill at each administration and must measure one underlying construct [e.g., they must be unidimensional, a basic assumption of many measurement techniques (Allen & Yen, 1979)]. The scale of the assessment must also remain consistent across administrations so that a student who has not learned anything relevant to the construct would receive the same score with each administration of an assessment. This requirement is met when either the same assessment is used at multiple time points or when the assessments have had their scores placed onto the same metric through a process called test equating (Singer & Willett, 2003).

If assessments have had their scores placed on the same scale so that we can directly compare scores over time, they are said to be vertically scaled. Because vertically scaled assessments yield comparable scores, they are useful for modeling student growth. Think of the vertical scaling procedure as placing the results of multiple years of data on the same equal interval "ruler" so that growth may be measured in the same metric. Height in inches yields an equivalent metric across time; a height of five feet references the same amount of height regardless of who is measured or the age at which they are measured. In the absence of vertical scaling, the difference between the two scores does not measure growth in any meaningful way because the two scores are on two different, unlinked scales. Other tests are scaled within the same specific content area but are not designed to place scores along the same metric across time points (e.g., the calculus 1, calculus 2, and calculus 3 test means could be equal, or could have different and unrelated values). Therefore, comparing a student's scores across time cannot provide information on student growth.

In addition to having a scale that provides a common metric across time, the validity of the assessment must remain consistent across multiple administrations of the assessment. For example, a multiplication and division assessment might be a reasonable test to determine the mathematics achievement of a third grader; however, it would not be a valid indicator of high school mathematics achievement. In this case, the assessments must be sensitive to, and valid indicators of, current mathematics instruction (Singer & Willett, 2003).

What Analytic Techniques Do We Use to Measure Change?

Modern models of change use Structural Equation Modeling (SEM) or Hierarchical Linear Modeling (HLM) frameworks to estimate individual growth curves (Kline, 2005). Both SEM and HLM individual growth models require the same specifications of basic growth models: at least three waves of data, a valid and reliable measure of time, and a psychometrically sound, unidimensional, equal interval scaled instrument. Both SEM and HLM individual growth models are incredibly flexible in their approach to modeling growth. In addition to being able to model linear growth, they can model data that exhibit any number of patterns. For example, individual growth models can be extended to incorporate polynomial, piecewise, or other non-linearities into the individual growth trajectories provided enough time points are present to support the complexity of the model. They also have the ability to capture the nested nature of educational data.

Recent developments in statistical modeling allow for a more exploratory approach to describe student growth. Both the SEM and HLM approaches assume that data are drawn from a single population. In contrast, Growth Mixture Modeling (GMM) techniques assume that there are a mixture of populations within the dataset, and they allow researchers to identify different classes of growth. Using GMM, we can identify different subpopulations and compare rates of change across them. In essence, GMM is conceptually a blend of latent class analysis and growth curve analysis. GMM techniques can also incorporate information from known covariates to help predict student membership in a particular group. It is important to be cautious when drawing conclusions from GMM. They are very exploratory in nature, and it is not always easy to determine how many different classes are present.

In the following sections, we provide a very brief overview of Hierarchical Linear Modeling (HLM), Structural Equation Modeling (SEM), and Growth Mixture Modeling (GMM), as three modern methods to examine systematic change over time.

HLM Models

HLM individual growth models allow for the measurement of time points to vary across students and have the ability to capture the nested nature of student data—measures within students, students within classes, classes within schools, and so forth (Kline, 2005; Raudenbush & Bryk, 2002). In HLM individual growth models, both individual and group trajectories are estimated (Raudenbush & Bryk, 2002). HLM individual growth models are incredibly flexible in their approach to modeling growth. The primary advantage to using HLM to model individual growth is that HLM allows for a great degree of flexibility in the structure of time. In HLM, time is explicitly entered into the model as an explanatory variable. Therefore, every person within a dataset can have his or her own unique data collection schedule (Stoel & Galindo-Garre, 2011). When the length of time between data collection points varies from person to person, we refer to the data as "time unstructured." Conventional multilevel models handle time unstructured data seamlessly because time is represented as an explicit independent variable within the dataset.

The basic two-level HLM model for linear growth

In an HLM individual growth model, level 1 describes an individual's growth trajectory across time. A simple two-level linear growth model is illustrated below.

Level 1:

$$y_{ti} = \pi_{0i} + \pi_{1i}(time_{ti}) + e_{ti}$$

Level 2:

$$\pi_{0i} = \beta_{00} + \beta_{01}(gender_i) + r_{0i}$$

$$\pi_{1i} = \beta_{10} + \beta_{11}(gender_i) + r_{1i}$$

The observations are nested within persons. The level-1 equation models individual trajectories or within student variability across time. The dependent variable (y_{ti}) is the score for student i at time t. We predict that y_{ti}, person i's score at time t, is a function of the intercept, π_{0i} (which is the predicted value of y_{it} when time = 0), $\pi_{1i}(time_{ti})$, and individual error. The time slope, π_{1i}, represents the linear rate of change over time. Notice that both the slope and the intercept contain a subscript i. This means that a separate slope and intercept are estimated for each person in the sample. The deviation of an individual from his or her predicted trajectory (e_{ti}) can be thought of as the measurement error associated with that individual's data at that time point. The pooled amount of error variability within individuals' trajectories is estimated by the variance of e_{ti} [$var(e_2) = \sigma_2$] (Bryk & Raudenbush, 1988; Raudenbush & Bryk, 2002).

The level-2 equation models the average growth trajectories across students and deviations from those averages. The second level of the multilevel model specifies that the randomly varying intercept (π_{0i}) for each individual (i) is predicted by an overall intercept (β_{00}), the effects of level-2 variables on the intercept, and r_{0i}, the level-2 residual, which represents the difference between person i's model predicted intercept and his or her actual intercept. Likewise, the randomly varying linear growth slope (π_{1i}) for each individual (i) is predicted by an overall intercept (β_{10}), the effects of level-2 variables on the linear growth slope, and r_{1i}, the level-2 residual, which represents the difference between person i's model predicted linear growth slope and his or her actual growth slope. In our current example, gender is coded as male = 0, female = 1. Time is coded 0, 1, 2. Therefore, the intercept, π_{0i}, represents the predicted initial status of person i. Thus, the intercept (π_{0i}) is predicted from the overall mean of male students on the initial measure (β_{00}) and the expected differential between males and females in initial scores (β_{01}). The linear growth parameter (π_{1i}) is predicted from the mean growth of all male students (β_{10}) and the expected differential in growth between males and females (β_{11}). The amount of variability in the intercept between students after accounting for gender is estimated by the variance of u_{0i} [$var(u_{0i}) = \tau_{00}$], and the amount of variability in the time slope between students after accounting for gender is estimated by the variance of u_{0i} [$var(u_{1i}) = \tau_{11}$] (Bryk & Raudenbush, 1988; Raudenbush & Bryk, 2002).

The level-2 model allows for person-specific variables to explain variation in the growth trajectory. In other words, individual growth patterns can be explained by person-level predictors such as gender, student socio-economic status, participation in a program. Ideally, person-level covariates should help to explain some of the inter-individual variability in terms of where people start (the intercept) or how fast people grow (the slope).

SEM Models

Like HLM models, SEM latent growth models require that the dependent variable be continuous and that the scores be in the same units across time. However, unlike HLM, SEM approaches have an additional requirement that the data are time structured. (There are some newer SEM techniques that allow researchers to relax the assumption of time structured data, but these are beyond the scope of this chapter. See Mehta and Neale (2005) for an excellent treatment of this topic.) As with HLM models, vertically scaled measures, which have equidistant units that can be used at multiple time points, make ideal dependent measures for SEM latent growth models.

The SEM approach models the parameters of the individual growth curves (the intercept and the linear growth rate) as latent variables. In this framework, time is introduced through the factor loadings for the latent variable representing the linear growth slope (Stoel & Galindo-Garre, 2011). This is why the standard SEM approach requires time-structured data. The time-structured nature requires that the interval between data collection points 1 and 2 and the interval between data collection points 2 and 3 are equal across all students in the sample (Kline, 2005), which can be difficult to control when data are collected from large numbers of students in multiple locations. The requirement for time structured for SEM latent growth models is a major difference between the SEM and HLM approaches to individual growth modeling. However, there are advantages to the SEM approach. First, it is easier to specify a wide variety of error covariance structures within

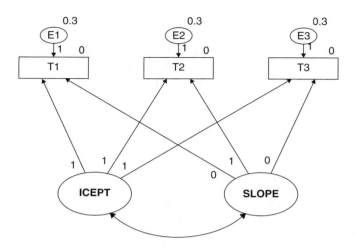

Figure 16.2 Graphic represents the estimation of a linear growth model from data collected at three time points using SEM

the SEM framework. Second, SEM provides the ability to build a measurement model for the dependent variable, allowing for the incorporation of multiple indicators at each time point. Third, SEM models allow for the simultaneous or sequential estimation of multiple growth models. Fourth, SEM allows for more flexibility in the incorporation of time varying covariates into the growth model. Finally, because the information about time is contained in the factor loadings, when there are at least four time points, it is possible to fix two-factor loadings and free the rest of the loadings, allowing for a very flexible expression of the growth trajectory. Thus, the SEM approach provides a great deal of flexibility in terms of its actual modeling capabilities. Additionally, SEM multi-level latent growth models have the ability to capture the nested nature of educational data.

Figure 16.2 provides a graphical depiction of a linear growth model with data collected at three time points, modeled within the SEM framework. This model contains two latent variables, the slope and the intercept. When using SEM to model growth, it is important to model means (and intercepts) as well as variances and covariances. This makes conceptual sense, as we are interested in modeling the change in level across time. The means of the latent variables provide the parameter estimates for the slope and the intercept. The variances of these latent variables provide information about the variability in the intercept and the slope. Again, all of the information about time is captured in the factor loadings for the slope variable. For an excellent and comprehensive book on latent variable growth curve modeling within an SEM framework, we recommend T.E. Duncan et al. (2006). A more advanced treatment of the topic is contained in Bollen & Curran (2006).

Growth Mixture Models

Growth Mixture Models (GMM) describe unobserved heterogeneity of participants and categorize participants based on growth trajectories (Muthén et al., 2002). Therefore, they can be likened to a cluster analysis or a latent class analysis conducted with longitudinal data. Growth models in an HLM or SEM framework allow researchers to easily examine group differences in the intercept or in the rate of change between observed groups—genders, ethnic groups, or between members of a treatment and a control group. However, GMM allows researchers to model differences in trajectories that are not readily captured by observed variables. For example, two different classes of students with varying rates of growth may exist in a dataset, but may go unnoticed with the HLM or SEM approaches because they are not explained by observed covariates. GMM allows researchers to uncover these patterns and to explore the relationship between class membership and measured covariates. Thus, it provides a mechanism to identify multiple unobserved groups (Ram & Grimm, 2009) through a sort of "post-hoc identification and description of group differences in change" (Ram & Grimm, 2009, p. 565).

In GMM, students that exhibit similar growth trajectories are hypothesized to be members of the same class whereas students who exhibit divergent patterns of growth are hypothesized to belong to different classes. For example, there might be two groups of low achieving freshmen—a flat class and a late bloomer class—that are followed for several semesters. The members of the flat class start with low GPAs and stay low for the duration of their time in college, and members of the late bloomer class start with low GPAs, but track upwards as time passes. One of the most challenging decisions in GMM is to determine the number of classes present in the data (Ram & Grimm, 2009). Deciding how distinct different growth patterns need to be to merit the creation of an additional class, or the minimum number of people or minimal percentage of the sample necessary to merit extraction of an additional class, is somewhat subjective. In this example, we expect that we have two classes present—a flat class and a late bloomer class. So we would want to test a variety of models. Minimally, we would examine at least three different models: the one class model (assuming one homogeneous population), the two class model (our hypothesized number of classes), and the three class model (which contains one more than our hypothesized number of classes.) The more complex the growth function is, the greater the number of estimated parameters. Thus, there are more ways in which people could differ from each other. Therefore, the number of extracted classes may increase as the number of time points and the complexity of the growth function increases.

To test how many classes best fit the data and the type of differences between and within classes for each model, researchers should first conduct a series of model comparisons using information criteria that indicate which model best fits the data given the number of parameters estimated. Some of the common information criteria that are used are the Bayesian Information Criterion (BIC), Akaiki Information Criterion (AIC), and the Adjusted BIC (Sclove, 1987). Information criteria are compared across models; models with the lowest information criteria values are considered to provide the best model-data fit. The Lo-Mendell-Rubin likelihood ratio test (Lo, Mendell, & Rubin, 2001) and Bootstrap LRT (BLRT; McLachlan, 1987; McLachlan & Peel, 2000) are also common tests used to help determine the appropriate number of classes to extract. Finally, researchers will also want to examine entropy, or the confidence with which students have been placed into classes. The higher the entropy, the better the model fits the data. For a full discussion about selecting the best model, see Ram & Grimm (2009), Tofighi and Enders (2008), and Wang and Bodner (2007). Ultimately, GMM is analogous to exploratory factor analysis. The determination of the number of classes to extract is at least somewhat subjective, and that decision affects the entire solution. Therefore, GMM is a very exploratory technique.

After the number of classes has been determined through model comparisons, then we examine the types of differences that exist between classes (Ram & Grimm, 2009). Assuming a linear model, classes would be most likely to differ in terms of their starting score means and their linear rates of growth. For our freshman example, we would assume that the classes would not differ at their starting point, or intercept, but would have different average GPAs as time passed. Therefore, we would assume that the two classes had the same average intercepts, but different average linear growth slopes. Next, we would check to see if classes differed in the amount of variability in each of the scores. In this group of tracked students, we might suspect that the members of the flat class have GPAs that do not differ much across time, but we expect that members of the late bloomer class vary a lot on their subsequent GPAs. Finally, classes could differ on the pattern of growth (e.g., linear or quadratic) (Ram & Grimm, 2009). For our freshman groups, we might suspect that the flat class has a linear, nearly flat trajectory while the late bloomer class experiences growth that rapidly accelerates during their junior and senior years of college. We can use GMM to model these two hypothetical classes and test all of our hypotheses about their performance (differences in means and linear growth, differences in variability across scores, and differences in type of trajectories). Finally, once we have used GMM to place students into classes, we could test our covariates to see if they help to predict class membership, e.g., student referrals to student support services, living arrangements of the student, student use of available tutoring services, or student participation in a campus organization.

It is important to remember that, in GMM, class membership is due to some unobserved categorical latent variable. We might have some suspicions as to why certain initially low performing students end up in either the flat class or late bloomer class, but ultimately class membership is due to differences between the classes on unobserved variables. Although GMM is an exploratory technique, it can provide useful information about different patterns of growth. Researchers who employ GMM strategies need to use common sense and be cautious in drawing conclusions from the analysis. It is often possible to find anomalies in a given dataset; however, those anomalies may not generalize to other samples. Also, it is helpful if researchers have covariates that they believe help predict group membership to validate their findings. Unfortunately, sometimes the use of covariates makes group membership even harder to detect or even changes the composition of the groups (Tofighi & Enders, 2008).

Issues and Pitfalls in the Measurement of Change

Assessing the growth of students presents a variety of issues and challenges. We address several key concerns in the remainder of this chapter: measurement of the dependent variable, regression to the mean, measurement error, floor or ceiling effects, the scale of the dependent variable, non-normal or non-interval level data, and changes in the distribution across time.

Measurement of the Dependent Variable

Even when scores are comparable over time (e.g., the same assessment is administered repeatedly or vertically scaled assessments are used), problems can easily still arise when assessing growth. With vertically scaled tests, if the content of the assessments varies even slightly from year to year, the ability to compare the scores received at two different levels is compromised (Martineau, 2006; McCaffrey, Lockwood, Koretz, & Hamilton, 2003). Even changing the relative weight that topics contribute to the total test score from year to year can change the construct being measured. Finally, vertically scaled assessments that span multiple years are not likely to measure constructs that are actually exactly the same content. This potential violation of unidimensionality threatens the validity of any estimate of growth obtained from the measure (McCaffrey et al., 2003).

Growth models with continuous variables require an assumption that the dependent variable is normally distributed at each time point. However, when using the same measure across time, the distribution of the dependent variable could change. For example, scores on an assessment could be positively skewed at time point 1, normally distributed at time point 2, and negatively skewed at time point 3. Imagine giving the same assessment to students across three time points. Perhaps on the first testing occasion, the test is difficult for most of the students, resulting in a positively skewed distribution. On the second testing occasion, students are fairly normally distributed. By the third testing occasion, many students have made so much growth that the assessment is now fairly easy for them, resulting in a negatively skewed distribution. Situations such as this are not uncommon, resulting in changes in the shape of the distribution of the dependent variable across time.

In this situation, transforming the dependent variable across all of the time points is problematic, as the transformation would alleviate the problem at one time point but exacerbate the problem at another time point. However, applying different transformations across the different time points is also not possible, as that creates different scales across time. Some have suggested standardizing the dependent variable at each time point to normalize the distribution and to try to ensure equatability of the variable across time. This is a poor idea. The fact that standardized scores have a mean of 0 and a standard deviation of 1 (and thus a variance of 1) leads to two important outcomes. First, because the mean across time points is standardized to be 0, growth models using standardized scores are not capturing growth per se; instead, they capture change in relative status. Second, and more importantly, standardizing scores at each time point constrains the variance of the measure to be equal across time, which is often an unrealistic assumption. Educational research has consistently shown that the variance in achievement, skills, or ability generally increases across time (Bast & Reitsma, 1998; Gangé, 2005; Kenny, 1974). "Such standardization constitutes a completely artificial and unrealistic restructuring of interindividual heterogeneity in growth" (Willett, 1988, p. 378) and constraining scores in this way is likely to produce distorted results (Thorndike, 1966; Willett, 1988). Thus, Willett (1988) recommends against the standardization of the dependent variable when conducting analyses of change.

Measurement Challenges

There are several measurement issues that should be considered before embarking on growth analyses. These challenges relate to the ability to adequately capture growth using any measure. The reliability of scores used as dependent variables in growth analysis is of particular concern. Factors that jeopardize reliability are discussed in this section. Regression to the mean, or the tendency for those with extreme initial scores to score closer to the average score on subsequent assessments, can bias growth measures, overestimating the growth of low achieving students and underestimating the growth of high achieving students. Measurement error, or the degree of imprecision in test scores, is also of concern for students who have an underlying ability or score that falls in the outside range of what is measured by the assessment. Most academic assessments are designed to measure more precisely students who fall near the mean. For students who fall in the extremes, there may be more error associated with their scores. Finally, the term floor or ceiling effects refers to problems that arise when student abilities are either below or beyond the skills captured by the test. When this occurs, students receive the lowest score or the highest test score possible, but this score does not reflect their true level of ability (Popham, 1999). Each of these challenges is discussed in detail below.

Regression to the mean

Regression to the mean is an important, but commonly misunderstood, statistical phenomenon. When using an independent variable (such as a test score at Year 1) to predict scores on a dependent variable (such as a test score at Year 2), errors in prediction will occur whenever the correlation between the two variables is less than perfect (+1.0 or -1.0) (Campbell & Kenny, 1999). These errors in prediction will make it appear that people with initially extreme scores have scores closer to the mean on the post-test. Therefore, the scores of high achieving students will grow at a smaller rate than low or average achieving students. Students who score very low on the initial assessment are more likely to demonstrate steeper growth rates than average or than those of high achieving students. There are two primary sources for this imperfection: lack of congruence between the two assessments (in format or in content tested), and measurement error.

Measurement error

The measurement of psycho-educational constructs is fraught with error. For example, educators use scores on achievement tests to infer a person's level of content mastery in a domain. However, a person's score on the test is *not* a perfect measure of his or her achievement level. There are a variety of factors that could cause the test score to be either an overestimation or an underestimation of the person's actual achievement level. The content sampling of items on the test, the format of the items, the testing conditions, and many other factors can cause the observed test score to deviate from the underlying trait value. All of these factors are subsumed under the general term measurement error. Reliability is a related concept in that it describes the consistency of scores across time, test forms, or internally within the test itself. Measurement error and reliability are inversely related: the greater the measurement error, the lower the reliability of the scores. The goal, of course, is to minimize the degree of measurement error in scores, but it is impossible to completely eliminate them.

Both unconditional and conditional errors of measurement influence the reliability with which we can estimate the scores of high ability students. Conditional errors of measurement are errors that depend on the location of a score on the scale (Lohman & Korb, 2006), whereas unconditional errors of measurement are evenly distributed across the entire range of scores. The reliability coefficient and the traditional standard error of measurement both assume errors of measurement to be constant across the score distribution. However, in general, the amount of error in test scores is not uniform across the distribution of scores (Lohman & Korb, 2006). Instead, it is U-shaped: the error is lowest for people in the middle of the score distribution and highest for the people at the extremes of the score distribution.

Floor or ceiling effects

A somewhat related issue is that of ceiling effects. A test may not contain questions to assess or distinguish among the lowest or highest scoring students. Obviously, this is a more extreme, more problematic scenario than the one described above. Now, instead of trying to distinguish among the highest scoring students with just a few questions or with very little information, there is no information with which to determine students' abilities. The same holds for students whose performance falls below the span of the assessment. When a student hits the ceiling of an assessment, the student has mastered all of the content on the administered test, but there is no way to assess how much more the student knows and can do. If a student's performance is far above or below the range of the assessment, even if the student makes gains we will not be able to accurately quantify the size of the gain. In some sense, floor and ceiling effects are an extreme scenario which leads to a very large conditional error of measurement at the tails of the distribution. Obviously, if the floor of a test is too high or the ceiling of a test is too low, then there is no way to accurately measure the achievement or the growth of the students whose performance falls outside the range of the assessment.

Attrition and Missing Data

One strength of individual growth modeling is that it can easily handle missing data, assuming "that the probability of missingness is unrelated to unobserved concurrent outcomes (conditional on all observed outcomes)" (Singer & Willett, 2003, p. 159). When data are missing completely at random or missing at random, individual growth modeling should still produce valid results (Singer & Willett, 2003). However, when attrition is systematic and is related to scores on the outcome variable of interest (after controlling for the independent variables in the model), the estimates of the growth parameters are likely to be biased, leading to invalid inferences about the phenomenon of interest. Thus, it is very important to examine the nature of the missingness within the sample prior to conducting growth analyses. The interested reader should consult Enders (2010) for an excellent introduction to the issue of missing data.

Recommendations

When a researcher is interested in capturing growth or change over time, it is best to collect three of more data points. The more complex the shape of the growth trajectory is expected to be, the greater the number of time points required to estimate the model. The timing and spacing of the measurements is also important. Researchers should consider the expected shape of the trajectory and their goals for conducting the analysis during the design phase, when they make determinations about how frequently and how many times they plan to measure participants on the outcome measure of interest. Further, it is critical to visually inspect the shape of the individual growth trajectories prior to conducting any statistical analyses in order to understand and correctly model the functional form of the data. No statistical analysis can supplant the information that is provided by the examination of individual growth trajectories.

Measurement issues are especially salient when analyzing change. The reliability of a measure of change is bounded by the reliability of the initial measure. Therefore, to accurately capture the nature of change, it is important to use measures that exhibit strong psychometric qualities. One possible solution to this issue is to use multiple indicators of the construct of interest and to impose a measurement model onto the analysis of change. This is easily accomplished in the SEM framework. While it is possible to build crude measurement models in an HLM framework under certain limiting assumptions, the SEM framework lends itself more naturally to the modeling of latent variables. Further, to increase the reliability of growth slopes, increase the number of data collection points.

We hope that this introduction to analyses of change and growth modeling provides useful advice for researchers who are interested in analyzing change or growth. Obviously, this overview just scratches the surface in terms of explicating issues regarding the analysis of change and growth. However, this chapter has provided a general overview of some of the more modern methods to analyze change as well as some of the most important issues and pitfalls in the analysis of change.

References

Allen, M. J., & Yen, W. M. (1979). *Introduction to measurement theory*. Long Grove, IL: Waveland Press.

Bast, J., & Reitsma, P. (1998). Analyzing the development of individual differences in terms of Matthew effects in reading: Results from a Dutch longitudinal study. *Developmental Psychology, 34*, 1373–1399.

Bollen, K. A., & Curran, P. J. (2006). *Latent Curve Models: A structural equation perspective*. Hoboken, NJ: Wiley Interscience.

Bryk, A. S., & Raudenbush, S. W. (1988). Toward a more appropriate conceptualization of research on school effects: A three-level hierarchical linear model. *American Journal of Education, 97*, 65–108.

Campbell, D. T., & Kenny, D. A. (1999). *A primer of regression artifacts*. New York: Guilford Press.

Cronbach, L. J., & Furby, L. (1970). How we should measure 'change': Or should we? *Psychological Bulletin, 74*, 68–80.

Duncan, T. E., Duncan, S. C., & Stryker, L. A. (2006). *An introduction to latent variable growth curve modeling: Concepts, issues, and applications* (2nd ed.). Mahwah, NJ: Lawrence Erlbaum and Associates.

Enders, C. K. (2010). *Applied missing data analysis*. New York: Guilford Press.

Gangé, F. (2005). From noncompetence to exceptional talent: Exploring the range of academic achievement within and between grade levels. *Gifted Child Quarterly, 49*, 139–153.

Kenny, D. (1974). A quasi-experimental approach to assessing treatment effects in the nonequivalent control group design. *Pyschological Bulletin, 82*, 342–362.

Kline, R. B. (2005). *Principles and practice of structural equation modeling* (2nd ed.). New York, NY: Guilford Press.

Lo, Y., Mendell, N. R., & Rubin, D. B. (2001). Testing the number of components in a normal mixture. *Biometrika, 88*, 767–778.

Lohman, D.F., & Korb, K.A. (2006). Gifted today but not tomorrow? Longitudinal changes in ability and acheivement during elementary school. *Journal for the Education of the Gifted, 29*, 451–484.

Martineau, J. A. (2006). Distorting value added: The use of longitudinal, vertically scaled student achievement data for growth-based, value-added accountability. *Journal of Educational and Behavioral Statistics, 31*, 35–62.

McCaffrey, D. F., Lockwood, J. R., Koretz, D. M., & Hamilton, L. S. (2003). *Evaluating value-added models for teacher accountability*. Santa Monica, CA: The RAND Corporation.

McLachlan, G.J. (1987). On bootstrapping the likelihood ratio test statistic for the number of components in a normal mixture. *Applied Statistics, 36*, 318–324.

McLachlan, G. J., & Peel, D. (2000). *Finite mixture models*. New York, NY: John Wiley.

Mehta, P. D., & Neale, M. C. (2005). People are variables too: Multilevel structural equations modeling. *Psychological Methods, 10*(3), 259–284.

Muthén, B., Brown, C. H., Masyn, K., Jo, B., Khoo, S.T., Yang C. C., . . . Liao, J. (2002). General growth mixture modeling for randomized preventative interventions. *Biostatistics, 3*, 459–475.

Popham, W.J. (1999). *Classroom assessment: What teachers need to know* (2nd ed.). Boston, MA: Allyn & Bacon.

Ram, N., & Grimm, K. J. (2009). Growth mixture modeling: A method for identifying differences in longitudinal change among unobserved groups. *International Journal of Behavioral Development, 33*, 565–576.

Raudenbush, S. W. (2001). Toward a coherent framework for comparing trajectories of individual change. In A. G. Sayer (Ed.), *New methods for the analysis of change* (pp. 35–64). Washington, DC: American Psychological Association.

Raudenbush S. W., & Bryk, A. S. (2002). *Hierarchical linear models* (2nd ed.). London, UK: Sage Publications.

Rogosa, D., Brandt, D., & Zimowski, M. (1982). A growth curve approach to the measurement of change. *Psychological Bulletin, 92*, 726–748.

Sclove, L. S. (1987). Application of model-selection criteria to some problems in multivariate analysis. *Psychometrika 52*, 333–343.

Singer, J. D., & Willett, J. B. (2003). *Applied longitudinal data analysis: Modeling change and event occurrence*. New York, NY: Oxford University Press.

Stoel, R. D., & Garre, F. G. (2011). Growth curve analysis using multilevel regression and structural equation modeling. In J. J. Hox, & J. K. Roberts (Eds.), *Handbook of advanced multilevel analysis* (pp. 97–111). New York, NY: Routledge.

Thorndike, R. L. (1966). Intellectual status and intellectual growth. *Journal of Educational Psychology, 57*(3), 121–127.

Tofighi, D., & Enders, C. K. (2008). Identifying the correct number of classes in growth mixture models. In G. R. Hancock, & K. M. Samuelson (Eds.), *Advances in latent variable mixture models*. Charlotte, NC: Information Age.

Wang, M., & Bodner, T. E. (2007). Growth mixture modeling: Identifying and predicting unobserved subpopulations with longitudinal data. *Organizational Research Methods, 10*, 635–656.

Willett, J. B. (1988). Questions and answers in the measurement of change. *Review of Research in Education, 15*, 345–422.

QUESTIONS AND EXERCISES
FOR SECTION 2

Note: Suggested answers are provided for selected questions. These questions are indicated by an asterisk (*).

(1) How could you explain "Classical Test theory" to another student in three to four sentences?
(2) What could be a rationale for choosing CTT over IRT in assessment of students' reading level?
(3) What could be the benefits of systematic formative evaluation in relation to students with a learning disability?

Scenario for Questions 4–10: In a hypothetical G study of written language proficiency, eight students completed brief written summaries of five news articles on current events. Each summary (here, called a task) was scored by two graders on a scale from 1 to 5. The data are presented in Table S2.1 below.

Table S2.1 Data for a Hypothetical G Study of Written Language Proficiency

Student	Grader	Task				
		1	*2*	*3*	*4*	*5*
1	1	5	5	4	2	3
	2	5	4	4	1	4
2	1	5	5	4	4	3
	2	5	5	4	4	4
3	1	3	4	2	3	2
	2	5	5	2	2	4
4	1	1	4	5	2	4
	2	2	3	5	2	3
5	1	3	3	2	2	4
	2	4	4	2	2	2
6	1	1	4	4	2	2
	2	2	4	4	3	5
7	1	2	2	2	1	2
	2	1	3	1	1	2
8	1	1	1	4	2	2
	2	2	2	4	2	4

(4)   Specify the G-study design and what assumptions you make about sampling.*
(5)   Carry out an analysis of variance, and calculate the estimated variance components.*
(6)   Array the results of the analysis in a table such as that shown in Table 10.2 of the chapter.*
(7)   Interpret the estimated variance components including whether there are any "surprises" or what you see follows trends in the literature.*
(8)   Calculate the estimated error variances and generalizability coefficients for the following numbers of graders and tasks: (1, 1), (1, 5), (1, 10), (2, 5), and (2, 10). Compare the results.*
(9)   In the decision study, the language proficiency of a large number of students will be evaluated. Describe the practical advantages of a D-study design in which graders are nested within tasks.*
(10)   One way to increase the generalizability is to fix the task facets. Describe the implications of this choice.*
(11)   Consider the two propositions below. Briefly defend one of them over the other.*

   •   ***Proposition A***: IRT explicitly contradicts basic assumptions about a true score central to CTT (classical test theory).
   •   ***Proposition B***: IRT merely, but significantly, extends CTT and does not contradict basic CTT assumptions.

(12)   Explain the two scales in the IRT figure illustrated in Figure S2.1.*
(13)   Explain the curve in Figure S2.1.*
(14)   A test developer is developing a test for evaluating the mathematics achievement of students in higher education. Different alternate forms of the test are going to be administered in two different years for security purposes. The alternate forms are going to be equated using the common item nonequivalent groups design. What are the most important considerations in choosing which items are to be common to the two forms?

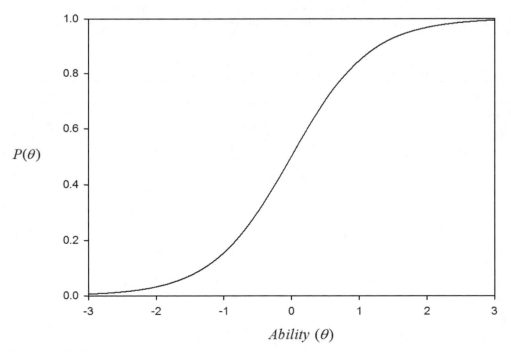

Figure S2.1 IRT item characteristic curve for one item

(15) A testing company is making plans to develop a new college admissions assessment. The assessment will have a raw score scale of 0-150, but the test developers want to report scores to examinees on a score scale with more inherent meaning. Discuss the ways that the test developers could incorporate meaning into the reported score scale.

(16) The formula for coefficient alpha includes three elements: (a) the number of items divided by the number of items minus 1, (b) the sum of the item variances, and (c) the variance of the total scores. The first element is a statistical correction factor. Does the correction factor always make the final estimate larger, or always smaller? What happens to the influence of the correction factor as the number of items gets larger? Does alpha get bigger or smaller, all other things equal, as the items variances get larger? Does alpha get bigger or smaller, all other things equal, as the variance of the total scores get larger? Conceptually, why does total score variance affect coefficient alpha in this manner?

(17) What happens if I make my test have k times (e.g., $k = 2$ or 3 or 4.5, or 0.5) as many items, assuming the new items I add are equivalent to the original items (or when $0 < k < 1.0$, the items I delete to make the test shorter are equivalent to the items I keep)? We can use the Spearman-Brown prophecy formula to make this determination. For example, if my original reliability coefficient is $r_{XX} = 0.40$, and I am willing to double the number of items ($k = 2.0$, e.g., from 50 to 100 items, or from 100 to 200 items), my expected new reliability coefficient, $r_{XX} =$

$$(k \star r_{XX})/(1+(k-1)\star r_{XX})$$
$$(2\star 0.40)/(1+(2-1)\star 0.40)$$
$$(0.80)/(1+(1)\star 0.40)$$
$$(0.80)/(1+0.40)$$
$$(0.80)/(1.40)$$
$$0.571$$

If $r_{XX} = 0.40$, and I am willing to use half as many items (i.e., $k = 0.5$), what is r_{XX}? Perform the same calculations for $k = 3, 4, 5,$ and 6. Is adding more items expected to improve the score reliability by a constant amount? What if the initial reliability was $r_{XX} = 0.90$, or 0.95?

(18) We can also algebraically rearrange the Spearman-Brown prophecy formula to solve for k rather than for $r_{XX'}$. For example, let's say that $r_{XX} = 0.60$, but we desire $r_{XX'} = 0.85$. For this situation, $k =$

$$((r_{XX'})\star(1-r_{XX}))/((r_{XX})\star(1-r_{XX'}))$$
$$((0.85)\star(1-0.60))/((0.6)\star(1-0.85))$$
$$((0.85)\star(0.40))/((0.6)\star(0.15))$$
$$0.34/0.09$$
$$3.777$$

What is k for this situation if I desire $r_{XX'} = 0.85, 0.90,$ and 0.95?

(19) Discuss the issues related to choosing an appropriate criterion for establishing predictive validity of a standardized admissions test. What are some of the technical issues that can affect the resulting correlation?

(20) Discuss the steps that should be followed in developing a placement exam. How would these procedures be different for a test used for program evaluation?

(21) Several statistical modeling strategies were introduced in Chapter 15: correlation/regression, multilevel modeling, structural equation modeling, and non–parametric methods. Compare and contrast them. List the salient characteristics of each strategy.[*]

(22) Under what circumstances would a simple difference score be sufficient to measure change? When would it be insufficient?[*]

(23) Assume that the basic requirements for measuring growth have been met. When studying growth, under what type of circumstance should a researcher prefer HLM? SEM? Growth mixture modeling?[*]

(24) Before employing a growth model, a researcher should check for several potential problems with the measure. What are some of those checks?[*]

Suggested Answers to Selected Questions

Answer/Response for (4)

The design is fully crossed (students × graders × tasks). The object of measurement is students; the error facets are graders and tasks. We assume that all sources of variation in the design are random.

Answer/Response for (5)

See Table S2.2.

Answer/Response for (6)

See Table S2.3.

Table S2.2 Solution for Section 2 Discussion Question 5

Source of Variation	df	Sum of Squares	Mean Square	Estimated Variance Component
Student (s)	7	43.18750	6.16964	0.41964
Grader (g)	1	1.51250	1.51250	0.01607
Task (t)	4	18.57500	4.64375	0.16607
s × g	7	4.58750	0.65536	0.04018
s × t	28	49.62500	1.77232	0.65893
g × t	4	2.67500	0.66875	0.02679
s × g × t,e	28	12.72500	0.45446	0.45446

Table S2.3 Solution for Section 2 Discussion Question 6

Source	Variance Component	Estimate	% of Total Variability
Student (s)	σ_s^2	0.41964	23.5
Grader (g)	σ_g^2	0.01607	0.9
Task (t)	σ_t^2	0.16607	9.3
s × g	σ_{sg}^2	0.04018	2.2
s × t	σ_{st}^2	0.65893	37.0
g × t	σ_{gt}^2	0.02679	1.5
s × g × t,e	$\sigma_{sgt,e}^2$	0.45446	25.5

Answer/Response for (7)

Student (s): Universe-score variance. The substantial estimated variance component for students shows that, averaging over graders and tasks, students in the sample differ in their writing proficiency.

Grader (g): Constant effect for all students due to stringency of graders. The small estimated variance component for graders shows that graders, on average, were equally stringent in their ratings of students' summaries.

Task (t): Constant effect for all students due to the difficulty of the task. The moderately large estimated variance component for the main effect of tasks shows that some tasks were more difficult than others.

sg: Inconsistencies of graders' evaluation of particular students' performance. The relatively small estimated variance component for the students-by-graders interaction shows that the relative standing of students on writing proficiency was fairly consistent from one grader to another.

st: Inconsistencies from one task to another in particular students' performance. The large estimated variance component for the students-by-tasks interaction shows that the relative standing of students on writing proficiency differed across tasks.

gt: Constant effect for all students due to differences in graders' stringency from one task to another. The small estimated variance component for the graders-by-tasks interaction shows that mean task scores had similar relative standing across graders.

sgt,e: Residual consisting of the unique combination of student, grader, task; unmeasured facets that affect the measurement; and/or random events. The large residual effect suggests a large students-by-graders-by-tasks interaction, unmeasured systematic or unsystematic sources of variation, or both.

Overall, more of the variability comes from tasks than from graders.

Answer/Response for (8)

See Table S2.4. For the same number of observations per student, slightly higher generalizability is obtained with more tasks and fewer graders.

Table S2.4 Solution for Section 2 Discussion Question 8

Source of Variation	n'_g	1	1	1	2	2
	n'_t	1	5	10	5	10
Student (s)		0.41964	0.41964	0.41964	0.41964	0.41964
Grader (g)		0.01607	0.01607	0.01607	0.00804	0.00804
Task (t)		0.16607	0.03321	0.01661	0.03321	0.01661
sg		0.04018	0.04018	0.04018	0.02009	0.02009
st		0.65893	0.13179	0.06589	0.13179	0.06589
gt		0.02679	0.00536	0.00268	0.00268	0.00134
sgt,e		0.45446	0.09089	0.04545	0.04545	0.02272
$\hat{\sigma}^2_\delta$		1.5357	0.26286	0.15152	0.19732	0.10871
$\hat{\sigma}^2_\Delta$		1.36250	0.31750	0.18688	0.24125	0.13469
$E\hat{\rho}^2$		0.27	0.61	0.73	0.68	0.79
Φ		0.24	0.57	0.69	0.63	0.76

233

Answer/Response for (9)

It would be logistically difficult for the same set of graders to carry out all of the ratings. In the nested design with graders nested within tasks, different graders would be assigned to different tasks. Thus, each grader would be responsible for rating the papers for only one task, constituting a more feasible design. With five tasks per student, and two graders rating each task, the estimated generalizability and dependability coefficients are .72 and .69, respectively. These coefficients are slightly higher than for the fully crossed design due to the larger total number of graders used in the nested design (10 graders).

Answer/Response for (10)

When task is treated as a fixed facet, the decision maker does not generalize beyond the five tasks used here and, consequently, no error of generalization due to tasks occurs. The only remaining source of error is graders. Because graders agreed quite highly, the levels of generalizability for the mixed design are high. For example, the estimated generalizability and dependability coefficients for one grader are .81 and .78; and the estimated generalizability and dependability coefficients for two graders are .89 and .88. This choice of design demonstrates a trade-off between the universe of generalization (limited) and the level of generalizability (high).

Answer/Response for (11)

For defense of Proposition A. CTT is built on the central notion of a true score for an examinee over a domain of knowledge, ability, or proficiency. That domain is sampled by the test's items/exercises; and, the more precisely the domain is defined and the more thoroughly and accurately it is sampled, the more exactly is known an examinee's true score (i.e., reliability is better). IRT does not view an examinee's ability (or proficiency, talent, etc.) as a domain that can be circumscribed at all. Rather, in IRT a cognitive function is conceived of a latent continuum, with a range of $\pm\infty$ and to which both examinees and items can be located by statistical means. The location on the continuum (with the right side of the continuum meaning higher) represents one's ability or proficiency—and, IRT makes no explicit allowance for a "true score" of a domain of knowledge. Hence, the IRT paradigm is explicitly contradictory of the basic notion of reliably measuring a true score as is done in CTT.

For defense of Proposition B. At their core, both IRT and CTT are methodologies useful to make reliable inferences about knowledge or abilities or proficiencies. CTT is a simpler approach, using an additive condition to sum responses to test stimuli. IRT employs much more sophisticated statistics for measurement in an approach called maximum likelihood estimation to locate responses along the theta continuum. Both approaches seek reliable measurement of mental attributes. Hence, IRT is merely a different, albeit more sophisticated methodology, and therefore extends CTT yielding more accurate inferences but it does not contradict it.

Answer/Response for (12)

The horizontal line is the abscissa and represents the ability or proficiency that is appraised, called theta (θ). Since ability has no theoretical limits, either low or high, the scale too has the range of an infinite continuum ($-\infty$, $+\infty$). However, by convention and for graphing, only the ±3 portion of the range is displayed. Although IRT values can be calculated in a normal metric, calculation is nearly always done in a logistic metric. Hence, this theta scale is shown in a logistic metric, centered at 0 and with standardized intervals. By ranging ±3 the scale captures nearly all (more than 99%) of the population. The vertical scale is the ordinate axis and represents the probability of observing a response on this item (i.e., the correct answer). It is a function of the ability or proficiency: hence, $P(\theta)$. Of course, probability can range from none to absolute, or 0 to 1.

Answer/Response for (13)

The curve in the figure represents characteristics of a test item (or exercise) relative to a population of values for an examinee (see response to Question (12) above for explanation of the scales). The curve is called an ICC (item characteristic curve) or, by some authors, an IRF (item response function). Notice that it is not a straight line, meaning that the function it presents is not linear along the range of theta values, and is called an ogive. The location of the ogive along the theta continuum (i.e., the left or right shifting) displays the ICC's difficulty parameter relative to the theta scale. Its slope shows the range of theta relative to probability, hence is an indicator of discrimination along theta. The inflection point is the theta value where the curve "inflects" or changes direction. Still, it is a monotonic function, always rising. The left-most portion of the ICC displays the probability of low ability examinees getting the item correct, which is generally (but not always) very low.

Answer/Response for (21)

A correlation is an index of the relationship between (usually two) variables. Depending on the types (measurement levels) of these variables, different correlation indices may be used. For example, with two interval variables, the most commonly used correlation is Pearson's r; with two ordinal variables, the most commonly used correlation is Spearman's ρ. While correlation is a useful way to describe variable relationships, it alone cannot be used to infer causality.

Regression is a statistical technique used to investigate relationships between a single outcome variable and one or more predictors. The outcome variable is sometimes called the dependent variable (DV), the criterion variable, or (less often) the effect variable. The predictor variable(s) are sometimes called the independent variable(s) [IV(s)]. In contrast to correlation, regression can help assess the one-to-many relationship, as well as assessing unique contributions of individual predictors. Regression is a special case of the broader general linear models (GLM). Similar to correlation, regression alone does not imply causality.

Multilevel modeling is appropriate when there is a nesting data structure. For example, students are nested within schools. If the outcome variable is at the student level, and the predictors come from both the student and the school levels, we have to consider the fact that students from different schools with the same characteristics may have different standings within their respective schools. Multilevel modeling can be thought of as regression models at different levels. Another advantage of multilevel modeling is that it can handle longitudinal data and "growth trajectories" can be compared across different subjects.

Structural equation modeling (SEM) examines multivariate relationships simultaneously. For example, the DV in a regression model may serve as an IV in another regression model. In SEM, we do not have to use two models. Instead, both relationships can be assessed simultaneously. Another advantage of SEM is that it can incorporate latent variables as in factor analysis. It allows the researcher to assess the substantive/conceptual models even if the same construct is operationalized differently (i.e., latent variables are less prone to measurement error). Many studies on model fit indices are conducted within the framework of SEM.

While less often used, non-parametric methods are proposed that usually do not assume certain statistical distributions of variables (e.g., normal distributions). Spearman's ρ can be thought of as the non-parametric version of Pearson's r; there are also non-parametric versions of t-test and ANOVA to compare group means. The statistical power (i.e., probability of correctly detecting an effect in the population) of non-parametric methods is usually lower than the corresponding parametric methods (e.g., t-test or ANOVA based on interval dependent variables) when the assumption of statistical distributions is met.

Answer/Response for (22)

Sufficient

- Participants were randomly assigned to groups
- Only linear trends were expected
- Data were missing at random

Insufficient

- Random assignment was not feasible
- Trend was expected to be non-linear
- Measurement error makes the true effect difficult to detect
- The researcher wanted to understand trends across time

Answer/Response for (23)

HLM. The data collection schedule varies across participants; the participants are nested into clusters.

SEM. The researcher wants a lot of flexibility in the manner in which the model is constructed, e.g., a need exists to specify a particular covariance structure, to allow flexibility when incorporating time varying covariates, to allow maximum flexibility when creating the growth trajectory, or to use a measurement model as the dependent variable.

GMM. (a) A single population growth trajectory is not assumed; (b) group membership is not determined by observed variables but is assumed to be based on unobserved characteristics; and (c) should be used only in an exploratory fashion.

All are capable of modeling curvilinear data provided enough data points have been collected (two more than the degree of the expected polynomial function: 3 for linear, 4 for quadratic, etc.).

Answer/Response for (24)

- Floor and ceiling effects—does the measure have a broad enough range to cover the sample of participants?
- Reasonable reliability across the range of scores
- Unidimensionality—does the construct being measured remain consistent across time?
- Normally distributed results across each time point

SECTION 3

Test Construction and Development

Louise Yarnall

Although few postsecondary professionals are likely to participate in a formal test design and development process, throughout their careers they will need to make many decisions about outcomes assessment that will be related to testing. To make these choices, having a good grounding in how tests are constructed can be a powerful tool. These chapters provide examples of how measurement principles inform the kinds of day-to-day decisions that practitioners increasingly will face as postsecondary institutions strive to attain wider success for more diverse populations of students.

As underscored in all the chapters in this section, good decisions around assessment begin with a clear understanding of the ultimate purpose and use of the assessment results. The following chapters immerse the reader in the ways assessment designers conduct their work. While sometimes dismissed as a chore, assessment design is logical, philosophical, and infinitely creative, encompassing both art and science. As a science, assessment is about measurement that is fair, precise, reliable, and valid. As an art, assessment might be likened to a jazz interpretation of an American standard, where there is a definitive structure that allows for, if not demands, the ability to improvise. In short, assessment is an art guided by rules and principles that fundamentally and palpably inform every decision in the design process.

All the chapters in this section provide specific examples of the many different kinds of assessments that postsecondary educators will encounter in their work. Knupp and Harris open the section with an elegant overview of content and statistical specifications (Chapter 17). They compare the varying standards for specifying classroom tests, large-scale assessments, and licensure exams. This chapter should help practitioners understand the importance of establishing a correspondence between domain knowledge and the items on a test.

Haertel, Wentland, Yarnall, and Mislevy review in Chapter 18 the evidence-centered design methodology for analyzing domain knowledge and identifying the forms of evidence of student learning. They illustrate these principles through two examples: The design of a driver-training test and the development of assessments for scenario-based curricula in career technician education classes in community colleges. While it is unlikely that any practitioner will need to implement all the steps of evidence-centered design, the system is a helpful framework for developing a critical eye for recognizing a valid assessment argument.

In Chapter 19, Yarnall and Ostrander describe an effort to engage community college faculty in thinking about their own classroom assessments using a reflection approach inspired by evidence-centered design. In this example, the technique was used to help faculty expand their vision of the content they were teaching beyond the narrowly technical to include 21st-century professional communication and teamwork skills. Even using just one or two of these concrete reflection approaches could have a beneficial impact on classroom and program assessment at the postsecondary level.

Clauser and Hambleton (Chapter 20) discuss some practical ways to ensure test items are fair and constructed well. They review the major procedures for examining how test items function, including: item difficulty, item discrimination between high achieving and low achieving examinees, effectiveness of distractors in multiple choice items, and item bias. They provide a quick primer on the core procedures for both dichotomously and polytomously scored items. Finally, they review the different major software packages currently available to conduct such analyses.

In Chapter 21, Carlton provides a thorough review of the history of bias reviews. She also describes two different ways of ensuring that test items are unbiased: the Fairness Review method conducted before a test is administered and the data-based Differential Item Functioning (DIF) method conducted after a test is administered.

Finally, Dolan and Burling (Chapter 22) provide a useful overview of the many ways that computer technology is advancing assessment at the postsecondary level. They describe how computers allow extended activities that can permit finer-grained assessment of student reasoning. They also discuss the range of student data reports provided by computer-based testing, advances in computer-based scoring of constructed response items, computer-adaptive testing, and some ways that computers are used to automate feedback to students for formative assessment. They close with an overview of universal design principles in computer-based testing that are permitting fairer and more precise assessment of students who are not fluent in English and students with learning disabilities.

After reading these chapters, administrators and practitioners should be better able to face with confidence the sundry decisions of their working lives: deciding whether to purchase online curricula with embedded assessments, leading committee meetings around student learning outcomes, outlining institutional research reports, and planning testing systems for academic placement and student support services.

17

BUILDING CONTENT AND STATISTICAL TEST SPECIFICATIONS

Tawnya Knupp and Deborah J. Harris

This chapter deals with building content and statistical specifications. Specifically, classroom assessments, large-scale educational assessments, and licensure and certification exams are discussed. Additionally, the content and statistical specifications for the ACT and the Praxis Series are detailed for illustration purposes. Finally, several practical issues are discussed, including factors affecting the specifications, polytomous items, and test mode considerations.

Perhaps one of the most important aspects of educational measurement is test development, which encompasses numerous activities and can require the participation of a variety of subject matter and measurement experts. In general, test development includes test design, item[1] development, field testing, item evaluation, test assembly, test review, scoring keys, item banking, quality control, and monitoring and improving the test development procedures. In this chapter, we draw attention to test design, one of the most important aspects of test development. In particular, we focus on the development of content and statistical specifications, a crucial component of test design.

The term *test content* indicates the subject matter of an item or test and references a particular ability measured by the item or test (Vaughn, 1951). Content specifications, then, provide a type of summary pertaining to the test content and typically include a list of general topics pertinent to a particular domain[2], with the possible addition of a set of cognitive levels. For instance, the National Board of Dental Examination (NBDE) Part I contains four general content areas (anatomical sciences, biochemistry and physiology, microbiology and pathology, and dental anatomy and occlusion) and three cognitive domains (understanding, application, and reasoning) (Neumann & MacNeil, 2007). Content specifications also include domain weights, which indicate the relative importance of each content area to the domain. Eventually, these weights are transformed into the number of items per category.

Closely tied to content specifications are the statistical specifications. Statistical specifications include summary information about the test items, such as the desired level of item difficulty and the ability of the items to discriminate the lower-achieving examinees from the higher-achieving examinees. Classical statistics, such as difficulty and discrimination indices (see Schaughency, Smith, van der Meer, & Berg, this volume) or IRT-related statistics, such as test information or precision (see Osterlind & Wang, this volume), can be included in the statistical specifications. The objective is that prior to the assembly of a test form, the test content is clearly explained and a plan has been constructed that lays out the intended statistical behavior of the set(s) of items and, possibly, the test scores.

The appropriate development of the content and statistical specifications is extremely important for two main reasons. First, when developing the content and statistical specifications, the construct[3] and test domain are defined and described, and this information is used to assist in the development of an assessment for a given purpose. In other words, content-related validity evidence (see Geisinger, Shaw, & McCormick, this volume) is established during this process. Briefly, content-related validity evidence illuminates "the relationship between a test's content and the construct it is intended to measure" (American Educational Research Association, American Psychological Association, & National Council on Measurement in Education, 1999, p. 11), and is crucial to the appropriate interpretation of test scores. Second, when issues such as item exposure, test security, and retesting situations occur, it is good practice to administer different but equivalent test forms. The content and statistical specifications help ensure that these forms cover the same material and are equally difficult. Test forms designed to be this similar are suitable for equating (see Kolen & Hendrickson, this volume) to adjust for the inevitable difficulty differences that occur, making the scores across forms comparable. Without a well-developed set of content and statistical specifications in place, establishing adequate and defensible validity evidence and interchangeable test scores across different forms becomes suspect.

Building Content and Statistical Specifications

The first step in test development, prior to constructing the content and statistical specifications, is to determine the purpose for the test. Tests can be used to evaluate students' mastery of curricula, assess the benefits of specific educational programs, or place students in particular classes. Tests can also determine scholarship awards, predict college success, or assist with career choice. Obtaining and maintaining licensure and certification in numerous job fields may also depend on test scores. The possible purposes for tests in educational settings are vast, with each purpose impacting test design, assembly, administration, and score use. For the purpose of this chapter, we limit our discussion to cognitive tests, specifically classroom assessments, large-scale educational assessments, and licensure and certification examinations.

Classroom Assessments

Building content and statistical specifications for classroom assessments is typically less formal and less technical compared to building specifications for large-scale, standardized assessments, but is, nonetheless, important. Tests used in the classroom can be administered for a variety of purposes, such as diagnosing students, rank ordering students, and assessing students for formative and summative reasons. For the purpose of this section, we focus on summative assessments. (For a more detailed discussion of classroom assessment, see Drezek McConnell & Doolittle, this volume.) Scores on classroom tests should represent an adequate sample of the material covered in class, which, in turn, should reflect the curriculum or syllabus. (See Appendix A for a discussion on population and samples.) Additionally, if a teacher or professor decides to create a different test form to administer to students who were absent from the original test administration, the second form should be as similar as possible to the first form, ensuring an equitable testing experience.

Classrooms ranging from kindergarten through postsecondary have a set of standards on which the material being presented in the classrooms is based. In elementary, middle, and secondary school systems, this information comes in the form of local or state curricula or from the Common Core State Standards. Postsecondary classrooms, however, can vary somewhat in how the course material is determined. This material can be outlined for the students in a syllabus or textbook or set of course objectives, depending on the institution. Whether the starting point is a specific curriculum or a list of course objectives, the development of content and statistical specifications is relatively similar.

As is the case with all test development, first, the purpose of the test must be clearly stated and understood by the test stakeholders. Purposes for tests used in the classroom can be diagnostic, formative or summative, to name a few, and the test specifications will depend on the purpose. Most frequently, the purpose for classroom tests is to determine how much of the presented material the students have mastered, and this mastery is quantified by the test score. Valid interpretations of the scores rely, in part, on the content representativeness of the test items relative to the material presented. In other words, the content specifications of the test should be a reflection of the course objectives addressed during class.

When developing the content specifications for classroom tests, two dimensions are most commonly referenced: a content dimension and a cognitive level dimension. The content dimension should include several mutually exclusive content categories that adequately summarize the domain. This dimension will typically include the standards[4] that were addressed in class. An appropriate amount of specificity of the standards would allow two different teachers to create two tests with similar content. The cognitive dimension identifies the intellectual processes required for a particular task. Perhaps the best known cognitive taxonomy was proposed by Bloom (Bloom, Englehart, Furst, Hill, & Krathwol, 1956), which includes six levels: knowledge, comprehension, application, analysis, synthesis, and evaluation. However, Bloom's taxonomy is somewhat difficult to employ when developing test specifications. Often the cognitive dimensions include levels such as recall, application, and evaluation. Adding a cognitive dimension to the content specifications further enables two different teachers to create very similar tests.

After the content and cognitive levels are decided, the domain weights must be determined. For classroom assessments, this process is typically based on one of two factors: the proportion of time spent on the particular dimension or the number of objectives subsumed by each dimension. Nitko (2001) advises that content representativeness and relevance can be achieved by (a) emphasizing the material that was taught, (b) representing the curriculum, (c) reflecting the current thinking about the subject area, and (d) including content worth learning.

Subjective judgment also plays a role. For instance, consider the scenario in which a class struggles on a particular objective, resulting in more time being spent on that topic. A second scenario also occurs where one content standard/dimension includes several specific objectives requiring factual recall only, and a second content standard/dimension includes a few general objectives requiring understanding and application of knowledge. In these two scenarios, judgment must be exercised, recognizing that time spent on an objective or the number of objectives must be considered in conjunction with the purpose of the test and the domain to which the scores will generalize.

When developing a classroom test, the domain weights—which reflect the importance of the content and cognitive categories to the domain—are often directly translated to the number of items per category[5]. For instance, if content category 1 has a weight of 40% and content category 2 has a weight of 20%, then category 1 will have twice as many items (or possible points) as category 2. The resulting weights, in the end, should indicate the influence of each content category on the overall score, which should reflect the importance of each category in the test domain to the purpose of the test.

Consider a test domain that includes content areas A, B, and C, and cognitive levels 1 and 2. The content specifications grid will include cells A1, A2, B1, B2, C1, and C2. The proportion of items in each cell should be a representative sample of the domain. Assume the domain indicates an equal importance across content and cognitive dimensions. A test that has one third of the items in area B but more emphasis in cognitive level 2 will not yield test scores that can be generalized to the domain because students with a stronger grasp of cognitive level 2 will potentially be able to compensate for a lower performance on the items in level 1 (see Figure 17.1). In other words, when the proportion of items—and in turn, the number of score points—attributed to the cells of the content specifications do not reflect the composition of the domain, the test scores and the subsequent interpretations will not be valid.

In a sense, the cognitive dimension informally begins to address the statistical specifications. In the case of classroom assessments, the statistical specifications are most likely not applicable in the

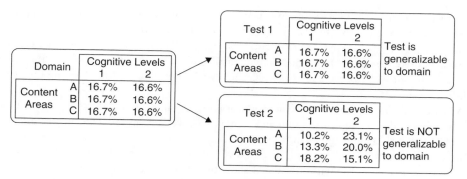

Figure 17.1 Depiction of two tests and the corresponding domain

technical sense of the word. Teachers most likely do not have the time or means to pretest items, calculate item statistics, and develop new tests based on those statistics. (See Nitko, 2001, for a detailed discussion on item analysis and classroom assessments.) However, teachers should consider the intended difficulty of the tests they develop. Certainly, items that involve knowledge level processes could be potentially less difficult than items that require evaluation type processes. Also, by nature, teachers have in their minds how difficult the test questions might be for their students. Perhaps items are chosen because all students should be able to answer them, and some items might be on a test to challenge the higher achieving students. These decisions are based on the teacher's experience and knowledge of the students' abilities and the purpose of the test. Regardless of the lack of technical evidence, the decision of how difficult to make the test should be an intentional process.

While the development of the statistical specifications is an informal process in the classroom, consideration should still be given to issues such as the difficulty and discrimination of the test items. In large-scale assessment programs, items are often designed to vary in difficulty in order to challenge students with differing abilities. However, it is highly possible that a classroom assessment designed to measure mastery of a set of specific learning objectives will have items to which most students respond correctly, assuming they have learned the material. Therefore the difficulty level plays less of a role in item selection and more of a role in describing the item after its administration (Millman & Greene, 1989). However, for tests designed to measure the relative achievement of students, multiple-choice items in which approximately 70% of the examinees respond correctly may be appropriate[6] (Nitko, 2001). Additionally, the items should be written such that the students who have mastered the material answer the items correctly and the students who have not mastered the material answer incorrectly. In other words, the test items should discriminate between passing and failing students. It is important to remember that the content and statistical specifications work simultaneously. Writing a difficult question that covers content not in the specifications may challenge the higher-achieving students. However, the resulting scores become less valid when making generalizations to the test domain. These considerations are also applicable when tests are developed to separate the class into multiple categories, such as earning an A, B, C, D, or F. (See Nitko, 2001, Popham, 2002, and Shepard, 2006 for a more detailed discussion of classroom assessment.)

To reiterate, the content and statistical specifications of classroom assessments allow for valid interpretation of test scores. If the test content includes a non-representative sample of the domain, then the scores do not reference the amount of the domain that has been mastered. For instance, a vocabulary test given in an English class will yield scores that are indicative of the students' vocabulary and not of other English-related abilities, such as writing prose or editing drafts. The specifications also allow for two forms of the same test to be similarly constructed. This is important when additional testing administrations occur and when the tests will be used in the course over multiple semesters. Finally, when the same classes and courses are being taught by multiple teachers, content and statistical specifications can be used to help ensure that the tests across classes and courses are as similar as possible. The goal is to ensure a fair testing experience for all students and to obtain valid interpretations and test scores.

Large-Scale Educational Assessments

Developing the content and statistical specifications for large-scale assessments is similar to the development of classroom assessments, except the process is much more formal. This increase in formality and technicality is a direct result of the differences in purpose of the tests and available resources for test development. For a classroom assessment, the material covered in the curriculum is available to the teachers prior to writing the test, and the delivery of the material is specific to a class or school. Large-scale assessments, on the other hand, are designed to reach a much wider audience. For instance, a science test might include material that is taught within and across states and is intended for a state-wide, multi-state or national audience. Additionally, inferences regarding the test scores need to be valid and useful because higher-stakes decisions are often made based on these scores, placing the validity of the scores under scrutiny. Therefore, the process of determining the content and statistical specifications are formally documented and supported with technical evidence.

Determining the domain for a large-scale assessment depends on the purpose for the assessment and the existing documentation pertinent to the domain and purpose. In some cases, pre-existing documents may be of great benefit. For instance, the development of a national mathematics exam for elementary school students might include collecting the math standards from the National Council of Teachers of Mathematics or obtaining a copy of the Common Core State Standards[7]. A state-wide assessment designed for accountability purposes will utilize the state's curricula. In these cases, the standards and objectives should be used in the development of the content specifications.

However, in many instances, a testing organization will need to gather additional information that best represents the purpose of the test. End-of-course (EOC) exams administered to high school students may be designed in such a way as to indicate not only mastery of curricula but also readiness for college success. QualityCore® (ACT, 2010) is a collection of teacher resources, formative items, and summative assessments specific to several high school course areas. The course and content information for this program were gathered, in part, from the results of a study (ACT & The Education Trust, 2004) that looked at high-minority, low-income schools with particularly large percentages of students who met or exceeded the ACT college readiness benchmarks, as these schools offered important information about the factors that played a role in the success of minority and low-income students. This information was used in conjunction with additional research to develop a set of course standards. Then, a group of teachers from high achieving high schools reviewed the standards. Through this process, the content specifications for the QualityCore® assessments were developed (ACT, 2010).

Norman Webb might have said it best: "Identifying the content of a test designed to measure students' content knowledge and skills is as much an art as it is a science" (2006, p. 155). The science part may include a standardized procedure for collecting, comparing, and synthesizing various curricula. However, determining the specificity of the content areas/categories in the content specifications is a bit of an art and, ultimately, depends on the purpose of the test. For academic achievement tests, content specificity can be established fairly easily, and like classroom assessments, the content specifications should enable the construction of two (or more) forms of a test that have very similar content (Millman & Greene, 1989). Additionally, for tests designed to measure mastery of a set of objectives, a greater degree of specificity of the test's content is necessary compared to tests designed to, say, distinguish between or sort students relative to their knowledge of a specific subject (Webb, 2006).

Collecting curricula, using state and national standards, and seeking the input of teachers are ways of ensuring the alignment between the domain and test content when developing content specifications. Webb (2006) discusses in detail four criteria used to align the content with the domain: categorical concurrence, depth-of-knowledge consistency, range-of-knowledge correspondence, and balance of representation. Categorical concurrence requires the test and the domain to address the same content categories. Depth-of-knowledge consistency is achieved when the complexity of a test item matches the intended task complexity, as listed in a curriculum or state's standards document, for example. Range-of-knowledge correspondence refers to the similarity between the breadth and/or depth of the knowledge on the test and in the domain. Finally, balance of representation is obtained when the emphasis of each objective on the test is similar to the objective's emphasis in the test domain.

Once the content categories are established, the domain weights are determined. Domain weights are indications of the relative importance of each category (Vaughn, 1951), and thus require judgments to be made. One method of establishing domain weights is to draft a set of weights and ask for feedback from a panel of experts. This initial draft of domain weights can involve documenting the number of pages allocated in the textbooks to a particular topic and then using the median number of pages to gauge the importance of that topic (Tinkelman, 1971; Vaughn, 1951), which is based on the, perhaps inaccurate, assumption that the number of pages indicates importance. However, instead of asking a panel to provide comments on a pre-established set of weights, it is also possible to ask a sample of experts, such as teachers or subject matter experts, to indicate the relative weight of each topic (Tinkelman, 1971), referred to as pooled judgments of authorities (Vaughn, 1951). In this case, the median percents could be used to initially establish the domain weights. Ultimately, the final decision regarding the content specifications typically involves the affirmation by a panel of experts.

Content specifications need to be regularly monitored. Collecting and examining curricula is perhaps the most common way to gauge content shifts. However, curriculum surveys administered to a representative sample of a particular population of teachers are also an effective way to elicit input. Every three to five years, ACT administers a national curriculum survey to keep abreast of what students need to know to be ready and able for college coursework (ACT, 2009). National surveys are also effective tools to determine how curricula change and evolve over time, such as the work by Russell and Stouffer (2005) in their examination of civil engineering curricula. These types of investigations are necessary for monitoring the stability of the content standards and aiding in future test development practices.

Special attention needs to be given to the sampling procedures used throughout the development of the content and statistical specifications, particularly when selecting survey participants, choosing the test content from the domain, and field testing items. First, when determining the participants of a large-scale survey, the sample should be proportionally representative of the population relative to predetermined characteristics, such as years of experience, job title, and location and size of place of work. Second, once the content specifications have been established, the selected content (or sample of standards) included in the content specifications should be representative of the test domain. Finally, consideration should also be given to the sampling procedure used to select the examinees taking the pretest items, making sure the examinees taking the pretest items are representative of the population of examinees potentially taking the future operational test. All of the information gathered above will be generalized to a larger population, and the validity of such interpretations depends upon the representativeness of the samples to the population.

Once the content specifications are established, the statistical specifications can be drafted. The statistical specifications indicate the desired behavior of the item scores, and this behavior can be based on classical test theory (CTT; see Shaughency et al., this volume) or item response theory (IRT; see Osterlind & Wang, this volume). The desired specifications may be of help to the item writers prior to creating the items, as the intended difficulty levels can provide targets toward which the writers work. However, after the items have been pretested[8], the statistical specifications can play a major role in item selection.

Pretested items are test items that are administered to a group of examinees but do not impact the test scores. In some cases, these items can be intermingled with the operational test questions[9]. In other cases, the items may be administered separately from the actual test. In either case, the goal is to acquire some insight as to how the items will behave when they are administered as part of an operational test. In other words, the item statistics are calculated and used to make decisions about the future use of the items to create test forms.

Once the responses are gathered from the pretest items, the statistical characteristics of the items can be determined. This process begins with scoring the examinees' responses. Multiple-choice questions are examples of dichotomously scored items. If the answer to a test item is correct, a score of 1 is given. An incorrect answer receives a score of 0. Each examinee's response string is scored, resulting in a vector (or string) of 0s and 1s. These score vectors are used to calculate the item statistics. Constructed-response items are examples of polytomously scored items, where there are more than two possible scores. For instance, the response to an open-ended mathematics item might be worth 0, 1, 2, or 3 points, depending on the degree of correctness. This section deals primarily with dichotomous items. Polytomously scored items are discussed later in the chapter.

In CTT, item statistics typically involve difficulty and discrimination indices. The most commonly used difficulty index is simply the proportion of correct responses for that particular item. This index can range from 0 (where all examinees respond incorrectly) to 1 (where all examinees respond correctly). Sometimes confusing, a relatively high difficulty index means that a relatively large proportion of examinees answered the item correctly. In other words, a large difficulty index implies the item was relatively easy. One of the simpler discrimination indices is the difference between the proportion of high-ability students responding correctly and the proportion of low-ability students responding correctly. Conceptually, this index is a measure of how well the item is discriminating between the high- and low-achieving students, and can theoretically range from –1 to 1. Typically, the index will take on positive values. The items with indices greater than 0 do a better job of discriminating between the upper and lower groups of students compared to the items with indices less than 0. Items with a negative discrimination index indicate that the examinees who performed poorly on the exam are correctly responding to the item more often than the examinees that performed well, and this situation should not occur with well-constructed tests. Difficulty and discrimination indices are often considered simultaneously when developing CTT statistical specifications because extremely easy (or extremely difficult) items can have lower discrimination indices compared to items with moderate difficulty levels.

There are several other difficulty and discrimination indices that can be calculated and used in item selection. For instance, a common discrimination index is the biserial correlation, which is a measure of the relationship between the item score and a criterion score, such as the total test score. Again, items with biserial correlations greater than 0 (especially those greater than 0.20) are considered to discriminate between the higher and lower achieving students. Regardless of the choice of indices, the goal with all item analyses is to find the items that are appropriately difficult[10] and are functioning in expected ways. (See Gulliksen, 1950, for a seminal discussion of item analyses.)

In IRT, determining the item statistics is more complicated, and while some of the same terminology is used, the interpretations are slightly different. (See Hambleton & Jones, 1993, for a comparison of CTT and IRT models.) Conceptually, the IRT models attempt to explain an examinee's performance on one or more parameters such as a difficulty parameter (b), a discrimination parameter (a), and a guessing parameter (c) (see Figure 17.2). In this case, difficulty is not the proportion

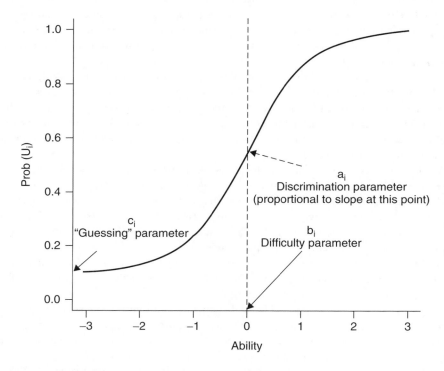

Figure 17.2 Item characteristic curve for a 3-parameter IRT model

of examinees with correct responses, but it is, in a sense, a measure of how difficult the item was. For example, in Figure 17.2, the item difficulty is 0. As *b* moves toward the positive values of the ability axis, the item becomes more difficult. Similarly, the discrimination indices in CTT and IRT are calculated in two very different ways; but, conceptually, both indices indicate the extent to which the high-ability students are responding correctly and the low-ability students are responding incorrectly. As the item's discrimination index increases, the slope of the item characteristic curve will increase. In other words, with highly discriminating items, the probability of a lower achieving examinee responding to an item correctly is considerably less than the probability of a higher achieving examinee responding correctly. The difficulty and discrimination indices are used in determining an item's information function[11]. This function can show for which examinee ability levels the item is most precisely estimating. The item information functions can be combined to determine the test's information function. The test's information function can be used to ensure that the most precise test scores are occurring at the most crucial parts of the score scale—at the cut score, for example.

An additional consideration is the consistency of the difficulty and discrimination indices across content areas. Consider the fairly simple example of a test comprised of two content categories, each with a domain weight of 50%. Now assume that the first category is comprised of very easy items, and the second category contains moderately difficult items. The scores for the first category will have a relatively small variance compared to the variance of the second category. This means that the variance of the total scores is most affected by the second category. In other words, the examinees' scores will be different because of the difference in the second category's scores, which means that the second category has a greater effective weight[12] than the first category even though the domain weights are equal.

The purpose of the test is, ultimately, the driving force when developing the statistical specifications for an assessment. For instance, it may be best when developing a norm-referenced, 7th grade mathematics test to choose items with large discrimination indices and average difficulty values (Millman & Greene, 1989), as it will spread out student scores the most. A high school exit exam with one cut score separating the passing from failing students might best be served with items that yield the highest test information at that cut point. Similarly, a test that classifies students into one of multiple categories will best be served with items with statistical variety at each cut score in order to reliably score examinees in all classification categories (Schmeiser & Welch, 2006). There is not a one-size-fits-all prescription for determining a test's statistical specifications for the wide variety of assessments. However, for all types of assessments administered to all types of students, the statistical specifications depend on the purpose of the exam. (See Ferrara & DeMauro, 2006, and Millman & Greene, 1989, for detailed discussions on developing tests of achievement and ability.)

Licensure and Certification Exams

Licensure and certification exams are used in a variety of occupations to determine candidates' levels of competency for a particular profession. (See Clauser, Margolis, & Case, 2006, for a more detailed discussion of testing in the professions.) For instance, in the United States, a nurse must pass a licensure exam in order to legally practice as a practical, vocational, or professional nurse (Oermann & Gaberson, 2009), and future teachers across the country often must pass at least one certification exam, such as the Praxis Series (Educational Testing Service, 2010), before obtaining a valid teaching license. These types of exams are extremely high-stakes in that the test scores and corresponding classifications are often used to protect the public when deciding on candidates' professional capabilities. Therefore, paying close attention to the development and implementation of the content and statistical specifications for licensure and certification exams is crucial.

Developing the content specifications for these licensure and certification exams may be somewhat more time intensive relative to academic achievement tests. Consider the situation in which a test is being developed to determine if an examinee has acquired a set of knowledge, skills and abilities (KSAs) necessary for appropriate (safe and ethical) participation in a particular profession. The test developers and measurement experts have many tasks to accomplish, including, but certainly not limited to (a) gathering information about the tasks and KSAs of the profession, (b) determining the importance of the tasks and KSAs relative to successful job performance, and (c) translating the importance of the tasks and KSAs into a test blueprint.

An exam that determines whether a person is ready or able to enter a profession not only covers content relevant to that profession, but also places emphasis on the most crucial aspects of the job. Typically, this type of information is gathered by the test developers via a practice analysis. There are several types of practice analyses, such as the critical incident technique (CIT; Flanagan, 1954), the functional job analysis (FJA; Fine & Wiley, 1971), the professional practice model (PPM; LaDuca, Downing, & Henzel, 1995), and the task inventory, to name a few. Each type of practice analysis can vary based on who is participating in the analysis and on the phrasing and specificity of the listed tasks and KSAs (Raymond, 2002). J. E. Knapp and L. G. Knapp (1995) suggest a general approach, which includes (a) creating an advisory committee, (b) reviewing the literature and documents relevant to the profession of interest, (c) interviewing practitioners, (d) constructing a survey instrument, (e) pilot testing the survey, (f) finalizing and administering the survey to a particular group of experts, and (g) analyzing the survey data and preparing a report.

Practice analysis surveys can vary a great deal, and depend on the purpose of the test. Typically, these questionnaires involve items about (a) job-related activities and tasks and/or (b) the KSAs that are required of the worker (Raymond, 2001). The former utilizes scales that focus on the *job* components. The latter utilizes scales based on the *person* components. Rating the job components often requires a judgment about (a) what is involved in the activity, (b) the time needed to complete the activity, (c) the activity's importance, and (d) the difficulty of the activity. Rating the person components often requires judgment about KSAs, specifically regarding (a) the frequency of use, (b) the importance of the particular KSA, and (c) the relationship between the KSA and job performance. Again, the type of development preference depends on the purpose of the test.

Certainly the format and content of the practice analysis questionnaires will also vary. However, there are some similarities across the instruments. Typically, the item responses are in a Likert-type format, requiring the participants to indicate their response on a scale of, say, 1 to 3. For example, a practicing dentist might have to indicate the criticality of the statement "Using an x-ray to identify a cavity" by indicating either "very important," "somewhat important," or "not important." The same statement may also require a response regarding the frequency of the skill's implementation, such as "often needed," "sometimes needed," or "rarely needed." The responses to all of the items on the questionnaires are combined in a systematic way—such as assigning numbers to the responses—and are eventually translated into content specifications. For instance, the items with the highest (sums of) ratings would be molded into sections of the content specifications, and items with the lowest (sums of) ratings would either be excluded altogether or combined with the other higher rated items. The domain weight assigned to each section should represent the importance of the skills necessary to be successful as an entry level professional.

For the purpose of this section, we assume the proper steps have been taken to finalize the survey instrument, and it is ready to be administered. (See J. E. Knapp and L. G. Knapp (1995), for a more detailed discussion of the entire process.) The selection of the survey participants should not be overlooked because the results from the survey will be generalized to a much larger population. Sample characteristics, such as the organization's size, the participants' years of experience, the company's location, and so forth, may impact the survey responses and, in turn, impact the content-related validity evidence of the test scores. For instance, the skills and abilities necessary to be a lawyer in a large city may not totally overlap with the skills and abilities needed in a less urban setting. However, if the candidates will be practicing law in urban and/or rural settings, the test's design should reflect that.

Once the surveys are administered and collected, the responses can be translated into content specifications. The content standards and cognitive levels have to be established along with the weights for each cell in the content specifications table. Before choosing a method to determine the weights, it is important to keep in mind that the point values for the survey responses are typically ordinal-level data. In other words, the difference between a score of 1 ("rarely") and 2 ("sometimes") is not the same as the difference between 2 ("sometimes") and 3 ("often"); the scores simply order the responses. Another complexity of these scores is that the same statement describing a task may be used to evaluate the frequency *and* importance of that particular task. Certainly a 3 ("often") on the frequency scale does not have the same meaning as a 3 ("extremely important") on the importance scale.

Mathematically speaking, because ordinal-level data define a position (e.g., 1 = least, 3 = most) and not a size or quantity, they should not be added or multiplied together. However, often the nature of ordinal level data is ignored[13]. For example, two simple methods of combining survey responses are to simply sum the ratings for each item (frequency + criticality + difficulty) or to multiply the item ratings (Raymond & Neustel, 2006). The weight of the objectives can then be determined based on the sums or products of each item. These results can then be used by a panel of experts in the revision and finalization of the content specifications.

More formalized analyses of the survey data can also be conducted. One example of how to deal with a survey's ordinal-level data is described by Spray and Huang (2000), which illustrates how to use an IRT model to convert the ordinal data[14] to interval data and then to item weights. This model is fairly complex and requires many assumptions of the data that may not be met. For example, the Rasch rating scale model (Andrich, 1978) assumes the survey is unidimensional; in other words, the survey should measure one, and only one, construct. Other analyses, such as reliability estimates or factor analyses, require interval[15] data; conducting such analyses with ordinal data yields results that are difficult to interpret. The important point is that careful consideration needs to be given to the methodology used to move from the domain to test content. The employed procedures must be defensible, both conceptually and statistically, given the high-stakes nature of these tests, and the decision regarding the appropriateness of the methodology varies. For instance, in the case mentioned above (Spray & Huang, 2000), the employment of the methodology of transforming ordinal to interval was defensible and effective, and IRT can be particularly useful when needing to work with and/or compare different subscores because the scores will be on the same scale.

As was the case with the large-scale achievement tests, the determination of the statistical specifications for licensure and certification exams depends on the purpose of the test. For instance, if the test is designed to separate examinees into two categories, pass or fail, then the statistical specifications should be designed to most effectively distinguish between the two classifications. More specifically, the items should discriminate best at the cut score, and, ideally, would be written such that half of the people with an ability level at the cut score answer correctly (Henrysson, 1971). However, if the purpose of the test is to determine specific degrees of mastery or levels of certification, then test items that efficiently separate the examinees across the spectrum of ability levels are necessary. More specifically, items with a range of difficulty levels—especially with an approximately equal number of items across the difficulty levels or ranges—most efficiently discriminate students with a wide range of abilities (Henrysson, 1971). Ultimately, the statistical specifications, content specifications, and available resources work cooperatively when test developers select items for test forms. Again, the goal is to choose items that most effectively establish reliable and valid test scores, relative to the purpose of the test.

Examples

Published tests should provide relatively detailed descriptions of the test development processes (AERA, APA, & NCME, 1999), allowing for the appropriate selection of tests given a specific purpose. Typically this information is presented in a technical manual, and most test publishers have their technical manuals publically available. In this section, details about the content and statistical specifications of two large-scale assessments, the ACT test and the Praxis Series, are summarized. This information can be read in detail by accessing the technical manuals from ACT (2007) and the Educational Testing Service, ETS (2008), respectively.

The ACT

The ACT test is part of ACT's larger Educational Planning and Assessment System (EPAS), which includes two other assessments administered at grades 8, 9, or 10. The ACT is designed to measure high school students' general educational development and readiness for college coursework. The foundations for the test's content are the knowledge and skills in the high school curricula that are prerequisite to success in entry-level postsecondary courses. While EPAS used in its entirety provides the most comprehensive information for students as they plan for their postsecondary education, this section will focus solely on the ACT, specifically the development of its content and statistical specifications.

The initial development of the ACT began with collecting information regarding the content typically covered in middle and high school courses in the domains of English, reading, math, and science. First, states' published curricula were gathered and textbooks were reviewed. Then, the curricula and textbook content was used to develop a survey, which was administered to a national sample of college and university personnel who were qualified to make judgments regarding the appropriateness of the content as it related to college success. Panels of content experts at the secondary and post-secondary levels were also consulted as the knowledge and skills in the four content areas were finalized.

The four tests comprising the ACT battery[16]—English, Reading, Mathematics, and Science—include dichotomously scored items[17]. The content specifications for these tests include four to six content categories with the number and proportion of items in each area. The statistical specifications are also described in the technical manual. The average difficulty is targeted at 0.58 (with item difficulties ranging from 0.20 to 0.89), and the item biserial correlations should be at least 0.20. Simply put, the tests have a medium difficulty level and discriminate well between the low- and high-achieving examinees. This information gives users important knowledge when determining the appropriateness of using ACT scores in decision making processes and when interpreting test scores.

The ACT has been administered for decades and, to ensure the continued adequacy of the test specifications, periodic reviews are conducted. This process involves reviewing textbooks, curriculum guides, and state standards, as well as convening panels of content experts. Most significantly, a large-scale research endeavor, called the ACT National Curriculum Survey, is conducted every three to five years (ACT, 2009). While the test developers work to ensure that the specifications remain stable across time, this newly gathered information is used to develop and refine item types within the specific content categories. For more information, see the ACT technical manual (ACT, 2007).

The Praxis Series

The Praxis Series is a nationally administered set of assessments designed to assist states in the licensing and certification of teachers new to the profession. The Praxis I tests measure basic academic competency in reading, writing and mathematics. The Praxis II tests assess specific content areas and professional knowledge. The content covered by the Praxis II tests is determined through committee work and job analysis surveys. Additionally, input from educators and state departments of education are used in item writing and revision. While all tests in the Praxis Series are available nationally, states can select the tests required for new teachers and set their own passing scores.

The development of a Praxis test begins with identifying a list of tasks and KSAs via a job analysis. The job analysis includes reviewing available documentation regarding the necessary KSAs pertinent to a particular test, utilizing input from a panel of experts to revise the KSA list, and confirming the importance of the KSA to the domain by consulting professionals. Special consideration is given to the selection of panelists and professionals giving input on the development process to ensure adequate representativeness.

The Praxis Series includes numerous content tests, and the specific content specifications for each test are not presented in the technical manual, but are available for free for those who register to take the exam(s). The statistical specifications of the tests are addressed. Specifically, extremely difficult items—those with low average scores—and items with low discrimination indices (correlation to a criterion) are flagged and reviewed by measurement experts prior to operational use. This includes both multiple choice and constructed response items.

Similar to the process for the ACT, the Praxis tests are periodically reviewed to make sure the content covered by the tests is applicable and appropriate for making valid interpretations. ETS refers to this as validity maintenance. Typically test content is reviewed about every five years, unless there is an anticipation that the content may evolve faster, especially in areas of science and technology. This review is conducted by National Advisory Committees. For more information regarding the test development process, see the Praxis Technical Manual (ETS, 2008).

Practical Issues

Developing content and statistical specification for assessments is often an involved and on-going process. This chapter has touched on some of the major aspects of test specifications. However, there are other issues worth mentioning that can influence the development process. This section addresses some additional factors affecting the content and statistical specifications, the inclusion of polytomous items, and the effect of test mode on specifications.

Factors Affecting Content and Statistical Specifications

Certainly the purpose of the test is the driving force behind the test design, and this chapter focuses on two test-design aspects: content and statistical specifications. However, there are several additional factors to consider, and they are worth mentioning because ultimately they could influence some of the details of the content and statistical specifications. First, establishing the connection between the purpose of the test and the test domain is crucial. For instance, assume an organization is building a test for the purpose of course placement for incoming freshmen students. Should the test domain be based on what the examinees learned in their high school course work, or should the test domain be based on the necessary knowledge and skills needed to be successful in a particular college course? The answer to this question will impact all subsequent test development issues, such as the content and format of the test items, the test specifications, and test assembly, to name a few.

A second important consideration is translating the domain weights to the number of items. In the simplest case, the domain weights (listed as percents) translate directly to the number of items. For instance, a content area with a domain weight of 25% would include 25 items. However, because the domain weights sum to 100%, the test form will have a total of 100 items. Therefore, this method is only appropriate if the examinees' age and the available administration time allows for a 100 item test form. A second method of translating the domain weights to the number of items is to use the domain weights as the percentage of items for each content area. For example, a domain weight of 25% would imply that 25% of the test form's items will belong to that content area. However, each content area should have enough items to obtain a reliable score, especially if content-area subscores will be reported. A third method is to use the domain weights as the percent of possible points for each content area. For example, a content area with a domain weight of 25% would include items that have a total score equal to 25% of the test's total score. An issue arises with these three methods when the difficulties of the items across the content areas vary considerably, which results in the different variances of the content category scores. When the variances are different, the effective weights do not reflect the domain weights. The final method of translating the domain weights is to choose the number of items for each content category that will yield effective weights that are similar to the domain weights (Vaughn, 1951). The technicalities of this process are beyond the scope of this chapter. Conceptually, however, the goal is to select the number of items such that the content categories' score variances and covariances can be determined. Then the effective weights can be estimated, and the number of items can be adjusted so that the effective and domain weights are comparable.

Ultimately, the number of items included in the test and in each subsection will impact the reliability of the test and subsections' scores. The number of items will depend on the administration time available, the age of the students, and the types of interpretations that will be made from the results. Additionally, reliability will increase when the differences between (a) the item/test scores *within* examinee ability groups are relatively small compared to (b) the item/test scores *between* examinee ability groups. Similarly, reliability will increase when the difficulties of the items are moderate for the ability of the group and there is a wide range of abilities within the examinee group. Finally, item discrimination and reliability also have an important relationship; "working to improve the discrimination of the individual items in most classroom tests is probably the most effective means of improving score reliability and, hence, test quality" (Ebel & Frisbie, 1991, p. 90).

A third important consideration affecting the content and statistical specifications is the group of intended test-takers. This group is the examinee population to whom the test will be potentially administered and for whom the scores will be used. Characteristics of this group—such as age, prior knowledge and experiences, and educational level, to name a few—will impact item format, item difficulty, test administration, and test mode. For instance, tests designed for college-level students typically have more options from which to choose on multiple-choice items, have longer testing sessions, and are more apt to be administered via computer compared to tests designed for younger, elementary school students (Schmeiser & Welch, 2006).

A fourth consideration is administration constraints. These constraints include issues such as available and appropriate testing time (how much testing time the examinees should have), test mode (paper and pencil versus computer), testing site (at school or a testing facility), security procedures (classroom environment versus a highly controlled, standardized administration), and administrative model (individual or group administration). Again, the administration constraints, once adequately defined, will influence the subsequent test design procedures.

Polytomous Items

The discussion of test item scores and calculating item statistics has been focused on dichotomously scored items only. Dichotomously scored items are those items that are either correct or incorrect, such as multiple choice or true-false questions. In these cases, the examinees receive a 1 for a correct response and a 0 for an incorrect response. However, polytomously scored items, such as constructed response items, have more than two score options. For instance, an open-ended mathematics problem might allow students to earn a score of 1, 2, 3, or 4. While including polytomously scored items may lessen the overall test reliability and increase administration time, these items may also be particularly relevant to the content specifications. When translating the domain weights in the table of content specifications to the number of items on a test form, caution should be used with polytomously scored items. These items require more time for examinees to respond completely and typically are worth more points (or have more weight) than dichotomously scored items. In other words, polytomously scored items can have great influence on the test scores, and this influence needs to be a purposeful decision, which relates back to connecting the purpose of the test with the content specifications.

Item analyses are also performed on polytomously scored items, but the calculations are a bit more complicated due to the increase in possible score points. Several IRT models are available for polytomously scored items (van der Linden & Hambleton, 2010), making it possible to establish IRT-related statistical specifications for these items. Often, simple descriptive statistics are used to determine the value of polytomously scored items, such as the item's score distribution, the percent of examinees at each score point, the average item score, the inter-rater reliability, or the correlation between the item score and the total test score. Similar to the dichotomously scored items, the goal is to select the items that are appropriately difficult and are effectively useful to the purpose of the test.

Test Mode Considerations

With the current technological advances, the role that computers play in testing has increased tremendously. In fact, computers can be used for a variety of activities, ranging from the collection of states' curricula during test development to exam administration and score reporting. (See Drasgow, Luecht, & Bennett, 2006, and Dolan & Burling, this volume, for a detailed discussion of the use of computers in testing and in higher education, respectively.) Here, we focus on the use of computers as a mode of test delivery, and examine how computer-based testing may affect the development of content and statistical specifications.

A computer may be used simply as a tool for administering an intact test form, and we refer to this as computer-based testing (CBT). For CBT, a paper and pencil version and a computer version of the test may be identical in the presentation and sequencing of items. Careful consideration must be given to how the computerized format might change the skills required to respond correctly. For instance, an examinee who is comfortable with technology, able to effectively navigate the display of the item (especially if the item contains a lengthy reading passage or large figure), and is aware of how to appropriately enter a response is likely to earn a higher score than an examinee with the same content knowledge but not having the same familiarity with CBT. This suggests that the paper and pencil and computer versions of a test are potentially not measuring the same abilities (scores are not interchangeable) even though the two tests are identical in content. Therefore, it is necessary to research and document the extent to which the scores from these two versions are interchangeable (AERA, APA, & NCME, 1999).

A computer may also be used, simultaneously, for item selection and test administration, called computer-adaptive testing (CAT). One distinction between CBT and CAT is that CAT selects items on-the-fly and typically bases this selection on the specified content specifications and the examinee's response(s) to the previous item(s). In order to achieve a precise measurement, CAT will administer an easier item if the previous response was incorrect and a more difficult item if the response was correct. Due to this feature, it is necessary to develop items with a wide range of difficulty levels (Way, 2005). Another distinction between CBT and CAT is that CBT is typically a tool for delivering a test form, and CAT delivers items that are selected from an item pool, requiring the item pool to meet the content and statistical specifications. This item pool could contain hundreds of items, and the computer selects an item from the pool (or from a subset of the pool). This design often results in the need for a specific list of item characteristics so that the computer does not randomly choose items that all have the same context (Way, 2005). For example, the item selection process for a CAT science test might ensure that a variety of animal species are presented to the examinees or that a relatively equal number of items referencing males or females—establishing a balance of gender references—are administered. This item specificity, in turn, could influence the specificity of the content specifications. While item selection for paper and pencil tests also considers such characteristics, CAT must do this on-the-fly.

Conclusions

This chapter has touched on some of the important aspects of developing content and statistical specifications for classroom, large-scale educational, and certification and licensure exams. As emphasized, the purpose of the test is central to all subsequent decisions regarding test development. This chapter has focused on summative assessments administered after learning has occurred. However, the same issues need to be addressed when creating tests for other purposes, such as formative (used to guide instruction) and diagnostic decisions.

The three types of assessments (classroom, large-scale, and licensure and certification exams) were used to draw attention to specific techniques used in developing test specifications. These techniques, however, can be used for tests across purposes. For instance, as described in the ACT example, surveys were used to seek the advice of content and professional experts when determining the importance of content relative to college success. It is also possible for classroom assessments to utilize IRT methods in item selection, especially when these assessments are computer-based.

While classroom, large-scale, and licensure and certification assessments are vastly different, the test development process associated with all three types is similar. Specifically, the test purpose should drive test development.

It is worth reiterating that developing and maintaining strong and consistent test specifications is extremely important for two main reasons. First, content-related validity evidence is collected during this process. This information is crucial to the appropriate interpretation and use of test scores. Additionally, and equally important, the content and statistical specifications allow for multiple, similar forms of a test to be developed. This ensures that the examinees have similar testing experiences across administrations of different forms, and assists in the creation of forms that cover the same material and are equally difficult. Forms of this type are necessary when the scores on different forms will be used interchangeably. In short, designing forms to be as similar as possible allows measurement experts to provide scores that are comparable across forms. These specifications are also extremely useful in the item development process and can be used in alignment studies, linking assessments to content standards. As stated earlier, without a solid set of content and statistical specifications in place, establishing adequate and defendable validity evidence and interchangeable test scores across different forms becomes suspect.

Many professionals in higher education will not formally participate in large-scale test development processes. However, most will be users of assessments to determine students' mastery of classroom material, make decisions about college and scholarship acceptance, award students college credit, or to prepare students for licensure and certification exams. Choosing an appropriate test and making valid inferences based on test scores depend on matching the purpose of the test to the test's content. Published content and statistical specifications make this connection clear.

Notes

1 An item is a question or statement on a test or survey that requires a response from an examinee or participant.
2 Domain refers to an overall area of study to which the test scores generalize. Domains can be as specific as one-digit multiplication facts and as general as the dentistry profession.
3 A construct is defined as an abstract (not directly observable) trait. An example of a construct would be readiness to practice law. The domain would be the set of all possible test items that could be used to indicate the degree to which an examinee possesses the construct.
4 A standard describes the knowledge and/or skills that are taught.
5 Determining the length of a test should also be based on other considerations, such as establishing adequate reliability, meeting time constraints, the age of the examinees, and so forth.
6 He lists items of varying types (true-false, 3-option MC, 4-option MC, and 5-option MC) with ranges of difficulty levels, and approximately 0.70 is included in the three MC item types.
7 Information about the Common Core State Standards can be found at http://www.corestandards.org/
8 Pretested items are sometimes referred to as field-tested items.
9 Operational test questions refer to those items on which the examinee's score is based.
10 Deciding on an appropriate level of difficulty is discussed later in this chapter.
11 Depending on the IRT model, additional parameters may also be used.
12 An effective weight is the percentage of contribution that a component has to the total variance.
13 The decision to treat these types of data as ordinal or interval is an unresolved debate between statisticians. For a detailed discussion on this issue, see Knapp (1990).
14 The authors also demonstrate how to convert ordinal data from multiple scales to ordinal data on a single scale.
15 Interval data have equally spaced values with an arbitrary zero point. An example is the Fahrenheit scale used to measure temperature.
16 A battery is a collection of tests used for the same purpose. Often individual test scores and a single battery score are reported.
17 An ACT writing test (polytomously scored) is offered as an optional supplement.

References

ACT (2007). *The ACT technical manual*. Iowa City, IA: Authors. Retrieved from http://www.act.org/aap/pdf/ ACT_Technical_Manual.pdf

ACT. (2009). *ACT national curriculum survey 2009*. Iowa City, IA: Authors. Retrieved from http://www.act. org/research/policymakers/pdf/NationalCurriculumSurvey2009.pdf

ACT. (2010). *QualityCore: Technical manual*. Iowa City, IA: Authors. Retrieved from http://www.act.org/ qualitycore/pdf/TechnicalManual.pdf

ACT & The Education Trust. (2004). *On course for success: A close look at selected high school courses that prepare all students for college*. Iowa City, IA: Authors.

American Educational Research Association, American Psychological Association, & National Council on Measurement in Education. (1999). *Standards for educational and psychological tests*. Washington, DC: American Educational Research Association.

Andrich, D. (1978). A rating formulation of ordered response categories. *Psychometrika, 43*, 561–573.

Bloom, B. S., Englehart, M. D., Furst, E. J., Hill, W. H., & Krathwohl, D. R. (1956). *Taxonomy of educational objectives: Handbook I: Cognitive domain*. New York: David Mckay.

Clauser, B. E., Margolis, M. J., & Case, S. M. (2006). Testing for licensure and certification in the professions. In R. L. Brennan (Ed.), *Educational measurement* (4th ed.; pp. 733–756). Westport, CT: Praeger Publishers.

Dolan, R., & Burling, K. (this volume). *Computer-based testing in higher education*.

Drasgow, F., Luecht, R. M., & Bennett, R. E. (2006). Technology and testing. In R. L. Brennan (Ed.), *Educational measurement* (4th ed.; pp. 471–515). Westport, CT: Praeger Publishers.

Drezek McConnell, K., & Doolittle, P. E. (this volume). *Classroom-level assessment: Aligning pedagogical practices to enhance student learning*.

Ebel. R. L., & Frisbie, D. A. (1991). *Essentials of educational measurement*. Englewood Cliffs, NJ: Prentice Hall.

Educational Testing Services. (2008). The praxis series: Praxis technical manual. Retrieved from http://www. ets.org/Media/Tests/PRAXIS/pdf/PraxisTechnicalManual.pdf

Educational Testing Services. (2010). *The praxis series information bulletin*. Retrieved from http://www.ets.org/ Media/Tests/PRAXIS/pdf/01361.pdf

Ferrara, S., & DeMauro, G. E. (2006). Standardized assessment of individual achievement in K-12. In R. L. Brennan (Ed.), *Educational measurement* (4th ed.; pp. 579–622). Westport, CT: Praeger Publishers.

Fine, S., & Wiley, W. W. (1971). *An introduction to functional job analysis*. Washington, DC: Upjohn Institute for Employment Research.

Flannagan, J. C. (1954). The critical incident technique. *Psychological Bulletin, 51*, 327–358.

Geisinger, K., Shaw, L. H., & McCormick, C. (this volume). *The validation of tests in higher education*.

Gulliksen, H. (1950). *Theory of mental tests* (pp. 363–398). New York, NY: John Wiley & Sons, Inc.

Hambleton, R. K., & Jones, R. W. (1993). Comparison of classical test theory and item response theory and their applications to test development. *Educational Measurement: Issues and Practices, 12*, 38–47.

Henrysson, S. (1971). Gathering, analyzing and using data on test items. In R. L. Thorndike (Ed.), *Educational measurement* (2nd ed.; pp. 130–159). Washington, DC: American Council on Education.

Knapp, J. E., & Knapp, L. G. (1995). Practice analysis: Building the foundation for validity. In J. C. Impara (Ed.), *Licensure testing: Purposes, procedures, and practices* (pp. 93–116). Lincoln, NE: Buros Institute of Mental Measurements.

Kolen, M. J., & Hendrickson, A. (this volume). *Scaling, norming, and equating*.

LaDuca, A., Downing, S. M., & Henzel, T. R. (1995). Systematic item writing and test construction. In J. C. Impara (Ed.), *Licensure testing: Purposes, procedures, and practices* (pp. 117–148). Lincoln, NE: Buros Institute of Mental Measurements.

Millman, J., & Greene, J. (1989). The specification and development of tests of achievement and ability. In R. L. Linn (Ed.), *Educational measurement* (3rd ed.; pp. 335–366). New York, NY: Macmillan Publishing Company.

Neumann, L. M., & MacNeil, R. L. (2007). Revisiting the national board dental examination. *Journal of Dental Education, 71*, 1281–1292.

Nitko, A. J. (2001). *Educational assessment of students* (3rd ed.). Upper Saddle River, NJ: Prentice-Hall, Inc.

Oermann, M. H., & Gaberson, K. B. (2009). *Evaluation and testing in nursing education*. New York, NY: Springer Publishing Company.

Osterlind, S. J., & Wang, Z. (this volume). *Item response theory in measurement, assessment, and evaluation for higher education*.

Popham, W. J. (2002). *Classroom assessment: What teachers need to know*. Boston, MA: Allyn and Bacon.

Raymond, M. R. (2001). Job analysis and the specification of content for licensure and certification exams. *Applied Measurement in Education, 14*, 369–415.

Raymond, M. R. (2002). A practical guide to practice analysis for credentialing examinations. *Educational Measurement: Issues and Practices, 21*, 25–37.

Raymond, M. R., & Neustel, S. (2006). Determining the content of credentialing examinations. In S. M. Downing, & T. M. Haladyna (Eds.), *Handbook of test development* (pp. 181–223). Mahwah, NJ: Lawerence Erlbaum Associates, Inc.

Russell, J. S., & Stouffer, W. B. (2005). Survey of the national civil engineering curriculum. *Journal of Professional Issues in Engineering Education and Practice, 131*, 118–128.

Schaughency, E., Smith, J., van der Meer, J., & Berg, D. (this volume). *Classical test theory and higher education.*

Schmeiser, C. A., & Welch, C. J. (2006). Test development. In R. L. Brennan (Ed.), *Educational measurement* (4th ed.; pp. 307–345). Westport, CT: Praeger Publishers.

Shepard, L. A. (2006). Classroom assessment. In R. L. Brennan (Ed.), *Educational measurement* (4th ed.; pp. 623–646). Westport, CT: Praeger Publishers.

Spray, J. A., & Huang, C. (2000). Obtaining test blueprint weights from job analysis surveys. *Journal of Educational Measurement, 37*, 187–201.

Tinkelman, S. N. (1971). Planning the objective test. In R. L. Thorndike (Ed.), *Educational measurement* (2nd ed.; pp. 46–80). Washington, DC: American Council on Education.

van der Linden, W. J., & Hambleton, R. K. (Eds.). (2010). *Handbook of modern item response theory*. New York, NY: Springer-Verlag.

Vaughn, K. W. (1951). Planning the objective test. In E. F. Lindquist (Ed.), *Educational measurement* (pp. 159–184). Washington, DC: American Council on Education.

Way, W. D. (2005). *Practical questions in introducing computerized adaptive testing for K-12 assessments* (Research Report 05–03). Retrieved from Pearson Educational Measurement website: http://www.pearsoned.com/RESRPTS_FOR_POSTING/ASSESSMENT_RESEARCH/AR6.%20PEM%20Prac%20Questions%20in%20Introl%20Computer%20Test05_03.pdf

Webb, N. L. (2006). Identifying content for student achievement tests. In S. M. Downing, & T. M. Haladyna (Eds.), *Handbook of test development* (pp. 155–180). Mahwah, NJ: Lawerence Erlbaum Associates, Inc.

Appendix A

Populations and Samples

Choosing a representative sample from a population—whether selecting survey participants from a national group of people or a choosing a set of items from an item pool or deciding on content specifications from a domain—is crucial to the validity of the results; the results based on the sample will be generalized to the population. When sampling from a population, the important and defining characteristics should be identified. For instance, when selecting a group of high school teachers to participate in a survey, the sample might be selected based on grade taught, courses covered, years of experience, school size, school type, and school location. The sample is considered representative of the population of all high school teachers if (a) all of the identified characteristics are included and (b) the proportion of teachers with each characteristic is the same in the sample and the population (see Figure 17.3).

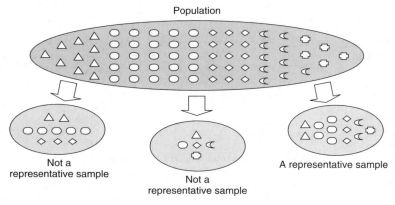

Figure 17.3 A depiction of a population and three potential samples

18

EVIDENCE-CENTERED DESIGN IN ASSESSMENT DEVELOPMENT

Geneva D. Haertel, Ellen Wentland, Louise Yarnall,
and Robert J. Mislevy

Evidence-Centered Design (ECD) is a view of assessment as evidentiary argument; it is an argument from what we observe students say, do, or make in a few circumstances to inferences about what they say, do or make more generally (Mislevy, Steinberg, & Almond, 2002). ECD can serve as a cornerstone of test validation, providing items that are well matched to the domain definition and inferences that can be drawn from students' performances. As the ECD process is implemented and the test is developed, the domain from which the content is drawn is delineated at both general and specific levels and items are created to assess the key aspects of the domain. Thus, both content and construct evidence for validity are built in during the development of the items (Ebel & Frisbie, 1991; Fuhrman, 1996). This chapter lays out the basic ideas of ECD and illustrates its use with two applications in the context of community colleges: (a) developing an assessment for students in commercial vehicle driver training programs (Wentland, 2008), and (b) designing assessments of 21st-century skills across disciplines in a community college curriculum (Yarnall & Ostrander, 2009; Yarnall, Toyama, Gong, Ayers, & Ostrander, 2007).

ECD has a broad range of applications that can offer the developers of outcomes assessments in higher education an opportunity to develop valid content and construct evidence during the construction of test items. The ECD approach can be applied to the development of testing for general education, testing for specific course examinations (especially in career/technical programs), tests used for licensure and certification, as well as tests used to evaluate the effectiveness of community college programs during accreditation reviews.

Layers in Evidence-Centered Assessment Design

ECD is organized around the five layers described in Table 18.1. The layers are referred to in terms of the roles they play in the assessment design and development process: Domain Analysis, Domain Modeling, Conceptual Assessment Framework, Assessment Implementation, and Assessment Delivery. Each layer involves the use of key concepts and entities, knowledge representations, workflow, and communications tools.

Because ECD enables test developers to refine, document, and implement the functions and design decisions within each of the five layers independently, the developers can carry decisions through the other layers to guarantee that the eventual pieces of the operational assessment are consistent with each other and with the intended assessment argument. As the examples in the chapter show, not all elements of all layers may be detailed in a given assessment; different projects,

Table 18.1 Layers of Evidence-Centered Design for Educational Assessments

Layer	Role	Key Entities	Selected Knowledge Representations
Domain Analysis	Gather substantive information about the domain of interest that has direct implications for assessment; how knowledge is constructed, acquired, used, and communicated.	Domain concepts, terminology, tools, knowledge representations, analyses, situations of use, patterns of interaction.	Representational forms and symbol systems used in domain (e.g., algebraic notation, Punnett squares, maps, computer program interfaces, content standards, concept maps).
Domain Modeling	Express assessment argument in narrative form based on information from Domain Analysis.	Knowledge, skills, and abilities; characteristic and variable task features; potential work products; potential observations.	Toulmin and Wigmore diagrams, PADI design patterns, assessment argument diagrams, "big ideas" of science and mathematics.
Conceptual Assessment Framework	Express assessment argument in structures and specifications for tasks and tests, evaluation procedures, measurement models.	Student, evidence, and task models; student, observable, and task variables; rubrics; measurement models; test assembly specifications; PADI templates and task specifications.	Algebraic and graphical representations of measurement models; PADI task template; item generation models; generic rubrics; algorithms for automated scoring.
Assessment Implementation	Implement assessment, including presentation-ready tasks and calibrated measurement models.	Task materials (including all stimulus materials, tools, affordances); pilot test data to hone evaluation procedures and fit measurement models.	Coded algorithms for rendering tasks; interacting with examinees and evaluating work products; tasks as displayed; IMS/QTI representation of materials; ASCII files of item parameters.
Assessment Delivery	Coordinate interactions of students and tasks; task-and test-level scoring; reporting.	Tasks as presented; work products as created; scores as evaluated.	Renderings of materials; numerical and graphical summaries for individuals and groups; IMS/QTI results files.

From "Implications of Evidence-Centered Design for Educational Testing," by R. J. Mislevy and G. D. Haertel, 2006, *Educational Measurement: Issues and Practice*, 25(4), 6–20. Copyright 2006 by John Wiley & Sons. Reprinted with permission.

depending on their nature and purpose, will focus more attention on some layers than on others. Below we will introduce each layer in the assessment design process.

Domain Analysis (Layer 1)

In Domain Analysis, the assessment designer gathers information about concepts, terminology, representational forms, ways of interacting, and so on in the domain to be assessed. Lists of content and process standards, statements of "big ideas," classroom experience, and cognitive research are examples of sources that can be helpful as background for constructing assessments.

In Wentland's (2008) certification test for commercial truck drivers, domain analysis built on a report that identified twenty-four topics in five major subject areas that were judged to be ". . . required subjects for the training of all entry-level drivers" (Commercial Vehicle Training Association & National Association of Publicly Funded Truck Driving Schools, 2007, p. 1).

In Yarnall et al.'s example, domain analysis is operationalized in the identification of the technical content covered in twenty-one classrooms that address five technical areas: computer programming (Python & Ajax), engineering, environmental studies, and bioinformatics (Yarnall, et al., 2007).

Domain Modeling (Layer 2)

In domain modeling, information that is gathered during domain analysis is organized along the lines of an assessment argument. This layer articulates the argument that connects observations of students' actions in various situations to inferences about what they know or can do. In domain modeling, the assessment argument takes a narrative form—the assessment designer may sketch descriptions of proficiencies of interest, observations that provide evidence of those proficiencies, and ways of arranging situations in which students can provide evidence of their proficiencies.

The concern of ECD at this layer is to encourage the assessment designer to relate the construct they are trying to assess to the components of an assessment argument. Toulmin (1958) provided a general structure for such arguments, in terms of claims, data, and warrants. These components provide a starting point for our work in domain modeling. Figure 18.1 illustrates the basic structure of Toulmin's argument form, where W = warrants, B = backing, C = claims, D = data, A = alternative explanations, and R = rebuttal data. The claim refers to the target of the assessment, such as level of proficiency in scientific problem-solving, or ability to use language appropriately in varying contexts. Data refers to the quality of responses to questions, or behaviors observed in particular situations and are provided to support the claims. The warrant is the logic or reasoning that explains why certain data should be considered appropriate evidence for certain claims. Much of the information for constructing the argument will have been marshaled during domain modeling, although cycling across layers is the norm in practice.

Design patterns are examples of a knowledge representation that supports work in the domain modeling layer (Mislevy et al. 2003; Mislevy & Haertel, 2006). Drawing on work in architecture (Alexander, Ishikawa, & Silverstein, 1977) and software engineering (Gamma, Helm, Johnson, & Vlissides, 1994), design patterns help organize information from domain analysis into the form of potential assessment arguments.

Design patterns help designers complete an assessment argument around some theme in the domain of interest, such as model-based reasoning in science or using negotiating apology situations in language testing. The structure of the design pattern is organized around the structure of an assessment argument. Filling in the design patterns thus renders explicit the relationships among the pieces of information in terms of the roles they will play in the argument. We can speak of the assessment structure as provided by the design pattern, and the assessment substance as determined by the assessment designer.

Table 18.2 shows the attributes of a design pattern and their connection to the Toulmin assessment argument, as well as to the student, evidence, and task models of the Conceptual Assessment Framework (CAF), which is discussed in the following section. Centered on the knowledge, skills and abilities (KSAs) in a content domain, a design pattern offers approaches to obtain evidence about those capabilities, organized in such a way as to lead toward designing particular tasks, scoring rubrics, measurement models, and other more technical elements of an assessment.

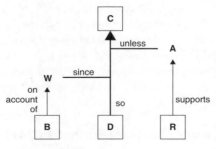

Figure 18.1 Toulmin's (1958) structure of arguments

Source: R. J. Mislevy. Substance and Structure in Assessment Arguments. *Law, Probability and Risk*, 2003, 2(4), 237–258. Reprinted by permission of Oxford University Press.

Table 18.2 Relationship among Assessment Argument Elements and Design Pattern Attributes

Assessment Argument Elements & Guiding Questions	Design Pattern Attribute	Definition of Design Pattern Attribute
	Name	Short name for the design pattern
	Summary	Brief description of the family of tasks implied by the design pattern
	Rationale	Nature of the KSA of interest and how it is manifest
Student Model/Claim	Focal KSAs	The primary knowledge/skills/abilities targeted by this design pattern
	Supported Benchmarks	State benchmarks that this design pattern supports
What construct (complex of student attributes) should be assessed?	Additional KSAs	Other knowledge/skills/abilities that may be required by tasks motivated by this design pattern
Evidence Model/Actions	Potential Observations	Things students say, do, or make that can provide evidence about the Focal KSAs
What behaviors should reveal the construct?	Potential Work Products	Features of Work Products that encapsulate evidence about the Focal KSAs
Task Model/Situation	Characteristic Features	Aspects of assessment situations likely to evoke the desired evidence
What tasks should elicit those behaviors?	Variable Features	Aspects of assessment situations that can be varied in order to control difficulty or target emphasis on various aspects of the KSAs
	Narrative Structures	Aspects of assessment situations that can be varied or combined to construct a scenario or storyboard outline

Wentland (2008) conducted domain modeling by specifying an overall model to guide the test development effort. She moved beyond the general description of the content domain provided in the *Proposed Minimum Performance Measures for Entry-Level Commercial Drivers* document (Commercial Vehicle Training Association & National Association of Publicly Funded Truck Driving Schools, 2007) and applied Zieky's (2006) interpretation of ECD. In this approach, the assessment designer is required to document: (a) the purpose of the test, (b) the inferences or claims that are to be made about students based on their test performance, and (c) the evidence needed to support the claim in terms of knowledge and skills associated with a particular topic.

Yarnall and colleagues use an extended structured interview to elicit information about particular attributes of the design pattern from community college instructors (Yarnall & Ostrander, 2009; Yarnall, et al., 2007). Based on assessment tasks that the instructors have already used in their classes, she elicits information from them about the learning objectives for the course (i.e., KSAs), additional KSAs, the instructional activities that provided students with learning opportunities, and the evidence that the instructor thinks will best demonstrate students' learning. She thus reverse-engineered an existing assessment from each instructor into the design pattern form as a means of documenting information that could be used in the future by other community college instructors to create assessments of problem-based learning.

Conceptual Assessment Framework (CAF) (Layer 3)

The work at Layer 3 focuses on technical specifications for the "nuts and bolts" of the assessment. Three models comprise the CAF: student, evidence, and task. These three models are specified by the assessment designer and are linked via the student-model variables, observable variables, work products, and task model variables (Mislevy & Riconscente, 2006). Detail about task features, measurement models, structures, and stimulus materials are expressed in terms of representations and data structures.

The Student Model identifies aspects of student proficiencies. The number, character, and grain size are determined to serve the purpose of the assessment. The Task Model describes the environment in which students say, do, or make something. It specifies the forms and key features of directives, stimulus materials, and features of the presentation such as simulation capabilities in technology-based tasks. A key decision is specifying the work products—the assessment designer may choose among alternative formats such as multiple choice, open-ended items, performance tasks, oral presentations, or essays. Other examples of task related decisions that assessment designers make include specifying the number, sequence, and complexity of steps to be completed in a multipart task such as an investigation, specifying the "look and feel" of the graphical interface that is used in online assessment tasks, or the degree of scaffolding provided for a task.

The Evidence Model bridges the student and task models. It consists of two sub-models: the evaluation component and the statistical component. The first component is task-level scoring: identifying and evaluating salient aspects of student work to produce values of observable variables. The component, test-level scoring, synthesizes data across tasks using a measurement model, such as simple number-right scores, Item Response Theory (IRT) modeling, or Rasch analyses.

Wentland's example establishes connections among the purpose of the test, the knowledge and skills in a topical content area that have been identified as desired student outcomes, and the test items that are written. These connections support the inferences to be made about the interpretation of a test-taker's score. Student, task, and evidence models are not formally specified, although the identification of the student model occurs in the specification of claims in Levels 2 and 3, and Level 3 foreshadows the observable variables, kinds of stimulus materials, and presentation sequence that will be needed to gather the information necessary to make the desired inferences.

Like Wentland, Yarnall (Yarnall & Ostrander, 2009; Yarnall, et al., 2007) focuses on domain modeling to guide the assessment design process. During the domain modeling process there is detailed documentation of the nature of the items (task features, item format) that will be administered, the scoring rubric to be used, and the scoring/grading procedures used by the instructor to assign a level of performance at the end of the course. The particulars of task specification are left to the teachers who create and implement the assessment tasks in their classrooms.

Assessment Implementation (Layer 4)

The work at this layer is about the construction and preparation of the operational elements specified in the CAF. This includes, authoring tasks, finalizing rubrics or automated scoring rules, estimating parameters in the measurement models, and producing fixed test forms or algorithms to assemble tailored tests. Because of the compatible data structures developed in the prior layers, the assessment designer can leverage the value of the design system for authoring or generating future tasks, calibrating items, presenting materials, or interacting with examinees.

Wentland uses the Levels 1–3 claims to develop multiple performance tasks for each Level 3 claim. The tasks developed are clearly related to the claims and purpose of the assessments developed during the Domain Modeling layer and ultimately to the Domain Analysis of the 24 topic areas (Wentland, 2008).

Yarnall's community college instructors developed items which were reviewed by her for their alignment to the information elicited during the interview. Feedback was provided to the instructors regarding the degree to which the assessments were aligned with the learning objectives, KSAs, and task features that were required to gather the evidence needed to make valid inferences about student performance (Yarnall & Ostrander, 2009; Yarnall, et al., 2007).

Assessment Delivery (Layer 5)

At this layer of ECD, the individual interacts directly with tasks, performances are evaluated, and feedback and reports are produced. The delivery system architecture that has been incorporated in ECD is the Four-Process Delivery System (Almond, Steinberg, & Mislevy, 2002). The Wentland example did not detail an assessment delivery system; the Yarnall example describes an online system for scoring and reporting assessment results.

Example 1. Developing an Assessment for Students in Commercial Vehicle Driver Training Programs

As a result of an association between principals in national truck driver training associations and administrators in a community college, an assessment specialist at the community college was asked to develop a knowledge and skills assessment of students completing commercial vehicle driver training programs in schools nationwide.

The starting point for this process was a report entitled, *Proposed Minimum Performance Measures for Entry-Level Commercial Drivers*, prepared by representatives from the Commercial Vehicle Training Association and the National Association of Publicly Funded Truck Driving Schools (2007). This report identified and outlined twenty-four topics in five major subject areas that were judged to be ". . . required subjects for the training of all entry-level drivers" (p. 1). An example of a subject is Basic Vehicle Operation with the associated topic of Backing. In terms of the ECD model, these subject areas and associated topics provided the Domain Analysis.

General Test Development Process

The first step in developing an assessment for the subject areas was to review the topic descriptions provided in the report, and decide whether the assessment method should be a written test, a yard test, a road test, or some combination. The next step in the process was to identify a model that would guide the test development efforts. The *Proposed Minimum Performance Measures for Entry-Level Commercial Drivers* provided a general description of the content domain, but it was necessary to move from this to a more detailed articulation of outcomes that could lead to item development in the case of written tests, or task descriptions in the case of performance tests. The model selected to structure and guide the assessment efforts was ECD (Zieky, 2006). This approach calls for decisions concerning:

- The purpose of the test. What is the overall goal?
- The inferences we want to make about test-takers. What claims do we want to be able to make about test-takers as a result of their test performance?
- The type of evidence needed to support the claims. What knowledge or skill demonstration concerning which topics would provide the needed evidence?
- The tasks that would provide the needed evidence.

Following this approach, the topics identified to be assessed were each outlined in a series of tables as follows:

- First, the overall purpose of each of the topic tests was defined. These statements typically followed the format: "The overall purpose of the test is to determine . . ." (followed by a specific description of the focus topic).

- Next, a series of three claims was developed, designated as Level 1, Level 2, and Level 3.
- The Level 1 claim was a re-statement of the purpose of the test in terms of the test-taker, and took the form: "A person who passes the test is able to . . ." (followed by a rewording of the test purpose).
- The Level 2 claim(s) identified the sub-topic(s) included in the Level 1 claim, and took the form: "A person who passes the test is able to . . ." (followed by a statement for each sub-topic).
- The Level 3 claim(s) identified the component(s) of the Level 2 claim, and took the form: "A person who passes the test is able to . . ." (followed by a statement for each component).

While the Level 1 claims were the most general claims on the topics, the Level 3 claims were the most specific. These claims were specific enough to point to particular items or tasks. In the case of written tests, these Level 3 claims were also general enough to facilitate the generation of multiple items—a necessary feature to consider for the eventual development of alternate test forms. The linkages from purpose to Level 3 claims were detailed for each test topic. As noted earlier, this series of claims specification is a representational form in Domain Analysis, which has been tailored to the needs of the project.

Once the Level 3 claims were identified, the next step was to specifically develop or specify the items or tasks that would provide the evidence to support those claims—Assessment Implementation, in ECD terms. This process with respect to the written test topics included the development of two multiple-choice items for each Level 3 claim. For the performance tests—the yard and road tests—task descriptions were developed. The specification of items and tasks in conjunction with the Level 3 claims again provided specific linkages between what we want to say about test-takers and the activities (answering items or performing tasks) that would provide the supporting evidence.

An important advantage of this approach is that it is a procedure that builds in validity as part of the test development process. According to Haladyna (1999, p. 222): "Central to the validation process is the idea of evidence. Validity evidence can come in many forms, including statistical, empirical, and even procedural."

The linkages among the claims and the test items support the inferences that will be made about test-takers. By developing items that flow from the Level 3 claims, and having Level 3 claims that flow from the Level 2 claims, and having Level 2 claims that flow from the Level 1 claim, the linkage is made between test items, topic content, and the overall purpose of the test. This connection supports the inferences that will be made concerning the test-takers based on their test results—the interpretation of test scores.

This procedure is a structured approach for creating the test items and tasks, ensuring that they relate to the defined test content. According to Ebel and Frisbie (1991)

> If the items have been written to match the domain definition precisely, the inferences we wish to make . . . can be highly valid. From this point of view, a major portion of the answer to the validity question is inherent in the test development process. That is, content related- evidence is furnished simultaneously with test development activities. The domain definition (boundaries of content to be included), judgments about the relevance of test items, and steps taken to achieve representativeness of content serve the dual purpose of guiding test development and documenting validation evidence. *(p. 104)*

The approach of building in validity during test development is a content validity approach, which was used in the development of this assessment. The content was carefully delineated, following the ECD model, at general and increasingly specific levels. Items and tasks were developed to link or relate to the identified content.

As noted above, some of the topics were judged to be best assessed by means of a written test, while for others performance tests were developed. The remainder of this section will offer a brief summary of the process used to develop the performance assessment.

Development of the Performance Tests

As noted above, the focus of this section will be the development of the performance tests. These are tests to evaluate student abilities with respect to actual vehicle maintenance and operation, both in "yard" and "road" environments. For the initial development of the yard and road test tables, including the identification of specific tasks, the textbooks and regulations manual were reviewed, followed by consultation with two subject matter experts.

All of the information was next subjected to a review via a series of three lengthy conference calls with the same panel of subject matter experts used for the written test reviews. In preparation for these calls, detailed memoranda were distributed along with the tables to be discussed during the calls. Again, the reviews were of the chain of claims as well as of the specific tasks identified. Suggestions were taken, revisions made, and then distributed for final review during a subsequent call. Ultimately, the subject matter experts verified the chain of claims and the relatedness of the tasks to the defined content. As noted above, this review of the entire content of the tables developed in this approach is essential to support the overall content validity of the test.

Figure 18.2 provides a description of the application of the ECD model, using the structure described in this section, to the topics included in the development of the performance tests, using the Backing Yard test topic as an example. In Figure 18.2, the process is represented as a series of sequential steps, or as a chain of claims. This chain can flow in either direction, somewhat equivalent to using an inductive or deductive approach.

Yard tests

Four topics were identified to be assessed at least in part via a yard test. Following the ECD methodology, two tables were developed for each of these topics, with the first table displaying the topic outline in the *Proposed Minimum Performance Measures for Entry-Level Commercial Drivers*. This was followed by a statement concerning the overall purpose of the test—a statement derived from the *Proposed Minimum Performance Measures for Entry-Level Commercial Drivers* descriptions. Also included in the first table was the equivalent of the written test topics for the Level 2 claim, where the overall topic is divided into major sub-topics. The second table for each yard test topic restated the Level 2 claim from the first table, and added the components or tasks related to each of the sub-topics. These task lists are the equivalent of the Level 3 claims for the written test topics. The number of tasks to be performed by the test-takers varied for each of the performance subjects, depending on the number of sub-topics and components associated with each.

Road test

Seven topics had been identified to be assessed, at least in part, via a road test. Two tables were again prepared for the road test, combining all of the topics to be covered. This combination was necessitated because a road test is conducted on one occasion, with all identified tasks to be performed in the context of this occasion. As with the yard tests, the second table included a specification of the tasks to be performed in conjunction with each of the road test topics. Also, as with the yard tests, the number of associated tasks varied depending on the number of associated sub-topics and components.

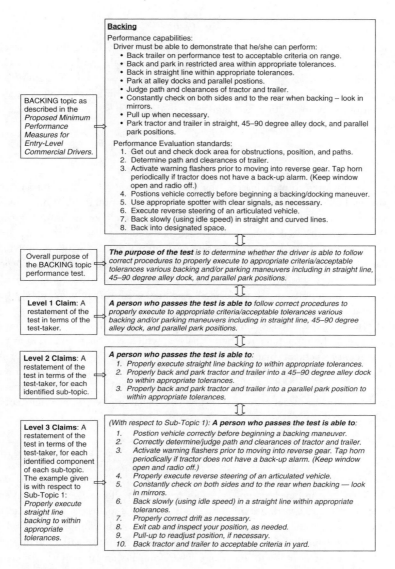

Backing

Performance capabilities:
Driver must be able to demonstrate that he/she can perform:
- Back trailer on performance test to acceptable criteria on range.
- Back and park in restricted area within appropriate tolerances.
- Back in straight line within appropriate tolerances.
- Park at alley docks and parallel postions.
- Judge path and clearances of tractor and trailer.
- Constantly check on both sides and to the rear when backing – look in mirrors.
- Pull up when necessary.
- Park tractor and trailer in straight, 45–90 degree alley dock, and parallel park positions.

Performance Evaluation standards:
1. Get out and check dock area for obstructions, position, and paths.
2. Determine path and clearances of trailer.
3. Activate warning flashers prior to moving into reverse gear. Tap horn periodically if tractor does not have a back-up alarm. (Keep window open and radio off.)
4. Postions vehicle correctly before beginning a backing/docking maneuver.
5. Use appropriate spotter with clear signals, as necessary.
6. Execute reverse steering of an articulated vehicle.
7. Back slowly (using idle speed) in straight and curved lines.
8. Back into designated space.

BACKING topic as described in the Proposed Minimum Performance Measures for Entry-Level Commercial Drivers.

Overall purpose of the BACKING topic performance test.

***The purpose of the test** is to determine whether the driver is able to follow correct procedures to properly execute to appropriate criteria/acceptable tolerances various backing and/or parking maneuvers including in straight line, 45–90 degree alley dock, and parallel park positions.*

Level 1 Claim: A restatement of the test in terms of the test-taker.

***A person who passes the test is able to** follow correct procedures to properly execute to appropriate criteria/acceptable tolerances various backing and/or parking maneuvers including in straight line, 45–90 degree alley dock, and parallel park positions.*

Level 2 Claims: A restatement of the test in terms of the test-taker, for each identified sub-topic.

A person who passes the test is able to:
1. *Properly execute straight line backing to within appropriate tolerances.*
2. *Properly back and park tractor and trailer into a 45–90 degree alley dock to within appropriate tolerances.*
3. *Properly back and park tractor and trailer into a parallel park position to within appropriate tolerances.*

Level 3 Claims: A restatement of the test in terms of the test-taker, for each identified component of each sub-topic. The example given is with respect to Sub-Topic 1: *Properly execute straight line backing to within appropriate tolerances.*

(With respect to Sub-Topic 1): ***A person who passes the test is able to:***
1. *Postion vehicle correctly before beginning a backing maneuver.*
2. *Correctly determine/judge path and clearances of tractor and trailer.*
3. *Activate warning flashers prior to moving into reverse gear. Tap horn periodically if tractor does not have a back-up alarm. (Keep window open and radio off.)*
4. *Properly execute reverse steering of an articulated vehicle.*
5. *Constantly check on both sides and to the rear when backing — look in mirrors.*
6. *Back slowly (using idle speed) in a straight line within appropriate tolerances.*
7. *Properly correct drift as necessary.*
8. *Exit cab and inspect your position, as needed.*
9. *Pull-up to readjust position, if necessary.*
10. *Back tractor and trailer to acceptable criteria in yard.*

Figure 18.2 Example of the application of the Evidence Centered Design model to the development of a performance test for students in truck driver training programs

Additional subject matter expert review—Scoring Guide creation

After the task lists were confirmed through expert review, the tasks were subjected to more detailed descriptions and explanations of terms. This was because the yard and road test scoring depended on instructor ratings. To help eliminate subjectivity from ratings assigned, tasks had to be described in such detail that the standards indicating correct performance of each of the tasks were clear. These detailed task descriptions were also subjected to review by the panel of subject matter experts until agreement was reached. The descriptions were used to create Scoring Guides which were then distributed to all schools volunteering to participate in the pilot of the performance test.

Rating forms

Along with the development of the instructors' Scoring Guides, rating forms were created which were designed to be conveniently used while testing students in the yard or on the road. The formats adopted for the rating forms approximated the formats generally used in the training schools as well as in commercial drivers' license testing. Also included on the rating forms, to ensure standardization of administration, were instructions to be given to students. These rating forms were also reviewed by the subject matter expert panel.

Pilot test

Five schools volunteered to participate in the performance test pilot study. Instructions were provided to these schools regarding general performance test administration. While validity was being established through the process selected to identify and define content, in order to estimate reliability, schools were directed to have two instructors independently rate each student assessed. Instructors were provided with information on preparation activities including studying the Scoring Guides, and testing out the process with another instructor before proceeding to the actual test. For the road test, to ensure standardization, schools were asked to take the students on a route where they would have an opportunity to perform all listed tasks. Also, they were asked to take approximately 30 minutes for this test.

Detailed data entry instructions and templates were provided. Students had ratings submitted by two raters enabling the inter-rater reliability analysis, which was operationalized as percent agreement. The percent agreements by task ranged from approximately 79% to 97%. Overall, the percent agreements are very high, and indicate a satisfactory level of inter-rater agreement or inter-rater reliability for these performance tests. As reported by Miller (1980), ". . . most researchers shoot for a total reliability of 90% or more. However, with a new behavior definition, a figure of 80% or more is acceptable" (p. 28).

Summary

The process from the development of the *Proposed Minimum Performance Measures for Entry-Level Commercial Drivers* to the development and pilot testing of performance tests was very structured, owing largely to the framework provided by the ECD model for test development. This structure facilitates not only an understanding of the test content, but the ability to use and interpret test results. The results from the pilot tests are very supportive of test quality, and also indicate that a test of this length is not a burden to test-takers. Therefore, all content important to require in truck driver training programs can be successfully covered and tested. This coverage followed by testing helps ensure that entry-level commercial drivers are well prepared for their work with the important knowledge and skill sets required.

Example 2. Designing Assessments of 21st-Century Skills Across Disciplines in a Community College Curriculum

The goal of this section is to illustrate to administrators and practitioners some key concepts of evidence-centered assessment design for use in a community college. This example describes the methods for using ECD to support community college instructors as they create a new type of instructional activity.[1] The instructional materials, scenario-based learning (SBL) tasks, were presented as workplace problems that student teams solve. The instructional materials present the problem through a series of email memos from a fictional supervisor, and provide links to resources that students can peruse as needed to support their learning as they solve the problem (http://www.learnpbl.com).

Development of the Assessments

A critical goal of this kind of "problem based" curriculum is to teach knowledge and skills within the context of application. The learning outcomes for this kind of curriculum are not isolated knowledge of technical facts or procedures, but metacognitive social-technical skills developed through planning, designing, and executing a problem solution and the related social skills of working on a team and communicating one's work to different audiences. Historically, technician educators in community colleges have focused on teaching technical facts and procedures rather than application of those skills to complex problems presented in the real world (Lynch, 2000). Consequently, the goal of this collaboration around evidence-centered design was to help technician educators measure the learning outcomes unique to this curriculum model: social-technical skills and social skills.

During this effort, a research team from SRI International in Menlo Park, CA, worked with five instructors (three community college technical instructors, one former community college instructor, and one 4-year university adjunct instructor) to codesign assessments using the evidence-centered approach. This chapter describes the overall approach; another chapter focuses on how the process worked with this particular set of constituents (see Yarnall & Ostrander, this volume).

The researcher-instructor teams designed 72 final and 44 in-class assessments associated with 13 scenario-based tasks in the technician education domains of computer programming (Python, Ajax), engineering, environmental studies, bioinformatics, and network security.

Domain Analysis (Layer 1)

To gather information about concepts, terminology, representational forms, and common interactions in each technical field, the SRI team created an Assessment Reflection Project Task Interview protocol. This interview permitted researchers to gather information from community college instructors to fill in the essential elements of the domain being covered, including the learning goals and the knowledge and skills that students needed to complete their work. In this example, the identification of the learning goals and associated knowledge and skills illustrates the Domain Analysis layer of ECD.

Domain Modeling (Layer 2)

In domain modeling, information that was gathered during domain analysis is organized along the lines of an assessment argument. In our case, the SRI team conducted the translation of the responses to the interview into a narrative document, a design pattern, which captures the key elements of the assessment argument. We created a set of design patterns for each SBL task and shared them with the instructors. The domain-modeling phase of this work involved the reverse engineering of SBL instructional tasks into design patterns.

At the Domain Modeling layer, the goal is to gather all the attributes of an evidence-based assessment argument as represented in a Design Pattern. These attributes include: Rationale; Focal Knowledge, Skills and Abilities (KSAs); Additional KSAs; Potential Work Products; Potential Observations; Potential Rubrics; Characteristic Task Features; and Variable Task Features (see Mislevy, et al., 2003, for a definition of each attribute). We gathered this information using the structured interview protocol presented below (see Appendix).

The language of the interview protocol avoids using the technical terminology of ECD in eliciting the assessment attributes. Instead, the SRI team used common language. For example, KSAs are described as "learning goals" and the community college instructor is asked, "What knowledge or skills do students need to complete this task?" The design pattern attributes, "Potential Observations" and "Work Products," were elicited by asking, "Let's now list the ways students demonstrate knowledge, skills, and abilities in your task." Most questions elicit attributes of the assessment argument. A subset of questions were drawn from the work of Jonassen (2000) to focus on the features of the problem that are central to the scenario-based task. These additional features provided more information about the type of knowledge and skills learned from the task—and measured by the assessment. In ECD terms, they are Variable Task Features that indicate which Focal KSAs are being emphasized in a given task generated with the support of a given design pattern.

Using this interview process, researchers teased out the target sets of 21st-century knowledge and skills that could be learned through scenario-based tasks across multiple technical fields. To capture the focus on "knowledge application" that was central to the scenario-based learning curricula, each design pattern captured multiple, complex sets of knowledge and skills. The goal was to identify knowledge and skill sets that were distinct and coherent so that the design patterns could be used to inform the development of assessments in other subject areas or in related subject areas. The effort resulted in the following seven 21st-century skill design patterns, which we found had applications across multiple domains of technician education (see Table 18.3).

Conceptual Assessment Framework (Layer 3)

The CAF contains the technical specifications for the "nuts and bolts" of the assessment. In this project, formal specifications of the CAF models (as described in Mislevy, Steinberg, & Almond, 2003) were not detailed, but classes of tasks were organized around particular kinds of work products and targeted knowledge and skills. These classes serve to guide the development of additional tasks, and could, if needed, be the basis for specifying formal student, evidence, and task models if this proved useful. This section describes the activities that produced the classes of tasks and generative descriptions of them. These products were defined through discussions and negotiations between researchers and instructors that eventually led to the production of assessments. After the production phase ended, the research team reviewed the resulting assessments and documented the features of the assessments produced.

Table 18.3 Design Pattern Foci Associated with Technical Disciplines

Design Pattern Foci: Problem Solving Skills	Technical Disciplines of Application
1. Research and analysis	Engineering, Environmental Studies, Bioinformatics, Network Security
2. Framing a problem	Programming, Engineering, Network Security
3. Generating a product or solution	Programming, Engineering, Network Security
4. Using tools★	Bioinformatics
5. Making inferences ★	Bioinformatics
Design Pattern Foci: Professional Knowledge and Skills	
1. Collaborating to solve a problem	Programming, Engineering, Network Security
2. Presentation and communication	Programming, Engineering, Environmental Studies, Bioinformatics

★ These were developed later and potentially are applicable to other technical fields

These processes served to link the design patterns to the production of actual assessment tasks. Typically, researchers discussed the initial set of design patterns that were relevant to the scenario-based task designed by the instructor. In these discussions, instructors provided feedback on how well they thought the design pattern matched the learning goals of their scenario-based task. This was typically the point when instructors revealed specific preferences for highly technical or more behavioral or attitudinal learning outcomes. In short, it was the time when instructors revealed what they valued most in this instructional approach and what they most wanted students to learn. For example, a programming instructor wanted to make sure students were learning programming skills and the ability to translate client requirements into a working program. An engineering instructor wanted to remove a focus on mathematics and emphasize the importance of design, testing, and revision. An environmental studies instructor wanted to build students' confidence in researching environmental problems and reflecting on how they could translate ideas into community action. These discussions usually clarified key assessment decisions for instructors. They embraced some design patterns and rejected others (see Yarnall & Ostrander, this volume).

The processes began with the researcher focusing on assessment production, asking the instructors how they measured their favored learning outcomes in past tests, quizzes, or formative assessments. For the more technical outcomes, instructors usually had a set of standard assessments they preferred to use. For the metacognitive and social-technical outcomes, they did not. In some cases, instructors brainstormed very productively with researchers to develop new assessments of non-technical outcomes. In other cases, instructors delegated the design of these non-technical assessments to the researchers.

The research team documented the results only after a collection of initial new assessments were devised with this approach. The final list of the kinds of work products students were asked to generate in the scenario-based assessments appears in Table 18.4.

Assessment Implementation (Layer 4)

In this project, the construction and preparation of assessment tasks and rubrics needed to occur in a form that would be useful to community college instructors. The research team collaborated with key community college instructors to develop an assessment template that provided the core features of each assessment task.

The assessment template provided the basic assessment task, examples of acceptable student responses, a simple 3-level scoring key (above proficient, proficient, below proficient), a summary of the knowledge and skills assessed and the relevant design pattern, a suggested form for the assessment task (pencil and paper, computer-based), and a suggested use for the assessment task (formative, summative). The research team generated both "in-class" assessment templates to highlight the formative assessments built into the original scenario-based learning tasks, and "final test" assessment templates of the assessments for use in the instructor's final examinations.

Assessment Delivery (Layer 5)

This layer of evidence-centered design focuses on the system for delivering assessments to students. In this project, the researchers worked closely with instructors to determine the best delivery method. In some cases, instructors chose to incorporate new final test items into their existing paper-and-pencil tests. In other cases, instructors chose to have SRI generate an online test that they could direct their students to take. The online system had the advantage of permitting easy access to student responses, but added an extra step for researchers who needed to aggregate and print the results for final hand scoring by the instructors. The assessment delivery process was developed using the four-process delivery-system architecture of the ECD process (Mislevy, Steinberg, & Almond, 2002), but is not detailed here.

Table 18.4 Kinds of Work Products to be Generated by Students in Scenario-Based Assessments

In-Class Item Types	Description of Work Product	Percentage of Total Assessments★
Tool Performance	Technical step-by-step procedural performance that demonstrates proficiency with tool, language, or system	36%
Check in	Brief questions or "on demand" performances requiring students to demonstrate important skills and knowledge	29%
Tracking Progress	Progress checklist to mark student performance against a pre-established schedule or set of benchmarks	20%
Presentation/Inference	Presentation of project, summary of findings, or formal argument based on data	17%
Final Item Types		
Short Answer Conceptual	Short-answer written or oral description of the principles or concepts relevant to a problem	40%
Short Answer Professional	Short-answer written or oral description of the strategies or tactics relevant to a social, or presentational or organizational problem	27%
Mapping	Concept map to illustrate understanding of an overall process or the full range of principles relevant to a problem	5%
Computation	Performance of mathematical or statistical procedure in the course of solving a problem	5%
Procedural with or without Tools	Demonstration of steps in a technical procedure; may involve actual tool or representation of tool	25%★

★ Some overlap of items

Validation of Assessment Tasks

The project also engaged in validity studies of the assessments, examining the construct validity through student think-alouds, content validity with expert reviews and ratings, instructional sensitivity with pretests and posttest change, and reliability with inter-rater agreement on scoring (instructor and another subject expert). By the time these data were gathered, most instructors had moved on and were not directly involved in the process of instructional design or the grant activities any longer, but interactions with one of the remaining instructors who agreed to conduct student think-alouds suggested this activity would be particularly productive for deepening instructors' knowledge of assessment. In addition, the information collected from each of the validation studies can be used to inform refinements of the SBL assessment tasks.

Summary

The ECD process provided a systematic approach for defining the primary learning objectives of the scenario-based learning tasks and the features of assessment tasks that will elicit student performances aligned with those learning objectives. The ECD framework permitted researchers to work with community college instructors across multiple technical fields to define common high-level problem solving and professional skills. It also provided a useful structure for specifying the specific technical knowledge and skills that practitioners in each field apply to problem solving situations. Subsequent validity studies indicated that the ECD-based assessments were aligned with key content knowledge relevant to each field and elicited the kinds of cognitive processes important for each field. These findings underscore the utility of ECD as a tool for informing the validity of a wide variety of skills using a varied range of assessments.

Discussion

As the examples in this chapter illustrate, evidence-centered design is a versatile approach that can be used to guide the design and development of a wide variety of assessments. These assessments can vary by domain (e.g., computer programming vs. commercial truck driving), purpose (e.g., licensing vs. academic course performance), format (e.g., multiple-choice vs. performance), grade level (e.g., adult learners, community college students vs. K-12) and delivery mode (online presentation of tasks vs. behavioral performance measure).

ECD, when used for the purposes of assessment design, typically proposes five layers of assessment development activity. The examples presented in this chapter illustrate that not all applications of ECD detail each of the five layers, and different projects tailor the processes and representational forms they use in order to best suit the needs and the contexts of the project. For example, the community college example does not set forth a statistical submodel for the CAF, although evaluative rubrics are used to score the assessment items and tasks. A more detailed implementation of a statistical submodel appears, for example, in Mislevy, Steinberg, Breyer, Johnson, & Almond (2002), for computer simulation tasks in the domain of dental hygiene. For the Implementation phase, a computer-aided system for designing simulation-based tasks in computer network design and troubleshooting, used in the Cisco Networking Academies; see Mislevy et al. (2010).

The two examples in this chapter supply evidence of how ECD can span the needs of technician education—in the examples, the domains analyzed include commercial truck driving, programming, bioinformatics, environmental studies, network security and engineering. ECD is able to guide the development of tasks in these diverse areas and help elicit the knowledge, skills and abilities that are the targets of measurement, the observations and evidence that need to be collected as well as the features of tasks and potential work products.

Note

1 The work was conducted as part of a grant to support innovative curriculum development from the National Science Foundation's Advanced Technological Education (ATE) program (DUE Grant No. 0603297). Any opinions, findings and conclusions or recommendations expressed in this material are those of the author and do not necessarily reflect the views of NSF.

References

Alexander, C., Ishikawa, S., & Silverstein, M. (1977). The multidimensional random co-efficients multinomial logit model. *Applied Psychological Measurement, 21*, 1–23.

Almond, R. G., Steinberg, L. S., & Mislevy, R. J. (2002). Enhancing the design and delivery of assessment systems: A four-process architecture. *Journal of Technology, Learning, and Assessment, 1*(5). Retrieved from http://escholarship.bc.edu/jtla/vol1/5/

Commercial Vehicle Training Association, & National Association of Publicly Funded Truck Driving Schools. (2007). *Proposed minimum performance measures for entry-level commercial drivers*. Springfield, VA: Author.

Ebel, R. L., & Frisbie, D. A. (1991). *Essentials of educational measurement* (5th ed.). Englewood Cliffs, NJ: Prentice-Hall.

Fuhrman, M. (1996). Developing good multiple-choice tests and test questions. *Journal of Geoscience Education, 44*, 379–384.

Gamma, E., Helm, R., Johnson, R., & Vlissides, J. (1994). *Design patterns*. Reading, MA: Addison-Wesley.

Haladyna, T. M. (1999). *Developing and validating multiple-choice test items*. Mahwah, NJ: Erlbaum.

Jonassen, D. (2000). Toward a design theory of problem solving. *Educational Technology Research and Development, 48*(4), 63–85.

Lynch, R. L. (2000). High school career and technical education for the first decade of the 21st century. *Journal of Vocational Education Research, 25*(2), 155–198.

Miller, L.K. (1980). *Principles of everyday behavior analysis.* Monterey, CA: Brooks/Cole.

Mislevy, R. J., Behrens, J. T., Bennett, R. E., Demark, S. F., Frezzo, D. C., Levy, R., . . . Winters, F. I. (2010). On the roles of external knowledge representations in assessment design. *Journal of Technology, Learning, and Assessment, 8*(2). Retrieved from http://escholarship.bc.edu/jtla/vol8/2

Mislevy, R. J., & Haertel, G. D. (2006). Implications of evidence-centered design for educational testing. *Educational Measurement: Issues and Practice, 25*(4), 6–20.

Mislevy, R. J., Hamel, L., Fried, R., Gaffney, T., Haertel, G., Hafter, A., . . . Wenk, A. (2003). *Design patterns for assessing science inquiry.* (PADI Technical Report 1). Menlo Park, CA: SRI International. Retrieved from http://padi.sri.com/downloads/TR1_Design_Patterns.pdf. Also presented at American Education Research Association (AERA) in April, 2003.

Mislevy, R. J, & Riconscente, M. M. (2006). *Evidence-centered assessment design: Layers, concepts, and terminology.* In S. Downing, & T. Haladyna (Eds.), Handbook of test development (pp. 61–90). Mahwah, NJ: Erlbaum.

Mislevy, R. J., Steinberg, L. S., & Almond, R. A. (2002). Enhancing the design and delivery of assessment systems: A four-process architecture. *Journal of Technology, Learning, and Assessment, 1*(5), 3–63.

Mislevy, R. J., Steinberg, L. S., & Almond, R. A. (2003). On the structure of educational assessments. *Measurement: Interdisciplinary Research and Perspectives, 1,* 3–62.

Mislevy, R. J., Steinberg, L. S., Breyer, F. J., Johnson, L., & Almond, R. A. (2002). Making sense of data from complex assessments. *Applied Measurement in Education, 15,* 363–378.

Toulmin, S. E. (1958). *The uses of argument.* Cambridge, UK: Cambridge University Press.

Wentland, E. (2008). *Project summary: The development of an assessment for students in commercial vehicle driver training programs.* Unpublished manuscript.

Yarnall, L., & Ostrander, J. (2009, April). *Principled assessments of 21st-century skills across disciplines in a community college curriculum.* Symposium presented at the annual meeting of the American Educational Research Association, San Diego, CA.

Yarnall, L., & Ostrander, J. (this volume). *The assessment of 21st-century skills in community college career and technical education.*

Yarnall, L., Toyama, Y., Gong, B., Ayers, C., & Ostrander, J. (2007). Adapting scenario-based curriculum materials to community college technical courses. *Community College Journal of Research and Practice, 31*(7), 583–601.

Zieky, M. (2006). *An introduction to evidence-centered design.* Princeton, NJ: Educational Testing Service.

Appendix

Interview Protocol to Elicit Design Pattern Attributes From Community College Instructors

Goals of Interview:

- Elicit instructors' principal learning goals to prioritize design pattern development.
- Elicit key content knowledge, skills, and abilities needed to solve problems.
- Elicit what students do when working in groups on the scenario-based tasks.

Overall guidelines:

- General goal is to let the instructor describe the learning task he/she has designed, taking up to 10 minutes to do so and then focus on the essential features of the problem solving tasks that students are learning.
- For developing design patterns for individual assessments, the interviewer should listen carefully to the instructor's description of the problem, and try to frame the problem type along three continua: well-structured to ill-structured; complex to simple; domain specificity to domain generality (see description bullet points below in interview).

- For developing design patterns for group tasks, the interviewer should listen carefully to the instructor's description of how he/she teaches students to work on teams, ensure individual ownership and contributions to the task, and ensure completion of a quality deliverable.
- By close of interview, interviewer will have identified the key features of the design pattern for review and discussion by assessment experts, which will be filled in after the interview on the Design Pattern Template.

Interview Protocol:

1. Please take up to 10 minutes to walk me through each step of the scenario-based task you have designed. (Let instructor provide full description, and ask minimal questions, only to resolve problems of clarity.)
2. Let's create a list of the learning goals in this task. (Do this jointly, noting points that seem like possible content learning elements if the instructor does not volunteer some that seem relevant to you.) What knowledge do they need to do it? What skills do they need? What abilities do they need? (Note each in writing and then review that list with the instructor and ask him/her to explain which KSAs are *prerequisites for the course* and which are *learned during the course.*)
3. Let's now list the ways students demonstrate knowledge, skills, and abilities in your task. (Do this jointly also, again prompting the instructor as needed to think of observable behaviors and work products.)
4. Where is problem solving occurring in this task? Please describe the one or two problems that you think are most important and why. (What's most important here is getting the instructor's framing of the problem – here is where your follow up questions might focus on its structuredness [e.g., how much information is given to the student to solve the problem; how much are rules provided? What is left for the student to formulate?], complexity [e.g., how many possible solutions are there to this problem? How will you determine which approach is more successful than another?], and domain specificity [e.g., how much is this a type of reasoning that only people in this field of work use?]) **Use the slider scales below to categorize the instructor's responses on a 7-point scale.**

Structuredness of the Task

- ○ *Tightly structured:*

  - *All elements of the problem are presented to learners*
  - *Application of limited number of regular rules and principles organized in a predictive/prescriptive way (Jonassen, 2000)*
  - *Knowable solution*

  VS.

- ○ *Loosely structured:*

  - *Possible relevant problem elements not known with confidence*
  - *Possible multiple solutions, solution paths, or no solution*
  - *Multiple evaluation criteria, uncertainty about rules, concepts, principles necessary for solution*
  - *Requires learner to make judgments and express opinions*

1	2	3	4	5	6	7

Complexity of the Task

◦ *Complex:*

- *Multiple issues, functions, or variables in problem*
- *High degree of connectivity among them*
- *Multiple functional relations among them*
- *Dynamic and changing problem states (Funke, 1991)*

VS.

◦ *Simple:*

- *A low number of issues, functions, or variables in problem*
- *Low degree of connectivity among them*
- *A few key functional relations among them*
- *Stable problem state*

1	2	3	4	5	6	7

Specificity of the Task

◦ *Domain specificity:*

- *Problems are situated, embedded, and therefore dependent on the nature of the context or domain*
- *Problems require a specific type of reasoning unique to a given domain*

VS.

◦ *Domain general:*

- *Problems are grounded in general logic*
- *Problems invoke "general or broad methods" or reasoning strategies*

1	2	3	4	5	6	7

5. Where does team work occur in this task? (Prompt instructor to discuss how he/she supports student learning about key aspects of teamwork: teamwork processes such as assigning roles, running meetings, teaching each other, communicating; deliverable management processes such as setting interim deadlines, tracking slipping tasks; and, individual team member account-ability processes, such as completing one's tasks, contributing.) **Use the slider scales below to categorize the instructor's responses on a 7-point scale.**

Teamwork Processes

◦ *Heavy teamwork process emphasis:*

- Instruction focuses on how teams divide, assign, and organize tasks
- Instruction focuses on having complementary expertise that students share with each other reciprocally
- Instruction focuses on strategies for communication and clarification around conflict

VS.

    ◦   *Low teamwork process emphasis:*

- Instruction does not address how teams divide, assign, and organize tasks; students can "figure out" as they go, and their success is not tracked
- Instruction does not strategically select students for teams so that there is a mix of skill or experience levels
- Instruction does not address the strategies for resolving conflict

1	2	3	4	5	6	7

Deliverable Management Processes

    ◦   *High deliverable management focus:*

- Instruction focuses on how teams set interim deadlines and organize tasks by complexity
- Instruction tracks students' interim progress

    VS.

    ◦   *Low deliverable management focus:*

- Instruction lets teams figure out own way of getting the project done
- Instruction does not track students' interim progress

1	2	3	4	5	6	7

Individual Team Member Accountability Processes

    ◦   *High student accountability focus:*

- Instruction focuses on how to ensure individual team members complete their work
- Grading takes into account individual contribution

    VS.

    ◦   *Low student accountability focus:*

- Instruction does not provide accountability strategies
- Grading is for whole team

6. Based on what you've told me, it sounds as though this is a _____ (tightly/loosely) –structured problem of _____ (high/medium/low) complexity that is solvable through reasoning that is _____ (strongly/loosely) associated with this field of work. It seems that knowledge of _____ and skills of _____ are most important to solving it. Would you agree with this characterization? (Get instructor to elaborate and provide more specificity.) Also, from what you've told me, it sounds as though you're teaching students _____ (some/no) strategies for teamwork, _____ (some/no) strategies managing deliverable deadlines, and _____ (some/no) strategies for individual team member accountability.

Next steps

1. Write up notes that debrief the instructor's responses to the above questions, and then propose an outline of 1–2 design patterns for review and development by assessment experts.

References

Funke, J. (1991). Solving complex problems: Exploration and control of complex systems. In R. J. Sternberg, & P. A. Frensch (Eds.), *Complex problem solving: Principles and mechanisms* (pp. 185–222). Hillsdale, NJ: Erlbaum.

Jonassen, E. H. (2000). *Computers as mindtools for schools: Engaging critical thinking* (2nd ed.). Upper Saddle River, NJ: Prentice-Hall.

19

THE ASSESSMENT OF 21ST-CENTURY SKILLS IN COMMUNITY COLLEGE CAREER AND TECHNICIAN EDUCATION PROGRAMS

Louise Yarnall[1] and Jane Ostrander

Community colleges have an extensive history of training technicians (Cohen & Brawer, 2002), but new 21st-century technical fields such as biotechnology, forensics, and environmental science call for new models of technician preparation. Traditionally, career and technical education (CTE) has emphasized hands-on training in basic procedures (Lynch, 2000). The new fields of the 21st century blend hands-on skills with two other elements: the application of advanced concepts from mathematics and science, and coordinated teamwork with professionals from multiple disciplines. To keep pace with these changes, community college educators are transforming CTE programs so students can engage in 21st-century professional activities that require interdisciplinary problem solving, teamwork, and strong communication skills.

This chapter describes how using *evidence-centered assessment reflection* (EC-AR) with technician educators can help align the learning goals of technician courses with the demands of the new high-technology workforce. This is an approach to assessment that grew out of foundational work in evidence-centered design (ECD) (Messick, 1994; Mislevy, 2007; Mislevy & Riconscente, 2006). Evidence-centered design is an alternative to the measurement models of classical test theory and item response theory. Unlike these models, which examine a test's technical features—such as item difficulty and latent traits measured (e.g., verbal skill)—*after* test design, ECD outlines the assessment argument *first*. The ECD "front loaded" approach allows assessment designers to capture more complex student performances in a wider range of assessment tasks.

Key Points

The EC-AR process helps instructors clarify the full range of skills involved in competent workplace performance, which includes not only technical skills but also "social-technical" and "social" skills:

- "Social–technical" skills are metacognitive in nature and focus on ways to link client needs to technical concepts through problem framing, solution design, and solution implementation.
- "Social" skills capture the communicative activities that help students leverage distributed networks of knowledge (Pea, 1993).

- "Social-technical" and "social" learning goals should supplement, rather than supplant, the traditional CTE classroom focus on hands-on, technical skills. Our research suggests they act as the cognitive equivalent of "bread starter": they raise the standards and outcomes of any CTE course.

While EC-AR's theoretical roots, tools, procedures, and summary findings are described in another chapter (Haertel, Wentland, Yarnall, & Mislevy, this volume), the present chapter will describe details that may be useful to the practitioner.

Background

The EC-AR process unfolded within the context of an instructional materials development project called Scenario-Based Learning (SBL) in Technical Education. This project involved instructors collaborating with industry experts to design curriculum activity modules that engage students in real world problems (http://learnpbl.com). These goal-based scenarios (Schank, 1997) challenge students to collaborate with their team members to solve authentic workplace problems, use the vocabulary of their target profession, and communicate their solutions to stakeholders. Each workplace problem was presented through a series of e-mails from a fictional supervisor (the instructor). The online materials contained tips and links to resources that students consulted as needed to solve problems. All problems required students to share their problem-solving approach in various forms of communication, both informally within a team and more formally before the class or an industry representative.

The SBL project was funded by the National Science Foundation's Advanced Technological Education (ATE) program. This federal program supports technician education for high-growth, high-demand fields in science, technology, engineering, and mathematics (STEM). In the initial phases of this work, the need for a focus on assessment emerged as we experienced challenges similar to those encountered by other innovators who incorporated problem-based learning into their programs (Alverno College, 1977; Woods, 2000; Yarnall, Toyama, Gong, Ayers, & Ostrander, 2007). Both community college instructors and students expressed discomfort with the less structured quality of SBL instruction. Community college technical students liked learning from team members, but demanded clearly defined learning goals, better evidence that they were learning, and instructor feedback. Instructors wanted to know how to manage teams and track individual student progress.

To address these concerns, the second phase of our work focused on assessment. To engage instructors in defining the new learning goals associated with SBL, we used the EC-AR process. This process involved:

- An initial interview that engaged instructors in *domain analysis*, a process that characterizes the range of knowledge, skills, and dispositions required in a technical field.
- A rough documentation phase called *domain modeling*, which describes the features of assessments that provide evidence that students have acquired the requisite knowledge, skills, and dispositions.
- A detailed documentation phase in which the *conceptual assessment framework* (CAF) defines the specific types of prompts, stimuli, performances, and scoring rubrics for assessments measuring the key learning outcomes.
- The final processes of assessment implementation and delivery system development, during which validity testing is performed (e.g., scoring reliability, construct validity, content validity, and instructional sensitivity).

In total, we codeveloped 72 final assessment tasks and documented 44 in-class formative assessments for SBL with community college instructors in the domains of computer programming (Python, Ajax), engineering, environmental studies, bioinformatics, and network security.

Theoretical Considerations

Central to the EC-AR process was an understanding that technician educators were trying to teach and assess more than the recall of technical facts and procedures. Instead, they were trying to teach and assess complex behaviors and skills associated with competent application of technical knowledge to real world problems. A conceptual model of the range of skills and their interrelationships that were to be taught and assessed appears in Figure 19.1.

This model illustrates the progression we saw occurring as we engaged technician educators in the EC-AR process. Most instructors saw their primary responsibility as teaching and testing technical knowledge. In the EC-AR process, the assessment team elicited instructors' knowledge of the professional activity context, which revealed essential social processes and social-technical processes and products.

A "figure-ground" relationship existed among these different forms of knowledge. Instructors saw the technical knowledge as the figure in the picture, and the social and social-technical knowledge as the background. Part of the goal of the EC-AR process is to put these background components into closer focus so they are not neglected in either teaching or testing.

List of New Skills for CTE Education

In this section, we will review the kinds of skills that technician educators in multiple domains identified as important to performing proficiently in the workplace. The technician educators identified these skills by participating in different steps in the EC-AR process. Each step and its associated findings are presented below.

The EC-AR Process: Step-by-Step

EC-AR Step 1

During the EC-AR process domain analysis and domain modeling phases, the instructors first described to the researcher the complex behaviors that are the mark of professional competence.

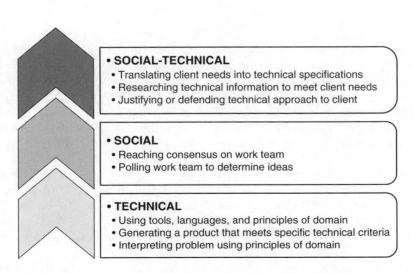

Figure 19.1 Model for expanding technical education learning outcomes using the EC-AR process

Table 19.1 Design Pattern Foci: Professional Behaviors Important in Technician Education

Problem-Solving Skills	Technical Disciplines of Application
1. Research and analysis	Engineering, Environmental Studies, Bioinformatics, Network Security
2. Framing a problem	Programming, Engineering, Network Security
3. Generating a product or solution	Programming, Engineering, Network Security
4. Using tools★	Bioinformatics
5. Making inferences ★	Bioinformatics
Professional Knowledge and Skills	
1. Collaborating to solve a problem	Programming, Engineering, Network Security
2. Presentation and communication	Programming, Engineering, Environmental Studies, Bioinformatics

★ These were developed later and potentially are applicable to other technical fields

These behaviors are listed above, in Table 19.1. Each complex behavior became a distinct *design pattern*, which is a document that lists the different attributes of an effective assessment of the professional behavior.

The list shows that instructors across multiple technical disciplines shared many common ideas about the core professional behaviors involved in applying technical knowledge in the workplace. Some of the skills they identified resembled phases of critical thinking or problem solving (Facione, 1990; Jonassen, 2000), including: preparatory activities, such as research and analysis and framing a problem; direct production activities, such as generating a product and using tools; and interpretive activities, such as making inferences. They also emphasized social activities such as teamwork and presentation. Often these critical thinking and social process skills are commonly associated with liberal arts and general education courses, but as can be seen, these technical instructors valued such skills as essential too. In the design pattern, the assessment reflection activity of defining the professional behaviors set the stage for instructors to move beyond a narrow focus on technical skills toward broader categories of problem solving and professional skills.

EC-AR Step 2

In the remaining steps of the EC-AR process, technician instructors thought about different aspects of each professional behavior, recording those details in the design pattern. Since these professional behaviors are complex, one of the first tasks in the EC-AR process involves identifying the elements that are most central to a quality performance. The EC-AR process engaged technician instructors in identifying the *focal* knowledge, skills, and abilities (KSAs) and *additional* KSAs. Focal KSAs comprise the specific principles and procedures that were the desired learning outcomes of the instructors. Additional KSAs represented the prerequisite knowledge and skills that the technician educators expected students to know before learning the focal KSAs.

In the EC-AR process, the activity of generating focal KSAs and additional KSAs became the place where instructors not only defined the relevant technical knowledge, but, more importantly, the specific social skills that students needed to apply that technical knowledge effectively.

To show how this worked, Table 19.2 compares the focal and additional KSAs for the same problem-solving behavior—framing a problem—in two different domains, programming and engineering.

These examples of KSAs show how competence in a technical field involves interplay of social skills and technical knowledge. As expected, the fields of engineering and programming differ in fundamen-

Table 19.2 Focal and Additional KSAs for Framing a Problem in Different Domains

Domain	Ajax programming	Engineering
Focal KSAs	• Skill of identifying and asking appropriate questions to specify user requirements • Skill of engaging in software design brainstorming by generating examples of possible user interactions with the Web site • Skill of documenting system requirements using a simplified use case format • Skill of addressing user needs in specifying system requirements questions to specify the core engineering	• Skill of identifying and asking appropriate problem and requirements • Skill of generating possible solutions using engineering principles • Skill of addressing engineering problem and requirements in specifying possible solutions
Additional KSAs	• Knowledge of possible options for Web site functions • Knowledge of user interface design • Skills of communication and writing • Ability to conduct simple Web searches • Ability to use graphic tools to create mockup of Web site's user interface design	• Knowledge of algebra, trigonometry and geometry • Knowledge of physics • Skills of presentation, communication and writing

tal technical principles and tools, but in both cases, technicians need to interview clients to understand the constraints and expectations that inform the technical solution. The Additional KSAs illustrate the importance of specific technical knowledge and tools for supporting clear communication and shared reasoning in a variety of social workplace contexts. These tools and knowledge help technicians interact effectively with other technicians and make presentations to non-technical audiences.

In practice, this step is challenging. Some instructors frame the course learning goals as a long list of many forms of knowledge and skill. At the other extreme, some instructors primarily seek to instill a general attitude or sense of confidence in their students, which they find difficult to specify for measurement. In one case, the problem is one of prioritization; in the other, specification. The goal of EC-AR Step 2 activity is to focus attention on prioritization—defining what is important according to what is fundamental. By this we mean to focus on those forms of knowledge and skill that have the most influence on performance. A helpful way of visualizing fundamental knowledge is to think of a flow chart with arrows stemming from each type of knowledge: Which type of knowledge will have the most arrows pointing to other kinds of skill or knowledge? They are the most fundamental! Another question that elicits reflection on fundamental knowledge is: "What does one have to know to perform the target skill?"

EC-AR Step 3

When judging a high-quality performance, people often say, "I know it when I see it." Capturing that intuitive sense of what it looks like to do something well is another key step in the EC-AR process. We asked instructors to describe what it looked like when a student could do the KSAs they wanted them to learn. Their descriptions were recorded under the design pattern attribute "observable behaviors." To show how this works, examples of how two different instructors described what it looks like when students know how to "frame a problem" in two different domains are presented in Table 19.3 below.

As can be seen from Table 19.3, in the two domains there are common elements of observable behaviors: (1) identifying user/client needs, (2) defining the user needs/problem in applicable technical terms, and (3) making a recommendation for a technical approach.

Table 19.3 Comparison of Observable Behaviors for Framing a Problem in Different Domains

Domain	Ajax programming	Engineering
Observable behaviors of the problem-solving design pattern "framing a problem"	The student will: • Define the user's primary needs for the Web site • Define the user's range of possible uses for the Web site • Determine Web functionalities that meet each of the user's needs/uses	The student will: • Focus on a problem by using the principles of engineering • Define a comprehensive range of possible engineering problems and requirements in a given case • Comprehensively and thoughtfully rationalize and justify problem framing decisions for a technical audience

As in the KSAs, we see here some mention of the technical elements unique to each domain. In Ajax programming, the students translate user needs into "Web functionalities;" in engineering, students translate user needs into "engineering principles."

We also see, at least in these specific SBL tasks, that the programming instructor underscores the importance of "alignment with user needs" as the primary index for judging the quality of students' professional performance, while the engineering instructor sees the "comprehensiveness" of the possible applications of engineering principles as the primary performance quality indicator. These slight variations—one toward the social dimension of the client and one toward the technical dimension of the engineering principles—demonstrate how the EC-AR process flexibly incorporates individualized instructor priorities.

Implementing this step in the reflection process should be easy. Instructors frequently have many examples of observations from their own workplaces or from years observing students in their classrooms.

EC-AR Step 4

After imagining what a skillful performance looks like, the next step is to imagine what "work products" students can produce to show evidence of learning. Table 19.4 presents the types of work products that instructors used across the domains. The work products are organized by whether they were used primarily in class for formative purposes or on the final test for summative purposes.

As the table below illustrates, most of the work products involve familiar assessment modes, such as short-answers, and familiar topics, such as concepts and principles. Yet some of the assessment modes are unfamiliar (e.g., mapping) and so are some of the topics (professional skills). Most of the work products require rubric scoring. They monitor student learning in highly technical areas (tool use procedures, computations, concepts), more social areas (professional skills), and combined social-technical areas that involve higher-order cognitive skills (presentation/inference, mapping, tracking progress).

In practice, this step works best by asking instructors to imagine different ways that students can show what they know. It helps to have instructors work alone or with a partner, imagining how any of the different examples of work products would provide evidence that students have learned the key skills of applying technical knowledge to a real world problem. We engaged instructors in a three-step process: (1) focusing on one learning outcome; (2) selecting three different assessment types from the list, preferably including one formative and one summative; and (3) envisioning what those three different assessments of the same outcome would look like. This process helps instructors cultivate fresh ideas for tracking student progress.

EC-AR Step 5

Over time, instructors develop a repertoire of different forms of test questions. In the design pattern, these preferred test question forms are recorded under the attribute "characteristic task features."

Table 19.4 Work Products by Percentage in Scenario-Based Learning

In-Class Item Types	Description of Work Product	Percentage of Total Assessments*
Tool Performance	Technical step-by-step procedural performance that demonstrates proficiency with tool, language, or system	36%
Check in	Brief questions or "on demand" performances requiring students to demonstrate important skills and knowledge	29%
Tracking Progress	Progress checklist to mark student performance against a pre-established schedule or set of benchmarks	20%
Presentation/ Inference	Presentation of project, summary of findings, or formal argument based on data	17%
Final Item Types		
Short Answer Conceptual	Short-answer written or oral description of the principles or concepts relevant to a problem	40%
Short Answer Professional	Short-answer written or oral description of the strategies or tactic relevant to a social or presentation organization problem	27%
Mapping	Concept map to illustrate understanding of an overall process or the full range of principles relevant to a problem	5%
Computation	Performance of mathematical or statistical procedure in the course of solving a problem	5%
Procedural with or without Tools	Demonstration of steps in a technical procedure; may involve actual tool or representation of tool	25%*

* Some overlap on items

These characteristic task features (see Table 19.5) represent the essential ingredients of technical educator assessments. As can be seen from this table, each assessment links some knowledge representation stimulus from the technical context to a specific prompt to the student to perform a cognitive or social operation. This list specifies the prompt and stimulus elements of each assessment task that will ensure each assessment elicits the desired student performance. In addition, the elements can be varied to make test questions harder or easier. These are documented under the attribute "variable task features."

In the EC-AR process, researchers gathered or created prompt and stimulus elements with instructors. In these discussions, we engaged in detailed consideration of the prompts with the instructors' input, sometimes weighing each word to ensure it elicited higher-level skills rather than simple recall. Sometimes we brainstormed how to focus student attention on social negotiation skills instead of technical matters.

To generate ideas for test item scenarios (stimuli), the assessment team asked instructors to provide some working technical knowledge representations. These included a log file, in which network security students would find anomalies and a hacker attack, and a snippet of computer programming code, which students would analyze and complete. In some cases, researchers created "end product" representations, such as the results of a bioinformatics database search or a newspaper article about, or transcript of, a planning commission meeting on an environmental issue.

Table 19.5 Characteristic Features of Assessment Tasks for Core Technician Education Professional Behaviors

	Characteristic Task Features	
Professional Behavior Assessed	Stimuli & Skill Requirements	Task Features
Research and analysis	Technical Context Stimulus	• Brackets a phenomenon for investigation
	Cognitive Operation Requirements	• Cues the use of procedures for searching, testing, or inquiring into the phenomenon of interest
		• Cues analysis and interpretation of the results of research or testing
Framing a problem	Technical Context Stimulus	• Contains constraints that students must recognize
	Social or Cognitive Operation Requirements	• Requires demonstration of social process for identifying client requirements
		• Cues summarization of problem goals
Generating a product	Technical Context Stimulus	• Engages students in using real world tools, procedures, and knowledge representations
	Cognitive Operation Requirements	• Requires students to make recommendations or summarizations of their intended (or enacted) design or solution process
Using tools	Technical Context Stimulus	• Engages students in using real world tools, procedures, and knowledge representations
	Cognitive Operation Requirements	• Contains different opportunities to demonstrate proficiency with different procedural elements of the tool
		• Scaffolds conceptual and interpretive knowledge as it is not the focus of this assessment
Making inferences	Technical Context Stimulus	• Presents student with multiple knowledge representations relevant to real world practice
	Cognitive Operation Requirements	• Cues interpretation, weighing evidence toward reaching a conclusion
Teamwork	Technical Context Stimulus	• Engages or presents student with a conflict or disagreement in a team
	Social Operation Requirements	• Cues summary of the relevant social negotiation processes to reach a solution
Presentation and communication	Technical Context Stimulus	• Engages student in, or presents student with a challenge around information organization for a specific technical or non-technical audience
	Cognitive Operation Requirements	• Cues student to summarize an approach for organizing information to meet the communication needs of that audience

In addition to describing the characteristic task features, the design patterns also included specific descriptions of how to increase or decrease the difficulty of assessments in the "variable task features" attribute. A brief list provides an indication of the common features of variable task features:

- Vary the number of features expected in a computer program (Python, framing a problem).
- Vary the number of GUI library or data storage systems for consideration (Python, generating a product).
- Programming performed by individuals or teams (Python, generating a product).
- Few or many user-defined Web site functions expected of the program (Ajax, framing a problem).
- Vary the Web development tools or functions needed by the fictional user/client (Ajax, generating a product).
- Programming from a worked example or "from scratch" (Ajax, generating a product).
- Use familiar or unfamiliar structural collapse scenario (Engineering, research and analysis).
- Vary the number of people on the team (Engineering, collaborating to solve a problem).
- Vary the degrees of feedback provided to the students during design testing (Engineering, generating a product).
- Presentations may be individual or team assignments (Engineering, presentation).

As can be seen from this list, variable task features increase or decrease problem complexity by adding or subtracting tasks, adjusting the emphasis on technical considerations, providing more or less feedback, or permitting team collaboration or individual performance.

In practice, this step can be challenging as it involves analyzing the details of the wording of a prompt. It helps to show examples of prompts and stimuli, sometimes contrasting cases of how a poorly worded prompt malfunctioned in pilot testing, whereas another precisely worded prompt worked well.

EC-AR Step 6

In technical education, the details matter. For this reason, when we put together our assessment templates, we did not simply set forth rubrics for scoring, we incorporated details from successful student responses to support scoring for each in-class and final test item. This kind of transparency is particularly important for complex tasks of technical knowledge application to real world problems. In pilot testing, we found considerable subjective differences in how different scorers (instructors) rated student work. We found that providing detailed examples of proficient student responses fostered consistency in scoring.

We engaged in two pilot-testing phases. In the first phase, we worked with a starter rubric based on our initial expectations. Based on the results from that pilot study, we used the student responses to anchor the rubrics for the second pilot test. This anchoring process involved first reviewing all student responses for all given items, and then grouping them as high, medium, and low performances. To revise the rubrics, we used student answers from each performance level to adjust the content and skill elements we included in each corresponding level of the rubric. In some cases, even the highest performing students failed to achieve the initial goals set forth by the instructors. We discussed those findings with instructors who made the final judgment about how to define the high performance expectations.

We established a three-level rubric that runs from "above proficient" to "proficient" to "below proficient." In general, more elaborate and technically correct responses for both problem solving and professional tasks attained an "above proficient" score. Responses that are basically correct but lacked some elaboration ranked as "proficient." Incorrect responses ranked as "below proficient." An example of a scoring rubric can be seen in the assessment template in Appendix A.

Applying rubrics can also be challenging. It helps to provide examples of how an instructor applied the rubric to actual student work. Some instructors have reported that sharing with students past student work and rubrics can be helpful for instruction. Rubrics are also helpful in clarifying "non-technical" performance standards, rendering them more objective and transparent.

Selected Validity Study Findings

After the technician educators participated in the EC-AR process, both instructors and assessment designers created test items. This section of the chapter will describe the content and construct validity of these new final test items. This section provides evidence of the value of teaching and testing social-technical skills in technician education classes.

Content Validity

Content validity analysis seeks to answer the question: Does what we're teaching and what we're testing reflect valued learning outcomes in the technical field? It answers this question by collecting content experts' judgments of the assessments on different dimensions and their qualitative comments about each of the assessment items. We engaged at least one educator and one industry professional to review each SBL task and its associated assessments.

The experts reviewed our assessments according to their relevance to the workplace and technician education, their alignment with the professional behaviors and KSAs set forth in the design patterns, and the accuracy and usability of the scoring rubrics. We also asked only the education experts to review the cognitive complexity of the assessments and their utility with students of diverse abilities and backgrounds. Finally, we asked all experts to review samples of student work to determine if they provided evidence of the target professional behaviors and KSAs.

In total, 22 expert reviewers (10 industry reviewers, 12 education reviewers) provided feedback on 9 SBL tasks and their associated 50 assessments (18 in-class formative assessments, 32 final test summative assessments). We had them review the posttest items only, not both pretest and posttest, to minimize the time required to complete the review. Both pretest and posttest prompts were structurally similar; they differed only in the specific contextual details of the stimulus. The expert feedback was solicited through an online rating system that presented experts with links to: (1) online SBL tasks, (2) downloadable representative samples of the assessment templates, (3) two samples of student in-class work (high performer, low performer), and, (4) links to two online surveys. One survey posed questions to the experts about the SBL tasks and the other, about the assessments. They were paid with gift cards for their services. The primary findings of interest for the purposes of this chapter focus on the educator experts' judgments of the cognitive complexity of the SBL assessments.

Experts generally endorsed the quality of the tasks, assessments, and the design patterns' professional behaviors and KSAs as relevant to real world work and technician education. Both sets of experts (i.e., industry and educator) had numerous suggestions for improvement too. Overall, the industry reviewers wanted *greater complexity* in both the SBL tasks and the assessments to reflect the difficulty of the workplace better. The educational reviewers called for *clearer specifications* of the learning goals for each task and *more succinct presentations of problems* in both the scenario-based tasks and the assessments.

We also asked education experts additional questions to judge to what degree the final test items were sufficiently cognitively complex to give students the opportunity to develop higher-level thinking skills and content knowledge. These ratings may be broadly interpreted as feedback on how difficult educators perceived the test items to be. Overall, educators saw most of the problem-solving and professional skills items as adequately challenging for students, and they gave higher ratings to those items that measured more social-technical and social skills rather than the purely technical.

The educators gave high ratings of cognitive complexity to all problem-solving items in the environmental studies, bioinformatics, and all but one of the engineering items, with scores ranging from greater than 2.5 to 3.0 on the three-point scale. These problem-solving items addressed the professional behaviors of research and analysis, framing a problem, making inferences, and using tools.

The educators gave slightly lower ratings (2.2 to 2.5) on cognitive complexity to the more traditional assessment items that focused on "generating a product" in programming and engineering. These tasks were the most consistent with what technician educators typically used in their final examinations. They required students to produce some operational programming code or to complete some fundamental computations.

The educators also gave high to moderately high ratings on the cognitive complexity of the professional skills items that were more focused on social skills of communication and teamwork. There were fewer final test items that tested professional skills as some instructors declined to test these skills in a summative fashion. The experts gave high ratings (2.5 to 3.0) to engineering professional skills items focused on teamwork and presentation, and gave ratings of 2.5 to environmental studies professional skills items focused on presentation.

The content validity results indicate the external experts, both from education and industry, gave high ratings to the assessments that required application of technical knowledge to real world problems. They also rated the items measuring social-technical and social skills as more cognitively complex than those measuring basic technical knowledge.

In practice, community college instructional leaders may find these results useful for conveying to technician educators the value of teaching "social" and "social-technical" skills—not only technical. These particular validity study results indicate that conveying purely technical knowledge represents only a starting point for CTE. According to these results, both technician educators and industry professionals see the task of applying technical knowledge to real world problems as much more valued learning outcomes than simply showing proficiency in executing a technical procedure.

Construct Validity

In a construct validity study, assessment designers try to find out if item stimuli and prompts are eliciting the target skills and knowledge. Think-aloud interviews provide one method for checking to see if the items are working as intended.

The construct validity analysis was conducted with 26 final test items, engaging an average of four students per item, for a total of 104 think-alouds. This methodology is used to reveal reasoning processes that are frequently unavailable for analysis (Clark, Feldon, van Merrienboer, Yates, & Early, 2008). For each task, we sought to engage two high-performing students and two low-performing students as nominated by their instructors based on classroom performance. In a think-aloud, a researcher briefly trains each student to verbalize thoughts while completing a task (such as tying a shoe or solving a simple math problem). Then, the researcher records the student solving problems on the test and closes with asking the student a brief set of retrospective questions about task difficulty and quality. The think-aloud sessions are transcribed and then analyzed.

For the purposes of this pilot study, we had a minimum of two raters review each transcript using a coding system to categorize students' statements in the think-aloud as either providing—or failing to provide—evidence of the desired knowledge and skills. In the code development phase of the work, researchers and domain experts reviewed transcripts and created codes based on the KSAs, rubrics, and possible responses in the assessment templates. In the code application phase, researchers coded the transcripts and then categorized examples of student statements that confirmed and/or disconfirmed the use of the target knowledge or reasoning. In cases where the KSAs were well defined in the design patterns, raters could engage in a traditional inter-rater agreement approach, where the goal is to reach 75% agreement. In cases where the original KSAs were less clearly delineated, raters jointly reviewed the transcripts and reached consensus on how to categorize statements based on alignment with emerging features of student answers that reflected key understandings or skills.

This analysis clarified the focal KSAs of the SBL tasks and informed revision of the assessments. In this summary, we will report on the descriptive findings of the construct validity analysis, documenting the nature of the skills measured. Overall, the construct validity study indicated that the prompts functioned fairly well for higher-performing students, who applied social-technical skills in a more coordinated and systematic way than lower-performing students, who often used a "trial and error" approach to technical problem solving (Hmelo, 1998) and who did not smoothly coordinate the social and technical elements.

In practice, community college instructional leaders may use this information to frame the overall EC-AR approach for improving technician education. This framing is easiest to explain if we step back and consider the full scope of the EC-AR process: First, the EC-AR process *reveals the instructors' ideas* about how to apply technical knowledge to real world problems. Then it *defines the technical, social, and social-technical learning goals* that lead to improved skill in solving real world problems. Then it *develops assessments* for tracking student development in meeting those learning goals. When this system is in place, instructors are likely to see variations in student performance along both the technical and social dimensions similar to those reflected in the construct validity results.

Specifically, they will see that some students have challenges coordinating the social and technical dimensions. In particular, the lower-performing students may have two types of problems: (1) understanding basic technical procedures and tools; and, (2) understanding how to use information from the social context (e.g., client needs, budget, client problems, team member expertise) to guide the application of technical knowledge. The instructional challenge becomes not only to teach technical principles and procedures, but also to teach students how to attend to the different dimensions of client needs that can constrain the solution approach to a technical problem (e.g., budget, time frame), and to teach students how to identify gaps in their own knowledge that need to be addressed by posing questions and seeking out the expertise of team members.

Problem-solving skills

FRAMING A PROBLEM: PYTHON PROGRAMMING, AJAX PROGRAMMING, NETWORK SECURITY

Framing a problem was defined in the EC-AR process as a social-technical skill that requires technicians to gather information about client needs and then translate those needs into technical specifications. For example, in programming, a client interview leads to specifying use cases and user requirements, which in turn help the programmer to code or select Web widgets to implement desired functions. In a similar vein, a client in a Network Security interview describes budgetary constraints and a list of mechanical symptoms that require the technician to diagnose the problem and recommend a course of repair or improved network protection.

The think-aloud analysis showed that items designed to measure the skill of framing a problem required the students to construct a partial mental representation of the client's needs, and then to identify the gaps in their own knowledge that inform further questions to the client.

The assessment items that stimulated this line of social-technical reasoning typically involved a scenario-based stimulus drawn from the real world, and then a prompt designed to focus students on applying the specific skill of asking questions of a client. Figure 19.2 illustrates an example from Network Security.

Evidence of student proficiency in the skill was reflected both in the number and technical relevance of the questions posed by the student. In Network Security, for example, one high-performing student generated several relevant questions to determine if the intrusion was still ongoing, whether the data had already been restored, and what the value of the lost data was. The student

Real World Stimulus	A health care agency that sends patient services information to over 100 insurance companies recently had its data corrupted by a hacker attack. This SQL injection attack allowed the hacker to create a database administrator account and corrupt the data, leading to inaccurate billing and statements. Your system's technical specifications include a cluster of HP blade servers running in a virtualized environment on VMWare Infrastructure 3—with a combination of Windows and Linux machines. This consolidation took them from 48 physical servers down to 8 physical hosts. The Web servers all run Apache and are designed for high availability. The company does not run an Intrusion Prevention system, but has recently purchased log analysis software to help with security management and forensic investigations. The IT department has a budget for materials and supplies of $10,000 a year and already plans hardware purchases of $20,000.
Prompts	a) List 3 additional questions you would need to have answered to understand the level of risk to the enterprise. b) Describe, given your remaining IT annual budget, the scope of security solution the enterprise can currently afford.

Figure 19.2 Example of a problem-framing assessment item for Network Security

also noted the small size of the budget available, a key constraint to the choice about the technical solution. By contrast, lower performing students tended to ask questions that either focused on information already given in the initial stimulus or that provided little, if any, relevant information to determining the technical choices that would need to be made.

GENERATING A PRODUCT: PYTHON PROGRAMMING, AJAX PROGRAMMING, NETWORK SECURITY

While some of the items designed to measure the students' proficiency in "generating a product" were more narrowly technical in nature, some involved the interplay of the social and technical dimensions. One such social-technical item type that was used in multiple domains asked students to link an initial client request to the specification of a technical solution.

In Network Security, for example, "generating a solution" was operationalized through the EC-AR process as "the skill of generating a solution that applies just the amount of resources needed, within the constraints of the configuration and budget, and selecting and assembling a configuration of components to adequately address a security problem." Figure 19.3 illustrates an item for assessing this skill.

In this and other similar questions, higher performing students were able to discern technical functions or requirements that met user requirements relatively quickly whereas lower performing students failed to make these links. For the Network Security item, the high-performing students showed evidence of checking off technical components that "belonged together," such as data mirroring and identifying LINUX, and the students also selected components that were within the client's specified budget. One of these students provided a detailed implementation description. In this performance, we see a smooth coordination of social and technical components. By contrast, one low-performing student instead guessed at the various components that "belonged together," and did not systematically defend the security budget or provide an implementation description.

Stimulus	Management at the medical agency described above has decided to provide additional funding of up to $15,000 to the IT budget to ensure the long-term security of the system.
Prompt	Given the higher budget, answer the following question: Briefly describe how you would implement the solution with the selected components. a) Which of the following network security components and measures would you recommend? • Switch to a Linux architecture • Run MySQL as a database • Use Perl for the scripting language • Run an Apache Web server • Purchase a second database and server • Mirror data to another machine • Purchase an Intrusion Prevention System • Outsource your data management and server management to a third party • Switching to Oracle instead of SQL Server • Fund a part-time security staff position and hire someone trained in use of open-source network security scanning tools and IT audit tools to assess and monitor the security of the system.

Figure 19.3 Example of a solution-generation assessment item for Network Security

RESEARCH AND ANALYSIS: BIOINFORMATICS

The assessment items designed to measure the skill of "research and analysis" required students to apply "strategic knowledge of how to plan a research strategy." This included applying knowledge of the relevant databases and biological concepts to guide research steps and search queries. It also included "knowledge of appropriate bioinformatics representations that aid in analyzing viral characteristics and evolutionary patterns." Figure 19.4 illustrates an item for assessing this skill.

The real test in this item was to see how far the students would move from the initial pointers (NCBI, TPMT) embedded in the item stimulus. Three out of the four students simply repeated the given information. Only one moved beyond it. These think-aloud responses indicate that, at least for the higher-performing student, the item elicited higher-order, metacognitive skills of planning a research strategy using particular databases (OMIM, PubMed) and identifying the correct search queries, but that most students need more support and guidance to generate a plan for a database search.

Professional skills

COLLABORATING TO SOLVE A PROBLEM: NETWORK SECURITY

The target professional behavior was operationalized as "the skills of identifying and discussing alternative solutions, building consensus with the team, tapping and sharing team expertise, and

Stimulus	The human enzyme thiopurine methyl transferase (TPMT) catalyzes the methylation of thiopurine compounds. Thiopurine compounds have been used successfully in the treatment of various conditions like leukemia or autoimmune disorders. Unfortunately, thiopurine compounds have also been found to have adverse effects for up to 25% of patients and extremely adverse effects for a small percentage of patients.
	You have been asked to locate information about the human TPMT gene and the protein encoded by this gene, and evaluate whether it would be reasonable to test for specific forms of the TPMT gene when prescribing drugs for conditions or diseases like leukemia or autoimmune disorders.
Prompt	Describe a step-by-step plan for using the National Center for Biotechnology Information (NCBI) databases to determine whether or not knowing a patient's TPMT genotype would be useful to doctors when they are considering treatments involving thiopurine compounds. Cite and justify specific search methods, databases, and ways of organizing data that you would use.

Figure 19.4 Example of a research–and–analysis assessment item for Bioinformatics

Stimulus	The health care agency has noted an increase in the use of electronic medical records and so the company has decided to make some upgrades in its services and functions. You have been asked to work with several technical and medical billing specialists to prioritize what changes will be made in the data sent to the insurance companies. While you are most concerned with security, other team members are most concerned with speed of the data feed, as well as the accuracy of the data feed. You have one week as a team to set your priorities, though your first two meetings have not yet yielded any agreement.
Prompt	Describe 3–5 steps you would take as the team leader to arrive at a list of priorities agreed upon by the team.

Figure 19.5 Example of a collaboration assessment item for Network Security

distributing and managing team work and work products in a timely way." Figure 19.5 illustrates an item for assessing this skill. This task focused on the extent to which students could integrate social problem-solving skills—such as consideration of different perspectives and polling—into the network troubleshooting process.

The findings from the construct validity tests show, overall, that the assessments developed had elicited coordinated responses that interwove social and technical elements of solving a real world problem. The results also show that the ability to coordinate the social and technical elements was not evident in the students consistently, which suggests that students need more opportunity to hone this skill.

As mentioned earlier, these results indicate the kinds of instructional challenges that technician educators will encounter when they shift from a narrow technical focus in instruction to one that teaches both social and social-technical skills for applying technical knowledge to real world problems. As can be seen, instructors may find they will need to support students in a range of skills. The example about bioinformatics research and analysis skills indicates that instructors may need to help students persist in tasks beyond what they may typically expect from school assignments. The examples indicate that students may need help knowing when to switch from a technical focus to a social focus, to how to use social input to guide the technical solution to a problem.

Challenges to the EC-AR Process

Engaging technician educators in this process was not easy. In this section, we will briefly summarize the range of challenges that emerged and describe how we addressed them.

Although the KSAs would seem to be the easiest to define, they were actually the hardest point of reflection. As mentioned earlier, the problem is partly one of prioritization, particularly for instructors who thoroughly list many forms of knowledge and skills they intend to teach; and it is partly a problem of specification, particularly for instructors who seek to instill a generalized sense of confidence or self-efficacy in students. We found that focusing instructors on describing the forms of knowledge that were most fundamental to performance supported prioritization. Although we did not get to test it in this project, we suspect this approach may also help instructors who care most about confidence building. For example, they may see how mastering such fundamental skills will contribute to students' sense of self-efficacy in a field.

Postsecondary instructors also expressed concern that assessment procedures might threaten student engagement in the SBL task. In our view, while poor assessment design can threaten student engagement, quality assessment should have the opposite effect. These concerns about student engagement are legitimate but addressing them required more specialized time and focus than our project permitted. In the future, instructors with these concerns might be encouraged to find ways to engage students in developing the learning goals and rubrics by which they are judged. Establishing student buy-in can make the assessment process more engaging.

Most instructors welcomed EC-AR as an opportunity to "unpack" what they were teaching and to understand better what they needed to do to help their students perform competently in the workplace. Still, it is challenging to extract and organize all this information. This is because technicians master their fields not just by gaining discrete technical knowledge, but by playing progressively more central roles in the core social, cognitive, and technical aspects of the work (Lave & Wenger, 1991). Such background does little to prepare technician educators for the analytic processes of curriculum and instructional design, nor does it prepare them to develop what Shulman (1987) has called pedagogical content knowledge—not just the technical knowledge, but the knowledge of what students find difficult to learn, why, and how to intervene to support their learning. Defining KSAs is hard precisely because it represents the first step toward breaking down the different components of technician educators' deeply integrated knowledge base.

To improve collaboration with these instructors, our team developed a KSA discussion process over time, taking cues from instructors about what supports they needed. Past cognitive research indicates that experts find it difficult to describe all the steps in any procedure partly because their expertise permits them to "chunk" discrete steps into automatic "super procedures." To avoid the instructors' "blind spots," we added some additional questions to the EC-AR interview to elicit from the instructors more details about what students were learning how to do. For example, we asked them to describe each step of a technical process in detail so we could probe deeper into areas where they took "shortcuts," and sometimes we acted as naïve students who did not understand how the instructors got from the proverbial point A to point B.

To assess social and social-technical skills, it helps to use rubrics to specify the elements of a good social performance in consistent ways. While the formative approach to teamwork and presentation works well as an informal instructional technique, it also can become a signal to students that the social aspects of the technical work are not central to the course, but "extra." In a high-stakes education context, where students are making decisions about where to invest their effort, too often what doesn't get assessed doesn't get learned.

Another difficulty surfaced in examining student work. Too often students provided relatively brief responses. It appeared that the assessments elicited the desired skills but not in a sufficiently elaborate manner. We might blame these sparse responses on pressures of the test-taking context— except that a similar lack of elaboration was also observed in some of the student in-class assignments. It may be that students need explicit prompting in both in-class and final test assessments to provide more detailed descriptions of their reasoning. We recommend more exploration of alternatives to writing, such as spoken and annotated hands-on performances.

In our work one-on-one and in professional development groups, we have found the EC-AR process to be one that gets faculty talking in thoughtful ways about how they teach. In our future work, we plan to engage faculty in action research applying the ideas of EC-AR in their own practice. We also plan to create an online tool to create a DIY version of EC-AR.

The Promise and Challenge of EC-AR in Technician Education

The EC-AR draws deeply on the instructors' technical knowledge and experience to inform new learning goals. Using EC-AR, technician educators successfully characterized the important learning goals for 21st-century workforce programs as comprising a range of skills: technical, social, and social-technical. In reviewing the results of our work, we can see the outlines of Vygotsky's theory of "activity" (Wertsch, 1985). In this theory, cognition is not in the head, but distributed across the tools, language, social systems, and knowledge representations of the everyday world. The EC-AR process helped elicit, document, and assess what technician educators see as the primary forms of evidence that their students can coordinate the technical tools, discourses, social norms, and representational systems of each technical field.

The validity studies confirmed the value of the EC-AR process as a basis for developing aligned and sensitive measurements of student learning in a complex technician education setting.

- The content validity study demonstrated that domain experts from education and industry endorsed the quality and difficulty of the items overall. Industry experts recommended greater difficulty and complexity, while education experts sought clearer definitions of learning outcomes and strong usability of the scoring rubrics.
- The construct validity study confirmed that the characteristic task prompts and stimuli effectively elicited metacognitive skills of planning and constraint monitoring. However, the study also indicated that additional direct guidance or prompting are required to support students in imagining the dynamic processes of social and real problem-solving contexts. Only the highest-performing students spontaneously engaged in such imaginative reasoning without additional prompting.

To keep pace with change in the technician workforce, the EC-AR process shows that technician instructors see the importance of going beyond teaching and testing the purely technical skills and incorporating social and social-technical learning goals. Our research also indicates the EC-AR process can serve as a first step to broadening two-year technical educators' assessment repertoire and a fundamental part of transforming technician education to meet the demands of the 21st-century workplace.

Note

1 The authors acknowledge the invaluable contributions of the following researchers in all phases of this project: SRI colleagues Geneva Haertel, Ruchi Bhanot, Bowyee Gong, Ann House, Ken Rafanan, Thomas Gaffney, Britte Cheng, Tina Stanford, Jasmine Lopez, Nathan Dwyer, Yesica Lopez, and Luisana Sahagun. The authors also acknowledge the cooperation of the community college instructors, four-year college instructors, and subject matter experts who assisted in this work: Elaine Haight, Sandra Porter, Richard Swart, Ralph Lantz, Tessa Durham Brooks, James "Jake" Jacob, Kristin Sullivan, and Lianne Wong. In addition, the authors thank the many instructors who participated in our workshops both online and at conferences. Finally, the authors extend appreciation to the industry and education experts who assisted in this work: Jas Sandhu, Claudia De Silva, Susan Hiestand, Debra F. McLaughlin, Joe Leizerowicz, Jill Mesonas, Warren Hioki, Mike Ogle, Jorge Rodriguez, Parthav Jailwala, Bruce Van Dyke, Elizabeth Murray, Konstantinos Belonis, Robert G. Pergolizzi, Mulchand S. Rathod, and Erin Sanders-Lorenz. This material is based on work supported by the National Science Foundation under DUE grant number 0603297. Any opinions, findings and conclusions or recommendations expressed in this material are those of the author and do not necessarily reflect the views of NSF.

References

Alverno College. (1977). *Faculty handbook on learning and assessment.* Milwaukee, WI: Author.

Clark, R. E., Feldon, D., van Merrienboer, J. J. G., Yates, K., & Early, S. (2008). Cognitive task analysis. In J. M. Spector, M. D. Merrill, J. J. G. van Merrienboer, & M. P. Driscoll (Eds.), *Handbook of research on educational communications and technology* (3rd ed.). Mahwah, NJ: Erlbaum.

Cohen, A. M., & Brawer, F. B. (2002). *The American community college* (4th ed.). San Francisco, CA: Jossey-Bass.

Facione, P. A. (1990). *Critical thinking: A statement of expert consensus for purposes of educational assessment and instruction—Research findings and recommendations.* Millbrae, CA: The California Academic Press.

Haertel, G., Wentland, E., Yarnall, L., & Mislevy, R. J. (this volume). *Evidence-centered design in assessment development.*

Hmelo, C. E. (1998). Problem-based learning: Effects on the early acquisition of cognitive skill in medicine. *Journal of the Learning Sciences, 7*(2), 173–208.

Jonassen, D. (2000). Toward a design theory of problem solving. *Educational Technology Research and Development, 48*(4), 63–85.

Lave, J., & Wenger, E. (1991). *Situated learning: Legitimate peripheral participation.* Cambridge, UK: Cambridge University Press.

Lynch, R. L. (2000). *New directions for high school career and technical education in the 21st century.* ERIC Clearinghouse on Adult, Career, and Vocational Education, Center on Education and Training, Information Series No. 384. Columbus, OH: The Ohio State University.

Messick, S. (1994). The interplay of evidence and consequences in the validation of performance assessments. *Educational Researcher, 23*(2), 13–23.

Mislevy, R. (2007). Validity by design. *Educational Researcher, 36*(8), 463–469.

Mislevy, R., & Riconscente, M. M. (2006). Evidence-centered assessment design: Layers, structures, and terminology. In S. Downing, & T. Haladyna (Eds.), *Handbook of test development* (pp. 61–90). Mahwah, NJ: Erlbaum.

Pea, R. D. (1993). Practices of distributed intelligence and designs for education. In G. Salomon (Ed.), *Distributed cognitions* (pp. 47–87). New York, NY: Cambridge University Press.

Schank, R. (1997). *Virtual learning. A revolutionary approach to building a highly skilled workforce.* New York, NY: McGraw-Hill.

Shulman, L. S. (1987). Knowledge and teaching. *Harvard Educational Review, 57*(1), 1–22.

Wertsch, J. V. (1985). *Vygotsky and the social formation of mind.* Cambridge, MA: Harvard University Press.

Woods, D. R. (2000, December). *Helping your students gain the most from PBL.* Paper presented at the 2nd Asia-Pacific Conference on PBL, Singapore.

Yarnall, L., Toyama, Y., Gong, B., Ayers, C., & Ostrander, J. (2007). Adapting scenario-based curriculum materials to community college technical courses. *Community College Journal of Research and Practice, 31*(7), 583–601.

Appendix A

Ajax Programming Task 1: Everest Hiking and Rock Climbing Club – Final Test Items

Question #1: TD 2

A small group of outdoors enthusiasts, the Everest Hiking and Rock Climbing Club, wants you to help design an interactive Web site for its members. The users want to have access to a variety of functions, including the ability to follow local and international hiking and rock climbing expeditions, find local hiking routes, look up wilderness first aid information, and find links to other local outdoor clubs.

Generate 3 questions for the Everest Hiking and Rock Climbing Club client so you can understand how the Web site will be used and what the end user's needs are. Your answer will be scored for how well you anticipate the end user's needs, and how well you articulate your questions to a non-technical person, keeping in mind that the client is not an engineer.

Possible Responses	<ul><li>Who are the different users of this system and what do you want them to accomplish with it?</li><li>What kinds of inputs do you want users to enter into the system?</li><li>What criteria will users want to search on?</li><li>What outputs do you want to be visible to the users?</li><li>How sophisticated are your users?</li><li>Is there an existing Web site that is something like what you want?</li><li>How are these users getting this information now?</li></ul>
Scoring Key	Above proficient **(Score: 2)** = Formed at least 3 questions whose answers would identify and articulate what end users or client want in the product; shows attention to primary technical concerns as they affect the end user, and clear articulation. Proficient **(Score: 1)** = Formed at least 1 good question whose answers would address an end user or client need; shows some attention to primary technical concerns as they affect the end user or client, and somewhat clear articulation. Below proficient **(Score: 0)** = End user or client needs are not included in any questions or addressed in the questions; attention only to pure technical concerns, and/or unclear.

Knowledge and Skills Assessed: Skill of identifying and asking appropriate questions to specify user requirements. This skill is part of **"Framing a problem and identifying design constraints."**
Suggested Form and Procedure: Paper and pencil test administered by instructor.

Figure 19.6 Example of an assessment template with scoring rubric

20

ITEM ANALYSIS PROCEDURES FOR CLASSROOM ASSESSMENTS IN HIGHER EDUCATION[1]

Jerome C. Clauser and Ronald K. Hambleton

Very few instructors working in higher education—and, for that matter, instructors working at any level of education—receive much, if any, formal training in the construction of classroom tests and their uses. This training, if it were provided, might include topics such as the development of test plans (e.g., the content emphases, test length), sometimes called "test specifications," preparation of various types of test items such as multiple-choice, true-false, short answer questions, and extended answer questions (sometimes called "constructed response items"); item analyses; test scoring; grading; and the evaluation of tests including the investigation of their test score reliability and validity (see, for example, Gronlund & Waugh, 2009). This lack of test development training is unfortunate because achievement tests for assessing student knowledge of test content are common in higher education and as a result these tests all too often fall short of the technical requirements that are needed to ensure that the scores produced by these tests demonstrate the properties of test score reliability and validity.

It would not take very much training to substantially improve the quality of an instructor's test development skills. Often universities and colleges handle this training through the preparation of easy-to-follow checklists and short handouts, and/or by offering courses on test development through a teacher improvement or institutional research center.

In a chapter by Drezek McConnell & Doolittle (this volume), the topic of classroom assessment is addressed. Our chapter will focus on one step in the classroom test construction process known as "item analysis." As you will read in the sections that follow, item analysis is a test development technique that is used in the development of many tests for use in higher education such as the *Scholastic Assessment Test* (SAT). That said, item analysis can be effectively used by classroom instructors to improve their own assessment practices. This topic is expanded upon in this chapter.

Item analysis is a process of calculating and interpreting statistics for individual items on a test. These analyses are probably most common with multiple-choice items but they are easily extendable, for example, to other types of items such as true-false and matching, and both short and extended answer type questions. These item statistics are often useful in judging the statistical merit of test items and in helping to identify flaws and potential biases. Item statistics are also useful in building tests but we will leave that application to several other authors in this handbook (see, for example, the chapter on Item Response Theory by Osterlind & Wang). It is the first two of these three uses that are of interest in this chapter.

The remainder of the chapter has been divided into three main sections: First, the topic of practical item statistics for classroom item review is addressed. Second, the topic of identifying potentially biased test items is considered. These analyses are often called studies of "differential item function-ing (DIF)." Finally, we provide readers with a description of the available software to help with their item analyses.

With important test development projects such as those associated with state achievement tests, or national tests such as the *Scholastic Assessment Test* (SAT), the *National Assessment of Educational Progress* (NAEP), and ACCUPLACER (college placement tests prepared by the College Board), item analyses are carried out with substantial numbers (often in the 100s and even 1,000s) of students during the test development process at the pilot testing or field-testing stages, before the final tests are put together. With classroom tests, there is simply not the time or opportunity or even the need to conduct item analyses of the scope we see for tests intended for wide university, state, and/or national use. No one would expect these classroom tests to be of equal quality to these national tests (see Downing & Haladyna, 2006), but there are consequences for students (e.g., grades) and so a reasonable level of test quality is required and expected.

Clearly, instructors will benefit considerably from the use of item analysis results following test administration when they have the item response data from a full set of students, sometimes in the 100s. Even with small classes, informal item analyses can be helpful. Throwing student answers away after scoring a test and re-administering the same test a year later can never be justified. The results from an item analysis following a test administration will point the instructor to strengths and weak-nesses in his or her test items so that those that are problematic can either be eliminated from any future use or the items can be edited before the next time they are used. Future classroom tests will be better, and the instructor may actually become a better test developer by paying close attention to the results. For example, a multiple choice test item may appear to be surprisingly easy to the instructor after a review of the item analysis until he/she realizes that a bit of deductive reasoning by students with little knowledge of the topic will lead them to the only possible answer. The next time, the instructor could try to improve the test item by adding a couple of plausible but incorrect answer choices. It is true that small samples of students can lead to unstable statistics, but this small sample can and should be considered in the interpretation of results. And, in many undergraduate classes, 50 or more students will be found, and this number is more than large enough to conduct item analyses.

Practical Item Statistics for Classroom Test Item Review

The choice and use of item statistics is often dependent on the type of test item to which the statistics are being applied. With multiple-choice items, for example, an item analysis can provide three types of statistics: statistics that reflect item difficulty, item discrimination, and effectiveness of distractors (incorrect answer options).

What is Item Difficulty?

Dichotomous data (items scored 0 or 1)

Item difficulty is the average performance of students on an item. If the item is scored 0 (for an incorrect answer) and 1 (for a correct answer), we say that the item is "binary-scored" or "dichoto-mously-scored" and the average item score is referred to as the p value for the item. "P" stands for proportion, and in the case of 0-1 scoring, item difficulty or item p value represents the proportion of students who answer the item correctly. It is unfortunate that the statistic is not called "item easi-ness" since high p values describe easy test items. "Item easiness" is a more meaningful description that goes with the definition. Calculating and interpreting this statistic is easy, but it is important to recognize that it is dependent on the sample of students. For example, if the sample of students in one classroom is unusually capable, the item difficulty statistic will not generalize to other groups of students coming along at later time periods. In fact, no item statistics will generalize to other groups of students unless the other groups are similar in ability to the group and range of ability scores on which the item statistics were calculated.

There is an approach for estimating item difficulty statistics that is independent of the particular sample of students, but the approach is complicated and requires fairly large samples of students. The approach is based on models and procedures from the field of item response theory (for an introduction, see Osterlind & Wang, this volume).

While the probability of producing a correct answer or response is the most common way to express item difficulty, it is only one of several methods. Another popular method for presenting item difficulty is through the use of "delta values," sometimes called ETS delta values because the statistic was introduced by ETS more than 50 years ago. A delta value is a nonlinear transformation of the p value to a normal distribution with a mean of 13 and SD of 4 (e.g., a p value = .84 corresponds to an ETS delta value of 9). This non-linear transformation allows difficulties to be expressed on an (assumed) equal interval scale from 1 to 25. This method results in item difficulty values which may be better understood than p values since higher delta values are associated with more challenging items. Even more importantly, with estimates of item difficulty on an equal interval scale (i.e., delta values), more manipulations of the item difficulty statistics can be carried out for purposes such as test score equating and the study of item bias.

Item p values are just about the most popular way to statistically describe test items. These p values provide the basis for understanding test difficulty (which items contribute to making a test hard or easy), and direct instructors to where students are having the most problems (i.e., the lower p values), or the least problems (i.e., higher p values). Items with unusually high or low p values relative to other test items are sometimes in need of careful review, and sometimes these and other p values can be useful in determining the strengths and weaknesses of instruction.

Polytomous data (data scored 0 to m where m is the maximum score on the item)

The majority of techniques for calculating item difficulties are reserved for dichotomously-scored data. (See Table 20.1 for a complete list.) There are, however, methods for expressing the difficulty of polytomously-scored items. Livingston (2006), for example, recommends using a series of probabilities associated with each possible item score obtained from the item administration. For an item that could be scored 0 to 4, the instructor would calculate the probability of achieving a 4, the probability of receiving a 3 or greater, the probability of receiving a 2 or greater, and so on. These cumulative probabilities often help item level interpretations. Based on the frequency for each score, the instructor can draw conclusions about item difficulty in a way not possible with the use of the simple item mean score. At the same time, the simple item mean score is also a way to communicate item difficulty information. Polytomous scoring is often used with short- or extended-answer test items or what are called "constructed response" test items.

What Is Item Discrimination?

Dichotomous data

Item discrimination is typically estimated by the correlation between scores on an individual item with some criterion of interest, most commonly total test score because of its utility and convenience. Item discrimination indicates the capability of a test item to distinguish between high- and low-achieving students, something we would like each test item to do. Discrimination indices (as calculated by the point biserial correlation or the biserial correlation) greater than 0.30 are consid-

Table 20.1 Item Difficulty Statistics

Statistic	Description	Item Types
p Value	p value is the average performance on an item for the group of students. For dichotomous items, it can be calculated by dividing the total number of correct answers on the item by the total number of students.	This technique is appropriate for dichotomously-scored item types such as multiple choice, short answer, and true/false.
p Value Corrected for Unreached Items	For tests in which many students do not complete all of the items, it is sometimes appropriate to correct for unreached items when calculating p values. In order to make this correction, p values are calculated by dividing the total number of correct answers by the number of students who attempted that item or any later item. This procedure will prevent unreached items at the end of the test from looking artificially difficult.	
p Value Corrected for Guessing (With Equal Distractors)	It is sometimes desirable to determine what proportion of students was able to answer the item correctly without guessing. To make this determination, p values must be corrected (downward) by eliminating the effects of guessing. When it is reasonable to assume that all distractors are approximately equally attractive to students, there is a straightforward method to make this correction. The corrected p value is calculated by dividing the number of incorrect responses by the number of distractors and subtracting this value from the number of correct responses. This difference is the theoretical number of students who answered correctly without guessing. Dividing this value by the total number of students results in the corrected p value (for guessing). Of course it is just an estimate and based on an untestable assumption.	
p Value Corrected for Guessing (With Unequal Distractors)	In the circumstance in which it is desirable to correct for the effects of guessing but it is not reasonable to assume that all distractors are equally attractive to students, there is an alternative method to correct p values for guessing. In this procedure, it is assumed that the proportion of students who selected the most attractive distractor is equal to the proportion of students who guessed and arrived at the correct answer. Therefore the corrected p value is calculated by subtracting the number of students who choose the best distractor from the number who choose the correct answer. This value, divided by total number of students, is the corrected p value.	
Delta	Another popular method for presenting item difficulty is through the use of delta values. A delta value is a nonlinear transformation of the p value to a normal distribution. This configuration allows difficulties to be expressed on an equal interval scale. This method can potentially mitigate some of the confusion with p values by moving away from the 0–1 scale. In addition, the transformation can flip the scale so that higher deltas are associated with more challenging items.	
p Value Divided by Item Weight	While the previous examples have all been for dichotomous data, there are methods for calculating difficulty for polytomously-scored items. p values for polytomously–scored items can be calculated by dividing the average score on the item by the maximum possible score for that item. This approach would restrict the difficulties of polytomously-scored items to between 0 and 1, making them more readily comparable to dichotomous items.	This technique is appropriate when the test contains polytomous items such as essay questions.

ered acceptable for most purposes. With classroom tests, the expectation is that the values are at least above 0.0. At this point, it is critical to remember that "discrimination," as it is used in this context, is not the same as "bias" which will be discussed later. While test developers wish to make each item fair for students by removing bias, they are also striving for items that most efficiently separate, or "discriminate between," those who have mastered material from those who have not. Table 20.2 provides a listing of several different statistics for describing item discrimination. Software applications for obtaining these statistics are described later.

Since item discrimination (often denoted by the symbol "r") is simply a correlation, many different measures of association can be used. The most common correlation statistics for dichotomous data are the biserial and point biserial correlations. Each of these correlations can be used when one variable is dichotomous (item score) and the other is continuous, usually the test score. The primary distinction is that the point biserial treats the dichotomous variable as truly binary, while the biserial correlation assumes that the dichotomous scores are simply a manifestation of a student's latent proficiency, and across the set of students these latent proficiencies are normally distributed. When this additional assumption is appropriate, researchers tend to prefer the biserial correlations because these statistics are likely to be consistent across different samples of students. We say that the item statistics are likely to be "invariant" in their values across groups of students and this makes them more useful when building tests. The proof and demonstration of this point, however, would require substantially more explanation involving complex statistics (Crocker & Algina, 1986).

Despite the popularity of the biserial and point biserial correlations, a wide variety of correlation statistics may be appropriate for use with dichotomous data. When both the item level and the test score variable are dichotomous (for example, the test score variable might be binary if students have been identified as passers and failers), the phi and tetrachoric correlations would be most appropriate. With both statistics, items are scored in a binary way, and students are assigned to two groups based on their level of proficiency.

Polytomous data

While the item discrimination statistics described above are exclusively appropriate for dichotomous data, there are correlation coefficients which can be used with polytomously scored data too. The two most common of these are the polyserial and polychoric correlations. The polyserial correlation is like the biserial correlation but can be used with polytomously-scored item level data. The polychoric correlation is in essence an extension of the tetrachoric correlation for polytomous data. Regardless of which correlation is used to calculate item discrimination, it is important that the data are appropriate for the technique chosen.

Sometimes in place of a correlation to represent item discrimination, the D statistic is used: It is the difference of the p value in the top and bottom performing groups of students. Of course the goal is for this item statistic to be positive. The D statistic has a simple interpretation and is often used to reflect the discriminating power of a test item. It is quick and easy to obtain, and can be used with either binary or polytomous response data.

In summary, whether items are binary or polytomously-scored, item discrimination indices estimated with the appropriately chosen correlations are an invaluable way to evaluate test items. Items with higher discrimination indices are widely valued because they contribute to the statistical usefulness of the test in which they are placed, leading to more reliable and valid test scores. With items matched on content, the more discriminating items are nearly always preferred. The choice of items for tests is more complicated when decisions need to be made between the best fitting items based on content considerations versus the best items based on statistical considerations. The choice usually depends on the purpose of the test being constructed (see Knupp and Harris, this volume).

Table 20.2 Item Discrimination Statistics

Statistic	Description	Item Types
Point Biserial Correlation	One of the most common techniques used to calculate item discrimination for a test with binary scored items. This technique is ideal for determining an item's tendency to correlate with total test score. This Pearson product moment correlation coefficient makes no assumptions with regard to the distribution of the variables.	This technique is appropriate exclusively for dichotomously-scored item types such as multiple choice, short answer, and true/false.
Biserial Correlation	Like the point biserial, this is another common technique used to calculate item discrimination for a test with binary scored items. This technique assumes that a normal distribution underlies the dichotomously scored item and the statistic tends to produce higher discrimination statistics than the point biserial. Like the point biserial correlation, it is appropriate for determining an item's tendency to correlate with total test score.	
Phi Correlation	This technique is used to calculate item discrimination with two dichotomous variables. This feature causes the statistic to typically be used to determine an item's tendency to correlate with another dichotomous decision such as pass/fail. This correlation makes no assumption with regards to the distribution of the variables. It is simply a special case of the Pearson product moment correlation coefficient.	
Tetrachoric Correlation	Like the phi correlation, this statistic is used to determine item discrimination with two dichotomous variables and is most commonly used to determine an item's tendency to correlate with another dichotomous decision such as pass/fail. This statistic assumes that both dichotomously-scored variables are normally distributed. Due to its computational difficulty, software is typically required for performing the calculations.	
D Statistic	This procedure is popular due in large part to its ease of calculation. The students are split into two groups: high achievers and low achievers (for small tests typically top half and bottom half). Then the difference in the proportion of students who got the item correct in each group is calculated. For items with high discrimination, the high achievers should have scored significantly better than the low achievers and the calculated difference will be high. For items with low or negative discrimination, the opposite is true.	
Polyserial Correlation	This is like the biserial correlation but is used to calculate item discrimination for a test with polytomously-scored items. This technique assumes that a normal distribution underlies the polytomously scored items.	This technique is appropriate when the test contains polytomously-scored items such as with essay questions.
Polychoric Correlation	This is a modified version of the tetrachoric correlation designed to deal with polytomously-scored items. Because the criterion is still dichotomous, this technique is most often used to correlate scores on a polytomous item with dichotomous decisions such as pass/fail. Like the tetrachoric correlation, this correlation assumes a normal distribution underlies both variables.	
Correlation With Item Removed	This is a method for modifying all of the above item discrimination statistics. For tests with relatively few items, it is often desirable to remove the effect of an item from the total score to eliminate the potential bias. This technique is typically applied with short tests. For tests greater than 20 items or so, the effect of this change will be minimal.	This correction can be made with all of the item discrimination statistics and for all item types.

Effectiveness of Distractors in Multiple-Choice Items

With multiple-choice test items, one of the keys to the success of the format is the care with which the distractors (i.e., the incorrect answers) are written. If the item contains two correct answers, or no correct answers, or if a distractor is not attracting any students, or if the item stem provides clues to the correct answer, the multiple choice item may not be serving its intended purpose as an indicator of student knowledge or skills (see Gronlund & Waugh, 2009). Of course, there are many more item flaws that are possible, and these can often be inferred from an analysis of the distractor information. Item statistics in these situations can be very revealing. Studying the statistics associated with incorrect answers is valuable too, and can lead to clues about the possible flaws in the test items.

Figures 20.1 and 20.2 contain statistical summaries for two items. Each figure shows a different test item, the number of students who were administered the test item, and the p and r values (point biserial) for each item.

In addition, for these 4-choice items, a display is provided of the performance of the top 1/3 of the students and bottom 1/3 of the students. Usually "top" and "bottom" is determined by total test scores, but another criterion could be instructor determination of the "best" and the "poorest" students. Sometimes if there are lots of students, an instructor might consider only the top 1/4 and the bottom 1/4, and when the sample size is small perhaps the groups might consist of the top and bottom halves of the students so as to use all of the limited data available. The percentages in each group (fractions in each group: 1/3, 1/4, or 1/2) are not important. What is important is that the two groups have a sizeable number of students in each and that they differ in their test performance. The reason for the focus on two extreme performance groups is to check to see how the item is discriminating in relation to all of the possible answer choices. For a well-constructed item, more of the top performing group than the bottom performing group will answer the item correctly. For the distractors (or incorrect answers), the reverse is true: More of the lower performing group than the higher performing group will choose each of the distractors.

Figures 20.1 and 20.2 represent the types of displays we would like to see instructors produce after each test administration. What appear in the evaluation section are the instructor's thoughts about the item analysis data, and how the item might be revised prior to any future use. At the same time, we caution instructors not to over interpret the item statistics. Item statistics based on 36 students are quite unstable and can suggest potential problem areas in items but they are certainly not definitive.

Item 1	Item Statistics			
Who was the primary author of the US Constitution? A. Alexander Hamilton B. James Madison C. Benjamin Franklin D. John Hancock	N = 36	p = 0.27	r = −0.23 D = −.42	

	Distractor Analysis				
Group	N	A	B	C*	D
Top 1/3	12	8%	83%	8%	0%
Bottom 1/3	12	25%	17%	50%	8%

Instructor Evaluation: The item appears very hard. Statistics suggest that probably choice B is correct not choice C (notice the high number of students in the top 1/3 who chose choice B and how very few students chose choice B in the lower performing group). In fact, choice B was correct after I took the time to read the item carefully again! Also, very few students chose choice D. I will come up with a more plausible choice for D before I use this item again. I'll also revise the scoring key to reflect that choice B is correct.

Figure 20.1 An instructor's item analysis highlighting a miskeyed item
The "★" marks the correct answer.

Item 2	Item Statistics					
Who is credited with first writing the phrase: "Life, Liberty, and the Pursuit of Happiness?"	N = 36		p = 0.67		r = 0.31 D =.33	
A. Thomas Jefferson	Distractor Analysis					
B. George Washington	Group	N	A*	B	C	D
C. John Locke	Top 1/3	12	75%	0%	25%	0%
D. Barack Obama	Bottom 1/3	12	42%	50%	8%	0%

Instructor Evaluation: Based on the item statistics, this item (choice A is the correct answer) seems to be functioning well. But, the distractor analysis indicates possibly a few problems. Choice C (which is incorrect) is being selected far more by the top third of students than the bottom third (25% versus 8%). This suggests that it may be at least a partially correct response. Second, choice D is not being selected by any of the students. I will come up with a better distractor. I need to check choice C to be sure it is not a correct answer, and I should try to revise choice D before I use this item again.

Figure 20.2 An instructor's item analysis showing a non-functioning distractor and two possibly correct answers The "★" marks the correct answer.

In Figure 20.1, choice C is marked as the correct answer and the item was very difficult for students (p = .08) and negatively discriminating (r = -.23). These are known as "bad" item statistics and indicative of one or more problems. A study of the statistical information suggests that there appear to be major problems with the item. If choice B were the correct answer, statistically the item would be functioning much better. A re-review of the test item shows clearly that this item was miskeyed and choice B should have been scored as the correct answer. One other observation is possible: Almost no one went to choice D. Perhaps it would be possible to come up with a better distractor before the test item is used again.

In Figure 20.2, two bits of statistical information stand out: No students in the bottom 1/3 were attracted to choice C, but many of the better performing students went to choice C. When a pattern like the one seen for choice C is observed, a suspicion is raised about the correctness of choice C. Perhaps choice C is a correct answer too. If the test item were worded more carefully to ensure that choice C is not correct and choice D made more plausible to lower performing students, it is likely that in a new test administration that the item would function as easier (not necessarily a goal for revision), and almost certainly the item would function with more discrimination (and this is a goal of revision).

Detecting Potentially Biased Test Items

Instructors should also worry about introducing items into their tests that may be unfair to some of their students—notably: females or males; Blacks, Hispanics, or Whites; international groups; religious groups; or even students from cities versus the suburbs or rural regions. With highly technical content, the likelihood of potentially biased test items is very low. But with many other content areas, investigation of potential problems of unfairness or bias should be investigated.

There are three common ways to reduce or eliminate the problem of unfairness or bias in test items. First, instructors need to be sensitive to aspects of test item development that might interfere with the fair evaluation of their students. Second, a more formal judgmental review of test directions, test items, and any related scoring rubrics might be carried out. Finally, there are both simple as well as more complex statistical methods that might be applied to any available item level test data. A few words about each follow.

The first approach is for instructors to use some judgment in the development or selection of the test items. Instructors are encouraged to think about the diversity of students in their classrooms. Would the use of certain words or situations put a subgroup of students in the classroom at a disadvantage and make it more difficult for them to show their achievement? Perhaps an item has a religious or political context that some students might find offensive. Another source of differential item functioning (DIF) might be due to limiting the time to complete a test. Students writing in a second language may be adversely affected because they simply need more time. The result is that items later in a test show some signs of DIF. In many instances, instructor scrutiny may be the only approach that is used to reduce or limit sources of item level bias, and so it is important this approach be used.

The second approach is a bit more formal and may involve the use of a checklist and may involve additional reviewers providing commentary on the test items and scoring rubrics. A sample of items that may appear on a checklist (see, for example, Hambleton & Rogers, 1995) follows:

1. Does the test item contain inflammatory, controversial, or emotionally charged content for one or more subgroups of students taking the test?
2. Does the test item contain language or material which is demeaning or offensive for one or more subgroups of students?
3. Does the test item make reference to a certain culture that may place members of one or more subgroups at a disadvantage?
4. Does the test item contain words which have different or unfamiliar meaning in different subgroups of students?
5. Does the format or structure of the test item present greater problems for students from some backgrounds more than others?

Even if an instructor is not in a position to have others apply the checklist, the instructor at least can use it to check that his or her own test is not in violation of good test practices to reduce or eliminate potentially biased items or unfair testing methods (such as a restrictive time limit). Of course these types of potential biases and stereotyping would be less likely to occur in science and mathematics tests, though the possibility is always present that faulty language and failure to represent cultural differences can be found in any set of test items.

Finally, if the instructor has more than 100 students in a class, it may be possible to carry out empirical analyses like those shown in Figures 20.3 to 20.7. Here, groups of interest need to be identified—for example, males and females in the class. The group about whom no problems would be expected is referred to as the "reference group," while the group that might be considered to be disadvantaged is called the "focal group." In practice, the labeling of groups does not matter as long as the direction of the findings is considered when interpreting the results. Then, based upon the overall test score (or some other criterion measure), the students in each group are divided into subgroups based upon their total test scores. In the example, five subgroups are formed based upon total test score: 0 to 8, 9 to 16, 17 to 24, 25 to 32, and 33 to 40. Not too many subgroups should be formed to ensure that there are reasonable numbers of students from each group in each test score interval. Within the test score intervals, the reference and focal groups are assumed to be "matched" on test score. There may be big differences between the groups on the total test score, but within each test score interval the reference group and focal group are closely matched in test performance, so any difference in performance must be due to some feature of the test item not related to the construct measured by the test.

In Figure 20.3, the focal group shows consistently lower performance than the reference group across the test score intervals. This would not be expected, and so the item would be designated as "DIF" (and usually called "Uniform DIF") and an effort would be made to explain the results. Figures 20.4, 20.5 and 20.6 show what is called "Non-Uniform DIF" and should receive careful scrutiny before being included in future tests. Figure 20.7 shows a no-DIF test item. The more

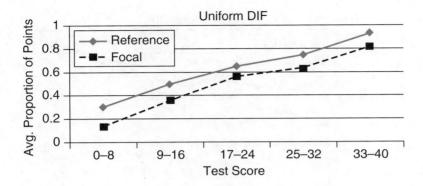

Figure 20.3 Display of reference and focal group data for an item showing uniform DIF

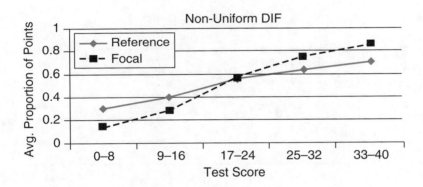

Figure 20.4 Display of reference and focal group data for an item showing non–uniform DIF—Example 1

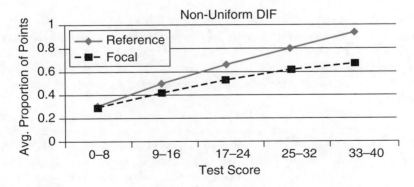

Figure 20.5 Display of reference and focal group data for an item showing non-uniform DIF—Example 2

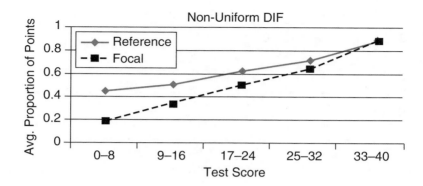

Figure 20.6 Display of reference and focal group data for an item showing non-uniform DIF—Example 3

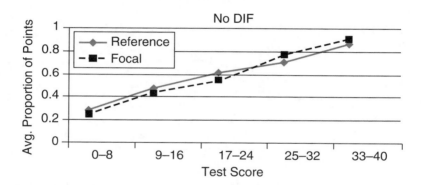

Figure 20.7 Display of reference and focal group data for an item showing no evidence of DIF

capable students answer an item with a higher level of performance than the less capable students, but reference and focal groups show no performance differences. These analyses are completed for all the test items and for the demographic variables of interest. The advantage of these displays is that instructors can view the results graphically. The disadvantage is that, with small samples, they can be quite unstable.

Of course, analyses like those highlighted in Figures 20.3 to 20.7 can be carried out with both large and small samples, but are more meaningful with larger samples. It is important to remember that sample size is important for both the reference and focal group; so, in a classroom with only one or two Asian students, an Asian versus white DIF analysis would not be reasonable. In addition, with either large or small samples, there are many statistical methods that can be applied to data like the data displayed in the figures (see Penfield, 2005). When DIF is possible in a set of test items, it is common to consider judgmental item reviews and either (or both) graphical and statistical methods to identify potential item problems.

Sample of Available Item Analysis Software

There are numerous benefits to performing item analysis on classroom tests. That said, calculating item statistics using a spreadsheet or within a complex statistical package can be time consuming and tedious. Fortunately, there are a number of dedicated item analysis software applications which can greatly simplify the process. This section will provide a brief overview of some of the available software and highlight a few potential use cases. See Table 20.3 for a sample of software and brief descriptions.

Classical Item and Test Analysis Spreadsheet (CITAS) is an excellent way to begin analyzing test items for anyone who is comfortable working within a spreadsheet like Microsoft Excel or OpenOffice Calc. CITAS is a custom spreadsheet with preprogramed formulas for calculating item difficulty and discrimination and overall test reliability. In addition, CITAS can also provide a simple distractor analysis to aid in the identification of poor distractors or errors in the answer key. The program is easy to use and is targeted specifically at small scale classroom examinations. Unfortunately, CITAS is limited to no more than 50 dichotomous test items and no more than 50 students. Because CITAS is free and works with commonly available spreadsheet software, it is an ideal starting point for any instructors interested in performing item analysis.

For instructors looking for slightly greater functionality, *Test Analysis Program* (TAP) is a free item analysis package for Microsoft Windows. Like CITAS, TAP is capable of calculating item difficulty, discrimination, and reliability. TAP is also able to perform advanced distractor analysis and generate student level reports. In addition, TAP is capable of supporting up to 200 students and as many as 90

Table 20.3 Brief Descriptions of Six Item Analysis Software Packages

Name	Platforms	Features	Item Type	Access
Classical Item and Test Analysis Spreadsheet (CITAS)	Windows Mac Linux	Difficulty Discrimination Test Reliability Distractor Analysis	Dichotomous Only	Available at no cost at: www.assess.com/xcart/home.php?cat=19
Test Analysis Program (TAP)	Windows	Difficulty Discrimination Student Reports Distractor Analysis	Dichotomous Only	Available at no cost at: http://oak.cats.ohiou.edu/~brooksg/tap.htm
ITEMAN	Windows	Difficulty Discrimination Reliability	Polytomous and Dichotomous	Available for purchase at: www.assess.com/xcart/home.php?cat=19
jMetrik	Windows Mac Linux	Difficulty Discrimination Reliability Decision consistency DIF Many advanced procedures	Polytomous and Dichotomous	Available at no cost at: www.itemanalysis.com
DIFAS	Windows	DIF statistics for several popular methods	Polytomous and Dichotomous	Available for purchase at: www.psychsoft.soe.vt.edu/listall3.php
Laboratory of Educational Research Test Analysis Package 5 (LERTAP 5)	Windows Mac	Difficulty Discrimination DIF Distractor Analysis	Polytomous and Dichotomous	Available at no cost at: www.assess.com/xcart/home.php?cat=19

dichotomously-scored test items. These features make TAP an ideal fit for many university tests. If an instructor's class size exceeds 200 persons, drawing a representative sample of students would still provide the basis for a very useful item analysis.

ITEMAN is one of the oldest commercial item analysis packages on the market for Windows PCs. It is capable of calculating item difficulty, discrimination, and reliability statistics for true/false, multiple-choice, and Likert-type items. In addition, ITEMAN can generate graphical displays of the total test and individual item statistics. The major advantage of ITEMAN over the above packages is that it is capable of handling as many as 750 items and imposes no limit on the number of students. Although, these higher limits will be excessive for many instructors, ITEMAN may be practical in some academic environments.

jMetrik is a free and feature rich program capable of item analysis for Windows, Mac, and Linux. The software has a wide variety of features which includes calculating item difficulty, discrimination, reliability, and decision consistency for both dichotomous and polytomously-scored items. In addition, jMetrik supports flexible scoring options, detection of differential item functioning (DIF), and many advanced psychometric procedures. jMetrik's extensive feature set means that it may be overwhelming for inexperienced users, but the feature set also makes it possible for instructors to perform more complex analyses as their interest and skill levels develop.

Differential Item Functioning Analysis Software (DIFAS) is an easy to use DIF analysis package for Microsoft Windows. DIFAS offers a wide variety of DIF detection methods for both dichotomous and polytomous items. Although this software does not provide detailed item analysis information, it may be ideal for instructors interested primarily in detecting potentially biased test items.

The Laboratory of Educational Research Test Analysis Package 5 (LERTAP 5) is a sophisticated commercial item analysis program that works with Microsoft Excel. LERTAP 5 is capable of calculating standard item analysis values as well as differential item functioning (DIF), Distractor Analysis, and Response Similarity Analysis. LERTAP 5 is very flexible and robust and capable of handling up to 10,000 items and over 1 million students. This program will be beyond the needs of most instructors but may be of interest to some instructors.

Follow-Up Readings

Nearly all texts on classroom test construction will include a very practical chapter or a section of a chapter on conducting item analyses (see, for example, Airasian, 2005; Gronlund & Waugh, 2009). For more advanced treatment of item analysis and the detection of differential item functioning, readers are referred to books by Crocker and Algina (1986) and Holland and Wainer (1993), and short chapters by Hambleton and Dirir (2003), Livingston (2006), Luecht (2006), and Wood (1988). The detection of potentially biased items via judgmental methods might be covered as an activity in the item writing and review process (see, for example, Hambleton & Rogers, 1995). For a detailed discussion of detecting item and test unfairness, see Carlton (this volume).

Note

1 Center for Educational Assessment Research Report No. 744. Amherst, MA: University of Massachusetts, Center for Educational Assessment. The authors appreciated the careful review of the chapter by Skip Livingston from ETS.

References

Airasian, P. (2005). *Classroom assessment: Concepts and applications* (5th ed.). Boston, MA: McGraw-Hill.
Carlton, S. (this volume). *Using content specialists for detecting item and test unfairness.*

Crocker, L., & Algina, J. (1986). *Introduction to classical and modern test theory*. Orlando, FL: Holt, Rinehart, & Winston.

Drezek McConnell, K., & Doolittle, P. E. (this volume). *Classroom-level assessment: Aligning pedagogical practices to enhance student learning*.

Gronlund, N., & Waugh, C. K. (2009). *Assessment of student achievement*. Upper Saddle River, NJ: Pearson.

Hambleton, R. K., & Dirir, M. (2003). Classical and modern item analysis. In R. Fernandez-Ballesteros (Ed.), *Encyclopedia of psychological assessment* (Vol. 1, pp. 188–192). Thousand Oaks, CA: Sage.

Hambleton, R. K., & Rogers, H. J. (1995). *Item bias review* (EDO-TM-95-9). Washington, DC: Clearinghouse on Assessment and Evaluation.

Holland, P., & Wainer, H. (Eds.). (1993). *Differential item functioning*. Mahwah, NJ: Erlbaum.

Knupp, T., & Harris, D. (this volume). *Building content and statistical test specifications*.

Livingston, S. (2006). Item analysis. In S. M. Downing, & T. M. Haladyna (Eds.), *Handbook of test development* (pp. 421–441). Mahwah, NJ: Erlbaum.

Luecht, R. (2005). Item analysis. In B. S. Everitt, & D. C. Howell (Eds.), *Encyclopedia of statistics in behavioral science* (Vol. 2, pp. 958–967). New York, NY: Wiley.

Osterlind, S. J., & Wang, Z. (this volume). *Item response theory in measurement, assessment, and evaluation for higher education*.

Penfield, R. D. (2005). DIFAS: Differential item functioning analysis system. *Applied Psychological Measurement, 29*(2), 150–151.

Wood, R. (1988). Item analysis. In J. Keeves (Ed.), *Educational research, methodology, and measurement* (p. 376–384). London, UK: Pergamon Press.

21

USING CONTENT SPECIALISTS FOR DETECTING ITEM AND TEST UNFAIRNESS

Sydell T. Carlton

The increasing diversity in the populations of most countries in the world has been accompanied by an equal diversity in the students taking tests. The number of female test-takers in most countries has grown, for example, as has the proportion of students from various ethnic and religious and regional groups, the proportion of students with disabilities, and the number of students of relatively low socioeconomic status. Testing, further, has increased in scope and is used by more and more institutions worldwide for more and more purposes: admission not only into universities and graduate and professional schools but also into several lower-level academic institutions, including primary schools, secondary schools, and technical schools; placement into courses at these schools; placement out of courses and for graduation; diagnosis of student strengths and weaknesses for remediation; certification and licensing for any number of professions from plumbing to psychiatry; providing a snapshot of a nation's level of academic accomplishment or a comparison of the academic levels of students from several nations; the granting of advanced standing to students or professionals; and so on (see for example, Carlton, 2001, 2005; Aina, 2005; UNESCO, 2005, 2006).

In confronting the difficulties arising from the convergence of an increase in testing and an increase in the diversity of test-taking populations, test publishers and academicians have responded in a variety of ways. They have initiated a series of accommodations for test-takers with disabilities, ranging from Braille editions of tests, to the use of readers and scribes, to the use of audio rather than written materials, or some combination of the above. For test-takers with learning differences, they offer tests with more liberal timing. Differential speededness for different ethnic or gender groups has been examined and, where feasible, changes to test content or to test timing have been made or at least investigated. In addition, for students for whom test-taking is a new experience—as is sometimes the case with students from lower socioeconomic groups—test preparation (or test familiarization) materials have been created or expanded. Other issues of differential access have also been cited and investigated. As well, myriad reasons for—and potential solutions for—the "Achievement Gap," as evidenced in divergent test scores, have been advanced. Most important, perhaps, test content and differential responding to test content have come under scrutiny.

Several decades ago, beginning in the late 1960s, test publishers developed several means of measuring actual differences in test-taking patterns of the various groups in the population. They also and further developed methods for determining whether any given test or set of tests is "fair," or appropriate, for all segments of the population and for trying to remediate these differences when such remediation is deemed necessary—either for social reasons or for reasons of test validity. In a world in which testing has so many purposes, it was deemed critical that each question in each test be examined for its contribution to the purpose of the test (hence, for its validity); it was equally critical that group differences in performance not directly attributable to a test's purpose but rather attributable to membership in a particular demographic group be identified and removed (validity again). From the 1970s and on, several statistical—or empirical—and after-the-fact techniques for identifying "unfair" questions were developed, and several methods to rid a test of such questions were put into place. Chief among these is the Differential Item Functioning (DIF) approach implemented at Educational Testing Service in the mid-1980s. DIF allows a test-maker to analyze the performance of test questions after they have been administered to determine whether examinees of similar ability in different gender or ethnic groups perform differentially. It helps to evaluate whether other information—for instance, the context in which a test question is posed—may be interfering with the original intent of the test question in a way that differentially favors or disfavors different groups. In brief, DIF occurs when people from different groups who have approximately equal knowledge and skill perform in substantially different ways on test questions. Corrective measures (e.g., changes in test formats or even test specifications) have been suggested and taken for some of the issues uncovered by the DIF statistic.

However, such statistical methods are administered *after* test administration, *after* test-takers have been subjected to a test. Another procedure has gained prominence over the years, one that is used *before* a test is administered. This procedure is usually known as Sensitivity Review or, simply, as Fairness Review. Unlike DIF, which is data-driven, Fairness Review is based on human judgment. Also unlike DIF, Fairness Review does not require large numbers of test-takers to implement—it is not at all dependent on test-takers. In Fairness Review, individual test questions and tests in their entirety are subjected to scrutiny in order, first, to remove offensive or upsetting materials, and second, to include material that represents the accomplishments of the diverse groups that make up the test-taking population. If DIF deals with how test questions *behave*, then Fairness Review deals with how test questions *look*—and for certain classes of test content, how test questions look can affect test-taking behavior (see, for example, Carlton & Harris, 1992; Tittle, 1982; Zieky, 2006). It is test specialists who are typically called upon to conduct these reviews.

The Fairness Review process promotes a general awareness of and a responsiveness to the cultural diversity of nations; the diversity of backgrounds, cultural traditions, and viewpoints to be found in the test-taking population; the changing roles and attitudes toward different groups in society; the contributions of various groups (including ethnic and minority groups, individuals with disabilities, and females) and the achievements of individuals within these groups; and the role of language in setting and changing attitudes toward various groups. This kind of review is best if it is done late in the process of test development; if it is carried out by trained reviewers following specific criteria or guidelines; if the process is documented; and if procedures are in place to deal with intractable disagreements (which, while relatively rare, are bound to come up when human judgment comes into play).

A few general comments about Fairness Review are worthy of mention. First, as is the case with most, if not all, issues dealing with fairness, the purpose of the test is a primary criterion; that is, while some materials may seem indefensible in *any* test, other materials may be more allowable in tests that specifically require certain kinds of content. For this reason, specific subject-matter tests, or content tests—which rely on specific curricula—have more latitude than do more general tests, or skills tests, in which the points tested are not reliant on any specific or short-term subject matter but rather on material learned over the course of years (as with vocabulary, for example). Second, Fairness Review is directly linked to test validity: if a valid test is one that does not contain construct-irrelevant materials, then a review process that removes construct-irrelevant material that may disrupt test performance and, thereby, falsify true ability or knowledge is a critical process that serves to enhance validity. The review is designed to remove aspects of a test question that are not related to what one wants to test and that may differentially impact different groups. The job of test-makers is to measure what a student knows or can do, not to measure what a student can do under conditions of extreme

311

agitation or distress; the review process works toward minimizing such adverse conditions. A third point is that the review process is always carried out from the perspective of the examinee, so that all parts of a question—the test, the correct answer, the incorrect choices—are subjected to review; all parts must meet the criteria or satisfy the guidelines.

How one sets up the criteria for Fairness Review, how one chooses and trains the reviewers, how one settles disagreements between question writer and question reviewer, along with other aspects of the Fairness Review process, are founded on common sense but in the end are judgmental, depending on values and in some cases on federal or state requirements. However, the general framework remains. Moreover, with many test publishers, the framework is one that has evolved over the course of nearly a half century, becoming broader and broader in scope at the same time as it has become finer and finer in its guidelines. The remaining discussion in this chapter will provide a brief description of the history of Fairness Review, along with a description of various methods for carrying it out.

History

In the early days of Fairness Review, reviews were typically informal and largely voluntary. Although practices differed from test publisher to test publisher, in general tests were assembled and then given to members of minority groups for what was then known as "minority review." There were usually no written criteria—certainly not elaborate ones—for these reviews and typically no formal documentation. Test developers would ask colleagues who were members of minority groups to review a test to determine whether any questions seemed "offensive" or "unfair" to members of minority groups. Women had not yet become a focus of the reviews. Changes in items deemed "unfair" were made at the discretion of the test developers. Reviews were most often internal, although it was not unknown for publishers to go to outside sources for such reviews. States had not yet mandated reviews by what have become known as "state bias committees."

In the very late 1960s and the 1970s, the Fairness Review process of many publishers was expanded to include women, as well as members of minority groups, and written guidelines were developed. In this period, the American Psychological Association (1977, 2001) included "Guidelines for Nonsexist Language" in its Publications *Manual*, and the McGraw-Hill Book Company published several sets of guidelines: among them were the *Recommended Guidelines for Multiethnic Publishing* (1968, 1974) and the *Guidelines for Equal Treatment of the Sexes* (1974). Educational Testing Service (ETS) issued *The ETS Guidelines for Testing Minorities* in 1974 and in 1976 came out with the *ETS Guidelines for Sex Fairness in Tests and Testing Programs*. In addition, other test publishers (e.g., American College Testing, Riverside, Science Research Associates, the Psychological Corporation), whether in explicit publications or in editorial and procedural processes, incorporated measures for Fairness Review of individual test questions and entire tests (see Berk, 1982, for examples; and Zieky, 2006).

Between the 1970s and now, Fairness Review has grown among test publishers. As ideas about fairness have evolved in society and as thinking about the relationship between test fairness and validity has increased, Fairness Review has successively become more inclusive and more comprehensive. Included in its purview are not only "minority group" members and females but also people who are disabled; people who are gay, lesbian, bisexual, and transgender; and people with limited English proficiency, among others. Reviews often are mandated not only for tests but also for ancillary publications, such as test-taker bulletins, test-user manuals, test supervisors manuals, research reports, and the like. At ETS, guidelines, or criteria, to be followed are typically explicit, reviewers are specifically trained, Fairness Review work is monitored and documented, and procedures are in place to deal with intractable disagreements between writer and reviewer. The details of each of these aspects may vary from publisher to publisher, but the purpose is the same: within the bounds of what is necessary to measure the construct of interest, to (a) include in tests the accomplishments of the various groups that make up the test-taking population, and (b) exclude from tests material that is stereotypical, sexist, racist, or otherwise demeaning or offensive or that is likely to cause upset among test-takers, particularly among subsets of test-takers. Individual questions we reviewed to be sure that groups are represented in a balanced way (e.g., relatively equal mentions of males and females) and that the accomplishments of each group are included, insofar as is feasible.

Test Reviewers

In making decisions about who conducts Fairness Review, publishers are typically in a position of compromise. The ideal situation is to have each test question and each test reviewed for fairness by a large group of reviewers, who among them represent all of the groups dealt with—minority members, females, and so forth. Reviewers would likely come from inside the publishing corporation and outside the publishing corporation, the former for feasibility and the latter for face validity. But such a system is not practical, either in terms of financial outlay or in terms of the time necessary to collect and reconcile all of the reviews. At the other end of the spectrum, it is possible to have only one reviewer, calling on others only when necessary. In the middle is considerable ground. Many states have specific bias review committees, all members of which are external to the test publisher; some publishers follow the more "streamlined" method, with only one reviewer unless serious issues arise. Often, these single reviews are supplemented by more expert and often external reviews if the expertise does not exist within the corporation. (For example, a reading passage about a Native American origin story might be sent externally to one or more Native Americans to review for fairness if Native Americans are not present within the testing organization.) Time and financial considerations will dictate how reviewers are chosen, whether or not they are internal or external, and whether or not they have to be members of the groups of concern (including, but not necessarily limited to, those with reference to ethnicity, race, age, gender, disability, national or regional origin, sexual orientation, religion, and socio-economic status). For rigorous reviews, however, it is critical that the reviewers be adequately and specifically trained, that records be kept of their performance, and that their reviews be a permanent part of the test record.

Disagreements

Because Fairness Review is subjective and judgmental, it is inevitable that disagreements about what is "fair" will arise. Two or more people who are equally "fair-minded" might well disagree about a particular item or test. To handle disagreements fairly, it is important to have a mechanism set up whereby third-party review or some other kind of adjudication is in place. Fairness coordinators who aid the process, steering committees that oversee the process, or other staff are ideal third-party judges. It is important that neither party—reviewer or question writer—feel aggrieved or browbeaten into submission. Disputes need to be handled quickly so that time and money do not become major issues. But most important, they need to be handled reasonably so that the process is viewed as fair. How the adjudication process is set up is not as important as that it *is* set up, that it is set up reasonably, and that it is adhered to.

Fairness Review Guidelines and Their Application

As mentioned earlier, the goal of Fairness Review is to ensure that test products will be designed and developed in ways that treat people equally and fairly regardless of differences in personal characteristics such as race, ethnicity, gender, disability, and so forth, that are irrelevant to the construct being measured. If inferences are made about people on the basis of their test scores, one wants to be sure that these inferences are accurate (valid). The extent to which Fairness Review helps ensure the accuracy of these inferences is the extent to which the test can be viewed as fair. How procedures do this can vary a great deal. The criteria that are used to apply to test questions and entire tests can be configured in many ways and, moreover, often overlap with each other; decisions about configuration and format are arbitrary. The critical aspects that need to be covered, however, are the following: (a) treat people with respect and represent diversity in depictions of people; (b) minimize the effects of construct-irrelevant knowledge or skills; (c) avoid construct-irrelevant material that is unnecessarily controversial, inflammatory, offensive, or upsetting to groups of people; and, of more recent origin in Fairness Review, (d) avoid construct-irrelevant physical barriers in test questions. All of these will be explained in more detail below, along with examples of test questions that violate the guidelines. The criteria cited, along with the examples provided, are drawn from the *ETS Fairness Review Guidelines* (2003) and the *ETS Guidelines for Fairness Review of Assessments* (2009) of Educational Testing Service, the copyright owner.

Treat People with Respect (Including Using Appropriate Terminology and Avoiding Stereotypes and Representing Diversity)

Treating test-takers with respect means using language and images that show respect for members of different groups, and avoiding language that is belittling, insulting, derogatory, condescending, or sarcastic. It means that test questions are to avoid stating or implying that the "majority group" or one's own group is superior to other groups, or is the reference point against which all other groups are measured. Material based on negative underlying assumptions about groups of people is to be avoided. Also to be avoided is language that assumes that test-takers or readers are citizens of the United States or are members of the "majority group" or are native speakers of the language of the tests.

Part of treating people with respect is using appropriate terminology in referring to people. In general, it is best to avoid unnecessary labels for people. If group identification *is* necessary, use the terms that people call themselves, recognizing that preferred terms change. It is best to recognize diversity *within* groups and to refer to individual groups whenever possible, rather than to broadly inclusive terms (e.g., Cuban American, Mexican American, Puerto Rican are preferable to Hispanic). Females or males over the age of 18 are "women" or "men," not "girls" or "boys." The use of the generic "he" or "man" to refer to all people is to be avoided. As of this printing, the following terms are generally acceptable for members of groups: Black, African American; Asian, Asian American, Asian/Pacific Island American, Pacific Island American (avoid "Oriental"); Hispanic, Latino/a, Chicano (although the last term in the Southwest and West can be used to refer to members of gangs and therefore might warrant special care); White, Caucasian. Care with terminology is also warranted in referring to all other groups, particularly to older people and to people with disabilities. It is necessary that negative terms and images be avoided; it is also necessary that condescending terms and images be excluded (e.g., disabled people who are heroic in "overcoming" their disabilities, older people who "surprisingly" can still learn to speak a foreign language).

Stereotypes, which are overgeneralized and oversimplified conceptions of the characteristics of groups of people and which attribute characteristics to groups on the basis of age, disability, ethnicity, gender, sexual orientation, and so forth, should be avoided in tests. This includes positive stereotypes as well as negative stereotypes. It also includes stereotypical statements that are then criticized or debunked, since the very mention of a stereotype can upset some groups of test-takers. In short, all stereotypes are to be avoided unless test blueprints specifically call for them (as might be the case in a sociology test).

Representing diversity simply means that in depictions of people in test questions, several groups should be shown when feasible and that, when possible, the status of the groups included should be equivalent. Men and women, along with members of several groups, should be represented and represented in ways that are equivalent.

Examples of guideline violations

Table 21.1 presents examples of violations of this Fairness Review guideline.

Table 21.1 Examples of Guideline Violations for Treating People with Respect

Guideline	Example	Violation
Treat people with respect	From a reading comprehension passage: *Many welfare mothers supplement AFDC (Aid to Families with Dependent Children) with wages from low-paying jobs; many get support from parents or boy friends; a few turn to selling drugs or to prostitution to narrow the gap between what AFDC pays and what they need to support their children.*	Negative, disrespectful attitude toward single parents and to people on public assistance.
Avoid stereotypes	From an essay prompt: *"Our society has many stereotypes regarding old people. We name them little old ladies, old geezers, and old fools. At the same time, we sometimes say that they are wise or serene."* *Discuss the extent to which you agree or disagree with this viewpoint.*	Stereotypes of old people.
Avoid stereotypes	From a math test: *Mary's home has four bedrooms of equal sizes. Mary can vacuum one bedroom in 30 minutes, and her mother can vacuum three bedrooms in 1 hour. How many minutes will it take Mary and her mother to vacuum the four bedrooms if they both vacuum together, each with her own vacuum cleaner?*	Unnecessarily stereotypical female behavior.
Represent diversity	Sentence in a writing ability test: *The pioneers and their wives suffered many hardships.*	Lack of equivalency between the males ("pioneers") and the females ("their wives"); assumption that pioneers were all male.

Minimize the Effects of Construct-Irrelevant Knowledge

Studies conducted over the years have demonstrated that some types of knowledge and skills that are not necessarily related to what we are trying to test are not always equally distributed across groups. These types of knowledge and skills are to be avoided in test questions unless they are clearly specified in test blueprints. Test questions required for valid measurement are allowable; those not required for valid measurement should be avoided. Subject matter in this category, shown to affect different groups differentially, includes the following: charts, maps, graphs, and other visual stimuli; unnecessarily difficult words or syntactic structures; figures of speech; idioms; elitism (that is, words or topics generally associated with wealthier groups, such as *arbitrage* or other uncommon financial vocabulary) or depictions of people spending large amounts of money on luxuries; religious knowledge; spatial skills; sports; military topics, including wars, weapons, conflict; regionalisms; and highly specialized words in several fields—farm-related, legal, political, scientific, technical, and associated with tools, machinery, transportation; and words or topics associated exclusively or largely with United States culture (coins, geography, holidays, measurement, slang, wildlife, entertainment, political systems, etc.). Any test requiring any of the above topics is free to make use of them; tests not requiring these topics would do best to avoid them.

An additional aspect of avoiding construct-irrelevant language is concerned with the use of accessible language. If "difficult" language is not needed to test a construct, then simple and straightforward language should be used. This is particularly important because so many test-takers now are not native speakers of the language of the tests. Again, with the need to test validly, any language necessary to test a construct is admissible; very hard vocabulary, therefore, is possible in a graduate test of verbal ability, for example. However, when "difficult" language is not part of the construct

Table 21.2 Examples of Guideline Violations for Minimizing the Effects of Construct-Irrelevant Knowledge

Guideline	Example	Violation
Avoid construct-irrelevant knowledge	Sentence in a writing ability test: *After he won the Heisman Trophy, he became one of the most productive running backs in the history of professional football.*	Unnecessary and construct-irrelevant mention of sports.
Avoid construct-irrelevant knowledge	An analogy in a verbal skills test: *HYMN: PRAISE:* *(A) waltz: joy* *(B) liturgy: rite* *(C) lullaby: child* *(D) dirge: grief* *(E) prayer: congregation*	Unnecessary and construct-irrelevant knowledge of religion.
Use accessible language	A sentence in a verbal skills test: *Though science is often imagined as a disinterested exploration of external reality, scientists are no different from anyone else, being passionate human beings enmeshed and circumscribed in a web of idiosyncratic and socially oriented circumstances.*	Language not accessible: sentence is too long and convoluted and vocabulary is difficult. (Note that if sentence structure and/or vocabulary is being tested intentionally as part of test specifications, the sentence is acceptable.)
Avoid idioms and colloquialisms	A sentence in a verbal skills test: *In a most impressive demonstration, the tenor sailed through the aria.*	"Sailed through" is idiomatic and likely not known by non-native speakers of English.

being tested, a few simple guidelines should be followed. First, short paragraphs and simple sentences, with specific and concrete words, should be used. Pronouns should have clear referents, and verb forms should be simple. The active voice is generally preferable to the passive voice. In addition, And colloquial expressions, idioms, and foreign expressions should be avoided, as should specialized words that are part of the vocabulary of special fields (as, for example, "tort," "lumen," "flange," "JPEG").

Examples of guideline violations

Table 21.2 presents examples of violations of this Fairness Review guideline.

Avoid Material that is Unnecessarily Controversial, Inflammatory, Offensive, or Upsetting

Unnecessarily upsetting or controversial material may serve as a source of construct-irrelevant, or invalid, difficulty and should be avoided when possible. (If such material *is* necessary, it should be handled in a conscientious manner.) Several topics, generally controversial and/or upsetting, should be steered away from (see ETS, 2009): abortion, abuse of people or of animals, experimentation on human beings or on animals that is painful or harmful, genocide, human sexual behavior, hunting or trapping for sport, rape, satanism, torture, witchcraft. Other topics, not as "inflammatory," should be handled with extreme care. These include: graphic depictions of accidents, illness, and the results of natural disasters; detailed discussion of death and dying; evolution of human beings from other species, except in science tests; views—positive or negative—on religion or religious practices; descriptions of slavery; suicide or other self-destructive behavior; violence or suffering. The point here is that one wants to test what students know and can do, not what they know and can do under stressful circumstances, which can be called up by discussion of many of the topics cited

Table 21.3 Examples of Guideline Violations for Avoiding Material that is Unnecessarily Controversial, Inflammatory, Offensive, or Upsetting

Guideline	Example	Violation
Avoid inflammatory or upsetting material	Sentence in a writing ability test: *When speaking of Napoleon and himself, Adolf Hitler was once quoted as saying, "We are both men born before our time."*	Unnecessarily inflammatory material for a skills test.
Avoid controversial material	Sentence in a verbal ability test: *The wonder of De Quincey is that although opium dominated his life, it never conquered him; indeed, he turned its use to gain when he published the story of its influence in the London Magazine.*	Unnecessarily controversial material for a non-literature test.

above. Materials suitable for classroom discussion need to be distinguished from material suitable for inclusion in tests. In the former, the teacher is present and presumably knows the sensitivities of the students; the teacher can mediate upset caused by the material; and the material in a discussion does not contribute to high-stakes decisions, as many tests do. In a test, anonymous test writers write questions for a very wide body of test-takers whose sensibilities they are not familiar with and who often view the test as having a large, sometimes permanent, effect on their lives. Unless it is needed to fulfill test specifications, presenting upsetting material or taking sides on controversial issues (e.g., evolution, conservation) serves no construct-relevant purpose.

Examples of guideline violations

Table 21.3 presents examples of violations of this Fairness Review guideline.

Avoid Construct-Irrelevant Physical Barriers

Relatively recently, Fairness Review has included the idea of avoiding physical barriers, that is, aspects of a test that pose problems for students with disabilities. In addition to producing what are called "alternate test forms" for students with more extreme kinds of disabilities (e.g., tests in Braille, large-type print, listening to tapes instead of reading material, etc.), some publishers are trying to make *all* tests more accessible to all students, particularly those with milder forms of disabilities. Some kinds of material are very difficult for students with seeing problems but are viewed as necessary or essential (e.g., graphs in a math test); some kinds are merely helpful (e.g., cartoons in language tests for non-native speakers); and some are unnecessary (e.g., illustrations in a reading test). It is clear that necessary materials should be retained and that unnecessary materials should be avoided. For material in the middle group (i.e, helpful, but not essential), decisions need to be reached that weigh the degree of helpfulness against the degree of difficulty posed. In general, it is best to avoid the following, if they are construct-irrelevant (see ETS, 2009): visual stimuli or stimuli requiring spatial skills, visual stimuli in the middle of a text, fine distinctions in shading (or lack of contrast), special symbols that are not needed, crowded graphics, letters that look or sound alike in labels (e.g., O,Q, and X,S), illustrations that are merely decorative, text that is not horizontal, and fonts that are hard to read. Recordings and material on computer screens need to be clear, and scrolling on the computer should not be required unless it is necessary.

Tests for special groups and for very young populations may have additional guidelines. States, in particular, may impose guidelines that reviewers will need to follow and that state "bias committees" need to adhere to. Review standards for younger populations (as in K-12 students) are in general more stringent; for older populations (e.g., graduate students) they are usually more relaxed. The age and experience of test-takers are important elements to take into consideration when guidelines are developed and applied.

Balance

Finally, a word should be said about *balance*, or about the totality of what is included in any one test. Although removing potentially problematic items is a vitally important goal, so too is including material relating to as many groups as feasible. During a Fairness Review, reviewers need to be concerned about overall balance of test questions—which groups are included and how these groups are portrayed. Questions asked here include: "What is the impression the test gives?" and "What is causing that impression?" Are males and females portrayed not only in more or less equal numbers but also in more or less important roles? Are all the men "important" (e.g., Beethoven) and all the women "trivial" (e.g., Susan)? Or, are both groups on a more equal footing? Similarly, are ethnic groups presented in relatively equal ways and with relatively equal emphases? Finally, individual test questions presenting people in traditional roles may occasionally be acceptable; the juxtaposition of several such questions, however, may well constitute stereotyping. Balance is far easier to achieve in general skills tests, where very specific content is seldom required, than in content or specific subject-matter tests, which often require materials that historically have not been balanced (as with famous authors in literature or leaders in history). Test specifications—which represent test purpose—must naturally take precedence in decisions about what to include in a test. However, test writers and test reviewers must try their best, within whatever strictures exist, to create tests with as much balance as the test purposes will allow.

Compared with other means that test publishers use to try to ensure equity, Fairness Review is relatively simple. Conducted as a test review in addition to "regular" content reviews, it recognizes that all kinds of students now take our tests, that these students come to the testing situation with anxieties and with sensitivities, and that exacerbating these sensitivities with unnecessarily problematic test material may disrupt behavior and, thereby, lead to invalid conclusions. Removing or revising offensive references and including positive cultural and gender references not only can increase examinee comfort during an anxious time but can also increase the probability that tests are testing what they purport to test. Fairness Review is rooted in these two aims: to accomplish a social goal at the same time as it enhances the psychometric goal of test validity.

Fairness Review in Context

As mentioned in the introduction to this chapter, Fairness Review is critical both in measurement terms and in social terms, but it is important to note that it is only one aspect of test fairness. While it is a major contributor to validity, it needs to be supplemented by other measures if equity is a goal (see ETS, 2009).

Equality of Treatment

In addition to treating people fairly in test material, people need to be treated fairly in terms of access to the test. Establishing test centers that make it possible for most if not all test-takers to get to a center and maintaining standardization of all procedures—before, during, and after the test—are important steps for test publishers. Offering special tests—or alternate test formats—for people with disabilities, and special arrangements—like extra time for dyslexic students or separate rooms for test-takers with psychological problems—are other means of providing equality of access.

Diversity of Contributors

To the extent possible, test publishers need to provide as diverse input as possible into their tests. This includes internal staff as well as external consultants at all stages of test-making, from deciding on test specifications, to writing and reviewing test questions, to assembling and reviewing tests, to scoring essays, to providing test scores and score interpretation, to providing guidelines and examples of proper—and improper—test use. At all of these stages, contributors of both genders and of as many ethnic and national groups as possible should be part of the process. If it is not feasible to have a very varied internal staff, external consultants can be hired, particularly for writing and reviewing individual test questions and for reviewing entire tests. The perspectives of the contributors to the test need to match insofar as possible the perspectives of those taking the test. Test-takers need to feel that they are "part of the world of the test" when they are taking the test; using staff with multiple views is one way of enabling this feeling.

Test Interpretation and Test Use

Since even the "fairest" test can be misused and, thereby, become "unfair" (consider, for example, the use of a spatial test for admission to a graduate program in the French language), it is important for test-makers to provide as much information as possible on how to interpret test scores, including what given scores mean and do not mean and on how to use test results fairly. Such information needs to be provided to all involved in the test, from test-takers to test users such as admission officers and other school officials. Remedies for perceived misuse ideally should be provided.

Validation

Test makers need to carry out methods of validation, that is, methods of showing that the interpretation of test scores is appropriate. One way of doing this is by showing that the varied contributors to the test are qualified to be contributors. Another way is to demonstrate that the various parts of the test relate to each other and to external criteria (e.g., freshman grade point average) in the way that one would predict. Further, test makers can show that the test relates closely to other accepted measures (e.g., other tests) of the construct being tested. As well, test makers can demonstrate that the material in the test is appropriate for inclusion: each question should be shown to be closely related to the purpose of the test. As mentioned earlier, validation and fairness are very closely linked. Since without validity, a test cannot be fair, it is critical that the validity of a test be demonstrated in as many ways as feasible.

Differential Item Functioning (DIF)

As spelled out earlier in this chapter, DIF is an empirical method of comparing two groups of test takers matched for ability and seeing how these matched test takers perform on each test question. DIF occurs when substantially different responses are given to a question by two groups shown to be substantially similar. When DIF occurs in test questions, trained reviewers ideally from several ethnic groups and both gender groups need to examine each such question to determine whether the differences are related more to what is being tested (in which case, the question is retained) or whether the differences are more related to being a member of a group (in which case, the question is dropped). DIF studies can demonstrate the kinds of subject matter most likely to cause unwarranted differences in test scores and can therefore be used to help set or adjust test specifications. If, for example, it were shown that males do substantially better than a matched-for-ability group of females on questions dealing with war, it would be possible to eliminate war questions from a skills test or to limit the number of war questions on a history test (or other test in which some mention of war is necessary). Many of the subject matters listed as possibly construct-irrelevant earlier in this chapter were derived from DIF studies that pointed out differences in responses between groups of equal ability to questions of various subject matters.

Research

The tradition of investigating causes of and remedies for differences in test scores between groups needs to continue. DIF studies, as mentioned above, have been valuable aids to the partial elimination of inequity among groups in test performance. Other methods of investigation need to be pursued to look at ways of overcoming differences. Although it is important to remember that fairness exists only in the context of test purpose, it is critical to be able to show that each question on each test has a distinct and equitable relation to that purpose. Continuing research can best serve that mission.

References

Aina, O. (2005, September). Introductory remarks. Presented at the 31st Annual Conference of the International Association for Educational Assessment, Abuja, Nigeria.

American Psychological Association. (1977). *Guidelines for non-sexist language in APA Journals.* Washington, DC: Author.

American Psychological Association. (2001). *Publication manual of the American Psychological Association.* Washington, DC: Author.

Berk, R. A. (Ed.). (1982). *Handbook of methods for detecting test bias.* Baltimore, MD: Johns Hopkins University Press.

Carlton, S. T. (2001, May). *The fairness review process in testing diverse populations.* Paper presented at the 27th Annual Conference of the International Association for Educational Assessment, Rio de Janeiro, Brazil.

Carlton, S. T. (2005, September). *Fairness review of assessments.* Paper presented at the 31st Annual Conference of the International Association for Educational Assessment, Abuja, Nigeria.

Carlton, S. T. & Harris, A. M. (1992). *Characteristics associated with differential item functioning on the Scholastic Aptitude Test: Gender and majority/minority group comparisons.* Research Report No. 92-64. Princeton, NJ: Educational Testing Service. Educational Testing Service. (1974). *The ETS guidelines for testing minorities.* Princeton, NJ: Author.

Educational Testing Service. (1976). *The ETS guidelines for sex fairness in tests and testing programs.* Princeton, NJ: Author.

Educational Testing Service. (2003). *ETS fairness review guidelines.* Princeton, NJ: Author.

Educational Testing Service. (2009). *ETS guidelines for fairness review of assessments.* Princeton, NJ: Author.

McGraw-Hill. (1968, 1974). *Recommended guidelines for multiethnic publishing.* New York, NY: McGraw-Hill.

McGraw-Hill. (1974). *Guidelines for equal treatment of the sexes.* New York, NY: McGraw-Hill.

Ramsey, P. (1993). Sensitivity review: The ETS experience as a case study. In P. Holland & H. Wainer (Eds.). *Differential item functioning* (pp. 367-388). Hillsdale, NJ: Erlbaum.

Tittle, C. K. (1982). Use of judgmental methods in item bias studies. In R. A. Berk (Ed.), *Handbook of methods for detecting test bias* (pp. 31–63). Baltimore, MD: Johns Hopkins University Press.

Zieky, M. (2006) Fairness reviews in assessment. In S. Downing & T. Haladyna (Eds.) *Handbook of Test Development* (pp. 359–376). Mahwah, NJ: Erlbaum.

22

COMPUTER-BASED TESTING IN HIGHER EDUCATION

Robert P. Dolan and Kelly S. Burling

In recent years changes in technology have begun to significantly alter the ways we assess students. Digital technologies have been used both as a solution to many of the challenges of current modes of testing, such as administration (Bennett, 2001; Kingston, 2009) and scoring (Shermis & Burstein, 2003; Wolfe, Matthews, & Vickers, 2010), as well as a means for ushering in a new generation of test administration options (Almond et al., 2010; Dolan & Hall, 2007). However, it is important to keep in mind that "technology" has always been an integral part of testing, even in the most "traditional" forms of testing. Given that direct measurement of latent properties such as knowledge and skill is difficult or impossible, reliance on various technologies has always been a necessity. For example, inferring from a student's choice of predetermined responses whether they have the knowledge and skills to effectively factor an equation involves the use of technology, as it requires a practical application of specific sciences. Of course, when we speak of "technology" in testing we are generally referring to the use of *digital* technologies, those that permit dynamic display of information to students, allow or require students to interact with and respond in potentially complex fashions, and enabled the collection of rich data about student interaction and response. While this more narrow definition of technology is distinct from the general term, it is important to recognize that technologies—digital or otherwise—do evolve, and that this evolution has greatly impacted assessment and testing through the past. As so much of our lives globally becomes impacted by the great changes in digital technology—including the ways in which we use digital technologies in learning—it is important to understand their current and potential impact on student assessment and testing.

Digital technologies can be used during testing in a host of ways, from authoring items to reporting student results. This chapter will be limited to the use of such technology in administering tests to students—commonly referred to as computer-based testing (CBT)—and the uses and reporting of digital assessment data. This chapter provides an overview of the use of CBT in higher education. Our intention is to provide an understanding of how digital technologies have impacted testing and how they likely will do so over the short-term future. We also hope to provide some insight as to how a longer range future of testing in higher education might play out. To accomplish this, the chapter is organized in four sections. The first provides a general overview of the potential CBT has for improving assessment systems in elementary, secondary, and higher education. This will be a fairly high-level introduction to some of the concepts and issues surrounding CBT. The second section provides a survey of how CBT is currently being used in higher education. In the third section, we describe possible future applications of CBT in higher education, with enough implementation details that readers get a sense of what is realizable and how it might impact them. Finally, we address how students with disabilities and students who are English learners will likely be affected by CBT in higher education.

The Potential for Computer-Based Testing in Education

The ways in which CBT can improve educational assessment fall into four general categories: (a) increasing the depth of student knowledge and skill that can be assessed, (b) improving the range of accuracy for test results, (c) increasing the efficiency of the assessment process, and (d) improving the fairness of testing. Note that these categories overlap. For example, tests that can be delivered more efficiently allow additional testing that will improve the quality of the measures; tests that are accurate across a range of students are inherently fairer than those that aren't. Nonetheless, discussing CBT in terms of these characteristics provides a convenient framework for understanding the impacts of technology on testing. For thoroughness, the focus of this section will span all levels of education: primary, secondary, and postsecondary. The discussion of technology will also include instructional considerations, since this is where digital technologies have a longer history and have made the greatest impact.

Testing Students to Greater Depths of Knowledge and Skills

As mentioned previously, knowledge and skill represent latent student characteristics that are difficult or impossible to assess directly. Instead, we assess these measures of learning by looking at indicators that presumably correlate with them. The art of measurement, as described throughout this book, is therefore one of choosing reasonable indicators and applying the best methods to the process of drawing inferences from them. Unfortunately, the process inherently favors measurement of more superficial representations of knowledge and skill, since these are the easiest to measure.

Various approaches have been proposed to represent the superficiality or depth of learning and its measurement, such as Bloom's Taxonomy (Bloom, Englehart, Furst, Hill, & Krathwohl, 1956) and Marzano's Dimensions of Thinking (Marzano et al., 1988). Another taxonomy, commonly used in assessment alignment studies is that of Webb's Depth of Knowledge (DOK), which proposes four levels of depth of knowledge and skill: (1) recall, (2) demonstration of skills and concepts, (3) strategic thinking, and (4) extended thinking (Webb, 1997). There are two general approaches to testing students to greater depths of knowledge and skill (i.e., Webb DOK levels three and four). The first is to increase the complexity of the tasks asked of students, and thus increase the opportunities for directly observing and measuring students' exhibition of these knowledge and skills. The second is to stretch our faith in our inferences. As an example of the latter, consider testing students on their strategic thinking skills by virtue of their ability to design a simple experiment to determine whether gravity affects root growth in plants. We could either have students describe such a study—perhaps orally or in writing—or we could give them a multiple choice problem in which they identify the best of four example study designs. Clearly the former is more likely to produce evidence that can be used to support valid inferences of students' strategic thinking skills, as it would be difficult for them to complete the task using recall or demonstration of skills and concept alone (i.e., Webb DOK levels one or two). In general, selected response items such as multiple choice generally cannot tap students to the same depths of knowledge and skills as can constructed response items (Jodoin, 2003; Shepard, 2008; Traxler, 1953). As a result, we frequently over-rely on correlations—whether actual or presumed—between students' low-level and high-level knowledge and skills.

A major challenge of direct assessment of students' deeper knowledge and skills is its resource intensiveness[1]. This is where digital technologies can help by lessening the gap between task and underlying constructs by providing students with extended, authentic tasks that more closely resemble learning experiences. These include simulations, constructed responses, and performance tasks

(Dolan, Goodman, Strain-Seymour, Adams, & Sethuraman, 2011; Quellmalz, Schank, Hinojosa, & Padilla, 1999; Zenisky & Sireci, 2002). While these more sophisticated types of tasks can be administered without the use of technology, this cannot be accomplished at scale without a large investment of resources.

Students are also increasingly using computers and other digital technologies to acquire, develop, and demonstrate their knowledge in and outside classroom settings. Trying to divorce students from these media for the sake of a controlled assessment environment risks testing them on irrelevant skills and is not representative of how students will be asked to demonstrate their knowledge and skills in the real world. Take, for instance, a student who has been studying ancient Greek architecture and has had access to blueprints, interactive tours of Grecian ruins, representations of the buildings as they would have appeared whole, and simulations of their use by people of various eras. For a final exam, consider two possibilities: (a) the student is given a series of prompts and an answer book into which he is to write essay responses during a 2-hour session, or (b) the student is allowed to create a digital response that includes written text, links to blueprints, tours, and simulations which he has annotated with text or voiced comments, and his own digital representations (animations, video, etc.) of his conclusions. In the second option, the student would be able to demonstrate at least as much content knowledge of ancient Greek architecture. Furthermore, he would be challenged to combine information from multiple sources of media, to use various media to make or break arguments, to create an engaging multi-sensory response, and to use technology in a way analogous to how he interacts with his world and to the expectations of employers who need technologically savvy employees.

The recent emphasis on 21st-century skills aligns well with this approach (see Yarnall & Ostrander, this volume, for a detailed description of 21st-century skills). The Partnership for 21st Century Skills, a leading advocacy organization in the 21st-century-skills movement, identifies the "4Cs" as the most critical skills necessary for students and workers currently and in the future. They are: (a) critical thinking and problem solving, (b) creativity and innovation, (c) communication, and (d) collaboration (Kay, 2010; Trilling & Fadel, 2009). According to the organization's policy statements, these skills must be applied across content areas such as reading, writing, mathematics, social studies, and science, and be undergirded by facility and expertise with technology. Simulations, authentic tasks, and constructed response assessments presented and captured via technology represent the marriage of these three domains: the 4Cs, core content knowledge, and expertise with technology.

Testing Students Where They Are

In addition to limitations in accurately assessing students' deeper levels of knowledge and skills, traditional testing is limited in its ability to accurately assess student performance across a range of proficiencies. In linearly administered traditional assessments, there is a direct trade-off between the length of a test, the range of performances it can measure, and the accuracy of its measurements. Most standardized tests, in fact, are designed to maximize the information captured for students who are performing near one or more cut scores or in the middle of the achievement distribution (Gulliksen, 1987; Zarin & Earls, 1993). Such tests are generally not focused on providing accurate information about students whose performance lies at each end of the scale.

One way to increase accuracy of measurement across a range of performance is to deliver test content dynamically as a function of continuously updated estimates of where a student likely lies on a scale of measurement, so called computerized-adaptive testing (CAT; Lord, 1970; Wainer et al., 2000). In CAT, tests adaptively present questions to students based on real-time estimation of their knowledge and skills. Thus, high-performing students will be presented with more challenging questions than would lower-performing students. This maximizes the collection of information that can be used to discern a student's location on a proficiency scale. This greater efficiently can be used to increase the accuracy of measurement and/or decrease testing time. Some of the most notable examples of CAT currently used within higher education are the Graduate Record Exam (Educational Testing Service) graduate school admission test and the ACCUPLACER (The College Board) and COMPASS (ACT) college placement tests.

Testing Students More Efficiently

Scoring of student responses can be a time- and resource-consuming process. As a result, educators are under pressure to minimize the use of constructed response items, in favor of faster- and easier-to-score selected response items. By collecting student responses digitally, however, we can rely on increasingly sophisticated technologies to support the process of scoring. For example, automated essay evaluation has been used operationally in a number of testing programs, either to provide a primary score of student work or as a supplemental score to a human evaluation (Shermis & Burstein, 2003). In addition, as a simpler, low-tech example, selected response item scoring can be accomplished more quickly, easily, and accurately by computer than it can by hand.

Even when student responses cannot be scored automatically, by collecting student performances digitally, we can streamline the process of scoring. In situations that are high stakes or that require moderated scoring to ensure validity and reliability, computer-based testing facilitates rapid and efficient scoring and feedback. There are several options for scoring and for recruiting and training scorers that should be considered.

For classroom-level scoring, digital student artifacts can be stored, accessed, and then scored on demand. When the collection of student responses is tied to a learning management system (LMS), scores and additional feedback can be immediately fed back to the student. Additional feedback can include comments from the instructor and/or be automatically generated. Automated feedback can be coded comments created by the instructor to respond to common errors in student work. Then, instead of creating written comments for each student individually, the instructor can assign codes based on the student responses. The students receive constructive, relevant textual feedback about their work but the instructor only needs to generate the textual feedback once.

In addition to the advantages technology can provide for scoring student responses, the opportunity for customized feedback is greatly enhanced in a digital environment. The concept of instructor-assigned comment codes was mentioned above. There can also be automatically assigned comment codes based on scores and responses in both selected and constructed response settings. Currently, this is most common in computer-based assessment and learning systems meant to provide formative feedback to students where it has been shown to increase student learning (e.g., Warnakulasooriya & Pritchard, 2005). Computer-based tests intended to monitor student progress and knowledge acquisition— whether part of an intelligent tutoring system or an interim assessment—can provide relevant feedback and references to learning materials targeted to individual student needs based on their responses (Koedinger, McLaughlin, & Heffernan, 2010; VanLehn, 2006; Woolf, 2008).

Reporting of student results can also be greatly enhanced through technology, both in terms of efficiency and effectiveness. Score report tables, charts, statistics, and so forth, can be automatically generated and distributed to stakeholders, such as instructors, students, and administrators. Furthermore, additional reporting capabilities become feasible, such as aggregation of results and additional analyses, distractor analysis for understanding student misconceptions, and trend lines for understanding changes in learning over time.

One additional benefit to CBT, both in terms of delivery and reporting, is that it reduces our reliance on limited resources, namely trees for paper and the fossil fuels necessary for its transportation. Furthermore, CBT will potentially decrease the carbon footprint associated with the assessment process.

Testing Students More Fairly

A fair test is one that provides all students with equivalent opportunity to demonstrate their relevant knowledge and skills, thus supporting accurate, bias–free inferences about them. To that extent, accurate tests are inherently fair. Unfortunately, inaccuracies in test scores often show up in terms of systematic error or bias that discriminates against certain groups of students, most notably students with disabilities (Kamata & Vaughn, 2004; Sireci, Li, & Scarpati, 2003; Thurlow & Johnson, 2000) and/or who are English learners (EL; Abedi, 2002). These students face particular barriers during instruction and testing due to inaccessibility of materials and methods. Consider, for example, the classic example of reading skills impacting scores of measures other than reading. This can occur whether or not students have an identified disability or have been classified as EL; students' reading skills or challenges can interfere with our ability to accurately, and fairly, measure intended knowledge and skills in content areas other than language arts. This issue is best framed in terms of the impact on the validity of interpretations drawn from test scores. One of the greatest threats to validity is the impact from construct-irrelevant variance, namely contamination of intended measures by orthogonal knowledge and skills (Helwig, Rozek–Tedesco, Tindal, Heath, & Almond, 1999; Messick, 1989). (Carlton, this volume, also discusses the issue of fairness in assessment.)

In both instruction and testing, specific solutions are available to reduce the impact of construct–irrelevant variance. Most of these are geared toward students with disabilities or students who are EL. Within instruction, various supports and scaffolds are made available to students to lessen the impact of barriers to learning. In primary and secondary education, federal law requires students to receive Individualized Education Program (IEP) or Section 504 plans as directed by the Individuals with Disabilities Education Act (IDEA; "Individuals with Disabilities Education Act," 1990) and the Americans with Disabilities Act (ADA; "Americans with Disabilities Act," 1990), respectively. Postsecondary students receive support and guidance from college and university disability services offices and resource centers. Within assessment, accommodations are used to lessen the impact of construct-irrelevant factors (Elliot & Thurlow, 2006; Hollenbeck, 2002; Tindal & Fuchs, 1999). For both instruction and assessment, in recent years a variety of digital technologies are commonly used to reduce the impact of barriers for students with disabilities and who are EL (Anderson-Inman, 1999; Edyburn, Higgins, & Boone, 2005; Freed & Rothberg, 2006; Rose & Meyer, 2002). Solutions such as read-aloud through text-to-speech, adjustable text size, and access to online dictionaries provide students with supports and scaffolds far more effectively and appropriately than can be done manually. Digital technologies thus provide improved opportunities for a wider range of students to both participate effectively in the general curriculum, as well as demonstrate their relevant knowledge and skills. As a result, students can be taught and tested more fairly. This topic will be discussed in greater detail below in the section *Supporting Students with Disabilities and English Learners.*

Current Use of Computer-Based Testing in Higher Education

CBT use in higher education applications, including progress monitoring, learning and assessment systems, course-based assessments, intelligent tutoring systems, progress monitoring, and remediation programs, is widespread and increasing. CBT use in more formal assessment programs is also increasing. At public and private two- and four-year institutions, many students are screened for remediation, placed in courses, or admitted to special programs using commercially available CBTs that provide immediate or nearly immediate results. Several states and large systems have also developed proprietary assessment programs for admission, placement, and diagnostics. Texas has a long standing assessment system, the Texas Higher Education Assessment, whose use and implementation has varied over time. The City University of New York also has its own assessment program, which includes assessments used to support decision making around admissions, placement, remediation, and graduation. These newer players in the higher education assessment market are in addition to the college entrance exams, International Baccalaureate assessments, Advanced Placement tests, and graduate school admissions tests. The ease of administration, scoring, and reporting resulting from their computer-based administration has facilitated their rapid growth.

Diagnostics and Remediation

Many open enrollment institutions, such as community colleges and some public four-year colleges and universities, are provided little information about the academic capabilities of the students they enroll. Additionally, increasing numbers of students come to school with significant deficiencies in academic content (Johnson, Rochkind, Ott, & DuPont, 2009; Vandal, 2010) so in many cases assumptions cannot be made about even basic skills competencies. The problem persists, although less dramatically, at private and even at selective institutions. In response, schools have begun administering competency and placement tests to whole and portions of incoming freshman classes. The aforementioned ACCUPLACER and COMPASS tests are two of the most widely used for course placement and identification of remediation needs. Morgan (this volume) provides additional details on the use of placement tests for new students.

In a report by Public Agenda prepared for the Gates Foundation, remediation is currently costing students and states approximately $2.3 billion annually (Johnson, et al., 2009). Due to the increasing burden of providing remediation and monitoring the progress of students in remedial programs, many schools are using online courses to supplement or replace traditional classes. These programs can provide remedial content and assessments to monitor the progress of students. In many cases these programs are integrated into schools' LMSs and instructors and/or counselors are provided access to students' data. In addition to reducing instructor and facilities costs, the online systems provide extra motivational benefits to the students. Currently, a student enrolled in remedial coursework is approximately 50% less likely to earn a degree than a student not in remediation (Johnson, et al., 2009). The stigma associated with being in a remedial class and the fact that remedial courses are not credit-bearing likely impact students' persistence in higher education. Participation in self-paced online remedial courses removes the social stigma and allows students to enroll in credit-bearing courses simultaneously with remediation.

The concept of remediation can also be applied to students in credit-bearing college courses. When students are struggling in a content area, instructors can assign students to remedial online work. Online assessments associated with the academic content provide instant feedback to students about the knowledge acquisition and allow instructors to monitor the progress of their students. Assessments themselves can also become learning tools when feedback is incorporated, as in intelligent tutoring systems, which are described in the next section.

Online Learning, Homework, and Quiz Systems

The use of online learning systems to supplement higher education instruction has grown tremendously over the past few years. Of particular note is the use of these systems as a means for delivering homework and quizzes. For instructors, these systems provide features such as construction of assignments, authoring of new questions, modification of existing questions, scheduling, automated and supported manual scoring, data analysis, and reporting. For students, various learning supports are available while working on assignments, including links to digital textbook content, instructional videos and animations, hints (such as interactive, step-by-step problem solving), and real-time feedback on responses (including analysis of incorrect responses). While designed and used primarily to supplement classroom-based instruction, use of these systems has increasingly been supporting other learning situations as well, including independent learning. Examples of commercial online learning systems currently in use in higher education include ALEKS (UC Regents and ALEKS Corporation), Carnegie Learning Developmental Math Software Solution, and MyLabs and Mastering (Pearson). Community-based solutions, such as those running on open-source platforms including Moodle, are also increasingly used. These programs exist as off-the-shelf products, but with little effort many allow instructors to create simple versions of their own automatic feedback systems by studying student response patterns, identifying common errors, and creating comments that can be automatically triggered by specific responses.

All of these online learning systems can be run in a quiz mode, during which student supports are unavailable. For student self-testing, this configuration can be used by students anywhere and independently, but for grading purposes a controlled environment must be provided to minimize opportunities for students to cheat by accessing supports or sharing information with each other. Recent research has shown that it may even be possible to detect some types of student cheating (i.e., copying other students' responses) based upon analysis of time on task (Palazzo, Lee, Warnakulasooriya, & Pritchard, 2010).

Accountability Systems

Easily consumable data is the cornerstone of accountability. Expectations can be defined by identifying relevant or important data points and success can be identified by measuring the distance between current states and the relevant data points. In American education, there has been a significant accountability trend primarily focused on the K–12 system through the assessment and reporting requirements in the reauthorization of the Elementary and Secondary Education Act, better known as No Child Left Behind ("No Child Left Behind Act," 2002). In higher education, the recent accountability debate has been defined by the Spellings Commission, which was charged with exploring accessibility, affordability, accountability, and quality. The commission concluded:

> Compounding all of these difficulties is a lack of clear, reliable information about the cost and quality of postsecondary institutions, along with a remarkable absence of accountability mechanisms to ensure that colleges succeed in educating students. *(The Secretary of Education's Commission on the Future of Higher Education, 2006, p. x)*

The commission's recommendations have led to an increased effort to gather data and an increased focus on accreditation policies. However, the data have primarily been limited to crude measures such as retention and graduation rates; there has been little effort to impose standardized assessments to measure the impact of higher education institutions on student learning. The effects of the economic recession that began in 2008, coupled with increased globalization and competition for jobs, have increased pressure on higher education outcomes.

While no comprehensive accountability model currently exists in higher education, political and policy-based pressure has spawned some recent efforts as institutions fight for federal funding and work to avoid an NCLB-like system (Carey, 2008). Two large organizations representing public institutions have joined to form the Voluntary System of Accountability (VSA) and an association of private institutions has started the University and College Accountability Network (U-CAN). While both focus on making data about the institutions publicly available and comparable, only the VSA includes an assessment component.

The idea of a common assessment of learning used across higher education institutions is difficult to envision. Even within a single institution different schools and programs of study have very different goals and expected outcomes for their students. In order for a common test to make sense, a common focus of measurement must be found. Some consensus has been reached about outcomes such as graduation and earnings, instructional quality, student engagement, and development of critical thinking and communication skills. There are several assessments of student learning in higher education, all computer-administered, currently in use for accountability purposes. They are the Collegiate Learning Assessment (Council for Aid to Education), the Collegiate Assessment of Academic Proficiency (ACT), Tasks in Critical Thinking (Educational Testing Service), Measures of Academic Proficiency and Progress (Educational Testing Service), Major Field Tests (Educational Testing Service), and the Area Concentration Achievement Test (Austin Peay State University). While none of these assessments independently or as a group has sufficient penetration in the higher education marketplace, or in the public's common knowledge base to represent a comprehensive accountability assessment, they do represent the trend in higher education accountability. Assessment results, in combination with common outcome measures, will need to be rapidly administered, collected, scored, and disseminated to meet accountability pressures from federal funding sources and the public, necessitating the use of digital platforms. The extensive use of and reliance upon such platforms in elementary and secondary education can provide initial guidance on solutions appropriate for use in higher education.

How Computer-Based Testing can Shape Higher Education

In the previous section, we described how computer-based assessment is currently being used in higher education and charted its rapid increase. We now turn to the future of CBT in higher education. Building from the current state described in the preceding section, we will describe some newer and more innovative uses in greater detail, using them as a basis to project a vision of the future state. In doing so, we will provide on-the-ground perspectives of how these potential uses of CBT will directly impact students and professors. As computers and other digital devices continue to penetrate the higher education classroom, opportunities for assessment and feedback will continue to evolve. Activities such as on-the-fly classroom-wide assessment—allowing instructors to more closely monitor student comprehension in real time—can make the classroom experience more relevant and effective for students. Other activities, such as peer collaboration, scoring, and feedback on digital content using electronic portfolios and distributed electronic scoring, can increase student investment in their own and others' work.

Classroom-Based Formative Assessment

Most of the assessment discussion so far in this chapter has focused on summative assessment, assessment designed to collect evidence to support decisions indirectly related to instruction, such as instructor and program evaluation and student promotion, retention, or graduation. By contrast, formative assessment is the process by which evidence is collected and used to directly support instructional decision making. Specifically, formative assessment is a process for gathering instructionally appropriate and actionable data that reflect ongoing student knowledge and skills—or lack thereof—within specific educational contexts, upon which subsequent instruction is based (Black & Wiliam, 1998b; Drezek McConnell & Doolittle, this volume; Shepard, 2000). Formative assessment can range from informal processes, such as on-the-fly evaluation of student affect to determine how to best keep students engaged in the moment, to more formal processes, such as semiweekly evaluations of student prerequisite knowledge and misconceptions in order to determine reading assignments. It is important to understand that the nature of assessment as summative or formative is not an inherent property of a test, but rather an indication of how the results from that test will be used, and therefore—hopefully—how the test has been designed (Heritage, 2010; Nichols, Meyers, & Burling, 2009).

Although formative assessment is a process, not an instrument, its successful implementation can be facilitated with the use of instruments, most notably digital technology-based tools. Two particularly promising uses of technology are student response systems and online learning systems. Student response systems represent the best example of how technology can improve formative assessment processes. Such systems are offered by companies including Promethean, Quizdom, and SMART Technologies. These systems are designed to support instructor-student interaction during lectures. Each student uses a dedicated "clicker," or in some cases their cell phone, to respond to instructor queries, with instant visual feedback provided to the instructor and optionally the students. In addition to encouraging active student participation, these systems provide a critical ingredient to effective formative assessment—instructionally actionable data—assuming that questions and answer options have been appropriately written. While responses are anonymous to other students, responses can be collected on an individual student basis by instructors for later analysis. Preliminary research findings have provided evidence for the pedagogical value of student information systems in the classroom (e.g., Griff & Matter, 2008; Hunter, Rulfs, Caron, & Buckholt, 2010; Miller, Ashar, & Getz, 2003; Moss & Crowley, 2011).

As mentioned previously, online homework systems facilitate the process by which instructors can shape instruction as a function of student knowledge and skills on a near-real-time basis. A typical usage pattern would be for instructors to review student work prior to class as a means for choosing and/or adapting instruction, and/or identify appropriate supports for students. As with student response systems, the onus is on the instructor to select and/or create questions and responses that will generate instructionally actionable data.

Summative and formative assessment need not be mutually exclusive processes. However, they do have distinct purposes, and as such conducting both simultaneously generally involves compromise. An exception is sought by those developing interim assessment, a hybrid approach in which testing occurs regularly, perhaps weekly or monthly, with results intended to support longer term instructional decision making and provide early predictive indicators of students' likelihood of course success (Perie, Marion, & Gong, 2009). Tests and assignments can be created in which some questions are designed to determine student grades, and others designed to serve diagnostic purposes. For example, multiple choice questions can be created with distractors carefully designed to uncover particular misconceptions. Also, items can be designed for automated scoring, although until more sophisticated tasks are extant this will generally be at the cost of tapping students only on lower-level knowledge and skills through overreliance on selected response items. The exception here is in automated scoring of essays, as previously mentioned.

Students as Active Participants

Digital technologies and LMSs are creating repositories of information which increasingly allow students to understand and manage their own learning in higher education. When students are able to see course expectations, identify a trajectory of learning that leads to meeting the expectations, and locate their learning on the trajectory, they can share ownership of the learning process. They are no longer passive recipients of knowledge transmitted by instructors, and instead can actively engage in inquiry and identify steps that can help them reach the course expectations (Bloom, 1980). Ideally, as students and instructors monitor student work, students will self-regulate their learning by identifying areas of understanding and confusion, and instructors will, similarly, gain insight into students' mastery of the objectives and thus adjust their teaching to guide students' inquiries (Black & Wiliam, 1998a). This concept can also be expanded to encompass a path of learning across a degree program. It is most powerful when the system includes mechanisms for students to check their understanding, such as automatically scored interim assessments, feedback, and additional resources to support areas in which students struggle (Blythe, 1998; Wiggins & McTighe, 2005).

In a system with clearly defined learning objectives, teaching and learning can be improved through a deeper and more individualized understanding of content that students can transfer to other classroom, assessment, or career situations. This is especially true when there are also criteria against which learning will be measured (as defined in syllabi, course expectations, and assessment blueprints) that are clear to both instructors and students, and designed to provide feedback in a timely manner. In higher education, students are expected to take ownership of their education with greater independence than most have previously faced. A digital learning management system can both scaffold this process for students and make it more powerful by providing access to greater detail about their progress and a better understanding of expected outcomes. Computer-based assessments that provide students and instructors information about knowledge acquisition and mastery are critical in this system, as they can provide immediate and relevant feedback, allow students and instructors to monitor participation in and the effectiveness of remediation, and track progress toward course objectives.

Aligning and implementing so many components in a higher education setting is a complex task. Yet, research from primary and secondary school settings suggests that in instances when such programs have been employed, from school level adoptions (Black, Harrison, Lee, Marshall, & Wiliam, 2002) to national programs (Maxwell, 2007; Stanley, MacCann, Gardner, Reynolds, & Wild, 2009), learning outcomes for students have been positive. In higher education settings, where students have greater autonomy and responsibility for their learning, and where faculty have less time dedicated to monitoring and supporting students, the positive impact could be even greater.

Supporting Students with Disabilities and English Learners

In the first section of this chapter, we described how students with disabilities and/or who are EL can benefit from the technologies in CBT. In this section, we will describe this in greater detail, and also consider the ways in which these—and all other—students can be negatively impacted by careless design and implementation of CBT. Since the use of education technologies to reduce barriers for students with disabilities and who are EL has been better developed in instruction than in assessment, we will focus on ways in which the former has informed the latter.

Accommodations, Universal Design, and Technology

Accommodations are the typical means by which students with disabilities and those who are EL can meaningfully participate in assessments (Thurlow, Thompson, & Lazarus, 2006). However, regardless of how well designed, administered, and utilized accommodations are, they are post-hoc retrofits and thus may fail to provide students adequate support and/or can compromise validity (Dolan & Hall, 2007). Furthermore, accommodations are typically provided as one-size-fits-all solutions that fail to account for the diverse ways in which students' challenges, disabilities, and/or linguistic skills present themselves (Rose & Meyer, 2000).

To move beyond accommodations as a means for accessible and accurate testing of a wide range of students, the principles of universal design (Mace, 1991; Mace, Hardie, & Place, 1996) have recently been applied to the assessment process. The central idea of universal design is to consider from the start the diverse ways in which individuals interact with their environment in order to create flexible solutions, and thus minimize the need for post-hoc adaptation. Various approaches exist for applying universal design to testing (Dolan & Hall, 2001, 2007; Ketterlin-Geller, 2005; Thompson, Johnstone, & Thurlow, 2002). Universal Design for Learning (UDL) is an educational framework that extends universal design from a physical space to a pedagogical space (Rose & Meyer, 2000, 2002), utilizing recent discoveries and advances in the cognitive sciences and digital technologies. It guides the design of flexible, accessible curricula, materials, and assessments that account for individual differences in how students recognize, strategize, and engage in learning situations. This is accomplished by providing alternative formats for presenting information (multiple or transformable accessible media), alternative means for action and expression (writing, drawing, speaking, switch, use of graphic organizers, etc.), and alternative means for engagement (background knowledge, options, challenge, and support).

UDL is particularly well-suited to guide the development and delivery of computer-based tests, especially those that include "innovative items," those that use digital technologies to test students on greater depths of knowledge and skill than traditional items and/or to embed accessibility supports, as mentioned previously. For the reasons already stated, it is imperative that such items be accessible, accurate, and fair for a diverse range of students (Almond, et al., 2010). To the extent that such items involve novel interfaces and tasks, they potentially introduce new forms of construct-irrelevant variance. A framework and guidelines for applying UDL principles to the creation of innovative items has recently been proposed (Dolan et al., 2006; Dolan, Rose, Burling, Harms, & Way, 2007) with emphasis on interactions between students and test features as a function of individual differences in perceptual, linguistic, motoric, cognitive, executive, and affective processing during item presentation, strategic interaction, and response action.

In all cases, it is imperative that students have adequate advance opportunities to familiarize themselves with the tools and strategies they will use during testing, especially to the extent they vary from those they are already familiar with. We otherwise risk introducing new forms of construct-irrelevant variance, in which we unfairly reward students who are adept at figuring out novel interfaces—generally an unintended construct—and penalize students who are not. Additional information on the specific supports necessary to make tests accessible for students with disabilities and those who are EL is provided, respectively, in Banerjee & Thurlow (this volume) and Kim, Hart, Abedi, & Vanneman (this volume).

Computerized Adaptive Testing and Students with Disabilities

Although CAT has shown great promise for improving assessment, the dynamic nature with which test items are presented may present a problem for some students. This is because some of the test-taking strategies used by students—particularly students with disabilities—during conventional, static testing may no longer work (Bennett, 1999; Thompson, Thurlow, & Moore, 2003). Changing strategic demands are likely to differentially impact students with disabilities, especially to the extent that the disabilities impact their executive function abilities. However, this should not be seen as an obstacle to introduction of CAT, only another call for the importance of providing students adequate opportunity to learn and practice CBT interfaces. Such practice aligns with the likely increasing use of adaptive learning situations as differentiated instruction and intelligent tutoring systems become more commonplace.

Examples of how CAT can—and has been—designed to not overly constrain students' test-taking strategies include the ability for students to return to previously answered questions and modify their responses, something that many students do (Lunz & Bergstrom, 1994). Another is to consider the constraints of timed tests on students with disabilities when testing them using CAT (Moshinsky & Kazin, 2005).

Conclusions

The widespread use of computer-based testing is likely to continue its rapid increase across higher education. While in some ways this represents an evolutionary step in the assessment field—one which can be met with evolutionary changes in our understanding—there are tremendous revolutionary opportunities coming as well. These can only be met with a willingness to reconsider many of our doctrines of learning and assessment—especially those habits of practice that isolate instruction and testing, fix instruction across students, and exclude the use of data to inform ongoing instruction.

The very disruptive nature of digital technologies may in fact empower new forms of assessment to usher in significant changes in higher education altogether (Christensen, Horn, & Johnson, 2008). Open debate and collaboration, with an emphasis on conducting and assimilating new research, are imperative to ensure this process occurs soundly.

Note

1 An additional challenge is due to the potential subjectivity of complex assessments, such as performance tasks. While a discussion of this topic is beyond the scope of this chapter, the validity threats due to any such subjectivity must be considered in light of the threats to validity due to construct underrepresentation, in which we fail to measure all that we intend.

References

Abedi, J. (2002). Standardized Achievement Tests and English Language Learners: Psychometrics Issues. *Educational Assessment, 8*(3), 231–257.

Almond, P., Winter, P., Cameto, R., Russell, M., Sato, E., Clarke, J.,…Lazarus, S. (2010). Technology-enabled and universally designed assessment: Considering access in measuring the achievement of students with disabilities—A foundation for research. *Journal of Technology, Learning, and Assessment, 10*(5), 1–52.

Americans with Disabilities Act of 1990, 101–336, 104 Stat. 327 (1990).

Anderson-Inman, L. (1999). Issues in technology computer-based solutions for secondary students with learning disabilities: Emerging issues. *Reading and Writing Quarterly, 15*(3), 239–249.

Banerjee, M., & Thurlow, M. L. (this volume). *Using data to find common ground between secondary and postsecondary accommodations for students with disabilities.*

Bennett, R. E. (1999). Computer-based testing for examinees with disabilities: On the road to generalized accommodation. In S. J. Messick (Ed.), *Assessment in higher education: Issues of access, quality, student development, and public policy* (pp. 181–191). Mahwah, NJ: Lawrence Erlbaum Associates, Inc., Publishers.

Bennett, R. E. (2001). How the Internet will help large-scale assessment reinvent itself. *Education Policy Analysis Archives, 9*(5).

Black, P., Harrison, C., Lee, C., Marshall, B., & Wiliam, D. (2002). *Working inside the black box: Assessment for learning in the classroom.* London, UK: King's College London School of Education.

Black, P., & Wiliam, D. (1998a). Assessment and classroom learning. *Assessment in Education: Principles, Policy & Practice, 5*(1), 7-74.

Black, P., & Wiliam, D. (1998b). Inside the black box: Raising standards through classroom assessment. *Phi Delta Kappan, 80*(2), 139–148.

Bloom, B. S. (1980). *All our children learning.* New York: McGraw-Hill.

Bloom, B. S., Englehart, M. D., Furst, E. J., Hill, W. H., & Krathwohl, D. (1956). *Taxonomy of educational objectives: The classification of educational goals; Handbook 1: Cognitive domain.* New York, NY: David McKay Company.

Blythe, T. (1998). *The teaching for understanding guide.* San Francisco, CA: Jossey-Bass.

Carey, K. (2008). *Graduation rate watch: Making minority student success a priority.* Washington, DC: Education Sector.

Carlton, S. (this volume). *Using content specialists for detecting item and test unfairness.*

Christensen, C. M., Horn, M. B., & Johnson, C. W. (2008). *Disrupting class: How disruptive innovation will change the way the world learns.* New York, NY: McGraw-Hill.

Dolan, R. P., Burling, K. S., Harms, M., Beck, R., Hanna, E., Jude, J., Way, W. (2006). Universal design for computer-based testing guidelines. Retrieved May 4, 2009, from http://www.pearsonassessments.com/udcbt

Dolan, R. P., Goodman, J., Strain-Seymour, E., Adams, J., & Sethuraman, S. (2011). *Cognitive lab evaluation of innovative items in mathematics and English language arts assessment of elementary, middle, and high school students* (Research Report). Iowa City, IA: Pearson.

Dolan, R. P., & Hall, T. E. (2001). Universal design for learning: Implications for large-scale assessment. *IDA Perspectives, 27*(4), 22–25.

Dolan, R. P., & Hall, T. E. (2007). Developing accessible tests with universal design and digital technologies: Ensuring we standardize the right things. In L. L. Cook, & C. C. Cahalan (Eds.), *Large-scale assessment and accommodations: What works* (pp. 95–111). Arlington, VA: Council for Exception Children.

Dolan, R. P., Rose, D. H., Burling, K. S., Harms, M., & Way, W. (2007, April 10). *The universal design for computer-based testing framework: A structure for developing guidelines for constructing innovative computer-administered tests.* Paper presented at the National Council on Measurement in Education Annual Meeting, Chicago, IL.

Drezek McConnell, K., & Doolittle, P. E. (this volume). *Classroom-level assessment: Aligning pedagogical practices to enhance student learning.*

Edyburn, D., Higgins, K., & Boone, R. (Eds.). (2005). *Handbook of special education technology research and practice.* Whitefish Bay, WI: Knowledge By Design.

Elliot, J. E., & Thurlow, M. L. (2006). *Improving test performance of students with disabilities.* Thousand Oaks, CA: Corwin Press.

Freed, G., & Rothberg, M. (2006, April). Accessible digital media: Design guidelines for electronic publications, multimedia and the web. Retrieved July 18, 2006, from http://ncam.wgbh.org/publications/adm/

Griff, E. R., & Matter, S. F. (2008). Early identification of at-risk students using a personal response system. *British Journal of Educational Technology, 39*(6), 1124–1130.

Gulliksen, H. (1987). *Theory of mental tests.* Hillsdale, NJ: Lawrence Erlbaum.

Helwig, R., Rozek-Tedesco, M. A., Tindal, G., Heath, B., & Almond, P. (1999). Reading as an access to mathematics problem solving on multiple-choice tests for sixth-grade students. *Journal of Educational Research, 93*(2), 113–125.

Heritage, M. (2010). *Formative assessment and next-generation assessment systems: Are we losing an opportunity?* Washington, DC: Council of Chief State School Officers (CCSSO).

Hollenbeck, K. (2002). Determining when test alterations are valid accommodations or modifications for large-scale assessment. In G. Tindal, & T. M. Haladyna (Eds.), *Large-scale assessment programs for all students: validity, technical adequacy, and implementation.* Mahwah, NJ: Lawrence Erlbaum Associates, Publishers.

Hunter, A., Rulfs, J., Caron, J. M., & Buckholt, M. A. (2010). Using a classroom response system for real-time data display and analysis in introductory biology labs. *Journal of College Science Teaching, 40*(2), 19–25.

Individuals with Disabilities Education Act of 1990, 101–476, 104 Stat. 1142(1990).

Jodoin, M. G. (2003). Measurement efficiency of innovative item formats in computer-based testing. *Journal of Educational Measurement, 40*(1), 1–15.

Johnson, J., Rochkind, J., Ott, A. N., & DuPont, S. (2009). *With their whole lives ahead of them.* New York, NY: Public Agenda.

Kamata, A., & Vaughn, B. K. (2004). An introduction to differential item functioning analysis. *Learning Disabilities—A Contemporary Journal, 2*(2), 49–69.

Kay, K. (2010). 21st century skills: Why they matter, what they are, and how we get there. In J. Bellanca, & R. Brandt (Eds.), *21st century skills: Rethinking how students learn.* Bloomington, IN: Solution Tree.

Ketterlin-Geller, L. R. (2005). Knowing what all students know: Procedures for developing universal design for assessment. *Journal of Technology, Learning, and Assessment, 4*(2), 1–23.

Kim, Y. Y., Hart, J., Abedi, J., & Vanneman, A. (this volume). *Testing and evaluation of English-language learners in higher education.*

Kingston, N. M. (2009). Comparability of computer- and paper-administered multiple-choice tests for K-12 populations: A synthesis. *Applied measurement in education, 22*(1), 22–37.

Koedinger, K. R., McLaughlin, E. A., & Heffernan, N. T. (2010). A quasi-experimental evaluation of an online formative assessment and tutoring system. *Journal of Educational Computing Research, 4*, 489–510.

Lord, F. M. (1970). Some test theory for tailored testing. In W. H. Holtzman (Ed.), *Computer-assisted instruction, testing, and guidance* (pp. 139–183). New York: Harper and Row.

Lunz, M. E., & Bergstrom, B. A. (1994). An empirical study of computerized adaptive test administration conditions. *Journal of Educational Measurement, 31*(3), 251–263.

Mace, R. L. (1991). *Definitions: Accessible, adaptable, and universal design (fact sheet).* Raleigh, NC: Center for Universal Design, NCSU.

Mace, R. L., Hardie, G. J., & Place, J. P. (1996). *Accessible environments: Toward universal design.* Raleigh, NC: Center for Universal Design.

Marzano, R. J., Brandt, R. S., Hughes, C. S., Jones, B. F., Presseisen, B. Z., Rankin, S. C., & Suhor, C.(1988). *Dimensions of thinking: A framework for curriculum and instruction.* Alexandria, VA: The Association for Supervision and Curriculum Development.

Maxwell, G. (2007). *Implications of proposed changes to senior secondary school syllabuses.* Spring Hill, Queensland: Queensland Studies Authority.

Messick, S. (1989). Validity. In R. L. Linn (Ed.), *Educational measurement* (3rd ed., pp. 13–103). Washington, DC: American Council on Education.

Miller, R. G., Ashar, B. H., & Getz, K. J. (2003). Evaluation of an audience response system for the continuing education of health professionals. *Journal of Continuing Education in the Health Professions, 23*(2).

Morgan, D. L. (this volume). *College placement testing of entering students.*

333

Moshinsky, A., & Kazin, C. (2005). Constructing a computerized adaptive test for uiversity applicants wth disbilities. *Applied Measurement in Education, 18*(4), 381–405.

Moss, K., & Crowley, M. (2011). Effective learning in science: The use of personal response systems with a wide range of audiences. *Computers & Education, 56*(1), 36–43.

Nichols, P. D., Meyers, J. L., & Burling, K. S. (2009). A framework for evaluating and planning assessments intended to improve student achievement. *Educational Measurement: Issues and Practice, 28*(3), 14–23.

No Child Left Behind Act of 2002, Pub.L. 107–110, 115 Stat. 1425 (2002).

Palazzo, D. J., Lee, Y.-J., Warnakulasooriya, R., & Pritchard, D. E. (2010). Patterns, correlates, and reduction of homework copying. *Physical Review Special Topics—Physics Education Research, 6*(1).

Perie, M., Marion, S., & Gong, B. (2009). Moving toward a comprehensive assessment system: A framework for considering interim assessments. *Educational Measurement: Issues & Practice, 28*(3), 5–13.

Quellmalz, E., Schank, P., Hinojosa, T., & Padilla, C. (1999). Performance assessment links in science (PALS). ERIC/AE Digest. *ERIC DIgest.*

Rose, D. H., & Meyer, A. (2000). Universal design for learning. *Journal of Special Education Technology, 15*(1), 67–70.

Rose, D. H., & Meyer, A. (2002). *Teaching every student in the digital age: universal design for learning.* Alexandria, VA: ASCD Press.

Shepard, L. A. (2000). *The role of classroom assessment in teaching and learning* (Technical Report No. 517). Los Angeles, CA: CRESST.

Shepard, L. A. (2008). The role of assessment in a learning culture. *Journal of Education, 189*(1/2), 95–106.

Shermis, M. D., & Burstein, J. C. (Eds.). (2003). *Automated essay scoring: A cross-disciplinary perspective.* Mahwah, NJ: Lawrence Ehrlbaum.

Sireci, S. G., Li, S., & Scarpati, S. (2003). *The effects of test accommodation on test performance: A review of the literature* (Center for Educational Assessment Research Report No. 485). Amherst, MA: University of Massachusetts Amherst, School of Education.

Stanley, G., MacCann, R., Gardner, J., Reynolds, L., & Wild, I. (2009). *Review of teacher assessment: Evidence of what works best and issues for development.* London, UK: Qualifications and Curriculum Authority.

The Secretary of Education's Commission on the future of higher education. (2006). *A Test of Leadership: Charting the future of U.S. higher education.* Washington, D.C.: U.S. Department of Education.

Thompson, S. J., Johnstone, C. J., & Thurlow, M. L. (2002). *Universal design applied to large-scale assessments* (NCEO Synthesis Report 44). Minneapolis, MN: University of Minnesota, National Center on Education Outcomes.

Thompson, S. J., Thurlow, M. L., & Moore, M. (2003). *Using computer-based tests with students with disabilities* (Policy Directions No. 15). Minneapolis, MN: University of Minnesota, National Center on Educational Outcomes.

Thurlow, M. L., & Johnson, D. R. (2000). High-stakes testing of students with disabilities. *Journal of Teacher Education, 51*(4), 305–314.

Thurlow, M. L., Thompson, S. J., & Lazarus, S. S. (2006). Considerations for the administration of tests to special needs students: Accommodations, modifications, and more. In S. M. Downing, & T. M. Haladyna (Eds.), *Handbook of test development* (pp. 653–673). Mahwah, NJ: Lawrence Erlbaum.

Tindal, G., & Fuchs, L. S. (1999). *A summary of research on test changes: An empirical basis for defining accommodations.* Lexington, KY: Mid-South Regional Resource Center/OSEP.

Traxler, A. E. (1953). *The IBM scoring machine: An evaluation.* Paper presented at the 1953 Invitational Conference on Testing Problems, Princeton, NJ.

Trilling, B., & Fadel, C. (2009). *21st century skills: Learning for life in our times.* San Francisco, CA: Jossey-Bass.

Vandal, B. (2010). *Getting past go: Rebuilding the remedial education bridge to college success.* Denver, CO: Education Commission of the States.

VanLehn, K. (2006). The behavior of tutoring systems. *International Journal of Artificial Intelligence in Education, 16*(3), 227–265.

Wainer, H., Dorans, N. J., Eignor, D., Flaugher, R., Green, B. F., Mislevy, R. J., ...Thissen, D. (2000). *Computerized Adaptive Testing: A Primer* (2nd ed.). Mahwah, NJ: Lawrence Erlbaum.

Warnakulasooriya, R., & Pritchard, D. (2005). *Learning and problem-solving transfer between physics problems using web-based homework tutor.* Paper presented at the EdMedia 2005: World Conference on Educational Multimedia, Hypermedia & Telecommunications.

Webb, N. L. (1997). *Criteria for alignment of expectations and assessments in mathematics and science education.* Washington, DC: Council of Chief State School Officers.

Wiggins, G., & McTighe, J. (2005). *Understanding by design.* Alexandria, VA: Association for Supervision and Curriculum Development (ASCD).

Wolfe, E. W., Matthews, S., & Vickers, D. (2010). The effectiveness and efficiency of distributed online, regional online, and regional face-to-face training for writing assessment raters. *Journal of Technology, Learning, and Assessment, 10*(1), 1–22.

Woolf, B. P. (2008). *Building intelligent interactive tutors: Student-centered strategies for revolutionizing e-learning.* Amsterdam, The Netherlands: Morgan Kaufmann/Elsevier.

Yarnall, L., & Ostrander, J. (this volume). *The assessment of 21st-century skills in community college career and technician education programs.*

Zarin, D. A., & Earls, F. (1993). Diagnostic decision making in psychiatry. *American Journal of Psychiatry, 150,* 197–206.

Zenisky, A. L., & Sireci, S. G. (2002). Technological innovations in large-scale assessment. *Applied Measurement in Education, 15*(4), 337–362.

QUESTIONS AND EXERCISES FOR SECTION 3

Note: Suggested answers are provided for selected questions. These questions are indicated by an asterisk (★).

Scenario for Questions 1–5: You have been hired as a new faculty member at a university. Your responsibilities include developing an end-of-course (comprehensive) exam for an undergraduate class titled Introduction to Measurement. This course is being taught by three other faculty members who are interested in administering a common final exam. Consider the fact that these students will continue onto an advanced measurement course during the following semester.

(1) What are the possible purposes of this final exam?★

(2) What steps would you use to determine the content coverage of the exam?★

(3) What are the advantages and disadvantages of including cognitive levels in the content specifications?★

(4) One of the faculty members has suggested that the purpose of the test scores should be to rank order the students taking the course. What argument could you use to contradict this opinion?★

(5) Informally, or in a non-technical fashion, describe what the desired statistical specifications would be for this end of course exam assuming that (a) there were three content categories with equal domain weights across categories, and (b) the test scores will be used to determine if students should receive an A, B, or C.★

(6) What kinds of assessments benefit most from the use of an Evidence-centered Design approach: (a) assessments of well-understood constructs that will be administered to large populations of students using traditional item types, such as multiple choice items?; (b) assessments of hard-to-assess constructs that require innovative item types and complex measurement models?; or (c) both? If both, in what ways might the two kinds of assessment benefit differently?

(7) Is evidence-centered assessment design a truly innovative approach to assessment design? Or is it the "same old wine in a new bottle"?

(8) Evidence-centered design comprises five layers of work. How is the validity of the assessment that is being developed enhanced at each layer? How does conducting a Domain Analysis enhance the quality of the assessment? What benefits are conferred on the assessment design process through the use of Domain Modeling, the articulation of the CAF, and the specification of the Implementation and Delivery layers? What unintended side effects might result from the use of evidence-centered design?

(9) What are the advantages of using evidence-centered assessment reflection (EC-AR) with postsecondary faculty?*

(10) What are the potential challenges of engaging faculty in using EC-AR and how would you address them?*

(11) In determining the strengths and weaknesses of particular items on a classroom test, explain the usefulness of: (a) item difficulty estimates (e.g., unusually high or low p values), (b) item discrimination indices (e.g., negative, near zero, or high), (c) information about the functioning of distractors (e.g., many high performing students choosing a distractor, no one choosing a distractor, and near equal numbers of students providing each possible answer), and (d) potential bias (e.g., Hispanic students performing poorly on a set of items positioned near the end of a test or assessing the meaning of a complex science passage).

(12) One way to convince yourself of the merits of conducting routine item analyses on your tests, is to do one, and see what you can learn from it. Before looking at the statistical results, try to predict the difficulties of the items and how well the items are discriminating. Try to predict the poorest distractors among the items in the test. We think you will be surprised with the findings. Most instructors are not very good at predicting how well the items in their tests are functioning, and nearly always, they can spot problems in the test (such as miskeyed items, multiple correct answers to items, distractors that aren't functioning, and so on) with the aid of an item analysis.

(13) One of the benefits of computer-based testing is the flexibility it affords in how students are presented with information and how they construct their responses. Might such flexibility represent a threat to comparability of test scores, since different students will essentially have different testing experiences? Also, can we assume students will always make the best choices when they have options available to them?

(14) Computerized-adaptive testing offers efficiency by eliminating questions that would provide little additional information about individual students' knowledge and skills. Are there times when it might be desirable for students to all be tested using the sets of test items, and thus computerized-adaptive testing is inappropriate?

Suggested Answers to Selected Questions

Answer/Response for (1)

(a) Determine examinees' mastery of the content covered in the course;

(b) Predict examinees' potential success in the advanced course;

(c) Assist in determining the final grade for the course;

(d) Evaluate the professors' teaching ability.

Answer/Response for (2)

(a) Compare the exams already created and in use by the faculty members and combine similar topics;

(b) Examine the syllabi (and course objectives) used by the three professors, again looking for similarities and differences in the major or unit topics;

(c) Collect and examine any texts or additional references that may be used to disseminate course material;

(d) Survey the faculty members about the prerequisites of the advanced measurement course and, perhaps, ask them to rank the importance of each prerequisite, allowing the prerequisites to be grouped into major categories;

(e)   Discuss with the faculty of the introductory course the topics covered during the semester and evaluate the importance of those topics; and

(f)   Use the results gathered from steps a–e to establish a single set of content categories.

Answer/Response for (3)

Advantages include: A varied set of response types may be needed to adequately meet the intended purposes; examinees are afforded the opportunity to demonstrate knowledge at a variety of levels; a variety of cognitive levels may be needed to establish an appropriate mapping to the curricula/syllabi/course objectives.

   Disadvantages include: Including items requiring higher cognitive levels may take longer in which to respond, longer to score, and the scoring may be somewhat subjective; the purposes of the test may not require the demonstration of multiple cognitive levels; writing items to meet cognitive levels such as "evaluation" can be difficult to develop effectively.

Answer/Response for (4)

(a)   The students have, in part, had similar classroom experiences, implying that perhaps their abilities are relatively similar as well. In other words, the ability levels of the group could be homogeneous, making it difficult to rank order students of similar abilities.

(b)   The test being developed is an end-of-course exam. At best, perhaps, the goal would be to have multiple classifications (A, B, C, D, F), and discriminating the students belonging to those categories is important, rank ordering all students would not fit the purpose of the test or aid in the interpretation of test scores.

(c)   Perhaps, instead of rank ordering the students, it would be a good idea to rank order across the four instructors (mean grades) to determine a teaching award.

Answer/Response for (5)

(a)   The content of the items should be based on the content specifications and written such that if the students mastered the material, then the responses would be correct. Considering there are three levels of mastery, the items should also be written in such a way as to discriminate between those three categories.

(b)   After deciding on the content of and the items on the test, the professors (and perhaps other experts) should decide on what set of skills determine if a student should earn an A, B, or C. In other words, the cut scores should be determined.

(c)   For the most part, the test items need to discriminate between the students in each of the three scoring categories. Ideally, students in the A category can answer items correctly that the other students cannot. Similarly, students in the C category, ideally, will not be able to answer all of the items that were answered correctly by students in the A category.

Answer/Response for (9)

Builds deeper understanding of what they're teaching and why, helps faculty prioritize key points of learning according to real world application, helps faculty integrate measurement of 21st-century skills into instruction, and helps the department chair provide evidence that a program is meeting needs of workforce and industry.

Answer/Response for (10)

Postsecondary faculty may resist management and accountability around their classroom instruction, prefer to do what they've always done, and question the value of what they perceive as additional work. To address such challenges, a program dean may consider submitting faculty assessment instruments for review by prospective employers and adult students to find out how useful these audiences perceive the tests to be for the teaching and learning of skills for the workplace and real world application. The results may be shared with faculty and used to inform process improvement.

SECTION 4

Testing and Assessment for Decision-Making

Charles Secolsky and D. Brian Denison

Decisions based on test results and program outcomes necessitate that there is a point on a relevant scale that separates the status of success from the status of failure. Section 4 of the handbook consists of six chapters that in some way reflect how these statuses are determined. For placement tests like the ACCUPLACER or COMPASS, cut scores are determined through a systematic set of processes. For program outcomes, benchmarks are often used to indicate what level of student success is required for the student to pass onto the next level.

Chapter 23, by Pitoniak and Morgan, provides details on the topic of setting and validating cut scores for tests and has applicability for success on program outcomes. It offers the higher education decision maker information on the most recent methods for how a passing score ought to be determined. The key element to all the standard-setting methods is that they rely on some sort of judgment.

Chapter 24, by Morgan, represents an application of a specific systematic procedure for finding a passing score for placement tests in higher education. The consequences of placement decisions are discussed in the context of assigning students to remedial coursework.

Chapter 25 by Zwick is a comprehensive treatment of admissions testing. The chapter examines the main higher education admissions tests used in the US today—the SAT and ACT, the Graduate Record Examinations, the Medical College Admission Test, the Law School Admission Test, and the Graduate Management Admission Test. The history of these tests is presented, followed by a discussion of test development, scoring, predictive validity evidence, and fairness issues. The chapter ends with key information for admissions personnel.

Chapter 26, by O'Neill and Murphy, is on postsecondary writing assessment. The authors review the theory and research that informs assessment practice. They argue that assessment methods must be consistent with current understandings of writing and writing development. In making this argument, the authors foreground the research in validity and writing assessment.

Chapter 27, by Yen and Hynes, discusses the validation of authentic assessment activities and decisions. The authors introduce a new tool for conceptualizing or mapping such undertakings: a heuristic rubrics cube. Just as Bloom's taxonomy is often used to convey the dimensions of cognitive abilities, the Yen and Hynes cube brings together cognitive level, stakes of an assessment, and reliability and validity for organizing efforts in program-level authentic assessment.

Chapter 28, by Tatsuoka, Kelly, Tatsuoka, and Dean, introduces cognitive diagnosis, a methodology for modeling how the application of cognitive skills and knowledge interfaces with test item responses. Assessments conducted with this methodology provide diagnostic profiles that include information about how well students perform on the underlying knowledge and cognitive process-ing skills required for answering test questions. The reader is encouraged to think about how this method might be applied for improving instruction and student learning in courses and programs.

The chapters in this section address a wide range of issues in which decisions must be made: dis-tinguishing between success and failure, the need for remedial education, whether or not someone should be admitted to a higher education institution or program, the validity and potential fallibil-ity of assessment results for postsecondary writing, and the existence or non-existence of cognitive misconceptions in relation to subject matter. They also incorporate different dimensions: cognitive level, high-level versus low-level stakes, and reliability and validity. Some of the decisions related to the issues discussed in this section are based on judgments relating to a neat dichotomy; others are based on judgments relating to more complex criteria. Taken together, the chapters in this section provide the reader with valuable concepts and insights into a variety of topics that are important in the higher education context. These are reinforced by the questions and exercises at the end of the section.

23

SETTING AND VALIDATING CUT SCORES FOR TESTS

Mary J. Pitoniak[1] and Deanna L. Morgan

Test scores are often used in decision making in higher education contexts. For example, examinees may be placed into a remedial course if their test scores are below a certain point, and into an entry-level course if their test scores are above a certain point. That certain point on the test score scale is termed the *cut score*, and the process used to define the location of the cut score is termed *standard setting* (Hambleton & Pitoniak, 2006; Kane, 1994; Cizek & Bunch, 2007).

The purpose of this chapter is to familiarize higher education professionals and faculty, institutional researchers, and students in higher education administration programs with the concept of a cut score, how they may be used, how they are determined, and how evaluations of their validity can be conducted. Because of length restrictions, this chapter can provide only an overview of key points, and is not intended to enable the reader to conduct a standard setting study without additional resources. Throughout the chapter, the reader will be referred to relevant references for more detailed information.[2]

Caveats for the Use of Cut Scores

Before reviewing the types of cut scores and the process for setting them, several caveats should be noted about the uses of cut scores in higher education decision making processes. The *Standards for Educational and Psychological Testing* (American Educational Research Association [AERA], American Psychological Association [APA], National Council on Measurement in Education [NCME], 1999) provides guidelines for the appropriate uses for tests in different contexts. Standard 13.7 states that "in educational settings, a decision or characterization that will have a major impact on a student should not be made on the basis of a single test score. Other relevant information should be taken into account if it will enhance the overall validity of the decision" (p. 146).

Therefore, the classification of an examinee made on the basis of a cut score should be one part of a collection of evidence. For example, the *Guidelines on the Uses of College Board Test Scores and Related Data* (College Board, 2010) note that admission test scores should be used "in conjunction with other indicators, such as the secondary school record (grades and courses), interviews, personal statements, writing samples, portfolios, recommendations, and so forth, in evaluating the applicant's admissibility at a particular institution" (Guideline 5.2, p. 7). Other relevant College Board guidelines suggest that test scores be used as approximate indicators rather than a fixed and exact measure of an examinee's preparation (Guideline 5.3) and that test scores and other relevant information should be evaluated in the context of their background and experiences, in addition to the context of the programs the examinee intends to pursue (Guideline 5.4).

Throughout this chapter, it should thus be kept in mind that the classification of an examinee based on a cut score should not on its own be the basis for an admission or placement decision. Other sources of information should be taken into account.

Types of Cut Scores Used in Higher Education

In the postsecondary setting, the two most common uses for cut scores are for admission decisions and placement decisions. Admission decisions generally aim to divide examinees into two categories—individuals meeting one or more standards that the institution or department has set for being part of the pool from which students are selected for admission, and those who do not meet the standards and are not part of the pool from which students are selected.

Other decisions, such as course placement, may require multiple cut scores on the score scale of an assessment. It may be desirable to separate examinees into multiple skill groups that are aligned to course placement. An example may be the use of two cut scores to separate examinees into three groups: (a) those who should begin in the entry-level, credit-bearing course, (b) those who should begin in the highest level developmental course for remediation, and (c) those examinees who should be placed into a lower level developmental course for even greater remediation. Figure 23.1 displays one typical use of two cut scores for placement decisions.

Within this chapter, for simplicity's sake, examples will feature the use of one cut score to separate examinees into two categories for placement purposes. For additional information on setting cut scores for admissions, see Morgan, 2006. For additional examples of setting multiple cut scores, see Morgan and Michaelides (2005) and Morgan and Hardin (2009).

Components of the Standard Setting Process

The following section presents information about the individual components of the standard setting process.

Role of Judgment in Standard Setting

Cut scores cannot be obtained by using a statistical formula.[3] There is no "true" cut score waiting to be discovered. Instead, standard setting involves informed judgment. The cornerstone of the process

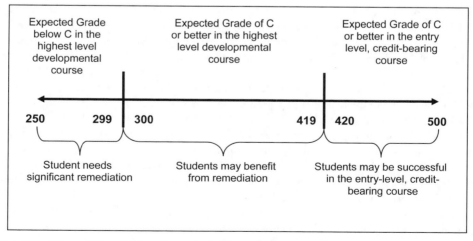

Figure 23.1 Diagram of hypothetical placement decisions using two cut scores

Note: The cut scores of 300 and 420 were arbitrarily chosen for this example and should not be interpreted as a recommendation for the placement of the cut scores in placement decisions.

lies with the judgments of experts about what the examinees who took the test need to know and be able to do to be classified into a certain category. For example, for a placement test, experts make judgments about what examinees need to know and be able to do to be placed into an entry-level course vs. a remedial one. As described later, the focus may be on the test items or the examinees themselves. But in either case, the experts will be asked to make informed judgments that are then used to calculate a recommended cut score. The focus of this chapter is on how to design the process so that these judgments can be made in as informed a manner as possible, with the benefit of clear and thorough training about the task they are being asked to do and an understanding of the context for their judgments.

Participants in the Standard Setting Process

The standard setting process consists of a standard setting study and a subsequent decision made on the basis of the study recommendation. Within the standard setting study itself, there are two key roles that must be filled. The first role is that of a facilitator who oversees the standard setting process, ensures that appropriate procedures are followed, and maintains documentation. The second role is that of the Subject Matter Experts (SMEs) who, after sufficient and appropriate training, serve as panelists and provide the judgments used to form the recommended cut score.

The outcome of a standard setting study is a recommendation that will be used by the individual, or group of individuals, who has the authority to make decisions on the final value(s) that will be used as the cut score. This individual or group is known as the policymaker. Each of these three roles—facilitator, SME, and policymaker—is described in the following subsections.

The facilitator

The facilitator is a person with specific skills and training in standard setting and has the ability to train the SMEs to perform an unfamiliar task, elicit full participation from each participant, and ensure no one participant or set of participants dominates the process. The facilitator must not have an immediate stake in the outcome of the standard setting to avoid the possibility or the appearance that the panel's recommendation is not independent of the facilitator.

The facilitator may be someone from the institution or an outside consultant. A facilitator chosen from within the institution may include, for example, the director of institutional research or testing at the institution or a faculty member in the department of educational psychology. The facilitator could also be someone from the placement office, however this may have the appearance of bias or lead to real bias in the process and results. Whether the facilitator comes from within the institution or is hired from without, it is critical that the individual has training and experience in standard setting and has no direct stake in the outcome of the study.

The facilitator's role is to (a) assist the policymaker in choosing a standard setting method and designing the study, (b) confirm that sufficient materials are produced and appropriate procedures and tasks will take place during the standard setting, and (c) ensure that procedures and tasks are performed as intended to maintain the validity of the process. This role includes not only overseeing the development and assembly of materials and data, but also (a) training the SMEs on the standard setting tasks they will be performing, (b) monitoring large and small group discussions, and (c) providing the SMEs with information they may need to consider in the standard setting process. The facilitator should not provide any personal opinions on test content or skills that may influence the judgments of the SMEs (Geisinger, 1991; Mehrens, 1986).

Subject matter experts

The SMEs (also called panelists throughout this chapter) should be knowledgeable about the examinee population and the skills and knowledge that are required of examinees in relation to the decisions being made. Given that the purpose of the standard setting is to categorize examinees with respect to performance in a specific content area, the SMEs should be experts in the content or proficiency of the area under consideration.

Ideally most of the SMEs will be faculty members currently teaching in the subject or proficiency area at the institution(s) that will use the resulting cut scores. The panel of SMEs should be representative of the college or institution for which the decisions are being made. SME representation should be considered in terms of gender, race/ethnicity, tenure (both veteran staff and those who have been there for a shorter length of time), and, in cases where the cut score may be intended for multiple campuses or locations, the geographical location and campus size. For example, if the cut score will be used system-wide, then representatives from around the system should be included, not just the main campus, and representatives from both 2-year and 4-year campuses are suggested.

The more representative the panel of SMEs, the more generalizable and valid the results will be. For that reason, stakeholders other than faculty may be considered for inclusion. However, anyone chosen to serve on the panel must be knowledgeable in the content or proficiency area in which the cut score will be set and have experience in working with examinees like those about whom the decisions are to be made.

As the process encourages discussion and interactions, the panel should ideally have at least 15 members for the purposes of representation. A panel with fewer than 10 members would be likely not to be representative, and a panel with more than 25 members may not allow every panelist to participate and contribute. However, it should be noted that panel size may vary based on the method chosen. For example, the Angoff (1971) method generally uses fewer panelists than the Bookmark method (Lewis, Mitzel, & Green, 1996), since activities conducted at multiple tables are an integral part of the Bookmark approach (both methods are described later in the chapter). In any case, it is important to set targets for different types of panelists (location, expertise, etc.) and not just assemble a "convenience" panel. After the study, it is also important to compare the convened panel to those targets. This is an important source of validity evidence when evaluating the results of the standard setting study, since the participation of non-representative or non-knowledgeable panelists may cast doubts on the appropriateness of the cut score.

The policymaker

The panelists convened for the standard setting are content experts and serve to provide a recommendation for the placement of the cut score that is based primarily on content and performance level descriptors (see next section for definition). However, the final cut score that will be adopted for use must be approved by someone with the authority to make policy decisions. The policymaker makes many decisions through the course of the standard setting process (with the input of the facilitator), which may include which method to use, what the make-up of the panel of SMEs will be, what data will or will not be provided to the SMEs, the criteria for making final decisions, and ultimately the location of the final cut score(s). Though the authoritative body makes several decisions related to the standard setting, they should not participate in the actual standard setting session since that could inhibit the participation of other panelists.

The policymaker may be a single person but generally is a small group of people. The identity of the policymakers will differ based on the policy and procedure at each institution; for example, the group may include the department head, dean of admissions, director of placement testing, president of the college, board of regents, and so forth. The key is to ensure that the person(s) selected has the authority and knowledge to evaluate the SME recommendations and other relevant material and then make the final decision on the location of the cut score(s).

Performance Level Descriptors

A key component of the standard setting process is the Performance Level Descriptors (PLDs), which define the rigor or expectations associated with the categories, or performance levels, into which examinees are to be classified. For example, for placement cut score(s), the PLDs may clearly delineate the difference in content and/or proficiency expectations for examinees in a developmental course versus an entry-level, credit-bearing course. The creation or refinement of PLDs facilitates the calibration of panelists by providing each panelist with the same working definition for each performance level. The PLDs may be created at the standard setting study or beforehand, with the latter perhaps allowing for a more thorough concentration on this key component of the process. More information about the development of PLDs is given in the section titled *Common Steps in a Standard Setting Study* (see also Perie, 2008, for further details).

The Borderline Examinee

The objective of the standard setting process is to identify the point on the score scale that separates examinees who meet the specified expectations from those who do not. Generally each group (those who meet or exceed the standard and those who do not meet the standard) contains some examinees who obviously belong in that specific group; for example, very low scorers or very high scorers. However, each group will also contain a number of examinees who either exhibit (a) just enough proficiency to be placed in the higher category or (b) who lack proficiency, but just barely, to keep them from being placed in the higher category. Examinees who exhibit just enough proficiency, as defined by the PLDs, for placement into a category are known as *borderline examinees*[4]. When setting a cut score, the SMEs should make decisions with the borderline examinee (and the PLDs) in mind. Specifically, the performance of the borderline examinee on the test is important because many standard setting methods use the test score obtained by the borderline examinees as the cut score.

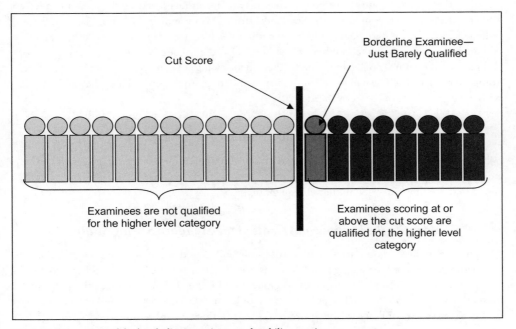

Figure 23.2 Location of the borderline examinee on the ability continuum

Figure 23.2 provides an illustration of the ability continuum and the location on the continuum of the borderline examinee.

Errors of Classification

All test scores represent inferences that we make about the examinee's knowledge, skills, and abilities (Cizek & Bunch, 2007). As such, they contain what is termed *measurement error*. This does not mean that mistakes were made in the design and administration of the test, but instead reflects the fact that we are unable to measure their "true ability" and are instead using test scores as a proxy. Sources of measurement error are extraneous factors that are not directly related to what we are intending to measure, and may include the particular items that a particular form of the test contains, leniency or severity in scoring of responses to constructed-response items, conditions related to the testing environment, and examinee-related factors such as fatigue. The statistical estimate of this quantity is termed the *standard error of measurement* (SEM; see Cizek & Bunch, 2007 for information on its calculation).

Given measurement error, it is likely that examinees whose tests scores are right below or right above the cut score actually have the same true ability (also termed true score) if we were able to measure it without error. As a result, two types of classification errors may occur when we set a cut score: (a) false positive errors, where an examinee whose true score is below the cut score is classified as being above the cut score, and (b) false negative errors, where an examinee whose true score is above the cut score is classified as being below the cut score.

Error will always be present, but it is the goal to optimize classification of examinees into categories such that the error deemed most egregious is reduced. Therefore, the policymaker may choose to raise or lower the recommended cut score to reduce one of these two types of classification errors. For example, in a placement context, the policymaker may consider it more important to (a) minimize the number of examinees placed into the remedial course who could have been successful in the entry-level course than to (b) place into the entry-level course an examinee who would be better served by the remedial course. The policymaker may then consider lowering the recommended cut score by some amount; commonly the Standard Error of Measurement (SEM) or Standard Error of Judgment (SEJ) are used to identify the range within which an acceptable adjustment may be made. Although this will reduce the number of examinees placed erroneously into the remedial course, it will increase the number of examinees placed erroneously into the entry-level course. Therefore, it is important that all of those involved in the standard setting process, including panelists, be familiar with the concept of errors of classification.

Common Steps in a Standard Setting Study

While each standard setting method has its own set of unique steps or features, in general 15 steps exist in the typical process for setting cut scores. These general steps are listed below in Table 23.1 and then more fully discussed in the subsequent text.

Identify the Purpose and Goals of the Standard Setting Study

The purpose of this section is to outline the decisions and steps that the policymaker should undertake before the method for setting a cut score has been determined or the panel has been convened. Many of these decisions will be made in conjunction with the facilitator, though the policymaker makes the final determination. The policymaker should carefully consider the implications and make final decisions on the following issues prior to the start of the standard setting session:

Table 23.1 General Steps in the Typical Process for Setting Cut Scores

Stage	Step
Prior to the Standard Setting Session	
	1 Identify the purpose and goals of the standard setting study.
	2 Choose an appropriate method for setting cut scores.
	3 Select a facilitator who has experience with the method chosen (the facilitator may also participate in the selection of the method).
	4 Choose a panel of subject matter experts and stakeholders to participate.
During the Standard Setting Session	
	5 Conduct an orientation to familiarize panelists with the goals of the meeting, what their task will be, and what the role of the facilitator is.
	6 Have the panelists take the test.
	7 Train panelists on the performance level descriptors (PLDs).
	8 Conduct discussion to define the characteristics of the borderline examinee.
	9 Train the panelists on the selected standard setting method.
	10 Compile item ratings or holistic judgments from the panelists that can be used to calculate cut score(s).
	11 Conduct panel discussions regarding the judgments and resulting cut score(s).
	12 Present normative, item–level and/or impact (consequences) data to the panel (optional).
	13 Obtain panelist feedback about the process and level of confidence in the resulting cut score(s).
After the Standard Setting Session	
	14 Compile technical documentation to support an evaluation of the validity of the process for setting cut score(s).
	15 Make recommendations to policymaker, who makes the final decision.

- What is the purpose of the standard setting session?
- What test will be used?
- How many cut scores will be needed, and does the design/length of the test support that many?
- When will the performance level descriptors be created—at the standard setting study or beforehand?
- Who will be the facilitator (faculty member, testing or research director, outside consultant)? (It is important that the facilitator be familiar with the standard setting method to be used.)
- What are the qualifications required of the SMEs?
- Will the performance level descriptors be considered confidential or will SMEs be able to take this information with them when they leave the session?
- What types of data will be presented between rounds (normative, item–level, and impact)?
- If impact data will be presented:

  o How much impact data will be presented and for which subgroups?
  o How will the results of the post-impact data recommendations from the panel be presented to and used by the decision makers?

- Will the recommended cut score from the final round of ratings be shared with the SMEs? (Although the policymaker may want to keep them confidential, this makes it difficult for the SMEs to evaluate the result of the process. However, in that case, the SMEs could be advised that cut scores do not generally change by a large amount from the next-to-last to the last round.)

The facilitator should participate in making the above decisions as needed, since the policymaker may not have sufficient knowledge and expertise in standard setting to do so without input. Before selecting a method to set cut scores, the facilitator should be clear on the general placement procedures (which test[s] and how many tests are to be used in the placement decision and any other data or information that is used in the placement decision) and the stakes attached to the test. Also, the facilitator should be provided with any historical information about previous standard setting studies or political concerns about the cut scores. As noted earlier, however, the final decisions described in this section are to be made by the policymaker.

Choosing a Cut Score Method

Many considerations go into the decision of which cut score method is the best for a specific placement decision and the specific population under consideration. Because of the importance of this decision, a separate section entitled *Selecting a Standard Setting Method* is presented later in the chapter.

Choosing a Standard Setting Panel

It is key to convene a set of panelists who are familiar with the content of the test and the examinees about whom placement decisions will be made. Further information about the selection of panelists can be found in the section on SMEs earlier in this chapter. However, it is worth repeating here the importance of setting targets for different types of panelists (location, expertise, etc.) before recruitment begins, and then comparing the convened panel to those targets. This is an important source of validity evidence when evaluating the results of the standard setting study since the participation of non-representative or non-knowledgeable panelists may cast doubts on the appropriateness of the cut score.

Conduct Orientation

At the start of the standard setting session, it is important that the panelists be given an orientation to the process so that they know what to expect. This orientation should include a review of the agenda and how much time is allotted for each activity. In addition, the panelists should be made aware of the context of the standard setting study. Information to be provided includes the purpose(s) of the assessment, how the assessment was developed and the content it contains, why performance standards are being set, what are the consequences of the performance standards, and what are the roles of the panel, facilitator, and policymaker (Raymond & Reid, 2001).

Have Panelists Take the Test

When possible, it is recommended that the panelists take the test on which cut scores will be set *before* they provide their cut score recommendations. (If the test contains performance or constructed response items, panelists may not be required to provide a complete response to the items, only a general outline or process that they might use as a response.) Taking the test provides the panelists with the opportunity to become familiar with the test content and structure. During the actual process of setting cut scores, panelists are provided with answer keys (correct response for a multiple-choice question or a rubric for a constructed-response item) and, where appropriate, a mapping of each item to the content standard or course objectives it is intended to measure. With the standards and answer keys in hand, an assessment can appear much easier than when panelists are faced with only the items and must provide the correct answers themselves. Taking the test without the key on hand can give the SMEs a more realistic view of item difficulty and the experience of the examinee for reference during the standard setting study. After taking the test, panelists should be given an opportunity to discuss the items and how they map onto the content standards or course objectives. An introduction to item difficulty and the features of an item that would make it more or less difficult (such as the attractiveness of the alternative answer choices) should also be a part of the training for item judgment methods.

Train Panelists on the Performance Level Descriptors

SMEs bring a diverse set of opinions about and experiences with both examinees and courses into the standard setting process. While this diversity increases the generalizability of the standard setting results, it may also introduce a variation in initial definitions of the examinees within a performance level. Consider, for instance, a group of faculty members teaching the same course at a college or university. The course may be the same and may use the same curriculum and materials, but it is not uncommon for the requirements necessary to earn a grade of 'A' from one professor to differ slightly or dramatically from the requirements necessary to earn a grade of 'A' from another professor. Therefore, it is likely that when asked to think of the examinees in a given performance level each SME will picture this hypothetical person differently. As a result, it is important that the SMEs have for their use in standard setting a set of *performance level descriptors* (PLDs). The set of performance level descriptors should:

- Describe what examinees at each level should reasonably know and be able to do.
- Relate directly to the content or proficiency standards, course prerequisites and course requirements.
- Distinguish clearly from one level (remedial course) to the next (entry-level course).
- Be written in positive terms.
- Be written in clear and concise language without using non-measurable qualifiers such as often, seldom, thorough, frequently, limited, and so forth. Knowledge and skills should be quantified as much as possible.
- Focus on achievement.

The creation of PLDs can be a very time-consuming enterprise and add up to a full day to the process of setting cut scores. For that reason, it may be preferable to convene a panel of experts expressly for the purpose of creating the PLDs prior to the cut score session, so that this critical part of the process is given full attention. Then, during the process of setting cut scores, panelists are given the prepared PLDs and provided an opportunity to discuss, edit, and refine them. The panelists convened to develop the PLDs may overlap in part or in full with those who serve on the standard setting panel.

The performance level descriptors will be a major part of the documentation provided to the policymaker and in the final report. The final set of performance level descriptors provides the meaning in words of the numeric cut score that will be set and adds to the validity of the standard setting process and the resultant cut score (Perie, 2008; Hambleton, 2001). For additional information on writing performance level descriptors and examples that have been used in standard setting studies, see Perie (2008), Cizek and Bunch (2007), Hambleton (2001), or Hansche (1998). For sample PLDs that could be used with the SAT Reasoning Test mathematics section, see Morgan (2006).

Define the Borderline Examinee

The PLDs describe the knowledge and skills for all examinees in a given performance level. For example, in a placement setting context, PLDs may describe the characteristics of (a) examinees who will succeed in a full-credit, entry level course and (b) examinees who will need remediation.

Within the first level, there will be examinees who have so much knowledge and skills that they will likely perform at the top of their class. There will also be examinees who perform at an average level within that category. Of interest in the standard setting process are those examinees who are on the *borderline* between the lower and higher categories. They are *just good enough* to be placed into an entry level course.

A key step in the standard setting process is to work with the panelists to define the borderline examinee. The goal is to discuss the PLDs and specify the level of knowledge and skills called for in that level that the borderline examinee will possess. The borderline examinee will not know or be able to do all of the things listed in the PLD for a given level, so discussion needs to take place so that the nature of the knowledge and skills can be refined. In essence, this definition is a second set of PLDs that are specific to those students at the border between the performance levels. It is helpful to have the facilitator or an observer record the definition of the borderline examinee so that this material can be copied and distributed to panelists for their reference as they are making standard setting judgments.

The process of setting cut scores should not proceed until the panelists feel comfortable with the definition of the borderline examinee, since in most methods it is the cornerstone of the judgments that panelists will make. For that reason, when panelist feedback is collected (see section titled *Obtaining Panelist Feedback*), panelists' confidence in their understanding of the borderline examinee should be collected, both before and after they provide their judgments.

Training Panelists on the Method

Training panelists is a critical component of any standard setting study. It is important for panelists to fully understand the process in which they are participating and the consequences that may result from any cut score recommendation produced by the panel. Well-trained panelists should be confident in both the process they use during the cut score session and their cut score recommendations. A key component of training includes an opportunity for the panelists to practice using the method, ask questions, and provide feedback on their understanding of the purpose of the session and the method being used, *prior to* working on the operational cut score placements. This practice step is essential to establish the validity of the process and, therefore, the resultant cut score. As part of the panelist feedback collection process, they should be asked after training whether they understand the task they are about to perform before they proceed with making their "real" judgments.

It is key not to underestimate the amount of time needed for training since it lays the groundwork for the successful execution of the required tasks. The schedule should allow at least a half day for training and practice in the method. Additional information about training in the standard setting process is given in Raymond and Reid (2001).

Compiling Ratings from Panelists

A common feature of all cut score sessions, regardless of method, is the need to collect data from each panelist regarding his or her recommendation for the placement of the cut score. The judgments provided by the panelists may appear in different formats. For example, as will be described below in the section on types of methods, in the Angoff method panelists provide a judgment for each item. In contrast, with the Bookmark method they provide one judgment for each cut score. So on a 100-item test with one cut score, for each round of the Angoff-method panelists provide 100 judgments, and for the Bookmark method panelists provide 1 judgment. However, all judgments ultimately lead to a performance standard defined by a certain score on the test.

Panelist judgments are typically collected three times during the standard setting process with panelist discussions occurring between each of the three rounds of judgments (Hambleton, 2001).

However, it is sometimes necessary to have only two iterations, or at other times more than three, depending on the circumstances and method in use. A single round of ratings with no opportunity to discuss and revise should be avoided. Multiple rounds of judgments typically result in less variance in panelist ratings. For reviews of the effects of multiple rounds of ratings and accompanying feedback, see Brandon (2004), Busch and Jaeger (1990), and Reckase (2001).

Conducting Panel Discussions

The purpose of discussions is to allow panelists to discuss the feedback they have received about their ratings, the ratings of others, and item-level and consequence data (see following section for description of data). This information usually stimulates useful conversations about how panelist ratings may reflect each individual's background and/or their conceptualization of the borderline examinee.

Panelist discussion may occur in small or large groups. Large-group discussion is valuable in that it allows all panelists to hear all discussion, bringing all viewpoints into play and ensuring that all panelists are hearing the same information. However, large-group discussion may sometimes result in more reticent panelists being hesitant to share their opinions. An overly aggressive or opinionated panelist could more easily influence the entire group, adding to the hesitancy of other panelists to speak up (for a review of influences of social interactions in group decisions, see Fitzpatrick, 1989). The facilitator should make every effort to create an atmosphere that is friendly and respectful of differing opinions and to insure that all panelists feel comfortable participating in the discussion.

Small-group discussions can encourage all panelists to express their opinions in a smaller forum and can help limit the influence of controlling panel members on the small group in which they are working. A drawback to the use of small discussion groups is that the small groups are not privy to the discussion of other panelist groups and will be making recommendations based on information that may differ across groups. For this reason, it is important that at some point, typically after round two, the small groups come together as a large group and share the discussions that took place in their groups. When working in a small group setting, it is useful for the facilitator to provide item-level and consequences feedback to the individual groups, rather than to the room as a whole, until it is time for the large-group discussion. Then, small-group cut scores as well as large-group cut scores can be shared.

Providing Normative, Item-Level, and Consequences Data to Panelists

After each round of ratings, panelists are generally given one or more of three types of data as appropriate, given the standard setting method being used: (a) normative, (b) item level, and (c) impact. The first type, normative data, gives each panelist a sense of where his or her ratings are located compared to those of other panelists. For example, a panelist may see that he or she has the lowest ratings (leading to the lowest cut score) of the entire panel, or may see that his or her ratings are at about the average for the panel. Normative data are often the focus of much panelist discussion, which can help to reveal issues such as differing conceptions of the borderline examinee or misunderstandings about the rating task.

The second type, item level data, is obviously only given when panelists are making item level judgments. In the Angoff method, for example, panelists may be given percent correct values for items. The feedback is not given so that panelists will change every rating to correspond to item difficulty, but instead to provide a sense of the relative difficulty of items in the group of examinees who took the test. Panelists often find this type of information very helpful in conjunction with other sources of information such as other panelists' ratings.

Third, panelists may be provided with impact data or some indication of the consequences that would result from the current cut score recommendation. Impact data may consist of overall information on the percentage of examinees who would be expected to perform within each performance level, or placed into each course, given the current cut score recommendations. For example, they may be provided with the percentages of examinees who would be placed into each type of course based on their test scores. Sometimes this information is provided in terms of specific subgroups that may be of interest at the institution, e.g. gender, race/ethnicity, socioeconomic status, disability, and so forth.

Provision of impact data may occur at different points in the process, but typically occurs just prior to the last round of judgments. Opinions vary as to what type of impact or consequence data should be provided to panelists and whether anything should be provided at all since it is viewed as taking a step away from the criterion-referenced, test-focused process engaged in during the earlier part of the standard setting process. However, many argue that setting a cut score in the absence of such information is unwise, and that such feedback may help panelists come to a common understanding of the level for the cut score (Reckase, 2001), and allow for panelists to be aware of the consequences of their recommendations and express their level of confidence in them (Cizek & Bunch, 2007; Zieky et al., 2008). Whether or not to provide impact data—if such data are available—is a policy decision and should be made by the policymaker, with input from the facilitator.

Obtaining Panelist Feedback

The evaluation of the process and resultant cut scores should be designed into the standard setting study. Evaluation should occur at major stages of the process. Panelists should be asked to give an indication of their level of understanding and confidence in the process, as well as to provide feedback on the type of information they found useful in their decision making. Evaluations serve two purposes: (a) to provide feedback on the clarity of the training and the level of the panelists' understanding, and (b) to determine the panelists' level of satisfaction with the process and final cut score (if provided), which is an important piece of evidence for establishing the validity of performance standards (Hambleton, 2001). Panelist feedback should be collected following the training session and reviewed prior to the next stage in the process so that any misunderstanding or confusion can be addressed prior to the panelists making any operational cut score recommendations.

The frequency with which the evaluations occur can vary. At a minimum, evaluation should occur following training and at the end of the cut score session. It is recommended that evaluation also occur after the first round of cut score recommendations, and sometimes it may be desirable to evaluate panelists' understanding following each round of cut score recommendations. Then, a final evaluation should be given at the end of the process to document panelists' comfort level with the outcome (Hambleton, Jaeger, Plake, & Mills, 2000). Sample evaluation forms are provided in Cizek and Bunch (2007), Morgan and Hardin (2009), and Zieky et al. (2008).

Documenting the Process

It is critical to document the process used for setting cut scores, and to evaluate the resulting validity information. These important issues are discussed in detail in the section *Documentation and Evaluation* later in the chapter.

Policymaker Makes the Final Decision

The involvement of so many people (e.g., panelists, facilitator, policymaker) in the standard setting study may result in confusion as to who actually set the cut score(s). The responsibility for the final cut score(s) which are implemented belongs to the policymaker—the college/university administrators or other policy-making body with the authority to implement the placement rules at the institution. The facilitator implements the standard setting study, maintains proper documentation, and ensures acceptable procedures are followed. The panelists provide subject matter expertise and knowledge of the target population and use this information to make recommendations for the placement of the cut score(s).

However, it is the policymaker who has the final say as to whether the cut score recommendations are adopted directly from the panelist recommendations or whether a modified version of the recommendations is adopted. The policymaker should make his or her determination only after a careful review of the technical report and all relevant validity information. As noted previously, the policymaker should take errors of classification into account, and reduce the type of error that is deemed the most serious.

Selecting a Standard Setting Method

As described in Morgan and Michaelides (2005), a distinction can be made between traditional and empirical standard setting studies. In traditional studies, panels of SMEs are employed to make judgments about either assessment materials or examinees and determine the level of content knowledge or proficiency that the examinee should demonstrate in order to be considered borderline for placement into a specified course. In empirical standard setting studies (sometimes referred to as validity studies), data are collected on actual examinee performance in courses as external criteria to determine the placement of the cut score. Within this chapter, the focus is on judgmental standard setting methods; the reader is referred to Morgan and Michaelides (2005) for information on empirical standard setting or validation studies.

Issues for Consideration

A variety of traditional standard setting methods exist from which to choose. No one method can be deemed the best for every situation. A review of several issues related to the use of the test and the decisions made on the basis of the cut scores should be undertaken to determine the best method for a given application. These issues are discussed in this section, after which specific types of methods are reviewed.

Tests used in the higher education context are comprised of various types of items, and information related to the items—such as the text of the item itself or information on its difficulty—may or may not be available to the institution. The characteristics of panelists who will be involved in the standard setting process will also vary across contexts. Availability of resources, previous use of standard setting methods at a given institution, and the extent of prior research on a method may also play a role. The issues that may influence the standard setting method chosen are described in the following subsections.

Types of items

Tests used in higher education may contain selected-response items (e.g., multiple-choice items) or constructed-response items (e.g., short answer or essay items), or a mixture thereof. The types of items used should be considered when selecting a standard setting method. For example, the Body of Work method was designed to be used with tests comprised mostly of constructed-response items that require examinees to provide a sample of their work. This method would be less effective if used with tests comprised mostly of selected-response items. Conversely, the Bookmark method may become unwieldy if used with a test containing many constructed-response items.

Availability of test-related information

As is described later in the chapter, different types of standard setting methods utilize different types of information. Some of the methods require items for panelists to rate. Also, for many methods, feedback is given to panelists during the process about how examinees performed on the items; in those cases, item-level performance data are required. Several methods require that test-level performance data—total test scores—be available for at least a subset of examinees. The degree to which these different sources of information are available will play a role in the selection of the standard setting method.

Knowledge of examinees

In the "examinee-centered" methods that are described below, panelists rate individuals whom they know in terms of the knowledge, skills and abilities that the individuals possess. They indicate, based on their knowledge, where the examinee lies in relation to the borderline between the performance levels. If panelists are not available who know enough about the examinees to make such judgments, some of the examinee-centered methods will not be able to be utilized.

Available resources

Standard setting methods vary in terms of the resources required in the areas of time, materials, and analysis. The type of rating task performed by the panelists will have a direct effect on each of these resource factors. For example, a method that calls for the panelists to rate each item individually (e.g., the Angoff method) may take more time at the session to implement than a method that does not (e.g., the Bookmark and Direct Consensus methods).

However, time is also an issue in terms of materials preparation before the session, and analysis of data both before and after the study. In the Angoff method, for example, materials preparation may not be as time consuming as with other methods because the panelists can be given intact test forms to rate. In contrast, with the Bookmark method the items must be ordered by difficulty level, requiring more data analysis and re-sorting of the test items. With methods such as the Body of Work, samples of examinee work must be obtained and organized before the session. If all possible samples are not photocopied before the session (which will result in wasted paper), materials may need to be created during the session. The availability of staff and equipment (such as photocopiers) should be considered before choosing a method that requires these resources.

Data analysis requirements may also play a role in the feasibility of implementation for a given method. With the Angoff method, for example, the data that may be used include percentage correct on each item, and percentage of examinees scoring at or above each total score level. Such data analysis is fairly simple. In contrast, the Bookmark method requires that items be sorted by difficulty level determined using an Item Response Theory (IRT) model (Hambleton, Swaminathan, & Rogers, 1991), which requires more specialized knowledge. The Body of Work method generally calls for logistic regression to be used in determining the cut score, though an alternative, less computationally intensive approach may be used (Morgan & Hardin, 2009). It is thus important to consider the level of availability of a statistician or psychometrician when choosing a standard setting method since the level of such technical knowledge required varies across approaches.

Consistency with previous standard setting studies

If standard setting studies have been conducted previously at an institution, there may be a desire for consistency across prior and current implementations (Morgan & Hardin, 2009). Such consistency could streamline the standard setting process and allow for lessons learned in prior studies to be applied to future ones. However, consideration of other issues discussed within this section, such as item type, may lead to a decision to change standard setting methods to better fit a different situation.

Degree of use, availability of research, and legal precedents

Standard setting methods vary in their frequency of use, as well as the extent to which they have been subjected to research and evaluation. The extent of research supporting the validity of the method and the degree to which the method is used play a role in establishing the method's legal defensibility. The Angoff method is generally seen as the most commonly used, particularly in licensure and certification settings (Meara, Hambleton, & Sireci, 2001) and is the most heavily researched (see, e.g., Brandon, 2004; Hurtz & Auerbach, 2003). As a result, it is seen as very legally defensible. The Bookmark method also has a high rate of use, particularly in statewide student testing (Council of Chief State School Officers, 2001). Until recently, however, it has not been subjected to a great deal of research, and the research that has been conducted has raised concerns (Hambleton & Pitoniak, 2006). Although the method is widely accepted and panelists indicate confidence in results obtained using the approach (Karantonis & Sireci, 2006) attention should be paid to continued research and its findings when determining the suitability of using the method in any given situation.

Types of Standard Setting Methods

Standard setting methods differ in terms of the task that panelists are asked to perform. There are several ways of classifying these tasks and methods. The simplest, to be used in this chapter, is to differentiate between test-centered methods and examinee-centered methods (Kane, 1998; a more complicated classification scheme can be found in Hambleton & Pitoniak, 2006).

The descriptions of methods provided below focus on the primary rating task. These ratings are provided within the context of the overall standard setting process, incorporating the steps described in previous sections.

Test-centered methods

In test-centered methods, the panelists' main focus is on the test items themselves. Panelists provide a rating as to how examinees will perform on the items—though the exact nature of those ratings differs as described below. Panelists must be familiar with the examinee population for which the cut score is being set. However, they are not required to provide ratings for specific examinees with whom they are familiar; that type of task is performed with the examinee-centered methods to be described later in the chapter.

ANGOFF

The Angoff method is named after William Angoff (1971), who noted that if one were to estimate the probability that a just-qualified candidate were to get a test item correct, one could then sum up those probabilities to get the cut score for the test.[5] The Angoff method is very widely used, and as indicated above has a strong research base. As a result, it has been found to be highly defensible when challenged in a court of law. There have been some criticisms of the Angoff method as being too cognitively challenging for panelists (Pellegrino, Jones, & Mitchell, 1999; Shepard, 1995; Shepard, Glaser, Linn, & Bohrnstedt, 1993), but those criticisms have been countered by defenders of the method (Hambleton, Brennan, et al., 2000; Kane, 1995). The Angoff method's continuing use suggests that there is a general consensus that the method is an acceptable approach to setting cut scores.

The Angoff method is commonly implemented as follows. Panelists are given sets of test items on which to provide their ratings. These may be intact test forms, or a bank of items. The panelists are asked to consider the knowledge, skills, and abilities that the borderline examinee possesses (if there is more than one cut score, the process is repeated for each cut score). Once they have a good understanding of the characteristics of the borderline examinee, they proceed to rate each item. They are asked to estimate the probability that the borderline examinee at a given cut score would answer the item correctly. They may also be told that they could instead estimate how many borderline examinees out of 100 would answer the item correctly. Both approaches yield a proportion between 0 and 1; for example, a rating of 0.75 indicates that the panelist estimated that there is a 75% probability that the borderline examinee would answer the item correctly, or alternatively, that 75 out of 100 borderline examinees would answer the item correctly. These proportions are summed for each panelist to yield a panelist's cut score. The panelists' cut scores are then averaged to yield an overall cut score for the panel.

The approach just described is used when rating multiple-choice items. The method may also be used with constructed-response items, and is then called either the Extended Angoff method (Hambleton & Plake, 1995) or the Mean Estimation Method (Loomis & Bourque, 2001). The panelist is asked to estimate the score that the borderline examinee would obtain on the task; for example, the panelist may estimate that for a group of borderline examinees, an average of 4.2 points would be obtained for a 6-point item.

Implementations of the Angoff method are often termed "modified Angoff" because Angoff's (1971) brief description of the method did not prescribe exactly how it was to be executed. It is often conducted across three rounds of ratings, with feedback given to the panelists after the first and second rounds of ratings. For example, they may be given item-level performance data such as percent-correct or p-values. They may also be given consequences data such as how many examinees would fall below or above a given cut score. Morgan (2006) has written a guide to using the Angoff method in setting local cut scores in an institutional context.

DIRECT CONSENSUS

The Direct Consensus standard setting method (Sireci, Hambleton, & Pitoniak, 2004) was developed in response to the needs of several organizations that license practitioners where an approach was needed in which standards could be set in a less time-consuming manner. In this method, items are grouped ahead of time into clusters, and panelists then provide a rating of how many items in the cluster the borderline examinee would answer correctly. The items are usually clustered by content to facilitate the rating process.

For example, if a given cluster has 7 items, the panelist may estimate that the borderline examinee will answer 5 of them correctly (non-integer ratings, such as 5.2, are also permissible if the panelist is estimating the average score of a group of borderline examinees). As in the Angoff method, ratings are then summed for each panelist to yield a cut score, and then averaged across panelists to get a panel-level cut score. The last step in the process is for the facilitator to attempt to bring the panel to consensus; if that is not possible, the panel average cut score can be used as the final panel recommendation.

The Direct Consensus method has been compared to the Angoff method in several studies and support for the validity of the results was found (Pitoniak, Hambleton, & Biskin, 2003; Pitoniak, Hambleton, & Sireci, 2002). An advantage of the approach is that it may take less time than the Angoff method. However, the method is not yet in wide use, and Cizek and Bunch (2007) discuss several limitations. They noted that (a) the method may be less adaptable to tests that cannot be divided into content-based subareas, (b) it is not always possible to bring the panelists to consensus (particularly if the facilitator is not skilled at consensus-building), and (c) group dynamics need to be carefully monitored since it is a very interactive process in which panelists can exert a more direct influence on the cut score recommendation.

BOOKMARK

The Bookmark method (Lewis, Green, Mitzel, Baum, & Patz, 1998; Lewis, Mitzel, & Green, 1996; Mitzel, Lewis, Patz, & Green, 2001) gets its name from the fact that items are organized in a "book" in order of their difficulty level. This ordering is based on an analysis conducted using an IRT (Hambleton et al., 1991) model that relates item difficulty to examinee proficiency. Panelists are asked to review the items in the ordered item booklet—moving from the easiest to the most difficult items—and to consider the knowledge, skills, and abilities that are called for by each item. They then place a bookmark at the point at which the borderline examinee has a defined probability of a correct response.[6] The cut score is determined by calculating the expected score for the borderline examinee based on where the bookmarked item is located.

As noted above, the Bookmark method is widely used (Council of Chief State School Officers, 2001) and panelists express confidence in the results (Karantonis & Sireci, 2006). However, the research base is just beginning to be built, and questions have arisen about the ordering of the items in the booklets and how well the panelists comprehend the probability of a correct response may affect the process (Davis & Buckendahl, 2009; Hambleton & Pitoniak, 2006). In addition, the method requires very large data sets, and if there are large gaps in the item difficulties when the items are ordered, the method should not be used.

Examinee-centered methods

Some standard setting methods focus on the examinees who took the test more than they do on the test items themselves. Alternatively, they may focus on samples of examinee work.

BORDERLINE GROUP

In the Borderline Group method (Livingston & Zieky, 1982), a set of panelists is assembled who have knowledge of a set of examinees for whom test scores are available. Before seeing those test scores, the panelists are asked to rate each examinee in terms of knowledge, skills, and abilities relative to the performance level definitions (PLDs). Each examinee is placed into one of three categories: (a) clearly below the borderline, (b) at the borderline between the two performance levels, or (c) clearly above the borderline. The median test score of those examinees judged to be at the borderline is determined to be the cut score.

The Borderline Group method requires that panelists have sufficient familiarity with a group of examinees in order to classify them into a category, which is not always the case; and, when it is possible, panelists may not be able to disregard their opinions on other characteristics of the examinee, such as personality, when making judgments, which yields biased ratings. Also, panelists may classify examinees into the borderline group when they are not sure of the knowledge and skills of the examinees (Livingston & Zieky, 1982; Jaeger, 1989). The group containing borderline examinees may also be very small, yielding an unstable score distribution on which to calculate the cut score (Mills, 1995); smoothing the data may be beneficial in such cases (see Zieky et al., 2008, for a description of smoothing). However, the method is otherwise easy to use, and easy to explain to panelists. Also, panelists' ratings can be collected prior to the administration of the test rather than after it, which is a benefit under tight time constraints.

CONTRASTING GROUPS

The Contrasting Groups method (Livingston & Zieky, 1982) also calls for panelists who have familiarity with the knowledge, skills, and abilities of actual examinees, and for test scores for those examinees.[7]

Instead of determining which examinees are in the borderline group, however, the panelist places each examinee into one of the performance categories. Analytic methods are then used to determine the cut score. The most basic approach involves taking the midpoint between the medians of the two distributions (Cizek & Bunch, 2007). Alternatively, approaches such as logistic regression (Cizek & Bunch, 2007) can be used to determine the test score at which membership in a given category has a probability of 0.50. As with the Borderline Group method, smoothing of the data is usually required.

The advantages and disadvantages of the Contrasting Groups method are similar to those for the Borderline Groups method, advantages including the ability to collect ratings before the test is administered and the simplicity of the rating task, and disadvantages including possible bias on the part of the panelists when making ratings about examinees they know. In addition, it is highly likely in the Contrasting Groups approach to have score distributions that overlap; without a clear demarcation between the groups, it is more difficult to determine the cut score. In addition, it is likely that the sizes of the two groups will differ dramatically, creating some issues due to differential baseline.

BODY OF WORK

The focus in the Body of Work method (Kahl, Crockett, DePascale, & Rindfleisch, 1994, 1995; Kingston, Kahl, Sweeney, & Bay, 2001) is on samples of examinee work, not on the examinees themselves. Therefore, the method does not require panelists who are familiar with a certain group of examinees. Instead, panelists review and rate sets of work from the pool of examinees. Each "body of work" is rated as falling into one of the performance categories. The method involves several rounds; initially panelists rate sets of work from across the score distribution (although those scores are not known to them). After finding the area in the score range where the boundary between the performance categories is seen as likely to fall, additional review activities are undertaken to pinpoint its location. The cut score is then located analytically using logistic regression (Kingston et al., 2001) or through averaging of ratings (Olson, Mead, & Payne, 2002).

The method is best suited for tests containing primarily constructed-response items for which work samples can be reviewed. It does require a lot of time for materials preparation, both before and during the meeting. A detailed guide to using the Body of Work method in the higher education context is provided in Morgan and Hardin (2009).

Other methods in which samples of examinee work are reviewed include Analytic Judgment (Plake & Hambleton, 2001) and Paper Selection (Loomis & Bourque, 2001). These and other methods are described in Hambleton and Pitoniak (2006).

Summary

There are many standard setting methods from which to choose. Those presented in this chapter are among the most commonly used approaches and may be most suitable for the higher education context; however, the lack of inclusion of a method does not indicate that it would not be appropriate. In addition, there are many variations on each method that have been implemented and for which research exists. As indicated at the beginning of this section, a careful review of the nature of the test and the resources available should be undertaken before a method is selected. Each method has its strengths and weaknesses, but some may be better suited than others to a particular situation.

The descriptions presented in this chapter are not comprehensive enough to guide one through implementing a method. For more detailed information on execution of the methods, the reader is referred to Zieky et al. (2008) and Cizek and Bunch (2007). These resources also describe additional methods not mentioned in the chapter. For a more thorough discussion of the advantages and disadvantages of the methods, as well as their research bases, see Hambleton and Pitoniak (2006), Cizek, Bunch, and Koons (2004, 2005), and Cizek (2001).

Documentation and Evaluation

It is critical to document all of the steps that were undertaken in designing and implementing the standard setting study. A technical report should be compiled indicating how the method was chosen, how it was carried out, and what the results were. Having such a report available positions the institution well to defend the cut score if the cut score is questioned. In addition, proper documentation facilitates the institution's repeating of the standard setting process if so desired, as well as improving upon it based on the lessons learned.

In addition to procedural documentation, an evaluation of the standard setting study is important so that it can be determined whether valid inferences can be made on the basis of the performance classifications. This evaluation information should be included in the technical report. It is also important that the *Standards for Educational and Psychological Testing* (AERA, APA, & NCME, 1999) is consulted so that the study and its documentation comply with best practice.

Documentation

Documentation of the preparations for and execution of a standard setting study should not be left until the completion of the study. Instead, it should be viewed as integral part of the planning process. After all, it is difficult to evaluate whether the study was executed as designed if the design is not clearly explicated before execution. The plan can then be used as a basis for documenting what actually did occur. Also, in the event that the cut score recommendations are ever challenged, the standard setting study documentation is the evidence of what occurred and of what the panelists recommended. Documentation should include, but should not be limited to, the following information:

- Technical Report
    - How the standard setting method was chosen (i.e., issues considered when making the decision)
    - Information on panelist recruitment and qualifications (i.e., the target characteristics that were set, and the degree to which they were attained)
    - Agenda for study (including notes on activities that took a much shorter or longer time than planned)
    - Performance level descriptions and description of process through which they were constructed
    - Detailed description of the method implemented
    - Types of feedback provided to panelists
    - Facilitator scripts, if used
    - Summaries of panelists' ratings and how they changed across rounds
    - Recommended cut scores after each round
    - Standard error of measurement
    - Standard error of judgment (which estimates the extent to which the cut score would vary if the study were replicated with many different samples of panelists)[8]
    - Summary of impact data[9]
    - Evaluation of validity information (see Evaluation section)
    - Suggestions for any recommended modifications to the process
    - Recommendation to authoritative body and their subsequent decision
- Materials
    - A full set of the materials used and handed out in the study (e.g., test items [to be stored in secure location], training materials, presentations, blank rating and evaluation forms, performance level descriptors, feedback information)

    o   Completed rating forms
    o   Spreadsheet with compiled ratings and any subsequent analyses
    o   Completed evaluation forms

It is advisable to document the process as soon after the study as possible. Having a written plan will facilitate completion of the technical report as much of the information will already be in place. Describing the results of the study immediately after its completion will ensure that no important details are forgotten. This is particularly helpful when the process is repeated, as lessons learned will have been recorded.

One of the final pieces of documentation may be provided by policymakers. Specifically, to the extent that the final cut score decision made by the policymakers deviates from the recommendation resulting from the standard setting session, a rationale for that decision should be documented.

Evaluation

An integral part of the documentation is an evaluation of the execution of the study and its results. This is essential to judging the validity of the inferences to be made on the basis of the categorizations made using the cut scores. Many sources of validity evidence have been discussed in the literature. Kane (1994, 2001) has described those as falling into three categories: procedural, internal, and external (see also Hambleton & Pitoniak, 2006). It is desirable to include information from each of these sources in the technical report.

Procedural

As noted above, the procedures for implementing the standard setting study should have been delineated in advance of the study. To the extent that they were not, and instead decisions were made midstream, the results may be less valid since it is difficult to properly consider all issues in that manner. Among the procedural aspects that should be evaluated are the extent to which the goals of the decision procedure were made explicit, and the degree to which (a) the selection and training of panelists, (b) the definition of the performance standards and the borderline examinee, and (c) the collection of data were implemented in a systematic and thorough fashion.

Panelist evaluations are another key source of information about the procedural validity of the process. Information to be collected from panelists includes topics such as the efficacy of the orientation, understanding of performance category descriptors and the borderline examinee, training in the rating task, the helpfulness of discussion and feedback, and the level of confidence in the resulting standards.

Internal

The *Standards for Educational and Psychological Testing* (AERA, APA, & NCME, 1999) indicates that "whenever feasible, an estimate should be provided of the amount of variation in performance standards that might be expected if the standard setting procedure were replicated" (p. 60). The most direct way in which to obtain this information would be to actually replicate the procedure; however, that may not be feasible in the higher education context. However, if the number of panelists is sufficiently large (greater than 15), the panel can be split after training and data from the separate panels can be used as an estimate of the replicability of the ratings. Alternatively, one can use the standard error of judgment as an estimate of the standard deviation of a large number of replications of the panel's recommendations; however, this is generally appropriate only for the first round of ratings since they are independent judgments.

Other sources of internal validity evidence include interpanelist and intrapanelist consistency. Interpanelist consistency refers to the degree to which ratings are consistent across panelists. While panelists are recruited to represent diverse opinions, and therefore their ratings may diverge, particularly before discussion and feedback, a very low estimate of interrater reliability would suggest that panelists may lack a common understanding of the performance level definitions, the borderline examinee, or the rating task. Intrapanelist consistency refers to both (a) the relationship between the panelist's rating and item-level data, if available, and (b) the extent to which the panelist's ratings change across rounds. Again, the goal is not to obtain panelist's ratings that perfectly correlate with item difficulty values, but if the relationship is very low the panelist's content knowledge may be called into question. In addition, if a panelist's ratings do not change at all across rounds, it suggests that he or she may have an agenda and/or is not considering the feedback provided.

External

There are several possible sources of external validity evidence. The first, comparing results of two standard setting methods, is not usually practical, particularly in the higher education context where resources may be limited. Information more readily available relates to the extent to which the categorization of examinees into performance levels aligns with other information available about those examinees' knowledge, skills, and abilities. For example, an institution can compare the performance level categorization of examinees to their performance on another measure of the same content area. Another approach, described by Morgan and Michaelides (2005), is to use logistic regression to examine the relationship between test scores and course grades.[10]

A final consideration that may be given to the external validity of a cut score is that of reasonableness. For example, questions may be raised about a placement cut score if it results in a very low percentage of examinees as being in need of remediation when historical data indicate otherwise.

Summary

The collection and documentation of validity evidence is a key component of the standard setting process, and should not be viewed as an afterthought. Important decisions are made on the basis of cut scores, and the validity of the inferences made on the basis of these classifications must be carefully evaluated.

As Zieky et al. (2008) noted, cut scores cannot be categorized as right or wrong, since the "rightness" of a cut score is a matter of values, and different stakeholders have different values. However, although validity evidence cannot establish that a cut score is appropriate, the lack of such evidence can cast doubts on its validity.

Notes

1 The authors wish to thank Daniel Eignor, Kevin Sweeney, Richard Tannenbaum, Michael Zieky, James Impara, Anthony Napoli, and Chuck Sekolsky for their comments on an earlier version of this chapter.

2 In general, Cizek (2001) and Hambleton and Pitoniak (2006) provide technical overviews of the methods and relevant research. Cizek and Bunch (2007) and Zieky, Perie, and Livingston (2008) provide more detailed information about the implementation of each method.

3 Norm referenced methods, designed to pass or fail pre-specified percentages of examinees and empirical methods often used in admissions decisions, are not discussed within this chapter. Here the focus is on criterion-referenced methods in which judgments about the knowledge, skills, and abilities for examinees in a given category are used to determine the cut score.

4 Other terms for the borderline examinee that are used in the standard setting literature include minimally competent examinee and just qualified examinee.

5 Angoff (1971) also suggested that one could count up the number of items that a just-qualified examinee was predicted to get correct. For a description of methods using that approach, see Impara and Plake (1997) and Loomis and Bourque (2001).

6 The probability of answering the item correctly is tied to what is called a Response Probability Criterion, or RP criterion. More information on the RP criterion, and the challenges it presents in the Bookmark method, can be found in Cizek and Bunch (2007), Hambleton and Pitoniak (2006), and Zieky et al. (2008).

7 Some authors (e.g., Zieky et al, 2008) consider approaches that call for review of examinee work to fall under the umbrella of Contrasting Groups methods. However, in this chapter a distinction will be made between those approaches.

8 For information on computing the SEJ see Zieky et al. (2008) and Morgan (2006).

9 It is helpful to provide estimates of the percentages of students in each performance category based on the cut scores +/- 2 SEJs and +/- 2 SEMs, for the total population and possibly for any subgroups of interest.

10 The organization that administers and scores the test may offer a service to assist with validating cut scores. These services include the Admitted Class Evaluation Service (ACES) offered by the College Board to users of its tests (http://professionals.collegeboard.com/higher-ed/validity/aces) and the Course Placement Service offered by ACT for its tests, including ACT, ASSET, or COMPASS (http://www.act.org/research/services/crsplace/). The policymaker may want to check to see if the test publisher for the test on which cut scores were set offers this service.

References

American Educational Research Association, American Psychological Association, & National Council on Measurement in Education. (1999). *Standards for educational and psychological testing*. Washington, DC: American Educational Research Association.

Angoff, W. H. (1971). Scales, norms, and equivalent scores. In R. L. Thorndike (Ed.), *Educational measurement* (2nd ed., pp. 508–597). Washington, DC: American Council on Education.

Brandon, P. R. (2004). Conclusions about frequently studied modified Angoff standard-setting topics. *Applied Measurement in Education, 17*, 59–88.

Busch, J. C., & Jaeger, R. M. (1990). Influence of type of judge, normative information, and discussion on standards recommended for the National Teacher Examinations. *Journal of Educational Measurement, 27*, 145–163.

Cizek, G. J. (2001). *Setting performance standards: Concepts, methods, and perspectives*. Mahwah, NJ: Erlbaum.

Cizek, G. J., & Bunch, M. B. (2007). *Standard setting: A guide to establishing and evaluating performance standards on tests*. Thousand Oaks, CA: Sage.

Cizek, G. J., Bunch, M. B., & Koons, H. (2004). Setting performance standards: Contemporary methods. *Educational Measurement: Issues and Practice, 23*(4), 31–50.

Cizek, G. J., Bunch, M. B., & Koons, H. (2005). Clarification for the ITEMS module, setting performance standards: Contemporary methods. *Educational Measurement: Issues and Practice, 24*(2), 43.

College Board. (2010). *Guidelines on the uses of College Board test scores and related data*. New York, NY: Author.

Council of Chief State School Officers. (2001). *State student assessment programs annual survey* (Data Vol. 2). Washington, DC: Author.

Davis, S., & Buckendahl, C. (2009, April). *Evaluating panelists' Bookmark standard setting judgments: The impact of random item ordering*. Paper presented at the annual meeting of the National Council on Measurement in Education, San Diego, CA.

Fitzpatrick, A. R. (1989). Social influences in standard setting: The effects of social interaction on group judgments. *Review of Educational Research, 59*, 315–328.

Geisinger, K. F. (1991). Using standard-setting data to establish cutoff scores. *Educational Measurement: Issues and Practice, 10*(2), 17–22.

Hambleton, R. K. (2001). Setting performance standards on educational assessments and criteria for evaluating the process. In G.J. Cizek (Ed.), *Setting performance standards: Concepts, methods, and perspectives*. Mahwah, NJ: Erlbaum.

Hambleton, R. K., Brennan, R. L., Brown, W., Dodd, B., Forsyth, R. A., Mehrens, W. A., ...Zwick, R. (2000). A response to "Setting reasonable and useful performance standards" in the National Academy of Sciences' "Grading the nation's report card". *Educational Measurement: Issues and Practice, 19*(2), 5–14.

Hambleton, R. K., Jaeger, R. M., Plake, B. S., & Mills, C. N. (2000). *Handbook for setting standards on performance assessments*. Washington, DC: Council of Chief State School Officers.

Hambleton, R. K., & Pitoniak, M. J. (2006). Setting performance standards. In R. L. Brennan (Ed.), *Educational measurement* (4th ed., pp. 433–470). Westport, CT: Praeger.

Hambleton, R. K., & Plake, B. S. (1995). Using an extended Angoff procedure to set standards on complex performance assessments. *Applied Measurement in Education, 8*, 41–55.

Hambleton, R. K., Swaminathan, H. R., & Rogers, J. (1991). *Fundamentals of item response theory*. Thousand Oaks, CA: Sage.

Hansche, L. N. (1998). *Handbook for the development of performance standards: Meeting the requirements of Title I*. Bethesda, MD: U.S. Department of Education, Council of Chief State School Officers. Retrieved May 18, 2005 from: http://www.ccsso.org/publications/details.cfm?PublicationID=131

Hurtz, G. M., & Auerbach, M. A. (2003). A meta-analysis of the effects of modifications to the Angoff method on cutoff scores and judgment consensus. *Educational and Psychological Measurement, 63*, 584–601.

Impara, J. C., & Plake, B. S. (1997). Standard setting: An alternative approach. *Journal of Educational Measurement, 34*, 353–366.

Jaeger, R. M. (1989). Certification of student competence. In R. Linn (Ed.), *Educational measurement* (3rd ed., pp. 485–514). Englewood Cliffs, NJ: Prentice-Hall.

Kahl, S. R., Crockett, T. J., DePascale, C. A., & Rindfleisch, S. I. (1994, June). *Using actual student work to determine cutscores for proficiency levels: New methods for new tests*. Paper presented at the National Conference on Large-Scale Assessment, Albuquerque, NM.

Kahl, S. R., Crockett, T. J., DePascale, C. A., & Rindfleisch, S. I. (1995, June). *Setting standards for performance levels using the student-based constructed-response method*. Paper presented at the annual meeting of the American Educational Research Association, San Francisco, CA.

Kane, M. (1994). Validating the performance standards associated with passing scores. *Review of Educational Research, 64*, 425–461.

Kane, M. (1995). Examinee-centered vs. task-centered standard setting. In *Proceedings of the joint conference on standard setting for large scale assessments of the National Assessment Governing Board (NAGB) and the National Center for Educational Statistics (NCES), Volume II* (pp. 119–141). Washington, DC: U. S. Government Printing Office.

Kane, M. (1998). Choosing between examinee-centered and test-centered standard-setting methods. *Educational Assessment, 5*, 129–145.

Kane, M. (2001). So much remains the same: Conception and status of validation in setting standards. In G. Cizek (Ed.), *Standard setting: Concepts, methods, and perspectives* (pp. 53–88). Mahwah, NJ: Erlbaum.

Karantonis, A., & Sireci, S. G. (2006). The bookmark standard setting method: A literature review. *Educational Measurement: Issues and Practice, 25*(1), 4–12.

Kingston, N. M., Kahl, S. R., Sweeney, K., & Bay, L. (2001). Setting performance standards using the body of work method. In G. J. Cizek (Ed.), *Standard setting: Concepts, methods, and perspectives* (pp. 219–248). Mahwah, NJ: Erlbaum.

Lewis, D. M., Green, D. R., Mitzel, H. C., Baum, K., & Patz, R. J. (1998, April). *The bookmark standard setting procedure: Methodology and recent implementations*. Paper presented at the meeting of the 1998 National Council on Measurement in Education, San Diego, CA.

Lewis, D. M., Mitzel, H. C., & Green, D. R. (1996, June). *Standard setting: A bookmark approach*. In D. R. Green (Chair), *IRT-based standard setting procedures utilizing behavioral anchoring*. Symposium presented at the Council of Chief State School Officers National Conference on Large-Scale Assessment, Phoenix, AZ.

Livingston, S. A., & Zieky, M. J. (1982). *Passing scores: A manual for setting standards of performance on educational and occupational tests*. Princeton, NJ: Educational Testing Service.

Loomis, S. C., & Bourque, M. L. (2001). From tradition to innovation: Standard setting on the National Assessment of Educational Progress. In G. J. Cizek (Ed.), *Standard setting: Concepts, methods, and perspectives* (pp. 175–217). Mahwah, NJ: Erlbaum.

Meara, K. C., Hambleton, R. K., & Sireci, S. G. (2001). Setting and validating standards on professional licensure and certification exams: A survey of current practices. *CLEAR Exam Review, 7*(2), 17–23.

Mehrens, W. A. (1986). Measurement specialists: Motive to achieve or motive to avoid failure? *Educational Measurement: Issues and Practice, 5*(4), 5–10.

Mills, C. N. (1995). Establishing passing standards. In J. C. Impara (Ed.), *Licensure testing: Purposes, procedures, and practices* (pp. 219–252). Lincoln, NE: Buros Institute of Mental Measurements.

Mitzel, H. C., Lewis, D. M., Patz, R. J., & Green, D. R. (2001). The bookmark procedure: Psychological perspectives. In G. J. Cizek (Ed.), *Standard setting: Concepts, methods, and perspectives* (pp. 249–281). Mahwah, NJ: Erlbaum.

Morgan, D. L. (2006). *Setting local cut scores on the SAT Reasoning Test™ Writing Section for use in college placement and admissions decisions* (College Board Special Report). New York, NY: The College Board.

Morgan, D. L., & Hardin, E. (2009). *Setting cut scores with WritePlacer®* (College Board Special Report). New York, NY: The College Board.

Morgan, D. L., & Michaelides, M. P. (2005). *Setting cut scores for college placement* (College Board Research Report No. 2005-9). New York, NY: The College Board.

Olson, B., Mead, R., & Payne, D. (2002). *A report of a standard setting method for alternate assessments for students with significant disabilities* (Synthesis Report 47). Minneapolis, MN: University of Minnesota, National Center on Educational Outcomes. Retrieved February 14, 2010, from http://education.umn.edu/NCEO/OnlinePubs/Synthesis47.html

Pellegrino, J. W., Jones, L. R., & Mitchell, K. J. (1999). *Grading the nation's report card: Evaluating NAEP and transforming the assessment of educational progress.* Washington, DC: National Academy Press.

Perie, M. (2008). A guide to understanding and developing performance-level descriptors. *Educational Measurement: Issues and Practice, 27*(4), 15–29.

Pitoniak, M. J., Hambleton, R. K., & Biskin, B. H. (2003). *Setting standards on tests containing computerized performance tasks* (Center for Educational Assessment Research Report No. 488). Amherst, MA: University of Massachusetts, Center for Educational Assessment.

Pitoniak, M. J., Hambleton, R. K., & Sireci, S. G. (2002). *Advances in standard setting for professional licensure examinations* (Center for Educational Assessment Research Report No. 423). Amherst, MA: University of Massachusetts, Center for Educational Assessment.

Plake, B. S., & Hambleton, R. K. (2001). The analytic judgment method for setting standards on complex performance assessments. In G. J. Cizek (Ed.), *Standard setting: Concepts, methods, and perspectives* (pp. 283–312). Mahwah, NJ: Erlbaum.

Raymond, M. R., & Reid, J. B. (2001). Who made thee a judge? Selecting and training participants for standard setting. In G. J. Cizek (Ed.), *Standard setting: Concepts, methods, and perspectives* (pp. 119–157). Mahwah, NJ: Erlbaum.

Reckase, M. D. (2001). Innovative methods for helping standard-setting participants to perform their task: The role of feedback regarding consistency, accuracy, and impact. In G. J. Cizek (Ed.), *Setting performance standards: Concepts, methods, and perspectives* (pp. 159–173). Mahwah, NJ: Erlbaum.

Shepard, L. A. (1995). Implications for standard setting of the National Academy of Education evaluation of the National Assessment of Educational Progress achievement levels. In *Proceedings of the joint conference on standard setting for large scale assessments of the National Assessment Governing Board (NAGB) and the National Center for Educational Statistics (NCES), Volume II* (pp. 143–160). Washington, DC: U.S. Government Printing Office.

Shepard, L. A., Glaser, R., Linn, R., & Bohrnstedt, G. (1993). *Setting performance standards for student achievement.* Stanford, CA: National Academy of Education.

Sireci, S. G., Hambleton, R. K., & Pitoniak, M. J. (2004). Setting passing scores on licensure exams using direct consensus. *CLEAR Exam Review, 15*(1), 21–25.

Zieky, M. J., Perie, M., & Livingston, S. (2008). *Cutscores: A manual for setting standards of performance on educational and occupational tests.* Princeton, NJ: Educational Testing Service.

24

COLLEGE PLACEMENT TESTING OF ENTERING STUDENTS

Deanna L. Morgan[1]

Placement testing of entering college freshmen is a common activity following admission into college; however, it may come as a surprise to the incoming student. Many 2-year and 4-year institutions require placement testing of incoming students to determine whether individual students have the knowledge and skills necessary to be successful in entry-level, credit-bearing courses or if remediation through some form of developmental education is required. While admissions standards may serve as a gateway to higher education at some institutions, many colleges, particularly community colleges, have adopted an open admissions model allowing access to higher education to a greater number of applicants than ever before. At these institutions the focus is placed more heavily on placement testing than on admissions testing. The question is not whether a student may attend college but in which class the student would be most appropriately enrolled in order to be successful during their college career. Frequently, incoming students have little knowledge, if any, of the need to take a placement test, the impact their performance on a placement test can have on their subsequent path of study, or how to prepare for the placement test.

The need for remediation through developmental coursework extends the time to graduation and increases the cost of a college education for those students who must pay for additional non-credit-bearing courses before even beginning the credit-bearing courses required for degree completion. The National Center for Education Statistics (NCES, 2004) estimates 95% of students who require remediation spend one year or less in developmental courses. As a result, it is possible that a student's time to graduation and subsequent entry into the workforce could be delayed by up to a year, or longer, increasing the amount of tuition and related costs from the extra enrollment time. Additionally, students needing remediation have a significantly lower probability of graduating (Camara, 2003). The Alliance for Excellent Education (2006) estimates the nation loses $3.7 billion a year because students are not acquiring in high school the knowledge and skills to be successful in college or the workforce. Approximately $1.4 billion of the total lost is associated with the provision of developmental education to students recently completing high school. However, proper placement is important to ensure students have the knowledge and skills to be successful without the coursework being so difficult that the student becomes frustrated, or so facile that the student is bored. Both possible scenarios, frustration and boredom, can lead to decreased motivation on the part of the student (Mattern & Packman, 2009).

This chapter will explore the need for placement tests, discuss characteristics of tests used for college placement, and offer guidelines for consideration in how placement tests and placement test results are used. Of note is the distinction between placement tests used for placement into entry-level, credit-bearing courses or developmental courses, and those used for placement into courses beyond the entry-level course. The College Board's Advanced Placement Program® (AP®) and College-Level Examination Program® (CLEP®) are examples of placement tests which focus on testing as a means to place students into a more advanced class beyond the entry-level, credit-bearing course. These credit-by-examination tests allow students to receive credit for the coursework by demonstrating sufficient proficiency in the subject area and thereby allow students the opportunity to complete college earlier or use the extra time to complete coursework of a more advanced level than may typically be encountered during an undergraduate program. Credit-by-examination tests are beyond the scope of this chapter which focuses on placement testing for entering college freshmen.

The Need for Placement Testing

A key factor in the need for placement testing lies in the difference between the level of knowledge and skills required for high school graduation and those required to be successful in entry-level, credit-bearing courses. To begin to understand the current disconnect between graduation from K-12 and entry into higher education, it is instructive to first examine how the assessment systems and the intent of those systems differ in the two groups. Assessment in the K-12 arena has typically focused on a minimum competency approach to determine whether students have the minimum level of knowledge and skills to be considered proficient in regards to the standards endorsed by each state board of education. Proficiency, which on the high school level may or may not count towards graduation, is defined differently depending upon the state in which the student matriculates, and test scores are validated for the purpose of determining proficiency. A key factor in the determination of proficiency is the identification of a point on the score scale that will be used to separate students who are proficient from those who are not. This identified point on the score scale is referred to as the *cut score* and the process of establishing the cut score is called *standard setting* (see Pitoniak & Morgan, this volume, for more information on cut scores and standard setting). Because the cut score is the location at which decisions must be made to discriminate among test taker ability, it is extremely important that the score at this location exhibits high precision, meaning the amount the score would be expected to fluctuate with repeated testing is small. As a result it will be important to ensure that a sufficient number of items of high discrimination indices, or r-biserial correlations, be present in the area surrounding the cut score(s).

Placement tests are used to determine the student's level of knowledge and skills so that appropriate placement can occur to allow the student to be successful in the course. Often the college will have developed multiple cut scores for the purpose of assigning students to varying levels of entry level or developmental education. The number of developmental courses that may be offered by a college can vary from one to as many as six levels per subject area, generally in the subjects of Reading, Writing, and Mathematics. To complicate factors, the cut scores used for placement are typically determined locally by the individual college or system and can vary widely from one college to the next both in terms of the number of cut scores used and the placement of the cut scores along the score scale.

Placement tests are commercially available from some test vendors, such as the College Board's ACCUPLACER® and COMPANION® tests, and ACT's COMPASS® and ASSET® tests. But the variability between the number of developmental courses offered and the different standards that the colleges deem appropriate for placement into their local courses makes it almost impossible to create a test that will serve the needs of all colleges. As a result, commercially available placement tests must be constructed to allow for discrimination across the entire score scale. Sufficient items of targeted difficulty that measure well defined content and skills must be available to assess the well-prepared student who is ready for the entry-level, credit-bearing course, the student who will need to begin with the most basic level of developmental education and work their way up to the entry-level, credit-bearing course, and all levels of student ability between these two extremes. This necessitates a different test building strategy than that used with the minimal competency tests typically encountered in the arena if high school assessments for graduation and/or No Child Left Behind (NCLB).

In addition to differences in test construction and purpose, the content being assessed by NCLB high school level assessments can vary widely between states both in terms of the breadth of the content being assessed and the level of rigor expected though there is considerable overlap in terms of very basic concepts, such as the need for computation skills. The common focus on minimal competency for graduation has traditionally been established with limited input from higher education (Kirst, 2005; The Education Trust, 1999; Venezia, Kirst, & Antonio, 2003) such that high school graduates have minimal life skills but are not necessarily prepared for entry into college (Achieve & The Education Trust, 2008). Too often the focus in high school is distilled down into the number of courses or credit hours needed in a subject area with little or no specification as to what students should know and be able to do to be successful in postsecondary education (ACT$_s$ 2007; The Education Trust, 1999).

Though only one example, the results from the Education Longitudinal Study in 2002 (ELS:2002) illustrate the disconnect between high school expectations and those of postsecondary education where a portion of even the students that should be best prepared are being placed into developmental coursework and determined to not be ready for college upon completion of high school. The study cohort was followed over multiple years beginning in the 10th grade during 2002. In 2004, the senior year of high school for the cohort, 35.6 % of students received a high school grade point average (HSGPA) of 3.0 or higher (National Center for Education Statistics, 2010a). An analysis of coursework by each student indicated that 26.8% of students in the cohort were identified as completing "high-level academic coursework", defined as a minimum of 4 years of English, 3 years of mathematics (including at least 1 year of coursework higher than Algebra II), 3 years of science (including at least 1 year of coursework higher than Biology), 3 years of social studies (including at least 1 year of US History or World History), and 2 years of a single non-English language. Within the cohort, 92.1% of the students planned to continue their education following high school with 61.7% planning to attend a 4-year institution, 22.5% planning to attend a 2-year community college, and 8% planning to attend Vocational, Technical, or Trade School (National Center for Education Statistics, 2010b).

A follow-up study of the ELS:2002 cohort in 2006 indicated that 16.2% of students who first attended a 4-year institution had taken a developmental reading course, 24.8% had taken a developmental writing course, and 25.8% had taken a developmental math course (National Center for Education Statistics, 2010a). Students first attending a 2-year institution showed slightly higher rates of remediation with 26.9%, 29.8%, and 38.7%, respectively. Within the subset of students identified as completing high-level academic coursework, rates of remediation were smaller than those for the general cohort attending college (which included these same students plus others not completing high-level academic coursework). However, the rates of 14.3% of students in the cohort first attending a 4-year institution taking a developmental reading course, 22.3 % taking a developmental writing course, and 21.6% taking a developmental mathematics course are still higher than what would be expected from the students that according to high school coursework should be the best prepared. Similar, but slightly higher rates of remediation (except for Writing) were reported for the students completing high-level academic coursework in high school and first attending a 2-year community college with rates of 19.6%, 21.1%, and 29.6%, respectively.

ACT (2007) reports similar results in an ACT-tested group of high school graduates in 2006. Of students taking a core curriculum, only 26% were ready for entry-level, credit-bearing college courses. Of graduates completing an extra year of math in addition to the core curriculum, 62%

369

were ready for college-level mathematics but after an extra year of science in addition to the core curriculum, only 38% were ready for college level sciences (ACT, 2006).

Work is under way by a number of organizations to attempt to bridge the gap between high school and postsecondary education. Two notable examples include the American Diploma Project and the Common Core Standards Initiative. In 2005, Achieve, in partnership with The Education Trust and the Thomas B. Fordham Foundation, launched the American Diploma Project (ADP) as a means to make college and career readiness a priority in states with the goals of aligning high school standards and assessments with the skills and knowledge needed to be college and/or workforce ready, requiring rigorous coursework of all graduates that will prepare them for success beyond high school, and streamlining the transition between high school and college or the workplace. In 2010, approximately 70% of states were participating members of the ADP Network (www.achieve.org).

The National Governor's Association Center for Best Practices (NGA Center) and the Council of Chief State School Officers (CCSSO) coordinated a national effort to develop a set of college- and career-readiness standards with the goal of identifying the knowledge and skills necessary for students to succeed in entry-level, credit-bearing, academic college courses and in workforce training programs. The college- and career-readiness standards were released for review in September 2009 with finalization expected in 2010. The final set of standards will align with college and work expectations, include rigorous content and application of knowledge through high-order skills, and build upon strengths and lessons of current state standards. Additionally, the standards are intended to be internationally benchmarked to prepare students for success in a global economy and society, and to be based on evidence and research (www.corestandards.org). An advisory board was established to provide guidance on the Common Core Standards Initiative including experts from Achieve, ACT, The College Board, the National Association of State Boards of Education, and the State Higher Education Executive Officers.

Until a seamless curriculum and pathway for students transitioning from high school into college or the skilled workforce can be devised and implemented, it will be necessary to continue placement testing of incoming students to ensure proper placement to allow the student the best opportunity for success. The remaining sections of this chapter address research, special topics, and best practices in regards to testing for placement into introductory college level courses.

Evaluating Tests for Use in Placement

A plethora of tests are in use by colleges throughout the United States for the purposes of college placement. Abraham (1992) reported nearly 125 combinations of 75 different placement tests were in use by colleges in the 15 states comprising the Southern Regional Education Board (SREB) in 1988. On the California Community Colleges Chancellor's Office (CCCCO) website, during the 2008–2009 academic year, 41 tests were listed as "second party assessments" and 142 were listed as locally developed assessments on the list of assessments approved for use in California Community Colleges. This number has continued to grow with ever increasing numbers of local "home-grown" assessments being used for placement in one or more subject areas. Sometimes the locally created assessments are used alone for placement while at other times the college may use a commercially developed placement exam in combination with locally created assessments. This is particularly true in the area of writing where some colleges may administer a commercially developed placement exam in Reading and Mathematics but prefer to use a locally developed and scored essay for Writing.

The most commonly used commercially available placement tests are ACT's COMPASS and The College Board's ACCUPLACER tests. Both assessments feature a suite of test titles in Reading, Writing, Mathematics, and English as a Second Language (ESL) using online computer adaptive technology that enables shorter but more targeted assessment to maximize information while minimizing testing time, and an electronically scored essay to provide immediate feedback to the student and their advisor about the student's placement and remediation needs, if any. However, paper and pencil tests are available in the form of the College Board's COMPANION tests and ACT's ASSET tests. As students may be required to take placement tests in one or multiple content areas, efficiency of testing is a key feature of both assessments. Both ACCUPLACER and COMPASS also offer a suite of diagnostics tests to provide additional information to examinees and instructors about the strengths and weaknesses of each student to allow for focused study or instruction. ACT's COMPASS provides default cut scores for initial use with the assessment but encourages users to evaluate how well the default cuts are functioning for placement and adjust as needed in subsequent testing years. The College Board's ACCUPLACER test does not provide default cut scores, preferring colleges to collect evidence specific to the college to validate use and inform the setting of cut scores early in the process using a standard setting methodology. Other, but less prevalent, commercially available tests are the Maplesoft-MAA suite of tests that assesses only mathematics content, and McGraw-Hill's ALEKS which focuses primarily on remediation and content but does include a placement test component. Additionally, the SAT and ACT admissions tests, as well as the SAT Subject tests, are used by some colleges in placement decisions as a screening tool thereby exempting students from placement testing in one or more content areas if the student has achieved a locally determined minimum score on the corresponding portion of the assessment.

Whether using a locally developed placement test, or a commercially developed test, the characteristics that a college should consider when deciding on which placement test(s) to use are the same. At a minimum, evidence of the following should be available and fully reviewed prior to selecting a placement test(s):

- Does the test measure content that is relevant for and aligned with the entry-level, credit-bearing course students will be placing into?
- Have the test scores been validated for the purpose to which you propose using the test?
- What evidence is available supporting the validity of the test for placement into the entry-level, credit-bearing course?
- What evidence is available supporting the reliability of the test scores? What are the reliability coefficients, standard error of measurement (SEM) for the test, and conditional standard errors of measurement (CSEMs) for each scale score and particularly those you may intend to use for cut scores?
- Have test items been reviewed for bias and sensitivity?
- Have studies been conducted to investigate Differential Item Functioning (DIF) of items? Do items disadvantage any subgroup when controlled for student ability?

Validity

Validity refers to the interpretation and use of assessment results and not to the test instrument being used, though the quality of the instrument does play an important role in the validity of the results. It is possible that a college may want to use the results from an assessment for multiple purposes—measuring students' knowledge and skills for proper course placement, describing students' growth from the beginning of class until the end of the course, evaluating instructor performance over the length of a course or a particular instructional program/strategy. While all of these goals may be admirable, it is unlikely that one assessment has been constructed and validated to produce scores serving all of these purposes. Therefore, it is prudent to identify the primary purpose and use of the assessment results and investigate the evidence that exists to validate that use. Commercial test developers should have information available about the validity of score interpretations for specific purposes and uses. Colleges choosing to use locally developed assessments need to conduct validity studies to provide this evidence themselves. Should a placement decision or other decision be made using the assessment results and then fall under scrutiny, it is certain that the validity of the test scores and score interpretations will be among the first points challenged. A lack of evidence to support the validity of using the score results will place the college on shaky ground in terms of defending themselves.

One important aspect of score validity concerns the content of the assessment. Does the assessment measure what the college needs it to measure? For example, placement into a math course should be accomplished using a test that measures mathematical skills and produces a score that reflects the students' knowledge of math. A math test should not be so confounded with reading level or other content that a student with sufficient skills in math is unable to demonstrate that knowledge because of a reading difficulty—this is sometimes an issue when math tests have a preponderance of word problems and result in a score reflective of math and reading ability rather than just math ability. It may be that the entry-level, credit-bearing mathematics course does require a particular reading level to be successful in addition to math skills and therefore, the score reflecting math and reading ability is appropriate for the intended use. However, this should be evaluated against the entry-level, credit-bearing math course content and requirements rather than just assuming that a math score from a particular instrument is appropriate for use in placement. The same holds true for the level of content being measured by the math test; if a student will need to have an understanding of trigonometry to be successful in the entry-level, credit-bearing math course then the test should be assessing trigonometry and not solely computation or Algebra I. It is a good practice to have faculty review operational, if available, or sample test items prior to endorsing the use of scores from any placement test.

In addition to evaluating what the assessment is measuring and what knowledge and skills are being reflected by the test score, it is also important to assess the validity of the use of test scores for placement into the entry-level, credit-bearing course. A placement test score is essentially a snapshot of the student's knowledge and skills in the content area relative to the knowledge and skills that were assessed. One test cannot measure everything that is found in a domain of study and this is particularly true of placement tests that are often subject to both limited resources to be spent on each student for testing, and limited time that can be devoted to each student given the number of students that must be assessed at a given point and time. Typically, colleges want an assessment that will give them the most information at the lowest price and using the least amount of time per student possible. This limits the number of test questions that may be administered to a student and has implications for both the validity and reliability of test scores (Kane, 2006; Nitko, 1996; Payne, 1992; Popham, 1999).

In the following section, score reliability and measurement error will be discussed to more fully outline the issue of test length. However, before moving to that discussion, it is important to think about the issue of test length in terms of content coverage and the validity of score use. Continuing with the idea that a test score is analogous to a snapshot of student knowledge and skills at that point in time, on the assessment given, and that it is unlikely that a single test, even a rather long one, would be able to fully assess every part of the content domain for a given subject, such as mathematics, it follows that the depth of knowledge being measured by the assessment is important. The depth of knowledge being assessed can be ascertained through a review of the test items and what each item is measuring; this is often part of an alignment study (Webb, 1997). But, the question still remains whether the test score is sufficiently valid for the purpose of placing students into the entry-level, credit-bearing course such that the student has a strong possibility of succeeding in the course. To answer this question, it is recommended that a predictive validity study be conducted to determine whether students placed into the courses are adequately prepared for success in the course where they are placed.

This may be accomplished by administering the assessment to incoming students prior to any coursework being undertaken in the subject area. Next, place students into courses using the method that has been used previously by the college to determine placement and without any regard to the students' performances on the placement test under consideration, which should be saved for use later in the process. When students finish the course into which they were placed using whatever placement rules were already in existence at the college, collect the students final course grade. It is important that the course grades collected be for the course into which they were placed and that no intervening coursework occurred between placement testing and entry into the course for which grades are being collected. Define what the college considers to be "success" in the course, typically a grade of 'B' or a grade of 'C' is used. Employing a statistical procedure known as logistic regression, it is possible to predict the probability of success for students achieving each score on the score scale. This information can then be used to evaluate whether the test scores are working as intended for placement into the courses (i.e., that most students placing into the course are able to successfully complete the course). Additionally, the information gained as to the probability of success for each score point on the test score scale can be used to inform decisions about the cut score that may be appropriate for use in placing students into the course. While not recommended for use in setting the initial cut score for use in placement testing due to the undefined relationship with content and what students should know and be able to do (see Pitoniak & Morgan, this volume), this method is a good way to evaluate how well the cut scores established are working as a follow up in subsequent years to the standard setting study where the initial cuts were established.

When conducting a validity study, it is important that test scores and grades be collected for all students enrolled in the course with no intervening training occurring between testing and the start of the course of interest. Otherwise, it is possible to have skewed results due to self-selection and range restriction. Range restriction occurs when a portion of the population being examined is excluded from the sample such that the resulting sample is no longer representative of the population. This restriction of the range of population members can lead to a reduction in the correlation and a biased interpretation of the results. For example, if testing is not required for all students during the study period, it is likely that only a small portion of the students will participate and this portion may not be representative of the typical group of incoming students that are placed into the entry-level, credit-bearing course. Additionally, for colleges that use ACT or SAT as a screening device to exempt students from testing, the sample is likely to include results based only on the population of students who have scores too low to allow for placement based on ACT or SAT score alone and the non-ACT or non-SAT takers. This group is typically of lower ability than those students submitting scores high enough to be used for exemption and the result is a decrease in representation of the higher ability students from what would be found in the total population of students entering college. Not only will a self-selected sample possibly result in skewed results for the validation study, but the restricted range will also cause the predictive power of the test scores to be underestimated. For a more thorough discussion of logistic regression, see Agresti (1996), or see Mattern and Packman (2009) for an overview of placement validity studies and range restriction. Commercial testing companies may provide validity study services to users of their test products. Information about the College Board's Admitted Class Evaluation Service (ACES) can be found at the following website: http://professionals.collegeboard.com/higher-ed/validity/aces/placement. ACT offers the Course Placement Service to users of ACT products with additional information available at their website: http://www.act.org/research/services/crsplace/. A more complete coverage of validity can be found in Geisinger, Shaw, and McCormick (this volume).

Reliability

When thinking of the reliability of test scores, it is helpful to think in terms of consistency. If the same student is tested multiple times with no intervening instruction or learning between test administrations, does the student get a similar score each time? Notice the use of the word "similar" rather than "same" in reference to the student's score with repeated testing. This wording is in recognition that error is frequently present in testing. Here the word "error" is used in the statistical sense of the term, indicating fluctuations in test scores due to factors unrelated to ability, not in the lay sense indicating a mistake. The error may be systematic, meaning it has the same influence on the student in repeated testing sessions or it affects all examinees on one occasion. For example, poor lighting or a disruption in connectivity to the Internet during testing one afternoon in the testing lab would have an effect on all students in the testing lab at that time. Error may also be unsystematic, showing no consistent pattern and fluctuating from one situation to the next. For example, the student may have different levels of motivation during one or more testing sessions due to fatigue, emotional distress, illness, or other such factors. As mentioned in the previous section on validity, a test score is a snapshot of student performance and ability on that test on that day at that time under those circumstances. Changing one or more of these factors could result in a change in the student's score. For example, any test form is simply a sampling of items from the domain of all possible items that could have been used. On a different set of items it is possible that a student could receive a higher, or lower, score because the item set administered is a better match to their skill set. As such, the more items on the assessment the greater the percentage of all possible items in the domain being represented. For this reason, longer tests with more items measuring the intended construct generally have higher score reliability than shorter tests with fewer items.

An exception to the positive correlation between test length and reliability may occur when one of the tests scores being compared results from a traditional paper and pencil exam while the other score is achieved on a computer adaptive test (CAT). In the case of the CAT, a smaller number of items can produce scores that are as reliable as the traditional paper and pencil test score, if not more so, due to the ability of the item selection algorithm to choose items that are specifically targeted in both content and difficulty to the ability of the student based on their performance on previous test items. This targeted item selection allows for an efficiency of measurement that often results in shorter test lengths producing scores with the same or higher reliability (Haertel, 2006; Hambleton, Swaminathan, & Rogers, 1991; Nitko, 1996; Payne, 1992; Popham, 1999; Traub, 1994).

Reliability estimates range from zero to one with estimates of one indicating that the test score is free of error and estimates closer to zero indicating the score is mainly a function of error. Many ways to measure reliability exist and include test-retest, internal consistency, and parallel forms. Higher reliability estimates are desirable but the exact size of an acceptable estimate will vary depending on the intended score use and the type of reliability being estimated (Traub, 1994). In addition to the reliability estimate, it is also advisable to consider the Standard Error of Measurement (SEM) reported for the scores. The SEM is an indicator of the consistency of an individual person's score and how much that score could be expected to vary in the event the student is tested multiple times. For example, if Jane scored 440 on an assessment and the SEM for scores on the assessment was $\pm$ 5 then Jane's scores on repeated testing would be expected to fall between 435 and 445 in 68% of retests (using $\pm$ 1 SEM) and between 430 and 450 in 95% of retests (using $\pm$ 2 SEM). Smaller values of SEM indicate greater precision in the score and are better than larger values of SEM which indicate less precision.

The precision of scores can vary at different points along the score scale due to factors such as not having sufficient numbers of items available at certain points on the score scale. For this reason, SEM values may be computed conditional upon the score of interest. These Conditional Standard Errors of Measurement (CSEMs) should be examined for the places on the score scale where a cut score may be located to ensure sufficient precision at the cut. Additionally, the SEM, or relevant CSEM for the score point, can be used when students score just below the cut score to evaluate whether it may be beneficial to have the student retest in the hopes of obtaining the extra points needed to score above the cut score. If the range of scores created by using the student's score $\pm$ 1 SEM, or $\pm$ 1 CSEM, includes the cut score then it is likely that the student, if retested, would score at or above the cut score and a retest would be worthwhile, though it is equally likely that a retest would result in a lower score. Using the SEM may help to save testing costs due to retesting large numbers of students that are unlikely to receive a passing score with a second chance. An exception may be in cases where the student did not exert sufficient effort during the initial testing as a result of a lack of understanding about the importance attached to doing well on the assessment. See Figure 24.1 for an example using the SEM to determine whether a student should be encouraged to retest. Reliability estimates, SEM values, and CSEMs should be provided by the test developer and evaluated whether the placement test is developed by a commercial testing company or a local test developer. More complete coverage on the topic of score reliability can be found in Thompson and Vache-Haase (this volume).

Bias of Results

An important part of evaluating an assessment for potential use as a placement test is ensuring the test results are free of bias. This begins by investigating the item development practices of the test developer. How are the items developed? Who develops the items and based on what specifications? Are

Hypothetical Placement Test Example	
Test SEM =	+/−4
Cut Score =	250
Allie's Score =	247
Lower Bound of Band (Score − 1 SEM) (247 − 4) =	243
Upper Bound of Band (Score + 1 SEM) (247 + 4) =	251
Allie's Score Band (+/- 1 SEM) =	(243 to 251)
Does the band include the score of 250?	YES
Conclusion:	It would be recommended for Allie to Retest.
Nick's Score =	243
Lower Bound of Band (Score − 1 SEM) (243 − 4) =	239
Upper Bound of Band (Score + 1 SEM) (243 + 4) =	247
Nick's Score Band (+/- 1 SEM) =	(239 to 247)
Does the band include the score of 250?	NO
Conclusion:	It would NOT be recommended for Nick to Retest.

Figure 24.1. Example using SEM to determine if retest would be worthwhile

the items field tested prior to use operationally to ensure that only items that are working as intended are administered to a student and used to compute the student's score? Are the test items reviewed by experts for potential bias or sensitivity issues? For example, do the items contain any content that could inadvertently upset the examinee in such a way that it would affect their performance on the exam? Other factors to watch out for with test items are words or contexts that may have nothing to do with the knowledge needed to correctly answer the item but which are not familiar to the examinee and cause the examinee to be unsure in their response due to the lack of familiarity with the context. For example, examinees in Miami, Florida may not perform as well on an item within the context of a snowy day but may be perfectly fine if asked to demonstrate knowledge on the same topic in the context of a sunny day or other context familiar to them. A bias and sensitivity review of all items should be part of any item and test development activities (Camilli, 2006; Camilli & Shepard, 1994; Crocker & Algina, 1986).

Another way to assess the potential bias in an assessment includes reviewing evidence for differential item functioning (DIF). A DIF analysis is a statistical procedure that compares the performance of examinees on each item who are the same or very similar in terms of ability levels and the overall test score but who differ in terms of subgroup membership (e.g., gender, race/ethnicity, SES, ESL). The assumption is that examinees scoring the same or very similarly on the total assessment should also perform the same or very similarly on each individual item. When examinees matched in ability are separated by subgroup and performance on an individual item differs such that members of one subgroup (females or Hispanic examinees, for example) are much more likely to answer an item incorrectly than the subgroup used as a reference group (in this case, males or White examinees), then the item needs to be examined more closely to try to determine why females (or Hispanic) examinees are performing differently on this particular item. If the contributing factor can be identified, then the item may be edited and field tested again for re-use on the exam. More often, the cause is not clear and the item is removed from the exam and not re-used (Camilli, 2006; Camilli & Shepard, 1994; Holland & Wainer, 1993).

Commercial test developers should perform DIF analyses on a regular basis and be able to provide additional information about their specific procedures or criteria for identifying biased items. Additionally, DIF results are often one of the pieces of information that must be provided when seeking approval of a test for a certain purpose such as the CCCCO list of approved exams, and Federal approval for use in Ability to Benefit (ATB, 1995) determination. In the event that an examinee or other entity ever challenges the use of a placement test at a college, it is very likely that evidence the test scores are free of bias will be one of the top considerations. Therefore, it is important to use an assessment with sufficient evidence to support that scores are free of bias and to maintain a copy of that evidence for the lifetime of the college's use of the assessment. More complete coverage of bias and differential item functioning can be found in Clauser and Hambleton (this volume).

Special Topics in Placement Testing

The following sections discuss special topics associated with placement testing for entry-level college students. Questions about these topics are frequently found among those posted on electronic discussion boards for test administrators and other professionals working with placement tests and their scores. The special topics covered include concordance tables, post-testing, and the use of college placement tests in high schools.

Concordance Tables

Placement testing of students entering college most often occurs at the institution where the student intends to enroll for classes. Therefore, a large number of students are tested on site using the institution's preferred placement test. However, for varying reasons, students may come to the institution with existing scores on an alternative test purporting to measure the same concept as the assessment instrument in use at the institution. Frequently this occurs either because the student visits multiple sites before actually enrolling for classes or has a change of mind about the institution into which they will enroll. Additionally, the institution may like to conserve resources and limit placement testing to only those students without sufficient supporting evidence of their proficiency from another source, such as the SAT, ACT, or SAT Subject tests. In these instances, institutions may look for ways to use the available information to make comparable decisions about student proficiency and proper course placement. Common questions of interest may include: What COMPASS score is equivalent to a score of 85 on ACCUPLACER? What SAT score is equivalent to a score of 28 on the ACT? What SAT score is equivalent to a score of 100 on ACCUPLACER? Concordance tables are used to answer questions of this type; however, concordance tables do have limitations that must be considered. Concordance tables provide a link between a score on one assessment and a score on another assessment that is purported to indicate the same level of student ability.

The use of a concordance table to estimate an examinee's score on one assessment based on their score from a different assessment implies that scores from the two assessments are interchangeable or have the same meaning. For this to be true, several characteristics of both tests must also be true. First, and most importantly, the tests must measure the same thing. Second, a correlation coefficient of at least 0.866 is needed between scores on the two tests. Third, the population of students used to create the concordance table should not differ in a meaningful way from the population of students to which the concordance table results will be applied (Dorans, 1999; Hanson, Harris, Pommerich, Sconing, & Yi, 2001; Schneider & Dorans, 1999).

Take into consideration the often requested concordance of the College Board's ACCU-PLACER and SAT tests. ACCUPLACER measures similar broad content areas as are measured on the SAT—Reading, Writing, and Mathematics. However, the exact breakdown of specific content within each area (e.g., sentence fragments, vocabulary, fractions, complex number) and the difficulty level of the items used in the assessments may vary drastically. It is a certainty that the SAT and ACCUPLACER, for instance, do not measure the same content at the same level of difficulty. Additionally, the number of tests in a content area for ACCUPLACER and the SAT varies and this makes alignment even more difficult. For example, ACCUPLACER has three separate mathematics assessments (Arithmetic, Elementary Algebra, and College Level Math) while the SAT has only one. The different breakdowns in terms of number of tests compounds the problem of aligning content between the tests since the SAT may cover the information on one or more ACCUPLACER tests. To create a concordance table between ACCUPLACER and the SAT when it is known that the content differs or between ACCUPLACER and another assessment without knowledge of the content alignment between the tests is untenable.

At a local institution level where knowledge exists to compare the content alignment between tests, a concordance table can be created for local use if it is determined that the content alignment between the two tests is similar. However, it is important to remember that a correlation coefficient of at least 0.866 between the two scores is recommended to reduce as much error in the results as possible. The examinee's scores used in the concordance study should be representative of the population of students at the institution where the concordance table will be used. For this reason, concordance tables developed by and for another institution are not likely to be applicable to your own institution and the use of concordance tables from another institution is strongly discouraged. Always remember that a concordance table can provide a suggested location for where an examinee may score if given the other assessment, but this is not a perfect predictor and the alignment of the content, correlation, and population are all potential sources of error. It is entirely possible, if not likely, that an examinee would get a different score, if they actually took the assessment, than what is predicted by the concordance table.

Posttesting

Institutions are often interested in using placement tests as posttests to measure the amount of learning that has occurred over the term of a course or, in some cases, over the length of many courses; for example, using the placement test as a gateway for student entry into upper level courses past the second year of college. This practice should be avoided unless the scores for the placement test have been validated for that purpose. In general, placement tests are designed to measure content that students entering college for the first time should know and be able to do in order to be successful in the entry level course. It is unlikely that a placement test has been developed for this purpose and with sufficient breadth and depth to cover the more advanced skills that a student may have acquired over the term of one or multiple courses.

One alternative would be the use of a placement test as a posttest to evaluate the effectiveness of a developmental course used to provide remediation. Given that placement test scores' validly measure what students should know and be able to do to be successful in the entry level course, and that the developmental course should improve the knowledge and skills of the student taking the course, then it would be expected that the student's placement test score would increase following the completion of the developmental course (Schiel & Sawyer, 2002). While the posttest results should not be used to evaluate the individual student, the aggregated results can be used by institutions interested in gathering evidence for the evaluation of the efficacy of the developmental courses being taught at the institution. It is important to remember that any evaluation of results should be considered in light of the SEM, as discussed previously, and the amount of change that could be expected and attributable to measurement error as opposed to real student growth in reaction to the remediation provided by the developmental course.

Using College Placement Tests in High Schools

Earlier in this chapter, the gap between student learning in secondary school and the skills necessary to be successful at the postsecondary level was identified as problematic and a major reason for the necessity of college placement testing for entering students. The use of college placement tests in high schools is a recent trend that has been growing over the past few years. Early efforts began with colleges, primarily community colleges, going into the high schools or arranging for high school students to come to the college campus to be tested for the purpose of early recruitment and/or identification of students who may have the necessary skills to be successful but had not considered higher education as an option. As commercially available placement tests became more portable by allowing the test proctor to access the testing platform from any computer via the Internet using an appropriate password, and as interest in increasing outreach efforts to the high schools continued to grow, the use of placement tests in high schools has become commonplace. Two overarching goals seem to be guiding the high school outreach efforts: (a) the recruitment of students in local high schools to the local community colleges, particularly those students who may not have traditionally considered themselves as "college material"; and (b) the early identification of student strengths and weaknesses while in high school to allow for remediation to occur prior to graduation rather than at cost to the student, and subsequently the college, after the student enrolls. Many of the high school outreach efforts have been quite successful and the number of programs utilizing placement tests in the high schools continues to grow with some use seen as early as the middle school years.

One caveat in regards to the use of placement tests in the high schools concerns the interpretation of results. Previously in this chapter, the lack of agreement and alignment concerning the number of developmental classes offered and the location of the cut score used to identify a student as "college ready" was discussed. The lack of alignment in the standards used by different institutions to determine if a student is ready for the entry-level, credit-bearing course can lead to confusion. If a student is determined to be "college ready" by the local community college using the local cut score and requirements, it is likely that the student will take away the message that they are "college ready." However, there is no guarantee that if this same student tests under the cut score and requirements of another institution that they will still be deemed "college ready" since the cut scores are not aligned and essentially become a moving target as the student considers multiple institutions. The result can be both confusing and frustrating to the student, in addition to expensive, should the student subsequently enroll in the college with a higher placement standard and be required to complete developmental courses before starting coursework for which they will earn college credit.

Some states have made great strides in reducing the potential for confusion due to the variable placement test cut scores in use across institutions by conducting statewide efforts to align course numbering systems, course curricula, and placement test scores used across the state for all institutions within the same system. Not only does this create an equal footing for the entering college student at all institutions in the state, but the common course numbering system and common curricula also provides an advantage to students that may have reason to transfer between institutions by increasing the likelihood that prior credits will be directly transferable.

Increasing Student Awareness

Too often, students are leaving high school to find they are not adequately prepared for success in college, often as a result of taking a placement exam and placing into a developmental course. Along with the confusion and frustration the student may feel at discovering they lack the necessary skills comes the realization that their college degree may take longer to earn and cost more than previously expected due to the cost of extra coursework needed for remediation. Approximately half of students first enrolling at a community college and a fourth of students at four year colleges do not return for their second year. Only 34% of students taking at least one developmental reading course eventually complete a degree (Venezia, et al., 2003).

Given the statistics, it is important that every effort be made to increase student awareness of the need to prepare for college beyond the preparation given by many students to admissions tests. In particular, students attending an open admissions institution that does not require an admissions test should be made aware of the likelihood that they will be given a placement test to determine the appropriate course placement. A large number of institutions report placement testing requirements on their website and provide written information to students who have applied for admission. Too often students, particularly in a community college, wait until the last moment to complete requirements for enrollment and may be entirely unaware of the need for the placement test until they are asked to report to the testing center. For this reason, placement test information and awareness must begin at the high school.

A large community effort is needed to prepare students to the extent possible and that effort needs to begin well prior to the end of the students' senior year of high school. High school teachers and counselors must be made aware of the placement tests students will need to take and be sure this information is transmitted to all students, not only those considered to be on a college preparatory track. Though the possible drawbacks and confusion that can result from placement testing in the high school were discussed earlier, the practice can be a very valuable one as long as students and high school faculty are adequately prepared to understand the variation in standards at different institutions and the need to continue learning and improving rather than taking a designation of "college ready" as a sign the student has reached the goal and may relax.

To follow up on this point, it is of utmost importance that students be encouraged and pushed to undertake the most challenging courses available throughout high school. Too often students choose to rest during the senior year with the thought that they have earned enough credits for graduation and can take it easy for the rest of the year, especially if they have already been accepted into a postsecondary institution. The prevalent "senioritis" or tendency to slack off during the senior year must be discouraged if the gap between secondary and postsecondary requirements is to ever be closed (Kirst, 2005).

Conclusion

In the current education system, placement testing of entering college freshmen serves a valuable role in identifying the course where the student will be best served when beginning their college career. Secondary and postsecondary educators working together to prepare students and align the requirements for exiting high school with those for entering college is absolutely essential to improving the current system. Placement testing does not bridge the gap between the two parts of the system—secondary and postsecondary—but it does allow for the identification of the students that are falling through the gap. While often considered of less consequence than denying admission to a student, course placement decisions can have a very large effect on the individual student's probability of success in the course and subsequently the student's persistence toward graduation. Therefore, it is imperative that placement decisions be made based upon valid and reliable score interpretations with as much precision as possible to reduce the risk of improper placement.

To afford the student the best chance possible for college success, rigorous preparation, frequent evaluation of academic strengths and weaknesses, and complete awareness of the college enrollment process, including placement testing, is needed by all students. At best, the students will be fully prepared to succeed in college and, at worst, those students not attending college will have solid skills to take into the workforce.

Note

1 The author wishes to thank Kevin Sweeney and Tom Proctor for their comments on an earlier version of this chapter.

References

Ability to Benefit Rule, 34 C.F.R. § 668 (1995).
Abraham, A. (1992). *College remedial studies.* Atlanta, GA: Southern Regional Education Board.
Achieve, & The Education Trust. (2008, November). *Making college and career readiness the mission for high schools: A guide for state policymakers.* Retrieved from http://www.achieve.org/files/MakingCollegeandCareerReadinesstheMissionforHighSchool.pdf
ACT. (2006). *ACT high school profile report: The graduating class of 2006: National.* Iowa City, IA: Author.
ACT. (2007). *Rigor at risk: Reaffirming quality in the high school core curriculum.* Iowa City, IA: Author.
Agresti, A. (1996). *An introduction to categorical data analysis.* New York, NY: Wiley.
Alliance for Excellent Education. (2006). *Paying double: Inadequate high schools and community college remediation.* Washington, DC: Author.
Camara, W. J. (2003, March). *College persistence, graduation, and remediation.* (College Board Research Note No. RN-19). New York, NY: The College Board.
Camilli, G. (2006). Test fairness. In R. L. Brennan (Ed.), *Educational measurement* (4th ed., pp. 220–256). Westport, CT: American Council on Education/Praeger.
Camilli, G., & Shepard, L. A. (1994). *Methods for identifying biased test items* (Vol. 4). Thousand Oaks, CA: Sage.
Clauser, J. C., Hambleton, R. K. (this volume). *Item analysis procedures for classroom assessments in higher education.*
Crocker, L. A., & Algina, J. (1986). *Introduction to classical and modern test theory.* Fort Worth, TX: Harcourt Brace.
Dorans, N. J. (1999). *Correspondence between ACT and SAT I Scores.* (College Board Research Report No. 99–1). New York, NY: The College Board.
Geisinger, K., Shaw, L. H., & McCormick, C. (this volume). *The validation of tests in higher education.*

Haertel, E. H. (2006). Reliability. In R. L. Brennan (Ed.), *Educational measurement* (4th ed., pp. 65–110). Westport, CT: American Council on Education / Praeger.

Hambleton, R. K., Swaminathan, H., & Rogers, H. J. (1991). *Fundamentals of item response theory.* Newberry Park, CA: Sage.

Hanson, B. A., Harris, D. J., Pommerich, M., Sconing, J. A., & Yi, Q. (2001). *Suggestions for the evaluation and use of concordance results.* (ACT Research Report No. 2001–1). Iowa City, IA: ACT.

Holland, P. W., & Wainer, H. (Eds.). (1993). *Differential item functioning.* Hillsdale, NJ: Erlbaum.

Kane, M. T. (2006). Validation. In R. L. Brennan (Ed.), *Educational measurement* (4th ed., pp. 17–64). Westport, CT: American Council on Education/Praeger.

Kirst, M. W. (2005). Rethinking admission and placement in an era of new K-12 standards. In W. J. Camara, & E. W. Kimmel (Eds.), *Choosing students: Higher education admissions tools for the 21st Century* (pp. 285–312). Mahwah, NJ: Erlbaum.

Mattern, K. D., & Packman, S. (2009). *Predictive validity of ACCUPLACER scores for course placement: A meta-analysis.* (College Board Research Report No. 2009–2). New York, NY: The College Board.

National Center for Education Statistics. (2004). *Remedial education at degree-granting postsecondary institutions in Fall 2000.* (Report No. 2004–010). Washington, DC: U.S. Department of Education.

National Center for Education Statistics. (2010a). *Academic preparation for college in the high school senior class of 2003–04.* (Report No. NCES 2010-169). Washington, DC: U.S. Department of Education.

National Center for Education Statistics. (2010b). *Postsecondary expectations and plans for the high school senior class of 2003–04.* (Report No. NCES 2010–170). Washington, DC: U.S. Department of Education.

Nitko, A. J. (1996). *Educational assessments of students* (2nd ed.). Englewood Cliffs, NJ: Prentice-Hall.

No Child Left Behind Act of 2001, Pub. L. No. 107–110, 115 Stat. 1425–2094 (2002).

Payne, D. A. (1992). *Measuring and evaluating educational outcomes.* New York, NY: Macmillan.

Pitoniak, M. J., & Morgan, D. L. (this volume). *Setting and validating cut scores for tests.*

Popham, W. J. (1999). *Classroom assessment: What teachers need to know* (2nd ed.). Needham Heights, MA: Allyn & Bacon.

Schiel, J. L., & Sawyer, R. (2002). *Using posttesting to show the effectiveness of developmental/remedial college course.* (ACT Information Brief No. 2002–3). Iowa City, IA: ACT.

Schneider, D., & Dorans, N. J. (1999). *Concordance between SAT I and ACT scores for individual students.* (College Board Research Note RN-07). New York, NY: The College Board.

The Education Trust. (1999, Fall). Ticket to nowhere: The gap between leaving high school and entering college and high performance jobs. *Thinking K-16, 3*(2).

Thompson, B., & Vache-Haase, T. (this volume). *Reliability.*

Traub, R. E. (1994). *Reliability for the social sciences: Theory and applications* (Vol. 3). Thousand Oaks, CA: Sage.

Venezia, A., Kirst, M. W., & Antonio, A. L. (2003). *Betraying the college dream: How disconnected K-12 and postsecondary education systems undermine student aspirations.* (Final Policy Brief). Retrieved from http://www.stanford.edu/group/bridgeproject/embargoed/embargoed_policybrief.pdf

Webb, N. L. (1997). *Criteria for alignment of expectations and assessments in language arts and science education.* (Council of Chief State School Officers and National Institute for Science Education Research Monograph No. 6). Madison, WI: University of Wisconsin, Wisconsin Center for Education Research.

25

ADMISSIONS TESTING IN HIGHER EDUCATION[1]

Rebecca Zwick

Standardized admissions testing first took root in the US more than 100 years ago, when college applicants were faced with a bewildering array of admissions criteria that varied widely across schools. In an attempt to impose order, the leaders of 12 top northeastern universities established the College Entrance Examination Board in 1900. The College Board created a set of examinations that were administered by the member institutions and then shipped back to the Board for scoring. Initially, the Board developed essay tests in nine subject areas; it later created a new exam that contained mostly multiple-choice questions—the Scholastic Aptitude Test. This precursor to today's SAT was first administered in 1926 to about 8,000 candidates.

Large-scale admissions testing became more feasible in 1939, when mechanical scoring of the SAT was initiated, eliminating many hours of tedious clerical work. The passage of the GI Bill in 1944 sent thousands of returning veterans to college, further boosting the SAT's popularity. In 1947, Educational Testing Service (ETS) was founded through the merger of the testing activities of three companies: The College Entrance Examination Board, the Carnegie Foundation for the Advancement of Teaching, and the American Council on Education. (All three continue to exist as separate organizations.) The ETS calendar of testing programs for 1949–50 listed 22 distinct exams. Although some have now faded into obscurity, such as "Knights of Columbus" and "National College Home Economics Testing Program," the list also included the College Entrance Examination Board (the SAT and related tests), the Graduate Record Examination, the Medical College Admission Test, and the Law School Admission Test (ETS, 1950, p. 43). As described below, the testing industry is now far less centralized and involves many more companies.

The first three sections of this chapter examine the main higher education admissions tests used in the US today. The first discusses the undergraduate admissions tests—the SAT and ACT, the second describes the Graduate Record Examinations (GRE), and the third provides information about the professional school admissions tests—the Medical College Admission Test (MCAT), the Law School Admission Test (LSAT), and the Graduate Management Admission Test (GMAT).[2] The remaining sections pertain to test development, scoring, predictive validity, fairness, and key information for admissions personnel.

Undergraduate Admissions Tests: The SAT and ACT

The SAT testing program is sponsored by the College Board; the tests are administered by ETS under a contract with the Board. The centerpiece of the program is the SAT Reasoning Test, which, according to the College Board Web site (www.collegeboard.com, May 2010), "measures critical reading, mathematical reasoning, and writing skills that students have developed over time and that they need to be successful in college." ("SAT" is no longer considered to be an acronym, but the actual name of the test. Originally, it stood for "Scholastic Aptitude Test," which was later changed to "Scholastic Assessment Test." More recently, the test was known as the "SAT I: Reasoning Test.")

In addition to the SAT Reasoning Test, the SAT program also includes the SAT Subject Tests (formerly called the College Board Achievement Tests and later, the SAT II: Subject Tests), which assess the candidates' knowledge in particular areas. Twenty SAT Subject Tests are available, in literature, US and world history, math, biology, chemistry, physics, and foreign languages. (When the new SAT writing test was unveiled in 2005, the SAT Subject Test in writing was eliminated.) The SAT Reasoning Test and the Subject Tests are all paper-and-pencil tests.

The SAT has been modified substantially since it was first administered in 1926 (complete with instructions indicating that the "pencil is preferable to the fountain pen for use in this sort of test"). A history of the changes in the content of the SAT is provided by Lawrence, Rigol, Van Essen, and Jackson (2004). The most recent changes occurred in 2005, following a nationwide controversy about the SAT that came to a head in 2001, with a speech by Richard C. Atkinson (2001), then the president of the University of California. Atkinson recommended the elimination of the SAT Reasoning Test as a criterion for admission to the University and advocated an immediate switch to college admissions tests that were tied closely to the high school curriculum. The newest version of the SAT consists of three sections: critical reading, math, and writing. The critical reading section substitutes short reading items for the analogy items that were formally part of the verbal section. The math section incorporates more advanced math content than its predecessor and eliminates certain item types. All critical reading questions and most math questions are multiple-choice. Each SAT includes some math questions that require "student-produced" answers—there are no response choices. The writing section includes both multiple-choice questions and an essay.

In 1959, ETS acquired a competitor in the college admissions test market. The American College Testing Program was founded in Iowa City by E. F. Lindquist, a University of Iowa statistician who was also the director of the Iowa Testing Programs (Peterson, 1983). (Today, the company is "ACT, Inc." and the test is simply "the ACT." Like "SAT," "ACT" is no longer considered an acronym.) From the beginning, the ACT was somewhat different from the SAT in terms of underlying philosophy: While the SAT consisted only of verbal and mathematical sections, the ACT was more closely tied to instructional objectives. Today, the content of the test is informed by regular surveys of secondary school teachers and curriculum experts. The ACT consists of four multiple-choice sections: English, mathematics, reading, and science. Students receive a score in each subject area, as well as a composite score. Seven subscores are also reported—two in English, three in mathematics, and two in reading. The ACT is a paper-and-pencil test.

In 2002, after the College Board announced that a writing component would be added to the SAT, ACT, Inc. announced that it would add a 30-minute essay test to the ACT. Unlike the SAT writing section, however, the ACT writing test, first administered in 2005, is optional. Students who elect to take it along with the ACT receive two additional scores, a writing test score and a combined English/writing score, as well as comments about their essays.

In its early years, the ACT was administered primarily in Midwestern states, but it is now considered interchangeable with the SAT by most institutions. To allow comparisons to be made between scores on the two tests, The College Board and ACT, Inc. have created tables of "concordance" between ACT and SAT scores. (Some institutions develop their own such tables as well.) The most recent large-scale concordance study was based on results from test administrations that took place between 2004 and 2006 (The College Board, 2009; Dorans & Petersen, 2010). Two separate concordance tables were developed: One provides a concordance between the ACT composite score and the sum of SAT critical reading and mathematics scores. The other provides a concordance between the ACT English/writing score and the SAT writing score. These linkages, however, are only approximate. In particular, because the content areas covered by the tests are not the same, the degree to which the SAT sum score and the ACT composite score are correlated is likely to depend on students' course background.

The role of standardized tests in undergraduate admissions varies widely over institutions. For candidates who pick an "open-door" college, for example, tests play no part in the admissions process: All that is required is to submit an application and, in some cases, show proof of high school graduation. In a survey conducted by ACT, Inc., the Association for Institutional Research, the College Board, Educational Testing Service, and the National Association for College Admission Counseling, 8% of the 957 four-year institutions that responded and 80% of the 663 two-year institutions[3] fell into the open-door category (Breland, Maxey, Gernand, Cumming, & Trapani, 2002, p. 15).

Of course, the degree to which standardized test scores and other academic criteria are considered useful in admissions decisions depends on the institution's goals. As Harvard public policy professor Robert Klitgaard pointed out in his thought-provoking 1985 book, *Choosing Elites*, the "first question to ask about selective admissions is why it should be selective at all" (p. 51). One justification for selectivity in college admissions is that it rewards academic excellence, motivation, and hard work. Another argument is that it encourages high schools to provide a quality education; the same argument could be extended to the graduate and professional school admissions process. But most institutions are selective for a more immediate reason: They wish to admit candidates who are likely to be able to do the academic work required of them. Standardized admissions test scores, along with other criteria, are intended to help in identifying these candidates.

How heavily are test scores weighted in undergraduate admissions decisions? One source of information is the annual admission trends survey conducted by the National Association for College Admission Counseling (NACAC; see Clinedinst, 2008), to which 382 colleges and universities responded in 2008.[4] According to the NACAC report, "[a]lthough an increasing number of colleges have adopted test-optional admission policies in recent years, NACAC survey data show that the importance of standardized testing across all four-year colleges and universities has increased over the past 15 years" (p. vii). (Similarly, a recent *Newsweek* article by Springen, 2010, noted that "[e]ven with more schools embracing test-free admissions, a record number of students took both the SAT and the ACT [in 2010].") The NACAC survey showed that, overall, responding institutions viewed test scores on the SAT or ACT as the third-most important factor, after grades in college preparatory courses and strength of curriculum. The percentage of institutions that viewed these test scores to be of "considerable importance" was 58.5; another 30.9% said test scores were of "moderate importance." By contrast, SAT Subject Test scores were viewed as being of considerable importance by only 6% of institutions.

Graduate School Admissions: The Graduate Record Examinations

The Graduate Record Examinations program of the Carnegie Foundation for the Advancement of Teaching administered its first exam in 1937. In 1948, the GRE program was transferred to the newly formed ETS. Today, the GRE, which is used to evaluate candidates for admission to graduate school, is developed and administered by ETS under the direction of the Graduate Record Examinations Board, an independent 34-member organization that is affiliated with the Association of Graduate Schools and the Council of Graduate Schools. The exam, which consists of the GRE General Test, as well as optional subject tests, is available in test centers around the world. (As a result of a marketing effort by ETS, an increasing number of business schools now accept the GRE as an alternative to the GMAT, which is no longer an ETS test; more than 400 were listed on the GRE Web site, www.gre.org, as of November 2010.)

The GRE has undergone several significant changes since its inception. The GRE General Test was the first major admissions test to be administered as a computerized adaptive test (CAT),beginning In a CAT, items are selected for administration from a pool in such a way as to target the difficulty of the exam to the test-taker's proficiency level. Therefore, a CAT can measure proficiency more efficiently than a conventional test. The test-takers's proficiency is re-estimated after the administration of each item. The item selection procedure choose for administration the item that, based on it's properties and the test-taker's proficiency level, will supply the most information about the test-taker's skills. Certain other constraints (involving item content and other features) ordinarily need to be met as well. CATs are discussed in further detail in Dolan and Burling (this volume). Among the more recent content modifications of the GRE was the incorporation of a writing assessment in 2002, replacing an analytical reasoning section.

In 2011, the GRE became a multistage test (MST; ETS, 2010a, p. 6): It is still adaptive, but at the level of subsections of the test, rather than individual items. The MST version, unlike the CAT version, allowss test-takers to revise previous answers (within a subsection). Like the CAT version, the revised GRE General Test includes separately scored verbal rasoning, quatitative reasoning, and analytical writing sections. However, the content of these sections has been modified, along with the scale on which verbal and quantitative scores are reporated. According to the GRE Bulletion (ETS, 2010b, p. 4), the verbal reasoning section of the revised test "more closely reflects the kind of thinking[that is done] in graduate or business school" and the quatitative reasoning section includes multiple-choice items and items that involve selecting a particular segment of a passage as a response. The quantitative section includes both multiple-choice items and those that require numerical entry. (Some multiple-choice items on the revised GRE require the test-taker to select one *or more* correct answer from a set of possible responses.) As before, the analytical writimg section consists of two essays, one involving the evaluation of a logical argument and on asking the candidate to express views on a critical issue.[5]

In addition to the General Test, eight GRE Subject Tests are available: biochemistry, cell and molecular biology; biology; chemistry; computer science; literature in English; mathematics; physics; and psychology. These exams are multiple-choice, and will continue to be administered in paper-and-pencil format only.

Surveys have shown that standardized admissions tests are widely used in graduate admissions, in combination with undergraduate grades and other factors (Kuncel, Hezlett, & Ones, 2001; Rigol & Kimmel, 1997). Many graduate programs require the GRE General Test; some require certain GRE Subject Tests as well. The Miller Analogies Test, developed by The Psychological Corporation, is accepted by a small percentage of graduate programs as an alternative to the GRE.

Although a great deal of self-selection by applicants takes place, graduate programs tend to be more selective than undergraduate programs at the same institution (Whitney, 1989). However, admissions policies and rates vary widely over the hundreds of fields of doctoral study available in the US. The weight accorded to standardized test scores in graduate school admissions is difficult to gauge. Graduate school admissions policies tend to be less formalized and less public than their undergraduate counterparts. Decisions are typically in the hands of faculty at the department level, rather than admissions officers, and admission procedures are typically very flexible. As a 1997 College Board report noted, "published statements about [doctoral] admissions provide ample latitude for almost any decision" (Rigol & Kimmel, 1997, p. 13).

The Professional School Admissions Tests: The MCAT, LSAT, and GMAT

The Medical College Admission Test, first given in 1946, is sponsored by the Association of American Medical Colleges, which currently represents 132 US medical schools, 17 Canadian medical schools, about 400 teaching hospitals, and various academic societies and medical professionals.

Since 2007, the MCAT has been administered as a (non-adaptive) computer-based test by Prometric, a technology-based testing company that is a subsidiary of ETS.

As described in an MCAT bulletin, the test assesses "the skills and knowledge that medical educators and physicians have identified as key prerequisites for success in medical school and the practice of medicine," including "mastery of basic concepts in biology, general and organic chemistry, and physics, . . . capacity for problem solving and critical thinking as well as general writing skills" (Association of American Medical Colleges, 2007). The test consists of three multiple-choice sections—verbal reasoning, physical sciences, and biological sciences—as well as a writing sample composed of two essay questions. A separate score is reported for each section of the MCAT.

The MCAT is required by nearly all American medical schools. College grades, the quality of the undergraduate institution, letters of recommendation, and interviews are also important factors in admissions decisions. In a survey of accredited US medical schools (Johnson & Edwards, 1991), the interview was rated as the most crucial factor in selecting among candidates, followed by undergraduate GPA in science courses, letters of recommendation, MCAT scores, and undergraduate non-science GPA, in that order.

The LSAT was conceived at a 1947 meeting between College Board staff and representatives of an association of nine law schools, the precursor of the Law School Admission Council (LSAC). In 1948, the first LSAT was administered by ETS. Since 1979, the LSAT has been developed by the LSAC itself, which today has more than 200 member institutions in the US and Canada.

The LSAT is a paper-and-pencil test "designed to measure skills that are considered essential for success in law school: the reading and comprehension of complex texts with accuracy and insight; the organization and management of information and the ability to draw reasonable inferences from it; the ability to reason critically; and the analysis and evaluation of the reasoning and argument of others" (www.lsac.org, April 2010). Four multiple-choice sections serve as the basis for a single score. Three item types are included: reading comprehension, analytical reasoning, and logical reasoning. In addition to the multiple-choice questions, the LSAT includes a writing sample, which is not graded, but is sent to the law schools to which the candidate applies.

All American-Bar-Association-approved law schools and most Canadian law schools require the LSAT, and many other law schools do as well. Test scores and undergraduate grades tend to be weighted heavily in law school admissions decisions; schools often use an index score that combines the LSAT score and undergraduate GPA.

The precursor to the Graduate Management Admission Test was first administered in 1954. Prior to that, the GRE was used to screen business school applicants (Schmotter, 1993). For five decades, the test that eventually became known as the GMAT was developed and administered by ETS for the Graduate Management Admission Council, which includes about 160 "governing schools" of business and management. In 2006, the GMAC began working with two new companies: ACT, Inc. now develops the test questions and Pearson VUE, a company specializing in computer-based testing, delivers the exam at test centers around the world.

Today's GMAT is "designed to measure verbal, mathematical, and analytical writing skills that have been developed over a long period of time through education and work" (www.gmac.org, April 2010). It does not measure knowledge of business or achievement in any other subject area. The test contains verbal and quantitative sections, both of which are multiple-choice, and an analytical writing section, which was added in 1994. The verbal and quantitative sections have been administered as a CAT (see the section on graduate school admissions) since 1997. The writing section requires the test-taker to produce essay responses to two questions, with half an hour allowed for each. Separate scores are reported for each of the three sections of the GMAT; a total score that reflects performance on the verbal and quantitative sections (but is not the total of the verbal and quantitative scores) is also reported. According to the GMAT Web site, a "Next Generation GMAT" will make its debut in 2012 (www.gmac.org, November 2010). The revised test will include a new 30-minute separately scored section called Integrated Reasoning, which is intended to assess how well candidates "analyze information, draw conclusions, and discern relationships between data points." The Analytical Writing Assessment will be revised to include only one essay instead of two, so that total test length will remain the same.

According to its Web site, the GMAT is used by "thousands of graduate management programs around the world." (As noted in the section on graduate school admissions, some business schools accept the GRE in place of the GMAT.) Undergraduate grades and math background are also important factors in business school admissions, and essays, letters of recommendation, and interviews may be considered as well.

Test Development

The sponsoring organization for each test (for example, the College Board in the case of the SAT, or the Graduate Management Admission Council in the case of the GMAT) makes the broad policy decisions about the purpose, content, length, and method of administration of the test. The next step in the process usually involves the development of a framework or blueprint that specifies the content areas—and sometimes the cognitive skills—that are to be included in the test, along with the importance to be accorded to each of these areas and skills. This framework is typically developed by a committee of testing professionals and subject-area experts and then submitted for review to numerous other individuals and panels. The tests have statistical specifications as well, typically including a target range of item difficulties and item discrimination indexes (measures of the relationship between an item score and a test or section score). In a CAT, test development involves the development of one or more pools of test items from which the candidates' items will be drawn, rather than the creation of a test form (e.g., see Rudner, 2010).

With the exception of the writing assessments, higher education admissions tests consist primarily of multiple-choice questions. The way items are created varies to some degree across tests and testing organizations. Some companies rely mainly on in-house staff, some contract with other testing companies, and others primarily use hired consultants—usually classroom teachers or university professors—to develop test questions. After the items are created, they are reviewed by expert panels and by test editors who check the grammar, spelling, and format of the items.

In addition, items are typically subjected to a "sensitivity" review to eliminate content that is thought to be offensive or disturbing. According to the guidelines used at ETS, for example, staff must "[e]nsure that symbols, language, and content that are generally regarded as sexist, racist, or offensive are eliminated, except when necessary to meet the purpose of the assessment . . ." (ETS, 2002, p. 19). Also prohibited, in general, is content that could be upsetting or inflammatory.

The items that pass muster are then field-tested. This may be done by embedding items (which typically do not count toward the test-taker's score) in a test that is given at a regular administration, or by conducting a separate experimental administration. The results of this field test are analyzed to determine whether the new items meet the established statistical specifications. Analyses of differential item functioning (see the section on fairness below and the chapter by Clauser & Hambleton, this volume) are typically conducted at this point too. The surviving items are deemed eligible for inclusion in a CAT pool or in a bank of items from which paper-and-pencil test forms can be constructed.

Scoring

How are admissions tests scored? These processes depend in part on the administration mode of the test. The main portions of the four nonadaptive tests (SAT, ACT, MCAT, and LSAT) are considered in the first part of this section, followed by the GMAT and GRE in the second part. The scoring procedures for the essay components of the SAT, ACT, MCAT, GRE, and GMAT are described in the third part of this section. (The essay that accompanies the LSAT is sent to the law schools unscored.)

Scoring the SAT, ACT, MCAT, and LSAT

For the admissions tests that do not have adaptive features, scoring consists of two basic steps, detailed further below.

- Step 1. A raw score is computed, based on test-taker responses.
- Step 2. The process of test equating is used to translate the raw score to the reporting scale (for example, the 200-to-800 scale for the sections of the SAT). The equating process adjusts for differences in difficulty between test forms.

For the ACT, MCAT, and LSAT, the raw score is simply the number of correct answers, but for the multiple-choice questions on the SAT Reasoning Test (and also the SAT Subject Tests and the GRE Subject Tests), a formula score is used. The formula score includes a "correction for guessing," which is intended to adjust the score to compensate for random guessing. The idea underlying the correction is that test-takers who guess randomly (in contrast to those who make informed guesses) should not be allowed to increase their scores by doing so. Specifically, the formula score is $R - W/(C-1)$, where R is the number of right answers, W is the number of wrong answers, and C is the number of response choices. No points are subtracted for omitted items. The formula score is intended to be an estimate of the number of items for which the test-taker actually knew the answer (see Gulliksen, 1987, pp. 246–249 for a rationale). The formula score, which can include a fraction, is rounded to the nearest whole number before proceeding to Step 2.

The raw score now needs to be translated to a scale score for reporting, and this translation involves an equating process. The purpose of equating is to assure that scores on new test forms can be used interchangeably with scores on earlier forms. Even though the intention of test-makers is to create new test forms that are equivalent in difficulty to the old ones, some differences will inevitably exist, requiring that score adjustments be made. In nonadaptive tests, adjustments are typically made through the use of "anchor" items that are included in more than one test form. Responses to these equating items allow the two forms to be put on the same scale.

As an example, consider the scoring and equating process for the critical reading section of the SAT Reasoning Test. Suppose a test-taker answered 61 of the 67 questions correctly, got 4 five-choice items wrong, and omitted 2 items. The test-taker's raw (formula) score would be computed by subtracting 1/4 point for each wrong answer from the number of right answers, yielding a score of 60. A test equating process would then be applied to determine the correspondence between raw and scaled scores for the particular SAT version at hand. Responses to items appearing in the "variable" section of the SAT (a special section that does not count toward test-takers' scores) would be used to determine the necessary adjustment. On a relatively easy form, the raw score of 60 would translate to a lower score on the 200–800 scale than it would on a harder form. Each testing program uses a somewhat different equating method. For further information on test equating, see Kolen and Hendrickson (this volume).

Scoring the GMAT CAT and the GRE MST

Adaptive and multistage tests are scored using an item response theory (IRT; see Osterlind & Wang, this volume) model that takes into account the fact that candidates receive tests that vary in terms of item difficulty and other item properties. For each main section of the exam, a test-taker's proficiency level is estimated based on his item responses and on the estimated parameters of the items he received. An item's parameters represent its characteristics—its difficulty, its discrimination (the association between the item score and the proficiency measured by the test) and its likelihood of being answered correctly by a low-proficiency candidate (e.g., through guessing).[6] On an adaptive test, therefore, two candidates who answer the same number of questions correctly will not, in general, be estimated to have the same level of proficiency. As a final step in score calculations, each test-taker's estimated proficiency level, which is initially expressed in terms of an arbitrary scale, is transformed to the desired reporting scale (e.g., 0–60 for the verbal section of the GMAT).

Scoring the SAT, ACT, MCAT, GRE, and GMAT Writing Assessments

The MCAT writing sample consists of two handwritten essays, which are scored by raters using conventional essay-grading procedures (see O'Neill & Murphy, this volume). Two raters score the overall effectiveness of each of the two essays on a 1-to-6 scale. Disagreements of more than one point are adjudicated by a third rater. The resulting four scores (two per essay) are summed and then converted to an alphabetic score that ranges from J to T.

On the Analytical Writing section of the GRE, each of the two essays is scored by two raters on a six-point scale. Raters are trained to score the essays in terms of their overall quality rather than focusing on grammar and mechanics. If the raters disagree by more than one point, the discrepancy is adjudicated by a third rater. Otherwise, the scores from the two raters are averaged to obtain the final score for each essay. To obtain the overall Analytical Writing score, the final scores on the two essays are averaged and rounded up to the nearest half-point. Essays are reviewed by ETS essay-similarity-detection software and by experienced raters during the scoring process to assure that they represent "independent intellectual activity" (www.ets.org/gre, October 2011).

In the GMAT writing assessment, as in the MCAT and GRE, test-takers respond to each of two essay questions. Each essay is evaluated by one human rater and by a computerized essay-scoring program, the Intellimetric Essay Scoring System of Vantage Learning. Both human and computer score the essay on a six-point scale. If the two scores differ by more than a point, another human rater resolves the disagreement. The candidate's writing score is the average of the four essay scores (two ratings for each of two essays), rounded to the nearest half-point. The agreement between Intellimetric ratings and human ratings of GMAT writing responses was found to be about as strong as the agreement between two human ratings (Rudner, Garcia, & Welch, 2005), a finding that is less remarkable in light of the fact that assigning a number to a piece of writing remains a complex and, to some degree, subjective task even for trained human raters.

Predictive Validity of Admissions Tests

Although they differ somewhat in the skills they are alleged to measure, all college, graduate school, and professional school admissions tests share one particular claim—that they are useful for predicting the first-year grades students will receive in the educational programs they enter. Research on the association between test scores and college grades began in the late 1800s. In 1939, T. R. Sarbin conducted a particularly interesting study that compared two methods of predicting first-quarter college grade-point averages of 162 college freshmen. One method used a regression equation that included the students' high school ranks and college aptitude test scores; the other was based on the judgments of counselors, who used the students' high school standings and test scores, plus additional background information and personal interviews to make the predictions. Sarbin found that the regression equation was more accurate—the counselors tended to overestimate the student's future grades (Sarbin, 1943; see Gough, 1962, p. 556). Although the superiority of the statistical approach in the Sarbin analysis was small, two studies of the prediction of academic performance conducted thirty years later—Dawes (1971) and Wiggins and Kohen (1971)—showed a substantial advantage for the statistical approach (see Dawes & Corrigan, 1974, p. 98).

A comprehensive evaluation of a test's validity must involve a consideration of the test's design, development, content, administration, and use (see Geisinger, Shaw, & McCormick, this volume, for a general discussion of validity). In practice, the validity of admissions tests as a selection tool for higher education institutions is judged largely by the degree to which test scores can predict students' grade-point averages in college, graduate school, or professional school (GPAs). This aspect of validity is the focus of the present section.

Conducting a predictive validity study requires that the GPAs for the cohort of interest be available so that the predicted GPAs can be compared to the GPAs actually earned by the admitted students. Predictive validity studies are usually conducted within a single institution, although results may later be averaged across institutions. Typically, linear regression analysis is applied to estimate an equation for predicting GPA. Most often, first-year grades are used. The predictors are ordinarily admissions test scores and high school grades (in the case of college admissions) or undergraduate grades (in the case of graduate or professional school admissions). The resulting multiple correlation, which can range from 0 to 1, provides an index of the effectiveness of the prediction equation. The regression analysis can then be repeated using prior grades alone as a predictor. Comparing the predictive effectiveness of the two equations gives an estimate of the value added by using admissions test scores. The simple correlations between test scores and subsequent GPAs are often examined as well.

A factor that complicates the interpretation of these correlations, or validity coefficients, is restriction of range: students whose test scores are too low to allow admission to a higher education institution will not have GPAs. Because of this restriction of range (of test scores, and, as a result, of other predictors and of GPAs as well), validity coefficients tend to be smaller for the admitted students than they would be for the entire population of applicants. (See the section titled *Effects of Range Restriction and Criterion Unreliability on Validity Coefficients* for further discussion.) Statistical corrections are often applied in an attempt to estimate how big the association would have been if the range had not been restricted. Except where noted, the correlations reported in this chapter have not been corrected for range restriction. Typically, the corrected correlations are larger by 0.15 to 0.20.

An examination of large-scale studies (focusing on multi-institution studies and reviews published in 2000 or later) reveals some consistent patterns in the findings on the predictive validity of admissions tests in college, graduate school, and professional school. (See Kuncel & Hezlett, 2007, for an excellent overview of graduate and professional school results.) The multiple correlation of the ACT or the SAT with college GPA is typically about 0.3 to 0.4 (ACT, Inc., 2007; Burton & Ramist, 2001; Camara & Echternacht, 2000; Kobrin, Patterson, Shaw, & Barbuti, 2008). In the case of the ACT, these results are based on analyses that use scores on the English, mathematics, reading, and science sections, considered together. In the case of the SAT, results are based on analyses that use math and verbal (or, after 2005, critical reading) scores considered together. The correlation between the admissions test (ACT or SAT) and college GPA is usually found to be slightly lower than the correlation between high school grades and GPA. Considering ACT or SAT scores as predictors along with high school grades yields correlations with GPA that average about 0.5.

A study of the SAT writing test, first administered in 2005, showed that scores were correlated about 0.3 with college GPA (Kobrin et al., 2008). These results supported the predictive validity of the writing test, but also showed that it added only a small amount (0.02) to the validity coefficient obtained using critical reading and mathematics scores alone. These results paralleled those obtained from an earlier study of a prototype version of the SAT writing test (Norris, Oppler, Kuang, Day, & Adams, 2005; see also Mattern, Camara, & Kobrin, 2007). Similarly, research on the ACT writing test (ACT, Inc., 2009) showed that scores were predictive of grades in "writing-intensive" college courses, but that inclusion of the writing test in the prediction equation increased the validity coefficient by only 0.02 over the value obtained using the ACT English test alone.

Most GRE validity research predates the substitution of the writing assessment for the analytical reasoning component in the main part of the test. Results from the GRE Validity Study Service collected between 1986 and 1990, which are based on more than 1,000 departments and more than 12,000 test-takers (ETS, 2003), as well as on other recent multi-institution studies (Burton & Wang, 2005; Kuncel et al., 2001), show that the predictive validity of the GRE (as formerly constituted) is quite similar to that of the SAT and ACT. GRE scores (verbal, quantitative, and analytical reasoning considered together) typically have a validity coefficient of 0.3 to 0.4, and this is usually similar to the correlation between undergraduate GPA and first-year graduate school GPA. When undergraduate GPA and GRE scores are considered in combination, their correlation with graduate school GPA is 0.4 to 0.5. Including scores on the GRE Subject Tests as predictors usually boosts the correlation to 0.5 to 0.6.

Separate validity analyses of the GRE writing assessment (before it was added to the main assessment) were conducted based on approximately 2,000 college juniors, college seniors, and first-year graduate students. Analyses showed that the writing assessment (the combined score on two essays) had correlations of about 0.3 with a GPA based on courses that "required considerable writing." Correlations with overall GPA were about 0.2, and correlations with GPA in the students' major field were smaller (Powers, Fowles, & Welsh, 1999, p. 33).

A study based on two student cohorts at each of 14 medical schools reported that the median correlation between MCAT scores and the average of first-year and second-year medical school GPA exceeded 0.4, higher than the median correlation between undergraduate grades and medical school GPA (Julian, 2005). According to a recent summary of results from 166 schools, the LSAT typically does a slightly better job of predicting first-year law school GPA than do undergraduate grades, yielding correlations averaging over 0.3 (Stilwell, Dalessandro, & Reese, 2007). The association between scores on the GMAT (verbal, quantitative, and analytical writing scores considered together) and business school GPA (evaluated halfway through the business school program) was investigated by Talento-Miller and Rudner (2005), based on results from 273 schools. They found a median multiple correlation of 0.5, substantially larger than the median correlation between undergraduate grades and business school GPA (0.3). (These correlations were adjusted for restriction of range.) In the case of the MCAT, LSAT, and GMAT, using test scores and undergraduate grades in combination to predict subsequent GPA was slightly more effective than using test scores alone.

In summary, college admissions test scores tend to be slightly weaker than high school grades as predictors of college GPA. Including test scores in addition to past grades in the prediction equation tends to increase the validity coefficient by about 0.1. In predicting graduate school grades, GRE scores and undergraduate grades tend to be equally effective. Test scores are frequently found to be more effective than undergraduate grades in predicting professional school grades.

Although first-year GPA is the most common criterion variable in admission test validity studies, other criteria have been studied as well. For example, there is considerable evidence that admissions test scores are helpful in predicting grades beyond the first year (Burton & Ramist, 2001; Kuncel & Hezlett, 2007; Zwick, 2006, 2007). The evidence on prediction of degree attainment is mixed (Zwick, 2006, 2007). The SAT appears to be useful for this purpose (Burton & Ramist, 2001; Carnevale & Rose, 2003), while graduate and professional school admission tests are less so (Kuncel & Hezlett, 2007). Some studies have examined prediction of other criteria, such as performance on licensing exams and measures of career success, with inconsistent results (see Zwick, 2006, for a summary).

Effects of Range Restriction and Criterion Unreliability on Validity Coefficients

A factor that complicates the interpretation of validity coefficients is selection, or restriction of range: A basic limitation of test validity research is that only a portion of the college, graduate school, or professional school applicants is available for analysis. For example, in a SAT validity study conducted by a particular college, students whose SAT scores were too low to allow admission will not, of course, have freshman GPAs. Some high-scoring applicants who were, in fact, admitted may also be unavailable for analysis because they chose another school. Because of this restriction of range of SAT scores (and, as a result, of other predictors and of FGPAs as well) validity coefficients tend to be smaller for the admitted students than they would be for the entire population of applicants. As a result, the apparent association between test scores and FGPA is smaller than it would be if the entire group of applicants could be considered. A simple correlation or regression approach to the analysis of test validity will, therefore, produce a more pessimistic picture than is warranted, given that the intended goal of a validity study is to estimate the usefulness of tests in selecting students *from the overall applicant pool*. The range restriction problems that affect validity analyses at the college level lead to even greater distortions in the case of graduate and professional school admissions, where the selection process is more stringent. To compensate for the effects of selection, statistical corrections are sometimes applied in an attempt to estimate how big the association would have been if the range had not been restricted (Gulliksen, 1987, chapters 12 and 13; see Sackett & Yang, 2000 for a typology of range restriction corrections). These adjustments generally rely on unverifiable assumptions and can only be regarded as approximate.

An additional drawback of traditional validity studies is that they ignore the inaccuracies and inconsistencies of GPA as a criterion of academic performance. As in the case of range restriction, statistical corrections can be applied to validity coefficients to adjust for the unreliability of grades. In evaluating the results of a validity analysis, it is important to determine whether validity coefficients have been adjusted for range restriction or criterion unreliability, since the effect of these corrections can be substantial. For example, Ramist, Lewis, & McCamley-Jenkins (1994) found the uncorrected multiple correlation of verbal and math SAT scores with FGPA to be .36; with adjustments for restriction of range and criterion unreliability, the correlation rose to .57, a sizable increase.

Several researchers have attempted to improve the precision of GPAs by taking into account the fact that some college courses are harder than others and that some fields of study have more stringent grading practices than others (see Johnson, 1997; Stricker, Rock, Burton, Muraki, & Jirele, 1994; and Willingham, Pollack, & Lewis, 2000, for reviews). Adjusting GPAs for course difficulty usually leads to a slight increase (up to .1) in the correlation between test scores and GPAs. Even a relatively simple refinement—achieved by using only specific academic courses as the basis for computing GPA—has been found to make GPAs more comparable across students and more highly correlated with test scores. A more troublesome question about the validity of GPAs is whether grades reflect biases against particular groups of students, such as people of color, individuals with disabilities, or foreign students. This issue is rarely investigated. In general, grades are subject to far less scrutiny than tests when it comes to investigating bias.

Another subtle and complex aspect of validity analysis is the problem of "underprediction" and "overprediction" of subsequent grades. This phenomenon is discussed further in the following section.

Fairness of Admissions Tests to Special Populations

Standardized admissions test results often reveal substantial average score differences across ethnic, gender, and socioeconomic groups. These differences are often regarded as sufficient evidence that these tests are biased. From a psychometric perspective, however, a test's fairness is inextricably tied to its validity. According to Cole and Moss (1989), test bias occurs (i.e., fairness is violated) "when a test score has meanings or implications for a relevant, definable subgroup of test takers that are different from the meanings or implications" for other test takers. ". . . [B]ias is differential validity of a given interpretation of a test score . . ." (p. 205).

A key component of a psychometric assessment of the fairness of an admissions test is an investigation of whether there is evidence of differential prediction of a criterion, usually a grade-point average. Two distinct questions are typically addressed. The first is a question of strength of association: Are the test scores equally predictive of later grades for all groups? The second pertains to systematic errors of prediction: If we obtain a single prediction equation for students as a whole, will this equation lead to predicted GPAs that are systematically too high or too low for some student groups?[7] Analyses of this kind often include key predictors in addition to test scores. For example, in the case of college admissions tests, high school GPA would typically be included in the regression equations.

Another common component of fairness assessment is an examination of item content. Before an item is approved for inclusion in an admissions test, it undergoes a "sensitivity review" to make sure its content is not disturbing to certain student groups or offensive in some other way (see the section above titled *Test Development*). Later, after the test is administered, a differential item functioning (DIF) screening is performed (see Clauser & Hambleton, this volume) to determine whether equally skilled members of different groups (e.g., men and women) have statistically different rates of correct response on some items. The ultimate purpose of the DIF analysis is to identify test items with content that may be problematic for some student groups. The item may include content that is irrelevant to the construct being assessed, and is more familiar to some student groups than others, such as sports content in a mathematics test. Items found to have DIF are either discarded immediately or "flagged" for further study. Typically, a flagged item is reviewed by panelists from a variety of backgrounds who are expert in the subject-matter of the test. If the question is considered legitimate despite the differential functioning, it remains on the test. If the item is determined to be biased, it is modified or eliminated.

In the first five parts of this section, findings on differential test performance, differential validity, and differential item functioning on admissions tests are summarized for key student groups. The final part of this section addresses fairness issues related to test coaching.

Test Performance Findings for People of Color

Performance differences among racial and ethnic groups on standardized tests, including admissions tests, have been pervasive. Typically, White and Asian-American test-takers perform better than African-American, Hispanic, and Native American test-takers. Researchers, social theorists, and politicians have offered an array of reasons for this score gap, including socioeconomic, instructional, cultural, linguistic, and biological factors, as well as test bias.

Psychometric research has yielded a complex set of results regarding the validity of admissions tests across ethnic groups. Two recurrent findings in SAT validity studies are that correlations of test scores with FGPA tend to be somewhat smaller for Black and Hispanic students than for White students (see Young, 2004, p. 291) and that, counterintuitively, the use of a common regression equation to predict FGPA using SAT scores and high school grades produces overpredictions (predicted grades higher than actual grades) for these groups. Based on 11 studies, Young (2004, pp. 293–294) found the average overprediction for African-American students to be .11 (on a 0–4 scale); based on eight studies, the average overprediction for Hispanic students was .08. The lower correlations and the tendency toward overprediction also occur when high school GPA only is used to predict FGPA. In fact, although high school GPA is usually more highly correlated with FGPA than is SAT, overprediction of grades for African-American and Hispanic students tends to be worse if only high school GPA is included in the prediction equation (e.g., Mattern, Patterson, Shaw, Kobrin, & Barbuti, 2008; Ramist et al., 1994; Zwick & Himelfarb, 2011; Zwick & Schlemer, 2004; Zwick & Sklar, 2005). The overprediction of subsequent college achievement for Black students (and often for Hispanic students too) has been found on the ACT (Noble, 2004), GMAT (Braun & Jones,

1981), MCAT (Koenig, Sireci, & Wiley, 1998), and LSAT (Wightman & Muller, 1990), but a 1985 study did not find similar evidence of overprediction on the GRE (Braun & Jones, 1985).

There are a number of theories about the reasons for the overprediction findings (see Zwick, 2002, pp. 117–124). One conjecture is that minority and White students are likely to differ in ways that are not fully captured by either their test scores or their high school grades. For example, a Black student and a White student who both have high school GPAs of 3.5 and ACT composite scores of 26 may nevertheless differ in terms of the quality of early schooling, the environment in the home, and the aspirations of the family, all of which can influence academic preparation. Zwick & Himelfarb (2011) found some support for the hypothesis that overprediction is partly attributable to the fact that Black and Hispanic students are more likely to attend high schools with fewer resources.

A related technical explanation is that overprediction occurs because both SAT scores and high school grades are imprecise measures of academic abilities. Under various sets of plausible statistical assumptions (see Snedecor & Cochran, 1967, pp. 164–166; Wainer & Brown, 2007), it can be shown that to the degree that the test score is affected by measurement error, groups with lower test scores will tend to be overpredicted while those with higher scores will tend to be underpredicted. One major finding, however, argues against this factor as an all-purpose explanation for the overprediction phenomenon: On standardized admissions tests, women often score lower than men, yet their later grades tend to be *underpredicted* (see the section below titled *Test Performance Findings for Women*).

Another hypothesis is that, once in college, minority students do not fulfill their academic potential, which is assumed to be accurately captured by the tests. This "underperformance" could occur because of racism, an inhospitable environment, or life difficulties. It has also been hypothesized that anxieties, low aspirations, or negative attitudes may interfere with the academic success of minority students (e.g., Bowen & Bok, 1998, p. 84).

It seems evident that unmeasured differences in academic preparedness between White students and Black and Hispanic students with the same test scores and previous grades play a role in the recurrent finding of overprediction. It seems plausible as well that a greater incidence among minority students of life difficulties in college, such as financial problems, contributes to the phenomenon.

Test Performance Findings for Women

Recent results show that, on average, men scored better than women on the SAT math and critical reading sections, the ACT math and science tests and the ACT composite; the MCAT verbal reasoning, physical sciences, and biological sciences tests; the GRE verbal, quantitative, and analytical writing tests; the GMAT verbal, quantitative, and analytical writing tests and GMAT total; and the LSAT. Women tended to score better than men on the SAT and ACT writing tests and the ACT English and reading tests, and the same as men on the MCAT writing sample.[8]

Countless reasons have been offered to explain the generally superior performance of men on higher education admissions tests, including test bias; biological differences; diverging interests, aspirations, and course background; and societal influences. It has also been suggested that this test score gap occurs in part because women and men differentially self-select to take these admissions tests, producing sex differences in average economic and academic background, which, in turn, are associated with test performance.[9]

Performance differences are sometimes attributed to test features as well: Women are assumed to perform more poorly because test content is oriented toward men, because they are afraid to guess, or because the multiple-choice format is disadvantageous to them. More recently, "stereotype threat"—the fear of inadvertently confirming a cultural stereotype—has been invoked as an explanation (Steele, 1997, p. 613). Each of these speculations has gleaned support in some studies, but none have held up consistently.

Regarding validity results, it is typical to find that validity coefficients are higher for women than for men on the SAT, although the reasons are not clear. In more selective colleges, validities for men and women tend to be more similar to each other (Young, 2004). Another recurrent finding is that, when a common regression equation, based on both men and women, is used to predict college grades using SAT scores and high school GPA, women's predicted grades tend to be lower than the FGPAs they actually earned, and the reverse is true for men (e.g., see Mattern et al., 2008). Based on consideration of 17 studies, Young (2004) found an average underprediction of .06 (on a 0–4 scale) for women. Unlike the prediction errors that occur for ethnic groups, underprediction of women's grades is less severe when high school GPA alone is used as a predictor than when both SAT and GPA are used (e.g., Mattern et al., 2008; see Zwick, 2002, p. 148 for discussion).

Research on the underprediction of women's grades dates at least as far back as 1972 (Young, 2001, p. 7). The SAT, the ACT, and most of the SAT Subject Tests have been found to under-predict women's college grades (see Leonard & Jiang, 1999; Ramist, Lewis, & McCamley-Jenkins, 2001; Willingham & Cole, 1997; and Young, 2004). What accounts for this phenomenon? Ramist et al. (1994) found that a portion of the underprediction of women's FGPAs could be explained by the fact that women are less likely than men to take college courses that are stringently graded. This conclusion is consistent with the recurrent finding that underprediction is slight or even absent at very high academic levels (Koenig et al., 1998; Ramist et al., 1994; Young, 1991, 2001), although the Leonard and Jiang (1999) research appears to be an exception. Researchers have speculated that underprediction is minimized at graduate and professional schools and at elite colleges because nearly all students at these institutions take difficult courses, minimizing differences between men and women in the grading stringency of their coursework. Some researchers (e.g., Pennock-Román, 1994) have found that including college major in the prediction equation served to decrease the underprediction of women's grades, although this did not occur in the Leonard and Jiang study. Stricker, Rock, and Burton (1993) found that underprediction at a large university could be reduced by including in the regression model various measures of academic preparation, attitudes toward mathematics, and studiousness (see also Dwyer & Johnson, 1997; Willingham et al., 2000).

Some interesting results on prediction accuracy emerged from a study of SAT validity by Bridgeman, McCamley-Jenkins, and Ervin (2000), who grouped students on the basis of both sex and ethnic background and then studied the patterns of over- and underprediction. Analyses revealed that it was primarily White women who were affected by the underprediction problem, while the college grades of men from all ethnic groups tended to be overpredicted.

From a statistical perspective, the claim that college admissions tests are biased against women could be considered more convincing than the case for ethnic bias: Women tend to receive lower test scores than men *and* (at least in the case of White women) to earn higher college GPAs than predicted by their test scores. The bias conclusion is mitigated, however, by the finding in several analyses that underprediction of women's grades is reduced when the grading stringency of college courses is taken into account. Also, some researchers have suggested that underprediction occurs because women are more serious than men about their studies, more diligent about attending class and doing assignments, and more likely to be neat and careful in their work. According to this conjecture, women actually do perform better in college than men with equivalent academic preparation, and this is appropriately reflected in their college grades.

Test Performance Findings for People with Disabilities

A standardized test is meant to be administered under uniform conditions and time constraints, but fairness dictates that test scores should not be affected by any limitations of the test-taker which are not relevant to the skills being assessed. In this spirit, various accommodations are made available to admissions test candidates with disabilities. Test-takers with visual impairments, for example, are offered Braille or large-type versions of the test, or are provided with assistants who read the test aloud. Other special arrangements that are typically available include scribes for individuals with physical impairments that make writing impossible and sign language interpreters who can relay spoken instructions to deaf test-takers. Extended time is also permitted for candidates with disabilities. The rationale for offering these accommodations is that "the standard procedures . . . impede [these] test takers from performing up to their ability" (Mandinach, Cahalan, & Camara, 2001, p. 5). Ideally, scores on the accommodated admissions tests should be comparable to scores obtained from nondisabled test-takers under standard conditions. The standard and accommodated assessments should measure the same cognitive abilities and should be of equivalent difficulty and precision for their respective populations of test-takers.

The provision of special testing arrangements gives rise to a vast array of questions. What should "count" as a disability in an admissions testing situation? How can we determine whether the difficulty of an accommodated test for a candidate with a disability is equal to the difficulty of the standard test for a nondisabled test-taker? Should scores that are sent to schools be "flagged" if they have been obtained under nonstandard conditions? Do admissions test scores predict grades as well for people with disabilities as for other test-takers?

During the 1980s, a four-year research program that focused on candidates with disabilities who took the SAT or the (paper-and-pencil) GRE was conducted under the sponsorship of Educational Testing Service, the College Board, and the Graduate Record Examinations Board (Willingham, Ragosta, Bennett, Braun, Rock, & Powers, 1988). In general, the researchers concluded that the scores of test-takers who received accommodations were roughly comparable to scores obtained by nondisabled test-takers under standard conditions.

The one major exception involved test-takers who were granted extended time. Willingham et al. (1988, p. 156) stated that, for SAT-takers who received extra time due to presumed learning disabilities, "the data most clearly suggested that providing longer amounts of time may raise scores beyond the level appropriate to compensate for the disability." These students were more likely to finish the test than candidates at standard test administrations and their subsequent college grades were lower than was predicted by their test scores. The college performance of these students was consistent with their high school grades, suggesting that their SAT scores were inflated by excessively liberal time limits. Similar conclusions have been obtained in more recent SAT analyses (Cahalan, Mandinach, & Camara, 2002), as well as studies of the ACT and LSAT (Wightman, 1993; Ziomek & Andrews, 1996).

A longstanding controversy about testing accommodations for people with disabilities is whether score reports should contain a "flag" indicating that the test was given under nonstandard conditions. Proponents of flagging, who include most college admissions officers and high school guidance counselors, according to a survey (Mandinach, 2000), say that information about testing conditions is needed to interpret test scores correctly. Test users, such as universities, are misled when this information is withheld, they contend, possibly to the test-taker's disadvantage. Advocates of flagging say that it can also help to discourage dishonest "game-players" from requesting undeserved extra time and can thus increase the fairness of the test to those who play by the rules. Those who argue against flagging, however, say that it stigmatizes test-takers with disabilities and constitutes both a privacy violation and a form of discrimination that is prohibited by law.

The *Standards for Educational and Psychological Testing* developed by the American Educational Research Association, American Psychological Association, and National Council on Measurement in Education (1999, p. 105) offer a reasonable guideline for determining when flagging is appropriate: "[I]mportant information about test score meaning should not be withheld from test users who interpret and act on the test scores . . . When there is sufficient evidence of score comparability across regular and modified administrations, there is no need for any sort of flagging." Because the comparability of scores from extended-time administrations for students claiming learning disabilities is not well supported by research, flagging the scores from these administrations seems appropriate. The flagging debate, however, has been more heavily influenced by legal than by psychometric considerations: Spurred by a federal lawsuit filed against ETS in 1999 by a GMAT test-taker with a disability (Hoover, 2002), most admissions testing programs have discontinued the use of flagging. The MCAT program, however, flags the scores of "tests that are administered under non-standard conditions" (www.aamc.org, November 2010) and the LSAT program flags the records of test-takers who received extra time (www.lsac.org, November 2010).

Test Performance Findings for English Language Learners

Findings on the performance of language minorities on admissions tests are quite mixed. In their study of a national sample of more than 150,000 students who entered college in 2006, Mattern et al. (2008) found that test-takers who said their best language was not English performed substantially worse than average on the SAT critical reading and writing sections, but somewhat better than average on the math section. For students whose best language was not English, the correlation between SAT and first-year college grades was somewhat lower than for other test-takers, and these students were underpredicted by an average of .19 when a common regression equation was used to predict college grades using SAT scores and high school GPA.

Some researchers have found that prediction is accurate for language minorities. For example, in a six-institution study of SAT validity for Hispanic and non-Hispanic students, Pennock-Román (1990) concluded that "persons with somewhat limited English proficiency are handicapped both on test scores and in college achievement . . . their achievement in the first year is commensurate with their lower SAT scores" (pp. 122–126). By contrast, Ramist et al. (1994), who analyzed data from 45 colleges, found that any combination of predictors that included SAT verbal score led to underprediction of FGPA for students whose best language was not English. Zwick and Schlemer (2004), however, found substantial overprediction of FGPA among language minorities at the University of California, Santa Barbara, when high school GPA alone was used to predict FGPA; this overprediction was mitigated by inclusion of SAT scores in the prediction equation. Zwick and Sklar (2005), using data from the High School and Beyond sophomore cohort of 1980, compared Hispanic students who said their first language was Spanish with Hispanic students who said their first language was English (among other comparisons). The "Spanish" group received higher FGPAs, on average, than members of the "English" group who had similar high school GPAs and SAT scores. This inconsistency in results across studies is probably due in part to the fact that language minority groups have been defined in varying ways; see Zwick & Sklar, 2005.

Differential Item Functioning Findings for People of Color and Women

In ethnic group DIF analyses, it has been a recurrent finding that African-American, Hispanic, and Asian-American test-takers do not perform as well as a matched group of Whites on verbal analogy items (Bleistein & Wright, 1987; Rogers & Kulick, 1987; Schmitt, 1987) or on test questions containing homographs—words that are spelt the same but have two or more completely different meanings (Schmitt & Dorans, 1988; O'Neill & McPeek, 1993). (As of 2005, verbal analogy items no longer appear in the SAT.) Schmitt and her colleagues also found that items containing similar words with common roots in English and Spanish—true cognates—favor Hispanic test-takers if the Spanish version is used more frequently than its English cognate. There is some evidence that Hispanic test-takers are disadvantaged by false cognates—similar words that have different meanings in the two languages.

DIF findings on math items are quite mixed. Some studies have found that students of color perform better than a matched group of Whites on "pure math" items—those involving algebraic manipulations in the absence of any context—and do worse on word problems. One speculation about the reason for this is that pure math items tend to resemble textbook problems, which may be the focus of instruction at schools with fewer resources (O'Neill & McPeek, 1993, p. 270).

Other studies have shown that questions on topics of "minority interest" show evidence of DIF in favor of people of color. For example, one study of the SAT found results of this kind on a reading comprehension passage about a Black mathematician and on passages about civil rights and poverty (Rogers & Kulick, 1987, p. 7; see also O'Neill & McPeek, 1993, pp. 262–263). These findings suggest that DIF can be caused by differences in test-takers' interest in the content of the test items.

Certain DIF findings have emerged fairly consistently from comparisons of men and women. Women tend not to do as well as a matched group of men on verbal SAT and GRE items about scientific topics or about stereotypically male interests, like sports or military activities. On the other hand, women tend to perform better than their male counterparts on questions about human relationships or questions about the arts (O'Neill & McPeek, 1993, p. 262). It seems likely that these performance disparities stem from differences in interests and pastimes, and perhaps high school coursework.

For the vast majority of items that show evidence of DIF based on gender, the reasons are murky at best, particularly for math questions. O'Neill and McPeek (1993) noted that on several ETS tests and on the ACT, women perform better on algebra questions than men with equivalent quantitative scores; men do better on geometry and mathematical problem-solving. Also, analyses of the GRE, GMAT, SAT, and ACT have shown that women do better on "pure mathematics" problems and men tend to perform better on word problems framed in terms of an actual situation (O'Neill & McPeek, 1993, p. 269). However, a later study found that women have an advantage on GRE items that require "modeling of a word problem as an algebraic expression" (Gallagher, Morley, & Levin, 1999).

Although evidence suggests that DIF items are not a major source of overall test score differences among ethnic and gender groups, at least on the SAT (E. Burton & N. W. Burton, 1993), DIF screening is important as a precaution against the inclusion of unreasonable test content and as a source of information that can contribute to the construction of better tests in the future.

Effect of Test Coaching on Fairness

The effectiveness and ethics of commercial test preparation for admissions tests, particularly the SAT, have long been the subject of controversy. Several well-designed studies appearing since 1990 have produced consistent results about the magnitude of score improvement that results from SAT coaching. Becker (1990), Powers and Rock (1999), and Briggs (2001, 2004) all concluded that the average gain from SAT coaching is between 6 and 8 points on the verbal section and between 14 and 18 points on the math section. Coaching studies on tests other than the SAT are quite scarce, and results are not yet available for the 2005 revision of the SAT. Research suggests that coaching produces small benefits on the ACT (Briggs, 2001; Scholes & McCoy, 1998), the paper-and-pencil GMAT (Leary & Wightman, 1983), and the quantitative section of the paper-and-pencil GRE (Powers, 1983), and essentially no effect on the MCAT (Koenig & Leger, 1997) or the verbal section of the paper-and-pencil GRE (Powers, 1983). Although many testing companies long maintained the position that test preparation programs were largely ineffective, the sponsors of all major admissions tests now produce test preparation materials, seemingly a tacit acknowledgment that preparation can be beneficial.

Currently, the coaching debate tends to focus on the question of whether coaching, because it is likely to be most accessible to those who have already benefited from a lifetime of educational advantages, presents an impediment to test fairness for poor and minority test-takers. Although average coaching effects are apparently quite small and studies of the demographic makeup of coached and uncoached candidates have been inconclusive, it is legitimate to question the fairness of a system in which some test-takers can afford coaching and others cannot. It is clear that coaching programs are here to stay, and that it is impractical, if not impossible, to create admissions tests that are not susceptible to coaching. Minimizing the impact of coaching on test fairness, then, requires that the availability of free and low-cost test preparation be increased. Several states sponsored programs of this kind during the 1990s.

Key Information for Admissions Personnel

According to the National Association for College Admission Counseling's *Statement of Counselor Competencies*, it is essential that college admissions counselors understand "the proper administration and uses of standardized tests and be able to interpret test scores and test-related data to students, parents, educators, institutions, agencies, and the public" (NACAC, 2000, p. 11). In order to develop a thorough understanding of test use and interpretation, counselors and other admissions personnel need to have a command of the fundamentals of educational measurement and statistics. However, they may not have had the opportunity to acquire training in the area of academic assessment and score interpretation.

One possible avenue for professional development for admissions personnel is the use of Web-based instruction in educational measurement and statistics, similar to the Web-based instructional modules that were developed for K–12 teachers and administrators as part of the Instructional Tools in Educational Measurement and Statistics (ITEMS) project (Sklar & Zwick, 2009; Zwick et al., 2008) under a grant from the National Science Foundation.[10] Other sources of instruction in educational measurement and statistics include workshops, university courses, and self-study materials, such as those developed by Popham (2006). Staying up to date on research findings about admissions tests is best achieved by subscribing to key journals in the field and by consulting the Web sites of the testing programs.

Finally, the *Standards for Educational and Psychological Testing* (American Educational Research Association, American Psychological Association, & National Council on Measurement in Education, 1999), mentioned previously, should be on the bookshelf of every admissions officer.[11] This important (though not always accessible) volume includes explanations of fundamental testing concepts, such as validity, reliability, measurement error, score scales, norms, and test fairness, as well as widely accepted professional guidelines for test use and interpretation. In general, the *Standards* cautions against over-reliance on test scores, noting that "[t]he improper use of tests . . . can cause considerable harm to test-takers and other parties affected by test-based decisions" (p. 1). On a more positive note, the *Standards* also states that, "[a]lthough not all tests are well-developed nor are all testing practices wise and beneficial, there is extensive evidence documenting the effectiveness of well-constructed tests for uses supported by validity evidence. The proper use of tests can result in wiser decisions about individuals and programs than would be the case without their use . . ." (p. 1).

Notes

1 Portions of this chapter are adapted from *Fair Game: The Use of Standardized Admissions Tests in Higher Education*, RoutledgeFalmer, 2002. Copyright © 2002 by Rebecca Zwick. The author thanks Charles Secolsky, Daniel Eignor, Shelby Haberman, and Richard Sawyer for their reviews.
2 Tests that are not discussed in this chapter include the Preliminary SAT/National Merit Scholarship Qualifying Test, which serves as a practice SAT for high school sophomores and juniors and is used in awarding National Merit Scholarships, the PLAN assessment, a "pre-ACT" test that is typically administered to high school sophomores, the Test of English as a Foreign Language, which is required of foreign students by some US colleges and graduate schools, and the Miller Analogies Test, which is accepted by a small percent of graduate programs as an alternative to the GRE.

3 Because survey respondents do not constitute random samples of the corresponding populations of institutions, the survey results should be interpreted with caution.

4 Because survey respondents do not constitute a random sample of the corresponding population of institutions, the survey results should be interpreted with caution. The response rate for the survey was 20% (Clinedinst, 2008, p. 5).

5 As is currently the case, a (non-adaptive) paper-and-pencil version of the GRE will be offered in areas of the world where computer-based testing is unavailable.

6 On the GRE, score calculations also take into account the number of questions answered www.ets.org/gre, October, 2011.

7 In a least squares regression analysis, the sum of the prediction errors across all observations must be zero, but this need not be true within each group of interest.

8 References for these findings are as follows. SAT: www.collegeboard.com (May, 2010), ACT: (www.act.org, May 2010), GRE: ETS (2008, 2010), MCAT, www.aamc.org (Data warehouse: applicant matriculant file as of 10/19/2010), LSAT: Dalessandro, Suto, & Reese (2008), GMAT: www.gmac.org (GMAC Interactive Research tool, November 2010).

9 Also, average score differences between males and females who have been "selected" on the basis of academic criteria are likely to be larger than the differences that exist before the selection criteria are applied. See Hoover & Han, 1995; Lewis & Willingham, 1995. Similar phenomena may apply in the case of ethnic group differences.

10 Three instructional modules and supplementary materials are freely available at http://items.education.ucsb.edu/pages/modules.html

11 The *Standards* document is currently under revision.

References

ACT, Inc. (2007). *The ACT Technical Manual.* Iowa City, IA: Author.

ACT, Inc. (2009). *The ACT Writing Test Technical Report.* Iowa City, IA: Author.

American Educational Research Association, American Psychological Association, & National Council on Measurement in Education. (1999). *Standards for educational and psychological testing.* Washington, DC: American Educational Research Association.

Association of American Medical Colleges. (2007). *2007 MCAT essentials.* Retrieved August 15, 2009 from http://www.aamc.org

Atkinson, R. (2001, February 18). *Standardized tests and access to American universities.* The 2001 Robert H. Atwell Distinguished Lecture, delivered at the 83rd annual meeting of the American Council on Education, Washington, DC.

Becker, B. J. (1990). Coaching for the Scholastic Aptitude Test: Further synthesis and appraisal. *Review of Educational Research, 60,* 373–417.

Bleistein, C. A., & Wright, D. J. (1987). Assessment of unexpected differential item difficulty for Asian-American examinees on the Scholastic Aptitude Test. In A. P. Schmitt, & N. J. Dorans (Eds.), *Differential item functioning on the Scholastic Aptitude Test* (ETS Research Memorandum No. 87–1). Princeton, NJ: Educational Testing Service.

Bowen, W. G., & Bok, D. (1998). *The shape of the river: Long-term consequences of considering race in college and university admissions.* Princeton, NJ: Princeton University Press.

Braun, H. I., & Jones, D. H. (1981). *The Graduate Management Admission Test prediction bias study* (GMAC Report 81–4). Princeton, NJ: Educational Testing Service.

Braun, H. I., & Jones, D. H. (1985). *Use of empirical Bayes methods in the study of the validity of academic predictors of graduate school performance* (ETS Research Report 84–34). Princeton, NJ: Educational Testing Service.

Breland, H., Maxey, J., Gernand, R., Cumming, T., & Trapani, C. (March 2002). *Trends in college admission 2000: A report of a national survey of undergraduate admissions policies, practices, and procedures.* (Sponsored by ACT, Inc., Association for Institutional Research, The College Board, Educational Testing Service, and the National Association for College Admission Counseling.) Retrieved October 6, 2003 from http://www.airweb.org

Bridgeman, B., McCamley-Jenkins, L., & Ervin, N. (2000). *Prediction of freshman grade-point average from the revised and recentered SAT I: Reasoning Test* (College Board Report 2000–1). New York: College Entrance Examination Board.

Briggs, D. (2001). The effect of admissions test preparation: Evidence from NELS: 88. *Chance, 14*(1), 10–18.

Briggs, D. C. (2004). Evaluating SAT Coaching: Gains, effects and self-selection. In R. Zwick, (Ed.), *Rethinking the SAT: The Future of Standardized Testing in University Admissions,* pp. 217–233. New York: RoutledgeFalmer.

Burton, E., & Burton, N. W. (1993). The effect of item screening on test scores and test characteristics. In P. W. Holland, & H. Wainer (Eds.), *Differential item functioning* (pp. 321–336). Hillsdale, NJ: Lawrence Erlbaum Associates.

Burton, N. W., & Ramist, L. (2001). *Predicting success in college: SAT studies of classes graduating since 1980* (Research Report 2001–2). New York, NY: College Entrance Examination Board.

Burton, N. W.& Wang, M. (2005). *Predicting long-term success in graduate school: A collaborative validity study* (Research Report 05–03). Princeton, NJ: Educational Testing Service.

Cahalan, C., Mandinach, E., & Camara, W. (2002). *Predictive validity of SAT I: Reasoning test for test takers with learning disabilities and extended time accommodations* (College Board Research Report RR 2002–05). New York, NY: College Entrance Examination Board.

Camara, W. J., & Echternacht, G. (2000, July). *The SAT and high school grades: Utility in predicting success in college* (College Board Research Note RN-10). New York, NY: College Entrance Examination Board.

Carnevale, A. P., & Rose, S. J. (2003). *Socioeconomic status, race/ethnicity, and selective college admissions*. A Century Foundation Paper. New York, NY: The Century Foundation.

Clauser, J., & Hambleton, R. K. (this volume). *Item analysis procedures for classroom assessments in higher education.*

Clinedinst, M. E. (2008). *State of college admission 2008*. Arlington, VA: National Association for College Admission Counseling. Retrieved May 5, 2010 from http://www.nacacnet.org

Cole, N. S., & Moss, P. A. (1989). Bias in test use. In R. L. Linn, (Ed.), *Educational Measurement* (3rd ed. pp. 201–219). New York, NY: American Council on Education/Macmillan.

Dalessandro, S. P., Suto, D. A., & Reese, L. M. (2008). *LSAT performance with regional, gender, and racial/ethnic breakdowns: 2001–2002 through 2007–2008 testing years* (LSAT Technical Report 08–03). Newtown, PA: Law School Admissions Council.

Dawes, R. M. (1971). A case study of graduate admissions: Application of three principles of human decision making. *American Psychologist, 26*, 180–188.

Dawes, R. M., & Corrigan, B. (1974). Linear models in decision making. *Psychological Bulletin, 81*(2), 95–106.

Dolan, R., & Burling, K. (this volume). *Computer-based testing in higher education.*

Dorans, N. J., & Petersen, N. (2010, April). *Distinguishing concordances from equatings*. Paper presented at the annual meeting of the National Council on Measurement in Education, Denver, CO.

Dwyer, C. A., & Johnson, L. M. (1997). Grades, accomplishments, and correlates. In W. W. Willingham, & N. Cole, *Gender and Fair Assessment* (127–156). Mahwah, NJ: Lawrence Erlbaum Associates.

Educational Testing Service. (1950). *Educational Testing Service annual report to the Board of Trustees (1949–1950)*. Princeton, NJ: Author.

Educational Testing Service. (2002). *ETS Standards for Quality and Fairness*. Princeton, NJ: Author.

Educational Testing Service. (2003). *GRE for Educators: The General Test*. Retrieved September 24, 2003 from http://www.gre.org

Educational Testing Service. (2008). *Factors that can influence performance on the GRE General Test*. Princeton, NJ: Author.

Educational Testing Service. (2010a). *The GRE revised General Test: Better by Design*. Princeton, NJ: Author.

Educational Testing Service. (2010b). *GRE Information and Registration Bulletin: 2011–2012*. Princeton, NJ: Author.

Educational Testing Service. (2010c). *Graduate Record Examinations guide to the use of scores, 2010–2011*. Princeton, NJ: Author.

Gallagher, A., Morley, M. E., & Levin, J. (1999). *Cognitive patterns of gender differences on mathematics admissions tests* (The GRE, FAME Report Series 3 pp. 4–11). Princeton, NJ: Educational Testing Service.

Geisinger, K., Shaw, L. H., & McCormick, C. (this volume). *The validation of tests in higher education.*

Gough, H. G. (1962). Clinical versus statistical prediction in psychology. In L. Postman (Ed.), *Psychology in the making: Histories of selected research problems* (526–584). New York, NY: Alfred A. Knopf.

Gulliksen, H. (1987). *Theory of mental tests*. Hillsdale, NJ: Lawrence Erlbaum Associates.

Hoover, E. (2002, July 26). "Removing the 'Scarlet Letter:' The College Board will no longer flag the SAT-score reports of students granted extra time because of disabilities." *Chronicle of Higher Education*. Retrieved May 10, 2010 from http://chronicle.com/weekly/v48/i46/46a04101.htm

Hoover, H. D., & Han, L. (1995, April). *The effect of differential selection on gender differences in college admission test scores*. Paper presented at the annual meeting of the American Educational Research Association, San Francisco, CA.

Johnson, V. E. (1997). An alternative to traditional GPA for evaluating student performance. *Statistical Science, 12*(4), 251–278.

Johnson, E. K., & Edwards, J. C. (1991). Current practices in admission interviews at U. S. medical schools. *Academic Medicine, 66*(7), 408–412.

Julian, E. R. (2005). Validity of the Medical College Admission Test for predicting medical school performance. *Academic Medicine 80*(10), 910–917.

Klitgaard, R. E. (1985). *Choosing elites.* New York, NY: Basic Books.

Kobrin, J. L., Patterson, B. F., Shaw, E. J., Mattern, K. D., & Barbuti, S. M. (2008). *Validity of the SAT for predicting first-year college grade point average* (College Board Research Report No. 2008–5). New York, NY: The College Board.

Koenig, J. A., & Leger, K. F. (1997). Test-taking behaviors and their impact on performance: A comparison of retest performance and test-preparation methods for MCAT examinees grouped by gender and race-ethnicity. *Academic Medicine, 72*(10), S100–S102.

Koenig, J. A., Sireci, S. G., & Wiley, A. (1998). Evaluating the predictive validity of MCAT scores across diverse applicant groups. *Academic Medicine, 73*(10), 1095–1106.

Kolen, M. J., & Hendrickson, A. (this volume). *Scaling, norming, and equating.*

Kuncel, N. R., & Hezlett, S. A. (2007). Standardized tests predict graduate students' success. *Science* 315, 1080–1081.

Kuncel, N. R., Hezlett, S. A., & Ones, D. S. (2001). A comprehensive meta-analysis of the predictive validity of the Graduate Record Examinations: Implications for graduate student selection and performance. *Psychological Bulletin, 127,* 162–181.

Lawrence, I., Rigol, G., Van Essen, T., & Jackson, C. (2004). A historical perspective on the content of the SAT. In Zwick, R. (Ed.), *Rethinking the SAT: The future of standardized testing in university admissions,* pp. 57–74. New York, NY: RoutledgeFalmer.

Leary, L. F., & Wightman, L. E. (1983). *Estimating the relationship between use of test-preparation methods and scores on the Graduate Management Admission Test* (ETS Research Report 83–22). Princeton, NJ: Educational Testing Service.

Leonard, D., & Jiang, J. (1999). Gender bias and the college prediction of the SATs: A cry of despair. *Research in Higher Education, 40*(4), 375–408.

Lewis, C., & Willingham, W. W. (1995). *The effects of sample restriction on gender differences* (ETS Research Report 95–13). Princeton, NJ: Educational Testing Service.

Mandinach, E. B. (2000, April). *Flagging: Policies, perceptions, and practices.* Paper presented at the annual meeting of the American Educational Research Association, New Orleans, LA.

Mandinach, E. B. & Cahalan, C., & Camara, W. J. (2001, April). *The impact of flagging on the admissions process: Policies, practices, and implications.* Paper presented at the annual meeting of the American Educational Research Association, Seattle, WA.

Mattern, K., Camara, W., & Kobrin, J. L. (2007). *SAT writing: An overview of research and psychometrics to date* (Research Note RN-32). New York, NY: The College Board.

Mattern, K. D., Patterson, B. F., Shaw, E. J., Kobrin, J. L., & Barbuti, S. M. (2008). *Differential validity and prediction of the SAT* (College Board Research Report No. 2008–4). New York, NY: The College Board.

National Association for College Admission Counseling (2000). *Statement on Counselor Competencies.* Retrieved May 10, 2010 from http://www.nacacnet.org

Noble, J. (2004). The effects of using ACT composite scores and high school averages on college admissions decisions for ethnic groups. In R. Zwick (Ed.), *Rethinking the SAT: The Future of Standardized Testing in University Admissions* (pp. 303–319). New York, NY: RoutledgeFalmer.

Norris, D., Oppler, S., Kuang, D., Day, R., & Adams, K. (2005). *The College Board SAT writing validation study: An assessment of the predictive and incremental validity.* Washington, DC: American Institutes for Research.

O'Neill, K. A., & McPeek, W. M. (1993). Item and test characteristics that are associated with differential item functioning. In P. W. Holland, & H. Wainer (Eds.), *Differential item functioning* (pp. 255–276). Hillsdale, NJ: Lawrence Erlbaum Associates.

O'Neill, P., & Murphy, S. (this volume). *Postsecondary writing assessment.*

Osterlind, S. J., & Wang, Z. (this volume). *Item response theory in measurement, assessment, and evaluation for higher education.*

Pennock-Román, M. (1990). *Test validity and language background: A study of Hispanic American students at six universities.* New York, NY: College Entrance Examination Board.

Pennock-Román, M. (1994). *College major and gender differences in the prediction of college grades* (College Board Report 94–2). New York, NY: College Entrance Examination Board.

Peterson, J. J. (1983). *The Iowa testing programs.* Iowa City, IA: Iowa University Press.

Popham, W. J. (2006). *Mastering Assessment: A Self-Service System for Educators.* New York, NY: Routledge.

Powers, D. E. (1983). *Effects of coaching on GRE aptitude test scores* (GRE Board Report 83–7). Princeton, NJ: Graduate Record Examinations Board.

Powers, D. E., Fowles, M. E., & Welsh, C. K. (1999). *Further validation of a writing assessment for graduate admissions* (GRE Board Research Report No. 96–13R, ETS Research Report 99–18). Princeton, NJ: Educational Testing Service.

Powers, D. E., & Rock, D. A. (1999). Effects of coaching on SAT I: Reasoning test scores. *Journal of Educational Measurement, 36*(2), 93–118.

Ramist, L., Lewis, C., & McCamley-Jenkins, L. (1994). *Student group differences in predicting college grades: Sex, language, and ethnic groups* (College Board Report 93–1). New York, NY: College Entrance Examination Board.

Ramist, L., Lewis, C., & McCamley-Jenkins, L. (2001). *Using Achievement Tests/SAT II Subject Tests to demonstrate achievement and predict college grades: Sex, language, ethnic, and parental education groups* (Research Report No. 2001–5). New York, NY: College Entrance Examination Board.

Rigol, G. W., & Kimmel, E. W. (1997, November). *A picture of admissions in the United States.* New York, NY: The College Board and Educational Testing Service.

Rogers, H. J., & Kulick, E. (1987). An investigation of unexpected differences in item performance between Blacks and Whites taking the SAT. In A. P. Schmitt, & N. J. Dorans (Eds.), *Differential item functioning on the Scholastic Aptitude Test* (ETS Research Memorandum No. 87–1). Princeton, NJ: Educational Testing Service.

Rudner, L. M. (2010). Implementing the Graduate Management Admission Test. In W. J. van der Linden, & C. A. W. Glas (Eds.), *Elements of adaptive testing* (pp. 151–165). New York, NY: Springer, 2010.

Rudner, L. M., Garcia, V., & Welch, C. (2005). *An evaluation of IntelliMetric essay scoring system using response to GMAT AWA prompts* (Graduate Management Admission Council Research Report RR 05–08). McLean, VA: GMAC.

Sackett, P. R., & Yang, H. (2000). Correction for range restriction: an expanded typology. *Journal of Applied Psychology, 85,* 112–118.

Sarbin, T. R. (1943). A contribution to the study of actuarial and individual methods of prediction. *American Journal of Sociology, 48,* 593–602.

Schmitt, A. P. (1987). Unexpected differential item performance of Hispanic examinees. In A. P. Schmitt, & N. J. Dorans (Eds.), *Differential item functioning on the Scholastic Aptitude Test* (ETS Research Memorandum No. 87–1). Princeton, NJ: Educational Testing Service.

Schmitt, A. P., & Dorans, N. J. (1988). *Differential item functioning for minority examinees on the SAT* (ETS Research Report 88–32). Princeton, NJ: Educational Testing Service.

Schmotter, J. W. (1993). The Graduate Management Admission Council: A brief history 1953–1992. *Selections, 9*(2), 1–11.

Scholes, R. J., & McCoy, T. R. (1998, April). *The effects of type, length, and content of test preparation activities on ACT assessment scores.* Paper presented at the annual meeting of the American Educational Research Association, San Diego, CA.

Sklar, J., & Zwick, R. (2009). Multimedia presentations in educational measurement and statistics: Design considerations and instructional approaches. *Journal of Statistics Education,* http://www.amstat.org/publications/jse/v17n3/sklar.html

Snedecor, G. W., & Cochran, W. G. (1967). *Statistical methods* (6th ed.). Ames, Iowa: The Iowa State University Press.

Springen, K. (2010, November 4). Going SAT-free. *Newsweek,* http://education.newsweek.com/2010/11/04/going-sat-free.html

Steele, C. M. (1997). A threat in thin air: How stereotypes shape intellectual identity and performance. *American Psychologist, 52*(6), 613–629.

Stilwell, L. A., Dalessandro, S. P., & Reese, L. M. (2007). *Predictive validity of the LSAT: A national summary of the 2005–2006 correlation studies.* Newtown, PA: Law School Admission Council.

Stricker, L. J., Rock, D. A., & Burton, N. W. (1993). Sex differences in predictions of college grades from Scholastic Aptitude Test scores. *Journal of Educational Psychology, 85*(4), 710–718.

Stricker, L. J., Rock, D. A., Burton, N. W., Muraki, E., & Jirele, T. J. (1994). Adjusting college grade point average criteria for variations in grading standards: A comparison of methods. *Journal of Applied Psychology, 79*(2), 178–183.

Talento-Miller, E. & Rudner, L. M. (2005). *GMAT validity study summary report for 1997 to 2004* (GMAC Research Report 05–06). McLean, VA: Graduate Management Admission Council.

The College Board (2009, October). *ACT and SAT concordance tables* (Research Note RN-40). New York, NY: The College Board.

Wainer, H., & Brown, L. M. (2007). Three statistical paradoxes in the interpretation of group differences: Illustrated with medical school admission and licencing data. In C.R. Rao, and S. Sinharay (Eds.), *Handbook of Statistics Vol. 26: Psychometrics* (pp. 893–918). Elsevier Science B.V: The Netherlands.

Whitney, D. R. (1989). Educational admissions and placement. In R. L. Linn (Ed.), *Educational Measurement* (3rd ed. pp. 515–525). New York, NY: American Council on Education/Macmillan.

Wiggins, N., & Kohen, E. S. (1971). Man vs. model of man revisited: The forecasting of graduate school success. *Journal of Personality and Social Psychology, 19,* 100–106.

Wightman, L. F. (1993). *Test takers with disabilities: A summary of data from special administrations of the LSAT* (LSAC Research Report 93–03). Newtown, PA: Law School Admission Council.

Wightman, L. F., & Muller, D. G. (1990). *Comparison of LSAT performance among selected subgroups* (Law School Admission Council Statistical Report 90–01). Newton, PA: Law School Admission Council.

Willingham, W. W., & N. Cole (Eds.). (1997). *Gender and Fair Assessment.* Mahwah, NJ: Lawrence Erlbaum Associates.

Willingham, W. W., Pollack, J. M., & Lewis, C. (2000). *Grades and test scores: Accounting for observed differences* (ETS Research Report 00–15). Princeton, NJ: Educational Testing Service.

Willingham, W. W., Ragosta, M., Bennett, R. E., Braun, H., Rock, D. A., & Powers, D. E. (1988). *Testing handicapped people.* Boston, MA: Allyn and Bacon, Inc.

Young, J. W. (1991). Improving the prediction of college performance of ethnic minorities using the IRT-based GPA. *Applied Measurement in Education, 4*(3), 229–239.

Young, J. W. (2001). *Differential validity, differential prediction, and college admissions testing: A comprehensive review and analysis* (Research Report No. 2001–6). New York, NY: The College Board.

Young, J. W. (2004). Differential validity and prediction: Race and sex differences in college admissions testing. In Zwick, R. (Ed.), *Rethinking the SAT: The future of standardized testing in university admissions* (pp. 289–301). New York, NY: RoutledgeFalmer.

Ziomek, R. L., & Andrews, K. M. (1996). *Predicting the college grade point averages of special-tested students from their ACT assessment scores and high school grades* (ACT Research Report 96–7). Iowa City, IA: ACT, Inc.

Zwick, R. (2002). *Fair Game? The Use of Standardized Admissions Tests in higher education.* New York, NY: RoutledgeFalmer.

Zwick, R. (2006). Higher education admissions testing. In R. L. Brennan, (Ed.). *Educational Measurement* (4th ed. pp. 647–679). Westport, CT: American Council on Education/Praeger.

Zwick, R. (2007). *College admissions testing.* (Paper Commissioned by the National Association for College Admission Counseling). http://www.nacacnet.org (accessed July 2007).

Zwick, R., & Himelfarb, I. (2011). The effect of high school socioeconomic status on the predictive validity of SAT scores and high school grade-point average. *Journal of Educational Measurement, 48,* 101–121.

Zwick, R., & Schlemer, L. (2004). SAT validity for linguistic minorities at the University of California, Santa Barbara. *Educational Measurement: Issues and Practice, 25,* 6–16.

Zwick, R., & Sklar, J. C. (2005). Predicting college grades and degree completion using high school grades and SAT scores: The role of student ethnicity and first language. *American Educational Research Journal, 42,* 439–464.

Zwick, R., Sklar, J., Wakefield, G., Hamilton, C., Norman, A., & Folsom, D. (2008). Instructional tools in educational measurement and statistics (ITEMS) for school personnel: Evaluation of three web-based training modules. *Educational Measurement: Issues and Practice, 27,* 14–27.

26

POSTSECONDARY WRITING ASSESSMENT

Peggy O'Neill and Sandra Murphy

Writing competency, often labeled as "written communication skills," is one of the fundamental learning outcomes identified by institutions of higher education. Consequently, general education curricula often include programs such as first-year composition and writing-across-the curriculum/ writing-in-the-disciplines. As notions of what it means to write are complicated by digital media, these programs have also expanded to include more than just traditional essayistic literacy as reflected in programs with names such as communication-across-the-curriculum. Even in institutions that do not have designated writing programs, competency in writing is still considered one of the important goals of undergraduate education. Although much of this focus occurs in the classroom or within specific courses, writing also plays a significant role in assessment beyond the classroom in composition placement, proficiency exams, and program reviews. While most psychometricians consider writing assessment to include indirect methods such as short-answer and/or multiple-choice exams of editing, writing teachers prefer exams that require students to write (e.g., Broad, 2003; Diederich, 1974; O'Neill, Moore, & Huot, 2009). In this chapter, we focus exclusively on these types of assessments, so-called direct writing assessments.

We begin by reviewing the theory and research that informs current approaches to writing assessment then review various practices that draw on these approaches. We believe that methods for collecting samples or scoring them should not be the driving force in designing writing assessments. Rather, assessment methods should be determined by linguistic and language theories as well as psychometric ones.

Writing assessment theory draws on theories about writing development as well as educational measurement. Both of these perspectives influence the validity of writing assessment results because, as Messick (1989) explained, both empirical evidence and theoretical rationales are needed to make the "integrated evaluative judgment" necessary "to support the adequacy and appropriateness of inferences and actions based on test scores and modes of assessment" (1989, p. 5). Below we outline some of the key theoretical frameworks that should be considered in writing assessments. Then we review issues of validity as manifested in writing assessment and discuss emerging consensus and implications. We conclude with a look to ongoing debates and developing trends in writing assessment, a field which includes a diverse pool of professionals, including academic researchers in education, measurement, and composition and rhetoric, as well as testing industry specialists.

Writing: A Socially Situated Cognitive Activity

Writing, like all language use, is a social and contextually bound activity. Gee (1996), for instance, explains that the meaning of all language depends on context, which includes ways of behaving, valuing, thinking, believing, speaking, reading, and writing (1996, p. viii). Although writing is often considered less context-bound than impromptu, spoken discourse, the meaning of texts is still heavily influenced by the context, including the time, place, writer, purpose, audience, topic, and other socio-cultural factors. This rhetorical context influences what a writer produces and how audiences understand it. From e-mails and letters, to reports and memos, to essays and novels, experienced readers and writers understand how the context in which the text was produced—as well as read—informs the interpretation.

Misreadings and misunderstandings highlight the role context plays in comprehension, whether involving historical or contemporary texts. Jonathon Swift's satirical essay, "A Modest Proposal" is a well-known example. Readers need to know about the historical and political context of Ireland, particularly in the 1720s, to comprehend the true meaning of Swift's essay. They need to be familiar with Swift's essay to fully appreciate the comments Steven Colbert (2010) made in a segment on his show, "The Word: Swift Payment," where he discussed a proposal by Ted Turner to limit all families to one child and allow the poor to sell their reproduction rights to the rich. While satire is a particularly strong example of how context is important to accurately understand written texts, the same principle holds true for all texts. Because of the significance of context in meaning-making, good writing, from this theoretical stance, is defined as that which effectively communicates to its audience. In contemporary society, school is a powerful context that shapes the production and interpretation of both spoken and written texts produced in classrooms and school-related activities (e.g., Cazden, 2001; Cook-Gumperez, 2006; Gee, 1996).

While this rhetorical perspective seems obvious, in assessment situations it can become complicated. For example, a test prompt might specify that the students address a specific audience about a certain topic for a particular purpose and in a specific genre. However, the actual rhetorical context of the task is the assessment situation. That is, the text is not an authentic text meant to communicate to the specified audience but rather constructed to communicate to an evaluator the writer's abilities. Savvy students understand that the prompt directions are not a genuine rhetorical situation but that the assessment is. Students have to satisfy expectations specified in the prompt as well as the assessment context. Students who don't understand how this works can have trouble succeeding on the assessment although they may have adequately addressed the prompt's directions according to their specific context. Murphy (2007) summarizes several studies that demonstrate how prompts can "misfire" when students interpret the task according to the specific context and don't understand it within the expectations of the assessment context. This type of problem, which highlights the rhetorical nature of writing, can create threats to the validity of an assessment's results.

Writing Development, Pedagogy, and Process

Writing, along with being a social activity, is also a cognitive activity. Writers use a process, or more accurately many processes, to write. These processes are unique to individual writers although most writers' processes share many similar features. Researchers and teachers describe these in various ways, but all share the basics of prewriting, drafting, and, when the situation allows it, revising. The writing process can be compressed or extended depending on the situation. Manipulating the writing situation can influence the writer's process and the product. Instruction in writing strategies can help students develop more effective processes and stronger products. Research shows that instructional approaches influence how students develop as writers and that explicit teaching of particular strategies can improve students' writing abilities (e.g., Graham & Perin, 2007; Hillocks,

1986). Researchers such as Hilgers, Hussey, and Stitt-Bergh (1999) argue that teaching student writers self-assessment strategies can improve their ability to do this and help them be more effective writers. Writers also use different processes for different tasks so that what a writer does to generate a lab report is different than what she may do to draft a philosophy essay. Writers may be adept at one genre but not so adept at another, which is one of the basic assumptions informing writing-in-the-disciplines programs. As writing tasks and expectations become more demanding, students may appear to backslide before learning how to meet expectations successfully. This can happen when the content challenges the student or when the task itself is challenging.

In postsecondary writing research, longitudinal, qualitative studies of students' development as writers show that the ability of students to write is strongly influenced by the tasks and challenges they encounter across the disciplines and throughout their educational careers; that first-year writing courses do not prepare students to succeed in all the subsequent writing tasks they encounter in college; that sometimes students appear to backslide as writers when they encounter new content, new genres, and new tasks, but through repeated practice they develop proficiency; and that learning to write in a discipline is part of the enculturation in a discipline (e.g., Beaufort, 2007; Carrithers & Bean, 2008; Carroll, 2002; Herrington, 1985; Herrington & Curtis, 2000; Sommers, 2008; Sternglass, 1997; Walvoord & McCarthy, 1990). For example, McCarthy (1987) described the biology major in her study as a "stranger in a strange land" as the student experienced the writing demands of biology classes. The student's generic writing course did little to prepare him for the demands of writing in biology. As he moved through his biology curriculum, he developed not just the content knowledge but the ways of thinking and writing that he needed to succeed in the writing tasks associated with biology. Sternglass (1997) concluded that given the appropriate time and support, underprepared writers can develop the writing competencies associated with college graduates, but the progress of many students will not follow a prescribed trajectory. Longitudinal studies such as those published by Herrington & Curtis (2000) and Sternglass (1997) also highlighted the role that the learning and social environments play in student writers' development.

This research in writing development and pedagogy has important implications for writing assessment. For example, because writing ability varies across genres and tasks, one writing sample does not provide an adequate representation of a student's abilities. Time limits, the medium for writing, and other situational components can also be important factors in student performance. Relatively short impromptu essay exams, typically used in most statewide assessments and many standardized exams, often don't allow students to draw on processes and approaches used for more extensive writing tasks and may reinforce a shortened, abbreviated process unlike the extended, intertwined reading and writing tasks that students are expected to complete in college. Various factors such as these make obtaining an accurate and valid assessment of writers' abilities challenging, a topic we return to in our discussion of validity and writing assessment below.

Assessment Theory

Postsecondary writing assessment scholars have focused on validity and reliability. Historically, reliability has received the most attention, with a particular focus on interrater reliability, the agreement between two or more independent raters (Cherry & Meyer, 1993; Diederich, French, & Carlton, 1961; Hayes & Hatch, 1999; Huot, O'Neill, & Moore, 2010). The use of different methods for calculating interrater reliability rates can lead to very different results and conclusions in terms of reliability. However, no one method for determining interrater reliability has become standardized. Although the issue of interrater reliability has not been resolved, traditional holistic, analytic, and primary trait scoring have remained useful rating methods. Holistic scoring, as advocated by White (1994), seems to be the most popular. The widespread use of portfolios created some challenges in using these methods for rating, but many researchers were able to meet the reliability threshold (e.g., Murphy & Underwood,

2000; Nystrand, Cohen, & Dowling, 1993; Sommers, Black, Daiker, & Stygall, 1993). Other research-ers have developed alternative methods of evaluating writing samples that did not rely on points on a scale, focusing on the concept of reliability more broadly (e.g., Durst, Roemer, & Schultz, 1994; Haswell, 1998, 2001; Hester, O'Neill, Neale, Edgington, & Huot, 2007; Smith 1992, 1993).

Recent discussions in the writing assessment literature have highlighted the role of validity in assessment, with reliability considered as one aspect of the validation argument. For example, Wil-liamson (2003) acknowledged that "automated scoring is reliable, efficient, fast, and cheap" (p. 88) but turned to validity to challenge the acceptability of contemporary approaches to automated scor-ing. Conceding that the automated scoring program *e-rater* produces reliable scores, he noted that "the real question for *e-rater* is whether the scores help make better decisions about students than cur-rent procedures used by a particular college or university" (Williamson, 2003, p. 98). This question reframes the issue as part of the validation process that gets at the use of the results instead of focusing on how the score was obtained. Williamson (2003) and others such as Moss (1994) advocated for shifting the emphasis away from reliability to validity inquiry.

Various definitions of validity exist in the assessment literature. Traditional educational and psy-chological measurement theory has typically identified content validity, criterion-related validity, and construct validity as key aspects. Content validity is the extent to which a test adequately rep-resents the domain that a test claims to cover, criterion-related validity the accuracy of a measuring procedure when it is compared to some other measurement procedure believed to be valid, and construct validity the extent to which a test or measurement procedure measures the constructs that it proposes to measure. In recent years scholars have also emphasized the importance of *contextual validation*, i.e. determining "the validity of procedures for the particular contexts in which they are used" (Williamson, 1997, p.15) and *authenticity*, "the degree of correspondence of the characteristics of a given language test task to the features of a target language use . . . task" (Bachman & Palmer, 1996, p. 23). In the field of writing, contextual validation and authenticity go hand in hand. In other words, writing specialists argue that writing tasks should represent the type of writing that examinees will be expected to employ in the context for which the assessment is designed. Finally, scholars also support the notion of consequence as a facet of validity. They argue that appraisal of both potential and actual social consequences of an assessment should be part of the evaluation of the validity of assessment results (Messick, 1989). More contemporary conceptions treat validity as a unified concept in which aspects such as content, criterion, and consequence are interdependent and subsumed under the general concept of construct validity (Messick, 1989). Writing assessment scholars in composition and rhetoric tend to favor the unified approach to validity.

As these comments suggest, determining the validity of an assessment is a complicated matter, as different types of evidence for various aspects of validity need to be gathered and interpreted. It is complicated further by the many potential threats to construct validity. Messick (1989, 1994) identifies two general kinds of threats: "construct under-representation" and "construct-irrelevant variance." When a "test is too narrow and fails to include important dimensions or facets of the con-struct," the construct is said to be underrepresented. In other words, the items or tasks in an assess-ment fail to include important facets of the construct. Construct-irrelevant variance, on the other hand, occurs when a "test contains excess reliable variance, making items or tasks easier or harder for some respondents in a manner irrelevant to the interpreted construct" (1989, p. 7). In other words, aspects extraneous to the test or task may lead to scores that are higher or lower for some groups of students than they would if the construct were measured accurately and appropriately.

Construct Under-Representation

As noted above, some direct assessments have been criticized for under-representation because they fail to represent the variety of types of writing that examinees will be expected to employ in the context for which the assessment is designed. For example, research has demonstrated that students in college are assigned a wide variety of writing tasks that vary on a number of rhetorical, practical, and textual dimensions, and that their frequency and type varies across disciplines, and graduate and undergraduate levels (Bridgeman & Carlson, 1983; Greene & Orr, 2007; Hale, et al., 1996; Sommers, 2008). Yet many placement tests assess "writing" via a single kind of task, one that may neither align in important ways with the kinds of tasks that college students may be asked to do nor adequately represent the construct of writing.

Textual features, for example, vary across writing done for different purposes and audiences. Comparing the textual features associated with two prompt types—(a) comparison/contrast and (b) take a position, describe, and interpret a chart or graph—Reid (1990) found significant differences in length, in vocabulary, and the use of pronouns. Crowhurst and Piche (1979) found that argumentative essays composed by 6th and 10th graders contained more complex syntax than either descriptive or narrative essays at both grade levels. When asked to write for audiences of high, medium, and low intimacy, 10th graders (but not 6th graders) produced texts with significant semantic and syntactic differences.

In addition to producing variations in textual features, different rhetorical purposes appear to require different processes. For instance, using observational data (pause time and hand movement) Matsuhashi (1982) found differences in composing processes for reporting and generalizing. Witte and Cherry (1994) showed not only that writers' composing processes differed across two broad purposes (to inform or explain on the one hand, and to persuade on the other), but also that processes differed across different writing tasks within each purpose.

Evidence also suggests that performance levels vary with the mode and/or genre required by the writing task. For example, in an early study, Godshalk, Swineford, and Coffman (1966) reported significant variation in ratings assigned to texts written in response to prompts calling for four different genres: an imaginative story, an argumentative essay supporting a position, an opinion essay, and a character analysis. They observed, "If the five topics had been assigned as alternate topics from which one or two could be chosen by students, a student's rating might depend more on which topic he chose than on how well he wrote" (Godshalk et al., 1966, p. 13). Freedman and Pringle (1981) found that students were far more successful in producing the structure of a story than the structure for an argument. Quellmalz, Capell, and Cho (1982), on the other hand, found that lower ratings were assigned to narrative essays than to expository essays. Although these studies are mixed in results about the impact of specific modes or genres in different assessment situations, they provide evidence that levels of writing performance may vary by topic and genre.

Time for writing also is an issue. Research conducted by Yancey, Fishman, Gresham, Neal, and Taylor (2005) indicated that college composition teachers expect complex, in-depth, and well-developed writing—writing that is very different from the kind of writing students are able to produce in the abbreviated time frames of the SAT and ACT (25 minutes for the SAT and 30 for the ACT). The report by the NCTE Task Force on SAT and ACT writing tests notes that the "validity of a short, impromptu, holistically scored essay is severely limited when it comes to predicting first-year course grades, first-year writing performance, or retention" (NCTE, 2005, p. 3). Many scholars have noted the disjunction between writing instruction that emphasizes a process of research, drafting, feedback, and revising, and tests that demand impromptu writing in a short period of time. Peckham (2010) compared students' performance on the ACT essay to a locally designed Online Challenge that gave students three days to read eight to ten articles on an issue and then three days to complete a writing task online based on those articles. Students' performances varied significantly on the two tasks, with a -.07 correlation between the students' scores on these tasks, tasks which were very different, and administered and scored under very different conditions.

Clearly, writing performance across situations and tasks varies in important ways. This variation has important implications for assessment validity. Early views of traits "as fixed, unchanging, underlying causal entities" have been challenged by social theorists because behavior varies across situations, and there is growing agreement that "in order to identify broad traits, we have to assess individuals across situations and aggregate the results" (Anastasi, 1986, p. 9). Situational variation thus limits the construct validity of any impromptu, single-sample assessment. Advocates for portfolios argue that they provide potential solutions to the problems associated with impromptu single-sample assessments. Portfolios offer opportunities to sample a range of genres produced under a variety of conditions of time and support, to engage students more directly in the assessment process in ways that give them responsibility for evaluating their own learning, and to collect samples under more natural and authentic conditions that are directly linked to instruction.

Construct-Irrelevant Variance

Direct assessments of writing have also been criticized for problems with construct-irrelevant variance, that is variations in scores that can be attributed to factors other than a candidate's writing abilities. Research on direct assessment has demonstrated that a variety of factors—including the nature and subject of the writing task; the scale and scoring procedures used; the characteristics of the texts, the raters, the knowledge, culture, and linguistic background of the writers; and various contextual factors—can systematically influence the way writing samples are evaluated (Freedman, 1981; Hamp-Lyons, 1990; Weigle, 2002).

For example, students who have more knowledge about the subject of a prompt tend to write better and more coherent essays (Langer, 1984). For this reason, test designers frequently turn to general knowledge topics because they are presumed to be accessible to the broadest range of participants. However, even the best general knowledge topics may disadvantage some students, particularly those from a non-mainstream culture. Although the evidence on this issue is mixed, for these writers prompts that draw on their specific expertise may ultimately be fairer than general knowledge prompts (Hamp-Lyons, 1990; Tedick, 1990).

Conflicts of language and culture also pose threats to assessment validity. For example, linguistic complexity can make multiple-choice tests more difficult for ELL (English Language Learner, also sometimes described as ESL, English as a Second Language) students. Several studies have demonstrated that reducing the linguistic complexity of test items can narrow the performance gap between ELL and non-ELL students in content based assessments (Abedi & Lord, 2001; Abedi, Lord, Hofstetter, & Baker, 2000; Abedi, Lord, Kim-Boscardin, & Miyoshi, 2000; Abedi, Lord, & Plummer, 1997). Similarly, in direct writing assessments, how a writer interprets the task can also influence the score he or she receives. ELL students and/or students with reading disabilities may interpret a topic very differently than a general community of readers and in ways that can adversely affect their scores (Ruth & Murphy, 1988).

Students' scores may also be adversely affected when the linguistic and rhetorical patterns of their home culture differ from the expectations of readers and the patterns that particular scoring rubrics value. Studies have demonstrated contrastive patterns at different linguistic and stylistic levels, across diverse student populations (Basham & Kwachka, 1991; Sullivan, 1997) and such patterns may not meet the expectations of their readers. Research has demonstrated variability in scores between raters who differ in their linguistic background (Ball, 1997; Brown, 1991; Brown, 1995; Chalhoub-Deville, 1995; Santos, 1988; Song & Caruso, 1996). Gamaroff (2000) found that raters from native and non-native speaker backgrounds differed in their assessments of second-language students' essays in the relative weight they gave to different types of errors and how severe they considered errors to be.

Scores may vary because of other rater characteristics, too. Research has demonstrated variability in scores between raters who differ in their level of experience (Keech & McNelly, 1982; Song & Caruso, 1996; Weigle, 1999), in their disciplinary or teaching background (Bridgeman & Carlson, 1983; Santos, 1988; Song & Caruso, 1996), and in their cultural background (Ball, 1997; Kobayashi

& Rinnert, 1999). Ball (1997) found different scoring patterns between white and African American raters who shared similar backgrounds, experiences, and training. R. H. Haswell and J. T. Haswell (1996) found that the raters' stereotypes about gender influenced their scoring of writing samples. The amount and kind of training raters receive also influences the scores they assign. For instance, Freedman (1981) found that more thoroughly trained raters generally gave higher scores than raters whose trainers simply discussed the meaning of a topic.

Research also suggests that raters may be influenced by their perception of the student and/or the task. For instance, research by Janopoulos (1992) suggests that professors in the university largely judge sentence level errors in the writing of non-native English speakers more leniently than comparable errors made by native speakers. Hamp-Lyons and Matthias (1994) found that raters tend to award higher scores to essays written by ELL writers when they judged the student-selected topic to be more difficult. On the other hand, Erdosy (2004) found that raters of ELL writing did not compensate for perceived biases in topics related to writing difficulty. Taken together, however, these studies suggest that in any scoring session complex interactions can take place among raters, tasks, and products that can influence the scores students receive.

Various other contextual factors may also influence scores. Research has demonstrated that the order of essays in a scoring session influences ratings. A composition will receive a higher score if preceded by weak compositions rather than strong ones (Daly & Dickson-Markman, 1982). Time for writing, in addition to being a source of construct under-representation, can be a source of construct irrelevant variance. When time is a serious factor for most of the test population, or for particular groups within that population, a test's validity is diminished. Several studies suggest that increased time for writing may provide a more valid picture of ELL students' writing abilities (Cho, 2003; Hilgers, 1992; Polio, Fleck, & Leder, 1998). The use of word processing technology can also affect student performance and scores. Wolfe, Bolton, Feltovich, and Niday (1996) found, for example, that in a timed writing assessment, students with medium or high levels of experience with word processing "wrote slightly more words with a word processor than with pen and paper" while those with limited experience wrote much less than they did with pen and paper (p. 132). Coaching or instruction specifically targeted at performance for the test can also be a factor. Hardison and Sackett (2008) conducted a study on the effects of coaching on student performance on standardized essay tests. They concluded that "after controlling for individual differences in ability and pre-test performance, short-term coaching can significantly increase essay test scores when compared to a control group" (Hardison & Sackett, 2008, p. 243).

Research demonstrates that the scores of native speakers are also influenced by the amount of time allowed for writing. Powers and Fowles (1996) found that students' writing performance on the 60-minute version of the trial Graduate Record Examination (GRE) essay test was significantly better than on the 40-minute version. Herman, Gearhart, and Baker (1993) found that raters' scores for students' portfolios of classroom work were higher than those for a standard writing assessment in which the students were given 30 to 40 minutes to write a story. In a comparison of timed writing samples and portfolio collections, Simmons (1992) found that the weakest writers and writers from the poorest schools were disadvantaged by the timed test. Taken together, these studies indicate that time impacts the quality of a writer's performance, affects some writers' performance more than others, and can threaten the validity of assessment results.

Consequential Validity

While multiple-choice assessments have been more widely criticized for their negative impact on teaching and curriculum, single-sample writing tests have also been blamed for negative consequences, especially when high stakes are attached. Some studies suggest that single-sample tests narrow the curriculum (O'Neill, Murphy, Huot, & Williamson, 2004; Scherff & Piazza, 2005; Wallace,

2002), encourage formulaic teaching (Hillocks, 2002; Johnson, Smagorinsky, Thompson, & Fry, 2003), and have a negative effect on student attitudes (Ketter & Poole, 2001; Loofbourrow, 1994). On the other hand, some studies indicate that teachers are likely to increase the time students spend writing when an assessment includes a writing sample, so the evidence on this issue is mixed (Almasi, Afflerbach, Guthrie, & Schafer, 1995; Koretz & Hamilton, 2003; Koretz, Mitchell, Barron & Keith, 1996; Stecher, Barron, Kaganoff, & Goodwin, 1998).

At the secondary level, studies of large-scale portfolio assessment programs have demonstrated positive effects on the educational environment. For example, nearly three-fourths of the principals interviewed in a study of Vermont's portfolio assessment program reported that the portfolio program produced positive changes, including "an increased emphasis on higher order thinking skills," "lessened reliance on textbooks and worksheets; an increase in writing overall and more integration of writing with other subjects; more work in cooperative groups. . ." (Koretz, Stecher, Klein, & McCaffrey, 1994, p. 31).

Evidence in the literature also suggests that participation in scoring sessions for curriculum embedded assessments such as portfolios may contribute to teachers' knowledge and expertise and, by extension, to curricular reform (e.g., Gearhart & Wolf, 1994; Storms, Sheingold, Nunez, & Heller, 1998; Sheingold, Heller, & Paulukonis, 1995). Portfolio assessments, however, have not exerted uniformly positive effects, in part because the design of portfolio assessment systems can work against instructional reform goals. One study at the secondary level, for example, found that because so many different types of writing were required, students had few opportunities to practice and refine any one type, had few decisions to make about the relative quality of different pieces of their work, and were, thus, unable to reflect on individual progress and goals (Murphy, Bergamini, & Rooney, 1997). Research on the Kentucky portfolio system revealed that high school English teachers saw the required portfolios "primarily as a stressful administrative task . . . . imposed from outside" (Callahan, 1999). In studying the perceptions of first-year students who had all completed the University of Kentucky's compulsory 12th grade portfolios, Spaulding and Cummins (1998) found that two-thirds of the students didn't think compiling the portfolio was "a useful activity" (p.191). Taken together, these findings suggest that the policies that surround an assessment, as well as the assessment design itself, influence its consequences.

At the postsecondary level, portfolios have been popular for local assessments including placement and proficiency (e.g., Borrowman, 1999; Durst, Roemer, & Shultz, 1994; Elbow & Belanoff, 1986; Haswell & Wyche-Smith, 1994; Hester, et al., 2007; Willard-Traub, Decker, Reed, & Johnston, 1999). Much of the literature on postsecondary writing portfolios argued that portfolio results were more valid than those obtained by evaluating one or even two impromptu samples. For example, Elbow and Belanoff (1986), who are often credited for initiating the postsecondary portfolio trend, explain the move from a traditional essay exam to a portfolio in their writing program by claiming that the essay exam cannot provide "a valid picture of a student's proficiency in writing" (p. 336). Although many writing programs embraced portfolios, White (1993) identified reliability as the major issue for the future of portfolios in large-scale writing assessment: "While reliability should not become the obsession for portfolio evaluation that it became for essay testing, portfolios cannot become a serious means of measurement without demonstrable reliability" (p. 105). Broad (1994) contended that scoring portfolios was antithetical to the whole notion of a portfolio and instead argued for alternative ways of evaluation.

Alternative Ways to Warrant Validity

Interest in alternative approaches to assessment has prompted some scholars to challenge traditional concepts of validity and reliability on theoretical and epistemological grounds. Carini (1994) emphasized the importance of context, both social and historical, in evaluation, criticizing impersonal assessment procedures that remove writing from the contexts within which they are created, and from their location "within a body of works, spanning time and genre, and the relationship of these works to a person—a self-history in the making" (p. 63). In her view, assessment should be personal, contextual, and descriptive to acknowledge the links between writing, personal history, and identity.

Several theorists have supported a move away from exclusive reliance on traditional psychometric evidence to the use of constructivist, expert reader, or hermeneutic social negotiation procedures (Broad, 2003; Gitomer, 1993; Moss, 1992, 1994). For example, Moss (1994) argued that traditional statistical measures ought to "be treated as only one of several possible strategies serving important epistemological and ethical purposes" (p. 5). Indeed, from a hermeneutic perspective, the most credible judges are those who are most knowledgeable about the context in which a performance occurred and the nature of the performance itself. Their judgments are grounded in the richest contextual and textual evidence available, including the observations of others in the interpretive community. Moss (1994) offered several ways to warrant a hermeneutic approach to assessment:

> . . . extensive knowledge of the learning context; multiple and varied sources of evidence; an ethic of disciplined, collaborative inquiry that encourages challenges and revisions to initial interpretations," and ". . . the transparency of the trail of evidence leading to the interpretations, which allows users to evaluate the conclusions for themselves. *(p. 7)*

Gitomer (1993) proposed ways to warrant the dependability of judges' scores, including gathering information about what sort of interactions went on among the judges during the scoring process, how well they understood the context in which the performance was done, who they were, and their relationship to the individuals being assessed.

Theorists have also called for the development of a new or expanded set of quality criteria for assessment (Frederikson & Collins, 1989; Gielen, Dochy, & Dierick, 2003; Gipps, 1994; Linn, Baker, & Dunbar, 1991). Frederikson and Collins (1989) maintain that systemically valid assessment systems should be designed to "induce curricular and instructional changes in education systems (and learning strategy changes in students) that foster the development of the cognitive traits that the tests are designed to measure" (p. 27). The challenge for higher education is to develop assessments that foster the skills and traits that they value in students.

Writing Assessment Theory

Historically, writing assessment scholarship has focused on practice, not theory (Faigley, Cherry, Jolliffe, & Skinner, 1985; Gere, 1980). Over the last 15 years or so, writing assessment scholars, especially those in postsecondary sites, have begun to more carefully articulate theory, with the goal of developing a theoretical base that draws across various areas of study including linguistics, literacy, and psychometrics (Broad, 2003; Haswell, 1998; Huot, 1996, 2002; Lynne, 2004). While there has been considerable debate in the literature, recent statements by professional organizations (CCCC, 2009; NCTE-WPA, n.d.) support the position that writing assessment should be locally controlled, context-sensitive, rhetorically-based, theoretically consistent, and accessible (Broad, 2003; Broad et al., 2009; Huot, 2002; O'Neill et al., 2009). The principles contained in the statements of these professional organizations assume that writing assessment is linked not only to writing instruction but also that its primary aim is to improve teaching and learning. Assessment scholars also acknowledge the power inherent in writing assessments—even those considered "low" stakes—to shape curricula, define values, influence pedagogy, and affect students' educational experiences and self-perception, as well as their instructors' careers. For example, Hillocks (2002) demonstrates how different types of state-mandated writing assessments affected the teaching in different types of schools, in different states. In postsecondary writing, for instance, Agnew and McLaughlin (1999, 2001) showed how writing exams negatively influenced the educational trajectory and self-perception of writing abilities of African American students.

Given this framework of assessment principles and the power inherent in assessment, postsecondary writing assessment scholars tend to support practices that are informed by the local context—that is, they prefer assessments that involve writing instructors, align with local curricula and pedagogy, are dynamic and not static, produce results useful for instructors and students, and reinforce what research supports in terms of language and literacy.

Approaches and Practices

An assessment's purpose should be the guiding principle in selecting practices and approaches in postsecondary writing assessment. Smith's (1992, 1993) research on placement into first-year composition illustrates this principle. Over a decade of research led Smith (1992, 1993) to develop an approach to placement that relied on teacher expertise for placing students directly into the appropriate course based on the teacher's reading of the essays instead of essay scores. Having raters score essays and set cut scores for each course added an unnecessary layer to the assessment procedures, Smith (1992, 1993) argued, and did not increase the likelihood of students being adequately placed. Smith (1992, 1993) found that by selecting readers based on their experience with the curriculum, he actually got much higher reliability rates and students were placed more accurately. He further reasoned that some students, who he called "tweeners," didn't fit into the curriculum neatly, which explained why the readers disagreed on their placements. The problem, then, wasn't with the readers' training or in getting them to agree (typical conclusions if one were focused simply on meeting the reliability threshold); rather the problem was that the curriculum did not fit some students. In placement, students have to go into one course or another, there isn't a "between" course. Follow up research showed how these students tended to remain tweeners as they progressed through the curriculum. Smith reasoned that over time, if a sustained, critical mass of tweeners developed, teachers and the curriculum would adapt to them.

Haswell and his colleagues (Haswell, 2001) took a similar approach to placement, developing procedures that depended on instructors and their level of expertise. The process was different than Smith's—for example, it used a two-tier reading approach—because Haswell's process was designed to accommodate the local needs at his institution. Examples such as these abound in postsecondary writing (e.g., Broad et al., 2009; Harrington, 1998; Hester et al., 2007; Yancey & Huot, 1997), although many of the locally designed assessments have not been as rigorously investigated as those designed by Smith (1992, 1993) and Haswell (2001).

Sampling Methods

As with all other aspects of writing assessment, purpose should determine sampling and collection procedures. Research indicates that one writing sample is not enough to make judgments about a student's overall writing ability (as discussed above in the section on Construct Under-Representation). Because one writing sample is not enough to determine writing ability, portfolios have been very popular in postsecondary writing assessment. Portfolio parameters, however, will differ depending on the program, the curriculum, the purpose, the resources, and other factors. Although the contents will vary, most composition and rhetoric scholars agree that in addition to including various types of writing selected from a larger pool, a distinguishing characteristic is that a portfolio includes a self-analysis, or reflection, that provides additional information about the contents (e.g., Hamp-Lyons & Condon, 2000; Yancey, 1992). Sometimes, for example, portfolios will include a timed impromptu essay written in a testing situation along with longer essays that included multiple drafts produced in classes, while in other cases the contents may all be connected to one course and the portfolio will include all process work associated with the assignment as well as an introductory letter (Hamp-Lyons & Condon, 2000).

Although composition and rhetoric specialists prefer multiple writing samples, many writing assessments still rely on impromptu essays written in response to an assigned prompt under testing conditions, whether the assessment is designed by local experts or by testing professionals at such corporations as the Educational Testing Service or Pearson. Many of these rely on paper and pencil, as the SAT writing essay exam does, while others take advantage of computer-based technologies. For example, Peckham (2009, 2010) and Perelman (2008) reported on the use of an online platform, iMOAT, that uses the Internet for administering writing assessments.

Scoring and Evaluation Methods

Traditionally, holistic scoring has been a popular method for rating writing samples whether essays or portfolios (White, 1993, 1994). Typically, this approach has relied on a rubric with a four- or six-point scale. Analytic rubrics have also been used, depending on the purpose. However, assessment scholars also have investigated, and in some cases, challenged the use of holistic scoring and rubrics (e.g., Broad, 1994, 2003; Huot, 1993; Pula & Huot, 1993). Some researchers have developed alternative methods for evaluating writing samples that they argue are more aligned with writing theory and practice (Broad, 2003; Haswell, 2001; Hester, et al., 2007; Smith, 1992, 1993). The evaluation of writers' self-reflection, self-assessment, or introductory material has also attracted the attention of writing scholars and researchers (e.g., Schendel & O'Neill, 1999; Scott, 2005; White, 2005). Most recently, the discussion has revolved around digital composition, especially compositions that include multimedia technologies (e.g., Neal, 2010; Penrod, 2005; Whithaus, 2005; Yancey, 2001).

While there are debates within the field about the best methods for evaluating student writing samples, composition and rhetoric specialists agree that the procedures should be locally controlled and, in most cases, constructed and defined locally (e.g., Broad et al., 2009; Haswell, 2001; Huot, 2002; O'Neill et al., 2009). Because of the contextual nature of writing, and writing programs, standardizing assessments across institutions is difficult. Pagano, Barnhardt, Reynolds, Williams, and McCurrie (2008) attempted to create a cross-institutional embedded writing assessment. They discovered the difficulty in developing not only a shared task but also a shared rubric. While they found the process of the inter-institutional assessment productive for the participants, especially in the construction of the rubric and the challenges they faced in using a shared rubric, they also acknowledged that the assessment "had serious threats to reliability" (Pagano et al., 2008, p. 311). Their work supported the argument made by writing assessment scholars such as Broad (2003) and Huot (2002): the value of writing assessment is not only tied to the results but also comes from the participation in the assessment process, including defining the evaluation criteria, scoring the writing samples, and interpreting and using the results.

Ongoing Concerns and Emerging Trends

Interest in assessment in higher education has increased since the publication of *A Test of Leadership* (Miller et al., 2006), the report issued by the commission on higher education convened by then–US Secretary of Education, Margaret Spellings. With this increasing emphasis on demonstrating what students learn in postsecondary education, there is no doubt that writing assessment will continue to be on the frontlines of these debates. Recent large-scale initiatives such as the American Association of Colleges & Universities VALUE project and the development of the Collegiate Learning Assessment show the role that writing plays not only in learning but also in demonstrating that learning (Adler-Kassner & O'Neill, 2010). Because of the centrality of writing in the academy and beyond it, there is also no doubt that writing assessment will continue to be an active scholarly field that draws researchers and practitioners from diverse areas, including educational measurement, K–12 and post-secondary literacy educators, and composition specialists, some of whom work within the academy and others who work for testing companies.

Researchers will continue to deal with the challenges associated with validity that we have outlined here. While these challenges are not new, current trends in composing and assessment will create new challenges or complicate existing ones. Technology, for example, continues to be a contentious area for debate. One issue is the machine scoring of essays, which has been criticized by some writing specialists (e.g., Ericcson & Haswell, 2006; Herrington & Moran, 2001; Neal, 2010; Whithaus, 2005) and endorsed by others (e.g., Shermis & Burstein, 2003). Automated scoring, of course, has already been used for both instructional and assessment purposes as ETS explains on its Web site. The *e-rater* scoring engine, according to the ETS Web site (2011), "provides a holistic score for an essay" and has been used by students "to practice and evaluate their essay-writing skills as well as identify areas that need improvement" and by teachers "to help their students develop their writing skills independently and receive automated, constructive feedback" (http://www.ets.org/erater/about). Related to the use of programs such as *e-rater* are the preponderance of indirect computer adaptive tests, such as ACCUPLACER and COMPASS, used for evaluating student abilities.

Other ongoing issues in writing assessment related to technology include changing literacy practices associated with digital technologies. Writing specialists, such as Whithaus (2005) and Neal (2010), articulated the limits of current writing assessment practices to produce valid results in dealing with multimodal digital texts. They highlight the disjunction between traditional essayist literacy that dominates current writing assessment and the evolving digital writing that is increasingly used both inside and beyond the academy. As Neal (2010) explained, we are using 20th-century assessment theories and practices to evaluate 21st-century literacies. This can be an especially contentious issue because of the power of assessment to influence what is valued and taught. If standardized, single sample, impromptu, essay exams continue to be used as gatekeeping devices, they will continue to promote a limited understanding of writing. Not only will this threaten the validity of the results because the construct of writing will be limited and incomplete, but also, perhaps, because of the consequences to teaching and learning. If the findings from Hillocks' (2002) research hold, the discrepancies will be unevenly experienced across socio-economic lines with the tests influencing—and limiting—the curriculum in schools serving lower socio-economic areas more than they do in wealthier schools. While Hillocks' (2002) findings were specifically referencing K–12 writing assessments, other exams, such as the timed, impromptu essay portions of the SAT and ACT, will influence secondary writing curricula as well. With the new assessments in development associated with the Common Core State Standards (CCSS), these issues will become even more important. For example, one of the nationwide assessment consortia recently funded to develop assessments linked to the CCSS, Partnership for the Assessment of Readiness for College and Careers (PARCC), originally planned to assess student writing four times a year, every year from grade 3 through 11 (for more specific information, see http://www.achieve.org/PARCC). Because these tests are intended to certify that students are ready for the demands of postsecondary writing, they carry a high stake for individual students, schools, and districts as well as the postsecondary institutions that students move on to after completing high school. As a result, they will assuredly affect both teaching and learning.

Clearly, writing assessment researchers and practitioners have many challenges to face. Learning to work across the disciplinary and institutional boundaries that currently divide many of the scholars in the field may be the most important one if our goal is to improve teaching and learning.

References

Abedi, J., & Lord, C. (2001). The language factor in mathematics tests. *Applied Measurement in Education, 14*, 219–234.

Abedi, J., Lord, C., Hofstetter, C., & Baker, E. (2000). Impact of accommodation strategies on English language learners' test performance. *Educational Measurement: Issues and Practice, 19*(3), 16–26.

Abedi, J., Lord, C., Kim-Boscardin, C., & Miyoshi, J. (2000). *The effects of accommodations on the assessment of LEP students in NAEP* (Tech. Rep. No. 537). Los Angeles, CA: University of California, National Center for Research on Evaluation, Standards, and Student Testing.

Abedi, J., Lord, C., & Plummer, J. (1997). *Language background as a variable in NAEP mathematics performance* (Tech. Rep. No. 429). Los Angeles, CA: University of California, National Center for Research on Evaluation, Standards, and Student Testing.

Agnew, E., & McLauglin, M. (1999). Basic writing class of '93 five years later: How the academic paths of blacks and whites diverged. *Journal of Basic Writing, 18*(1), 40–54.

Agnew, E., & McLaughlin, M. (2001). Those crazy gates and how they swing: Tracking the system that tracks African-American students. In G. McNenny, & S. H. Fitzgerald (Eds.), *Mainstreaming basic writers: Politics and pedagogies of access* (pp. 85–100). Mahwah, NJ: Erlbaum.

Adler-Kassner, L. & O'Neill, P. (2010). *Reframing writing assessment to improve teaching and learning.* Logan, UT: Utah State University Press.

Almasi, J., Afflerbach, P., Guthrie, J., & Schafer, W. (1995). *Effects of a statewide performance assessment program on classroom instructional practice in literacy* (Reading Research Report No. 32). University of Georgia: National Reading Research Center.

Anastasi, A. (1986). Evolving concepts of test validation. *Annual Review of Psychology, 37*, 1–15.

Bachman, L. F., & Palmer, A. S. (1996). *Language testing in practice.* Oxford,UK: Oxford University Press.

Ball, A. F. (1997). Expanding the dialogue on culture as a critical component when assessing writing. *Assessing Writing, 4*, 169–202.

Basham, C. S., & Kwachka, P. E. (1991). Reading the world differently: A cross-cultual approach to writing assessment. In L. Hamp-Lyons (Ed.), *Assessing second language writing in academic contexts* (pp. 37–49). Norwood, NJ: Ablex.

Beaufort, A. (2007). *College writing and beyond: A new framework for university writing instruction.* Logan, UT: Utah State University Press.

Borrowman, S. (1999). Trinity of portfolio placement: Validity, reliability, and curriculum reform. *Writing Program Administrator, 23*, 7–27.

Bridgeman, B., & Carlson, S. (1983). *Survey of academic writing tasks required of graduate and undergraduate foreign students* (TOEFL Research Report No. 15; ETS Research Report No. 83–18). Princeton, NJ: Educational Testing Service.

Broad, R. L. (1994). 'Portfolio Scoring': A contradiction in terms. In Black, L., Daiker, D.A., Sommers, J., & Stygall, G. (Eds), *New directions in portfolio assessment: Reflective practice, critical theory, and large-scale scoring.* Portsmouth, NH: Boynton/Cook Heinemann.

Broad, R. (2003). *What we really value: Beyond rubrics in teaching and assessing writing.* Logan, UT: Utah State University Press.

Broad, R., Adler-Kassner, L., Alford, B., Detweiler, J., Estrem, H., Harrington, S., & McBride, M. (2009). *Organic writing assessment: Dynamic criteria mapping in action.* Logan, UT: Utah State University Press.

Brown, A. (1995). The effect of rater variables in the development of an occupation-specific performance test. *Language Testing, 12*, 1–15.

Brown, J. D. (1991). Do English and ESL faculties rate writing samples differently? *TESOL Quarterly, 25*, 587–603.

Callahan, S. (1999). All done with best of intentions: One Kentucky high school after six years of state portfolio tests. *Assessing Writing 6*(1), 5–40.

Carini, P. F. (1994). Dear Sister Bess: An essay on standards, judgment and writing. *Assessing Writing, 1*, 29–65.

Carrithers, D., & Bean, J. C. (2008). Using a client memo to assess critical thinking of finance majors. *Business Communication Quarterly, 71*(1), 10–26.

Carroll, L. A. (2002). *Rehearsing new roles: How college students develop as writers.* Carbondale, IL: Southern Illinois University Press.

Cazden, C. B. (2001). *Classroom discourse: The language of teaching and learning* (2nd ed.). Portsmouth, NH: Heinemann.

Chalhoub-Deville, M. (1995). Deriving assessment scales across different tests and rater groups. *Language Testing, 12*, 16–33.

Cherry, R., & Meyer, P. (1993). Reliability issues in holistic assessment. In M. M.Williamson, & B. A. Huot (Eds.), *Validating holistic scoring: Theoretical and empirical foundations* (pp. 109–41). Cresskill, NJ: Hampton Press.

Cho, Y. (2003) Assessing writing: Are we bound by only one method? *Assessing Writing, 8*(3), 165–191.

Colbert, S. "The word: Swift payment" Colbert Nation. Originally aired Dec 13, 2010. http://www.colbert-nation.com/the-colbert-report-videos/368379/december-13-2010/the-word---swift-payment   Accessed March 31, 2011

Conference on College Composition and Communication. (Nov. 2009). *Writing assessment: A position statement* (Rev. ed.). National Council of Teachers of English. Accessed 1 April 2010. Available at http://www.ncte.org/cccc/resources/positions/123784.htm

Cook-Gumperz, J. (2006). *The social construction of literacy* (2nd ed.). Cambridge, UK: Cambridge University Press.

Crowhurst, M., & Piche, G. L. (1979). Audience and mode of discourse effects on syntactic complexity in writing on two grade levels. *Research in the teaching of English, 13*, 101–109.

Daley, J. A., & Dickson-Markham, F. (1982). Contrast effects in evaluating essays. *Journal of Educational Measurement, 19*(4), 309–316.

Diederich, P. B. (1950). *The 1950 College Board English validity study*. Princeton, NJ: Educational Testing Service. R. B. Nos. 50–58.

Diederich, P. B., French, J. W., & Carlton, S. T., (1961). *Factors in judgments of writing quality*. Princeton, NJ: Educational Testing Service, 1961. RB No. 61–15 ED 002 172.

Durst, R. K., Roemer, M., & Schultz, L. (1994). Portfolio negotiations: Acts in speech. In Black, L., Daiker, D. A., Sommers, J., & Stygall, G. (Eds.), *New directions in portfolio assessment: Reflective practice, critical theory, and large-scale scoring*. Portsmouth, NH: Boynton/Cook Heinemann.

Educational Testing Service. (2011). About the *e-rater®* Scoring Engine. Retrieved April 1, 2011 from http://www.ets.org/erater/about.

Elbow, P., & Belanoff, P. (1986). Staffroom interchange: Portfolios as a substitute for proficiency examinations. *College Composition and Communication 37*, 336–39.

Erdosy, M. U. (2004). *Exploring variability in judging writing ability in a second language: A study of four experienced raters of ESL compositions* (TOEFL Research Report 70). Princeton, NJ: Educational Testing Service.

Ericcson, P. F., & Haswell, R. A. (Eds.). (2006). *Machine scoring of student writing: Truth and consequences*. Logan, UT: Utah State University Press.

Faigley, L., Cherry, R., Jolliffe, D. A., & Skinner, A. (1985). *Assessing writers' knowledge and processes of composing*. Norwood, NJ: Ablex.

Frederickson, J., & Collins, A. (1989). A systems approach to educational testing. *Educational Researcher, 18*(9), 27–32.

Freedman, A., & Pringle, I. (1981). *Why students can't write arguments*. Unpublished manuscript, Carleton University, Linguistics department, Ottawa, Canada.

Freedman, S.W. (1981). Influences on evaluators of expository essays: Beyond the text. *Research in the Teaching of English, 15*(3), 245–255.

Gamaroff, R. (2000). Rater reliability in language assessment: The bug of all bears. *System, 28*, 31–53.

Gearhart, M., & Wolf, S. (1994). Engaging teachers in assessment of their students' narrative writing: The role of subject matter knowledge. *Assessing Writing, 1*, 67–90.

Gee, J. P. (1996). *Social linguistics and literacies: Ideology in discourses* (2nd ed.). London, UK: Taylor and Francis.

Gere, A. R. (1980). Written composition: Toward a theory of evaluation. *College English 42*, 44–48, 53–58.

Gielen, S., Dochy, F., & Dierick, S. (2003). In M. Segers, F. Dochy, & E. Cascallar, (Eds.), *Optimising new modes of assessment: In search of qualities and standards*. Dordrecht, Netherlands: Kluwer.

Gipps, P. (1994). *Beyond testing: towards a theory of educational assessment*. London, UK: The Falmer Press.

Gitomer, D. (1993). Performance assessment and educational measurement. In R. Bennett, & W. Ward (Eds.), *Construction vs. Choice in cognitive measurement: Issues in constructed response, performance testing, and portfolio assessment*. (pp. 241–293). Hillsdale, NJ: Erlbaum.

Godshalk, F., Swineford, E., & Coffman, W. (1966). *The measurement of writing ability*. New York, NY: The College Entrance Examination Board.

Graham, S., & Perin, D. (2007). A meta-analysis of writing instruction for adolescent students. *Journal of Educational Psychology, 99*(3), 45–476.

Greene, S., & Orr, A. (2007). First-year college students writing across the disciplines. In P. O'Neill (Ed.), *Blurring boundaries: Developing writers, researchers and teachers*. Cresskill, NJ: Hampton Press.

Hale, G., Taylor, C., Bridgeman, B., Carson, J., Kroll, B., & Kantor, R. (1996). *A study of writing tasks assigned in academic degree programs* (TOEFL Research Report #54). Princeton, NJ: Educational Testing Service.

Hamp-Lyons, L. (1990). Second language writing: Assessment issues. In B. Kroll (Ed.), *Second language writing: Research insights for the classroom* (pp. 69–87). New York, NY: Cambridge University Press.

Hamp-Lyons, L., & Condon, W. (2000). *Assessing the portfolio: Principles for practice, theory, and research.* Cresskill, NJ: Hampton Press.

Hamp-Lyons, L., & Matthias, S. (1994). Examining expert judgments of task difficulty on essay tests. *Journal of Second Language Writing, 3*(1), pp. 49–68.

Hardison, C. M., & Sackett, P. R. (2008). Use of writing samples on standardized tests: Susceptibility to rule-based coaching and resulting effects on score improvement. *Applied Measurement in Education, 21,* 227–252.

Harrington, S. (1998). New visions of authority in placement test rating. *WPA: Writing Program Administration 22,* 53–84.

Haswell, R. H. (1998). Multiple inquiry in the validation of writing tests. *Assessing Writing, 5,* 89–109.

Haswell, R. H. (Ed.). (2001). *Beyond outcomes: Assessment and instruction within a university writing program.* Vol. 5, Perspectives on Writing Theory, Research and Practice. Westport, CT: Ablex.

Haswell, R. H., & Haswell J. T. (1996). Gender bias and critique of student writing. *Assessing Writing, 3,* 31–84.

Haswell, R. H., & Wyche-Smith, S. (1994). Adventuring into writing assessment. *College Composition and Communication, 45,* 220–236.

Hayes, J. R., & Hatch, J. A. (1999). Issues in measuring reliability: Correlation versus percentage of agreement. *Written Communication, 16,* 354–367.

Herman, J., Gearhart, M., & Baker, E. (1993). Assessing writing portfolios: Issues in the validity and meaning of scores. *Educational Assessment, 1*(3), 201–224.

Herrington, A. J. (1985). Writing in academic settings: A study of the contexts for writing in two chemical engineering courses. *Research in the Teaching of English, 19,* 331–361.

Herrington, A., & Curtis, M. (2000). *Persons in process: Four stories of writing and personal development in college.* Urbana, IL: National Council of Teachers of English.

Herrington, A., & Moran, C. (2001). What happens when machines read our students' writing? *College English, 63,* 480–499.

Hester, V., O'Neill, P., Neal, M., Edgington, A., & Huot, B. (2007). Adding portfolios to the placement process: A longitudinal perspective. In P. O'Neill (Ed.), *Blurring boundaries: Developing researchers, writers, and teachers* (pp. 261–290). Cresskill, NJ: Hampton Press.

Hilgers, T. (1992). *Improving placement exam equitability, validity, and reliability.* Paper presented at the Conference on College Composition and Communication, Cincinnati, Ohio.

Hilgers, T. L., Hussey, E. L., & Stitt-Bergh, M. (2000). The case for prompted self-assessment in the writing classroom. In J. B. Smith, & K. B. Yancey (Eds.), *Self-assessment and development in writing: A collaborative inquiry.* Cresskill, NJ: Hampton Press.

Hillocks, G., Jr. (1986). *Research in written composition: New directions for teaching.* Urbana, IL: National Council of Teachers of English.

Hillocks, G., Jr. (2002). *The Testing trap: How states writing assessments control learning.* New York, NY: Teachers College Press.

Huot, B. A. (1993). The influence of holistic scoring procedures on reading and rating student essays. In M. M. Williamson, & B. A. Huot (Eds.), *Validating holistic scoring: Theoretical and empirical foundations* (pp. 206–236). Cresskill, NJ: Hampton Press.

Huot, B. (1996). Toward a new theory of writing assessment. *College Composition and Communication 47,* 549–566.

Huot, B. (2002). *(Re)Articulating writing assessment for teaching and learning.* Logan: Utah State University Press.

Huot, B., O'Neill, P., & Moore, C. (2010). A usable past for writing assessment. *College English, 7*(2), 495–517.

Janopoulos, M. (1992). University faculty tolerance of NS and NNS writing errors: A comparison. *Journal of Second Language Writing, 1*(2), 109–121.

Johnson, T. S., Smagorinsky, P., Thompson, L., & Fry, P.G. (2003). Learning to teach the five-paragraph theme. *Research in the Teaching of English, 38,* 136–176.

Keech, C. L., & McNelly, M. E. (1982). Comparison and analysis of rater responses to the anchor papers in the writing prompt variation study. In J. R. Gray, & L. P. Ruth (Eds.), *Properties of writing tasks: A study of alternative procedures for holistic writing assessment.* Berkeley, CA: University of California, Graduate School of Education, Bay Area Writing Project. (ERIC Document Reproduction Service No. ED230576)

Ketter, J., & Pool, J. (2001). Exploring the impact of a high-stakes direct writing assessment in two high school classrooms. *Research in the Teaching of English, 35,* 344–393.

Kobayashi, H., & Rinnert, C. (1996). Factors affecting composition evaluation in an EFL context: Cultural rhetorical pattern and readers' background. *Language Learning, 46,* 397–437.

Koretz, D., & Hamilton, L. (2003). *Teachers' responses to high-stakes testing and the validity of gains: A pilot study* (CSE Tech.Prep.610). Los Angeles, CA: Center for Research on Evaluation, Standards, and Student Testing.

Koretz, D., Mitchell, K., Barron, S., & Keith, S. (1996). *Perceived effects of the Maryland School Performance Assessment Program* (Technical Report 409). Los Angeles, CA: National Center for Research on Evaluation, Standards, and Student Testing, University of California, Los Angeles.

Koretz, D., Stecher, B., Klein, S., & McCaffrey, D. (1994). *The evolution of a portfolio program: The impact and quality of the Vermont program in its second year (1992–93)* (CSE Technical Report 385). Los Angeles, CA: National Center for Research on Evaluation, Standards, and Student Testing, University of California, Los Angeles.

Langer, J. (1984). The effects of available information on responses to school writing tasks. *Research in the Teaching of English, 18*(1), 27–44.

Linn, R., Baker, E., & Dunbar, S. B. (1991). Complex, performance-based assessment: Expectations and validation criteria. *Educational Researcher, 20*(8), 15–21.

Loofbourrow, P. (1994). Composition in the context of the CAP: A case study of the interplay between composition assessment and classrooms. *Educational Assessment, 2*(1), pp.7–49.

Lynne, P. (2004). *Coming to terms: A theory of writing assessment.* Logan, UT: Utah State University Press.

Matsuhashi, A. (1982). Explorations in the real-time production of written discourse. In M. Nystrand, (Ed.), *What writers know: The language, process, and structure of written discourse* (pp. 269–290). New York, NY: Academic Press.

McCarthy, L. P. (1987). A stranger in a strange land: A college student writing across the curriculum. *Research in the Teaching of English, 21*, 233–265.

Messick, S. (1989). Meaning and values in test validation: The science and ethics of assessment. *Educational Researcher, 18*(2), 5–11.

Messick, S. (1994). The interplay of evidence and consequences in the validation of performance assessments. *Educational Researcher, 23*(2), 5–11.

Miller, C., et al. (2006). *A test of leadership: Charting the future of U.S. higher education.* Washington, DC: U.S. Department of Education.

Moss, P. (1992). Shifting conceptions of validity in educational measurement: Implications for performance assessment. *Review of Educational Research. 62*(3), 229–258.

Moss, P. (1994). Can there be validity without reliability? *Educational Researcher, 23*(2), 5–12.

Murphy, S. (2007). Culture and consequences: The canaries in the coal mine. *Research in the Teaching of English, 42*, 228–244.

Murphy, S., Bergamini, J., & Rooney, P. (1997). The impact of large-scale portfolio assessment programs on classroom practice: Case studies of the New Standards field-trial portfolio. *Educational Assessment, 4*(4), 297–333.

Murphy, S., & Underwood, T. (2000). *Portfolio practices: Lessons from schools, districts and states.* Norwood, MA: Christopher Gordon.

National Council of Teachers of English. (April, 2005). *The impact of the SAT and ACT timed writing tests: Report from the NCTE task force on SAT and ACT writing tests.* Urbana, IL: NCTE.

National Council of Teachers of English/Council of Writing Program Administrators. (n.d.). *NCTE-WPA white paper on writing assessment in colleges and universities.* Retrieved from http://wpacouncil.org/whitepaper

Neal, M. (2010). *Writing assessment and the revolution in digital texts and technologies.* New York, NY: Teacher's College Press.

Nystrand, M., Cohen, A., & Dowling, N. (1993). Addressing reliability problems in the portfolio assessment of college writing. *Educational Assessment, 1*(1), 53–70.

O'Neill, P., Moore, C., & Huot, B. (2009). *A guide to college writing assessment.* Logan, UT: Utah State University Press.

O'Neill, P., Murphy, S., Huot, B., & Williamson, M. (2004). *What high school teachers in three states say about high stakes writing assessments.* Paper presented at the annual conference of the National Council of Teachers of English, Indianapolis.

Pagano, N., Barnhardt, S., Reynolds, D., Williams, M., & McCurrie, M. K. (2008). An inter-institutional model for college writing assessment. *College Composition and Communication, 60*, 285–320.

Peckham, I. (2009). Online placement in first-year writing. *College Composition and Communication, 60*, 517–540.

Peckham, I. (2010). Online challenge versus offline ACT. *College Composition and Communication, 61*(4), 718–745.

Penrod, D. (2005). *Composition in convergence: The impact of new media on writing assessment.* Mahwah, NJ: Erlbaum.

Perelman, L. (2008). Assessment symposium: Information illiteracy and mass market writing assessments. *College Composition and Communication, 60*(1), 128–141.

Polio, C., Fleck, C., & Leder, N. (1998). "If I only had more time": ESL learners' changes in linguistic accuracy on essay revisions. *Journal of Second Language Writing, 7*(1), 43–68.

Powers, D. E., & Fowles, M. E. (1996). Effects of applying different time limits to a proposed GRE writing test. *Journal of Educational Measurement, 33*(4), 433–452.

Pula, J. J., & Huot, B. A. (1993). A model of background influences on holistic raters. In M. M. Williamson, & B. A. Huot (Eds.), *Validating holistic scoring: Theoretical and empirical foundations* (pp. 237–265). Cresskill, NJ: Hampton Press.

Quellmalz, E., Capell, F., & Chou, C., (1982). Effects of discourse and response mode on the measurement of writing competence. *Journal of Educational Measurement, 19*(4), 241–258.

Reid, J. (1990). Responding to different topic types: A qualitative analysis from a contrastive rhetoric perspective. In B. Kroll (Ed.), *Second language writing: Research insights for the classroom.* New York, NY: Cambridge University Press.

Ruth, L. & Murphy, S. (1988). *Designing writing tasks for the assessment of writing.* Norwood, NJ: Ablex

Santos, T. (1988). Professors' reactions to the academic writing of nonnative-speaking students. *TESOL Quarterly, 22*(1), 69–90.

Schendel, E., & O'Neill, P. (1999). Exploring the theories and consequences of self-assessment through ethical inquiry." *Assessing Writing 6*(1), 199–227.

Scherff, L., & Piazza, C. (2005). The more things change, the more they stay the same: A survey of high school students' writing experiences. *Research in the Teaching of English 39*(3), 271–304.

Scott, T. (2005). Creating the subject of portfolios: Reflective writing and the conveyance of institutional perogatives. *Written Communication, 22,* 3–35.

Sheingold, K., Heller, J., & Paulukonis, S. (1995). *Actively seeking evidence: Teacher change through assessment development* (MS#94–04). Princeton, NJ: Educational Testing Service.

Shermis, M. D., & Burstein, J. (Eds.). (2003). *Automated essay scoring: A cross-disciplinary perspective.* Mahwah, NJ: Erlbaum.

Simmons, J. (1992). Don't settle for less in large-scale writing assessment. In K. Goodman, L. B. Vird, & Y. M. Goodman, *The whole language catalog: Supplement on authentic assessment* (pp. 160–161). Santa Rosa, CA: American School Publishers.

Smith, W. L. (1992). The importance of teacher knowledge in college composition placement testing. In J. R. Hayes (Ed.), *Reading empirical research studies: The rhetoric of research* (pp. 289–316). Norwood, NJ: Ablex.

Smith, W. L. (1993). Assessing the reliability and adequacy of using holistic scoring of essays as a college composition placement technique. In M. Williamson & B. Huot (Eds.), *Validating holistic scoring: Theoretical and empirical foundations* (pp. 142–205). Cresskill, NJ: Hampton Press.

Sommers, J., Black. L., Daiker, D., & Stygall, G. (1993). The challenges of rating portfolios: What WPAs can expect. *WPA Journal, 17*(1/2), 7–29.

Sommers, N. (2008). The call of research: A longitudinal view of writing development. *College Composition and Communication, 60*(1), 152–163.

Song, B., & Caruso, L. (1996). Do English and ESL faculty differ in evaluating the essays of native-English speaking and ESL students? *Journal of Second Language Writing, 5,* 163–182.

Spaulding, E., & Cummins, G. (1998). It was the best of times. It was a waste of time: University of Kentucky students' view of writing under KERA. *Assessing Writing, 5*(2), 167–200.

Stecher, B. M., Barron, S. I., Kaganoff, T., & Goodwin, J. (1998). *The effects of standards based assessment on classroom practices: Results of the 1996–97 RAND survey of Kentucky teachers of mathematics and writing* (CSE Tech. Rep. 482). Los Angeles, CA: Center for Research on Evaluation, Standards, and Student Testing.

Sternglass, M. (1997). *Time to know them: A longitudinal study of writing and learning at the college level.* Mahwah, NJ: Erlbaum.

Storms, B. A., Sheingold, K., Nunez, A., & Heller, J. (1998). *The feasibility, comparability, and value of local scorings of performance assessments.* Technical report. Princeton, NJ: Educational Testing Service, Center for Performance Assessment.

Sullivan, F. (1997). Calling writers' bluffs: The social production of writing ability in university placement-testing. *Assessing Writing, 4*(1), 53–82.

Tedick, D. J. (1990). ESL writing assessment: Subject matter knowledge and its impact on performance. *English for Specific Purposes, 9,* 123–143.

Wallace, V. L. (2002). Administrative direction in schools of contrasting status: Two cases. In G. Hillocks, Jr. (Ed.), *The testing trap: How state writing assessments control learning* (pp. 93–102). New York, NY: Teachers College Press.

Walvoord, B. E. & McCarthy, L. P. (1990). *Thinking and writing in college: A naturalistic study of students in four disciplines.* Urbana, IL: National Council of Teachers of English.

Weigle, S. C. (1999). Investigating rater/prompt interactions in writing assessment: Quantitative and qualitative approaches. *Assessing Writing 6*(2), 145–178.

Weigle, S. C. (2002). *Assessing writing.* Cambridge, UK: Cambridge University Press.

White, E. M. (1993). Holistic scoring: Past triumphs and future challenges. In M. Williamson, & B. Huot (Eds.), *Validating holistic scoring: Theoretical and empirical foundations* (pp. 79–108). Cresskill, NJ: Hampton Press.

White, E. M. (1994). *Teaching and assessing writing* (2nd ed.). Portland, ME: Calendar Islands.

White, E. M. (2005). Scoring of writing portfolios: Phase 2. *College Composition and Communication, 56,* 581–600.

Whithaus, C. (2005). *Teaching and evaluating writing in the age of computers and high stakes testing.* Mahwah, NJ: Erlbaum.

Willard-Traub, M., Decker, E., Reed, R., & Johnston, J., (1999). The development of large-scale portfolio placement at the University of Michigan 1992–1998. *Assessing Writing, 6,* 41–84.

Williamson, M. M. (1997). Pragmatism, positivism, and program evaluation. In K. B. Yancey, & B. Huot (Eds.), *Assessing writing across the curriculum: Diverse approaches and practices.* (pp. 237–259). Greenwich, CT: Ablex.

Williamson, M. M. (2003). Validity of automated scoring: Prologue for a continuing discussion of machine scoring student writing. *Journal of Writing Assessment, 1,* 85–104.

Witte, S., & Cherry, R. (1994). Think-aloud protocols, protocol analysis, and research design: An exploration of the influence of writing tasks on writing processes. In P. Smagorinsky (Ed.), *Speaking about writing: Reflections on research methodologies.* Thousand Oaks, CA: Sage.

Wolfe, E. W., Bolton, S., Feltovich, B., & Niday, D. M. (1996). Influence of student experience with word processors on the quality of essays written for a direct writing assessment. *Assessing Writing, 3,* 123–146.

Yancey, K. B. (Ed.). (1992). *Portfolios in the writing classroom: An introduction.* Urbana, IL: National Council of Teachers of English.

Yancey, K. B. (2001). Digitized student portfolios. In B. L. Cambridge (Ed.), *Electronic Portfolios: Emerging practices in student, faculty, and institutional learning* (pp. 15–30). Washington, DC: American Association for Higher Education.

Yancey, K. B., Fishman, T., Gresham, M., Neal, M., & Taylor, S. S. (2005). *Portraits of composition: How writing gets taught in the early 21st century.* Paper presented at the Conference on College Composition and Communication Annual Convention. San Francisco, CA.

Yancey, K. B., & Huot, B. (Eds.). (1997). *Assessing writing across the curriculum: Diverse approaches and practices.* Greenwich, CT: Ablex.

27

AUTHENTIC ASSESSMENT VALIDATION: A HEURISTIC RUBRICS CUBE

Jion Liou Yen and Kevin Hynes

Authentic assessment entails judging student learning by measuring performance according to real-life-skills criteria. This chapter focuses on the validation of authentic assessments because empirically-based, authentic assessment-validation studies are sparsely reported in the higher education literature. At the same time, many of the concepts addressed in this chapter are more broadly applicable to assessment tasks that may not be termed "authentic assessment" and are valuable from this broader assessment perspective as well. Accordingly, the chapter introduces a heuristic, rubrics cube which can serve as a tool for educators to conceptualize or map their authentic and other assessment activities and decisions on the following three dimensions: type and level of taxonomy, level of assessment decision, and type of validation method.

What is a Rubric?

The call for accountability in higher education has set the tone for campus-wide assessment. As the concept of assessment gains prominence on campuses, so do questions about how to conduct meaningful, reliable, and valid assessments. Authentic assessment has been credited by many as a meaningful approach for student learning assessment (Aitken & Pungur, 2010; Banta, Griffin, Flateby, & Kahn, 2009; Eder, 2001; Goodman, Arbona, & de Rameriz, 2008; Mueller, 2010; Spicuzza & Cunningham, 2003). When applied to authentic assessment, a rubric guides evaluation of student work against specific criteria from which a score is generated to quantify student performance. According to Walvoord (2004), "A rubric articulates in writing the various criteria and standards that a faculty member uses to evaluate student work" (p.19).

There are two types of rubrics—holistic and analytic. Holistic rubrics assess the overall quality of a performance or product and can vary in degree of complexity from simple to complex. For example, a simple holistic rubric for judging the quality of student writing is described by Moskal (2000) as involving four categories ranging from "inadequate" to "needs improvement" to "adequate" to "meet expectations for a first draft of a professional report." Each category contains a few additional phrases to describe the category more fully. On the other hand, an example of a complex rubric is presented by Suskie (2009) who likewise describes a four-category holistic rubric to judge a student's ballet performance but utilizes up to 15 explanatory phrases. So, even though a rubric may employ multiple categories for judging student learning, it remains a holistic rubric if it provides only one overall assessment of the quality of student learning.

The primary difference between a holistic and an analytic rubric is that the latter breaks out performance or product into several individual components and judges each part separately on a scale that includes descriptors. Thus, an analytic rubric resembles a matrix comprised of two axes—dimensions (usually referred to as criteria)—and level of performance (as specified by rating scales and descriptors). The descriptors are more important than the values assigned to them because scaling may vary across constituent groups. Keeping descriptors constant would allow cross-group comparison (S. Hatfield, personal communication, 2010). Although it takes time to develop clearly defined and unambiguous descriptors, they are essential in communicating performance expectations in rubrics and for facilitating the scoring process (Suskie, 2009; Walvoord, 2004).

To further elucidate the differences between holistic and analytic rubrics, consider how figure skating performance might be judged utilizing a holistic rubric versus how it is judged utilizing an analytic rubric. If one were to employ a holistic rubric to judge the 2010 Olympics men's figure skating based solely on technical ability, one might award a gold medal to Russian skater Evgeni Plushenko because he performed a "quad" whereas American skater Evan Lysacek did not. On the other hand, using analytic rubrics to judge each part of the performance separately in a matrix comprised of a variety of specific jumps with bonus points awarded later in the program, then one might award the gold medal to Evan rather than Evgeni. So, it is possible that outcomes may be judged differently depending upon the type of rubric employed.

Rubrics are often designed by a group of teachers, faculty members, and/or assessment representatives to measure underlying unobservable concepts via observable traits. Thus, a rubric is a scaled rating designed to quantify levels of learner performance. Rubrics provide scoring standards to focus and guide authentic assessment activities. Although rubrics are described as objective and consistent scoring guides, rubrics are also criticized for the lack of evidence of reliability and validity. One way to rectify this situation is to conceptualize gathering evidence of rubric reliability and validity as part of an assessment loop.

Rubric Assessment Loop

Figure 27.1 depicts three steps involved in the iterative, continuous quality improvement process of assessment as applied to rubrics. An assessment practitioner may formulate a rubric to assess an authentic learning task, then conduct studies to validate learning outcomes, and then make an assessment decision that either closes the assessment loop or leads to a subsequent round of rubric revision, rubric validation, and assessment decision. The focus of the assessment decision may range from the classroom level to the program level to the university level.

While individuals involved in assessment have likely seen "feedback loop" figures reminiscent of Figure 27.1, these figures need to be translated into a practitioner-friendly form that will take educa-

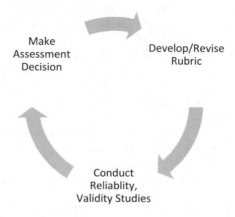

Figure 27.1 Rubric assessment loop

tors to the next level conceptually. Accordingly, this chapter introduces a heuristic, rubrics cube to facilitate this task.

Rubrics Cube

Figure 27.2 illustrates the heuristic rubrics cube where height is represented by three levels of assessment stakes (assessment decisions), width is represented by two methodological approaches for developing an evidentiary basis for the validity of the assessment decisions, and depth is represented by three learning taxonomies. The cell entries on the face of the cube represented in Figure 27.2 are the authors' estimates of the likely correspondence between the reliability and validity estimation methods minimally acceptable for each corresponding assessment stakes level. Ideally, the cell entries would capture a more fluid interplay between the types of methods utilized to estimate reliability and validity and the evidentiary argument supporting the assessment decision.

As Geisinger, Shaw, and McCormick (this volume) note, the concept of validity as modeled by classical test theory, generalizability theory, and multi-faceted Rasch Measurement (MFRM) is being re-conceptualized (Kane, 1992, 1994, 2006; Smith & Kulikowich, 2004; Stemler, 2004) into a more unified approach to gathering and assembling an evidentiary basis or argument that supports the validity of the assessment decision. The current authors add that as part of this validity reconceptualization, it is important to recognize the resource limitations sometimes facing educators and to strive to create "educator-friendly validation environments" that will aid educators in their task of validating assessment decisions.

Moving on to a discussion of the assessment-stakes dimension of Figure 27.2, the authors note that compliance with the demands posed by such external agents as accreditors and licensure/

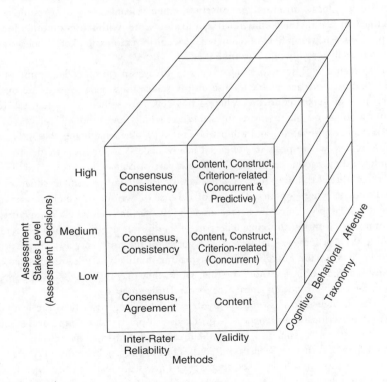

Figure 27.2 Rubrics cube

certification boards has created an assessment continuum. One end of this continuum is characterized by low-stakes assessment decisions such as grade-related assignments. Historically, many of the traditional learning assessment decisions are represented here. The other end of the assessment-stakes continuum is characterized by high-stakes assessment decisions. Licensure/certification driven assessment decisions are represented here, as would the use of portfolios in licensure/certification decisions. Exactly where accreditation falls on the assessment-stakes continuum may vary by institution. Because academic institutions typically need to be accredited in order to demonstrate the quality and value of their education, the authors place accreditation on the high stakes end of the assessment-stakes dimension of Figure 27.2 for the reasons described next.

While regional accreditors making assessment decisions may not currently demand the reliability and validity evidence depicted in the high-stakes methods cells of Figure 27.2, the federal emphasis on outcome measures, as advocated in the Spellings Commission's report on the future of U.S. higher education (U.S. Department of Education, 2006), suggests accrediting agencies and academic institutions may be pressured increasingly to provide evidence of reliability and validity to substantiate assessment decisions. Indeed, discipline-specific accrediting organizations such as the Accreditation Council for Business Schools and Programs, the Commission on Collegiate Nursing Education, the National Council for Accreditation of Teacher Education, and many others have promoted learning-outcomes based assessment for some time. Because many institutions wishing to gather the reliability and validity evidence suggested by Figure 27.2 may lack the resources needed to conduct high-stakes assessment activities, the authors see the need to promote initiatives at many levels that lead to educator-friendly assessment environments. For example, it is reasonable for academic institutions participating in commercially based learning outcomes testing programs to expect that the test developer provide transparent evidence substantiating the reliability and validity of the commercial examination. Freed from the task of estimating the reliability and validity of the commercial examination, local educators can concentrate their valuable assessment resources and efforts on triangulating/correlating the commercial examination scores with scores on other local measures of learning progress. An atmosphere of open, collegial collaboration will likely be necessary to create such educator-friendly assessment environments.

Returning to Figure 27.2, some of the frustration with assessment on college campuses may stem from the fact that methods acceptable for use in low-stakes assessment contexts are different from those needed in high-stakes contexts. Whereas low-stakes assessment can often satisfy constituents by demonstrating good-faith efforts to establish reliability and validity, high-stakes assessment requires that evidence of reliability and validity be shown (Wilkerson & Lang, 2003). Unfortunately, the situation can arise where programs engaged in low-stakes assessment activities resist the more rigorous methods they encounter as they become a part of high-stakes assessment. For example, the assessment of critical thinking may be considered a low-stakes assessment situation for faculty members and students when conducted as part of a course on writing in which the critical thinking score represents a small portion of the overall grade. However, in cases where a university has made students' attainment of critical thinking skills part of its mission statement, then assessing students' critical thinking skills becomes a high-stakes assessment for the university as it gathers evidence to be used for accreditation and university decision-making. Similarly, while students can be satisfied in creating low-stakes portfolios to showcase their work, they may resist high-stakes portfolio assessment efforts designed to provide an alternative to standardized testing.

Succinctly stated, high-stakes assessment involves real-life contexts where the learner's behavior/performance has critical consequences (e.g., license to practice, academic accreditation, etc.). In contrast, in low-stakes assessment contexts, the learner's performance has minimal consequences (e.g., pass-fail a quiz, a formative evaluation, etc.). Thus, from a stakeholder perspective, the primary assessment function in a low-stakes context is to assess the learner's progress. On the other hand, from a stakeholder perspective, the primary assessment function in a high-stakes context is to assess that the mission-critical learning outcome warrants, for example, licensure to practice (from the stakeholder perspective of the learner) and accreditation (from the stakeholder perspective of an institution). Lastly, a medium-stakes context falls between these two end points. Thus, from a stakeholder perspective, the primary assessment function in a medium-stakes context is to assess that moderating outcomes (e.g, work-study experiences, internship experiences, volunteering, graduation, etc.) are experienced and successfully accomplished.

For the low-stakes assessment level, at a minimum, a content validity argument needs to be established. In the authors' judgment, while content, construct and concurrent validity evidence would typically need to be assembled for a validity argument at the medium-stakes assessment level, no such need exists for predictive validity evidence. In order to demonstrate a validity argument at the high-stakes assessment level, all types of validation methods such as content validity, construct validity (i.e., convergent and discriminant), and criterion-related validity (i.e., concurrent validity and predictive validity) need to be demonstrated (see Thorndike & Hagen, 1977, for definitional explanations).

With regard to inter-rater reliability estimation, for the low-stakes assessment level, percentage of rater agreement (consensus) needs to be demonstrated. For the medium- and high-stakes assessment levels, both consensus and consistency need to be demonstrated. Needless to say, there are a variety of non-statistical and statistical approaches to estimate these types of reliability and validity. For those having the software and resources to do so, the MFRM approach can be an efficient means for establishing an evidentiary base for estimating the reliability and validity of rubrics. The important consideration in validation is that it is the interpretation of rubric scores upon which validation arguments are made.

Before examining the interplay of learning taxonomies with assessment decisions, a few additional comments on methods may be helpful. First, the reliability methods portrayed in the rubrics cube ignore such reliability estimates as internal consistency of items, test-retest, parallel forms, and split-half. Instead, the chapter focuses on inter-rater reliability estimates because it is critical to establish inter-rater reliability estimates whenever human judgments comprise the basis of a rubrics score. In creating the methods dimension of the rubrics cube, the authors adapted the Stemler (2004) distinction between consensus, consistency, and measurement approaches to estimating inter-rater reliability. Figure 27.2 indicates that at a low-assessment-stakes level, consensus is an appropriate method for estimating inter-rater reliability. Estimating the degree of consensus between judges can be as simple as calculating the percent of agreement between pairs of judges or as intricate as collaborative quality filtering which assigns greater weights to more accurate judges (Traupman & Wilensky, 2004). Figure 27.2 also shows that as the assessment stakes level moves to the "medium" and "high" levels, then both consistency and consensus are relevant methods for estimating inter-rater reliability. Among the more popular approaches, consistency can be estimated via an intraclass correlation derived utilizing an analysis of variance approach. In the analysis of variance, judges/raters form the between-factor source of variation and the within-ratee source of variation is a function of both between judge/rater variation and residual variation (Winer, 1971, pp. 283–89). Consistency can also be estimated utilizing an item response theory (IRT) approach (see Osterlind & Wang, this volume) as well as Linacre (2003). Because reliability is a necessary, but not sufficient condition for validity, it is listed first on the methods dimension.

Having discussed the contingency of the various types of validation methods on the assessment-stakes-level dimension of the rubrics cube, a few general comments on validation methods as they relate to rubrics are warranted here. Detailed definitions and discussions of the types of validity are available in the *Standards for Educational and Psychological Testing* (American Education Research Association, American Psychological Association, National Council Measurement in Education, 1999). In order for others to benefit from and replicate the validation of rubrics described in the assessment literature, it is essential that the rubric scaling utilized be accurately described. Researchers need to describe the way in which content validity evidence was assembled (rational, empirical, Delphi technique, job analysis, etc.). Likewise, researchers' discussions of efforts to establish construct validity should describe any evidence of positive correlations with theoretically related (and not simply convenient) constructs (i.e., convergent validity), negative or non-significant correlations with unrelated constructs (i.e., discriminant validity), or results of multivariate approaches (factor analysis, canonical correlations, discriminant analysis, multivariate analysis of variance, etc.) as support for construct validity. Central to the concept of predictive validity is that rubric scores gathered prior to a theoretically relevant, desired, end-state criterion correlate significantly and therefore predict the desired end state criterion. At the high-stakes assessment level, assembling information regarding all of these types of validity will enable stakeholders to make an evidentiary validity argument for the assessment decision.

With regard to predictive validity, the authors note that it is possible to statistically correct for restriction in the range of ability (Hynes & Givner, 1981; Wiberg & Sundstrom, 2009; also see Geisinger et al., this volume). For example, if the adequacy of subsequent work performance of candidates passing a licensure examination (i.e., restricted group) were rated by supervisors and these ratings were then correlated with achieved licensure examination scores, this correlation could be corrected for restriction in range, yielding a better estimate of the true correlation between performance ratings and licensure examination scores for the entire, unrestricted group (pass candidates and fail candidates).

Assessment Decisions (Assessment Stakes Level) by Taxonomy

The levels of each of the learning taxonomies as they relate to rubric criteria and assessment decisions are explicated through fictional examples in the tables that follow. Figure 27.3 represents an assessment-decision-focused slice of the three-dimensional heuristic rubrics cube for Bloom's (1956) cognitive learning taxonomy involving creative/critical thinking (CT). Five rubric criteria are crossed with three assessment decisions in a fictional, medium-stakes authentic assessment adapted from Smith and Kulikowich (2004).

The pluses and minuses in Figure 27.3 represent 'Yes'/'No' analytic assessment decisions regarding students' mastery of critical thinking criteria. For example, the assessment decisions for students who received minuses in all five CT criteria would be to take remedial CT training. On the other hand, students who received a majority of pluses would need to take targeted CT training until they

Cognitive Taxonomy: Evaluation/Critical Thinking (CT)			
Rubric Criteria*	Assessment Decisions		
	Remedial CT Training	Targeted CT Training	Advanced CT Training
Planning	−	−	+
Comparing	−	−	+
Observing	−	+	+
Contrasting	−	+	+
Classifying	−	+	+

*Criteria were adapted from Smith & Kulikowich (2004)

Figure 27.3 Rubrics cube applied to medium-stakes decisions, Cognitive Taxonomy

master all criteria. Lastly, students who earned all pluses are ready to move on to the advanced CT training.

Figure 27.4 represents an assessment-decision-focused slice of the three-dimensional heuristic rubrics cube for the behavioral/psychomotor taxonomy level (operation) with two rubric criteria crossed with three assessment decisions in a fictional, authentic assessment of pilot performance adapted from a study by Mulqueen, Baker, and Dismukes (2000). The 4-point scale in Figure 27.4 represents analytic assessment decisions regarding students' ability to apply knowledge in two criteria. For example, an assessment decision could be made whereby students need to repeat simulation training if they scored a total of less than '5'. Similar assessment-decision logic could apply to the supervised practicum and solo flight where advancement is based on meeting or surpassing specified cutoff scores.

Figure 27.5 represents an assessment-decision-focused slice of the three-dimensional heuristic rubrics cube for the valuing level of Krathwohl's (1964) affective taxonomy. Figure 27.5 involves authentic assessment because students are involved in a real-life context and are asked to self assess their community service experiences using holistically judged reflection. For some students, their self-assessment decision would be to engage in additional community service to increase their valuing of community to the level they deem appropriate.

Behavioral/Psychomotor Taxonomy: Operating Equipment/Work Performance (WP)			
Rubric Criteria*	Assessment Decisions		
	Repeat Simulation	Supervised Practicum	Solo Flight
Technical	1 2 3 4	1 2 3 4	1 2 3 4
Team Work	1 2 3 4	1 2 3 4	1 2 3 4
*Decision rule**	*Total < 5*	*Total >= 5 &< 8*	*Total = 8*

*Criteria were adapted from Mulqueen et al. (2000)

**Decision rule represents a cutoff score for each assessment decision.

Figure 27.4 Rubrics cube applied to high-stakes decisions, Behavioral/Psychomotor Taxonomy

Affective Taxonomy: Value/Attitudes Towards Community (VATC)	
Rubric Criteria	Assessment Decisions
	Self-Assessment Question
Reflection	Describe how your community service has affected your values and attitudes toward the community and decide whether additional community service would be beneficial.

Figure 27.5 Rubrics cube applied to a low-stakes decision, Affective Taxonomy

Assessment Stakes Level (Assessment Decisions) by Methods

Thus far, in discussing Figure 27.2, the learning taxonomy dimension has been discussed as it relates to the assessment-stakes level dimension and the assessment decisions, but the methods dimension has not yet been addressed. It is critical to note that valid assessment decisions can be made only if the reliability and validity of the rubrics (i.e., methods dimension) involved have been established. Without an evidentiary validity argument, the decisions may be called into question, or in a worst-case, high-stakes assessment scenario, challenged "in a court of law" (Wilkerson & Lang, 2003, p. 3).

Central to the heuristic value of the rubrics cube is the notion that the methods employed to estimate inter-rater reliability and validity are contingent on the assessment stakes level. If the assessment-stakes level is low, then the authors suggest only consensus reliability (percentage of agreement between raters) and content validity need to be established. On the other hand, as represented by the authors in Figure 27.2, if the assessment-stakes level is high, then consensus and consistency inter-rater reliability as well as content, construct, and criterion-related validity evidence need to be assembled. The realities of the medium-stakes assessment level will determine how much evidence may be gathered in support of the assessment decision. Because the establishment of adequate reliability estimates is a necessary condition for the establishment of validity (and, indeed, the size of a validity coefficient is limited by the size of the reliability estimate), the estimations of validity and reliability are both included in the methods dimension of the rubrics cube. Currently, in the higher education literature, it can be difficult to locate exemplars where evidentiary validity arguments have been made for rubrics. But this does not justify describing the task of validating rubrics as an insurmountable one, because some exemplars are beginning to surface in the higher education literature. With this in mind, Figure 27.6 presents six key studies highlighting the types of inter-rater reliability and validity demonstrated for low, medium, and high-stakes assessment decisions. The studies summarized in the figure are next discussed in greater detail.

Low-Stakes Assessment

Study 1

Faced with the need to judge the quality of research presentations by 204 undergraduate, masters, and doctoral students across multiple disciplines, Bresciani et al. (2009) address what may be termed a low-stakes assessment task because consequences to the student presenters were never specified and appeared to be nil. Based on an extensive review of internal rubrics as well as rubrics for the review of publication submissions, a multidisciplinary team of 20 faculty members devised a rubric comprised of four content area constructs (organization, originality, significance, and discussion/summary) and a fifth construct for presentation delivery that was applied by judges with no formal training in the use of the rubrics. Thus, two taxonomies (cognitive and behavioral) were involved and therefore dealt with all cells of the lowest layer of the rubrics cube portrayed in Figure 27.2 with the exception of those associated with the affective taxonomy. In developing their five-construct rubric, the researchers employed a 5-point Likert scale with unambiguous, construct-specific descriptors labeling each point of the scale deemed equally applicable across multiple disciplines. Inter-rater reliability/internal consistency was estimated using intraclass correlations which were computed for each of 40 multiple-presenter sessions based on an inter-rater data structure where 3 to 7 judges rated 6 to 8 student presentations per session. Bresciani et al. (2009) reported moderately high intraclass correlations. It could be argued that Bresciani et al. (2009) made good-faith efforts to establish the content validity of their rubrics. Although the researchers did not report any construct validity or criterion-related validity results, the validity argument they presented was adequate for their low-stakes assessment situation.

	Reliability • Consensus • Consistency	Content Validity	Construct Validity • Convergent • Discriminant	Criterion-related Validity • Concurrent • Predictive
Low Stakes Assessment				
Study 1—Research Quality (Bresciani, et al., 2009)	Consistency	Yes	No	No
Medium Stakes Assessment				
Study 2—Delphi method (Allen & Knight, 2009)	Consensus / Agreement	Yes	No	No
Study 3—Comparing generalizabilty & multifaceted Rasch models (Smith & Kulikowich, 2004)	Consistency	Not described	Yes	No
High Stakes Assessment				
Study 4—Multifaceted Rasch model study of rater reliability (Mulqueen, et al., 2000)	Consistency	Not described	Not described	No
Study 5—Performance assessment (Pecheone & Chung, 2006)	Consistency	Yes	Yes	Yes (Concurrent)
Study6—Minimum Competency Exam (Goodman, et al, 2008)	Not described	Yes	Yes	Yes (Concurrent/ Predictive)

Figure 27.6 Key studies highlighting stakes assessment dimension/decisions by methods

Medium-Stakes Assessment

Study 2

In a medium-stakes assessment context, Allen and Knight (2009) presented a step-by-step, iterative process for designing and validating a writing assessment rubric. The study involved assessment activities concentrated on Bloom's cognitive taxonomy as displayed in Figure 27.2. It was considered a medium-stakes assessment because the decisions had some effects on learners' knowledge and skills but were not determinants of critical decisions. In this study, faculty and professionals worked in collaboration to develop agreed-upon criteria that were in accordance with intended learning outcomes and professional competence. Using content-related evidence resulting from baseline data, the rubric was further refined and expanded. The Delphi method, a qualitative research methodology which extracts knowledge from a panel of experts (Cyphert & Gant, 1970), was adopted by these authors as a means for developing group consensus to assign scoring weights for each category in the rubric. Accordingly, the method was implemented with separate groups of professionals and faculty in order to reach consensus on the weights of each rubric category so as to improve the construct validity of the rubric.

The study then utilized two-way Analysis of Variance (factorial ANOVA) techniques to identify the sources of variability in rubric scores. Student writing samples were first grouped into two piles based on quality of writing. Faculty and professionals used the scoring rubric to grade writing samples that were randomly selected from each pile. Significant differences between the average scores for the two piles of writing samples indicated that the rubric differentiated the quality of student writing, while non-significant differences between average scores given by faculty and professionals indicated that there was rater agreement in scoring. The same data were reanalyzed using an ANOVA to measure rater agreement within the faculty and professional group. Discrepancies in scores were discussed throughout the scoring process. The authors concluded that smaller estimated variance in rubric scores existed in higher quality writing samples. They also raised concerns over various interpretations of rubric categories that had affected rating consistency. It was suggested that descriptors for each level of performance needed to be added to each category in the rubric to help clarify the scoring category and guide the scoring process. The evidentiary validity argument presented by Allen and Knight (2009) could be improved by the inclusion of concurrent validity estimates.

Study 3

Two approaches—Generalizability theory (G-theory; see Webb, Shavelson & Steedle, this volume) and Multi-Faceted-Rasch Measurement (MFRM)—were used to explore psychometric properties of student responses collected from a simulated assessment activity involving the cognitive taxonomy (problem-solving skills) and medium-stakes assessment decision (students would be selected as the coach of a fictional kickball team). Five questions that measured the complex problem-solving skills of observing, classifying, comparing, contrasting, and planning were given to 44 students and scored by two judges at two points in time with a three-month interval (Smith & Kulikowich, 2004). The authors first adopted G-theory to explicitly quantify multiple sources of errors and the effect of errors on the ranking order of subjects. In their first-stage Generalizability analysis, estimates of the variability of four facets (subject, item, judge, and occasion) were first obtained from the fully crossed, random-effects model. The estimates—Generalizability (G) coefficients—were used as sample estimates. The second stage of analysis illustrated how different components of measurement errors could be reduced in repeated studies for the purpose of obtaining optimal generalizability for making decisions.

These authors continued their study by employing MFRM analysis with the same data to further estimate variance accounted for by differences in subjects, judges, items, and occasions. Since MFRM is an extension of the basic Rasch model for which unidimensionality and local independence are two assumptions, Smith and Kulikowich (2004) noted that if these assumptions are met, the data should "provide a precise and generalizable measure of performance" (p. 627). Using associated fit statistics—infit and outfit—Smith and Kulikowich (2004) investigated the extent to which data fit the model (model-data fit) and identified the degree of consistency for each element within each facet. FACETS (Linacre, 1988), a computer program, was used to calculate reliability of separation and chi-square statistics in providing the information on individual elements (subjects, items, raters, occasions) within each facet (subject, item, rater, occasion). The FACETS results indicated that planning was the most difficult item, followed by comparing, observing, contrasting, and classifying. They further reported that complex problem-solving skills were different from student to student. In particular, differences in perceptions on the items were found for five students. The significant reliability of separation ($p = 0.00$) and non-significant associated chi-square ($p = 0.2$) indicated that judges were very consistent in "their ratings and overall severity level, and their influence on the estimation of person measures is minimal" (p. 635). Consistency between occasions also provided acceptable calibration fit statistic values of 0.5 to 1.5 for the mean square, reliability of separation (p = 0.00), and chi-square statistics (p = .05). Because judges consistently rated items in accordance with item difficulty, this supported the underlying construct of the complex problem-solving skills. Also, the Rasch model essentially establishes construct validity because any items not fitting the model constitute instances of multidimensionality and are subject to modification or deletion. Therefore, Smith and Kulikowich (2004) demonstrated construct validity and, indeed, indicated that the findings may provide additional information on the hierarchy of the complex problem-solving skills. However, the evidentiary validity argument presented by Smith and Kulikowich (2004) could be improved by describing content validity estimates and by presenting some concurrent validity estimates.

High-Stakes Assessment

Study 4

In contrast to study 1 which provided raters with no formal training, study 4 by Mulqueen et al. (2000) not only provided rater training but also measured the effectiveness of the training in addition to other factors (i.e., ratee ability, task performance difficulty, and rater severity/leniency/bias) utilizing a MFRM approach. Mulqueen et al. (2000) addressed what may be termed a high-stakes assessment task involving pilot training (job simulation) with trainee consequences being flight certification or additional training. Based on a series of three videotaped aircrew scenarios, airline pilot instructors were trained to rate the teamwork and technical ability of each member of a two-person crew utilizing a four-point Likert scale with each point described by a one-word, assessment-decision-focused descriptor (i.e., repeat-debrief-standard-excellent). Although the events being rated were only described in general terms (teamwork and technical ability), the researchers indicated performance was being rated and presumably involved the cognitive and behavioral taxonomies and therefore dealt with all cells of the highest layer of the rubrics cube portrayed in Figure 27.2 with the exception of those associated with the affective taxonomy. The researchers did not describe how they developed their rubric and provided no rational content or construct validity for the training program. However, Mulqueen et al. (2000) reported that the training program displayed "separation reliability" because the three crews videotaped were judged to be low, moderate, and high in their ability. The multi-faceted Rasch analysis identified raters who were too lenient or too harsh. Mulqueen et al. (2000) noted that while the multi-faceted Rasch model has many advantages, the startup involves cumbersome data and programming by an individual trained in the multi-faceted Rasch modeling. Because Mulqueen et al. (2000) did not present an evidentiary argument that included content, construct, and criterion-related validity estimation, additional work is needed in order to meet the stringent validity standards associated with a high-stakes assessment decision.

Study 5

Pecheone and Chung (2006) reported a study that proposed meeting state credentialing mandates with utilization of authentic assessment. The study addressed a high-stakes assessment context across all three taxonomies (cognitive, behavioral, and affective) and therefore dealt with the top layer of the rubrics cube portrayed in Figure 27.2. In a pilot effort to promote an alternative assessment to state credentialing, the Performance Assessment for California Teachers (PACT) was created by a coalition of California colleges and universities. Because this is a high-stakes assessment, PACT was required by the state to report reliability and validity estimates for the measures. Pecheone and Chung (2006) defined validity as referring ". . . to the appropriateness, meaningfulness, and usefulness of evidence that is used to support the decisions involved in granting an initial license to prospective teachers" (p. 28). Thus, a series of studies was conducted in order to collect evidence of content, construct, and concurrent validity along with rater consistency on PACT scores from pilot samples since 2002. Using expert judgment from teacher educators, the content representation and job-relatedness of the Teaching Event (TE) elements (e.g. rubrics) was examined and validated. Factor analysis was performed to determine whether or not clusters of interrelated elements loaded into hypothesized TE categories. The results from separate factor analyses conducted in two pilot years supported the underlying TE construct categories. To further substantiate the construct validity of PACT, Pecheone and Chung (2007) conducted correlation analyses between mean task scores and documented the results in a PACT Technical Report (2007). Pecheone and Chung (2006) concluded significant correlations between mean scores across PACT tasks demonstrated that ". . . scorers can differentiate their judgments of teacher competence across scoring tasks and that there is reasonable cohesiveness across the dimensions of teaching" (p. 32).

Pecheone and Chung (2006) conducted an additional two sets of studies to examine the external validity of PACT scores—namely, their ability to validly differentiate candidates who met minimum teaching performance standards from those who did not. In the first study, the authors found strong agreement between TE analytic-rubric scores and holistic ratings of candidate performance used to grant preliminary teaching credentials. The second study reported 90% agreement between TE scores and candidate competency as evaluated by their faculty and supervisors. Consensus estimates, obtained by calculating percent agreement between raters, resulted in 90% to 91% level of agreement within one point (on a 1–4 point scale) across a two-year preliminary study. In the second pilot year, the authors also investigated inter-rater reliability for each task and the full year by using the Spearman-Brown Prophecy reliability statistic and the standard error of scoring (SES) to quantify the amount of variation associated with raters. The inter-rater reliability for the 2003–04 year was 0.88 and across TE tasks was in the range of 0.65 to 0.75. In addition, PACT adopted an evidence-based three-stage standard setting model to determine cut-off scores for granting teaching credentials. Using a consensus based process, the passing standards have been continuously reviewed and revised and were adopted in 2007. Although Pecheone and Chung (2006, 2007) proposed a predictive validation study to see if TE scores predicted candidate performance in a real-job context, the analysis had yet to be implemented since PACT was not approved as a high-stakes assessment in the state of California. To summarize, Pecheone and Chung (2006, 2007) presented a convincing evidentiary validity argument that would be strengthened by the inclusion of the proposed predictive validity study.

Study 6

In a teacher-education study involving 150 teacher candidates, Goodman et al. (2008) also addressed a high-stakes assessment context across all three taxonomies displayed in Figure 27.2 as was done in Study 5. Next, consider the methods these researchers employed in developing two sets of performance-based rubrics. One 20-item rubric designed to assess professional attributes had a maximum score of 100. Although student performance was judged by faculty members and master school-based teacher educators (SBTE), no inter-rater reliability estimates were reported. Nor was an internal consistency reliability estimate reported in the study. The authors reported significant concurrent validity estimated by a Pearson correlation ($r = .39$) between the professional attributes rubric and portfolio scores. The authors also reported significant predictive validity estimated by a Pearson correlation ($r = .34$ and $r = .25$) between the professional attributes rubric and two teacher certification examinations.

The second rubric, designed to assess student teaching performance via a portfolio, had a maximum score of 300 based on student presentation rated by a cluster coordinator. Although Goodman et al. (2008) referred to the domains being assessed, they did not describe the methods utilized in creating the rubric criteria for these domains, nor did they provide descriptors for the scoring. As noted above, the authors reported significant concurrent validity estimated by a Pearson correlation between the portfolio scores and the profession attributes rubric scores (r = .39). Goodman et al. (2008) also reported significant predictive validity estimated by a Pearson correlation between the portfolio scores and one teacher certification examination (r = .27). Thus, Goodman et al. (2008) presented a sound evidentiary validity argument that will be strengthened by increased reliability estimates which should improve the validity estimation evidence.

Discussion and Summary

The issue of rubric score generalizability is one that warrants discussion. Unlike psychological test development efforts intended to be universally applicable (such as tests designed to measure needs or motivations), rubrics upon initial consideration appear to be domain-specific and often are drawn from small, convenience samples. If indeed, the rubrics are domain-specific, then perhaps the heuristic rubrics cube introduced in this chapter can also serve a categorizing/coding role as was done in the discussion of the studies summarized in Figure 27.6. In other words, the rubrics cube itself may serve as a rubric for judging the evidence being generated by rubric validation studies. Through systematic recording of rubric findings according to the rubrics cube three dimensions, generalizable findings may eventually be deduced from the patterns of evidence that emerge from taxonomic-domain-specific findings. Studies that directly assess the variability associated with a task facet (or a rubric facet) may be particularly helpful in increasing the generalizability of findings.

The issue of the small, convenience samples serving as the basis of rubric validation efforts can be addressed from a variety of approaches. For one thing, metastudies of rubric validation will eventually be feasible as the field progresses. Also, the findings of state-wide initiatives (such as Study 5—Pecheone and Chung, 2006, 2007, and Study 6—Goodman, et. al., 2008) begin to increase the scope of the inference space that is generalizable. A suggested role for research sponsored by the Department of Education would be to gather requests for proposals to systematically study a high-stakes assessment "setting" (such as university systems, states, accreditation agency jurisdictions, etc.) facet for critical areas such as authentic teacher certification efforts. It would be reasonable for consortia of colleges of education to conduct rubric validation studies in the high-stakes assessment area of authentic teacher certification measures. Accreditation agencies could foster these efforts by serving as a dissemination vehicle for promising rubrics. Such efforts would help foster an educator-friendly validation environment and would supplement efforts by institutional research and assessment offices.

The issue of fairness in the high-stakes assessment context was raised in Study 5 and Study 6; they are to be commended for testing effects of race/ethnicity on performance scores. The authors emphasize that in accordance with the *Standards for Educational and Psychological Testing* (AERA, APA, and NCME, 1999), valid assessment rubrics should apply equally across gender and ethnicity subgroups. Rubrics displaying gender/ethnicity subgroup differences need to be revised as per Figure 27.1 until they apply equally across these subgroups.

In summary, learning goals are not formulated and rubrics are not utilized in theoretical vacuums. Indeed, one way of making sense of rubrics is to acknowledge that they are methodological tools framed by one of the assessment-stakes levels depicted in the heuristic rubrics cube (Figure 27.2). Using the rubrics cube as a conceptual organizer, this chapter systematically cited examples from the literature and compared/categorized how researchers utilized and validated rubrics. Lastly, from a utilitarian-assessment perspective, a rubric will have served its purpose well if accreditors (in the case of high-stakes educational assessments) or other stakeholders accept the evidentiary argument of valid learning gathered by the rubric as the basis for a positive assessment decision. Otherwise, the rubric will not have served its purpose and would need to be revised as part of a continuous quality improvement process.

References

Aitken, N., & Pungur, L. (2010). Authentic assessment. Retrieved January 11, 2010 from http://education. alberta.ca/apps/aisi/literature/pdfs/Authentic_Assessment_UofAb_UofL.PDF

Allen, S., & Knight. J. (2009). A method for collaboratively developing and validating a rubric. *International Journal for the Scholarship of Teaching and Learning, 3*(2). Retrieved from http://academics.georgiasouthern. edu/ijsotl/v3n2/articles/PDFs/Article_AllenKnight.pdf

American Educational Research Association, American Psychological Association, and National Council of Measurement in Education. (1999). *Standards for educational and psychological testing.* Washington, DC: American Educational Research Association.

Banta, T. W., Griffin, M., Flateby, T. L., and Kahn, S. (2009). *Three promising alternatives for assessment college students' knowledge and skills.* Retrieved January 3, 2010 from http://learningoutcomesassessment.org/documents/AlternativesforAssessment.pdf

Bloom, B. S. (Ed.). (1956). *Taxonomy of educational objectives: Handbook 1, Cognitive domain.* New York, NY: Longman.

Bresciani, M. J., Oakleaf. M., Kolkhorst. F., Nebeker, C., Barlow. J., Duncan, K., & Hickmott, J. (2009). Examining design and inter-rater reliability of a rubric measuring research quality across multiple disciplines. *Practical Assessment, Research & Evaluation, 14*(12). Retrieved from http://pareonline.net/pdf/v14n12.pdf

Cyphert, F. R., & Gant, W. L. (1970). The Delphi technique: A tool for collecting opinions in teacher education. *Journal of Teacher Education, 31,* 417–425.

Eder, D. J. (2001). Accredited programs and authentic assessment. In C. A. Palomba, & T. W. Banta (Eds.), *Assessing student competence in accredited disciplines: Pioneering approaches to assessment in higher education* (pp. 199–216). Sterling, VA: Stylus.

Geisinger, K., Shaw, L. H., & McCormick, C. (this volume). *The validation of tests in higher education.*

Goodman, G., Arbona, C., & de Rameriz, R. D. (2008). High-stakes, minimum-competency exams: how competent are they for evaluating teacher competence? *Journal of Teacher Education, 59*(1), 24–39.

Hynes, K., & Givner, N. (1981). Restriction of range effects on the New MCAT's predictive validity. *Journal of Medical Education, 56,* 352–3.

Kane, M. T. (1992). An argument-based approach to validity. *Psychological Bulletin, 112,* 527–535.

Kane, M. (1994). Validating the performance standards associated with passing scores. *Review of Educational Research, 64*(3), 425–461.

Kane, M. (2006). Validation. In R. L. Brennan (Ed.), *Educational measurement* (4th ed. pp. 17–64). Washington, DC: American Council on Education/Praeger.

Krathwohl, D. R., Bloom, B. S., & Masia, B. B. (1964). *Taxonomy of educational objectives: Handbook II: Affective domain.* New York, NY: David McKay.

Linacre, J. M. (1988). *FACETS.* Chicago, IL: MESA Press.

Linacre, J. M. (2003). *A user's guide to Winsteps Rasch-Model computer programs.* Chicago, IL: www.Winsteps. com

Moskal, B. M., & Leydens, J. A. (2000). Scoring rubric development: validity and reliability. *Practical Assessment, Research & Evaluation, 7*(10). Retrieved December 17, 2009 from http://PAREonline.net/getvn. asp?v=7&n=10

Mueller, J. (2010). *Authentic assessment toolbox.* Retrieved December 22, 2009 from http://jonathan.mueller. faculty.noctrl.edu/toolbox/rubrics.htm

Mulqueen, C., Baker, D., & Dismukes, R. K. (2000). *Using multifacet Rasch analysis to examine the effectiveness of rater training.* Retrieved February 8, 2010 from http://www.airteams.org/publications/rater_training/multifacet_rasch.pdf

Osterlind, S. J., & Wang, Z. (this volume). *Item response theory in measurement, assessment, and evaluation for higher education.*

Pecheone, R. L., & Chung, R. R. (2006). Evidence in teacher education: the performance assessment for California teachers (PACT). *Journal of Teacher Education, 57*(1), 22–36.

Pecheone, R. L., & Chung, R. R. (2007). *Technical report of the performance assessment for California teachers (PACT): Summary of validity and reliability studies for the 2003–04 pilot year.* Retrieved March 24, 2010 from http://www.pacttpa.org/_files/Publications_and_Presentations/PACT_Technical_Report_March07.pdf

Smith, E. V., Jr., & Kulikowich, J. M. (2004). An application of generalizability theory and many-facet Rasch measurement using a complex problem-solving skills assessment. *Educational and Psychological Measurement, 64*(4), 617–639.

Spicuzza, F. J., & Cunningham, M. L. (2003). Validating recognition and production measures for the bachelor of science in social work. In T. W. Banta (Ed.), *Portfolio assessment: Uses, cases, scoring, and impact.* San Francisco, CA: Jossey-Bass.

Stemler, S. E. (2004). A comparison of consensus, consistency, and measurement approaches to estimating inter-rater reliability. *Practical Assessment, Research & Evaluation, 9*(4). Retrieved February 16, 2010 from http://PAREonline.net/getvn.asp?v=9&n=4

Suskie, L. (2009). *Assessing student learning.* San Francisco, CA: Jossey-Bass.

Thorndike, R. L., & Hagen, E.P. (1977). *Measurement and evaluation in psychology and education.* New York, NY: Wiley.

Traupman, J., & Wilensky, R. (2004). *Collaborative quality filtering: establishing consensus or recovering ground truth?* Retrieved March 22, 2010 from http://maya.cs.depaul.edu/webkdd04/final/traupman.pdf

U.S. Department of Education. (2006). *A test of leadership: charting the future of U.S. higher education.* Washington, DC.

Walvoord, B. E. (2004). *Assessment clear and simple: a practical guide for institutions, departments, and general education.* San Francisco, CA: Jossey-Bass.

Webb, N. M., Shavelson, R. J., & Steedle, J. T. (this volume). *Generalizability theory in assessment contexts.*

Wiberg, M., & Sundstrom, A. (2009). *A comparison of two approaches to correction of restriction of range in correlation analysis.* Retrieved March 22, 2010 from http://pareonline.net/pdf/v14n5.pdf

Wilkerson, J. R., & Lang, W. S. (2003). *Portfolios, the pied piper of teacher certification assessments: Legal and psychometric issues.* Retrieved January 3, 2010 from http://epaa.asu.edu/ojs/article/viewFile/273/399

Winer, B. J. (1971). *Statistical principles and experimental design* (2nd ed.). New York, NY: McGraw Hill.

28

COGNITIVE DIAGNOSTIC METHOD: RULE SPACE, Q-MATRIX THEORY AND APPLICATIONS

Kikumi K. Tatsuoka, Curtis Tatsuoka, Anthony E. Kelly, and Michael Dean

Psychometric advances have been made in modeling how the application of cognitive skills and knowledge interfaces with test item responses. This area of research is known as cognitive diagnosis. Cognitively diagnostic assessment holds the promise of yielding useful and detailed information about student knowledge in areas such as mathematics, language, and other areas of higher education. In turn, this information can help in guiding individualized learning, allow for insight into how learning progresses longitudinally, and even give precise feedback with curriculum development. Pioneering and fundamental research in this area has been done under a framework known as the Rule Space Method (RSM). RSM has been successfully applied to create diagnostic scoring reports for the Preliminary SAT/National Merit Scholarship Qualifying Test (PSAT/NMSQT) and they have been distributed to several million students since 2003.

It is important to note that statistical methods such as factor analysis, cluster analysis, and traditional latent class modeling produce factors, clusters and classes of similar student responses, but it is often difficult to give researchers clear interpretation of the resulting groups. Ideally, diagnostic analyses of test results should be descriptive, objective, and free from ambiguous interpretations, and most importantly expressing an individual's true state of knowledge. To achieve these goals, a new methodology is presented that will transform many unobservable knowledge and skills variables, that is, attributes into measurable variables without losing their original meanings.

Cognitive Diagnosis and the Rule Space Method

In 2009, K. K. Tatsuoka published a book entitled *Cognitive Assessment: An Introduction to the Rule Space Method*. The preface of her book starts with the statement,

> The methodology portrayed in this book is central to current missions in education in the United States. The "No Child Left Behind" Federal Government initiative requires that each state develop diagnostic tests of basic skills that not only assess overall educational progress but also identify areas of individual student weakness that will lead to tailored educational experiences. *(p. xi)*

In this chapter, RSM will be introduced with few mathematical terms. We will describe how it works with an actual state assessment, and how the diagnostic results can be used. Valuable conclusions to improve further learning activities at schools are identified.

In recent years, each state has developed assessments that attempt to not only assess overall educational progress but also to identify areas of an individual student's weaknesses and strengths. Measuring underlying knowledge and cognitive skills is not an easy task because it is impossible to directly observe them. Still, it would be very valuable to provide diagnostic profiles that include information about how well students perform on the underlying knowledge and cognitive processing skills required for answering problems. Cognitive skills and knowledge can be viewed as unobservable variables called "attributes". They can be measured as "mastered" or "not mastered," but RSM also provides individual mastery probabilities for all attributes involved in a test item. In other words, RSM converts item scores for each student into his/her mastery probabilities for all attributes. These are different from the more standard notion of a continuously-valued, unidimensional latent trait variable θ that has been used as an ability measure in what is called Item Response Theory (IRT). (For an introduction to IRT, see Osterlind & Wang, this volume.) IRT is a statistical model that tries to explain student responses on test items by using a mathematical function on a latent variable, θ, called IRT ability. However, numerous latent variables can arise in cognitive diagnosis, and perhaps not just one unidimensional variable. For example, when we closely examine students' performances on a standardized verbal test, we frequently observe individual differences in attribute mastery profiles on items. Although students may have exactly the same scores, they could have entirely different profiles of strengths and weaknesses.

Consider the following example. For two students, Jason and Juliana, suppose they have very different individual attribute profiles, yet both attain 500 on the verbal scale score. Jason is not good at bringing material together from two passages and processing grammatically complex texts. He also does not understand the main idea when it is not explicitly stated. On the other hand, Juliana is not good at synthesizing scattered information and applying general background knowledge; however, her global understanding of the passage is good. Juliana can still have the same IRT ability value, and hence the same scale score, as Jason.

RSM can determine an individual's strengths and weaknesses, such as has been applied to the PSAT to generate scoring reports. These reports on attribute mastery can be used to inform schools, teachers and parents, and elaborate more precisely what a total score of, say, 500 means for each individual student. For example, analogy items in language assessment involve skills to process difficult vocabulary, ability to process complex concepts and relationships, skills to process multiple meanings (semantic ambiguity, syntactic ambiguity), skills to process negative rationale, complex rationale, skills to analyze and contrast concepts, ability to deploy background knowledge in the realm of scientific discourse, and the ability to discount the influence of emotive language. These skills are termed "attributes" in this chapter. Table 28.1 contrasts two test takers A and B who scored the same scaled score of 500. The attribute mastery probability values listed in the column named "Norm" are computed from the population of test takers. Student A has better probabilities of mastery for Attributes 3, 6, 8, 11, 12, and 13, while Student B obtained higher than the Norm for Attributes 1, 2, 4, 5, 6, 9, and 11. The detailed information for explaining how each student performed on a test may be useful for remediation, future instructional planning and curriculum design.

Q-Matrix Theory in RSM as a Tool for Describing the Relationship Between Two Spaces: Unobservable Attributes and Observable Item Scores

As we stated earlier, RSM follows in the framework of statistical pattern recognition and classification methods (e.g., Fukunaga, 1990). This approach is not that familiar to psychometricians in the field of educational measurement, but it has been widely used in engineering and science.

Table 28.1 Comparison of Analogy Attribute Mastery Probabilities for Two Students

Ability to process difficult vocabulary	A	B	Norm
1. Lowest frequency in stem	.78	.99	.90
2. Lowest frequency in key	.12	.99	.80
3. Average of lower frequency Words in four distracters	.99	.91	.98
4. Number of syllables in 4 key	.90	.99	.92
5. Number of syllables in 4 distracters	.34	.99	.81
6. Number of characters in stem	.99	.99	.91
Ability to process complex concepts			
7. Multiple meanings, semantic ambiguity	.99	.99	.99
8. Multiple meanings, syntactic ambiguity	.96	.89	.93
9. To process negative rationale	.01	.60	.35
10. To process complex rationale	.80	.80	.82
11. To analyze and contrast concepts	.99	.99	.92
Ability to deploy background knowledge			
12. To process scientific topics	.71	.40	.40
13. To discount the influence of emotive Language	.99	.50	.75

Note: Although both students have the same scores on the verbal section of the SAT, their patterns of analogy attribute mastery probabilities are different.

Statistical pattern recognition approaches are fairly free from many complicated constraints and unrealistically strict assumptions like unidimensionality of data in IRT. Human cognition is extremely complex and impossible to observe and measure directly unlike test scores or heights or weights of students. Therefore, it makes sense to put forth a methodology with a minimal amount of constraints and assumptions, and RSM provides flexibility in describing how underlying cognitive processing skills, thinking skills, and knowledge (i.e. attributes) are involved in correctly responding to an item. RSM has two phases:

1. Application of Q-matrix theory, which allows for specification of linkages between attributes and item responses, and systematically identifies which mastery profiles of attributes cannot be distinguished from a given item pool (K. K. Tatsuoka, 1990, 1991a, 1991b, 1995, 2009); and
2. Rule space classification, which allows for diagnosis of student item response patterns by associating the patterns to profiles of attribute mastery status (K. K. Tatsuoka, 1983, 1985, 1990, 1995, 2009; K. K. Tatsuoka, & M. M. Tatsuoka, 1987; M. M. Tatsuoka & K. K. Tatsuoka, 1989). A mastery pattern of attributes is called a knowledge state, and each knowledge state can be expressed by a unique item score pattern termed as an ideal item score pattern (K. K. Tatsuoka, 1991a, 1995, 2009).

In practice, Q-matrix theory starts with identifying and coding test items with attributes required to answer an item correctly (K. K. Tatsuoka, 1991a, 1995). Then all possible knowledge states are generated by applying what is known as a Boolean Description Function (BDF) to the Q-matrix. BDF is a mapping of all possible knowledge states generated from a Q-matrix. Suppose that we consider three attributes, A1, A2, and A3 in fraction problems:

- Attribute A_1: Getting the lowest common denominator of two different denominators;
- Attribute A_2: Converting a whole number to a simple fraction; and
- Attribute A_3: Adding two fractions with the same denominator.

Suppose we have three problems:

- i1: Find the lowest common denominator of 2/3 and 1/4,
- i2: Add 2/5 and 1/5, and
- i3: Add 2 and 1/2.

Solutions for these items are:

i1: Common denominator of 2/3   Finding the lowest common A_1
     and 1/4 is 12   denominator

i2: 2/5 + 1/5   = 3/5   Add the numerator and get 3/5 A_3

i3: 2 + 1/2   = 4/2 + 1/2   Converting 2 to 4/2 A_2
                  = 5/2   Add the numerator and get 5/2 A_3

Then, the Q-matrix for these items is:

$$Q = \begin{matrix} & A_1 & A_2 & A_2 \\ i1 & \begin{pmatrix} 1 & 0 & 0 \\ i2 & 0 & 0 & 1 \\ i3 & 0 & 1 & 1 \end{pmatrix} \end{matrix}$$

Let us use this Q-matrix for further discussions. There are three row and three column vectors in this Q-matrix. Attribute A_1 is involved in item 1, Attribute 3 is required in item 2, Attributes 2 and 3 are required in solving item 3. In a Q-matrix, the attributes are represented by vectors (columns) in which 1 is involvement, and 0 is lack of involvement. Therefore, for the attributes A_1, A_2, and A_3, the column vectors of the Q-matrix are given by

$$A_1 = \begin{pmatrix} 1 \\ 0 \\ 0 \end{pmatrix} A_2 = \begin{pmatrix} 0 \\ 0 \\ 1 \end{pmatrix} A_3 = \begin{pmatrix} 0 \\ 1 \\ 1 \end{pmatrix}$$

Let us assume Mary cannot convert a whole number into a simple fraction but can do A_1 and A_3, in other words, Mary has the attribute mastery pattern of (1, 0, 1). Then her most plausible response pattern of three items will be i1 = 1, but i2 = 1, and i3 = 0, because the Q-matrix indicates i1 and i2 do not require A_2 but i3 requires application of A_2 correctly. We get the ideal item score pattern of (1, 0, 1) that corresponds to attribute mastery pattern of (1, 0, 1).

The conceptual framework of the RSM and the Q-matrix theory may not be easy to grasp intuitively. Figure 28.1 (from K. K. Tatsuoka, 2009) shows complicated but elegant abstract relationships among a space of attribute-mastery patterns, and a space of item responses. In this figure, the shapes in the lower left (attribute pool, attribute-mastery patterns, etc.) represent variables that are impossible to observe directly, while those in the upper left (item pool, ideal-item score pattern, etc.) are observable variables. The item pool on top is connected to the attribute pool on the bottom through a Q-matrix (the box in the middle, labeled as incidence matrix) that represents latent variables. By applying a BDF to this Q-matrix, we can connect the ideal-item score patterns above to the attribute-mastery patterns below. In other words, the Q-matrix serves as a tool for constructing the relationship between two spaces: the unobservable attribute-mastery patterns and the observable ideal item score patterns.

However, the number of potential knowledge states expressed by binary attribute patterns is a large number, up to 2^k for K attributes. To understand this, one must recognize that there is mastery (correct status) and a non-mastery (incorrect status) for each attribute. To deal with this issue, K. K. Tatsuoka (1991a, 1995, 2009) introduced several statistical and mathematical properties that reduce

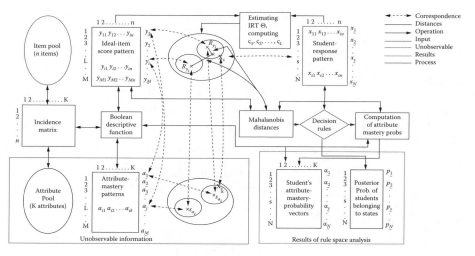

Figure 28.1 Conceptual framework of the rule space methodology

From *Cognitive assessment: An introduction to the rule space method* (p. 163), by K. K. Tatsuoka, New York, NY: Routledge Academic. Copyright 2009 by Taylor & Francis Group, LLC. Reprinted with permission.

the number of knowledge states generated from the Q-matrix to a manageable number, and yet, BDF establishes the one to one correspondence between ideal item score patterns and attribute mastery patterns. This relationship is very important when we estimate probabilities of attribute mastery. For more detailed discussions of various mathematical theorems and properties in the Q-matrix theory, see K. K. Tatsuoka (2009). See also C. Tatsuoka (1996, 2002) and C. Tatsuoka and Ferguson (2003).

Since unobservable latent attribute mastery patterns are connected to ideal item score patterns, one can make inferences about the performances on attributes from performances on the observable items. Now we classify a given student's item response pattern into one of a list of knowledge states generated from our Q-matrix. Rule space refers to the classification space.

Rule Space Classification

Suppose we have a student's item response pattern and want to determine which knowledge states may account for it. A plausible approach is to match the student's response pattern (upper right in Figure 28.1) one-by-one, to all the ideal item score patterns (upper left in Figure 28.1) in a list of patterns (not illustrated) generated by BDF from the Q-matrix (incidence matrix in Figure 28.1). In practice, this approach is difficult and prone to error. We need a good decision rule based on statistical theory.

Rule space is a classification space spanned by IRT θ as the X-axis and Zeta as the index, on the Y-axis (K. K. Tatsuoka, 1983, 1984, 1985). The Zeta index is the standardized covariance, f(xi) of two residuals for a given person i: or, $f(x_i) = \Sigma_{j=1,n}[\text{cov}(P_j(\theta_i) - x_i)(P_j(\theta_i) - T(\theta_i))]$ where $P_j(\theta_i)$ is item response function of item j, xi is person i's item response pattern, $T(\theta_i)$ is the mean of $P_j(\theta_i)$ for all items. The standardized covariance can be thought of as the relationship of the difference between a given item response function of one latent attribute and its observed counterpart standardized by the difference for the average or mean of all the item response functions. This index works to differentiate the item response patterns with the same IRT ability value θ into scattered points in the rule space. By so doing the examples in Table 28.1 can be diagnosed as having two different attribute mastery patterns. Since the estimation of θ_i and computation f(x_i) are linear continuous operations, two close item response patterns should be two close points in the rule space. In Chapter 5 in K. K. Tatsuoka (2009), the 39 knowledge states are found in fraction subtraction problems. Since f(x) is considered as one of the person-fit statistics (K. K. Tatsuoka, 1997), the points located the upper part and lower part of the rule space correspond to unusual item response patterns. Therefore one can interpret the characteristics of any knowledge states located in the rule space. Some knowledge states are popular among high scoring students while others are not.

It is well known (e.g., Fukunaga, 1990; M. Tatsuoka, 1988) that for the multihypothesis test for many classification groups, say M groups, Bayesian decision rules give the best results with respect to minimizing the classification errors. Bayesian decision rules take into account prior information about the probability of errors of classification. Under a loss function that assigns 0 for a correct classification, and a 1 for an incorrect one, the Bayes decision rule is to select the state with the maximum posterior probability values among M groups after observing data and updating. Posterior probabilities can be thought of as probabilities that are obtained after prior information is taken into account. In order to obtain updated posterior probabilities, the prior distribution and the conditional density functions are required to employ Bayes theorem. For readers not familiar with the meaning of a conditional density function, they should think of it as similar to a plot of the simple frequency distribution of posterior probabilities.

For Rule Space, classification decision rules are based on computed Mahalanobis distance (weighted Euclidian distance or orthogonal distance) of two points in the Rule Space, one being the empirically determined by a student's response data, the other generated from an ideal response pattern. (To think of it another way, the Mahalanobis distance is like the X and Y axis but is shifted somewhat off right angles.) This is optimal under the assumption of normality of the Rule Space indices. The detailed discussion on the classification decision rule in the Rule space is given in Chapters 6, 7 and 8, from pages 165 to 239 of K. K. Tatsuoka (2009), so we just state the classification criteria for our example in this chapter. Note that these posterior probabilities among the classification states embody our best, updated knowledge of the identity of a student's cognitive profile.

In review, the rule space classification determines membership probabilities of the student to their closest ideal item response patterns. Then, a vector of attribute mastery probabilities can be given as this student's diagnosis, obtained by averages of mastery profiles weighted by respective posterior probabilities. One of the innovative characteristics of RSM is that it entails developing correspondences between an examinee's observed item response pattern and the corresponding ideal item score pattern(s). By so doing, we can make an inference about how well an individual has performed on latent (unobservable) attributes from his/her performance on observable item responses. This pattern of mastered and non-mastered attributes is referred to as the student's "knowledge state." Diagnosed knowledge states are vectors summarizing combinations of attributes mastered and not mastered by students. Results of the RSM are stored in a dataset consisting of an attribute mastery vector for each student. Because an RSM analysis converts a dataset of specific test item responses for each student into a vector of attribute mastery probabilities, one can merge the item response patterns of several different tests into a single dataset of students by attributes, as long as tests share the same set of attributes. This property of the RSM is particularly suitable to the sampling design of the TIMSS, or NAEP because the RSM results from several exam booklets can be merged into a single dataset of students by attribute mastery.

Application of RSM to Large Scale State Assessment

We have introduced the outline of RSM and Q-matrix Theory in the previous section. This section introduces how this cognitively diagnostic methodology can be applied to a large-scale state math assessment, and what kind of information can be obtained. Also, discussion of the diagnostic results and their implications for future improvement of students' learning and teaching, and more efficient educational practices are described. For this example, students all come from a county-wide school district (N = 14,969).

Content, Process Attributes, and Special Skills of the Mathematics Items in Some State Assessment

The source of potential attributes for Rule Space analysis in the mathematics items of this test is from a painstaking task analysis and study of written protocols (K. K. Tatsuoka, Kelly, C. M. Tatsuoka, Varadi, & Dean, 2007). In the first instance, all math items are solved by our team of experts, and then solutions are compared. This is the first step in identifying the content and process skills needed in solving each item.

Math attributes previously obtained from the analysis of items from the SAT and GRE, along with TIMSS-R (Birenbaum et al., 1993; Chen et al., 2008; Dogan & K. K. Tatsuoka, 2010; Guerrero, Yamada, & K. K. Tatsuoka, 2004; K. K. Tatsuoka et al., 2000, 2004, 2006, 2009), are also used as the original pool of our potential cognitive attributes. Figure 28.2 demonstrates how mathematics items are decomposed into several attributes, and Table 28.2 is a brief summary description of attributes.

Then a Q-matrix—n items by k attributes of the binary incidence matrix—is coded using the attributes described in Table 28.2. This set of attributes is very similar to the attributes involved in SAT/GRE/TIMSS items (including content, and process attributes).

Example 1. *A dairy farmer is filling his cylindrical storage tank with fresh milk. The tank has been filled with 45 gallons as shown below. Which of the following is the best estimate of the number of gallons the entire tank will hold?*

F. 45 gallons: G. 90 gallons: H. 180 gallons: I. 270 gallons

A geometrical figure is given--S3(Geometry)
This item asks estimation from the figure given above. This is a cylinder storage and the volume must be estimated.--C4
We estimate about ¼ of the tank is filled with milk. --------------------------------S5
We supposed to get the "best" estimate by multiply 4 to 45---------------------P10
"best" is quantitative reading.

Example 2. *Xavier spent his $10.00 allowance at the county fair. He brought a hot dog and soda for $2.00 and went on n rides, which cost $0.50 each. The equation below can be used to find the number of rides Xavier went on.*
      2.00 + 0.50n = 10.00
How many rides did Xavier go on?

A.   4
B.   8
C.   16
D.   20

Solution and coding: This problem uses a variable and equation------------------------c3
The relationship of the variable and cost, expense is explained in verbal----------------p1
(P1 usually expects a student derive the relationship expressed in
Equation of n for Grade 8, we coded because the meaning of the equation
must be understood by a 7th grader.)
The question asks to get n, which means he/she must solve the equation----------------p4
Plugging a number in n and find the solution may occur.///

Figure 28.2 Example of attribute coding for mathematics items.

Table 28.2 Modified List of Knowledge, Skill, and Process Attributes Derived to Explain Performance on Mathematics Items from the TIMSS–R (1999) for Population 2 (8th graders) for FAC Project

Label	Attribute
CONTENT ATTRIBUTES	
C1	Basic concepts and operations in whole numbers and integers
C2	Basic concepts and operations in fractions and decimals
EXP	Powers, Roots and Scientific expression of numbers are separated from C2
C3	Basic concepts and operations in elementary algebra
C4	Basic concepts and operations in 2–dimensional geometry
C5	Data, and basic statistics
PROB	Probability and combinatorics are separated from C5
PROCESS ATTRIBUTES	
P1	Translate/formulate/understand (only for 7th graders) equations and expressions to solve a problem
P2	Computational applications of knowledge in arithmetic and geometry
P3	Judgmental applications of knowledge in arithmetic and geometry
P4	Applying rules in algebra and solving equations (plugging in included for 7th graders)
P5	Logical reasoning—includes case reasoning, deductive thinking skills, if–then, necessary and sufficient conditions, generalization skills
P6	Problem search; analytic thinking, problem restructuring; inductive thinking
P7	Generating, visualizing and reading figures and graphs
P8★	Applying and evaluating mathematical correctness
P9	Management of data and complex procedures, and be able to set multi goals
P10	Quantitative and logical reading (less than, must, need to be, at least, best etc.)
SKILL (ITEM TYPE) ATTRIBUTES	
S1	Unit conversion
S2	Apply number properties and relationships; number sense/number line
S3	Using figures, tables, charts and graphs
S3g	Using geometric figures
S4	Approximation/estimation
S5	Evaluate/verify/check options
S6	Patterns and relationships (inductive thinking skills)
S7	Using proportional reasoning
S8	Solving novel or unfamiliar problems
S9	Comparison of two/or more entities

★ Omitted due to the lack of requirement in a RSM analysis

Summary Statistics of RSM Classification Results

A large percentage of students are successfully classified into one of the predetermined knowledge states generated from the Q-matrix; Table 28.3 summarizes the descriptive statistics of the RSM results. However, these descriptive statistics alone may not be useful enough in their current form for teachers who may want to improve their quality of teaching.

Since RSM provides individual diagnostic scoring reports for students, Figure 28.3 has an example of a hypothetical student's scoring report. The student with ID of 46672 in School 21 obtained his score of 28, which belongs to the 27th percentile. Norms for attribute mastery probabilities are

Table 28.3 Descriptive Statistics of Attributes for the School District

Attribute	N	Minimum	Maximum	Mean	Std. Deviation
C1	14969	.00	1.00	.7163	.33448
C2	14969	.00	1.00	.8507	.30150
C3	14969	.00	1.00	.7831	.27770
C4	14969	.00	1.00	.9304	.23515
C5	14969	.00	1.00	.7919	.34211
C6	14969	.00	1.00	.3873	.30332
expont	14969	.00	1.00	.5222	.30874
prob	14969	.00	1.00	.4093	.31788
S1	14969	.00	1.00	.6992	.36235
S2	14969	.00	1.00	.8593	.28897
S3	14969	.00	1.00	.9458	.18448
S3g	14969	.00	1.00	.9481	.20400
S4	14969	.00	1.00	.6850	.30891
S5	14969	.00	1.00	.7552	.32937
S6	14969	.00	1.00	.7252	.31940
S7	14969	.00	1.00	.6329	.31494
S9	14969	.00	1.00	.8087	.28439
P1	14969	.00	1.00	.7386	.32956
P2	14969	.00	1.00	.9085	.21866
P3	14969	.00	1.00	.7744	.29775
P4	14969	.00	1.00	.5543	.29360
P5	14969	.00	1.00	.8249	.28549
P6	14969	.00	1.00	.5441	.25316
P7	14969	.00	1.00	.8858	.24545
P9	14969	.00	1.00	.8635	.25721
P10	14969	.00	1.00	.6691	.33826
	14969				

calculated, where a norm is the respective average of an attribute mastery probability among students with the same score. In this example, content and process attributes are listed with their attribute mastery probabilities next to the norms derived from the total sample. Attribute C4, Geometry, has probability of mastery to be 0.99 while the norm is only 0.82. The graph below shows this student's performance on the attributes as compared to the norms. This student performed better than the norm for C2, C4, P1, P9, and P10, but not for C5, prob (Probability), and P2. This student excels in the problems dealing with language (word problems).

An Example of Application of Diagnostic Assessment to School Practice

A common educational practice in the United States is to group students into several different levels of courses. RSM allows for analysis of cognitive differences across course level. In the school district they group students into twelve courses (M/J = Middle school/Junior high school): Applied Math I, Math 6–8, M/J Intensive Math, M/J Math 1 & 2, M/J Math2 Advanced, M/J Math 3, M/J Math 3 Advanced, Algebra, Algebra Advanced, Algebra Honors, and Geometry 7th Algebra. Table 28.4 describes courses into which students are classified and their mean scores and standard deviations—M/J Math 2 is further split into two groups (IDs 5 and 6), making a total of 13 IDs. Courses for Algebra Honors, Algebra Advanced, and Geometry 7th Algebra have smaller standard deviations than the M/J Math and Algebra courses. Figure 28.4 shows the trend of the average scores for Course IDs 1 through 13. It shows classes corresponding to Course IDs 11 (Algebra Honors) and 13 (Geometry 7th Algebra), respectively, have the highest and second highest scores.

DIAGNOSTIC SCORING REPORT FOR 7th Grade Mathematics Test		student	Norm
Student ID: 46672			
School ID: 21			
Score : 28/90 (27th percentile from the conversion table)			
CONTENT ATTRIBUTES		student	Norm
C1	Able to use knowledge, basic concepts and operations in whole numbers and integers	0.52	0.58
C2	Able to apply knowledge (K), basic concepts and operations in fractions & mixed numbers	0.99	0.7
EXP	Able to use knowledge, operations and concepts in powers, roots of numbers	0.33	0.51
C3	Able to use knowledge, basic concepts and operations in elementary algebra	0.49	0.69
C4	Able to use basic concepts and operations in plane geometry, & analytic geometry	0.99	0.82
C5	Able to use basic statistics and handle data	0.15	0.59
PROB	Able to understand and use probability and combinatorics	0.15	0.4
PROCESS ATTRIBUTES			
P1	Able to Translate/formulate/understand equations and expressions	0.92	0.54
P2	Able to compute by applying operational rules and K in arithmetic and geometry	0.42	0.76
P3	Able to apply the right properties & K in arithmetic and geometry	0.66	0.63
P4	Apply rules in algebra and solving equations (plugging in included for 7th graders)	0.25	0.45
P5	Able to use logical reasoning such as deductive thinking skills in problem solving	0.58	0.7
P6	Able to do problem search, problem restructuring & inductive thinking skills	0.25	0.45
P7	Able to do generating, visualizing and reading figures and graphs	0.5	0.71
P9	Able to manage several procedures, to set multi goals to solve complex problems	0.99	0.67
P10	Able to do Quantitative and logical reading (less than, must, need to be, at least, best etc.)	0.99	0.64

Comparison between student and norm

Comment: You did a good job for P1, P9, P10, and C2, C4.
You should study EXP, C3, C5, Probability and P5 and P6.

Figure 28.3 Individual diagnostic scoring report for a hypothetical student

Table 28.4 Assessment Results for the Mathematics Courses

Course ID	Course Name	n	M	SD
1	Applied Math 1	18	29.8	5.4
2	Math 6–8	440	23.8	6.6
3	M/J Intensive Math	565	32.2	10.6
4	M/J Math 1	33	36.0	12.4
5	M/J Math 2	7,028	41.1	13.5
6	M/J Math 2	915	33.6	11.7
7	M/J Math 2 Advanced	3,395	61.6	13.0
8	M/J Math 3	98	45.9	15.8
9	M/J Math 3 Advanced	143	53.9	16.9
10	Algebra	158	46.3	18.4
11	Algebra Honors	32	75.5	7.9
12	Algebra Advanced	237	69.8	10.5
13	Geometry 7th Algebra	1,906	63.6	10.8

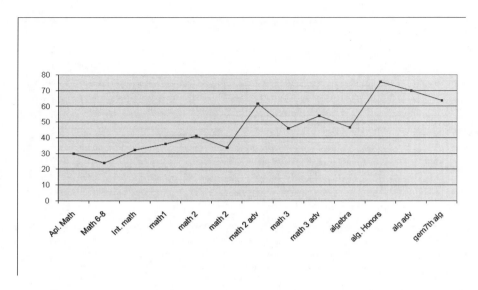

Figure 28.4 Plot of mean scores across mathematics courses

In order to extract the characteristics of student performances on 26 attributes by course, a discriminant analysis was performed. Discriminant analysis is a statistical classification technique to determine hyperplanes that serve to divide up a space into regions. For a discriminant analysis consisting of three different attributes, the space will be two-dimensional. For twenty-six attributes by course, there are twenty-five dimensions, and so on. Vector values, such as those representing student attribute probabilities, are classified according to which region they lie in. This is a standard technique in multivariate analysis (see, for instance, M. Tatsuoka, 1988). The group centroids of the students in the 13 courses are given in Table 28.5 and the coordinates given by the most influential first two discriminant functions are plotted in Figure 28.5. The line for Function 1 (diamonds) is increasing across the courses, which indicates the students in Course 13 have the highest followed by Course 11 and 12. In contrast, the line for Function 2 (squares) is rather flat across the 13 courses.

In order to find out the characteristics of the discriminant functions 1 and 2, the coefficients of the two functions are standardized and listed in Table 28.6. Sorting the standardized canonical discriminant

Table 28.5 Group Centroids by Course for the Discriminant Functions

Course	Function 1	Function 2	Function 3	Function 4	Function 5	Function 6
1	−1.38	−0.54	0.80	−0.01	0.63	0.01
2	−1.86	−1.75	−0.45	0.04	−0.07	0.00
3	−1.30	−0.24	0.26	−0.15	0.03	0.10
4	−0.91	−0.19	0.15	−0.23	−0.21	0.68
5	−0.62	0.21	0.06	0.03	−0.02	0.00
6	−1.18	−0.27	0.06	−0.02	0.10	−0.08
7	0.92	0.14	−0.26	−0.02	0.00	0.00
8	−0.24	0.04	−0.24	0.10	0.49	0.35
9	0.37	0.11	−0.03	−0.45	−0.20	0.13
10	−0.13	−0.09	0.27	−0.54	0.11	−0.21
11	1.44	−0.05	−0.19	0.07	0.10	0.10
12	1.08	0.07	−0.35	0.00	0.18	−0.02
13	1.91	−0.41	0.30	0.04	−0.01	0.00

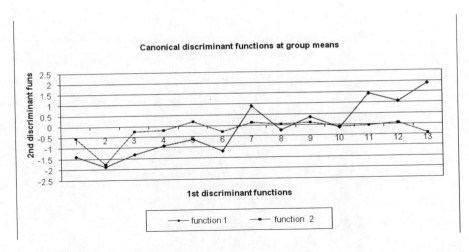

Figure 28.5 Plotting of two discriminant function values at 13 centroids

function coefficients by the magnitude of the first coefficients, we get the Figure 28.6. The bar lines represent the first discriminant function and the second bar lines are for the second discriminant function. The two curves clearly indicate the students in Course 13, "Geometry 7th Algebra" have higher scores

Table 28.6 Standardized Canonical Discriminant Function Coefficients for the 26 Attributes

Attribute	Function			
	1	2	3	4
p10	0.39	−0.37	0.67	0.03
p5	0.33	−0.04	−0.16	−0.57
p3	0.28	−0.16	0.29	0.03
p2	0.26	0.02	0.11	0.15
p1	0.21	−0.11	−0.18	0.04
p9	0.18	0.03	−0.13	0.24
c4	0.17	0.19	0.32	−0.31
s5	0.16	−0.10	−0.05	0.16
p4	0.15	−0.07	−0.22	0.00
s1	0.14	−0.09	−0.28	−0.31
c1	0.13	−0.11	0.21	0.08
c3	0.13	−0.14	0.19	−0.09
p7	0.12	0.06	0.26	0.08
c5	0.11	0.10	0.03	0.30
c2	0.10	0.01	−0.09	0.35
c6	0.09	−0.13	−0.25	−0.37
prob	0.06	−0.11	0.32	0.52
s2	0.04	0.20	0.01	0.12
s7	0.04	−0.03	−0.01	0.01
p6	0.02	0.05	0.08	−0.03
s9	−0.01	0.09	−0.14	−0.09
s3	−0.02	0.25	0.11	−0.20
expont	−0.02	0.01	0.01	0.10
s4	−0.02	0.08	−0.03	0.40
s3g	−0.03	0.52	0.12	0.08
s6	−0.10	0.20	−0.25	0.10

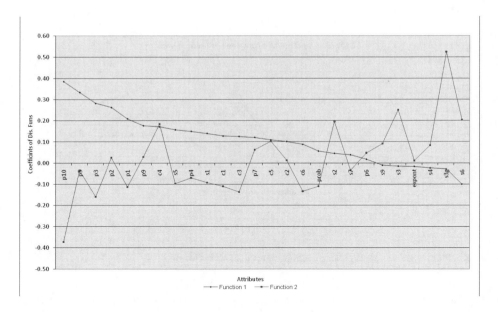

Figure 28.6 Comparison of the effects of the discriminant coefficients on attributes for two functions

in processing skills such as reasoning, dealing with complicated problems, quantitative reading, applying knowledge well in judging the next steps, translating words into algebraic and geometric expressions, and computational skills. The students (Figure 28.6) in Courses 12, 9, 7, and 5 excel in special skills, but not in process attributes. These results are similar to the findings in our TIMSS study.

Conclusions

K. K. Tatsuoka, Corter & C. Tatsuoka (2004) revealed by investigating an international dataset (TIMSS-R; Mullis et al., 2000, 2001) based on 20 countries, that geometry coursework seems to teach thinking skills such as P5, P3, P9, and P6 to eighth graders more effectively than teaching algebra. Also, a factor analysis of 23 attribute mastery probabilities resulted in geometry falling into the same factor as important mathematical thinking skills while algebra falls into the same factor as estimation, evaluation and computational skills. It is interesting to note that Course 13 is the only course teaching geometry and the students in Course 13 are portrayed by good performances on these thinking skill attributes, more so than those in the Algebra Honors and Algebra Advanced courses. Dean (2006) investigated the TIMSS 12th graders advanced mathematics achievement, and found a tendency that mastering mathematical thinking skills in early ages gives some advantages in learning advanced algebra, calculus, and trigonometry in later years. It is thus seen how diagnostic models can provide information about the impact of instruction and curriculum design. In other applications in assessment, these approaches can be applied.

References

Birenbaum, M., Kelly, A. E., & Tatsuoka, K. K. (1993). Diagnosing knowledge states in algebra using the rule-space model exponents. *Journal of Research in Teaching Mathematics, 24*(5), 442–449.

Chen, Y.-H., Gorin, J. S., Thompson, M. S. & Tatsuoka, K. K. (2008). Cross-cultural validity of the TIMSS-1999 mathematics test: Verification of a cognitive model. *The International Journal of Testing, 8*, 251–271.

Dean, M. (2006). *Explaining performance in the Third International Math and Science Study (TIMSS) 1995 Advanced Mathematics Test*, Ph.D. dissertation, Columbia University.

Dogan, E., & Tatsuoka, K. K. (2010). An international comparison using a diagnostic testing model: Turkish students' profile of mathematical skills on TIMSS-R. *Educational Studies in Mathematics, 68*(3), 263–272.

Fukunaga, K. (1990). *Introduction to statistical pattern recognition* (2nd ed.). New York, NY: Academic Press.

Guerrero, A., Yamada, T., & Tatsuoka, K. K. (2004). *Learning paths in mathematics and their relation to teacher background variables for the United States, Japan, and Chile* (Technical Report to NSF REC-0126064). New York, NY: Teachers College, Columbia University.

Mullis, I. V. S., Martin, M. O., Gonzales, E. J., Gregory, K. D., Garden, R. A., O'Connor, K. M., . . . Smith, T. A. (2000). *TIMSS 1999 International Mathematics Report*. Chestnut Hill, MA: International Study Center, Boston College.

Mullis, I. V. S., Martin, M. O., Gonzales, E. J., O'Connor, K. M., Chrostowski, S. J., Gregory, K. D., ... Smith, T. A. (2001). *Mathematics Benchmarking Report: TIMSS 1999-Eighth Grade*. Chestnut Hill, MA: International Study Center, Boston College.

Osterlind, S. J., & Wang, Z. (this volume). *Item response theory in measurement, assessment, and evaluation for higher education*.

Tatsuoka, C. (1996). *Sequential classification on partially ordered sets*. Ph.D Thesis, Department of Mathematics. Ithica, NY: Cornell University

Tatsuoka, C. (2002). Data analytic methods for latent partially ordered classification models. *Journal of the Royal Statistical Society. Series C (Applied Statistics), 51*, 337–350.

Tatsuoka, C., & Ferguson, T. (2003). Sequential classification on partially ordered sets. *Journal of the Royal Statistical Society. Series B (Statistical Methodology), 65*(1), 143–157.

Tatsuoka, K. K. (1983). Rule Space: An approach for dealing with misconceptions based on Item Response Theory. *Journal of Educational Measurement, 20*(4), 345–354.

Tatsuoka, K. K. (1984). Caution indices based on item response theory. *Psychometrika, 49*(1), 95–110.

Tatsuoka, K. K. (1985). A probabilistic model for diagnosing misconceptions in the pattern classification approach. *Journal of Educational Statistics, 10*(1), 55–73.

Tatsuoka, K. K. (1990). Toward an integration of item–response theory and cognitive error diagnoses. In N. Frederiksen, R. L. Glaser, A. M. Lesgold, & M. G. Shafto (Eds.), *Diagnostic monitoring of skill and knowledge acquisition* (pp. 453–488). Hillsdale, NJ: Erlbaum.

Tatsuoka, K. K. (1991a). *Boolean Algebra applied to determination of the universal set of misconception states* (ONR-Technical Report, RR-91–44). Princeton, NJ: Educational Testing Service.

Tatsuoka, K. K. (1991b). *Item construction and psychometric models appropriate for constructed responses* (Research Report 91–49–ONR). Princeton, NJ: Educational Testing Service.

Tatsuoka, K. K. (1995). Architecture of knowledge structures and cognitive diagnosis: A statistical pattern classification approach. In P. Nichol, S. Chipman, & R. Brennan (Eds.), *Cognitively Diagnostic Assessment* (pp. 327–359). Hillsdale, NJ: Erlbaum.

Tatsuoka, K. K. (1997). *Use of Generalized person-fit indices ζs for statistical pattern classification* (The College Board Research Report). Princeton, NJ: Educational Testing Service.

Tatsuoka, K. K. (2009). *Cognitive assessment: An introduction to the Rule Space Method*. New York, NY: Routledge Academic.

Tatsuoka, K. K., & Boodoo, G. (2000). Subgroup differences on the GRE quantitative test based on the underlying cognitive processes and knowledge. In D. Lesh, & W. E. Kelly (Eds.), *Handbook of research design in mathematics and science education* (pp. 827–857). Hillsdale, NJ: Erlbaum.

Tatsuoka, K. K., Corter, J. E., & Guerrero, A. (2004). *Coding Manual for identifying involvement of content, context, and process subskills for the TIMSS-R 8th Grade and 12th Grade General Mathematics Test Items* (Technical Report # MES 2004–1). New York, NY: Teachers College, Columbia University.

Tatsuoka, K. K., Corter, J. E., & Tatsuoka, C. (2004). Patterns of diagnosed mathematical content and process skills in TIMSS-R across a sample of 20 countries. *American Educational Research Journal, 41*(4), No. 4, 901–926.

Tatsuoka, K. K., Guerrero, A., Corter, J. E., Tatsuoka, C., Yamada, T., Xin, T., . . . Im, S. (2006). International comparisons of mathematical thinking skills in TIMSS-R (NSF Technical Report III). *Japanese Journal of Research on Testing, 2*(1), 3–39.

Tatsuoka, K. K., Kelly, A. E., Tatsuoka, C.M., Varadi, F., & Dean, M. (2007). *Rule Space and Associated Analysis of the Broward County Schools Benchmark FCAT (B-FCAT) Test*. Technical Report II to National Science Foundation, Tanar Software, Ohio.

Tatsuoka, K. K., & Tatsuoka M. M. (1987). Bug distribution and pattern classification. *Psychometrika, 52*(2), 193–206.

Tatsuoka, M. (1988). *Multivariate Analysis: Techniques for Educational and Psychological Research*. New York, NY: Macmillan.

Tatsuoka, M. M., & Tatsuoka, K. K. (1989). Rule space. In S. Kotz, & N. L. Johnson (Eds.), *Encyclopedia of statistical sciences* (pp. 217–220). New York, NY: Wiley.

QUESTIONS AND EXERCISES
FOR SECTION 4

Note: Suggested answers are provided for selected questions. These questions are indicated by an asterisk (*).

Data: The data for Questions 1 and 2 is presented below in Table S4.1.

(1) What is the recommend panel cut score for the data shown in Table S4.1?
(2) What is the interrater reliability of the panelist ratings for the data shown in Table S4.1?
(3) In which situations would using a test-centered standard-setting method be advisable? When would an examinee-centered method perhaps work better? What are the factors to take into consideration when choosing between the two types of methods?
(4) Discuss the benefits and drawbacks of placement testing in the high schools from the perspective of the high school student.
(5) The use of standardized tests in higher education admissions has been very controversial in the United States. If you were charged with designing a test-free college admissions system that would yield an academically capable and diverse student body, what procedures would you propose for screening applicants? What would be the advantages and disadvantages of your proposed system compared to a more traditional system that places considerable weight on test scores?

Table S4.1

						Panelist						
Item	A	B	C	D	E	F	G	H	I	J	K	L
1	0.60	0.70	0.60	0.60	0.60	0.70	0.60	0.65	0.60	0.60	0.55	0.70
2	0.40	0.50	0.60	0.55	0.55	0.75	0.60	0.50	0.60	0.50	0.45	0.70
3	0.50	0.60	0.65	0.55	0.55	0.70	0.60	0.60	0.70	0.55	0.50	0.70
4	0.70	0.60	0.85	0.85	0.55	0.80	0.75	0.75	0.80	0.70	0.85	0.90
5	0.60	0.70	0.80	0.70	0.65	0.70	0.65	0.80	0.80	0.70	0.70	0.80
6	0.60	0.60	0.65	0.80	0.65	0.75	0.75	0.65	0.70	0.65	0.65	0.70
7	0.60	0.50	0.65	0.75	0.50	0.70	0.65	0.60	0.60	0.60	0.55	0.70
8	0.80	0.70	0.80	0.95	0.80	0.90	0.80	0.90	0.80	0.90	0.90	0.90
9	0.30	0.60	0.50	0.60	0.55	0.75	0.50	0.50	0.60	0.70	0.40	0.80
10	0.70	0.50	0.60	0.65	0.60	0.50	0.65	0.50	0.60	0.60	0.50	0.80

Note: This table is for illustrative purposes only. A test with only 10 items would not be advisable for reasons of reliability and validity.

(6) What validity issues are of particular concern in direct writing assessment?

(7) What are the different theoretical perspectives that need to be considered in conducting validity inquiry for a writing assessment? What implications do they have for assessment practices?

(8) Your colleague in the Service Learning Office seeks your advice about how to measure the impact of service learning upon students. She presents you with a study proposal that links service learning to first-year academic achievement. She hypothesizes and finds a positive association between students' participation in community-based service learning and their first-year cumulative grade point average (GPA). You are asked to provide input on the research design and scope as well as measurement methods to assist the office in assessing the outcomes of service-learning courses. How would you utilize the rubrics cube in formulating your advice?*

(9) You are approached by a department chair who asks you how to validate a rubric which individual instructors in the department are utilizing to grade students' Capstone projects. What are your suggestions for assisting the department in improving the rubric validation process and scoring consistency?*

(10) Currently, your institution invests large amounts of assessment resources in gathering indirect measures of student learning such as course evaluations, surveys, etc. As the person responsible for coordinating assessment activities for the entire institution, how would you utilize the rubrics cube to strategically plan for the efficient utilization of assessment resources on campus in order to yield the greatest amount of direct evidence of student learning?*

(11) Five questions from a personality test are selected. These questions are developed to test three personality types: *Introverted*, *Extroverted* and *Highly Experimental* personalities. A list of keys for this test indicates Introverted persons (I) choose 1 for Questions 1 and 3, Extroverted persons (Ex) select 1 for Questions 2 and 4, and Highly Experimental persons (HE) choose 1 for Questions 2, 3 and 5. The Q-matrix of five items and three attributes will be as follows:

		I	Ex	HE
	i1	1	0	0
	i2	0	1	1
Q-Matrix =	i3	1	0	1
	i4	0	1	0
	i5	0	0	1

Now Mary answered the five questions and her response pattern is (10101). What is her personality type?*

Suggested Answers to Selected Questions

Answer/Response for (8)

Are components of one dimension of the rubrics cube currently under-represented in the study proposal? Do certain components of the rubrics cube hold more promise than others in demonstrating the impact of service learning upon students?

Answer/Response for (9)

Assuming a medium-stakes level applies to the Capstone project, the recommendation is that inter-rater reliability, content and construct validity should be estimated to substantiate the evidentiary basis of the assessment decision.

Answer/Response for (10)

Is a reallocation of assessment resources warranted? If so, how can you reallocate assessment resources to yield direct evidence of student learning? As part of efforts to establish a "culture" of assessment, you may need to involve relevant committees and administrators in the process.

Answer/Response for (11)

Her personality is *Introverted* and *Highly Experimental*.
   Key:

1.   Assume all personality types such as *Introverted*, *Extroverted*, etc., by creating all combinations of attributes.
2.   Find the ideal item score patterns corresponding to these attribute patterns by using the Q-matrix.

SECTION 5

Approaches to Evaluation in Higher Education

Thomas E. Grayson

Evaluation in higher education is fundamentally about generating evidence or valid information that helps various stakeholders in making judgments of merit or worth about a program, service, policy or whatever is being evaluated, i.e., an evaluand. This section offers very diverse methodological approaches for evaluating such programs, services, policies or other evaluands in the context of higher education.

Though careful and rigorous professional evaluation is valuable for making informed decisions on improving programs, determining cost effectiveness, or being accountable for results, in practice the conduct of evaluation also proves to be demanding, costly and time-consuming. Further, higher education policy and management environments are typically complex and institutional and program goals and strategies are often poorly defined. Given these realities, evaluators are often challenged to identify the appropriate focus necessary for selecting the right methodological approach for evaluating a program, service, policy or other evaluand.

In years past, many evaluators would typically consider using process evaluation (i.e., formative evaluation) approaches to improve a program, service, or policy or using an outcomes-based approach (i.e., summative evaluation) to determine and report impact. Today, professional evaluators have come to resist conducting such evaluations without a measure of exploratory evaluation understanding. More and more, evaluators are heeding the advice of Joseph Wholey (2010) to rather than proceed to a particular evaluation approach, to first consider conducting a rapid, low-cost "exploratory evaluation," such as an "evaluability assessment," which assesses the extent to which programs are ready to be evaluated, or a "rapid feedback evaluation," which is an extension of evaluability assessment that begins only after consensus on goals on which a program is to be evaluated has been reached. Such exploratory evaluation will produce preliminary evaluation findings; help evaluators and their clients identify priorities; help stakeholders reach consensus on evaluation goals, criteria, and intended uses of evaluation information; and ensure feasibility and usefulness of further evaluation efforts. In addition, exploratory evaluation can guide the evaluator in making appropriate choices as to what particular evaluation approach to employ.

All the chapters in this section describe realistic approaches to evaluation and deserve appreciation of their similarities and differences. Some of the similarities in the approaches can be categorized as questions and/or methods oriented evaluation approaches or as improvement and/or accountability oriented evaluation approaches. Regardless of the approach, each is a discrete and unique way to conduct an evaluation. Brief descriptions of each chapter in this section follow.

Chapter 29, *Program Evaluation in Higher Education*, by Grayson, offers a clear definition of what a program evaluation is, describes its types and purposes and how to design and conduct such an evaluation. Grayson's program evaluation approach is question oriented and theory-based in nature. Using examples, he describes seven necessary areas for a professional evaluator to reflect on while designing a program evaluation: (a) learn the institutional context of the program under study; (b) clarify the program's theory; (c) identify stakeholders; (d) clarify the purpose of the evaluation; (e) identify evaluative questions and criteria; (f) locate, collect and analyze data; and (g) report evaluation findings. The chapter concludes with a statement on program performance measurement.

Chapter 30, *Qualitative Evaluation*, by Pondish, describes a questions and methods oriented approach to collecting and analyzing data when the use of predetermined variables is not able to neatly render an understanding of the merits and shortcomings of a program or service via standard quantitative proofs. A qualitative approach typically includes open-ended questions and responses that can be summarized by categorization of emergent themes. This grounded method of issue identification and analysis is best used for exploratory investigation. While not providing mathematical inferences, the rich narratives associated with qualitative methods can lead to in-depth understanding of institutional phenomena.

Chapter 31, *Naturalistic Evaluation*, by Erlandson, describes the principles of designing a naturalistic evaluation inquiry which is methods oriented. Naturalistic evaluation rests on the assumption that reality is messy and cannot be embodied by research tools that constrain that reality by imposing a theoretical design on the flow of circumstances that occur in the setting or environment. This type of evaluation represents a shift in paradigmatic thinking from traditional evaluation research. Erlandson goes into detail on a toolbox of methods useful for the naturalistic evaluator that ensures such evaluation criteria as credibility, trustworthiness, and verifiability.

Chapter 32, *Responsive Evaluation*, by Godfrey and Finkelstein, discusses the history and development of responsive evaluation, as well as its uses. Responsive evaluation is a questions as well as improvement oriented evaluation approach which is client-centered and charges the evaluator with interacting closely with, and responding to, the evaluative needs of various clients, as well as other stakeholders. By successive questioning about findings and triangulating those findings from the data collected, responsive evaluators can conduct the evaluation in stages depending on what is found previously. For the most part, it differs from any standards-based assessment because the nature of the data collected is often difficult to quantify. While some assessments are practically dynamic like computer-adaptive testing, responsive evaluation can be even less restrictive. This makes considerable sense; however, a different way of thinking about evaluation results is required so that the evidence collected is valued.

Chapter 33, *Case Studies and Validity*, by Cisneros-Cohernour, offers insight into the nature of validity in the conduct of case studies. A case study is a focused, in-depth description, analysis, and synthesis of a particular program or other evaluand. This chapter relates various understandings of validity from the measurement literature and applies those understandings in the context of a case study analysis. For example, one important factor in a case study is to let the findings resonate off the reader whether it is a stakeholder or other decision making constituent. Validation takes the form of triangulation and the case study brings different forms of evidence together for that purpose. An actual case study is used in the chapter for demonstrating the understanding of validity in a case study analysis.

Chapter 34, *Mixed Methods Specialists in Action*, by Harnisch, Creswell, and Guetterman, presents a unique approach to evaluation that is different from a stand-alone quantitative or qualitative study. It is considered to be a question and/or methods oriented approach to evaluation. Harnisch et al. model different sequences of qualitative and quantitative combinations with each separate sequence having a different ramification. In short, this chapter advances a framework and process for applying qualitative, quantitative, and mixed methods methodology to evaluation, learning, and classroom assessment. It provides a unique application of mixed methods to classroom assessment and discusses its potential for scholarly inquiry. Harnisch, et al., provide a set of findings that will serve as a basis for continued discussion about the use of these approaches to the accountability assessment facing our educational system. A case study is presented that links mixed methods research to learning and classroom assessment.

Chapter 35, *Survey Use in Academic Contexts*, by Wentland, discusses various considerations for developing surveys and survey items for purposes of assessment in the conduct of an evaluation. The chapter is intended not so much as a method for analyzing survey results but as a means for outlining important considerations for data collection, reducing measurement error, and ensuring data quality and integrity. As Wentland indicates, it is important to clearly specify the purpose of the survey and intended use of information by primary stakeholders.

Discussion exercises for these chapters appear at the end of the section. The next section (Section 6) is on issues in assessment and evaluation in higher education and is generally more applied than the more purely methodological evaluation chapters presented in the present section.

References

Wholey, J. S. (2010). Exploratory evaluation. In J. S. Wholey, H. P. Hatry, & K. E. Newcomer (Eds.). *Handbook of practical program evaluation* (3rd ed., pp. 81–99). San Francisco, CA: Jossey-Bass.

29

PROGRAM EVALUATION IN HIGHER EDUCATION

Thomas E. Grayson

During the 1990s, in professional program evaluation in higher education, the most probable task for a program evaluator would have been to document and report "program fidelity" between an approved proposal for program services and actual services delivered and whether program activities were in accordance with legislation or regulations. Funding agencies and program administrators focused on questions about use of resources and program implementation: Were program resources used as intended? Was the program implemented as proposed? What was the number of products or services that were delivered? How many clients were served? Were clients satisfied with the deliverables or services? These types of questions, which were more research-oriented than evaluative in nature, directed evaluation efforts in that era.

Today, professional program evaluators are asked to do much more. Program evaluation is increasingly being used to meet the demand for information about the performance of public and nonprofit schools as well as private, for-profit educational programs. Institutional leaders, elected officials, funders, and citizens want to know about the quality and value of programs and services they support. Professional program evaluators are now asked to systematically conduct evaluations that have either a learning orientation emphasizing program improvement or development, or a results orientation emphasizing accountability for achieving intended results and determining impact.

Typical evaluative questions now include: What is working well in the program, and how might we improve it? What difference does the program make, for whom and under what circumstances? Is the program a justifiable expense? Does the program contribute to achieving the core mission of the organization? What is being developed in the program, and what are its merits? These questions require evaluators to think and work in ways that necessitate understanding institutional and departmental missions and goals, identifying program stakeholders and engaging them in exploring and articulating a program's rationale and theory, and specifying stakeholder evaluative-information needs. If answering such questions is to usefully inform individuals with vested interests in the program, then understanding the nature of program evaluation is necessary for identifying evaluative questions that are critical for planning, designing, and conducting a useful evaluation.

The reality is that higher education administrators and program managers need to manage the meaning (why they exist and how they work) of their programs just as much as they must manage program information, e.g., to support resource allocation and other policy decision making. Therefore, the role of the professional evaluator must be not only to enhance the quality and accuracy of evaluation data through systematic social science methods but also to help build the capacity of program executives to *think evaluatively and critically and to be able to appropriately interpret findings to reach reasonable and supportable conclusions* (Patton, 2011). Understanding why a program works or does not work is essential for making informed decisions, and making sense of evaluative program data is no easy task in a rapidly changing environment. Our institutions of higher education are very complex, dynamic systems encompassing multiple academic and developmental programs, some working independently, yet side by side, others in collaboration across their various disciplines. Today's evaluators must be professionally competent, possessing the necessary knowledge and skills to conduct such complex program evaluations (Russ-Eft, Bober, de la Teja, Foxon, & Koszalka, 2008), and they must also be sensitive, perceptive, analytical, and dedicated.

This chapter provides a basic overview of what is meant by program evaluation, a discussion of the types and purposes of program evaluations, a description of the fundamental considerations in designing and conducting a program evaluation, and presentation of various ways of measuring program performance.

What is Program Evaluation?

This chapter is about program evaluation. Thus, we must begin by asking ourselves: what is a program, and what is evaluation? In the *Handbook of Practical Program Evaluation, 3rd Edition*, by Wholey, Hatry, and Newcomer (2010), a program is defined as: ". . . a set of resources and activities directed toward one or more common goals, typically under the direction of a single manager or management team" (p. 5).

Further, in *The Program Evaluation Standards* (2011), it is emphasized that programs entail more than just activities. They consist of multiple components, including

- contexts and how they interact with programs and program components;
- participants and other beneficiaries as well as those who encounter costs or loss of benefits;
- needs, problems, and policy spaces in programs and their contexts;
- goals and objectives;
- resources and costs of all kinds, including staff, facilities, materials, and opportunity costs;
- activities, procedures, plans, policies, and products;
- logic models, beliefs, assumptions, and implicit and explicit program theories explaining why and how programs should work; and
- outputs, results, benefits, outcomes, and impacts. *(p. xxiv)*

As we use the term in this chapter, a program may encompass a set of activities in one institutional unit or it may be a multidisciplinary effort involving partnerships across two or more units. Further, a program typically is more than activities and may, in fact, consist of multiple components as described above.

In Michael Scriven's *Evaluation Thesaurus*, 4th edition (1991), evaluation is defined as ". . . the process of determining the merit, worth, or value of something, or the product of that process," the purposes of which are to make improvements in whatever is being evaluated or to determine the overall quality of what is being evaluated. The 2nd edition of *The Program Evaluation Standards* (Joint Committee, 1994, p. 3) similarly defines evaluation as: ". . . a systematic investigation of the worth or merit of an object." Here, "object" refers to the program under review. These notions of merit, worth, value, and quality are expanded upon in the recent 3rd edition *of The Program Evaluation Standards* (Joint Committee, 2011) by combining the two terms, program and evaluation, rendering a definition for program evaluation that includes:

- the systematic investigation of the quality of programs, projects, subprograms, subprojects, and/ or any of their components or elements, together or singly, for purposes of decision-making, judgments, conclusions, findings, new knowledge, organizational development, and capacity building in response to the needs of identified stakeholders;

- leading to improvement and/or accountability in the users' programs and systems; and
- ultimately contributing to organizational or social value. *(p. xxv)*

Clearly, then, professional program evaluation is to be methodologically systematic, addressing questions that provide information about the quality of a program in order to assist decision making aimed at program improvement, development or accountability and to contribute to a recognized level of value. Such evaluations may include guided monitoring of a program or services by program personnel, building the capacity of program administrators and staff to understand the value of evidence and to conduct their own evaluations. Good professional program evaluations help key stakeholders answer specific evaluative questions necessary for sound decision making about their programs and/or services.

Types and Purposes of Program Evaluations

There are many reasons for conducting a program evaluation. Sometimes debated, but generally agreed upon by most evaluators, are three broad categories of evaluation that generally describe the nature and purposes of program evaluations: *formative* program evaluation, *summative* program evaluation, and *developmental* program evaluation (Alkin, 2004; Davidson, 2005; Patton, 2011; Rossi, Lipsey, & Freeman, 2004; Scriven, 1991). Each type of evaluation has a unique focus and within each lies its own rationale as to why program evaluation is valuable and important.

Formative program evaluation has as its purpose *improvement by providing constructive feedback* to program implementers and clients (Alkin, 2004; Davidson, 2005; Scriven, 1991). This type of evaluation is aimed at helping a new program "get up to speed" or "find its feet," or it may be aimed at helping a mature program try out new strategies to improve its performance. In other words, formative evaluation informs program managers about ways to improve program quality or the delivery of program services. Formative evaluation asks how well the program meets the needs of its intended program recipients or how the initial outcomes achieved for program recipients compare with outcomes achieved by others in similar programs elsewhere (Davidson, 2005). Some designs for conducting formative evaluation include *implementation evaluation, process studies,* and *evaluability assessment* (Patton, 2008; Wholey, et al., 2010).

Summative program evaluation has as its purpose *measuring program performance in terms of outcomes and impacts* during ongoing operation or after program completion. It determines the overall quality or value of a program (Scriven, 1991; Wholey, et al., 2010). Summative evaluation asks whether the program was worth what it cost in terms of time, money, and other resources, or it asks, compared to other similar programs, whether this program was the most cost-effective (Davidson, 2005). A main reason for conducting a summative evaluation is to inform decision makers (administrators and funders) about whether the program was successful, which may lead to decisions about continuing or discontinuing the program or about implementing the program more widely (Alkin, 2011).

Developmental program evaluation has as its purpose *informing social program innovators* who intend to bring about major change through the development of new program models. It asks what is getting developed and with what implications (Patton, 2011), and it facilitates knowledge generation (Rossi et. al., 2004); that is, the focus is on exploring the nature and effects of a program as it is being developed, so as to contribute to the existing knowledge base.

Developmental evaluation is intended to facilitate innovation by: "Helping those engaged in innovation examine the effects of their actions, shape and formulate hypotheses about what will result from their actions, and test their hypotheses about how to foment change of uncertainty in situations characterized by complexity" (Patton, 2011, p. 14).

As Patton (2011) tells us, developmental evaluation is aimed at holding social innovators accountable as they explore, create and adapt new program models *before* there is a program which can be improved upon or whose performance can be measured. The role of the evaluator in developmental evaluation is to become part of the program innovator team, facilitating team discussions by suggesting evaluative questions, data and logic, and assisting decision making during the developmental process. Developmental evaluative questions may include: What's being developed? How is what's being developed or what's emerging to be judged and valued? Given what has been developed or has emerged, what is next?

Recapping the three primary types of program evaluation, then: formative program evaluation relates to gathering information that is useful for improving existing programs; summative program evaluation relates to gathering information useful for reporting on a program's intrinsic merits or determining its worth to participants or the associated organizations or institutions; and developmental program evaluation relates to the continuous gathering of information useful for making adaptations in the course of developing a program.

Designing and Conducting a Program Evaluation

The overarching goal of evaluating a program is to create an evidence and information database through which administrators and managers are informed so as to allow them to identify aspects of the program that require improvement in order to achieve intended strategic goals or to communicate the value of their program to key vested stakeholders. To these ends, much has been written about the processes for planning, designing, and conducting program evaluations. Prominent authors on the topic include: Rossi et al. (2005), wherein they propose "a tailored approach" which involves assessing the need for the program, the design of the program, program implementation and service delivery, program impact or outcomes, and program efficiency; Wholey et al. (2010), who devote the first ten chapters in their 3rd edition program evaluation handbook to describing a variety of approaches to planning and designing program evaluations; Alkin (2011), who outlines a set of essential cross-disciplinary skills for planning and conducting a program evaluation; Davidson (2005), who clearly and succinctly spells out the nuts and bolts of doing program evaluation; Patton (2008, 2011), who describes in detail a "utilization-focused" approach to planning, designing and conducting a program evaluation; Fitzpatrick, Sanders, and Worthen (2004), who provide a classic treatment to approaches and practices in program evaluation; and Funnell and Rogers (2011) who provide the most definitive understanding and use of program theory and logic models for planning, designing and conducting program evaluations.

In writing this chapter, I have borrowed bits and pieces from all of these major works and, based upon my own experience in the context of higher education, I have condensed the process of designing and conducting a program evaluation, into seven necessary areas for reflection:

1. Learn the institutional context of the program under study.
2. Clarify the program's theory.
3. Identify stakeholders.
4. Clarify the purpose of the evaluation.
5. Identify evaluative questions and criteria.
6. Locate, collect and analyze data.
7. Report evaluation findings.

Area 1: Learn the Institutional Context of the Program

The organizational, political, and social context of a program matters. Socrates has been credited with the saying, *"before we start talking, let us decide what we are talking about,"* and Yogi Berra is credited with, *"If you don't know where you are going, you won't know when you get there."* Useful program evaluation practice must begin with an understanding of *why* the program is thought to be necessary and *what* needs are being addressed. Both the *why* and *what* are intrinsic to institutional values and are (or should be) articulated in its mission and goal statements. Thus, in higher education, systematic program evaluation must begin with understanding the nature and purpose of the institution.

The difficulty and complexity of learning the institutional context of a program is expounded upon in an article titled, *The Art of the Presidency*, by Frank H. T. Rhodes (1998), well-respected President of Cornell University from 1977 to 1995. He wrote:

> The most important task, and also the most difficult one, is to define the institution's mission and develop its goals. That is the first task of the president. Everything else follows from that; everything else will depend upon it. The mission and goals must be ambitious, distinctive, and relevant to the needs and interests of campus constituents.
>
> The vision drives the goals, as the president establishes the benchmarks and articulates the values on which the day-to-day life of the institution will depend. Those goals, developed item by item, unit by unit, set the agenda, the blueprint for action, the mandate for change. This, too, is a joint effort: Trustees, provosts, vice presidents, deans, faculty, staff members, students, alumni, the public, advisors, and consultants—all have a role and a proportionate voice—actively influencing decisions, motivating effort, and channeling resources. *(p. 13)*

This is a keenly decided statement. It is inclusive; it implies complexity in the process of achieving particularized goals, recognizes multiple perspectives, suggests a reality of organizational politics and competing administrative goals, invites various power relationships, and has a focus on social change. As has been noted by Greene (2007), evaluation is inherently a political activity and the evaluator is, whether he or she realizes it or not, part of that activity. As such, the program evaluator is not completely independent and must keep an eye on institutional purpose and organizational structures, so as to understand what programs and services are contributing in meaningful ways towards achieving institutional goals. The evaluator must recognize and reflect on various stakeholder positions and points of view. Alkin (2011) stresses careful listening and observing to ensure that the program and its issues are understood from multiple stakeholder perspectives. Where are they coming from? How do they view the program? Such understandings will promote better communication, professional collegiality, and cooperation across all stakeholders. As Alkin (2011) states, "programs reflect a political consensus—a compromise—and an accommodation of multiple views" (p. 56). The evaluator must be attuned to these multiple views.

An example illustrates the complexity and challenge of understanding the organizational and political context of a particular program under study. The University of Illinois, located in Champaign-Urbana, Illinois, is a large Midwest public research university. The campus has several "living and learning" communities, of which Weston Hall Exploration is one. Weston Hall Exploration is managed and operated by University Housing, which is itself administered by the University's Office of the Vice Chancellor for Student Affairs. Table 29.1 lists the vision, mission, and goal statements for each of these four administrative levels.

Let's assume for the sake of illustration that Weston Hall Exploration is being evaluated for the purpose of determining its quality and worth (i.e., is this program worth what it costs?). The evaluator has the complicated task of, first, determining who the primary stakeholders are and, then, deciding which of them should be engaged in the evaluation. Selection should be made by prioritizing according to both practical and political reasons. This means that the evaluator must be able to communicate effectively with key individuals at all four administrative levels. The evaluator must cross all four organizational boundaries wherein the Weston Hall Exploration program resides in order to obtain relevant information about the program's worth from key individuals. As one can surmise,

Table 29.1 Vision and Mission Statements at Four Administrative Levels: University, Divisional, Departmental, and Program

University of Illinois at Urbana-Champaign

Vision: Become the preeminent public research institution.
Mission: The University of Illinois will transform lives and serve society by educating, creating knowledge, and putting knowledge to work on a large scale and with excellence.
Goals: Leadership for the 21st century; Academic excellence; Breakthrough knowledge and innovation; Transformative learning environment; and Access to the Illinois experience.

Division of Student Affairs

Vision: Student Affairs successfully transforms the lives of students, preparing them for citizenship in a global community. Its programs and services will attain a preeminence that will serve as a model for other universities.
Mission: Student Affairs transforms lives. We provide quality programs, services, facilities and living environments that create the Illinois experience at Urbana-Champaign which empowers students to achieve the greatest potential in their personal and academic development.
Goals: Enhanced knowledge & appreciation of diversity; Environmentally sound and culturally relevant facilities; clarity and enhancement of the student experience at Illinois; and Creation and sustainment of collaborative partnerships.

University Housing

Vision: Communities improving the world.
Mission: University Housing cultivates a safe space for the Illinois community to achieve its full human and academic potential. We are unified in purpose—to create memorable experiences and valued services.
Goals: Stewardship of resources; Create and maintain exceptional facilities; Hire and retain a qualified, diverse workforce; and Create a leadership culture.

Weston Hall Exploration Living and Learning Community

Mission: Weston Hall Exploration opened in Fall 1997 with the mission to bring together classroom and living experiences to provide opportunities for students to discover areas of interest and abilities and how they relate to academic majors and careers. Students entering Liberal Arts and Sciences General Curriculum may find Weston Hall Exploration a particularly supportive and stimulating environment in which to begin their Illinois experience. Weston students from all majors can utilize the resources to identify and prepare for careers.

References: University of Illinois website: http://illinois.edu/; Office of the Vice Chancellor for Student Affairs website: http://studentaffairs.illinois.edu/; University of Illinois Housing website: http://www.housing.illinois.edu/; University of Illinois Living and Learning Communities website: http://www.housing.illinois.edu/Current/Living-Learning.aspx

there is no "one size fits all approach"; the evaluation of Weston Hall Exploration must be tailored to the University's unique organizational and political context and to its specific set of circumstances.

Program context matters. The practice of program evaluation in higher education begins with knowledge and understanding of the institution's organizational structure and culture and the political context in which the program resides. A good starting point is to identify institutional values as expressed in stated vision, mission, and goals. Fleshing out context, administrators and program managers must be purposive about the program information they collect and clear about how it will be used to inform decision making at various levels, e.g., institutional, divisional, and unit. During this phase, the program evaluator is a facilitator as well as participant in the evaluation process. The overall intent is to engage primary stakeholders in the creation of an evidence and information framework through which the evaluation questions can be answered.

Area 2: Clarify the Program's Theory

Kurt Lewin's famous maxim, ". . . there is nothing as practical as a good theory" (1951, p. 169), exemplifies the importance of program theory in evaluation. As it suggests, the intent is to integrate theory with practice, and the best use of theory is to facilitate an understanding of applied aspects of social science. In this sense, program theory can serve as feedback to inform and enlighten program administrators, policy makers and practitioners, as well as those who created and funded the program.

Programs are results of deliberate allocations of resources in support of specific strategies or activities to produce defined services or products. These services or products are intended to address strategic problems or issues and may be considered necessary to fulfilling the institution's mission. In other words, programs are intended to produce desired outcomes. Describing a program along a continuum of resources, program activities, outcomes, and impact is a program's logic. This description of a program's *logic* has been referred to as an "espoused theory of action" (Argyris & Schon, 1974; Patton, 1997) or a program's theory of change. The theory then becomes a reference point against which progress towards achieving desired outcomes can be systematically assessed (Coffman, 1999).

In the course of conducting an evaluation, it is difficult, at best, to interpret evaluation findings without a clear understanding of a program's theory. Program theory is inextricably tied to the evaluation questions about the quality of a program and to the value of its intended effects, that is, a level of performance required for satisfactory functioning (Davidson, 2007). Thus, learning about and understanding the program's theory is essential before evaluation begins. In sum, the evaluator must learn about the purpose of the program, who the program serves, what the program intends to do, what it intends to accomplish, and what kinds of resources are needed to operate and manage the program.

To accomplish this, the evaluator should seek out existing written documents and conduct formal interviews with program staff and administrators and knowledgeable observers or experts in the program area who can provide insights. Alkin (2011) suggests five types of documents that might be examined: the written program proposal materials, guidelines of the funding agency, program materials, management documents, and past evaluation reports. Prior research and monitoring reports are also good sources of information. Alkin suggests that the most important of these documents is the program proposal as typically it will contain the goals of the program and particular activities that are expected to lead to accomplishing those goals. The proposal will also describe the resources (personnel and materials) needed in order to operate and manage the program. Interviewing key stakeholders, such as staff, administrators and program developers also can provide important information on a program's "raison d'être," its goals and its strategies to reach those goals.

A useful graphic for presenting a logical understanding of the program's expected performance is the *logic model*. As McLaughlin and Jordan (1999, 2010) and Bickman (1987) explain, a logic model will help describe the program by presenting a plausible and sensible rationale for how the program will work, under certain conditions, to meet unmet needs and solve identified problems. The logic model presents a clear graphic of the program, depicting linkages between a program's resources, activities/components, and the change those activities/components are intended to produce in the targeted participants. The logic model tells "*why*" a program exists and "*how*" the program works, at the same time that it identifies *external factors* influencing, positively or negatively, program operations or achievement of intended and unintended outcomes (McLaughlin and Jordan, 2010).

Program logic models may vary, but most likely would include the following elements:

- *Resources*—Resources dedicated to or consumed by the program. Resources may include such things as staff, volunteers, time, money, facilities, and so forth. The guiding question is: *What must this program have in order to operate effectively?*
- *Activities and components*—What the program does with the vested resources to fulfill its strategic intent. These include such things as conducting workshops, taking field trips, establishing partnerships, and so forth. The guiding question is: *What is to be done to achieve the intent of the program (e.g., its goals or outcomes)?*

- **Outputs**—Direct products of program activities or components and typically measured in terms of volume of work accomplished. This may include such things as workbooks produced, number of training seminars held, participants reached, and so forth. The guiding question is: *How much or how frequent and for how many clients?*
- **Participants**—The individuals, groups, organizations or institutions that receive the direct products or services from program activities and functions. The guiding question is: *Who do we serve and why?*
- **Outcomes**—The intended or unintended changes for individuals, groups, or organizations during or after participating in program activities. Outcomes may include changes in participants' knowledge, skills, or attitude; changes in behavior, practice or decision making; or changes in conditions (e.g., social, economic, civil, environmental). The guiding question is: *What changes in our participants or in a condition are we trying to effect?*
- **External and Contextual Factors**—Constraints on a program or unexpected outcomes (e.g., social, political, economic, environmental) over which administrators or program managers typically have little or no control.

When we place these elements together in such a way as to show relationships between resources and program activities (*how* the program is supposed to work), between program activities and expected benefits or changes in program participants, or between benefits or changes in program participants and addressing a problem or issue (*why* the program exists), we can readily see multiple realities involving all these elements. Figure 29.1 is a graphic depiction of a generic program logic model using the above elements. As it is displayed, the logic model provides a narrative along the line of "we use these resources [#1] to do these things [#2, #3] for these people [#4] in order to change them in these ways [#5, #6] so as to achieve these ultimate program goals [#7]. More simply stated, a program logic model displays how resources are linked to results which address a major issue or need for the program.

To illustrate with a more descriptive program logic model, Figure 29.2 displays the basic elements with typical descriptors that tell the program's story of why the program exists and how it intends to operate. This illustration can be used to answer an essential question: *Can the program, with these resources, through these action plans, yield these products and deliverables, which meet the needs of participants (short term and intermediate outcomes), so that various deleterious conditions are changed or issues of concern are addressed (impact)?*

Describing such theories of action is actually a very common occurrence for many of us. Most administrators create budget or funding proposals on a regular basis. Each proposal describes a program or service that we think will address a certain problem, issue, or priority. Often, in other

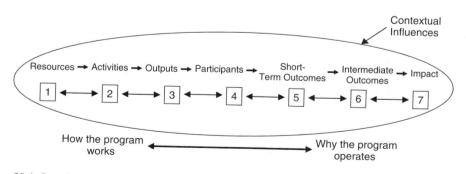

Figure 29.1 Generic program logic model

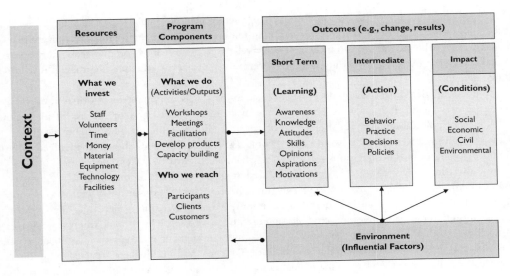

Figure 29.2 A program's logic or story

situations, we are asked to describe the strategic aim of a program or its purpose. Sometimes we are asked to justify the existence of a program; that is, we are asked to answer the question, "is the program necessary?" When we carry out any of these activities we are describing program theory; we are saying, "if we do these things, we should get these results," and exploratory evaluation, for example, evaluability assessment and rapid feedback evaluation (Wholey, 2010) can help to test or validate the theory.

Developing a program's logic can yield benefits beyond those that accrue to the evaluation process. As was mentioned above, there are usually many individuals with vested interests in any particular program. Those close to a program (i.e., managers, staff, and participants) may have different understandings about how the program should operate. Engaging these individuals in describing the program and building its logical framework can lead them to a greater understanding and shared vision of the program. Further, as they gain understanding, they may well decide to make important changes in the program (Alkin, 2011).

Summarizing Area 2, the logic model identifies the resources dedicated to or consumed by the program, describes what the program does with the resources to fulfill its mission and goals, identifies direct products or level of program activities, describes the benefits or changes for participants during or after program activities, and identifies the constraints on the programs, that is, external or contextual factors. Deciding which evaluative questions are to be addressed is facilitated by considering each element in the logic model as it relates to the intended use of performance-based information by primary users of the evaluative findings (Patton, in Coffman, 2002).

Area 3: Identify Stakeholders

Programs are about people: their values, behavior, relationships, and attitudes. They work as individuals and in groups and they partner with other groups within and outside their organizations. Every evaluation is political in that it is socially constructed, consisting of various interacting individuals and/or groups, each imbued with differing values, cultures, and intentions. Individuals may include but are not limited to: senior management, policy makers, community members, program managers, staff, participants, partners, advocates, adversaries, program sponsors and/or funders. At times, any of these may seek information helpful in making decisions or in understanding the program. For example, a trustee might need information to inform policy; a senior manager might have a strategic planning focus and need information that justifies allocating resources to a program; a program manager may seek ways for the program to run more cost effectively; a program staff person may seek information on how to improve program quality; and, funders may want to know whether the program is worth investing in.

Once a list of primary stakeholders has been identified, it is important to prioritize the list of stakeholders by whether they are critical to the evaluation's success and/or the use of findings. Practical or political implications should also be considered in determining who will be engaged in the evaluation process. Once a list of key stakeholders is established, they should be involved early in developing evaluation questions (focusing the evaluation). Further, stakeholders should be continuously and actively engaged in determining design and data collection methods, analyzing data and interpreting findings, and developing recommendations and action plans. A goal is to ensure that stakeholders feel ownership in and are committed to the evaluation, increasing the odds of evaluation findings being relevant, credible, and useful. Perhaps more important, when you engage stakeholders, they learn about evaluation. Their active engagement increases their knowledge of evaluation, encourages them to value a culture of evidence, and builds their capacity to conduct evaluations themselves. As Patton maintains, along with completing evaluation themselves, a parallel aim of evaluation activities is to have an impact on those involved (Coffman, 2002). Individuals who participate in the evaluation should learn to use and apply the logic, reasoning, and values that underlie the evaluation process.

Area 4: Clarify the Purpose of the Evaluation

As is noted elsewhere in this chapter, clarifying the purpose of the evaluation is often complicated. It involves practical and political strategies for communicating with primary stakeholders and engaging them in non-adversarial discussions to determine the purpose and focus of the evaluation. This is particularly true in complex situations and organizational structures where various primary stakeholders have competing evidentiary and informational needs.

The purpose of the evaluation is not always easily ascertained, but the evaluator must not begin the evaluation without a clear understanding of its purpose. As was described earlier, purposes may include: *program improvement*, where the focus is on bettering the quality and operation of a program; *accountability*, where the focus is on determining whether program expectations have been met; *program impact*, where the focus is on determining whether the program made a difference and is worthwhile; and on *knowledge generation*, where the focus is on exploring the nature and effects of a program as a way to contribute to the existing knowledge base or to develop a new program.

Area 5: Identify Evaluation Questions and Criteria

Program evaluations cannot produce relevant, credible, and useful findings unless they have a set of good questions that can guide the evaluation process. Questions should be formulated in consultation with primary stakeholders and should solicit information that the stakeholder needs. In addition, questions should be evaluative in nature, addressing the actual merit, value or worth of a program (Davidson, 2005). A set of carefully thought-out evaluation questions is the lynchpin upon which a professional program evaluation hinges.

Table 29.2 lists sets of sample evaluative questions that can guide an evaluation. The questions are not meant to be exhaustive; rather, they are intended to be broad in nature. The questions are presented in a manner intended to show their linkage to various elements (e.g., resources, activities/components, outputs, outcomes, and impacts) in a program's logical framework.

Table 29.2 Potential Evaluative Questions in a Program's Logical Framework

Program Resources	Program Activities/ Components	Program Outputs	Program Outcomes	Program Impact
Evaluative Questions	Evaluative Questions	Evaluative Questions	Evaluative Questions	Evaluative Questions
Did the program have adequate resources? Did the program employ qualified staff? Did the program have the necessary (right kind) of resources? To what extent did the program demonstrate the best possible use of available resources?	How well has the program been implemented? What is the quality of the program's activities or components? What are the barriers and enablers that have made a difference between success and failure in program implementation? How might we improve the program?	Did the program produce quality products? Were products delivered in a timely manner so as to be meaningful and useful? How beneficial were the products to the program participants? What are the merits of this program as compared to other similar programs?	Did this program make a difference in participants (e.g., knowledge gained, behavior changed)? What is the quality of those changes? How valuable or beneficial are intended or unintended outcomes for program participants?	Was this program worth implementing, i.e., did long-term outcomes outweigh the costs (resources used)? Did the program have any influence or impact on the conditions (e.g., social, economic, environmental) sought to be addressed by its implementation?

Identifying, constructing, and/or clarifying evaluation questions are by no means simple exercises. Questions must comport closely with the purpose of the evaluation. It is helpful to start by asking the primary stakeholders what type of information they will need as they make decisions about the program. Clearly articulated evaluation questions give structure to the evaluation, lead to thoughtful planning, and facilitate the choosing of appropriate methods to gather data to answer those questions.

If an evaluation's purpose is to judge the overall success of a program in order to make decisions about program continuation or expansion, criteria that will be used to judge the success of the program must also be identified. The evaluator should involve stakeholders in the identification of these criteria and should share with stakeholders the full evaluation plan in order to get their feedback, consensus, and support for its implementation.

In sum, good evaluation questions establish the boundary and focus of the program evaluation. They make clear to everyone concerned what the evaluation will and will not address. Further, good questions will be aligned with a program's logic providing actionable answers for program decision makers.

Area 6: Locate, Collect and Analyze Data

Upcraft and Schuh (1996) describe [evaluation] assessment as "any effort to gather, analyze, and interpret evidence, which describes institutional, divisional, [program], or agency effectiveness" (p. 18). Once evaluation questions are identified, the next steps should be to determine where the information to answer those questions is located, how best to collect it, and then how to analyze it. As has been stated in multiple areas above, it is important to involve stakeholders in all these steps.

The evaluator will want to select evaluation methods that can generate the most reliable and useful information pertinent to the overall evaluation purpose and then identify the sources of such information. Relevant information may already exist in readily available form (e.g., existing evaluation and/or status reports, existing data collected for other purposes, other public documents and databases).

Some of the more frequently used data collection methods include: *interviews* (one-to-one), *focus groups* (a group interview or discussion), *surveys, observations,* and *expert panels*. In some instances, data collection will consist simply of locating existing data files. There are many excellent texts on designing and conducting interviews (Colton & Covert, 2007; Dillman, 2000; Fink, 2003), and on designing and conducting focus groups (Krueger & Casey, 2009; Morgan & Krueger, 1998). Regarding observations, Creswell (2007) and Stake (1995, 2010) provide in-depth understanding on the nature and challenges in making observations of various programs under study.

It should go without saying that, in order to identify and eliminate bugs in the process of constructing a new instrument, one should pilot test the newly developed data collection procedures before full implementation. Usually, data collection procedures are piloted on selected segments of the program. For example, in conducting surveys with program staff, only one or two units in the program might be engaged to test meaningfulness and understandability of items.

All data in an evaluation, whether quantitative or qualitative in nature, should be appropriately and systematically analyzed, so that evaluation questions are fully and effectively answered. Further, any conclusions reached should be explicitly justified by the data, so that stakeholders can assess their validity.

Area 7: Report Evaluation Findings

How evaluation findings are reported is just as important as what is reported. Often, *tables and pictures*, such as graphs or bar charts, are useful to present a concise and clear summary of findings. The goal is to present evaluation findings in such a way that they will be easily understood. Presentation of findings may not be in a formal written form but, rather, findings may be presented orally or interactively depending on the intended use and/or intended users of the findings. Conclusively, as Patton (1997) cautions, it is important to realize that dissemination of findings is different from use of findings.

Lastly, as noted by Davidson (2007), "*weave the findings together to create a cohesive answer to a real question*" (p. v). This weaving of findings is known as "triangulation" and is standard professional practice in both the field of applied social sciences and the field of evaluation. Triangulation is using different types of data and from different sources, the purpose of which is to get different perspectives on the answer to the same question. When this is done, weaving the data together in the analysis, the results should be a cohesive answer to an evaluation question. This is the ultimate aim in reporting program evaluation findings.

Performance Measurement

In planning evaluations intended to improve program performance, it is possible to begin by identifying the program's *performance spectrum*, i.e., the logical ordering of program outcomes, including immediate outcomes, intermediate outcomes, and impact-associated performance indicators (types of evidence) by which the program will be evaluated (McLaughlin & Grayson, 1999). Again, a program's logical framework can be quite useful for identifying performance measures.

According to Friedman (2001), performance measurement essentially describes program achievements in terms of outputs and outcomes within a given time frame against a pre-established goal. It asks: Is progress being made toward achieving strategic goals? Are appropriate activities being undertaken to promote achieving those goals? Are there problem areas or issues that need attention? Are there successful efforts that can serve as a model for others?

Friedman (2007) also posits that all performance measures involve two sets of interlocking questions. The first set of interlocking questions relates to *quantity* (how much did we do?) and *quality* (how well did we do it?). The second set of questions relate to the work itself: *effort* (how hard did we try?) and *effect* (is anyone better off?). Figure 29.3 displays these interlocking questions in four quadrants.

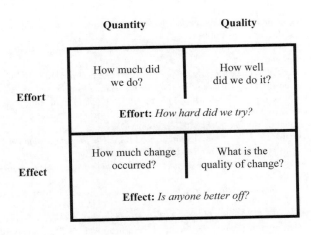

Figure 29.3 Quadrants of performance measures

Using a program's logic model, as can be seen in the quadrants, if we focus on program activities and outputs elements in the logic model, we can identify indicators that describe volume (quantity) of work accomplished, and quality of services delivered. This type of information can help us answer the questions, *"What are we doing and how much did we do?"* and *"How well did we do it?"* If we focus on the outcome elements, we can identify indicators that describe the effects of our program. This type of information can help us answer the questions, *"How much change or effect did we bring about?"* and *"What is the quality of the change or effect we brought about?"*

In summary, then, learning about institutional context, engaging stakeholders, identifying evaluation questions, and articulating a program's theory or logic are critical prerequisites to identifying performance indicators. Once these necessary pieces are in place, indicators by which the program will be evaluated can be identified, and data can be located, collected, analyzed, and reported.

References

Alkin, M. C. (2004). *Evaluation roots: Tracing theorists' views and influences.* Thousand Oaks, CA: Sage.

Alkin, M. C. (2011). *Evaluation essentials: From A to Z.* New York, NY: Guilford Press.

Argyris, C., & Schon, D. A. (1974). *Theory in practice: Increasing professional effectiveness.* San Francisco, CA: Jossey-Bass.

Bickman, L. (Ed.). (1987). *Using program theory in evaluation.* San Francisco, CA: Jossey-Bass.

Coffman, J. (1999). *Learning from logic models: An example of a family/school partnership.* Cambridge, MA: Harvard Family Research Project, Harvard Graduate School of Education.

Coffman, J. (2002). A conversation with Michael Quinn Patton. *Evaluation Exchange, 8*(1), 10–11.

Colton, D., & Covert, R. W. (2007). *Designing and constructing instruments for social research and evaluation.* San Francisco, CA: Jossey-Bass.

Creswell, J. W. (2007). *Qualitative inquiry & research design: Choosing among five approaches* (2nd ed.). Thousand Oaks, CA: Sage.

Davidson, E. J. (2005). *Evaluation methodology basics: The nuts and bolts of sound evaluation.* Thousand Oaks, CA: Sage.

Davidson, E. J. (2007). Editorial: Unlearning some of our social scientist habits. *Journal of Multidisciplinary Evaluation, 4*(8), iii–vi.

Dillman, D. D. (2000). *Mail and internet surveys: The tailored design method* (2nd ed.). New York, NY: Wiley.

Fink, A. (2003). *The survey kit* (2nd ed.). Thousand Oaks, CA: Sage.

Fitzpatrick, J. L., Sanders, J. R., & Worthen, B. R. (2004). *Program evaluation: Alternative approaches and practical guidelines* (3rd ed.). New York, NY: Allyn and Bacon.

Friedman, M. (2001). *The results and performance accountability implementation guide.* Located at: http://www.raguide.org/

Friedman, M. (2007). *Trying hard is not good enough: How to produce measurable improvements for customers and communities.* Bloomington, IN: Trafford Publishing.

Funnell, S. S., & Rogers, P. J. (2011). *Purposeful program theory: Effective use of theories of change and logic models.* San Francisco, CA: Jossey-Bass.

Greene, J. C. (2007). Method choices are contextual, contingent, and political. In G. Julnes & D. J. Rog (Eds.). *Informing federal policies on evaluation methodology: Building the evidence base for method choice in government sponsored evaluation.* New Directions for Evaluation, 113 (pp. 111–113). San Francisco: Jossey-Bass.

Joint Committee on Standards for Educational Evaluation. (1994). *The Program Evaluation Standards: How to assess evaluations of educational programs* (2nd ed.). Thousand Oaks, CA: Sage.

Joint Committee on Standards for Educational Evaluation. (2011). *The Program Evaluation Standards: A guide for evaluators and evaluation users* (3rd ed.). Thousand Oaks, CA: Sage.

Krueger, R. A., & Casey, M. A. (2009). *Focus groups: A practical guide for applied research* (4th ed.). Thousand Oaks, CA: Sage.

Lewin, K. (1951). *Field theory in social science; selected theoretical papers* (Edited by D. Cartwright). New York, NY: Harper & Row.

McLaughlin, J. A. & Grayson, T. E. (1999). *Planning and conducting performance-based evaluations.* Annual Meeting of Model Project Directors sponsored by the National Transition Alliance, University of Illinois at Urbana, IL, Washington, DC.

McLaughlin, J. A., & Jordan, G. B. (1999). Logic models: A tool for telling your program's performance story. *Evaluation and Program Planning, 22*(1), 65–72.

McLaughlin, J. A., & Jordan, G. B. (2010). Using logic models. In J. S. Wholey, H. P. Hatry, & K. E. Newcomer (Eds.), *Handbook of practical program evaluation* (3rd ed., pp. 55-80). San Francisco, CA: Jossey-Bass.

Morgan, D. L., & Krueger, R. A. (1998). *The focus group kit.* Thousand Oaks, CA: Sage.

Patton, M. Q. (1997). *Utilization-focused evaluation* (3rd ed.). Thousand Oaks, CA: Sage.

Patton, M. Q. (2008). *Utilization-focused evaluation* (4th ed.). Thousand Oaks, CA: Sage.

Patton, M. Q. (2011). *Developmental evaluation: Applying complexity concepts to enhance innovation and use.* New York, NY: Guilford Press.

Rhodes, F. H. T. (1998). The art of the presidency. *The Presidency, 1*(1), 12–18.

Rossi, P. H., Lipsey, M. W., & Freeman, H. E. (2004). *Evaluation: A systematic approach* (7th ed). Thousand Oaks, CA: Sage.

Russ-Eft, D., Bober, M. J., de la Teja, I., Foxon, M. J., & Koszalka, T. A. (2008). *Evaluator competencies: Standards for the practice of evaluation in organizations.* New York, NY: Wiley.

Scriven, M., (1991). *Evaluation thesaurus* (4th ed.). Thousand Oaks, CA: Sage.

Stake, R. E. (1995). *The art of case study research.* Thousand Oaks, CA: Sage.

Stake, R. E. (2010). *Qualitative research: Studying how things work.* New York, NY: Guilford Press.

Upcraft, M. L., & Schuh, J. H. (1996). *Assessment in student affairs: A guide for practitioners.* San Francisco, CA: Jossey-Bass.

Wholey, J. S. (2010). Exploratory evaluation. In J. S. Wholey, H. P. Hatry, & K. E. Newcomer (Eds.), *Handbook of practical program evaluation* (3rd ed., pp. 81-99). San Francisco, CA: Jossey-Bass.

Wholey, J. S., Hatry, H. P., & Newcomer, K. E. (Eds.). (2010). *Handbook of practical program evaluation* (3rd ed.). San Francisco, CA: Jossey-Bass.

30

QUALITATIVE EVALUATION

Christopher Pondish

Qualitative methods can be of great value as stand-alone procedures or in conjunction with quantitative strategies. On their own, qualitative methods can be effective in offering resonant descriptions of multifaceted phenomena, following exceptional or unanticipated events, describing and translating experiences via participant perspectives, allowing for the expression of minority and/or unique opinions, and conducting exploratory research. Qualitative methods have much to contribute to educational research, especially when the research deals with rapid change or seeks to develop a more robust knowledge base or research agenda (Sofaer, 1999). As the primary instrument of data collection and analysis, the researcher is required to assume an empathic stance exhibiting sensitivity, respect, awareness, responsiveness, and openness toward the subject and participants. The yield of this approach ought to be the inclusion of meaning to research often dominated by the urge to measure (Scott, 2002).

Qualitative methods are often either overlooked by institutional researchers or are assigned to the realm of non-rigorous activities and thus not given their due as a useful tool. The inability of qualitative results to provide meaningful predictions can also be seen as sufficient to forego their use. However, when properly executed and applied, qualitative methods and the data they produce can be a valuable means of gaining greater insight into the context and understanding of a given situation and ultimately presenting a valid path for the building of models and the development of quantitative strategies.

Reflection on this particular paradigm presents the yin yang relationship between quantitative and qualitative methodologies and attests to their mutual but compatible raison d'etre. For those unfamiliar with the Chinese philosophy, yin yang is used to describe how seemingly disjunctive or opposing forces are interconnected and interdependent in the natural world, giving rise to each other in turn. The preciseness of numbers can be complemented by the fuzziness of words. Good research design and execution integrates the strengths and weaknesses of both approaches and is able to capitalize on each, given appropriate circumstances.

Definitions

What do we mean by qualitative methods? At a base level, we are speaking about any method of data collection and evaluation whose primary building block is words rather than numbers. Qualitative methods use real-life context for uncovering certain phenomena, lend themselves to multiple approaches, and provide a comprehensive research strategy. In qualitative research the precise design of the research is emergent, depending on the requirements of the study as it evolves (Bogdan & Biklen, 1998; Ely, Anzul, Friedman, Garner, & Steinmetz, 1991; Merriam, 1998; Yin, 2002).

Research Perspective

Qualitative researchers attempt to make sense of, or provide an interpretation of, observed phenomena relative to meanings attributed to these phenomena by individuals involved in specific incidents or situations. Therefore, qualitative researchers spend the majority of their time in the field, working closely with participants in their natural surroundings, giving rise to the term naturalistic inquiry. The methodological orientation that guides this methodology is interpretist. The emphasis of the research is on understanding the meaning of the processes that led to the development of the subject being studied. The knowledge is derived from an inductive mode of inquiry and builds toward theory from observations and intuitive understanding of the data (Merriam, 1998). Contextualization is achieved by examining the perspectives and experiences of individuals with a close connection to the event or culture. The research perspective is concerned with developing explanations for the particular social phenomena that led to the unfolding of the event or the development of the culture.

Researcher Role

Some social science researchers (Guba, 1987; Lincoln & Guba, 1985; Schwandt, 1989; Smith, 1983a, 1983b; Smith & Heshusius, 1986) perceive qualitative and quantitative approaches as incompatible. Often the argument is that submission to whatever means works to achieve the end ignores the incongruity of the competing positivistic and interpretivist paradigms that undergird quantitative and qualitative methods (Howe, 1988). The paradigm can be emphasized by the difference in the role played by the researcher (for a different perspective on this see Howe, 1988, or Mislevy, Moss, & Gee, 2008).

The quick summation of the role of the researcher in qualitative methods is embodied in the following three phrases: personal involvement, partiality, and seeks to portray empathic understanding in the presentation of the data in narrative form. Contrastingly, the quantitative research role can be characterized as detached, impartial, and seeks an objective portrayal of the data and its interpretation.

For the institutional researcher studying her/his own campus, the data collection role will always be at some level of a participant. This is in direct contrast to the role played by the researcher using quantitative methods where the role is most often that of an outsider. The researcher can be considered an instrument in the qualitative research process as an element of the culture or event under study. Therefore, readers of the resulting report need to know about the researcher, their relation to the culture or event under study, level of participation, biases and assumptions, expectations, and other relevant history, and so forth. In this regard, the keeping and analysis of researcher notes can be as important to the study as the observation, interview, or document data. Levels of participation can be plotted on a scale running from emic (an insider view) to etic (an outsider view). Within the improvisational nature of qualitative methodology, the researcher can expect to move continuously along the emic-etic continuum depending on circumstance and/or task.

Operational Definitions

The following are some terms commonly used in conjunction with qualitative methods. Naturalistic can refer to the manner in which the research is conducted, that is, within the raw environment rather than in a manipulated situation, observing naturally occurring events rather than controlling them. Patton (1980) states, "Naturalistic inquiry is thus contrasted to experimental research where the investigator attempts to completely control the condition of the study" (p. 42). Qualitative observational research is naturalistic because it studies a group in its natural setting. For more on naturalistic evaluation, see Erlandson (this volume). The assumptions underlying naturalism and positivism can be contrasted in nature as illustrated in the following chart.

Naturalism	Positivism
Multiple constructed realities that can be understood to some extent but cannot be predicted or controlled.	Single reality, that is: can be empirically observed, predicted, and controlled.
The inquirer and the object of inquiry interact and influence each other.	The inquirer and the object of inquiry are discrete entities.
Separating cause from effect is difficult if not impossible if cause and effect are viewed as non-linear and evolving rather than static.	Actions can be explained in a cause and effect, linear manner even when the potential for multiple causes and timeframes is included.
Knowledge is idiographic as a working hypothesis that only describes an individual case.	Knowledge is nomothetic that can be generalized and replicated within limits and the variability within those limits can be predicted.
Inquiry is perceived as value-laden and subjective.	Inquiry is perceived as value-free and objective.

Figure 30.1 Underlying assumptions of naturalism and positivism

Holistic is somewhat synonymous with naturalistic and is used to describe the examination, in total, of what unifies a phenomenon by establishing context through the identification of the various internal and external systems involved and exploring the nature of their interactions/relationships. Context sensitivity, also related to naturalism and holism, emphasizes the many aspects of social, historical, and physical context that affect culture and phenomena and make them distinctive. Thick description is used to illustrate the narrative style of quantitative methods characterized by its abundance of, and attention to, detail.

Methods of Data Collection

In contrast to quantitative methods, there are no random subjects in the sample selected for a qualitative study. Because *n* is small for this type of design, only purposeful means of participant selection are appropriate. Purposeful sampling can be defined as non-random sampling where information-rich cases are selected for in-depth study. This model suggests that for the study of a particular socio-economic stratum, a great deal more can be learned by in-depth focusing on understanding the needs, interests, and incentives of a small number of carefully selected individuals within that stratum than by gathering standardized information from a large, statistically significant sample (Patton, 2001). Some examples of participant selection criteria appear below. Another distinctive aspect of qualitative sampling is the ability, indeed the necessity, to follow up with participants. The argument can be made that panel or cohort studies function similarly, but the improvisational nature of qualitative methods provides a distinct difference to both approach and application. In addition to posing additional questions, this recursive activity allows for clarification and participant validation either verbally or via review of notes/transcripts. A non-exhaustive typography or categories used to determine subject suitability can include:

- Typicality—participants that represent the midpoint on a variability scale;
- Maximum variation or extreme cases—participants that represent the end points on a variability scale, either low or high points;

- Uniqueness—participants that exhibit some discrete combination of characteristics;
- Snowball or networking—individuals recommended by other participants; and
- Experts—participants whose experience and or education qualify them as authorities in the field.

One of the chief distinguishing aspects of qualitative methodology is the ability to use multiple avenues of date collection. Figure 30.2 presents a brief synopsis of three of the most common approaches and their sources.

These three kinds of data collection (interviews, one-to-one or focus groups; observations; and document analysis) produce three kinds of data (quotations, descriptions, and excerpts of documents) resulting in a singular narrative, albeit sometimes with the inclusion of charts and/or diagrams.

The topic of the qualitative interview is the interviewee's world and their relationship to it. The focus should be on the interviewee's lived experiences, not just their beliefs or attitudes about issues. The interview attempts to obtain open, nuanced, rich descriptions of specific situations (Steinar, 1996). The interview seeks to describe the meanings of central themes in the life world of the interviewee on both factual and meaning levels. The main task in interviewing is to understand the meaning of what the interviewee says (Kvale, 1996).

The form of the interview can run the continuum from completely scripted (with little to no variation from the script) to completely ad hoc (with no pre-scripted questions). To take advantage of the improvisational opportunities qualitative methods offer, the researcher must be prepared to ask follow-up questions based on the interviewee's answers. It is important to be aware of the difference in effort for interviewees to respond orally as opposed to in writing. The "if not, why?" sequence often seen but seldom answered on questionnaires takes a different flavor in the conversational context of the interview regardless of one-on-one or group format.

Observations can generally be characterized as participant or non-participant, although institutional researchers studying their own campus will be participants to some degree. The act of observing is conflicting in nature to the necessity of scribing, akin to—although perhaps not quite as severe as—listening and simultaneous note taking. Only experience imparts the balance of skills necessary to observe, reflect, and record in an efficient manner. Novice observers can work toward proficiency by engaging in limited observance exercises without taking notes during the observation. Directly thereafter, the observer should avail themselves of a quiet environment and record their impressions. Starting with the standard who, what, where, when, how, and why questions provides a solid framework for recording observations and impressions. As important as recording is the act of revisiting written notes and editing. This recursive editing process needs to be repeated regularly over the term of the research.

Research Methods	Sources
Interviews (individual or group)	Faculty, administration, students, alumni, prospects/suspects, persons indirectly associated with an event or culture, persons associated with education or higher education, etc.
Observations	Time spent during an event or within a culture.
Document analysis	Literature—internal, external, published, unpublished, hardcopy, electronic, etc.

Figure 30.2 Most common qualitative data collection approaches and their data sources

The use of documents should not, in this day and age, be limited to traditional forms of hard copy. Audio or video recordings as well as electronic communications of any sort whose relevance to the research can be established are fair game. As with interviews, the use of quotations rather than paraphrasing is paramount to achieving a true picture. As a general rule, quoting should be the bulk of any data presentation section while paraphrasing has its place in the analysis.

Methods of Analysis

Categorization of data elements or typology is essential to qualitative analysis. Typology is recognizing the emergence of patterns, themes or other kinds of groups of data. The matrix for data categories presented in Figure 30.3 is an example of how visual elements can help to organize data and consequently create an analysis path.

Constant comparison or grounded theory method of analysis has been in wide use since the late 1960s. It searches for indicators of categories in events and behavior. Traditionally, a code is developed for the categories and assigned to relevant passages. It is important to note that passages are more often than not overlapping in their categorical nature. Re-reading field and researcher notes can result in additional coding. This review process is an essential component of the data sifting (one might almost say mining) mechanism used to allow emergent meaning. Categories saturate when a careful review results in no additions. This is an indicator that data collection is near its end. There are numerous software programs that are specifically designed to aid the qualitative analysis effort. The American Evaluation Association provides an extensive list at: http://www.eval.org/Resources/QDA.asp

Analytic induction looks at an event and develops a hypothetical statement. Examination of similar events results in testing whether the hypothesis fits or the possibility of hypothesis revision when

Cultural Dimensions			
Structure	Environment	Values	
Cultural Framework			
The institution itself Subcultures within the institution Subcultures within subcultures	Externalities	Individual actors and roles Mission	
Cultural Windows			
Rituals	Symbols	Saga	Heroes
Continuity Socialization Leadership Strategy	Beliefs Information	History Accomplishments	Ideals

Figure 30.3 Sample matrix for data categories

necessary. Similarities strengthen the hypothesis, exceptions call for hypothesis rework. Elasticity of the hypothesis is essential for encompassing all the results—in a manner somewhat akin to understanding that even ill-fitting suits fit to some extent.

Phenomenology or heuristic analysis emphasizes how individuals experience the world by focusing on idiosyncratic meaning rather than shared constructions. The effort here is to understand how the world appears to others. Self-phenomenological study can lead to the uncovering of biases and help establish the researcher's place within the culture or event under examination.

Higher education researchers frequently feel comfortable with the concept of quasi-statistics in which the researcher counts the number of times something is mentioned in field or researcher notes as an estimate of frequency. Often enumeration is used as validation for categories.

Reliability and Validity

The intention of reliability and validity in qualitative methods is to support the argument that the inquiry's findings are "worth paying attention to" (Lincoln & Guba, 1985, p. 290). This is in stark contrast to the quantitative method of attempting to demonstrate validity, or soundness of the interpretations of results, or plausibility of an argument. In qualitative methodology, four issues of trustworthiness require thought: credibility, transferability, dependability, and confirmability. These issues "replace the usual positivist criteria of internal and external validity, reliability, and objectivity" (Creswell, 2003; Denzin & Lincoln, 2000, p. 21).

A means of achieving some measure of accuracy and reliability is the use of repeated observations or repeated asking of the same or similar questions. Reliability can, to a relatively reasonable extent, be determined by noting the generalization of observations. If similar activities or reactions are noted at similar times or under similar circumstances, within the qualitative paradigm, these may be deemed reliable. Accuracy is often approached by allowing participants to review transcripts and/ or notes, whether written or verbal, coupled with questions addressed to how well the researcher captured the essence, tone, or other aspects of the participant's response. Both these techniques are included in the recursive nature of processes: data gathering, data interpretation, data gathering, data interpretation, and so forth.

Questions can be posed regarding reliability of data derived from different sources. The nature and use of triangulation requires different sources of data at least in a broad sense of the term. While sources can differ in the traditional sense of participants, it can also refer to differences in time. A combination of time and participants is a common approach in recursive techniques. Questions of reliability and accuracy can also be posed in regard to ambiguous interpretation. Within a naturalistic paradigm, ambiguity must be a legitimate interpretation. If we subscribe to the required subjective world view that is inherent to qualitative methods, an ambiguous interpretation of data is a natural occurrence. As human beings, how often are we completely sure of anything? Finally, questions can be posed regarding all of the above as being no more than the substantiation of error. Such a question runs contrary to the qualitative paradigm in which there is no right or wrong in the quantitative sense, hence no error. There is only interpretation.

Credibility is an evaluation of whether or not the research findings represent a "credible" conceptual interpretation of the data (Lincoln & Guba, 1985, p. 296). Transferability is the degree to which the findings of this inquiry can apply or transfer beyond the bounds of the project. Transferability should not be confused or compared with reliability in the quantitative sense. Rather, transferability is more a sense of what can be learned from the emergent patterns and themes resident in a particular study and can then be recognized in another. The idea is to seek similarity in context rather than similarity in outcome. Dependability is an assessment of the quality of the multiple methods and recursive processes of data collection, data analysis, and theory emergence. Confirmability is a measure of how well the inquiry's findings are supported by the data collected and is in that sense related to validity (Lincoln & Guba, 1985). Validity in quantitative methods asks whether or not the analysis and interpretation make sense. Likewise, in qualitative methods the idea again is context bound, i.e. given the circumstance and person involved, is the conclusion logical?

The researcher can find validity in qualitative research by examining the divergence from initial expectations, that is the review of researcher notes kept from the beginning to see how the data has pushed the researcher from initial assumptions. Convergence with other sources of data by using various kinds of triangulation and comparisons with the literature are also useful. Triangulation refers to convergent points of data gathered at different times or places, at different levels, and/or between multiple observers of the same phenomenon. Triangulation is also possible between quantitative and qualitative methods and their respective data. The researcher can also look to patterns within extensive quotations from field notes, transcripts of interviews, or researcher notes. Archival data, recordings (video or audio), or documents provide additional resources for data validation.

Adding to the qualitative paradigm of validity, Stake (2010) writes, "Because no one can know it, there is no objective truth," (p.165). We make decisions on a daily basis without any available objective truth, yet there are reasonable assurances inherent in the knowledge we process via our collective experience. The previous statement presents a valid, if that term has any relevance within the subject realm, definition of reliability. Bolstering the essence of qualitative validity, House (1980) paraphrasing Campbell notes, "Things out of context are not interpretable" (p. 84). We only know what we know by observing what we have observed. As we cannot observe everything, our knowing is bound by relativity. By this logic, the descriptive terms used in making arguments and corresponding proofs are either ambiguous or contextually defined. Given that assumption, House notes, "Rational analysis is possible in evaluation but only rarely will it assume syllogistic form," (p.85). The use of multiple researchers allows for a team perspective and additional sources of verification. Member checking, the act of returning to subjects at various points during the study for the purpose of transcript verification or comment upon constructs, hypotheses, and so forth, presents another opportunity for data validation. Finally, the use of recursive techniques in data examination can attest to the validity of initial responses or present new insights and paths to explore. Recursive in this regard refers to the process of reading and re-reading. It is often suggested that to enhance the effectiveness of this process, the order of material be varied from reading to reading. Think about the effectiveness of reading the same list in the same order over and over again. Before long, you are no longer reading the list but relying on memory. By varying the order of the list, you are forced to refocus. The same principle applies here. By reordering the material, you are forced to refocus and often new insights emerge.

Within the context of research methodology, reliability tends to be equated with the ability to replicate results under similar circumstances. The context bound nature of qualitative methods, however, is somewhat antithetical to the idea of reliability. Indeed, high reliability may suggest a systematic bias at work in data, a bias shared by multiple researchers or across observations by the same researcher. Qualitative researchers, therefore, tend to emphasize validity rather than reliability. It is important to realize that low reliability can be consistent with high validity because cultures or phenomena are constantly in flux, that is, people might see things differently within different contexts. Comparison of varying accounts is a holistic activity and can result in a better understanding than singular examinations of separate accounts.

Application to Institutional Research and Other Higher Education Administrators and Student Affairs Personnel

Institutional researchers as well as other higher educational administrators and student affairs personnel frequently come from social science backgrounds and consequently have been exposed to qualitative methods of data analysis. Departmental responsibilities can afford them opportunities to put this training into practice. Additionally, the easy access to non-qualitative campus data allows for the triangulation deemed necessary for validity and reliability. They are also customarily required to distribute their research findings to the campus community. By conducting a cultural analysis and sharing the findings with relevant persons and committees, the research can help shape policy and practice, which ultimately lends purpose and direction to the researcher's activities.

Unlike most quantitative institutional research, qualitative research typically does not measure (what is the institution's retention rate after the freshman year?), produce a quantified product (75% of our students are satisfied with the services of the Registrar), or seek to establish a causal relationship (attendance of the Freshman Seminar increases the likelihood of completing the baccalaureate degree). Qualitative methods can be of use when the topic is unmeasureable or concerned with interaction and/or process. The method is also appropriate for dealing with small *n*, exploring a topic so as to provide the basis for a quantitative follow-up, to interpret cultures, and illuminate or illustrate phenomena.

Harper and Kuh (2007) suggest institutional researchers shun qualitative methods for several reasons. To begin with, they are often more comfortable with quantitative methods, the types of questions these methods address, the tools available to answer these questions, and statistical forms of understanding. They can be uncomfortable with the assumptions of qualitative methods, standards of rigor, and trustworthiness. They have also been conditioned to accept the hypothetical superiority of quantitative methods. On the other hand, the use of qualitative approaches can help answer some of the multifaceted, difficult questions that affect stakeholders in higher education. Despite the growing recognition of the strength and efficacy of qualitative methods, many institutional researchers remain reluctant to employ them.

The importance of campus culture in shaping the behavior and experiences of individuals and groups on campus has long been documented. The values, norms, beliefs, and assumptions that constitute campus culture shape the behavior and experiences of faculty, staff, and students (Feldman & Newcomb, 1969; Kuh, 2001, 2002, 2003; Kuh & Love, 2000; Kuh & Whitt, 1988). Campus culture has been described as "the collective, mutually shaping patterns of institutional history, mission, physical settings, norms, traditions, values, practices, beliefs, and assumptions which guide the behavior of individuals and groups in an institution of higher education and which provide frames of reference for interpreting the meanings of events and actions on and off campus" (Kuh & Hall, 1993, p. 2). Institutional researchers can use qualitative cultural assessments to better understand the role that their campus cultures play in shaping individual and group behaviors and experiences. The following is an example of how an ethnographic study of a campus can lead to a better understanding of its culture and ultimately contribute to achieving its goals (Museus, 2007).

Often mission and/or vision statements express an institution's dedication to student success, but what exactly is meant by student success and who defines it for the campus? This is a good example of the type of questions qualitative methods were designed to answer. Various answers can be expected from conducting a series of semi-structured interviews among faculty, administration, and staff.

The selection of interviewees should correspond to the guidelines referenced earlier. The informed institutional researcher should be aware of campus strata in terms of common bio-demographic characteristics and participants selected should reflect this knowledge. Likewise, the institutional researcher's familiarity with campus personnel allows for the choice of experts, extreme, typical, and atypical cases.

Only three questions are necessary for beginning each interview: (a) How do you define student success? (b) What does the institution do to foster student success? (c) What could it do better? Note that the structure of the questions does not invite one word answers. Responses will often require probing for additional clarity or examples. The interviewer also has the opportunity to ask, "Why?" As noted earlier, the inclusion of "why" in written questionnaires frequently results in few responses, often for the reason that writing out a full explanation can be a somewhat arduous task. Attempting to answer the "why" question in oral form, however, is much less taxing on the interviewee and the interviewer can rephrase and probe until an exhaustive answer is achieved. The ability to follow up via additional questions or interviews is another advantage of qualitative methods not available in the quantitative realm.

Because the institutional researcher is a participant in campus life, the prospects for conducting observations will be more frequent and less obtrusive. Institutional researchers are commonly on committees and in attendance at various meetings and events. By entering such activities with an eye towards participant observation, data can be collected. Even the most trivial of activities, such as lunch in a campus cafeteria, is an opportunity to observe and collect data.

The third method of data collection is also enhanced by the nature of the institutional researcher's role. Traditionally, many public documents are influenced by the department. The process of assembling data also requires access to non-departmental documents and archives not usually associated with other members of the campus community.

In addition to establishing cultural definitions of student success as noted above, qualitative methods can be used in the assessment of courses (Van Note Chism & Banta, 2007). Qualitative method based assessment for courses mostly centers on written or oral narrative activities. An assessment question is posed to students by the faculty member. A typical question might ask to identify the most important thing the student learned in the previous class. Students respond either in a focus group like situation or in writing. As noted earlier, there are disadvantages to the written approach mostly dealing with the effort required, although faculty may choose to incorporate such activities as part of writing intensive initiatives. Similarly, student generated journals or portfolios are typical qualitative data–gathering methods which can provide insights unavailable via standard course assessment surveys.

Interviews, whether individual or group, can provide valuable and detailed information on the effectiveness of student services. Similar to the student success example noted above, the choice of participants should represent an array of student types and situations. Counterbalancing of this effort can be provided by a similar effort aimed at student services personnel. Comparing and contrasting the perception of services presented to the perception of services received offers a truer picture of effectiveness than one-sided surveys.

Student services such as counseling, tutoring, or mentoring programs can play a strong role in an institution's efforts to enhance student success as can initiatives like first year seminars and learning communities. Each student brings a unique story to these activities and will result in a variety of outcomes. Therefore, only a multifaceted approach to data gathering and analysis can be adequate for determining effectiveness at the individual, program, and institutional level.

Summary

Qualitative methodology is a valuable implement that should be resident in every institutional researcher's toolbox. But like any tool, it works best when applied properly in circumstances for which it was designed. Because institutional research is focused on specific campuses, findings must always be context bound. The predictive ability of quantitative methods conducted at singular institutions is limited by both context and sample size. Therefore, having the ability to temper findings via contextualization is necessary for understanding both the true nature of analytical results and their applicability.

References

Bogdan, R. C., & Biklen, S. K. (1998). *Qualitative research for education: An introduction to theory and methods.* Boston, MA: Allyn and Bacon.

Creswell, J. W. (2003). *Research design: Qualitative, quantitative and mixed methods approaches.* Thousand Oaks, CA: Sage.

Denzin, N. K., & Lincoln, Y. S. (2000). Introduction: The discipline and practice of qualitative research. In N. Denzin, & Y. S. Lincoln (Eds.), *Handbook of qualitative research* (2nd ed., pp. 1–28). Thousand Oaks, CA: Sage Publications.

Ely, M., Anzul, M., Friedman, T., Garner, D., & Steinmetz, A. M. (1991). *Doing qualitative research: Circles within circles.* New York, NY: RoutledgeFalmer.

Erlandson, D. A. (this volume). *Naturalistic Evaluation.*

Feldman, K., & Newcomb, T. (1969). *The impact of college on students* (2 Vols.). San Francisco, CA: Jossey-Bass.

Guba, E. (1987). What have we learned about naturalistic evaluation? *Evaluation Practice, 8*(1), 23–43.

Harper, S. R., & Kuh, G. D. (2007). Myths and misconceptions about using qualitative methods in assessment. *New Direction for Institutional Research, 136* (Winter 2007), 5–14.

House, E. R. (1980). *Evaluating with validity.* Beverly Hills, CA: Sage Publications.

Howe, K. R. (1988). Against the quantitative-qualitative incompatibility thesis or dogmas die hard. *Educational Researcher, 17*(8), 10–16.

Kuh, G. D. (2001). *The college student report.* Bloomington, IN: Indiana University, National Survey of Student Engagement, Center for Postsecondary Research and Planning.

Kuh, G. D. (2002). *The college student report.* Bloomington, IN: Indiana University, National Survey of Student Engagement, Center for Postsecondary Research and Planning.

Kuh, G. D. (2003). What we're learning about student engagement from NSSE: Benchmarks for effective educational practices. *Change, 35*(2), 24–32.

Kuh, G. D., & Hall, J. E. (1993). Using cultural perspectives in student affairs. In G. D. Kuh (Ed.), *Cultural perspectives in student affairs work* (pp. 1–14). Lanham, MD: American College Personnel Association.

Kuh, G. D., & Love. P. G. (2000). A cultural perspective on student departure. In J. Braxton (Ed.), *Rethinking the departure puzzle: New theory and research on college student retention* (pp. 196–212). Nashville, TN: Vanderbilt University Press.

Kuh, G. D., & Whitt, E. J. (1988). *The invisible tapestry: Culture in American colleges and universities.* San Francisco, CA: Jossey-Bass.

Kvale, S. (1996). *Interviews: An introduction to qualitative research interviewing.* Thousand Oaks, CA: Sage.

Lincoln, Y., & Guba, E. (1985). *Naturalistic inquiry.* Thousand Oaks, CA: Sage.

Merriam, S. B. (1998). *Qualitative research and case study applications in education.* San Francisco, CA: Jossey-Bass.

Mislevy, R. J., Moss, P. A., & Gee, J. P. (2008). On qualitative and quantitative reasoning in validity. In K. Ercikan & W-R. Roth (Eds.), *Generalizing from educational research: Beyond qualitative and quantitative polarization* (pp. 67–100). New York, NY: Routledge.

Museus, S. D. (2007). Using qualitative methods to assess diverse institutional cultures. *New Direction for Institutional Research, 136* (Winter 2007), 29–40.

Patton, M. Q. (1980). *Qualitative evaluation methods.* Thousand Oaks, CA: Sage.

Patton, M. Q. (2001). *Qualitative research and evaluation methods.* Thousand Oaks, CA: Sage.

Schwandt, T. (1989). Recapturing moral discourse in evaluation. *Educational Researcher, 18,* 11–16.

Scott, D. (2002). Adding meaning to measurement: The value of qualitative methods in practice research. *British Journal of Social Work, 32*(7), 923–930.

Smith, J. K. (1983a). Quantitative versus interpretive: The problem of conducting social inquiry. In E. House (Ed.), *Philosophy of evaluation* (pp. 27–52). San Francisco, CA: Jossey-Bass.

Smith, J. K. (1983b). Quantitative versus qualitative research: An attempt to clarify the issue. *Educational Researcher, 12*(3), 6–13.

Smith, J. K., & Heshusius, L. (1986). Closing down the conversation: The end of the quantitative-qualitative debate among educational researchers. *Educational Researcher, 15*(1), 4–12.

Sofaer, S. (1999). Qualitative methods: What are they and why use them? *Health Services Research, 34*(5 Part 2), 1101–1118.

Stake, R. E. (2010). *Qualitative research: Studying how things work.* New York, NY: Guilford Press.

Van Note Chism, N. & Banta, T. W. (2007). Enhancing institutional assessment efforts through qualitative methods. *New Direction for Institutional Research, 136* (Winter 2007), 15–28.

Yin, R. K. (2002). *Case study research: Design and methods* (3rd ed.). Newbury Park, CA: Sage.

31

NATURALISTIC EVALUATION

David A. Erlandson

Naturalistic inquiry begins with a number of paradigmatic assumptions that distinguish it from traditional positivistic inquiry. The most fundamental of these rests on its conception of reality and how information about that reality can be obtained. Positivistic science assumes that reality is objective and can be ascertained by objective methods and measures. The naturalistic paradigm is agnostic about the nature of reality but assumes that human knowledge cannot completely comprehend reality, and since a human researcher is part of that reality, he cannot be truly objective about it. This assumption of naturalistic research is based upon the axiom that reality is infinite in time and space (at least as humans calculate them) and comprehension is finite. Not only is this the case, but the naturalistic researcher would maintain that reality contains major components that are outside time and space. Furthermore, the naturalistic researcher claims that objective methods are inherently flawed in that they impose classifications that are limited in what they uncover. Part of this has to do with the nature of human language as an abstracting, simplifying, stabilizing device that can never say everything about anything. Another part of it has to do with the inquiry paradigms that are imposed upon reality in trying to understand it. This latter problem is essentially the difficulty portrayed in Thomas S. Kuhn's *The Structure of Scientific Revolutions* (1970).

This fundamental difference has clear epistemological implications that will guide research design and method. The positivistic researcher wants to use valid, reliable, objective measures that provide accurate, generalizable, reliable, objective results. The naturalistic researcher would not deny that this quest may produce valuable results but that, by their very nature, they can produce only approximations that at best give general direction to those who would use them to make decisions. They focus on a few specific research (or evaluation) topics and inevitably ignore many contextual elements that make a difference in how these results can be applied. This problem cannot be totally solved by improving objective methods for research and evaluation in organizations because organizations are social structures and the innumerable interrelations between people in a social context are constantly changing and the context itself continues to change. Social contexts are always messy because of the many human variables that are interacting in unpredictable ways. The positivistic researcher prefers orderly sets of data to analyze and, in an inherently disorderly social context, attempts to impose order upon it. As part of this desire for order he likes to identify linear cause and effect relationships that make analysis easier, even though in doing so he may grossly distort what's really happening in the context. This imposition of a priori order upon a disorderly conduct is in itself a flight from the objectivity he prizes. The naturalistic researcher, by contrast, attempts to understand the messiness and rather than isolating herself by her research methods from the messiness, gets down in the messiness so that she can better understand it. Instead of identifying linear cause and effect relationships, she recognizes that among the elements of the social context there is mutual simultaneous shaping. In other words, every cause is changed by its effect.

Although naturalistic inquiry uses primarily (although not exclusively) qualitative methods, it cannot be equated with qualitative inquiry. The term "qualitative" refers to the methods that are used; "naturalistic" refers to the underlying assumptions that are made and the implications these assumptions have for what can be expected as the result of the research. Much qualitative research is essentially positivistic in that it assumes that objectivity is possible, and it attempts to classify and categorize data and then reduce the meaning of these data to verbal statements of central tendency. One of the clearest indicators that much qualitative research is different from naturalistic research is that it insists that questions, observation protocols, and other data collection procedures be kept uniform throughout the study. Interview subjects are asked the same questions, the same way, in the same order. By contrast, the naturalistic researcher will adjust questions to reflect what the interviewee brings to the interview and will change direction when comments from interviewees indicate that this may lead to fertile new information. While the various classification and categorization schemes used by the positivistic qualitative researcher purport to be objective, they actually reflect the a priori assumptions of the researcher. Furthermore, in reducing a large mass of complex data to a relatively short verbal summary, much of the richness and meaning of those data are essentially ignored.

By contrast with traditional positivistic research, the researcher engaged in naturalistic research focuses first on the context. She begins with a basic question that is something like: "What's happening here?" The naturalistic researcher attempts to expand the meaning of the setting being described to include all that is reasonably possible to include within the limits of the researcher's resources and the comprehension of the audience for whom it is intended. Generally, a rich, naturalistic description of a human context reveals conflicting data that are hard to reconcile and forces that seem to be interacting in chaotic ways. As unsettling as this may be for the researcher who would like to reach a much neater picture of what is happening, it may be an excellent representation of what is actually occurring in that context. Ignoring this messiness in the analysis of data may impair decisions that are made based upon that data.

Naturalistic inquiry is omnivorous in acquiring data that can be used in understanding the human context being studied. Though it starts with the basic question of "What's happening here?" and other robust probing questions, it invites a wide variety of data acquired in a wide variety of ways. It creates an interactive atmosphere among inquiry participants that invites them to expose and explore elements of the context of which the researcher was not originally aware. From interviews, informal conversations, observations, and written artifacts, it acquires the materials for interpreting the basic question ("What's happening here?") with which the researcher began. From this mass of data emerge numerous little stories which merge into a large narrative that is credible to the persons within that context and meaningful to persons outside the context who would wish to understand it.

This rich presentation of the institutional context of a college or university can be used to more fully understand and appropriately apply the information obtained by traditional positivistic methods. What does it mean for an institution that sees that an unacceptable number of students are dropping out after the first semester of their freshman year? What can conceivably be done about perceived grade inflation? What can be done if many graduating students cannot gain admission to graduate school? What can be done to improve equity in faculty ranks and salaries? What can realistically be done to improve faculty performance in teaching and research? How do we effectively diversify our faculty and student body? In considering answers to each of these questions, we must ask: What is likely to be the impact on students, faculty, and other stakeholders if a proposed solution is initiated?

In constructing solutions to these questions, institutions of higher education typically look to what they've done in the past or to what other institutions have done or proposed in similar situations.

But what was done in the institution's past may not be entirely relevant to its present situation, and what was done in the past may in fact be part of the present problems. Furthermore, solutions that were tried (and perhaps worked) at other institutions may not work or at best be marginally effective in the institution that decides to adopt them. Every human institution has its own unique history, and the traditions, customs, norms, and mores that have come out of that history are also unique and are interactive with each other and with the forces for change that are brought on the institution by new faculty, new students, new programs, and changes in the political, financial, and social environments in which the institution operates.

A broad ranging, diverse picture of an institution provided by a naturalistic evaluation can provide college and university decision makers with a context for understanding their institution in a more complete way and with the basis for making effective decisions. Typically, however, college and university administrators will reject the need for generating such a context. Most feel that they already fully understand the traditions, customs, norms, and mores that operate in their institution. But this is generally an illusion. The fact is that, even though they have spent years in the institution, the odds are that they will hold a perception that diverges considerably from what is actually operating. In many cases new faculty and administrators may have a more precise assessment of some aspects of the institution because they stand out in sharp contrast to the institutional environment from which they came. Longtime members of an institution are so accustomed to the regularity of the cultural patterns of their institution that they fail to see them for what they are. How many people are constantly aware of the oxygen they breathe, which is so critical for their very existence? Is a fish aware of the water in which it is swimming? Familiarity dulls the cultural and interpersonal senses. We often need a different look at what's happening in order to recognize it for what it is.

Quality in a Naturalistic Evaluation

If the results of research or evaluation are to be taken seriously, they must meet certain quality criteria. In typical positivistic research these criteria are internal validity, external validity (generalizability), reliability, and objectivity. Internal validity speaks to how accurately the data collected conform to the reality they claim to represent. External validity, or generalizability, reflects how well the results obtained from the inquiry represent the external population to which they will be applied. Reliability refers to the stability of the methods used. If they were to be repeated with the same sample would they produce the same results? Objectivity refers to the degree to which the results are free of contamination by the researcher's biases.

Naturalistic inquiry is also concerned that its findings be taken seriously. However, the methods used by the positivistic researcher cannot readily be applied by the naturalistic researcher. Since, in order to adapt to emerging information and a changing situation, the naturalistic researcher will modify interview questions, observation techniques, and other data collection methods as the inquiry proceeds, the possibility of using instruments that have been determined to be valid before the investigation began makes internal validity, as positivists have defined it, totally impossible. Since methods constantly shift, reliability is also impossible. External validity is not even sought by the naturalistic researcher because generalizations from one complex context to another are simply absurd. Finally, since the research paradigm of the naturalistic researcher denies that true objectivity exists, objectivity cannot be a goal.

Trustworthiness

But if naturalistic inquiry is to be used for any practical purposes, it must demonstrate that it is trustworthy. However, if it is to do this, it is obvious that the standards it uses to demonstrate trustworthiness must be different from those used in positivistic research. Toward this end a set of criteria for establishing the trustworthiness of naturalistic investigation has been developed by Egon Guba and Yvonna Lincoln (Guba, 1981; Guba & Lincoln, 1981, 1989; Lincoln & Guba, 1985). They have proposed four criteria: *credibility, transferability, dependability*, and *confirmability*. These standards are roughly equivalent to the four standards used by positivistic researchers, though quite different in their epistemological foundations. Over the past three decades these criteria have provided the standards by which naturalistic studies may be judged as trustworthy. We will examine each of them in some detail.

Credibility

Credibility attempts to do the equivalent of what internal validity attempts to do for the positivistic researcher, though in a very different way. It attempts to determine if the information obtained by the researcher accurately reflects what is happening in the context being studied. This criterion may be conceived in another way: "Are the results of the inquiry credible to the people in the context being studied?" Or alternatively: "Do the findings and conclusions of the study ring true for the native?" There are several strategies, applied during and after the investigation, that the researcher may apply to achieve this.

First of these is the need for the *prolonged engagement* of the researcher in the research setting. The researcher needs to spend enough time in the setting being investigated to diminish distortion caused by the researcher's presence, to build rapport and relationships with the people there, to obtain a wide scope of data that describe the richness of the setting, and to be able to distinguish between typical behavior and temporary aberrations in that behavior. How long this period will be depends a lot upon the ability and previous experience of the researcher and also upon how familiar she is with settings similar to the one she is examining. If the researcher herself has spent a considerable amount of time working in an institution of higher education, she is likely, other things being equal, to be able, in researching a college or university, to achieve the required rapport and sensitivities more rapidly than a researcher who has not had that background.

If prolonged engagement serves to diminish the distortion caused by the researcher's presence in the setting, *persistent observation* serves to protect the autonomy of the researcher's presence and enables her to actively seek out sources of data identified by the purposes of her investigation. She deliberately uses different tools and different sources to provide different ways of looking at the setting she is investigating. As the researcher learns more about the setting she is studying, persistent observation enables her to raise pointed questions that can sort out relevancies from irrelevancies.

Triangulation refers to the process of substantiating the accuracy of information by having it corroborated by multiple sources. When different persons from different backgrounds and often with conflicting views agree that some information is accurate, it helps make the case for its credibility. In the same way, when information obtained through different means such as interviews, observations, and written documents, all affirm something, its credibility is enhanced.

Referential adequacy materials, generally, are artifacts of human behavior in the context being studied that exist independently of the inquiry, such as brochures, catalogs, yearbooks, photos, or memos that furnish unedited slices of life from the setting being investigated. Since they exist independently from the intrusion of the investigation, they can provide unbiased data that support, refute, or refine interpretations made from data collected from other sources.

Every naturalistic inquiry should provide for *peer debriefing*. Peer debriefing allows one or more persons who are knowledgeable about the inquiry process, but who are not directly involved with the work of the researcher, to analyze materials, question procedures, test hypotheses and emerging designs, listen to the researcher's ideas and concerns, and critique tentative conclusions. The peer debriefer should ask probing questions of the researcher and challenge interpretations with negative case scenarios. Negative case analysis considers alternative interpretations of the data, particularly those emanating from elements in the collection and analysis of data and in the data themselves, that would tend to refute or call into question the researcher's analysis. Through a process not too dissimilar to what happens in a court of law, the researcher, with the assistance of her peer debriefer, critiques her work and seeks to refine her original analysis.

Member checks allow the participants in the investigation to test categories, interpretations, and conclusions that have been made by the researcher. Member checking typically occurs at several times during the process. The interviewer should allow time at the end of each interview to review what she has learned from the interviewee. In subsequent interviews she can verify and expand information gained in earlier interviews. Member checking of data from observations and interviews can also occur in informal conversations during the conduct of the study. Written summary statements can be sent to participants asking for written or oral commentary on the researcher's findings. A draft copy of the final report of the research should be submitted to participants for their confirmation of or disagreement with the findings. In the latter case, the researcher should get further information from participants and make changes in the report if they are necessary.

Another very important tool of the naturalistic researcher (not only for the credibility of the inquiry but also for its transferability, dependability, and confirmability) is the *reflexive journal*. The reflexive journal is something like a diary that the researcher uses to record information about her schedule and logistics, her insights, and her reasons for methodological decisions. The reflexive journal also serves as the main organizer of the researcher's work, showing how decisions were made, why they were made, and the interaction of the researcher with the other elements in her research environment.

Since the naturalistic researcher interacts so personally with the participants she contacts, with the data she collects, and with the interactive processes in the setting being investigated, she should use the reflexive journal to keep track of her own cognitive and emotional development and determine if this is affecting her conduct of the research. If she thinks that this is happening, her peer debriefer and others should work with her to help her get back on track.

Transferability

A study that tells us only about a single social context may be very well done and be highly credible, but if it cannot provide direction for other settings or for the same setting at some point in the future, it has very limited value. As we have noted, the positivistic researcher wants his results to have external validity, that is, to be generalizable to other settings. But the naturalistic researcher believes that true generalizability is impossible. Does this mean that naturalistic research has no application for other settings or for the same setting in the future? The naturalistic researcher would claim that her work can be applicable to other settings, but not in the same way as the positivist sees it. In this regard, we may consider how in normal everyday life we apply what we have learned from our own past or from the experiences of others to our present situation, to situations in the future, and to new situations. Though they make mistakes in this process, most human beings are pretty adept at it. And they do it without the use of any statistical tools. What we need for learning from other situations is an understanding of what is happening in the other situation, an understanding of what our own situation is like, and an understanding of how the two are related. We do this constantly, usually without even thinking about it, and we usually do a fairly good job. Thus we transfer information from one situation to another, and the better understanding we have of both situations, the better the transfer will be.

Naturalistic inquiry seeks to meet the applicability criterion by providing for transferability. If a person leaves one university to take a job in another, his initial behavior in the new institution is conditioned by his learnings from his former institution. He immediately notices things that are similar and things that are different and makes adjustments accordingly. The better he understood his former institution, and the more effectively he learns about his new institution, the better the transfer will be.

The naturalistic researcher does her work with transferability in mind. The goal of transferability is to enable the person in the receiving context to understand how the research can be applied to his situation. The researcher enables this in two ways: (a) by choosing a representative sample from the setting she's researching so that people in other settings can make judgments about its applicability to their own setting, and (b) by describing the research setting in vivid language that enhances the reader's understanding of it by vicariously bringing him into it. To accomplish the first she uses *purposive sampling*. To accomplish the second she uses *thick description* in the presentation of her findings.

Purposive sampling seeks a sample that is as knowledgeable, as diverse, and as articulate as possible but still small enough to be manageable within the resources of the research effort. This guiding principle of efficiently seeking diverse, rich data that represent the breadth and depth of the setting being studied applies not only to the selection of participants for interviews but also to the scheduling of observations and to the identification of documents and records for review.

Thick description enables transferability by using multiple layers of low level abstractions to describe the inner workings of the setting in which the study takes place. The goal is to bring the reader into the setting in such a way that he is given the confidence that he can make his own judgments about it. The researcher must give the reader the same information that brought her to the conclusions she reached. Yet her thick description provides for independence for the reader in two ways—in the interpretation of that information and in the application of that information to the reader's own setting.

Dependability

As previously noted, the positivistic researcher seeks to demonstrate that the data he collected are reliable, that is, if were to do it again, he would substantially replicate the results obtained through the original data collection effort. The naturalistic researcher, who works with a complex, fluid setting, knows that precise replication is impossible. Nevertheless, she recognizes the need to give users of her research the assurance that the methods she used and the way she used them are consistent with the results she obtained. By doing this she can show the *dependability* of her research. In order to provide potential users of her research with an assurance of dependability, she makes provision for a *dependability audit* by constructing an *audit trail* that provides documentation (through interview notes, documents, citations from records, etc.) and a running account of the process (such as excerpts from her reflexive journal) that she followed through her inquiry.

Confirmability

Just as the positivistic researcher wants to show that the results of his research are free of contamination from his own biases, the naturalistic researcher also works to demonstrate a similar freedom from bias contamination in her work. However, she does not believe that the objectivity that the positivist works to demonstrate is really possible, particularly not in a fluid, complex setting in which she has worked closely and personally with the participants in her study. So rather than attempting to show that the results of her research are free of contamination, she relies on showing the *confirmability* of the results themselves. It is something like what is done by an expert descriptive linguist who, by initiating interaction and language with a person whose language was previously unknown to him, can in a relatively short time be communicating effectively (though perhaps still somewhat awkwardly) with that person. To arrive at this point he uses a systematic method of analyzing phonetic sounds and sound sequences as they are reflected in actions and responses. Admittedly, he also uses his intuition to provoke breakthroughs in his work and, in order to elicit responses, he establishes a close relationship with his partner in the venture. It is certainly a process that is filled with bias, but the bias is directed toward obtaining a result—learning a language and being able to communicate with this person whose language he had not previously known. If an intuitive move does not work, he discards it; but if it does, he is one step further to accomplishing his goal. His process is confirmed by its results.

In a similar way the naturalistic researcher confirms her findings by clearly documenting the evidence from her study that supports them. The reasoning behind her findings is contained in her reflexive journal and the supporting evidence is organized in such a way as to make possible a *confirmability audit*.

Authenticity

For decades positivistic researchers were able to take necessary measures to meet validity, reliability, and objectivity without paying too much attention to the possible negative impact of their research efforts. Obviously, it has never been acceptable to deliberately cause pain or suffering to the human subjects of the research efforts (though there are some notorious examples of when this was done "in pursuit of knowledge"). But in recent years researchers have faced much greater scrutiny of their research efforts in terms of their negative or even possible negative impact on human subjects. Institutional review boards (IRBs) at colleges and universities carefully screen all research performed in the institutions and face heavy penalties, including the loss of funding, for failing to sufficiently monitor the quality of research for potential infractions.

These restrictions, of course, apply to naturalistic research as well, and in one sense naturalistic research is even more dangerous because it brings researchers into such close personal contact with the participants in their studies. However, totally aside from what institutional review boards require, naturalistic research has its own standards regarding the treatment of human subjects, which are more stringent than those of the IRB. Unlike positivistic research, which refers to the participants in its studies as subjects, naturalistic research considers its participants as partners. The naturalistic researcher recognizes that these partners should benefit from the research being done as much as the researcher benefits from it. It is not enough to protect the participants from harm; they must also gain value from the research. This requirement is met by five criteria for authenticity: *fairness, ontological authenticity, educative authenticity, catalytic authenticity,* and *tactical authenticity* (Guba & Lincoln, 1989). These are equally as important as the trustworthiness criteria. Some authorities would say they are even more important.

Fairness

Fairness requires that the views of all stakeholders have equal access to the research process, that this access remains open throughout the conduct of the research, and that it contains an appeal mechanism for stakeholders who believe that the process has been compromised. Informed consent is obtained at the beginning of the research but must be renewed continually. The dynamics of any social setting are in continuous flux, and as they change in a research process, the power dynamics of the research process will change. Accordingly, the stakeholders' perceived impact of the research also changes and may require that the original agreement be renegotiated. This is a condition that the typical positivist researcher would reject.

But to the experienced naturalistic researcher such vulnerability is seen as an asset in conducting the research. One benefit is that it enables the researcher to recognize emerging problems in their early stages while they are still manageable. Further it keeps the process fresh and personal and frees up the flow of information. These are factors that enhance the value of the researcher's work.

Ontological Authenticity

Ontological authenticity relates to the way that individuals construct the world around them and bring it to the social context. The naturalistic research process should clarify those constructions and should enable participants in a study to improve the way they experience the world around them. Testimonies from participants regarding the changes they've experienced because of their participation in the study provide evidence that the ontological authenticity criterion has been met.

Educative Authenticity

Educative authenticity reflects the ways in which the constructions of participants have been enriched and enhanced by the constructions of their peers and by their experiences in the study. Participation in the study should broaden participants' understanding of what their fellow participants bring to the social context. Here again their testimonies provide the evidence that this has happened.

Catalytic Authenticity

Catalytic authenticity is reflected in the extent that participants' expanded constructions enable decisions and actions. This can be demonstrated by the participants' expressed desire to use these expanded constructions and by evidence that they have used them.

Tactical Authenticity

Tactical authenticity is represented by the degree to which participants actually act to have an impact on their social context. This can be shown by later evidence of how they have affected their organizations and by evidence of their empowering during the research process.

These quality criteria for building trustworthiness and authenticity into a naturalistic inquiry are not something additional that the researcher must insert into her design and methodology. They are essential parts of that design and methodology and are intrinsic to the way the inquiry is conducted. The very way the naturalistic researcher selects and applies the tools she uses in her in research should testify to the paramount role of these quality criteria.

Data Collection and Data Analysis in Naturalistic Inquiry

In the previous section on the quality criteria of naturalistic inquiry, we made reference to the methodological tools that serve the purposes of that research and the quality criteria by which they are judged. Much more could be added about each of these tools but limitations of space prevent us from explaining each of them in depth here. The reader who is interested in learning more about them should consult sources that deal with them in greater depth. However, two of those methods, interviews and observations, are also used in positivistic research; but their form and purpose in a naturalistic inquiry are markedly different. Accordingly, we will take some space here to describe the naturalistic interview and the naturalistic observation in greater depth. Following that we will briefly describe the major features of the analysis process used by the naturalistic researcher.

The Naturalistic Interview

A positivistic interview generally starts with the premise that the researcher knows what questions he will ask, the order in which he will ask them, and the type of answers he will get to those questions. As a lead question, he may ask a professor: "Approximately how many hours a week do you spend in preparing for each of your classes?" and follow this with questions like "Do you find that this is sufficient?" Or another lead question: "What has your publication record been over the past 12 months?" This might be followed up with "How many journal articles have you had published during this period?" to which he might then add: "In what journals have these been published?"

The naturalistic interviewer may ask similar questions, but none of them will be scheduled and will probably be chosen in response to something the interviewee has brought into the conversation. The naturalistic researcher is looking at a broad range of information that will help her understand a complex social context, and she selects interviewees and will propose basic research questions with this in mind. A lead question might be: "What do you consider to be the role of a professor at this university?" She might follow up with a question: "Which aspects of this role do you find most rewarding?" And, if the information is not supplied in the original response, she might continue: "Why do you find these aspects rewarding?" The naturalistic researcher wants first of all to get the interviewee's big picture interpretation of the social context in which he is operating and then work with him to fill in the specifics that make the big picture come alive. The positivistic researcher sees the interviewee as a source of data from which he wants to extract information in order to answer the researcher's questions. The naturalistic researcher sees the interviewee as a partner in her research who can help her understand the meaning of a social context from the inside.

As a result, the naturalistic researcher goes into an interview with a limited number of robust basic questions which, if answered in depth, will provide a tentative sketch of a social context as seen through the interviewee's eyes. Prior to going into the interview she imagines probable ways the interviewee may answer her question and possible follow-up questions to which these may lead; but she is not bound by them. As the interviewee talks, the researcher's main goal is to let him feel in charge and to go on to answer the basic question as fully as he can. With short, gentle responses, or even the nod of her head, she keeps the conversation on track and moving forward until she feels reasonably satisfied that she has obtained as full a description as she can at that time. If the interviewee wanders into answering what the researcher has identified as belonging to another basic question, she makes note of that and encourages the interviewee to continue his thoughts on that question until he comes to a pause. If she feels there is still more to find out about the first basic question, she then may direct the conversation back to it. She may also use the interviewee's meandering into another basic question to use it as a bridge, at that point or later in the interview, to bring the conversation around to that basic question.

The important thing here is to allow the interviewee to tell his own story. The naturalistic researcher does not want to override it with hers. If she really wants to understand a social context as insiders understand it, she must let them define the parameters of that context and fill in the details that they feel are most relevant. At the end of the interview, the naturalistic researcher takes a few minutes to review what she has learned from the interviewee and to allow that person to make corrections in her understanding. She wants to make sure that she has been faithful to the interviewee's interpretation and has not imposed her own.

After the interview, the naturalistic researcher reviews the notes she has taken or listens to the tape recording of the interview if she has made one. From this she identifies what she has learned and what she has not learned. If any of her basic questions were not fully answered, she structures new questions that will help her lead the interviewee back to these unanswered areas in her next interview. Perhaps more important, she may find that she has uncovered whole new areas of relevant information that she hadn't anticipated and that may lead to the forming of new basic questions for subsequent interviews.

How long does the naturalistic researcher continue with subsequent interviews of a single interviewee? The simple but uncertain answer is: As long as she believes she is still getting productive information. Realistically, given the restraints of time and other resources, she cannot go on indefinitely conducting interviews, but she must never shut off the possibility of additional interviews with an individual if she can help it. The general rule regarding follow-up interviews should be: Never lock the door behind you when you leave. You may need to go back.

What we've described here is very different from the type of interview that is typically used in positivistic qualitative research. The naturalistic researcher needs to realize that the interview is the joint enterprise of two partners, designed to use the rich understandings of one partner, the interviewee, to educate the understandings of the other partner, the researcher.

The Naturalistic Observation

In selecting sites for observation the researcher takes much the same stance she took with regard to interviews. She is open to a wide range of information that can help her understand the social context. She wants to look at diverse settings, but especially those where she can observe human interaction. She will want to observe faculty meetings, meetings of student organizations, casual conversations, gatherings of people at various phases—all with a view toward enriching her understanding of the organization she is observing.

She will use all of her senses to the fullest extent possible. She will listen, look, and even smell what's happening in the various settings she observes. At times she may even close her eyes, so that the powerful vehicle of sight does not mask what she can hear or smell. She pays attention to who talks to whom about what. She wonders about those persons who isolate themselves in their own offices. She makes notes about what she observes and what meanings she extracts from these observations.

She allows the meaning she has obtained from her observations to interact with the meanings she has gleaned from her interviews and other sources. She will use what she has observed to form new basic research questions, to structure her future interview questions, and to select additional interviewees. Her observations may raise questions that lead her back into an examination of documents and records. She will also consider how non-human factors, such as the architecture of a building, interact with the human activity she observes. She must never ignore the impact of her own presence as an observer and must consider that impact in making her interpretations. She is, in fact, analyzing data at the same time she is collecting them. As we will note in the following section, for the naturalistic researcher, the two processes are inextricably intertwined.

Analysis in a Naturalistic Study

Many of the techniques we've described in discussing what the naturalistic researcher can do to assure trustworthiness in her work are tools for both data collection and data analysis, including the interviews and observations which we have just discussed. Further, as we have noted, in naturalistic research data collection and data analysis cannot entirely be separated. By contrast, in positivistic research the processes of data collection and data analysis are separated, and usually data analysis does not begin until data collection stops. The two processes are separated primarily because of the positivistic researcher's concern for objectivity. If analysis done by the researcher, after data have been collected, affects future data collection, how can that data collection be objective?

But for the naturalistic researcher who does not think objectivity is even possible, interaction between data collection and data analysis is not only inevitable, but it is also desirable. If a researcher learns from her first interview that her question could be worded in a much better way, why would she blindly use the same inefficient question with her second interview?

The constant comparative method of analysis was introduced by Glaser and Strauss (1967) as a means for deriving theory from the data that are grounded in the social context being studied. Naturalistic inquiry uses this method, or something similar to it, in analyzing the data it collects. As soon as her first data are collected, the naturalistic researcher analyzes them and forms working hypotheses that she feels best represent what she has learned. As she proceeds, she uses every bit of new data she collects to shape and be shaped by the analysis that has preceded it. The process may be summed up: Collect, Analyze, Hypothesize, Collect, Analyze, Revise Hypotheses, Collect, and so on, until the process has been brought to its conclusion.

When does the process come to its conclusion? Ideally, it will not be concluded until new data add nothing to what has already been collected and analyzed. If, because of deadlines, lack of funding, or for whatever reason, this point never is reached, the researcher, in transparency and in fairness to those who read her final report, discloses that limitation in reporting her work. During the course of the study the researcher faithfully records the changing nature of the hypotheses she forms and indicates in her reflexive journal why she has formed them and why she modifies them. She does this in order to allow for an audit of her work and to enable future researchers to build upon her work.

Conducting a Naturalistic Evaluation

Conducting a naturalistic evaluation in a college or university immediately raises the question of who will do this. A comprehensive naturalistic evaluation of a large research university will take a lengthy period of time and will be too great a task for a single evaluator to assume. By the time she has finished the work, much of her earlier data will be out of date. However, it would be possible for a large university to employ an experienced naturalistic researcher full time and use that evaluator to review various elements and processes of the institution one at a time in a series of smaller case study evaluations. A smaller unit within the university might initiate its own naturalistic evaluation using a single evaluator. But as the size of a unit increases, it is more feasible to use a team rather than a single individual to perform a naturalistic evaluation. Although it is difficult to identify just when a given institution or unit of an institution is too large to be evaluated by a single individual, a rule of thumb might be to consider the number of 100 full-time employees as the point at which a team should be used rather than an individual. However, this is not a magic number, and the complexity of the organization being studied, the purposes of the evaluation, and similar considerations will affect whether the situation is more suitable for evaluation by a single naturalistic researcher or by a team. In either case the same general principles of data collection, data analysis, and the requirements for meeting trustworthiness and authenticity criteria will remain essentially the same.

With this in mind we will follow a naturalistic evaluation team through the stages of the evaluation from the initiation of the evaluation through the completion and delivery of the final report of the evaluation. We have chosen to describe the processes for a naturalistic evaluation team rather than for a single evaluator because the processes are slightly more complex due to the need for coordinating the efforts of multiple individuals. However, the tasks described for the team and the way they are approached are essentially the same for a single evaluator as they are for an evaluation team. Even the development of a time line, which is described below and which is especially important for a team evaluation because of its additional complexities, should be included in the early stages by the individual naturalistic evaluator.

Initiating a Naturalistic Evaluation

Before a naturalistic evaluation is begun or even planned in an educational organization it must be absolutely clear that the person or persons who hold formal authority in the organization have endorsed it and fully understand its implications. More than one such evaluation has failed because the president, dean, department head, or unit director never fully realized everything that the evaluation entailed. After the decision has been made to initiate a naturalistic evaluation, this person in authority then commissions the evaluation and assigns one person to take responsibility for overseeing the evaluation, to select a team to design and conduct the evaluation, to identify broad goals for the evaluation within the charge given by the commissioning agent, to develop a plan for the evaluation, and then report back with that plan to the commissioning agent.

Identifying a Team for a Naturalistic Evaluation

In bringing together a team for a naturalistic evaluation, two characteristics are important: diversity and compatibility. The team should be selected from a diversity of positions in the organization so that a full range of experience and institutional knowledge is available to the team. Equally important is a diversity of skills on the team. The team will be involved in interviewing, observing, analyzing, and reporting the results of the evaluation. All of these skills should be well represented on the team. All team members should be able to demonstrate empathy with the full range of participants in the organization and be able to apply the criteria for trustworthiness and authenticity in their work. Finally, since the team members will be sharing their work with each other, and in some cases will be serving as peer debriefers for each other, it's important that they be reasonably compatible and that they recognize the strengths of their fellow team members. They can disagree about religion, politics, and nearly everything else, but they must be committed to working together to produce a quality evaluation.

Designing a Plan for a Naturalistic Evaluation

After the original team for designing and implementing the evaluation has been formed (the team's membership may change somewhat over time, as additional members with special skills or unique points of view are identified, or as original members decide to drop out), the team's first task is to put together a tentative design for the evaluation. They must address several questions:

1. What information do we know that we'll need?
2. What sources can supply us with this information?
3. What procedures can be most effectively used to tap the information that these sources possess?
4. How do we best schedule our resources to collect and analyze the data we receive?
5. What time line can we establish for answering these questions and completing the final report?
6. How do we report this information back to the stakeholders?
7. In designing the evaluation process, have we taken steps to ensure that we address the quality criteria of trustworthiness and authenticity?

As we begin our planning for the evaluation, we can, in response to the first question, probably identify certain types of information that we know we'll need. But we must also realize that there are other types of information that we don't know now that we'll need, but which will arise most certainly as our inquiry proceeds. The team must make plans for being sensitive to these information needs as they emerge during the course of the evaluation. This reality reminds the team that, when they consider establishing a time line, a certain amount of slack must be built into the evaluation design to accommodate unforeseen needs for new knowledge. Similarly, in answering the second question regarding the identification of probable sources of information, the team must recognize that, as the evaluation proceeds, additional sources will emerge, and allowance must be made for including them.

In answering the third and fourth questions, the team will identify the procedures they will use, including interviews, observations, examination of documents and records, reflexive journals, and collection of referential adequacy materials. They must also consider how they may use these procedures in conjunction with one another so that each procedure may be informed from what is learned from previous procedures. Observations may inform subsequent interviews, and interviews may inform subsequent observations. Group interviews may precede individual interviews in order to identify the potential value of subsequent individual interviews. Or conflicting data obtained from individual interviews may be clarified by a group interview. Examination of documents and records may lead to better interview questions, and information obtained from interviews may give direction in examining documents and records. Referential adequacy materials may suggest anomalies that can be investigated by interviews and observations. Few of these relationships can be fully known in advance, and that is why the team must anticipate that they will occur and must allow time in their schedule for accommodating them.

The tentative time line must allow reasonable time for the events it schedules to take place. An arbitrary schedule that does not allow for the emerging time requirements of data collection and analysis (including time for peer debriefing and for team meetings where collected data can be disseminated throughout the entire group, where team members have a chance to share their experiences, and where systematic evaluation of data can take place) is certain to run into disaster. As we've noted, time must be allowed to take advantage of data collection opportunities that were not evident earlier. And, most important, adequate time must be scheduled for individual, small group, and large group analysis. Researchers of all stripes tend to emphasize data collection over data analysis. This is particularly true for the naturalistic researcher since data collection and data analysis interact throughout the research process. The evaluation team must specifically plan for substantial and frequent periods when team members can look at the data they've collected and ask: "What meanings are coming out of the data we've collected?" They then need to ask: "What does our analysis suggest we must do in our future data collection efforts?" In addition to planning for team analyses, the team should make plans and personnel assignments for enabling team members to serve as peer debriefers for each other's work and also assign some team members to serve the same function by critiquing and suggesting negative case scenarios for the team's analyses.

Since the final report represents the culmination of the entire process, all earlier questions must be considered with it in mind. As data are collected and analyzed, the team should be tentatively considering how the information gleaned from the data will be most effectively communicated in the final report. Tentatively building the report as the evaluation proceeds significantly saves time and energy in writing the report at the end of the evaluation.

All of these considerations must be built into the time line. Although we have listed our seven design questions in a logical order, it must be kept in mind that they are not discrete. The first six questions remain open almost until the end, and while the earlier questions are being answered, the team must keep in mind the subsequent questions and begin to consider them in their relation to the earlier questions.

The seventh question regarding the quality criteria of trustworthiness and authenticity must be in the forefront of the evaluation team's thoughts and evident in all its design decisions as they answer the first six questions. In addition to making plans to ensure that the evaluation process is open and transparent to all stakeholders, individual members must plan for individual and group roles in developing ontological, educative, catalytic, and tactical authenticity. Also, to enable outsiders to evaluate the processes and findings of the evaluation team, plans must be made for constructing an audit trail throughout the duration of the evaluation process.

All of these plans are tentative of course and will change as new information is obtained and external circumstances (e.g., an unexpected event occurs in the organization or its environment) require it.

Implementing the Evaluation

Once an evaluation team has designed and developed a plan for a naturalistic evaluation and the plan has been approved by the commissioning agent, the first step is to reach an understanding among all stakeholders about the purposes of the evaluation and the way in which it will be implemented. It must be made clear to all stakeholders that the purpose of the evaluation is to identify ways in which the organization can be improved and how those ways will affect all stakeholders. These stakeholders must be given the opportunity to ask questions and express their reservations about the evaluation and explain why they have their reservations. These questions and reservations must be taken seriously and responded to honestly by those who are seeking to initiate the evaluation. Furthermore, it must be clear that the process will be entirely transparent and that with the help of all stakeholders it will be modified if changes are considered desirable. There must be an appeals process in place if any stakeholder feels that the process has been compromised. The standards for informed consent may need to be renegotiated throughout the process to protect stakeholders who feel that the process is likely to harm them. Any person who wishes to drop out of the evaluation process may do so at any time.

Why is all of this necessary? Isn't this going to bog the evaluation down in endless wrangling? Why not just get informed consent at the beginning and then don't deviate from the original plan for the execution of the evaluation? There's no doubt about it that to most positivistic evaluators, what we've proposed sounds unnecessary and dangerous. But the naturalistic evaluator is likely to see things differently and should have no problem with these conditions. Rather than seeing them as obstacles, she sees them as opportunities. After all, she knows that she is about to begin a process in which she will need to get below surface responses and obtain the full range of honest, detailed, often emotional information that the people in the organization have and which is so important for the success of the evaluation. She knows also the reaction of most people when they hear they are going to be evaluated. She knows that many people consider that an evaluation is something that someone does to someone else, with unpleasant consequences for the persons being evaluated. She wants to allay these fears and she wants to be able to trust the participants in the study. She also wants them to know that they can trust her. Once the process has begun and the participants can see that she really means what she promised, things will go faster and much easier. The depth and honesty of the information she receives will more than offset any difficulties she experienced in getting the evaluation process started.

It cannot be stressed enough how important it is to make participants true partners in the evaluation. Their support and cooperation is essential. Once obtained, the naturalistic researcher must do everything possible to preserve the bond of trust which has been established with the study's participants. The author can personally testify to the value of this bond of trust. He was pleasantly surprised more than once when participants in an evaluation study, with whom he had formed a bond of trust, initiated contact with him to furnish him with information that he had not overtly sought but which they believed would be important to the study. He found out important information that may have been lost to his evaluation if the participants had not felt as though they were true partners in the process.

As suggested in the previous section, designing the evaluation does not stop at the end of the formal designing stage. As the evaluation team commences on their first round of data collection and analysis, its members need to begin to ask a question that will recur throughout the entire process: "What are we learning that can improve the way we are conducting this evaluation?" As they use their early learning to inform future data collection efforts, they begin to ask questions like: "How well has the trustworthiness of our data been established?" and "How can we confirm, refute, or modify our hypotheses through triangulation methods or member checks?"

As their evaluation matures through successive rounds of data collection and analysis, they begin to ask questions such as: "How fertile have our analysis sessions been?"; "How can we improve our analysis sessions?"; "Is peer debriefing effective among our team members?"; "Do we need to strengthen the peer debriefing process?"; "Are the reflexive journals being maintained and are they serving their intended purpose with each of our team members?"; "Are we supporting the authenticity of our participants?"; "How can we better ensure that authenticity criteria are being met in our evaluation?; "Are we building support for a final report that can impact and strengthen the organization?"; and "Are we collecting thick descriptive material that will enable us to write our final report in a way that will enable the stakeholders in the organization to take positive action to enhance their effectiveness?"

As the evaluation approaches its conclusion, an increasing amount of time is spent on analysis, seeking particular pieces of information that seem to be missing, and obtaining additional support for tentative conclusions through triangulation techniques and member checks. The team reviews its works, particularly the meanings it has arrived at, and as necessary makes modifications. These final processes are important and should not be rushed. The team's time line should have allowed sufficiently for this final review process, and if the time line has been managed properly, this should not be a problem.

Reporting the Results of the Evaluation

As the team begins to work on the final report of the evaluation, they should take time as a team to carefully consider what they want to say in the report, to whom they want to say it, and how it can most effectively be said. These three considerations are closely related.

Who is their audience? Certainly one primary audience is the initiating agent to whom the first copy of the report will be delivered. But another audience that is equally important is the stakeholders in the social context that the team has been evaluating, the evaluation participants who have become their trusted partners in the evaluation. Secondary audiences include other institutions and organizations that want to learn from the findings of the evaluation, other evaluators who are interested chiefly in learning from the process, and the general public.

What does the team want to say to their primary audiences? They want to present these audiences with what they have found, the certainty of their findings, and direction for applying what they learn from these findings to the real world in which they operate.

How can they most effectively communicate their findings and the implications of those findings to their primary audiences? Although the evaluation team's identification of what they need to say to their primary audiences may be right on target, the team's efforts will have little impact unless they can report their findings in such a way that they are not only understood but enthusiastically embraced by both the initiating agent and the stakeholders within the evaluated unit. And this is not any easy task.

Many people have learned to make efficient and effective formal reports that say very precisely what they want to say. But more is expected here. Anyone who has read large numbers of institutional reports know how generally dull they are, even when they are saying some very valuable things. The people who can together translate the findings and recommendations of the naturalistic evaluation into action (i.e., the initiating agent and the other internal stakeholders) must be motivated by the report to actually take action. This means that the report must make the findings come alive and stimulate them to action. This takes special writing skills. Of all the skills that are required by members of an evaluation team, the ability to write in this way is perhaps the most rare. In selecting team members, it is desirable to include persons with this skill.

Any report of a naturalistic study should read almost like a good novel and should provide specific details that bring the reader into the setting being studied and make him feel confident that the report reflects an understanding of the human dynamics of the setting. Readers must also see how what is written in the final report applies to their current situation. For the primary audiences of a naturalistic evaluation this should be relatively easy since the transferability that is sought is not from another institution, but from their own institution at a not too distant earlier date. Nevertheless, the report must inspire and motivate the reader to fully comprehend the report in language that is so specific and so credible that it is impossible for anyone familiar with the setting to deny it. As noted, not everyone has the writing skill to accomplish this effect upon the report's readers. At least one member with this skill should be made part of the evaluation team and should take the lead in drafting the final report.

After a draft of the final report has been completed and has been reviewed by the evaluation team, it is time to send it out to those participants whose views have contributed to the report for a final member check. Depending upon the number of participants who have provided data for the report, the draft of the final report may or may not be sent to all the participants. However, it is crucial that the report is reviewed by all major contributors to it, to representatives of every stakeholder group, and to individuals whose views were clearly different from those of the majority of participants. Essentially, the report should be credible to all the stakeholders, and it should not compromise or potentially harm anyone. All stakeholders should be invited to submit their concerns in writing or in person to the evaluation team.

In reviewing what participants have submitted in response to the report, the team should consider them carefully and get back to the participants who have submitted them to see how an issue may be better reported. In many cases, the objections to the report will be merely disagreement about reported facts that are relatively unimportant to the main message of the report. These can be corrected relatively easily. In cases where individuals believe that either they or other persons may be harmed by the report, team members will work with them to use wording that does not have these harmful effects. Where there are differences in interpretation about significant portions of the report, team members will work with the participants to resolve the differences satisfactorily, and, if they cannot do so, include these divergent views as a minority report. If a majority of the participants hold a significantly different view regarding an interpretation the team has made, the team needs to reconsider what they have written, work with stakeholders to resolve the differences if possible, and then rewrite the conflicting portion to bring it into line with the interpretation of the stakeholders. Although this is always a possibility that must be kept in mind, in this author's personal experience this has never happened, nor has he heard of a case where it has happened. If the evaluation has been conscientiously done, it is very unlikely that the draft of the final report will, as a whole, not be seen as highly credible by the stakeholders. This credibility in the eyes of the stakeholders is the key to whether or not the naturalistic evaluation will be of value to them in determining the future direction of their institution.

Final Thoughts

Within a relatively few pages this chapter has attempted to provide the reader with an understanding of what naturalistic inquiry is, what it provides, and how a naturalistic evaluation can be implemented. It does not provide sufficient direction for a person or organization to actually perform such an evaluation, though it may have sufficiently presented naturalistic inquiry's unique contributions to motivate readers into exploring it further. If conducted in the way it's designed, naturalistic research and evaluation can do a remarkably effective job of answering many of the institutional questions that keep administrators and other stakeholders in colleges and universities awake at night. It is aimed at the human questions, and not only the questions about individuals, but about the total interactions between humans in a social context.

The interested reader is encouraged to read other sources. Some of these have already been identified in this chapter. For a general understanding of what naturalistic inquiry is and what it can do, we recommend particularly two books by Egon Guba and Yvonna Lincoln: *Naturalistic Inquiry* (Lincoln & Guba, 1985) and *Fourth Generation Evaluation* (Guba & Lincoln, 1989). Another book that may be useful because it was written specifically with application of naturalistic inquiry in mind is *Doing Naturalistic Inquiry* by the present author and three of his former doctoral students (Erlandson, Harris, Skipper, & Allen, 1993).

There are also a number of other sources that can be of great value in the implementation of naturalistic inquiry. Two of these that can help build specific skills of data collection and data analysis are James P. Spradley's *The Ethnographic Interview* (1979) and *Participant Observation* (1980). Another book that the author found quite useful when he was getting started using naturalistic inquiry is the collection of essays edited by Robert W. Habenstein, *Pathways to Data* (1970). Still another is *Participatory Action Research*, edited by William Foote Whyte (1991). The basic source, cited earlier, for understanding the process of analysis in naturalistic and similar studies is Barney Glaser and Anselm Strauss's *The Discovery of Grounded Theory* (1967). And there are many other sources that can provide direction for those who would like to implement naturalistic studies. An excellent overview of related material is contained in the third edition of *The Sage Handbook of Qualitative Research*, edited by Norman Denzin and Yvonna Lincoln (2005). Finally, for the institution or individual researchers who would like to apply naturalistic evaluation in their own settings, but who feel in need of further guidance, these sources may provide help in identifying individuals who can assist them in getting started.

References

Denzin, N., & Lincoln, Y. (Eds.). (2005). *The Sage handbook of qualitative research.* Thousand Oaks, CA: Sage.

Erlandson, D., Harris, E., Skipper, B., & Allen, S. (1993). *Doing naturalistic inquiry.* Newbury Park, CA: Sage.

Glaser, B., & Strauss, A. (1967). *The discovery of grounded theory.* Hawthorne, NY: Aldine.

Guba, E. (1981). Criteria for assessing the trustworthiness of naturalistic inquiries. *Educational Communication and Technology Journal, 29,* 75–92.

Guba. E., & Lincoln, Y. (1981). *Effective evaluation.* San Francisco, CA: Jossey-Bass.

Guba. E., & Lincoln, Y. (1989). *Fourth generation evaluation.* Newbury Park, CA: Sage.

Habenstein, R. (Ed.). (1970). *Pathways to data.* Chicago, IL: Aldine.

Kuhn, T.S. (1970). *The structure of scientific revolutions* (2nd ed.). Chicago, IL: University of Chicago Press.

Lincoln, Y., & Guba, E. (1985). *Naturalistic inquiry.* Beverly Hills, CA: Sage.

Spradley, J. P. (1979). *The ethnographic interview.* New York: Holt, Rinehart, & Winston.

Spradley, J. P. (1980). *Participant observation.* New York: Holt, Rinehart, & Winston.

Whyte, W. F. (Ed.). (1991). *Participatory action research.* Newbury Park, CA: Sage.

32

RESPONSIVE EVALUATION

Kelly E. Godfrey and Doreen B. Finkelstein

Today's evaluation professionals are facing the same challenges and theoretical conundrums that evaluators have been facing since the beginnings of the profession: What should be paid attention to in an evaluation—processes, outcomes, or both? What data should be gathered, and how? What methods of analysis should be used? What claims do evaluators want ultimately to be able to make, and what constitutes evidence of those claims? Who should judge the value of the program? And finally, what role should stakeholders play, and how should results be communicated to them? How evaluators answer these questions depends upon a multitude of factors, including program goals, client needs and the evaluator's own philosophical outlook. Any given evaluation can take many different paths, and understanding those paths along with their accompanying trade-offs is an important component of modern evaluation practice.

The value of evaluation is widely recognized by funders. Large foundations and granters such as the Bill and Melinda Gates Foundation, the National Science Foundation, and the U.S. Department of Education all require that proposals for the development and implementation of educational programs include an evaluation component. A good evaluation not only can provide program personnel (and funders) with the information they need to judge the success of a program; it can also give valuable feedback for future program improvement. However, education professionals do not always understand the value of evaluation, and sometimes they even view it as an unnecessary burden, a mandated system for collecting unneeded information that consumes valuable time and resources. One of the first challenges of any evaluator is therefore to connect with program providers and other stakeholders in order to ensure that the full value of the evaluation is being communicated and understood.

This chapter covers the principles of responsive evaluation, a distinct approach to program evaluation that foregrounds this important principle of understanding and being responsive to the viewpoints of stakeholders. Along with discussing responsive evaluation and its relation to other evaluation approaches, the chapter will explore the notion of what it means to be "responsive," looking at the evaluation choices that are made and relating those choices to ongoing issues of measurement and practice in such realms as academic assessment, survey methodology, and qualitative data analysis.

Historical Context and Comparison to Other Approaches

In 1967, Robert Stake published a seminal paper entitled *The Countenance of Educational Evaluation* (Stake, 1967) where he argued that for an evaluation to be valuable, concentration on outcome measures is not enough; in order for an educational program to be fully understood, its evaluation must include description in addition to judgment. Also, as Stake pointed out, educators of the time relied little on formal evaluation, partly due to a natural resistance to opening themselves up to criticism by outsiders, and partly due to the fact that most formal evaluations did not address the questions that the educators themselves were most interested in getting answered. In 1972, Stake again addressed this issue of an evaluation where the processes of describing and judging are both essential components (Stake, 1972). In a time when publication and circulation of formal evaluations were scarce and usually oriented solely around student outcomes, Stake made an argument for a form of evaluation that focused on understanding program activities and communicating results to stakeholders in ways that fit their natural understandings. Over the years these initial conceptions of responsive evaluation have been added to and refined (see Abma, 2006; Abma & Stake, 2001; Stake, 1975; Stake, 2003) to evolve into an approach that is very different in outlook and philosophy from other popular evaluation methodologies used today (Worthen, Sanders, & Fitzpatrick, 1997).

One approach with stark differences to responsive evaluation is Tyler's objective-oriented evaluation. Conceived in the 1930s, Tyler's design emphasizes identifying a program's intended outcomes and measuring the extent to which the program obtains these goals and objectives (Tyler, 1950). Another popular evaluation approach is Stufflebeam's CIPP model, which focuses on the four components of context, input, process, and product. This approach, oriented towards serving decision makers, still places an emphasis on the objectives of the program and measuring success in intended outcomes (Stufflebeam, 1971). In Stake's perspective, these methods can overlook different meaningful perspectives and be limited due to adherence to structure and insensitivity to issues that emerge later in the evaluation (Stake, 1975). Scriven's evaluation approach (Scriven, 1967) also stands in contrast to responsive evaluation, as he calls for evaluators to serve as experts and make judgments on the value of a program. Meanwhile, advocates of responsive evaluation value plurality of viewpoints, seeing the evaluator's opinion as no more important or "expert" than that of stakeholders (House, 2001; Stake, 2003).

Essential Components and Distinguishing Features

What makes an evaluation responsive? Unlike its predesigned methodological counterparts, responsive evaluation focuses more on the process and activities of the program's implementation than on predetermined objectives and intended outcomes. Stake (1975) specifies three distinct characteristics of the responsive evaluation: it focuses on the activities more than the objectives, emphasizes providing information to audiences, and reflects the different values present among stakeholders of the program. The responsive evaluator relies on a system of actions and reactions, obtaining statements of value and input from multiple sources related to the program, and presenting multiple perspectives to interested audiences. Another important distinction between responsive evaluation and other evaluation approaches is that rather than relying on preordinate questions—questions that are determined prior to the start of the evaluation—questions are allowed to develop during the course of the evaluation as information is gathered and issues are uncovered (Abma & Stake, 2001; Stake, 1975).

The first main trait of responsive evaluation is the focus on activities more than objectives. This does not mean that being responsive requires ignoring the objectives of the program; rather, the role of the evaluator is to investigate implementation and processes alongside measuring the program's outcomes. There are numerous reasons why even a summative, objectives-oriented evaluation benefits from looking at program activities in addition to outcomes. For example, let's say you are given the task of evaluating an English curriculum that is to be implemented on campuses across a system. Unbeknownst to the administration, the program is largely being ignored, with many campuses leaving the materials on a shelf, still wrapped in cellophane. If the evaluation is focused solely on the academic outcomes intended by the program, there is a strong likelihood that critical information regarding the lack of implementation will be lost, and incorrect conclusions on the program's efficacy will be made. Understanding the *process* of the program is crucial to fully understanding its *impact*. An evaluation that focuses on implementation can help determine the match between program goals and participants' needs, identify strengths and challenges in developing and implementing the program, measure perceptions, and assess the adequacy of resources for sustaining a program (Kellogg Foundation, 2004). It also increases the likelihood of uncovering a program's unintended outcomes, which may be just as strong and desirable as the intended outcomes.

The second characteristic of a responsive evaluation is that it provides information to required audiences. Education professionals rely on evaluation experts to help them understand the impact of their efforts. Stakeholders, including program personnel and management as well as funders and participants, are invested in the findings and deserve solid and accurate reporting of the processes and outcomes. All evaluation provides information to audiences, but it is a particular concern in responsive evaluation to present information in a form that is accessible and understandable to all necessary audiences, such as through the use of anecdotes or descriptive portrayals of illustrative cases (Stake, 1975). In the case of our curriculum program still sitting on the shelf, the responsive evaluator would be responsible for alerting program management and funders of the lack of implementation and the reasons behind it, helping them to understand the issues before more financial resources are spent, and wasted, on a program that is not being used. All too often, an evaluation that fails to prioritize meaningful communication with stakeholders leaves the audience with a binder full of tables, graphs and crosstabs that are unlikely to convey what stakeholders most want to know about a program, or even be fully understood. Also, while this information is useful for making summary judgments about the program's effects, it does not provide the reader with an understanding of the program's implementation or the experiences of the participants, and thus misses out on information important for helping stakeholders to assess the program's underlying value.

The third main trait of a responsive evaluation is the reflection of different values among the program's stakeholders and to present these viewpoints along with the viewpoint of the evaluator. Most evaluation approaches ask the evaluator to assume the role of "expert," casting interpretations and judgments from a deliberately outsider (and therefore presumably unbiased) perspective. In contrast, responsive evaluation takes the view that multiple values and viewpoints should be reflected in the evaluation's findings. In this way, the approach is similar to democratic evaluation where the evaluator is more of a facilitator who gathers, organizes, and presents information rather than an expert who stands in judgment (House, 2001). In order to focus on the process of the program, one must also gather the perspectives and viewpoints of the people involved in its implementation. With our example of the unimplemented curriculum program, this characteristic of responsive evaluation would mean that the evaluator would gather the perspectives and opinions of the various campuses, thus presenting the audience with as many viewpoints as possible on why the program is not being implemented and what changes could be made to make implementation more attractive and/or feasible. This, in itself, is valuable information.

A final distinguishing feature of responsive evaluation is that instead of determining a set of preordinate questions to be answered, it takes a flexible approach, allowing the questions and issues of the evaluation to emerge as evaluators become familiar with the program, the local contexts and the concerns of stakeholders. Non-responsive evaluation approaches, particularly those that are concerned with measuring program outcomes, typically value the establishment of preordinate questions and view them through the lens of generally accepted practices of hypothesis-testing within empirical social science research. In this viewpoint, preordinate questions are seen as necessary for appropriate evaluation design, and also serve as a way of controlling for bias on the part of the evaluator. In contrast, responsive evaluation views preordinate questions as questions that have been developed without the necessary prerequisite understandings and contexts of the program. While a responsive evaluator may form ideas about preordinate questions, he or she would remain open to changing these ideas as new information is gathered. In our example of the unimplemented curriculum, if the evaluator in this situation begins with preconceptions regarding the program's implementation and is not responsive at all – that is, is not able or willing to change the course of the evaluation—then he or she will likely fail to gather feedback on *why* the program is not being implemented, which does not serve the purpose of the evaluation in providing useful information to the program's management, funders and other stakeholders. In this case, an evaluation that ignores the emergence of the issue of the program's non-implementation will have failed the audience.

Theoretical Considerations

In what situations is it preferable to allow for the development of issues in our investigations, and in what situations should questions and methods be preordinate? Can methods be responsive and rigorous at the same time? Is responsive evaluation subjective, objective, or both? Can it be summative, or is it always formative? What does it mean to be responsive in other measurement areas, such as assessment design? This section approaches these considerations and presents a responsive viewpoint to common issues in evaluation, measurement, and assessment.

Evaluation Methods

An important theoretical consideration behind responsive evaluation is the question of objectivity versus subjectivity. Outcomes-based assessments that judge the extent to which a program has met a set of predetermined goals are often based on "objective" measures, usually defined as data that are easily replicable and do not rely upon individual, subjective experience and interpretation. Frequently, objective data are quantitative in nature, while subjective data are qualitative. This polarization of data and methods into qualitative/quantitative, subjective/objective dichotomies has a long history in education research, reaching back to sharp divides on epistemology. Responsive evaluation tends to take a constructivist approach, stating that all measurements—even so-called "objective" ones—are ultimately subjective in that they depend upon choices made by the evaluator in terms of what data to gather and how to interpret them. In this view, obviously subjective data are valued no less than ostensibly objective data, as responsive evaluation brings out and makes explicit the inherent subjectivity of any evaluation activity (Stake, 2003). Traditionally objective approaches, such as attempting to control for bias and gather data that allow for generalization, are seen as less important and/or unreachable goals (Abma & Stake, 2001; Stake, 2003).

Being responsive indisputably includes collecting various viewpoints and value perspectives, data that are obviously quite subjective in nature. However, as Stake (2003) says, "There is a common misunderstanding that responsive evaluation requires naturalistic inquiry, case study, or qualitative methods" (p 64). Any and all methods of data collection are possible within a responsive evaluation, up to and including the use of measures that are traditionally seen as being very objective, such as standardized assessments. The question is not so much which methods are used, but how they are chosen. As long as data collection follows the needs and concerns of stakeholders and is responsive to emerging issues, then it can be called "responsive" regardless of whether it is objective or subjective in nature. Furthermore, objectivity does not have to refer solely to quantitative data; the evaluator can gather qualitative data in an objective manner, using rigorous, complete, and transparent approaches for collection and analysis with the goal of making them more replicable to other contexts. If the methods are technically sound, instruments are reliable and valid, and multiple perspectives are included in reporting results, then there is a level of objective credibility to the evaluation.

Because responsive evaluation is best applied when information about the processes involved in the program are important, a natural fit for the responsive approach is in formative evaluation—evaluation whose primary goal is providing information geared towards program improvement. If the program is still in flux, if details, approaches, and materials are still under development and feedback is needed for further improvement, then flexible, more exploratory approaches to the evaluation are appropriate. However, *summative* evaluation—evaluation whose primary goal is providing information on whether program objectives were reached—seems, on the surface at least, to be less of a natural fit.

To the extent that a summative evaluation begins with preordinate questions such as "Were goals and objectives reached? Was the program effective?" it can never be entirely responsive. However, responsive evaluation means being responsive to the context of the evaluation and the needs of stakeholders, and a desire to assess program effectiveness is not precluded. A responsive approach would take into consideration that there are different viewpoints on "effectiveness," and it would examine the quality of processes and not focus solely on definitively answering preordinate questions. In addition, while most summative evaluations are heavily centered around preordinate questions and measures of outcomes, the experiential aspect of responsive evaluation can be incorporated into them. For example, flexibility in the design and process of the evaluation might allow for the development and pursuit of additional questions that arise during its course. Responsive evaluation's focus on processes and activities are as appropriate for a summative evaluation as for a formative one, and when stakeholders express a need for outcome measures, they are not only possible in a responsive evaluation, but appropriate. Finally, an emphasis on communicating results to multiple stakeholders in such a way that the information is understood would benefit a summative evaluation, and while many summative evaluations require the evaluator to take on the role of expert judge, the inclusion of multiple stakeholder viewpoints is certainly possible, particularly when they are presented along with the evaluator's own judgments.

Assessment and Measurement

The field of evaluation long ago moved from an emphasis on outcomes to also looking at the processes that produce those outcomes. In contrast, the field of assessment and measurement is only more recently starting to investigate the extent to which intermediary information can be used to improve the validity and reliability of outcome measures. One example is computer adaptive testing, or CAT. In CAT, the test items that a test-taker receives depends upon his or her responses to previous items—test-takers who get an item wrong are next presented with an easier item, while test-takers who get the same item correct are next presented with a harder item. Thus, the content and coverage of the exam is dependent upon continuous input from the test-taker, and each test is individualized in such a way that the exam narrows in as quickly as possible to the set of items that are most useful in determining the examinee's true ability level. There are several benefits to using CAT: a fewer number of items have to be delivered to the examinee with greater precision, item security is more easily controlled by monitoring item exposure and setting constraints, scores are automatically calculated on scale without the need for equating, and performance is oftentimes rated immediately, with scores given at the close and submission of the exam. While fixed form tests, typically given in paper-and-pencil format, require a preset form to be created, adhering to preordinate constraints, the adaptive test uses feedback from performance on previous items to determine the next item the examinee sees. This type of assessment, with constant feedback on the ability level of the examinee, is responsive. By design, there is no one-size-fits-all approach, and continuous collection of feedback determines the next steps of the assessment process.

The issue of formative versus summative approaches arises not only in program evaluation, but in assessment as well. Formative assessment is designed to give feedback regarding examinees' knowledge and performance in order to monitor progress and make adjustments in teaching as necessary. Often the goal in formative assessment is to gather information that bears on the process of teaching as opposed to information that bears on whether a given student has or has not reached a given benchmark. Being responsive in formative assessment is fairly straightforward: use assessment to measure the level of knowledge and skill the students have achieved and share this feedback with the teacher so further instruction can be guided by this information. It is flexible enough to account for what has not yet been reached (units that have not been covered, but will be by the end of the course) and allows the teacher or test-user to judge what level of understanding is acceptable.

Summative assessment, like summative evaluation, is given at the end of a course or curriculum to assess the skills and knowledge of the examinee according to the purpose of the class, assuming the assessment has been designed in such a way as to reflect the values and objectives of the curriculum. To be responsive here is perhaps less relevant than with formative assessment, as findings cannot be used to change the process of curriculum delivery according to the feedback received. However, there are ways to be responsive in these situations.

In both formative and summative assessment, there are ways to collect information beyond the question, "Did this student master this skill, yes or no?" For instance, when skills and knowledge are cumulative, such as in mathematics, items can be constructed in such a way to determine the level of mastery on a continuum. Constructed response items, where the thought-process of the examinee is more readily apparent than with traditional multiple-choice question types, can allow the teacher to more deeply understand the skills of the student. When multiple-choice style items are unavoidable or even preferable (due to ease of grading), having purposeful distracters (the incorrect response options) can help to better understand the thought process of the examinee. This can provide valuable feedback regarding the interaction of the curriculum and teaching methods with the students' learning style and prior knowledge.

Stake's notion of responsiveness, although described within the realm of educational evaluation, can be helpful in other areas as well, depending on one's values and intentions. The *Standards for Educational and Psychological Testing* (American Educational Research Association, American Psychological Association, & National Council on Measurement in Education, 1999) even call for some elements of responsiveness. For instance, Standard 5.10 requires that "appropriate interpretations" in simple language be provided along with scores to all relevant audiences so that they may understand what those scores mean and how they are used. Standards 4.16 and 4.19, and several others, discuss the need for test publishers to document their scoring and delivery processes as well as any changes to procedures (AERA, APA, & NCME, 1999). If you are trying to understand the process just as much, if not more, than the outcomes, and if you are trying to give feedback and provide information to the audience, then your investigation, or at least components of it, can be responsive.

Practical Applications

Conducting a responsive evaluation is not without its challenges and obstacles. How does one deal with the tendency of potential funders to require an evaluation plan in place before funds are secured? Can an evaluator propose an approach before the program's implementation and still be responsive? If the evaluation plan is prescribed before it begins, then it is preordinate, as opposed to responsive. However, it is possible to plan your evaluation approach and incorporate room for flexibility and change, and to gather robust and thorough data on the participants' perspectives and values. The following sections discuss ways of gathering information in a responsive manner.

Survey Research

One of the most common forms of data collection is the administration of surveys. Surveys can be used for descriptive purposes (e.g., the U.S. Census), exploratory purposes (e.g., needs assessment), and other reasons (Nardi, 2003). Surveys can be relatively inexpensive to develop and administer, covering a larger sample of participants in a shorter amount of time more efficiently compared to other research methods, such as observations and interviews. It is often important for the evaluator to gather reliable data from a representative sample of the target population, and surveys are an attractive method for this.

There are two key components of responsive evaluation that can benefit from the use of survey methods in the evaluation design: collecting information on the process of implementing the program, and gathering various values and perspectives from different participants involved. Surveys can gather information not only on the attitudes and beliefs of the respondents, but also the behaviors within the realm of implementation. Commonly, changes in behavior are measured using a pre-post survey design, where the same survey is administered before the program's implementation and again after, or by asking participants to reflect back on the changes made over a specified period of time. Some evaluators may choose to survey participants multiple times throughout the life of the evaluation, gathering continual information on behaviors related to implementing and participating in the program. The survey approaches depend largely on the needs and scope of the evaluation. However, the same standards of survey research apply, no matter the situation: the instrument should be reliable, show evidence of validity, and should be written and delivered in a manner that is appropriate to the participants and is considerate of their time.

Surveys are useful in responsive evaluation, but can survey research itself be considered "responsive"? A good survey, by design, is built with research questions and a sampling plan determined beforehand, and analyses planned as items are constructed. Therefore, in this vein, survey research would be considered preordinate: determined beforehand. However, like constructed response items in assessment, survey questions can be purposefully designed to be flexible in the information gathered. That is to say, a researcher does not always have to plan exactly how participants will respond when he or she is developing the items. For example, closed-ended questions with a "check all that apply" answer option can stand to benefit from an "other" category that allows respondents to fill in an additional answer that is not already listed. Likewise, not all items need to be closed-ended. Certain situations may call for questions that ask for respondents to write a sentence or more, or to explain why they responded a particular way on a previous item. This kind of open flexibility can help evaluators avoid alienating respondents by omitting viable response options or missing valuable information because it was not foreseen when the instrument was being developed.

With today's advanced technology and the proliferation of personal computers with internet access, many evaluators choose to administer surveys via the World Wide Web. There are even several online survey tools to choose from, making this mode a more viable option for collecting information. Like computer adaptive testing, web-based surveys can be built to deliver subsequent questions based on previous responses. This branching technique is useful in creating efficient instruments where non-applicable items are not presented to participants, thus saving them time and frustration. This also allows researchers to arrange for highly relevant follow-up questions that ask for further explanation and clarification. In this sense, surveys can be presented as flexible and interactive data collection techniques, using the principles of responsiveness.

Qualitative Analyses

Quantitative measures aren't the only techniques useful to evaluators. Stake (Abma & Stake, 2001) advocates a more localized realm, as opposed to focusing on generalizing to a universe. While a distinct advantage of quantitative research methods is the generalizability, qualitative methods offer something of a different merit: an opportunity for individualized and in-depth perspective. These methods include interviews, observations, discussion forums, and so on. While quantitative methods have well-prescribed analytic approaches, the field of qualitative analysis is less concrete.

One popular theory of approach is grounded theory. This allows an understanding or theory to emerge from the data, as opposed to having a preconceived notion of the relationships between variables that you seek to verify with the data being analyzed (Dey, 2004). While not often used in program evaluation, grounded theory is a valuable approach in contexts where an evaluator is aiming to develop or expand upon theory, such as a theory of change model for a new program. A responsive evaluator can use a grounded theory approach, along with qualitative data collection methods such as observations and interviews, to gain an understanding of the process of implementation, as well as various perspectives and experiences from the program's participants. Rather than analyze the narratives, transcripts, and responses with a given hypothesis in mind, the evaluator allows key concepts and themes to emerge directly from the voices themselves. Another major component of grounded theory is the sampling selection approach: rather than select the sample beforehand, the evaluator is flexible in determining sources of information, selecting sources based on developing ideas (Dey, 2004). These key components make grounded theory a very responsive theoretical approach to collecting and designing the analysis of qualitative data.

Methods for analyzing qualitative data have evolved over the last thirty years. Prior to the invention and growth in prevalence of the personal computer, qualitative analysts largely worked in groups, agonizing over and analyzing various pieces of information over long periods of time, deliberating meanings and context until consensus was reached. Fortunately, researchers now have the benefit of computer assistance in their analyses, allowing for faster coding, more efficient management of information, and faster sharing (and comparing) of ideas and interpretations (Kelle, 2004).

There are several popular qualitative analysis software programs on the market today, including ATLAS.ti, MAXQDA, and NVivo. The benefits to using computer software to assist qualitative analysis are great: analysis can be conducted in a more efficient manner; there is greater transparency in the interpretation of data; and researchers can better synthesize various types and sources of information into one framework. Software platforms such as NVivo allow the researcher to analyze text, picture, video, and sound from a grounded theory perspective: the researcher builds major themes, or *nodes*, from the data, allowing patterns to emerge and ideas to develop directly from the data. Because the software allows for multiple researchers to simultaneously analyze data (and subsequently compare analyses) and helps organize information in systematic ways, a responsive evaluator can make changes as data are collected and ideas are created (e.g., moving and changing nodes), sharing those changes with others (e.g., exports into HTML), and presenting findings in an accessible form (e.g., graphs and models).

Mixed Methods

Qualitative methods, on their own, can be a powerful approach to gathering information about a program's impact and implementation. However, these methods can be time consuming and costly, and their inherent subjectivity can make them difficult to defend to some audiences. Because evaluators often need to make causal inferences, quantitative methods using a pre-post design and/or comparison groups are usually preferable in determining the efficacy of a program. Many argue that these inferences simply cannot be made using qualitative methods alone. However, qualitative proponents argue that quantitative methods alone cannot accurately capture the culture and experiences of a program's implementation and effect. With regard to the field of responsive evaluation, a mixed methods approach can be a way to incorporate an element of responsiveness into an otherwise preordinate design. The strongest argument for the effects and realities (both intended and unintended) of a program comes from using multiple views of data: both quantitative and qualitative. For more information on the benefits and challenges of mixed methods design, see Creswell and Plano Clark (2007).

Innovative Data Collection Methods

Many data collection techniques discussed here and in other evaluation references are the same general approaches that have been around for decades. With the growth of technology and the ever-increasing access to web-connected personal computers, there are a growing number of more innovative methods of data collection that can be beneficial to a responsive evaluator. Electronic resources such as wikis, social networking sites, and academic course software such as Blackboard are valuable sources of information that can often be overlooked by evaluators focusing only on traditional data collection methods.

A wiki is a website often used for sharing information and communication between group members on any given topic. Each accessing member can upload files, make changes to content, add calendar events, and so on. Social networking sites seem to be an unlikely place to gather information, but in today's technology-driven age, much socializing and communicating occurs electronically and can be a valuable source of real-time data for a responsive evaluator. In addition to socializing online, many of today's college courses are taught with an online component using academic software. These help instructors provide students with resources and course materials, encourage out-of-classroom discussion, and assess learning and progress. These resources are becoming another layer of implementation of programs in higher education and provide access to types of data that were not previously available.

Reporting to Audiences

A responsive evaluator can find him- or herself reporting to policymakers, faculty, students, parents, funders, academics, and/or the general public. Although methodology and data are very important to the integrity of the evaluation, reporting the evaluation's findings is just as critical. Responsive evaluation places particular emphasis on reporting results in a manner that is understandable and accessible for all relevant audiences so that they can make appropriate conclusions and value judgments (Abma & Stake, 2001; Stake, 1972, 1975). The responsive evaluator will provide his or her own judgments, but will not assert that these judgments are the only correct interpretations of the data, and will aim to provide additional information and multiple viewpoints for others to draw conclusions.

Oftentimes, audiences respond to personal accounts and anecdotes presented in the evaluation. They provide the outsider with an insider perspective of the experience of participating in the program. However, many audiences are looking for more than anecdotal evidence of a program's impact and efficacy. Some evaluation theorists may argue that the evaluator is the ultimate expert and is the only professional capable of judging a program's value. Stake, on the other hand, claims that it is *not* the role of the evaluator to cast judgment, but instead to explore the program and its participants in a complete and sufficient manner, presenting understandable results and value perspectives in such a way that the audiences can make judgments themselves (Stake, 1975).

An evaluator is given the task of presenting rigorous outcomes and results, while simultaneously providing audiences with an understanding of the various experiences, perspectives, and values involved in the program's implementation. A responsive evaluator presents methodology and findings in a clear, concise manner, covers multiple viewpoints with evidence to back up claims, and provides a straightforward presentation of information to promote the audience's full understanding of the program.

Summary and Conclusion

A responsive approach is not the only option an evaluator has at his or her disposal but, in appropriate situations, it can be a powerful tool in responding to stakeholders' needs. By focusing on the processes of the program, the viewpoints of the stakeholders, and by presenting information in a clear and understandable manner appropriate for all intended audiences, the evaluator can present a series of findings that allow the audience to understand the experience of participating in and implementing the program and to draw sound conclusions on the value of the program. However, evaluators are not the only professionals that can benefit from being responsive. By incorporating a responsive methodology, researchers and test developers can understand the thought processes and experiences of the participant or examinee on a deeper and more meaningful level, and can present results in a way that is useful to multiple audiences, further aiding the field of professionals in their efforts.

References

Abma, T. A. (2006). The practice and politics of responsive evaluation. *American Journal of Evaluation, 27*(1), 31–43.

Abma, T. A., & Stake, R. E. (2001). Stake's responsive evaluation: Core ideas and evolution. *New Directions for Evaluation, 92*, 7–21.

American Educational Research Association, American Psychological Association, & National Council on Measurement in Education (1999). *Standards for educational and psychological testing*. Washington, DC: American Educational Research Association.

Creswell, J. W., & Plano Clark, V. L. (2007). *Designing and conducting mixed methods research*. Thousand Oaks, CA: Sage.

Dey, I. (2004). Grounded theory. In C. Seale, G. Gobo, J. Gubrium, & D. Silverman (Eds.), *Qualitative research practice* (pp. 80–93). London, UK: Sage.

House, E. R. (2001). Responsive evaluation (and its influence on deliberative democratic evaluation). *New Directions for Evaluation, 92*, 23–30.

Kelle, U. (2004). Computer-assisted qualitative data analysis. In C. Seale, G. Gobo, J. Gubrium, & D. Silverman (Eds.), *Qualitative research practice* (pp. 443–459). London, UK: Sage.

Kellogg Foundation (2004). *W. K. Kellogg Foundation evaluation handbook*. Battle Creek, MI: Kellogg Foundation.

Nardi , P. M. (2003). *Doing survey research: A guide to quantitative methods*. Boston, MA: Pearson.

Scriven, M. (1967). The methodology of evaluation. In R. Stake (Ed.), *Curriculum evaluation* (American Educational Research Association Monograph Series on Evaluation, No. 1, pp. 39–83). Chicago, IL: Rand McNally.

Stake, R. E. (1967). The countenance of educational evaluation. *Teachers College Record, 68*(7), 523–540.

Stake, R. E. (1972). *Responsive evaluation*. Urbana-Champaign, IL: University of Illinois. (ERIC Document Reproduction Service No. ED075487)

Stake, R. E. (1975). To evaluate an arts program. In R. E. Stake (Ed.), *Evaluating the arts in education: A responsive approach* (pp. 13–31). Columbus, OH: Merrill.

Stake, R. E. (2003). Responsive evaluation. In T. Kelleghan, & D. L. Stufflebeam (Eds.), *International handbook of educational evaluation* (pp. 63–68). Dordrecht, Netherlands: Kluwer.

Stufflebeam, D. L. (1971). The relevance of the CIPP evaluation model for educational accountability. *Journal of Research and Development in Education, 5*, 19–25.

Tyler, R. W. (1950). *Basic principles of curriculum and instruction*. Chicago, IL: University of Chicago Press.

Worthen, B. R., Sanders, J. R., & Fitzpatrick, J. L. (1997). *Program evaluation: Alternative approaches and practical guidelines*. White Plains, NY: Longman.

33

CASE STUDIES AND VALIDITY

Edith J. Cisneros-Cohernour

This chapter is about qualitative case studies and validity. The purpose is to provide the reader with a better understanding of case study as a research strategy and about its usefulness for examining issues of validity, as well as for understanding how a specific reality can illuminate a general problem.

Case Study Characteristics

The term *case study* is used by different people with different meanings. For some, they are an intervention developed for improving the conditions of a patient, a school, a unit, and so forth. For others, they are a teaching strategy for helping students to apply theoretical or legal principles in the analysis of a particular situation. Others see case studies as a research strategy or design.

This chapter centers on case studies as a qualitative research strategy focusing on the study of a particular bounded social system, such as a classroom, a school, a unit, a program, and so forth. The essential characteristic of case studies as a qualitative strategy is its emphasis on particularity. As Stake (2005) asserts, the focus is on what is true about a particular classroom, school, or situation that we attempt to understand rather than on trying to compare it with other similar or different entities.

Case study also shares the following characteristics with other qualitative methods:

(a) They are naturalistic and empirically oriented. They are conducted in the natural setting in which the phenomenon takes place, and center on complexity and situationality. They involve a detailed exploration, for a long period of time, sufficient enough for us to acquire an in-depth understanding of the case and its context with all its complexity (Creswell, 2008).

(b) Meanings and interpretations are built in context. The focus is on deep understanding rather than on explanation. As Lincoln and Guba (1985) state, most qualitative researchers are not concerned with establishing cause-effect relations among variables. It is difficult to establish causal links when everything that is studied happens in a place in which many things take place at the same time; it is difficult and sometimes even impossible distinguishing among cause and effect(s).

(c) Case researchers recognize the subjectivity of research. While in quantitative studies there are strong claims of objectivity, in qualitative research there is recognition of subjectivity because the researcher is the main human instrument. Each researcher brings his or her background and experiences to the conduct of the study. This influences the types of questions that he or she asks, and the general inquiry process. The researcher and the case interact and influence each other.

(d) Case researchers believe that reality is constructed and are aware of multiple realities and interpretations. They work hard at honoring different voices and interpretations. The researcher provides the reader with different perceptions, voices, and value commitments of different stakeholders.

In addition, case study design is emergent, not preordinate. The researcher identifies critical issues for the study as he or she gets acquainted with the context and through its involvement with the case. The issues focus on the phenomenon, events, relations, and so forth, that are studied in the case. Then, he or she uses multiple methods and sources of information to identify and study critical issues and pays attention to expressed and tacit knowledge as well as multiple realities during data collection.

Data analysis is inductive and starts with the beginning of the study; interpretation is ideographic. The goal of the research is to develop ideographic knowledge in the form of hypotheses in process that describe the individual cases under study.

Because of its characteristics, cases can be useful for understanding problems, processes, relationships, and situations within their context and complexities. This is why case studies are also valuable for understanding issues of validity (Stake, 2005).

Case Studies and Validity

Validity is concerned with the questions: Are we measuring what we think we are measuring? Are our inferences and actions about the assessed object supported by evidence? Because validity is linked to the meaning, value, and appropriateness of interpretation, validity is the most critical consideration in research and evaluation.

Messick (1989, 1995) presents six important aspects of construct validity to be used for all educational and psychological assessments to identify sources of invalidity: construct, substantive, structural, external, generalizability, and consequential. The issues and sources of evidence emphasized by each of the aspects are (Messick, 1994, pp. 11–12);

- **Content aspect**: Includes evidence of content relevance, representativeness, and technical quality (Lennon, 1956; Messick, 1989).
- **Substantive aspect**: Refers to theoretical rationales for the observed consistencies in test responses, including process models of task performance (Embretson, 1983), along with empirical evidence that the theoretical processes are actually engaged by respondents in the assessment tasks.
- **Structural aspect**: Appraises the fidelity of the scoring structure to the structure of the construct domain at issue (Loevinger, 1957).
- **External aspect**: Includes convergent and discriminant evidence from multitrait-method comparisons (Campbell & Fiske, 1959), as well as evidence of criterion relevance and applied utility (Cronbach & Glesser, 1965).
- **Generalizability aspect**: Examines the extent to which score properties and interpretations generalize to and across population groups, and tasks (Cook & Campbell, 1979; Shulman, 1970), including validity generalization of test-criterion relationships (Hunter, Schmidt, & Jackson, 1982).
- **Consequential aspect:** Appraises the value implications of score interpretation as a basis for action as well as the actual potential consequences of test use, especially in regard to sources of invalidity related to issues of bias, fairness, and distributive justice (Messick, 1980, 1989).

Next, three of Messick's aspects of construct validity (content, substantial, and consequential) are used in a case study for examining validity related issues.

An Exemplary Case

The case study was developed around David, an assistant professor who taught mathematics-related courses at the College of Sciences of an American university. David was forty years old, athletic and had received several awards for his research, including the Fulbright fellowship and an award from the National Science Foundation.

He was recommended by a specialist from the Office of Instructional Resources of the university as ideal to participate in the study because he was an instructor who had significantly improved his teaching over the last years. At the beginning of his work at the university, he received very low student ratings, but after receiving support from the Office of Instructional Resources, David significantly improved in his ratings.

Once David agreed to participate in the study, data collection started and lasted for an academic semester. This involved semi-structured interviews with David and other faculty members who taught the same course, the department head, the college dean, vice-chancellor of academic affairs, the head of instructional resources and the instructional specialist who provided David with advice on how to improve his teaching. In addition, classroom observations and focus group interviews with David's students were conducted during the semester. Document analyses were conducted on all evaluation forms collected from his students during a period of five years, as well as on his class materials and instructional resources. The data collected provided valuable information about David's teaching style, instructional methodology, classroom interaction with students, as well as student interactions.

During the interviews, David was asked how the feedback from the ratings had influenced the activities taking place in his classroom. Interviews with the faculty and department head were centered on the main issues. Each of these interviews was conducted in the faculty private offices and lasted approximately an hour. Student ratings and evaluation forms and a variety of documentary data were available to the researcher. Because the records are considered private, access was gained after obtaining the consent of the parties involved in the study.

The researcher used traditional ways for validating observations. She took care to use more than one medium—combining observation, interviews, and document review. Data collection resulted in multiple statements, testimony, documents, and observations. Data analysis in this study, as in most qualitative studies, commenced as data collection continued. Throughout the study, data analysis helped to redefine the issues. To organize the data in a form that facilitates analysis and interpretation, the researcher used a thematic approach. The researcher analyzed her field notes around the key questions. She also showed her notes to the participants and improved the accuracy of quotes and descriptions. The methods of data collection used, the length of time devoted to data collection on site, and the use of multiple sources of evidence contributed to a better understanding of the context under which teaching took place—that is, validity.

David's Teaching

David taught in a large classroom, with excellent illumination, air conditioning and heat, located at the technical part of the campus. During the time of the study, he was teaching a calculus course to twelve students[1]. The following is an excerpt that illustrates some of David's teaching:

> As is his custom, David arrives at the classroom early and waits for his students by the classroom door; he greets them as they enter the room. His tone is cordial and informal; he tries to maintain the same tone during all the session.
>
> He follows a routine as he teaches his course. As is his custom, he spends the first part of the session explaining the topic and the last part supervising students while they work in teams. During the presentation, David reminds his students of what they learned the

former session, states the objectives of the session, stresses the main points of the topic, and asks questions of students in order to verify their understanding of the lecture.

At the beginning of the lecture, he divides the blackboard into three sections, then writes in order from left to right all the main points that he presents in his lecture. While he writes on the blackboard, his students take notes. He then asks students if they have questions about the topic. If someone asks a question, he responds using real life examples to illustrate his response. Then he asks questions to check for student understanding on the topic. Only when all students have participated and responded correctly to his questions, does he provide them with more information about the course content.

During the session, David continues teaching in this way; he keeps summarizing the main points and uses diagrams, drawings, graphs or examples to illustrate the topic that is being taught.

Every time he finishes explaining a concept, he erases the blackboard, always from top to bottom, from left to right as was taught him at the Office of Instructional Resources. Once he finishes his lecture, he asks students to work in teams solving problems about the learned concepts. He supervises students' work, provides feedback to the teams, and assigns additional homework. The class meets once more during the week to work in the lab. Between sessions, David keeps in touch with students via e-mail and provides advice to those who require it.

During the focus group interview with David's students, some indicated that this was a hard course. Some experienced problems with lab assignments. A few students had problems understanding homework indications (assignments?), but stated that they did not have problems in the course because David always clarified all their questions later.

During classroom observations, it was evident that David was a skillful communicator, well-organized, kept good visual contact with students, and tried to create a casual atmosphere that favored student learning. He also demonstrated many of the attributes promoted by many faculty development programs including: good organization, clarity, good tone of voice, good coverage of topics, and so forth.

During interviews, David indicated that he did not have pedagogical training prior to joining his department. The only formal pedagogical training he learned was from the Office of Instructional Resources at his university. He looked for help at this office after obtaining very low scores in the first student evaluations of his teaching.

During his first three years at the university, both David and his department chair were concerned about the very low scores that he obtained from his students. His department chair had stressed that the university took very seriously the end-of-the-course evaluations of teaching. When professors obtained scores lower than the campus mean, they were asked to find help to improve their scores; usually, they were asked to go to the Office of Instructional Resources or another resource, sometimes a mentor, to receive help for improving their teaching.

According to the specialist from the Office of Instructional Resources who worked with David, at the beginning David had very little contact with his students; he just lectured and asked them to solve calculus problems, similar to those explained in class. Because of this, the specialist recommended David be more personal in his interaction with his students, to use more examples and summarize the main points of the lecture in different moments during the session. The specialist believed that since the university was making a strong effort towards increasing the number of women and students from diverse ethnic groups, it was seen as important for the faculty to create a cordial environment in the classroom for all students.

Contrary to David's expectations, his ratings did not significantly increase after he made the changes recommended by the instructional specialist. Then, a semester before the study was conducted, he obtained very high ratings for his teaching and was ranked among the best instructors of the university by his students.

The analysis of the evaluation forms filled by David students over the last four years indicated that he received very poor evaluations during three years and slight improvement took place during the fourth year, just after receiving advice from the instructional specialist. Students rarely made comments about his teaching strengths or weaknesses on the evaluation forms. However, during the first three years, they commented that there was certain content in the course that was particularly difficult. Students requested this content be eliminated from the course, as well as the mathematics' software that was used in the course. More than 80% of the forms included student comments along these lines.

During the year that David was going to have his tenure review, his department head told him that his scores were still below the campus norm, so he needed to improve his ratings in order to make his case for tenure. David's students were still complaining about the content and use of the software.

Under pressure to increase his ratings, David decided to eliminate both the software and the content that was hard for his students. He did not feel good about this decision because he believed students would need that knowledge later in their studies but felt that if he did not change it, the ratings were not going to increase. After David made the changes, his scores increased significantly. A few months later, he was granted tenure.

Pressures for increasing student ratings above the campus mean were also a matter of concern of David's colleagues. Two of his peers were particularly concerned about the university policy that treated students as clients, on the grounds that it was ignoring the responsibility that the institution had with the general society. Faculty members in the department stressed their concern about the use of student ratings for making tenure decisions and about the impact the ratings had on the quality of teaching. As one instructor said:

> Student ratings are not always good for improving teaching. Students are not always in the best position to provide the instructor with meaningful feedback. Unfortunately, our Department makes decisions based only on the ratings. I believe this is a mistake because this is based on the assumption that the score is synonymous with instructional quality. If an instructor increases his ratings it doesn't necessarily mean that he has improved his instructional quality. There are faculty members that teach all the course content with the required rigor, but obtain just average or slightly low ratings. However, there are others who only teach 80% of the course content and do it superficially. They use activities and group techniques that students like. Then they obtain the highest ratings, but does this really mean that they are the best teachers?
>
> Giving all the weight to the numeric score creates other problems; there is the danger that some instructors manipulate students in order to obtain "good ratings". Students are beginning to realize the power they have in the evaluation process and they are using it.

Another of David's colleague added: "One of the problems of comparing instructors is that different courses need to be assessed differently. It is unfair to compare instructors who teach different subjects."

During the focus groups with David's students, those who selected a major in the social sciences and humanities said that they found his course to be very difficult because they lacked prerequisite knowledge. They added that they register for the course to fulfill a requirement from their college. Students who selected the course voluntarily had a better perception of its usefulness. When asked about David's teaching style, students indicated that he was clear but a little bit repetitive. However, they liked the way he interacted with them.

Next, we will analyze the validity issues raised in David's case regarding the use and interpretation of student ratings of his teaching.

Validity Issues and the Case Study

Here we discuss how David's case is useful for examining three aspects of Messick's construct validity: concept, substantive, and consequential.

Content validity issues

A fundamental aspect of construct validity is the capacity of the evaluation to reflect the content on the construct that it is intended to measure, in this case *good teaching*. Two main sources of invalidity can be associated with content aspects: construct underrepresentation and construct-irrelevant information. Construct underrepresentation takes place when the evaluation too narrowly or too simply represents the construct being measured. Construct-irrelevant variance takes place when the assessment is sensitive to information that is irrelevant to the construct being measured.

Our analysis of the case study indicates that in the evaluation of David's teaching, the evaluation system focused only on student ratings, thus narrowly representing the construct *teaching quality* and providing an example of construct underrepresentation. The case study helps us understand many complexities of the assessment of teaching that are essential for understanding David's teaching. It is not possible to understand critical events using the traditional quantitative approach. The concept of "good teaching" used by the Office of Instructional Resources put emphasis on a narrow definition of good teaching: on the use of pedagogical techniques, improving structure and course organization, planning, and faculty and student interactions. Many of these aspects are consistent with Chickering and Gamson's (1987) *Seven Principles for Good Practice in Undergraduate Education*. There are also other aspects that the specialists from that office did not take into account, such as ethics, course content coverage, and following student interests. In David's case, he teaches a course that is a prerequisite for other courses in the department. The depth of knowledge required for covering the course content is important since it provides a needed background for students.

In addition, the specialist that helped David to improve his teaching observed his class only on a few occasions. It was difficult for her to judge the connection among sessions, the relation of the teaching with the course objectives, and contexts that influenced student learning. Even though the specialist reviewed the student ratings of David's teaching and made suggestions for improvement, these suggestions were not based on complete information about the teaching context.

Substantive and consequential validity

Examining the substantive aspects of construct validity is important because "response consistencies or performance regularities are reflective of the domain processes" (Messick, 1994, p. 13). Ory and Ryan (2001) note that when items on a test are actually assessing the quality of teaching, we can assert that there is evidence for the validity of the scores. However, in David's case the analysis of his evaluation forms and the interview with his current and former students indicated that although he had made important changes in his teaching, this was not reflected in a significant change in his student ratings. The ratings remained below average and only improved after he eliminated the course content disliked by students, thus providing an example of consequential validity. It was evident that students based their ratings on the content change rather than on the evaluation of the characteristics of good teaching listed in the evaluation form:

- Presentation of course materials;
- Statement of course objectives and purposes;
- Focus on placing responsibility for learning on students;
- Instructor's accessibility and interaction with students;
- Clarity of instructor presentations;
- Enthusiasm;
- Instructor provision of supplementary handouts, problem sets or other visual aids, or
- Exam grading.

There are questions of consequential validity when evaluation results can lead to interpretations that could affect the instructor's career and professional future. There is a problem when over negatively decisions about the quality of teaching are based only on student ratings. Decisions about tenure, hiring, or rewarding faculty performance in teaching based on a single source of information will be problematic. The numeric score does not adequately reflect the way in which different interests, background and needs of students influence their perceptions of the importance of the course and the teaching quality of the instructor.

The tendency to reduce the evaluation of teaching to a single numeric score resulted in the department chair placing over-reliance on them. By focusing only on this score, David's department head and the administrative system eliminated potentially important content from the course. Using evaluation results in this way may lead to serious consequences, such as diminution of quality of student preparation. In addition, it made faculty members put more emphasis on how to increase their scores instead of improving their teaching (Cisneros-Cohernour, 2001; Stake & Cisneros-Cohernour, 2004).

Conclusions

David's case was part of a larger study on the use of evaluation results for improving college teaching. In general, findings of the case study helped to identify problems in the way the Office of Instructional Resources used evaluation results. The decision to use numeric reports based on the ratings obtained by the instructor and later comparing this score with the mean score obtained by faculty at the campus level did not provide sufficient scope of data for valid conclusions that can be used for the improvement of faculty teaching and of educational administration. For the faculty, this report was not sufficiently useful because it did not provide information for instructional improvement.

In addition, the narrow scope of the evaluation data led to confusion about the real meaning of the scores. David's department head, as well as other administrators later interviewed at the campus level, assumed that if an instructor obtained a score of 2 points in the evaluation system, he was half as good in his teaching than another instructor who obtained 4 points in the evaluation.

The case study also helped provide understanding of the context of teaching and to identify critical issues for faculty development that could not be detected by the traditional student ratings system or by the instructional specialist who provided support to David. The case was particularly useful for understanding the validity issues of a standardized evaluation system that is not sensitive to the context of teaching. Moreover, the analysis of the case illustrates how a particular or specific reality can illuminate the general problems of the main evaluation system.

Note

1 There were 11 male students and one female student. David's peers indicated that the average class size in the department was 12 students but there were also courses with 35 or even more than 100 students.

References

Campbell, D. T., & Fiske, D. W. (1959). Convergent and discriminant validation by the multitrait matrix. *Psychological Bulletin, 56*, 81–105.

Chickering, A.W., & Gamson Z. F.(1987). Seven Principles for Good Practice in Undergraduate Education. *American Association of Higher Education Bulletin, 39*(7), 3–7.

Cisneros-Cohernour, E. J. (2001). *The evaluation of teaching in the context of a research university: Different meanings, trade-offs and equity concerns.* Unpublished research dissertation, University of Illinois, Urbana-Champaign, EE.UU.

Cook, T. D., & Campbell, D. T. (1979). *Quasi-experimentation: Design and analysis for field settings.* Chicago, IL: Rand McNally.

Creswell, J. (2008). *Research design. Qualitative, quantitative and mixed method approches* (3rd ed.). Thousand Oaks, CA: Sage.

Cronbach, L. J., & Glesser, G. C. (1965). *Psychological and personnel decisions* (2nd ed.). Urbana, IL: University of Illinois Press.

Embretson (Whitely), S. (1983). Construct validity: Construct representation versus nomothetic span. *Psychological Bulletin, 93*, 179–197.

Hunter, J. E., Schmidt, F. L., & Jackson, C. B. (1982). *Advanced meta-analysis: Quantitative methods of cumulating research findings across studies.* San Francisco, CA: Sage.

Lennon, R. T. (1956). Assumptions underlying the use of content validity. *Educational and Psychological Measurement, 16*, 294–304.

Lincoln, Y., & Guba, E. (1985). *Naturalistic inquiry.* Newbury Park, CA: Sage.

Loevinger, J. (1957). Objective tests as instruments of psychological theory (Monograph), *Psychological Reports, 3*, 635–694.

Messick, S. (1980). Test validity and the ethics of assessment. *American Psychologist, 35*(11), 1012–1027.

Messick, S. (1989). Validity. In R. L. Linn (Ed.), *Educational measurement* (3rd ed., pp. 13–103). New York, NY: American Council on Education, and Macmillan.

Messick, S. (1994). *Alternative modes of assessment: uniform standards of validity.* Paper presented at a conference on Evaluating Alternatives to Traditional Testing for Selection, Bowling Green: OH, October.

Messick, S. (1995). Validity of psychological assessment: Validation of inferences from persons' responses and performances as scientific inquiry into score meaning. *American Psychologist, 50*(9), 741–749.

Ory, J., & Ryan, K. (2001). How do student ratings measure up to a new validity framework? *New Directions in Institutional Research, 109*, 27–44.

Shulman, L. S. (1970). Reconstruction of educational research. *Review of Educational Research, 40*, 371–390.

Stake, R. E. (2005). Qualitative case studies. In N. Denzin, & Y. Lincoln (Eds.), *Handbook of qualitative research* (3rd ed., pp.443–466). Thousand Oaks, CA: Sage.

Stake, R. E., & Cisneros-Cohernour, E. J. (2004). The quality of teaching in higher education. *Lithuanian Journal of Higher Education, 1*, 94–107.

34

MIXED METHODS SPECIALISTS IN ACTION: LINKING MIXED METHODS RESEARCH TO LEARNING AND CLASSROOM ASSESSMENT

Delwyn L. Harnisch, John W. Creswell, and Timothy Guetterman

A revolution is taking place in the way that research techniques are being used and applied in the social sciences and education. In addition to the traditional use of quantitative techniques in education, qualitative approaches to gathering data have been added. More recently, the combined use of quantitative and qualitative data has been emphasized, and its use heralds a new methodology called mixed methods research. Mixed methods involves the collection and analysis of both quantitative and qualitative data and its integration (Creswell & Plano Clark, 2011). The basic assumption is that the combination of data provides a better understanding of a research problem or practical situation than either type of data by itself. This more comprehensive way of studying research problems holds tremendous potential for utilizing the strengths of both quantitative and qualitative research. It also has application for a more systematic use of data in fields such as evaluation and assessment. The evaluation of student performance in the classroom, for instance, has traditionally been based on the quantitative outcome or performance data gathered from student evaluation forms. More recently, quantitative data has been augmented by qualitative data. Examples of this include written comments on student evaluation forms, portfolio data, or teacher observations. Teachers in higher education, we feel, are engaged as mixed methods specialists in action, gathering both quantitative and qualitative data. Although there is a long tradition of mixed methods in evaluation, little has been written about how it provides a systematic approach to classroom assessment.

This process lies mostly at an intuitive level, an informal process at best, in which the classroom teachers assemble a picture of the overall student performance based on quantitative and qualitative indicators. As an alternative, the teachers could be introduced to the mixed methods perspective, which: involves systematic procedures for gathering and using data, relies on the combination of the strengths of both types of data, and provides methodology for how such data collection and analysis might be designed and proceed. In this chapter we explore the use of mixed methods as a tool for evaluation and assessment in higher education. This exploration will first detail an overview of mixed methods research as a relatively new methodology. Next, we will discuss how mixed methods has played a central role in evaluation through the last four decades and is ideally suited to be a methodology useful to teachers as they assess student learning. We will then detail how mixed methods might be used in classroom assessment at many levels of education, including specific applications in higher education. Finally, we will offer specific recommendations for the use of mixed methods in student learning and assessment. In conveying these topics, this chapter represents the first known application of the emerging field of mixed methods methodology to student assessment literature, and identifies ways in which classroom assessors become mixed methods specialists in action.

An Overview of Mixed Methods Research

Discussing the application of mixed methods to a new area or field, such as student assessment, is not unusual. In fact, mixed methods application is expanding rapidly through many fields. It has been extensively applied in the social sciences (e.g., education, sociology, psychology, family science, management, marketing, and geography, to mention a few), has seen a surge of interest in the health sciences (e.g., family medicine, nursing, pharmacy, and health services research), and is becoming popular in funding initiatives at the U.S. federal level, such as at the National Science Foundation (Frechtling, 2002), the National Institutes of Health (2001), and the Robert Wood Johnson foundation (Cohen & Crabtree, 2008). It has expanded internationally, been marketed through the emergence of journals devoted to it, and has been described through more than 15 different books in education, evaluation, nursing, sociology, and psychology (Creswell, 2010).

All of this development has occurred rapidly and in a relatively short period of time. Mixed methods, which is around twenty years old, began with several social scientists working from different fields and nations who all came up with the same idea between 1985 and 1990. They had independently seen the rapid rise of qualitative research amidst the traditional quantitative modes of inquiry and began pondering how they might combine quantitative and qualitative approaches that would capture the best of both approaches to inquiry. Although early designs related to capturing both quantitative (i.e., instrument) data and qualitative (i.e., interview) data (Greene, Caracelli, & Graham, 1989), soon the idea of combining or integrating the data emerged as a dominant mode of thinking (e.g., Creswell, 1994; Tashakkori & Teddlie, 1998). Through the 1990s and into the 2000s considerable effort was spent detailing the types of mixed methods designs and the procedures that researchers might use to conduct a mixed methods investigation (Creswell, Plano Clark, & Guttmann, 2003).

Mixed methods research is not appropriate for all projects. It is important that the methods fit the problem. Problems most suitable for mixed methods are those in which the quantitative approach or the qualitative approach, by itself, is inadequate to develop a comprehensive understanding of the problem. In some fields a tradition does not exist for combining quantitative and qualitative data. In other cases it is more efficient to use only one procedure. Journals, for example, may be better suited for the shorter articles afforded by a single approach. Lack of knowledge about either quantitative or qualitative research may also cause an investigator to bypass the use of mixed methods.

The argument has long been made that the combined strengths of quantitative and qualitative data contribute to a stronger understanding of the research problem and hypotheses than a single data source. Using mixed methods also demonstrates a breadth of methodological skills from the researcher. Mixed methods research encourages interdisciplinary work, as investigators often come from different methodological persuasions. Individuals in the health sciences often view the benefits of mixed methods as they relate to the advantages of qualitative research. They value studying new questions and initiatives, complex initiatives, and interactions in natural—as opposed to experimental—settings. As mixed methods has developed, the purposes or rationale for using it have multiplied. The two most prevalent reasons for using mixed methods research are to develop a more complete understanding through the combination of both quantitative and qualitative data, and to extend or expand thinking by having one database build on the other (qualitative building on quantitative or vice versa). In addition to these two primary purposes, are the combinations and refinements of these purposes; for example, using qualitative data to help explain quantitative findings, or beginning a study with a qualitative data exploration in order to design an instrument to measure specific constructs.

Defining Mixed Methods

Mixed methods research bridges quantitative and qualitative approaches to scientific research. Mixed methods research can be considered a distinct methodology apart from traditional intervention studies, case studies, or ethnographies. Methodological developments involve a systematic approach to the use of mixed methods (as exemplified in specific designs), a language of procedures, and techniques for integrating quantitative and qualitative data. These are couched within specific books, journals, and funding opportunities at the federal level, and in private foundations. Methodologists come to mixed methods from diverse starting points. Some investigators focus on methods and the data collection process, some on combining quantitative and qualitative research across the entire process of research, and others based on the importance and framing of mixed methods from philosophical positions and theories. At a basic level mixed methods research involves gathering evidence through open-ended means (e.g., focus groups) as well as closed-ended means (e.g., surveys or instruments) and then combining or integrating the data to best understand a research problem or question. This definition is one of many available, but includes the basic elements involved in mixed methods research. Mixed methods research can be described in terms of four core characteristics that follow a logical order of steps: (1) collecting and analyzing, persuasively and rigorously, both qualitative and quantitative data; (2) using these procedures in a single study or in multiple phases of a program of study; (3) framing these procedures within philosophical worldviews and theoretical lenses; and (4) combining the procedures into specific research designs that direct the plan for conducting the study by mixing the two forms of data concurrently, sequentially, or embedding one within the other and giving priority to one or both forms of data (Creswell & Plano Clark, 2011).

From these characteristics, it follows that mixed methods starts with the assumption that an investigator, in understanding the social and behavioral world, gathers evidence and makes sense of it based on participant (subject) information as well as frameworks, scales, or perspectives drawn from the literature. Thus, mixed methods research is more than simply collecting qualitative data from focus groups; it involves the intentional collection of both quantitative and qualitative data and combining the strengths of each. Moreover, this collection is followed by data analysis in which investigators do not keep the databases separate, but integrate or combine them in a meaningful manner. This integration separates current views of mixed methods from older perspectives in which investigators collected both forms of data but kept them separate, or casually combined them rather than using systematic integrative procedures. The assumption is made that a synergy results from combining the strengths (or minimizing the weaknesses) of both quantitative and qualitative data.

Understanding the Use of Quantitative and Qualitative Evidence

Basic to understanding mixed methods procedures is knowledge of both quantitative and qualitative research. Quantitative research involves the testing of objective theories by examining the relationship among variables. These variables are measured, typically on instruments, in such a way that numbered data can be analyzed using statistical procedures. This measureable evidence helps to establish (probable) cause and effect, results in efficient data collection procedures, creates the possibility of replication and generalization to a population, facilitates the comparison of groups, and provides insight into a breadth of experience using a small number of variables or constructs. Typical quantitative designs are survey procedures, correlational techniques, and the use of various forms of experiments from randomized controlled tests to single subject time series designs.

Qualitative research, on the other hand, is used for exploring and understanding the meanings that individuals or groups ascribe to a single phenomenon. Researchers pose general questions, gather text data (e.g., transcriptions from interviews) or image data (e.g., pictures, videotapes, etc.), and analyze this data for general themes. These themes are then described, arrayed into a chronology to form a story, organized into an emerging theory, or assembled into a detailed picture of cultural life. In this way, qualitative data helps understand processes (especially those that emerge over time), provides detailed information about setting or context, emphasizes the voices of participants through quotes, facilitates the collection of data when measures do not exist or are confounding, and provides a deeper understanding of concepts. Typical qualitative research approaches include narrative inquiries, phenomenologies, grounded theory studies, ethnographies, and case studies.

Conducting Single or Multiphase Mixed Methods Studies

The two forms of data, quantitative and qualitative, are often combined in a single study, similar to the type that is conducted by a graduate student, single investigator, or teacher. In the case of student assessment in the classroom, a teacher might gather survey data as well as written qualitative documents to demonstrate a student's accomplishments in the classroom. At other times, the two forms of data are collected in a multiphase evaluation project that spans a period of time and interweaves quantitative and qualitative projects together in order to make sense of a common project objective. In evaluation, for instance, the overall purpose might be to develop, test, implement, and evaluate a health prevention program. This type of design would call for multiple projects—one quantitative, one qualitative, one quantitative, and so forth—conducted over time with links in place so that one phase builds on another (Natasi, et al., 2007).

Framing the Study within a Philosophical Worldview

In qualitative research much attention has been given to the worldview or philosophy that underpins a study (Guba & Lincoln, 1988). Quantitative researchers are less likely to convey their philosophical positions because they are understood, but quantitative philosophy, found in the form of post-positivist thinking, has been recently discussed among quantitative researchers (Phillips & Burbules, 2001). A lively debate has occurred since the early 1990s among mixed methods researchers about the worldview underpinning mixed methods research. Different stances have emerged, with a dominant discussion about the possibility of a single worldview for mixed methods. In 2003, Tashakkori and Teddlie announced that 13 writers had embraced pragmatism as the major worldview for mixed methods research. This philosophy is an American philosophy built on the premises of using multiple methods to study problems. Behind the philosophy is the idea that mixed methods research should document "what works" in a practical manner, and that the research question holds primacy in leading any mixed methods inquiry. Others have introduced alternative philosophies into the discussion, such as the transformative perspective, which suggests an orienting framework for a mixed methods study based on creating a more just and democratic society that permeates the entire research process from the problem to the conclusions and the use of results (Mertens, 2003). More recently, critical realism, based on assessing both an objective reality and a subjective interpretation, has discussed in mixed methods literature. In contrast to these perspectives is the view that mixed methods researchers might use multiple philosophies (Greene, 2007), link philosophy to design type (Creswell & Plano Clark, 2011), or vary the philosophy depending on the types of questions and methods used in a particular scholarly community (Morgan, 2007).

Using a Specific Type of Mixed Methods Design

Perhaps no discussion has dominated the literature in mixed methods research more than the identification and specification of mixed methods designs. Several possibilities exist, and there is no common adopted set of designs among the numerous typologies being discussed in the literature. Creswell and Plano Clark (2011) identified 12 different classifications of mixed methods designs.

Of these, two general methods are available: merging the two datasets, and/or having one dataset build on the other. These are known as convergent (or concurrent) approaches and sequential approaches.

When the intent is to merge quantitative and qualitative data, the investigator combines both quantitative and qualitative research. This design is known as a *convergent* or parallel design. For example, an investigator might collect quantitative correlational data as well as qualitative focus group data and combine the two to best understand a research problem or to have one dataset validate another dataset. Some challenges in this design involve having adequate sample sizes for both forms of data collection, explaining contradictions when they occur, and merging the two datasets. Several popular approaches for merging are comparing the results from the analyses of both datasets, transforming one dataset (e.g., transforming qualitative data into numeric data) so that it can be compared with the other dataset, or developing results tables or graphs that directly present a comparison. Another design possibility is to have one dataset build on the results from the other. These are known as *sequential* designs, and they may begin by a qualitative exploration followed by a quantitative follow up called an *exploratory sequential design*. A useful application of this design is to first collect qualitative data, use the results to develop an instrument with good psychometric properties, and then to quantitatively test the instrument with a sample from a population. Alternatively, an initial quantitative phase can be extended by a qualitative follow up. This is known as an *explanatory sequential design*. A popular approach is using qualitative data to help explain quantitative results in more depth.

A popular design in experimental research uses quantitative and qualitative approaches in tandem and to embed one in the other to provide new insights or more refined thinking. These designs are called *embedded* or nested designs. A prototype would be to conduct an experimental study and to embed qualitative data within the intervention procedures. Qualitative data may be used prior to the intervention to best recruit individuals or to develop the intervention, during the experiment to examine the process being experienced by subjects, or after the experiment to follow up and better understand the quantitative outcomes.

Another design seeks to either merge the data or to build on it sequentially, but the entire investigation is framed within a larger philosophical or theoretical framework. This is called a *transformational design*. For example, a community action study may be conducted to change attitudes toward bullying, and the research would employ a quantitative needs assessment followed by in-depth interviews with community members to more deeply understand their needs. The framework might be a transformational model in which the intent is to assist and bring about change. Finally, as mentioned earlier, a mixed methods design can be longitudinal with multiple projects conducted over time and linked together by a common purpose. These *multiphase* designs are frequently used in evaluation research.

How does an evaluator or assessor decide which design is appropriate to use? To decide which general approach might be used investigators need to consider which approach best answers the research questions or hypotheses in the study; which approach is workable given time, resources, and skills; what emphasis might be given to one database or the other (or both); the skills of the investigatory research team; and the overall intent of the study. A consideration needs to be made of the challenges in using a selected design. Issues that may arise include: knowing how to interface the quantitative and qualitative data (either in merging it or using it sequentially); difficulties in finding publishing outlets, given the word limits of medical journals; and the availability of resources, such as time, money, and personnel with skills in both quantitative and qualitative research.

Mixed Methods and Evaluation

In order to best understand the specific application of mixed methods to assessment we need to first detail how mixed methods has intersected with the field of evaluation. Some would say that mixed

Table 34.1 Six Research Strategies

	Approach	Data Collection	Data Analysis
Pure Paradigm	Experimental design	Quantitative Measurement	Statistical analysis
	Naturalistic inquiry	Qualitative Measurement	Content analysis
Mixed Form	Naturalistic inquiry	Qualitative Measurement	Statistical analysis
	Naturalistic inquiry	Quantitative Measurement	Statistical analysis
	Experimental design	Qualitative Measurement	Statistical analysis
	Experimental design	Qualitative Measurement	Content analysis

methods began in the field of evaluation that has for years gathered both quantitative and qualitative data (Creswell, in press). As we look back over the last 30 years, we can see that mixed methods has had a prominent presence and increased in use in evaluation. To review this development, it is important to assess the inception of mixed methods evaluation designs, the conceptual framework that developed, the philosophical debates that ensued, the paradigmatic debates, the advancement of mixed methods through reports and applications, and the developments in multiphase evaluation designs.

The Inception of Mixed Methods in Evaluation

In 1980, Patton wrote about qualitative methods in evaluation. Patton also broached the use of mixed methods in evaluation, discussing mixing at the levels of data, design, and analysis. He described six research strategies (see Table 34.1). Patton argued that the overall paradigms (i.e., inductive naturalistic inquiry or deductive experimental design) were not mixable. Rather, evaluators could combine strategies. For example, researchers could study a freshman retention program in which students were randomly assigned to the intervention or control group. To evaluate the program, researchers might conduct qualitative interviews and transform the data to numbers to subsequently conduct analysis to assess statistically significant differences between the intervention and control group. This would constitute a design consistent with Patton's description of experimental design with qualitative measurement and statistical analysis. Ultimately, researchers should consider the purpose of the evaluation study (e.g., actionable information for decision-making) when selecting a design. Although mixing paradigms within evaluation may have been inconceivable in the nascent years of mixed methods development, authors challenged this notion in later years.

Researchers continued to employ mixed methods in evaluation studies, as evidenced by its proliferation after 1980. Prominent evaluators continued to broach the notion of mixing methods. Fetterman and Pitman (1986) provided a discussion on how to integrate qualitative and quantitative data within a single study. Nevertheless, through this period, researchers typically sought designs that mixed methods to triangulate findings. Designs used three primary manifestations of triangulation: triangulation of measures (i.e., agreement between measures), triangulation of conclusions within a study, and triangulation of findings across studies (Kidder & Fine, 1987). This period culminated with a seminal iteration of the mixed methods evaluation methodological literature in the late 1980s.

A Conceptual Framework for Mixed Methods Designs

Challenging the notion of triangulation as the sole purpose of mixing methods within evaluation studies, Greene, Caracelli, and Graham (1989) developed a conceptual framework for mixed methods evaluation designs from a review of 57 empirical evaluation studies in the literature from 1980 to 1988. Their basic framework was to advance a purpose for mixed methods research and then to suggest a design that would match the purpose. Greene et al. advanced a framework of five purposes for applying mixed methods to evaluation and designs aligned with those purposes. The five purposes and designs were triangulation, complementarity, development, initiation, and expansion. Seven characteristics evince the Greene et al. designs. The characteristics are methods, phenomena, paradigms, status (importance and role of the qualitative and quantitative methods), implementation independence, implementation timing, and study (one or more than one study). By first identifying a mixed methods purpose, researchers can select a design with matching characteristics.

The logical question arose as to how to analyze the data given a purpose and research design. In addition to the design planning, however, evaluators must concurrently plan for data analysis. Filling a gap in the literature about integrating qualitative and quantitative data at the analysis stage, Caracelli and Greene (1997) furthered the development of the Green et al. (1989) conceptual framework and presented four strategies for integrated data analysis in mixed methods evaluation studies:

- Data transformation: convert data from one type into another (e.g., qualitative to quantitative) for concomitant analysis.
- Typology development: develop a typology from one data type as a framework for analyzing the other data type.
- Extreme case analysis: identify extreme cases from one strand and analyze in the other strand to test and refine the description.
- Data consolidation/merging: concurrently review both data types to develop new variables for datasets.

Many studies can have both a qualitative and quantitative strand. Nevertheless, a hallmark of mixed methods evaluation is the integration of the strands to serve an end purpose. Caracelli and Greene (1997) organized the ways to integrate strands at the analysis level. Researchers subsequently applied these techniques in evaluation studies.

Philosophical Debates in Evaluation

Despite pragmatic advances in conducting mixed methods evaluation studies, paradigmatic debates continued to linger. Writing about qualitative approaches to educational evaluation, Fetterman (1988), who would later become president of the American Evaluation Association, discussed the potential of combining approaches within an evaluation study. Fetterman (1988) discussed the quantitative-qualitative debate and observed the tendency of the terms quantitative and qualitative to become synonymous with conflicting paradigms and their methods. He noted, however, that the paradigms themselves rely on both quantitative and qualitative methods. In an attempt to reconcile the dissonant paradigms, Shadish (1993) discussed mixed methods program evaluation through a lens of critical multiplism, understanding that use of a single method (i.e., only quantitative or only qualitative) is a limitation. Critical multiplism is defined as the systematic application of the tenets of multiple operationalism to all components of research (Figueredo, 1993). Shadish described those components as question formation, theory or model selection, research design, data analysis, and interpretation of results. Ultimately, combining qualitative and quantitative strands can strengthen inferences within a body of knowledge.

Researchers continued to debate the issues of mixing paradigms within evaluation studies. The major beliefs were: (a) researchers should not mix paradigms (i.e., purist stance), (b) paradigms are helpful in conceptualizing research but methodological decisions remain pragmatic (i.e., pragmatic stance), and (c) paradigms are important and the discordance of multiple paradigms potentially yields more insightful evaluations (i.e., dialectical stance) (Greene & Caracelli, 1997). Greene and Caracelli urged focusing on the compatible characteristics of inquiry and embracing dialogue on "multiple ways of knowing and acting" (p. 15). The overall premise that arose through this period is that mixing methods is beneficial to evaluation studies, yet researchers must undertake mixing with intentionality.

Concurrent work continued to advance the typology of mixed methods designs. Caracelli and Greene (1997) generally classified mixed methods evaluation designs into component and integrated designs. The difference between these classifications rests in the level of methods of integration. In the component designs—which include triangulation, complementarity, and expansion—the qualitative and quantitative strands operate distinctly through the study or program of inquiry (Caracelli & Greene, 1997), and the integration or mixing occurs at interpretation or in the conclusion. Integrated designs differ in that integration or mixing can occur throughout the process of inquiry, including mixing characteristics of unique paradigms (Caracelli & Greene, 1997). Integrated designs encompass iterative, embedded, holistic, and transformative designs. Addressing integrated designs marked a significant contribution to the methodological literature on mixed methods evaluations and elucidated the interplay possible between qualitative and quantitative strands within an evaluation. Additionally, this provided a framework to consider the design choices and rationale for mixing methods.

Advancement of Mixed Methods

The themes of the next era of mixed methods evaluation appear to be proliferation and greater acceptance. A major funding source ostensibly accepted mixed methods when the National Science Foundation released a publication (Frechtling & Sharp, 1997) to provide general guidance to researchers conducting mixed methods evaluations. The guidebook gives pragmatic advice for researchers who would like to conduct mixed methods evaluation studies.

The National Science Foundation continued its support of mixed methods. Drawing from the mixed methods publication, the National Science Foundation released *The 2002 User-Friendly Handbook for Project Evaluation*, which included a chapter on both quantitative and qualitative data collection methods (Frechtling, 2002). The chapter reviewed the philosophical issues undergirding qualitative and quantitative approaches and focused on pragmatic advice for program managers. The chapter concluded with a section on mixing in which the authors felt, "a strong case can be made for including qualitative elements in the majority of evaluations of NSF projects" (Frechtling, 2002, p. 46). In this section, Frechtling (2002) explained benefits for mixed methods, which relate closely with purposes for mixing (Greene, Caracelli, & Graham, 1989). The benefits are enhanced validity (triangulation purpose), better instruments (development purpose), and a more complete understanding (complementarity purpose). In addition, Frechtling (2002) presented an example sequential design using a focus group followed by a survey followed by interviews (Qual → Quan → Qual) but stressed it is only one of several approaches. Finally, Frechtling (2002) emphasized the mixed methods design's role in both summative and formative evaluations and summarized the handbook's philosophy as, "The evaluator should attempt to obtain the most useful information to answer the critical questions about the project and, in so doing, rely on a mixed-methods approach whenever possible" (p. 48).

In the *Handbook of Mixed Methods in Social & Behavioral Research*, Rallis and Rossman (2003) noted that the applied nature of evaluation, providing information to its stakeholders, distinguishes it from theoretic research. They provided a pragmatic framework and examples of mixed methods evaluations that engage in three central tasks: description, comparison relative to a control or standard, and prediction. Regarding description, combining qualitative and quantitative strands for data collection and analysis produces a richer description with more data in evidence. Rallis and Rossman provided further examples supporting mixed methods for comparison purposes. For example, qualitative and quantitative data can complement one another in comparisons or build on one another through qualitatively identifying outcomes of interest and quantitatively comparing those outcomes. Finally, mixed methods assist with prediction in evaluation. As Rallis and Rossman described, evaluations arise from the need to make recommendations about the future of a program. Engaging stakeholders, for instance, through the qualitative strand has encouraged better use of findings. Although mixed methods is more resource intensive, it can enhance an evaluations ability to achieve its stated purpose.

Mixed methods evaluations further iterated with the proliferation of transformative evaluation designs. Transformative designs operate through a paradigm worldview that strives to actuate change and promote social justice for underrepresented or marginalized individuals (Creswell & Plano Clark, 2011). The topics of inquiry range from social programs in the third world to education in the United States, and examples exist throughout the literature. In fact, Mertens (2009) argued that researchers could conduct almost any mixed methods study with a transformative or advocacy purpose. Researchers have applied mixed methods to impact evaluation of international public policy issues, such as a World Bank project on rural electrification in Laos, basic education in Ghana, and self-help groups in Andhra Pradesh, India (White, 2008). Mertens (2010) discussed the mixed methods evaluation of the Shared Reading Project in which a specific goal was to assess its impact on underserved groups. Combining persuasive qualitative and rigorous quantitative strands, the goal of transformative mixed methods evaluations is social change, which can occur at a variety of levels (Mertens, 2010).

Developments in Multiphase Evaluation Designs

Another recent development is the multiphase design. The multiphase mixed method design involves a series of qualitative and quantitative strands that connect and compile in sequence (Creswell & Plano Clark, 2011). These designs typically involve large multiyear projects, such as the Wabash National Study of Liberal Arts Education (Seifert, Pascarella, Erkel, & Goodman, 2010). Researchers have used the multiphase design for formative evaluation, instrument development, and summative evaluation all within a single program of research. Natasi, et al. (2007) conducted a multiyear mixed methods study to guide development and evaluate a culturally specific intervention, the Sri Lanka Mental Health Promotion Project. Based on that multiphase project, the authors proposed five designs:

- Formative research (Qual →/+ Quan)
- Theory development or modification and testing (Qual → Quan →/+ Qual → Quan . . . Qual → Quan)
- Instrument development (Qual → Quan)
- Program development and evaluation (Qual →/+ Quan →/+ Qual →/+ Quan . . . Qual →/+ Quan, or Qual →← Quan)
- Evaluation research (Qual + Quan)

Furthermore, it is easy to envision extant literature as part of a multiphase design. For instance, Arnon and Reichel (2009) used mixed methods to identify characteristics of a good teacher. This could serve as the basis for further evaluation or assessment in a multiphase design. Other implementations already exist in the literature. Waysman and Savaya (1997) conducted an evaluation of a non-profit agency, SHATIL, which provides direct assistance to other non-profit organizations. The purpose of the study was to map characteristics of client organizations seeking assistance, map the services provided to those organizations, assess the perceived contribution of SHATIL's service to development and goal attainment of the organizations, and evaluate the satisfaction of the services. Waysman and Savaya conceived a three-phase study: qualitative focus groups and personal interviews, followed by a survey questionnaire derived from the qualitative phase, followed by qualitative focus groups to explore satisfaction issues.

Health Sciences Extensions

The field of health sciences has continued to extend mixed methods into evaluation. Researchers have recently been relying on mixed methods as a mode of evaluation throughout fields of health, including medicine, nursing, behavioral health, and public health. Mixed methods designs have assisted health sciences evaluators in identifying outcomes and understanding mechanisms of an intervention, in addition to conducting formative and summative evaluations.

Evaluators and stakeholders face the challenge of identifying the key outcomes or variables to measure. King et al. (2009) conducted a mixed methods study of the continuity of cancer care and its impact on health outcomes. In this study, the researchers conducted qualitative interviews with patients, individuals close with the patients, and health professionals; the researchers coded and analyzed the interviews to develop a standardized instrument to measure the experience of continuity of care. Next, King et al. (2009) administered the instrument to assess the relationship between continuity of care (i.e., as measured through the instrument) and health needs, psychological needs, quality of life, and satisfaction with care. Thus, within a single mixed methods study, researchers can identify key variables and use those variables within a quantitative phase.

Other evaluation designs have focused on the "how" question of evaluation through an examination of the mechanisms of change within an intervention. Citing 98,000 inpatient deaths and $9 billion in costs per year, Miller and LaFramboise (2009) reported an evaluation of a classroom intervention for senior-level nursing students designed to ultimately improve patient safety and care quality. Comparing a control group to two different intervention groups, the quantitative strand included student survey data of competency perceptions and repeated measures of analysis of variance. The qualitative strand consisted of data from case study focus group discussions and content analysis. While the quantitative strand examined the effect of the intervention on student perceptions of their knowledge, skills, and attitudes, the content analysis yielded critical insight into how students conceptualized the case. In another example, researchers conducted a mixed methods evaluation of a therapeutic community services for individuals with personality disorders (Barr et al., 2010; Hodge et al., 2010). While the overall aim of the study was to assess the effectiveness of the intervention, the qualitative strand identified the specific changes that enabled individuals to achieve the outcomes evident in the quantitative strand. Researchers have also used mixed methods to understand the experiences of intervention participants. For example, researchers conducted a mixed methods evaluation of an intervention to increase condom use and HIV disclosure among women diagnosed with HIV/AIDS (Teti et al., 2010). The quantitative strand relied on hierarchical general linear modeling of repeated measures of outcome variables. The qualitative strand consisted of a Grounded Theory approach to interview a subset of participants. Thus, the authors were able to evaluate the intervention in terms of quantitative outcomes and further explain the experience of the intervention and mechanisms of the intervention that led to the outcomes. In these examples, the use of mixed methods provided a more in depth understanding of the intervention.

Mixed methods research can also serve a formative evaluation purpose, identifying best practices to inform an existing program. Use of mixed methods designs for evaluation has further extended into public health interventions. For example, Besculides, Zaveri, Farris, and Will (2006) studied five heterogeneous projects implementing the WISEWOMAN (Well Integrated Screening and Evaluation for Women Across the Nation) program, which provided risk factor screening for cardiovascular disease and lifestyle interventions for women aged 40–64. In the WISEWOMAN study,

Besculides et al. (2006) first piloted data collection methods and then refined procedures, which helped the researchers anticipate issues that may arise. The study relied on quantitative analysis to identify high and low performing sites. Subsequently, the researchers collected qualitative data through interviews, focus groups, and observations for thematic analysis. In the final integration of the strands, the authors applied an algorithm that mixed quantitative data performance data with specific practices noted within qualitative themes in order to identify the best practices within the program. Serving a formative evaluation aim, the dissemination plan included a toolkit for both current and new WISEWOMAN projects.

Finally, use of mixed methods research is also beginning to show up within evidence-based practice databases, such as the Cochrane Collaboration Library. Systematic reviews of health interventions now integrate qualitative research with quantitative studies in systematic reviews of health interventions. Reviewers conduct a traditional meta-analysis of quantitative data within studies, apply qualitative analysis to the text data reported within the qualitative studies, and integrate findings (Harden, 2007; Thomas et al., 2004). This type of review both relies on mixed methods and includes multiple types of studies to build a body of knowledge around a particular condition or intervention.

Clearly, mixed methods within the field of evaluation has undergone significant transformations as it has been used. From Patton's (1980) discussion of mixed methods evaluation designs, the literature has grown through paradigmatic discussions and pragmatic discussions. A focus has been on the purpose and the types of designs available to evaluators (Greene, Caracelli, & Graham, 1989). This discussion has extended into data analysis strategies used for mixing data (Caracelli & Greene, 1997). More extensive discussions then appeared from federal funding agencies, such as the National Science Foundation's handbook on evaluation, which addressed mixed methods (Frechtling, 2002; Frechtling & Sharp, 1997). The link to how stakeholders might use mixed methods data emerged as a conversation in the field of evaluation (Rallis & Rossman, 2003). More recently, using mixed methods as a transformative evaluation for underrepresented groups illustrates a new way to link mixed methods and the field of evaluation (e.g., Mertens, 2009). Additionally, writers have begun to discuss how to apply mixed methods to multiphase evaluation designs that span several years and multiple projects (Natasi, et al., 2007). The next phase, then, is to link mixed methods to stakeholders in classrooms and in the field of assessment.

Mixed Methods and Assessment

Mixed methods has not only been developed as a method of research and found useful in the context of evaluation, but is also becoming a key resource in the field of assessment. In this section we will: detail the need for mixed methods in assessment, examine the importance of integrating assessment into planning, describe the way in which assessment relates to various types of motivation, discuss including the classroom as a site for mixed methods, and finally illustrate assessment using mixed methods in a higher education setting.

Need for Mixing Assessment and Methods

The current push for educational accountability suggests a concern about the ability of the educational system to prepare citizens to meet the challenges of a global economy. We all recognize that today's world is different—increasingly interconnected, interdependent and insecure. We also have unprecedented opportunities to collaborate and find solutions to global problems, such as hunger and poverty; and we have growing global markets for our ideas, goods, and services to reach the broad audiences of stakeholders in an evaluation context. We need to continue to play a leading role in the world; whether or not we do that wisely will depend in significant part on the education of our citizens. An educated citizenry is the lifeblood of a democracy. Now more than ever before education requires knowledge and understanding of the people around the world.

Several reports (*America's Perfect Storm: Three Forces Changing our Nation's Future* by Kirsch, Braun, Yamamoto, & Sum, 2007; *Tough Choices or Tough Times: The Report of the New Commission on the Skills of the American Workforce* by National Center on Education and the Economy, 2006; and *Rising Above the Gathering Storm: Energizing and Employing America for a Brighter Economic Future* by Committee on Prospering in the Global Economy of the 21st Century, 2007) claim that the U.S. education system is in danger of failing to produce the skilled and productive labor pools needed for tomorrow. The data from the Organization for Economic Co-operation and Development (OECD) Program for International Student Assessment (PISA) shows that U.S. 15-year-olds performed below the OECD average in math literacy, science literacy, and problem-solving (i.e., below the average for the industrialized nations with which the United States competes economically, Lemke et al., 2004). These conditions have raised the call for increased use of assessment as a tool for educational accountability to evaluate educational effectiveness and to provide the data to make informed decisions about how to improve the system. Citizens, educators, and policymakers need such assessments in order to identify the groups, schools, and learners that require attention.

The subjects of reading, math, and more recently, science have been the focal areas for assessment. The enactment of the No Child Left Behind Act has impacted instructional practices, creating an urgency to narrow curriculum, both in terms of content and the types of skills and understanding that are taught (Bennett & Gitomer, 2008). Shepard (2000) argues that the cognitive models underlying these assessments are out of date and result in a single proficiency score when the nature of the domain performance is much more complex.

Many experts in assessment and instruction claim that we have created a system of accountability assessment grounded in an outdated scientific model for conceptualizing proficiency, teaching it, and measuring it. In this next section we discuss the use of mixed methods in formative and summative assessment measures where inferences are made on student competency, followed by actions that are taken to help achieve learning goals (Forman & Damschroder, 2007). This concept of formative assessment proves itself fit to be used for instructional decision-making.

The power of mixed methods applied to assessment and assessment experience itself must be shown to be educationally worthwhile in order to succeed. As a priority on the national educational agenda, greater accountability assessment is both desired and required from all states. We must ask ourselves whether we can rethink assessment as a system that serves both local learning needs and the policy purposes of the nation. As assessment professionals, we have an obligation to do our best to find out if we can grow in our understanding of an assessment system that uses mixed methods to enhance learning indicators.

Quality Quantitative and Qualitative Criteria

Educators have nearly complete control over the information they gather and use to evaluate and improve their students' learning. Along with that independence come the professional responsibility to perform these tasks appropriately and the desire to perform them effectively. Educators must follow professional standards of practice and ethical principles of behavior as they fulfill their responsibilities and evaluate and assess their students.

Formative and summative assessment tools (mixed methods) help teachers gather useful information for making decisions about their students; decisions that may have serious ramifications. Correct or not, each of a teacher's decisions will have positive or negative consequences for their students. Decisions and consequences can vary in degree of seriousness. An example of a high-stakes decision would be giving a student a low final grade in physics that lowers the student's chances of being admitted as a physics major at a particular college. Less serious consequences occur when a low-stakes decision is made. In these situations a student loses something less valuable and readily recovers from an incorrect initial decision. When the consequences of a decision are serious, a teacher must be sure to use the best available information: information which is often procured through assessment.

Assessment is the process of gathering appropriate information for making educational decisions, drawing on both quantitative and qualitative data. Before making a decision it is important to ensure that one's information is highly valid, of high quality, and highly reliable for the particular decision. Using high quality information does not guarantee that a decision will be correct. Using poor quality or erroneous information, however, is more likely to lead to an incorrect decision, which may be harmful to a student. Causing harm to a student, either deliberately or through negligence, is unethical, unprofessional, and illegal.

The National Council on Measurement in Education's (NCME) *Code of Professional Responsibilities in Educational Measurement* (CPR) assumes that an informed user of educational assessment will behave in accordance with other assessment-related professional standards. These include the *Code of Fair Testing Practices in Education* (Revised, Joint Committee on Testing Practices, 2004) and the *Standards for Educational and Psychological Testing* (American Educational Research Association, American Psychological Association, and National Council of Measurement in Education. (1999). [See http://www.theaaceonline.com/codefair.pdf for a copy of these fair testing practices.]

Assessment Planning

Assessment should not be viewed as a conclusive measurement of teaching, but ought to be integrated into the entire teaching and learning process. Lesson plans are incomplete and risk being ineffective if they do not include plans for purposeful assessment. Assessment can take place at various intervals and might be integrated into lessons that are planned for a specific unit, marking period, term, or year. When teachers build assessment in their lesson plans they can more easily create an assessment blueprint that includes both higher-order and lower-order thinking. Sharing the blueprint with students gives the teacher the chance to make assessments more student-centered and allows the students to feel more prepared.

As a teacher improves their knowledge of classroom assessments they can expect the following quantitative cause and effect relationships (Nitko & Brookhart, 2007):

- Knowledge of how to choose or to craft quality assessment *increases the quality of teaching decisions*.
- The subjects a teacher assesses and the manner in which they assess *communicate in a powerful way what the teacher really values in their students' learning*.
- Learning to craft assessment tasks *increases freedom to design lessons*.
- Knowledge of assessment *improves the validity of interpretations and use of assessment results*.
- Knowledge of assessment *improves appreciation of the strengths and limitations of each type of assessment procedure*.

Teachers should learn to apply both formative and summative purposes with different assessment methods. Formative uses of assessment help teachers to guide or monitor student learning as it is in progress. The use of high-quality formative assessment and feedback increases student learning (Black & Wiliam, 1998). Qualitative types of teacher feedback involve providing information and understanding about the tasks that make a difference in light of what the student already understands, misunderstands, and constructs. Student feedback often involves providing information and understanding about the tasks that make a difference in light of what the teacher already understands, misunderstands, and constructs about the learning of his or her students. The goal is that the teacher will begin to see learning through the lens of the student who is grappling to construct beliefs and knowledge about the learning target for the lesson. This usually requires the ability to learn and learn again, necessitates a great amount of feedback, involves purposeful and deliberate practice, often leads to errors and misunderstandings or misdirections, calls for time to integrate prior knowledge and conceptions, and demands a sense of excitement and joy of learning.

Hattie (2009) offers six signposts towards excellence in education that direct attention to assessment using multiple methods. The extent to which teachers exemplify these requirements correlates to the extent to which they multitask and use multiple methods of assessment in their classroom:

- Teachers are among the most powerful influencers in learning.
- Teachers need to be directive, influential, caring, and actively engaged in the passion of teaching and learning.
- Teachers need to be aware of what each and every student is thinking and knowing, in order to construct meaning and meaningful experiences. Teachers must also have proficient knowledge and understanding of their content so they can provide meaningful and appropriate feedback such that each student moves progressively through the curriculum levels.
- Teachers need to know the learning intentions and success criteria of their lesson, gauge how well they are attaining these criteria for all students, and understand where to go next in light of the gap between students' current knowledge and understanding and the success criteria required to answer the question, "Where are you going?"
- Teachers need to move from a single idea to multiple ideas, and to relate and extend these ideas in such a way that learners construct and reconstruct knowledge and ideas.
- School leaders and teachers need to create school, staffroom, and classroom environments where error is welcomed as a learning opportunity, in which the learners can feel safe to learn, re-learn, and explore knowledge and understanding.

The Variety of Methods in Motivating Communities of Learners

Assessment can be done in a number of ways, employing a variety of methods to document learning in the classroom. To better understand the impact of methods for improving learning and student achievement, we establish quantitative benchmarks for progress (e.g., effect sizes preferably .40 or higher for every student). In other words, teachers and principals need to collect quantitative effect sizes within their schools and then ask "What is working best?"; "Why is it working best?"; and "Who is it not working for?" Having this type of discussion among teachers about teaching requires a caring community of learners who trust, respect, and share a passion for learning from other teachers. Trust fosters a set of organizational conditions that facilitate teachers' efforts to be innovative in their classrooms and to develop more effective instruction. It also facilitates public problem solving within a school and creates a moral resource that leads to commitment and greater effort to implement successful innovations. Creating a shared knowledge system that will make a difference requires investment from teachers who are learning about their teaching and about what is working and for whom (Harnisch, Shope, Hoback, Fryda, & Kelberlau, 2006). Together these teachers share evidence of the effectiveness of their methods. For the past decade cohorts of teachers/leaders have reflected on the evidence they collected and on how successful students were in achieving learning targets. Hattie (2009) refers to this kind of reflection as "visible learning."

When reviewing the methods chosen by teachers and the impact these methods have on learners we see marked differences. For example, a comparison of active and passionate teachers who used facilitative and inquiry methods revealed a marked contrast with an effect size of .60 for teacher as "activator" versus .17 for teacher as "facilitator" (Hattie, 2009). Results revealed that active and guided instruction is more effective than unguided, facilitative instruction (see Table 34.2). When

Table 34.2 Effect Sizes for Teacher as Activator and Teacher as Facilitator

Teacher as Activator	d	Teacher as Facilitator	d
Reciprocal teaching	.74	Simulations and gaming	.32
Feedback	.72	Inquiry-based teaching	.31
Teaching students self-verbalizations	.67	Smaller class sizes	.2
Metacognitive strategies	.67	Individualized instruction	.20
Direct instruction	.59	Problem-based learning	.15
Mastery learning	.57	Different teaching for boys and girls	.12
Goals—challenging	.56	Web-based learning	.09
Frequent/effects of testing	.46	Whole language—reading	.06
Behavioral organizers	.41	Inductive teaching	.06
Average Activator	.60	Average facilitator	.17

From *Visible Learning: A Synthesis of Over 800 Meta-Analyses Relating to Achievement* (p. 243), by J. A. C. Hattie, 2009, New York, NY: Routledge. Copyright 2009 by Routledge. Adapted with permission.

considering the variety of methods available, it is important to note that small increases in student achievement were noted for minimally guided methods such as discovery learning, problem-based learning, inquiry learning, experiential learning, and constructivist learning.

Bransford, Brown, and Cocking (2000) provide a set of three principles for improving achievement, which include many qualitative concepts. These principles should be taken into account when teachers are planning lessons, choosing methods, and designing assessments. They document: that culture matters, that individual student stories need to be gathered, that learning is collaborative and interactive, and that the processes of small group work need to be identified. The three principles are:

- Students come into classes with preconceptions about the world and need to be engaged by teachers in order to grasp new concepts and information.
- Students need to have a deep foundation of factual knowledge and understand ideas in the context of a conceptual framework that allows for knowledge retrieval and application.
- Students need to learn to take control of personal learning goals and monitor progress in achieving them.

The Classroom as a Site for Mixed Methods Approaches

The conditions of teaching require that teachers are adaptive learning experts that have high levels of flexibility which allow them to innovate when routines are not enough. Teachers need to be able to determine when certain students are not learning the targets for the course, discern the instruction that is needed, and adapt the resources and instructional strategies in order to assist students in meeting learning targets. A teacher might also alter the classroom environment in order to assist students in attaining the learning goal. Teachers are mixed methods specialists in action. They are often asked to be empathetic, to take the perspective of a student and to show both cognitive and affective domains of empathy. Teachers are required to characterize the learning targets for a course and to present complex and challenging problems to students who are being asked to attain difficult goals.

Teachers are agents of managing complex relationships. A teacher's role as a mixed methods specialist is best seen by the way that teachers choose worthwhile and appropriately challenging tasks even as they place a high value of importance on relationships, trust, caring, and safety with the community of learners. The evidence from the meta-analyses does not provide us with rules for action but does highlight the key questions that need to be explored with this mixed-methods approach. In short, evaluating the impact of learning in a classroom requires asking questions of "what works best?"; "when?"; "for whom?"; "to what ends?"; and "how?"

A Case Study of Mixed Methods in College Student Learning

Mixed methods has been used to assess various types of learning and the progress of individual, group, and programmatic achievement. The following is a case study of mixed methods as it was used to assess the implementation of iCUBED (Informatics and Computation through Undergraduate Baccalaureate Education), an innovative program that was developed at the University of Illinois Urbana-Champaign (UIUC) in 2008. [Sponsored by Illinois Informatics Institute and a grant from NSF (iCUBED, NSF #CNS 07-22327).]

Developers and directors designed iCUBED to introduce the cutting-edge field of informatics to students and faculty at UIUC. The primary goal of the program is to "transform undergraduate Computer Science(CS)/Informatics education at UIUC to prepare a more diverse and informatics-engaged workforce, including scientists, social scientists, artists, and educators." Program developers and implementers sought to do this in three ways. They would: (a) increase engagement in informatics by creating and institutionalizing new pathways to application-oriented CS/Informatics from other majors, from K-14, and from CS at UIUC; (b) improve preparation of application area informatics specialists by expanding CS instruction and building inter- and cross-disciplinary collaborations, courses, and curricula; and (c) increase retention of students by creating a student-focused CS immersion program and developing application-oriented informatics instruction and community building through extracurricular activities, service courses, and extensive internship opportunities. As these actions are being carried out, iCUBED is using mixed methods research, including qualitative site data, pre- and post-surveys, and observations, to document the UIUC transformational model. This approach is using a convergent design to triangulate the various sources of data to understand the use of the model and to evaluate its implementation. Once the primary goal of the program is met, they will leverage UIUC CS and NCSA leadership status to challenge and support other programs via aggressive dissemination; in doing so, they will meet their second goal of transforming education on a national level. By meeting this goal, inside reform, interdisciplinary reform, and institutional reform will be achieved.

Mixed Methods Evaluation in the Project

Mixed methods principles were used in evaluating the progress that has been made toward attaining the second objective, interdisciplinary reform. Evaluation of the effectiveness of the program was done through qualitative site visits, analysis of informatics course development proposals, and interviews with faculty members and student focus groups, along with quantitative surveys and document analysis from evaluators. Evaluators assessed the growth of existing informatics-infused courses, the addition of new discipline-based informatics-infused courses, the progress of the informatics minor, and the recent addition of the Informatics PhD (finalized in December of 2010). Student surveys, focus groups, and interviews aided evaluators in assessing student interest, student learning, and student transformation.

Quantitative Phase of the Study

As of fall 2010, 155 students representing just under 50 major fields of study had elected the informatics minor. These students participated in new and renovated courses. A quasi-experimental design was used to document their impact. Students who declared the minor as of fall 2010 were the target group. A matched group of students was used to evaluate the impact of the Instructional Informatics Program. Data was collected on a semester basis.

A profile of the learners at UIUC was developed using data from student transcripts, including gender, ethnicity, college, and GPA. A matched comparison sample was also created. Profiles of learners in the program were developed based on transcript review with the institutional research team.

In assessing interdisciplinary reform, evaluators compared a group of informatics students (students who enrolled in any of a dozen different INFO courses) with a matched group of non-INFO students. Students were matched based on five variables and sorted by a random variable. If the five-variable match did not work, age was not accounted for and a 4-variable match was attempted. The end result of the matching process allowed evaluators to review the GPAs from the greater community of learners with matched samples in the target community of learners.

Surveys

Both quantitative data (item responses) and qualitative data (open-ended questions) were acquired from the pre- and post-surveys that were used to monitor students who participated in INFO courses. Surveys provided evaluators with valuable information regarding student learning and transformation. Post-surveys comprised a series of focused questions. A subset of questions and the themes that emerged in student responses are shared below. That subset includes:

- What does the term "Informatics" mean to you?
- How do you think Informatics functions in the workplace?
- Describe the kind of career you see yourself in and how this course might help you to achieve your goals.
- If this course was a car or an animal, what kind would it be and why?
- Describe how you believe this course is integrated with real-life experiences. Give some examples.
- In general, how do you rate the Informatics program quality?
- If you have further comments at this time about any aspect of the program, please write them in your own words.

Based on survey data collected over two years, informatics courses are having a profound effect on students. Many of these students have little to no background in computer science, while others are well versed in the field. Courses have changed the perspectives of both groups.

Qualitative Themes in the Evaluation

Courses introduced many students to a field of which they were previously unaware. Students developed definitions and understandings of informatics, which ranged from "*the study of how computers are applied in the daily lives of people,*" to "*the study of the intersection and interaction of human users, information, and communication technologies and societies,*" to "*[how we] interpret, share, and discuss information among people over a wide range of services and technologies.*" Students came to understand that informatics is not a fixed discipline, but a continually developing field.

In conjunction with understanding the subject, students also learned its applicability. They noted the practical relevance that makes informatics courses fundamentally different, remarking that most people interact with technology on a daily basis. Students reported that INFO courses increased their skill base, giving them new knowledge of how to represent problems and structure processes. Courses also boosted students' personal knowledge and understanding of the capabilities and limitations of computers and information technology.

Students also reported having gained a better understanding of the ways informatics coincides with their principal areas of study. A sociology major reported that informatics is not a brief overview of human-techno interactions, but a means of understanding where all of those concepts are going. A student pursuing a career in health care observed that informatics is guiding the process of human-technology interaction in the medical field. Many other students remarked that informatics is personally beneficial in the practical skills that it teaches them, even if it is not directly related to their primary field of study.

Some of the students who had a positive experience in one INFO course took a shine to the field as a whole. "*I don't know what the percentage is*," an instructor remarked, "*but a decent number of them [students] have actually decided to minor in informatics because of taking the course [Writing Across the Media].*" Other student responses indicated that their first INFO course convinced them to take additional classes and enroll as informatics minors.

Some students have begun to view informatics as a shrewd career move. One of them reported, "*More than ever technology is essential for jobs and careers. This minor will help me be more marketable.*" Other students made similar comments, remarking that their experience in informatics will give them an edge as they develop their careers. Students are learning that informatics is essential in the workplace and applies to the ways we use technology to communicate with co-workers and to access, manipulate, organize, store, and share information.

One of the purposes of using a convergent model in mixed methods research is to integrate findings from all databases. We observed from elective student surveys that the majority of those who participate in informatics education feel better prepared to engage in additional informatics courses and pursue internships and careers following graduation. Overall, students reported having gained valuable knowledge that equips them to succeed in a competitive work environment.

Qualitative Focus Group Interviews on Authentic Learning

In addition to the elective post-surveys, focus group interviews were a valuable means of gaining student input and feedback. During a survey with a small group of vested informatics minors, evaluators garnered a more detailed understanding of what students have gleaned from the program. Students valued the pertinence of the material presented in courses that revolve around issues with which students engage as soon as they leave the classroom. "*We're seeing the changes or hearing about [them] as they happen,*" one student observed. Consequently, courses are constantly evolving. Unique to the field is the amount of impact that students themselves have on their learning. "*We as students . . . are going to change the field,*" one of the group asserted, excited at the prospect of impacting a field as he studies it.

Students reported having been told that a minor in informatics will be a huge asset and have taken classes to equip themselves with a unique and useful skill set. Informatics, however, is still finding its way as a program—a fact that both excites and frustrates the students who take part in the field. Students were frustrated to discover that this "cutting edge" component in their education is so little known among the greater populace. In time, these students hope to see the payoff for trailblazing the way as members of an innovative and emerging field.

Some of the focus group were members of the Informatics Club, a "fairly loose" group of roughly 25 informatics minors who seek to develop and utilize their skills outside the classroom. The group's largest activity is visiting a community of senior citizens once a week to help them work with technology. "*They love it,*" one club-member said. Senior eLearner Esther Steinberg affirms his statement. "*The program is fantastic,*" she said, "*and there's a tremendous amount of interest in it among residents. I'm so pleased that these young people are helping us. I really am delighted and very positive, as you can tell.*"

Interviews evidenced that taking informatics into the community teaches students the applicability of what they are learning in class and shows them a way they can use their new knowledge to benefit and serve others. Club members have also been active in leading the way to better IT on campus for students. They seek to promote the intelligent use of information technology based on the feedback they receive from the campus community.

Integrating and Interpreting the Qualitative and Quantitative Data

Based on student responses gathered from interviews and surveys, students are satisfied with the theory taught and skill set acquired in the classroom, but would like to gain more practical experience and a better explanation of how they might use what they have learned in class. They realize that informatics is important, but struggle with knowing how to use it.

Those with minors also feel the department needs to improve in its marketing, not just to students, but to the campus, faculty, and recruiters as well. They would like to see informatics gain more prominence on UIUC's campus.

Data collected using a mixed methods design is helping evaluators develop a holistic perspective of student learning. As UIUC seeks to prepare its students to engage with and excel in a society that is becoming increasingly dependent on information technology, programs like iCUBED are essential. Utilizing the correct method of assessing and evaluating this program is equally important. As UIUC's informatics department grows and changes based on evaluations, more and more students will graduate better prepared to enter and transform their world.

Conclusion

A more comprehensive way of studying research problems, mixed methods is a revolutionary development in methodology. In the past twenty years it has developed practically and philosophically, and now holds tremendous potential for utilizing the strengths of both quantitative and qualitative data and research. This is true in the health sciences, social sciences, and more recently in education. Due to its systematic use of data, mixed methods has gained prominence as a means of evaluation and assessment. It has incredible potential in the field of education, where student performance has traditionally been based on quantitative outcomes alone. As educators supplement quantitative test scores with qualitative student feedback, they soon realize the need to understand how mixed methods works, and to become mixed methods specialists in action.

Despite the evident need for educators to understand the mixed methods techniques that many of them use on a daily basis, little has been written about mixed methods as it applies to learning and classroom assessment. This chapter has advanced a framework and process for applying qualitative, quantitative, and mixed methods methodology to evaluation, learning, and classroom assessment. It has provided a unique application of mixed methods to classroom assessment and discussed its potential for scholarly inquiry. It is hoped that these findings will serve as a basis for continued discussion about the use of these approaches to the accountability assessment facing our educational system. In doing so, they will provide opportunities for critique and innovation, and open the possibilities to rethink assessment as a system that serves both local learning needs and national policy purposes.

References

American Educational Research Association, American Psychological Association, and National Council of Measurement in Education. (1999). *Standards for educational and psychological testing*. Washington, DC: American Educational Research Association.

Arnon, S., & Reichel, N. (2009). Closed and open-ended question tools in a telephone survey about "the good teacher". *Journal of Mixed Methods Research, 3*, 172–196.

Barr, W., Kirkcaldy, A., Horne, A., Hodge, S., Hellin, K., & Göpfert, M. (2010). Quantitative findings from a mixed methods evaluation of once-weekly therapeutic community day services for people with personality disorder. *Journal of Mental Health, 19*, 412–421. doi: 10.3109/09638230903469145

Bennett, R. E., & Gitomer, D. H. (2008). *Transforming K–12 assessment: Integrating accountability testing, formative assessment, and professional support*. Princeton, NJ: ETS.

Besculides, M., Zaveri, H., Farris, R., & Will, J. (2006). Identifying best practices for WISEWOMAN programs using a mixed-methods evaluation. *Preventing Chronic Disease, 3*(1), A07. Retrieved from http://www.cdc.gov/pcd/issues/2006/jan/05_0133.htm

Black, P., & Wiliam, D. (1998). Assessment and classroom learning. *Assessment in Education, 5,* 7–74.

Bransford, J., Brown, A., & Cocking, R. (2000). *How people learn: Brain, mind, experience, and school.* Washington, DC: National Academy Press.

Caracelli, V. J., & Greene, J. C. (1997). Crafting mixed-method evaluation designs. In J. C. Greene, & V. J. Caracelli (Eds.), *Advances in mixed-method evaluation: The challenges and benefits of integrating diverse paradigms* (New Directions for Evaluation, no. 74, pp. 19–32). San Francisco, CA: Jossey-Bass.

Cohen, D., & Crabtree, B. (2008). *Robert Wood Johnson, Qualitative research guidelines project.* Retrieved from http://www.qualres.org/.

Committee on Prospering in the Global Economy of the 21st Century. (2007). *Rising above the gathering storm: Energizing and employing America for a brighter economic future.* Washington, DC: National Academies Press.

Creswell, J. W. (1994). *Research design: Qualitative and quantitative approaches.* Thousand Oaks, CA: Sage.

Creswell, J. W. (2010). Mapping the developing landscape of mixed methods research. In A. Tashakkori, & C. Teddlie (Eds.), *SAGE handbook of mixed methods in social & behavioral research* (pp. 45–68). Thousand Oaks, CA: Sage.

Creswell, J. W. (in press). Controversies in mixed methods research. In N. Denzin, & Y. Lincoln (Eds.), *SAGE handbook on qualitative research.* Thousand Oaks, CA: Sage.

Creswell, J. W., & Plano Clark, V. L. (2011). *Designing and conducting mixed methods research* (2nd ed.). Thousand Oaks, CA: Sage.

Creswell, J. W., Plano Clark, V., & Guttmann, M. (2003). Advanced mixed method research designs. In A. Tashakkori, & C. Teddlie (Eds.), *Handbook of mixed methods research in social and behavioral research* (pp. 209–240). Thousand Oaks, CA: Sage.

Fetterman, D. M. (1988). Qualitative approaches to evaluating education. *Educational Researcher, 17*(8), 17–23.

Fetterman, D. M., & Pitman, M. A. (Eds.). (1986). *Education evaluation: Ethnography in theory, practice, and politics.* Newbury Park, CA: Sage.

Figueredo, A. J. (1993). Critical multiplism, meta-analysis, and generalization: An integrative commentary. *New Directions for Program Evaluation, 60,* 3–12.

Forman, J., & Damschroder, L. (2007, February). *Using mixed methods in evaluating intervention studies.* Presentation at the Mixed Methodology Workshop, VA HSR&D National Meeting, Arlington, VA.

Frechtling, J. (2002). *The 2002 user friendly handbook for project evaluations* (NSF 02-057). Arlington, VA: National Science Foundation.

Frechtling, J., & Sharp, L. (1997). *The user-friendly handbook for mixed-method evaluations* (NSF 97–153). Arlington, VA: National Science Foundation.

Greene, J. C (2007). *Mixed methods in social inquiry.* San Francisco, CA: Jossey-Bass.

Greene, J. C., & Caracelli, V. J. (1997). Defining and describing the paradigm issue in mixed method evaluation. In J. C. Greene and V. J. Caracelli (Eds.), *Advances in mixed-method evaluation: The challenges and benefits of integrating diverse paradigms* (New Directions for Evaluation, no. 74, pp. 5–17). San Francisco, CA: Jossey-Bass.

Greene, J. C., Caracelli, V. J., & Graham, W. F. (1989). Toward a conceptual framework for mixed-method evaluation designs. *Educational Evaluation and Policy Analysis, 11,* 255–274.

Guba, E., & Lincoln, Y. S. (1988). Do inquiry paradigms imply inquiry methodologies? In D. M. Fetterman (Ed.), *Qualitative approaches to evaluation in education* (pp. 89–115). New York, NY: Praeger.

Harden, A. (2007). *Using mixed methods in research synthesis.* A discussion forum presented at the Mixed Methods Conference, Fitzwilliam College, Cambridge, UK 8th to 11th July.

Harnisch, D., Shope, R., Hoback, M., Fryda, M., & Kelberlau, D. (2006). Connecting high-quality local assessment to teacher leadership. In K. Jones (Ed.), *Democratic school accountability a model for school improvement* (pp. 29–54). Lanham, MD: Rowman & Littlefield Education.

Hattie, J. A. C. (2009). *Visible learning: A synthesis of over 800 meta-analyses relating to achievement.* New York, NY: Routledge.

Hodge, S., Barr, W., Göpfert, M., Hellin, K., Horne, A., & Kirkcaldy, A. (2010). Qualitative findings from a mixed methods evaluation of once-weekly therapeutic community day services for people with personality disorder. *Journal of Mental Health, 19,* 43–51. doi: 10.3109/09638230903469152

Kidder, L., & Fine, M. (1987). Qualitative and quantitative methods: When stories converge. Multiple methods in program evaluation. *New Directions for Program Evaluation, 35,* 57–75.

King, M. M., Jones, L. L., Richardson, A. A., Murad, S. S., Irving, A. A., Aslett, H. H., & . . . Nazareth, I. I. (2009). The relationship between patients' experiences of continuity of cancer care and health outcomes: a mixed methods study. *British Journal of Cancer, 98,* 529–536. doi: 10.1038/sj.bjc.6604164

Kirsch, I., Braun, H., Yamamoto, K., & Sum, A. (2007). *America's perfect storm: Three forces changing our nation's future.* Princeton, NJ: ETS.

Lemke, M., Sen, A., Pahlke, E., Partelow, L., Miller, D., Williams, T., . . . Jocelyn, L. (2004). *International outcomes of learning in mathematics literacy and problem solving: PISA 2003 results from the U.S. perspective* (NCES 2005-003). Washington, DC: National Center for Education Statistics.

Mertens, D. M. (2003). Mixed methods and the politics of human research: The transformative-emancipatory perspective. In A. Tashakkori, & C. Teddlie (Eds.), *Handbook of mixed methods in social and behavioral research* (pp. 135–164). Thousand Oaks, CA: Sage.

Mertens, D. M. (2009). *Transformative research and evaluation.* New York, NY: Guilford Press.

Mertens, D. M. (2010). *Research and evaluation in education and psychology: Integrating diversity with quantitative, qualitative, and mixed methods.* Thousand Oaks, CA: Sage.

Miller, C., & LaFramboise, L. (2009). Student learning outcomes after integration of quality and safety education competencies into a senior-level critical care course. *Journal of Nursing Education, 48,* 678–85. doi: 10.3928/01484834-20091113-07

Morgan, D. L. (2007). Paradigms lost and pragmatism regained: Methodological implications of combining qualitative and quantitative methods. *Journal of Mixed Methods Research, 1*(1), 48–76.

Nastasi, B. K., Hitchcock, J., Sarkar, S., Burkholder, G., Varjas, K., & Jayasena, A. (2007). Mixed methods in intervention research: Theory to adaptation. *Journal Mixed Methods Research, 1,* 164–182.

National Institutes of Health, Office of Behavioral and Social Sciences Research. (2001). *Qualitative methods in health research: Opportunities and considerations in application and review.* Washington, DC: National Institutes of Health.

Nitko, A. J., & Brookhart, S. M. (2007). *Educational assessment of students* (5th ed.). Upper Saddle River, NJ: Pearson Merrill Prentice Hall.

Patton, M. Q. (1980). *Qualitative evaluation methods.* Beverly Hills, CA: Sage.

Phillips, D. C., & Burbules, N. C. (2000). *Postpositivism and educational research.* Lanham, NY: Rowman & Littlefield.

Rallis, S. F., & Rossman, G. B. (2003). Mixed methods in evaluation contexts: A pragmatic framework. In A. Tashakkori, & C. Teddlie (Eds.), *Handbook of mixed methods in social and behavioral research* (pp. 491–512). Thousand Oaks, CA: Sage.

Seifert, T. A., Pascarella, E. T., Erkel, S. I., & Goodman, K. M. (2010). The importance of longitudinal pretest-posttest designs in estimating college impact. *New Directions for Institutional Research,* Issue S2, 5–16.

Shadish, W. R. (1993). Program evaluation: A pluralistic enterprise. *New Directions for Program Evaluation, 60,* 13–57.

Shepard, L. A. (2000). The role of assessment in a learning culture. *Educational Researcher, 29*(7), 4–14.

Tashakkori, A., & Teddlie, C. (1998). *Mixed methodology: Combining qualitative and quantitative approaches.* Thousand Oaks, CA: Sage.

Tashakkori, A., & Teddlie, C. (Eds.). (2003). *Handbook of mixed methods research in the social & behavior sciences.* Thousand Oaks, CA: Sage.

Teti, M., Bowleg, L., Cole, R., Lloyd, L., Rubinstein, S., Spencer, S., ... Gold, M. (2010). A mixed methods evaluation of the effect of the protect and respect intervention on the condom use and disclosure practices of women living with HIV/AIDS. *AIDS and Behavior, 14,* 567. doi: 10.1007/s10461-009-9562-x

Thomas, J., Harden, A., Oakley, A., Oliver, S., Sutcliffe, K., Rees, R., . . . Kavanagh, J. (2004). Integrating qualitative research with trials in systematic reviews. *BMJ (Clinical Research ed.), 328*(7446), 1010–1012. doi:10.1136/bmj.328.7446.1010

Waysman, M., & Savaya, R. (1997). Mixed method evaluation: A case study. *American Journal of Evaluation, 18,* 227–237.

White, H. (2008). *Of probits and participation: The use of mixed methods in quantitative impact evaluation.* Network of networks on impact evaluation (NONIE). Working Paper No. 7. World Bank.

35

SURVEY USE IN ACADEMIC CONTEXTS: CONSIDERATIONS AND GUIDELINES

Ellen Wentland

Four developments in recent years have led to an increase in academic settings in the use of surveys to gather information related to diverse areas of interest (Gansemer-Topf & Wohlgemuth, 2009; Schuh, 2009). These developments include:

1. the need to investigate and provide evidence related to student achievement of defined learning outcomes;
2. the expansion of outcomes-driven investigations in higher education to areas outside of academic affairs, such as student affairs and institutional support services;
3. the overall focus on data-driven/evidence-based decision making, and the need for transparency; and
4. the availability of a number of easily accessible and user-friendly on-line survey tools.

The first development regarding learning outcomes assessment is significant in terms of its widespread application to all institutions of higher education and its requirement by regional accrediting bodies. Whether initiated on a voluntary basis, or in response to a need to comply with accreditation demands, all accredited institutions, and those that aspire to accreditation, must develop some system for assessing and documenting student success in terms of defined learning outcomes. Although direct assessment methods, such as written tests or skills demonstrations may be preferred, indirect methods such as surveys are also useful for investigating student attitudes and opinions, related to, for example, the adequacy with which certain course content areas were addressed, the efficacy of particular instructional methods, and the extent to which the educational experience provided sufficient preparation for employment and/or postgraduate studies. While useful in itself, this feedback can also serve to complement and perhaps inform the information gathered from direct approaches.

The second development is an extension of the first as outcomes-driven investigations have expanded to areas of an institution outside academic affairs. As partners in the overall goal of student success, many of these areas are included in accreditation standards and are required to evaluate the extent to which they achieve their purposes, and in general respond to and support students' and institutional needs. Student affairs or services is an area that has received much attention in this regard, and includes functions such as enrollment management, advising, student orientation, residence life, financial aid, career services, health services, counseling, and student activities. Given that an important purpose of these functions is to support students' retention and persistence through facilitating college entry, supporting continuing involvement, increasing student engagement, and assisting in postgraduate planning, it makes sense to evaluate the extent to which these goals are being achieved though the current structures and processes. In this area, surveys become an important method to assess the level of student participation in and satisfaction with these functions, and can serve as a valuable tool in program evaluation and improvement efforts.

Institutional support services include such functions as security, buildings and grounds maintenance, and event planning. These functions can also be at least partially evaluated using the survey method, as both internal and external "customers" can provide feedback related to current performance or with respect to planned changes.

The third development concerns the increased focus on evidence-based decision making. In its broadest sense, this focus encompasses the first two developments because outcomes assessment and program evaluation have as eventual goals the development of action plans for strengthening or improving the educational, co-curricular, and overall institutional experience for students—decisions concerning which are based on the information collected. In a different sense, surveys can serve a valuable role in collecting information related to program needs, or concerning initiatives being contemplated. Needs assessments or feasibility studies can readily include survey data to gauge potential use, or perceptions concerning planned changes. Examples include issues related to whether academic programs should be added or discontinued, or whether new student services should be offered.

The fourth development related to the increase in attention to survey methodology concerns the ease of survey construction, dissemination, and data analyses afforded by the variety of on-line survey construction and delivery tools available at no or low cost. The fact of likely universal possession of e-mail addresses by intended respondents contributes to the attractiveness of these tools.

To satisfy the various quality and accountability requirements and demands, faculty, staff, and administrators look to the survey method as a perhaps efficient tool which can be tailor-made to elicit the information needed to address a variety of questions. Often, however, certain considerations and tasks that are fundamental to survey product quality are inadequately addressed. These include the:

- identification of the problem or issue to be addressed;
- applicability of the survey method to the problem or issue being addressed;
- clear specification of the general purpose and specific objectives of the survey;
- description of the appropriate respondent group;
- detailing of methods to introduce the survey;
- overall quality of the survey instrument in terms of question construction, overall content, and format;
- conduct of a pilot study;
- selection of the delivery method;
- determination of an acceptable response rate;
- appropriateness and correct application of the analyses methods used; and
- interpretation and evaluation of the usefulness of findings vis-à-vis the stated purpose of the survey.

This situation may perhaps result from a failure to appreciate the many details that must be considered to ensure that a survey will be effective for the purpose. In addition, the ready availability of easy to use on-line tools may contribute to a false sense of expertise and decisions to use the survey method in the absence of adequate planning.

A detailed discussion of the large number of elements that can impact the validity of surveys is well beyond the scope of this chapter, the purpose of which is to outline some very basic and important considerations that should accompany survey planning discussions. Systematic attention to these elements can inform decision making, beginning with the initial one concerning whether this method is appropriate for the specific purpose and continuing to the data analyses and interpretation stages. The entire effort can be viewed as a process with important decisions at each of the highly interrelated steps. If the process is successful, the end product will be information that directly addresses the original problems or issues, in a type of feedback loop. In other words, the test of a survey's success is the developer's ability to deliver with confidence responses to the specific objectives that formed the basis for the survey (Ray & Ravizza, 1988).

The considerations will be addressed in the form of questions with the goal of providing a type of map or checklist to guide faculty, staff and administrators in their use of the survey method.

What is a Survey?

A survey is a means of collecting information from individuals concerning a topic or topics of interest through asking them to respond to questions about themselves or others (Schutt, 2009). These questions often relate to perceptions as represented in opinions, attitudes, or behavioral intentions although surveys may also concern facts and recollections, as for example, concerning respondent characteristics and current or past status or behavior (Grinnell, Jr., 2001). Questions on a survey offer fixed response formats—such as multiple choice, yes–no, ranking, or rating—or may be open-ended in the form of "fill-in-the-blank", or short answer.

What is the Problem?

The word "problem" is used to describe an area of discrepancy—between the information needed for decision making or action taking and the adequacy of the information currently available that can be brought to bear on this decision or action. The basic questions are, "What do you want or need to know?" and "What information is at hand or can be accessed that will contribute to your knowing?" If there is a gap, then perhaps the survey method can be used to address this gap. At this very important stage, it is necessary to define as concisely and precisely as possible the specific information that is needed and why, and where it can best be obtained.

When Would a Survey be an Effective Method to Consider?

A survey might be an effective data gathering method to consider when respondents are the best or perhaps the only possible source of the needed information, or when other possible sources are judged to be somewhat lacking. An example of the former includes information on attitudes, such as levels of satisfaction with services, or behavioral intentions, such as concerning whether a proposed program or service will attract students. An alternative would be to explore experiences of other institutions, and assuming similarity of student bodies, perhaps generalize to your site. Given the many unique internal and external features of many institutions, however, and depending on the extent of resource commitment involved, surveying your own constituents may be a good choice.

Surveys may also be a good choice if the information needed concerns highly private or sensitive information, known only to individuals. Depending on the method of administration, surveys may offer the anonymity and confidentiality necessary to support free and honest responding to questions (Cooper, 2009).

It is possible that the data needed can be obtained through structures that can be set up to gather information over time, such as over a semester or year or even longer. The suitability of these structures would depend on the ability to systematize accurate and comprehensive data collection, the immediacy of the information need, and the relevance of the information once it is collected. For example, information on graduate career success would perhaps ideally be obtained through tracking graduate employment and job advancement over time, but this would be, for various reasons, an impossible task. Even if obtained, the information would likely be untimely, and difficult to interpret and attribute, and therefore not useful for such interests as curriculum development.

In addition to information quality, decision acceptance must also be considered. Factual data may support a particular decision, but acceptance by relevant campus constituencies is not guaranteed. Their input in the form of survey responses may not only contribute to decision quality but also support its eventual implementation. A survey in this sense can function as a means to ensure that those affected by decisions are able to participate in making them, which may increase their commitment (McShane & Glinow, 2009). Although findings may not show uniform positions, results which support a certain direction can serve to persuade and mitigate any possible resistance. Consider, however, that surveying can have the effect of priming the respondents in that expectations may be formed. Unmet expectations may lead to disgruntlement if feelings and thoughts expressed are not considered in action planning or decision making.

Also to be considered is whether the information needed can be requested through the use of rather straightforward questions requiring simple responses, or through short answer formats. If an issue is complex and cannot be reduced to a simpler format, then perhaps other methods such as focus groups or in-depth interviews would better suit the purpose. At times, these approaches serve as starting points for gathering information and identifying themes or common concerns, which can then be used to develop questions for survey delivery. Also, if the number of respondents is small, it may be better to use interviews or focus groups, depending on time and confidentiality concerns.

Even if it is determined that the information needed is only available through asking people, a survey may still not be the best approach if it is concluded that the use of optimal approaches would be unlikely to interest or motivate targeted individuals to commit time and energy to the project. In the absence of resources for intensive follow-up work, perhaps it would be best to select a sample to approach directly for in-person or telephone interviews.

What is the Overall Purpose of This Survey?

If a decision is made to use the survey method to address the problem or issue, then the next step is to clearly specify the general as well as the specific objectives of this survey (Ray & Ravizza, 1988). These very detailed specifications will assist with the later development of survey question items and formats.

Who will be the Respondents?

Assuming that a decision has been made to use a survey because it has been determined that what needs to be known can only be supplied by certain readily identifiable groups of people, that there are sufficient numbers of them to support the delivery of an instrument to gather the information, and there is a reasonable expectation that cooperation can be achieved, the next step is to precisely define this group of respondents. These are individuals whose level of familiarity with or interest in the topic is high enough that their input would be relevant and sufficient to provide the information being sought. Inclusion and exclusion become important issues. The defined set should be inclusive enough so that all relevant perspectives have a chance of being included and exclusive in that non-affected or disinterested parties' offerings won't affect the interpretation of results.

With respect to awareness of the issue, a survey can serve an educational purpose as potentially affected respondents are alerted to possible future changes, and are provided an opportunity to explore their own reactions to this. There are, however, other situations where respondents, though not familiar with the topic, remain disinterested even after being alerted. Respondents perceive that there will be little personal or professional impact, and so may not be motivated to respond, or may provide replies based on perceived social desirability or simply to appear informed. To avoid contaminating results with irrelevant information, only those persons who have been a part of or will be affected by the information being gathered should be included in the respondent pool.

Surveys solely designed to obtain information about respondent characteristics and/or related to such topics as satisfaction with services contain challenges related to respondent motivation. In these cases, respondents are likely to see little direct advantage or reward/benefit while there is a clear cost associated with spending time answering the questions. To provide some balance to these cost/benefit relationships, various techniques such as providing incentives or rewards have been suggested, as well as appeals to respondent values connected with helping behavior and community responsibility (Dillman, 2000; Gansemer-Topf & Wohlgemuth, 2009). Clear messages to respondents concerning the purpose of the questions and their intended use are important to include in this regard, and will be discussed further.

Whether the entire target respondent group will be surveyed, as opposed to a sample, involves considerations such as representativeness, possible reactions of members not surveyed, and resources such as money, time, and expertise. A first step would be defining and listing potential respondents. In some cases, this may be fairly simple, as, for example, lists of program graduates. It would be more difficult, however, to create a list of potential employers, even when restricted to particular geographic areas, due to the difficulty of precisely defining who would be a potential employer.

Obtaining contact information is more difficult for some groups than for others. While individuals internal to an organization can often readily be contacted through e-mail, for external groups, such as graduates, the task is more difficult. And in the case of potential employers, even if specific employing companies were identified, for example, the identity of contact persons is not obvious. Failure to receive replies may be a consequence of the request not finding its way to the appropriate persons in the organizations. A considerable amount of time would be required to personally contact an organization to identify ahead of time a key party to designate as a respondent, and this level of cooperation is unlikely. Further, stake in the topic is probably low at best, leading to predictably low response rates. A better approach would be to target those employers with some relationship or history with the institution, to ensure replies and the offering of relevant information. Using a "snowball" sampling approach, perhaps these employers can then suggest other employers, and offer assistance in contacting them (C. A. Faulkner & S. S. Faulkner, 2009).

While it is certainly desirable to include all possible respondents in the survey distribution, if the potential respondent group is quite large, the costs associated with survey delivery and data analyses must be considered. Distribution choices are considered below, but costs associated with data entry and analyses must also be considered. Large amounts of numerical data require time for data entry and analyses. Responses to short answer inquiries also require data entry and qualitative analyses to investigate possible themes. Both types of analyses require considerable training and expertise, and the amount of time needed increases dramatically if large numbers of questions requiring qualitative analyses are included. If these types of questions are necessary and if resources are limited, then perhaps the number of respondents needs to be reduced. If this is the case, a random sampling method to ensure representativeness should be used. For example, if graduates are from a number of different programs, perhaps sampling from each program while including sufficient numbers in each program could be accomplished through using a stratified random sampling approach (Gansemer-Topf & Wohlgemuth, 2009).

How Should a Survey be Introduced?

The relevant questions include, "How will you get potential respondents attention?" and "How will you motivate people to reply?" The first task of any survey irrespective of the delivery method is to generate interest by communicating its purpose (Grinnell, Jr., 2001). For e-mail surveys to internal audiences, the subject line must be concise and attention getting, followed in the body of the e-mail by a professionally constructed and appealing introduction and cover letter. If the e-mail delivery is to external constituents, perhaps a cover letter can precede that delivery. This serves not only as an introduction but also as an alert to what will be coming, perhaps decreasing the possibility that the e-mail will be deleted, overlooked, or relegated to spam. For internal constituents, publicity about the study can help (Grinnell, Jr., 2001). Local announcements through meetings, student publications such as newspapers, or bulletin boards will alert respondents. By calling attention to the survey, the hope is that response rates will increase.

For mailed surveys, a professionally prepared cover letter is essential, not only to inform about the purpose, but importantly to increase response rates (Schutt, 2009). These efforts also highlight the importance of the survey effort and communicate its seriousness. Introducing a survey is part of creating interest, and this should continue in the body of the survey itself. Introduce sections of the survey with concise but explicit text that communicates the purpose behind the questions being included, and perhaps how the information being requested will be used. Creating interest in this way also provides a context for the questions which can aid in encouraging and framing responses, and helping respondents focus on what actually is being asked.

Any survey makes demands on people's time, and if respondents are familiar with or potentially personally impacted by the topic, and/or if they clearly see that an important purpose will be served, and if they believe that their input will make a difference, they will more likely spend the time needed to complete the survey.

How Should a Survey be Constructed?

The construction of a survey includes not only writing the individual questions, but also carefully attending to question grouping and sequencing, as well as formatting. Overall, the goal is to obtain the needed information, and this is best accomplished by providing questions which are directly tied to the information gap, and which are clearly and concisely written, logically grouped and sequenced so as to maximize cuing effects and facilitate recall, and through formatting that also helps to minimize cognitive demands. Drafting questions and making format decisions so as to obtain the information needed in the simplest and least demanding way requires skill and creativity.

The heart of the survey effort lies in the questions put to respondents. Each question must be carefully crafted so as to elicit the specific piece of information needed, and the questions must flow in some logical order. Each question must clearly and unambiguously ask for just one piece of infor-mation—no "double-barreled" questions—and include appropriate and comprehensive response choices. Questions are prompts to replies, and to obtain accurate replies, questions must be writ-ten so that respondents understand precisely what is being asked, and also in a way that facilitates respondents' access to the requested information. The respondents must be able to see a connection between the questions and the described purpose of this survey. Further, there should be a reason-able expectation that the respondents have the information and are thus able to provide a thoughtful response (Grinnell, Jr. 2001).

In this regard, it is important to conduct some type of "audience analysis," to obtain information about what the respondents are likely to know and also be able to understand in terms of language, vocabulary and jargon, as well as their general reading ability level.

The logical order of question presentation facilitates recall as it helps to provide a context for the questions being presented. Research has shown that respondents will provide accurate responses to items, if they can (Wentland, 1993). The overall question context affects accessibility, as does the time frame of the questions posed. Asking people to retrieve information, for example, on past behaviors lacking salience, such as attendance in certain activities during the past six months or year, may yield inaccurate information. Limiting the time period to recent events may be a simpler approach, as is offering temporal contexts or cues.

Including "skip" patterns assists in providing overall organization, and also ensures that respondents only provide information to questions relevant to them (Schutt, 2009). If some respondents, for example, never attended an orientation session, it makes no sense to ask them their level of satisfaction with the session. Failure to offer the "opt out" or "skip" alternative can frustrate respondents, who may answer the irrelevant question anyway!

Not only must the questions be precise, but the response choices, if offered, must be appropriate, and also exhaustive and mutually exclusive. Some response formats include "Yes–No", multiple choice, rating scales, ranking, and short answer. With "Yes–No" formats, make sure that these are really the only possible choices. Sometimes a reasonable response is, "Not sure" or "Don't know." If so, they should be included. With multiple choice, responses such as "Not Applicable" or "Not Sure" may be reasonable choices as is "Other". Including all possible response options helps insure that people are making real as opposed to forced choices.

Often, respondents are presented with rating scales which they are to use a number of times in responding to survey questions. For example, a Likert type scale might be presented for respondents to use in indicating the extent of agreement or satisfaction with certain items or services. If so, the rating scale should be prominent and connected to the list of items or services, for example, by being included as column headings as opposed to being presented independent of the list. In this way, the scale is easy to reference, and helps ensure that the rating intended is what is assigned.

It is also important that all scale points be clearly labeled, as opposed to just the end points. While not assuring that scale point descriptions will be similarly interpreted by all respondents, labeling does help support this similarity. The more guidance provided to respondents as to the meaning of the scale points, the more confidence you can have in interpreting the ratings assigned.

Ranking is used as a response format when there are many possible choices, and the intent is to find those that most would select. If there are a large number of choices, asking respondents to rank them all may prove to be too demanding, and may not in fact be useful for the survey's purposes. On the other hand, selecting a top five may serve just as well.

Open ended or short answer formats are used when the appropriate set of response choices cannot be provided because of the likelihood of substantial and meaningful variation across respondents which cannot be adequately captured in predetermined categories. For example, these formats are typically used when respondents are asked to explain why they did or didn't take an action, or to ask questions concerning the number of times a service was used, or a class attended. Unless respondents are able to consult records, the latter type questions are dependent on adequacy of recall which, considering the time interval involved and the salience of the experience, has been found to have its limitations. If using questions that call on respondent recollections, you may need to build in cues in the context to assist accessibility. On the other hand, if general estimates will serve your purpose, then perhaps some intervals can be provided in the form of response choices, again making certain that the list is exhaustive and the categories mutually exclusive. Often, response choice intervals are constructed as a means to obtain certain information which may be considered private or sensitive, such as concerning income.

When should you use each format type? The answer to this question concerns how effective a particular format type will be in providing you with the information you are seeking. If you simply want to take a ballot, then "Yes–No" formats will likely work. If on the other hand you are interested in the intensity of reactions to certain items, then rating scales may be best. With multiple choice formats, you need to consider the number of viable options that need to be included. Multiple choice items are useful if the number of choices is limited.

Overall, the guiding question is, "What is simplest way to present the request that gets at the exact information you need?" In this same vein, do not overload a survey with unnecessary questions, or questions that you would have difficulty analyzing or interpreting.

In terms of formatting, white space is important. It helps to simplify the instrument because it isolates questions or question groups. This visual "chunking" makes the task seem more manageable.

After the questions are written, and the format is drafted, it may be helpful to compare the information you expect to receive with the information that you had determined you needed. After summarizing across respondents, will the answers to your questions give you all of the information you need? Will it be sufficient for your action planning or decision making? Is it too much, or too little? In the terminology used above, will the information gap now be filled?

Should You Conduct a Pilot Study?

Conducting a pilot study is essential for a number of reasons, the most important being to determine through respondent feedback whether the questions are clearly worded and similarly interpreted, the response choices adequate and appropriate, and whether there is any difficulty navigating the questions (Ray & Ravizza, 1988). In this regard, the appropriate individuals for the pilot test are individuals that are members of the respondent population. Information concerning the relationship between the questions asked and the overall and specific objectives of the survey can be obtained by pilot testing the instrument with those familiar with the purposes, such as the end users of the information (Grinnell, Jr., 2001). A pilot study will also enable you to collect time estimate data, which is important to communicate in distribution materials. This feedback may lead to content and/or length modification. Finally, this testing can inform decisions about choice of administration method. Low response rates in a pilot test, for example using an e-mail method, can suggest that a different method, perhaps regular mail, may be more successful.

Another purpose served by piloting an instrument, if a sufficient number of respondents is included, is to perhaps get a sense of the variety of responses that will be provided to open ended questions. This information could become the basis for creating categories which will be simpler to analyze, and which place less of a demand on a subject as opposed to exact recall.

How Will the Survey be Administered?

Survey delivery methods include mail, in-person, telephone, on-line, or via e-mail. Deciding which method is best to ensure that the survey is received and responded to requires a knowledge of the audience. Although it is tempting to just select the method that is perceived to be quickest and least expensive—namely e-mail—there are many considerations. E-mails with attachments or links to on-line tools are inexpensive and efficient time wise, but may for various reasons be overlooked by potential respondents. As mentioned earlier, alerts via mailed letters or campus advertisements and an attention-getting subject line may help in stemming the tendency of especially students to ignore e-mail requests.

In certain other situations, paper surveys can be distributed for self-administration. This can work well in many academic situations, such as for surveying students in classrooms or following advising sessions, or for faculty members, staff persons, and administrators when mailboxes and intercampus delivery services are readily available. For external constituents whose stake in the outcome is likely to be minimal, and when a connection between their replies and the decisions or actions to be informed is not readily apparent, in-person or telephone strategies may be more effective. If mailed surveys are used, costs associated with paper, copying, and return envelopes must be considered, as well as costs associated with follow-up efforts to increase replies, including additional mailings.

What is an Acceptable Response Rate?

Response rate is a key issue in survey work, and there is evidence that respondents may differ from non-respondents in important ways. Whether the number of responses received is sufficient is a common concern. Many of the recommendations included in this chapter, such as related to selecting respondents, introducing the survey, and properly crafting the instrument can help to increase survey response rate. That is, responding is encouraged by promoting interest in the task; being straightforward about time demands; posing questions that are clear; and providing cues, context and formatting that help minimize cognitive demands.

The recommendations referred to above are all part of the "up-front" work that is so critical to the success of the survey effort. Increasing response rate after a survey due date is also possible, through steps such as follow-up e-mails or telephone calls, but then additional time and resources are required.

In a balance between "real" and "ideal," consider whether you have gathered a sufficient number of completed surveys to enable the data analyses work that has been outlined. Desirable return rates may be affected by a number of considerations. For example, a lower return rate may suffice if the population surveyed is relatively homogeneous. This holds for determination of sample size as well (Schutt, 2009).

What Analyses Methods will be Used?

For various reasons, decisions about how the data will be analyzed should be made hand in hand with survey construction and before the survey is distributed. One reason is that often surveys are distributed with little attention to the perhaps large volume of information that will be collected. Surveyors may then find themselves faced with large amounts of information that they lack the time or expertise to filter through and analyze. Developing analyses templates also aids in understanding how well the specific questions being asked will provide the information needed. Data analyses discussions concern not only data entry but importantly how information will be summarized and displayed. These discussions also assist in understanding how well the questions have been crafted so as to facilitate analyses, and may lead to important revisions.

This is an important step for another reason and that has to do with making sure that what you need to know has been addressed in a way that leads as precisely as possible to that knowing. This helps ensure the relatedness of the information gathered to the information needs, as opposed to discovering after the fact that what you have gathered is not precise enough or related enough to inform the topic.

How will You Interpret Results?

Results of the data collection and analyses should map quite directly onto the major goals of the survey, and, in their entirety, show a direct relationship with the overall survey purpose. At this point, hopefully, the questions that were to be addressed have been addressed in a satisfactory way. With all of the effort that has gone into investigating the need for this survey, developing it, administering it, and analyzing the data collected, it would be very unfortunate to find that the data gathered does not answer the questions, or that the response rate is insufficient to support any conclusions. The deliverables at this point should be a professionally drafted report including an introduction, description of purpose and methods, data analyses and interpretation summary, limitations, and conclusions and recommendations, with the actual instrument used included in an appendix.

Should a Published Survey be Considered for Use?

To this point, the discussion has been directed to efforts to develop surveys locally. Another choice to consider is to use an already constructed published survey. In this regard, it is important to carefully evaluate the purpose of the published survey in general and as represented in the specific questions vis-à-vis your purposes or objectives (Saunders & Cooper, 2009). Further, it is important to determine as precisely as possible the extent to which your information needs will be satisfied by the information obtained in the published survey or whether that instrument can serve effectively in another setting. Some questions on the published survey may be not applicable to your purposes, or inappropriate in terms of content or wording for your particular respondent group. Presenting this survey to your respondents could cause confusion and affect their overall level of motivation to participate.

Whether you use a locally developed or published instrument, there are costs and benefits. Costs associated with the published instruments include the purchase and possible misalignment with local purposes and audience. Locally developed instruments require time and resources in the form of expertise. Other more subtle costs and benefits have to do with perceptions of respondents as to motives of test developers and applicability to the local context. Locally developed instruments may be seen as directly related to the local interest and as a product of internal investment, which may motivate respondents to provide thoughtful replies. On the other hand, local developers may be seen as having a bias or agenda. Published instruments may be seen as irrelevant to local purposes, and also biased. On the other hand, perhaps the published instrument may be viewed as more "professional" or "objective." While these factors need to be considered, the main concerns are the match with purpose.

Summary

Certain considerations related to decisions concerning the use of surveys in academic contexts have been presented in the form of questions intended to serve as guides in planning discussions. These questions provide an overall context for the decision making, and are important to systematically address in the interests of ensuring survey quality. Each of the questions can be represented as a step in the process, and as previously noted, the steps are highly interrelated. Starting with basic questions related to information needs and specification of purposes, the questions lead to other topics including ultimately the analyses and interpretation, and presentation of the information collected. As noted above, if the effort is successful, the end product will be information that directly addresses the original problems or issues. Although there are many other factors and topics related to surveys that have been extensively investigated and reported, the important considerations outlined in this chapter should provide a solid base for efforts related to developing and using surveys in academic contexts.

References

Cooper, R. M. (2009). Planning for and implementing data collection. In J. H. Schuh, & Associates (Eds.), *Assessment methods for student affairs* (pp. 51–75). San Francisco, CA: Jossey-Bass.

Dillman, D. A. (2000). *Mail and internet surveys.* New York, NY: Wiley.

Faulkner, C. A., & Faulkner, S. S. (2009). *Research methods for social workers: A practice-based approach.* Chicago, IL: Lyceum.

Gansemer-Topf, A. M., & Wohlgemuth, D. R. (2009). Selecting, sampling, and soliciting subjects. In J. H. Schuh, & Associates (Eds.), *Assessment methods for student affairs* (pp. 77–105). San Francisco, CA: Jossey-Bass.

Grinnell, R. M., Jr. (2001). *Social work research and evaluation: Qualitative and quantitative approaches* (6th ed.). Belmont, CA: Brooks/Cole.

McShane, S. L., & Von Glinow, M. A. (2009). *Organizational behavior* (2nd ed.). New York, NY: McGraw-Hill/Irwin.

Ray, W. J., & Ravizza, R. (1988). *Methods toward a science of behavior and experience.* Belmont, CA: Wadsworth.

Saunders, K., & Copper, R. M. (2009). Instrumentation. In J. H. Schuh, & Associates (Eds.), *Assessment methods for student affairs* (pp. 107–139). San Francisco, CA: Jossey-Bass.

Schuh, J. H. (2009). Looking to the future of assessment. In J. H. Schuh, & Associates (Eds.), *Assessment methods for student affairs* (pp. 231–248). San Francisco, CA: Jossey-Bass.

Schutt, R. K. (2009). *Investigating the social world: The process and practice of research* (6th ed.). Thousand Oaks, CA: Pine Forge Press.

Wentland, E., & Smith, K. W. (1993). *Survey responses: An evaluation of their validity.* San Diego, CA: Academic Press.

QUESTIONS AND EXERCISES
FOR SECTION 5

(1) What are the major types of program evaluation and what are the associated evaluative questions for each?

(2) Thinking about the IPEDS data that is gathered every year, how might qualitative methods be used to enhance your institution's understanding of a bio-demo student characteristic endemic to your institution?

(3) Thinking about an assessment measure that has not met a particular academic goal, how might qualitative methods be used to tailor a plan designed to achieve better results?

(4) In trying to define an institution's culture and climate, what are the shortcomings of using strictly quantitative methods? In this same case, how could the quantitative results of a culture study be enhanced by the use of qualitative methods?

(5) What kinds of evaluation questions can be best answered by naturalistic methodology? What kinds of questions can be best answered by positivistic methodology?

(6) Why does the naturalistic researcher refer to the persons in the context being evaluated as "participants" rather than as "subjects?" What differences does this make in the way the evaluation is conducted?

(7) What are the major obstacles to conducting a naturalistic evaluation in an institution of higher education? How can these obstacles be overcome?

(8) Individuals in assessment and evaluation often collect both qualitative (interview) and quantitative (survey) data. Is mixed methods defined solely by the presence of these two types of data, or is an additional element necessary? Aside from the presence of qualitative and quantitative data, what else needs to be present in a good mixed methods study?

(9) We believe that American education is best served by an integrated system where summative and formative components are built from common frameworks and provide coherent information. Discuss how a mixed methods approach might be used to study student learning regarding the common core standards for high school youth. Integrate a mixed methods approach as you come up with an introduction, purpose statement, research questions, assessment design, and specific forms of data collection.

(10) As noted, mixed methods designs are relevant for assessment, formative evaluation, and summative evaluation. Researchers have also used methods to aid in the development of educational programs. How might mixed methods be applied to an educational program from conception through termination? Which specific mixed methods designs are applicable and what are the characteristics of those designs? When would mixing or integration occur?

(11) Review the questions included in a survey that is being or has been used at your institution. Critique the survey in terms of question clarity, appropriateness of sequencing, inclusion of statements concerning the purpose of the questions, and with respect to other factors discussed in the chapter.

(12) Why is it important to make decisions regarding how data will be analyzed and interpreted before the survey is actually administered?

SECTION 6

Issues in Assessment and Evaluation in Higher Education

April L. Zenisky

For those who wish to use the results of assessment instruments and program outcomes effectively in higher education, considerations of context are necessarily central to communicating this information to stakeholders at all levels. The characteristics of testing and evaluation populations, small or large, matter, as do the means by which results are communicated, disseminated and used with integrity. With high-quality assessments being produced to reflect standards for best practices, test developers, assessment specialists, and evaluators also have a responsibility to ensure that the data and any conclusions drawn thereof are thoughtfully presented, and that intended interpretations are clear, principled, and supported by the data. The seven chapters contained within the *Issues in Assessment and Evaluation in Higher Education* section connect the technical specifics of assessment development outlined throughout this Handbook with the bigger picture of how assessments can and indeed *should* be designed, used, and interpreted for maximum impact and effect on higher education practices.

Chapter 36 by Banerjee and Thurlow focuses on the critically important subpopulation of students with disabilities. Awareness of these students, their needs, and how their performance of assessments can and cannot be interpreted in the setting of higher education assessment has come to the forefront as essential. Relating data from secondary and postsecondary testing involving these students provides mechanisms for understanding and using results based on these students.

Chapter 37 from Kim, Hart, Abedi, and Vanneman addresses a similarly important subpopulation, that of English-language learners. Given shifting demographics, persons involved with assessment at many colleges and universities must be aware of a number of important considerations that come into play with testing these students as well and using data based on their test performance.

Chapter 38 from Knight offers an overview of assessment and evaluation issues that relate to teacher quality. Efforts in this regard are politically challenging and a highly debated area within the measurement and evaluation fields, and careful attention must be paid to the methods employed for this purpose as well as appropriate interpretation and use. It is interesting to note that colleges and universities have become particularly concerned about the readiness of students to do college-level work. Yet, the colleges and universities are the learning institutions that prepare the teachers of the students.

Chapter 39 by Zenisky and Laguilles presents a pragmatic perspective on reporting assessment results for individuals, groups, and institutions by describing steps and strategies for preparing assessment reports, including considerations of content and formatting.

The following chapter (40) by Provezis and Jankowski likewise details reporting in the realm of student learning outcomes with an eye toward addressing improvement and accountability goals. A framework for evaluating the quality of student learning assessment information is presented to help guide users toward quality communication of results.

Chapter 41 from LeCompte and Aguilera–Black Bear reinforces the essential importance of two central qualities in measurement and evaluation: reliability and validity. Adherence to rigor in methodology promotes quality, and establishing and maintaining standards directly impacts the utility and effectiveness of assessment or evaluative findings. The reader should find their treatise on evaluation research useful for understanding how reliability and validation efforts take into consideration the presence of the researcher/evaluator. Story telling is one such method introduced. Arguments are presented on how validity is achieved for this method

The final chapter in this section (42) by Finley echoes the call for standards in assessment and evaluation. Referencing the role of higher education 'assessor' as a researcher tasked with at times multiple jobs with multiple masters, considerations of ethics in this setting involve professional objectivity, structural ambiguity, and communication and use of data-based findings.

In sum, the chapters in this section all strive to push persons involved in measurement, assessment, and evaluation to consider the broader view of their work, particularly at the point of presenting assessment data, results, and interpretations to a potentially wide range of intended users and audiences. This Handbook is testament to the many dimensions of 'quality' that define a quality assessment instrument or evaluative process, but in this section and through this section's accompanying exercises the emphasis is on the public face of the field and how communication and interpretation of results can be used effectively both by and for institutions.

36

USING DATA TO FIND COMMON GROUND BETWEEN SECONDARY AND POSTSECONDARY ACCOMMODATIONS FOR STUDENTS WITH DISABILITIES

Manju Banerjee and Martha L. Thurlow

Students with disabilities are attending postsecondary education institutions more than ever before. In the 1970s, not long after the passage of the *Education for All Handicapped Children Act* (1975), 2.6% of undergraduates were reported to have a disability (Gajar, 1992). In 2008, according to census data, 3.0% of students in undergraduate colleges had a disability (U.S. Census Bureau, 2009). Most of these students had learning disabilities (NCES, 2007). The current profile of college students with disabilities is diverse, with increasing numbers having psychiatric disabilities, autism spectrum disorders, and post-traumatic stress disorders (Government Accountability Office, 2009; Hart, Grigal, & Weir, 2010; Wagner, Newman, Cameto, Garza, & Levine, 2005). The 2009 report by the Government Accountability Office (GAO) noted that in 2008 nearly 11% of all postsecondary students had a disability. The number of two- and four-year college undergraduates is expected to reach 16 million by 2015 (Gregg, 2009). These kinds of enrollment numbers parallel the population of students with disabilities in the K–12 public education system, where about 11% of all students ages 6–17 have a disability (Data Accountability Center, 2010; Kessler Foundation and the National Organization on Disability, 2010). Yet these numbers fall far short of the numbers of students without disabilities transitioning to college (Wagner, Newman, Cameto, Garza, & Levine, 2005; National Center for Learning Disabilities, 2009).

For many high school students entering college, successful transition, retention, and graduation depends on eligibility and the provision of appropriate accommodations (Gregg, 2009). This chapter focuses on *accommodations* for students with disabilities and the accommodation gap between secondary and postsecondary education. Understanding the accommodation decision-making process between the two educational institutions can help facilitate the secondary to postsecondary experience for these students.

Accommodations are changes in materials or procedures to provide individuals with access to instruction and assessments (Elliott & Thurlow, 2006; Thurlow, Elliott, & Ysseldyke, 2003). Accommodations enable students to overcome and/or compensate for specific impairments due to their disability and, thereby, provide equal opportunity for access as their non-disabled peers. For example, a student with slow processing speed due to a specific learning disability may need extended time accommodation on an exam to demonstrate mastery of course content. Unfortunately, data used to inform accommodations at the secondary level are not always in alignment with data that serve the same purpose at the postsecondary level. Identification, eligibility, and provision of accommodation is a process that is guided by multiple and different drivers for secondary and postsecondary education. Students are often surprised to learn that accommodations received in high school do not automatically transfer to college.

The purpose of this chapter is two-fold. First is to trace the apparent disparity in purpose, definition, historical precedence, and practices regarding accommodations and the accommodation decision-making process between secondary and postsecondary education. Second is to demonstrate that data-based decision-making is at the heart of the accommodation process at both institutional levels. The difference is often the result of varying policies, practices, and emphases on data. Specifically, this chapter describes three categories of data: objective data (e.g., standardized test scores within disability documentation), authentic data (e.g., Individualized Education Program, Child Study Team report), and relevant data (e.g., state or institutional policies and practices) in bridging the accommodation gap. To keep the chapter focused, only *assessment accommodations*—that is, accommodations provided to students on state-wide and other high-stakes assessments—are addressed. Assessment accommodations for students with disabilities in postsecondary and graduate/licensure exams will be referred to as *test accommodations*, in keeping with convention.

Setting the Stage: Evidence of Growing Disparity

Analyses of the relationship between earnings and educational attainment show that the gap has increased between those with postsecondary degrees and high school diplomas; individuals with postsecondary degrees earned 3.7 times as much as high school graduates in 2003 (Baum & Payea, 2005), compared to 2.6 times as much in 1999, and 1.8 times as much in 1975 (Day & Newburger, 2002). Such job market changes have pushed all students, including those with disabilities, to seek education credentials beyond the high school diploma.

A federal emphasis on the transition of youth with disabilities to postsecondary education and work placements has resulted in increased attention to what happens to these students. States now are monitored on the percentage of youth ages 16 and above with Individualized Education Programs (IEPs) who have coordinated, measurable, annual IEP goals and transition services that will reasonably enable them to meet postsecondary goals. In the most recent data available, only 15 states and U.S. territories (25% of those monitored) met the compliance criteria, and this was up 8% from the year before (NSTTAC, 2009). Despite these improvements in transition planning, and some evidence that there has been progress in the transition outcomes of students with IEPs (Cameto, Levine, & Wagner, 2004), there continue to be inconsistencies in focus and implementation within states and across the U.S. (Johnson, Stodden, Emanuel, Luecking, & Mack, 2002), and much remains to be accomplished (Johnson, in press).

Emerging Trends in K-12

A renewed focus not just on transition but also on access to the general education curriculum emerged in the 2004 amendments to the *Individuals with Disabilities Education Act*. Educators began to realize more than ever that students with disabilities were general education students first. The implication of this new focus was that all students with disabilities needed to receive instruction in standards-based academic content for the grade in which they were enrolled (Thurlow & Quenemoen, 2011).

At the foundation of the attention to accommodations in the K-12 education system has been the desire to ensure that students with disabilities have access to the general education curriculum and are ready to move into postsecondary education. Yet events in the K-12 system have gone on without much consideration of the definitions, driving forces, and perspectives of accommodations in the postsecondary system.

Emerging Trends in Postsecondary Education

Within postsecondary education, accommodations have historically been part of the non-discrimination mandate defined by the *Americans with Disabilities Act of 1990* (ADA, 1990). In recent years, court cases, documentation guidelines, technological innovations, and Universal Design for Instruction (UDI) have shaped the provision of test accommodations for college students with disabilities. In the legal arena, an expanded definition of disability as outlined by the *ADA Amendments Act of 2008* (ADA AA, 2008) has led to greater awareness and more targeted requests for accommodations (Enyart v. National Conference of Bar Examiners, 2010). Institutions of higher education are re-examining their policies regarding disability documentation to be in compliance with the amendments' broader definition of disability and considerations describing episodic disabilities and mitigating measures (Association on Higher Education and Disability [AHEAD], n.d.).

In turn, technological innovations and adoption of the principles of Universal Design in assessment (Thompson, Thurlow, & Malouf, 2004) have enabled the inclusion of many accommodations into the testing environment with increasing ease. Computer-based tests are particularly amenable to built-in features such as screen readers, Braille displays, screen magnification, and self-voicing (i.e., text-to-speech) capabilities (Banerjee, 2007), but the availability of such accommodations for *all* students with disabilities is still emerging (Thurlow, Lazarus, Albus, & Hodgson, 2010). In summary, accommodation determination at the postsecondary level is guided not only by considerations that are different from secondary education, but are influenced by systemic changes within higher education, which make the need for uniformity and data-based decision-making even more pertinent.

Understanding the Accommodation Disparity

Accommodations in K-12 Education

As a foundation for understanding accommodations in the K-12 system, it is important to think about the nature of students in the public special education system in the U.S. With the students as a foundation, it is then possible to examine the purpose and definition of accommodations in K-12 assessments, historical perspectives on accommodations, how the assignment of assessment accommodations is determined, and current trends in K-12 assessment accommodations.

Special education students in K-12 public education

It has become clear during the past decade through analyses that the majority of special education students are those with learning disabilities, speech-language impairments, and emotional or behavioral disabilities. In these analyses, categories of disability have been used as a proxy for exploring the nature of students who have disabilities (see Figure 36.1). Only a small percentage of students with disabilities (10 to 15%), most often those with intellectual disabilities, autism, and multiple disabilities, have disabilities that require them to meet different achievement standards than the standards targeted for other students. This means that 80 to 85% of students with disabilities can meet the same achievement standards as other students—as long as they receive specially designed instruction, appropriate access, supports, and accommodations, as required by IDEA. Thus, no longer are special education students seen as a group that is to be pitied and protected from the content of instruction, but instead are seen as students who can achieve what other students achieve when given appropriate supports and services and the accommodations that they need to have access to the curriculum (Thurlow, Quenemoen, & Lazarus, in press).

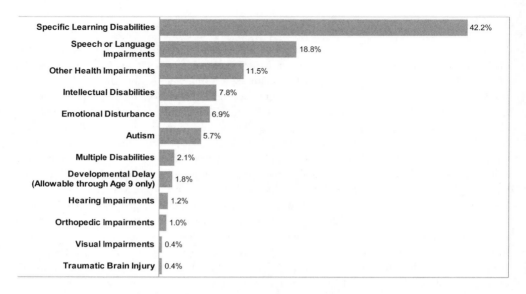

Figure 36.1 Distribution of disability categories among students served under IDEA (Fall 2009)

Source: Data Accountability Center. 2009 Part B Child Count, Tables 1–1 and 1–3 (Students ages 6–21, 50 States, DC, PR, BIE schools). Retrieved from www.ideadata.org/arc_toc11.asp#partbCC. Note: Students in the "Deaf-blindness" category accounted for only 0.02% of students served and are not displayed.

Purpose and definition

In the context of assessments, the purpose and definition of accommodations has been refined over time. In 1997, when the IDEA reauthorization, for the first time, required that special education students participate in state- and district-wide assessments, the purpose of accommodations was to provide those students with access to assessments so that all would be able to participate in the assessments. Over time, more emphasis was placed on the goal of improving the validity of assessment results for students with disabilities. The focus on validity was enforced through regulations that accompanied both the reauthorization of IDEA in 2004 and the *Elementary and Secondary Education Act of 2001* (known as the No Child Left Behind Act).

At the same time that the purpose and definition of accommodations were refined, so was the language that surrounded the concept of accommodations (Thurlow, 2007). Specifically state assessment policies for K-12 testing began to distinguish between *accommodations*—those changes that resulted in valid scores—and *modifications*—those changes that resulted in invalid scores because they changed what the test was intended to measure. Some states distinguished between the two concepts by referring to standard and non-standard accommodations while other states used terms such as approved accommodations and non-approved accommodations. A few other states referred to conditional accommodations, which were changes that they viewed as *possibly* altering the intent of the assessment, but that would still count for accountability purposes as producing valid scores. Still, as used most often today by states and districts for educational assessments, accommodations are changes in test materials or procedures that *do not* alter the content being measured (Lazarus, Thurlow, Lail, & Christensen, 2009).

Historical perspectives on K-12 accommodations

Few topics have received the attention that accommodations have received as policymakers and educators have thought about and addressed the inclusion of students with disabilities in K-12 assessments. The topic has been the focus of entire books and numerous chapters (e.g., Bolt & Roach,

2009; Elliott, Braden, & White, 2001; Laitusis & Cook, 2007; Thurlow, Lazarus, & Christensen, in press; Thurlow, Thompson, & Johnstone, 2007). They also have been the topic of lawsuits challenging state accommodation policies (e.g., Disability Rights Advocates, 2001, 2008; *Noon v Alaska State Board of Education & Early Development*, 2004; Volz, 2004).

The identification of challenges in the decision-making process for K-12 assessment accommodations was followed by requirements that states had to meet to justify their accommodations for their ESEA accountability assessments (U.S. Department of Education, 2004). Several tools were developed to help states meet the peer-review criteria for accommodations (Christensen, Lail, & Thurlow, 2007; Christensen, Thurlow, & Wang, 2009; Thurlow, Christensen, & Lail, 2008). These and other efforts increasingly recognized that appropriate accommodation practices in K-12 education depended on more than just setting policy (Crawford, 2007).

Legal challenges and the pressures of federal reviews of state assessments used for ESEA accountability (Christensen, Lail, & Thurlow, 2007) have promoted the generation of state-level documents detailing policies for the use of assessment accommodations (Christensen, Lazarus, Crone, & Thurlow, 2008; Clapper, Morse, Lazarus, Thompson, & Thurlow, 2005; Lazarus, Thurlow, Lail, Eisenbraun, & Kato, 2006; Thurlow, House, Boys, Scott, & Ysseldyke, 2000; Thurlow, Lazarus, Thompson, & Robey, 2002; Thurlow, Scott, & Ysseldyke, 1995; Thurlow, Seyfarth, Scott, & Ysseldyke, 1997; Thurlow, Ysseldyke, & Silverstein, 1993). Still, the most frequently mentioned accommodations in state testing policies are not necessarily the most frequently used (Bolt & Thurlow, 2004; Thurlow, 2007). Braille, large print, sign language interpretation and other accommodations for sensory disabilities are frequently included in accommodations policies as allowed accommodations. Still, they are among the least frequently used (Thurlow, Bremer, & Albus, 2008).

It is difficult to determine the most frequently used accommodations for a couple of reasons. First, federal data reporting requirements ask only that states report the *number* of students using accommodations, not the specific accommodations that they are using. Second, state data generally are not publicly available. Although most states have the ability to examine their data to determine which accommodations are most frequently used (Thompson, Johnstone, Thurlow, & Altman, 2005), they generally do not make these data available to the public (Albus, Thurlow, & Bremer, 2009).

Attempts by the National Center on Educational Outcomes to examine the use of accommodations prior to the enactment of the federal reporting requirements resulted in data from just a few states (Thompson & Thurlow, 1999). Those data suggested the existence of wide variability in the use of accommodations (from 8 to 82%) across states, and a general trend for decreasing percentages of students using accommodations across school levels (elementary to middle, to high school; see also Johnson, Kimball, Brown, & Anderson, 1996), except perhaps for exit exams where the numbers increased.

States, districts, and schools continue to be challenged by the need that many K-12 special education students seem to have for assessment accommodations. Not all states have reacted in the same way, as is evident from the significant variation that exists in state policies on some of the same accommodations (see Figure 36.2 for policies on the read aloud questions accommodation for reading tests). As illustrated in this figure, eight states allow questions to be read on a test of reading. Fifteen states prohibit this accommodation. The rest of the states are somewhere in between, with some states allowing the read aloud questions under certain circumstances (such as at higher grade levels) and other states allowing students to use the accommodation but with implications for scoring (such as not counting those items that measure decoding). This type of variability exists for many accommodations that are currently in state assessment accommodation policies (Christensen, Thurlow, & Scullin, 2010). Similar variability exists within states across time (Lazarus, Thurlow, Lail, & Christensen, 2009).

As might be expected with the variation in state policies, there continues to be considerable variation in the percentage of special education students receiving accommodations. Figure 36.3 shows

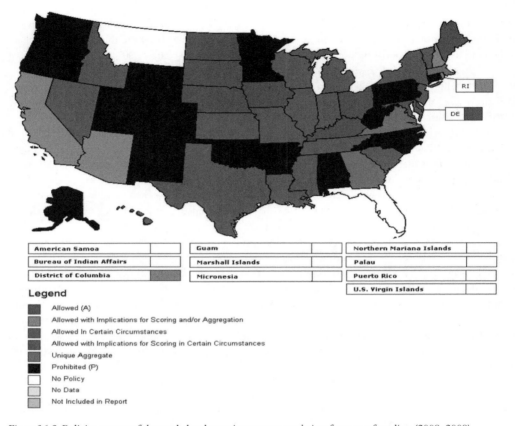

Figure 36.2 Policies on use of the read aloud questions accommodation for tests of reading (2008–2009)

Source: DataViewer (www.nceo.info/dataviewer). Reprinted with permission from the National Center on Educational Outcomes.

the percentage of students in each state who received one or more accommodations for the state elementary reading test. The percentage ranged from less than one percent to 88% of all students with disabilities using accommodations for elementary reading assessments. The same type of variability exists at other school levels (middle school and high school) and for mathematics.

Although research on the effects of K-12 assessment accommodations has increased (Cormier, Altman, Shyyan, & Thurlow, 2010; Zenisky & Sireci, 2007), it has not provided specific directions for state policy. The research has focused on whether an accommodation changes the construct being measured, and whether a differential boost is created for students with disabilities compared to students without disabilities (Laitusis, 2007; Sireci, Scarpati, & Li, 2005). One of the critical findings of the research has been that it is essential to have defined carefully the content to be assessed—what we are really trying to measure. Only then do the results of research begin to have implications for individual state policies.

Determination of K-12 accommodations

Accommodations for students receiving special education services are determined by each student's IEP team. This team makes decisions about both accommodations for instruction and accommodations for assessments. The team reviews the student's characteristics and needs, and, in light of the nature of the test and state policies, determines the accommodations that the student will receive for testing. IEP teams have to differentiate between instructional accommodations that provide access

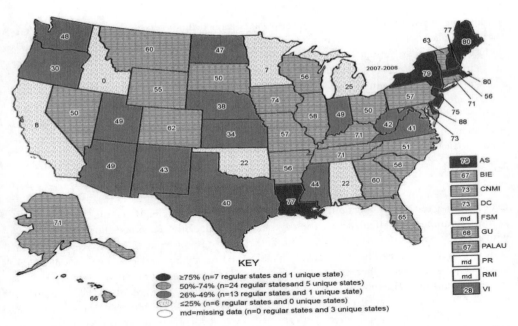

Figure 36.3 Percentages of special education students using accommodations on an elementary reading assessment (2007–2008)

Source: Annual Performance Reports: 2007–2008 State Assessment Data (www.nceo.info/OnlinePubs/APRreport2007–2008. pdf). Reprinted with permission from the National Center on Educational Outcomes.

to the content and assessment accommodations that provide both access to the assessment and valid results (Thurlow, Lazarus, & Christensen, 2008). For students with disabilities on 504 accommodation plans, the decision-making process used to determine accommodations is less clear. There is no consistent formalized group or process for indicating who may receive accommodations and what those accommodations might be (Madaus & Shaw, 2008).

Considerable discussion about how to make good accommodation decisions can be found in the literature (Elliott & Thurlow, 2006; Salend, 2009). This discussion was prompted, in part, by several findings that questioned decision-making about accommodations needed by individual students, and the extent to which they were implemented once decisions had been made (DeStefano, Shriner, & Lloyd, 2001; Rhode Island Department of Education, 2003). Researchers have also shown that some decision-making and implementation issues can be addressed through training (Shriner & DeStefano, 2003). Still, there continues to be documentation of the difficulties encountered in the K-12 system in decision making and implementation (Ketterlin-Geller, Alonzo, Braun-Monegan, & Tindal, 2007).

Accommodation in Postsecondary and High Stakes Tests

Beyond the K-12 system, accommodations are not directly guided by program of study or even student support services. At its core, postsecondary accommodations are academic adjustments to ensure that an institution does not discriminate on the basis of a disability (U.S. Department of Education, Office of Civil Rights, 2007).

Purpose and definition

Postsecondary accommodations are individualized changes and/or adaptations to the planning and delivery of instruction, and assessment of learning. Accommodations such as extended time, breaks during a timed test, use of a note-taker, reader, and assistive technology provide students with alternate or parallel options for receiving information, demonstrating mastery, and performing tasks without the impediments due to a disability. The objective of accommodations is "access" to higher education and not a part of special education services, since there is no such mandate in college.

High-stakes test accommodations, in particular, are changes to the design and standardization protocol of a test that provide students with disabilities equal opportunity to access the test (Sireci, Li, & Scarpati, 2003). Tindal and Fuchs (2000) define test accommodations as "changes in standardization assessment conditions introduced to level the playing field for students by removing construct-irrelevant variance created by their disabilities" (p. 8).

Historical perspective

In determining test accommodation, an important consideration is eligibility and the appropriateness of the accommodation. High-stakes testing agencies are particularly concerned about score validity with and without accommodations. Prior to 2001, scores on non-standard high-stakes tests taken with accommodations used to be "flagged." In 2001, the Briemhorst case led to the removal of flagging on high-stakes tests, where it was determined that the accommodation did not lead to changes in the test construct (Briemhorst v. ETS, 2001). Scores received under accommodated conditions must satisfy two fundamental psychometric properties of assessment. One, the scores must be a valid representation of the examinee's performance. Two, the scores must be comparable to scores received by other examinees under non-accommodated conditions. Sireci, Li, & Scarpati (2003) observed that:

> In many cases, researchers argue against test accommodations in the name of fairness to the majority of examinees who must take the test under perceivably stricter, standardized conditions. In many other cases, researchers argue that test accommodations are the only way to validly measure the knowledge, skills, and abilities of significant numbers of students. *(pp. 3–4)*

A test score is valid if it leads to an accurate interpretation of an individual's performance on the test (Sireci et al., 2003). For example, scores produced under inaccessible conditions, such as a print-only version for a test-taker who is blind, are clearly invalid. The reality of interpreting accommodated test scores is more nuanced than the presented example suggests. It is difficult to determine the extent to which an accommodation accurately compensates for the functional limitations of a given disability. An accommodation becomes an unfair advantage or disadvantage if: (a) it overcompensates or undercompensates for the disability, and/or (b) others can also benefit from receiving the given accommodation (Banerjee, 2007). Given the high stakes, data used to determine accommodation eligibility for college admissions and/or licensure exams must meet a high standard of scrutiny.

Determination of postsecondary accommodations

To receive accommodations in college, students must self-disclose their disability to the appropriate office and be deemed eligible as an individual with a disability under the ADA. The ADA identifies an individual with a disability as someone who has a substantial impairment in one or more major life activities, has documentation of the impairment, and is regarded as having the impairment (see http://www.eeoc.gov/policy/docs/902cm.html#902.2). The statutory definition of disability under the Amendment Act of the ADA includes a list of major life activities and bodily functions that serve as a reference for determining eligibility and, in turn, appropriate accommodations. The regulatory definition of disability, on the other hand, does not include such a list, but describes the type of condition that may constitute an impairment under the ADA (http://www.eeoc.gov/policy/docs/902cm.html#902.2b). For example, a student with poor reading skills because of inconsistent formal instruction is not considered as having an impairment requiring ADA accommodations.

The definition of disability under the ADA is not specific to any type or nature of disability, as is the case under IDEA. The ADA does not require identification or diagnosis of a disability category such as learning disability or traumatic brain injury. The description and identification of a "qualified student with a disability" is therefore different between K–12 and postsecondary education. In K–12, a qualified student with a disability is a student who is:

> of an age at which students without disabilities are provided elementary and secondary educational services; of an age at which it is mandatory under state law to provide elementary and secondary educational services to students with disabilities; or a student to whom a state is required to provide a free appropriate public education under the Individuals with Disabilities Education Act (IDEA). *(Retrieved from http://www2.ed.gov/about/offices/list/ocr/504faq. html)*

In postsecondary education, a qualified student with a disability is one who meets the academic and technical standards for admission and participation in the college's programs and activities, and is an individual with a disability under the ADA definition.

The process of determining eligibility for accommodations is subjective and varied across postsecondary institutions (Lindstrom, 2007). Generally speaking, identification of individual accommodations is based on responses to four fundamental queries. First, does the student have an impairment that affects one or more major life activities as identified under the ADA; second, does the impairment rise to the level of a disability; third, what is the impact of the impairment on performance in the area for which accommodations are being considered; and fourth, what are the appropriate accommodations, given a specific test or assignment.

Answers to the above questions are sought from the disability documentation provided by the student. The documentation is the primary source for determining fair and reasonable accommodations at the postsecondary level. The disability documentation is a report, usually a psychoeducational, neuropsychological, or medical evaluation conducted by a credentialed professional, to assess the current status of a student's reported impairment(s). To bring a level of uniformity to the documentation review process, postsecondary institutions and testing agencies have established guidelines and procedures for reviewing documentation. However, there are variations across institutions and testing agencies as to how extensive the disability documentation needs to be to support the accommodations requested. Most institutional guidelines are some variation of the guidelines established by the Association on Higher Education and Disability (AHEAD) which serve as the standard for documentation compliance at the postsecondary level (Madaus, Banerjee, & Hamblet, 2010). AHEAD's "Seven Essential Elements of Quality Disability Documentation" provide stipulations regarding: (a) the credentials of the evaluator, (b) diagnosis and diagnostics statement identifying the disability, (c) diagnostic methodology used, (d) description of current functional limitations, (e) expected progression or stability of the disability, (f) description of current and past accommodations, services and/or medications, and (g) recommendations for accommodations, adaptive devices, assistive services, compensatory strategies, and/or collateral support services.

Understanding the Accommodation Gap

From the K–12 education perspective, good accommodations practices depend on decision makers who understand the nature of the content being assessed and the assessment itself, the student's characteristics and needs, and the accommodations policies, and in that order (Elliott & Thurlow,

2006; Thurlow, Lazarus, & Christensen, 2008). Further, there is general agreement on the need for training for decision makers and students (e.g., NCEO, 2009; Thompson, Morse, & Sharpe, 2005), as well as for monitoring procedures to ensure that proper accommodations implementation is occurring (Christensen, Thurlow, & Wang, 2009).

Despite the move toward somewhat greater standardization in thinking about accommodations, there clearly is still a lot of variability when it comes to K–12 accommodations. Several of the variations that characterize K–12 assessments have implications for postsecondary education accommodations:

- It is not just special education students who may use accommodations in K–12 assessments. In all states (Christensen, Thurlow, & Scullin, 2010), students who are on 504 accommodation plans also may use accommodations for assessments. And, in the majority of states, English language learners (ELLs) also may use accommodations (on the basis of policies that usually are different from those for students with disabilities). In a small number of states, all students have access to accommodations, as long as there is a documented need.

- No certification by a psychologist or other diagnostic professional is required for accommodations to be designated for a student in K–12 assessments. For those students in special education, the IEP team determines the accommodations. In most states, this team can select accommodations that the state may not consider appropriate for the assessment (and, thus, would call them modifications). There may be implications for the scoring or reporting when modifications are used, but students may still use them. For 504 plan students, a team may be available to make decisions about accommodations, but in most cases it is an individual teacher or principal who determines the accommodations. For ELLs, a designated team or teacher determines the accommodations. And, in those states where all students have access to accommodations, an IEP team, teacher, principal, or other educator may determine assessment accommodations.

- K–12 assessments are being designed from the beginning to be more appropriate for all students and hopefully to decrease the need for accommodations (Thompson, Thurlow, & Malouf, 2004; Johnstone, Thompson, Miller, & Thurlow, 2008). Often referred to as universal design, this approach has changed the nature of many assessments and led to the hope that computer-based tests can move the field even further forward toward assessments that are more appropriate for all students (Thurlow, Lazarus, Albus, & Hodgson, 2010).

Postsecondary institutions and testing agencies have a responsibility to establish disability status and subsequent eligibility for test accommodations (Keiser, 1998). Unfortunately, neither the ADA nor the federal regulations on disability discrimination has been explicit in describing what constitutes "evidence" of a disability (Frierson, 1998). As a result, there are variations in established policy statements and guidelines for disability documentation across testing agencies and postsecondary institutions, which can be confusing.

The following observations are worth highlighting:

- Specific test accommodations are determined on a case-by-case basis through an institutional documentation review process. Models for documentation review are varied across institutions (Lindstrom, 2007), as well as, by demographic characteristics of the reviewers (Banerjee, 2009). Testing agencies such as the Educational Testing Service (ETS) have internal documentation review criteria that inform the documentation review process (Brinckerhoff & Banerjee, 2009). As noted by Banerjee and Shaw (2007), "Documentation review criteria are like checkpoints used by testing agencies to verify the existence of the claimed disability status, functional limitations due to the disability, and the need for each requested accommodation. Potential for conflict arises when evidence of disability in grade school does not measure up to the evidence of disability considered essential by high-stakes test administration agencies" (p. 172).

- Not all impairments constitute a disability that warrants accommodation. For example, test anxiety may constitute an impairment for the individual, but unless it rises to the level of a disability (such as generalized anxiety disorder), it is not protected by ADA accommodations.
- Accommodations must be "reasonable" and not cause "undue burden." For example, a test accommodation must not alter the integrity or construct of the test in which accommodations are being requested. Determination of "reasonableness of accommodation" can be a negotiated process between the institution and the individual. Faculty members and high-stakes testing agencies have the right to determine the form, format, and mode of delivery of a test.
- Accommodations are not automatically transferrable. Accommodations received in K-12 schools or at a specific institution do not automatically transfer to another college or a testing agency. Test modification such as rephrasing of test questions are rarely, if at all, provided at the undergraduate or graduate level.

Finding Common Ground Between Secondary and Postsecondary Accommodations

Decisions regarding accommodations for students with disabilities are different between secondary and postsecondary education for a variety of reasons. Yet the broad objectives are similar. It would appear that much of the difference lies in the varying emphases placed on the components of evidentiary information (i.e., data) in determining accommodations. Data for accommodation decision-making come from multiple sources such as the IEP and child study team report, diagnostic evaluation, disability documentation and guidelines, Summary of Performance (SOP), state and local educational policies, historical precedence, and legal mandates. Understanding the way different types of data inform the accommodation process is key in identifying common ground between secondary and postsecondary education.

For the purpose of accommodation decision-making, data can broadly be classified into three categories: (a) objective evidence, (b) authentic evidence, and (c) relevant evidence (Banerjee & Shaw, 2007).

Objective evidence is described as data that are independently verifiable. In other words, any qualified individual reviewing the evidence can independently interpret the reported information and draw the same conclusion. Examples include scores on standardized evaluation instruments and self-assessment inventories, medical tests, nationally normed state-wide assessments, and high stakes tests. Authentic evidence is described here as observational and/or field based data. This category includes curriculum-based, teacher-made assessment of the student's level of performance in academic, vocational, and social settings. Other examples include self-reporting by the student of learning difficulties encountered in school or at work, description of coping strategies used that may explain the absence of formal special education services, parent and teacher report on performance in various settings, IEP and transition plan documents, SOP, and reported observations by other individuals. Relevant evidence as described here constitutes policies and procedures, legal and otherwise, that have a bearing on accommodation determination. Stipulations of the ADA and special education mandates, institutional disability documentation guidelines, are examples of this type of evidence.

Data from within each of these three categories are important in making accommodation decisions for students with disabilities. The differing emphases on the categories of data by secondary and postsecondary institutions have resulted in the accommodation gap (Banerjee & Shaw, 2007). Clearly, if accommodation decisions are primarily driven by standardized scores, the data become vulnerable to criticism commonly leveled at standardized tests (Popham, 2001) that do not reflect authentic evidence. On the other hand, data that are primarily self-reported, interpretive, or subjective, and lack independent verifiability create skepticism. Banerjee and Shaw (2007) suggest the following approach for a cohesive framework for accommodation determination:

1. *Multiple sources.* Is there data from multiple sources demonstrating the impairment(s) experienced by the student? Different types of data (such as from an IEP and disability documentation) and awareness of the source or use of such data in decision-making can facilitate the accommodation process across educational institutions.

2. *Cross validation.* Do the data demonstrate a consistent pattern of academic difficulties over time? Evidence that spans the academic career of a student from grade school to postsecondary builds credibility. Authentic data describing coping strategies, teacher-based activities in K-12 schools may help explain why no accommodations may have been used in the past, but are needed on a high-stakes test. Cross validation of data from multiple sources can be compelling.

3. *Effectiveness of accommodations.* Is there a past history of accommodations and support for effectiveness of these accommodations? In other words, do the data address current eligibility for test accommodations and efficacy of specific accommodations in various assessment contexts? While not conclusive in and of itself, data that attest to prior effectiveness of accommodations can further serve to build a case for accommodations at the next educational level.

4. *Context.* Is there data demonstrating use of specific accommodations in similar circumstances or context? In other words, is there any evidence of performance with accommodations in situations that are close simulations of high-stakes test environments?

Despite acknowledgment of the challenges, students with disabilities are slipping through the support system designed to facilitate their educational transition. Accommodations play a key role in effective participation in all levels of education. The accommodation gap between secondary and postsecondary education leaves many students at a disadvantage. Understanding of the "apparent" disparity and leveraging data for decision-making can help bridge this gap.

References

Albus, D., Thurlow, M., & Bremer, C. (2009). *Achieving transparency in the public reporting of 2006–2007 assessment results* (Technical Report 53). Minneapolis, MN: University of Minnesota, National Center on Educational Outcomes.

Americans with Disabilities Act of 1990 (ADA), 42 U.S.C.A. § 12101 *et seq.* Retrieved February 20, 2011 from http://www.ada.gov/pubs/ada.htm

Americans with Disabilities Amendments Act of 2008 (ADA AA). Retrieved February 20, 2011 from http://www.ada.gov/pubs/ada.htm

Association on Higher Education and Disability (AHEAD), n.d. Retrieved January 30, 2011 from http://www.ahead.org/resources/best-practices-resources

Banerjee, M. (2007). *Examinee choice in test development: Implications for universally designed high stakes tests* (Unpublished doctoral dissertation). University of Connecticut, Storrs.

Banerjee, M. (2009). *2008 grant funded study on documentation review: Implications for testing agencies.* Paper presented at the 7th Annual Testing Agency Disability Forum, Princeton, NJ.

Banerjee, M. & Shaw, S. F. (2007). High-stakes test accommodations: Documentation review by testing agencies in an era of change. *Assessment for Effective Intervention, 32*(3), 171–180.

Baum, S., & Payea, K. (2005). *The benefits of higher education for individuals and society* (rev. ed) . Washington, DC: The College Board, College Entrance Examination Board.

Bolt, S., & Roach, A. T. (2009). *Inclusive assessment and accountability: A guide to accommodations for students with diverse needs.* New York, NY: Guilford Press.

Bolt, S. E., & Thurlow, M. L. (2004). A synthesis of research on five of the most frequently allowed testing accommodations in state policy. *Remedial and Special Education, 25*(3), 141–152.

Briemhorst v. ETS, (N.D. Cal, March 27, 2001). Retrieved February 3, 2011 from http://www.dralegal.org/cases/education_testing/breimhorst_v_ets.php

Brinckerhoff, L. & Banerjee, M. (2009). *Understanding the complexities of disability documentation: In the shadow of IDEA 2004 and in light of the ADA Amendments Act of 2008*. Workshop presented at the Postsecondary Training Institute, Center for Postsecondary Education and Disability, Philadelphia, PA.

Cameto, R., Levine, P., & Wagner, M. (2004). *Transition planning for students with disabilities: A special topic report of findings from the National Longitudinal Transition Study-2* (NLTS-2). Menlo Park, CA: SRI International.

Christensen, L. L., Lail, K. E., & Thurlow, M. L. (2007). *Hints and tips for addressing accommodations issues for peer review*. Minneapolis, MN: University of Minnesota, National Center on Educational Outcomes.

Christensen, L. L., Lazarus, S. S., Crone, M., & Thurlow, M. L. (2008). *2007 state policies on assessment participation and accommodations for students with disabilities* (Synthesis Report 69). Minneapolis, MN: University of Minnesota, National Center on Educational Outcomes.

Christensen, L. L., Thurlow, M. L., & Scullin, S. (2010). *2009 state policies on assessment participation and accommodations for students with disabilities* (Synthesis Report). Minneapolis, MN: University of Minnesota, National Center on Educational Outcomes.

Christensen, L. L., Thurlow, M. L., & Wang, T. (2009). *Improving accommodations outcomes: Monitoring instructional and assessment accommodations for students with disabilities*. Minneapolis, MN: University of Minnesota, National Center on Educational Outcomes.

Clapper, A. T., Morse, A. B., Lazarus, S. S., Thompson, S. J., & Thurlow, M. L. (2005). *2003 state policies on assessment participation and accommodations for students with disabilities* (Synthesis Report 56). Minneapolis, MN: University of Minnesota, National Center on Educational Outcomes.

Cormier, D. C., Altman, J., Shyyan, V., & Thurlow, M. L. (2010). *A summary of the research on the effects of test accommodations: 2007–2008* (Technical Report 56). Minneapolis, MN: University of Minnesota, National Center on Educational Outcomes.

Crawford, L. (2007). *State testing accommodations: A look at their value and validity*. New York: National Center for Learning Disabilities.

Data Accountability Center. (2010). Data tables for OSEP state reported data (Number of children and students served under IDEA) https://www.ideadata.org/arc_toc10.asp#partbCC

Day, J. C., & Newburger, E. (2002). The big payoff: Educational attainment and synthetic estimates of work-life earnings. In *Current Population Reports* (pp. 23–210). Washington, DC: U.S. Census Bureau.

DeStefano, L., Shriner, J. G., & Lloyd, C. A. (2001). Teacher decision making in participation of students with disabilities in large-scale assessment. *Exceptional Children, 68*(1), 7–22.

Disability Rights Advocates. (2001). *Do no harm—High stakes testing and students with learning disabilities*. Oakland, CA: Author.

Disability Rights Advocates. (2008). *Chapman v. California Department of Education*. Retrieved on September 20, 2009 from http://www.dralegal.org/cases/education_testing/chapman_v_ca.php

Education for All Handicapped Children Act, Pub. L. No. 94–142, 89 Stat. 773 (1975).

Elliott, J. E., & Thurlow, M. L. (2006). *Improving test performance of students with disabilities*. Thousand Oaks, CA: Corwin Press.

Elliott, S. N., Braden, J. P., & White, J. (2001). *Assessing one and all: Educational accountability and students with disabilities*. Alexandria, VA: Council for Exceptional Children.

Enyart v. National Conference of Bar Examiners (NCBE). (2010). Retrieved February 16, 2011 from http://www.dralegal.org/cases/index.php

Frierson, J. G. (1998). Legal requirements for clinical evaluations. In M. Gordon, & S. Keiser (Eds.), *Accommodations in higher education under the Americans with Disabilities Act* (pp. 73–97). New York, NY: Guilford Press.

Gajar, A. (1992). University-based models for students with learning disabilities: The Pennsylvania State University in Mode. In F. R. Rusch, L. DeStefano, J. G. Chadsey-Rusch, L. A. Phelps, & E. Szymanski (Eds.), *Transition from school to adult life: Models, linkages, and policy*. Sycamore, IL: Sycamore Publishing Company.

Government Accountability Office (GAO). (2009). Higher education and disability: Education needs a coordinated approach to improve its assistance to schools in supporting students. Retrieved October 20, 2010 from http://www.gao.gov/products/GAO-10–33

Gregg, N. (2009). *Adolescents and adults with learning disabilities and ADHD: Assessment and Accommodation*. New York, NY: Guildford Press.

Hart, D., Grigal, M., & Weir, C. (2010). Expanding the paradigm: Postsecondary education options for individuals with autism spectrum disorder and intellectual disabilities. *Focus on Autism and Other Developmental Disabilities, 25*(3), 134–150.

Johnson, D. R. (in press). Policy and adolescent transition. In M.L. Wehmeyer, & K. Webb (Eds.), *Handbook of transition for youth with disabilities*. Rutledge, Taylor and Francis.

Johnson, D. R., Stodden, R. A., Emanuel, E. J., Luecking, R., & Mack, M. (2002). Current challenges facing secondary education and transition services for youth with disabilities: What research tells us. *Exceptional Children, 68*(4), 519–531.

Johnson, E., Kimball, K., Brown, S., & Anderson, D. (1996). A statewide review of the use of accommodations in large-scale, high-stakes assessments. *Exceptional Children, 67* (2), 251–264.

Johnstone, C. J., Thompson, S. J., Miller, N. A., & Thurlow, M. L. (2008). Universal design and multi-method approaches to item review. *Educational Measurement: Issues and Practice*, 27 (1), 25–36.

Keiser, S. (1998). Test accommodations: An administrator's view. In M. Gordon, & S. Keiser (Eds.), *Accommodations in higher education under the Americans with Disabilities Act* (pp. 46–69). New York, NY: Guilford Press.

Kessler Foundation and the National Organization on Disability, Harris Interactive. (2010). *The ADA, 20 years later.* New York, NY: Retrieved February 20, 2011 from http://www.2010disabilitysurveys.org/

Ketterlin-Geller, L. R., Alonzo, J., Braun-Monegan, J., & Tindal, G. (2007). Recommendations for accommodations: Implications of (in)consistency. *Remedial and Special Education, 28*(4), 194–206.

Laitusis, C.C. (2007). Research designs and analysis for studying accommodations on assessments. In C. C. Laitusis, & L. L. Cook (Eds.), *Large-scale accommodations: What works?* (pp. 67–79). Arlington, VA: Council for Exceptional Children.

Laitusis, C. C., & Cook, L. L. (2007). *Large-scale assessment and accommodations: What works?* Arlington, VA: Council for Exceptional Children.

Lazarus, S. S., Thurlow, M. L., Lail, K. E., & Christensen, L. (2009). A longitudinal analysis of state accommodations policies: Twelve years of change 1993–2005. *Journal of Special Education, 43* (2), 67–80.

Lazarus, S. S., Thurlow, M. L., Lail, K. E., Eisenbraun, K. D., & Kato, K. (2006). *2005 state policies on assessment participation and accommodations for students with disabilities* (Synthesis Report 64). Minneapolis, MN: University of Minnesota, National Center on Educational Outcomes.

Lindstrom, J. H. (2007). Determining appropriate accommodations for postsecondary students with reading and written expression disorders. *Learning Disabilities Research and Practice, 22*(4), 229–236.

Madaus, J. W., Banerjee, M., & Hamblet, E. (2010). Learning disability documentation decision making at the postsecondary level. *Career Development for Exceptional Individuals, 33*(2), 68–79.

Madaus, J. W., & Shaw, S. F. (2008). The role of school professionals in implementing Section 504 for students with disabilities. *Educational Policy, 22*(3), 363–378.

NCEO (National Center on Educational Outcomes). (2009). *Training guide for Minnesota manual of accommodations for students with disabilities.* Minneapolis, MN: University of Minnesota, National Center on Educational Outcomes. Available at http://www.cehd.umn.edu/nceo/OnlinePubs/MNmanuals/MNtrainingguide.pdf

NCES (National Center for Education Statistics). (2007). *The condition of education 2007.* Washington, DC: U.S. Department of Education.

National Center for Learning Disabilities. (2009). *The state of learning disabilities.* Retrieved from http://www.ncld.org/images/stories/OnCapitolHill/PolicyRelatedPublications/stateofld/StateofLD2009-final.pdf

NSTTAC (National Secondary Transition Technical Assistance Center). (2009). *Analysis of 2007–2008 state annual performance reports for indicator 13.* Retrieved January 8, 2011 from http://www.nsttac.org/sites/default/files/assets/pdf/StatePerformanceReportSummary2009.pdf

Noon v. Alaska State Board of Education & Early Development, No. A04–0057 (filed D. Alaska Mar. 16, 2004). [The complaint can be found at http://www.wrightslaw.com/law/pleadings/ak.highstakes.complaint.pdf and the settlement agreement can be found at http://www.eed.state.ak.us/tls/assessment/general/noon_settlementagreementfinal.pdf

Popham, W. J. (2001). *The truth about testing: An educator's call to action.* Alexandria, VA: Association for Supervision and Curriculum Development.

Rhode Island Department of Education. (2003). *Rhode Island assessment accommodation study: Research summary.* Minneapolis, MN: University of Minnesota, National Center on Educational Outcomes. Retrieved from http://www.cehd.umn.edu/nceo/topicareas/accommodations/RhodeIsland.htm

Salend, S. J. (2009). *Classroom testing and assessment for all students: Beyond standardization.* Thousand Oaks, CA: Corwin Press.

Shriner, J. G., & DeStefano, L. (2003). Participation and accommodation in state assessment: The role of individualized education programs. *Exceptional Children, 69*(2), 147–161.

Sireci, S. G., Li, S., & Scarpati, S. (2003). *The effects of test accommodations on test performance: A review of the literature* (Center for Educational Assessment Research Report no. 485). Amherst, MA: Board on Testing and Assessment of the National Research Council of the National Academy of Sciences.

Sireci, S. G., Scarpati, S. E., & Li, S. (2005). Test accommodations for students with disabilities: An analysis of the interaction hypothesis. *Review of Educational Research, 75*, 457–490.

Thompson, S. J., Johnstone, C. J., Thurlow, M. L., & Altman, J. R. (2005). *2005 State special education outcomes: Steps forward in a decade of change.* Minneapolis, MN: University of Minnesota, National Center on Educational Outcomes.

Thompson, S. J., Morse, A. B., & Sharpe, M. (2005). *Accommodations manual: How to select, administer, and evaluate use of accommodations for instruction and assessment for students with disabilities.* Washington, DC: Council of Chief State School Officers. Available at www.nceo.info/OnlinePubs/AccommodationsManual.pdf

Thompson, S. J., & Thurlow, M. L. (1999). *1999 state special education outcomes: A report on state activities at the end of the century.* Minneapolis, MN: University of Minnesota, National Center on Educational Outcomes.

Thompson, S. J., Thurlow, M. L., & Malouf, D. (2004). Creating better tests for everyone through universally designed assessments. *Journal of Applied Testing Technology, 6*(1). Retrieved from http://www.testpublishers.org/journal-of-applied-testing-technology

Thurlow, M. L. (2007). State policies and accommodations: Issues and implications. In C. C. Laitusis , & L. L. Cook (Eds.), *Large-scale assessment and accommodations: What works?* (pp. 13–22). Arlington, VA: Council for Exceptional Children.

Thurlow, M. L., Bremer, C., & Albus, D. (2008). *Good news and bad news in disaggregated subgroup reporting to the public on 2005–2006 assessment results* (Technical Report 52). Minneapolis, MN: University of Minnesota, National Center on Educational Outcomes.

Thurlow, M. L., Christensen, L., & Lail, K. E. (2008). *An analysis of accommodations issues from the standards and assessments peer review* (Technical Report 51). Minneapolis, MN: University of Minnesota, National Center on Educational Outcomes.

Thurlow, M. L., Elliott, J. L., & Ysseldyke, J. E. (2003). *Testing students with disabilities: Practical strategies for complying with district and state requirements* (2nd ed.). Thousand Oaks, CA: Corwin Press.

Thurlow, M., House, A., Boys, C., Scott, D., & Ysseldyke, J. (2000). *State participation and accommodation policies for students with disabilities: 1999 update* (Synthesis Report 33). Minneapolis, MN: University of Minnesota, National Center on Educational Outcomes.

Thurlow, M., Lazarus, S. S., Albus, D., & Hodgson, J. (2010). *Computer-based testing: Practices and considerations* (Synthesis Report 78). Minneapolis, MN: University of Minnesota, National Center on Educational Outcomes.

Thurlow, M. L., Lazarus, S. S., & Christensen, L. L. (2008). Role of assessment accommodations in accountability. *Perspectives on Language and Learning, 34*(4), 17–20.

Thurlow, M. L., Lazarus, S. S., & Christensen, L. L. (in press). Accommodations for assessment. In B. Cook, & M. Tankersley (Eds.), *Effective practices in special education.* Iowa City, IA: Pearson.

Thurlow, M. L., Lazarus, S., Thompson, S., & Robey, J. (2002). *2001 state policies on assessment participation and accommodations* (Synthesis Report 46). Minneapolis, MN: University of Minnesota, National Center on Educational Outcomes.

Thurlow, M. L. & Quenemoen, R.F. (2011). Standards-based reform and students with disabilities. In J. M. Kauffman, & D. P. Hallahan (Eds.), *Handbook of special education* (pp. 134–146). New York, NY: Routledge.

Thurlow, M. L. Quenemoen, R. F. & Lazarus, S. S. (in press). Leadership for student performance in an era of accountability. In J. Crockett, B. Billingsley, & M. Boscardin (Eds.). *The handbook of leadership & administration for special education.* London, UK: Routledge.

Thurlow, M. L., Scott, D. L., & Ysseldyke, J. E. (1995). *A compilation of states' guidelines for accommodations in assessments for students with disabilities* (Synthesis Report 18). Minneapolis, MN: University of Minnesota, National Center on Educational Outcomes.

Thurlow, M., Seyfarth, A., Scott, D., & Ysseldyke, J. (1997). *State assessment policies on participation and accommodations for students with disabilities: 1997 update* (Synthesis Report 29). Minneapolis, MN: University of Minnesota, National Center on Educational Outcomes.

Thurlow, M., Thompson, S., & Johnstone, C. (2007). Policy, legal, and implementation issues surrounding assessment accommodations for students with disabilities. In L. Florian (Ed.), *The Sage handbook of special education* (pp. 331–346). Thousand Oaks, CA: Sage

Thurlow, M. L., Ysseldyke, J. E., & Silverstein, B. (1993). *Testing accommodations for students with disabilities: A review of the literature* (Synthesis Report 4). Minneapolis, MN: University of Minnesota, National Center on Educational Outcomes.

Tindal, G., & Fuchs, L. S. (1998). *A summary of research on test changes: An empirical basis for defining accommodations.* Lexington, KY: University of Kentucky, Mid-South Regional Center.

U.S. Census Bureau. (2009). *Current population survey: Type of college and year enrolled.* Washington, DC: Author. Retrieved January 10, 2011 from www.census.gov/population/www/socdemo/school/cps2008.html

U.S. Department of Education. (2004). *Standards and assessments peer review guidance: Information and examples for meeting requirements of the No Child Left Behind Act of 2001.* Washington, DC: Office of Elementary and Secondary Education.

U.S. Department of Education, Office of Civil Rights. (2007). *Students with disabilities preparing for postsecondary* education: Know your rights and responsibilities.* Retrieved February 20, 2011 from http://www2.ed.gov/about/offices/list/ocr/transition.html

Volz, M. (2004, August 3). *Disabled students in Alaska to get special accommodations during high school exit exams in settlement.* Retrieved September 20, 2009 from www.SignOnSanDiego.com

Wagner, M., Newman, L., Cameto, R., Garza, N., & Levine, P. (2005). *After high school: A first look at the postsecondary experiences of youth with disabilities. A report from the National Longitudinal Transition Study-2* (NLTS-2). Menlo Park, CA: SRI International.

Zenisky, A.L., & Sireci, S.G. (2007). *A summary of the research on the effects of test accommodations: 2005–2006* (Technical Report 47). Minneapolis, MN: University of Minnesota, National Center on Educational Outcomes.

37

TESTING AND EVALUATION OF ENGLISH-LANGUAGE LEARNERS IN HIGHER EDUCATION

Young Yee Kim, James Hart, Jamal Abedi, and Alan Vanneman

This chapter discusses issues related to testing and evaluation of English-language learners (ELL) in higher education. Higher education typically refers to both undergraduate and graduate education. While ELL issues can apply to both undergraduate and graduate school students who "learn English" for their academic success and future careers, this chapter discusses only the issues related to undergraduate level ELL students, including community colleges.

The ELL population has received increasing notice among policymakers and educational researchers for its size, its rate of growth, and the fact that there is typically a performance gap between ELL and non-ELL students. In U.S. public schools, ELL students are the fastest growing subgroup of students, with an annual increase of about 10% per year and a 72% overall increase from 1992 to 2002 (Zamora, 2009). From 1979 to 2007, the number of school-age children ages 5–17 who spoke a language other than English is estimated to have increased from 3.8 to 10.8 million, or from 9 to 20% of the population (Planty et al., 2009). This growth, coupled with the fact that ELL students typically score lower than non-ELL students, has made this group an increased focus of concern in K-12 education policy.[1] However, the percentage of ELL students tends to decrease as grade level increases. According to the grade 12 data from the 2009 National Assessment of Educational Progress (NAEP), only about 3% of grade 12 students were identified as ELL students, while about 10% of grade 4 students were identified as ELL students.

While the definition of ELL in the K-12 education context seems to be unambiguous at first glance, the term "ELL" covers a diverse population that includes both immigrants and native-born students whose home language is other than English. In addition, the classification of ELL students is not consistent across states, districts, or schools. This suggests that similar challenges exist in defining ELL students in higher education. Defining ELL students in higher education is directly related to the issues of how to best serve their educational needs, including accurate assessment with appropriate accommodations.

The rest of this chapter begins with a discussion of how to define the ELL population in higher education, followed by a brief treatment of the general issues related to testing and evaluation of ELL students in that context. Next, several major topics related to testing ELL students in higher education are discussed: college entrance exams; English language class placement exams, including placement decisions; tests in English language classes and evaluation of such classes/programs; and finally, testing ELL students in academic subject classes.

Who are ELL Students in Higher Education?

The term English-language learners or ELL students was first popularized in the context of K–12 education, where it has been widely used to denote students who are not native English speakers and who are still developing proficiency in English.[2] It has been applied to K–12 students because the term ELL was used in the Elementary and Secondary Education Act as reauthorized by the No Child Left Behind Act of 2001 (NCLB, 2002). The term "English language learner (ELL)" may seem to be a general term that can be used for any students learning English as a second language, i.e. ESL students. However, the only clear and operational definition of the term occurs in NCLB 2002, and this definition applies exclusively to K–12 students. The identification process for K–12 students starts with a "Home Language Survey" as the initial step for identifying potential ELLs. Those who are identified as potential ELLs (speak a language other than English at home) are then tested by English language proficiency (ELP) assessments that are developed specifically by consortia of states and some test publishers for this purpose. If students who are identified as potential ELLs do not reach the "proficiency level" on the tests, they are labeled as ELLs and often provided with ELL services. On the other hand, ESL students who did not attend K–12 schools in the United States have not gone through such a systematic approach of identification. The term "ELL" was employed at the K–12 level instead of "students with limited English proficiency" (LEP) to emphasize the process of learning rather than deficiency. Because the term was first widely used in the context of NCLB, research on the issues related to ELL students, including classifying, educating, and assessing them, has focused on K–12 students. Hector-Madison and Bardack (2010), for example, provide a comprehensive overview of research on issues related to ELL students, mostly in the K–12 education.

While there is a well developed definition for ELL in K–12 education, it cannot directly translate to higher education. In the case of K–12 students, a detailed list of definitions of ELL can be provided, as outlined in NCLB 2002 (Abedi, 2007). This definition includes students who are enrolled or preparing to enroll in elementary or secondary schools and who are at age 3 through 21. This is straightforward. There are, however, two additional important criteria used in NCLB 2002 that have application beyond the K–12 context: "not born in the United States or whose native language is not English" and "has difficulties in speaking, reading, writing, or understanding the English language that may deny the individual the ability to meet the state's proficient level of achievement and the ability to successfully achieve in classrooms where English is the language of instruction, or to participate fully in society" (Abedi, 2007, p. 3). These two criteria can serve as guidelines for defining ELL students in higher education.

Higher education in this chapter will be defined as postsecondary education provided by colleges or community colleges where at the end of a prescribed course of study, a degree, diploma, or certificate is awarded, excluding graduate school programs. This means that ELL students in higher education as discussed in this chapter do not include ELL adults who are enrolled in English language programs for the purpose of learning "functional" English independent of a degree program or students who are enrolled in English language programs without enrolling in a college or community college for the purpose of pursuing a degree or certificate. This restriction is important in discussing testing and evaluation of ELL students in higher education because these groups compose different populations who need different approaches to their educational needs and evaluation.

The term ELL has not become rooted in higher education; instead, the term "English as a Second Language" (ESL) students is more often used to describe students who "need special assistance in using English effectively in their academic work" (California Intersegmental Committee of Academic Senates [CICAS], 2006, p.3). While the CICAS report uses the term ESL rather than ELL to describe those students with limited English proficiency who need special assistance in using English effectively in their academic work in higher education, the term ELL will be used throughout this chapter to refer to students who are in the process of acquiring English for academic learning, and whose primary language is not English (or who are not mono-lingual English native-speakers).

In higher education, the term "ESL students" typically refers to students in ESL programs who traditionally have been considered as someone whose first language is not English. Obtaining a reliable definition of "English as second language" is not as easy as it might appear. A study of English language learners in the California postsecondary system (CICAS, 2006) classified ELL students according to three categories, as follows:

- They are either immigrants or the children of immigrants who received the majority, if not all, of their K–12 education in U.S. schools, but who have grown up in non-English linguistic communities and have not achieved college-level proficiency in oral or written work. Such students are sometimes called "1.5 generation students."
- They are recent immigrants, who have completed only a few years of K–12 education in U.S. schools. These students have not achieved proficiency in English and may or may not have academic proficiency in their native language.
- The third group consists of international students, who typically have academic proficiency in their native language but not in English.

Classifying ELL students into three distinct groups is important because each group needs different approaches for testing and evaluation.

The first category, also referred to as language minority students by some researchers, mostly consists of Latino students who graduated from a high school in the United States (Bunch & Panayotova, 2008). According to the CICAS report, these students may try to avoid taking or being placed into ESL classes because of the potential stigma associated with ESL. While these students are not mono-lingual English native speakers, they are not learning English as a second language, implying that they are not ESL students by definition. Some researchers use a term, "circumstantial bilingual," for this type of student (Bunch & Panayotova, 2008). This group of ELL students is dominantly served by community colleges. In both four-year colleges and community colleges, identification of this group is made by self-identification or through placement tests or other similar measures. In the case of the California State University system, for example, all entering freshmen take the English Proficiency Test developed by Educational Testing Service (ETS). Issues related to identifying ELL students based on placement tests or other measures will be discussed in the placement exam section.

The second category can be classified broadly into two types: (a) those who developed first language literacy and (b) those who did not. Common to these two types is the fact that they speak a language other than English as their first language. In this they differ from the first category of ELL and resemble the third category of ELL. This category of ELL students can be found in both four-year colleges and community colleges.

The third category consists mostly of international students who are enrolling directly in U.S. colleges from their home countries. These students are typical ESL students and might need ESL classes for listening and speaking even though they are good at the major academic English skills—that is, reading and writing. Many colleges issue conditional admissions to international students who are qualified to enroll in terms of their academic ability, but have limited English proficiency. Placement of these students into ESL classes is typically determined by standardized test scores used for admission decisions or a separate placement test given by the institution. These students may also require accommodations for testing in academic classes.

There is another type of international ESL student which is being served in postsecondary institutions, mostly community colleges. These students come to the United States to learn English, and therefore enroll in ESL-only programs (non-academic). These students can return to their home country after a short period of ESL instruction, or try to enter postsecondary education in the United

States once they develop sufficient English proficiency to begin academic programs. This group of international ESL students is not included in the definition of ELL as used in this chapter. If these students enter into higher education for an academic degree, they will be covered by the discussion of the third category, i.e., international ESL students who are full-time or part-time college students.

In this chapter, ELL students refer to those who belong to any one of the three categories as defined above.

Issues Related to Testing English Language Learners

Issues related to testing ELL students can be classified broadly into two categories: (a) testing ELL students for academic subjects; and (b) testing ELL students for English proficiency (this includes identifying or classifying ELL students).

The major issue related to the first category is a concern about construct-irrelevant variance. Construct-irrelevant variance refers to error variance that arises from systematic error (Haladyna & Downing, 2004). Because test instruments might not be perfect measures for the constructs of knowledge and skills that are intended to be measured, observed test scores would contain certain "errors." When factors which are irrelevant to the construct being measured affect test results systematically in an individual or group specific way, errors included in observed test scores are defined as systematic errors. In relation to ELL students, unnecessary linguistic complexity of assessments, for example, can make ELL students attain "systematically" lower observed scores than their true ability or achievement. When construct-irrelevant factors affect test scores, as *Standards for Educational and Psychological Testing* (hereinafter *Standards*) states, ". . . test results may not reflect accurately the qualities and competencies intended to be measured" (American Educational Research Association, American Psychological Association, & National Council on Measurement in Education, 1999, p. 91). As *Standards* indicates, it is important to recognize the possible impact of language abilities and skills on test performance (p. 92). The potential effects of construct-irrelevant factors on test results call for the development of fair and valid subject area assessments for ELL students and careful interpretation and use of test results. In addition, to remove or minimize the effects of construct-irrelevant factors on test results in testing ELL students, appropriate testing accommodation should be provided.

Considering ELL status in testing and evaluation of subject-specific content knowledge and skills is very challenging in the development of a wide variety of large-scale standardized assessments, for example: college entrance exams such as SAT reasoning and subject tests or ACT subject tests; college placement tests such as COMPASS® by American College Testing (ACT); or collegiate achievement tests such as CAAP by ACT or MAPP tests by ETS;[3] as well as individual instructor-developed subject specific assessments.

Pitoniak et al. (2009) provide some useful guidelines for developing and administering subject assessments other than English proficiency which are "fair and valid" to ELL students. While detailed guidelines are not discussed in this chapter,[4] the most important consideration is that assessments for evaluating content-specific knowledge and skills should be developed to measure an individual's ability in the content area being assessed, while minimizing the potential impact of English proficiency on test results. Because it might not be possible to completely remove the impact of English proficiency on test scores in subject area assessments, it is important to provide ELL students with appropriate accommodations.

The primary goal of providing ELLs with testing accommodations is, according to Pitoniak et al. (2009), "to ensure that they have the same opportunity as students who have English as their first language to demonstrate their knowledge or skills in a content area" (p. 22). While accommodation policies for students with disabilities have been relatively well developed, there are not any uniform guidelines or policies at the federal level regarding the use of accommodations for ELL students (Pitoniak et al., 2009). The most important consideration in making a decision on accommodations is that they should not change the construct being assessed, which requires in turn a clear definition of the construct. For example, in NAEP, reading aloud is not permitted in the reading assessments because it will change an assessment of reading comprehension into an assessment of listening comprehension. This accommodation, however, can serve a valid accommodation for other academic subjects. In the case of NAEP, at grade 12 reading, the accommodations most commonly used are "extended time" and "small group" administration instead of large group administration.[5]

As Pitoniak et al. (2009) indicate, the choice of accommodations should allow ELL students to demonstrate their knowledge and skills to the greatest extent possible. As a way of ensuring this outcome, Pitoniak et al. recommend using the greatest degree of linguistic support accommodations—such as a glossary or bilingual dictionary.

The major issue related to the second category, "testing ELL students for English proficiency," is what "constitutes English language ability and performance," that is, the construct of English proficiency and the measurement of that construct. English proficiency has been used to refer to language abilities for those whose first language is not English, while verbal ability can be used to refer to English language abilities for all (Duran, 1989).[6]

While there is a quite bit of research on testing ELL students in a K–12 context since 2003 when the testing requirements of the NCLB 2002 began to take effect, there is not much research on testing ELL students in higher education. One major problem with testing ELL students for English proficiency is that the construct of English proficiency is multidimensional: reading, writing, speaking, and listening. While speaking and listening are more related to social language, reading and writing are more typically related to academic English. This fact raises additional challenges to the assessment and evaluation of ELL students' English proficiency.

Construct of English Proficiency: Theoretical Approach

In the United States, the earliest English proficiency testing for non-native English speakers was developed in the 1950s, and large-scale language testing began in 1961 with the launch of the Test of English as a Foreign Language (TOEFL). TOEFL was developed "as a standardized measure that could be used to determine if foreign student applicants possessed a suitable level of English proficiency that would allow them to pursue university-level academic work" (Chalhoub-Deville & Deville, 2006, p. 519). TOEFL still functions as a major screening tool for this purpose. According to ETS, the test developer, the TOEFL test measures the ability of nonnative speakers of English to communicate in English in the college or university classroom. Test scores are used in the admissions process at more than 8,000 academic institutions throughout the world (ETS, n.d.).

The construct of English proficiency needs to be examined from a broader perspective of a language proficiency construct because English (as a second or foreign language) proficiency tests have been developed from broad academic areas. "Theories and practices of second/foreign language learning, teaching, and testing have been influenced by dominant and popular paradigms from psychology, education, and linguistics" (Chalhoub-Deville & Deville, 2006, p. 522). According to Chalhoub-Deville and Deville (2006), the construct of language proficiency has evolved from a cognitive, psycholinguistic perspective to a social, interactional competence perspective.[7]

The cognitive, psycholinguistic perspective represented by Lado (1961) provided language tests with a way of formulating a construct. According to Chalhoub-Deville and Deville (2006, p. 523), for Lado, "language knowledge is essentially examined in terms of skills (reading, writing, listening, and speaking) and elements (e.g., grammatical structure, vocabulary, pronunciation, cultural understanding)." Since the early 1960s, several variations of this perspective developed, giving more attention to language use and performance (e.g., Oller, 1979; Canale & Swain, 1980; Canale, 1983).

More recently, the so called communicative language model (CLA) has been developed (Bachman & Palmer, 1996). This approach tries to model both language knowledge and language use. However, the CLA model is "essentially a psycholinguistic representation of language ability and performance" (Chalhoub-Deville & Deville, 2006, p. 524), trying to build "all-inclusive, generic models of ability". In contrast to this approach, some researchers have proposed "local theories of language proficiency" (Chalhoub-Deville, 2003; McNamara, 2003). This position emphasizes "ability-in-language-user-in-context". In other words, rather than pursuing the construct of language ability as generalizable (or applicable) beyond specific contexts, this position emphasizes notions of interaction and co-construction of communication among participants (Kramsch, 1986). According to this position, language ability and skills are local and jointly constructed by participants.

Therefore, as Chalhoub-Deville and Deville (2006) indicate, developing language tests which can be applicable to more general contexts will be challenging and may not be possible. This position, relatively new as a theory of language construct and still being developed, has yet to function as an overarching framework to guide language tests. While it may be difficult to develop any large-scale standardized language tests which aim at being generalizable to larger contexts based on this approach, developing specific, context-bound tests might be more feasible. For example, the English language ability needed to function as a good nurse might be different from that needed to function as a good computer engineer. The English proficiency needed to become a capable nurse can be developed based on clinical evidence and incorporated as a part of a nursing program requirement. In summary, a test can be used for a special purpose as far as it serves the goal supported by good validity evidence. The same test can be used for a different interpretation and use, but it needs a separate validity argument supported by validity documentation.

ELL Students and College Admissions

ELL students seeking admission to higher education, to a four-year college in particular, typically need to take college entrance exams such as the SAT or ACT. Are these exams fair to ELL/ESL students? Does the SAT or ACT provide any kind of validity evidence?

According to the College Board, about 11% of the 2010 college-bound seniors who took the SAT reported that they learned a language other than English as their first language. Among this category of students, those proficient in English are by definition not ELL students. The rest of this group are potential ELL students who could be affected in the college entrance exam and admission process because of their ELL status. This category will include many international students who come to study in U.S. colleges and universities after graduating from high school in their home country. The majority of them will be ELL students by definition. While it is not possible to estimate reliably the size of the ELL student population who take college entrance exams such as the SAT or ACT, based on available data, it is important to evaluate the validity of college entrance exams for this type of ELL student.

According to Kobrin, Patterson, Shaw, Mattern, & Barbuti (2008), the SAT has typically underpredicted ELL student performance in college, as measured by the first-year college grade point average. This finding was consistent with the results from the previous study by Ramist, Lewis, & McCamley-Jenkins (1994). Patterson, Mattern, & Kobrin (2009) confirmed these findings from the previous studies. These findings suggest that the SAT might be an unfair measure for college entrance decisions for ELL students. However, some studies (e.g., Pennock-Román, 1990) report that the prediction of the SAT is accurate for language minorities. Zwick (this volume) indicates that there is an inconsistency in the results across studies of SAT validity for language minorities. According to Zwick, this inconsistency might have resulted from the fact that language minority groups have been defined in varying ways. Similar findings might be expected for the ACT, but it was not possible to find any similar validity studies on the ACT. The ACT might have conducted those studies internally. But if the results are not publically available, there is no way to evaluate the validity of ACT as a measure of college success for ELL students. The ACT technical manual (p. 107) reports that "Validity evidence for using ACT test scores for predicting first-year college GPAs of different population groups was developed using data for ACT-tested first-year students from colleges that participated in the ACT Prediction Research Service for two consecutive years (1992–93 and 1993–94)."[8] ACT reports predictability validity evidence for racial groups and for students with disabilities (SD), but not for ELL students.

Neither the SAT nor ACT provides any accommodations in academic subject tests to ELL students, even though they do provide them for students with disabilities. Test developers such as ETS and ACT are responsible for documenting validity evidence that the impact of construct-irrelevant factors on ELL students' test scores does not invalidate the use of the test scores for admission decision purposes; or they need to provide a caution about the interpretation of test scores for ELL students. Higher education programs also need to consider the potential impact of construct-irrelevant effects on ELL students' test scores in non-English subject areas. This need is increasing especially because of the growing number of ELL students taking these tests—international students as well as U.S. high school seniors. According to the Institute of International Education, 690,923 international students received education in the United States in 2009/2010, more than in any previous year, and a 2.9% increase over the figure for 2008/2009.[9] About 300,000 of these students are undergraduate students seeking a degree. A majority of these undergraduate students are expected to take ELL/ESL classes. Currently, colleges take other measures than the SAT or ACT standardized college entrance exams into account in their college admission review process, mitigating the potential "unfairness" of these test scores for ELLs.

In addition to college entrance exams such as the SAT or ACT, groups 2 and 3 ELL students are typically required to take a separate English-language proficiency test. Three representative tests are the Test of English as a Foreign Language (TOEFL), the International English Language Testing System (IELTS), and the Michigan English Language Assessment Battery (MELAB). According to ETS, the developer of the test, TOEFL is the most widely used English-language test in the world. The TOEFL test measures listening, reading, speaking and writing skills as used in academic settings.[10] IELTS is also used around the world, recognized by more than 6,000 institutions in over 135 countries.[11] According to the IELTS website, over 3,000 institutions and programs in the USA accept IELTS scores as proof of English language skills.[12] IELTS tests all four language skills—listening, reading, writing and speaking. The speaking test is a face-to-face interview with a certified examiner. MELAB is another English-language proficiency test used for admission purposes. The MELAB consists of three parts: a composition; a listening test; and a written test which contains grammar, cloze,[13] vocabulary, and reading comprehension problems. An optional speaking test is also available. According to the website of the test developer, the University of Michigan English Language Center, many educational institutions in the United States, Canada, the United Kingdom, and other countries accept the MELAB as an alternative to the TOEFL.[14]

The principal function of these tests is, as Chalhoub-Deville and Deville (2006) adequately indicate, to provide information on whether or not "test takers have achieved a linguistic threshold that enables them to approach academic work in English in a meaningful manner" (p. 520). This suggests that there is no single threshold cut-point applicable to all institutions. As a specific example, while most four-year colleges require the minimum TOEFL score of 500 or 550, the University of Michigan requires a minimum TOEFL score of 570. When institutions set their own cut-scores or adopt a widely used test score such as 550 of TOEFL or equivalent scores in other tests, they are responsible for providing validity evidence to support the minimum scores they have established. This is especially important because establishing a rigorous standard without adequate grounds might deprive some ELL students of the opportunity for succeeding in their chosen academic career.[15] Another important point to be noted in relation to these English proficiency tests is that there is no expected positive correlation between English proficiency and academic ability in specific subject areas. In other words, these tests are not designed to assess ability of academic language in English for content learning. Developing academic language ability in English for content learning is a separate "educational" issue which might need more attention from higher education, but is not directly related to the issues of testing and evaluation of ELL students.

ELL Students and Placement Exams

There are two issues that need to be considered in relation to placement exams for ELL students: (a) the validation of the English proficiency test scores used to evaluate the level of English proficiency and educational needs of ELL students; and (b) the consideration of construct irrelevant provisions of accommodations for ELL students when taking placement exams in subjects other than English.

Placement Tests in Academic Subject Areas

Placement testing for entering freshman students to determine whether they are ready for college-level academic course work is common in 2-year and 4-year institutions[16]. Placement testing is typically given in mathematics and English. Many 2-year and 4-year colleges use standardized placement tests developed by professional testing institutions such as the College Board, ETS, and ACT. COMPASS is the computer-adaptive college placement test developed by ACT. Specific testing content areas are reading, writing skills, essay writing, mathematics, and ESL. According to their website, ACT provides not only reporting services such as individual and institution specific reports but also research services to help the institutions evaluate the effectiveness of their programs. The College Board's ACCUPLACER® is a set of computer-adaptive tests intended to provide test takers with useful information about their academic skills in math, English, and reading. All questions are multiple choice, except the essay. The test scores are expected to give useful information to academic advisors and counselors for determining student course selection. The College Board, however, does not provide information on how to interpret specific test scores. There is research documenting some validity evidence of the tests for placement purposes (Mattern & Packman, 2009). The California State University (CSU) system uses placement tests developed by ETS, the English Placement Test (EPT) and the Entry-Level Mathematics Test (ELM). CSU requires all entering freshmen to take these placement tests unless they demonstrate their proficiency in these subjects. The decision for exemption from taking a placement test is based on external measures such as SAT or ACT scores: e.g., a score of 500 or above on the critical reading section of the College Board SAT Reasoning Test exempts students from taking the EPT. Some universities/colleges, such as Michigan State University develop their own placement tests.[17]

The basic principle in considering ELL status in placement tests in academic subject areas and evaluation is that ELL students need to be provided with appropriate accommodations and that validity evidence for ELL students needs to be documented. While it is difficult to expect individual institutions to possess such capability, higher education institutions need to be aware of this issue and should try to make placement assessments as valid as possible for ELL students in order to maximize their academic learning opportunity.

Placement Tests for English Proficiency

In the K–12 education context,

> Assessment impacts ELL students' academic lives in many different ways. In the classroom, assessment of ELL students affects planning of their curriculum and instruction. In par-

ticular, ELP [English language proficiency] assessment plays a major part in the classification and grouping of ELL students. A student's level of English proficiency serves as the most important criterion for the classification that determines their level of proficiency in English and guides the prescription of any needed instruction and instructional materials. *(Abedi, 2008, p. 4)*

This is increasingly true at the postsecondary level as well, particularly for less selective institutions.

Postsecondary institutions have a variety of sources to consider in evaluating student proficiency in English. If incoming students are U.S. high school graduates, high school graduation exams can be used.[18] This approach, however, has comparability problems because the high school graduation exams of the 50 states are not comparable. However, they still can provide valuable data for screening purposes if the data are available. Even when a high school diploma is not required, as at many community colleges, students without diplomas should have some records on their ELL status and/or the level of English proficiency from their high schools, given that NCLB Title II requires states to assess ELL students' level of English language proficiency using reliable and valid measures (Abedi, 2008).

International students' English proficiency can be measured by tests like the TOEFL and IELTS assessments. Some universities, such as University of Michigan, encourage international students to take the SAT rather than ACT to demonstrate their English proficiency in addition to TOEFL or IELTS.

Placement of enrolled ELL students is a particular concern in California, which has the largest state-operated postsecondary education system in the United States and also has the nation's largest population of ELL students (Abedi, 2009). The CICAS survey of ESL students in California higher education draws on the experiences of a large, multi-tier postsecondary system consisting of California community colleges, California State University (CSU), and University of California (UC), (CICAS, 2006). The responses indicated a variety of approaches to the identification and placement of ELL students. Students could self-identify at the time of application, through the selection of a placement test, or through the selection of ELL-specific courses. The effectiveness of self-identification is limited, according to some respondents to the CICAS survey: students may feel that ESL status carries a stigma, or, if they are high school graduates, they may feel that, since they completed their ESL courses in high school and graduated, they can no longer be considered ESL students.

ELL students can also be identified by a placement test administered to all students. Community colleges responding to the CICAS survey frequently mentioned the use of the Combined English Language Skills Assessment (CELSA), approved by California for use as an ESL instrument, although some said that the test did not discriminate effectively in placing students in specific courses offered by the community college. At many community colleges, students can challenge the imposition of required ESL courses.

Within the California State University system, all entering freshmen take the English Proficiency Test developed by ETS. About a quarter of survey respondents said that an additional assessment was available for second language learners, which includes international students and immigrants. One college said that all freshmen composition courses had students write a diagnostic essay in the first class session. "Essays with possible ESL markers are evaluated by ESL specialists, and students are directed to other courses as appropriate" (CICAS, 2006, p. 28). Freshmen are exempted from taking the EPT if they meet any of the following criteria:

- a score of 500 or above on the critical reading section of the College Board SAT Reasoning Test;
- a score of 22 or above on the American College Testing (ACT) English Test;
- a score of 3 or above on either the Language and Composition, or Composition and Literature examination of the College Board Scholastic Advanced Placement Program;

- completion and transfer to CSU of the credits for a college course that satisfies the CSU General Education requirement in English Composition, provided such a course was completed with a grade of C or better; or
- a score of "Exempt" or "Ready for college-level English courses" on the CSU Early Assessment Program (EAP) taken along with the English Language Arts California Standard Test in grade 11.

At the University of California, all entering freshmen must take the UC Systemwide Analytical Writing Placement Exam (AWPE). Students can place out of the AWPE by meeting any of the following criteria: 30 or better on the ACT Combined English/Writing test; 680 or better on the College Board SAT Reasoning Test, Writing section; 3 or above on either Advanced Placement Examination in English; 5 or above on an International Baccalaureate High Level English Exam; 6 or above on an International Baccalaureate Standard Level English Exam.[19] Students with non-passing scores may be given an "E" designation for essays that exhibit "non-native English linguistic or rhetorical features contributing to the non-passing score" (CICAS, 2006, p. 24). Five of the eight UC campuses with ESL programs reported that ESL or writing program faculty re-read the examinations of these students to make placement decisions for the students, which may include either ESL or mainstream courses. This is a desirable practice to ensure the reliability of the scoring system.

Many higher education institutions operate independent ELL programs mainly targeted at ELL students, while other offer ELL programs, including remedial English classes, run by English departments rather than a separate ELL program. Initial decisions on placement in these classes usually depend on test scores on assessments recognized by the institution. There is not much research evidence documented for validity of these cut-scores. While it is an expensive procedure, it is important to collect data on the validity of such cut-scores and on the scoring system as well, especially when the scoring is subject to human subjectivity. In addition, it is recommended that the test-making companies conduct a joint study to establish a concordance table or function[20] across tests to determine if their tests can be used equivalently.

ELL Students and Tests in ELL Program/Classes

In California, UC and CSU students are generally placed in ESL writing courses with the implicit assumption that other aspects of English proficiency are exclusively the student's responsibility. Community colleges, in contrast, offer a wide variety of courses, in writing, reading, speaking, listening, and note-taking: courses that address a broad range of linguistic issues and skills needed for academic success (CICAS, 2006). Students initially placed in mainstream English composition courses may be directed to take ESL-specific programs, depending on their performance in class. This means that all three types of ELL students might be served through ESL programs, which were "originally" designed to serve ESL students. It is not clear, however, whether the effects of such programs are adequately evaluated.

According to CICAS (2006), about 60% of the California community colleges and California state university sites answering the survey, and 87.5% of the University of California sites, had some means of tracking the progress of students who were identified as ELL students, by whatever means, at least through their freshman year. The tracking methods were not consistent or complete, and the CICAS report concluded that "it is clear that data collection specifically about ESL learners [ELL students] is lacking" (p. 24).

In 2000, the California Community Colleges Chancellor's Office prepared a report, *California Pathways: The Second Language Student in Public High Schools, Colleges, and Universities*. In addition to providing an extensive review of existing practices for ELL/ESL students, the report also developed

"Second Language Writing Proficiency Descriptors," explaining the development of writing skills through four different levels, "Novice," "Intermediate," "Advanced," and "Distinguished." The report states that "The descriptors have yet to be anchored to language samples or compared to existing assessment instruments used in the four segments addressed in this document. Once this formal validation process has been completed, the descriptors will fill acute needs:

- They will provide ESL and English professionals a means by which to discuss the complete range of second language proficiency irrespective of segment, curriculum, or any other issue unrelated to language proficiency.
- The descriptors will also assist in the development and enhancement of articulated curricula. Ideally, courses supporting students' second language development will follow a smoother and more sensible transition from one segment to another.
- Intersegmental assessment instruments tied to an agreed-upon continuum of second language development will be created. Development of such instruments will assist in providing a standard for second language instruction throughout the state. *(p. v)*

However, at this writing it does not appear that the formal validation process has occurred. In any event, individual postsecondary sites in California are typically given a wide discretion in developing and implementing programs of instruction for their students. Crusan (2002) argues that colleges and universities use direct and indirect measures (or a combination of both) for assessing ESL students' writing skills without having much quantitative evidence to support their choice. It is important that higher education institutions try to prepare procedures to evaluate the validity of initial placement decisions and effectiveness of ELL programs.

ELL Students and Tests in Academic Classes

There is little research on testing and evaluating ELL students in regular academic classes in higher education. While most instructors are aware of the need to accommodate students with disabilities in instruction and evaluation, there is little if any corresponding procedure or awareness for ELL students. In approaching accommodations in testing ELL students, it is important to make sure that accommodations do not change the construct being assessed. Pitoniak et al. (2009) emphasize the importance of the choice of accommodations that will allow ELL students to demonstrate their knowledge and skills as fully as possible. While it is important to allow ELLs to receive the greatest degree of linguistic support accommodations—such as a glossary or bilingual dictionary—as Pitoniak et al. indicate, indirect linguistic accommodations such as extended time and small group administration are also important. These two types of accommodations are in fact the most commonly used in the NAEP Grade 12 assessments.[21]

The same principles discussed in the context of placement tests applies to assessing ELL students in academic subject areas using individual, instructor-developed assessment measures, including in-class exams and papers or reports as well as commercially available academic achievement tests such as the Collegiate Assessment of Academic Proficiency (CAAP), the Measure of Academic Proficiency and Progress (MAPP), and the Collegiate Learning Assessment (CLA). CAAP is the standardized, nationally normed assessment program from ACT that enables postsecondary institutions to assess, evaluate, and enhance student learning outcomes and general education program outcomes. MAPP, developed by ETS, is designed to assess general education student learning in two- and four-year colleges and universities in order to improve the quality of instruction and learning. CLA is a product of the Council for Aid to Education (CAE). While the Voluntary System of Accountability (VSA) initiative[22] approved three test instruments, CAAP, CLA, and MAPP, for measuring student learning outcomes (Klein et al., 2009), there is no separate investigation on validity of the tests for ELL students.

In general, it is difficult to standardize testing procedures in individual academic classes because it is instructors' "professional" responsibility to prepare valid processes for evaluating and testing their students. It is not possible to request instructors to conduct any validation studies demonstrating "construct equivalence among various language and cultural backgrounds" (see *Standards*, p. 93). It is important, however, to make instructors aware of the need to accommodate ELL students in testing and to take the language factor into account in interpreting test results and evaluating their students' knowledge and ability in a particular construct of interest.

Conclusion

While educational accountability is defined as "[making] all students reach proficiency in academic subjects" in K-12 education, higher education has been less subject to requirements of "educational accountability." Colleges and universities are responsible for educating students, but "failure or success" has been considered as a student's individual responsibility rather than as an educational system's responsibility. This means that achieving English proficiency to be successful in higher education might be more challenging for ELL students in higher education, compared to K-12 students. Part of the reason why research on ELL issues, including testing and evaluation, has not been focused on in higher education as compared to K-12 is the relatively large proportion of ELL students in K-12, especially in the early grades. The growing size and thus importance of ELLs in higher education requires higher education to pay more attention to this student group's educational needs and valid evaluation.

Recently, colleges and universities have increasingly been called upon to demonstrate their accountability.[23] Accountability in higher education began to be formulated around performance-based accountability in the late 1970s (Alexander, 2000). According to Alexander (2000), there is an increasing societal requirement that colleges and universities become more responsive to national economic needs and new governmental demands for increased performance. In response to these accountability requests for students' learning outcomes, many higher education institutions began to utilize standardized assessment programs such as CAAP, MAPP, or CLA. It is important that each testing program makes it clear what constructs the tests are targeted to measure and how the test scores can be interpreted, with appropriate validity documentation. Research on the potential impact of construct-irrelevant factors on ELL performance on the tests is a necessity. They also need to be clear about allowable accommodations for ELL students in non-English subject area assessments. When an institution tries to use a test for a purpose other than the testing program allows, it needs to document evidence of validity for the specific use and interpretation. It is possible for higher education institutions to collaborate with professional testing programs or institutions in developing valid score use and interpretations such as setting a cut-score for passing remedial English classes.

If an institution develops an English proficiency test for placement, it needs to conduct appropriate validation research and document validation evidence which supports the use of the test for the particular purpose and make the results publicly available. In the case of individual classes where instructors develop their own assessment instruments, it is difficult to expect instructors to conduct any type of validation study for their own classroom tests. Institutions, however, need to make sure that instructors recognize the importance of the validity of their assessment tools as well as their evaluation criteria for ELL students. The most important consideration relating to testing and evaluating ELL students in higher education is that each institution and instructor should make a clear definition of the construct they are trying to measure and minimize the role of construct-irrelevant factors in testing and other evaluation processes. Each institution needs to establish and implement ELL testing policies, including the evaluation of validity and reliability of such tests and accommodation policies, which will regularly evaluate the ELL program's effectiveness based on scientific research.

There might not be one correct theory of the English proficiency construct. English proficiency can be defined differently depending on what potential test takers are expected to know and be able to do. Learning and testing might need to be defined from the "local theories of language" perspective; that is, "specific English skills needed" and types of validation research for test and evaluation measures will vary.

Notes

1 According to NAEP results for grade 12 students in 2009, 81% of ELL students were below *Basic* in mathematics, compared to 36% of non-ELL students, and 78% of ELL students were below *Basic* in reading, compared to 25% of non-ELL students. Data were obtained from NAEP Data Explorer, http://nces.ed.gov/nationsreportcard/naepdata/

2 Similarly, the National Education Association uses ELL to refer to "a person who is in the process of acquiring the English language and whose first language is not English". Source: http://www.nea.org/home/32346.htm

3 CAAP stands for Collegiate Assessment of Academic Proficiency and MAPP stands for the Measure of Academic Proficiency and Progress.

4 Refer to the document for specific guidelines for the assessment of ELLs.

5 For more NAEP accommodation policy, see http://nces.ed.gov/nationsreportcard/about/inclusion.asp#rates

6 Duran (1989) distinguishes English proficiency for English language learners from verbal ability for native English speakers.

7 Discussion of the construct of English proficiency in this section heavily relies on Chalhoub-Deville and Deville (2006).

8 The technical manual can be downloaded in here http://www.act.org/aap/pdf/ACT_Technical_Manual.pdf

9 The document for these data can be downloaded from http://www.iie.org/en/Research-and-Publications/~/media/Files/Corporate/Open-Doors/Special-Reports/Fast%20Facts%202010.ashx

10 For more information of TOEFL, see http://www.ets.org/ell/products/assessments

11 From http://www.ielts.org/default.aspx

12 From http://www.ielts.org/ielts_in_the_usa.aspx

13 According to Wikipedia, A cloze test (also cloze deletion test) is "an exercise, test, or assessment consisting of a portion of text with certain words removed (cloze text), where the participant is asked to replace the missing words. Cloze tests require the ability to understand context and vocabulary in order to identify the correct words or type of words that belong in the deleted passages of a text. This exercise is commonly administered for the assessment of native and second language learning and instruction". Retrieved Jan 23, 2011 from http://en.wikipedia.org/wiki/Cloze_test

14 For more information, see http://www.lsa.umich.edu/eli/testing/melab

15 Some highly selective colleges such as Harvard, Yale, and Stanford do not require international applicants to submit any separate English proficiency test scores such as TOEFL other than regular required scores for all applicants.

16 For more detailed general discussions, see the Placement chapter in this Handbook.

17 Michigan State University uses its own developed mathematics placement tests. The validity of the test is currently unknown, even though there might be some validity evidence documented internally.

18 See http://www.cehd.umn.edu/NCEO/onlinepubs/archive/AssessmentSeries/MnReport13.html

19 For source, see http://www.ucop.edu/elwr/index.html

20 Concordance refers to a scaling approach which produces direct links between the scores on the two tests. Tests linked by concordances typically measure similar constructs but they are not intended to be interchangeable. A concordance table between SAT and ACT is a good example of this linking approach. The table can be located from here http://www.act.org/aap/concordance/. For more information on concordances, see Pommerich & Dorans (2004).

21 These data are based on the most recent assessments released. For more information, refer to http://nces.ed.gov/nationsreportcard/about/inclusion.asp#rates

22 The Voluntary System of Accountability (VSA) is an initiative by public 4-year universities to supply basic, comparable information on the undergraduate student experience to important constituencies through a common web report—the College Portrait. The VSA was developed in 2007 by a committed group of university leaders and is sponsored by two higher education associations—the Association of Public and

Land-grant Universities (APLU) and the American Association of State Colleges and Universities (AASCU). From http://www.voluntarysystem.org/index.cfm
23 For more discussion on this topic, see Banta and Pike (this volume).

References

Abedi, J. (2007). English language proficiency assessment and accountability under NCLB Title II: An overview. In J. Abedi (Ed.), *English language proficiency assessment in the nation: Current status and future practice* (pp. 3–12). (Report). Davis, CA: University of California. Retrieved May 7, 2010, from http://education.ucdavis.edu/research/elp_report.pdf

Abedi, J. (2008) Classification system for English language learners: Issues and recommendations. *Educational Measurement, Issues and Practice, 27*(3), 17–31. Retrieved August 28, 2010, from ProQuest Education Journals. Document ID: 1559992711

Abedi, J. (2009). Computer testing as a form of accommodation for English language learners. *Educational Assessment, 14*, 195–210.

Alexander, F. K. (2000). The changing face of accountability: Monitoring and assessing institutional performance in higher education. *The Journal of Higher Education, 71*(4), 411–431. Stable URL: http://www.jstor.org/stable/2649146

American Educational Research Association, American Psychological Association, & National Council on Measurement in Education (1999). *Standards for educational and psychological testing.* Washington, DC: American Educational Research Association.

Bachman, L. F., & Palmer, A.S. (1996). *Language testing in practice.* Oxford, UK: Oxford University Press.

Banta, T. W., & Pike, G. R. (this volume). *The bottom line: Will faculty USE assessment findings?*

Bunch, G. C., & Panayotova, D. (2008). Latinos, language minority students, and the construction of ESL: Language testing and placement from high school to community college. *Journal of Hispanic Higher Education, 7*(6), 6–30.

California Community Colleges Chancellor's Office. (2000). *California pathways: The second language student in public high schools, colleges, and universities.* Sacramento, CA: Author. http://www2.bakersfieldcollege.edu/jfulks/basicSkills%20course_coding/pathways.pdf (Accessed 11/19/2010 11:35.)

California Intersegmental Committee of Academic Senates, ESL Task force. (2006). *ESL students in California public higher education.* Sacramento, CA: Author. http://www.academicsenate.cc.ca.us/icas.html (Accessed: 11/19/2010 11:15.)

Canale, M. (1983). On some dimensions of language proficiency. In J. W. Oller, Jr. (Ed.), *Issues in language testing research* (pp. 333–342). Rawley, MA: Newbury House.

Canale, M., & Swain, M. (1980). Theoretical bases of communicative approaches to second language teaching and testing. *Applied Linguistics, 1*(1), 1–47.

Chalhoub-Deville, M. (2003). Second language interaction: Current perspectives and future trends. *Language Testing, 20*, 369–383.

Chalhoub-Deville, M., & Deville, C. (2006). Old, borrowed, and new thoughts in second language testing. In R. L. Brennan (Ed.), *Educational Measurement* (4th ed., pp. 517–30). Westport, CT: American Council on Education and Praeger Publishers.

Crusan, D. (2002). An assessment of ESL writing placement assessment. *Assessing Writing, 8*, 17–30.

Duran, R. (1989). Testing of linguistic minorities. In R. L. Linn (Ed.), *Educational measurement* (3rd ed., pp. 573–587). New York, NY: American Council on Education and Macmillan.

Educational Testing Service. (n.d.). [TOEFL Home Page]. Retrieved from http://www.ets.org/toefl/

Haladyna, T. M., & Downing, S. M. (2004). Construct-irrelevant variance in high-stakes testing. *Educational Measurement: Issues and Practice, 23*(1), 17–27.

Hector-Madison, A., & Bardack, S. (2010) *English language learners: Annotated bibliography.* Downloaded July 2010 from http://www.air.org/files/ELL_Annotated_Bibliography.pdf

Huisman, J., & Currie, J. (2004). Accountability in higher education: Bridge over troubled water? *Higher Education, 48*(4), 529–551. Stable URL: http://www.jstor.org/stable/4151570 (Accessed: 21/09/2010 09:22.)

Klein, S., Liu, O.U., Sconing, J., Bolus, R., Bridgeman, B., Kugelmass, H., . . . Steedle, J.(2009). Test validity study (TVS) report. Retrieved from http://www.voluntarysystem.org/docs/reports/TVSReport_Final.pdf

Kobrin, J. L., Patterson, B. F., Shaw, E. J., Mattern, K. D., & Barbuti, S. M. (2008). *Validity of SAT for predicting first year college grade point average* (Research Report No. 2008-5). New York, NY: College Board.

Kramsch, C. (1986). From language proficiency to interactional competence. *The Modern Language Journal, 70*, 366–372.

Lado, R. L. (1961). *Language testing: The construction and use of foreign language tests—A teacher's book*. New York, NY: McGraw-Hill.

Mattern, K. D., & Packman, S. (2009). *Predictive validity of ACCUPLACER® scores for course placement: A meta-analysis* (College Board Research Report No. 2009-2). New York, NY: College Board.

McNamara, T. (2003). Looking back, looking forward: Rethinking Bachman. *Language Testing, 20,* 466–473.

Oller, J. W., Jr. (1979). *Language tests at school: A pragmatic approach*. London, UK: Longman.

Patterson, B. F., Mattern, K. D., & Kobrin, J. L. (2009). *Validity of the SAT for predicting FYGPA: 2007 SAT validity sample* (Statistical Report). New York, NY: College Board.

Pennock-Román, M. (1990). *Test validity and language background: A study of Hispanic American students at six universities*. New York, NY: College Entrance Examination Board.

Pitoniak, M. J., Young, J. W., Martiniello, M., King, T. C., Buteux, A., & Ginsburgh, M. (2009). *Guidelines for the assessment of English Language Learners*. Princeton, NJ: Educational Testing Service. Retrieved from http://www.ets.org/Media/About_ETS/pdf/ELL_Guidelines.pdf

Planty, M., Hussar, W., Snyder, T., Kena, G., KewalRamani, A., Kemp, J., . . . Dinkes, R. (2009). *The Condition of Education 2009* (NCES 2009-081). Washington, DC: National Center for Education Statistics, Institute of Education Sciences, U.S. Department of Education.

Pommerich, M., & Dorans, N. J. (Eds.). (2004). Concordance [Special issue]. *Applied Psychological Measurement, 28*(4).

Ramist, L., Lewis, C., & McCamley-Jenkins, L. (1994). *Student group differences in predicting college grades: Sex, language, and ethnic groups* (College Board Report 93-1). New York, NY: College Entrance Examination Board.

Zamora, P. (2009). Minorities in special education: A briefing before the United States Commission on Civil Rights held in Washington, DC, December 3, 2007. *Minorities in special education* (pp. 93–96). Washington, DC: U.S. Commission on Civil Rights.

Zwick, R. (this volume). *Admissions testing in higher education*.

38

EVALUATION OF TEACHER QUALITY

Stephanie L. Knight

Teacher quality is a concept that has dominated discussions of educational policy and practice since publication of *A Nation at Risk: The Imperative for Educational Reform* in 1983 (http://www2. ed.gov/pubs/NatAtRisk/index.html). The National Center for Accreditation in Teacher Education (NCATE) cites weaknesses in all areas of the teacher quality system—preparation, entry, and professional development (Cibulka, 2009). Despite this intensive focus, little agreement exists among educators or researchers about what constitutes teacher quality and how it should be operationalized and measured. Since evaluation of teacher quality impacts educational decision-making in a number of important areas including compliance with state and national initiatives, teacher recruitment and incentives for performance, and choices about distribution of teachers and resources within our educational system, the discussion of the definition, measurement, and impact of teacher quality is important. While the emphasis to date has been primarily on K-12 classrooms, there is some indication that this focus also could be extended to higher education (Clawson, 2009; Wood & DesJarlais, 2006). For example, a consortium of 19 states currently is participating in the development and testing of a common performance-based assessment for teacher candidates (Sawchuk, 2010) that could ultimately be used to determine the quality of teacher preparation programs and faculty in higher education institutions.

Background

Historically, discussions of teacher quality were embedded in debates over the relative impacts of school versus home, and student characteristics on student outcomes. Despite studies in the 1960s highlighting the impact of socioeconomic and other home and societal factors on students, the Coleman Report ultimately established school as an import influence on student outcomes (Coleman et al., 1966) and suggested the methodology to be used in numerous, subsequent studies of this type. Reports in the 1980s and 1990s called for setting higher standards for students at all levels, which ultimately involved consideration of the classrooms in which they were taught (Wenglinsky, 2000).

More recently, interest has shifted to the teacher as the most important factor in student performance, probably as a confluence of a number of events. First, we know that teachers make a difference in student outcomes. The Tennessee study (Sanders & Horn, 1998), a landmark longitudinal study involving random assignment of teachers and students to classrooms of different sizes and staffing composition, firmly established the advantages of having a high quality teacher over a period of years and, more poignantly, the disadvantages throughout and beyond the school years that persisted for students of similar ability and background who had a poor teacher for several consecutive years. Second, after many years of addressing seemingly intractable socioeconomic factors related to poor student performance, teacher quality appeared to be manipulable. Not only do teachers make a difference, but their effectiveness can potentially be assessed, rewarded and improved—either through recruitment, incentives for performance and retention, professional development, or a combination of these approaches. Since the Tennessee study also suggested that low SES and minority students benefitted more from high quality teachers, providing high quality teachers for all students, particularly those in settings that placed them at risk of academic failure, constituted a viable approach for closing student achievement gaps between poor and minority students and their more advantaged counterparts. The third event that served to institutionalize the focus on teacher quality was passage of the *No Child Left Behind* (NCLB) legislation which used empirical data to advocate for this teacher-centered approach (Cohen-Vogel & Hunt, 2007). NCLB requirements focus on the provision of highly qualified teachers in all K-12 core subjects, particularly in settings with high numbers of poor and minority students, and specify the type of entry qualifications needed for teachers to be considered "highly qualified" (Haskins & Loeb, 2007). Following the lead of NCLB, one of the four major areas of *Race to the Top* also focuses on teacher quality and equitable distribution of teachers among poor and minority settings (http://www2.ed.gov/programs/racetothetop/index.html) and provides opportunities for funding to implement the focus, including linking teacher pay to student performance. The requirements for teacher quality in *Race to the Top* are very similar to those of NCLB (Newton, Darling-Hammond, Haertel, & Thomas, 2010).

Definitions of Teacher Quality

While the mechanisms that produced teacher effects on student achievement in the Tennessee study are not well understood, the implication is that variations in teacher quality make a difference. But what constitutes teacher quality? Two areas typically have been considered by researchers and policymakers as candidates for describing teacher quality: (a) teacher inputs including teacher characteristics, professional preparation, and licensure and (b) classroom effectiveness, frequently measured in terms of student performance on standardized tests (Heck, 2007). According to NCLB, highly qualified teachers are those that have a bachelor's degree, full state licensure, and proof from either a test or major or minor in a field that they have knowledge of the content they will teach. Veteran teachers can demonstrate quality in a number of ways linked to experience and professional development as described in the provisions under HOUSSE (High, Objective, Uniform State Standard of Evaluation) (http://www2.ed.gov/nclb/methods/teachers/hqtflexibility.html). However, an important distinction not considered under NCLB can be made between "highly qualified" and high quality teachers since teachers may have similar qualifications but may not be similarly effective in the classroom. Can we determine teacher quality outside of measures of classroom processes and student performance? *Race to the Top* adds the connection to student performance not explicitly mandated by NCLB (http://www2.ed.gov/programs/racetothetop/index.html). However, both NCLB and *Race to the Top* initiatives provide narrow definitions of quality and obscure the role that institutional and organizational factors play in teacher and student performance (Little & Bartlett, 2010).

Differences in definitions of teacher quality appear to be related to differences in perspectives on the purposes of education. Little and Bartlett (2010) characterize the dominant approach to teacher quality taken by NCLB as a result of a human capital or social efficiency view of education related to global competition of our workforce—in other words, we need to prepare and sort students for vocational purposes and ensure U.S. success in world labor and economic markets. From that perspective, differentiation of teacher quality based on intellectual ability and content knowledge and students' subsequent performance in areas valued by labor markets makes sense (see e.g., Hanushek, 2009). However, the set of skills required of teachers would necessarily be different for different purposes. For example, educators interested in preparing students for a democratic society would define high quality teachers according to their dispositions toward democratic ideals and their ability to foster student dispositions and behaviors related to civic engagement. A discussion of different aims of education and their relation to definitions of teacher quality is beyond the scope of this chapter, particularly since they involve differences in value judgments not easily resolved, but these differences are often the basis of disagreement between educators and policymakers seeking to improve education.

Even when educators and policymakers have similar views on the broad aims of education, differences in what constitutes teacher quality exist. Cohen-Vogel and Hunt (2007) distinguish current views of teacher quality from the perspectives of "professionalists" versus "deregulationists" (p. 137). Professionalists advocate acquisition of a set of professional standards as a prerequisite for quality while the opposing group advocates deregulation of certification requirements as the antidote to poor quality. Instead, deregulationists champion alternate pathways to attract high quality teachers with high intelligence and subject content knowledge. Professionalists define high quality in relation to certification while deregulationists focus on intellectual ability and subject matter knowledge. While NCLB appears to combine the two definitions in its requirements, analysis of documents and rhetoric associated with implementation of the requirements appears to favor the deregulationist perspective (Cohen-Vogel and Hunt, 2007).

Professionalist and deregulationist perspectives are similar in that they both take a view of quality that depends on teacher characteristics or inputs. Teacher inputs have been defined conceptually and operationally as general ability measured by intelligence tests or achievement tests such as the SAT or ACT (see Zwick, this volume, for more on admissions testing); content and/or pedagogical knowledge measured by major or minor degree, licensure tests, certification type and status, degree type and level; and years of experience. As reviewed in the section on findings, their relationship to student achievement is mixed. Furthermore, teacher characteristics or inputs provide a very narrow view of teacher quality.

Given the complexity of the concept of teacher quality, teacher qualities, rather than teacher quality, may be the more appropriate focus (Kennedy, 2008). While educators interested in recruitment or distribution of highly qualified teachers across student populations focus on licensure tests, credentials, and experience, others are interested in teaching practices, ability to increase student achievement, and teacher beliefs and dispositions (Kennedy, 2008). According to Kennedy, these interests fall into three categories: personal resources that teachers bring with them, classroom performance, and effectiveness or impact on students. Berliner (2005) expands the discussion when he makes the distinction between good teaching, teaching that exhibits the standards of the profession, and effective teaching which refers to reaching student achievement goals. Both are needed in a high quality teacher and encompass the three categories highlighted by Kennedy. However, districts do not typically keep or share the kind of data needed to determine effective classroom practice and the performance assessments needed to assess "good" teaching are difficult to construct and expensive to administer. Nevertheless, the studies described in the section on findings that describe National Board certification in relation to student achievement provide a proxy for assessment of individual teacher's implementation of standards of good teaching within the classroom context.

The distinction in various definitions of teacher quality is not just an academic exercise since some definitions result in unequal distributions of high quality teachers, particularly in high poverty and minority schools (Choi, 2010). A comparison of three definitions of teacher quality in elementary schools in Los Angeles—fully accredited teachers, teachers meeting NCLB requirements, and a composite variable called Teacher Quality (the first two levels plus 5 years experience and 42 units beyond the bachelor's degree)—revealed that schools within the same district with higher percentages of low SES and Hispanic and Black students had less highly qualified teachers. However, using minimal definitions of quality revealed no differences in the distribution and masked the uneven distribution (Choi, 2010). Given that high teacher quality can offset socioeconomic disadvantages in student achievement to some extent (Hanushek & Rivkin, 2006), this finding is troubling.

The issue of equitable distribution of highly qualified teachers is addressed in both the NCLB and *Race to the Top* initiatives which urge states to remedy the inequities that lead to a teacher quality gap. Students who are most at risk of academic failure due to socioeconomically disadvantaged backgrounds are most likely to be taught by the least qualified and least experienced teachers (Lankford, Loeb, and Wyckoff, 2002). Investigation of patterns in different states reveals that inexperienced teachers are twice as likely to be assigned to high poverty and minority schools (Peske & Haycock, 2006). In addition, teachers in high poverty and minority schools are more likely to have failed the licensure test of basic skills at least once and are more likely to be teaching a subject outside of their field (Peske & Haycock, 2006). A study of National Board Certified teachers in North Carolina revealed that the NBCT teachers, a designation that conveys high quality, are more likely to be in advantaged settings at all levels—district, school, and classroom—than in settings where poor and minority students are placed (Goldhaber, Choi, & Cramer, 2007).

An issue that impacts definitions of teacher quality emerges when we look across contexts and conditions to examine the construct. Is a teacher who is classified as highly qualified in general equally effective across different levels and types of classes and students? In a study of mathematics and language arts teachers in the San Francisco area, evidence suggests that teacher quality is related to students' race/ethnicity, SES, mathematics ability, and language status, and that teacher quality varies across courses, years, and to a lesser degree, the type of statistical model employed (Newton et al., 2010). The context-specificity of teacher quality may be a factor in the mixed findings outlined in subsequent sections, particularly for variables like experience and education level which may be temporally and contextually sensitive (Heck, 2007).

Research on Teacher Quality

Two types of studies traditionally have been conducted to study the impact of teacher quality: (a) studies that investigate variation in teacher effects by measuring differences between classes in residualized achievement gains after controlling for background characteristics (see e.g, Sanders & Rivers, 1996; Wright, Horn, & Sanders, 1997), and (b) regression studies that determine the relationship between specific teacher characteristics and student achievement after controlling for background characteristics (see e.g., Coleman et al., 1966; Monk, 1994). The first set of studies determined that teachers differ in effectiveness and that these differences are related to student achievement (Phillips, 2010). However, since there is little information about specific qualities comprising effectiveness in these studies, they have been of limited use to policymakers (Darling-Hammond, 2000).

The second type of study, usually referred to as production function studies, provide more information about specific characteristics such as preparation or certification related to student achievement. However, the findings have been inconsistent (Wayne & Youngs, 2003). Current and past factors affecting achievement that are omitted from the equations, often because data are not available or are not measured adequately, can impact findings (Hanushek & Rivkin, 2004). In addition to contributing to mixed findings, these potential biases affect interpretation of the causal directions of the findings (Heck, 2007). Do higher-quality teachers result in higher-performing students or are higher-quality teachers attracted to schools characterized by higher-performing students? Some evidence exists that teachers prefer settings with relatively few low SES and minority students and will select these workplaces when provided the opportunity (Little & Bartlett, 2010).

More recently, studies that use value-added modeling depending on measurement of gain scores pre and post rather than at the end of the year have been used to counter problems associated with previous production function approaches (Hanushek & Rivkin, 2006; Phillips, 2010). However, since most of these studies also obtain their data from surveys and administrative records, they suffer from similar problems due to the limited kinds of teacher characteristics that can be included, the limitations of achievement tests, non-random assignment of students and teachers to schools and classes, and confounding of multiple influences on student achievement (Hanushek & Rivkin, 2006; Newton et al., 2010). Researchers disagree about which value-added models are most appropriate and express concerns about ceiling effects that might occur when minimum competency or proficiency tests are used as the measure of student achievement (Koedel & Betts, 2009). Educators have concerns that teachers of English Language Learners (ELLs) and special education students, for whom standardized tests present a challenge due to language or level of assessment, will be unfairly disadvantaged by the value-added approach to evaluation of teacher quality.[1]

Given the problems associated with the methods used to determine the relationship between teacher quality characteristics and student achievement, it is not surprising that the findings are inconsistent, contradictory, and often controversial in interpretation (Wayne & Youngs, 2003). Advocates of professionalization or deregulation can find support or opposition depending on the set of studies they choose to review. While many studies found links between teacher inputs and student outputs, many others did not (Wenglinsky, 2000). Teacher experience (Hanushek, 1997, 2003; Rivkin, Hanushek, & Cain, 2005), scores on licensing exams, and combinations of teacher qualities (Darling-Hammond, 2000) emerge as positive correlates in a number of studies, but not in others. Teacher experience is stronger for novice teachers, with gains occurring particularly after the first year of teaching (Hanushek & Rivkin, 2006). Knowledge of teaching and learning and type of certification typically exhibit mixed outcomes (Darling-Hammond, 2000), although using survey data from the Schools and Staffing Survey (SASS) and the National Assessment of Educational Progress (NAEP), Darling-Hammond (2000) found that measures of teacher certification and preparation were the strongest correlates of student achievement in reading and math after controlling for poverty and language status. While several studies have attempted to examine differences between traditional certification and alternate pathways, the inability to adequately define and differentiate these two approaches has resulted in mixed findings (Wilson, Floden, & Ferrini-Mundy, 2002; Zumwalt & Craig, 2005). Subject matter knowledge, measured by degrees, coursework, and tests, emerges more positive for math and for secondary students (Bolyard & Moyer-Packenham, 2008; Phillips, 2010), but also exhibits inconsistencies across studies. Generally, however, students of teachers who are teaching math out-of-field score lower on standardized tests than their counterparts in classes where teachers are qualified to teach mathematics (Goldhaber & Brewer, 2000). Neither master's degrees nor salaries exhibit many positive relationships to student outcomes (Hanushek & Rivkin, 2004; Wenglinsky, 2000), despite the fact that many districts tie salary schedules to attainment of advanced degrees.

Since teacher characteristics have not been particularly helpful in determining the relationship between teacher quality and student achievement, some researchers have focused attention on classroom factors as possible determinants of differential student achievement (Wenglinsky, 2000). Wenglinsky (2000) investigated a combination of teacher inputs, classroom practices, and professional development using the NAEP results for math and science. Results indicated that having a major or minor in math or science, professional development in specific topics in math and science, hands-on learning and point-in-time tests for math and science, and emphasis on higher order skills in math, all were related to student performance.

Other researchers have investigated the relationship between National Board teacher certification, which serves as a proxy for high quality classroom practice, and student achievement (Cavaluzzo, 2004; Goldhaber, Perry, & Anthony, 2004). Cavaluzzo (2004) found that teacher certification in math, teaching in field, and National Board certification were the three strongest correlates of achievement for secondary math students in Miami. However, some evidence suggests that National Board certification impact may differ by subgroup and grade level (Goldhaber et al., 2004). In a study in North Carolina, a state with a large number of board-certified teachers, more impact emerged for third grade reading and math and for minority and high poverty students (Goldhaber et al., 2004).

More recent studies have also investigated expanded definitions of teacher quality. While most research has focused on individual teacher quality at the classroom level, the concept of collective teacher quality may be useful in explaining differences in student achievement by schools. Heck (2007) characterized collective teacher quality as the percent of fully certified teachers who passed content knowledge tests and met state professional standards. While a minimal definition of teacher quality was used, findings indicated positive impact on student achievement in reading and math. In addition, certain subgroups benefitted more from collective teacher quality than their peers—collective teacher quality acted as a mediator of SES and ethnicity variables (Heck, 2007).

Typically, studies of teacher quality have ignored the institutional and organizational influences that impact both teacher performance and student achievement (Little & Bartlett, 2010). Expanding the notion of teacher quality as both an individual and collective characteristic, Bryk and his colleagues conducted a longitudinal, mixed methods study of approximately 200 schools in Chicago that focused on teacher quality within the organizational culture of the school (Bryk, Sebring, Allensworth, Luppescu, & Easton, 2010). They characterized teacher quality as professional capacity consisting of the quality of staff, professional development opportunities, work orientation, and professional community. Professional capacity consistently predicted changes in student achievement. Although few examples exist, more complex definitions of teacher quality, which include individual, collective, and organizational or institutional variables, hold promise for improvement of the evaluation of teacher quality.

Improving Teacher Quality

The 1983 report from the National Commission on Excellence in Education, *A Nation at Risk*, focused educators on the role of the teacher in the poor performance of our nation's schools. The reasoning since that time has been that since our students are not performing well, particularly in international comparisons, teacher quality must be an issue. If we can raise the quality of our teachers, then we can raise the quality of student performance. An examination of the teacher workforce using the *Teacher Follow Up Study* (TFS) for 2000–2001 and the *Schools and Staffing Survey* (SASS) for 2000 provides a picture of the workforce at the millennium (http://nces.ed.gov/programs/coe/2005/analysis/index.asp). Of almost three and a half million teachers, 75% were female, with the percentage of males higher at the secondary level but still below that of females. The workforce was highly educated, with only about 1% with less than a bachelor's degree. However, approximately 12% of teachers were teaching in areas outside their field, and the percentage was highest for mathematics. Turnover was approximately 16%, a larger turnover rate than in previous reports of teacher demographics. About 17% of the teacher workforce, a large enough percentage to change the nature of the existing group, were new hires. Overall, the new hires were more likely to be young and teach out of field and less likely to have both a major and certification in the field in which they were teaching. Given the demographics of the workforce, the NCLB requirements for highly qualified teachers were predictable. However, with the possible exception of out-of-field teaching, few of the NCLB target characteristics were related to student performance and unlikely to consistently improve students' scores on state, national, or international assessments.

Another approach to improving teacher quality involves attempts to attract teachers who have high intellectual ability. The popular refrain has been any of a number of variations of: "Many of the best and the brightest are less likely to enter teaching compared to other fields" (Glazerman, Goldhaber, Loeb, Staiger, & Whitehurst, 2010, p. 1). In general, those who aspire to teaching do not score as high on aptitude and achievement tests as those in other fields (Gitomer, 2007), and standardized test scores of teachers have fallen over time (Hanushek & Rivkin, 2006). Teacher salaries, relative to other professions requiring similar education levels, also fell during the 1940–2000 time period—a pattern that many see as related (Angrist & Guryan, 2008; Hanushek & Rivkin, 2006). However,

Gitomer (2007) notes that the academic ability of Praxis II takers (as measured by GPA and SAT scores) increased between the 1994–1997 and 2002–2005 periods, but with African Americans, Hispanics, elementary education, special education and physical education majors still displaying weaker academic profiles. While teacher IQ has not been a consistent predictor of student performance (Darling-Hammond, 2000), the trend of lower ability and lower salaries has implications for recruitment and retention of "the best and the brightest" math and science teachers and teachers of color who are likely to accept positions in other sectors due to salaries (Hanushek & Rivkin, 2006). The use of market incentives in *Race to the Top*, such as linking teacher pay to student performance, provides one approach to countering the ability-salary trend. Districts in some states have already implemented increased teacher pay for improvement in student test scores (Podgursky & Springer, 2007).

Summary

Teacher quality has been the focus of intense national debate for over two decades. Despite this emphasis, educators and policymakers often disagree over the definition of teacher quality, how it should be evaluated, and how it should be interpreted and used. Federal initiatives such as NCLB and *Rise to the Top* have driven the definitions of teacher quality over the past 10 years and influenced the educational research agenda. However, research has not provided much support for the impact of variables related to these definitions in relation to student achievement, particularly when the measures involve teacher input variables and student standardized tests. More complex definitions of teacher qualities which include the nature of the organizational or institutional context, combined with more sensitive and multiple measures of both teacher qualities and student performance are needed.

Notes

1 See Kim, Hart, Abedi, & Vanneman (this volume) for a discussion of testing and evaluation of English-language learners in higher education; see also Banerjee & Thurlow (this volume) for a discussion of accommodations for students with disabilities.

References

Angrist, J., & Guryan, J. (2008). Does teacher testing raise teacher quality? Evidence from state certification requirements. *Economics of Education Review, 27*, 483–502.

Banerjee, M., & Thurlow, M. L. (this volume). *Using data to find common ground between secondary and postsecondary accommodations for students with disabilities.*

Berliner, D. C. (2005). The near impossibility of testing for teacher quality. *Journal of Teacher Education, 56*(3), 205–213.

Bolyard, J., & Moyer-Packenham, P. A review of the literature on math and science teacher quality. *Peabody Journal of Education, 83*(4), 509–535.

Bryk, A. S., Sebring, P. B., Allensworth, E., Luppescu, S., & Easton, J. Q. (2010). *Organizing schools for improvement*. Chicago. IL: University of Chicago Press.

Cavaluzzo, L. (2004). *Is National Board Certification an effective signal of teacher quality?* Alexandria, VA: CNA Corporation.

Choi, D. (2010). The impact of competing definitions of quality on the geographical distribution of teachers. *Education Policy, 24*, 359–397.

Cibulka, J. (2009). The redesign of accreditation to inform the simultaneous transformation of educator preparation and P-12 schools. *Quality Teaching, 18*(2), 1–4.

Clawson, D. (2009). Tenure and the future of the university. *Science, 324*(5931), 1147–1148.

Cohen-Vogel, L., & Hunt, H. (2007). Governing quality in teacher education: Deconstructing federal text and talk. *American Journal of Education, 114*, 137–163.

Coleman, J. S., Campbell, E. Q., Hobson, C. J., McPartland, J., Mood, A. M., Weinfeld, F. D., York, R. L. (1966). *Equality of educational opportunity*. Washington, DC: U.S. Government Printing Office.

Darling-Hammond, L. (2000). Teacher quality and student achievement: A review of state policy evidence. *Education Policy Analysis Archives, 8*(1), 1–44.

Gitomer, D. (2007). *Teacher quality in a changing policy landscape: Improvements in the teacher pool.* Princeton, NJ: Educational Testing Service.

Glazerman, S., Goldhaber, D., Loeb, S., Staiger, D., & Whitehurst, G. (2010). *America's Teacher Corps.* Washington, DC: Brookings Institution.

Goldhaber, D., & Brewer, D. (2000). Does teacher certification matter? High school certification status and student achievement. *Educational Evaluation and Policy Analysis, 22*(2), 129–145.

Goldhaber, D., Choi, H.-J., & Cramer, L. (2007). A descriptive analysis of the distribution of NBPTS-certified teachers in North Carolina. *Economics of Education Review, 26,* 160–172.

Goldhaber, D., Perry, D., & Anthony, E. (2004). National Board Certification : *Who applies and what factors are associated with success?* Washington, DC: The Urban Institute.

Hanushek, E. (1997). Assessing the effects of school resources on student performance: An update. *Educational Evaluation and Policy Analysis, 19*(2), 141–164.

Hanushek, E. (2003). The failure of input-based schooling policies. *Economic Journal, 113*(485), 64–98.

Hanushek, E. (2009). School policy: Implications of recent research for human capital investments in South Asia and other developing countries. *Education Economics, 17*(3), 291–313.

Hanushek, E., & Rivkin, S. (2004). *How to improve the supply of high quality teachers.* Washington, DC: Brookings Institution.

Hanushek, E., & Rivkin, S. (2006). Teacher quality. In E. Hanushek, & F. Welch (Eds.), *Handbook of the economics of education* (Vol. 2, pp. 1051–1078). Amsterdam, The Netherlands: North-Holland.

Haskins, R., & Loeb, S. (2007) A plan to improve the quality of teaching. *The Education Digest, 73*(1), 51–56.

Heck, R. (2007). Examining the relationship between teacher quality as an organizational property of schools and students' achievement and growth rates. *Educational Administration Quarterly, 43*(4), 399–432.

Kennedy, M. (2008). Sorting out teacher quality. *Phi Delta Kappan, 90*(1), 59–63.

Kim, Y. Y., Hart, J., Abedi, J., & Vanneman, A. (this volume). *Testing and evaluation of English-language learners in higher education.*

Koedel, C., & Betts, J. (2009). Value added to what? How a ceiling in the instrument influences value-added estimation. *Education Finance and Policy, 5*(1), 54–81.

Lankford, H., Loeb S., & Wyckoff, J. (2002). Teacher sorting and the plight of urban schools: A descriptive analysis. *Educational Evaluation and Policy Analysis, 24*(1), 37–62.

Little, J., & Bartlett, L. (2010). The teacher workforce and the problem of educational equity. *Review of Research in Education, 34,* 285–328.

Monk, D. H. (1994). Subject matter preparation of secondary mathematics and science teachers and student achievement. *Economics of Education Review, 13*(2), 125–145.

Newton, X., Darling-Hammond, L., Haertel, E., & Thomas, E. (2010). Value-added modeling of teacher effectiveness: An exploration of stability across models and contexts. *Educational Policy Analysis Archives, 18*(23). Retrieved from http://epaa.asu.edu/ojs/article/view/810

Peske, H., & Haycock, K. (2006). *Teaching inequality: How poor and minority students are shortchanged on teacher quality.* Washington, DC: Education Trust.

Philips, K. (2010). What does "Highly Qualified" mean for student achievement? Evaluating the relationships between teacher quality indicators and at-risk students' mathematics and reading achievement gains in first grade. *Elementary School Journal, 110*(4), 464–493.

Podgursky, M., & Springer, M. (2007). Teacher performance pay: A survey. *Journal of Policy Analysis and Management, 26,* 909–950.

Rivkin, S., Hanushek, E. A., & Kain, J. (2005). Teachers, schools and academic achievement. *Econometrica, 73*(2), 417–458.

Sanders, W., & Horn, S. (1998). Research findings from the Tennessee value-added assessment system (TVAAS) database: Implications for educational evaluation and research. *Journal of Personnel Evaluation in Education, 12*(3), 247–256.

Sanders, W., & Rivers, J. (1996). *Cumulative and residual effects of teachers on future student academic achievement.* Knoxville: University of Tennessee Value-Added Research and Assessment Center.

Sawchuk, S. (2010, September 1). State group piloting teacher prelicensing exam. *Education Week, 30*(2), 1.

Wayne, A. J., & Youngs, P. (2003). Teacher characteristics and student achievement gains: A review. *Review of Educational Research, 73,* 89–122.

Wenglinsky, H. (2000). *How teaching matters: Bringing the classroom back into discussions of teacher quality.* Princeton, NJ: Educational Testing service.

Wilson, S. M., Floden, R. E., & Ferrini-Mundy, J. (2002). Teacher preparation research: An insider's view from the outside. *Journal of Teacher Education, 53*(3), 190–204.

Wood, M., & DesJarlais, M. (2006). When post-tenure review policy and practice diverge: Making the case for congruence. *The Journal of Higher Education, 77*(4), 561–588.

Wright, S., Horn, S., and Sanders, W. (1997). Teacher and classroom context effects on student achievement: Implications for teacher evaluation. *Journal of Personnel Evaluation in Education, 11*, 57–67.

Zumwalt, K., & Craig, E. (2005). Teachers' characteristics: Research on the indicators of quality. In M. Cochran-Smith, & K. M. Zeichner (Eds.), *Studying teacher education: Report of the AERA Panel on Research and Teacher Education* (pp. 157–260). Mahwah, NJ: Erlbaum.

Zwick, R. (this volume). *Admissions testing in higher education.*

39

REPORTING ASSESSMENT RESULTS IN HIGHER EDUCATION

April L. Zenisky and Jerold S. Laguilles

Clearly reporting results to the intended users of data matters. High-quality tests or other measurement instruments, superior data collection methodologies, and sophisticated statistical analyses—none of these are likely to make much of a difference if the information obtained is not communicated clearly (or at all) and in a way that it can be readily interpreted and used to shape policy or practice. Unfortunately, communication of these findings to stakeholders, ranging from individual examinees to various users of group-level assessment data, has too often been relegated to being an afterthought in the process, though this is changing in many assessment contexts as measurement instruments and other empirical results are increasingly being used for evaluative purposes. In the realm of achievement testing, from K–12 through higher education, to certification and licensure assessment, more and more tests have high stakes associated with them. These stakes include promotion to the next grade, graduation, admissions to university for undergraduate and postgraduate study, entrance into a profession, and program quality monitoring. Also, many colleges and universities use a range of surveys, rubrics, and other data collection methods for assessment purposes and for gathering data to inform institutional policy decisions, and these results often have important implications for policy and practice.

Indeed, within the landscape of higher education, assessment certainly occurs in a variety of forms and for numerous important purposes. For example, college and universities may use tests (in the traditional sense of individually administered measurement instruments) to assess student learning and academic achievement; they also conduct assessments to satisfy the requirements of regional accreditation groups and/or for accountability purposes as established by federal or state/local governing bodies. In some cases, reporting is for internal purposes only, but in others results are disseminated more widely, including audiences that may be external to an individual institution. Ultimately, as Volkwein (2003) notes, institutions increasingly need to demonstrate their accountability, effectiveness, and efficiency, and an important part of that is not only the assessment of outcomes that fall into those categories, but also the communication of those findings.

Furthermore, assessment—and reporting of assessment results—within higher education can and does occur at several levels (in effect, units of analysis). In other words, these activities may take place at the *institution-level* (e.g., measuring institutional effectiveness via benchmarking with peer schools), the *school/program-level* (e.g., finding out if students in a school of education or a chemistry program are more or less satisfied with the experience in their respective academic departments than students from other schools or programs), *other relevant grouping levels* (e.g., are certain demographic groups or types of students more likely to be retained after their first-year?), and at the *individual level* (e.g., qualifying exams for majors or graduation requirements).

Institutions also have several options available for collecting data for assessment purposes. They can use existing data that is already being reported to external agencies (such as the U. S. Department of Education's Integrated Postsecondary Education Data System [IPEDS]). Alternatively, in some applications, it is possible to create and utilize "home-grown" assessment tools (e.g., tests, surveys, and other evaluative rubrics). Lastly, assessment tools developed by third-party organizations can be administered or employed as needed.

In terms of reporting results, it seems safe to say that a "one-size-fits-all" approach to assessment (and ultimately reporting assessment data) is extremely difficult in higher education given the myriad institutional types ranging from public research universities, to private not-for profit colleges, to community colleges (and, correspondingly, a multitude of institution-specific missions). However, regardless of the assessment purpose, unit of analysis under consideration, or type of evaluative instrument used, the current economic and social climate is such that all institutions share the common need for reporting their assessment results, and doing so in ways that are *accessible, useful,* and *understandable* to intended audiences (Zenisky, Hambleton, & Sireci, 2009).

The purpose of this chapter is to provide an overview of what is involved in assessment reporting strategies and methods in higher education, but in a practical, hands-on sense. While determining an assessment purpose, defining outcomes, selecting an instrument, and analyzing results are the central and most time-consuming aspects of assessment activity, reporting is often an afterthought, though many institutional researchers know that this is an equally important step to "closing the assessment loop" (Banta & Blaich, 2011). The framework used here for understanding these issues around reporting performance data in higher education is adapted from the Hambleton and Zenisky (in press) model that is rooted in a more traditional psychometric perspective and designed to reinforce the need to be careful, purposeful, and explicit in both informal and formal data reporting efforts. We begin here by defining what is meant by "reporting" as it relates to the range of higher education assessment activities, and then discuss how different reports may be structured and used in higher education, including information about the kinds of data that different reports may contain. From there, the focus turns to a formal model for report development, and what persons involved in reporting assessment data at colleges and universities can do to help ensure that reports containing assessment data are again accessible, understandable, and ultimately useful for their various intended audiences. In each of those steps, we provide illustrative examples to connect this report development approach to the different kinds of assessment reporting activities that occur in higher education. We then conclude with a discussion of how reporting occurs in one exemplar area of considerable importance for colleges and universities (retention) to provide a further frame of reference for the approach to reporting presented here.

What are Assessment Reports?

As noted earlier and evidenced by numerous other chapters in this handbook, assessment in higher education takes place for a wide variety of purposes and involves various units of analysis. It follows, then, that the reporting of these data likewise involves a range of reporting formats, contents, intended audiences, and levels of formality. It is this variation that can cause the topic of reporting to come off as difficult to pin down, as it were. At the same time, the outcomes of importance in higher education are not so esoteric that the principles of good reporting cannot apply.

Also mentioned in other chapters, there are a number of ways in which instruments that can be thought of as "tests" in a very traditional, psychometric sense are used in higher education. Among these applications are admissions, the placement of entering students, evaluating writing skills, cognitively diagnostic assessment, and classroom assessment. With these, reporting typically occurs at both the level of individual students and across groups. The intended audiences may be the students themselves, faculty, and/or college/university administrators, though at each of these levels the uses of the data may be quite different.

Moving to a broader view of assessment and reporting, as Volkwein (2003) describes, assessment activities involving surveys, rubrics, and quantitative data at the institutional level typically focus on accountability, efficiency, and effectiveness. Again, the corresponding reports of results take different forms and formats depending on the purpose and audience. One important determining factor in the type of report is whether the analysis is descriptive or analytical. Descriptive analyses typically yield more reports that are more straightforward in nature, especially if the primary intended audience is comprised of senior administrators. In such cases, an executive summary followed by data tables and well-developed graphs may be sufficient. Another increasingly common mechanism for reporting institutional effectiveness is the use of dashboards to provide summative information on specific institutional metrics, such as the number of inquiries and applications of prospective students or fall enrollment. Reporting dashboards like these typically include simple tables and/or graphs and provide administrators with highly accessible information in easily understandable pieces. Other descriptive reporting examples include institutional benchmarking or reporting the results of a survey of alumni on their postgraduate outcomes.

Reports of analytical analyses, on the other hand, may be more technical in nature, depending on the complexity of statistical analyses. Take, for example, an institutional survey used for accreditation purposes that seeks to measure student engagement both inside and outside the classroom across all class years. The reporting of these results could entail comparing mean responses between first-year and senior students via the use of t-tests. Such reports would not only require clear language in denoting statistically significant mean differences but also in noting mean differences that are not statistically significant, especially if the potential audience is unfamiliar with such terms. An analytic report need not employ advanced statistical methods either. For example, in trying to determine enrollment projections based on previous data, the analysis may employ using a straight average or a rolling average. Either way, the reporting of this information must clearly denote which method was employed and why. This is an important feature of analytic reporting because more than simply displaying results, these types of reports should also provide background on the methodology used in the analysis.

The above examples focus on the types of institutional- or group-level reports that occur within many colleges and universities. In addition, institutional research offices typically report information on the individual level usually to improve institutional processes or efficiency. For example, during registration period, institutions may be interested in seeing which students have *not* registered for the subsequent semester even though they were eligible to register. In such cases, a simple list can be generated, but since the goal of this report is to enable college staff to follow-up with individual students the list may need to be packaged differently. It could be sorted by department, academic advisor, or even residence hall and perhaps include relevant information such as phone number, e-mail address, and information regarding any academic or financial holds. While the purpose of this report seems basic, the various components require systematic thought and deliberation.

The Process for Developing Reports

As noted at the outset of this chapter, reporting results in many educational contexts (not the least of which is higher education) is typically not carried out according to any formal model for report creation. Rather, this has too often been regarded as something just done by a statistician, psychometrician, or institutional researcher on-the-fly to descriptively summarize data for a narrow institutional—or agency—specific purpose. To step back for a moment, however, reporting data across these settings can (and should) actually be conceptualized as an integral part of what Downing (2006) defined (from a psychometric perspective) as the test development process (which includes not only higher education assessment activities, but also K–12 achievement testing, licensure and certification assessment, and psychological evaluation). This is not to say that reporting data has not been done (or done quite well!) in any of these settings, but rather, too often, the activities associated with decisions about the kinds of results data provided to intended users and how these data are structured and formatted have not been given the same level of priority as other aspects of assessment development and validation, such as item development, item analysis, and standard-setting, among others.

In fact, reporting results is an assessment activity that lends itself to a formal development process quite easily. Just as test items are developed according to plans involving test specifications and are subject to multiple levels of review (content validity, technical quality, sensitivity/fairness), so too is it critical that reports of educational data are developed with clearly articulated ideas about their purposes and intended users in mind, and with a procedure in place to obtain feedback from stakeholders about report quality (and, perhaps more importantly, to ensure that a strategy exists to integrate any substantive comments received into revisions). Thus, Hambleton and Zenisky (in press) have developed a model in the context of educational and psychological testing for score report development that can be expressed in terms of a sequence of seven steps detailed in Table 39.1 that has broader application in the context of reporting results in a variety of educational settings, including higher education.

Before any data report is drafted, there are three activities that should take place that inform report development. These three steps (which can occur concurrently) involve defining report purpose, identifying the intended audience, and reviewing existing reports and the psychometric reporting literature for examples and ideas. As with test development, data report development starts out in Step 1 by *defining the purpose of the report*: what is the report to be used for? The answer to this question for any given assessment activity is influenced by both the assessment purpose and in standardized testing the validity evidence that has been collected to support score and data interpretations. Thus, a key consideration that should be the starting point for report creation concerns what the stakeholders need to know from the assessment data and/or what a testing agency defines in the test's technical manual as the appropriate use(s) of test scores. The report should be conceptualized at the outset as a means to an end to communicate data that supports the inferences that are supported by the data.

As mentioned previously, assessment in higher education can occur at multiple levels, and the defined purpose of the assessment activity will also drive relevant aspects of reports. For example, when conducting institutional benchmarking, it is common to report one's own institution's data in relation to a group of selected peer schools. If the purpose is to compare changes in tuition and fees, then the report will need some measure of central tendency (e.g. mean or median) and the ability to display trends over time. In this case, the institutional-level data is most relevant in comparison to the data from other schools.

The second step outlined in Table 39.1 is *identifying the likely audience or intended users* of the report. In K-12 achievement testing, the data that an individual parent receives about a student (and, more specifically, how that information is presented) is typically different than that which is made available to a classroom teacher or what a state education official is concerned with. Likewise, in higher education, data for individual faculty members might be different from the kind of information a department focuses on, which is yet again different from the kind of data that allows for comparisons of

Table 39.1 Steps in the Hambleton & Zenisky Model of the Score Report Development Process

Step	Task
1	Define purpose of the report
2	Identify intended audience(s)
3	Review report examples/literature
4	Develop reports
5	Data collection/field test
6	Review and redesign
7	Ongoing maintenance

Note: The full model is described in Hambleton & Zenisky (in press).

performance across institutions. While this consideration is somewhat related to report purpose, it is an important issue in its own right because different consumers of data have different familiarity with evaluative results and data as well as levels of quantitative literacy, so acknowledging such differences and integrating those types of considerations into report development supports efforts to create reports that are valid (in the sense of actually being understood and used appropriately by stakeholders).

Thus, identifying the audience in the reporting of higher assessment results is critically important. Institutions of higher education have many stakeholders including trustee boards, accreditation agencies, administrators, faculty committees, staff, parents, students, and alumni. Thus, it is quite common for institutional researchers to create multiple versions of certain reports for different audiences. Consider the administration of a post-graduation survey of a college's recent graduates to gauge satisfaction with one's college experience and to obtain outcomes data. When reporting this data for accountability purpose, extra attention should be paid towards describing the survey methodology in addition to reporting information such as job placement rates. Administrators and faculty may be most interested in the satisfaction data especially if it can be reported at the school, department, or other relevant group levels. However, when reporting this data to prospective students and parents, it may be more important to provide examples of specific types of employment.

Step 3 in Table 39.1 corresponds to the report development equivalent of a literature review, and involves *research to identify and review relevant report examples and the published literature on reporting*. In many assessment and evaluative contexts, reports similar to the information to be communicated already exist. Reports for individual test-takers exist in every testing context, and, similarly, reports for classes, department, and institutions can likewise be found. The purpose of this step in the report development process, then, is to consider the kind of information to be communicated and to look at ways in which other agencies have handled similar reporting efforts from several perspectives. The areas to focus on in this aspect of review include both report contents (what are the report elements that are typically included in various kinds of reports?) and report format and structure (what are the layout, format, and design decisions that agencies have made to facilitate report use and understanding?). In most report development contexts, the wheel need not be completely reinvented.

Researching sample reports as a means to inform one's own reporting needs is clearly useful in the realm of higher education. Overall, the institutional research community is noted for its collegiality, and colleagues at other colleges and universities are often willing to share report samples or ideas upon request. Furthermore, many institutions belong to one or more higher education associations such as the Association of American Colleges and Universities (AAC&U), which often provide resources in support of institutional activities, including assessment.

With the data collected from Steps 1, 2, and 3 in hand, the process of *drafting reports* begins (Step 4). The report development team should integrate the information gathered involving reporting goals, the intended audience(s), and report examples to come up with at least one draft report for each purpose/audience combination (and preferably multiple versions of each). It is likewise important to particularly highlight the team aspect of report development. There may have been a time where report creation involving an individual in a room with a computer, a word processing program, and an array of assessment results to be displayed was passable, but today most report development efforts should be viewed as considerably more interdisciplinary activities involving a range of professional expertise. In addition to psychometricians and/or statisticians, report development may also involve graphic designers for layout and design expertise, content people for familiarity with the domain of results being communicated, public relations experts for communications strategies, and information technologists to facilitate quality control in the automation of report creation and dissemination (and this goes for either paper-based or electronic reporting).

Hambleton and Zenisky (in press) have developed a review sheet for educational score report settings to use in this step, with 32 specific elements spread across seven topic areas to consider. The seven topic areas of interest are summarized in Table 39.2. By taking the types of issues listed in

Table 39.2 into account in the broader sense of reporting that is under consideration in this chapter, some of the potential issues with report drafts can be avoided or caught and changed at this stage of the report development process. Of course, the topic areas in Table 39.2 can be matched up to rough analogues in the context of a typical report of higher education outcomes (such as a document containing an executive summary and introduction/purpose statement, a results section, and a discussion that focuses on conclusions, interpretations, and limitations).

To start, at the outset of pulling together a report, the document should be defined clearly and completely. In both an executive summary and in the introductory pages, the evaluative activity for which results are being presented should be explained in full. When it comes time to show findings, whether the results are test scores, performance levels, or other data, report developers must give context and provide clear explanation for that data being provided.

Score scales as report elements. As an aside, to date one of the most challenging aspects of interpreting some assessment reports involves scores and score scales, which are how some tests and other instruments quantify results. For intended users of assessment results, the numerical scores used to describe performance on one assessment are often quite different from those used on other similar assessments, and keeping track of these values and what they mean from assessment to assessment is difficult at best. Take, for example, the SAT and the ACT college entrance examinations. The sections of the SAT are scored from 200 to 800 in increments of 10, and the mean is a score of about 500. The ACT, on the other hand, is reported using a 1 to 36 scale. While concordance tables have been developed to facilitate comparisons between scores on these two assessments (available at http://professionals.collegeboard.com/data-reports-research/sat/sat-act), understanding the details of what students who receive any particular score on the SAT *or* the ACT know and can do in a relatable way is a question that stakeholders are interested in. Each instrument's score scale has a

Table 39.2 Summary of Score Report Review Considerations

Topic Area	Description
Report Introduction and Descriptions	*It is necessary to define reports clearly and completely.* Reports should be labeled as to report purpose/goal, assessment name/label, the unit of analysis being reported (individual, class, department, etc.), and assessment purpose.
Scores and Performance Levels	*These are the main data included in many reports.* Where scores are included, some indication of the score scale should be included, as should data about precision of scores. Where performance level classifications are reported, those should be described sufficiently for the intended users. Report developers should consider describing how these results should and should not be used, and examples may be helpful in this regard.
Other Performance Indicators	*This addresses other kinds of quantitative and qualitative results that may be included in reports.* On the report document, interpretations should be explicit. Care should be taken in making reference group comparisons, and likewise with subscale-level reporting.
Language	*The language of the report should be suitable for the intended users.* Statistical and technical jargon should be avoided, and in cases where reports are translated/adapted into more than one language, appropriate care must be taken to ensure the quality of the translation/adaptation.
Design	*Reports should be structured clearly and have a logical flow to the information being communicated.* The layout of the report should be arranged in an orderly way (a "highlights" sections can be helpful in this regard), graphics should be clear and well labeled, and care should be taken to ensure a balance of information and white space. A mix of tables, texts, and graphics can be useful as a strategy to communicate data.
Interpretive Guides and Ancillary Materials	*Many testing agencies prepare separate interpretive guide documents to facilitate data use and understanding.* If such materials are made available, they should be written clearly and provide acceptable and unacceptable interpretations of results (field-testing with some intended users can help with this).
Other Content	*Reports should also provide ways for users to follow-up to get more information.* Contact information for the report author(s) (phone, email, or a Web address) can be included on the report.

score range and real-life values can be associated with different points on that scale, but users must be advised of that information to use the data effectively and as intended. So, in the course of reporting, considerations of scores and score scales should be articulated clearly and understood in the context of the subject/topic being reported.

Report "language" is an important element that must be addressed in report development. When discussing educational statistics, it is all too easy to rely on jargon and highly technical terms, but this approach can reduce the accessibility of a report to the very people for whom it is intended. The appearance, format, and structure of a report are likewise necessary considerations. The review of prior reports can be helpful in this regard for examples of how other groups have presented similar results effectively.

The last two areas of the Hambleton & Zenisky (in press) checklist are more directly related to educational score reports, but there may be occasions in higher education reporting too where providing ancillary materials is necessary, and/or where offering audiences opportunities to follow up on the data and findings is the recommended course of action.

Moving on to Step 5 from Table 39.1, *data collection and field-testing* is not as ominous or necessarily as formal as it sounds. It is the obtaining of feedback by informal or formal means, but also is the part of the process that Hambleton and Zenisky (in press) strongly encourage agencies to take seriously. The drafts that come out of Step 4 can often be quite good, especially when Steps 1–3 have been a part of the report development process and the reports have been reviewed accordingly to the topics and issues outlined in Table 39.2. However, there is no substitute for obtaining feedback on how the information is communicated from actual, intended users of the reports. Are they understandable? Can users use the data presented to inform decisions and set policy, in accordance with test purposes and inferences based on validity evidence? This aspect of report development can be formal or informal. In this context, "formal" refers to the carrying out of evaluative research studies using principles of research design and research methods. Focus groups have been used effectively for this purpose (Jaeger, 2003; Zenisky, Delton, & Hambleton, 2006; Zenisky, Hambleton, & Smith, 2006), as have interviews and think-aloud protocols (Wainer, Hambleton, & Meara, 1997; Zenisky & Hambleton, 2007). These approaches typically involve seeking out random samples of intended users and developing full research protocols. However, depending on the reporting context, informal data collection can be both valuable and provide score report developers with the kind of information needed. Here, methods may include the use of convenience samples and reviews that may or may not be guided by specific evaluative questions. Ultimately, the priority associated with Step 5 is to ensure that report developers have draft reports reviewed by prospective users to identify problems, potential sources of confusion, and other issues, *before* wider dissemination of the materials occurs.

Following review of draft reports, Step 6 in this process is *revision and redesign of reports* as necessary. The feedback obtained via Step 5 should be reviewed and evaluated by the report development team, and integrated into the reports. This may lead to a second round of formal or informal report review (or not) as shown in Table 39.1.

Lastly, the final step, Step 7, in the Hambleton and Zenisky (in press) model involves *ongoing review and maintenance*. Once reports have been released and are used in practice, it can be useful to monitor how they are used over time and check in with intended users about their understanding of the data at different points in time. Where problems are found, ancillary interpretive materials can be produced and shared with various audiences to clarify some of the issues, or reports can be updated or revised to reflect changes made to improve understanding of the data.

Reporting in Higher Education: Retention as an Example

To better understand how integral reporting is within the field of institutional research, it is helpful to use student retention as a concrete example. Almost all colleges and universities are mindful of their retention, which is typically defined as the percentage of a fall entering cohort (first-year) that remains enrolled the following fall (sophomore year). Student retention is also important to various stakeholders within higher education. An institution's retention rate can be viewed as a measure of students' educational progress and success. It is also an indirect measure of institutional effectiveness as more students retained means more students on track to graduate. From an economic perspective, institutions do not want to "lose" students they have enrolled as this may increase their instructional cost per student. Because of these reasons, external agencies, such as accrediting organizations and the federal government, require institutions to report their retention rate.

So, how can high-quality report development activities aid in providing accurate information to college officials and administrators? It is important to remember that the reasons why some students leave and why students stay is complex, and may even be institution specific. With that in mind, several different reports can be used to better understand this phenomenon. Take, for example, a college with a 75% retention rate. This value by itself is not useful to an institution until it is placed in the proper context. In other words, how does this retention rate compare to the national retention rate or to the retention rate of the same institutional type or even to a handpicked list of peer institutions? Thus, a benchmarking approach would be one useful strategy to employ here, in which a specific institution's retention rate can be compared to the retention rates of a peer group of institutions in a data table. The mean or median retention rate of the group could also be used. Finally, it might also be useful to graph several years' worth of retention rates to uncover any trends.

Going beyond an institutional-level report of retention rates, a school may want to report the retention rates of a number of subgroups to better understand retention from a more in-depth perspective, in addition to a global view. In other words, retention rate comparisons of interest could include female students versus male students, students in honors programs versus students not in honors programs, or declared versus undeclared majors. The obvious way to report this type of information is via simple bar graphs which will reveal any retention "gaps" between specific subgroups.

To provide even more in-depth retention information, institutions can report on retention at the individual level. Institutions can generate simple lists of students who were retained or even conduct statistical analysis, such as regression, to determine the relevant characteristics of retainers. This information can be reported in a descriptive fashion (i.e. students who were retained typically live in-state, or have first-year GPA greater than 2.5, or play a varsity sport etc.). Another individual-level report can be generated using services from the National Student Clearinghouse, which can provide subsequent enrollment at other institutions for students who left their initial institution. In other words, institutions can determine whether students who left ultimately enrolled or transferred to another college and university. Using frequency counts, this type of data can be presented to show to which schools you "lose" students. Still another way to better understand institutional retention is to match individual student data with any institutional surveys conducted during the first year. For example, comparing data from the National Survey of Student Engagement (NSSE) can provide some insight on student behaviors that may differ between student retainers and student leavers.

In summary, student retention is an apt example within institutional research that requires deliberate and systematic thought in reporting results. As shown in the Hambleton and Zenisky (in press) model, institutions need to consider their institutional goals in reporting about retention, consider who is going to be reviewing the data, and look at how other colleges and universities use statistics, graphs, tables, and text to communicate retention results. With some draft reports in hand, reporting results can be discussed in-house (administratively speaking) or in some cases shown to members of relevant intended audiences for feedback. Revision may be needed, and then follow-up can occur as needed. The main point to be made here is that as one example of higher education reporting, many different constituencies both inside and outside higher education are interested in retention data, and, thus, the reports for retention (as with any other area) must be mindful of intended audience.

Moreover, retention data can be reported on multiple levels: institutional, group, and individual; and the unit of analysis ultimately impacts the type of information to be displayed. Finally, various types of data are used to generate retention reports ranging from publicly available data, to institutional records, to survey research data, and this too will affect how one approaches constructing reports.

Conclusions

To *demonstrate* their accountability, effectiveness, and efficiency, as most higher education institutions are expected to do these days, it is not sufficient to implement good (or even very good) institutional research methods. The results must be presented in ways that are accessible, useful, and understandable, and, in this regard, recent efforts in the area of educational test score reporting can be informative to broader reporting efforts in all areas of education, including higher education. The model presented here provides a structure for report developers to be deliberative and purposeful throughout the process of preparing materials that describe the findings for the range of qualitative and quantitative studies, and is intended to be broadly applicable across institutional types, aims, and audiences. Ultimately, as decisions in higher educational become increasingly more data-driven, reporting mechanisms that allow college and university administrators to draw on results efficiently will be at a premium. Starting with good data analyses and sound interpretations of findings, clear presentations of results as informed by the steps discussed here can help promote efforts to use data effectively.

References

Banta, T. W., & Blaich, C. F. (2011, January/February). Closing the assessment loop. *Change: The Magazine of Higher Learning, 43*(1), 22–27.

Downing, S. M. (2006). Selected-response item formats in test development. In S. M. Downing, & T. M. Haladyna (Eds.), *Handbook of test development* (pp. 287–301). Mahwah, NJ: Erlbaum.

Hambleton, R. K., & Zenisky, A. L. (in press). Reporting test scores in more meaningful ways: Some new findings, research methods, and guidelines for score report design. In K. F. Geisinger (Ed.), *APA handbook of testing and assessment in psychology.* Washington, DC: American Psychological Association.

Jaeger, R. M. (2003). *NAEP validity studies: Reporting the results of the National Assessment of Educational Progress* (Working Paper 2003–11). Washington, DC: U.S. Department of Education, Institute of Education Sciences.

Volkwein, J. F. (2003). Using and enhancing existing data to reporting to campus challenges. In F. K. Stage, & K. Manning (Eds.), *Research in the college context: Approaches and methods* (pp. 183–210). New York, NY: Brunner-Routledge.

Wainer, H., Hambleton, R. K., & Meara, K. (1999). Alternative displays for communicating NAEP results: A redesign and validity study. *Journal of Educational Measurement, 36*(4), 301–335.

Zenisky, A. L., Delton, J., & Hambleton, R. K. (2006). *State reading content specialists and NAEP reporting: Use and understanding of selected data displays.* Technical report for the Comprehensive Evaluation of NAEP. [Also Center for Educational Assessment Report No. 596. Amherst, MA: University of Massachusetts, School of Education.]

Zenisky, A. L., & Hambleton, R. K. (2007). *Navigating "The Nation's Report Card" on the World Wide Web: Site user behavior and impressions.* Technical report for the Comprehensive Evaluation of NAEP. [Also Center for Educational Assessment Report No. 625. Amherst, MA: University of Massachusetts, School of Education.]

Zenisky, A. L., Hambleton, R. K., & Sireci, S. G. (2009). Getting the message out: An evaluation of NAEP score reporting practices with implications for disseminating test results. *Applied Measurement in Education, 22*(4), 359–375.

Zenisky, A. L., Hambleton, R. K., & Smith, Z.R. (2006). *Do math educators understand NAEP score reports? Evaluating the utility of selected NAEP data displays.* Technical report for the Comprehensive Evaluation of NAEP. [Also Center for Educational Assessment Report No. 587. Amherst, MA: University of Massachusetts, School of Education.]

40

PRESENTING LEARNING OUTCOMES ASSESSMENT RESULTS TO FOSTER USE

Staci J. Provezis and Natasha A. Jankowski

Imagine a several year study of an institution and the programs within it that involves a large number of committees articulating goals, making a plan, executing parts of the plan, and writing a report that is shared with an accreditation peer review team. After the team leaves, the committees are disbanded and the report is filed away without further thought or consideration as to how it might be used to improve student learning. A significant amount of time and energy was extended for the study and report, but quickly it is all forgotten. Unfortunately this scenario is all too common on many college campuses, as most simply use assessment information to fulfill accreditation requirements (Kuh & Ikenberry, 2009). Be it for an accreditation study or for another reason, information about educational quality is often not reported broadly to different audiences, whether internal or external to the institution. This break down of communication with varied audiences is unfortunate because it does not foster using assessment information for institutional improvement in so much as it simply reports the activities to a small internal group. Instead, documents and reports, whether created for accreditation or for another reason, could be used to tell a story about the institutional efforts to explore student learning, inform subsequent iterations of assessment, and lead to the improvement of student learning. While we do not advocate that all accreditation information should be made public, we do believe that information from this activity as well as other activities involving assessment should be communicated more broadly than is currently the case. Dissemination and availability of assessment results that are tailored to specific audiences may help with the utility of the results.

Currently, assessment information, for accreditation and other institutional purposes, focuses on understanding student learning outcomes. Student learning outcomes, "the competencies or attainment levels reached by students on completion of an academic program" (Ewell, 2001, p. 7), should be of utmost interest to institutions, given that learning is the foundation upon which colleges rest. Purposes and uses of student learning outcomes assessment include improvement of student learning and accountability to external constituents. While faculty members regularly assess students' skills at the course level, institutions have been asked to understand their impact upon student learning at the program and institutional levels and to report on these findings. In other words, institutions are asked to be more transparent by reporting to broader audiences. To be transparent, reporting should provide information about student learning outcomes assessment and institutional performance that is meaningful, understandable, and readily available to external audiences such as potential students, families, and policymakers as well as to internal audiences such as students, staff, and faculty.

To that end, this chapter begins by describing how reporting assessment information can serve both assessment purposes—improvement of student learning and accountability. The various transparency initiatives created by national organizations provide one method of reporting, while dashboards and benchmarking provide others. Next, the chapter offers strategies to consider when reporting, such as minding the audience, the presentation style, and the structure of the report. The chapter continues with a discussion of the National Institute for Learning Outcomes Assessment (NILOA)'s Transparency Framework, which is a guide for institutions to use as they examine their institutional websites for transparent information on student learning. The chapter concludes by explaining that assessment information needs to be placed in context and available to facilitate use the data. The primary goal of this chapter is to promote reporting on assessment to tell an institutional story about student learning at a campus and using the data gleaned from assessment to improve said institution.

Accountability and Improvement

As mentioned, assessment activities are often conducted for compliance reasons, specifically accreditation, according to a survey administered to chief academic officers (Kuh & Ikenberry, 2009). Assessment should serve to address accountability as well as institutional improvement, and yet too often these two functions are seen as independent of one another. No one talks about this tension better than Ewell (2009), who suggests there are two "paradigms" (p. 8). Assessment for improvement is an ongoing process that engages the internal stakeholders, whereas assessment for accountability is summative and requires that the institutional players comply with strict reporting strategies and timelines (Ewell, 2009). Often transparency is associated with accountability, but reporting assessment strategies and results can be useful for improvement as well. Instead of wrestling with these two uses of assessment results, institutions must instead find a balance of reporting for both improvement and accountability that is also transparent. Users of assessment information depend in part on the level at which the assessment occurs such that classroom level assessment will most likely be used by faculty for improvement of student learning in the classroom while institutional level assessment will most likely be used by external constituents accountability purposes. However, communicating to internal and external constituents involves consideration of similar aspects of presentation including audience, language, and structure of the report. As such, presenting assessment information to faculty not familiar with assessment for improving student learning in the classroom is similar to reporting to external audiences on institutional quality.

More attention has been given to transparent reporting for accountability purposes since the National Commission on the Future of Higher Education (2006) report *A Test of Leadership* (commonly referred to as the Spellings report, after the Secretary of Education who commissioned the report). This report explains that "there is inadequate transparency and accountability for measuring institutional performance, which is more and more necessary to maintain public trust in higher education" (p. 14). At the same time, it highlighted the need for "consumer-friendly information" that would allow for institutional comparisons. Moreover, of importance to some audiences, particularly government agencies and politicians, are comparisons between institutions that do not obscure differences between institutional types (Kelly & Aldeman, 2010). Many colleges resist these types of comparisons as they undervalue the diversity of institutions and state settings, and yet several national organizations are creating transparency templates to address the request of the Spellings report. For instance, the Voluntary System of Accountability (VSA), developed by the American Association of State College and Universities (AASCU) and the Association of Public and Land-grant Universities (APLU) communicates information on the undergraduate student experience through a common web-based reporting template, the College Portrait. The College Portrait alleges to demonstrate accountability and stewardship to the public; measure educational outcomes to identify effective practices; and assemble information that is accessible, understandable, and comparable. Another initiative, specifically for independent colleges and universities, is the University and College Accountability

Network (U-CAN), which is also a web-based resource designed to give both prospective and current students and their families concise, consumer-friendly information in a common format. U-CAN was developed and is managed by the National Association of Independent Colleges and Universities (NAICU). Another web-based student learning outcomes assessment and transparency initiative is Transparency by Design (TbD), developed by the Presidents' Forum, to foster accountability and transparency by colleges and universities. The initiative's members comprise a consortium of regionally accredited, adult-serving, distance educational institutions. And, finally, the American Association of Community Colleges (AACC) has created the Voluntary Framework of Accountability (VFA), which as of spring 2011 is in the pilot stage.

Some believe that these initiatives allow for institutional comparisons, which help facilitate consumer choice by providing relevant market based information to potential students and their families. But Kuh (2007) argues that the templates should strive to do more, as he explains that templates should: allow institutions to describe how they will improve if students are not meeting the goals of the institution; show information on student performance, among other areas; and be accountable to policymakers, through answering questions about the institution's achievements of graduating students and demonstrating student gains in learning. Following Kuh's (2007) advice, institutions could focus on how reporting and providing transparent information on their own websites to internal and external audiences may lead to institutional improvement from market pressure. Providing comparable transparent information on assessment in multiple reporting formats may or may not be effective in leading to institutional improvement, since a market approach to reporting depends on potential students: acting as rational economic decision-makers; having access to relevant information; understanding said information; and having the ability to gain admission and travel to the college of choice. However, transparent reporting is about more than providing consumers with the necessary or desired information to make decisions on attendance from assessment of student learning. It also speaks to the integrity of the institution to describe the quality of its fundamental activity—student learning—and, more importantly, to address ways that the institution evaluates and measures that quality for continuous improvement.

Reporting Assessment

Reporting involves communication among those involved in student learning (such as students and faculty, as well as those interested in student learning, such as external stakeholders), about what improves or hinders learning (Blaich, 2011). As Walvoord (2004) explains, assessment reports should explain not only what steps an institution has taken to assess student learning, but should also describe the changes that will be made to improve student learning. The reports should tell an important, coherent, interesting story that provides context for what is being measured and the next steps for institutional or program improvement. As Suskie (2009) states, "Assessments are worthwhile only if the results are put to good use, and those uses can take place only after careful consideration and discussion" (p. 273). This careful consideration and discussion is possible when results of assessment are communicated clearly and effectively.

Whether for paper or on-line reports, several authors offer guidance to effectively present assessment information to multiple audiences as well as present the information in ways to potentially enhance use. For instance, recommendations include consideration of the audience and tailoring reports and findings to their specific interests (Volkwein, 2010); presenting findings in text and graphic form (Walvoord, 2004); keeping the report simple and short (Middaugh, 2010); using a variety of formats, media, and locations (Ketcheson, 2001); and including a section on next steps and potential further actions (Suskie, 2009). The reports provide a means of transforming data into information for potential users (Middaugh, 2010) and offer information on what institutions or programs have done, are doing, and what they plan to do because of the findings (Walvoord, 2004).

Contextualization of the findings to the institution to reflect the mission and specific institution is important as well (Suskie, 2009). This section presents information on how to be transparent in reporting assessment information by focusing on audience, presentation of results, structure of the report, and dissemination of the information.

Audience

When designing reports on the assessment of student learning, consideration of the audiences to which this information is addressed is vital to effective communication. Different audiences have different interests and stakes in assessment information. For faculty and administrators as well as others situated within the university, assessment information can inform decisions that improve student learning. A governing board oversees the quality of the institution as a whole, so it may want to know what assessment activities are in place, what the results of the assessment are and what is being done to improve the quality of learning (AGB, 2011). The same is true for upper level administrators, such as the president and the chief academic officer, who are responsible for the academic quality of the institution. Deans, department chairs, and program directors all have the responsibility to improve upon learning at the institution, so they need to understand assessment data to use the information for program decisions as well as curricular development. These internal audiences would likely be more interested in baseline information about the institution and programs and would want to be able to disaggregate the data and "drill down" to learn more and make informed decisions. Further, to better assure use of the data, prior to writing assessment reports and ideally before conducting assessment activities, potential internal audiences and users of the assessment information should be contacted. By considering this audience prior to reporting, potential users can be involved in the assessment process and consulted about what information would be most useful, what problems they would like to address with the data, and to what use they might put the information. Such involvement will help tailor reports and foster use of results to improve student learning.

Communicating assessment information beyond internal audiences serves to establish public trust and meet the demands of accountability. External audiences want to know what students learn and what steps institutions are taking to further student learning. For instance, students and their families may use assessment information in deciding which institution to attend. Policymakers may use assessment information to justify institutional budgets. The general public may be assured that their tax dollars are well spent. Employers may use assessment information to know what skills students gain from a particular institution or program. Whatever the use, the fact is that external audiences typically want a brief overview that includes relevant information that is important to them. This overview should not be bogged down with more details than necessary, but should provide enough information to substantiate the claims made by the institution. It should be coherent, understandable, and use graphics as well as text to tell a story of institutional performance. In short, when designing reports, those charged with assessment reporting should consider reporting assessment information and findings to: those who are conducting assessment and want to know more about it, those interested in examining their teaching processes, or those outside of the institution who want to know about institutional performance and effectiveness.

Presentation of Results

To present results of assessment to potential users, employ clear, lay person's language in an easy to understand format. Crafting such reports is difficult and is an artistic skill. The use of charts and graphs as opposed to tables of numbers or lists of percentages can enhance user understanding (Middaugh, 2010). Sometimes, it is not important to state in a report that results are statistically significant or to list the statistical analysis used; instead, it is more important to present key findings, preferably in a graphical form. As Volkwein (2010) claims, using simple descriptive statistics, charts, counts, or percentages conveys a more understandable message than factor loadings or covariates.

Graphics can tell a story in a picture. Using arrows to show change over time and providing trend data can help readers better understand the data (Walvoord, 2004). Presenting key findings in text form as well as graphic, using bullets, clear language, and keeping the findings short will foster understanding (Volkwein, 2010). Most importantly, as with any report using graphics, the presentation of the graphics for an assessment report is as important as the data itself in assisting the various audiences understanding of the material. Several writers provide pointers on how to design graphs including: Bers and Seybert, 1999; Sanders and Filkins, 2009; and Tufte, 2001. Other steps to make the information meaningful can include disaggregating the results by major field, year in school, gender, ethnicity and so on, or by providing longitudinal analyses and comparisons with peer institutions. Disaggregated data provide more potentially useful information for programs and faculty as well as improvement decisions than institutional level aggregated data (Kuh, 2007).

While assessment may not be conducted with the rigor associated with scientific studies, nonetheless those assessing and reporting on it should take steps to assure that the data are accurate and include information on accuracy in the reports (Judd & Keith, this volume). One way to show accuracy is to provide a clear description of the assessment activities. Banta and Pike (this volume) describe using the AERA-APA-NCME standards which include describing the study with detailed information about the sample process, characteristics of those studied, and contextual information about the assessment strategies. Overall, it is important to present results in a variety of ways such as bulleted key findings, narratives, graphics, and tables. Once all the pieces are ready to be placed into a report, it is time to craft the story they will tell.

Structure of the Report

Reports should be written to tell a short, coherent, and simple story (Middaugh, 2010). To do this, Suskie (2004) stresses starting with interesting or unanticipated findings to enhance user interest. Further, the reports should include contact information with the offer to make additional information available for those that would like the in-depth story. Results presented within the report should include both positive and negative findings (Volkwein, 2010). Further, results should be contextualized to the institution and its mission. In Judd and Keith's chapter on student learning outcomes assessment (this volume), they discuss the importance of the institutional mission and the complexity of assessment processes which occur at many layers within an institution including classroom, program, department, college, and institution-wide. This complexity leads to the need for discussions on what the assessment results mean for the institution. Reports should include information on how the assessment activities and results relate to the institutional mission so as to address the unique aspects of the individual institution.

An important section of an assessment report is the potential areas for further action and explanations of the results. In addition, incorporated in the reports should be a discussion of the findings and their implications for the institution (Volkwein, 2010). The report may list areas for additional research or outline recommendations for action. However, whether the report includes this information depends on the institutional knowledge of the author writing the report, as well as the purpose and audience of the report. For this reason, multiple, short, focused reports may be a good option to reveal the results of certain assessment activities for specific audiences as opposed to one long report for an amorphous audience. A communication strategy should be in place to share the information presented with the intended readers. For additional information on structuring assessment reports, see Zenisky and Laguilles (this volume).

Dissemination of Reports

Reports may be disseminated in a variety of ways including the Internet, internal e-mail, newsletters, face-to-face communication, and paper. One reason that assessment information should be made available broadly is to widen the net of potential users. In addition, by communicating assessment results, institutions can establish a culture of evidence where institutions look to data to make institutional improvements. As Banta and Blaich (2011) explain, institutions should review and strengthen their assessment communication plans because if people on campus cannot state the learning goals for the institution, or point to the same few strengths or weaknesses, then the communication plans are not effective. Assessment information should be clear to students, staff, and faculty on a campus, and if it is not, a communication plan should be put in place allowing anyone who has the faintest interest in assessment to be able to receive the information easily and to know who to contact with questions.

The work of the National Institute for Learning Outcomes Assessment (NILOA) has focused on what information institutions show on their institutional websites and where this information can be found. A central finding is that institutions say that they are doing more than what can be found on their websites, and when this information can be found, it is typically on chief academic officer Web pages or institutional research pages (Jankowski & Makela, 2010). External audiences, or internal ones for that matter, may not even be aware that these pages exist or that information on assessment can be found on them. Thus, the information could be posted and technically available and publically shared, but unless a clear directive is given to look at the information, it may be hidden in plain sight. Therefore, a goal should be to not only share the information, but also to make the campus community aware that the information is available and understandable.

Reporting Strategies

Multiple avenues exist for reporting assessment information as discussed briefly above including on-line, paper, and face-to-face meetings or presentations. In addition, besides the previously mentioned transparency initiatives such as the VSA, some institutions use dashboards and benchmarking for reporting assessment information, often at the request of a state system for accountability purposes. Dashboards allow institutions to use a centralized web location to show indicators of institutional performance as it relates to student learning as well as other factors. Ideally, interested parties can see at a glance how each institution in the system is performing. Benchmarking is similar to dashboards in that institutions provide certain information on performance indicators, but benchmarking allows for a comparison of institutions (Seybert, Weed, & Bers, this volume, discuss this concept in detail). Some states ask institutions to report on measures of student progress that is then shared on the state's website. Understanding the context behind reporting and the various places where information is reported on student learning is important given the rising demand for this information, but this chapter will continue with a discussion of ways an institution can provide transparent assessment information for its own publications, internal or external communications, or website.

While assessment information can be reported in various paper forms, many institutions look to their own institutional website to communicate this information. The Internet provides a venue for reporting information to multiple audiences in varying formats and presentation styles. As mentioned previously, NILOA has conducted several systematic analyses of website communication in regard to student learning outcomes assessment information and has found that institutions should more proactively utilize their websites to communicate information on assessment results. Recommendations on how this may be done include: prominently posting student learning outcomes statements and resources in multiple places on the website and updating the information regularly, communicating the various ways that student learning outcomes assessment occurs on the campus, providing examples to help multiple audiences understand the outcomes specific to the institution, and explaining the meaning and use of results in layperson's language (Jankowski & Makela, 2010). From the work done on examining website communication, a Transparency Framework (NILOA, 2011) was developed to support institutions in sharing evidence of student learning on and off campus (see Figure 40.1).

Institutions may use NILOA's (2011) Transparency Framework[1] to examine their institutional websites and to gauge the extent to which evidence of student learning is readily accessible and potentially useful and meaningful to intended audiences. The Transparency Framework identifies six key components of student learning outcomes assessment:

1. student learning outcomes statements;
2. assessment plans;
3. assessment resources;
4. current assessment activities;
5. evidence of student learning; and
6. use of student learning evidence.

The components of the Framework serve as an outline of information on student learning assessment, and the details following each describe ways to advance public understanding. Institutions would be well served to go through each component to assure that they are fully describing their assessment activities. But for brevity, let us only discuss the second component, assessment plans, as

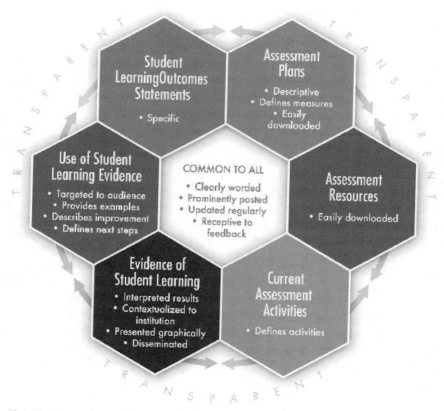

Figure 40.1 The NILOA Transparency Framework

Copyright (2011) by the National Institute for Learning Outcomes Assessment. Reprinted with permission.

a detailed example. First, the Framework provides a definition of the component; in this case, assessment plans are defined as: "Campus plans for gathering evidence of student learning might include institution-wide or program specific approaches that convey how student learning will be assessed, the data collection tools and approaches that will be used, and the timeline for implementation." Next, the Framework provides characteristics of a transparent assessment plan:

- descriptive of institutional assessment processes, procedures and activities;
- inclusive of assessment measures including what they are, how they are applied, and frequency of gathering evidence;
- clearly expressed and understandable by multiple audiences;
- prominently posted at or linked to multiple places across the website;
- updated regularly to reflect current activities;
- downloaded or accessed in a timely fashion by multiple web browsers and Internet download speeds; and
- receptive to feedback or comments on the quality and utility of the information provided. (*NILOA's Transparency Framework*, 2011)

Definitions and characteristics are offered for each of the components. Regardless of the component, some characteristics are common to all in the effort to be transparent, including prominently posting the information, updating it regularly, being receptive to feedback on the presentation and information provided, and clearly wording the information for easy comprehension. However, posting information on the Internet does not necessarily mean that internal audiences are aware of the information and will engage with it nor does the sending of reports to multiple audiences mean they will read and understand them (Blaich, 2011). Once reports are completed and ready to be read and potentially used, there are still multiple steps which must be undertaken prior to the occurrence of institutional improvement. These additional steps include the interpretation of the report or data and its subsequent use, non-use, or potential mis-use.

Interpreting and Using Assessment Information

Evidence from assessment can be used in a variety of ways. As Judd and Keith (this volume) point out, by assessing student learning outcomes institutions can show how they meet their stated mission, improve instruction, and plan effectively. Moreover, assessment information can communicate the institution's successes and goals and can be used to improve student learning. Assessment information can provide more than a "customer service" but can show that an institution is serious about its educational mission and that it is working towards using evidence to improve the central function of the institution (McCormick 2010). However, before the information is used it must be interpreted and transformed into usable information.

The process of determining what the data mean is vital to the potential use of assessment data. Data do not speak for themselves; as Shavelson (2010) points out, they "are open to interpretation along social and political lines" (p. 129). This means that data need to be interpreted before they can be used. Judd and Keith (this volume) discuss how it is difficult to determine cause and effect from assessment results in terms of what the institution did to a student to achieve a particular result. There must be a process of making sense of student learning outcomes assessment data as well as discussions about problem-solving and potential changes to improve student learning. Solutions are not intuitive and must be explored by those involved in the learning process. Of course, the ethical implications of determining what counts as "good evidence" or "actionable data" must be considered, and Finley (this volume) provides a discussion of the ethical responsibility involved with the use and implementation of data within an institution.

An additional aspect of the interpretation and use of assessment data is that multiple points of assessment data may not lead to one specific area of concern—triangulation may not lead to corroboration or a "right" answer. The "right" answer may differ depending on who is involved in the process. This makes it vitally important to bring a diverse group of people—faculty, administrators, staff, and students—together to discuss the meaning of the results as well as potential areas of concern and ways to improve. A common complaint among chief academic officers, according to a NILOA survey, is that faculty involvement and support for assessment is a challenge (Kuh & Ikenberry 2009). In the chapter by Banta and Pike, *Will Faculty USE Assessment Findings?* (this volume), the authors state that if faculty are involved in the assessment activities as well as the review of the multiple measures and the interpretation of the results, then they are more inclined to use the assessment information. This process of meaning-making involves discussing how the results are related to and impact student learning.

Data-informed decision-making assists administrators in determining institutional successes in terms of teaching and learning as well as identifying areas of improvement, as Krishnan, Yin, Mahler, Lawson, Harris, & Ruedinger (this volume) describe in more detail. These authors caution that the availability of information, such as having access to reports or assessment data, does not necessarily lead to a solution for a problem or enhanced decision-making per se. Instead, a space must be created within the institution for internal audiences to make sense of the data and determine next steps prior to direct use in decision making.

At the same time, if institutional leaders commit to using assessment for institutional improvement, then information on assessment, particularly the learning objectives, should be prevalent and easily found on a campus, or as Ewell (2009) states, they should be "inescapable" (p. 16). In so doing, institutions show a commitment to the stated standards and improvement. Institutions:

> demonstrate their commitment to evidence-based management and improvement to their members and their stakeholders by constantly referencing—and taking seriously—their goals for learning and the evidence they have about the extent to which these goals are being achieved. *(p. 17)*

Access to the information is only one part of the puzzle of how to use assessment information, but it is an important piece. Other pieces involve interpretation and meaning-making processes with the data. In the interpretation and use of assessment data, remember that regardless of whether assessment was conducted for improvement or accountability purposes, it can yield valuable information and useful results.

Conclusion

At the beginning of this chapter, we asserted that the primary goal for this chapter was to promote reporting on assessment, through the telling of an institutional story about student learning at a campus and to use the data gleaned from assessment for institutional improvement. Reporting on assessment should provide meaningful, understandable, and readily available information to external audiences as well as to internal audiences, which will speak to both accountability and improvement. Further, information is meaningful and understandable through contextualizing student learning outcomes assessment to the institution. While some reporting efforts focus on providing a common display of information, such as the national transparency initiatives, others focus on providing outcome measures such as graduation rates, or on transparent reporting (meaning that the reports are easily understandable and provide relevant information to potential readers). As the NILOA (2011) Transparency Framework outlines, regardless of the strategy employed, a goal for institutions is to share assessment information in a transparent way that informs other people as to what is going on, how it is being done, and what has come of it all rather than to tuck the information away unused.

Note

1 For more information on the Framework or to see institutional examples, see http://www.learningoutcome-assessment.org/TransparencyFramework.htm

References

Association of Governing Boards. (2011). *AGB statement on board responsibility for the oversight of educational quality*. Washington, DC: Author. http://agb.org/news/2011-04/agb-statement-board-responsiblity-over-sight-educational-quality

Banta, T. W., & Blaich, C. (2011). Closing the assessment loop. *Change, 43*(1), 22–27. doi: 10.1080/00091383.2011.538642

Banta, T. W., & Pike, G. R. (this volume). *The bottom line: Will faculty USE assessment findings?*

Bers, T. H., & Seybert, J. A. (1999). *Effective reporting*. Tallahassee, FL: Association for Institutional Research.

Blaich, C. (2011, January). *Can you see me now? Taking the pulse of transparency efforts*. Paper presented at the Annual Meeting of the Association of American Colleges and Universities, San Francisco, CA.

Ewell, P. (2001). *Accreditation and student learning outcomes: A proposed point of departure*. (CHEA Occasional Paper). Washington, DC: Council for Higher Education Accreditation.

Ewell, P. (2009). *Assessment, accountability, and improvement: Revisiting the tension* (NILOA Occasional Paper No.1). Urbana, IL: University of Illinois and Indiana University, National Institute for Learning Outcomes Assessment (NILOA).

Finley, A. (this volume). *Ethical assessment and institutional advancement: Connecting good practice with the need to move campuses forward.*

Jankowski, N., & Makela, J. P. (2010). *Exploring the landscape: What institutional websites reveal about student learning outcomes activities*. Urbana, IL: University of Illinois and Indiana University, National Institute for Learning Outcomes Assessment (NILOA).

Judd, T., & Keith, B. (this volume). *Student learning outcomes assessment at the program and institutional levels.*

Kelly, A. P., & Aldeman, C. (2010, March). *False fronts? Behind higher education's voluntary accountability systems.* Washington, DC: American Enterprise Institute and Education Sector.

Ketcheson, K. A. (2001). Public accountability and reporting: What should be the public part of accreditation? *New Directions for Higher Education, 113*, 83–93.

Krishnan, S., Yin, C., Mahler, W., Lawson, A., Harris, M., & Ruedinger, K. (this volume). *Using national, state, and local data for administrative decision-making.*

Kuh, G. D. (2007, September/October). Risky business: Promises and pitfalls of institutional transparency. *Change, 39*(5), 30–35.

Kuh, G., & Ikenberry, S. (2009). *More than you think, less than we need: Learning outcomes assessment in American higher education*. Urbana, IL: University of Illinois and Indiana University, National Institute for Learning Outcomes Assessment (NILOA).

McCormick, A. C. (2010, November/December). Here's looking at you: Transparency, institutional self-presentation, and the public interest. *Change, 42*(6), 35–43.

Middaugh, M. F. (2010). *Planning and assessment in higher education: Demonstrating institutional effectiveness*. San Francisco, CA: Jossey-Bass.

National Commission on the Future of Higher Education. (2006). *A test of leadership: Charting the future of U.S. higher education*. Washington, DC: U.S. Department of Education.

National Institute for Learning Outcomes Assessment. (2011). *Transparency Framework*. Urbana, IL: University of Illinois and Indiana University, National Institute for Learning Outcomes Assessment (NILOA). Retrieved from: http://www.learningoutcomeassessment.org/TransparencyFramework.htm

Sanders, L., & Filkins, J. (2009). *Effective reporting* (2nd ed.). Tallahassee, FL: Association for Institutional Research.

Seybert, J., Weed, E., & Bers, T. (this volume). *Benchmarking in higher education.*

Shavelson, R. J. (2010). *Measuring college learning responsibly: Accountability in a new era*. Stanford, CA; Stanford University Press.

Suskie, L. (2004). *Assessing student learning: A common sense guide*. Boston, MA: Anker.

Suskie, L. (2009). *Assessing student learning: A common sense guide*. (2nd ed). San Francisco, CA: Jossey-Bass.

Tufte, E. (2001). *The visual display of quantitative information* (2nd ed.). Cheshire, CT: Graphics Press.

Volkwein, J. F. (2010). Reporting research results effectively. *New Directions for Institutional Research, S1,* 155–163.

Walvoord, B. E. (2004). *Assessment clear and simple: A practical guide for institutions, departments, and general education.* San Francisco, CA: Jossey-Bass.

Zenisky, A., & Laguilles, J. S. (this volume). *Reporting assessment results in higher education.*

41

REVISITING RELIABILITY AND VALIDITY IN HIGHER EDUCATION RESEARCH AND PROGRAM EVALUATION

Margaret D. LeCompte and Dorothy E. Aguilera-Black Bear

Good evaluation requires good research practice. In this chapter, we argue that any canons of quality that apply to scientific investigation also apply to evaluative investigation. Similarly, threats to reliability and validity in pure research also affect evaluation research. Moreover, though evaluation and research traditionally are viewed as differing somewhat with regard to the role of stakeholders and participants in formulating research questions, we hold that *any* research project has stakeholders and participants with vested and privileged interests in research results and how they are used. Participants in research increasingly are true participants, working with researchers to reformulate and modify salient questions and data sources, and validate the findings and interpretations of investigations (Schensul & LeCompte, 1999). Since the boundaries between evaluation and research are significantly blurred, we often do not distinguish between processes engaged in during "research" and those involving "evaluation."

Although evaluation research is often built around value judgments and designed to help practitioners make choices about the "best" or "most effective" course of action, starting with attempts to "test for the best" often is premature. One cannot know what is best until one first knows what is "out there." Preliminary qualitative or ethnographic research to identify problems, map out context, conflicts, constituencies, and alternatives, and explore constraints often must precede more experimental approaches. We argue that the construct and external validity of current approaches to evaluation in higher education suffer from the narrowness of criteria used in evaluation as well as the limited constituencies who participate in decisions about what to evaluate, the evidence needed to substantiate valid claims, and who should conduct the evaluation. In this chapter, we discuss how issues of data quality, scale, definition, and purpose can affect validity and reliability of program evaluation in higher education, both because the field of higher education has not been as well documented as has K-12 education and its characteristics are changing rapidly. We also examine meta-evaluative and critical approaches to what the purposes of higher education are and should be, whom it should serve, and how its programs should be implemented in the 21st century.

Our thinking here is foreshadowed in three works by the authors (Aguilera, 2003; LeCompte & Goebel, 1987; LeCompte & Goetz, 1982). We begin with the assumption that issues of reliability and validity are critical to the credibility and quality of any research, regardless of the setting, research question, research design, or purpose. Many authors have written about how reliability and validity may, or may not, be implemented adequately in both qualitative and quantitative research and evaluation. However, some settings and contexts create more obstacles to assuring reliability and validity than others, and qualitative designs in research and evaluation require that reliability and validity be defined somewhat differently from their application in quantitative research. Further, critical and post-structural epistemologies have broadened the way reliability and validity are currently defined and assessed (Eisenhart & Howe, 1992; Lather, 1986). All of these factors affect research and program evaluation in higher education, even though higher education presents some uncharted territory that mandates qualitative research and evaluation; changes in the purposes and constituencies of higher education similarly mandate a postmodern definition for validity.

We argue that the same issues we have addressed elsewhere on reliability and validity also more generally apply to research done in and on higher education. However, while research and evaluation done *in* higher education on particular programs internal to an individual campus or institution poses fewer special or unusual problems to researchers, research *on* higher education as an institution creates some special problems with regard to these canons for research quality. We first review a set of issues involving the range of research designs appropriate for research in and on higher education.

Adapting Reliability and Validity for Qualitative Research Designs

Prior to the 1980s, the rigor and validity of non-experimental research in education was seriously called into question by positivists. LeCompte and Goetz (1982), however, argued that ethnographic research was no less rigorous than experimental design. Their article, *Reliability and Validity in Ethnographic Research*, along with Robert Stake's (1978) discussion of case study methods, laid the foundation for legitimating and necessitating alternatives to experimental design in educational research. Both LeCompte and Goetz and Stake suggested that current notions of what constituted "scientific" research were obsolete and/or unduly narrow and argued that many significant questions about educational processes could not be answered without the use of case studies, ethnographies, and other qualitative research designs.

LeCompte and Goetz (1982) were writing in the vanguard of shifts in educational research from entirely experimental and quantitative research. These shifts called into question the rigidity of experimental designs and the validity of their results. They suggested that the rigid controls required by such designs often were impossible to obtain in the natural world, and also were inappropriate for many important questions asked by researchers and evaluators. Rather than insist on experimental designs and randomized clinical trials as the gold, and the only, standard for high quality research, epistemological shifts changed the focus to processes that occurred during experiments, descriptions of hitherto poorly understood phenomena, research done when experiments were not possible, and explorations of what actually worked in the real world. Such postpositivistic (Lincoln & Guba, 1985; Phillips & Burbules, 2000) notions began to mandate case studies and more qualitative, process-oriented, and ethnographic analyses. These studies provided crucial insights into how and why schools worked as they did, and why anticipated results from evaluation did not always prove workable in real-world classrooms. Qualitative and ethnographic evaluation pointed out that:

- Product evaluation never could explain *why* a particular set of results occurred (Patton, 1986, 1992; Stake, 1978); process and formative evaluation was needed in addition to product evaluation.
- Complete control of experimental conditions was impossible in natural settings.
- Laboratory results often did not translate into real-world settings.
- Using true control groups is unethical in many real-world contexts and control of such groups can be achieved no more easily than in treatment groups.
- More often than not, experimental research was built on assumptions about how the world operated, or on hypothesized relationships, not on empirical descriptions or phenomena or well-documented associations between and among variables.

- The preliminary fieldwork needed to simply find out *what* was happening often had not been done, usually because what was being studied and manipulated was so familiar—like schools and classrooms—that its dynamics were assumed to be understood.
- Additionally, preliminary studies sometimes were not performed because remedies to problems seemed so obvious as to be incontrovertible; for example, studies asserting that more homework, higher standards and expectations, and increased parent involvement would improve student achievement.
- In other cases, proposals were so ideologically congenial to policymakers that alternatives never were explored. Instead, policies calling for closing "failing" schools, imposing higher and higher stakes tests, and eliminating first language support for English Language Learners simply were decreed without studying research to the contrary or assessing whether implementation was even feasible. Perhaps most important, experimental researchers did not always ask questions of people in the field who wanted answers. Practitioners needed to know more than just that an innovation failed to produce the desired results; they also needed to know why an innovation did not work and what could be changed.

LeCompte and Goetz (1982) suggested that the battle between "quantoids" and "ethnoids" was misplaced; the issue was not which approach was better, but which one most appropriately produced answers to the questions asked. Experiments could not answer the question, "Why did we get these results?" or "What solutions have been tried in the past?" Specific kinds of questions—such as "What happened?"—*required* case studies to identify problems, determine how practitioners actually were implementing innovations, and document processes. Thus, as recognition grew that good evaluation necessitated more than experimental designs alone, research and program evaluation increasingly evaluated processes in what were called "ethnographic components." Notwithstanding the utility of these designs, they still were criticized because they could not adhere to traditionally defined canons for reliability and validity.

Applying Canons of Reliability and Validity to Qualitative Research and Evaluation

LeCompte and Goetz (1982) suggested that while the canons of reliability and validity could not be applied to ethnographies and case studies in exactly the same way as they were to experiments[1], researchers could reasonably apply other principles to accomplish the same degree of rigor.

Reliability

Reliability refers to whether a study, if replicated, will achieve the same results as the first iteration. It also refers to whether tests yield the same results if retested with a similar population, or if two sets of coders will code a given set of data the same way. Obviously, since case studies are designed to document and explore relatively unknown or unique phenomena, it is difficult to replicate them exactly, if only because historical effects—the passage of time—will render a site or population different in its second exploration. However, LeCompte and Goetz (1982) posit that the real issue is not how to hold history constant, but whether or not the conditions in the original site, the characteristics of the original population, the methods used, and the researcher's stance and role have been documented with sufficient care that another researcher, given the same or similar conditions, could replicate the study. Once differences between the first and second study are described, researchers could apply a principle of "*comparability*," arguing that similar results could be expected to the extent that conditions and methods used in site two were similar to those in the original. Deviation from the original results also could be explained, given the careful documentation of what the initial differences were.

The key, then, to establishing *comparability*—an analog to reliability—is the care with which investigators describe how they conducted the study. This is facilitated either by using standard and well-understood methods, or by fully explaining those that might be unique or idiosyncratic.

Validity

Validity is the principle that requires that the instruments used actually measure the intended concept (construct validity), that hypothesized causes actually do produce the effects observed (internal validity), and that results obtained with one population can be generalized to another (external validity). LeCompte and Goetz's 1982 work identified how these three notions of validity apply to qualitative investigation.

Construct validity

Conventionally, construct validity refers to whether or not responses to a test item actually measure the underlying concept assumed to be embodied in that item. Thus, math items in a test which reflected concepts children were not taught or which were addressed in unfamiliar terminology would not have construct validity.

Establishing construct validity for qualitative investigations, by contrast, requires using questions and items that are meaningful to and make sense for the population being studied, which means investigators must acquire adequate knowledge of the culture, practices, and language of the people being studied *before* they begin constructing research instruments and protocols. Further, investigators are well advised to withhold formulating evaluative or research questions until they know whether or not the problems identified and questions asked actually make sense to the populations under study. For example, asking Latin American university professors how much a full-time faculty member earns or what their teaching load is would be meaningless, since full-time faculty positions seldom exist in Latin American countries. Too often investigators simply assume that terms mean the same in any setting; construct validity requires that this assumption be set aside even in what appear to be familiar settings. Further, problems that exist in one setting may not exist, or may exist differently, in different settings. "Success" in mainstream US education means high teacher-assigned grades, high scores on standardized tests, graduation from high school, and going away to college. Among Native Americans, however, these measures of success may denote failure to be a "good" citizen in one's own community if it also is accompanied by the loss of one's native language, moving away from one's home and family, and being unable to participate in important traditional rituals (Aguilera, 2003).

Internal validity

In experimental research, internal validity refers to whether the effect observed really is caused by the innovation or treatment under consideration. Internal validity facilitates prediction of future effects; to achieve it, all alternative or spurious causes must be ruled out. For qualitative research, internal validity also facilitates prediction of future behavior or belief, but it is assured by the extent to which researchers make sure that the results obtained and concepts used authentically explain what the participants do and believe. Thus, not only must the data, or evidence, represent real and meaningful concepts the participants use in their own lives, it must also be assembled into explanations or predictive statements that are ruled credible by participants. Just as experimental research rules out spurious or false causes with researcher controls, qualitative researchers rule out false explanations by triangulating reports of participants and seeking confirmation of hypotheses and explanations. They confirm results by member checks, sharing hunches and explanations with participants, and triangulating them with other explanations from participants to make sure that the story is "right." Results that are congruent with participant explanations can be considered authentic or valid in this sense, and they can be used to explain or predict events in the participants' world as they see it. If such assurances cannot be made, the results will be invalid, no matter how well the study is constructed.

External validity

It has been argued that the uniqueness of the populations in many case studies and ethnographies means that generalizability, or whether or not the results obtained from a small sample also describe accurately the larger population, is difficult to obtain. However, since qualitative researchers must assure that what their key informants and initial participants say is not totally idiosyncratic, good qualitative researchers also use ethnographic surveys (S. Schensul, J. J. Schensul, & LeCompte, 1999) to see if the "sense" being made or the stories told by initial respondents actually are shared by all constituents or clients under consideration. Confirmatory surveys not only can confirm consensus, but also can identify multiple opinion groups and outliers. For example, practices defined as "socially just" by an accrediting agency and "reasonable" by faculty and administrators may be defined as neither just nor reasonable when viewed by minority students and faculty whom a university or college is attempting to recruit.

Causality

Qualitative research also was criticized by positivists for its inability to confirm causal relationships. However, qualitative studies do not, in fact, ignore issues of causality; they simply do not seek to confirm it experimentally. Qualitative researchers advocate modus operandi approaches (Patton, 1990) that work backward in a post hoc fashion to seek out plausible antecedents of a particular phenomenon. Such approaches are increasingly convincing and legitimated among scholars, but politicians and policymakers who are poorly trained—if at all—in research methods often find them unfamiliar and insufficiently rigorous. Even many educational researchers remain unconvinced as to the legitimacy of non-experimental research, given the hegemony of experimental and quasi-experimental approaches and its privileged position in scholarly journals and professional associations. Conservative policymakers and politicians, positivistic researchers, and medical modelers have lined up against more progressive educators, evaluators, researchers, and practitioners in a series of skirmishes over rigor—or lack thereof—in educational research. The former argue that randomized clinical trials are the only basis for ensuring the "scientific" validity of studies in education, even though the conditions for such trials rarely, if ever, exist in K–12 and post high school educational settings. The latter continue to fight a rearguard action calling for a more nuanced view of educational complexity, including the need for varying research designs to match the types of questions asked.

Evaluation IN, or Evaluation OF, Higher Education?

We believe that while research and evaluation *in* higher education might well utilize experimental research for specific purposes, research *on* and evaluation *of* higher education is as yet exploratory, with too little of the context and variability known for much valid experimental research to be carried out. Thus, the rush to test hypotheses and verify the efficacy of programs has been premature in many educational settings, and, in particular, in higher education. Evaluation results deriving from experiments simply cannot be considered believable if the conditions needed for valid experiments cannot be obtained. Questions posed by outsiders to higher education participants may make no sense, given their insider perspectives and understanding of the purposes of university life. Further, if believable results can only be obtained in hothouse laboratories, they are of little use to practitioners. Nonetheless, as we shall indicate, policymakers still are calling for conservative and positivistic approaches to evaluation in higher education (ACTA, 2007; Ramirez, 2009). But if such approaches have produced less than stellar results in the relatively simple and more homogenous settings of K–12 public education, they have little chance for producing useful results in the infinitely more complex and diverse settings in higher education. In the pages that follow, we discuss those details.

Data Quality, Reliability and Validity

In 1987, LeCompte and Goebel called into question the validity of much school-based research, saying that many of its conclusions were both unreliable and invalid because data themselves were of such questionable quality. Based on five years of work in one of the nation's largest and most diverse school districts, their article documented missing data, lack of construct validity in tests, use of and adding of scores from incommensurate tests, inappropriate statistical manipulations, and inappropriately constituted cohorts. LeCompte and Goebel argued that making sense of and using such data for program planning, evaluation, and development was a questionable enterprise, though often a necessary expedient given the lack of better data.

Nearly 20 years later, Aguilera (2003) compared 14 schools "in need of improvement" that also served predominantly Native American students. She sought to investigate which reform models were most successful: the seven mainstream, "scientifically based" Comprehensive School Reform (CSR) models, or the seven using models developed by the indigenous community. Aguilera's initial question addressed whether or not the standards used to measure success in public schools were culturally congruent with the norms and values of American Indian communities. Soon, however, Aguilera discovered the same problem LeCompte and Goebel had; it was very difficult to evaluate the success of programs if the data available were flawed, missing, misused, or misinterpreted.

Without exception, the quality of the data available for assessing student performance was so poor that longitudinal analysis of performance was difficult even within a school and virtually impossible across schools. Standardized tests changed from one year to the next or were not administered to all children who should have been tested. Scores of incommensurate tests were aggregated. Often schools reported combining reading and mathematics scores or reporting scores of the entire school population even though special needs students—generally from 15 to 50% of Native American children—had not been tested. Most subject areas—especially those that addressed cultural issues and language—were not tested at all, and even when they were, the tests often lacked construct validity.

The CSR models measured success on performance on English-language standardized tests of reading, mathematics, and sometimes writing. By contrast, the indigenously based reform programs stressed not only these external measures, but also measures of student pride in their own culture, fluency in their native language, and the degree to which the programs provided linkages between the knowledge of their heritage possessed by elders in their community and what current students were learning. However, no tests assessed this content; such measures did not exist. Aguilera's research suggested that when native ways of knowing and control over their children's education were respected, Native American children tended to perform better in school and not to drop out. The CSR definitions of "success" were too narrow and often entirely inappropriate for the community or program under study, and the approaches, particularly the mandated pedagogy and curriculum contained in the "canned" reform models, actually impeded student learning.

Moreover, her research indicated several other factors important to evaluation in higher education. First is the complexity of the contexts within which reforms are implemented, and how external events and both cultural and political dynamics can sabotage a program, no matter how committed the reformers are. Second is the degree of variation among programs—even ones alleged to use the same model. Programs varied widely, not only in their approach, but also in their longevity and in fidelity of implementation. Populations also differed widely in background and preparation.

Third is that data on key problems such as retention and dropout rates, school climate, suspensions, discipline, and teacher satisfaction were defined in myriad incommensurate ways and collected haphazardly.

Finally, Aguilera vividly described how hegemonic pressures from No Child Left Behind mandates tended to crowd out instruction in anything other than reading and mathematics in English. The high stakes attached to student test performance meant low-performing schools could be shut down, teachers fired, principals and superintendents forced to resign, funds cut, and programs ended, all based on the level of student performance on math and language tests in English. High stakes testing in English transformed both native language programs and cultural instruction into expendable luxuries. Many culturally relevant curricular materials, including those that were thematic and content-specific, were tossed out or put in store rooms, creating more time for reading and math in English. As in other communities, teachers taught "to the test," and teachers who were not certified in the subject they taught could not be hired. Elders who had spent decades in local schools trying to maintain language and cultural history instruction were no longer permitted to enter the classrooms. This narrowed the curriculum to subjects in which teachers were certified, obviating instruction in anything having to do with native language, culture, and identity. In turn, this had a devastating effect on both elders and children, increasing language loss and a failure to develop positive cultural identity across entire tribal communities. Without these two components of indigeneity—native language fluency and cultural identity—no Native child can reasonably be expected to acquire sufficient self-esteem for high academic performance (see Deyhle, 1992, 1995; Deyhle and Swisher, 1997; Indian Nations at Risk Task Force, 1991). Further, under such conditions, the effectiveness of programs promoting culturally responsive instruction could not be evaluated validly.

Compromising Validity

We believe that the above examples provide important lessons for research on and evaluation of higher education. First, validity is seriously compromised when it cannot be assumed that valid data—or any data at all—exist to answer the research and evaluation questions asked. Most institutions of higher education do not collect data systematically on many topics of interest, including student retention rates and program quality (Miller, 2008; Walker, Golde, Jones, Conklin Bueschel, & Hutchings, 2008). As a consequence, the validity of cross-institutional comparisons cannot be easily or even validly assured. Second, as was the case in schools serving American Indians, external factors will seriously complicate and even compromise any assessment and evaluation efforts in higher education.

Third, competing goals and standards, and even competing cultural norms, will complicate efforts to determine what constitutes "success." Aguilera's research made it clear that what constitutes a good program for one set of stakeholders may be considered outright failure to another. Her findings are no less applicable to higher education than they were to K-12 schools. Particularly in the early 21st century, "culture wars" (LeCompte, 2010) over the mission and purpose of universities and how they should be organized pit a corporate agenda against the more traditional academic agenda, such that what the former calls success is labeled catastrophic by the latter (LeCompte, 2010; LeCompte & Bonetti, 2010; Washburn, 2005; Wilson, 1995). This dichotomy between academic and corporate cultures creates tensions regarding what is defined as success and how it is measured in traditional universities, just as definitions of success utilized by indigenous communities around the world conflict with conventional academic standards in universities.

Native students—and minorities in general—and their communities often feel that the "normal" commitments, standards, and behavior expected in universities conflict with, and even destroy, family and community ties because they interfere with tribal members' ability to learn and maintain native languages, cultural traditions and values, and interfere with participation in traditional roles important to the social fiber of the tribal nation or community. The ability of tribal members to carry on language, knowledge systems, and cultural traditions is a measure of sovereignty for tribal nation communities, and sovereignty itself is a measure of achievement. If sovereignty is compromised, so also is the validity of an assessment measuring success because it no longer conveys a story that makes sense to participants. Obviously, how success is defined or gets measured for tribal nation members will not be adequately or validly measured by standardized mainstream educational instruments. For example, a school whose success story lauds its students' very high test scores in English and math but coexists with another story about how its students can no longer communicate with their grand-parents, play key roles in cultural ceremonies, or remember the lore of their ancestors cannot be considered truly successful because it fails to support the cultural traditions, knowledge systems, and language needed to build tribal sovereignty for Native students. In a related vein, factors outside a reform initiative very often will provide more meaningful explanations of what really happened than factors internal to the initiative itself. Thus, small-scale research on individual programs, innovations, and colleges may be more feasible in higher education, have greater validity, and be more reliable than research seeking to compare across programs and institutions. Further, research and evaluation projects that work within a particular cultural milieu will be more valid than those that simply ignore the existence of cultural differences and use standard methods across cultural boundaries.

A fourth factor is the difficulty of determining what the "right" problem is or which questions are relevant to ask, given ideological pressures to implement specific programs in higher education with-out really knowing their efficacy. For example, the growing pressures to create uniform standards and consistent ways to measure the impact of college and university education and the increasing calls for accountability echo those of No Child Left Behind and Race to the Top for K–12 education (ACTA, 2007; Gabriel, 2011; Hess, 2010; Hess & Rotherham, 2007). However, even administrators who have expertise in both qualitative and quantitative research and who see the value in mixed methods approaches for finding ways to close gaps between program content and services, tend to privilege quantitative research over qualitative designs for evaluating these efforts. In part, this prac-tice derives from the hegemony of the former, at the expense of the latter.

Given the above, three guiding principles can be articulated for research in higher education. First, no single research design will suffice to answer complex questions. In an era such as the early 21st century, in which good "science" in education has been narrowly defined once again as controlled experimentation and randomized clinical trials, and the term "evidence-based" has come to mean strictly numeric data, adhering to the first guiding principle can be politically unpopular and research following it can be difficult to render convincing. The reliability and validity of alternative means for investigation must be made clear and legitimate to inhabitants of a different professional culture—the politicians, policymakers, and corporate leaders who increasingly direct the course of higher education and influence its goals. The second principle mandates that the quality of the data available must be evaluated before any attempts to engage in "data-driven" program planning begin. Investigators even must be open to the possibility that the needed data do not exist. A corollary is that researchers need to determine the multiple reasons for undertaking specific initiatives. Far too often, initiatives are under-taken for reasons that have everything to do with ideology and nothing to do with scientifically vali-dated prior practice. Thus, researchers can find themselves in the unenviable position of trying to find the good in programs about which meta-questions such as "Should we even be doing this in the first place?" and "Is this initiative congruent with our core mission and culture?" have never been asked.

The third principle mandates that researchers and evaluators exercise care when doing research on prespecified or a priori questions on which little prior fieldwork has been conducted. Before begin-ning an evaluation, they must find out whether the question being asked is valid in the context; they must identify the cultural, historical, political, and institutional conditions in which the question is embedded; and, most importantly, they must determine whether or not the program is being imple-mented as intended—or even being implemented at all! Addressing these issues, of course, requires qualitative research or process evaluation.

What Is the Existing Context for Evaluation in Higher Education?

We now move to a cursory examination of the existing state of data collection in higher education. All educational institutions seek to determine how effective their instruction is and how well their students perform once they graduate. They also have reporting obligations to federal and state agencies, engage in strategic planning, make enrollment and budgetary projections, participate in accreditation processes, and determine ways to raise funds and assess the performance of their faculty and staff. Higher education institutions also measure the quality of their employees, the success of their recruitment and retention efforts among desirable students, and, to the extent possible, the success of their graduates. This research is characterized as:

1. Evaluation of individual programs, usually done in house or across a few participating institutions. These tend to be relevant to a particular discipline, set of related disciplines, or a field, or ways to better assess teacher performance.
2. Rankings of programs within fields by professional associations. These also use varying criteria for assessing quality, ranging from the prestige of placement of graduates to the number of publications and amount of grant funding earned by faculty members. These criteria are not consistently applied across all programs or by associations employing them. For example, some evaluating agencies give heavy weight to the opinions of alumni about their educational experience, while others collect no alumni information at all.
3. IRB data collection and other ethical watchdogs (HAZMAT, protection of animals, research misconduct, etc.). These data are collected primarily to substantiate conformity to federal and state regulations, establishing the level of care that must be accorded to participants in research. They can, however, serve as a partial measure of the kinds and quantity of research carried out in an institution.
4. Fiscal accounting. All institutions of higher education are held accountable to their governing boards, taxpayers, and donors for how their funds are used. Like corporations, they must regularly report their budgets and expenditures. More often than not, however, these documents are not treated as research, and are not released to a wide public.
5. Accreditation—disciplinary and institutional—that uses a combination of internal self-studies and external "inspections" from respected practitioners and scholars in the field. Accrediting agencies set standards to which colleges and universities are held accountable, using people who have been researchers and educators in the field and who presumably understand the context and constraints of those under scrutiny.
6. Tenure and promotion of faculty and instructors. These deliberations assess quality of teaching (students questionnaires, observations, interviews with students, participation in professional development, advising, other non-classroom activities, and, less often, analysis of syllabi), and accessibility.
7. Measures that include quantity and quality of research, types and amount of service, lists of publications, types and quality of service, and measures of pedagogical excellence. As is the case with K–12 education, efforts now are emerging to apply "value-added" models to assessment of university teaching, so that the value of a program or a set of faculty is measured by how much more individual students in programs taught by specific teachers know after being taught by them. Still in the embryonic stages of implementation in K–12 education, value-added models have not yet appreciably improved assessment of teaching (Paulson & Marchant, 2009), and in fact can only be implemented where valid standardized measures of what was taught exist. These conditions rarely if ever exist in higher education.
8. Faculty course evaluations, used widely as a measure of course quality. Notwithstanding their popularity, they are more a measure of student satisfaction than of student learning. They also are

of questionable validity; considerable evidence demonstrates that students use these instruments to punish professors whose personality, rigor, ethnicity, or politics they dislike. Thus, faculty of color and those who teach difficult or required courses are more likely to receive poor course evaluations than white teachers and teachers of electives (Anas, 2011; Martinez, 2002).

9. Student grades, used to evaluate whether or not students have mastered prerequisites, are deserving of scholarships, should be retained, promoted, or graduate. However, the validity of these grades is compromised because the grading system does not factor in students' ability to apply and practice the knowledge learned in classrooms in real-world settings.

10. Administrators and staff evaluations. These individuals are subject to varied measures of quality including supervisory evaluations that are standard to the job, but they are seldom held accountable to the university's primary clients, the students—or assessed regarding whether their actions provide adequate support systems to permit faculty to effectively teach and serve all of their diverse students' needs.

11. External ratings and rankings of quality, such as those conducted by *US News and World Report, London Times Higher Education, Forbes College Rankings, Newsweek College Ranking*, and others. These vary in the criteria they use and in terms of what they "count," such that programs may rank quite high in one rating system and poorly in another. Schools of education, for example, are evaluated by superintendents in public schools; since alumni tend to rank their own alma mater highly, schools of education lacking an administrator training program do not have those enthusiastic alumni to boost their rankings.

12. Data on incoming students. Universities maintain records for admissions purposes and for assessments of student body diversity. These data probably are the most consistently collected and aggregated data in higher education; they consist of demographic information and test scores, as well as the essays students produce to justify their admission.

13. Records of graduation rates. These are not kept by most schools in a systematic and consistent way, and most schools lack records of where students go after graduation from all levels—whether from undergraduate, MA, postgraduate, or doctoral programs. While career counseling offices maintain records of the job seeking efforts of former students who use the service, many students do not. The number of graduates from programs in any given year can be found, but this does not reflect the percentage of a cohort that ever graduates from any given program. Especially in graduate programs, struggling students tend simply to fade away and be lost (Miller, 2008; Walker, Golde, Jones, Conklin Bueschel, & Hutchings, 2008).

Threats to Validity and Reliability in the Higher Educational Context

Problems of Data Quality and Quantity

Our earlier work (LeCompte & Goetz, 1982) did not directly address the threats to reliability and validity posed by problems of faulty databases or gaps in the available information. However, we have become aware of these issues and have addressed them as above regarding K–12 education. Even greater threats to the validity of research are posed by these same issues in higher education because it is light years behind K–12 education in the assembly and maintenance of consistent databases. In a very real sense, the status of higher education assessment and accountability resembles that of public education in the 1920s and 1930s, prior to the inception of scientific management, standardized testing, and the advent of computerized record keeping. The data enumerated above may answer some questions about the status of programs and their successes in a narrow sense, but it may be difficult to implement research *on* higher education overall, especially research that tries to assess the responsiveness of higher education to socioeconomic and demographic changes and concomitant demands for services.

The Problem of Standard Setting: Accrediting Agencies and Evaluative Bodies

Independent private and state-level certifying agencies set the standards for quality to which institutions of higher education are held accountable, but, while those standards purport to be congruent with "best practices," they are often supported by little hard research and instead influenced by political interests and ideological fads (e.g., Hess, 2010). The standard of "diversity" is a good case in point; initially, it referred to the degree to which an institution was able to recruit Black, Asian, Hispanic and Native American students to predominantly white colleges. As open support for affirmative action plans came under legal and political fire, those words could no longer be used; they were too progressive. The term "diversity" originally served as a gloss for multiraciality, but came to include socioeconomic, religious, and ideological variation as well—thus depriving the term of its original meaning and making any measurement of its existence or effectiveness unreliable and invalid.

Accreditation organizations often apply a single set of standards, regardless of the type of institution and its programs, and the background and demographic characteristics of the students and faculty; further, the focus of evaluations often is limited to quantitative measures of students entering and leaving programs and the grades they accrue in various classes. While such data can describe over time how many students passed the class, graduated from the program, and earned degrees, that information alone is not sufficient to rank the quality of schools or provide insight into why students failed to complete their work or to attain a degree.

Competing agendas regarding evaluation of quality in higher education: Who does the evaluation?

Another issue is whether or not the principles and goals to which various agencies hold institutions accountable are valid for that institution. While state departments of higher education and national certifying agencies such as NCATE and NCAA have long conducted regular accreditation visits to colleges and universities, the conservative political climate in the early 2010s has spawned other agencies, such as the *National Council on Teacher Quality* (NCTQ), an independent advocacy group affiliated with the news magazine, *US News and World Report*. This agency purports to supplant NCATE and other accrediting groups and to hold teacher education programs accountable to implementing practices resembling those mandated for K–12 schools under No Child Left Behind and its successors. NCTQ "originally told schools that if they did not voluntarily supply data and documents, the teacher quality group would seek the information under open-records laws. If that did not work, the raters planned to give the schools an F" (Gabriel, 2011). In fact, NCTQ *has* posted Fs on their public website for schools that did not voluntarily provide the data requested by NCTQ. Deans of many schools of education, including the largest and most prestigious in the USA, have protested NCTQ's agenda, arguing that it is even less appropriate and feasible for higher education than it already is for pre-baccalaureate education (Gabriel, 2011). One of the most controversial requirements proposed by NCTQ involves mandating the same forms of "value-added" assessment for college faculty as are now becoming mandates in K–12 education.

Competing notions of the proper goals and purposes for higher education

Customarily, what actually is evaluated depends on what the goals and objectives of those programs and institutions are, especially if the evaluation is assessing quality. Evaluation simply involves asking questions about whether the goals are being achieved, under which standards, and how well the standards are being met. This is relatively unproblematic if agreement has been achieved on the purposes and standards, but not if various stakeholders and constituencies disagree on the goals. Disagreements require deciding which goals are legitimate and feasible and should guide the research.

Currently, however, not only is disagreement growing between institutional and public and private sectors as to who should set and enforce standards for higher education and what those standards should be, but current culture wars (LeCompte, 2010) over the purposes of higher education pit corporate support and a vocational orientation outside the academy against the intellectual/academic orientation of university faculty and most academic administrators inside the academy. This conflict is exemplified by the differences in approach between that of the American Council of Trustees and Alumni (ACTA; http://www.goacta.org), a neoconservative pressure group seeking to privilege instruction based on a Western Euro-American canon, reduce the influence of so-called "liberals," weaken the role of faculty in governance and curriculum, and restructure university governance into a more top-down less participatory corporate model, and the American Association of University Professors (AAUP; http://www.aaup.org/aaup), whose manifestoes on academic freedom and faculty rights have been signed on to by nearly all institutions of higher education in the US, and which serve as a template guiding academic culture (see AAUP, n.d.). Faculty view the monitoring of the political orientations of faculty and the content of their courses and research to be gross violations of academic freedom; ACTA interprets these activities as a way to streamline the university, make it more accountable, and restore rigor in instruction.

Concerns over the measures used to assess conformity to specific standards

Another threat to validity and reliability in higher education research is the self-study, the primary mode for assessing institutional or program quality and adherence to accreditation standards. Self-studies are structured by questions and guidelines laid out by accrediting agencies and by colleges in their own periodic review processes. Essentially, they are "inside jobs," both in the sense that the questions are designed by individuals who already are participants in the higher educational system, and because the kind of evidence that is to be provided often is left up to the institution to decide. Self-studies too often involve having institutions repackage what they already are doing to maintain the appearance of compliance. While many institutions do take the accreditation process very seriously, others may not. A cynical approach might ask, "What are we doing already that more or less looks like what we are supposed to be doing, and how can we describe what we already are doing so we satisfy the accrediting agency?" For example, a mandate that requires doctoral level graduate instruction to include training in both qualitative and quantitative methods of research can be "satisfied" by a 10-day summer intensive course, a two-semester course in qualitative methods, and a similar course in quantitative methods, or a required series of specific methods classes (e,g., survey research, ethnography, discourse analysis, several levels of statistics, a course in measurement, and a course in proposal writing). Though all three might satisfy the accreditation or review standard, the competence achieved by students in each program will vary considerably, and reports stating that all three programs adequately met the standard would be invalid. Similarly, the depth of commitment to a specific motto could be measured by whether or not students and faculty can, when asked, rattle off what the motto says, rather than really investigating whether or not those same faculty actually walk the talk. A further problem is that such results seldom are monitored; when the review process stops, the concern over accountability in higher education also tends to stop until the next round of auditors arrive.

Cynicism and its impact aside, questions remain as to what *isn't* being measured by the existing system. What outside-of-the-box questions are not being asked, simply because the interlocutors are themselves still inside of the box? These can include meta-questions, such as "Is this program really doing what it should be doing?" "What *is* its purpose?" and "What should its goals be and how should they be met?" These questions rarely can be answered unless new perspectives enter the evaluative arena. One could argue that new agencies such as the NCTQ fill exactly that niche, but such agencies pose exactly the same political problems as that of ACTA. Its actual goals for higher education (disguised in the rhetoric of excellence and quality) differ drastically from what educators and practitioners believe they should be.

How good the standards of performance in higher education actually are also is problematic. Accreditation programs do not assess what is not being measured by the existing system, and they do not raise meta-level questions such as, "Is this program really doing what should be done to solve this problem?" "Does the institution really understand—from the perspective of key target populations—how the target population defines the problem and what it feels should be done?" And "What should the institution's goals be and how should they be met?" Too often the "evaluation" consists of counting exercises—how many students of which kind entered, how many graduated, and how many publications were produced by a faculty member. Rarely do such evaluations ask whether a program was adequately funded for its purposes and scope, or whether it provided the services needed to solve the problems for which it was initiated.

Aguilera's (2004) evaluation of a higher education program exemplifies the need for, and lack of, such a broader perspective on evaluation. She studied a federally funded program that purports to both encourage and prepare first-generation, low-income undergraduates and students of color to attend graduate school and earn PhDs in their respective disciplines. While the funding agency required only that the program report the number of students served and the retention rates according to the types of services provided, that information could not explain either the patterns of retention for diverse students or the effectiveness of the program components. Further, gaps in data existed across cohorts from three of the four years of the funding cycle because the program lacked funding resources to train staff in coding and entering data. The program director had expected the researcher to both provide credible findings and describe what these meant in terms of the program and the students, but the data to do so were lacking. Later, the program director decided to study the program for her own dissertation, which involved designing an ethnographic study that collected data beyond what the funding institute required. It included case studies investigating the backgrounds, conditions, and circumstances of current program students to understand their intellectual strengths, motivations, preparedness for graduate school, family and community support (especially mentors), financial situation, social networks, and cultural and academic identities. The dissertation demonstrated that all of the above were important indicators of retention and success among underrepresented groups of students (Aguilera, 2004; Beal, 2007), and confirmed that the data that had hitherto been required was insufficient for such a task.

The Lack of Measurement Instruments

While most disciplines have created tests and measures of graduate achievement, these remain internal to programs and colleges. Many educators and policymakers would like to go further, comparing the quality of higher education *across* institutions. Efforts are now under way to create some ways to reasonably compare institutions on similar bases. The Voluntary System of Accountability (VSA; http://www.voluntarysystem.org), a national on-line report card for colleges and universities, is a joint initiative of the Association of Public and Land-grant Universities (APLU; http://www.aplu. org/page.aspx?pid=280) and the Association of State Colleges and Universities (ASCU). Currently, it consists of establishing many measures of quality for higher educational institutions, the most hotly contested of which is a testing program to see how much general knowledge college seniors have gained during their education. This test purports to facilitate value-added comparisons between colleges and universities similar to the method proposed for K-12 schools. However, problems arise when attempts are made to determine the "value added" to a student's knowledge base by attendance at a given institution of higher learning.

University administrators argue that small liberal arts colleges, whose offerings generally are designed to build on and enhance knowledge in the same areas already initiated in high school, might be suitable units to compare with such tests. However, they are inappropriate for the highly varied and multiple training and educational purposes of university education. Many colleges and all universities are composed of multiple programs, each preparing students for specific professional careers or preparatory programs. In addition, the field of higher education is increasingly diverse, both in the structure and range of offerings, and how they deliver instruction. A test of general knowledge such as VSA proposes lacks construct validity for advanced professional training and graduate schools, and for technical institutes and other non-university post-baccalaureate training. It also penalizes institutions with high admission standards, since students already scoring at the top of a test of general knowledge such as the SAT or GRE cannot be expected to show dramatic gains over a pretest. Nonetheless, supporters of No Child Left Behind have advocated not only high stakes tests, but also a national curriculum with associated high stakes testing for higher education similar to the one proposed for K-12 education. University faculty and administrators hotly resist these proposals on the grounds that they lack construct validity, penalize top colleges, and stifle both academic freedom and faculty control over curriculum, instruction, and assessment.

The Variability in Higher Education

Research and evaluation in K-12 education deal with a universe far simpler than that of higher education. Organization and control structures in K-12 public education are relatively consistent across schools, districts, and states. The subject matter is limited, even if schools do organize multiple versions of the same course ranging in difficulty from advanced honors to remedial instruction. And while quite varied, the K-12 purposes still are the inculcation of foundational knowledge in the arts, humanities, and sciences, preparatory to a student's entry to the world of work or further study. Therein lies one of the problems: A fair degree of agreement can be obtained on what those K-12 foundational subjects should be and the performance levels required for modest proficiency. Past the senior year of high school, however, "higher education" becomes a wildly diverse assemblage of incommensurate entities. Higher education can mean anything from proprietary schools offering short courses in business, health, computers, cosmetology, and repair of all sorts of vehicles and equipment, to two-year community colleges, public and private four-year liberal arts colleges, on-line and partially on-line degree programs in every field imaginable, to full service residential colleges and universities offering a wide range of professional and other degrees in both public and private sectors.

What Is the Population? What Is the Unit of Analysis?

The preceding raises an important problem. Higher education is not a monolith. Nor is it an entity like water that cannot be disaggregated. If one is set on evaluating higher education, from which vantage point should the investigation begin? What should be the population or unit of analysis? Clearly, appropriate units of analysis must be isolated, with research questions appropriate to the scale, scope, purpose, and operations of each unit. What level or type should be approached? The program? The institution? The college? If the latter two, which kind of college or institution? Or if the questions are about the entire phenomenon, where does one start? The issue of defining units of analysis and operational measures is critical to issues of reliability and validity; if units are not defined and operationalized in ways that are comparable or commensurate, researchers will be comparing apples and oranges.

What Do Reliability and Validity Mean in a Postmodern Era?

Just as the terms reliability and validity had to be reinterpreted in the late 20th century for applicability to qualitative research and evaluation, we must address what they mean in the 21st century. Can standards and practices delineated—and contested—in the mid-20th century still be applied reasonably to new situations, populations, institutions, and historical eras? Can criteria that seemed reasonable as measures of quality in the 1980s and 1990s remain uncontested now? Entities that were recognized as arbiters of high quality in past decades no longer may be accorded the same legitimacy as they once were. Providing "equal educational opportunity," for example, once meant eliminating de jure prohibitions against admission of students of color to public schools. That standard no longer is considered a sufficient measure of equity or social justice in an era in which simple admission provides no guarantee of equal or equitable treatment once the gates of education are opened.

Similarly, practices that are seen as appropriate for one level of education may not be appropriate, or even feasible, for another. For example, it may not be possible to "scale up" standardized testing for higher education. Institutions of post-baccalaureate education may be too different from one another for that to be possible. Even the question of whether professors can be subjected to the same kinds of "value-added" assessments now being implemented for K–12 teachers is contestable. Given that many reform efforts current in K–12 public education are being proposed for or imposed on public institutions of higher education (ACTA, 2007; Ramirez, 2009), we believe it is appropriate to ask what those experiences teach us about the validity of research and evaluation conducted on such efforts. For example, questions about what is being evaluated, for what purposes, by whom, and for whom may need to be addressed before any evaluation begins.

Decolonizing Validity in Higher Education

A contemporary examination of research quality—or reliability and validity—needs to be framed within an understanding that the Academy, broadly speaking, is an institution imported to the Western Hemisphere from Europe, and that it increasingly serves a population that no longer resembles the exclusively white, male, Christian, and English speaking population it originally served. Evaluation *in* and *of* higher education must consider the hegemonic content of questions such as the following:

- Given the diverse populations enrolled, what are the varied criteria for success in higher education?
- Who defines what "success" is, and for whom?
- How are different definitions of success defined and operationalized?
- What research/evaluation designs are used to measure success?
- To what extent are different designs used to capture the diverse realities and goals encompassed in contemporary higher education?
- Which sectors in the population benefit from higher education, and why?

It also must be recognized that virtually every aspect of the world in which higher education exists has changed in the last 100 years. Notwithstanding that electronic technologies have changed everything from how investigations are done to how we amass data and communicate with one another, perhaps the most dramatic changes in higher education have been in the demography of its constituents. Once almost exclusively the province of white males, female graduates now outnumber males and are equal in number to males in many professions. Further changes have meant that many minority and first-generation students have graduated from colleges and become faculty and researchers themselves. These changes in the "face" of the Academy (LeCompte, 2002) also have dramatically changed what these constituents believe is and should be the Academy's purpose and role. These ideas clash with the fact that many of the criteria used by accreditation agencies to evaluate higher education may do more to reinforce past practice than to inform new approaches to teaching and learning; they do little to clarify the relationship of higher education to other structures in the society. As research in the mid- and late 1990s has made clear, universities play a key role in reinforcing existing social status hierarchies. Marginalized populations are not viewed by the Academy as legitimate participants (Lave & Wenger, 1991) because they might alter how universities allocate status and control information. However, insofar as the marginalized have gained access to and benefitted from university training, they have served as catalysts for transformation both in higher education and the world outside (Boudon, 1974; Bourdieu & Passeron, 1977; Foucault, 1980). Thus, contemporary canons for reliability and validity must take into consideration the definitions of reality held by marginalized constituencies in the Academy, not just those definitions that provide context for traditional programs. Additionally, higher educational institutions cannot assume that what works for mainstream populations will work as well for marginalized populations, whose beliefs, needs, realities, and life experiences differ radically from those of white mainstream populations.

We are, in effect, calling for "decolonizing" the way concepts of reliability and validity are conceived of and applied. This means holding mainstream and non-mainstream populations alike accountable for a completely revised set of standards, one not limited to what counts for success solely among European-Americans. One might begin by assessing the quality of student performance in areas such as service to one's community, respect and care for elders (valued by indigenous communities), and being able to perform at a high level in a language other than one's mother tongue. Assessment of knowledge of other cultures also would level the playing field for ethnically diverse groups. Requiring that students know about more than their own culture and language[2] could provide a more central arena in which once silenced or marginalized constituencies could be heard as well.

Decolonizing in Action: An Example

In rethinking who sets standards for whom and what these standards might be in higher education, we use the experience of Native Americans for a perspective on how to discuss issues of validity in research and program evaluation. Our premise is that what constitutes value in a program and whether or not its goals are valid for a population often privileges Western knowledge and values over Indigenous knowledge, values, and educational goals. Higher education leaders must decolonize higher education by acknowledging how higher education frames diversity hegemonically as a problem, rather than a strength. These approaches are, in fact, constructed consciously through relationships of power held by white people and non-whites; these approaches erroneously "blame the victim," positing that assimilation of native people is the *sole* solution to problems of diversity in education institutions. However, for example,

> The "Indian Problem" is not a problem of children and families but rather, first and foremost, a problem that has been consciously and historically produced by and through the systems of colonization: a multidimensional force underwritten by Western Christianity, defined by White supremacy, and fueled by global capitalism. *(Grande, 2004, p. 19)*

Hegemony and Success for Indigenous Students

To be successful, a contemporary student or program must conform to a hegemonic set of norms and values that may, in fact, seriously disrupt or destroy traditional values. Kincheloe (2006) argues that Western knowledge is so engrained with "cultural supremacy and exclusionary practices" that it fails to acknowledge the "genius" of indigenous knowledge (p. 181). Further, higher educational institutions cannot be said to provide equitable education for indigenous and other non-mainstream populations if the entire public educational system, from kindergarten through higher education, is based on epistemologies, knowledge, and assessment procedures from the mainstream. Bergstrom (2009) points out that many American Indian students and other minorities are greatly disadvantaged in college by the great disjuncture between traditional tribal cultural norms and expectations for success and how to achieve it on one hand, and what colleges and universities hold to be normative behavior for students and faculty on the other. While tribal colleges in some states do hire native scholars and experts in indigenous knowledge systems, tribal colleges more often than not are located in rural areas, inaccessible to urban Native Americans who actually constitute the majority of indigenous residents of the U.S. Further, tribal colleges themselves are marginalized within the larger system of higher education (Pavel, Inglebret, & Banks, 2001).

Perhaps most heinous is the deficit perspective that higher education institutions take with respect to non-mainstream students, their parents, and their communities. Most colleges and universities have indeed established student services offices for diverse populations, but such offices tend to focus on deficits, rather than on the assets these students bring with them. Locating student problems in the students themselves serves both the students and the institution poorly; it trivializes the true problems students have, including serious physical disabilities and illnesses (Beal, 2007), minimizes the kind and quantity of support such students actually need, and even prescribes as remedies services students really do not need, instead of what they actually could use. In such circumstances, "failure" of students can be reliably measured, but the reasons for such failure cannot be validly explained without a highly critical and culturally informed analysis of the measures used to assist them. Goals for the undergraduate program, evaluated by Aguilera (2004), for example, included that successful students would enter and graduate from PhD programs. This devalued the success of first-generation and minority students who completed MA degrees but did not pursue a PhD, prevented the program from counting completion of an MA degree as successful, and justified the program in continuing to hire (cheaper) graduate student ABDs to train undergraduates for the methodological rigor of PhD research instead of full-time faculty. As the director of one such program complained, "No wonder I can't figure out how to teach these children how to complete a PhD. I can't even figure out how to do it for myself! Maybe once I have my own degree I'll be better at it, but right now, I don't know . . ." (Beal, personal communication, 2007).

Indigenous peoples have not simply sat on their hands, waiting for the Academy to change itself. As more indigenous researchers/scholars/graduate students have entered higher education and begun to illustrate gaps in investigation, unasked research questions, and flaws in how previous research paradigms and methodologies have been used (LeCompte, 2002), the Academy has begun to transform. Indigenous methodologies have emerged alongside self-determination and revitalization projects among indigenous communities; both have facilitated and raised new research questions. When unimpeded, these methodologies have evolved collaboratively with proactive efforts of individual researchers, evaluators, activities, and community groups; where appropriate, they help build and protect the sovereignty of indigenous groups and promote their programs of nation building and social justice (Aguilera-Black Bear, 2011).

All these efforts have served to enlighten the Academy, not diminish its quality. What stultifies evaluation and research is not when new ideas are welcomed, but when hegemonic forces adopt an orthodoxy that legitimates only a few research designs, and rules out specific questions and interpretations. The most significant tenets of research and evaluation require principled skepticism regarding the rectitude of current theories and answers, openness to alternative explanations, flexibility with regard to which questions are worth asking, and openness with regard to which designs are legitimate. During the 2009 national conference of the American Anthropological Association, indigenous scholars challenged Eurocentric epistemologies and paradigms about education and research. In two sessions, "What Counts as Knowledge? Conflicting Ends of Schooling for Indigenous Peoples" and "Research in the Era of Self-Determination and Revitalization: Who Writes the Story?" the critique by indigenous scholars of current empirical research was clear. An example is Tuck's (2009) critique of damage-centered research:

In damaged-centered research, one of the major activities is to document pain or loss in an individual, community, or tribe. Though connected to deficit models—frameworks that emphasize what a particular student, family, or community is lacking to explain underachievement or failure—damage-centered research is distinct in being more socially and historically situated. It looks to historical exploitation, domination, and colonization to explain contemporary brokenness, such as poverty, poor health, and low literacy. Common sense tells us this is a good thing, but the danger in damage-centered research is that it is a pathologizing approach in which the oppression singularly defines a community. *(p. 413)*

For indigenous peoples, decolonizing frameworks enhance sovereignty and are vital to reclaiming and accessing indigenous knowledge systems as viable. They are, in fact, essential to indigeneity and native ways of viewing the world. While decolonizing education and research methodologies do not wipe the slate clean, they still challenge scholars to critique Western paradigms, pedagogies, and worldviews—the hegemony sustained by the Academy—and to value other epistemologies, knowledge, and pedagogies, especially indigenous knowledge systems which have been in existence for millenniums. At her keynote presentation, Konai Helu Thaman (2003) discusses colonization of Pacific Islanders peoples:

> . . . decolonizing Pacific studies is about our struggles, from kindergarten to university, to learn the dominant study paradigms and worldviews of western peoples who lived in other places at other times . . . [this] challenges us to look at our western educational legacies, their philosophies, ideologies, and pedagogies, which for nearly 200 years have not fully recognized the way Oceanic peoples communicate, think, and learn—ideologies that sought to destroy the values and belief systems underpinning indigenous education systems in which the majority of Oceanic peoples were and continue to be socialized. *(p. 2)*

Indigenous peoples throughout the world have named their struggles in ways similar to Konai Thaman's. She continues:

> For me, decolonizing Pacific studies is important because (1) it is about acknowledging and recognizing the dominance of western philosophy, content, and pedagogy in the lives and the education of Pacific peoples; (2) it is about valuing alternative ways of thinking about our world, particularly those rooted in the indigenous cultures of Oceanic peoples; and (3) it is about developing a new philosophy of education that is culturally inclusive and gender sensitive. *(p. 2)*

For far too long indigenous knowledge, languages, and cultural practices have been rejected, silenced, misrepresented, mocked, and even condemned in educational institutions.

Ethics, IRBs, and Decolonization

Decolonizing research has required revising protocols and guidelines for the protection of human participants in research studies. Based on medical models and the concept of the individual, rather than communal or group rights, the Belmont Report (National Commission, 1978), the Helsinki Accords (1975), and the Nuremburg Code (1947) inform the ethical principles to which researchers are bound in treating participants in research in equitable, humane, socially just, and respectful ways. However, these principles protect the privacy and identity of *individuals*, and expect that consent to conduct research resides with *individuals*, not the groups or communities to which individuals belong. These principles are inappropriate for more communally oriented indigenous communities, and may also be inappropriate for more mainstream institutions. In recognition of the differences between mainstream and indigenous communities, the University of Victoria Faculty of Human and Social Development created a new set of ethical principles, the "Protocols and Principles for Conducting Research in an Indigenous Context" (2003), to guide researchers studying indigenous communities. It included major revisions concerning ethical considerations, accountability, the use of participatory approaches, issues of consent and who has the capacity to provide it, who retains the rights to intellectual property generated by the research, and how research outcomes will be used (pp. 5–8) for research conducted with and on indigenous populations. Since that time, other guidelines have been developed, but they still are seen as specific to research on the "other," not as guidelines that also should govern studies of mainstream populations conducted by non-indigenous researchers. However, we hold that guidelines appropriate for indigenous populations are equally appropriate for non-indigenous populations; they simply raise issues that had not been considered important in the hegemonic framework of Western science. Decolonization will require that more general guidelines be developed for use by Institutional Review Boards in higher education, and that they be generalized for use with all populations.

The Need for Methods that Elicit More Valid Data

In addition to ethical guidelines, research designs and methodologies that enhance the validity and reliability of data elicited from non-mainstream populations need to be developed for diverse populations, conditions, and contexts. Conventional research often has resulted in further marginalization of Tribal communities because it has failed to examine and represent the contextual information in a meaningful and valid way. The research paradigm often used to study American Indians is based on measurable or quantitative data. While useful in some ways, such a deductive, a priori approach often makes assumptions which are largely irrelevant for contemporary native people, and, as such, is culturally inappropriate. For example, a common assumption is that cultural practices and beliefs no longer need to be considered in studies of urban indigenous people because they have "lost their culture." However, studies increasingly are showing that culture is critical in unpacking how indigenous people think, learn, and act, and how these differ from the patterns of white people (Bang & Medin, 2010).

Pepion (in press), a Blackfeet anthropologist, recently described the logic behind the designs and methods he used for examining conceptual ideas and the roles of leadership among Blackfeet leaders. His methods assured the validity of his findings through triangulation of data collection sources and types of primary and secondary data:

> The interviews and information from the contemporary tribal people validate that knowledge has persevered from early times . . . the triangulation of ethnographic records, ceremony, and oral tradition has merit in a validation process . . . the contemporary interviewees have been able to symbolically depict tribal culture, ceremony, and knowledge as a way of communicating the past and present. *(p. 37)*

Aguilera–Black Bear's (Aguilera–Black Bear, Figueira, Gelman, & Ryan-Fear, 2010; Aguilera–Black Bear, Ryan, & Figueira, 2009) study of school leaders, teachers, and ethnically diverse youth in three Oregon high schools that implemented Youth Participatory Action Research is an example of a culturally responsive initiative for equity and social justice. Inviting youth to the decision-making tables shifted the balance of power in these schools, raised important questions that had not been anticipated, and highlighted the ability of youth to emerge as leaders in their school community. Giving the youth opportunity to voice their perspectives in collective dialogues made it possible to identify inequities and resolve problems in new and different ways and brought to light considerations which adults previously had not anticipated. While these activities involved teenagers and their teachers, it is clear that the same processes can be used in institutions of higher education with faculty, administrators, and students.

Self-determination is at the core of decolonizing methodologies. These require indigenous methodologies such as those used by Pepion (in press) and other native scholars; they are culturally sensitive and relevant for the conduct of credible studies with diverse populations worldwide. Research utilizing participatory approaches and methods inclusive of and familiar to Native American communities allows participants to be involved in developing the data collection instruments, such as interview and focus group protocols and framing of dialogues. Reclaiming and reframing situations in tribal communities based on indigenous knowledge systems are important to counter ill-defined misrepresentations of indigenous peoples, past and present. In her book, *Decolonizing Methodologies*, Linda Tuhiwai Smith (1999) writes:

> It galls us that Western researchers and intellectuals can assume to know all that is possible to know of us, on the basis of their brief encounters with some of us. It appalls us that the West can desire, extract and claim ownership of our ways of knowing, our imagery, the things we create and produce and then simultaneously reject the people who created and developed those ideas and seek to deny them further opportunities to be creators of their own culture and own nations. *(p. 1)*

Contextualizing research requires specialized knowledge about indigenous communities which is often overlooked and difficult to attain by non-native researchers. Without this specialized indigenous knowledge, how could outsider non-native researchers, for example, answer Thaman's (2003) questions:

> What relationship do your ideas have to locally recognized concepts of knowledge and wisdom? And how are globally available, academically generated ideas able to articulate with the needs of Oceanic peoples and communities such that they can foster a better way of living at this time, let alone the future? *(p. 14)*

Aguilera-Black Bear & Bogard's (2010) evaluation of a regional initiative for leadership and wellness in five tribal nation communities by the Native Wellness Institute suggests that indigenous research approaches, methodologies, and localized knowledge are essential for assuring validity of data findings and interpretations. In this evaluation, activities such as storytelling, "talk abouts" (talking circles), and "play another" (skits, role play) were conceptualized differently by different community and age groups. Elders framed their participation in cultural traditions, acting on behalf of the community, while non-native participants framed their interactions according to power relations and as individuals, not a community. Depending on the community context, school or youth council/groups initially interacted and participated differently based on power relations. Once the facilitators saw the dynamics among youth, they stepped up mentoring and modeling to incorporate local knowledge and practices. As the initiative moved forward, youth participation in one school changed along with the culturally responsive curricula and pedagogy to look more like that of the elders, which was community-oriented and reflective of cultural traditions and protocols. Evaluators also found that research methods and approaches that resonated with one community might not with another; these differences significantly compromised the collection of data, scheduling, and the validity of the data. Because the facilitators were familiar with localized knowledge and practices, they could alter their procedures and the study itself was not jeopardized. This example demonstrates why localized knowledge is crucial to the validity of such studies.

Multiple Causality: What's the "Right" Story?
or Is There a "Right One" Out There?

Traditional research and evaluation required sifting data until a single story, set of predictions, or explanation of the phenomenon under study could be created. To achieve this, quantitative researchers attempt to control all sources of spurious, or alternative, explanations to come up with a "right answer." By contrast, qualitative investigation has used triangulation of data from multiple sources, fieldwork of significant duration, and checking for validity with participants. However, in many cases, 21st-century notions of validity must embrace an epistemology that legitimates multiple "stories" or explanations of phenomena that cannot be reconciled or crunched into a single tale. Such cases are especially common when working across cultures. LeCompte and McLaughlin (1994), investigating how Navajo and Anglo participants in the Navajo Nation explained a series of misfortunes befalling the school district, found a deep divide: Navajos argued that violation of cultural taboos by local people had caused disharmony in the community, which had led to the suicide of a teacher, the collapsed roof of a new gymnasium, and high rates of failure among high school students. By contrast, district administrators blamed the troubles on bad behavior, malfeasance, and mental illness, rather than pinpointing any systemic or collective origins. Since their explanations differed radically, neither side could agree on how to stop what seemed like a never-ending saga of catastrophes. Consequently, each acted upon its own set of explanations. The Navajo community held a Blessing Way Ceremony to restore harmony. The Anglo assistant superintendent fired the contractor who had installed the roof, instituted a tighter screening system for hiring staff, and commissioned a study to find out why so many high school students were failing.

We argue that because each set of participants in the story above constructed and acted upon a reality legitimately based on their own experiences and interactions, a "consensus" could only be achieved by suppressing one or another of the realities in which people lived. Denying legitimacy to those realities is, in fact, denying validity to their way of life, which is why LeCompte and McLaughlin (1994) sought to present, and theorize, both stories as valid. Complex institutions such as universities have no fewer constituencies than tribal communities, and the realities which they construct and in which they live are no less incommensurate. Researchers and evaluators, then, must approach their field sites with the expectation that what they observe may be seen differently by different groups in that site, and that such differences ultimately will lead to differing future consequences.

Conclusion

At the beginning of this chapter, we argued that good evaluation requires good research, and that good research requires following canons for rigor, regardless of the design and methods used. Now, we have come full circle to posit that in this increasingly diverse universe, good research and evaluation requires re-examination of how validity and reliability are defined and applied. We are not tossing out the basic principles underpinning those canons of rigor, but we argue that they should be broadened to include legitimate current understandings and realities. The world of science has not constructed just one form of reality, and the people and groups who live within our constructed universe understand and interact within it in different ways. In 21st-century institutions, multiple realities are a fact of life; researchers and evaluators can only document and try to explain them in all their complexities and contradictions. Trying to reconcile the differences, as we have argued above, serves only to silence someone's story or reality.

Notes

1 LeCompte and Goetz used the article, "Experimental and Quasi-Experimental Designs in Educational Research" by James Campbell and Julian Stanley (1963) as a model, translating the threats to reliability and validity described in that classic work into canons that would create much the same degree of rigor in qualitative and ethnographic research.

2 Here we understand that current higher education reinforces and assesses knowledge of a Eurocentric world. Decolonizing requires mainstream students to recognize the bias in their own funds of knowledge (Velez-Ibanez & Greenberg, 2005; Moll and Greenberg, 1990) and to demonstrate knowledge of other cultures' knowledge as well.

References

Aguilera, D. E. (2003). *Who defines success? An analysis of competing models of education for American Indian and Alaskan Native Students*. Dissertation: School of Education, University of Colorado.

Aguilera, D. E. (2004, July). *Four-Year Evaluation Report for U.S. Department of Education, Ronald McNair Post Baccalaureate Achievement Program: McNair Post Baccalaureate Achievement Program Evaluation Report for 1999–2003; Progress and Plan Report*, University of Colorado, Boulder.

Aguilera-Black Bear, D. E. (2011). Expanding notions of culturally responsive education with urban Native youth: Culturally relevant pedagogy for equity and social justice. In Scherff, L., & Spector, K. (Eds.), *Culture, relevance, and schooling: Exploring uncommon ground*. Lanham, MD: Rowman and Littlefield.

Aguilera-Black Bear, D. E., & Bogard, T. (2010). *All Native Training evaluation report: Report to the Native Wellness Institute and the Administration for Native Americans*. Unpublished manuscript.

Aguilera-Black Bear, D. E., Figueira, A., Gelman, C., & Ryan-Fear, A. (2010). *Participatory action research as pedagogy for equity and social justice in education: Intersections of youth voice, reflection, action in Lake High School*. Research Report to Oregon Department of Education and to school district.

Aguilera, D. E., Ryan, A., & Figueira, A. (2009). *Participatory action research as pedagogy for equity and social justice in education: Intersections of youth voice, reflection, action in River Valley High School*. Research Report to Oregon Department of Education and to school district.

American Association of University Professors. (n.d.). *Policy Documents and Reports (the Redbook) > Contents*. Retrieved from http://www.aaup.org/AAUP/pubsres/policydocs/contents/default.htm

American Council of Trustees and Alumni. (2007). *The Spellings Commission and you: What higher education trustees can do in light of the Department of Education's recent report*. Washington, DC: Author. Retrieved from https://www.goacta.org/publications/downloads/SpellingsFinal-Trustees.pdf

Anas, B. (January 3, 2011). Study: College students lie on faculty evaluations. *Daily Camera*, p. A1.

Bang, M., & Medin, D. (Nov 2010). Cultural processes in science education: Supporting the navigation of multiple epistemologies. *Science Education, 94*(6), 1008–1026.

Beal, R. (2007). *You mean they'll pay me to think?* Unpublished Doctoral Dissertation, University of Colorado School of Education, Boulder, CO.

Bergstrom, A. (2009). *Ji-AAnjichigeyang 'to change the way we do things': Retention of American Indian students in teacher education*. Published Dissertation, University of Minnesota.

Boudon, R. (1974). *Education, opportunity and social inequality: Change prospects in western society*. New York, NY: Wiley.

Bourdieu, P., & Passeron, J.-C. (1977 [1970]) *Reproduction in education, society and culture*. Richard Nice (tr.). London, UK: Sage.

Campbell, J. S., & Stanley, J. (1963). Experimental and quasi-experimental designs in educational research. In N. Gage, (Ed.), *The Handbook of research on teaching* (pp. 171–246). New York, NY: Rand McNally.

Deyhle, D. (1992). Constructing failure and maintaining cultural identity: Navajo and Ute school leavers. *Journal of American Indian Education, 31*(2), 24–47.

Deyhle, D. (1995). Navajo youth and Anglo racism: Cultural integrity and resistance. *Harvard Educational Review. 65*, 403–444. Reprinted in: Beauboeuf-Lafontant, T. & Smith, A. D. (1995).

Deyhle, D., & Swisher, K. G. (1997). Research in American Indian and Alaska Native Education: From assimilation to self-determination. *Review of Research in Education, 22*, 113–194.

Eisenhart, M., & Howe, K. (1992). Validity in educational research. In M. D. LeCompte, W. L. Millroy, & J. Preissle (Eds.), *The handbook of qualitative research in education* (pp. 643–680). San Diego, CA: Academic Press.

Foucault, M. (1980). *Power/Knowledge: Selected interviews and other writings, 1972–1977* (edited by C. Gordon). New York, NY: Pantheon Books.

Gabriel, T. (February 8, 2011) Teachers' colleges upset by plan to grade them. Retrieved from *New York Times* online.

Grande, S. (2004). *Red pedagogy*. Lanham, MD: Rowman & Littlefield.

Helsinki Accords: Declaration on Human Rights. The Final Act of the Conference on Security and Cooperation in Europe, August 1, 1975, 14 I.L.M. 1292. Retrieved February 16, 2011 from http://chnm.gmu.edu/1989/items/show/245

Hess, F. M. (December 6, 2010). Not Yet Sold on NCATE's "Transformative" clinical vision. *Teachers College Record*, Date Published: December 06, 2010. Retrieved from http://www.tcrecord.org/Home.asp ID Number: 16253. (Also available from http://www.aei.org/article/102974)

Hess, F. M., & Rotherham, A. J. (June 2007). Can NCLB survive the competitiveness competition? *Education Outlook*. Retrieved February 16, 2011 from http://www.frederickhess.org/5102/no-child-left-behind-what-the-public-thinks

Indian Nations at Risk Task Force. (1991). *Indian nations at risk: An educational strategy for action*. Washington, DC: U.S. Department of Education.

Kincheloe, J. L. (2006). Critical ontology and indigenous ways of being: Forging a postcolonial curriculum. In Y. Kanu (Ed.), *Curriculum as cultural practice*. Toronto, Canada: University of Toronto Press.

Lather, P. (1986). Research as praxis. *Harvard Educational Review, 56*(3), 257–277.

Lave, J., & Wenger, E. (1991). *Situated learning: Legitimate peripheral participation*. Cambridge, UK: Cambridge University Press.

LeCompte, M. D. (2002). The transformation of ethnographic practice: Past and current challenges. *Qualitative Research, 2*(3), 283–299.

LeCompte, M. D. (2010) *Higher education and the cult of efficiency: Fiscal crises, conservative ideology and academic culture*. Poster presentation given at the annual meetings of the American Educational Research Association, Denver, CO: April.

LeCompte, M. D., & Bonetti, K. (2010). Notes from ground zero: Budgetary crises and academic freedom at the University of Colorado. *Theory In Action, 3*(3), 7–20.

LeCompte, M. D., & Goebel, S. D. (1987). Can bad data produce good program planning? An analysis of record-keeping on school dropouts. *Education and Urban Society, 19*(3), 250–269.

LeCompte, M. D., & Goetz, J. P. (1982). Problems of reliability and validity in educational research. *Review of Educational Research, 52*(2), 31–60.

LeCompte, M. D., & McLaughlin, D. (1994). Witchcraft and blessings, science and rationality: Discourses of power and silence in collaborative work with Navajo schools. In A. Gitlin (Ed.), *Power and method: Political activism and educational research* (pp. 147–166). New York, NY: Routledge.

Lincoln, Y., & Guba, E. (Eds.). (1985). *Naturalistic inquiry*. Newbury Park, CA: Sage.

Martinez, I. (2002). *Taking it the wrong way: An examination of issues of diversity in the teacher licensure program at CU-Boulder*. Unpublished MA comprehensive paper, School of Education, University of Colorado, Boulder, CO, April 26.

Miller, C. (August 2008). *Doctoral student success? Negotiating a field of practice*. Doctoral Dissertation. Department of Educational Leadership, School of Education, University of Colorado, Denver.

Moll, L. C., & Greenberg, J. B. (1990). Creating zones of possibilities: Combining social contexts for instruction. In L. C. Moll (Ed.), *Vygotsky and education instructional implications and applications of sociohistorical psychology* (pp. 319–349). Cambridge, UK: Cambridge University Press.

National Commission for the Protection of Human Subjects of Biomedical and Behavioral Research. (1978). *The Belmont Report: Ethical guidelines for the protection of human subjects of research*. Washington, DC: Department of Health, Education and Welfare. Retrieved from the National Institutes of Health website: http://videocast.nih.gov/pdf/ohrp_belmont_report.pdf

Nuremberg Code. (1947). In *"Permissible Medical Experiments." Trials of War Criminals before the Nuremberg Military Tribunals under Control Council Law No. 10. Nuremberg October 1946–April 1949*, (Vol. 2., pp. 181–182). Washington. U.S. Government Printing Office (n.d.). Retrieved from Library of Congress website http://www.loc.gov/rr/frd/Military_Law/pdf/NT_war-criminals_Vol-II.pdf

Patton, M. Q. (1986). *Utilization-focused evaluation* (2nd ed.). Newbury Park, CA: Sage.

Patton, M. Q. (1990). *Qualitative evaluation and research methods*. Newbury Park, CA: Sage.

Patton, M. Q. (1992). *Qualitative evaluation and research methods*. Newbury Park, CA: Sage

Paulson, S. E., & Marchant, G. J. (2009). Background variables, levels of aggregation, and standardized test scores. *Education Policy Analysis Archives, 17*(22). Retrieved February 16, 2011from http://epaa.asu.edu/epaa/v17n22/

Pavel, D. M., Inglebret, E., & Banks, S. R. (2001). Tribal colleges and universities in an era of dynamic development. *Peabody Journal, 76*(1), 50–72.

Pepion, D. (in press). Exploring traditional Blackfeet leadership concepts. In D. E. Aguilera-Black Bear,

J. Tippeconnic, & T. Begaye (Eds.), *Leadership for self-determination: A compilation of new research and literature examining indigenous epistemologies and contextual systems of leadership.* University of Oklahoma Press.

Phillips, D. C., & Burbules, N. (2000). *Postpositivism and educational research.* New York, NY: Rowman & Littlefield.

Ramirez, E. (Feb 3, 2009). Arne Duncan: The lesson plan for education: Can the new education secretary's hands-on style jumpstart nationwide school reform? *US News and Education,* Retrieved February 16, 2011 from http://www.usnews.com/education/articles/2009/02/03/arne-duncan-the-lesson-plan-for-education

Schensul, J. J., & LeCompte, M. D. (Eds.). (1999). *Ethnographer's toolkit (Vols. 1–7).* Walnut Creek, CA: AltaMira Press.

Schensul, S., Schensul, J. J., & LeCompte. M.D. (1999). *Essential ethnographic methods.* Lanham, NJ: AltaMira Press.

Smith, L. T. (1999). *Decolonizing methodologies.* Dunedin, New Zealand: Zed Books & University of Otago Press.

Stake, R. E. (1978). The case study method in social inquiry. *Educational Researcher, 7*(2), 5–8.

Thaman, K. H. (2003). Decolonizing Pacific studies: Indigenous perspectives, knowledge, and wisdom in higher education. *The Contemporary Pacific, 15*(1), 1–17.

Tuck, E. (2009). Suspending damage: A letter to communities. *Harvard Educational Review, 79*(3), 409–428.

University of Victoria Faculty of Human and Social Development created a new set of ethical principles, the "*Protocols and principles for conducting research in an indigenous context*" (2003), (pp. 5–8).

Velez-Ibanez, C., & Greenberg, J. (2005). Formation and transformation of funds of knowledge. In N. Gonzales, L. Moll, & C. Amanti (Eds.), *Funds of knowledge: Theorizing practices in households, communities and classrooms* (pp. 47–70). Mahwah, NJ: Lawrence Erlbaum.

Walker, G., Golde, C. M., Jones, L., Conklin Bueschel, A., & Hutchings, P. (2008). *The formation of scholars: Rethinking doctoral education for the Twenty-First Century.* San Francisco, CA: Jossey-Bass. Retrieved February 16, 2011 from http://www.carnegiefoundation.org/previous-work/professional-graduate-education

Washburn, J. K. (2005). *University Inc: The corporate corruption of American higher education.* New York, NY: Basic Books.

Wilson, J. K. (1995). *The myth of political correctness: The conservative attack on higher education.* Durham, NC: Duke University Press.

42

ETHICAL ASSESSMENT AND INSTITUTIONAL ADVANCEMENT: CONNECTING GOOD PRACTICE WITH THE NEED TO MOVE CAMPUSES FORWARD

Ashley Finley

If one is interested in the ethics of assessment, there are a number of places to go to find a basic framework to guide the processes of inquiry. Foremost among these are the recommendations and guidelines on ethical conduct established by the Joint Committee on Standards for Educational Evaluation (JCSEE, 2011; see Yarbrough, Shulha, Hopson, & Caruthers, 2011) and the American Evaluation Association's (AEA) task force (2008). Resources can also be found among major professional associations, such as the American Sociological Association, the American Psychological Association, and the National Council on Measurement in Education, to name a few. A brief review of the ethical codes advanced by these associations will be offered in this chapter. These sources provide valuable foundations for engaging in assessment and decision guidelines to assist inquiry.

The difficulties that come with conducting assessment often pose ethical considerations, as well. This is not to suggest that most forms of assessment will directly confront ethical guidelines or pose an ethical quandary. Rather, the challenge with ethics in assessment refers to the nuances of conducting an inquiry about learning and student success within the environment of most postsecondary institutions. It is an environment in which the demarcations between objective researcher and subject are not always clear, where objectivity may not necessarily be desirable, and where evidence might only need to be good enough—not perfect. Albert Einstein said, "Relativity applies to physics, not ethics." The implication is that ethics are not circumstantial or malleable. Ethics are absolutes. But Einstein was not assessing the questions, programs, and processes at the heart of institutional change and advancement in higher education.

To conduct assessment for the good of institutional advancement, evaluators will likely encounter the grey areas that surround many ethical principles. First, there are the ambiguities raised by focusing on students and products of student learning as the subjects of assessment. This chapter reviews guidelines for confidentiality, anonymity, voluntary participation, the assumption of separation between researcher and subject—and the challenges that can arise from the strict adherence to such "standards."

Additionally, evaluators must also navigate ambiguities around the guidelines and principles regarding the ethical use and implementation of data on campuses for the goals of institutional advancement. Here campus practitioners must consider the ways in which data has been collected, the degree to which it is representative of the intended population, and the extent to which it can be constructively analyzed for empirical use. At the core of these issues is the question of what evidence, with regard to student learning and success, is needed or is "good enough" to help inform institutional advancement? And correspondingly—other than institutional research professionals—who should be empowered to use and interpret evidence to assess the implications for campus policy and practice? Commonly, and increasingly, the work of assessment to advance institutional goals is being carried out by faculty members, assessment committees, and other campus personnel in areas such as student development and academic affairs. When institutional assessment is inclusively conceived as the assessment of student learning, engagement, and development, the circle of evaluators must necessarily include a range of constituencies, including faculty and students themselves. Thus, the ethical considerations pertaining to the use and interpretation of data become a shared responsibility.

While ethical principles provide invaluable guidance for undertaking assessment, the aim of this chapter is to question the applicability of those principles within the context of institutional success and advancement. The issue is not that ethics and institutional advancement are at odds with one another, but rather that, contrary to Einstein's thinking, ethics are, in fact, relative. Our ability to challenge ethics, to invite others into this conversation, and achieve reconciliation on these matters serves a vital role in institutional assessment and advancement.

The Consensus on Ethics: A Review of Standards and Principles

"Every profession has distinct ethical obligations to the public. These obligations include professional competency, integrity, honesty, confidentiality, objectivity, public safety and fairness, all of which are intended to preserve and safeguard public confidence" (Schmeiser, 1995, p. 1). These tenets reflect similar thinking on ethics among many disciplinary associations (e.g., American Sociological Association; the American Psychological Association) and professional associations (such as counseling and education).

The preceding list also mirrors a common core of ethical standards established for assessment by task force committees and non-profit interest groups, as well (see Schmeiser, 1995, for an inclusive list of these bodies). For example, the AEA's task force on ethics has established a set of five interdisciplinary principles for evaluators. These principles are *systematic inquiry, competence, integrity/honesty, respect for people*, and *responsibility for general and public welfare* (American Evaluation Association, 2008). Overall, the AEA's principles stipulate processes of inquiry pertaining to conduct of evaluators toward interest groups and stakeholders, uses of data, and the treatment of subjects.

The standards advanced by the JCSEE cover five similar core areas and contain significant overlap with the AEA's principles (the AEA co-sponsors the JCSEE). The JCSEE's standards recognize *utility, feasibility, propriety, accuracy*, and *educational accountability* (see Yarbrough, et al., 2011). Overall, the principles outlined by the JCSEE refer to (a) the need for evaluation to be attentive to use and accuracy of data, (b) responsible implementation and documentation of the evaluation design and methods for data collection, and (c) legal and ethical treatment of subjects and users of the evaluation (Yarbrough, et al., 2011).

This chapter posits that across these commonly held and communicated guidelines are two distinct layers of complexity in the application of these ethical principles. These layers serve as lenses through which considerations for carrying out and communicating assessment to and with stakeholders can be viewed. The first layer refers to the ethical treatment and consideration of human subjects in assessment. The second layer refers to the use and interpretation of data. These ethical assessment "lenses" will be examined in the following pages, as will their practical implications for institutional advancement.

The Human Side of Ethics: Considerations for Students as Participants and Faculty (and Other Institutional Sympathizers) as Evaluators

Students have rightfully been at the center of educational research. To gauge institutional success, campuses must consider the markers of students' success, such as retention, persistence, performance (i.e., GPA)—and aspects of student experience, such as participation in study abroad and internship programs. As accreditation focuses increasingly on meaningful assessment of student learning, evaluation is more inclusively incorporating these markers of learning. Moreover, this student centrality is likely to make evaluation more complicated over time. Issues of confidentiality will grow more complex as we attempt to track learning gains over time and gather information on various types of learning experiences. Faculty will be drawn into the role of evaluator as essential intermediaries of the learning experience and institutions will look to involve students in evaluation, without coercing them to do so.

In his book, *Evaluation Ethics for Best Practice*, Michael Morris (2007) cites a study of AEA membership in which nearly two-thirds (65%) of respondents indicated they had faced an ethical dilemma in conducting an evaluation (p. 15). Additionally, the number of conflicts experienced by a particular evaluator corresponded directly with the number of evaluations they had conducted. Among the ethical dilemmas faced by respondents was a concern for confidentiality. "Being pressured by a stakeholder . . . to identify the source of a specific piece of information or request data sets that could permit identification [is one problem] . . . when the evaluator is concerned that reporting certain findings represents a violation [is another problem]" (p. 20). Morris further notes that these concerns are most prominent when sample sizes are so small that even basic demographic characteristics could be enough to reveal students' identities.

There may also be instances in which it is in the *best interest* of the students for their identities to be known. Specifically, institutional assessment of student success on campus must consider not only markers of student learning, but also markers of student *living*. How are students learning and developing on campus, in both academic and social contexts? These markers tend to refer most often to the dimensions of risk that students encounter (i.e., alcohol use, mental health issues) and the support services and programs aimed at keeping students safe and healthy.

For example, some years ago I was involved in a project assessing the correlates of student participation in a first-year learning community program in relation to factors that impact student learning, including the indicators of depressive symptomology. Though student participation in the study was confidential (as stipulated in the approved IRB proposal), I was challenged by the school's legal counsel to reveal the name of any student who responded with high levels of depressive symptoms or who indicated they frequently had suicidal thoughts. These students would then be "flagged" and referred to the counseling center. Bound by my professional ethics as a sociologist and the guarantee of confidentiality, I identified an alternate depression scale. The consent form was amended to include contact information for the counseling center. The study was given institutional clearance and, to the best of my knowledge, ran the entirety of its four-year duration without any negative consequences to students. I was confident that by following the ethical principles of my discipline, I was serving my ethical obligation to the students as participants. However, in retrospect, I now question whether protecting their identity was in the best interests of their health, safety, and ability to thrive.

Along with obligations to maintain confidentiality, a fundamental ethical obligation for researchers and evaluators alike is to assure participants that their participation is voluntary. This may be accomplished using consent forms and other written and oral statements informing students that participation is voluntary and not tied to any other form of evaluation, like grades or class standing. Complicating that message, however, is the practical reality that some form of incentive is likely to be offered in exchange for their participation. Because achieving high response rates is a challenge for campus assessment, and poses a threat to reliable data, incentives are commonplace. Most incentives that are offered are viewed with little concern. For example, students might be given free drink tickets for the campus coffee shop, or offered chances to enter into a random drawing for a larger prize, such as an iPod or gift certificate. What then is the threshold? At what point does incentivizing impact individual agency? To what degree is this further complicated when linking participation to access to some necessity of student life, such as registering for classes or picking up gowns for graduation?

Furthermore, institutional assessment of student learning depends upon knowing where students are at any given point in time and how they have developed over time. The latter calls for multiple points of participation from the same students to gather evidence of their progress in learning and engagement (i.e., a panel design). This type of assessment is particularly effective when assessing the long-term impact of campus programs or interventions or even whole segments of the curriculum (i.e., general education). This type of ongoing assessment may raise additional concerns about the use of incentives, as evaluators seek ways to keep students engaged across multiple administrations.

Voluntary participation is further challenged by the role of faculty within the assessment process. The faculty presence within evaluation occurs by virtue of their roles as researcher/evaluator or as gatekeeper for in-class evaluation. In both instances, students are likely to be aware of a faculty member's overt or implicit support of the assessment. This faculty "double agency" conflates their roles as teachers, researchers, and authority figures, posing additional concerns as to the boundaries of voluntary participation (Ferguson, Yonge, & Myrick, 2004; Ridley, 2009).

Just as the role of the faculty member as teacher/evaluator complicates ethical considerations, so too does that of non-faculty evaluators employed at institutions. The proximity and subjective ties of both to institutional goals and advancement speak to the challenges to unbiased reporting. Originating with the work of Max Weber, the ethic of positivism states that researchers conduct inquiry without bias and "value-free" so as not to let personal associations influence outcomes or the interpretation of data. More recently, the JCSEE guidelines specifically indicate that evaluations should "guard against misperceptions, biases, distortions, or errors."

Scholars have questioned whether it is necessary or even possible to adhere to positivism within social science (see Hunt, 1985, p. 73). "The disparity between the roles of investigator and advocate makes for a curious paradox: a social researcher may understand a social problem better than anyone else, but if he publicly advocates policies based on that special knowledge, he has to be prepared for attacks by both the public and the academic community on his reputation" (Hunt, 1985, p. 83). Nevertheless, given the relatively close quarters of the campus, there is reason to question what it means for assessment when the line between objective evaluator and institutional advocate becomes blurred.

The Data Side of Ethics: Considerations for Methodology and Evidence Gathering

In addition to the complications that arise from the ethical treatment of human subjects, data and the construction of evidence must also be carefully considered. It is potentially murky methodological and analytical factors that form the empirical basis for institutional decision making. Simply stated, what counts as evidence? On this point, the JCSEE highlights ethical considerations for "accuracy," defined briefly as the responsibility to "convey technically adequate information" (JCSEE, 2011). Specifically, the ethical guideline entails attentiveness, in part, to "justified conclusions and decisions," valid and reliable information, proper storage of data, and sound methodology of data collection (Yarbrough, et al., 2011). Similarly, the AEA (2008) identifies among its guiding principles the need for "systematic inquiry" based upon "[adherence] to the highest technical standards," "[exploration of] . . . shortcomings and strengths of evaluation questions and approaches," and "[communication] of approaches, methods, and limitations of the evaluation. . . ." How should evaluators determine what qualifies as "valid and reliable" data, the "highest" standard of inquiry, and employment of "sound" methodology in complying with these standards?

Generally speaking, the approach to increasing the reliability of data is twofold: reduce sample error and eliminate confounding factors. Reducing sample error can be achieved in two ways. Samples can be drawn using a purely random sampling procedure, or by using several types of pseudo-random sampling designs, all of which have some procedural element of randomization. As with any sample methodology, response rates should be around 60% (Hunt, 1985). Sample error can also be reduced by gathering "large" samples, or comparison groups within a sample, typically defined as being greater than 100 cases. In order to eliminate confounding factors, analyses should consider and control for characteristics that may impact outcomes, such as students' demographic characteristics, environmental influences (e.g., work responsibilities, club or sports participation), even dispositional influences (i.e., positive or negative effect, disciplinary records). Confounding factors can also be addressed through the use of a quasi-experimental design. In these designs, comparison groups are utilized to identify outcomes unique to students engaged in a particular program or activity, thereby distinguishing them from students not so engaged (see Grunwald & Mayhew, 2008, p. 758).

Whether considering the ethics of assessment as they pertain to human subjects or to the proper usage of data, the true challenge for evaluators is the translation of these considerations to the practical environment of the campus and the practical uses of assessment for institutional advancement. To what degree might our efforts to maintain ethical boundaries be impediments to institutional improvement? In what ways might a better understanding of ethical ambiguities facilitate campus conversations about assessment and enable institutions to move forward?

Practical Ethics: Balancing Ethical Boundaries with Institutional Advancement

As evaluators confront the practical complexities of implementing ethical assessment, there is an opportunity also to consider the ethical use of data to assess institutional goals for advancement. Just as there is an ethical responsibility to consider students as participants, to consider faculty as researchers, and to consider data for its limitations, is there also an ethical responsibility to maintain institutional integrity through assessment? If so, what is our ethical responsibility to use data for the purpose of institutional accountability and improvement in the interest of students, other campus stakeholders, and to the public?

To consider the role of "practical ethics" is to reconsider how an evaluator's adherence to common standards can paradoxically slow or impede the work of improving institutional success around student learning. It is not an endorsement of bad practice. In this sense, are there instances in which bias can be good? Can sampling procedures fail to be random but still be useful? To what degree can small sample sizes provide meaningful conclusions? How much can we know about student identity and background before violating confidentiality? How many incentives can students be offered before we need to question the voluntary nature of their participation? And, most fundamentally, how much assessment is needed to create incremental change on campus, whether that change is in the form of a conversation, a policy revision, or a holistic reframing of the curriculum?

The Human Side of Practical Ethics

Can Bias Be Good?

Despite the ideal of remaining value free, the campus context inherently blurs divisions between subject and researcher. For example, faculty bring multiple layers of potential bias into their role as evaluators with regard to their position to assess individual student performance, conduct departmental assessment of programmatic success, and engage in discussion around the use of data for institutional advancement. The use of assessment in considerations of promotion and tenure decisions can also influence faculty views on the use and interpretation of data (McCormack, 2005). Persons who engage in assessment work (i.e., institutional researchers) and for whom teaching is not a primary responsibility must similarly balance institutional ties and their own investment in institutional success in their approach to data interpretation. However, rather than presume that the interests and experiences of assessors may bias the reporting of assessment, we might ask how these same perspectives and experiences could provide valuable insight to assist institutional advancement?

The perspective and experience of faculty and others leading campus assessment should not be distanced from data analysis and interpretation. Assessing student learning and pathways to student success is complicated and multifaceted. It is critical to illuminate what happens within the learning environment to understand why data may or may not produce the expected or intended outcomes. "Too often we researchers—from our privileged standpoints—look but still do not see, listen but do not hear, touch but do not feel" (Symonette, 2009, p. 279). Perspectives of faculty, other institutional professionals, and students provide context for data, flushing out ambiguities and inconsistencies, and explaining counterintuitive findings.

Is Confidentiality Always Best or Even Mandatory?

A cornerstone of conducting ethical research is protecting participants by providing them with either anonymity or confidentiality. Because anonymity is often impossible or undesirable, confidentiality is more commonly offered. With regard to learning and institutional advancement, there are conceivable instances in which confidentiality might be a hindrance. For example, learning is developmental; it is non-linear; it is understood through reflection; and it is engaged at various levels of complexity as we mature as learners. As a developmental process, faculty must have the means by which to gauge students' growth, not just within a course but also over time. While confidentiality is undoubtedly significant for certain types of institutional assessment, it is less so when knowing who students are, what they need to succeed, and where they are as learners is essential to the assessment. "Ultimately, evaluation belongs in the hands of the person most affected, the client, who should testify whether a conventionally evaluated intervention has attained his or her desired goal, as well as demonstrate that he or she can perform this intervention independently" (Bloom, 2010, p. 1).

Investigating student success may mean going beyond the classroom to better understand the circumstances of student living environments, and how those environments impact learning. As we become more inclusive of the indices that measure student success and the significance of connecting student experiences across campus to gauge institutional advancement, we will need to revisit the issue of confidentiality. If we hope to bring students into this discussion, to allow them to be participants in assessment, and to provide space for their reflections on the meaning of results for institutional success, we will need to find ways to protect their voice beyond assurances of confidentiality or anonymity.

What Constitutes Voluntary Participation?

The notion of voluntary participation falls somewhere between ethical considerations for human subjects and ethical responsibilities to data. An undefined (or perhaps *under*defined) boundary exists between allowing participants to opt into assessment and using incentives to encourage their participation. To ensure the integrity of data, evaluators must maintain response rates high enough to ensure that information from the sample is representative of the population. With the increase in campus surveys and the resulting survey fatigue among students (and faculty), incentives have become a common accompaniment to assessment efforts. How can the dual interests of advancing institutional assessment and gathering reliable evidence be balanced with the need to ensure that students are not "coerced" into participating? Unfortunately, it is impossible to know the boundary at which incentives do more ethical harm than good.

One solution is to make clear to students that eligibility for incentives is based upon *submission*, not *completion*, of the survey. But there are many forms of assessment beyond surveys for which students may be asked to take part (i.e., focus groups, one-on-one interviews). To address the issue of incentives and voluntary participation more globally, evaluators need to reduce their reliance on incentives by more effectively communicating to students the need for surveys. For example, survey fatigue might be countered by giving more thought to how surveys are administered and how students are informed about the relevance of the survey to their lives (see Porter, Whitcomb, & Weitzer, 2004). In the case of panel designs, some evidence suggests that by informing participants at the beginning that future participation will be required to collect follow-up data, response rates were increased for subsequent administrations (Porter, et al., 2004). Informing students at the outset what is expected of them and why they should care about the study may have a significant impact on their participation. Ultimately, evaluators need to ask themselves if their use of incentives may be functioning more as compensation for the failure to communicate with students about the need for a particular assessment than as compensation for students' time.

Good (Enough) Data and Practical Ethics

Researchers have ethical responsibilities not only to human subjects but also to represent data accurately and to draw conclusions commensurate with the type and amount of data collected. It is not uncommon when analyzing and reporting institutional data for researchers to demur on drawing conclusions citing sample sizes "too small to warrant meaningful conclusions." The rationale for this "shying away" is that the characteristics of a small sample are likely to be unrepresentative of the population and/or to contain high levels of sample error. As sample error increases, the likelihood of drawing false conclusions also increases and, as a result, external validity is compromised; findings cannot be generalized beyond the sample to the population the sample is intended to represent.

Yet, sample size limitations are rarely noted when reporting summative assessment outcomes for the general student body, such as overall retention or completion rates. When this statement is used with regard to assessment, it is most often because the focus of the assessment was on a particular learning experience—a campus program (i.e., learning communities), a targeted pedagogy (i.e., service-learning or experiential learning)—or the learning experiences of a population of students (i.e., underserved student groups): the very pockets of campus life and learning that institutions need to know more about. Ethical standards regarding the use of data would suggest small samples should be rendered inconclusive due to the likelihood that they are unrepresentative of the population and prone to sample error. However, is there not also an ethical obligation to acknowledge and understand the learning experiences of that small sample of students? A similar consideration applies to the ethical obligation to examine data gathered from students from underrepresented groups, particularly ethnic or minority groups, and from women in specific majors (i.e., science and engineering), for which sample sizes are also likely to be small on campuses.

The nature of practical ethics suggests that, through the lens of institutional advancement, we need to consider how findings from even small sample sizes can be represented. In trying to understand variation in student learning, we may not always be able to acquire sample sizes large enough to perform certain statistical tests. Nevertheless, findings drawn from small samples can be represented descriptively and used to generate conversation about student experiences. Too often campus assessment data are filed away and, in some cases, it is because the data is deemed to be unrepresentative. Campuses may be better served by considering the relative trade-off between knowing more about student experiences at the institution and attaining external validity. Moreover, by keeping these types of assessment visible, campuses may be more likely to follow up with additional assessments which would eventually provide sufficient cases to allow for robust statistical analysis.

Finally, the failure to share data, regardless of how much there is, underestimates the cumulative effect that can be gained from communicating findings with faculty, administrators, and the student community. This is not to suggest that data from small or non-random samples should be presented without caution. With the communication of data comes the responsibility to be clear as to the limitations of those data. However, if we are too quick to discount the data altogether, we undervalue its utility to generate conversations, illuminate student experience, and increase understanding of the diversity of those experiences.

Conclusion: What Does it Take to Move the Needle?

The preceding discussion is not meant to imply there is a difference between ethical assessment and the practical application of those ethics. Difference implies a dichotomy; one is good and the other is bad. Rather, the argument is that there is a way of viewing the ethics of assessment such that while upholding ethical principles, we also acknowledge and respect the grey areas in which the practical implications of those ethics lie. We further appreciate that those grey areas often hold specific relevance to the work of institutional improvement.

As evaluators we need to provide opportunity within the implementation of ethics for conversation about the nuances that complicate institutional assessment. As we include others in the assessment process—student affairs professionals, faculty, administrators, and even students—we gain clarity as to what the ethical boundaries are and how we might navigate them. This perspective also suggests that we might recognize the parameters around the ethical use of data, particularly small or non-random samples. Rather than being restricted by data from these samples, by inviting others into conversation about the caveats and opportunities, we can use even limited findings to build assessment knowledge.

As practitioners of assessment we need to be courageous when confronted by these issues, rather than simply defaulting to the ethical standard. In my own ethical confrontation, by considering only the ethical ramifications and solutions to the issue of student confidentiality, I missed the opportunity for a rich and robust dialogue. How might a counselor or student affairs professional have advised me to better support students struggling with mental health issues or to provide them with material and resources without their asking? Might I have provided contact information within the survey itself or more effectively drawn out students' experiences? And how might we have, as a research team, better communicated with students to aid their understanding of our intentions and purposes?

John Dewey (1916/1980, p. 147) said that when we learn from experience, "doing becomes a trying; an experiment with the world to find out what it is like; the undergoing becomes instruction—discovery of the connection of things." While Dewey said this about student learning, the same might be said for the way in which we learn from assessment. "Doing becomes trying" as we think through the meaning and application of ethical principles in the context of campus life and institutional goals. When we invite others into that discovery process, ethics need not be viewed as a limitation, but rather as a catalyst.

References

American Evaluation Association. (2008). Guiding principles for evaluators. *American Journal of Evaluation, 29*(4), 397–398. doi: 10.1177/1098214008290040601

Bloom, M. (2010). Client-centered evaluation: Ethics for 21st century practitioners. *Journal of Social Work Values and Ethics, 7*(1), 1–7.

Dewey, J. (1980). Democracy and education. In J. A. Boydston (Ed.), *John Dewey: The middle works, 1899–1924* (Vol. 9). Carbondale, IL: Southern Illinois University Press. (Original work published 1916.)

Ferguson, L. M., Yonge, O., & Myrick, F. (2004). Students' involvement in faculty research: Ethical and methodological issues. *International Journal of Qualitative Methods, 3*(4), 1–14. Retrieved from http://www.ualberta.ca/~iiqm/backissues/3_4/pdf/ferguson.pdf

Grunwald, H. E., & Mayhew, M. J. (2008). Using propensity scores for estimating causal effects: A study in the development of moral reasoning. *Research in Higher Education, 49*, 758–779.

Hunt, M. (1985). *Profiles of social research: The scientific study of human interactions.* New York, NY: Russell Sage Foundation.

Joint Committee on Standards for Education Evaluation. (2011). *Program Evaluation Standards Statements.* Retrieved from http://www.jcsee.org/program-evaluation-standards/program-evaluation-standards-statements

McCormack, C. (2005). Reconceptualizing student evaluation of teaching: An ethical framework for changing times. *Assessment and Evaluation in Higher Education, 30*(5), 463–476.

Morris, M. (Ed.). (2007). *Evaluation ethics for best practice: Cases and commentaries.* New York, NY: Guilford Press.

Porter, S. R., Whitcomb, M. E., & Weitzer, W. H. (2004). Multiple surveys of students and survey fatigue. In S. R. Porter (Ed.), *Overcoming survey research problems* (New Directions for Institutional Research, No. 121, pp. 63–73). San Francisco, CA: Jossey-Bass.

Ridley, R. (2009). Assuring ethical treatment of students as research participants. *Journal of Nursing Education, 48*(10), 537–541.

Schmeiser, C. (1995). *Ethics in assessment.* ERIC Digest. Retrieved from http://www.ericdigests.org/1996-3/in.htm (ED391111).

Symonette, H. (2009). Cultivating self as responsive instrument: Working the boundaries and borderlands for ethical border crossings. In D. Mertens, & P. Ginsberg (Eds.), *The handbook of social research ethics* (pp. 279–294). Thousand Oaks, CA: Sage.

Yarbrough, D. B., Shulha, L. M., Hopson, R. K., & Caruthers, F. A. (2011). *The program evaluation standards: A guide for evaluators and evaluation users* (3rd ed.). Thousand Oaks, CA: Sage.

QUESTIONS AND EXERCISES FOR SECTION 6

(1) Describe the differences that guide accommodation decision making between secondary and postsecondary institutions. Suggest ways for high school students with disabilities to better prepare for transition to college given some of the differences between K–12 and postsecondary institutions.

(2) Discuss the importance of data-based decision making in determining eligibility for accommodations both at the secondary and postsecondary levels. What types of evidence would you consider compelling for extended time accommodation on high stakes exams, in school and college?

(3) In discussing the testing and evaluation of ELLs, higher education institutions tend to consider ELL testing procedures along with their developmental, remedial, and other disability-related testing procedures. In this approach, ELL students are often treated as "remedial" students. Do you agree with this approach or would you suggest a different approach to ELL students? Identify your position and discuss why your position might be more appropriate than the other, using the contents from chapter 37 and your own knowledge and experiences.

(4) Chapter 37 in this section classifies major issues related to testing ELL students into two categories: (a) testing ELL students for academic subjects; (b) testing ELL students for English proficiency (this includes identifying or classifying ELL students). Discuss these issues separately for each category and explain how they should be addressed.

(5) Define what construct-irrelevant variance is and discuss how these sources of variance can be controlled in the assessment of ELL students.

(6) Identify two issues that need to be considered in relation to placement exams for ELL students and briefly discuss how those issues might need to be addressed.

(7) Discuss what test publishers can do to make assessments more accessible for ELL students.

(8) What can be learned from existing assessment data in order to improve reliability and validity of assessments for ELL students?

(9) Discuss how one can differentiate between linguistic features that are related to the focal construct and those irrelevant or unnecessary.

(10) It is often argued that colleges and universities need to ensure the validity of testing and the evaluation of ELL students. However, this can raise the issue of "autonomy of professorship" versus "institutional regulation." Discuss how much "institutional regulation," i.e. intervention from the college and university authorities you think might be necessary and why.

(11) Consider the various measures being used to assess teacher quality in the K–12 system. How might these be used to improve student assessment and program evaluation in college and university teacher education programs?

(12) What does it mean to effectively report assessment results to multiple audiences?

(13) How can institutions foster transparent communication on student learning outcomes assessment?

(14) Can reporting designed for internal communication be used to satisfy external requirements for accountability?

(15) What can an institution gain from being transparent regarding assessment information?

(16) How can institutions create opportunities for discussions on assessment reports so as to foster using the assessment data?

(17) Given the complex ethical considerations that apply to both the treatment of participants and the ethical use of data in higher education assessment, can a case be made for weighing one set of considerations more heavily than another? For example, do campus researchers have an obligation to consider the ethical responsibility to participants more so than to the gathering of empirically "sound" data? Why or why not? To what degree might the weighing of these considerations depend upon who the researcher is—a faculty member, an institutional research professional, or a campus administrator?

(18) The Voluntary System of Accountability (VSA) was developed in reaction to the 2006 Spellings Commission report on accountability in higher education. The VSA is intended to provide a common portal through which public, four-year universities can "supply clear, accessible, and comparable information on the undergraduate student experience" (http://www.voluntarysystem.org/index.cfm). What types of data should be considered reflective of the "undergraduate experience"? To what degree should ethical considerations regarding evidence that may not be statistically robust but may be "good enough" factor into this type of reporting? Do considerations for the type of evidence reported depend upon whether the intended use of the data is for national comparability as opposed to institutional advancement?

CONCLUDING REMARKS

Charles Secolsky and D. Brian Denison

The information presented in the forty-two chapters of this handbook was organized with a particular focus on the interests and needs of higher education personnel, including administrators, assessment coordinators, institutional researchers, evaluators, and faculty members. The information presented can be summarized as follows:

- First, up-to-date information on higher education issues as they pertain to assessment, accountability, and accreditation was spelled out in detail.
- The sections on measurement theory and test construction addressed issues that are often left to measurement theorists and practitioners whose expertise exists mostly outside the realm of higher education administration. Now, hopefully, these concepts and theories will be more understandable and useful to higher education decision makers.
- Using the information provided, decision makers will now be able to work more collaboratively with their staffs, and be better equipped to ask and answer the most appropriate questions that need to be addressed and solved.
- There is a section that directly addressed testing and assessment for decision making. While more applied in nature, these chapters discussed the history and development of the fields of standard-setting and validation, placement testing, admissions testing, the assessment of writing skills, authentic assessment, and cognitive diagnostic assessment—information which can support a richer understanding of these applications.
- An extensive treatment of evaluation methodologies was presented to enable administrators and others to gain a more comprehensive understanding of what has led to the development and differences of approaches in this field and how they might be better applied to higher education.
- The reader is encouraged to understand the distinctions among qualitative, quantitative, and mixed methods approaches to research and evaluation. The approaches appear together in this one volume, to enhance their usefulness and value to higher education administrators for fostering greater informed decision making. By gaining insight into the latest developments and thinking in these three fields, the administrator should be at a distinct advantage by having a great array of assessment tools at her/his disposal.

The handbook contains chapters with a great deal of relevance for current and future issues on nearly every aspect of measurement, assessment, and evaluation as these topics relate to higher education.

The administrator will find that debates in the field which currently exist in the form of different positions or arguments regarding subdisciplines of these major fields are aptly portrayed in non-technical language. The chapters were purposely written with the "on-the-go" higher education executive in mind, filling a long existing gap between the latest advancements in measurement, assessment, and evaluation and even the most recent training offered to higher education professionals.

All of the topics in the handbook are closely tied to the business of higher education administration. The set of exercises that appears at the end of each section, often discussion questions, have hopefully helped to solidify one's understanding of each topic and its importance.

With recent attention given to the most appropriate ways of communicating results to various constituencies and stakeholders, separate chapters were devoted to assessment of test scores and assessment of learning outcomes. The flow of thought from the first section of the handbook on assessment to the last section on assessment results makes the point of distinguishing between the two burgeoning fields of assessment: one emanating from a more measurement-oriented perspective and the other emanating from a higher education outcomes assessment perspective. Together, these two topics work to carry out the ideas of assessment, defined two different ways in the handbook. Common to both these perspectives is how to improve reporting to different audiences. In assembling this handbook, the main purpose has been to provide the higher education administrator with both high-level and detailed views into contemporary theories and practices in measurement, assessment, and evaluation, supplemented with guidance on how to apply them for the benefit of students and institutions.

ABOUT THE CONTRIBUTORS

Jamal Abedi is a Professor at the School of Education of the University of California, Davis. Abedi's research interests include studies in the area of psychometrics and test and scale developments. Among his interests and his recent work are studies on the validity of assessments and accommodations and opportunity to learn for English language learners (ELLs). Abedi holds a Master's and a Ph.D. degree from Vanderbilt University in psychometrics.

Dorothy Aguilera-Black Bear (Choctaw) received her MA and Ph.D. in Education from the University of Colorado-Boulder. A former professor in Educational Leadership, she has produced extensive publications and presentations on research methods, culturally responsive education, educational leadership, Youth PAR, Indigenous wellness and leadership and Native American school communities. Dr. Aguilera-Black Bear is affiliated with the Native Wellness Center, and currently working as an independent consultant and evaluation researcher.

Isabel Arbesú (Ph.D. in Education) is a Research Professor at Universidad Autónoma Metropolitana, Campus Xochimilco (UAM-X), in Mexico City. Her research and teaching interests include the study and evaluation of the "modular system" pedagogical model taught at UAM-X, analysis and evaluation of teaching in higher education, and qualitative research methodology. She is the author of numerous books and articles.

Manju Banerjee received her Ph.D. in Special Education from the University of Connecticut. She is currently Associate Director of the Center for Students with Disabilities and Associate Research Scholar for the Center on Postsecondary Education and Disability at the University of Connecticut. Her research interests include learning technology and universal design, transition to college, disability documentation, and high-stakes testing. She can be reached at manju.banejee@ uconn.edu

Trudy W. Banta is Professor of Higher Education and Senior Advisor to the Chancellor for Academic Planning and Evaluation at Indiana University-Purdue University Indianapolis. She also serves as the founding editor of *Assessment Update*, a bi-monthly publication of Jossey-Bass of San Francisco. She is the author or editor of 18 published volumes on outcomes assessment in higher education.

David Berg is a teacher educator at the University of Otago, New Zealand. He has taught in elementary schools in England, Nepal, and New Zealand. David's research interests include initial teacher education, assessment, and international education.

Trudy H. Bers (Ph.D., Political Science, University of Illinois-Urbana) is the Executive Director of Research, Curriculum and Planning at Oakton Community College in Des Plaines, Illinois. She is a Data Facilitator for Achieving the Dream, a consultant-evaluator for the Higher Learning Commission, and teaches a course on institutional effectiveness and assessment for the University of Maryland University College doctor of management in community college leadership program. She has edited or co-edited four issues of *New Directions for Community Colleges*, co-authored two AIR online professional development courses, and written *Effective Reporting* for the Association for Institutional Research.

Kelly S. Burling directs educator effectiveness solutions for Pearson, using its products and services to help schools, school leaders, and teachers better understand the impact of the complex work of teaching on student outcomes. She also leads Pearson's work with the National Board for Professional Teaching Standards. Kelly joined Pearson as a Research Scientist in the Test, Measurement and Research Services division where she led contracts and research projects on innovation in assessments, curriculum embedded assessment, and the formative use of assessment information.

Sydell T. Carlton is an Assessment Specialist at Educational Testing Service (ETS), where she has worked on a variety of testing programs and on a variety of fairness-related projects. She has written books and papers and has made presentations in the United States and abroad on a wide range of topics, including policy matters, test fairness concerns, procedures to detect and eliminate test bias, gender and ethnic differences in test performance, assessment as linked to improving instruction, and techniques for test preparation. She is the past president of the International Association for Educational Assessment (IAEA).

Edith J. Cisneros-Cohernour (Ph.D., University of Illinois) is a full professor at the College of Education, Universidad Autonoma de Yucatan, Mexico. Her research interests are evaluation and higher education administration.

Jerome C. Clauser is a doctoral student in psychometrics at the University of Massachusetts Amherst and a research fellow at the Center for Educational Assessment. His research interests include setting performance standards, innovative score reporting, and measuring change in examinees.

Gloria Contreras received her Doctorate in Education from the Pontificia Universidad Católica de Chile. She is Director of the Masters in Education program in the School of Education at Pontificia Universidad Catolica de Valparaíso. Her teaching and research interests focus on the evaluation of teaching and learning in higher education, particularly the formative use of evaluation to improve learning and teaching.

John W. Creswell is a Professor of Educational Psychology at the University of Nebraska-Lincoln. He has authored numerous articles and books on research design, mixed methods research, and qualitative inquiry. He works across the social and human sciences as an applied research methodologist.

Michael Dean is the Head of Research at the International Baccalaureate and serves as an adjunct professor of statistics at Teachers College, Columbia University. His research interests are in the area of statistics, cognitive diagnostic assessment models of mathematical thinking, international education, and quality assurance.

D. Brian Denison received his M.A. (Education) in Student Personnel Services in Higher Education from the University of Maine at Orono and his Ph.D. in Educational Psychology from McGill University. He is currently the Institutional Research Analyst for Champlain Regional College, Quebec, Canada, where he has also served in such functions as the coordination of student success initiatives and coordination of strategic planning. He has presented or co-authored articles on such topics as graduate supervision, criteria and indicators for quality and excellence, students' conceptions of learning, evaluation of undergraduate education, initial challenges in the transition to university, and student goals and retention outcomes.

Robert Dolan is a Senior Research Scientist in the Assessment and Information group at Pearson. His work focuses on the research, design, development, and evaluation of innovative, technology-based formative and summative assessment and instruction systems for use in elementary, secondary, and postsecondary education. He received his Ph.D. from MIT in Brain and Cognitive Sciences in 1992.

Peter E. Doolittle is Director of the Center for Instructional Development and Educational Research (CIDER), Associate Professor of Educational Psychology in the Department of Learning Sciences and Technology (LST), and the Director of the Educational Psychology Research Program (EPRP) at Virginia Tech, Blacksburg, Virginia. He is also the Executive Editor of the *International Journal of Teaching and Learning in Higher Education* and Associate Editor of the *International Journal of Cyber Behavior, Psychology and Learning*. His current research focus includes the investigation of learning efficacy in large classes and multimedia learning environments.

Kathryne Drezek McConnell is Assistant Director with the Office of Assessment & Evaluation at Virginia Tech and adjunct faculty for the educational psychology program in Virginia Tech's School of Education. She is an Associate Editor of the *International Journal of Teaching and Learning in Higher Education* and currently serves as President of the Virginia Assessment Group, the nation's oldest continuing professional higher education assessment organization. Her current work involves campus customization of assessment tools like the AAC&U VALUE rubrics, learner-centered assessment of high-impact practices, and the assessment of interdisciplinary learning experiences.

David A. Erlandson (Ed.D, University of Illinois) is Professor Emeritus of Educational Administration at Texas A&M University. His primary academic interests are naturalistic inquiry and organizational learning. He is the lead author of *Doing Naturalistic Inquiry* (1993).

David Fetterman is president and CEO of Fetterman & Associates, an international evaluation consulting firm. He has 25 years of experience at Stanford University in the School of Education and School of Medicine. He is also concurrently a Professor of Education at the University of Arkansas at Pine Bluff and the Director of the Arkansas Evaluation Center. He is a past-president of the American Evaluation Association.

Doreen B. Finkelstein has worked for many years as an educational researcher and evaluator, including serving as a program evaluator for the College Board and as an external evaluator for NSF grants. She is currently an independent consultant affiliated with Haynie Research and Evaluation. She has areas of expertise in school reform, STEM education, assessment, informal learning, and college readiness.

Ashley Finley (Ph.D., Sociology, University of Iowa) is the Senior Director of Assessment and Research at AAC&U and the national evaluator for the Bringing Theory to Practice (BTtoP) Project. Her work, at both the campus and national levels, focuses on the development, implementation, and communication of meaningful assessment strategies to facilitate depth of learning at the student, faculty, and institutional levels. Before joining AAC&U, she was a faculty member at Dickinson College, where she taught courses in quantitative methods, social inequality, and gender inequality.

Kurt Geisinger is a psychometrician who formerly chaired Fordham University's Psychology Department and served as a Dean and an Academic Vice-President/Provost. As director of UNL's Buros Center for Testing and Buros Institute of Mental Measurements and Meierhenry Distinguished University Professor, he oversees one of the world's foremost research groups involved in test review and consultation.

Kelly E. Godfrey is an Associate Research Scientist at the College Board. She received her doctoral degree from the Educational Research Methodology department at UNC Greensboro. Her research focuses primarily in psychometrics, including IRT and test equating, and program evaluation, including mixed methods and responsive evaluation approaches.

Thomas E. Grayson (Ph.D., University of Illinois) is an evaluation consultant and a recent retiree from the University of Illinois at Urbana-Champaign (UIUC), where he was Director of Evaluation and Assessment in Student Affairs and adjunct professor in the College of Education. He has 35 years of experience in evaluation, including 18 years at the Illinois State Board of Education and 10 years at the Transition Research Institute located at UIUC. He is an active member of the American Evaluation Association, having served as Chair of both the Higher Education TIG and the AEA International Committee.

Timothy Guetterman is a doctoral student in Quantitative, Qualitative, and Psychometric Methods at the University of Nebraska-Lincoln. His professional interests and research writings are in research methodology, namely mixed methods, general research design, and evaluation. His professional experience is in the field of evaluation with a focus on education and healthcare programs.

Geneva D. Haertel is currently Director of Assessment Research and Design at the Center for Technology in Learning at SRI International. Her research interests include evidence-centered assessment design and universal design for learning in the assessment context. She has conducted research on influences on student learning and assessment for over 25 years. She can be reached at geneva.haertel@sri.com

Ronald K. Hambleton holds the titles of Distinguished University Professor and Executive Director of the Center for Educational Assessment at the University of Massachusetts. His research interests are in the areas of psychometric methods and, specifically, setting of performance standards on tests, reporting of test scores, large-scale assessment, and applying item response models to solve educational testing problems.

Delwyn Harnisch is directing an Assessment and Leadership for Learning Center at University of Nebraska Lincoln. He has had 25 years of experience at University of Illinois at Urbana-Champaign College of Education directing evaluation and assessment research projects. He is currently a Professor of Education at the University of Nebraska Lincoln College of Education and Human Sciences and has focused his efforts on integration of technology into the teaching and learning process with

653

a particular emphasis on mathematics while having been honored with NCME's Excellence in Classroom Assessment Training Award in Teacher Education for Assessment Cohort Program at University of Nebraska.

Deborah J. Harris is Assistant Vice-President for Measurement and Reporting Services at ACT, Inc., a not-for-profit organization that provides a broad array of assessment and other solutions geared toward helping people achieve education and workplace success. She holds a doctorate from the University of Wisconsin–Madison and is an adjunct at the University of Iowa. Her research interests center around comparability of scores, including equating, linking, scaling, data forensics, and context and mode effects.

Michael Harris (Ph.D., Public Policy, Indiana University) serves as the Chancellor of Indiana University, Kokomo, and as a Professor of Public and Environmental Affairs, Education and Business. He is a graduate of two of the Harvard Graduate School of Education's leadership programs (IEM and MDP), and has published four books and close to 40 articles in a variety of journals. Dr. Harris has been recognized for his teaching excellence, research, and service.

James Hart received his M.A. in Applied Linguistics from Montclair State University. He currently teaches Spanish, English as a Second Language, and Intercultural Communication at County College of Morris in Randolph, NJ, where he also coordinates the ESL, International Studies and Study Abroad Programs.

Amy B. Hendrickson (Ph.D., Educational Measurement and Statistics, University of Iowa) is a Psychometrician at The College Board. Her research interests include psychometrics, equating, large-scale assessment, and rater reliability.

Kevin Hynes directs the Office of Institutional Research and Educational Assessment for Midwestern University with campuses in Downers Grove, Illinois and Glendale, Arizona. His research interests include educational outcomes assessment and health personnel distribution.

Natasha A. Jankowski is a Research Analyst with the National Institute for Learning Outcomes Assessment, which is located at the University of Illinois Urbana-Champaign. Her current research interests include examining the use of evidence of student learning in institutional decision making and developing deeper understandings of institutional transparency of assessment efforts.

Thomas Judd is an Assistant Dean for Academic Assessment and Assistant Professor in the Behavioral Science and Leadership Department at the United States Military Academy at West Point. Prior to his current affiliation he held administrative positions in institutional research and planning.

Bruce Keith is a Professor of Sociology and Associate Dean for Academic Affairs at the United States Military Academy. His research activities center on the organization of higher education and the corresponding influence of such structures on individuals' outcomes.

Anthony E. Kelly earned his doctorate in Psychological Studies in Education at Stanford University. He taught at Rutgers University and George Mason University and spent a number of years as a program manager at the US National Science Foundation. He was a Fulbright Scholar (2009–2010). His interests include research method design, assessment theory, and innovation studies.

Young Yee Kim is a research scientist with NAEP ESSI at the American Institutes for Research. Dr. Kim's major research interests are in educational assessment policy and multidimensional item response theory (MIRT), applying MIRT to large-scale assessment data such as NAEP in particular. She worked as a lead statistical data analyst for the NAEP reading framework comparison study and the NAEP Grade 12 mathematics framework comparison study. She is also interested in ELL students' achievement issues and has authored and co-authored multiple papers on this subject.

Stephanie L. Knight is Professor in the Department of Educational Psychology at The Pennsylvania State University. Her research interests include classroom processes and preservice and inservice professional development. She has been an editor of the *American Educational Research Journal* and is currently editor of the *Journal of Teacher Education*.

Tawnya Knupp is a Research Associate for the Measurement Research Department at ACT, Inc. She received her doctorate from the University of Iowa in Educational Measurement and Statistics. Her research interests include decision consistency and accuracy estimation, equating methods, reliability, and classical test theory.

Michael J. Kolen is Professor of Educational Measurement and Statistics at the University of Iowa. Dr. Kolen is Past-President of the National Council on Measurement in Education (NCME), received an NCME Career Award in 2008, is a member of the Joint Committee for the Revision of the Standards for Educational and Psychological Testing, is a Fellow of the American Educational Research Association, is a Fellow of the American Psychological Association, and serves on technical advisory committees for State testing programs and testing organizations. Dr. Kolen has numerous publications in journals and books on the subjects of test scaling, linking, and equating.

Sathasivam 'Kris' Krishnan is the Associate Dean for Institutional Research and Planning at Hudson County Community College. He has over 20 years of experience leading Institutional Research offices at the state as well at the college. His research interest spans a number of areas including examining the factors and policies that help students succeed at college, student learning outcomes, institutional assessment, and performance indicators.

Jerold S. Laguilles is the Coordinator of Institutional Research at Springfield College in Massachusetts. His primary research interests focus on college retention, student and alumni outcomes, and survey research methods.

Albertha H. Lawson (Ph.D., Higher Education Administration, University of New Orleans) currently serves as the Assistant Vice-President of Institutional Research and Planning for the Louisiana Community and Technical College System. Prior to joining Louisiana's 2-year college system, she served as the Director of Institutional Research and Planning for the Louisiana State University System. Her research interests include community college student success measures, accountability in higher education, and formula funding.

Margaret D. LeCompte received her MA and Ph.D. in education from the University of Chicago. She is emerita professor of education and sociology in the School of Education, University of Colorado-Boulder. She has authored and edited 14 books and many articles on qualitative research methods, school reform and school organization, and school success among at-risk, ethnically diverse, gifted, artistically creative and language minority students. Dr. LeCompte was president of the Council on Anthropology and Education of the American Anthropology Association and Editor of the journal, *Review of Educational Research*, from 2003 to 2006.

William Mahler is the Director of Institutional Effectiveness at Kettering University. He has led institutional research, assessment, and planning efforts at a liberal arts college and two universities and has been a full-time faculty member, a research psychologist, an administrator in several positions, and an IPEDS trainer for the Association for Institutional Research and the National Center for Educational Statistics. His Ph.D. in Psychology is from Stanford University.

D. Betsy McCoach is an associate professor of measurement, evaluation, and assessment in the Educational Psychology department in the Neag School of Education at the University of Connecticut. Her research interests include longitudinal modeling, structural equation modeling, multilevel modeling, factor analysis, and instrument design.

Carina McCormick is a Ph.D. student in Educational Psychology at the University of Nebraska-Lincoln, and works as a Graduate Assistant in the Buros Institute for Assessment Consultation and Outreach (BIACO). Her research interests include test fairness, test accommodations, Universal Test Design, validation, and accountability policy.

Robert J. Mislevy is the Frederic M. Lord Chair in Measurement and Statistics at Educational Testing Service. His research applies developments in technology, statistics, and cognitive psychology to practical problems in educational assessment.

Deanna L. Morgan is a Research Scientist at the College Board. She received her Ph.D. in Research, Evaluation, Measurement, and Statistics from the University of Georgia in 2001. Her research interests include standard setting, placement testing, generalizability theory, and assessing students with disabilities.

Sandra Murphy, Professor of Education Emerita, University of California, Davis, researches literacy and assessment. She has co-authored several books including *Designing Writing Tasks for the Assessment of Writing* (with Leo Ruth), *Portfolio Practices: Lessons from Schools, Districts and States* (with Terry Underwood) and a series of books *Using Rubrics to Improve Student Writing* (with Sally Hampton and Margaret Lowry). Besides publishing widely, she has been a consultant on a range of educational programs such NAEP, the New Standards Project, and the National Writing Project.

Peggy O'Neill, Professor of Writing, directs the composition program and teaches in the Writing Department at Loyola University Maryland. Her scholarship focuses on writing pedagogy, assessment, and program administration and has appeared in several journals and edited collections. She has co-authored two books, *A Guide to College Writing Assessment* (with Cindy Moore and Brian Huot) and *Reframing Writing Assessment to Improve Teaching and Learning* (with Linda Adler-Kassner), edited or co-edited four books, and currently co-edits the *Journal of Writing Assessment*.

Steven J. Osterlind is Professor of Educational Psychology at the University of Missouri. His research interests include psychometrics, applied statistical procedures of academic achievement, and test development.

Jane Ostrander is Director of the Experiential Learning Center Projects at Truckee Meadows Community College in Reno, NV and Principal Investigator of the Destination: Problem-Based Learning, a National Science Foundation Advanced Technological Education project. She is also a Ph.D. candidate at Oregon State University, College of Education. Her research areas include problem-based learning, faculty inquiry, principled assessments, professional development for community college faculty, and building knowledge sharing communities to support instructional innovation.

James C. Palmer is a Professor of Higher Education at Illinois State University (ISU). Prior to joining the ISU faculty in 1992, he served as acting director of the Center for Community College Education at George Mason University, Vice-President for Communications at the American Association for Community Colleges, and assistant director of the ERIC Clearinghouse for Community Colleges at the University of California, Los Angeles. At ISU, Palmer teaches courses on the American community college, adult and continuing education, and the history of American higher education. He currently serves as editor of the *Community College Review*.

Gary R. Pike (Ph.D., Ohio State University, 1985) is the Executive Director of Information Management and Institutional Research at Indiana University-Purdue University Indianapolis. He is also an Associate Professor of Higher Education and Student Affairs at IUPUI.

Mary J. Pitoniak is a Strategic Advisor in the Statistical Analysis, Data Analysis, and Psychometric Research area within the Research and Development Division at Educational Testing Service. One of Dr. Pitoniak's areas of expertise is standard setting, having published, conducted research, and provided training in this area, including in numerous venues worldwide.

Christopher Pondish has been a higher education researcher for over 20 years in the greater New York City area at a range of institutions from small private colleges to large public university systems. Currently serving as the applications architect for the City University of New York's PeopleSoft implementation, he is also an adjunct assistant professor at Baruch College's School of Public Affairs. His research focuses on institutional distinctiveness, and the relationship between institutional saga, culture, and student success.

Staci J. Provezis is the Project Manager and Research Analyst with the National Institute for Learning Outcomes Assessment, which is located at the University of Illinois Urbana-Champaign. Her research examines the role of accreditation in institutional assessment and maps institutional responses to the nationwide call for transparency in student learning outcomes assessment.

Karen E. Rambo is an assistant professor in research and assessment in the School of Education at Colorado State University. She received her Ph.D. in Educational Psychology from the University of Connecticut and specialized in Measurement, Evaluation, and Assessment. Her research interests include student academic growth, gifted education, academic acceleration, multilevel modeling, and longitudinal growth modeling.

Karen Ruedinger (MBA, University of Michigan) is the Coordinator of Planning and Market Understanding at Northwestern Michigan College in Traverse City, Michigan. In this capacity Karen manages the process for both strategic and operational planning for the College and informs the process through regular environmental scans and market studies. Her particular areas of interest include understanding learner needs, strategic planning, and innovation.

Elizabeth Schaughency is Senior Lecturer in the Department of Psychology at the University of Otago, New Zealand. Her research interests focus on investigation of methods to promote evidenced-based practice and decision making as a means to develop ecologically valid prevention/intervention strategies for improved translatability, adoption, and sustainability with the goal of improved behavioral and academic outcomes for children and youth.

Charles Secolsky is Director of Institutional Research & Planning at County College of Morris in New Jersey. He received a Ph.D. in Education from University of Illinois at Urbana-Champaign, an

MA in Sociology and a Specialist Diploma in Educational Administration from Queens College. He has served as a measurement statistician at Educational Testing Service. He specializes in institutional research, statistics, measurement, assessment, and program evaluation. He has many publications and presentations in the areas of measurement and assessment.

Jeffrey A. Seybert is director of the National Higher Education Benchmarking Institute at Johnson County Community College in Overland Park, KS. Prior to assuming directorship of the Institute, Jeff served in the JCCC Office of Institutional Research for 27 years, the last 20 of which as director of the office. Jeff has also had experience as a full-time university faculty member and consultant to more than 120 colleges and other non-profit and governmental organizations in the areas of assessment of student learning outcomes and institutional effectiveness, benchmarking and peer comparisons, institutional research, strategic planning, and institutional and program evaluation.

Richard J. Shavelson is a Partner at SK Partners, LLC, the Margaret Jacks Professor of Education (Emeritus) and Professor of Psychology (by courtesy) at Stanford University and the I. James Quillen Dean of the Stanford University School of Education (Emeritus). His current research focuses on the measurement of learning and performance, especially in higher education and science education, and the statistical modeling of assessment scores. He has authored or co-authored *Measuring College Learning Responsibly: Accountability in a New Era, A Brief History of Student Learning: How We Got Where We Are and a Proposal for Where to Go Next, Statistical Reasoning for the Behavioral Sciences (3rd ed.), Generalizability Theory: A Primer* (with Noreen Webb), and *Scientific Research in Education* (with Lisa Towne).

Leslie H. Shaw is a Ph.D. student in Educational Psychology at the University of Nebraska—Lincoln, and works as a Graduate Assistant in the Buros Institute for Assessment Consultation and Outreach (BIACO). Her research interests include multilevel modeling and longitudinal data analysis, test validation, teachers' perceptions of standardized tests, K–12 assessment and policy.

Jeffrey K. Smith holds a chaired professorship in the College of Education at the University of Otago, New Zealand. For 29 years, he taught at Rutgers University where he was Chair of the Educational Psychology Department and Associate Dean of the Graduate School of Education. He conducts research in assessment in schools, and the psychology of aesthetics.

Robert E. Stake (Ph.D., Psychology, Princeton University) is Director of the Center for Instructional Research and Curriculum Evaluation (CIRCE) at the University of Illinois at Urbana-Champaign. He has been deeply engaged in educational program evaluation since the 1960s, developed an approach known as "responsive evaluation," and has authored many articles and books, including *Standards-Based and Responsive Evaluation* and *Multiple Case Study Analysis*. Stake is the recipient of the Lazarsfeld Award from the American Evaluation Association, the President's Citation from the American Educational Research Association, and a Lifetime Achievement Award from the International Congress of Qualitative Research.

Jeffrey T. Steedle is a Measurement Scientist at the Council for Aid to Education where he manages research and development projects and assists in operational aspects of the Collegiate Learning Assessment. His research interests include performance assessment, psychometrics, student motivation, and college readiness.

Curtis Tatsuoka received his Ph.D. in Statistics from Cornell University. Currently, he is Director of Biostatistics of the Neurological Institute and Neurological Outcomes Center, Case Western

Reserve University and University Hospitals, Cleveland, OH. His interests include statistical models of cognition and brain imaging analysis.

Kikumi K. Tatsuoka retired from Teachers College, Columbia University, as Distinguished Research Professor Emerita. Before arriving at Teachers College, she worked at Educational Testing Services developing PSAT diagnostic scoring reports, and applying her programmatic research on the Rule Space Method and Q-Matrix Theory that she had developed at the University of Illinois. She has published many papers and books that have been cited frequently in journals of measurement, psychometrics, and computer science.

Bruce Thompson is Distinguished Professor of Educational Psychology, and Distinguished Professor of Library Sciences, Texas A&M University, and Adjunct Professor of Family and Community Medicine, Baylor College of Medicine (Houston). He has edited four journals and a book series. He is the author/editor of 211 articles, and several books, including the recently published *Foundations of Behavioral Statistics*.

Martha L. Thurlow is Director of the National Center on Educational Outcomes at the University of Minnesota. In this role she addresses the implications of contemporary U.S. policy and practice for students with disabilities and English Language Learners, including national and statewide assessment policies and practices, standards-setting efforts, and graduation requirements.

Tammi Vacha-Haase is a professor in the Department of Psychology at Colorado State University. Her research interests include geropsychology and reliability generalization (RG) meta-analysis. She has published numerous professional articles and book chapters, and recently authored her first book, *Psychotherapy with Older Men*.

Jacques van der Meer was Senior Lecturer in the Higher Education Development Centre and Coordinator of the Student Learning Centre at the University of Otago, New Zealand, during preparation of the chapter for this book. He currently serves as Associate Dean (Academic) in the College of Education at the University of Otago. His research and related interests include the transition into University and the experience of first-year students, student retention, peer-learning, equitable access and participation in higher education, and pedagogical/andragogical approaches to enhancing student engagement.

Alan Vanneman is a senior writer/analyst with the American Institutes for Research in Washington, DC. He is co-author of *Achievement Gaps: How Black and White Students in Public Schools Perform in Mathematics and Reading on the National Assessment of Educational Progress* and *Achievement Gaps: How Hispanic and White Students in Public Schools Perform in Mathematics and Reading on the National Assessment of Educational Progress*, both published by the National Center for Education Statistics, as well as author of many shorter NCES publications.

Ze Wang (Ph.D., Educational Psychology, University of Missouri) is assistant professor in educational psychology at the University of Missouri. Her research interests include quantitative methods and academic achievement.

Noreen M. Webb is Professor of Social Research Methodology in the Graduate School of Education & Information Studies at the University of California, Los Angeles, with a joint appointment in the UCLA Department of Applied Linguistics & Teaching English as a Second Language. Her research spans domains in learning and instruction, especially the measurement and study of teaching and learning processes and performance of individuals and groups in mathematics and science classrooms. With Richard Shavelson, she co-authored *Generalizability Theory: A Primer*.

Ellen J. Weed (Ph.D., University of Michigan) is Vice-President for Academic Affairs at Nashville State Community College in Nashville, Tennessee. She has worked within the Tennessee Board of Regents system for more than 30 years, with experience at the community college, university, and governing board levels. She has been actively involved in regional accreditation activities through the Commission on Colleges of the Southern Association of Colleges and Schools, serving on more than 40 committees. In 2002 she received a Meritorious Service Award from the Commission on Colleges.

Megan Welsh is an Assistant Professor in the Measurement, Evaluation and Assessment Program of the Neag School of Education, University of Connecticut, where she teaches courses in assessment, evaluation, and educational statistics. Her primary areas of research interest include the use of tests as an educational reform lever, evaluation of educational programs, and assessment.

Ellen Wentland is Assistant Dean of Academic Program Review, Outcomes Assessment, and Educational Effectiveness at Northern Essex Community College in Haverhill, Massachusetts. She currently serves as a member of the AMCOA (Advancing a Massachusetts Culture of Assessment) team created by the Massachusetts Department of Higher Education. Her professional interests include outcomes assessment in higher education curricular and co-curricular areas.

Louise Yarnall (Ph.D., Education, University of California, Los Angeles) is a senior researcher at SRI International's Center for Technology in Learning. She specializes in assessment design, evaluation design, community college education research, and journalism education research. Her assessment work is grounded in evidence-centered design.

Edward J. Yaw (Ed. D., Columbia University) has been President of County College of Morris in New Jersey since 1986. He has served as Chair of the New Jersey Presidents' Council and was a member of the New Jersey Commission on Higher Education. He has also led accreditation evaluation teams on behalf of the Middle States Commission on Higher Education.

Jion Liou Yen is Executive Director of Institutional Research and Planning at Lewis University in Romeoville, Illinois. She provides leadership in university-wide assessment of student learning and institutional effectiveness as a member of the Assessment Office. Her research interests focus on college student access and persistence, outcomes- and evidence-based assessment of student learning and program evaluation.

Chengbo Yin is the Director of Institutional Research at Middlesex County College in Edison, New Jersey. He is also the Project Director of the *New Jersey's Community Colleges Fact Book and Directory*.

April L. Zenisky is Senior Research Fellow and Director of Computer-Based Testing Initiatives at the Center for Educational Assessment in the School of Education at the University of Massachusetts Amherst. Her research interests include score reporting, computer-based testing, test translation, and large-scale performance assessment.

Rebecca Zwick is a distinguished presidential appointee at Educational Testing Service and professor emerita at the University of California, Santa Barbara. Her areas of specialization are educational measurement and statistics, test validity and fairness, and higher education admissions testing.

INDEX